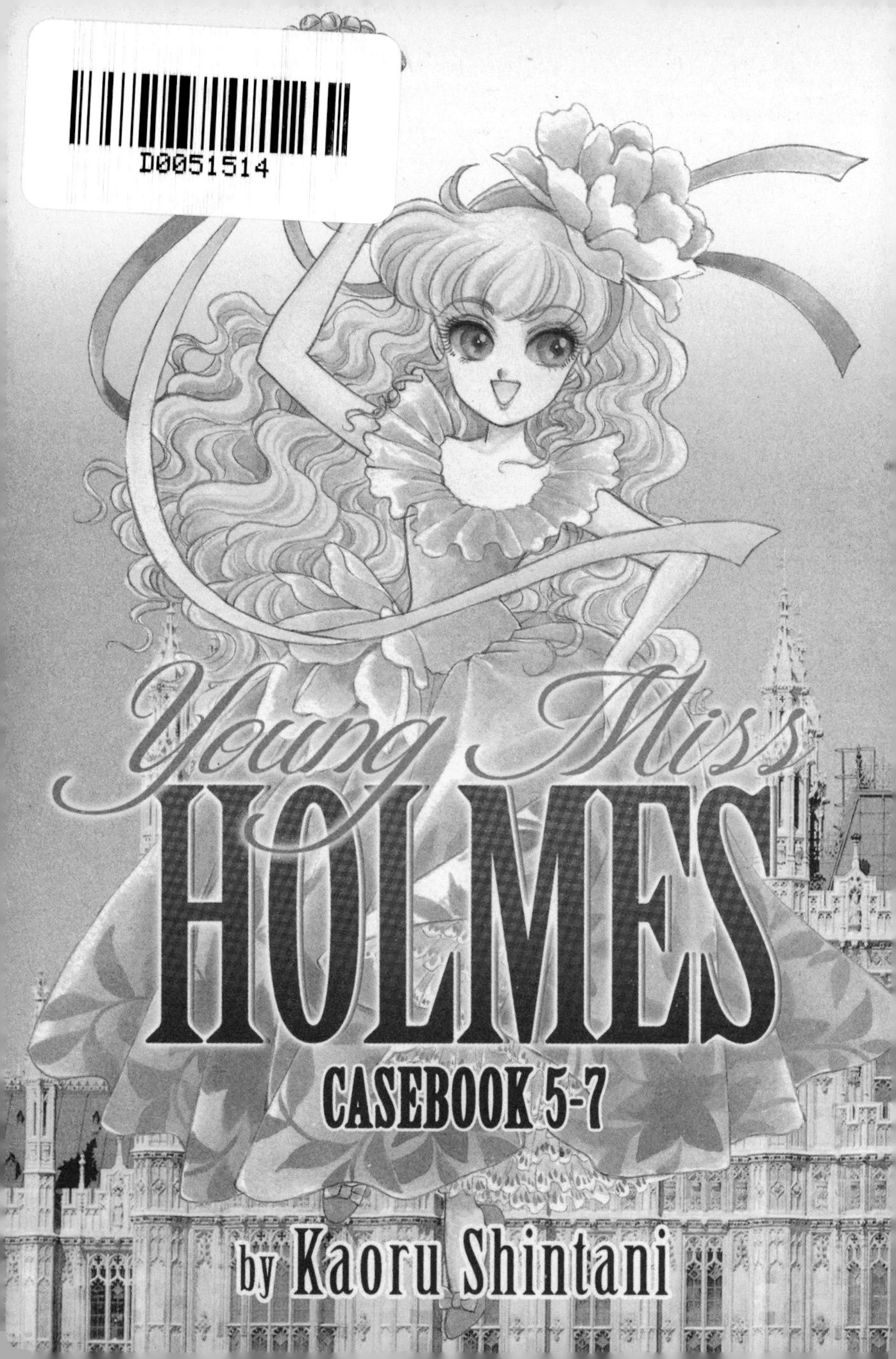
Young Miss
HOLMES
CASEBOOK 5-7
by Kaoru Shintani

Young Miss HOLMES

CASEBOOK 5-7

story & art by **Kaoru Shintani**

STAFF CREDITS

translation	**Adrienne Beck**
adaptation	**Shanti Whitesides**
lettering/layout	**Mia Chiresa**
cover design	**Nicky Lim**
proofreader	**Janet Houck**
editor	**Adam Arnold**
publisher	**Jason DeAngelis**
	Seven Seas Entertainment

YOUNG MISS HOLMES CASEBOOK 5-7
Originally published in Japan as CHRISTIE: HIGH TENSION Vol. 5-7
Copyright © 2010-2011 Kaoru Shintani
First published in 2010-2011 by MEDIA FACTORY, Inc., Tokyo, Japan.
English translation rights reserved by Seven Seas Entertainment, LLC.
under the license from MEDIA FACTORY, Inc., Tokyo, Japan.

ISBN: 978-1-937867-42-3

Printed in Canada

First Printing: September 2013

10 9 8 7 6 5 4 3 2 1

Seven Seas

FOLLOW US ONLINE: www.gomanga.com

READING DIRECTIONS

This book reads from *right to left*, Japanese style.
If this is your first time reading manga, you start
reading from the top right panel on each page and
take it from there. If you get lost, just follow the
numbered diagram here. It may seem backwards
at first, but you'll get the hang of it! Have fun!!

ONE HUNDRED POUNDS A YEAR?

The Adventure of the Solitary Cyclist (1)

YES. THE PAY IS TRULY ASTOUNDING.

BUT IT HAS COME WITH A LITTLE BIT OF A PROBLEM ...

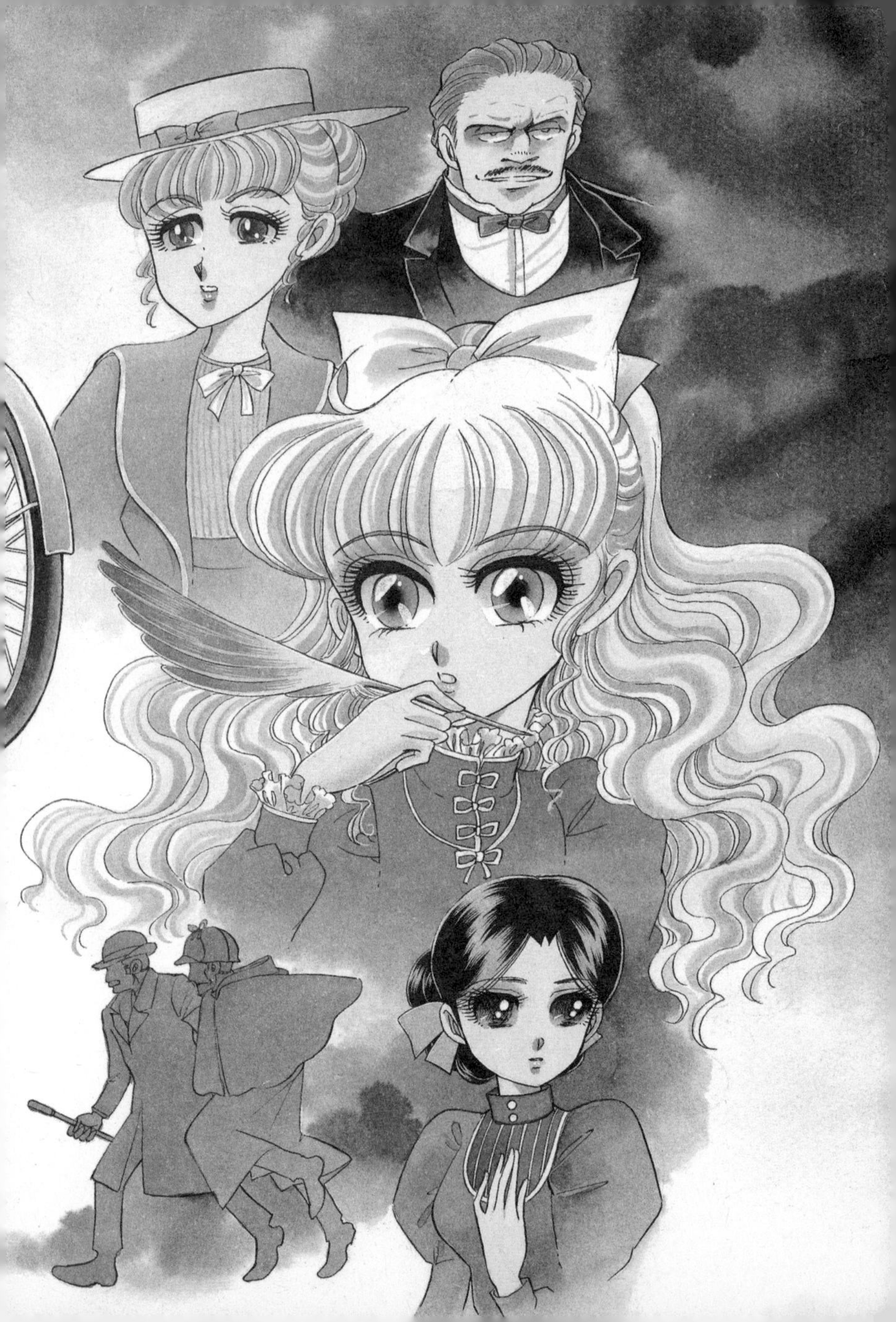

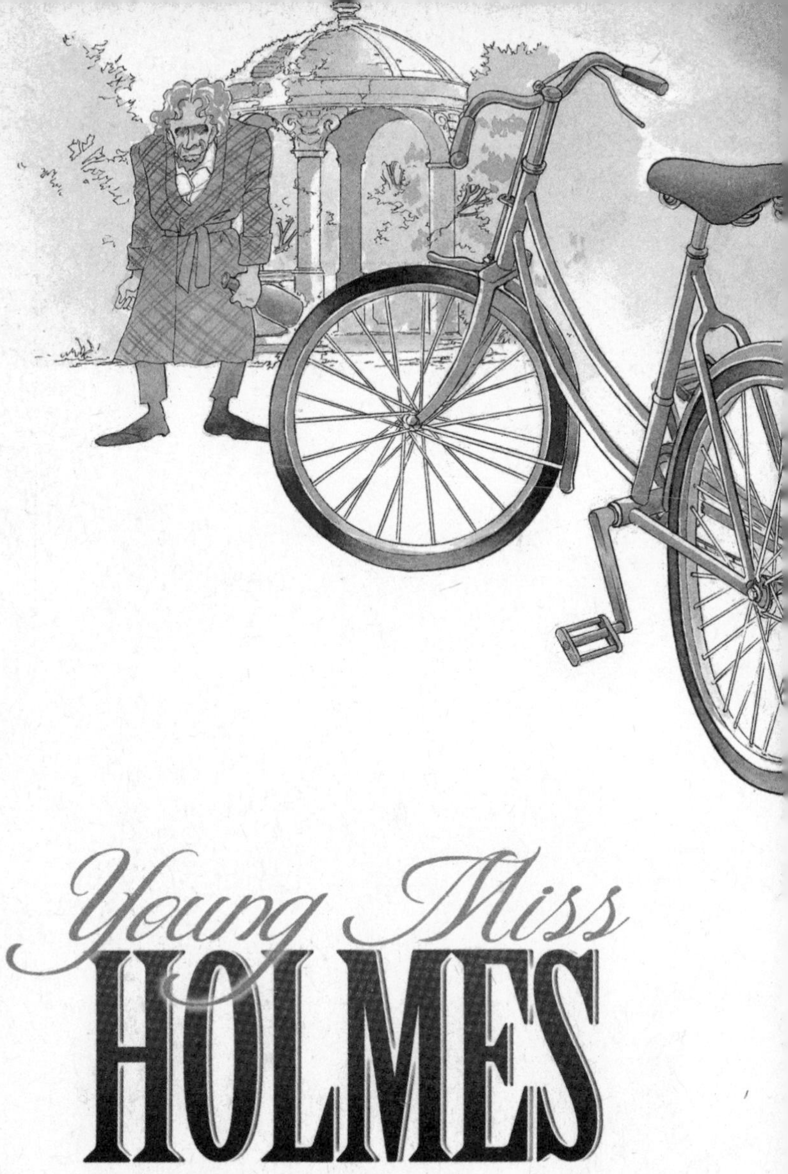

Young Miss HOLMES

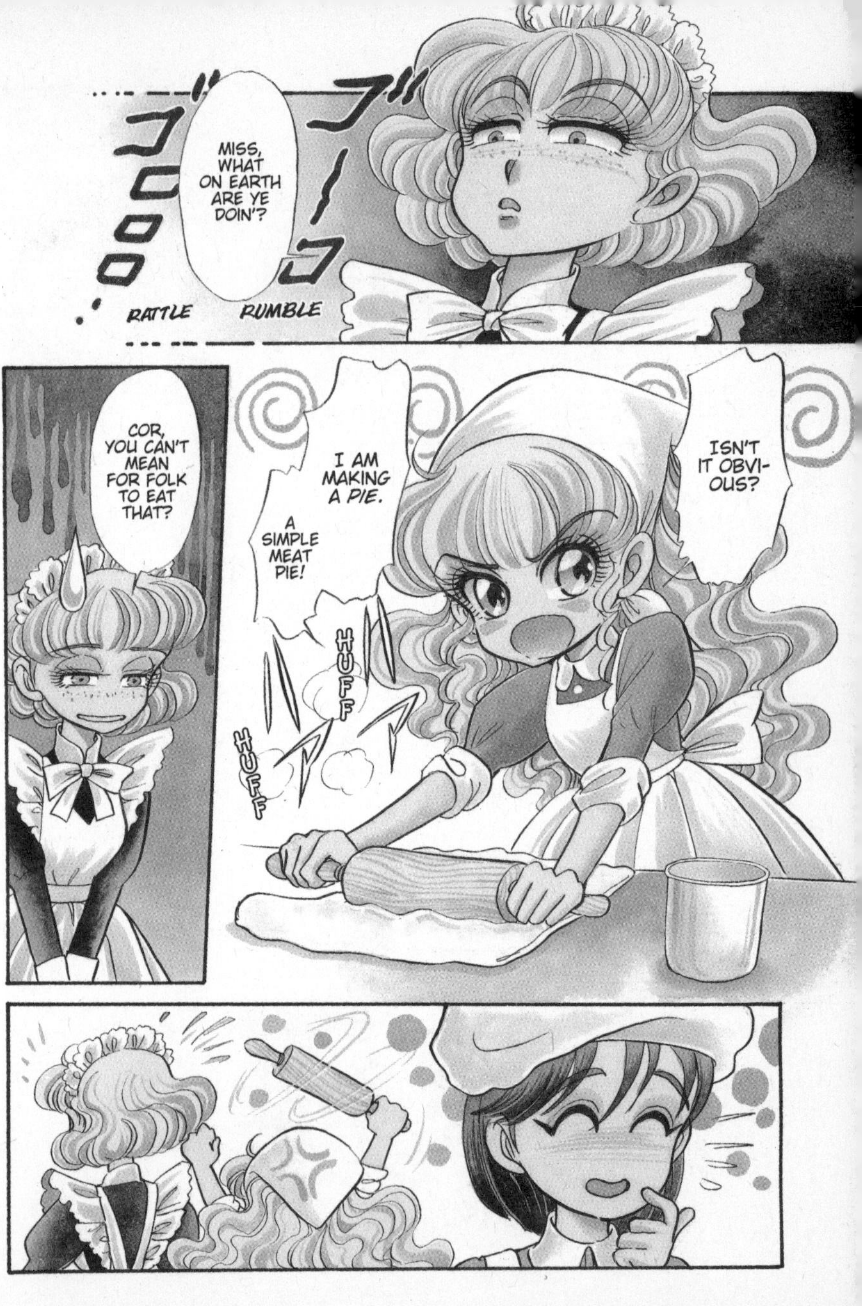
MISS, WHAT ON EARTH ARE YE DOIN'?
RUMBLE
RATTLE
ISN'T IT OBVIOUS?
I AM MAKING A PIE.
A SIMPLE MEAT PIE!
HUFF
HUFF
COR, YOU CAN'T MEAN FOR FOLK TO EAT THAT?

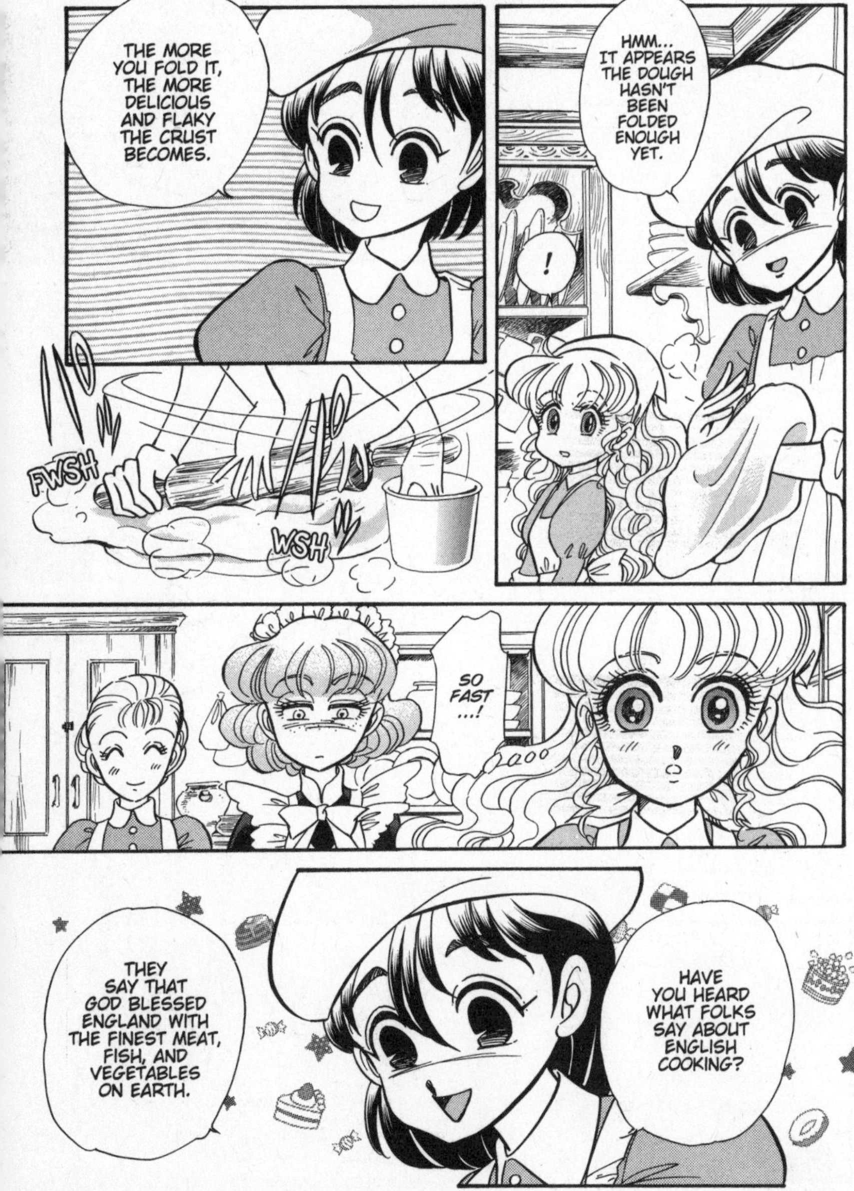
HMM... IT APPEARS THE DOUGH HASN'T BEEN FOLDED ENOUGH YET.
!
THE MORE YOU FOLD IT, THE MORE DELICIOUS AND FLAKY THE CRUST BECOMES.
FWSH
WSH
SO FAST ...!
HAVE YOU HEARD WHAT FOLKS SAY ABOUT ENGLISH COOKING?
THEY SAY THAT GOD BLESSED ENGLAND WITH THE FINEST MEAT, FISH, AND VEGETABLES ON EARTH.

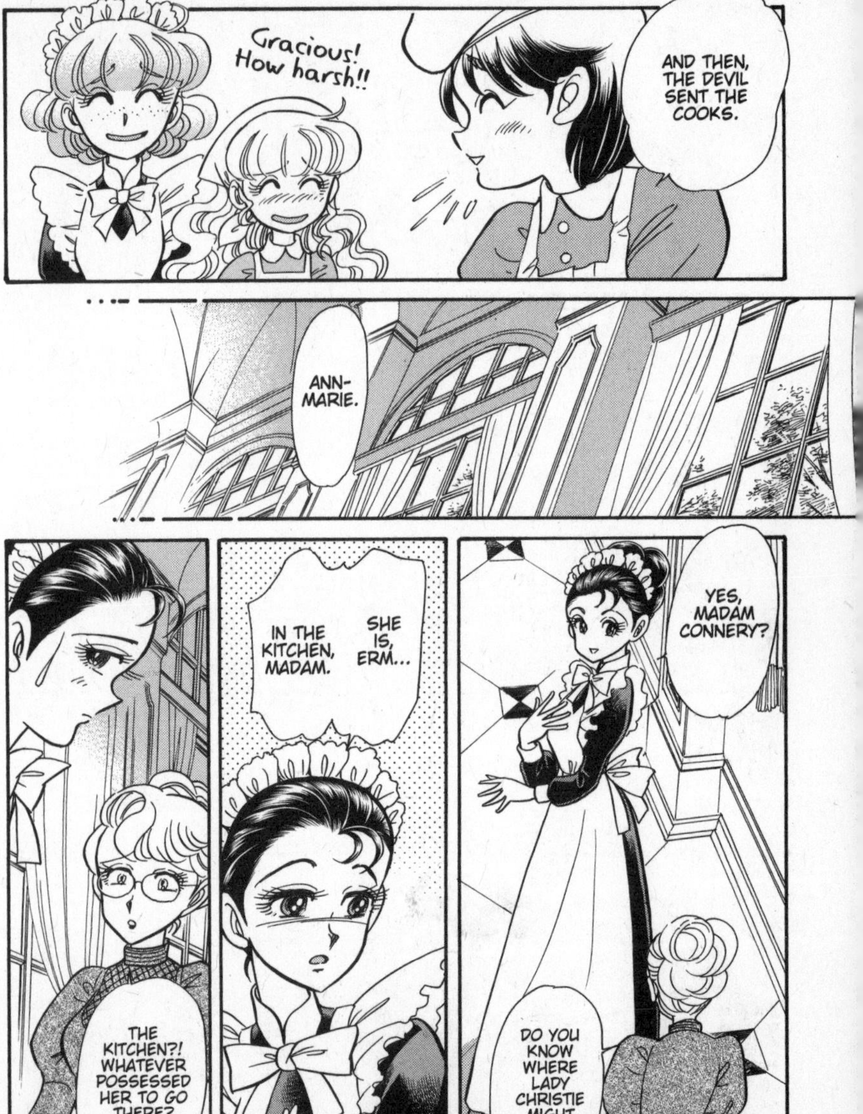
AND THEN, THE DEVIL SENT THE COOKS.
Gracious! How harsh!!
ANN-MARIE.
YES, MADAM CONNERY?
DO YOU KNOW WHERE LADY CHRISTIE MIGHT BE?
SHE IS, ERM...
IN THE KITCHEN, MADAM.
THE KITCHEN?! WHATEVER POSSESSED HER TO GO THERE?

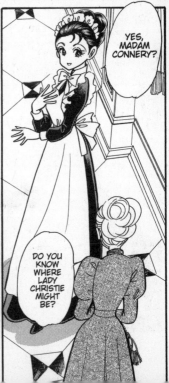

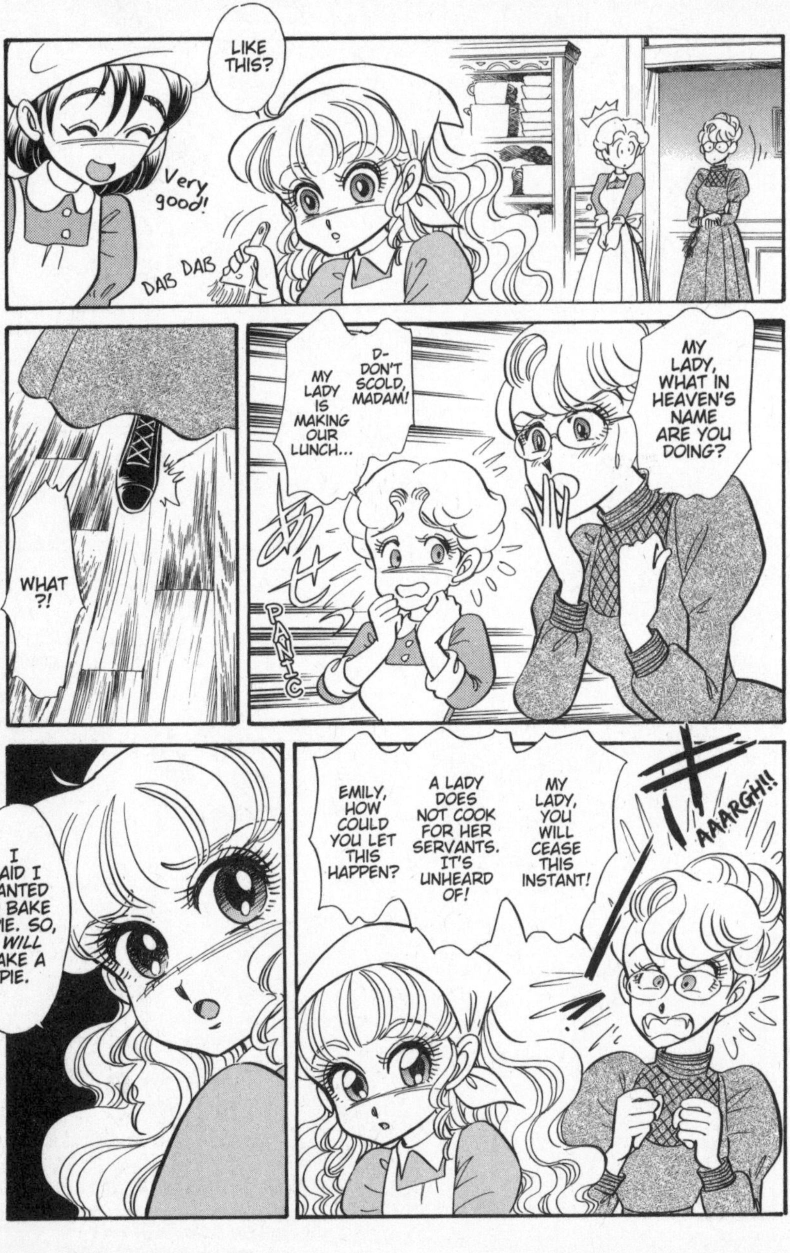
LIKE THIS?
Very good!
DAB DAB
MY LADY, WHAT IN HEAVEN'S NAME ARE YOU DOING?
D-DON'T SCOLD, MADAM!
MY LADY IS MAKING OUR LUNCH...
あせっ
PANIC
WHAT?!
AAARGH!!
MY LADY, YOU WILL CEASE THIS INSTANT!
A LADY DOES NOT COOK FOR HER SERVANTS. IT'S UNHEARD OF!
EMILY, HOW COULD YOU LET THIS HAPPEN?
I SAID I WANTED TO BAKE A PIE. SO, I *WILL* BAKE A PIE.

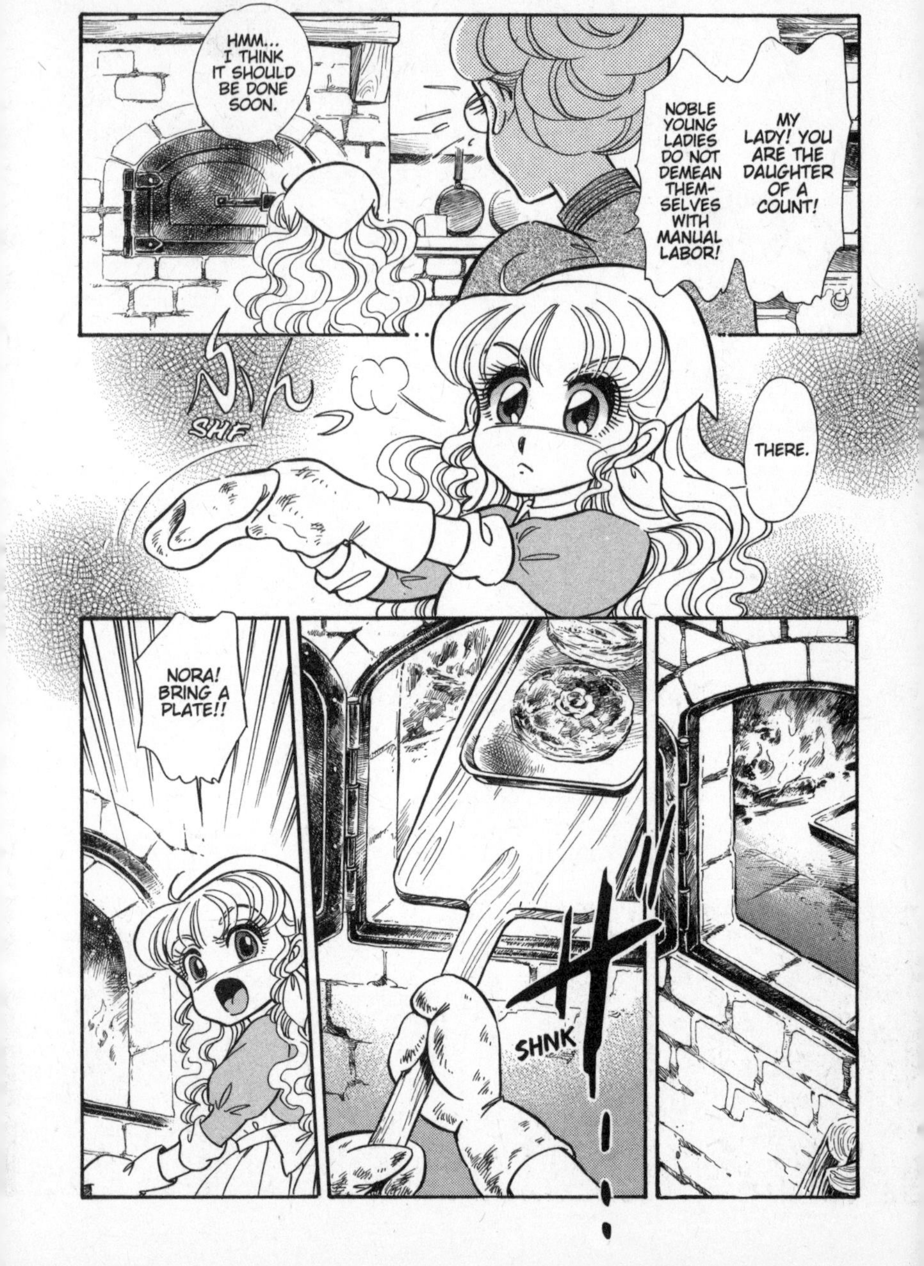
MY LADY! YOU ARE THE DAUGHTER OF A COUNT!
NOBLE YOUNG LADIES DO NOT DEMEAN THEMSELVES WITH MANUAL LABOR!
HMM... I THINK IT SHOULD BE DONE SOON.
THERE.
ふん
SHF
SHNK
NORA! BRING A PLATE!!

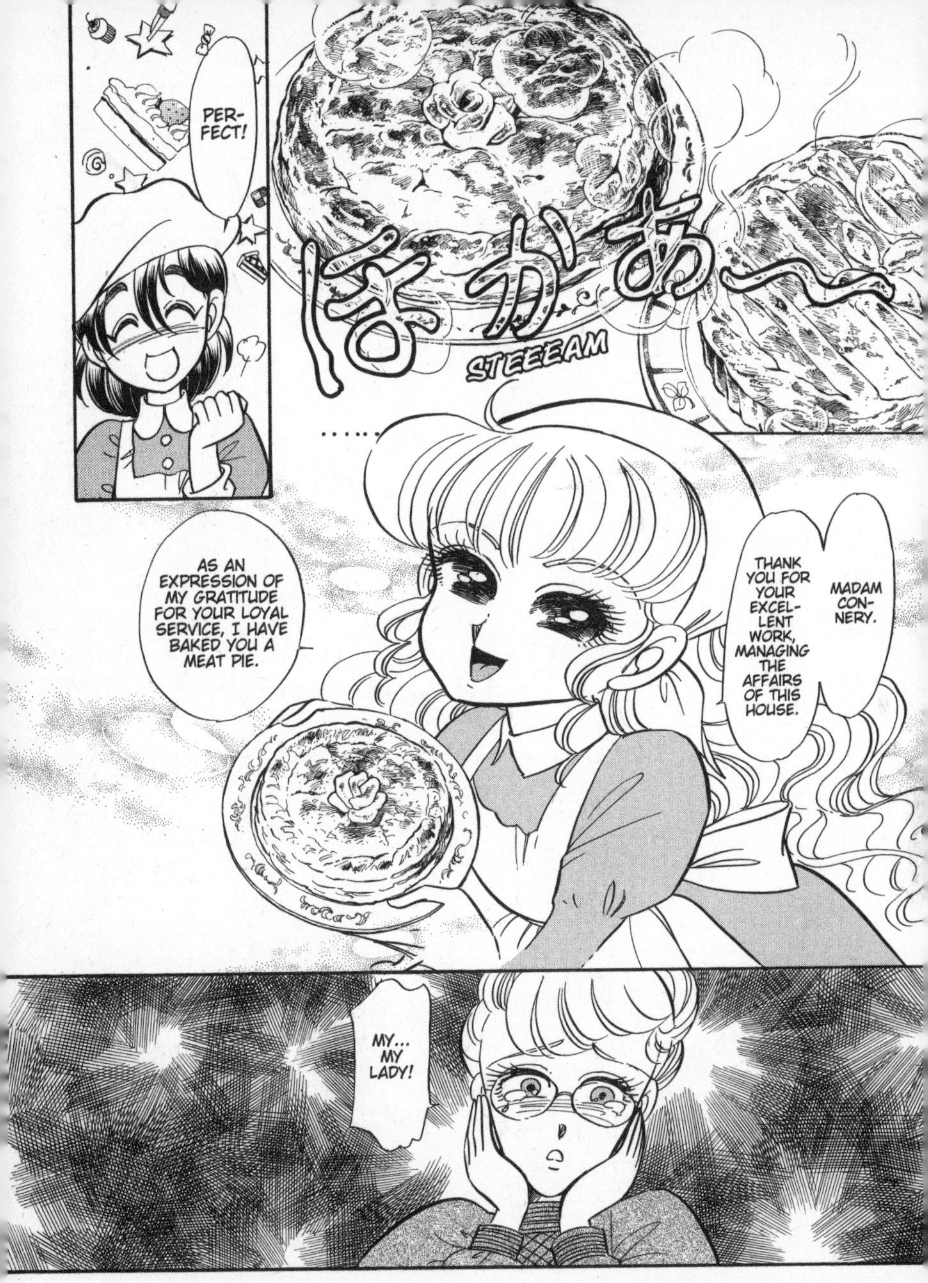
STEEEAM
PERFECT!
......
MADAM CONNERY.
THANK YOU FOR YOUR EXCELLENT WORK, MANAGING THE AFFAIRS OF THIS HOUSE.
AS AN EXPRESSION OF MY GRATITUDE FOR YOUR LOYAL SERVICE, I HAVE BAKED YOU A MEAT PIE.
MY... MY LADY!

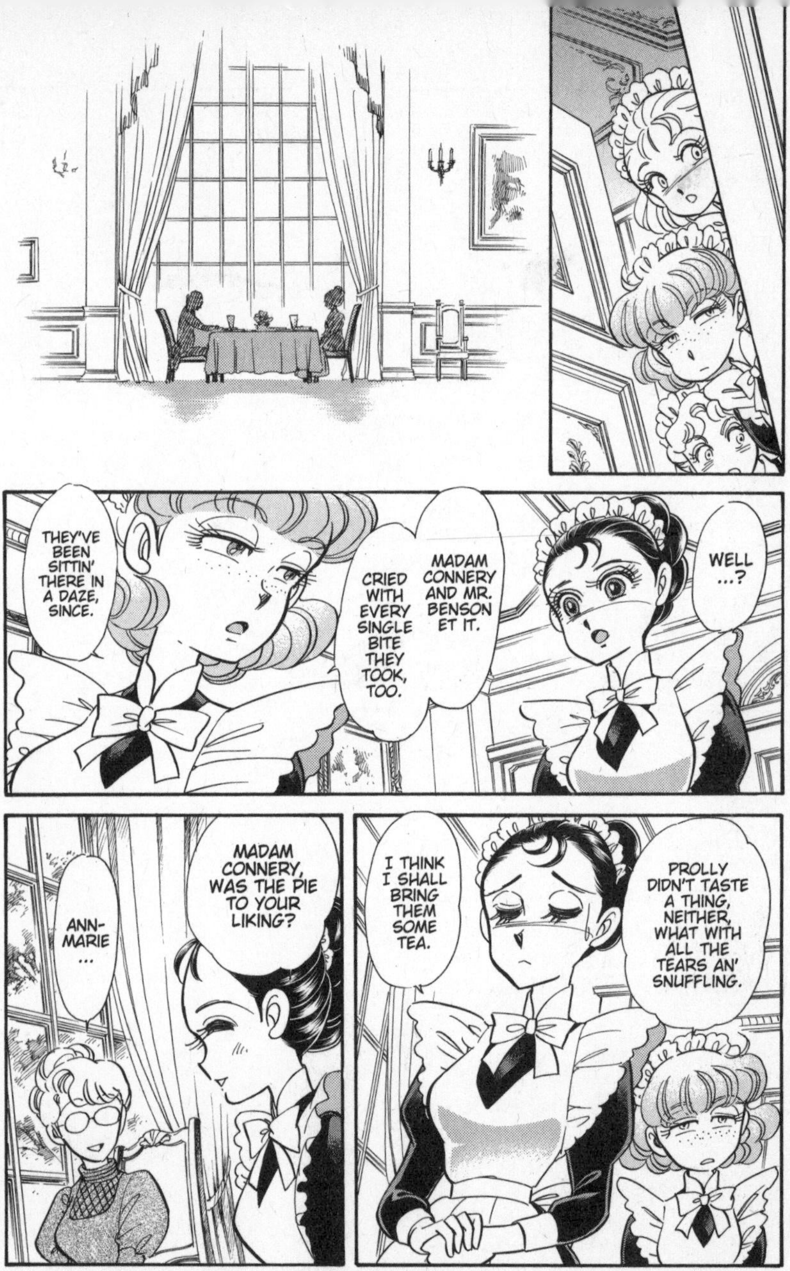
WELL ...?
MADAM CONNERY AND MR. BENSON ET IT.
CRIED WITH EVERY SINGLE BITE THEY TOOK, TOO.
THEY'VE BEEN SITTIN' THERE IN A DAZE, SINCE.
PROLLY DIDN'T TASTE A THING, NEITHER, WHAT WITH ALL THE TEARS AN' SNUFFLING.
I THINK I SHALL BRING THEM SOME TEA.
MADAM CONNERY, WAS THE PIE TO YOUR LIKING?
ANN-MARIE ...

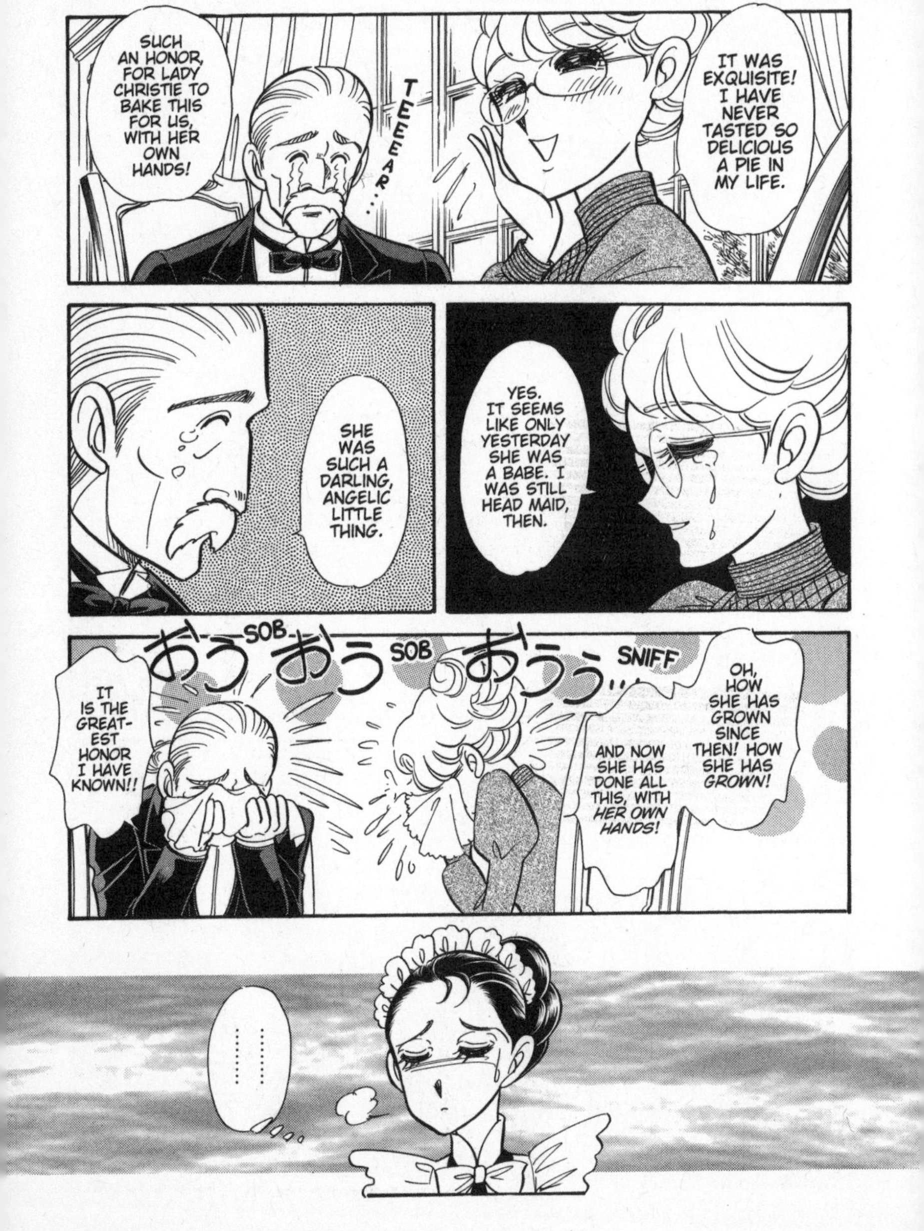
IT WAS EXQUISITE! I HAVE NEVER TASTED SO DELICIOUS A PIE IN MY LIFE.
TEEEEAR...
SUCH AN HONOR, FOR LADY CHRISTIE TO BAKE THIS FOR US, WITH HER OWN HANDS!
YES. IT SEEMS LIKE ONLY YESTERDAY SHE WAS A BABE. I WAS STILL HEAD MAID, THEN.
SHE WAS SUCH A DARLING, ANGELIC LITTLE THING.
OH, HOW SHE HAS GROWN SINCE THEN! HOW SHE HAS GROWN!
AND NOW SHE HAS DONE ALL THIS, WITH HER OWN HANDS!
おううぅ... SNIFF
おう SOB
おう SOB
IT IS THE GREATEST HONOR I HAVE KNOWN!!
......

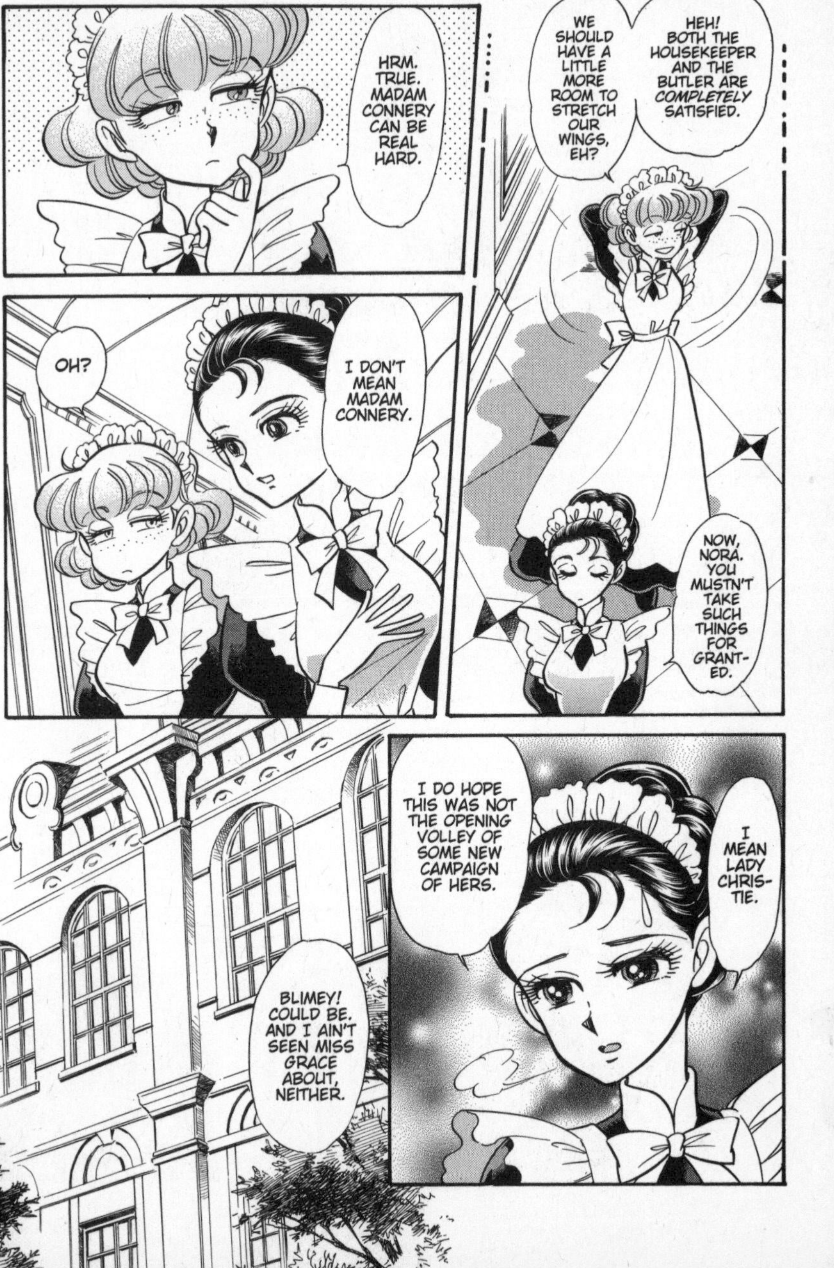
HEH! BOTH THE HOUSEKEEPER AND THE BUTLER ARE COMPLETELY SATISFIED.
WE SHOULD HAVE A LITTLE MORE ROOM TO STRETCH OUR WINGS, EH?
NOW, NORA. YOU MUSTN'T TAKE SUCH THINGS FOR GRANT-ED.
HRM. TRUE. MADAM CONNERY CAN BE REAL HARD.
I DON'T MEAN MADAM CONNERY.
OH?
I MEAN LADY CHRIS-TIE.
I DO HOPE THIS WAS NOT THE OPENING VOLLEY OF SOME NEW CAMPAIGN OF HERS.
BLIMEY! COULD BE. AND I AIN'T SEEN MISS GRACE ABOUT, NEITHER.

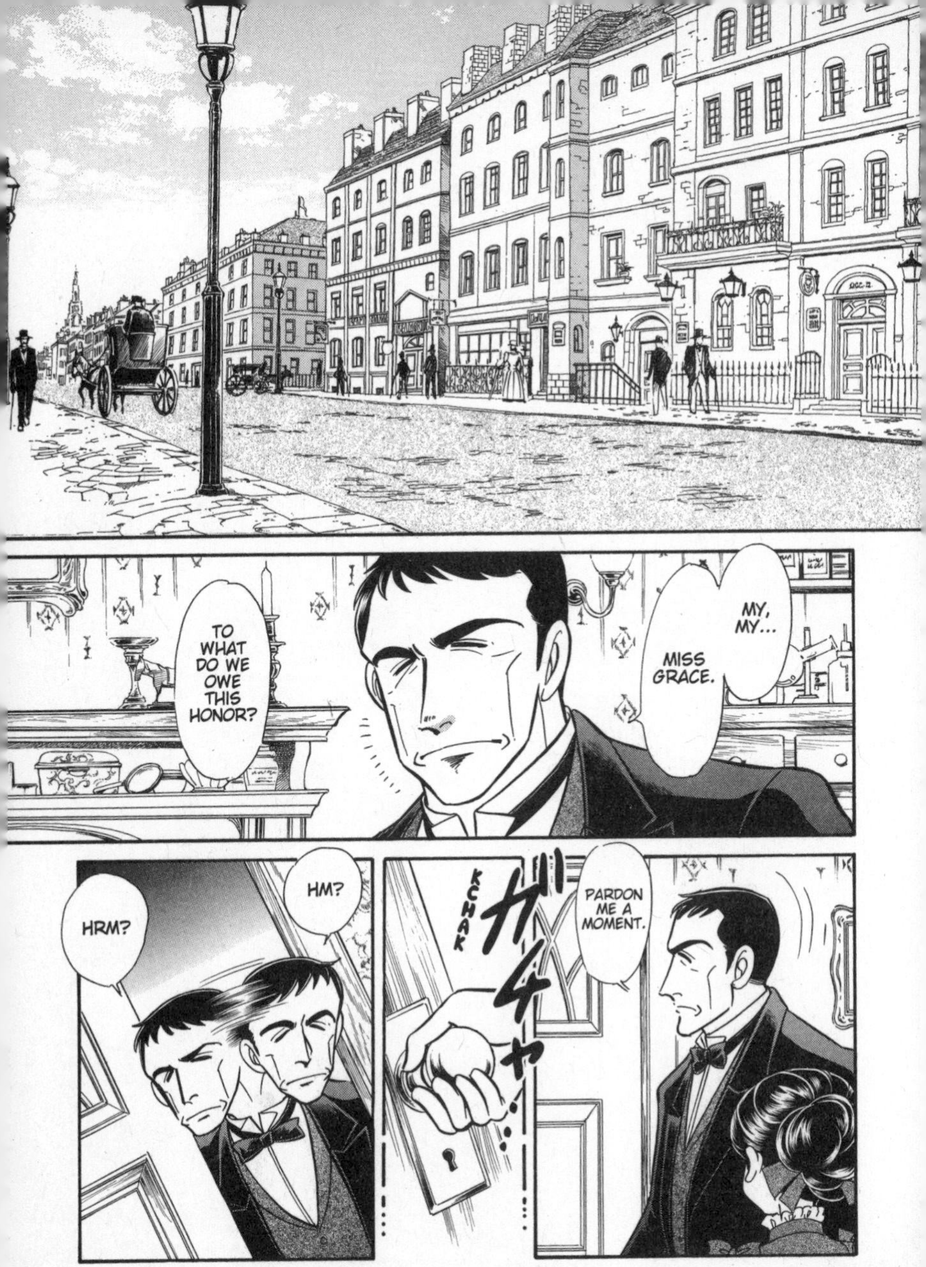
MY, MY... MISS GRACE.
TO WHAT DO WE OWE THIS HONOR?
PARDON ME A MOMENT.
KCHAK
HM?
HRM?

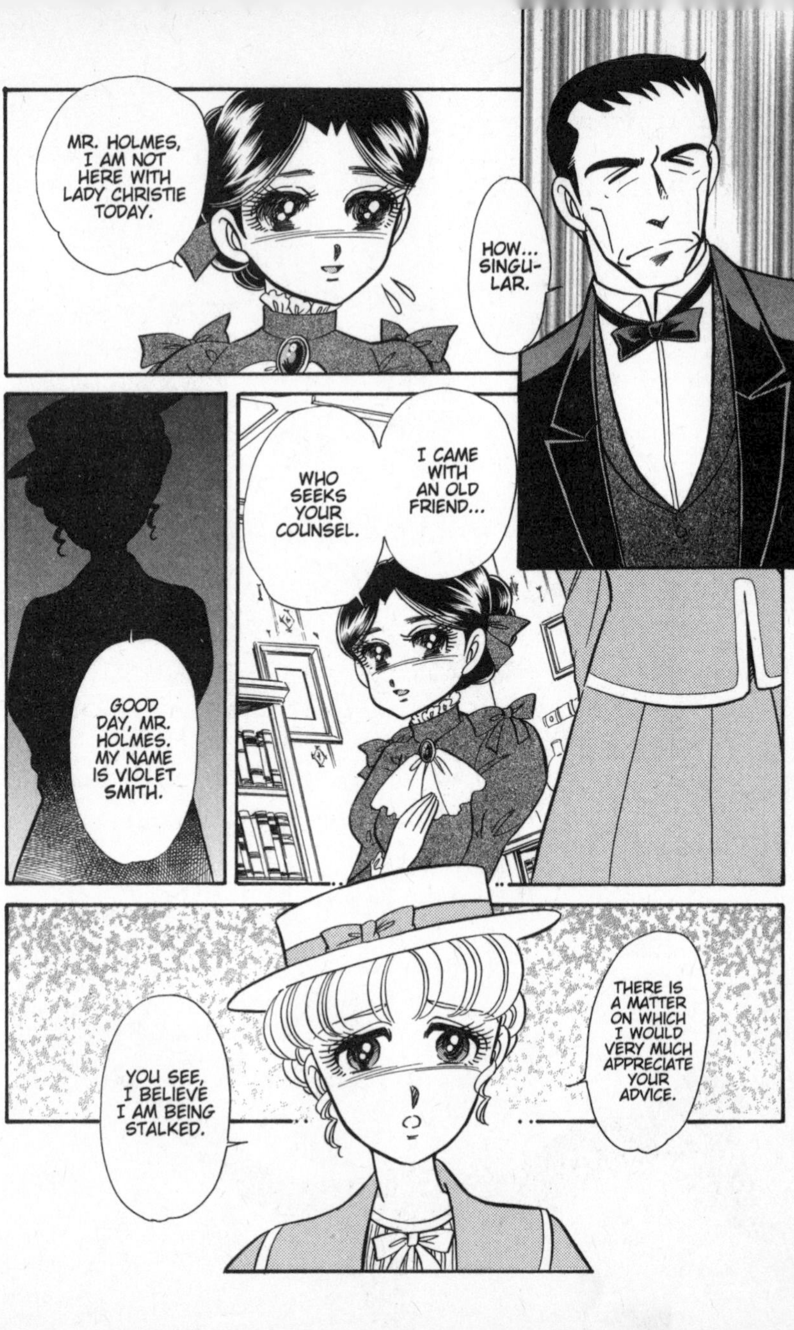
HOW... SINGU-LAR.
MR. HOLMES, I AM NOT HERE WITH LADY CHRISTIE TODAY.
I CAME WITH AN OLD FRIEND...
WHO SEEKS YOUR COUNSEL.
GOOD DAY, MR. HOLMES. MY NAME IS VIOLET SMITH.
THERE IS A MATTER ON WHICH I WOULD VERY MUCH APPRECIATE YOUR ADVICE.
YOU SEE, I BELIEVE I AM BEING STALKED.

The Adventure of the Solitary Cyclist (2)

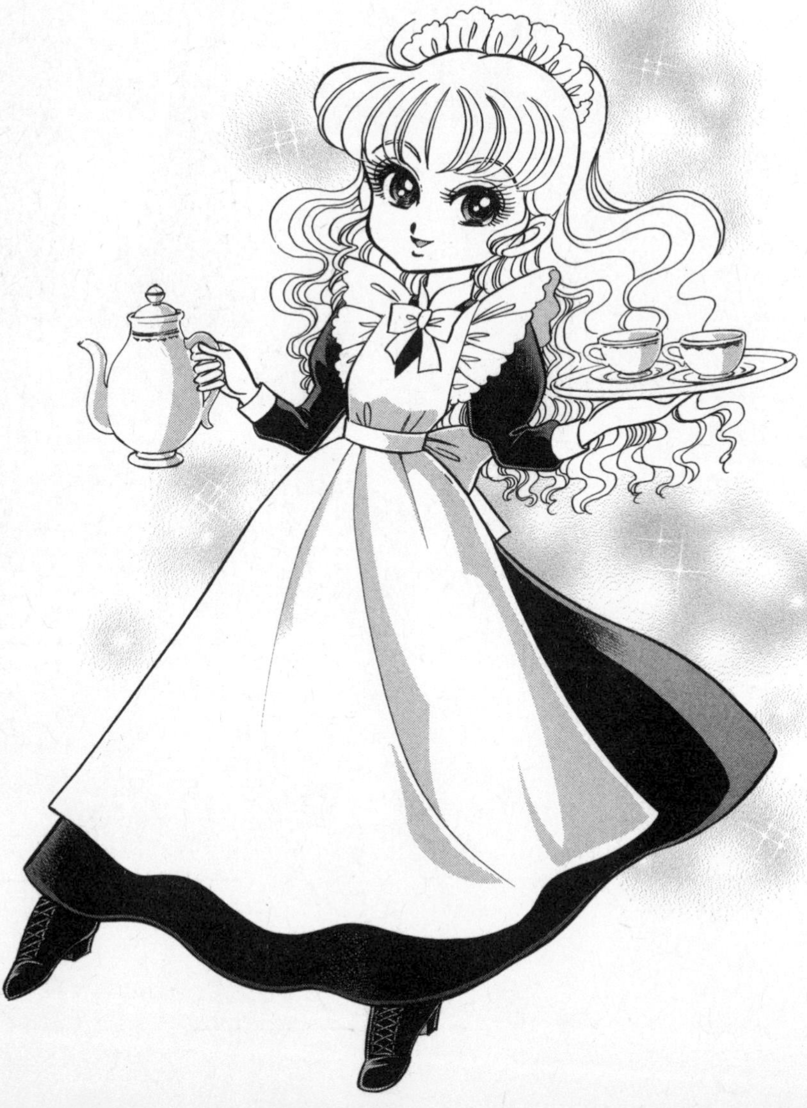

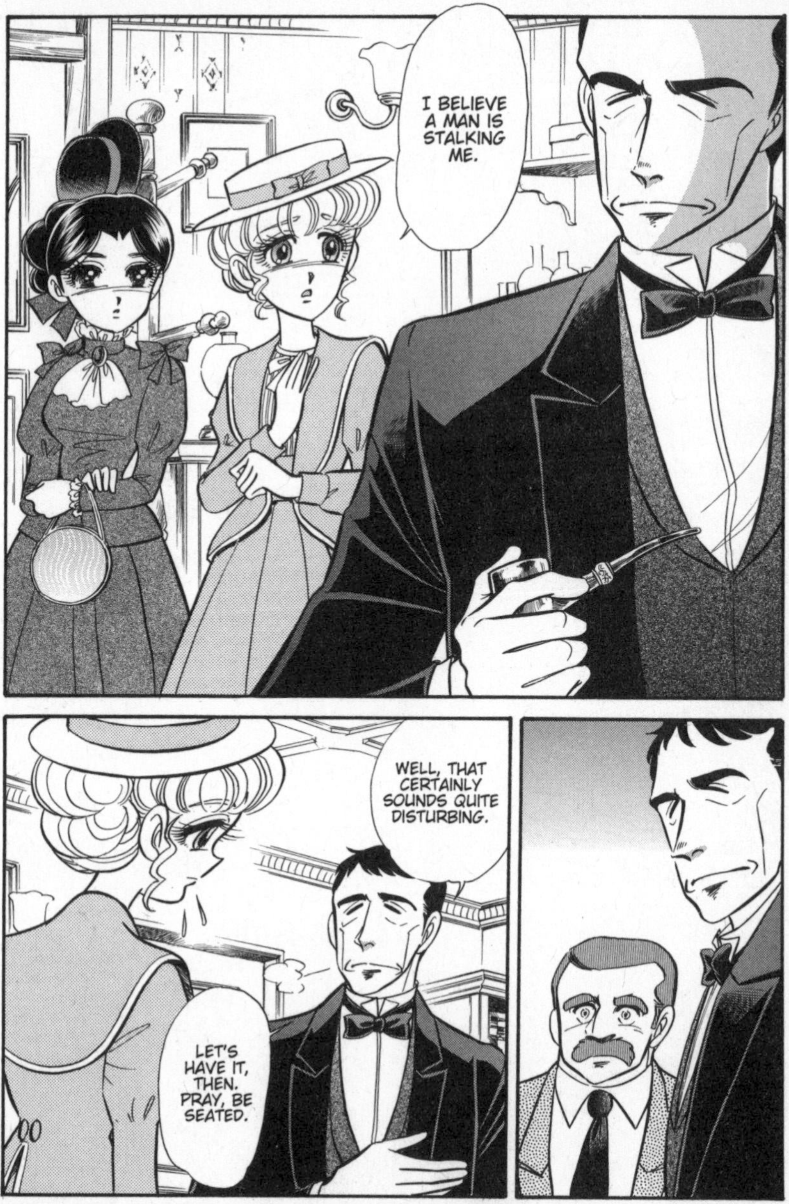
I BELIEVE A MAN IS STALKING ME.
WELL, THAT CERTAINLY SOUNDS QUITE DISTURBING.
LET'S HAVE IT, THEN. PRAY, BE SEATED.

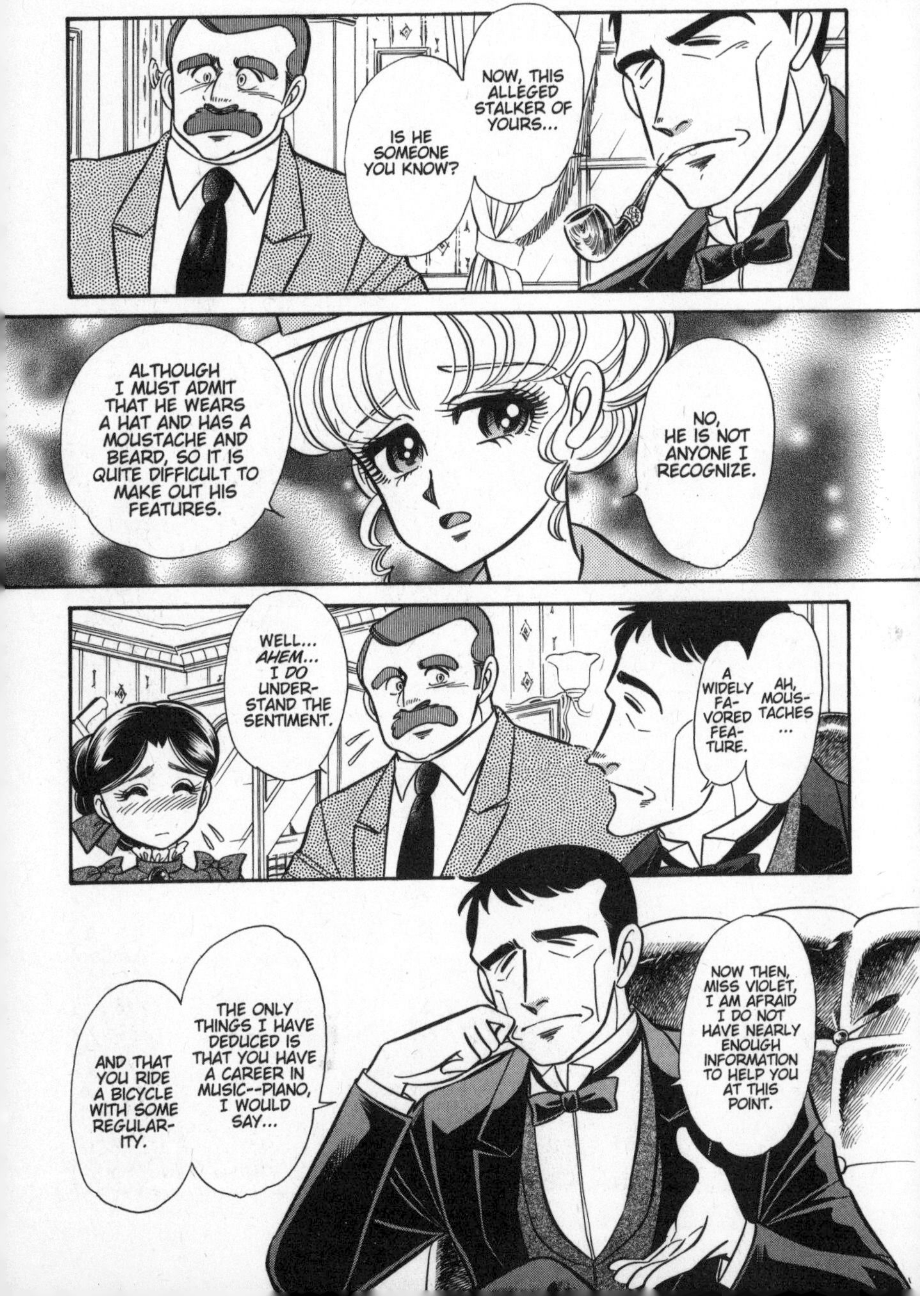
NOW, THIS ALLEGED STALKER OF YOURS...
IS HE SOMEONE YOU KNOW?
NO, HE IS NOT ANYONE I RECOGNIZE.
ALTHOUGH I MUST ADMIT THAT HE WEARS A HAT AND HAS A MOUSTACHE AND BEARD, SO IT IS QUITE DIFFICULT TO MAKE OUT HIS FEATURES.
AH, MOUS-TACHES...
A WIDELY FA-VORED FEA-TURE.
WELL... *AHEM*... I DO UNDER-STAND THE SENTIMENT.
NOW THEN, MISS VIOLET, I AM AFRAID I DO NOT HAVE NEARLY ENOUGH INFORMATION TO HELP YOU AT THIS POINT.
THE ONLY THINGS I HAVE DEDUCED IS THAT YOU HAVE A CAREER IN MUSIC--PIANO, I WOULD SAY...
AND THAT YOU RIDE A BICYCLE WITH SOME REGULAR-ITY.

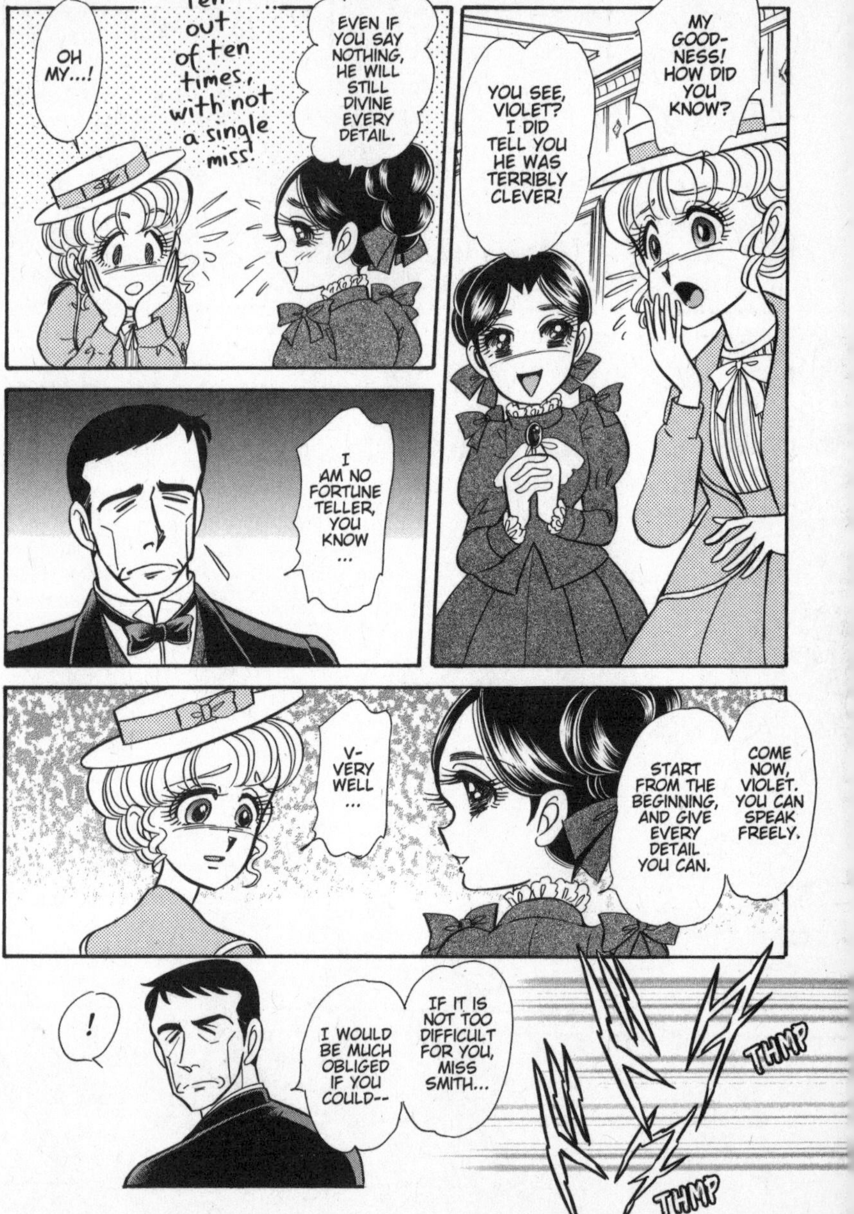
MY GOODNESS! HOW DID YOU KNOW?
YOU SEE, VIOLET? I DID TELL YOU HE WAS TERRIBLY CLEVER!
EVEN IF YOU SAY NOTHING, HE WILL STILL DIVINE EVERY DETAIL.
Ten out of ten times, with not a single miss!
OH MY...!
I AM NO FORTUNE TELLER, YOU KNOW ...
COME NOW, VIOLET. YOU CAN SPEAK FREELY.
START FROM THE BEGINNING, AND GIVE EVERY DETAIL YOU CAN.
V-VERY WELL ...
THMP
THMP
IF IT IS NOT TOO DIFFICULT FOR YOU, MISS SMITH...
I WOULD BE MUCH OBLIGED IF YOU COULD--
!

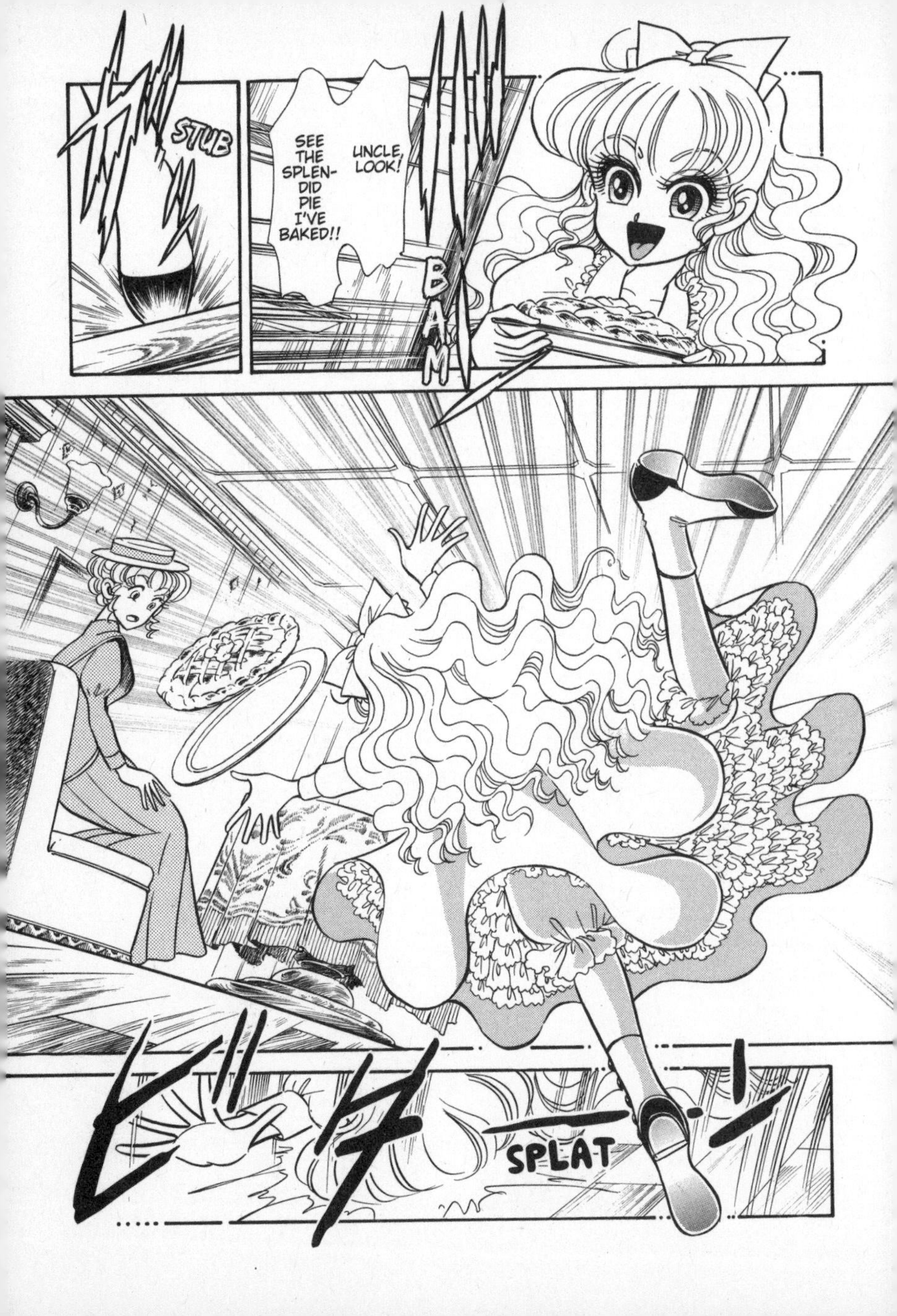
UNCLE, LOOK!
SEE THE SPLEN-DID PIE I'VE BAKED!!
BAM
STUB
SPLAT

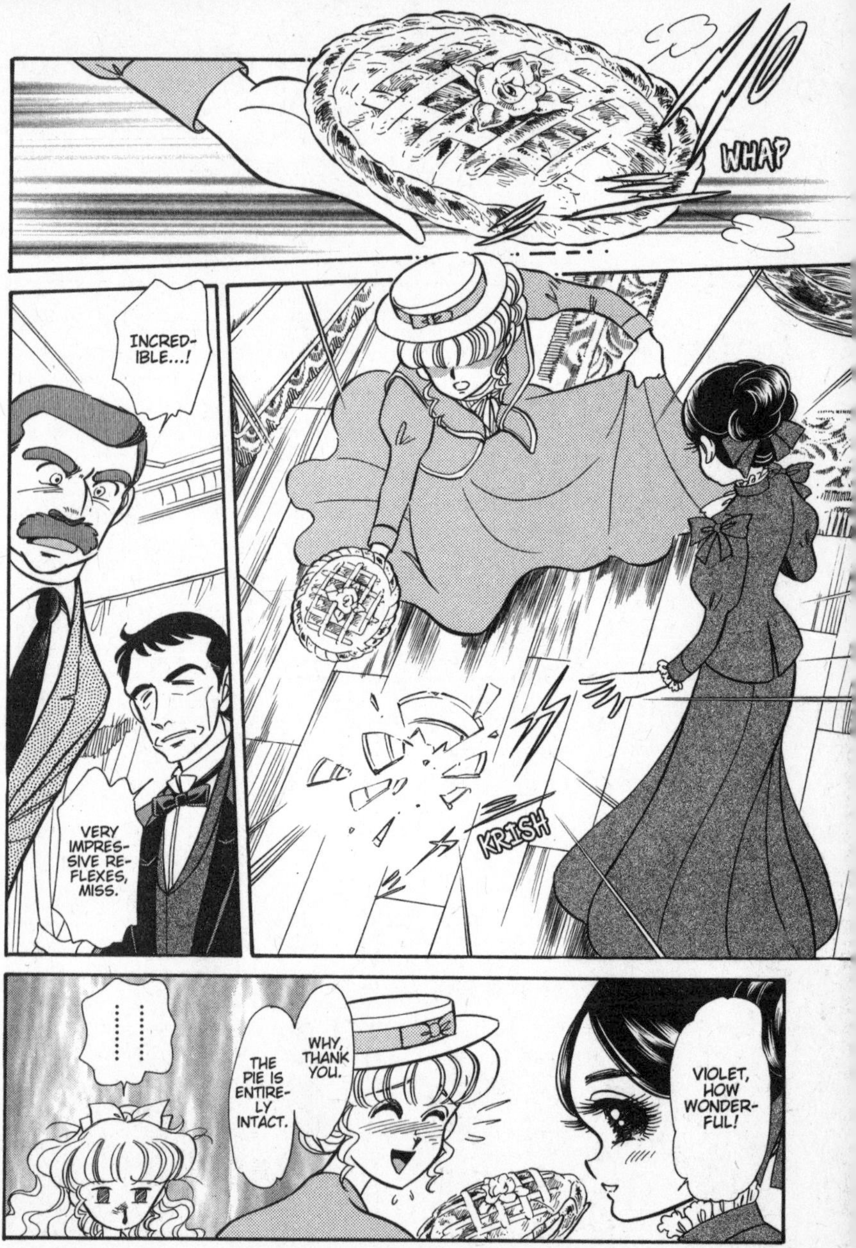
WHAP
KRISH
INCREDIBLE...!
VERY IMPRESSIVE REFLEXES, MISS.
VIOLET, HOW WONDERFUL!
WHY, THANK YOU.
THE PIE IS ENTIRELY INTACT.
......

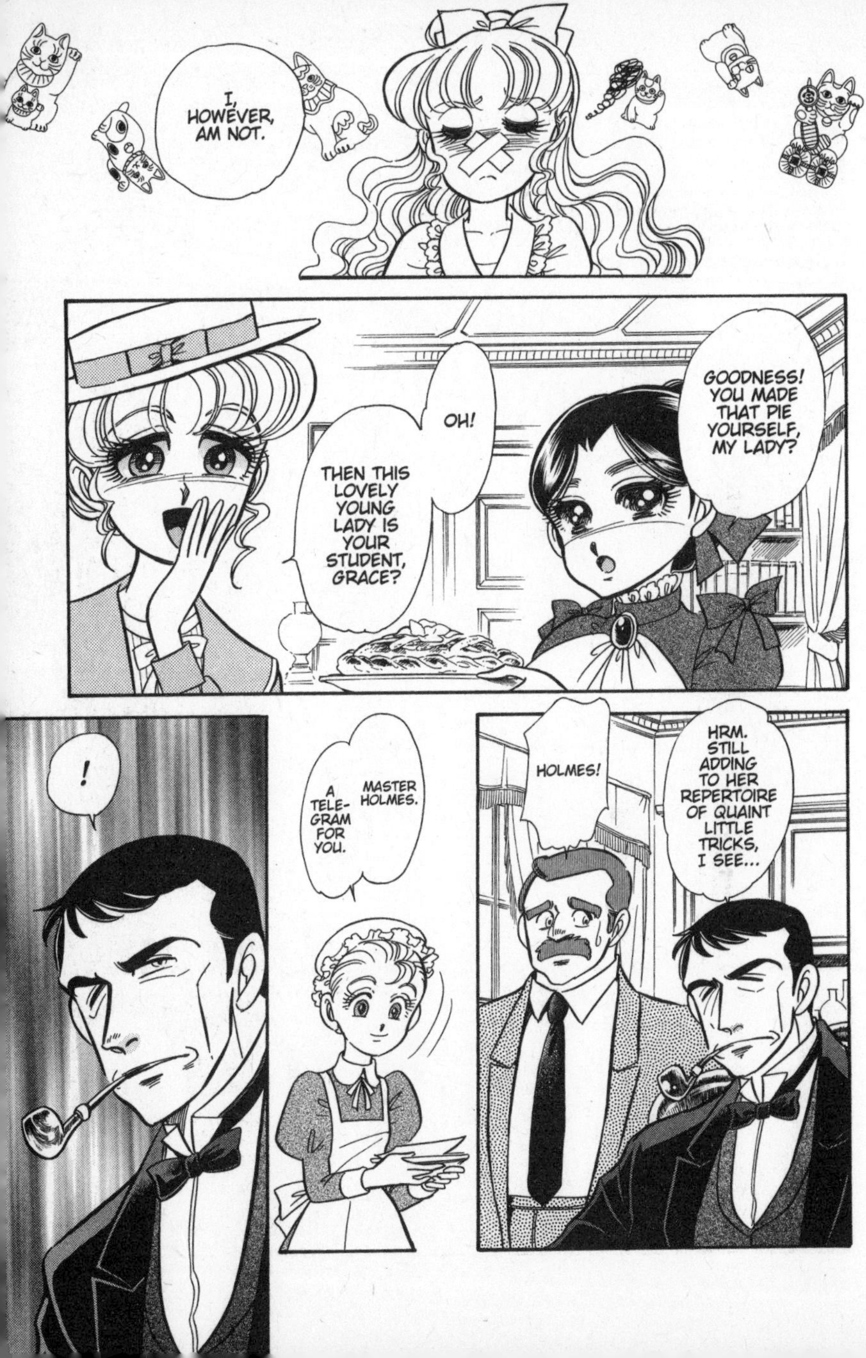
I, HOWEVER, AM NOT.
GOODNESS! YOU MADE THAT PIE YOURSELF, MY LADY?
OH!
THEN THIS LOVELY YOUNG LADY IS YOUR STUDENT, GRACE?
HRM. STILL ADDING TO HER REPERTOIRE OF QUAINT LITTLE TRICKS, I SEE...
HOLMES!
MASTER HOLMES.
A TELE-GRAM FOR YOU.
!

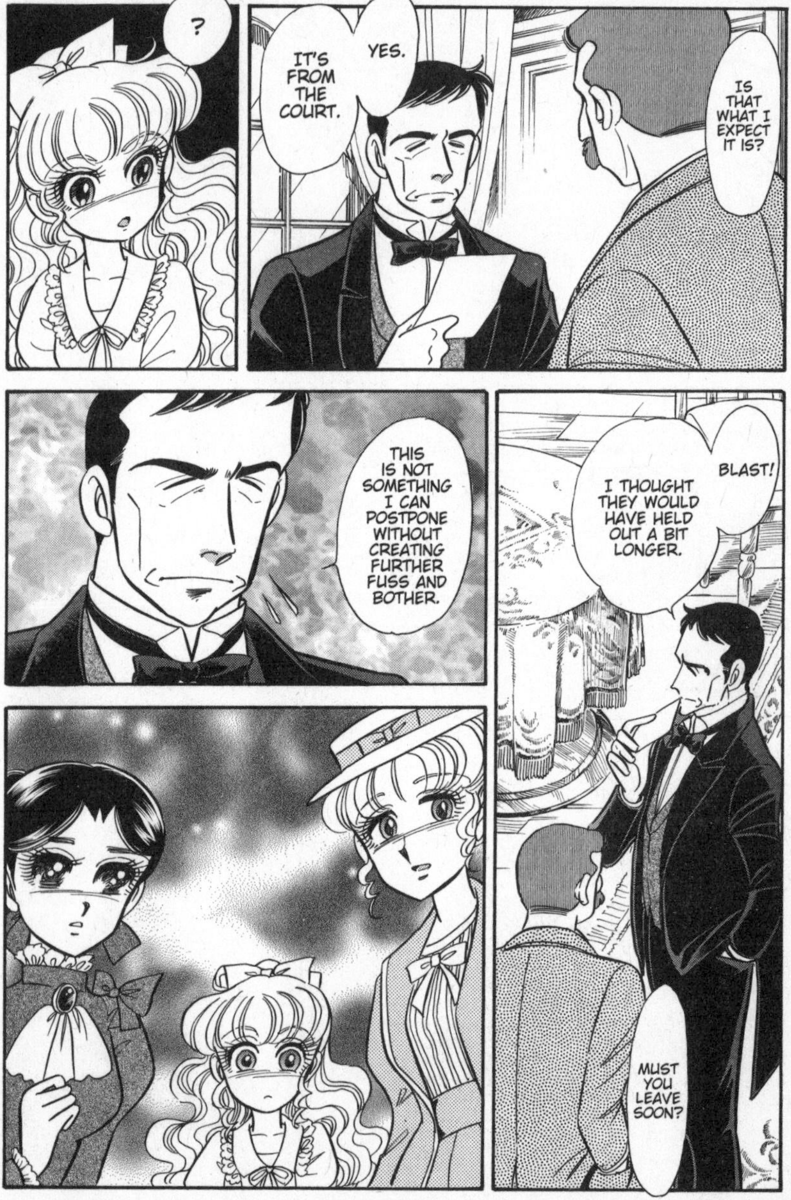
IS THAT WHAT I EXPECT IT IS?
YES.
IT'S FROM THE COURT.
?
BLAST!
I THOUGHT THEY WOULD HAVE HELD OUT A BIT LONGER.
MUST YOU LEAVE SOON?
THIS IS NOT SOMETHING I CAN POSTPONE WITHOUT CREATING FURTHER FUSS AND BOTHER.

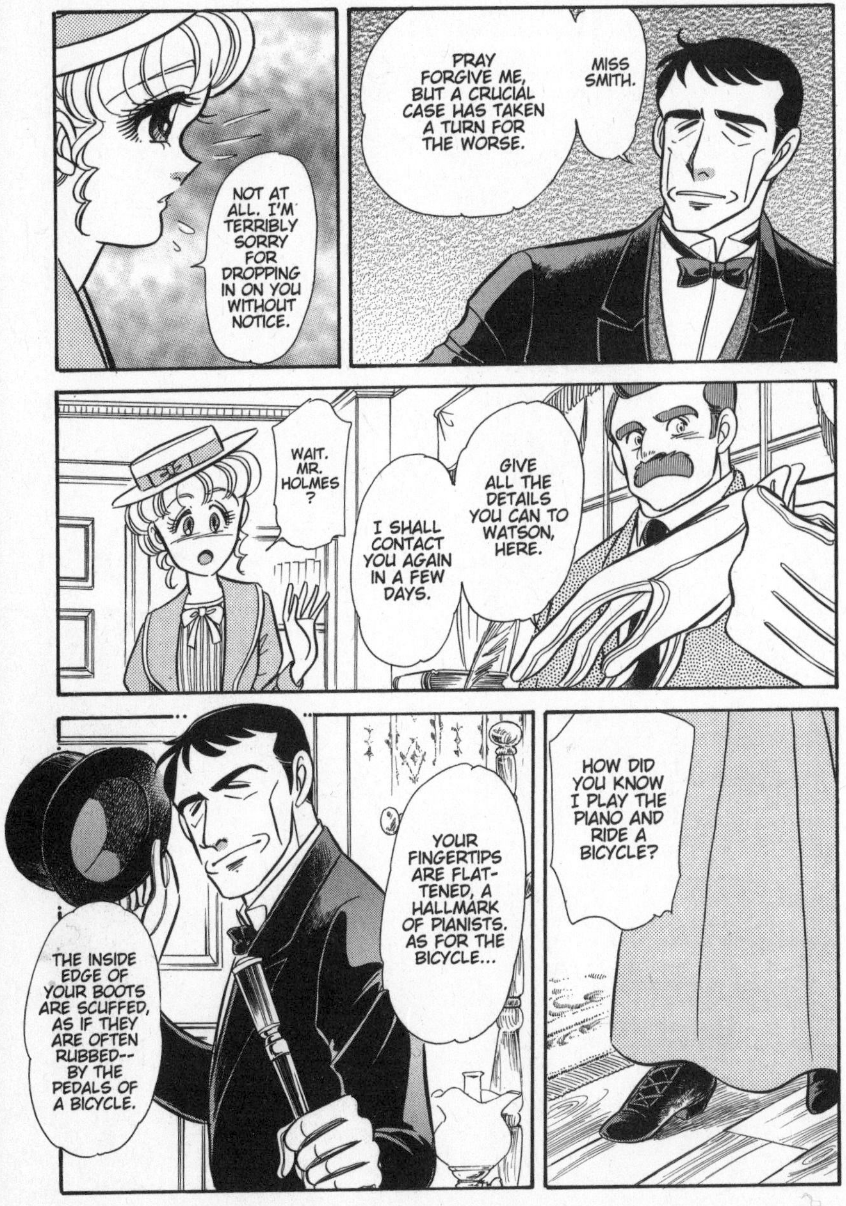
MISS SMITH.
PRAY FORGIVE ME, BUT A CRUCIAL CASE HAS TAKEN A TURN FOR THE WORSE.
NOT AT ALL. I'M TERRIBLY SORRY FOR DROPPING IN ON YOU WITHOUT NOTICE.
GIVE ALL THE DETAILS YOU CAN TO WATSON, HERE.
I SHALL CONTACT YOU AGAIN IN A FEW DAYS.
WAIT. MR. HOLMES?
HOW DID YOU KNOW I PLAY THE PIANO AND RIDE A BICYCLE?
YOUR FINGERTIPS ARE FLAT-TENED, A HALLMARK OF PIANISTS. AS FOR THE BICYCLE...
THE INSIDE EDGE OF YOUR BOOTS ARE SCUFFED, AS IF THEY ARE OFTEN RUBBED-- BY THE PEDALS OF A BICYCLE.

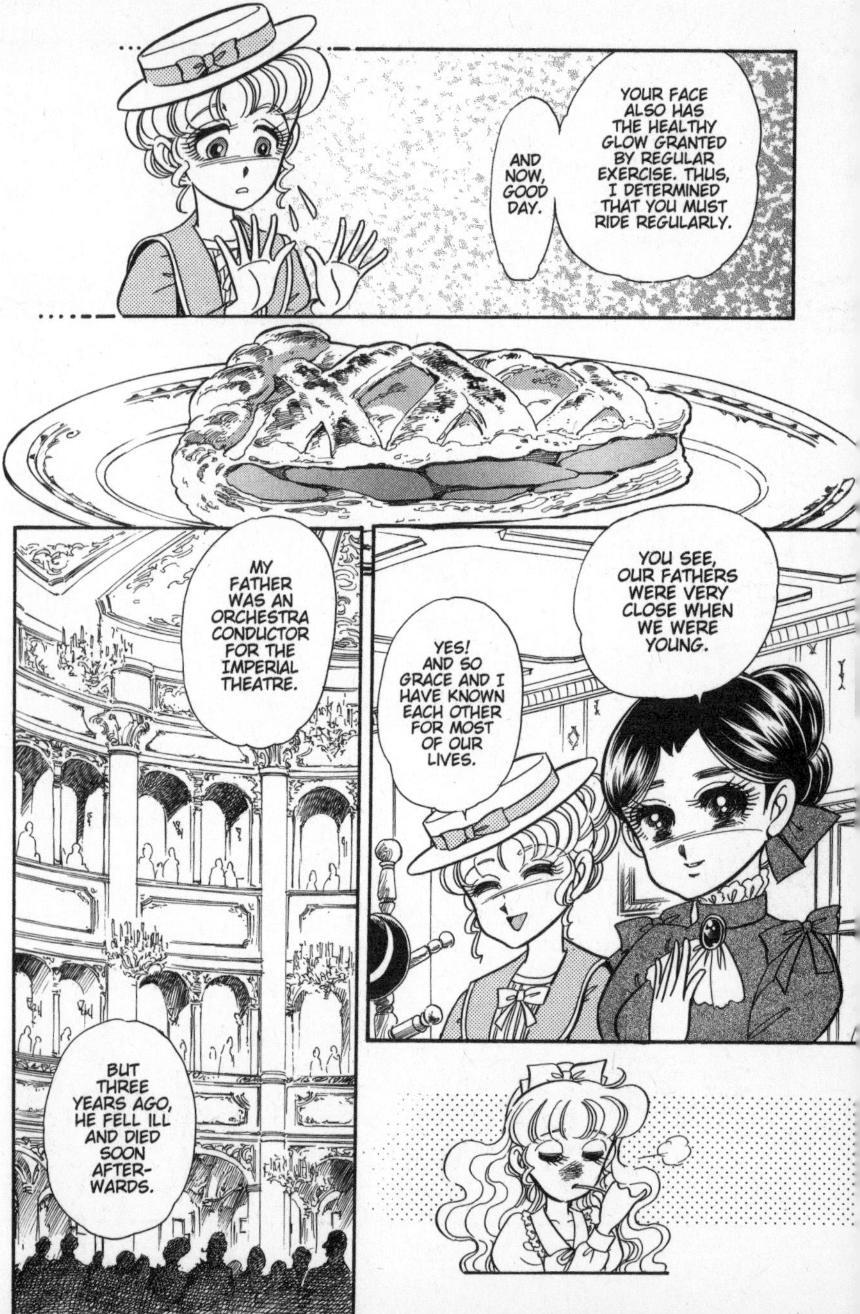
YOUR FACE ALSO HAS THE HEALTHY GLOW GRANTED BY REGULAR EXERCISE. THUS, I DETERMINED THAT YOU MUST RIDE REGULARLY.
AND NOW, GOOD DAY.
YOU SEE, OUR FATHERS WERE VERY CLOSE WHEN WE WERE YOUNG.
YES! AND SO GRACE AND I HAVE KNOWN EACH OTHER FOR MOST OF OUR LIVES.
MY FATHER WAS AN ORCHESTRA CONDUCTOR FOR THE IMPERIAL THEATRE.
BUT THREE YEARS AGO, HE FELL ILL AND DIED SOON AFTER-WARDS.

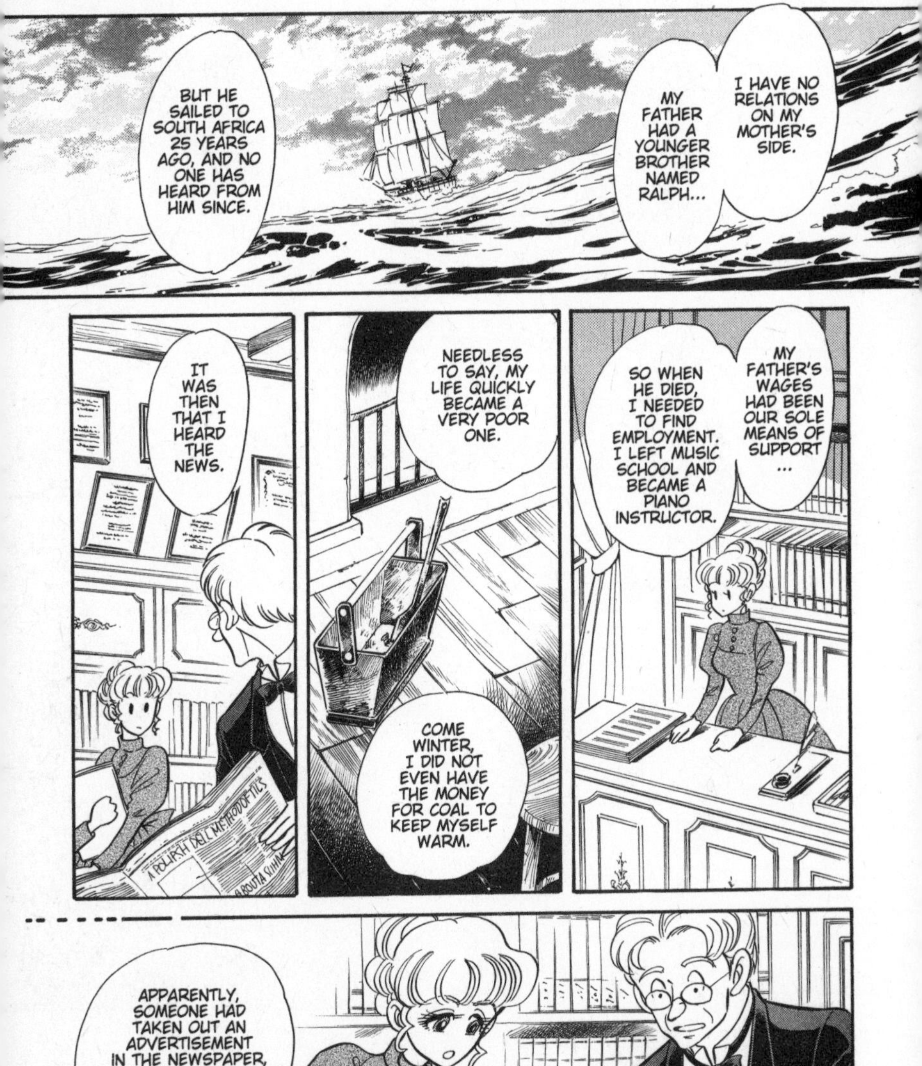
I HAVE NO RELATIONS ON MY MOTHER'S SIDE.
MY FATHER HAD A YOUNGER BROTHER NAMED RALPH...
BUT HE SAILED TO SOUTH AFRICA 25 YEARS AGO, AND NO ONE HAS HEARD FROM HIM SINCE.
MY FATHER'S WAGES HAD BEEN OUR SOLE MEANS OF SUPPORT ...
SO WHEN HE DIED, I NEEDED TO FIND EMPLOYMENT. I LEFT MUSIC SCHOOL AND BECAME A PIANO INSTRUCTOR.
NEEDLESS TO SAY, MY LIFE QUICKLY BECAME A VERY POOR ONE.
COME WINTER, I DID NOT EVEN HAVE THE MONEY FOR COAL TO KEEP MYSELF WARM.
IT WAS THEN THAT I HEARD THE NEWS.
APPARENTLY, SOMEONE HAD TAKEN OUT AN ADVERTISEMENT IN THE NEWSPAPER, LOOKING FOR MY FAMILY'S WHERE-ABOUTS.

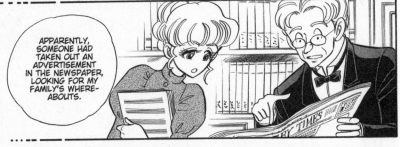

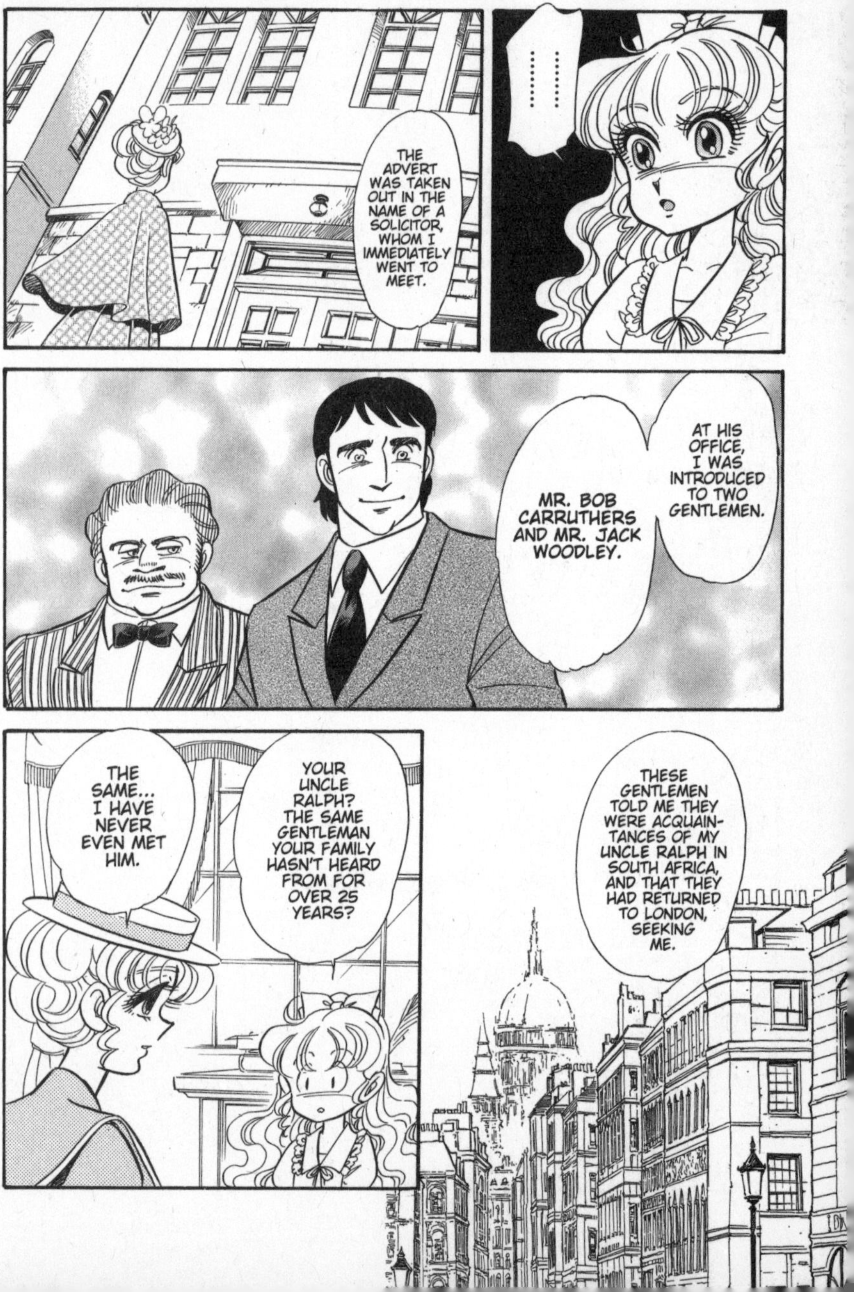
......
THE ADVERT WAS TAKEN OUT IN THE NAME OF A SOLICITOR, WHOM I IMMEDIATELY WENT TO MEET.
AT HIS OFFICE, I WAS INTRODUCED TO TWO GENTLEMEN.
MR. BOB CARRUTHERS AND MR. JACK WOODLEY.
THESE GENTLEMEN TOLD ME THEY WERE ACQUAIN-TANCES OF MY UNCLE RALPH IN SOUTH AFRICA, AND THAT THEY HAD RETURNED TO LONDON, SEEKING ME.
YOUR UNCLE RALPH? THE SAME GENTLEMAN YOUR FAMILY HASN'T HEARD FROM FOR OVER 25 YEARS?
THE SAME... I HAVE NEVER EVEN MET HIM.

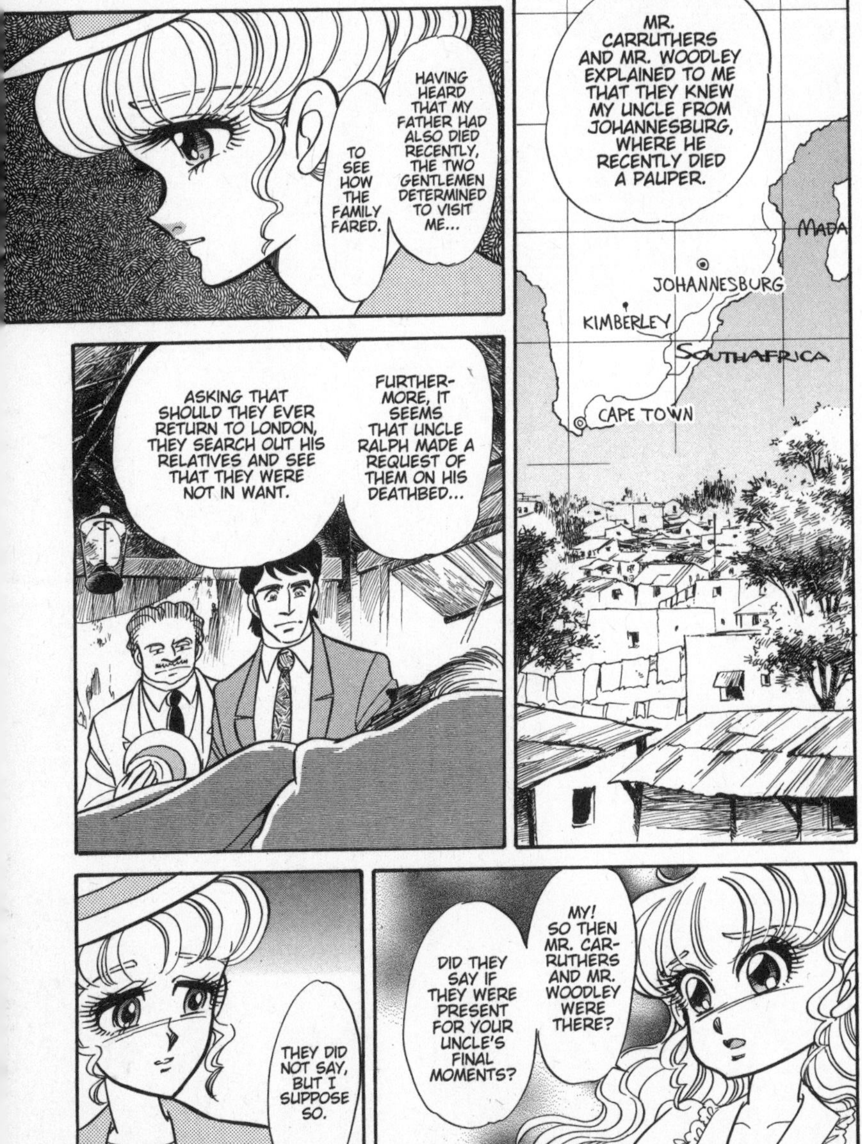
MR. CARRUTHERS AND MR. WOODLEY EXPLAINED TO ME THAT THEY KNEW MY UNCLE FROM JOHANNESBURG, WHERE HE RECENTLY DIED A PAUPER.
MADA
JOHANNESBURG
KIMBERLEY
SOUTHAFRICA
CAPE TOWN
HAVING HEARD THAT MY FATHER HAD ALSO DIED RECENTLY, THE TWO GENTLEMEN DETERMINED TO VISIT ME...
TO SEE HOW THE FAMILY FARED.
FURTHERMORE, IT SEEMS THAT UNCLE RALPH MADE A REQUEST OF THEM ON HIS DEATHBED...
ASKING THAT SHOULD THEY EVER RETURN TO LONDON, THEY SEARCH OUT HIS RELATIVES AND SEE THAT THEY WERE NOT IN WANT.
MY! SO THEN MR. CARRUTHERS AND MR. WOODLEY WERE THERE?
DID THEY SAY IF THEY WERE PRESENT FOR YOUR UNCLE'S FINAL MOMENTS?
THEY DID NOT SAY, BUT I SUPPOSE SO.

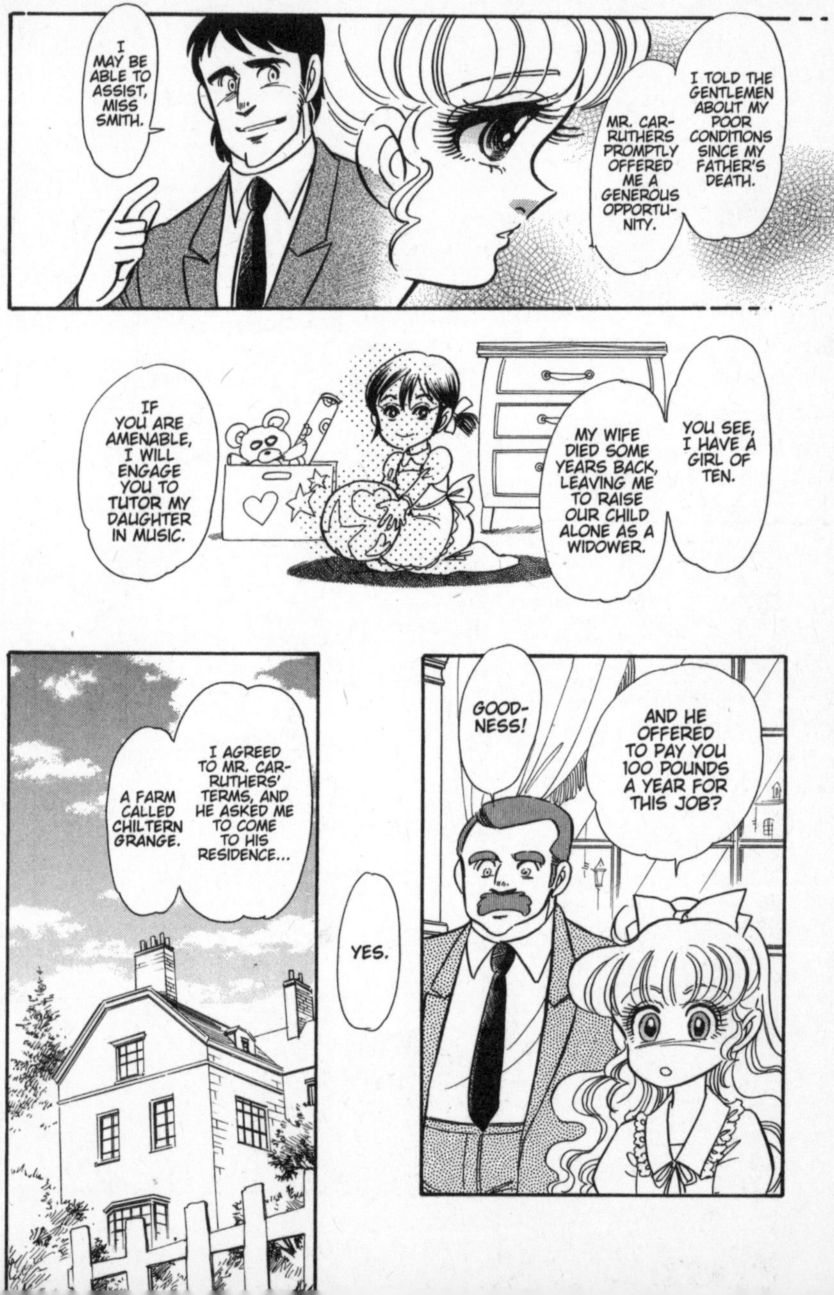
I TOLD THE GENTLEMEN ABOUT MY POOR CONDITIONS SINCE MY FATHER'S DEATH.
MR. CAR-RUTHERS PROMPTLY OFFERED ME A GENEROUS OPPORTU-NITY.
I MAY BE ABLE TO ASSIST, MISS SMITH.
YOU SEE, I HAVE A GIRL OF TEN.
MY WIFE DIED SOME YEARS BACK, LEAVING ME TO RAISE OUR CHILD ALONE AS A WIDOWER.
IF YOU ARE AMENABLE, I WILL ENGAGE YOU TO TUTOR MY DAUGHTER IN MUSIC.
AND HE OFFERED TO PAY YOU 100 POUNDS A YEAR FOR THIS JOB?
GOOD-NESS!
YES.
I AGREED TO MR. CAR-RUTHERS' TERMS, AND HE ASKED ME TO COME TO HIS RESIDENCE...
A FARM CALLED CHILTERN GRANGE.

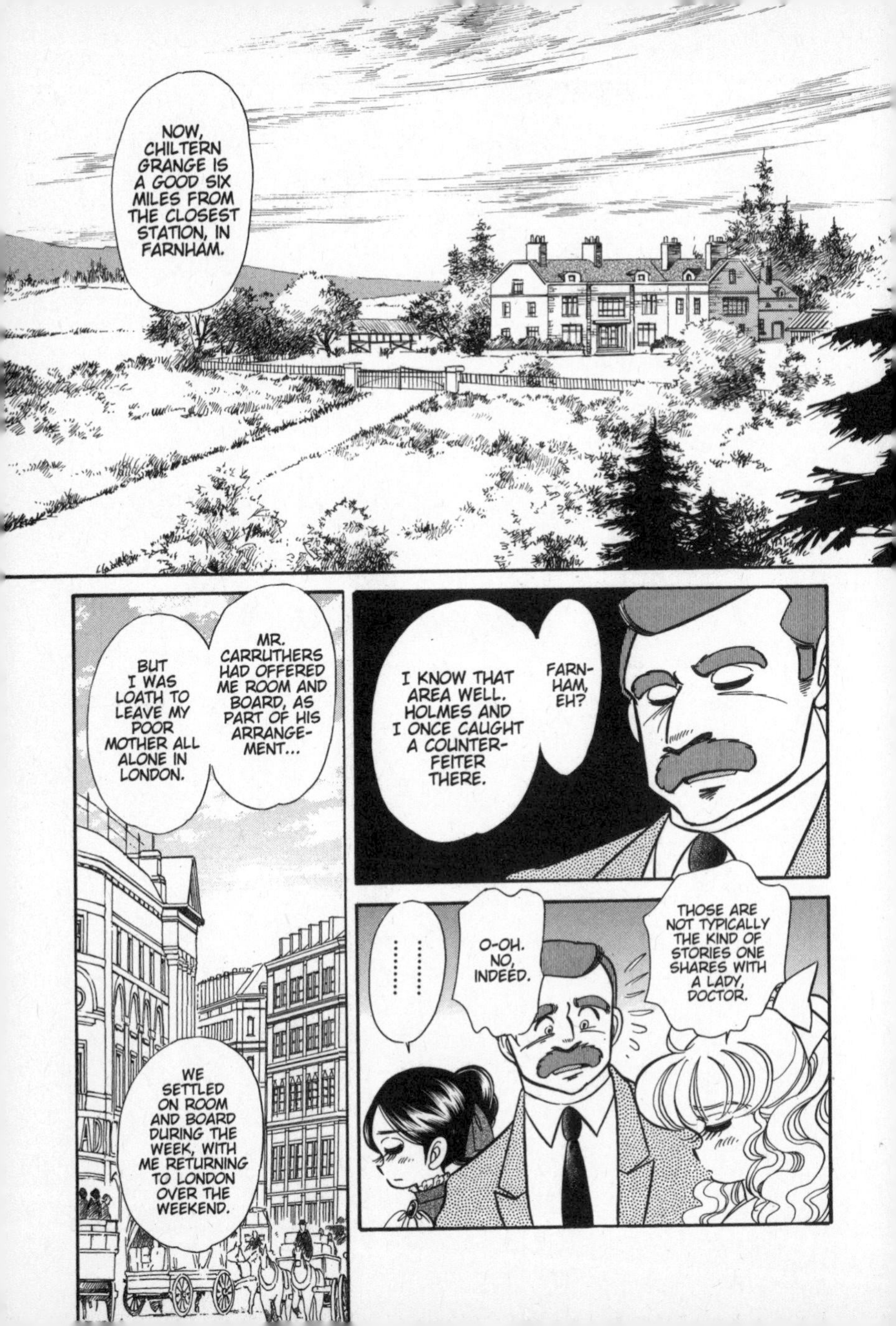
NOW, CHILTERN GRANGE IS A GOOD SIX MILES FROM THE CLOSEST STATION, IN FARNHAM.
FARN-HAM, EH?
I KNOW THAT AREA WELL. HOLMES AND I ONCE CAUGHT A COUNTER-FEITER THERE.
THOSE ARE NOT TYPICALLY THE KIND OF STORIES ONE SHARES WITH A LADY, DOCTOR.
O-OH. NO, INDEED.
......
MR. CARRUTHERS HAD OFFERED ME ROOM AND BOARD, AS PART OF HIS ARRANGE-MENT...
BUT I WAS LOATH TO LEAVE MY POOR MOTHER ALL ALONE IN LONDON.
WE SETTLED ON ROOM AND BOARD DURING THE WEEK, WITH ME RETURNING TO LONDON OVER THE WEEKEND.

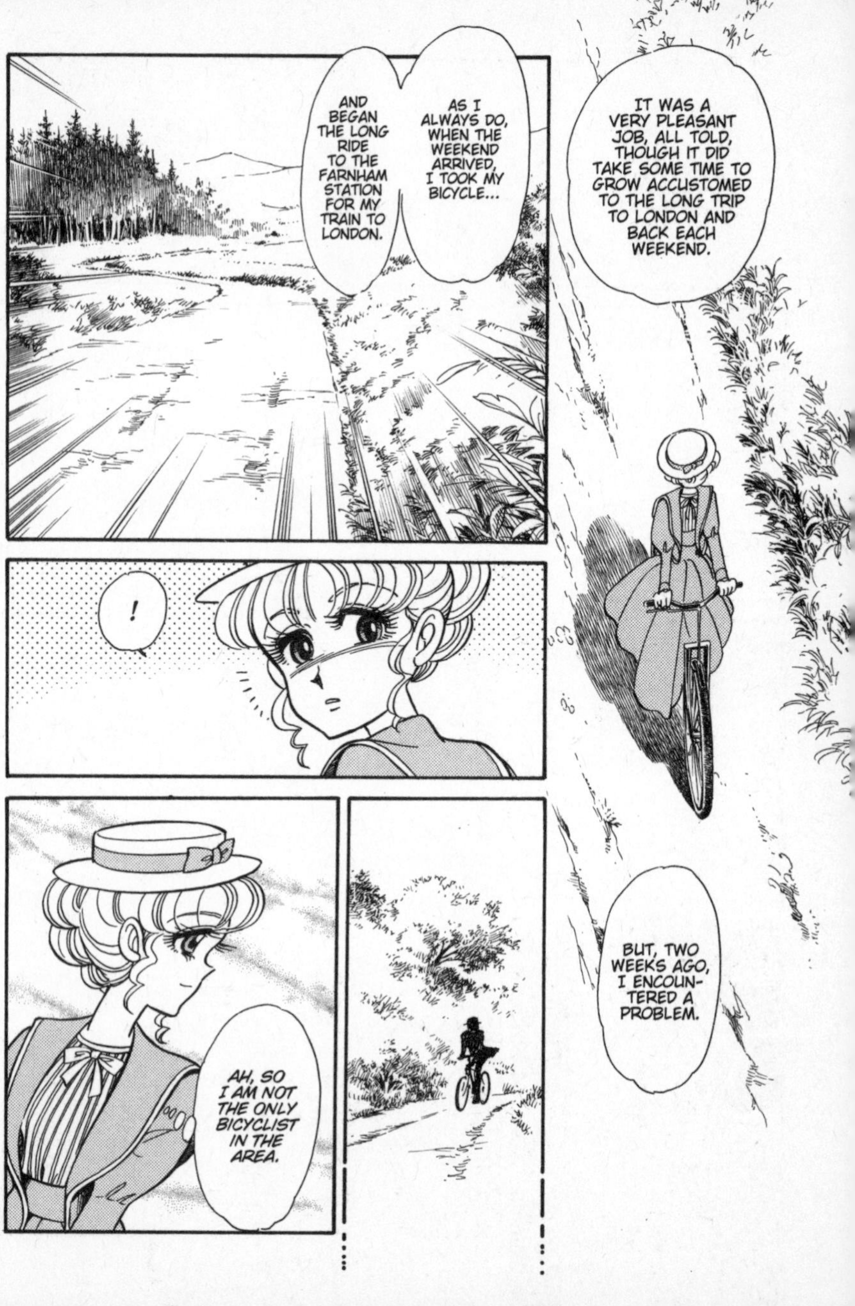
IT WAS A VERY PLEASANT JOB, ALL TOLD, THOUGH IT DID TAKE SOME TIME TO GROW ACCUSTOMED TO THE LONG TRIP TO LONDON AND BACK EACH WEEKEND.
BUT, TWO WEEKS AGO, I ENCOUN-TERED A PROBLEM.
AS I ALWAYS DO, WHEN THE WEEKEND ARRIVED, I TOOK MY BICYCLE...
AND BEGAN THE LONG RIDE TO THE FARNHAM STATION FOR MY TRAIN TO LONDON.
!
AH, SO I AM NOT THE ONLY BICYCLIST IN THE AREA.

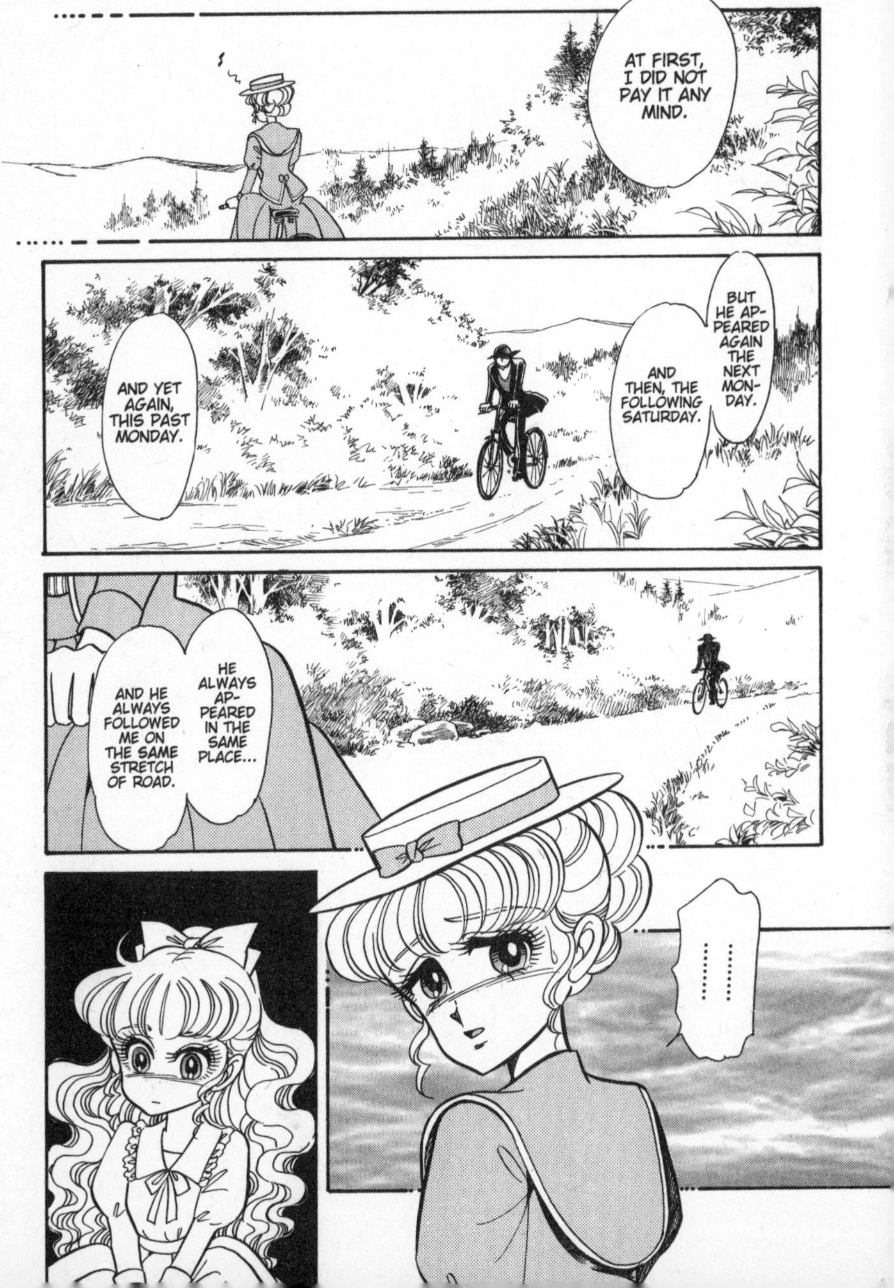
AT FIRST, I DID NOT PAY IT ANY MIND.
BUT HE APPEARED AGAIN THE NEXT MONDAY.
AND THEN, THE FOLLOWING SATURDAY.
AND YET AGAIN, THIS PAST MONDAY.
HE ALWAYS APPEARED IN THE SAME PLACE...
AND HE ALWAYS FOLLOWED ME ON THE SAME STRETCH OF ROAD.
......
......

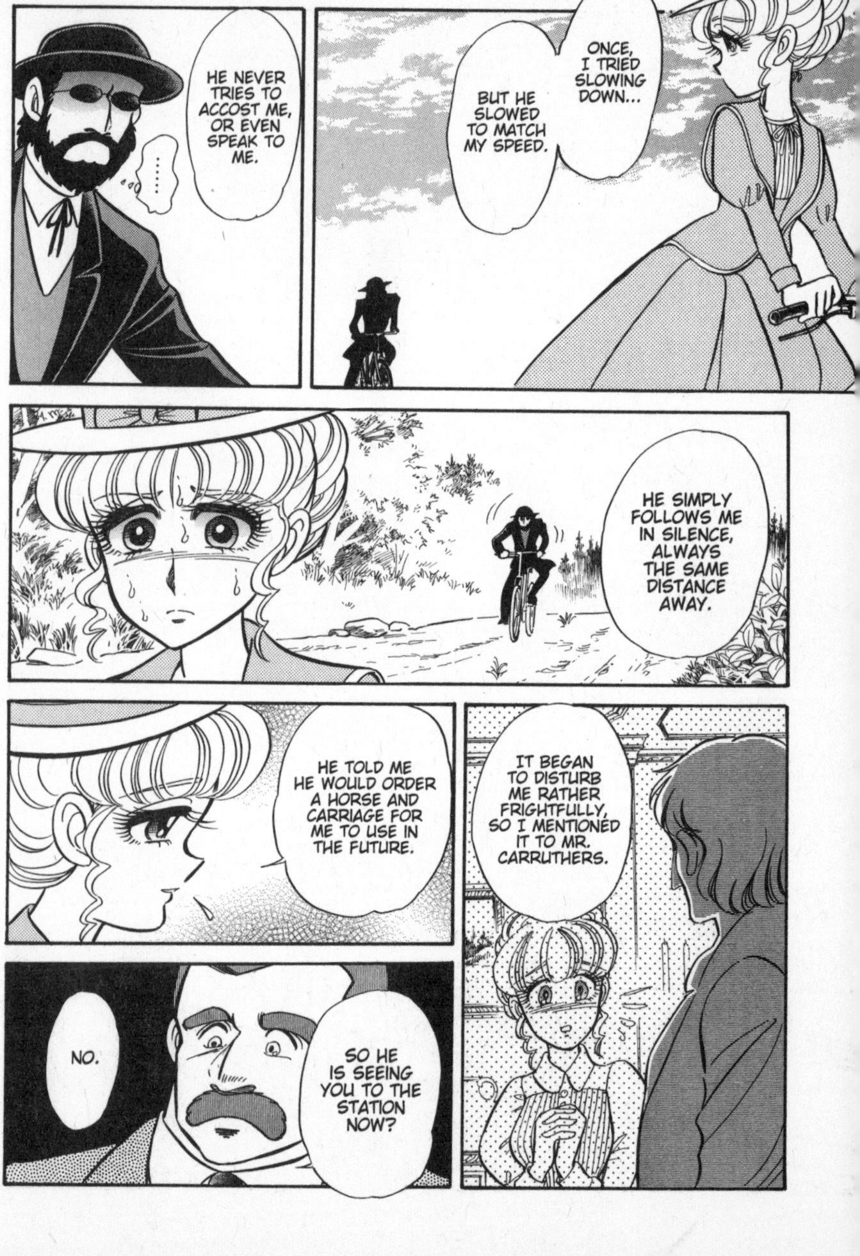
ONCE, I TRIED SLOWING DOWN...
BUT HE SLOWED TO MATCH MY SPEED.
HE NEVER TRIES TO ACCOST ME, OR EVEN SPEAK TO ME.
.....
HE SIMPLY FOLLOWS ME IN SILENCE, ALWAYS THE SAME DISTANCE AWAY.
IT BEGAN TO DISTURB ME RATHER FRIGHTFULLY, SO I MENTIONED IT TO MR. CARRUTHERS.
HE TOLD ME HE WOULD ORDER A HORSE AND CARRIAGE FOR ME TO USE IN THE FUTURE.
SO HE IS SEEING YOU TO THE STATION NOW?
NO.

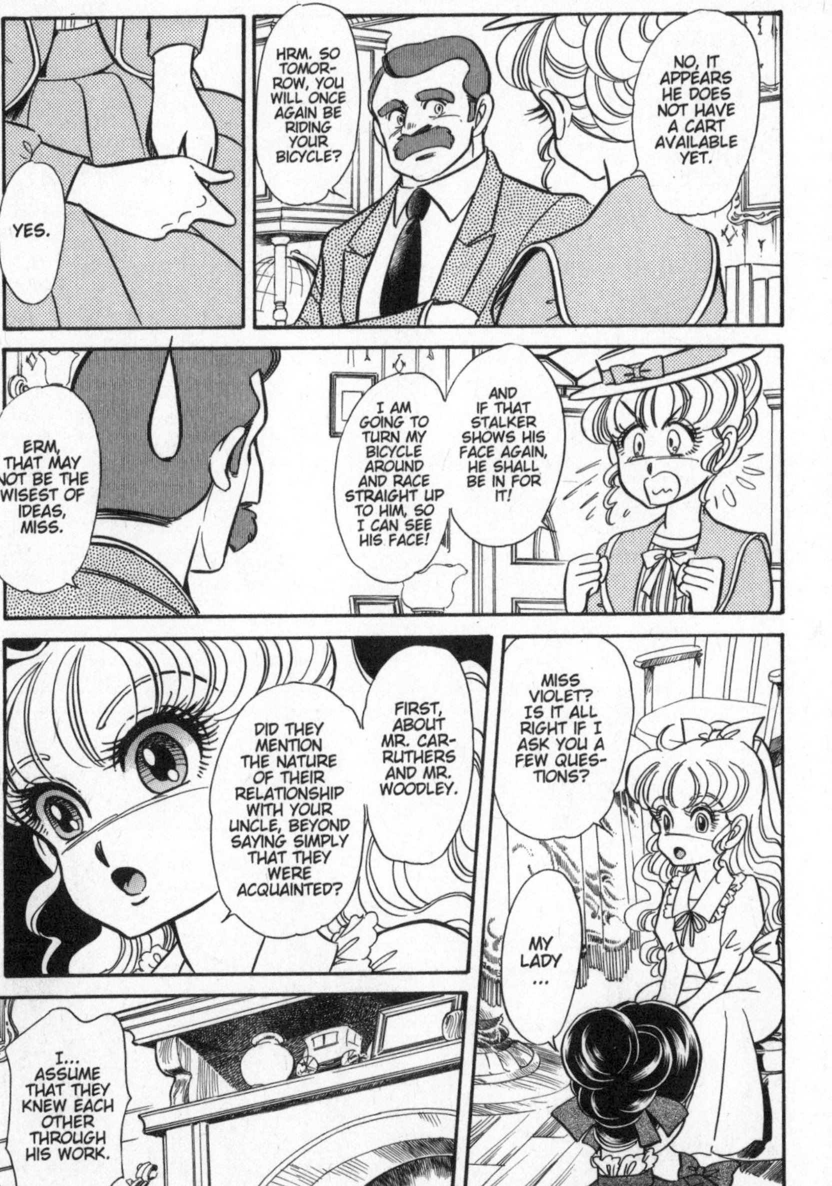
NO, IT APPEARS HE DOES NOT HAVE A CART AVAILABLE YET.
HRM. SO TOMOR-ROW, YOU WILL ONCE AGAIN BE RIDING YOUR BICYCLE?
YES.
AND IF THAT STALKER SHOWS HIS FACE AGAIN, HE SHALL BE IN FOR IT!
I AM GOING TO TURN MY BICYCLE AROUND AND RACE STRAIGHT UP TO HIM, SO I CAN SEE HIS FACE!
ERM, THAT MAY NOT BE THE WISEST OF IDEAS, MISS.
MISS VIOLET? IS IT ALL RIGHT IF I ASK YOU A FEW QUES-TIONS?
MY LADY ...
FIRST, ABOUT MR. CAR-RUTHERS AND MR. WOODLEY.
DID THEY MENTION THE NATURE OF THEIR RELATIONSHIP WITH YOUR UNCLE, BEYOND SAYING SIMPLY THAT THEY WERE ACQUAINTED?
I... ASSUME THAT THEY KNEW EACH OTHER THROUGH HIS WORK.

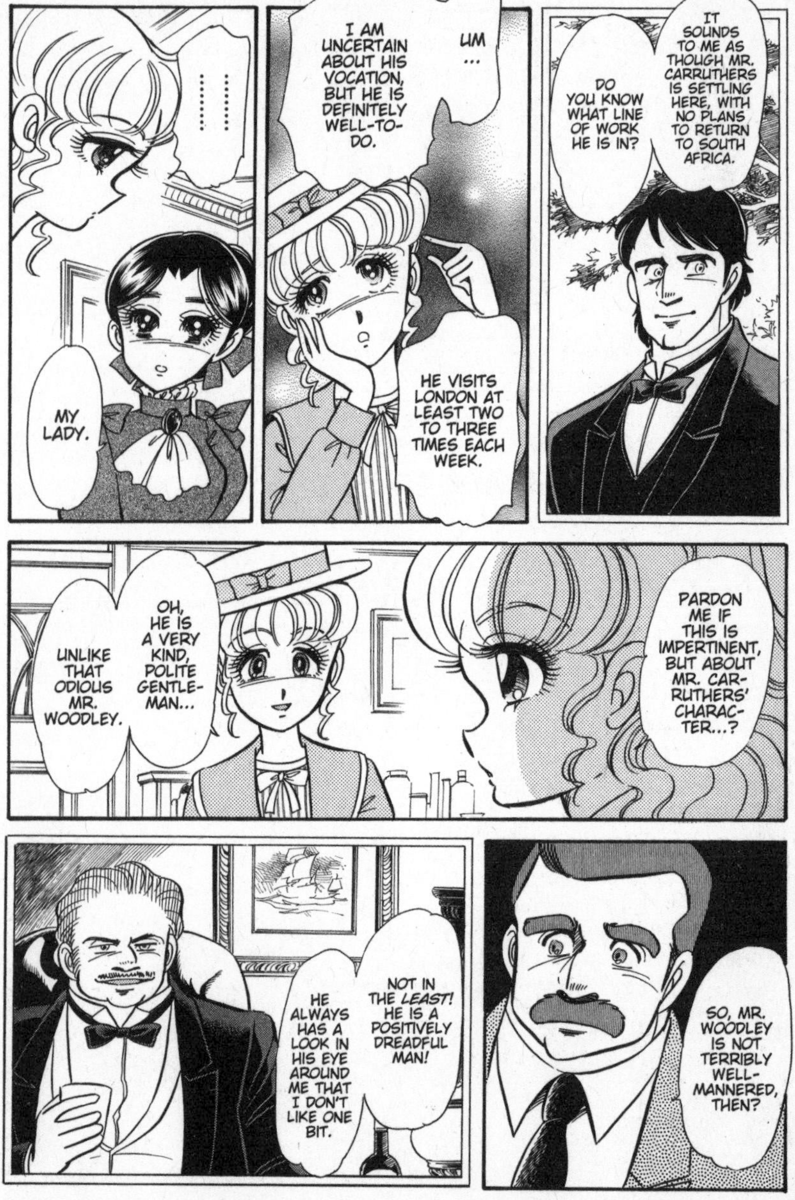
IT SOUNDS TO ME AS THOUGH MR. CARRUTHERS IS SETTLING HERE, WITH NO PLANS TO RETURN TO SOUTH AFRICA.
DO YOU KNOW WHAT LINE OF WORK HE IS IN?
UM ...
I AM UNCERTAIN ABOUT HIS VOCATION, BUT HE IS DEFINITELY WELL-TO-DO.
HE VISITS LONDON AT LEAST TWO TO THREE TIMES EACH WEEK.
……
MY LADY.
PARDON ME IF THIS IS IMPERTINENT, BUT ABOUT MR. CARRUTHERS' CHARACTER...?
OH, HE IS A VERY KIND, POLITE GENTLEMAN...
UNLIKE THAT ODIOUS MR. WOODLEY.
SO, MR. WOODLEY IS NOT TERRIBLY WELL-MANNERED, THEN?
NOT IN THE *LEAST*! HE IS A POSITIVELY DREADFUL MAN!
HE ALWAYS HAS A LOOK IN HIS EYE AROUND ME THAT I DON'T LIKE ONE BIT.

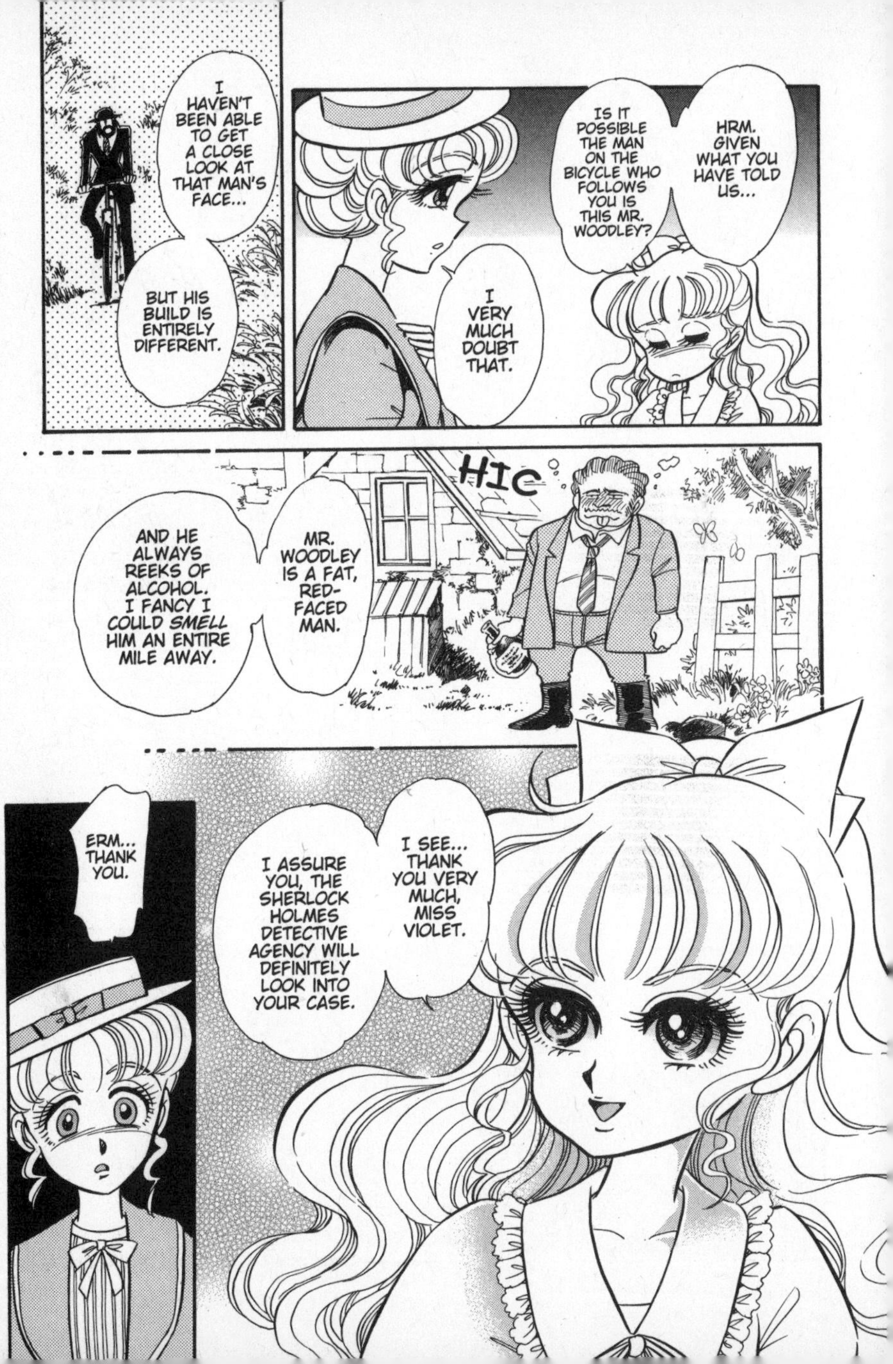
HRM. GIVEN WHAT YOU HAVE TOLD US...
IS IT POSSIBLE THE MAN ON THE BICYCLE WHO FOLLOWS YOU IS THIS MR. WOODLEY?
I VERY MUCH DOUBT THAT.
I HAVEN'T BEEN ABLE TO GET A CLOSE LOOK AT THAT MAN'S FACE...
BUT HIS BUILD IS ENTIRELY DIFFERENT.
HIC
MR. WOODLEY IS A FAT, RED-FACED MAN.
AND HE ALWAYS REEKS OF ALCOHOL. I FANCY I COULD *SMELL* HIM AN ENTIRE MILE AWAY.
I SEE... THANK YOU VERY MUCH, MISS VIOLET.
I ASSURE YOU, THE SHERLOCK HOLMES DETECTIVE AGENCY WILL DEFINITELY LOOK INTO YOUR CASE.
ERM... THANK YOU.

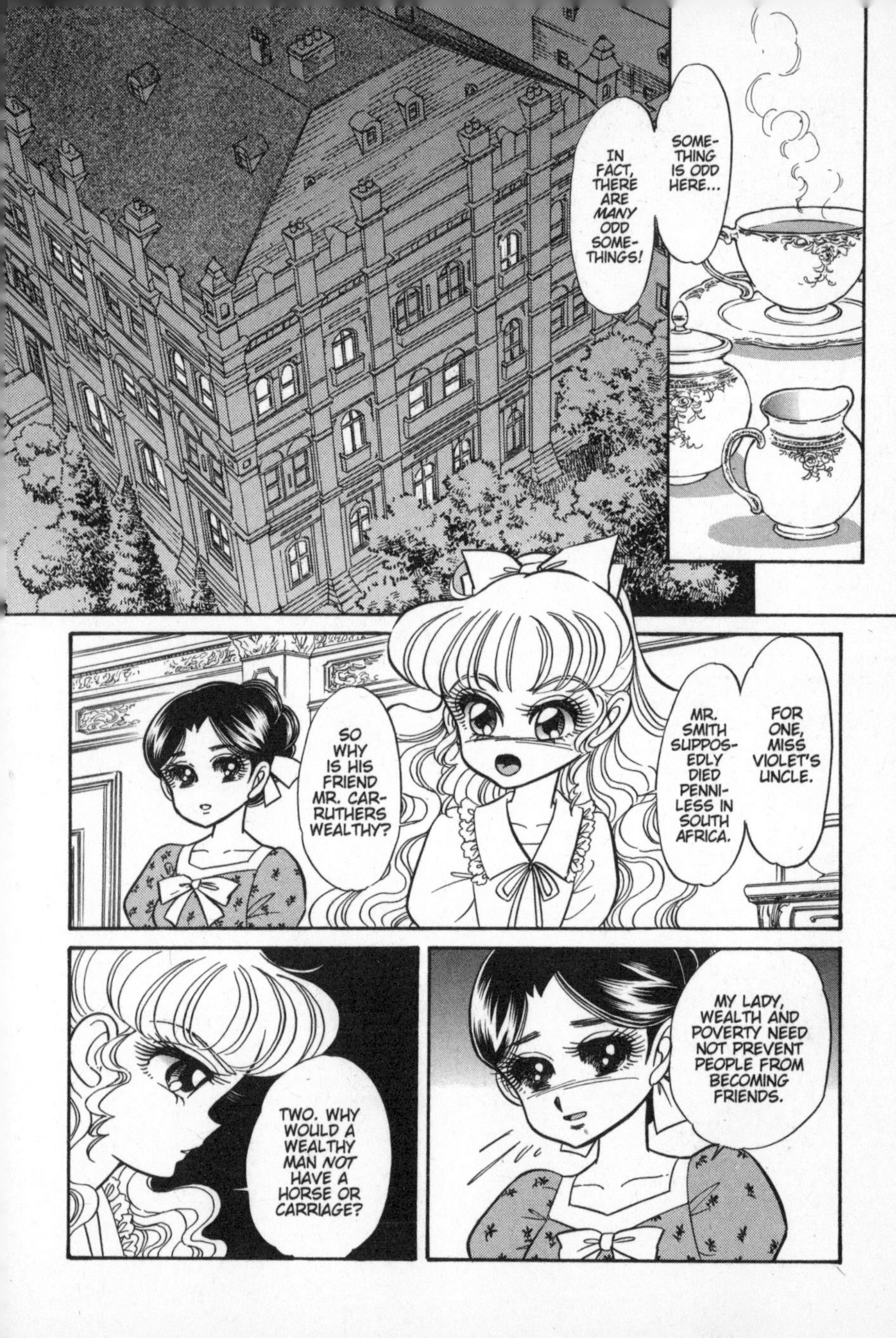
SOMETHING IS ODD HERE...
IN FACT, THERE ARE *MANY* ODD SOMETHINGS!
FOR ONE, MISS VIOLET'S UNCLE.
MR. SMITH SUPPOSEDLY DIED PENNILESS IN SOUTH AFRICA.
SO WHY IS HIS FRIEND MR. CARRUTHERS WEALTHY?
MY LADY, WEALTH AND POVERTY NEED NOT PREVENT PEOPLE FROM BECOMING FRIENDS.
TWO. WHY WOULD A WEALTHY MAN *NOT* HAVE A HORSE OR CARRIAGE?

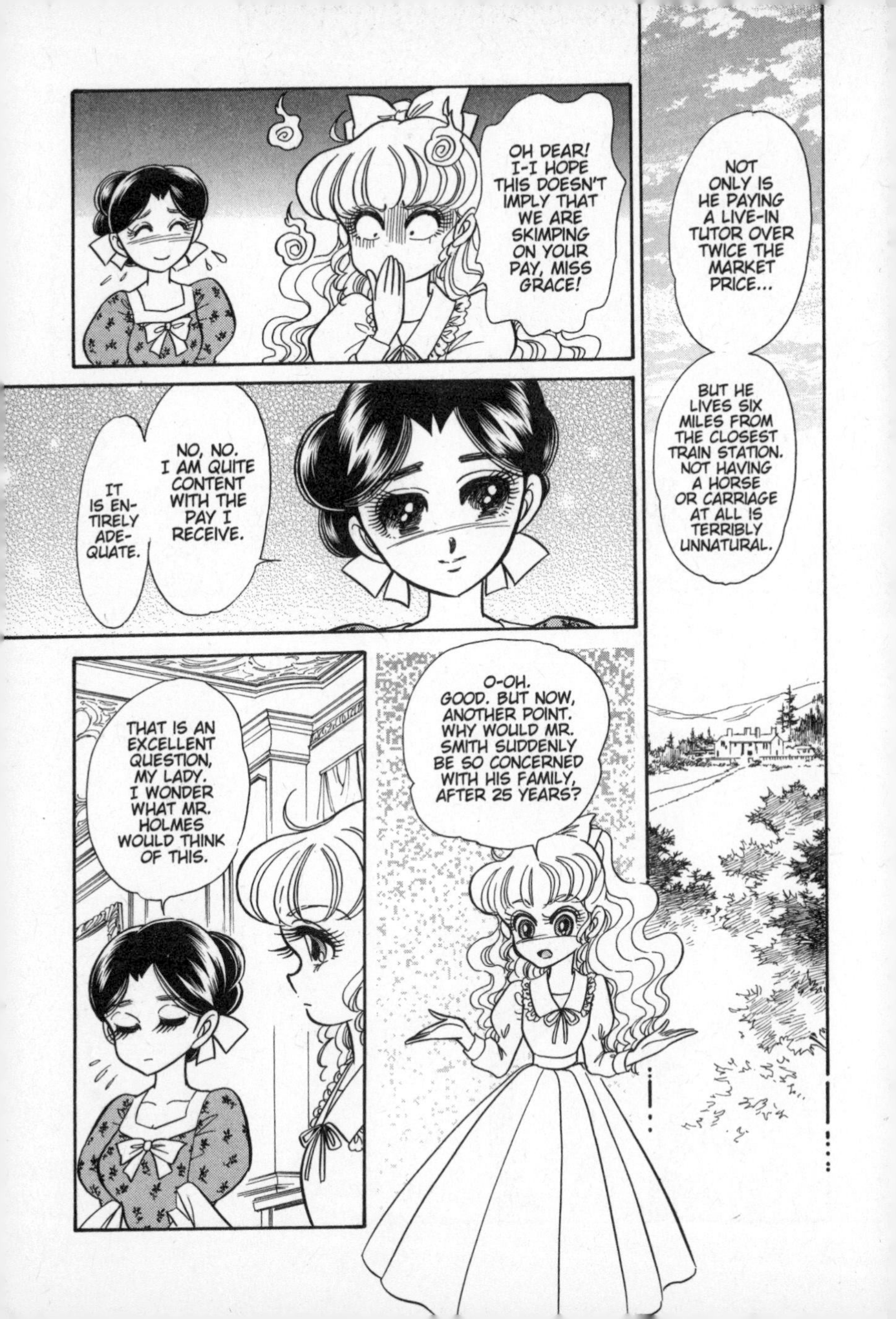
NOT ONLY IS HE PAYING A LIVE-IN TUTOR OVER TWICE THE MARKET PRICE...
BUT HE LIVES SIX MILES FROM THE CLOSEST TRAIN STATION. NOT HAVING A HORSE OR CARRIAGE AT ALL IS TERRIBLY UNNATURAL.
OH DEAR! I-I HOPE THIS DOESN'T IMPLY THAT WE ARE SKIMPING ON YOUR PAY, MISS GRACE!
NO, NO. I AM QUITE CONTENT WITH THE PAY I RECEIVE.
IT IS EN-TIRELY ADE-QUATE.
O-OH. GOOD. BUT NOW, ANOTHER POINT. WHY WOULD MR. SMITH SUDDENLY BE SO CONCERNED WITH HIS FAMILY, AFTER 25 YEARS?
THAT IS AN EXCELLENT QUESTION, MY LADY. I WONDER WHAT MR. HOLMES WOULD THINK OF THIS.

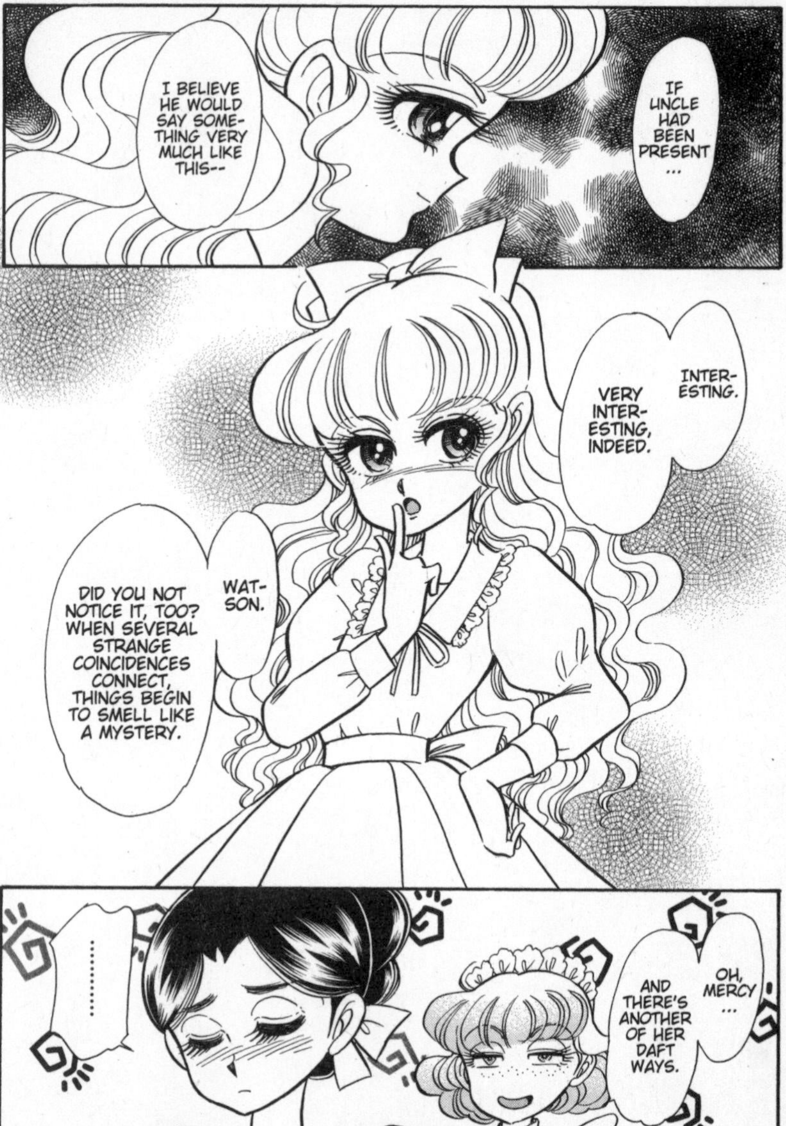
IF UNCLE HAD BEEN PRESENT ...
I BELIEVE HE WOULD SAY SOME-THING VERY MUCH LIKE THIS--
INTER-ESTING.
VERY INTER-ESTING, INDEED.
WAT-SON.
DID YOU NOT NOTICE IT, TOO? WHEN SEVERAL STRANGE COINCIDENCES CONNECT, THINGS BEGIN TO SMELL LIKE A MYSTERY.
OH, MERCY ...
AND THERE'S ANOTHER OF HER DAFT WAYS.
....

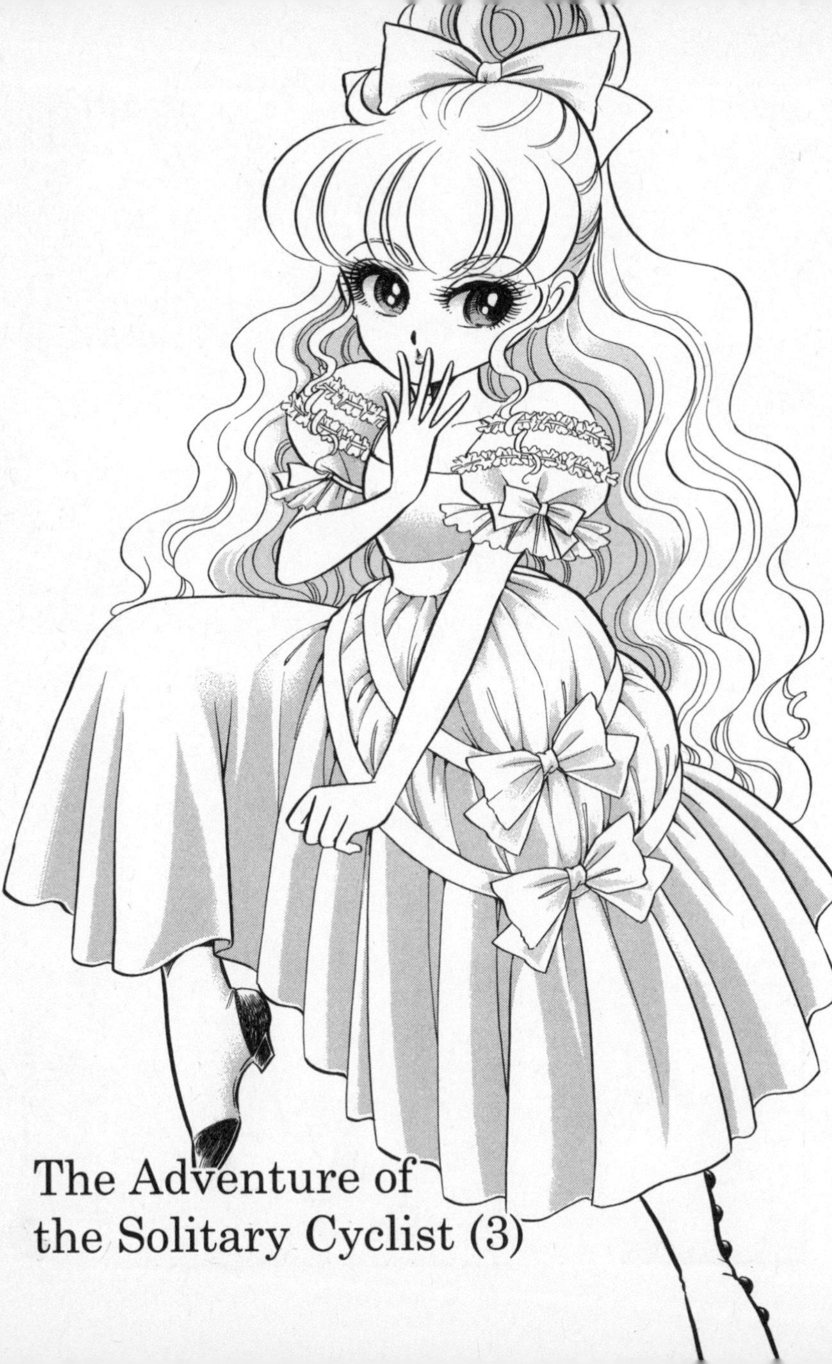

The Adventure of the Solitary Cyclist (3)

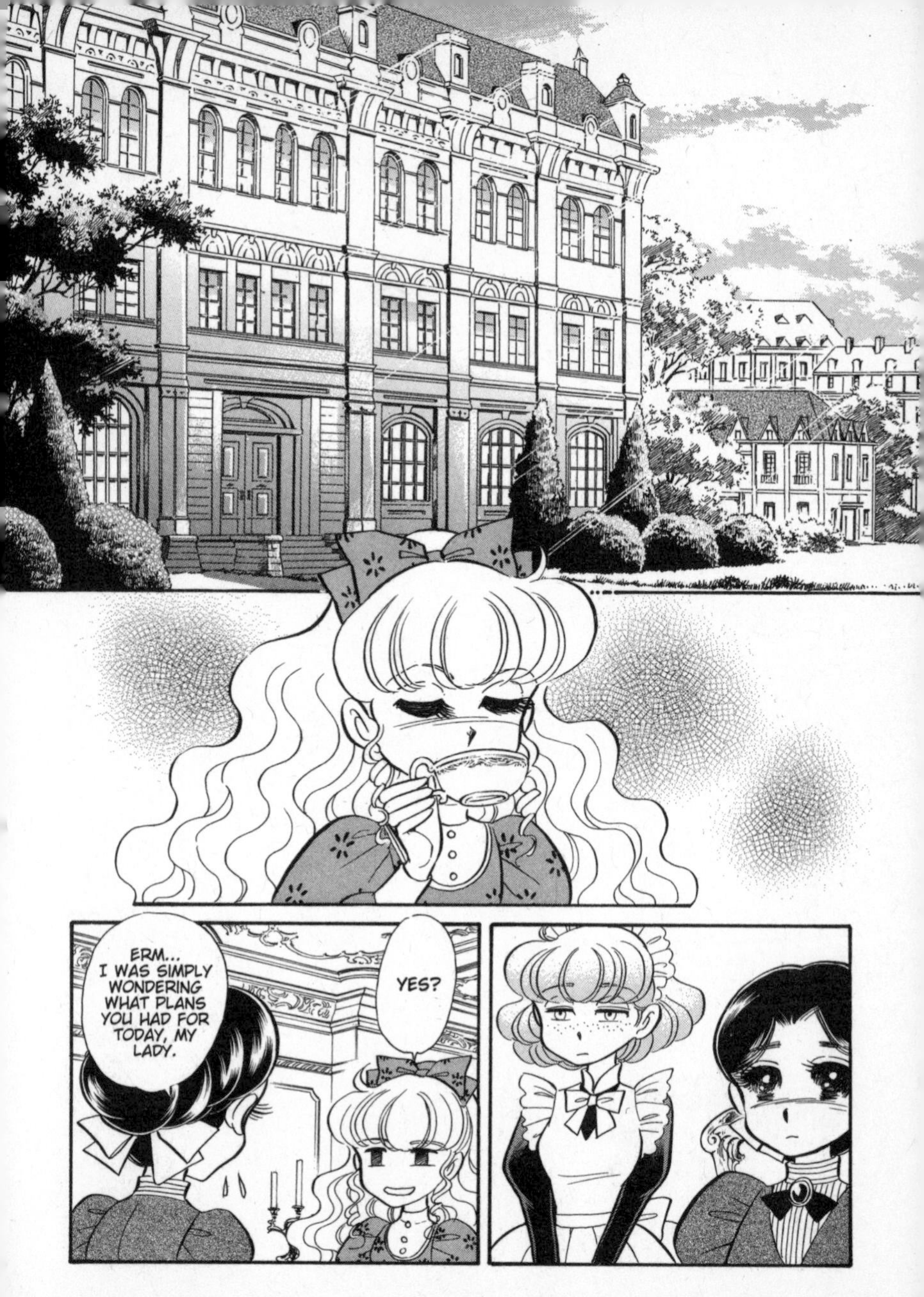
YES?
ERM... I WAS SIMPLY WONDERING WHAT PLANS YOU HAD FOR TODAY, MY LADY.

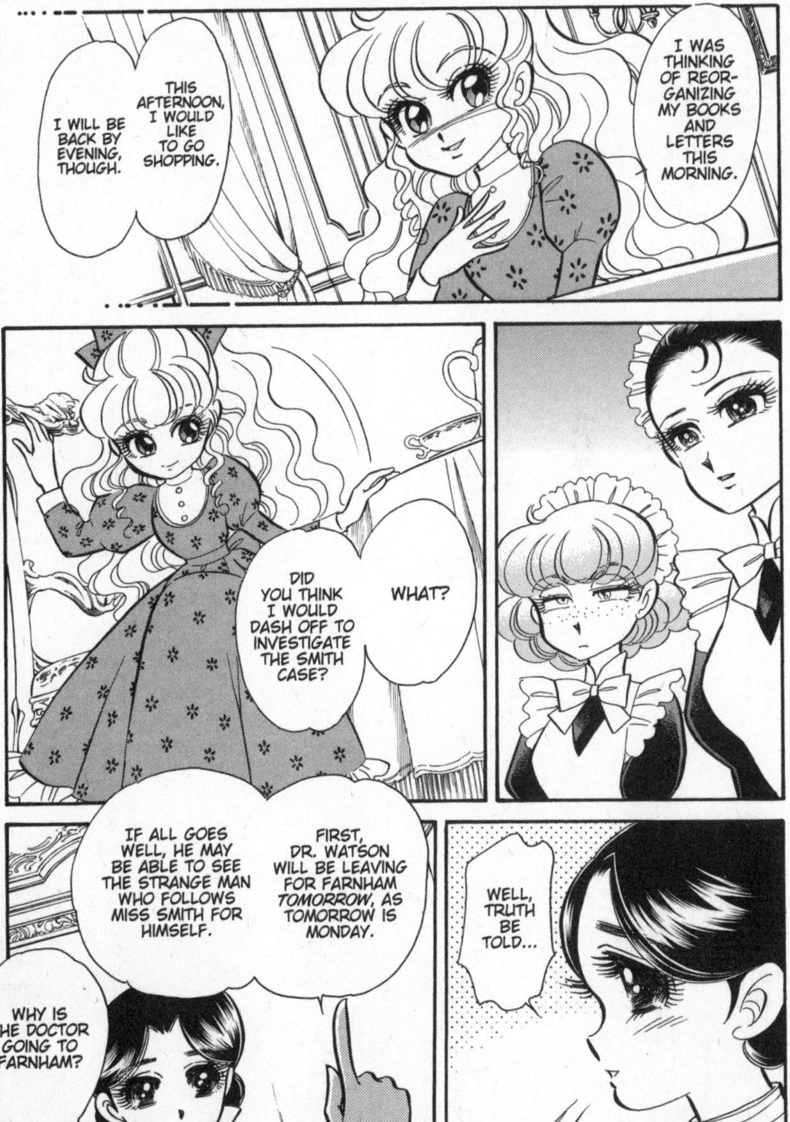
I WAS THINKING OF REORGANIZING MY BOOKS AND LETTERS THIS MORNING.
THIS AFTERNOON, I WOULD LIKE TO GO SHOPPING.
I WILL BE BACK BY EVENING, THOUGH.
WHAT?
DID YOU THINK I WOULD DASH OFF TO INVESTIGATE THE SMITH CASE?
WELL, TRUTH BE TOLD...
FIRST, DR. WATSON WILL BE LEAVING FOR FARNHAM *TOMORROW*, AS TOMORROW IS MONDAY.
IF ALL GOES WELL, HE MAY BE ABLE TO SEE THE STRANGE MAN WHO FOLLOWS MISS SMITH FOR HIMSELF.
WHY IS THE DOCTOR GOING TO FARNHAM?

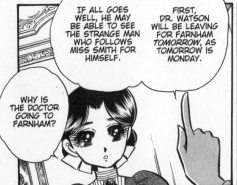

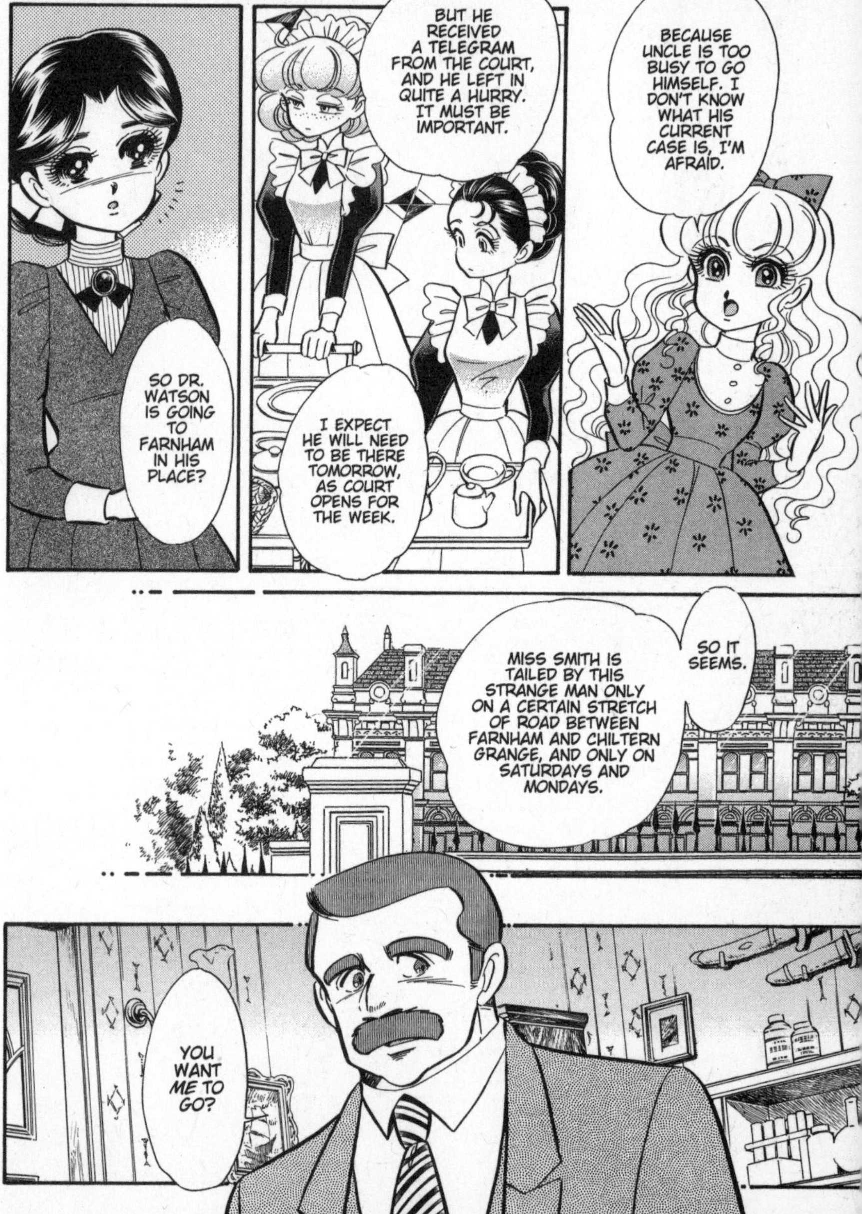
BECAUSE UNCLE IS TOO BUSY TO GO HIMSELF. I DON'T KNOW WHAT HIS CURRENT CASE IS, I'M AFRAID.
BUT HE RECEIVED A TELEGRAM FROM THE COURT, AND HE LEFT IN QUITE A HURRY. IT MUST BE IMPORTANT.
I EXPECT HE WILL NEED TO BE THERE TOMORROW, AS COURT OPENS FOR THE WEEK.
SO DR. WATSON IS GOING TO FARNHAM IN HIS PLACE?
SO IT SEEMS.
MISS SMITH IS TAILED BY THIS STRANGE MAN ONLY ON A CERTAIN STRETCH OF ROAD BETWEEN FARNHAM AND CHILTERN GRANGE, AND ONLY ON SATURDAYS AND MONDAYS.
YOU WANT ME TO GO?

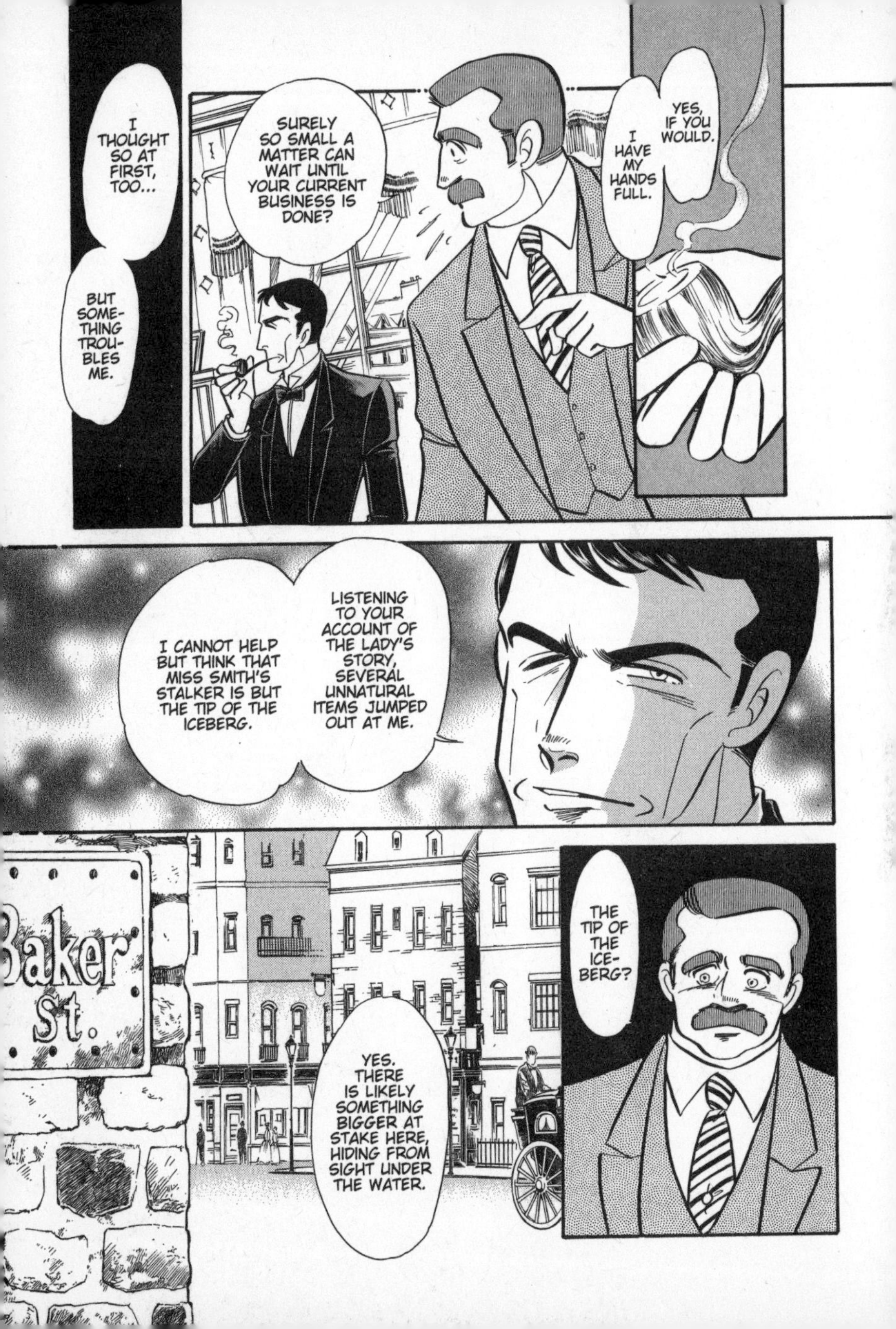
YES, IF YOU WOULD.
I HAVE MY HANDS FULL.
SURELY SO SMALL A MATTER CAN WAIT UNTIL YOUR CURRENT BUSINESS IS DONE?
I THOUGHT SO AT FIRST, TOO...
BUT SOME-THING TROU-BLES ME.
LISTENING TO YOUR ACCOUNT OF THE LADY'S STORY, SEVERAL UNNATURAL ITEMS JUMPED OUT AT ME.
I CANNOT HELP BUT THINK THAT MISS SMITH'S STALKER IS BUT THE TIP OF THE ICEBERG.
THE TIP OF THE ICE-BERG?
Baker St.
YES. THERE IS LIKELY SOMETHING BIGGER AT STAKE HERE, HIDING FROM SIGHT UNDER THE WATER.

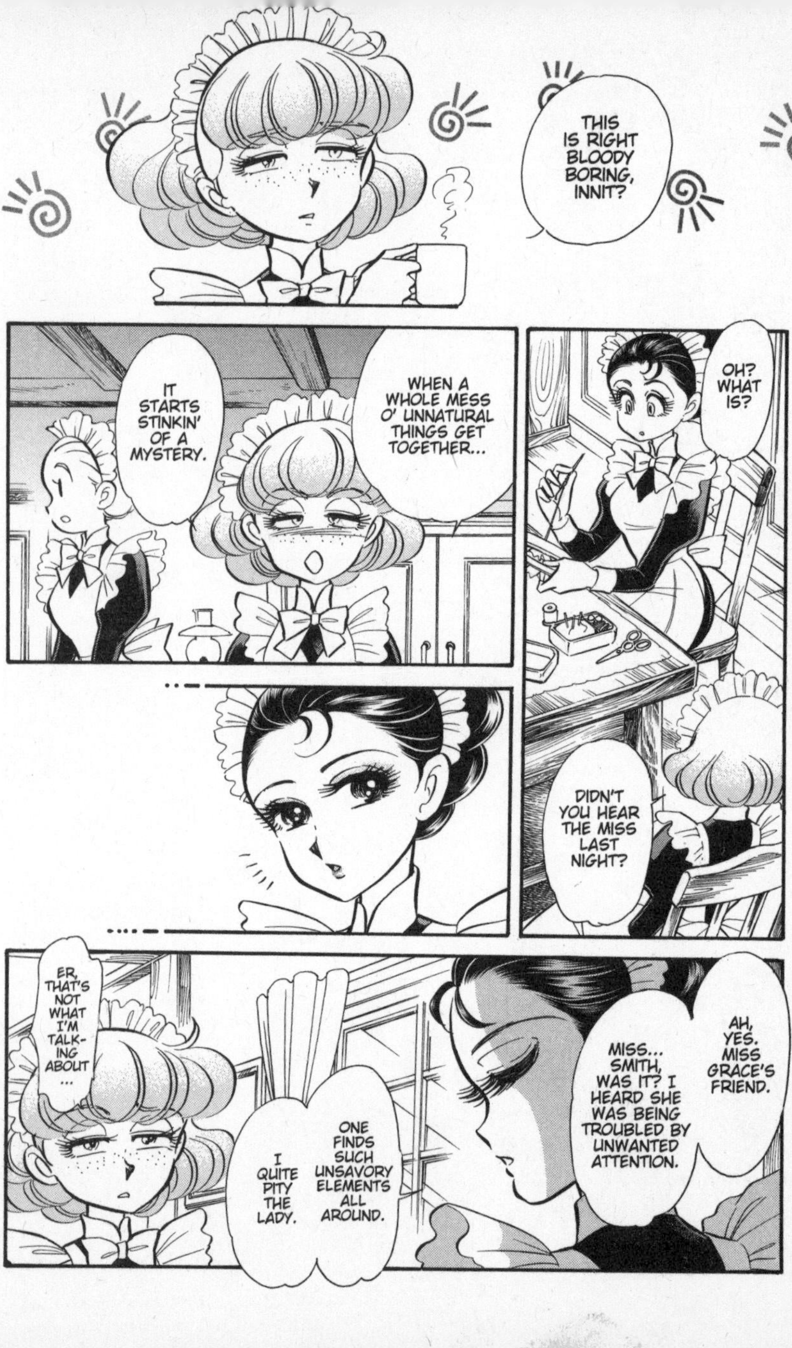
THIS IS RIGHT BLOODY BORING, INNIT?
OH? WHAT IS?
WHEN A WHOLE MESS O' UNNATURAL THINGS GET TOGETHER...
IT STARTS STINKIN' OF A MYSTERY.
DIDN'T YOU HEAR THE MISS LAST NIGHT?
...—
AH, YES. MISS GRACE'S FRIEND.
MISS... SMITH, WAS IT? I HEARD SHE WAS BEING TROUBLED BY UNWANTED ATTENTION.
ONE FINDS SUCH UNSAVORY ELEMENTS ALL AROUND.
I QUITE PITY THE LADY.
ER, THAT'S NOT WHAT I'M TALK-ING ABOUT...

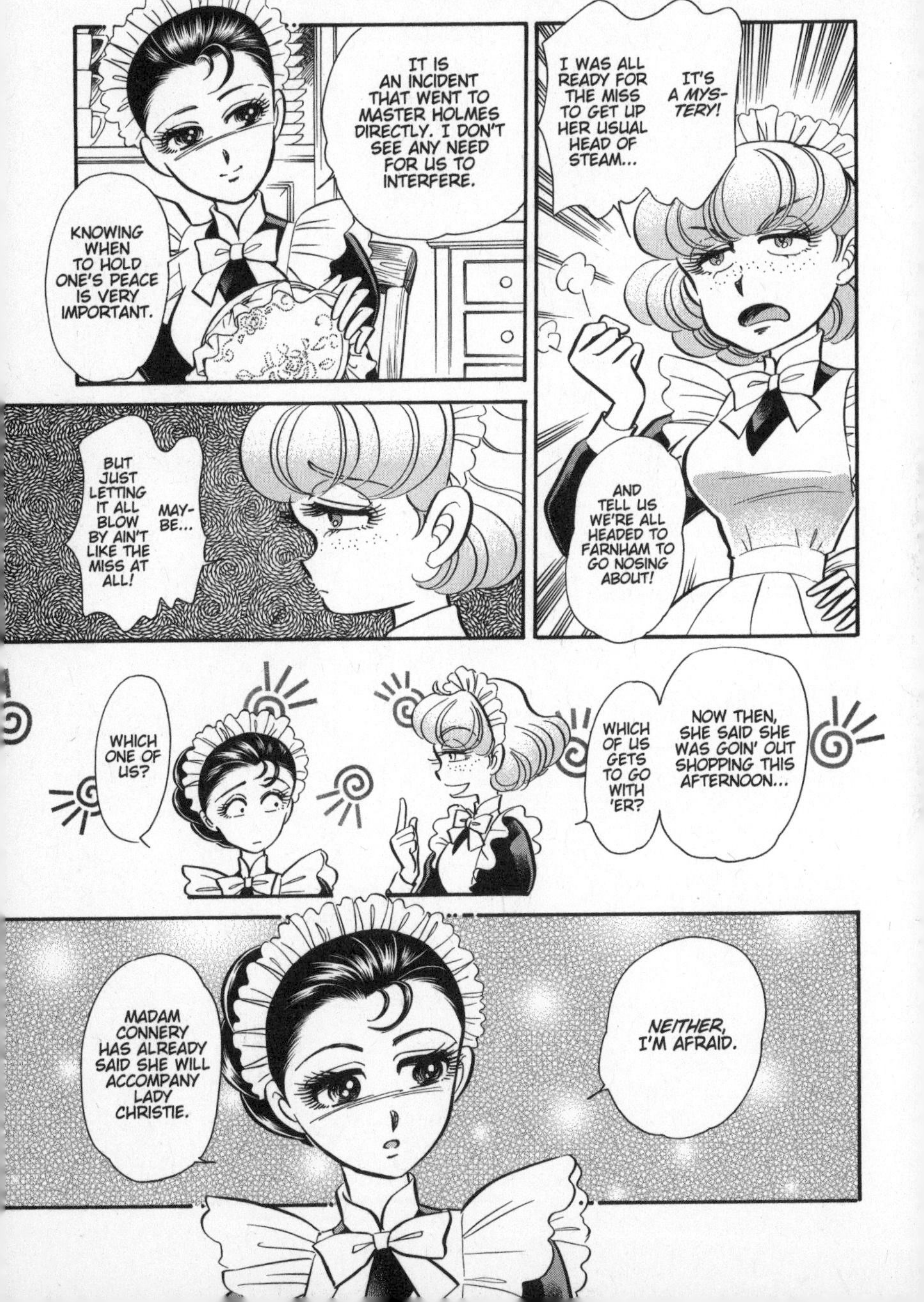
IT'S A *MYSTERY*!
I WAS ALL READY FOR THE MISS TO GET UP HER USUAL HEAD OF STEAM...
AND TELL US WE'RE ALL HEADED TO FARNHAM TO GO NOSING ABOUT!
IT IS AN INCIDENT THAT WENT TO MASTER HOLMES DIRECTLY. I DON'T SEE ANY NEED FOR US TO INTERFERE.
KNOWING WHEN TO HOLD ONE'S PEACE IS VERY IMPORTANT.
MAY-BE...
BUT JUST LETTING IT ALL BLOW BY AIN'T LIKE THE MISS AT ALL!
NOW THEN, SHE SAID SHE WAS GOIN' OUT SHOPPING THIS AFTERNOON...
WHICH OF US GETS TO GO WITH 'ER?
WHICH ONE OF US?
NEITHER, I'M AFRAID.
MADAM CONNERY HAS ALREADY SAID SHE WILL ACCOMPANY LADY CHRISTIE.

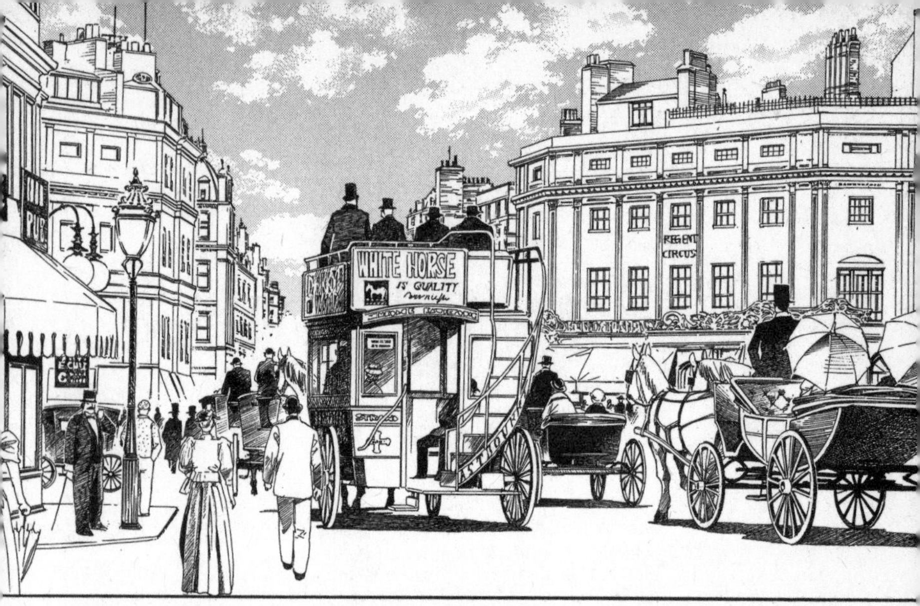
WHITE HORSE
IS QUALITY
REGENT
CIRCUS
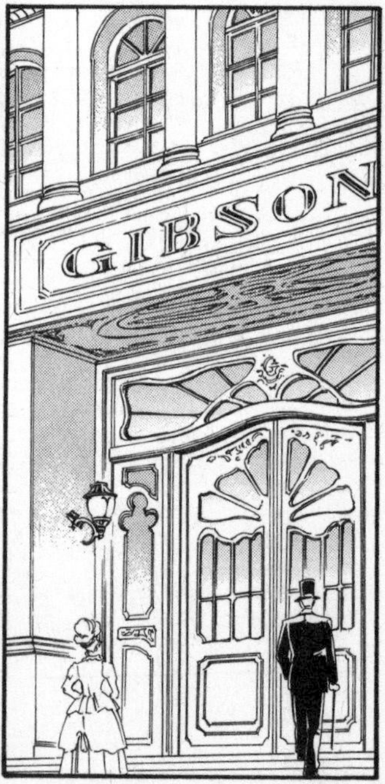
GIBSON
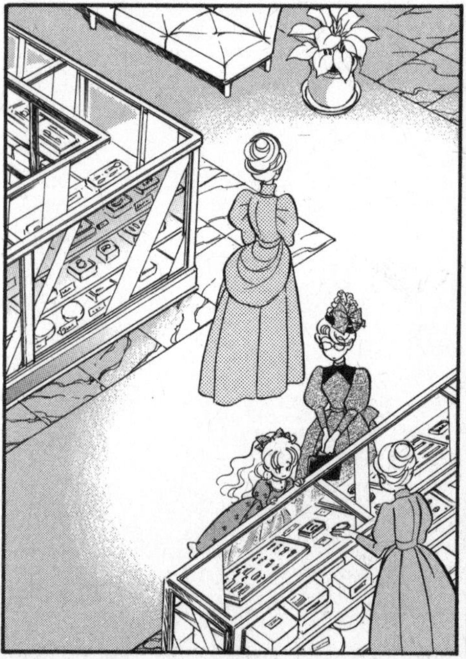

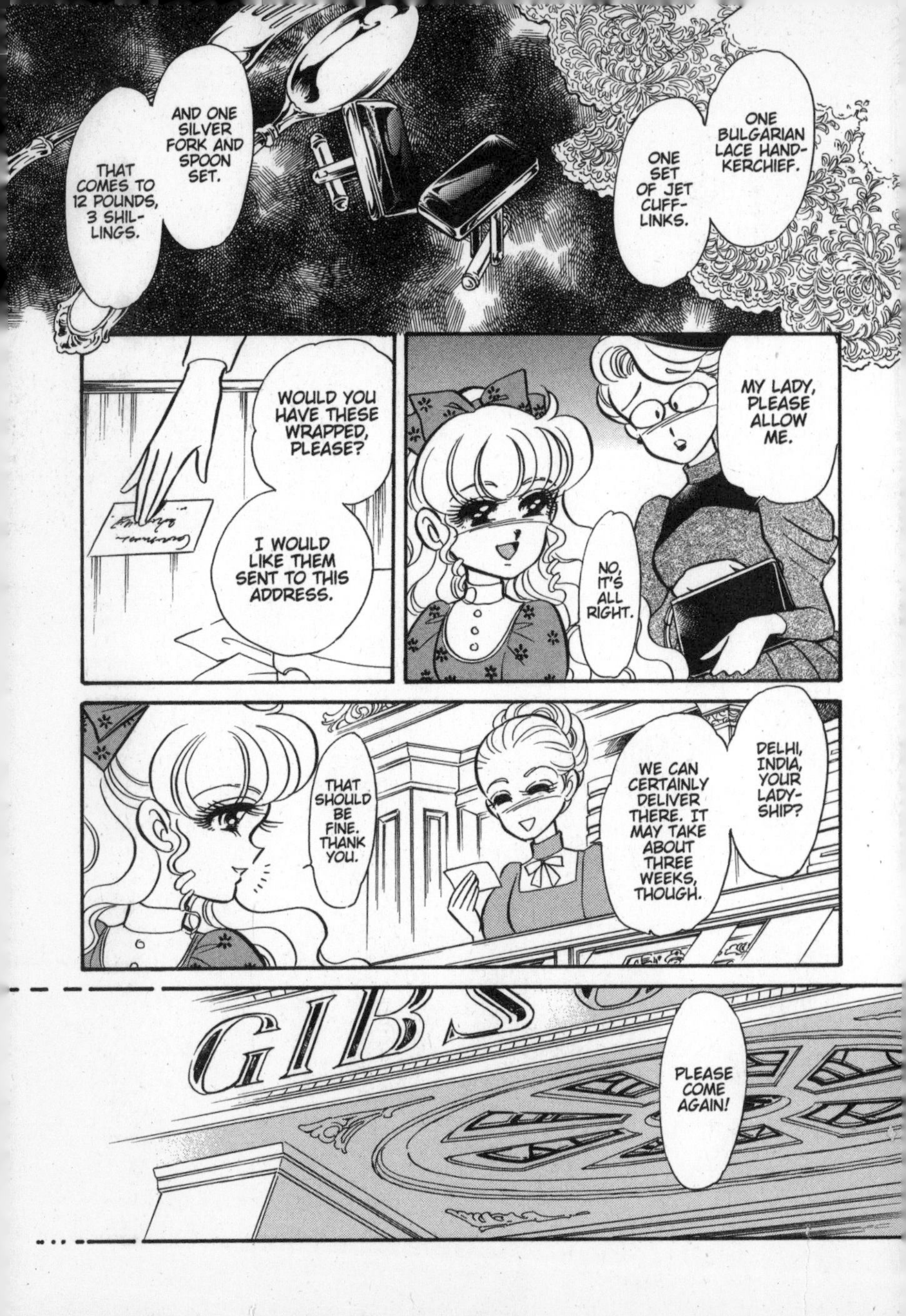
ONE BULGARIAN LACE HANDKERCHIEF.
ONE SET OF JET CUFF-LINKS.
AND ONE SILVER FORK AND SPOON SET.
THAT COMES TO 12 POUNDS, 3 SHILLINGS.
MY LADY, PLEASE ALLOW ME.
NO, IT'S ALL RIGHT.
WOULD YOU HAVE THESE WRAPPED, PLEASE?
I WOULD LIKE THEM SENT TO THIS ADDRESS.
DELHI, INDIA, YOUR LADYSHIP?
WE CAN CERTAINLY DELIVER THERE. IT MAY TAKE ABOUT THREE WEEKS, THOUGH.
THAT SHOULD BE FINE. THANK YOU.
PLEASE COME AGAIN!

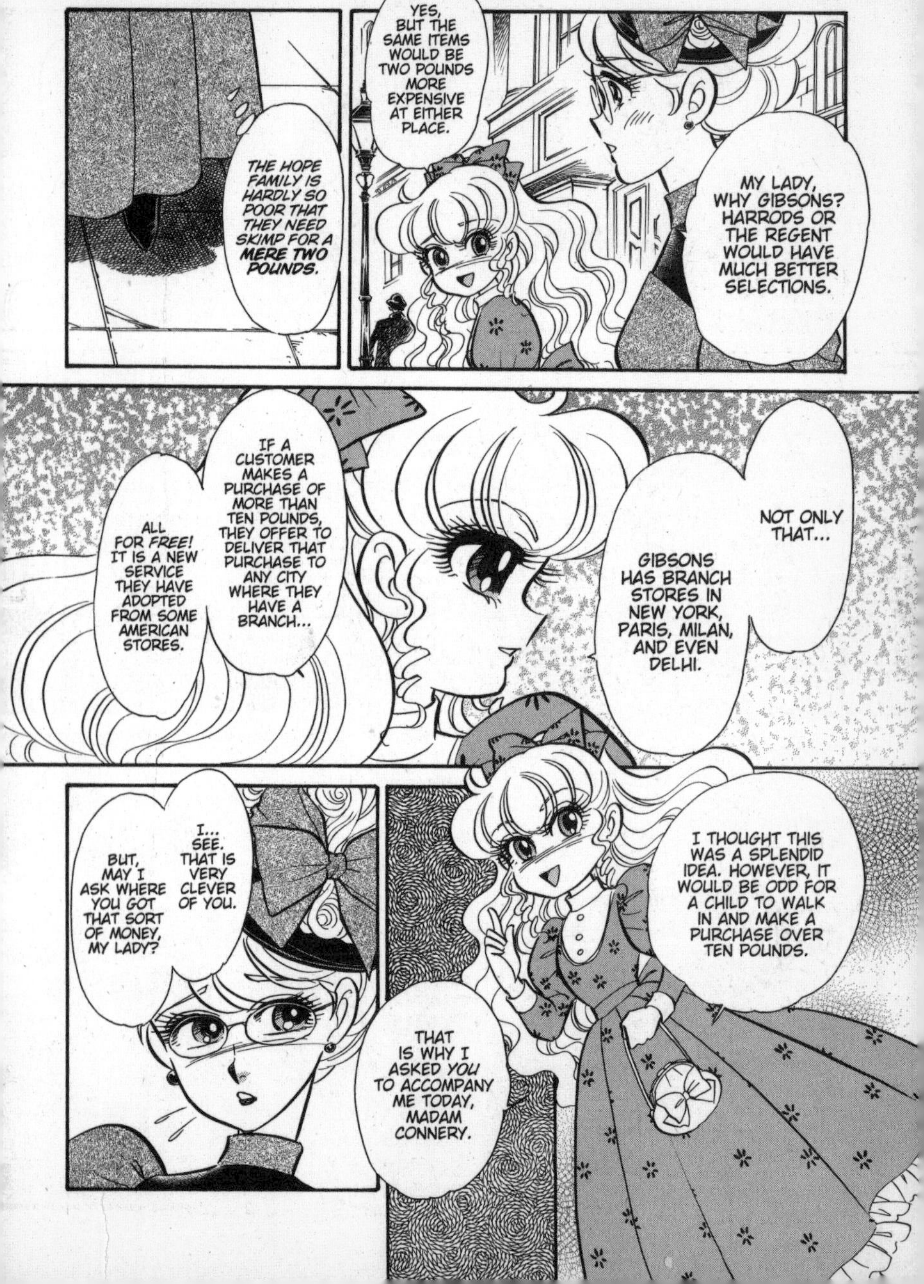
MY LADY, WHY GIBSONS? HARRODS OR THE REGENT WOULD HAVE MUCH BETTER SELECTIONS.
YES, BUT THE SAME ITEMS WOULD BE TWO POUNDS MORE EXPENSIVE AT EITHER PLACE.
THE HOPE FAMILY IS HARDLY SO POOR THAT THEY NEED SKIMP FOR A **MERE TWO POUNDS.**
NOT ONLY THAT...
GIBSONS HAS BRANCH STORES IN NEW YORK, PARIS, MILAN, AND EVEN DELHI.
IF A CUSTOMER MAKES A PURCHASE OF MORE THAN TEN POUNDS, THEY OFFER TO DELIVER THAT PURCHASE TO ANY CITY WHERE THEY HAVE A BRANCH...
ALL FOR *FREE!* IT IS A NEW SERVICE THEY HAVE ADOPTED FROM SOME AMERICAN STORES.
I THOUGHT THIS WAS A SPLENDID IDEA. HOWEVER, IT WOULD BE ODD FOR A CHILD TO WALK IN AND MAKE A PURCHASE OVER TEN POUNDS.
THAT IS WHY I ASKED *YOU* TO ACCOMPANY ME TODAY, MADAM CONNERY.
I... SEE. THAT IS VERY CLEVER OF YOU.
BUT, MAY I ASK WHERE YOU GOT THAT SORT OF MONEY, MY LADY?

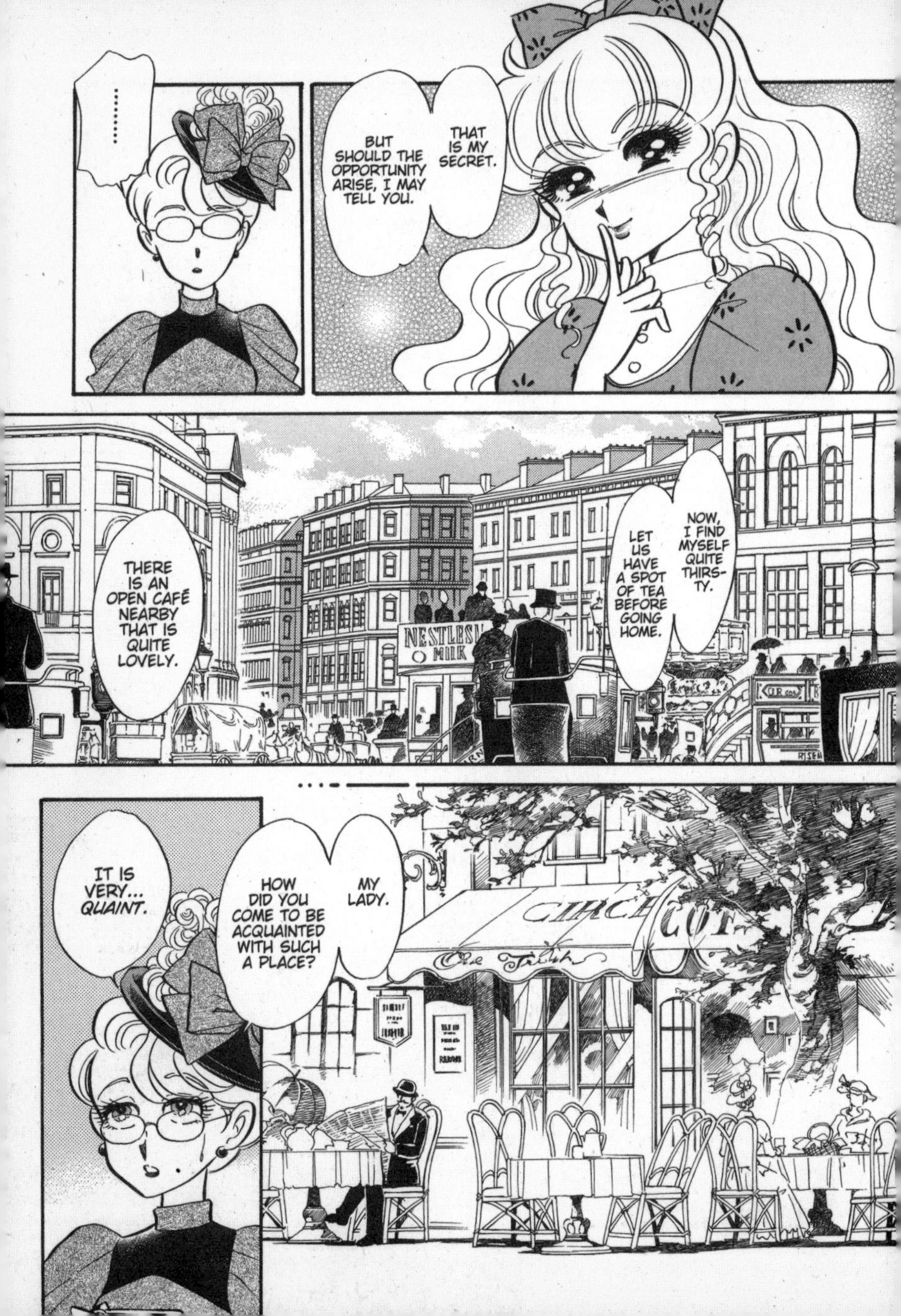
THAT IS MY SECRET.
BUT SHOULD THE OPPORTUNITY ARISE, I MAY TELL YOU.
......
NOW, I FIND MYSELF QUITE THIRSTY.
LET US HAVE A SPOT OF TEA BEFORE GOING HOME.
THERE IS AN OPEN CAFÉ NEARBY THAT IS QUITE LOVELY.
MY LADY.
HOW DID YOU COME TO BE ACQUAINTED WITH SUCH A PLACE?
IT IS VERY... *QUAINT*.

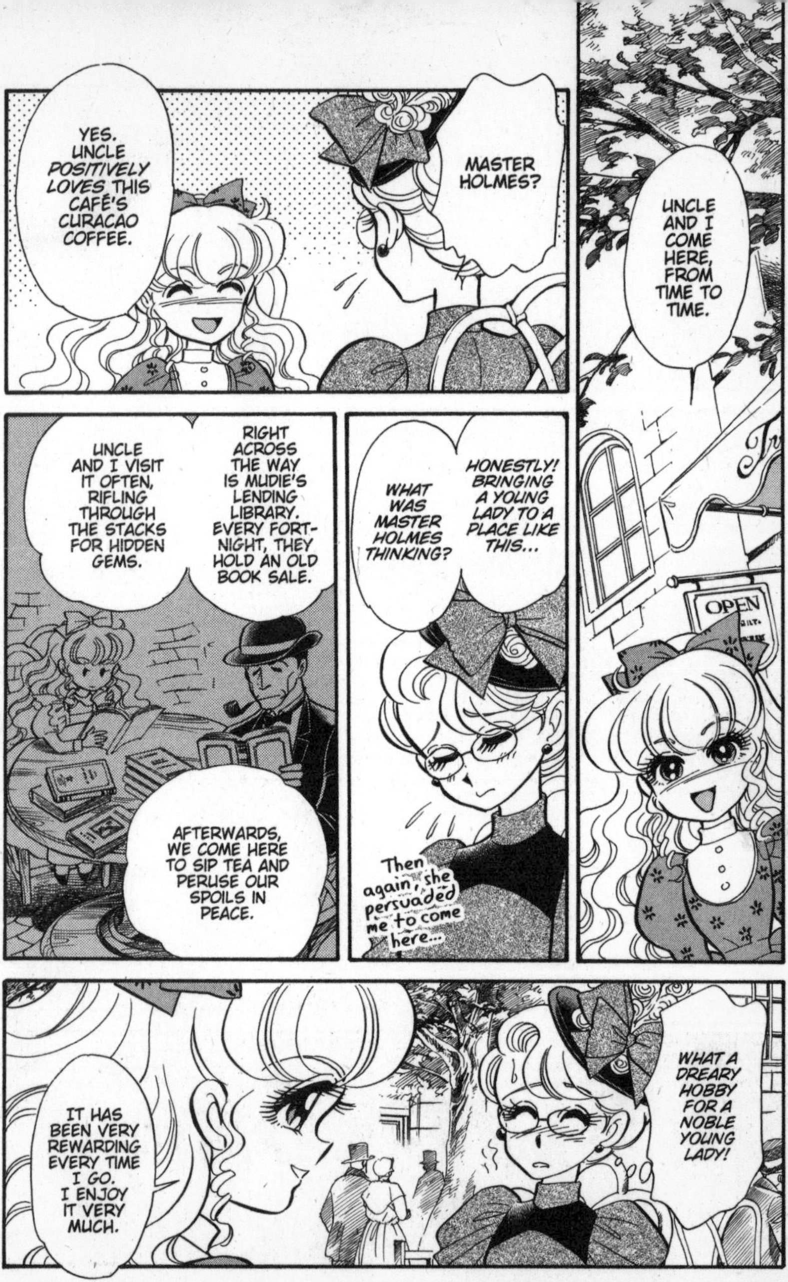
UNCLE AND I COME HERE, FROM TIME TO TIME.
MASTER HOLMES?
YES. UNCLE POSITIVELY LOVES THIS CAFÉ'S CURACAO COFFEE.
HONESTLY! BRINGING A YOUNG LADY TO A PLACE LIKE THIS...
WHAT WAS MASTER HOLMES THINKING?
Then again, she persuaded me to come here...
RIGHT ACROSS THE WAY IS MUDIE'S LENDING LIBRARY. EVERY FORT-NIGHT, THEY HOLD AN OLD BOOK SALE.
UNCLE AND I VISIT IT OFTEN, RIFLING THROUGH THE STACKS FOR HIDDEN GEMS.
AFTERWARDS, WE COME HERE TO SIP TEA AND PERUSE OUR SPOILS IN PEACE.
OPEN
WHAT A DREARY HOBBY FOR A NOBLE YOUNG LADY!
IT HAS BEEN VERY REWARDING EVERY TIME I GO. I ENJOY IT VERY MUCH.

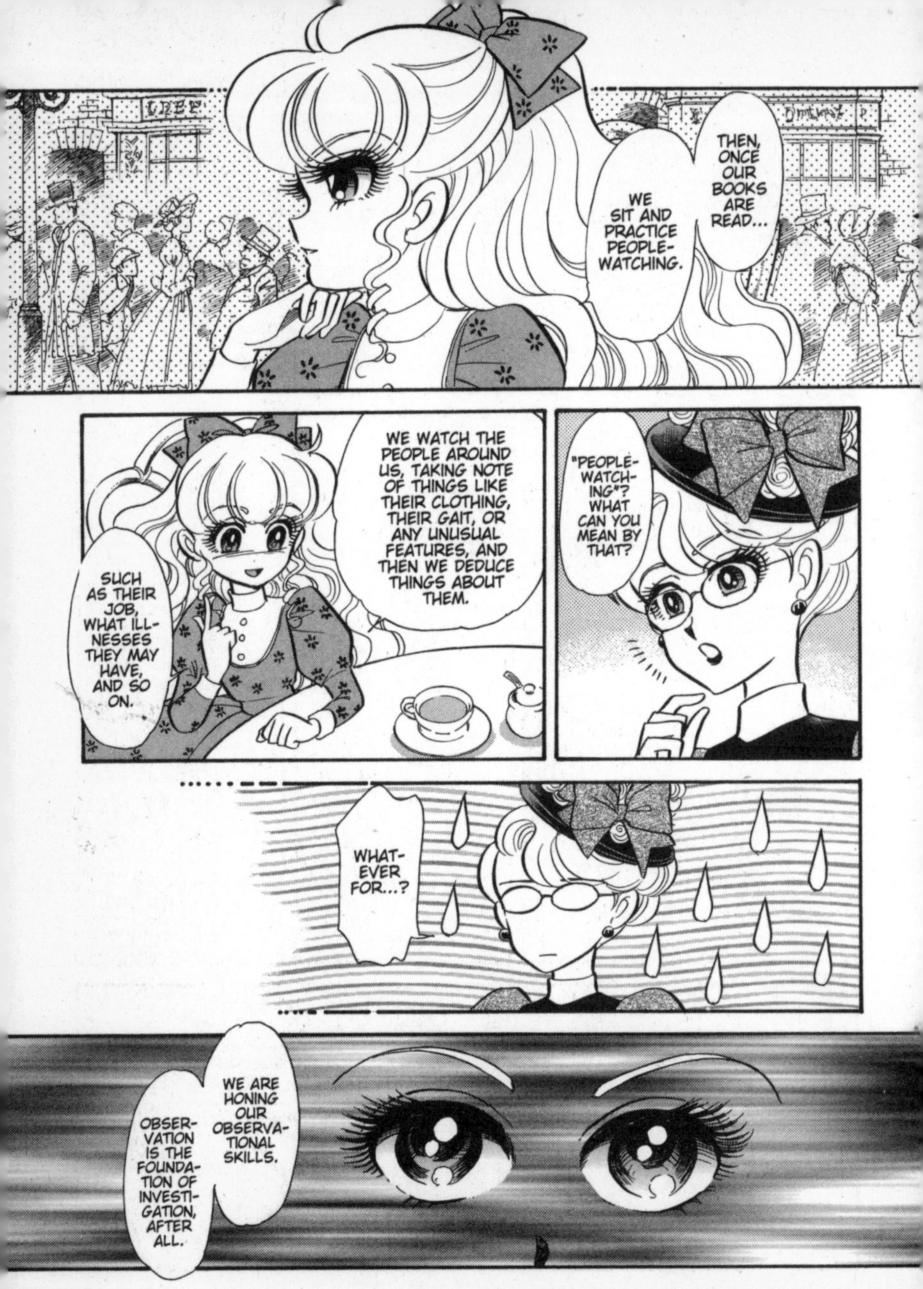
THEN, ONCE OUR BOOKS ARE READ...
WE SIT AND PRACTICE PEOPLE-WATCHING.
"PEOPLE-WATCHING"? WHAT CAN YOU MEAN BY THAT?
WE WATCH THE PEOPLE AROUND US, TAKING NOTE OF THINGS LIKE THEIR CLOTHING, THEIR GAIT, OR ANY UNUSUAL FEATURES, AND THEN WE DEDUCE THINGS ABOUT THEM.
SUCH AS THEIR JOB, WHAT ILLNESSES THEY MAY HAVE, AND SO ON.
WHATEVER FOR...?
WE ARE HONING OUR OBSERVATIONAL SKILLS.
OBSERVATION IS THE FOUNDATION OF INVESTIGATION, AFTER ALL.

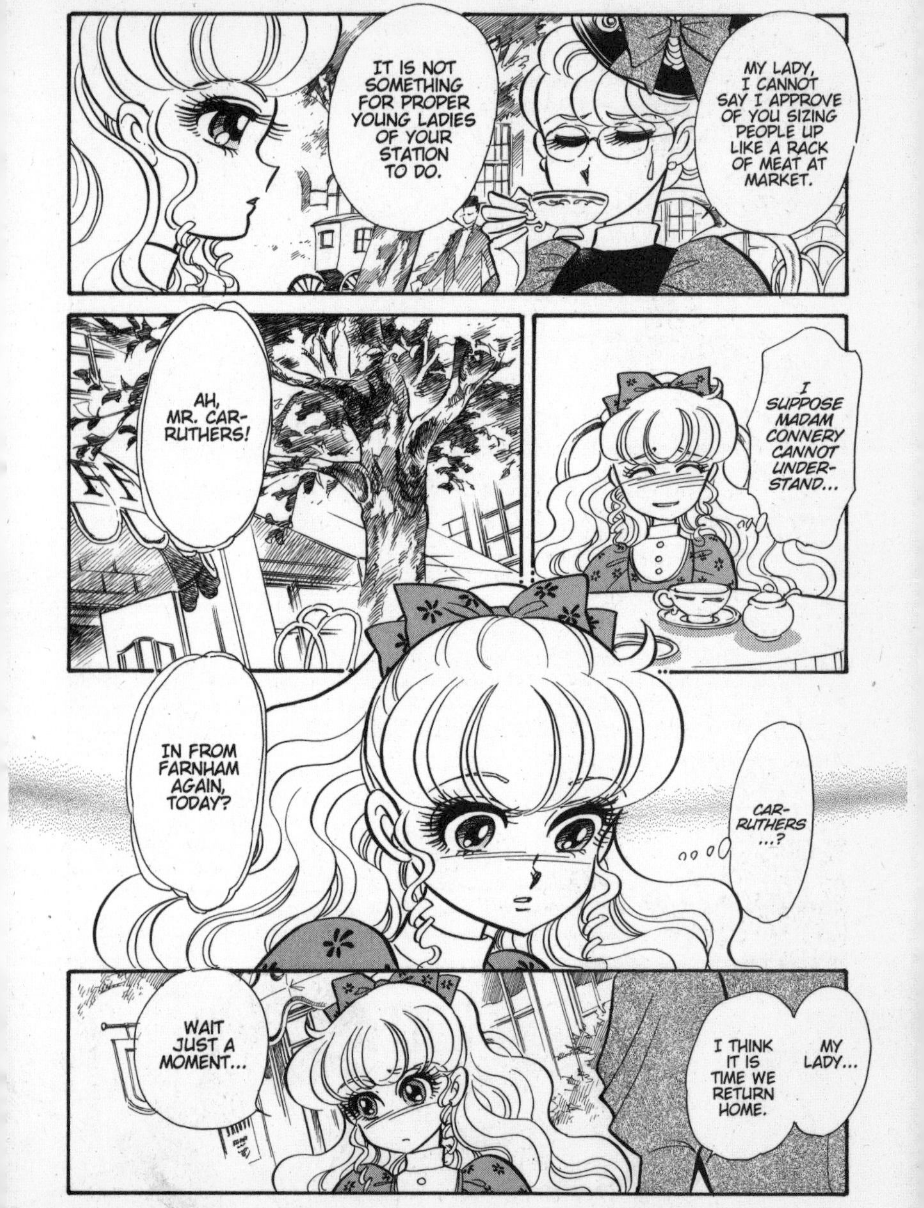
MY LADY, I CANNOT SAY I APPROVE OF YOU SIZING PEOPLE UP LIKE A RACK OF MEAT AT MARKET.
IT IS NOT SOMETHING FOR PROPER YOUNG LADIES OF YOUR STATION TO DO.
I SUPPOSE MADAM CONNERY CANNOT UNDER-STAND...
AH, MR. CAR-RUTHERS!
CAR-RUTHERS ...?
IN FROM FARNHAM AGAIN, TODAY?
MY LADY...
I THINK IT IS TIME WE RETURN HOME.
WAIT JUST A MOMENT...

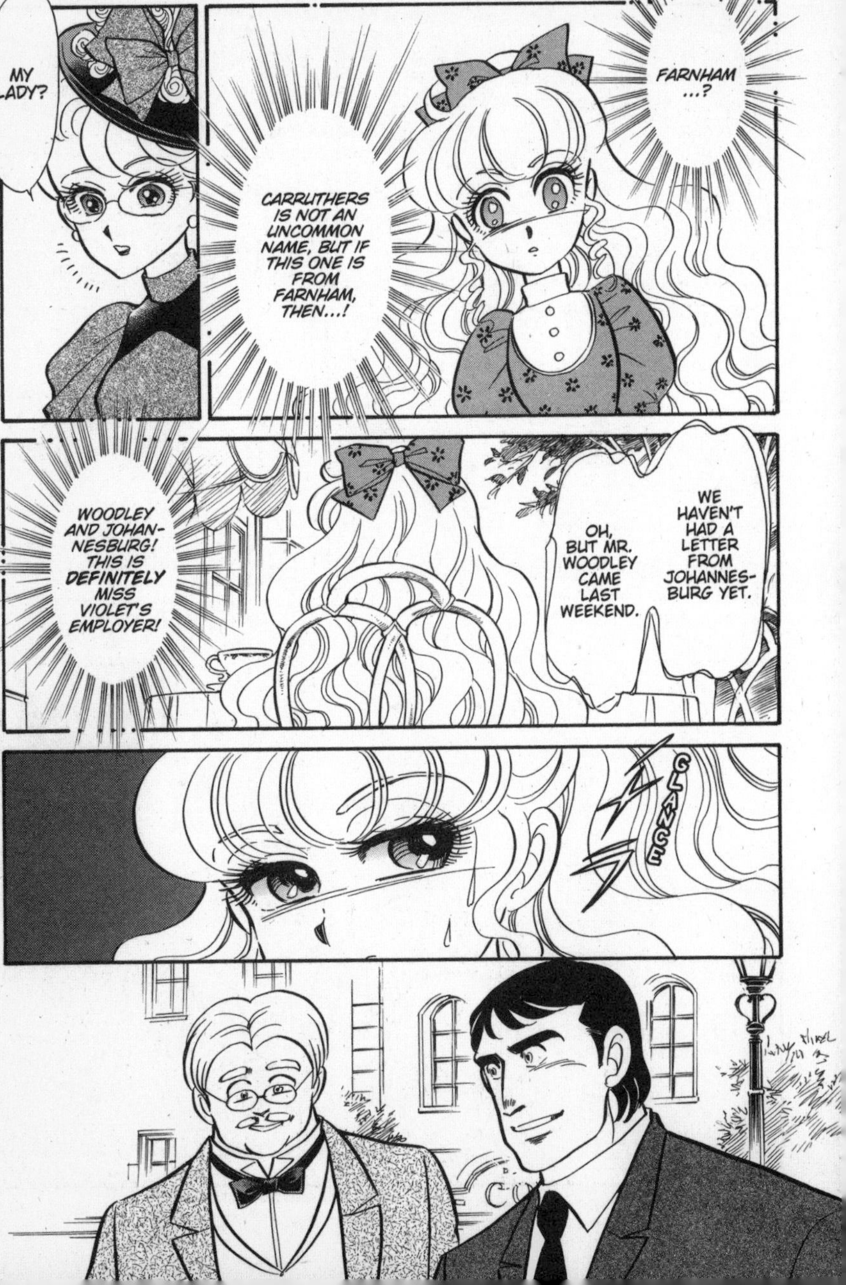
FARNHAM ...?
CARRUTHERS IS NOT AN UNCOMMON NAME, BUT IF THIS ONE IS FROM FARNHAM, THEN...!
MY LADY?
WE HAVEN'T HAD A LETTER FROM JOHANNESBURG YET.
OH, BUT MR. WOODLEY CAME LAST WEEKEND.
WOODLEY AND JOHAN-NESBURG! THIS IS **DEFINITELY** MISS VIOLET'S EMPLOYER!
GLANCE

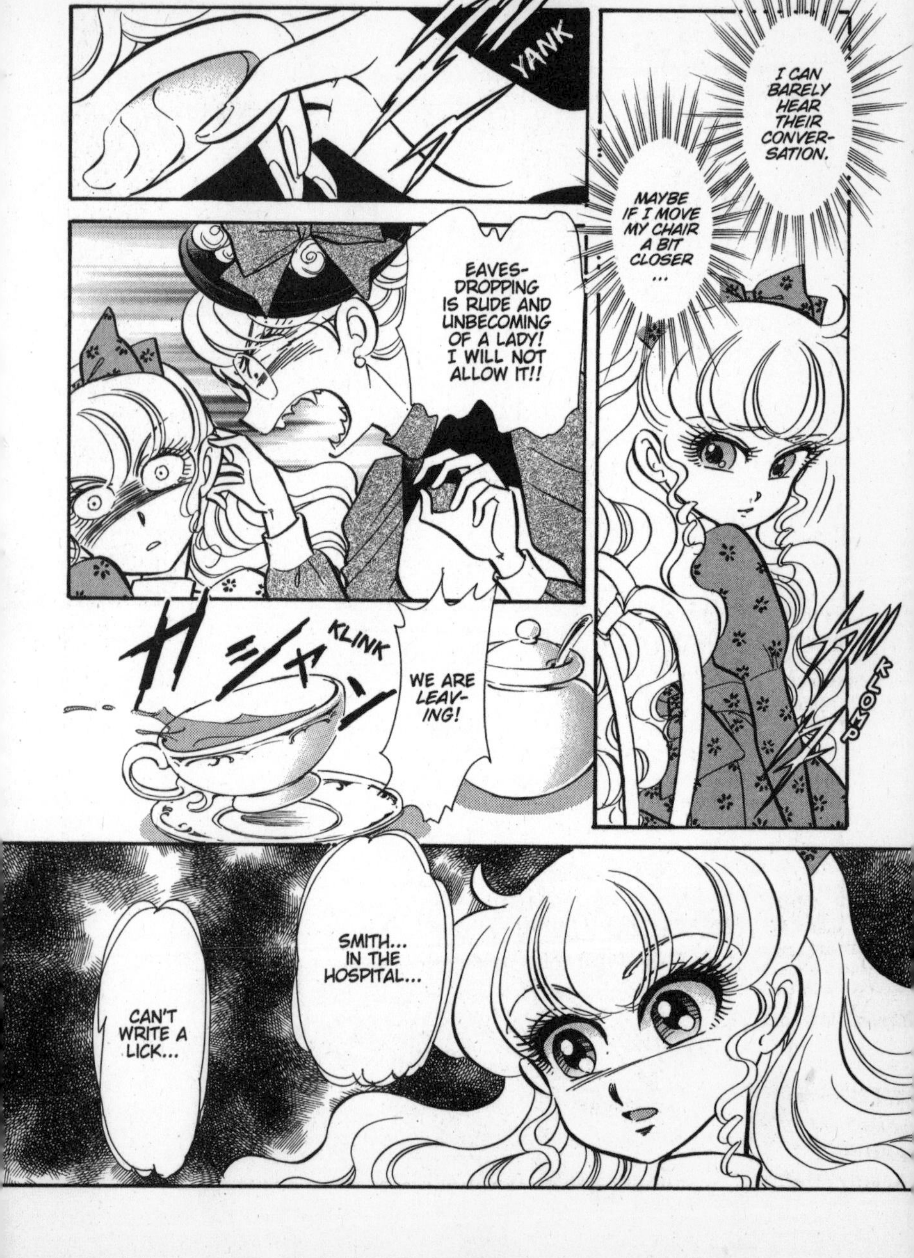
I CAN BARELY HEAR THEIR CONVER-SATION.
MAYBE IF I MOVE MY CHAIR A BIT CLOSER ...
YANK
EAVES-DROPPING IS RUDE AND UNBECOMING OF A LADY! I WILL NOT ALLOW IT!!
KLINK
WE ARE LEAV-ING!
SMITH... IN THE HOSPITAL...
CAN'T WRITE A LICK...

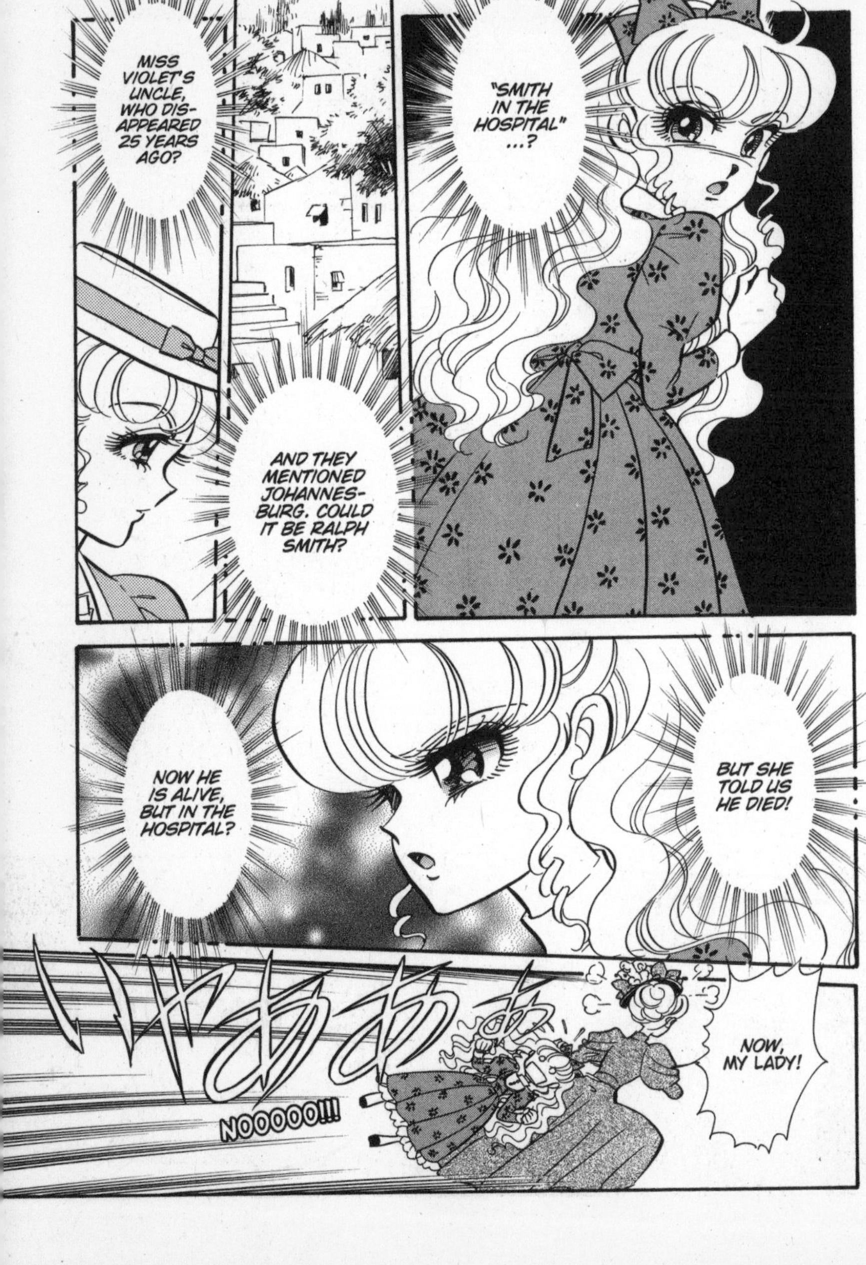
"SMITH IN THE HOSPITAL" ...?
AND THEY MENTIONED JOHANNES-BURG. COULD IT BE RALPH SMITH?
MISS VIOLET'S UNCLE, WHO DIS-APPEARED 25 YEARS AGO?
BUT SHE TOLD US HE DIED!
NOW HE IS ALIVE, BUT IN THE HOSPITAL?
NOW, MY LADY!
いやあああ
NOOOOO!!!

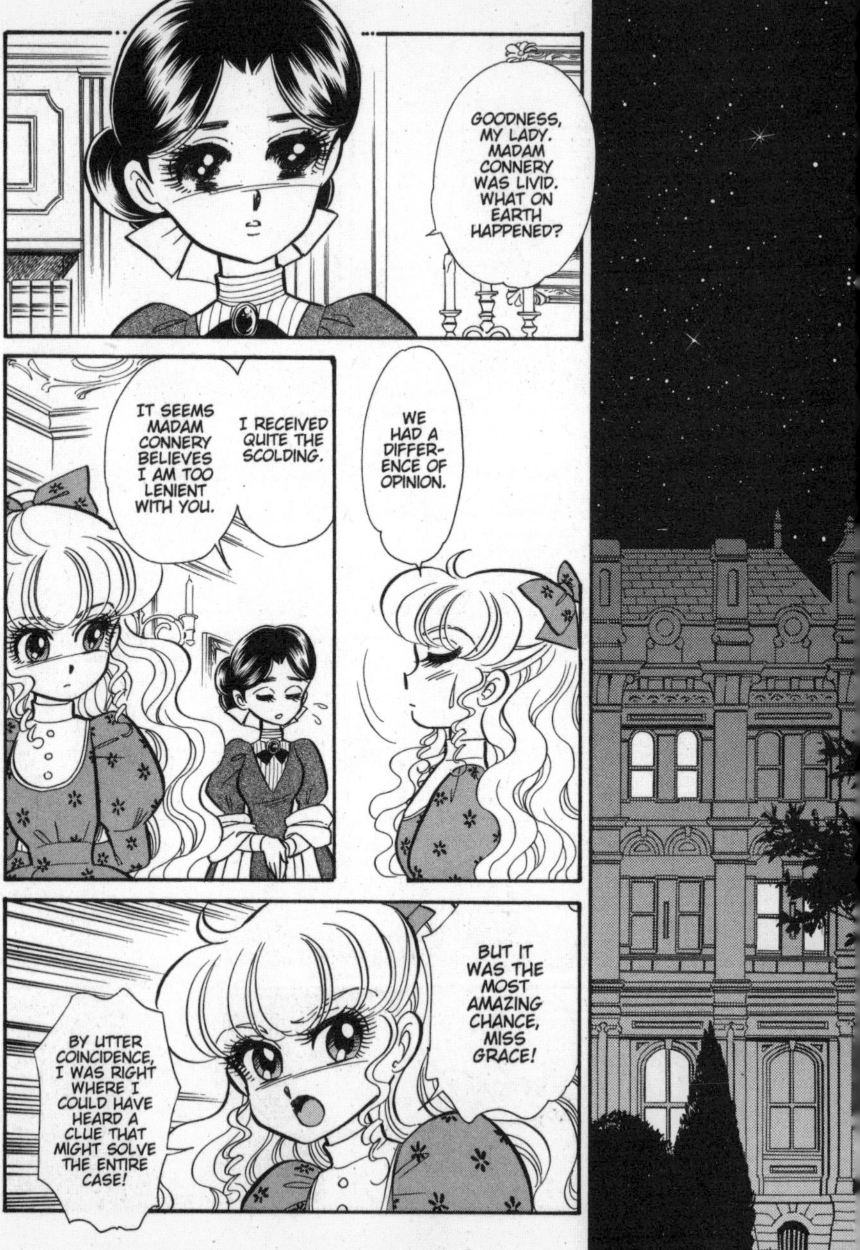
GOODNESS, MY LADY. MADAM CONNERY WAS LIVID. WHAT ON EARTH HAPPENED?
WE HAD A DIFFERENCE OF OPINION.
I RECEIVED QUITE THE SCOLDING.
IT SEEMS MADAM CONNERY BELIEVES I AM TOO LENIENT WITH YOU.
BUT IT WAS THE MOST AMAZING CHANCE, MISS GRACE!
BY UTTER COINCIDENCE, I WAS RIGHT WHERE I COULD HAVE HEARD A CLUE THAT MIGHT SOLVE THE ENTIRE CASE!

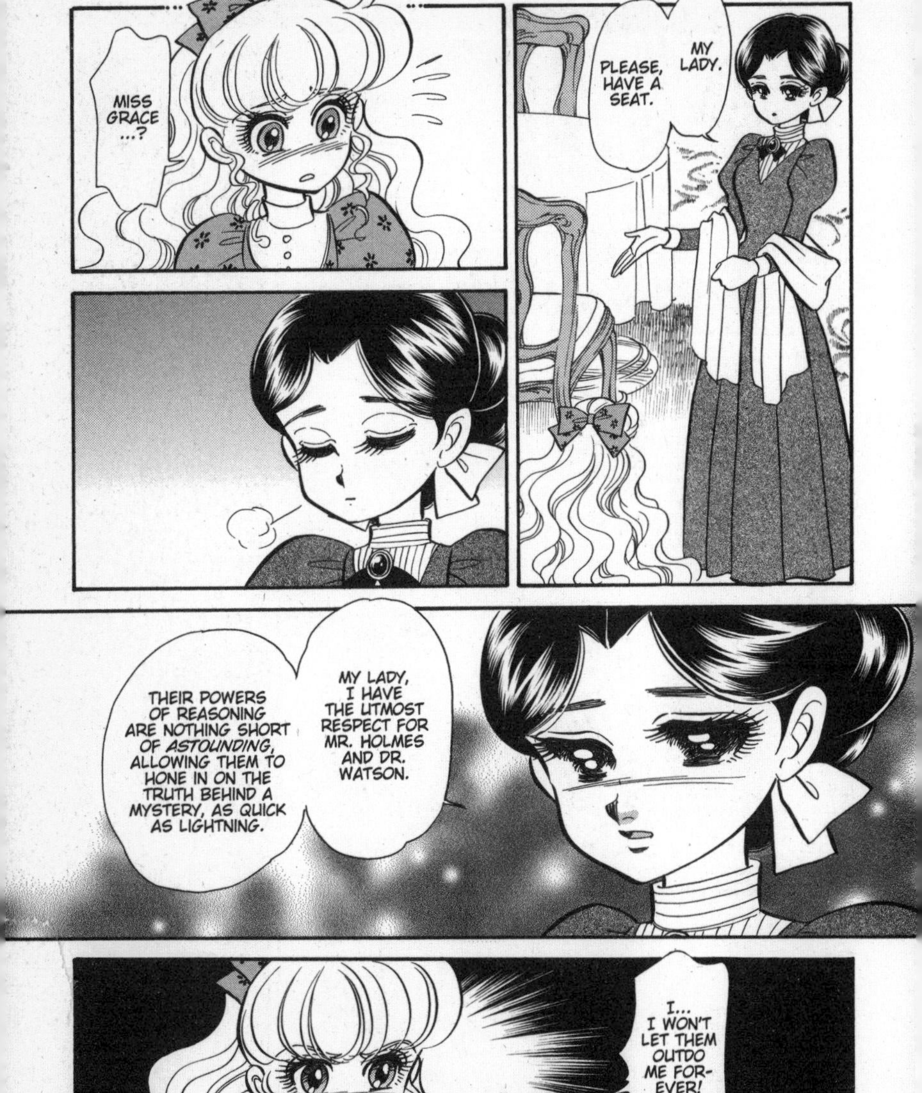
MY LADY.
PLEASE, HAVE A SEAT.
MISS GRACE ...?
MY LADY, I HAVE THE UTMOST RESPECT FOR MR. HOLMES AND DR. WATSON.
THEIR POWERS OF REASONING ARE NOTHING SHORT OF *ASTOUNDING*, ALLOWING THEM TO HONE IN ON THE TRUTH BEHIND A MYSTERY, AS QUICK AS LIGHTNING.
I... I WON'T LET THEM OUTDO ME FOR-EVER!

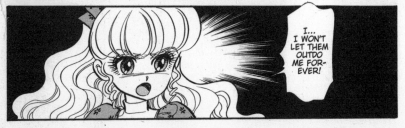

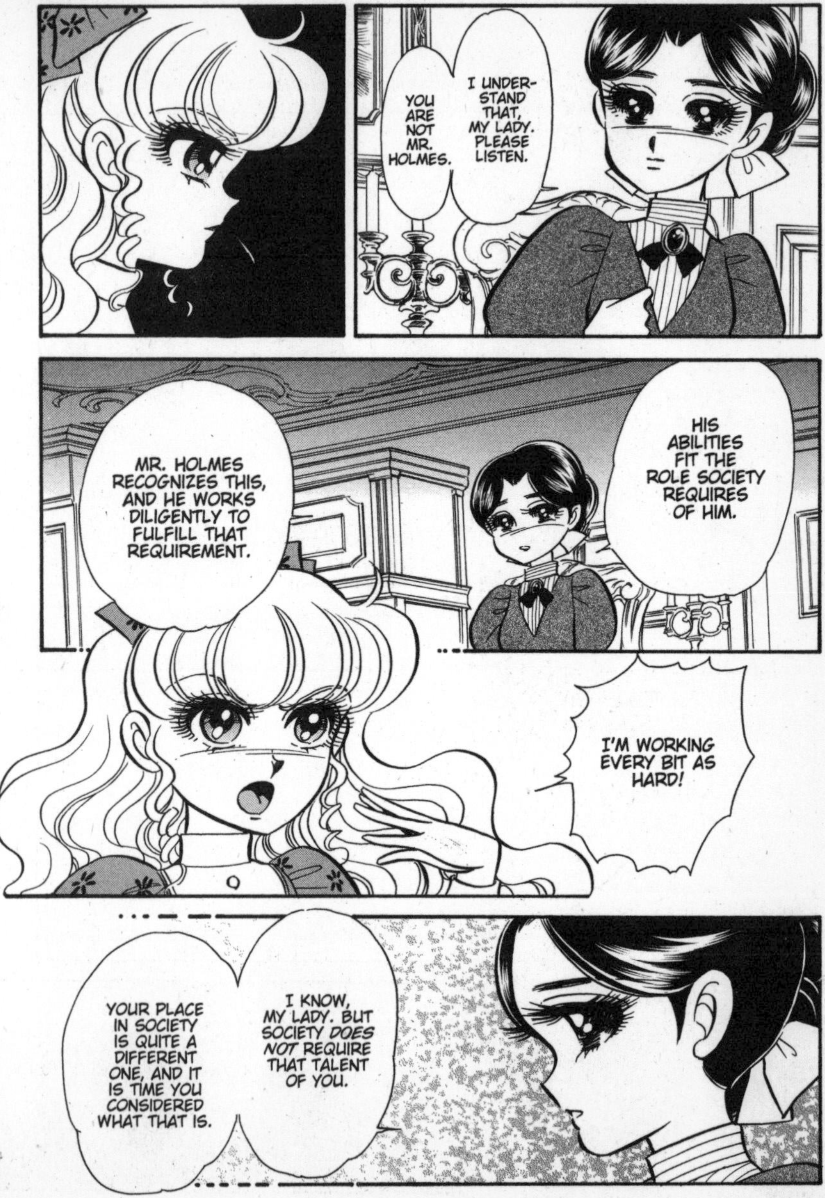
I UNDERSTAND THAT, MY LADY. PLEASE LISTEN.
YOU ARE NOT MR. HOLMES.
HIS ABILITIES FIT THE ROLE SOCIETY REQUIRES OF HIM.
MR. HOLMES RECOGNIZES THIS, AND HE WORKS DILIGENTLY TO FULFILL THAT REQUIREMENT.
I'M WORKING EVERY BIT AS HARD!
I KNOW, MY LADY. BUT SOCIETY *DOES NOT* REQUIRE THAT TALENT OF YOU.
YOUR PLACE IN SOCIETY IS QUITE A DIFFERENT ONE, AND IT IS TIME YOU CONSIDERED WHAT THAT IS.

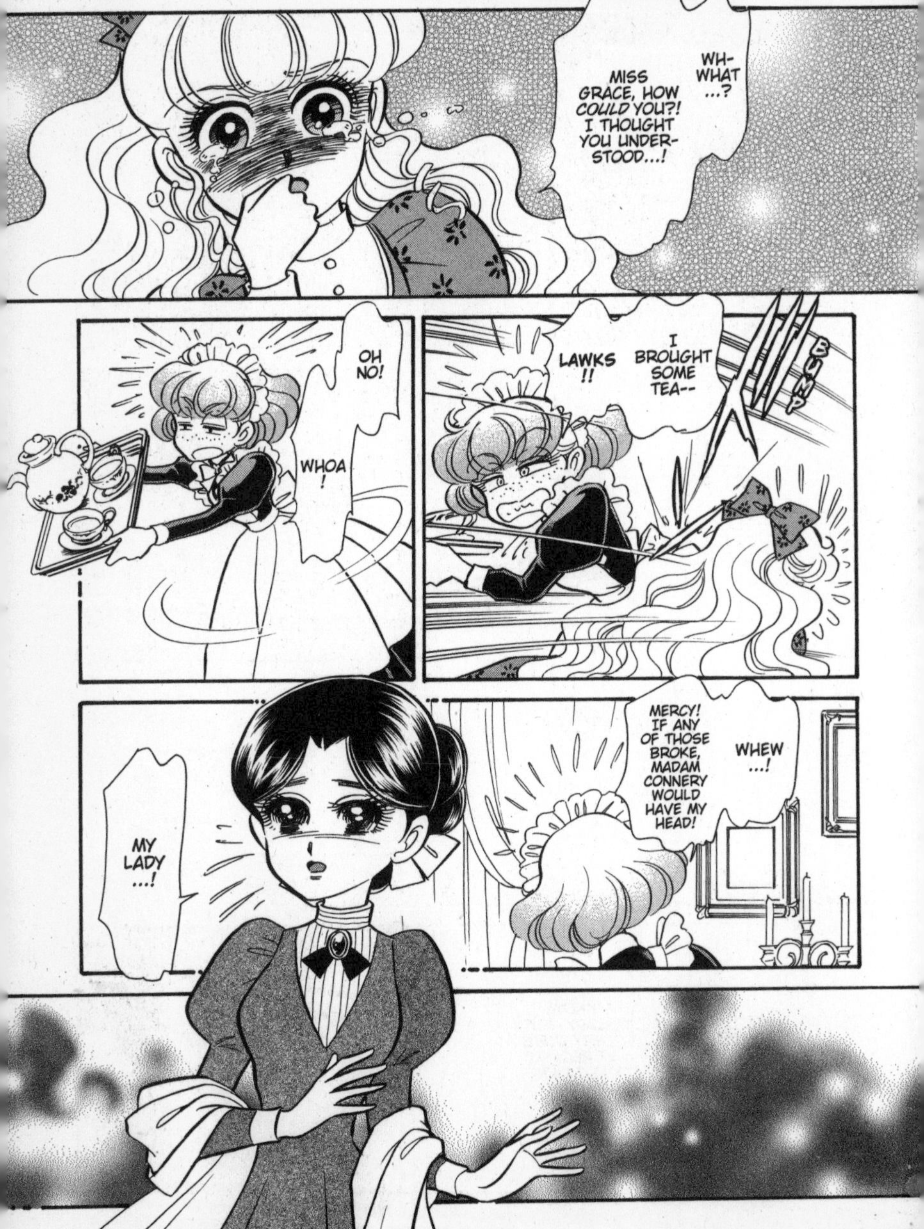
WH-WHAT ...?
MISS GRACE, HOW COULD YOU?! I THOUGHT YOU UNDER-STOOD...!
BUMP
I BROUGHT SOME TEA--
LAWKS !!
OH NO!
WHOA !
WHEW ...!
MERCY! IF ANY OF THOSE BROKE, MADAM CONNERY WOULD HAVE MY HEAD!
MY LADY ...!

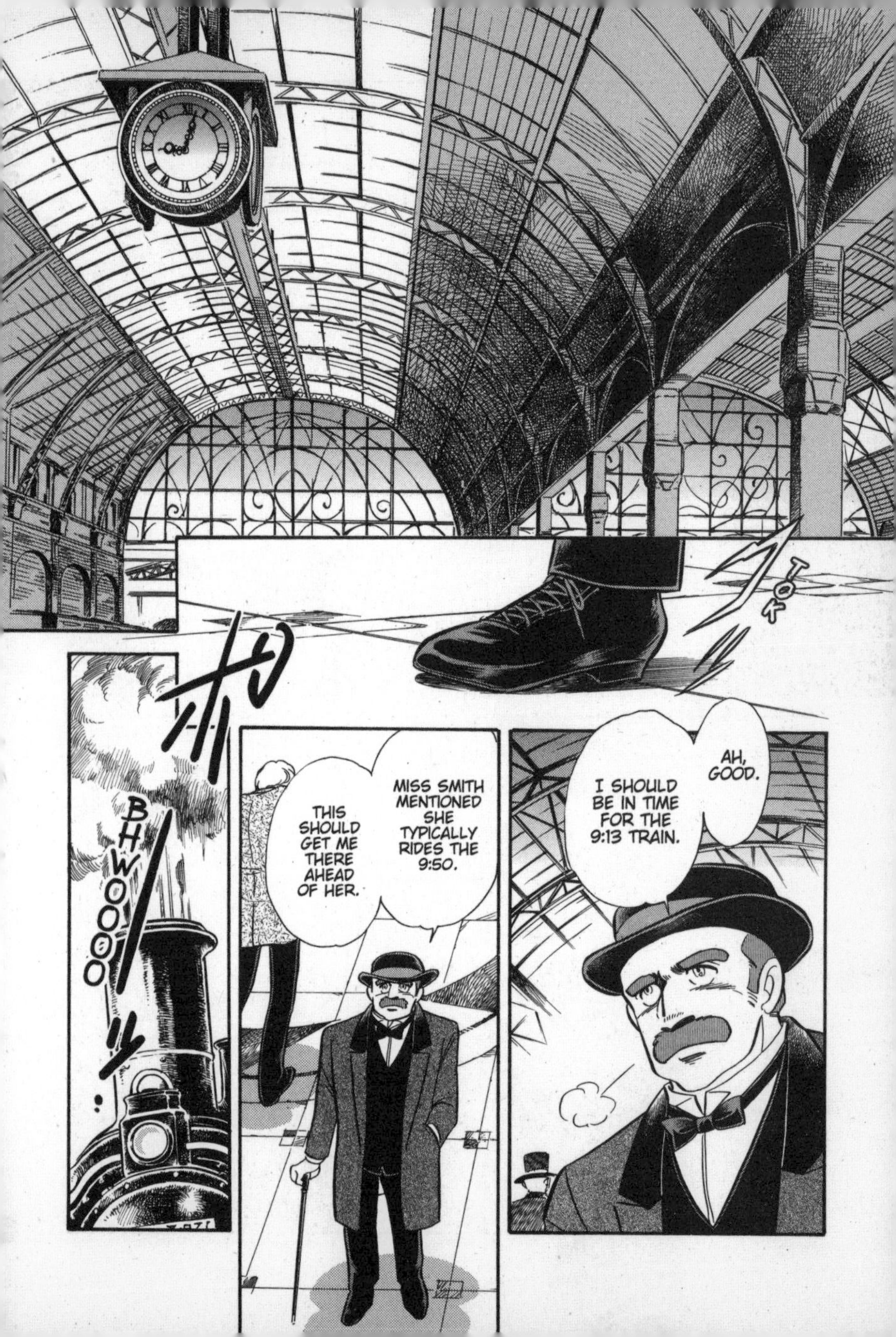
TOK
AH, GOOD.
I SHOULD BE IN TIME FOR THE 9:13 TRAIN.
MISS SMITH MENTIONED SHE TYPICALLY RIDES THE 9:50.
THIS SHOULD GET ME THERE AHEAD OF HER.
BHWOOOOO

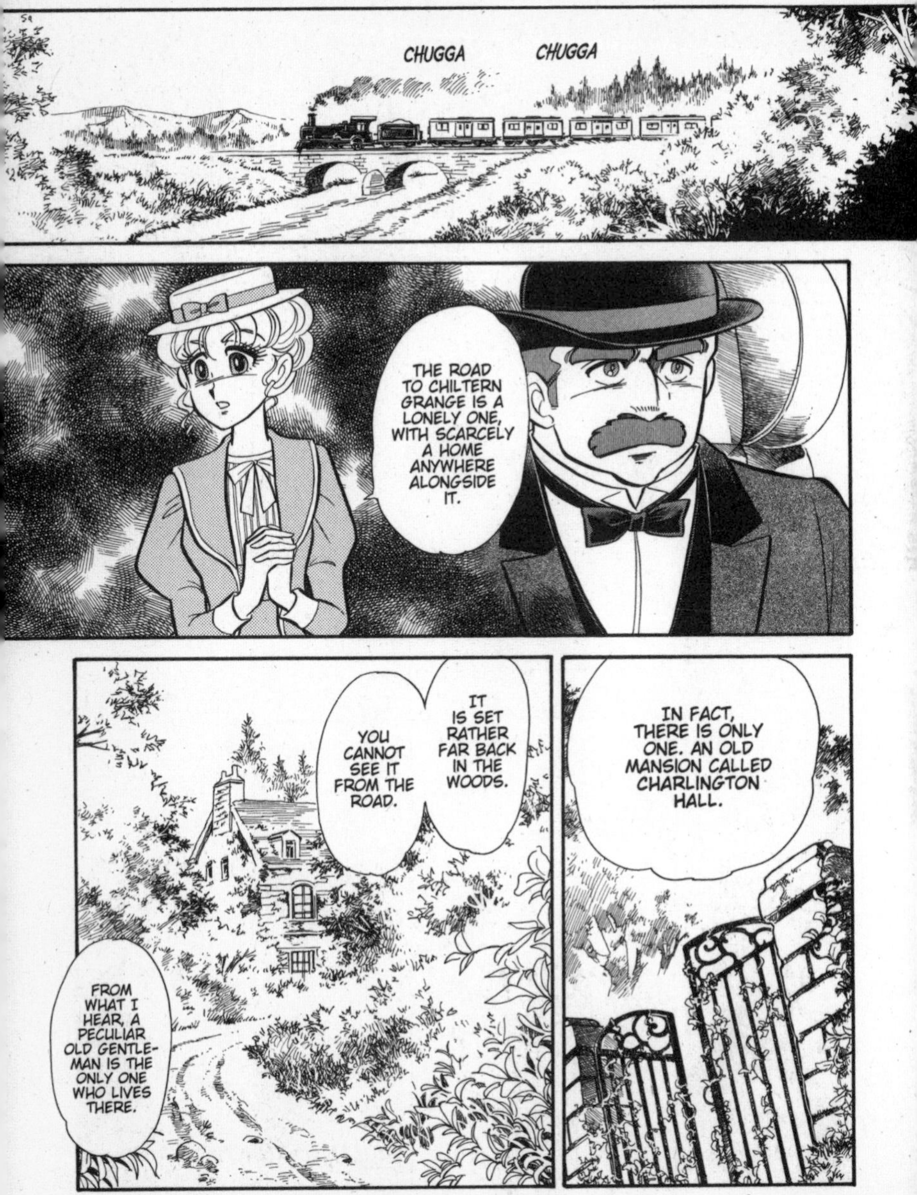
CHUGGA CHUGGA
THE ROAD TO CHILTERN GRANGE IS A LONELY ONE, WITH SCARCELY A HOME ANYWHERE ALONGSIDE IT.
IN FACT, THERE IS ONLY ONE. AN OLD MANSION CALLED CHARLINGTON HALL.
IT IS SET RATHER FAR BACK IN THE WOODS.
YOU CANNOT SEE IT FROM THE ROAD.
FROM WHAT I HEAR, A PECULIAR OLD GENTLEMAN IS THE ONLY ONE WHO LIVES THERE.

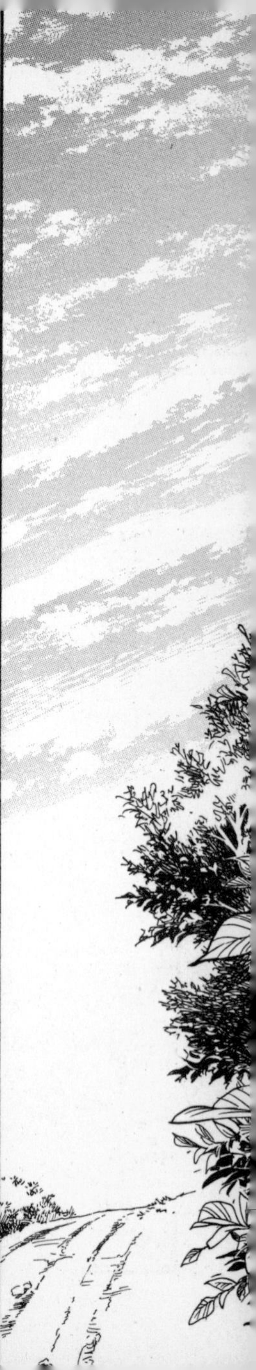

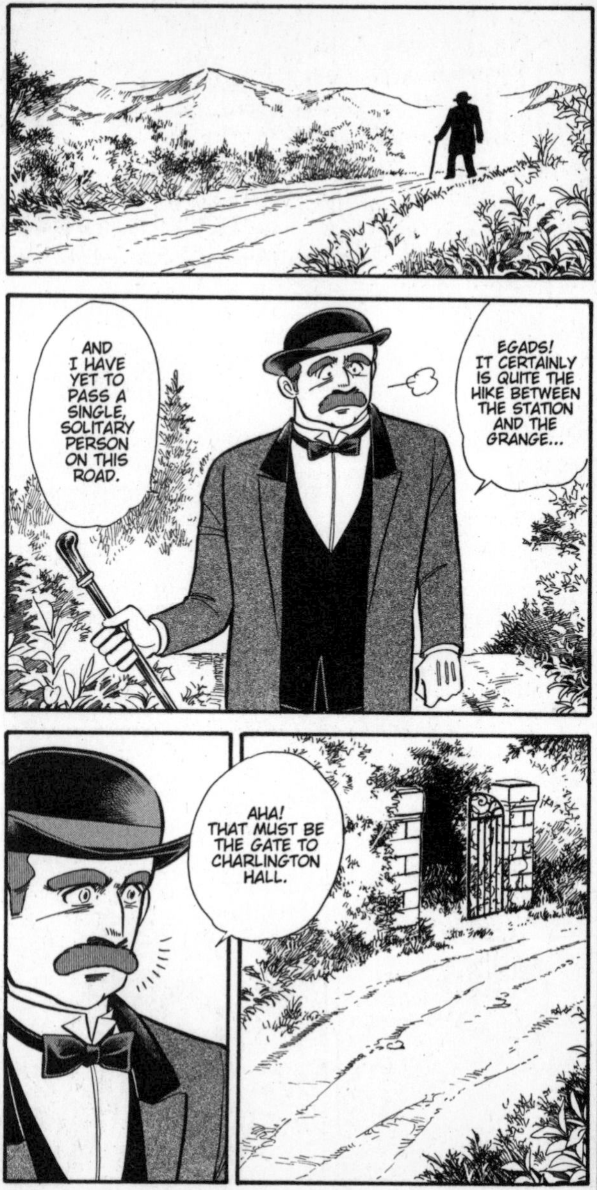
EGADS! IT CERTAINLY IS QUITE THE HIKE BETWEEN THE STATION AND THE GRANGE...
AND I HAVE YET TO PASS A SINGLE, SOLITARY PERSON ON THIS ROAD.
AHA! THAT MUST BE THE GATE TO CHARLINGTON HALL.

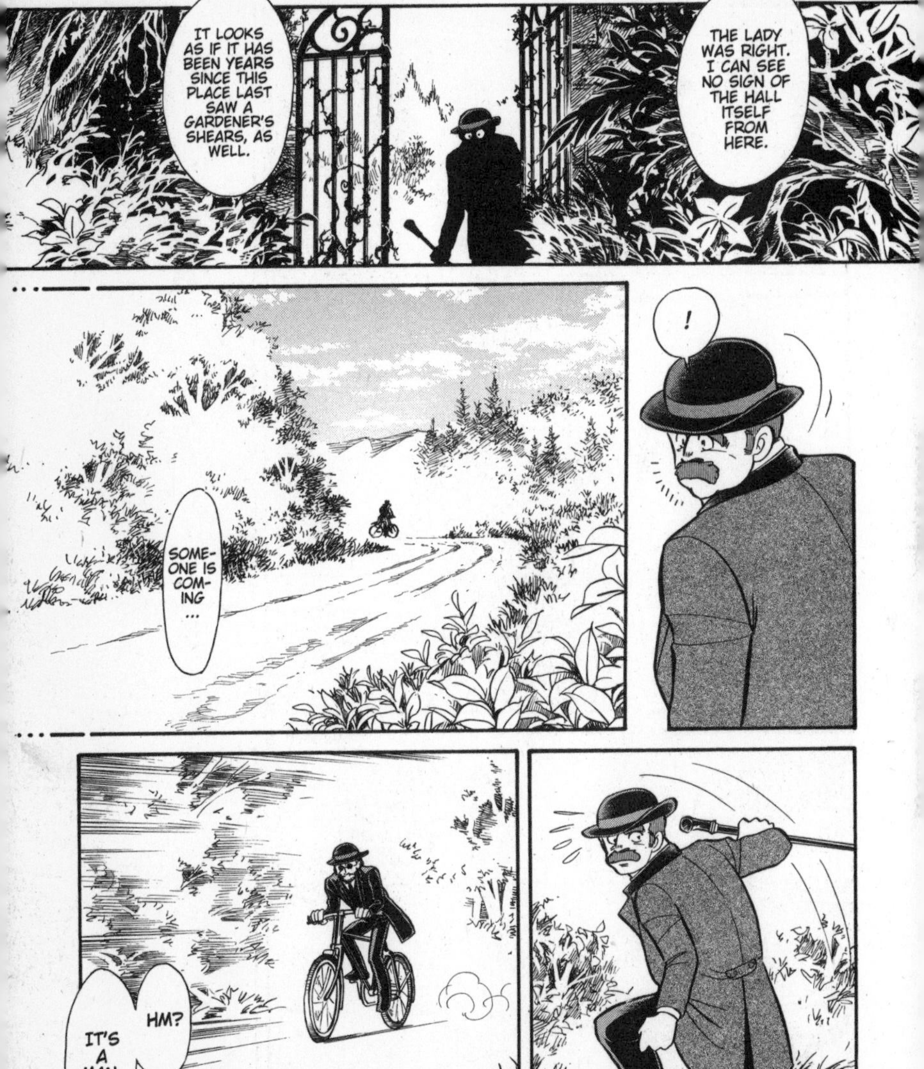
THE LADY WAS RIGHT. I CAN SEE NO SIGN OF THE HALL ITSELF FROM HERE.
IT LOOKS AS IF IT HAS BEEN YEARS SINCE THIS PLACE LAST SAW A GARDENER'S SHEARS, AS WELL.
!
SOME-ONE IS COM-ING ...
HM?
IT'S A MAN.

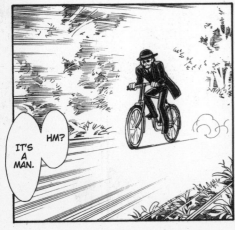

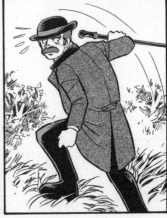

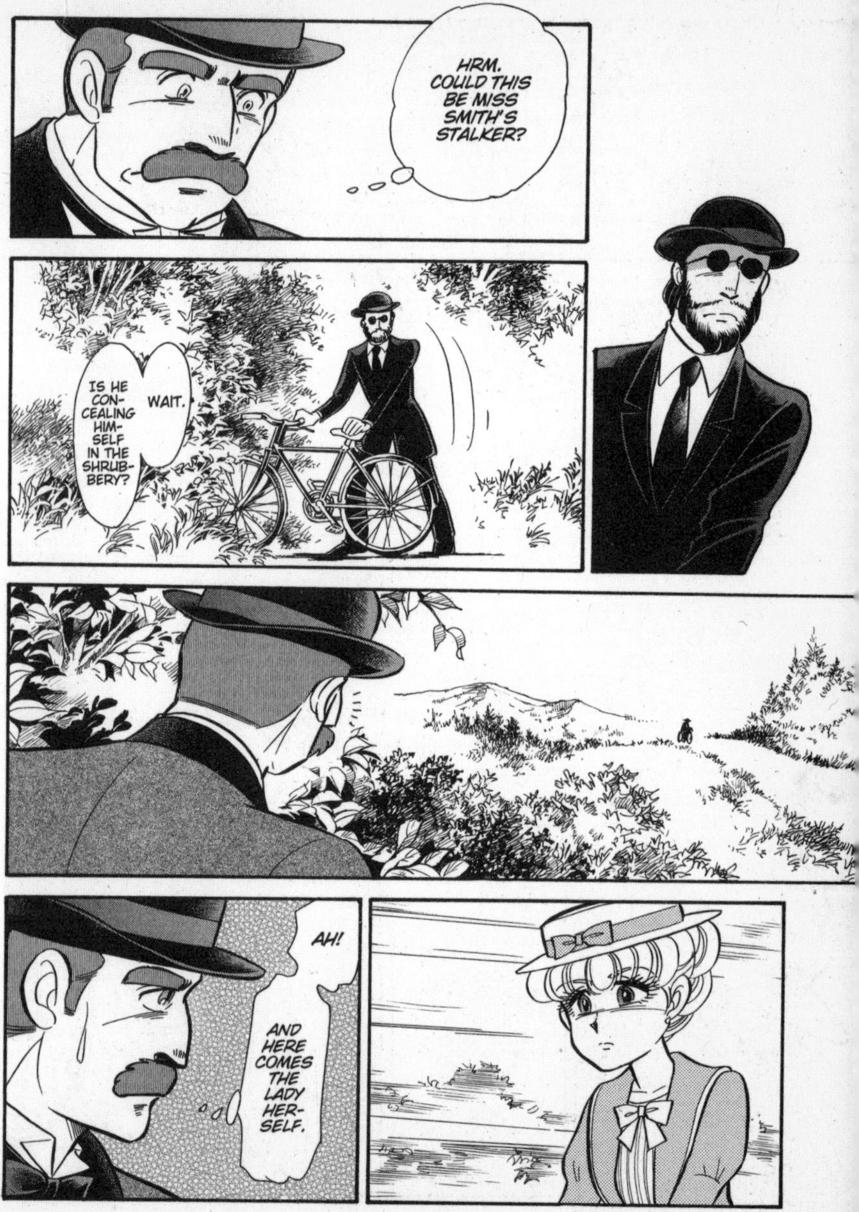
HRM. COULD THIS BE MISS SMITH'S STALKER?
WAIT.
IS HE CONCEALING HIMSELF IN THE SHRUBBERY?
AH!
AND HERE COMES THE LADY HERSELF.

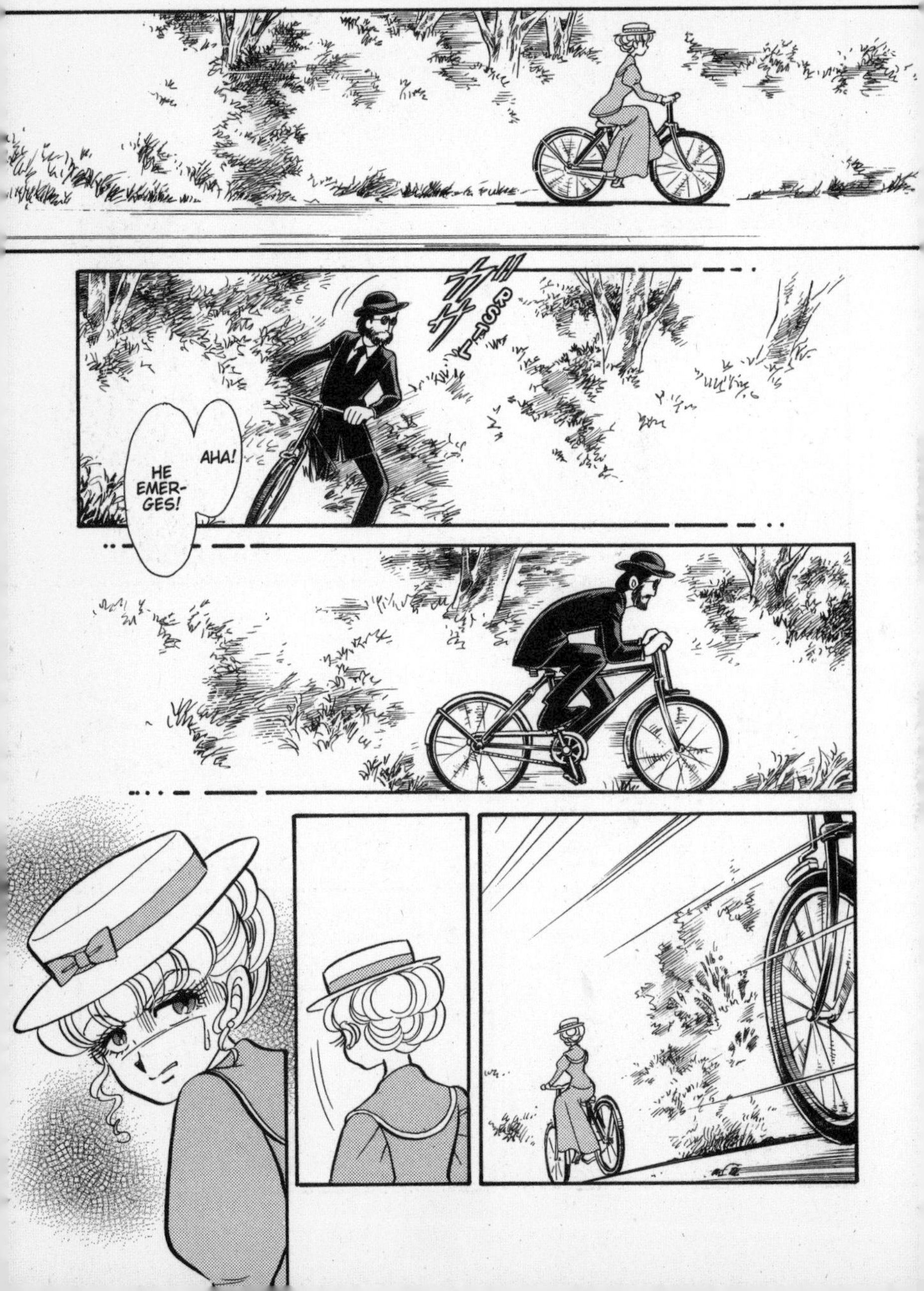
RUSTLE
AHA! HE EMERGES!

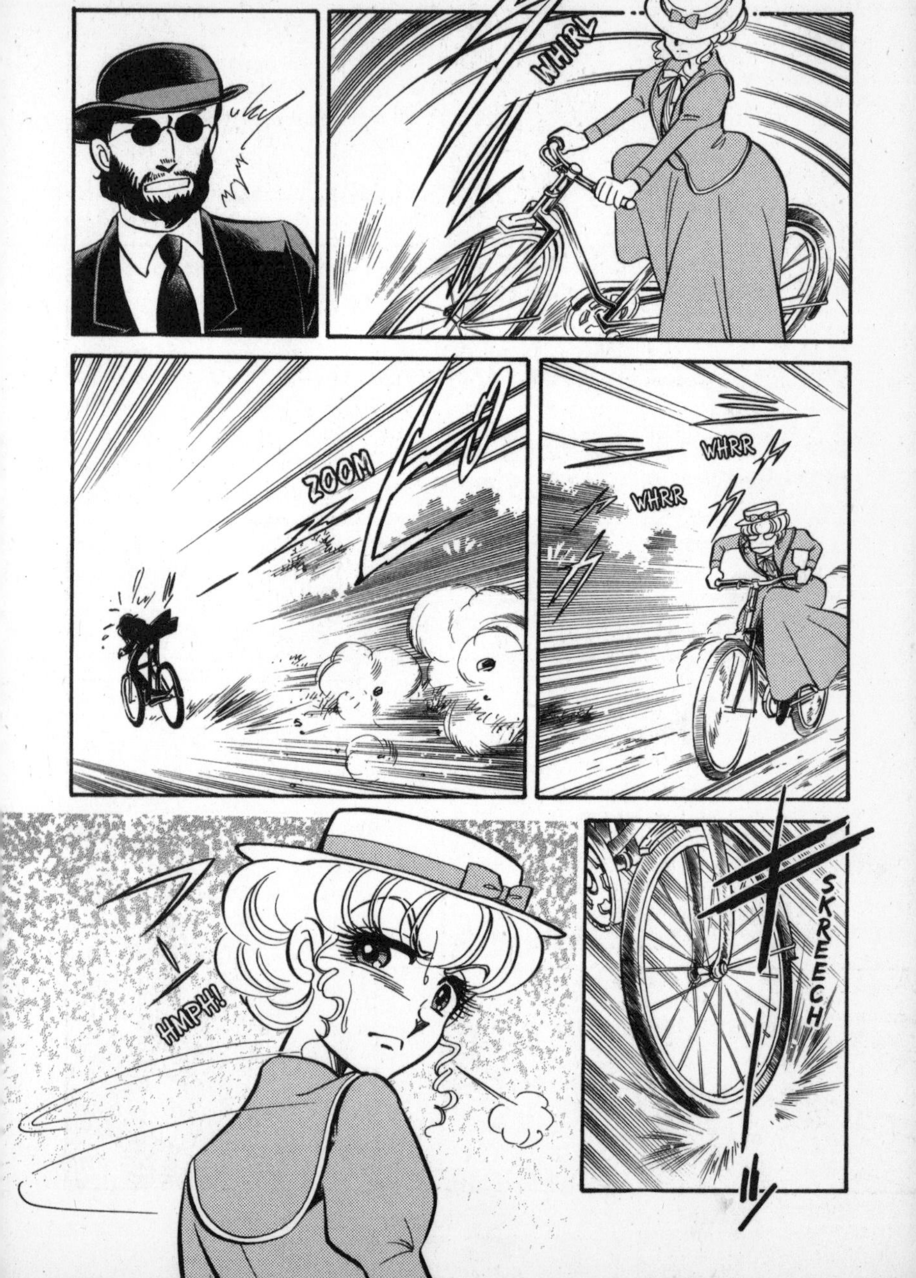
WHIRL
WHRR
WHRR
ZOOM
SKREECH
HMPH!

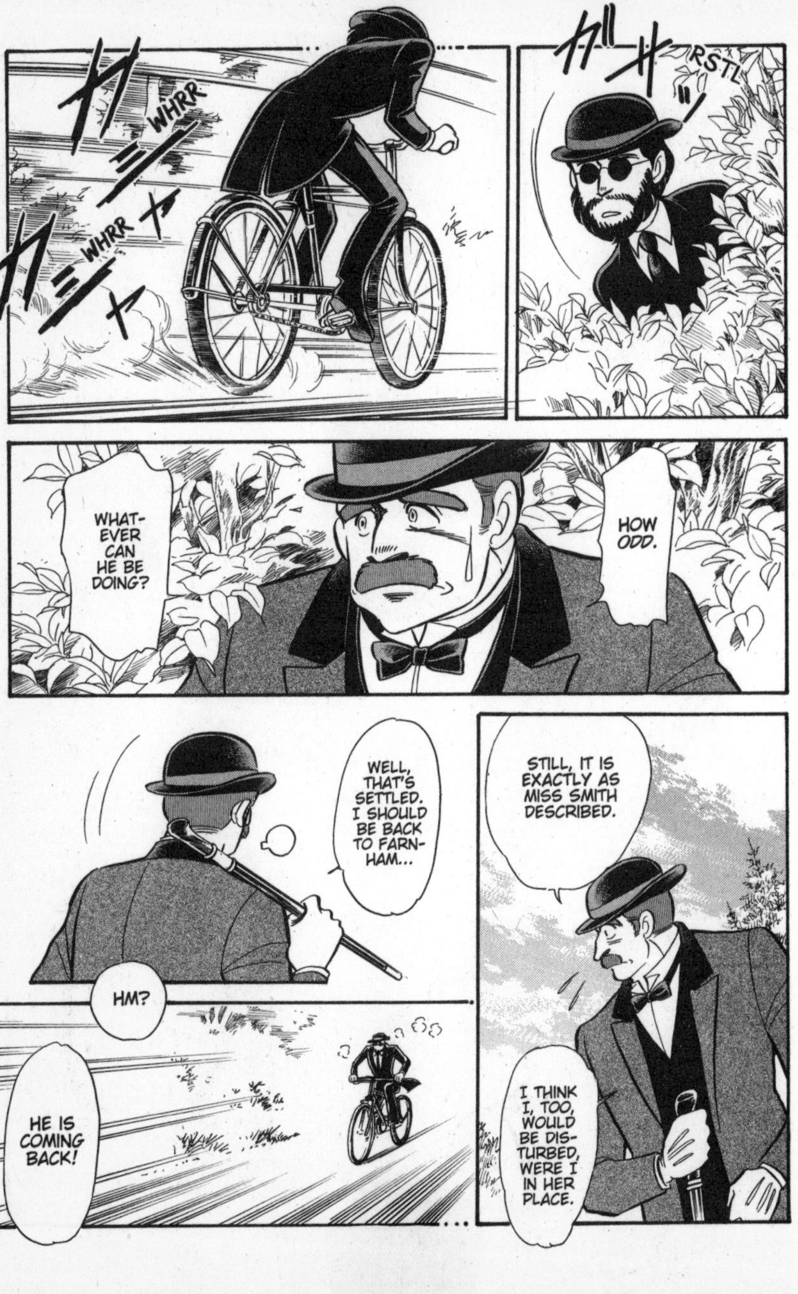
RSTL
WHRR
WHRR
HOW ODD.
WHAT-EVER CAN HE BE DOING?
STILL, IT IS EXACTLY AS MISS SMITH DESCRIBED.
I THINK I, TOO, WOULD BE DIS-TURBED, WERE I IN HER PLACE.
WELL, THAT'S SETTLED. I SHOULD BE BACK TO FARN-HAM...
HM?
HE IS COMING BACK!

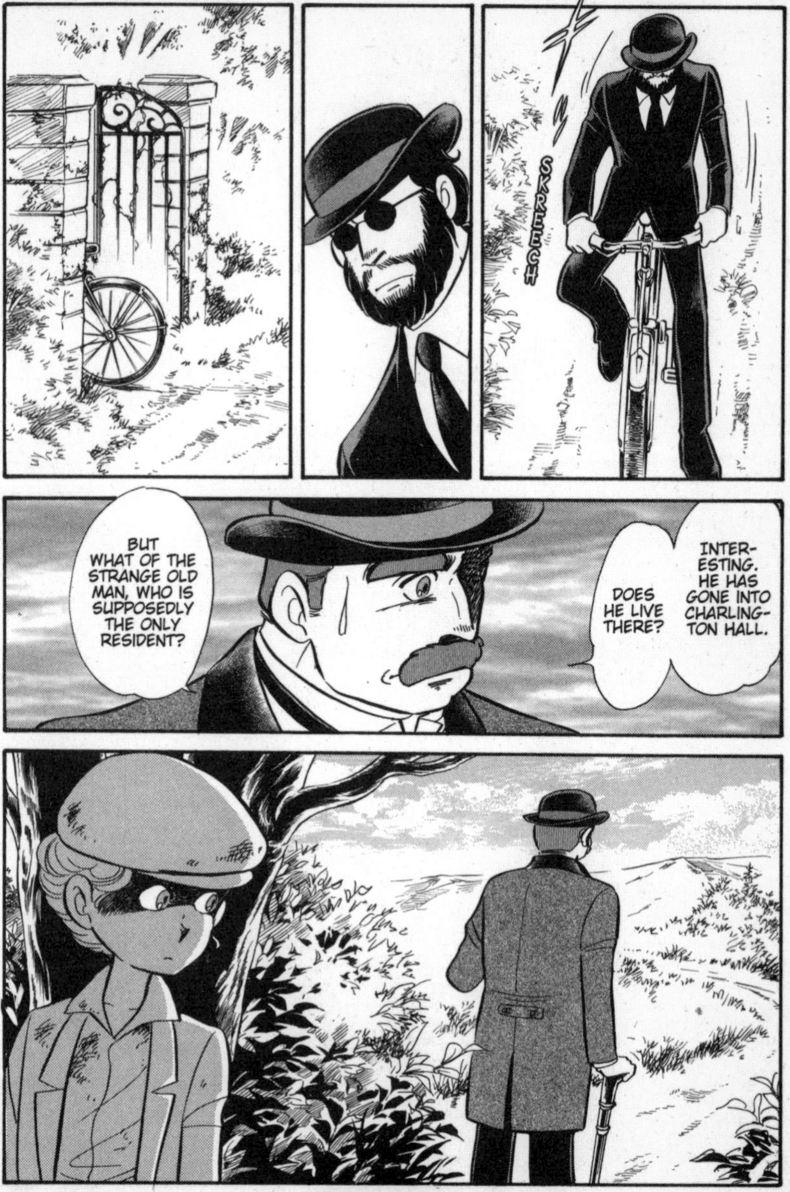
SKREECH
INTER-ESTING. HE HAS GONE INTO CHARLING-TON HALL.
DOES HE LIVE THERE?
BUT WHAT OF THE STRANGE OLD MAN, WHO IS SUPPOSEDLY THE ONLY RESIDENT?

The Adventure of the Solitary Cyclist (4)

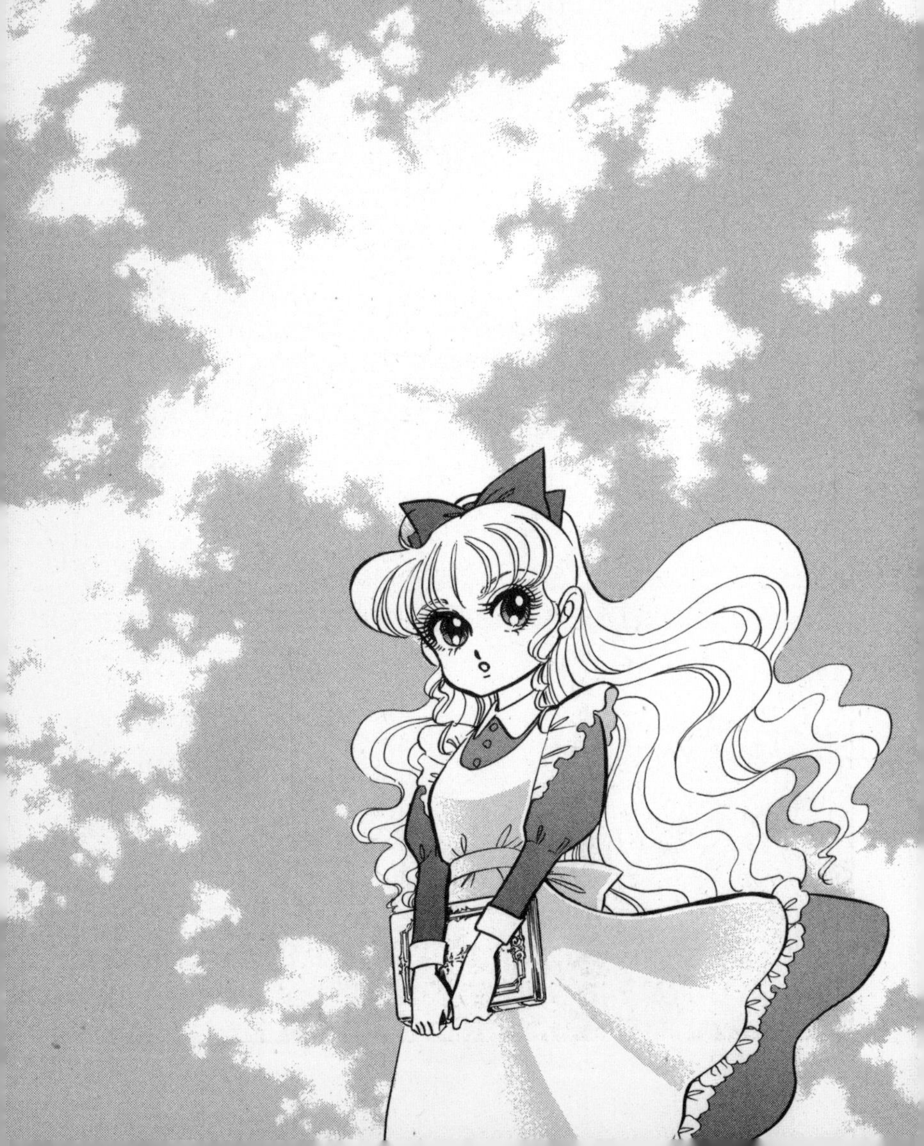

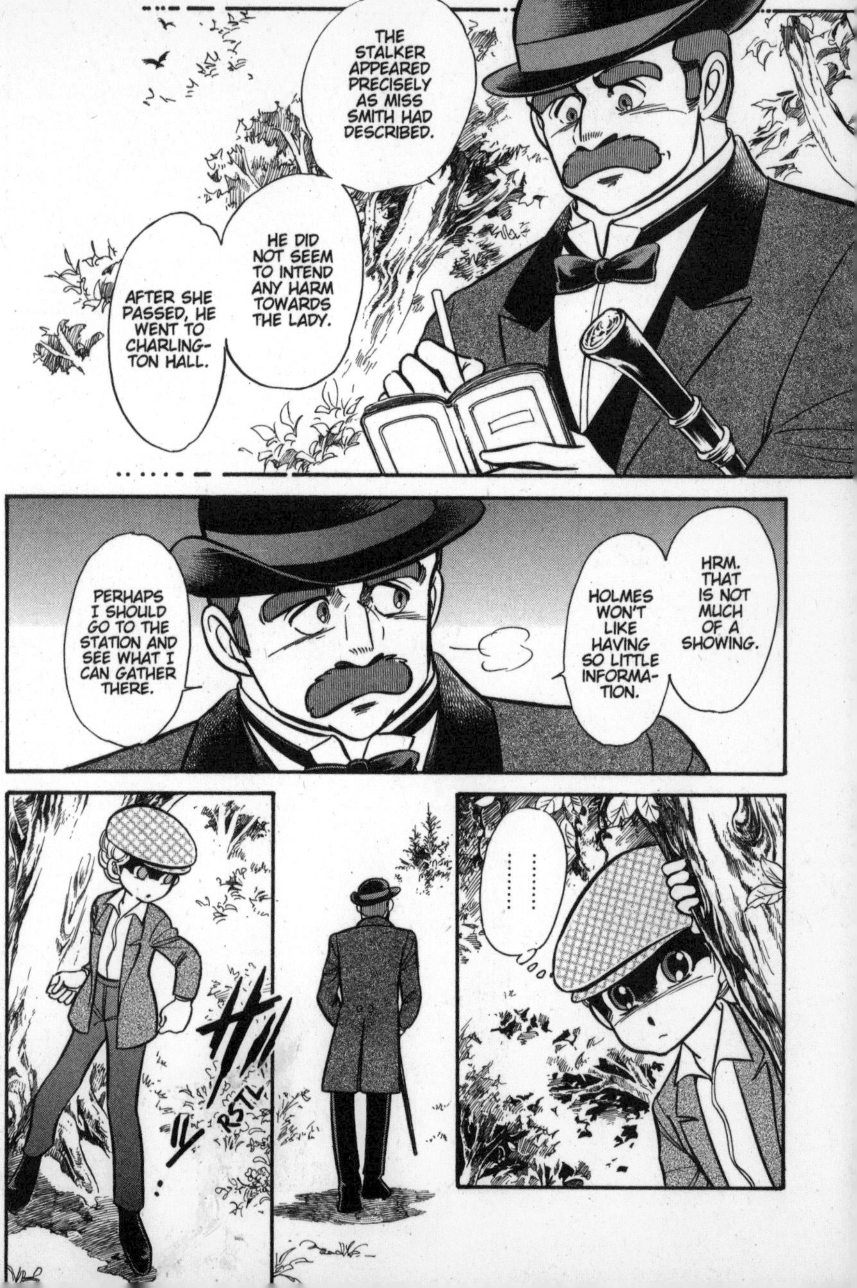
THE STALKER APPEARED PRECISELY AS MISS SMITH HAD DESCRIBED.
HE DID NOT SEEM TO INTEND ANY HARM TOWARDS THE LADY.
AFTER SHE PASSED, HE WENT TO CHARLING-TON HALL.
HRM. THAT IS NOT MUCH OF A SHOWING.
HOLMES WON'T LIKE HAVING SO LITTLE INFORMA-TION.
PERHAPS I SHOULD GO TO THE STATION AND SEE WHAT I CAN GATHER THERE.
......
RSTL

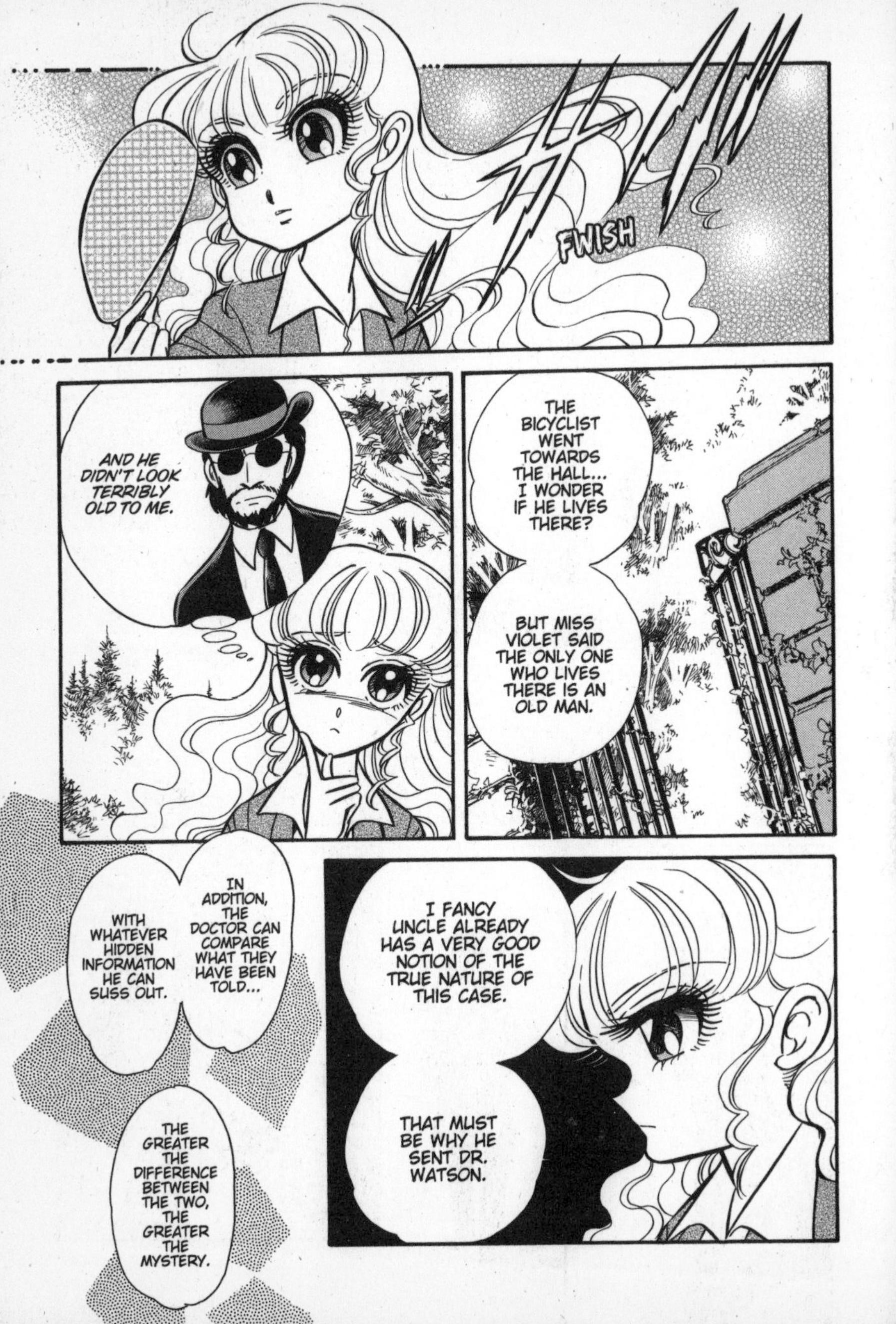
FWISH
THE BICYCLIST WENT TOWARDS THE HALL... I WONDER IF HE LIVES THERE?
BUT MISS VIOLET SAID THE ONLY ONE WHO LIVES THERE IS AN OLD MAN.
AND HE DIDN'T LOOK TERRIBLY OLD TO ME.
I FANCY UNCLE ALREADY HAS A VERY GOOD NOTION OF THE TRUE NATURE OF THIS CASE.
THAT MUST BE WHY HE SENT DR. WATSON.
IN ADDITION, THE DOCTOR CAN COMPARE WHAT THEY HAVE BEEN TOLD...
WITH WHATEVER HIDDEN INFORMATION HE CAN SUSS OUT.
THE GREATER THE DIFFERENCE BETWEEN THE TWO, THE GREATER THE MYSTERY.

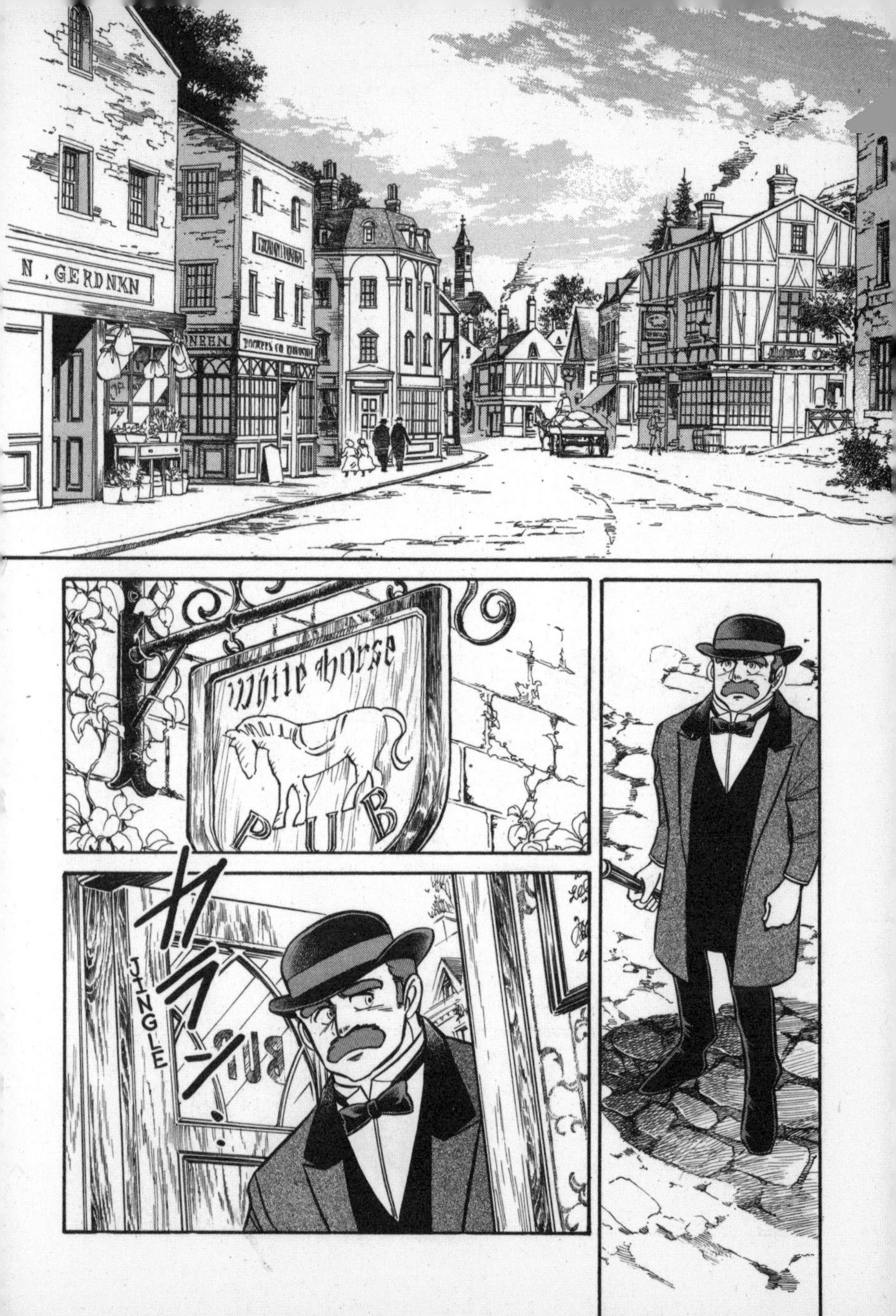
White horse
PUB
JINGLE

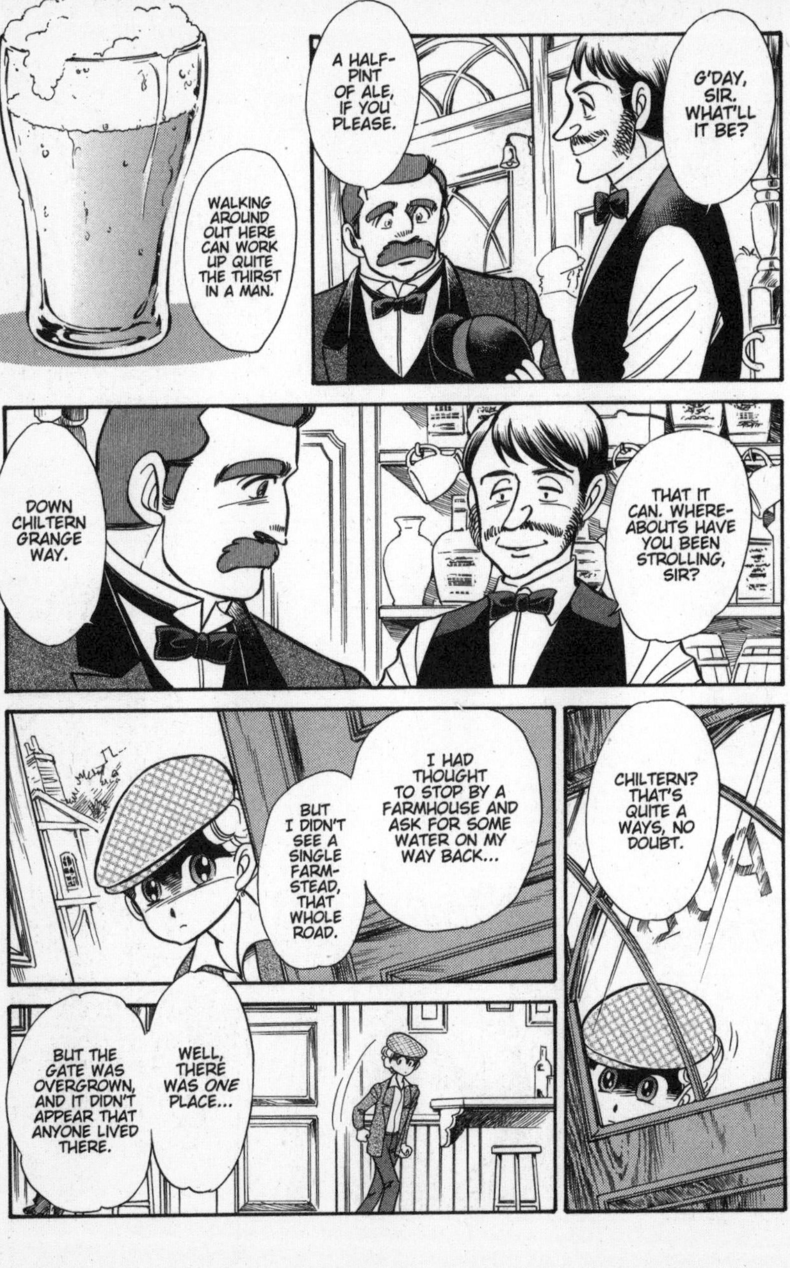
G'DAY, SIR. WHAT'LL IT BE?
A HALF-PINT OF ALE, IF YOU PLEASE.
WALKING AROUND OUT HERE CAN WORK UP QUITE THE THIRST IN A MAN.
THAT IT CAN. WHEREABOUTS HAVE YOU BEEN STROLLING, SIR?
DOWN CHILTERN GRANGE WAY.
CHILTERN? THAT'S QUITE A WAYS, NO DOUBT.
I HAD THOUGHT TO STOP BY A FARMHOUSE AND ASK FOR SOME WATER ON MY WAY BACK...
BUT I DIDN'T SEE A SINGLE FARMSTEAD, THAT WHOLE ROAD.
WELL, THERE WAS ONE PLACE...
BUT THE GATE WAS OVERGROWN, AND IT DIDN'T APPEAR THAT ANYONE LIVED THERE.

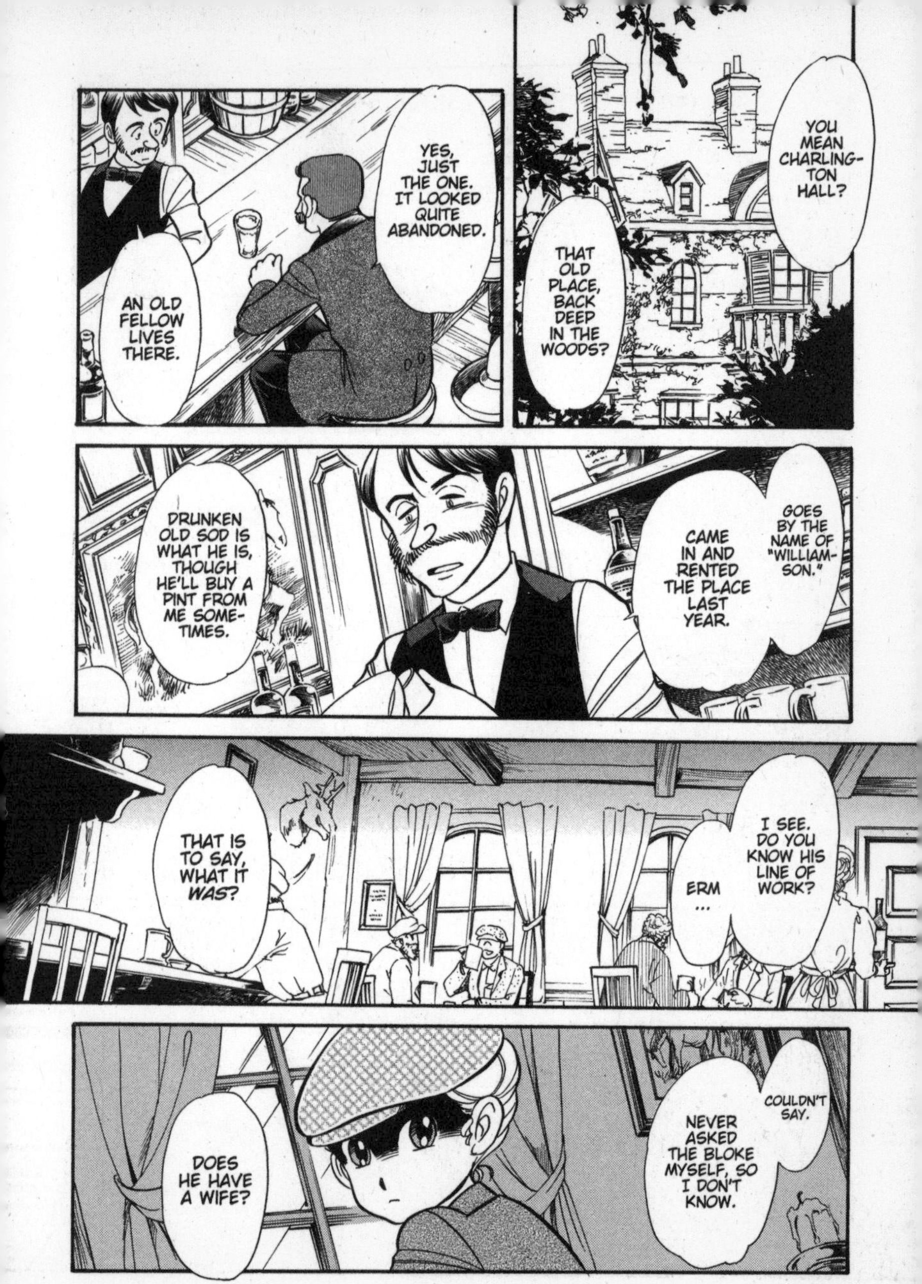
YOU MEAN CHARLINGTON HALL?
THAT OLD PLACE, BACK DEEP IN THE WOODS?
YES, JUST THE ONE. IT LOOKED QUITE ABANDONED.
AN OLD FELLOW LIVES THERE.
GOES BY THE NAME OF "WILLIAMSON."
CAME IN AND RENTED THE PLACE LAST YEAR.
DRUNKEN OLD SOD IS WHAT HE IS, THOUGH HE'LL BUY A PINT FROM ME SOMETIMES.
I SEE. DO YOU KNOW HIS LINE OF WORK?
ERM ...
THAT IS TO SAY, WHAT IT *WAS*?
COULDN'T SAY.
NEVER ASKED THE BLOKE MYSELF, SO I DON'T KNOW.
DOES HE HAVE A WIFE?

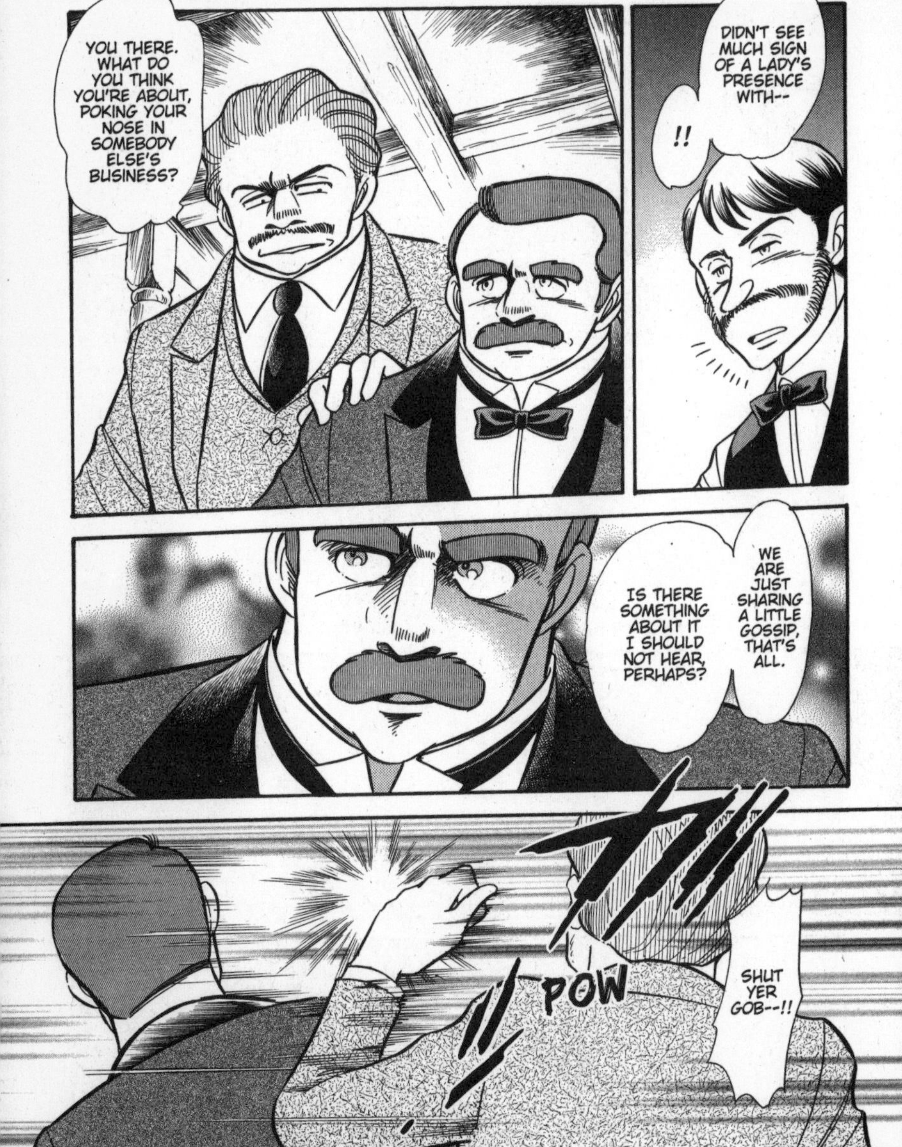
DIDN'T SEE MUCH SIGN OF A LADY'S PRESENCE WITH--
!!
YOU THERE. WHAT DO YOU THINK YOU'RE ABOUT, POKING YOUR NOSE IN SOMEBODY ELSE'S BUSINESS?
WE ARE JUST SHARING A LITTLE GOSSIP, THAT'S ALL.
IS THERE SOMETHING ABOUT IT I SHOULD NOT HEAR, PERHAPS?
SHUT YER GOB--!!
POW

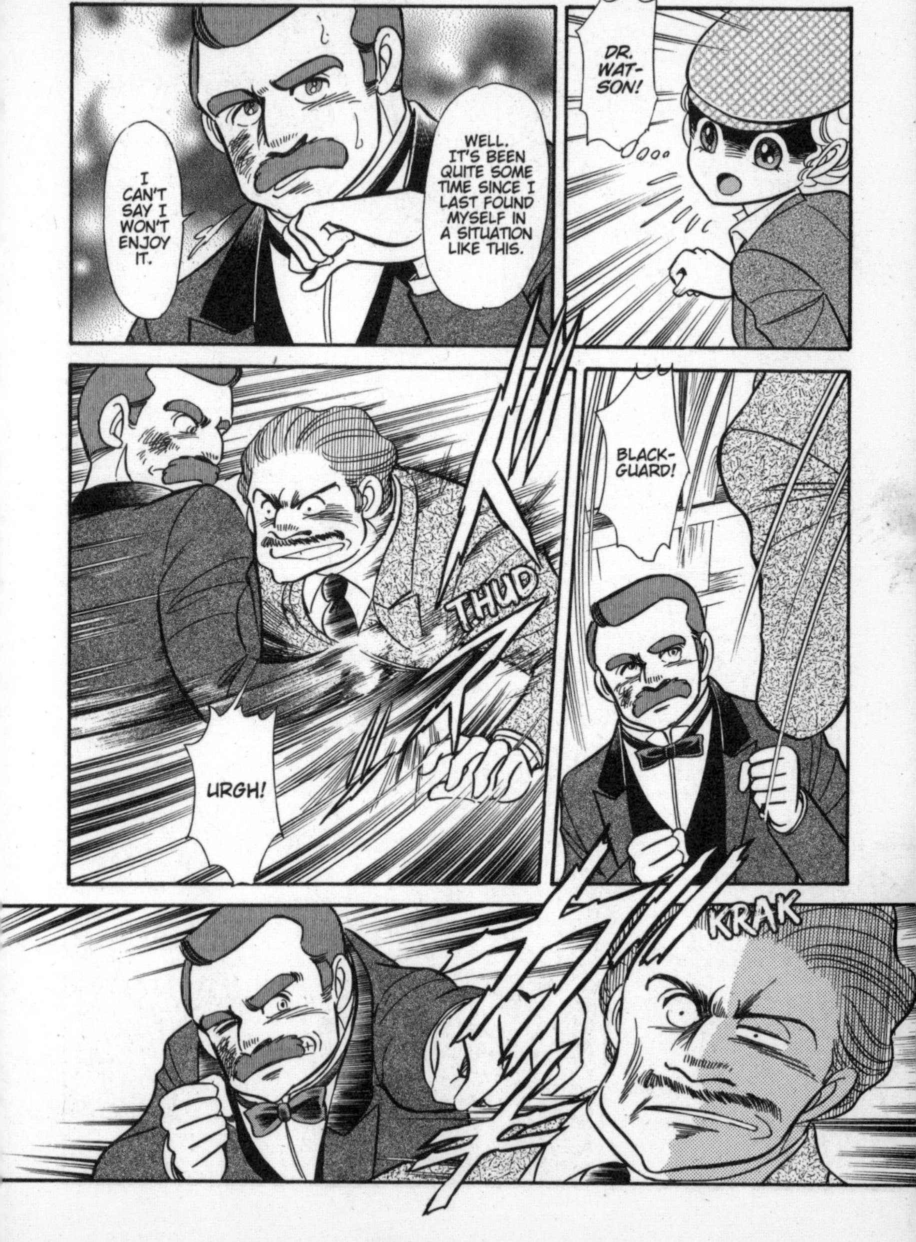
DR. WATSON!
WELL. IT'S BEEN QUITE SOME TIME SINCE I LAST FOUND MYSELF IN A SITUATION LIKE THIS.
I CAN'T SAY I WON'T ENJOY IT.
BLACKGUARD!
THUD
URGH!
KRAK

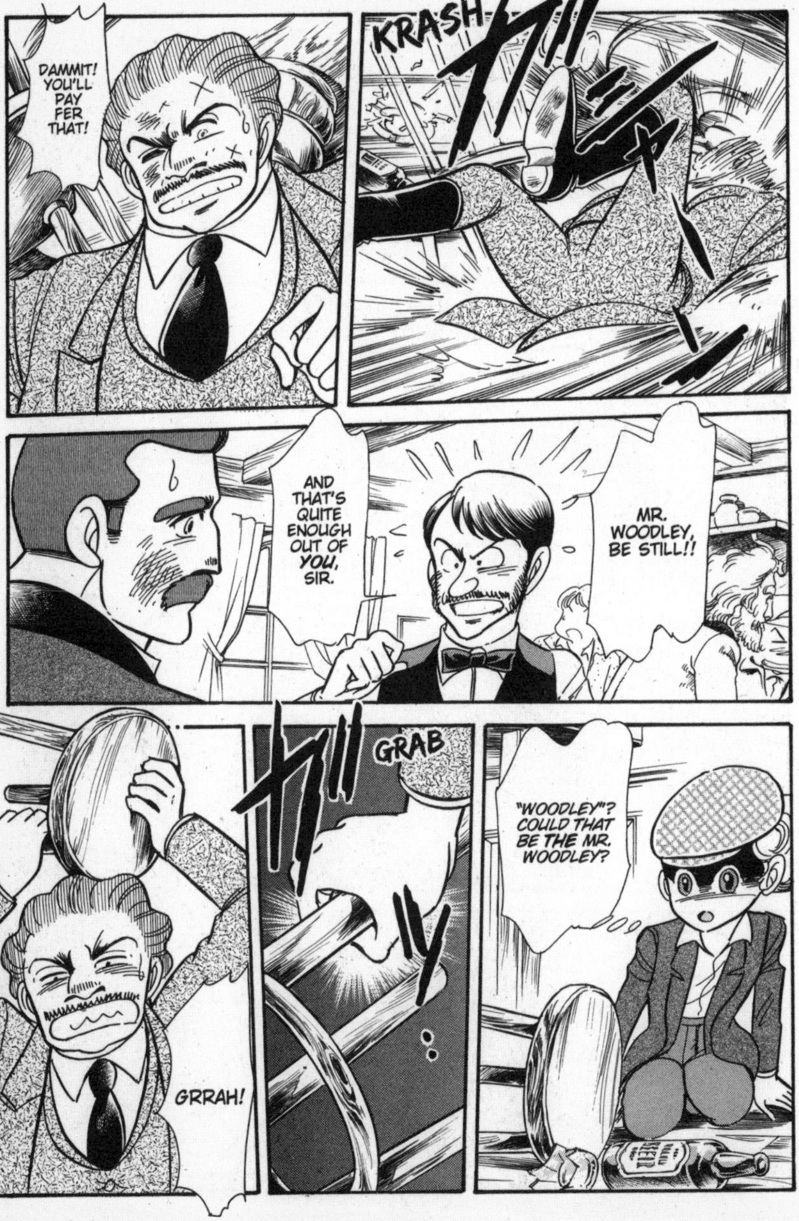
KRASH
DAMMIT! YOU'LL PAY FER THAT!
MR. WOODLEY, BE STILL!!
AND THAT'S QUITE ENOUGH OUT OF *YOU*, SIR.
"WOODLEY"? COULD THAT BE *THE* MR. WOODLEY?
GRAB
GRRAH!

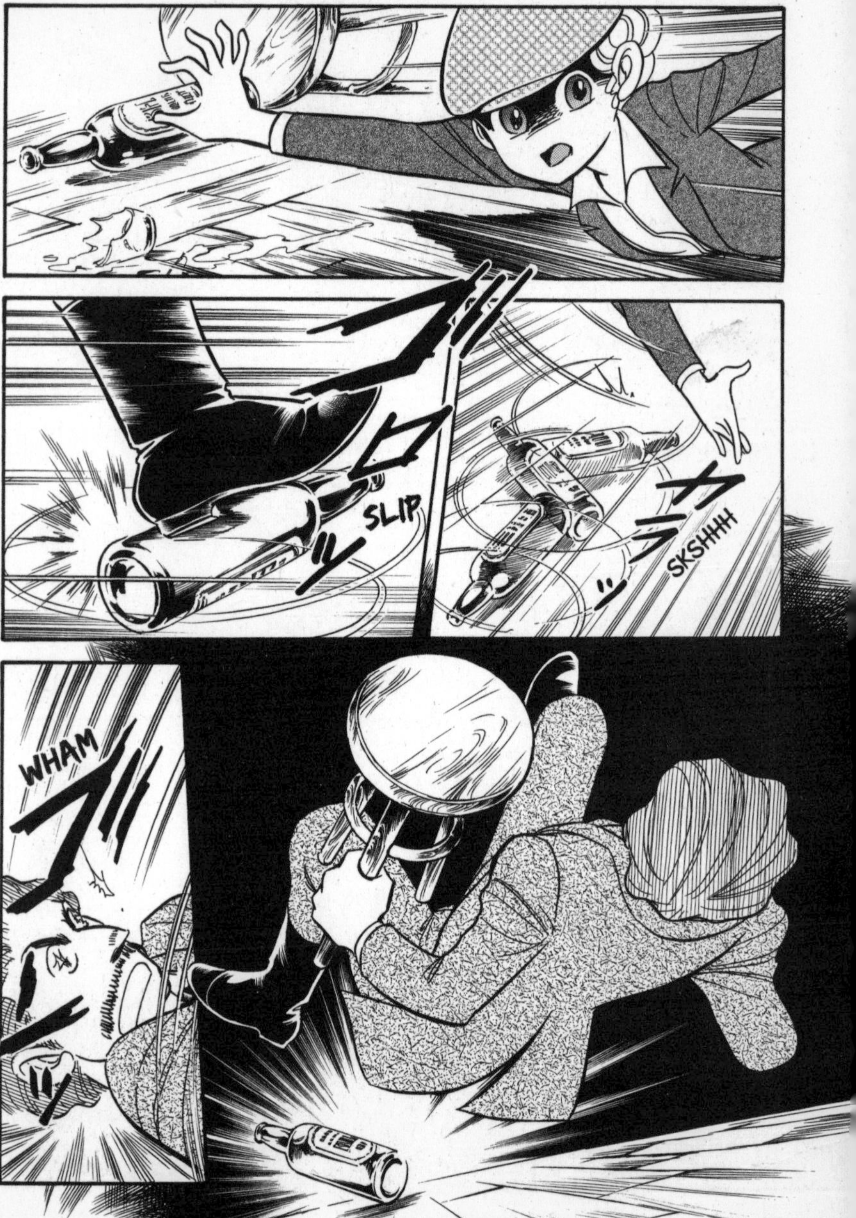
SKSHHH
SLIP
WHAM

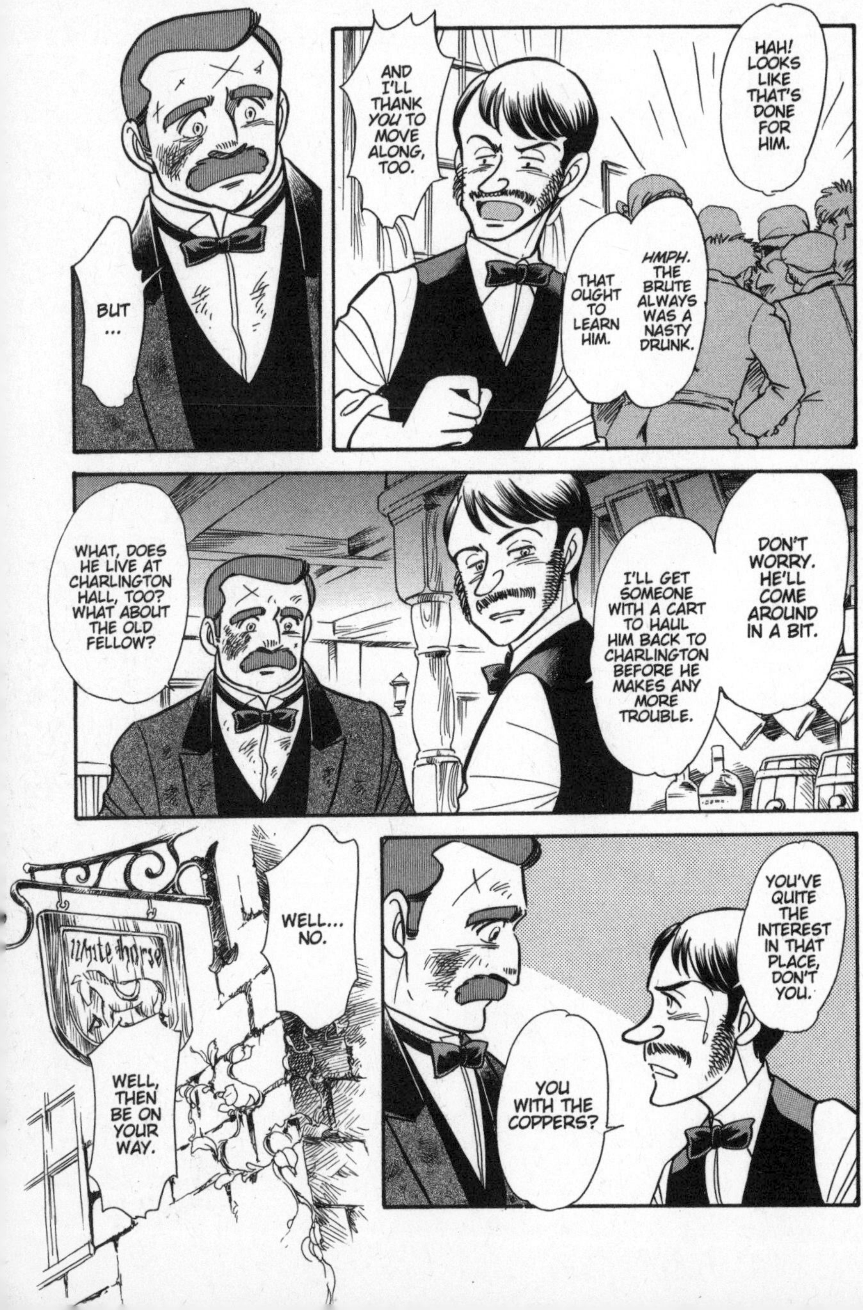
HAH! LOOKS LIKE THAT'S DONE FOR HIM.
HMPH. THE BRUTE ALWAYS WAS A NASTY DRUNK.
THAT OUGHT TO LEARN HIM.
AND I'LL THANK *YOU* TO MOVE ALONG, TOO.
BUT ...
DON'T WORRY. HE'LL COME AROUND IN A BIT.
I'LL GET SOMEONE WITH A CART TO HAUL HIM BACK TO CHARLINGTON BEFORE HE MAKES ANY MORE TROUBLE.
WHAT, DOES HE LIVE AT CHARLINGTON HALL, TOO? WHAT ABOUT THE OLD FELLOW?
YOU'VE QUITE THE INTEREST IN THAT PLACE, DON'T YOU.
YOU WITH THE COPPERS?
WELL... NO.
White horse
WELL, THEN BE ON YOUR WAY.

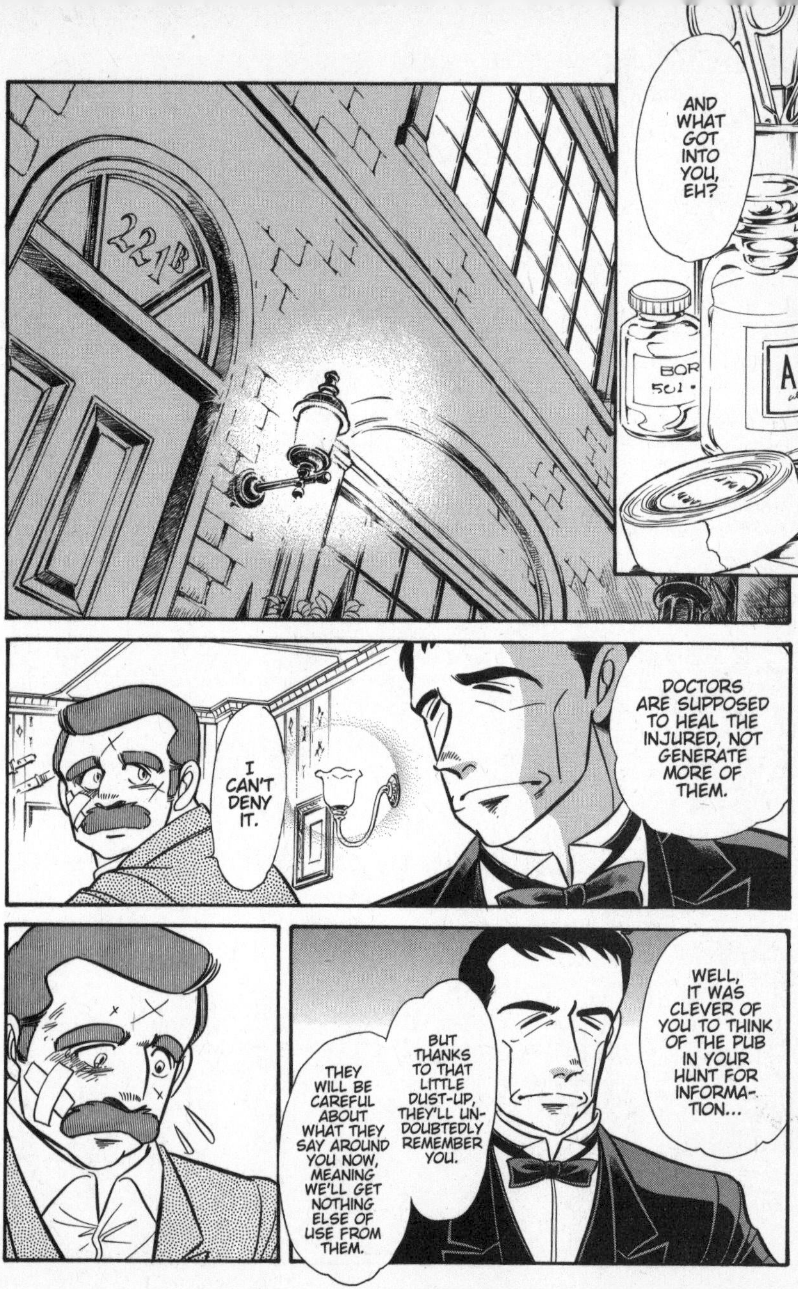
AND WHAT GOT INTO YOU, EH?
BOR 501
AIC
DOCTORS ARE SUPPOSED TO HEAL THE INJURED, NOT GENERATE MORE OF THEM.
I CAN'T DENY IT.
WELL, IT WAS CLEVER OF YOU TO THINK OF THE PUB IN YOUR HUNT FOR INFORMA-TION...
BUT THANKS TO THAT LITTLE DUST-UP, THEY'LL UN-DOUBTEDLY REMEMBER YOU.
THEY WILL BE CAREFUL ABOUT WHAT THEY SAY AROUND YOU NOW, MEANING WE'LL GET NOTHING ELSE OF USE FROM THEM.

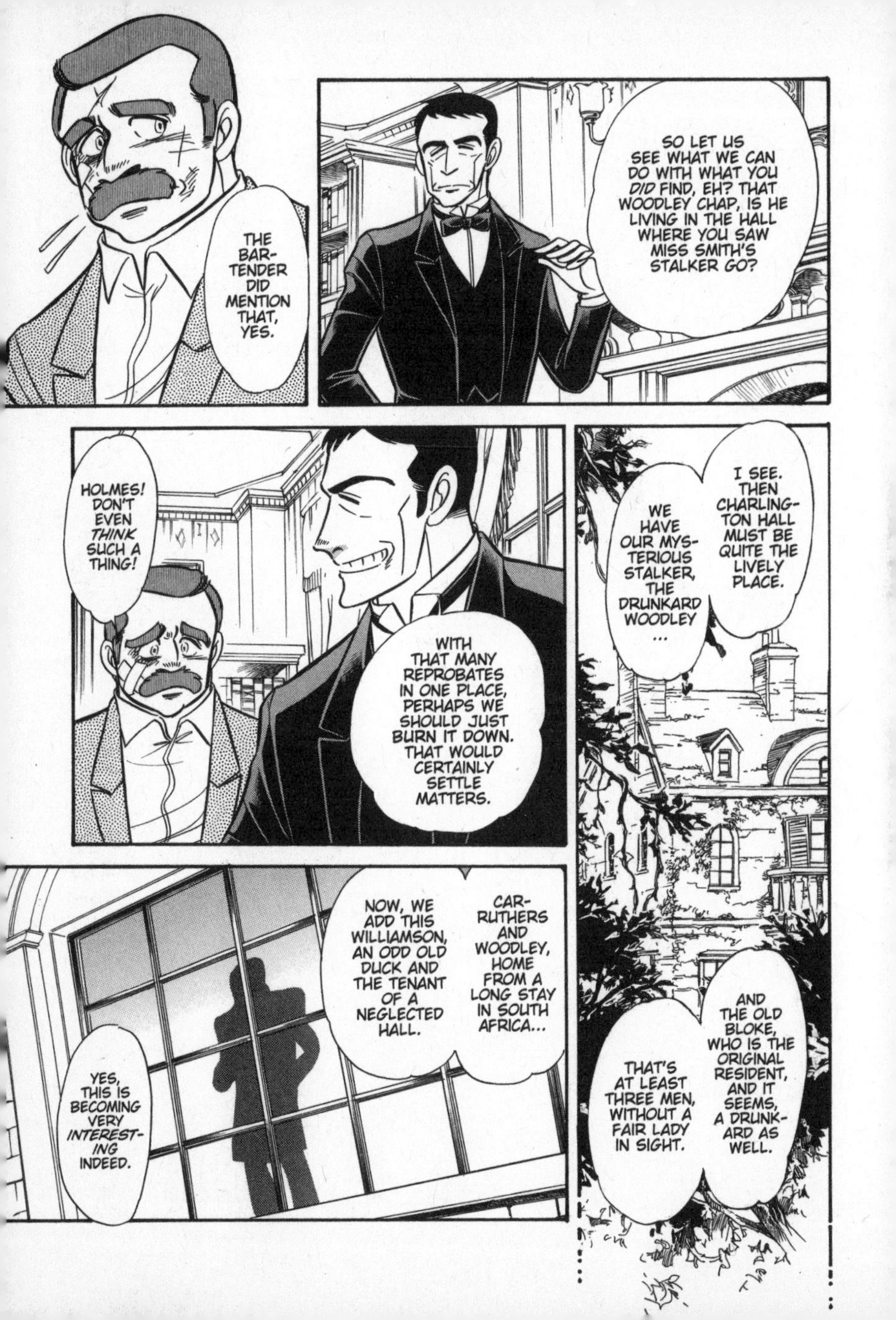
SO LET US SEE WHAT WE CAN DO WITH WHAT YOU *DID* FIND, EH? THAT WOODLEY CHAP, IS HE LIVING IN THE HALL WHERE YOU SAW MISS SMITH'S STALKER GO?
THE BARTENDER DID MENTION THAT, YES.
I SEE. THEN CHARLINGTON HALL MUST BE QUITE THE LIVELY PLACE.
WE HAVE OUR MYSTERIOUS STALKER, THE DRUNKARD WOODLEY ...
AND THE OLD BLOKE, WHO IS THE ORIGINAL RESIDENT, AND IT SEEMS, A DRUNKARD AS WELL.
THAT'S AT LEAST THREE MEN, WITHOUT A FAIR LADY IN SIGHT.
WITH THAT MANY REPROBATES IN ONE PLACE, PERHAPS WE SHOULD JUST BURN IT DOWN. THAT WOULD CERTAINLY SETTLE MATTERS.
HOLMES! DON'T EVEN *THINK* SUCH A THING!
CARRUTHERS AND WOODLEY, HOME FROM A LONG STAY IN SOUTH AFRICA...
NOW, WE ADD THIS WILLIAMSON, AN ODD OLD DUCK AND THE TENANT OF A NEGLECTED HALL.
YES, THIS IS BECOMING VERY *INTERESTING* INDEED.

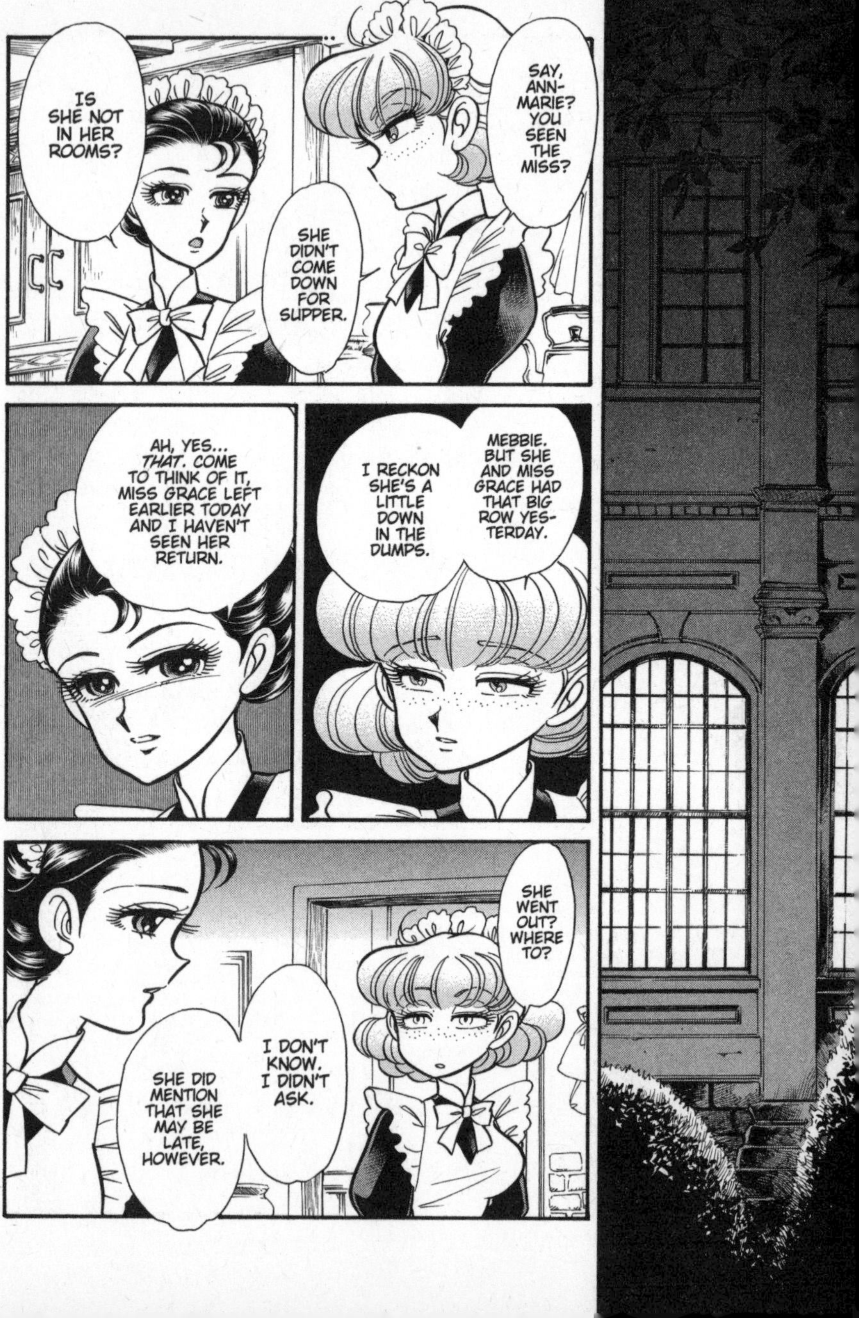
SAY, ANN-MARIE? YOU SEEN THE MISS?
IS SHE NOT IN HER ROOMS?
SHE DIDN'T COME DOWN FOR SUPPER.
MEBBIE. BUT SHE AND MISS GRACE HAD THAT BIG ROW YES-TERDAY.
I RECKON SHE'S A LITTLE DOWN IN THE DUMPS.
AH, YES... *THAT*. COME TO THINK OF IT, MISS GRACE LEFT EARLIER TODAY AND I HAVEN'T SEEN HER RETURN.
SHE WENT OUT? WHERE TO?
I DON'T KNOW. I DIDN'T ASK.
SHE DID MENTION THAT SHE MAY BE LATE, HOWEVER.

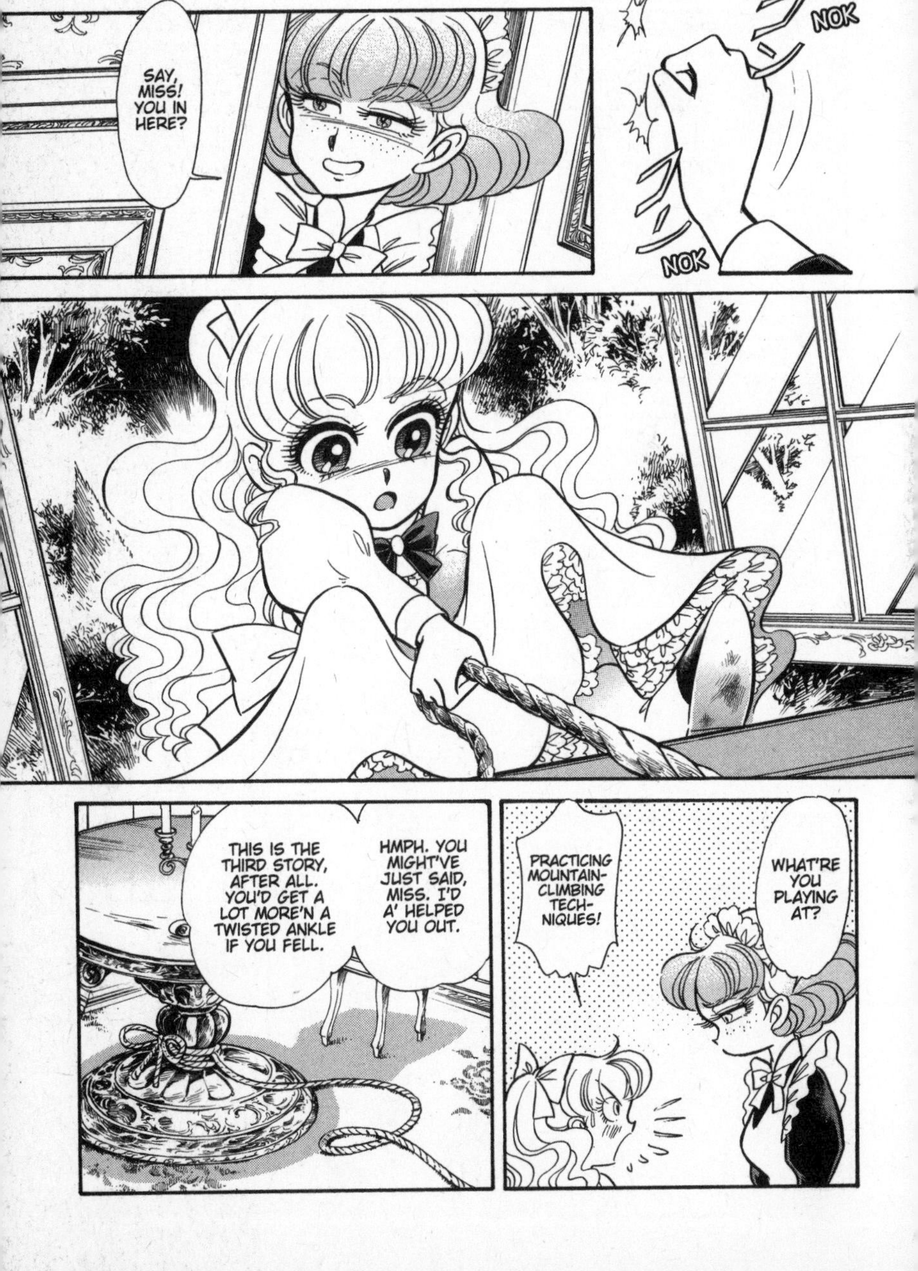
NOK
NOK
SAY, MISS! YOU IN HERE?
WHAT'RE YOU PLAYING AT?
PRACTICING MOUNTAIN-CLIMBING TECH-NIQUES!
HMPH. YOU MIGHT'VE JUST SAID, MISS. I'D A' HELPED YOU OUT.
THIS IS THE THIRD STORY, AFTER ALL. YOU'D GET A LOT MORE'N A TWISTED ANKLE IF YOU FELL.

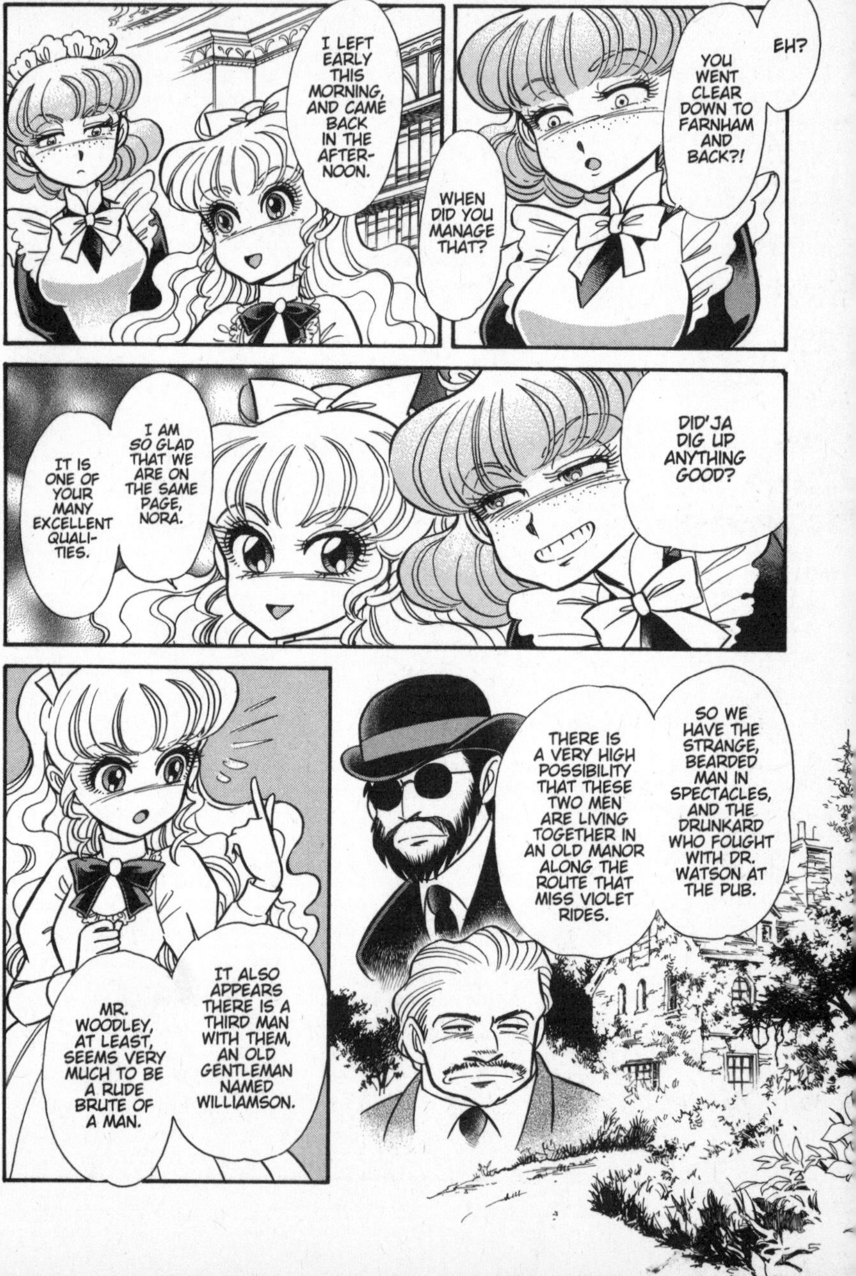
EH?
YOU WENT CLEAR DOWN TO FARNHAM AND BACK?!
WHEN DID YOU MANAGE THAT?
I LEFT EARLY THIS MORNING, AND CAME BACK IN THE AFTER-NOON.
DID'JA DIG UP ANYTHING GOOD?
I AM SO GLAD THAT WE ARE ON THE SAME PAGE, NORA.
IT IS ONE OF YOUR MANY EXCELLENT QUALI-TIES.
SO WE HAVE THE STRANGE, BEARDED MAN IN SPECTACLES, AND THE DRUNKARD WHO FOUGHT WITH DR. WATSON AT THE PUB.
THERE IS A VERY HIGH POSSIBILITY THAT THESE TWO MEN ARE LIVING TOGETHER IN AN OLD MANOR ALONG THE ROUTE THAT MISS VIOLET RIDES.
IT ALSO APPEARS THERE IS A THIRD MAN WITH THEM, AN OLD GENTLEMAN NAMED WILLIAMSON.
MR. WOODLEY, AT LEAST, SEEMS VERY MUCH TO BE A RUDE BRUTE OF A MAN.

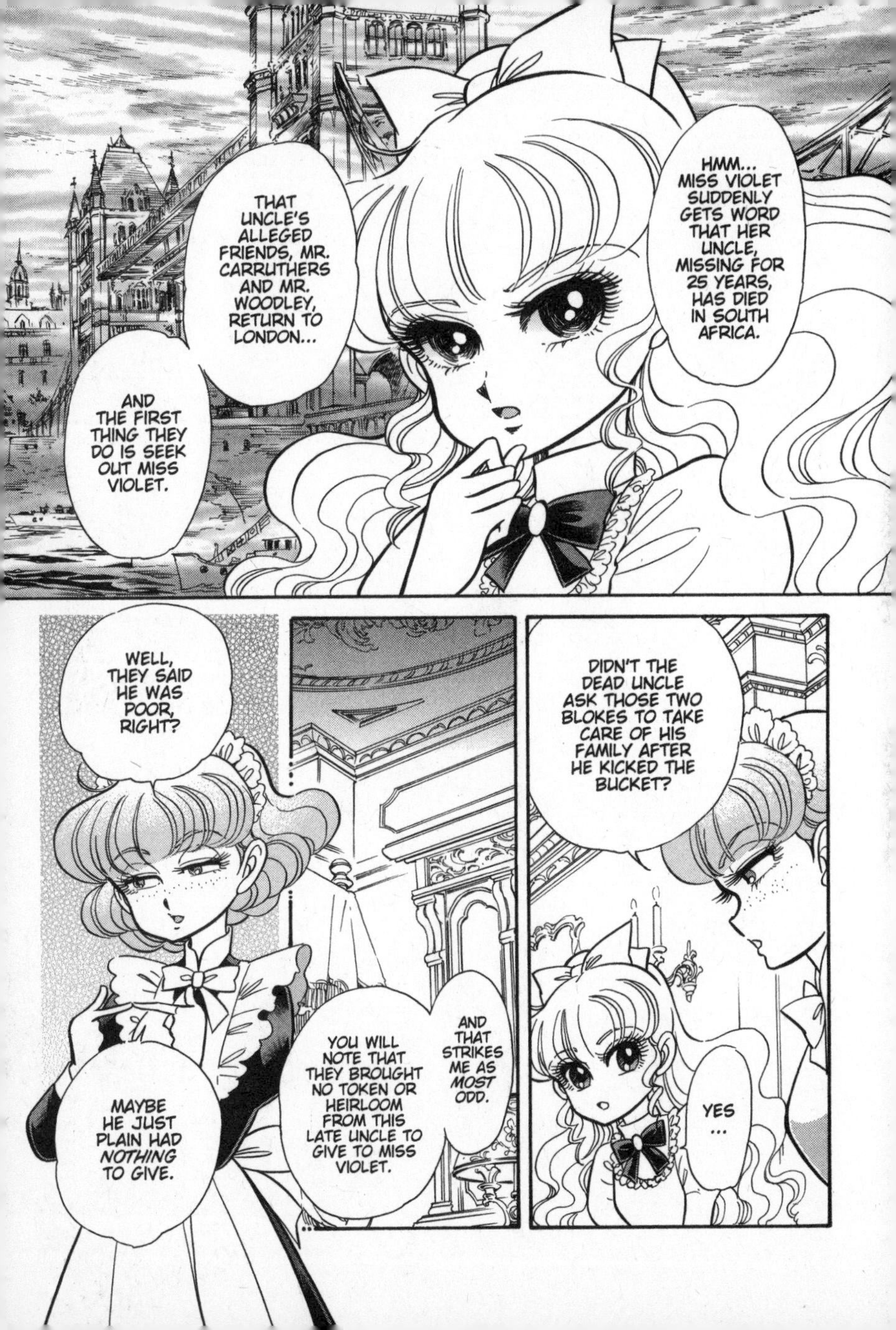
HMM... MISS VIOLET SUDDENLY GETS WORD THAT HER UNCLE, MISSING FOR 25 YEARS, HAS DIED IN SOUTH AFRICA.
THAT UNCLE'S ALLEGED FRIENDS, MR. CARRUTHERS AND MR. WOODLEY, RETURN TO LONDON...
AND THE FIRST THING THEY DO IS SEEK OUT MISS VIOLET.
DIDN'T THE DEAD UNCLE ASK THOSE TWO BLOKES TO TAKE CARE OF HIS FAMILY AFTER HE KICKED THE BUCKET?
YES ...
YOU WILL NOTE THAT THEY BROUGHT NO TOKEN OR HEIRLOOM FROM THIS LATE UNCLE TO GIVE TO MISS VIOLET.
AND THAT STRIKES ME AS *MOST* ODD.
WELL, THEY SAID HE WAS POOR, RIGHT?
MAYBE HE JUST PLAIN HAD *NOTHING* TO GIVE.

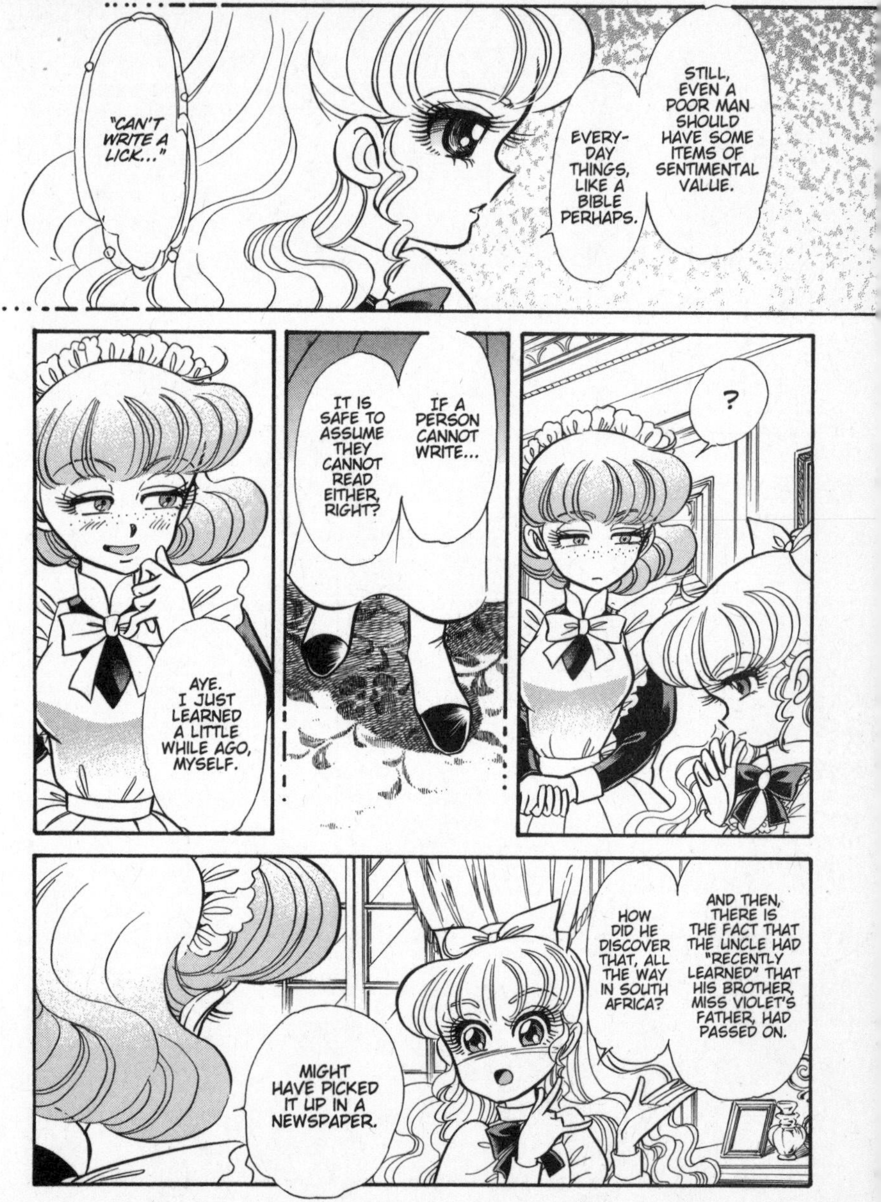
STILL, EVEN A POOR MAN SHOULD HAVE SOME ITEMS OF SENTIMENTAL VALUE.
EVERY-DAY THINGS, LIKE A BIBLE PERHAPS.
"CAN'T WRITE A LICK..."
?
IF A PERSON CANNOT WRITE...
IT IS SAFE TO ASSUME THEY CANNOT READ EITHER, RIGHT?
AYE. I JUST LEARNED A LITTLE WHILE AGO, MYSELF.
AND THEN, THERE IS THE FACT THAT THE UNCLE HAD "RECENTLY LEARNED" THAT HIS BROTHER, MISS VIOLET'S FATHER, HAD PASSED ON.
HOW DID HE DISCOVER THAT, ALL THE WAY IN SOUTH AFRICA?
MIGHT HAVE PICKED IT UP IN A NEWSPAPER.

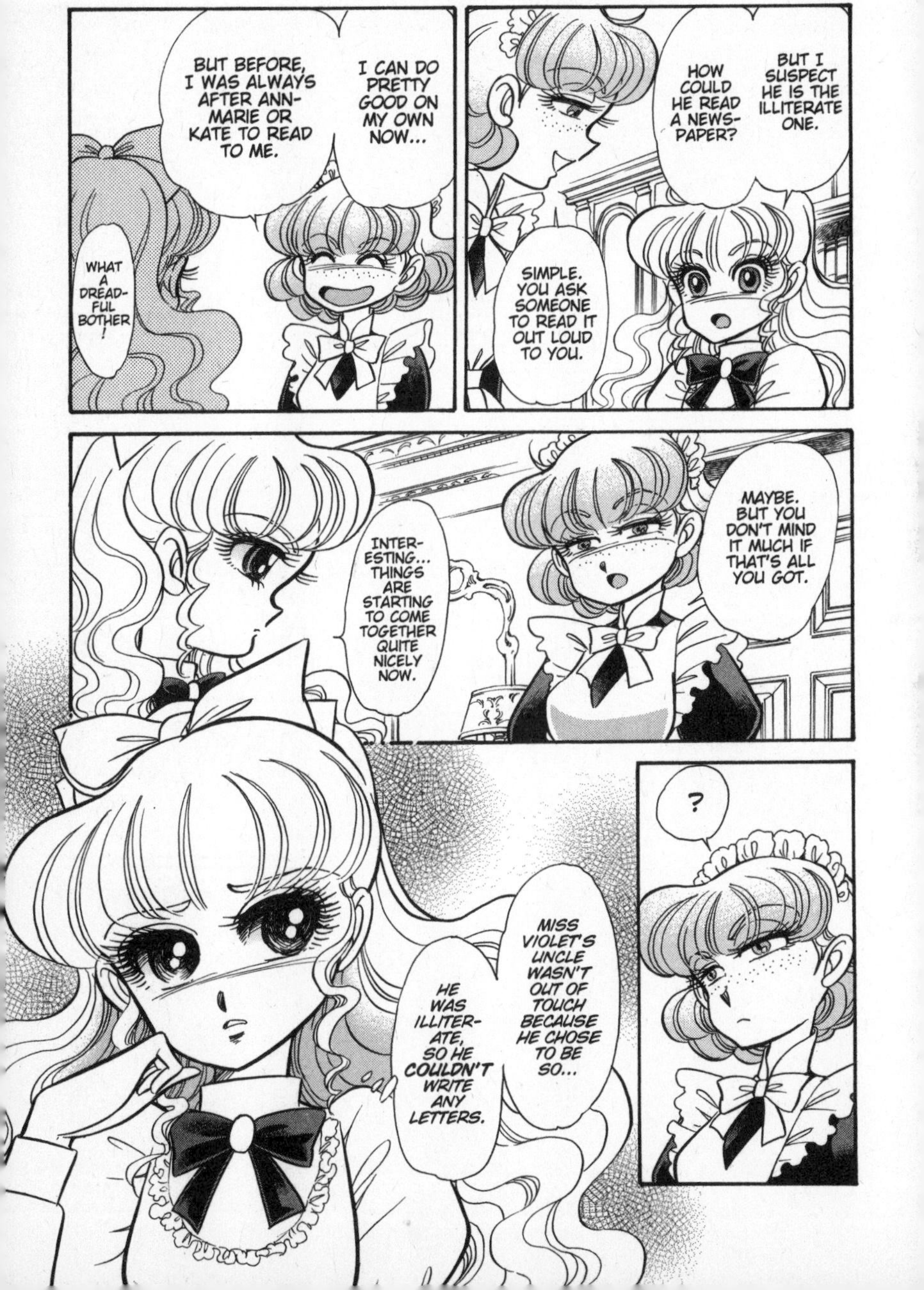
BUT I SUSPECT HE IS THE ILLITERATE ONE.
HOW COULD HE READ A NEWSPAPER?
SIMPLE. YOU ASK SOMEONE TO READ IT OUT LOUD TO YOU.
I CAN DO PRETTY GOOD ON MY OWN NOW...
BUT BEFORE, I WAS ALWAYS AFTER ANN-MARIE OR KATE TO READ TO ME.
WHAT A DREADFUL BOTHER!
MAYBE. BUT YOU DON'T MIND IT MUCH IF THAT'S ALL YOU GOT.
INTERESTING... THINGS ARE STARTING TO COME TOGETHER QUITE NICELY NOW.
?
MISS VIOLET'S UNCLE WASN'T OUT OF TOUCH BECAUSE HE CHOSE TO BE SO...
HE WAS ILLITERATE, SO HE **COULDN'T** WRITE ANY LETTERS.

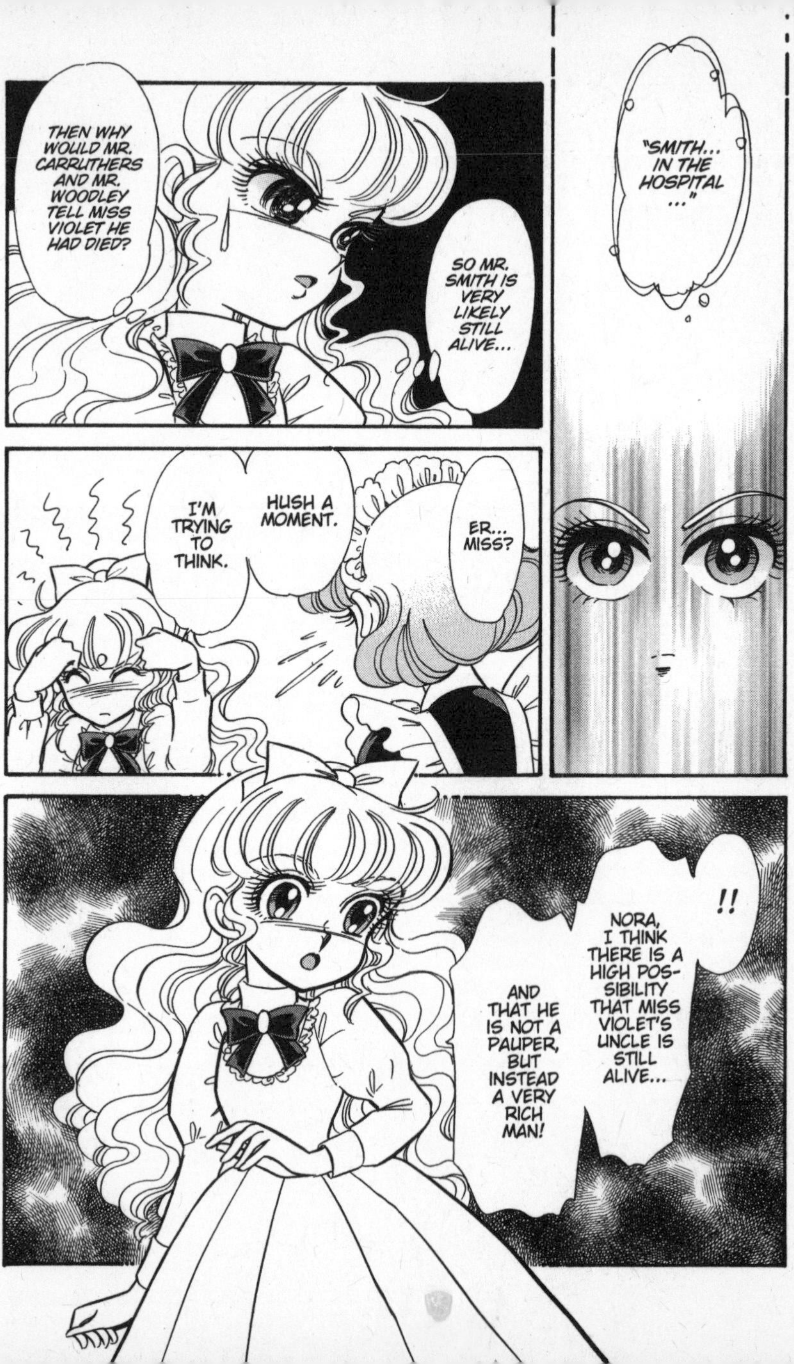
"SMITH... IN THE HOSPITAL..."
SO MR. SMITH IS VERY LIKELY STILL ALIVE...
THEN WHY WOULD MR. CARRUTHERS AND MR. WOODLEY TELL MISS VIOLET HE HAD DIED?
ER... MISS?
HUSH A MOMENT.
I'M TRYING TO THINK.
!!
NORA, I THINK THERE IS A HIGH POSSIBILITY THAT MISS VIOLET'S UNCLE IS STILL ALIVE...
AND THAT HE IS NOT A PAUPER, BUT INSTEAD A VERY RICH MAN!

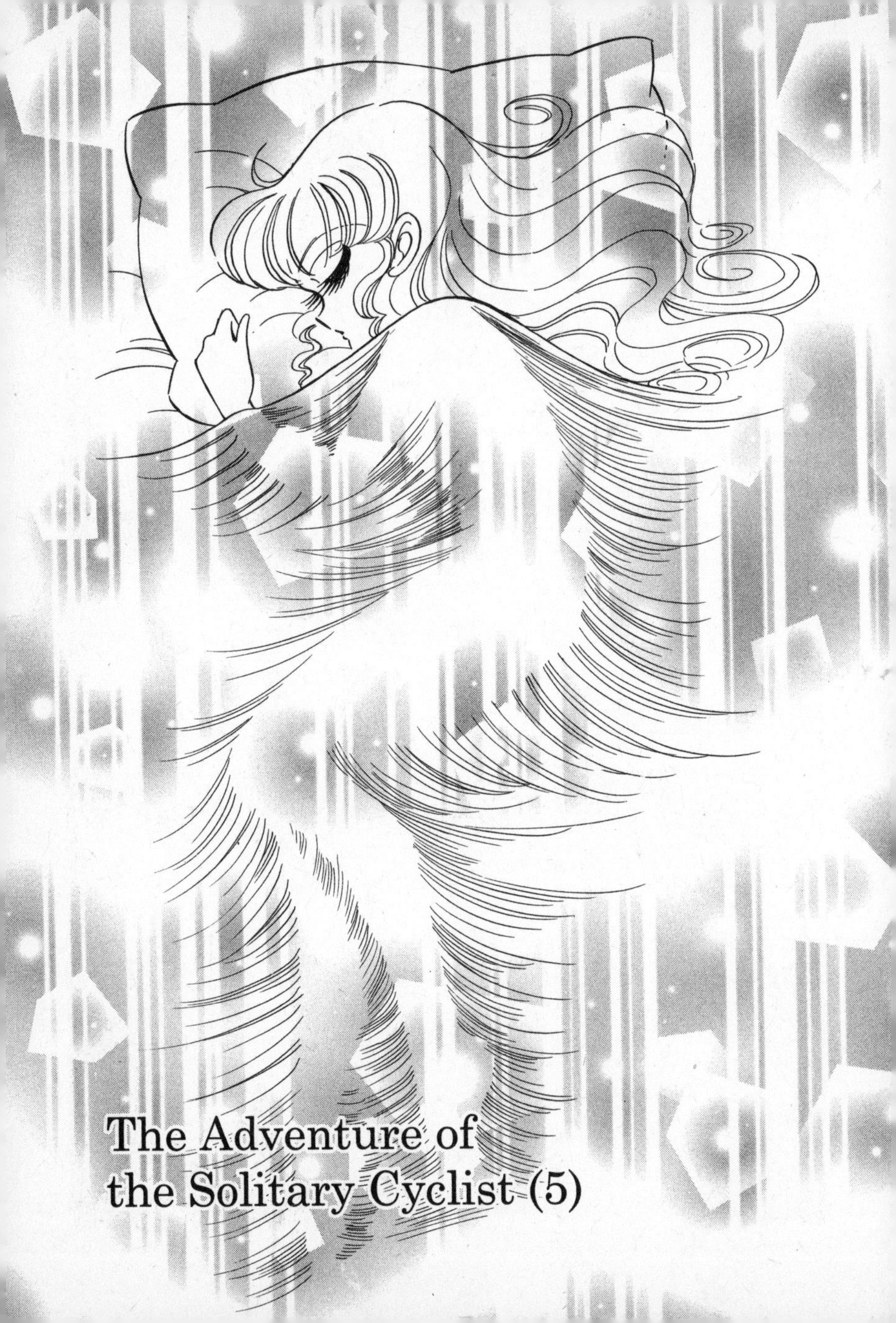

The Adventure of the Solitary Cyclist (5)

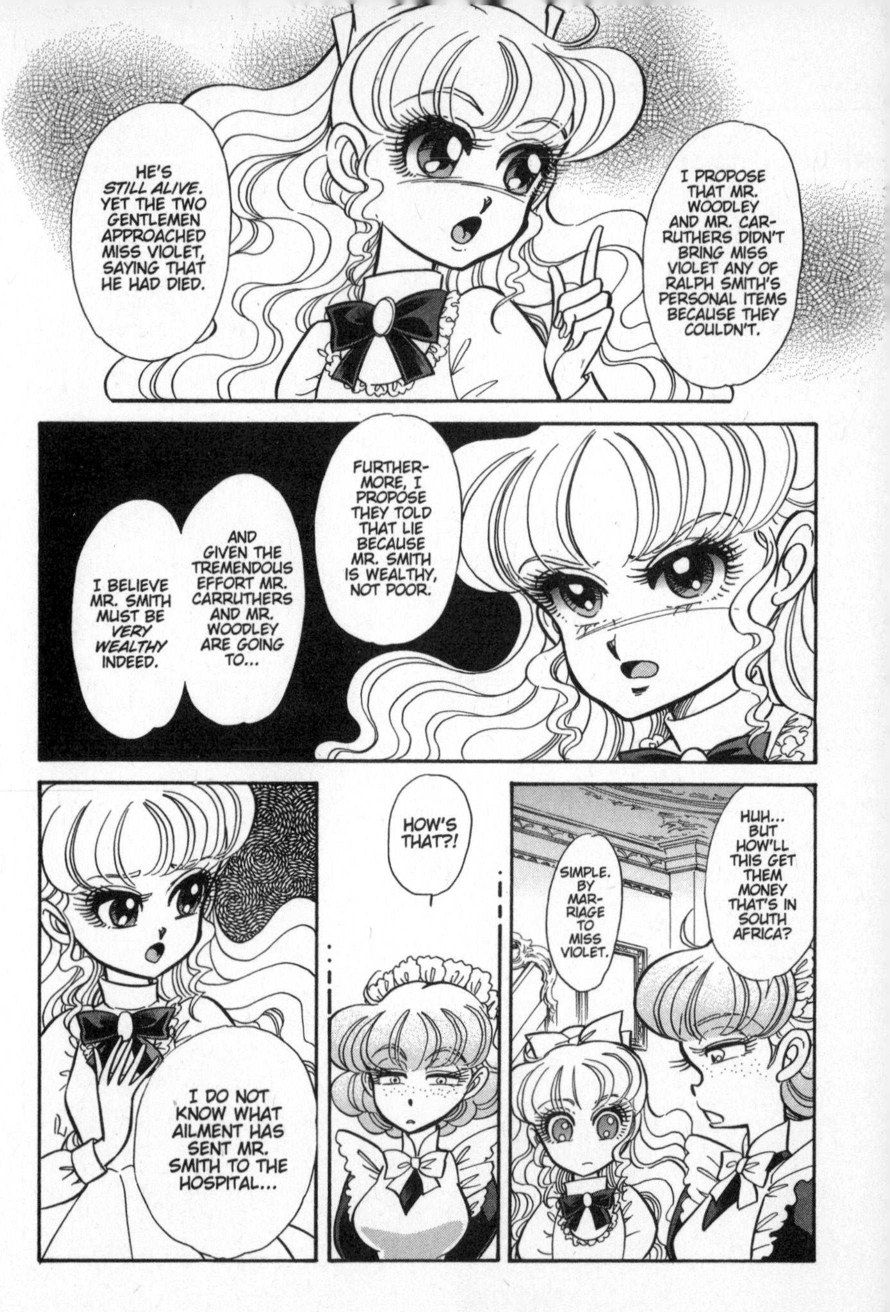
I PROPOSE THAT MR. WOODLEY AND MR. CARRUTHERS DIDN'T BRING MISS VIOLET ANY OF RALPH SMITH'S PERSONAL ITEMS BECAUSE THEY COULDN'T.
HE'S *STILL ALIVE*. YET THE TWO GENTLEMEN APPROACHED MISS VIOLET, SAYING THAT HE HAD DIED.
FURTHERMORE, I PROPOSE THEY TOLD THAT LIE BECAUSE MR. SMITH IS WEALTHY, NOT POOR.
AND GIVEN THE TREMENDOUS EFFORT MR. CARRUTHERS AND MR. WOODLEY ARE GOING TO...
I BELIEVE MR. SMITH MUST BE *VERY WEALTHY* INDEED.
HUH... BUT HOW'LL THIS GET THEM MONEY THAT'S IN SOUTH AFRICA?
SIMPLE. BY MARRIAGE TO MISS VIOLET.
HOW'S THAT?!
I DO NOT KNOW WHAT AILMENT HAS SENT MR. SMITH TO THE HOSPITAL...

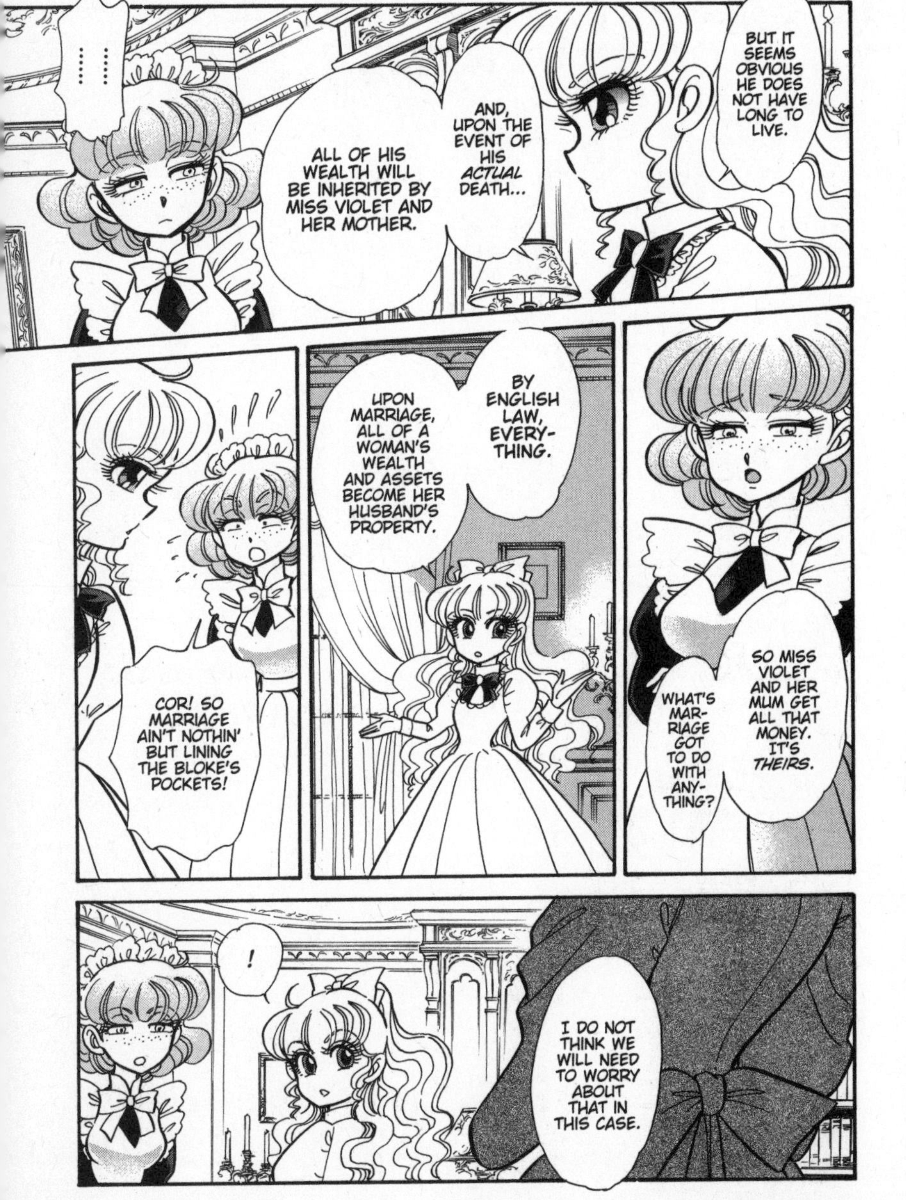
BUT IT SEEMS OBVIOUS HE DOES NOT HAVE LONG TO LIVE.
AND, UPON THE EVENT OF HIS *ACTUAL* DEATH...
ALL OF HIS WEALTH WILL BE INHERITED BY MISS VIOLET AND HER MOTHER.
......
SO MISS VIOLET AND HER MUM GET ALL THAT MONEY. IT'S *THEIRS*.
WHAT'S MARRIAGE GOT TO DO WITH ANYTHING?
BY ENGLISH LAW, EVERYTHING.
UPON MARRIAGE, ALL OF A WOMAN'S WEALTH AND ASSETS BECOME HER HUSBAND'S PROPERTY.
COR! SO MARRIAGE AIN'T NOTHIN' BUT LINING THE BLOKE'S POCKETS!
I DO NOT THINK WE WILL NEED TO WORRY ABOUT THAT IN THIS CASE.
!

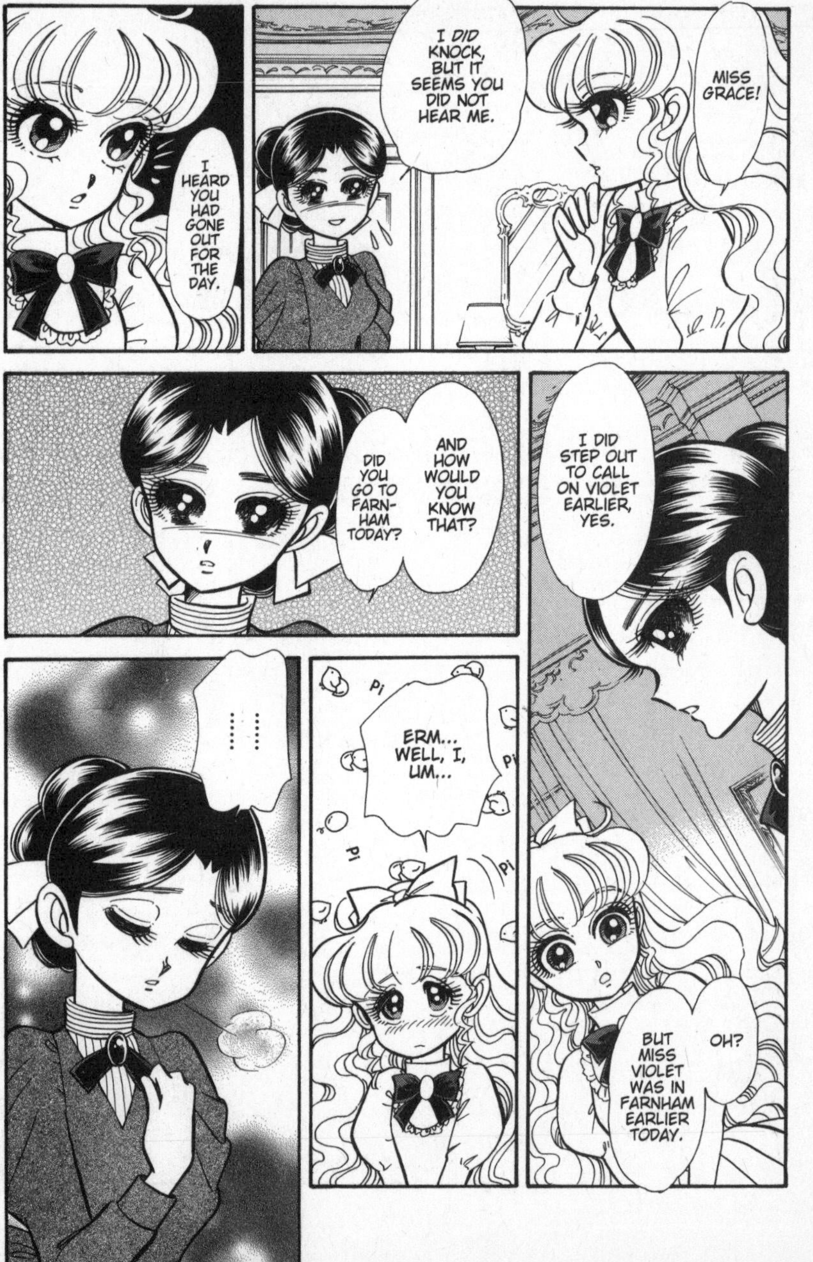
MISS GRACE!
I DID KNOCK, BUT IT SEEMS YOU DID NOT HEAR ME.
I HEARD YOU HAD GONE OUT FOR THE DAY.
I DID STEP OUT TO CALL ON VIOLET EARLIER, YES.
OH?
BUT MISS VIOLET WAS IN FARNHAM EARLIER TODAY.
AND HOW WOULD YOU KNOW THAT?
DID YOU GO TO FARNHAM TODAY?
Pi
Pi
ERM... WELL, I, UM...
Pi
Pi
......

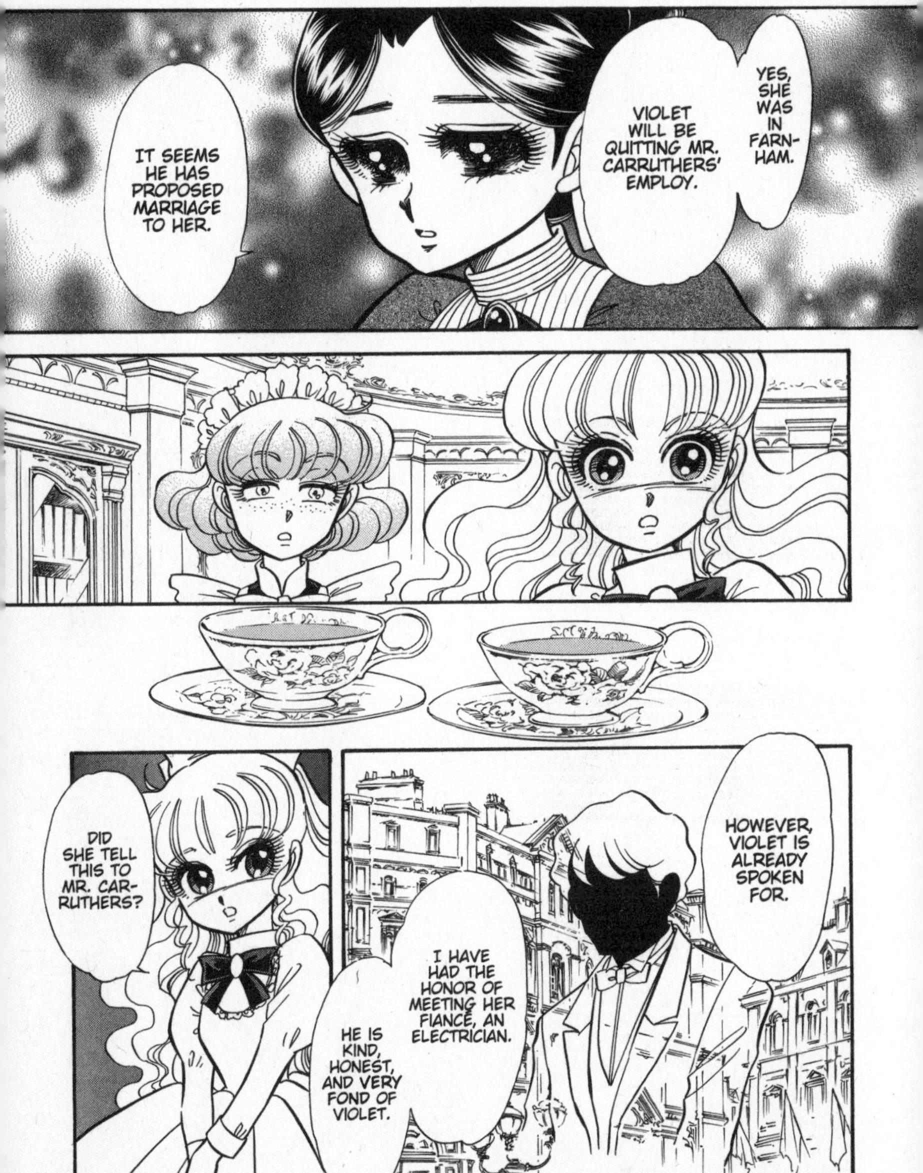
YES, SHE WAS IN FARNHAM.
VIOLET WILL BE QUITTING MR. CARRUTHERS' EMPLOY.
IT SEEMS HE HAS PROPOSED MARRIAGE TO HER.
HOWEVER, VIOLET IS ALREADY SPOKEN FOR.
I HAVE HAD THE HONOR OF MEETING HER FIANCÉ, AN ELECTRICIAN.
HE IS KIND, HONEST, AND VERY FOND OF VIOLET.
DID SHE TELL THIS TO MR. CARRUTHERS?

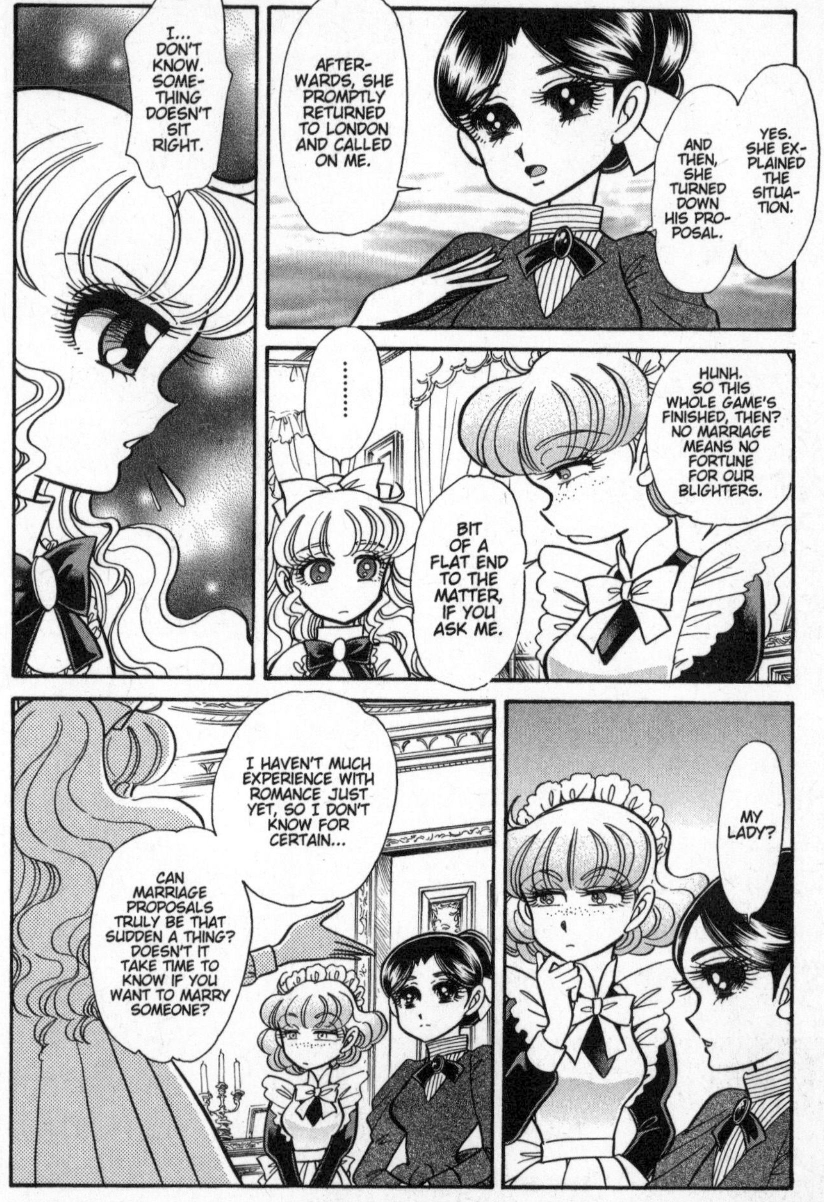
YES. SHE EXPLAINED THE SITUATION.
AND THEN, SHE TURNED DOWN HIS PROPOSAL.
AFTERWARDS, SHE PROMPTLY RETURNED TO LONDON AND CALLED ON ME.
HUNH. SO THIS WHOLE GAME'S FINISHED, THEN? NO MARRIAGE MEANS NO FORTUNE FOR OUR BLIGHTERS.
BIT OF A FLAT END TO THE MATTER, IF YOU ASK ME.
....
I... DON'T KNOW. SOMETHING DOESN'T SIT RIGHT.
MY LADY?
I HAVEN'T MUCH EXPERIENCE WITH ROMANCE JUST YET, SO I DON'T KNOW FOR CERTAIN...
CAN MARRIAGE PROPOSALS TRULY BE THAT SUDDEN A THING? DOESN'T IT TAKE TIME TO KNOW IF YOU WANT TO MARRY SOMEONE?

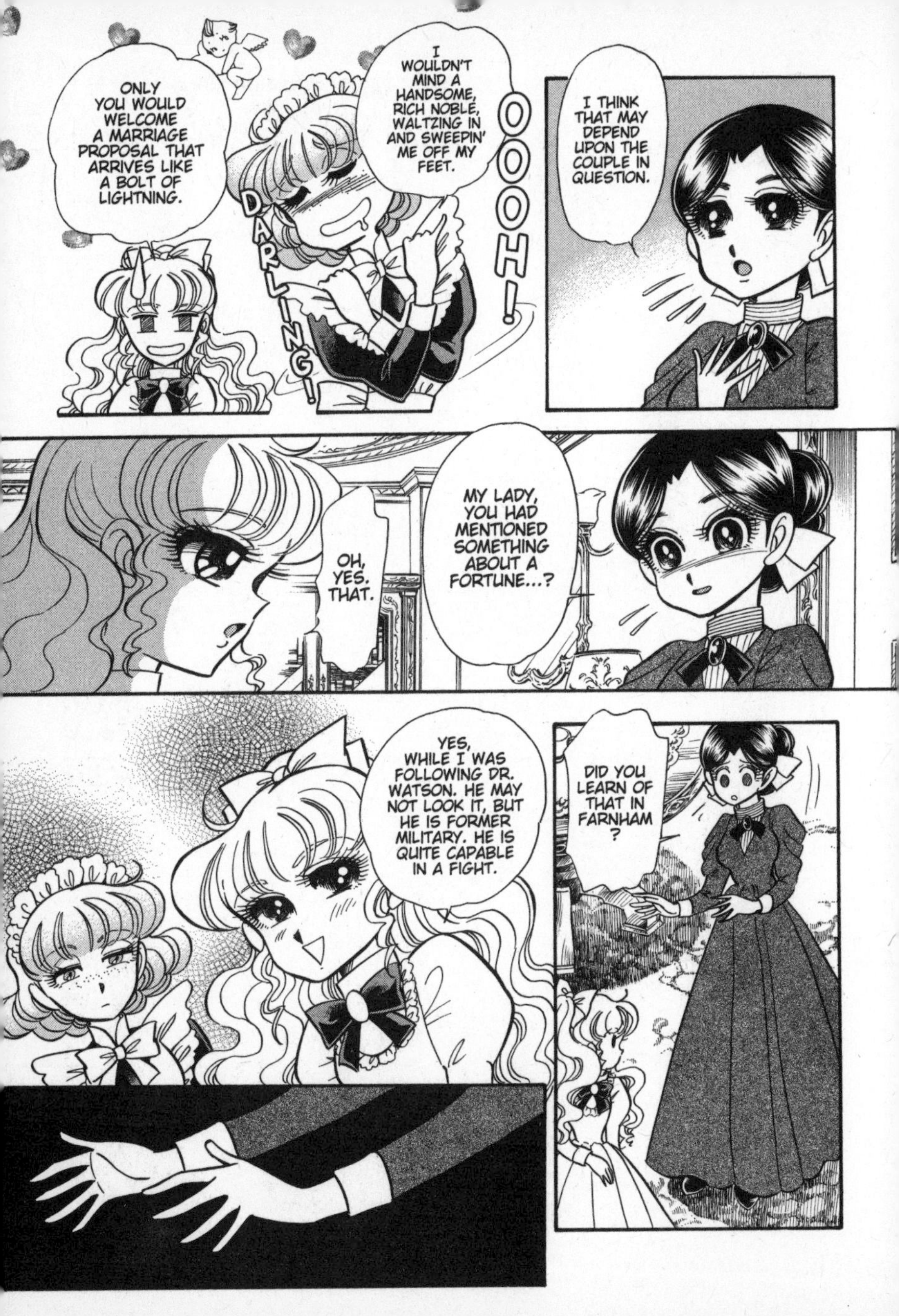
I THINK THAT MAY DEPEND UPON THE COUPLE IN QUESTION.
I WOULDN'T MIND A HANDSOME, RICH NOBLE, WALTZING IN AND SWEEPIN' ME OFF MY FEET.
OOOOH!
DARLING!
ONLY YOU WOULD WELCOME A MARRIAGE PROPOSAL THAT ARRIVES LIKE A BOLT OF LIGHTNING.
MY LADY, YOU HAD MENTIONED SOMETHING ABOUT A FORTUNE...?
OH, YES. THAT.
DID YOU LEARN OF THAT IN FARNHAM?
YES, WHILE I WAS FOLLOWING DR. WATSON. HE MAY NOT LOOK IT, BUT HE IS FORMER MILITARY. HE IS QUITE CAPABLE IN A FIGHT.

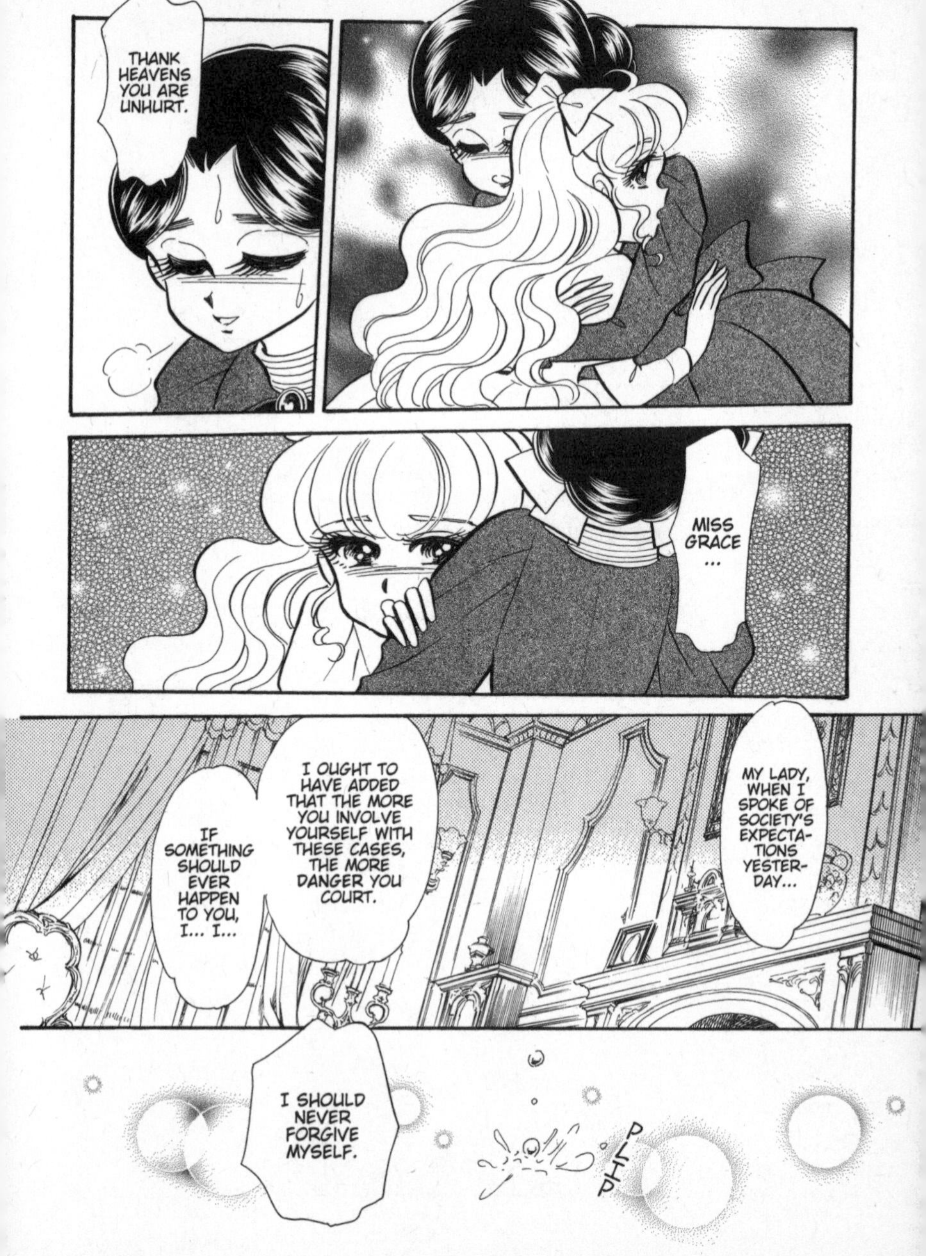
THANK HEAVENS YOU ARE UNHURT.
MISS GRACE ...
MY LADY, WHEN I SPOKE OF SOCIETY'S EXPECTATIONS YESTERDAY...
I OUGHT TO HAVE ADDED THAT THE MORE YOU INVOLVE YOURSELF WITH THESE CASES, THE MORE DANGER YOU COURT.
IF SOMETHING SHOULD EVER HAPPEN TO YOU, I... I...
I SHOULD NEVER FORGIVE MYSELF.
PLIP

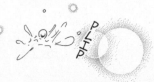

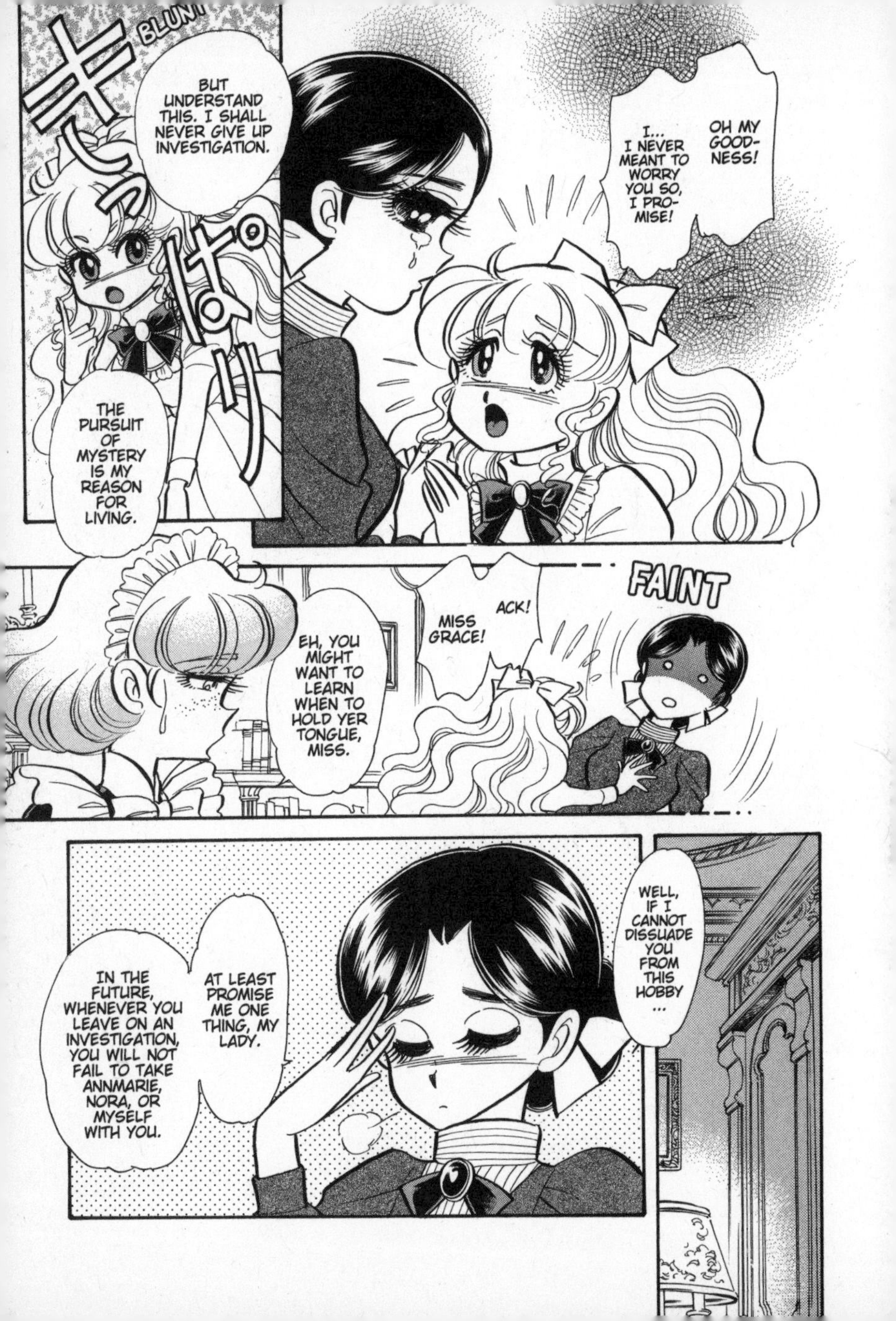
OH MY GOODNESS!
I... I NEVER MEANT TO WORRY YOU SO, I PROMISE!
BLUNT
キッぱり
BUT UNDERSTAND THIS. I SHALL NEVER GIVE UP INVESTIGATION.
THE PURSUIT OF MYSTERY IS MY REASON FOR LIVING.
FAINT
ACK!
MISS GRACE!
EH, YOU MIGHT WANT TO LEARN WHEN TO HOLD YER TONGUE, MISS.
WELL, IF I CANNOT DISSUADE YOU FROM THIS HOBBY ...
AT LEAST PROMISE ME ONE THING, MY LADY.
IN THE FUTURE, WHENEVER YOU LEAVE ON AN INVESTIGATION, YOU WILL NOT FAIL TO TAKE ANNMARIE, NORA, OR MYSELF WITH YOU.

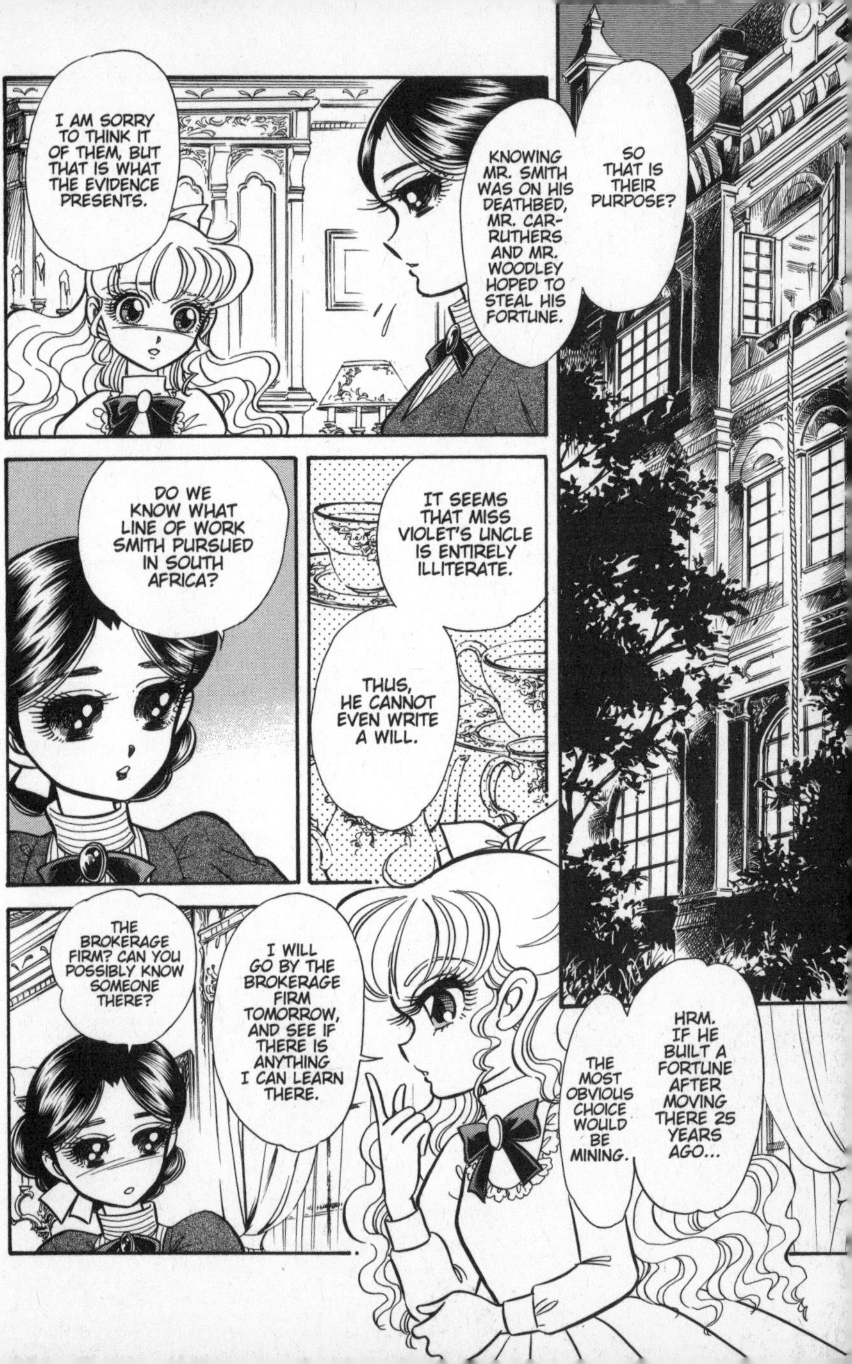
SO THAT IS THEIR PURPOSE?
KNOWING MR. SMITH WAS ON HIS DEATHBED, MR. CARRUTHERS AND MR. WOODLEY HOPED TO STEAL HIS FORTUNE.
I AM SORRY TO THINK IT OF THEM, BUT THAT IS WHAT THE EVIDENCE PRESENTS.
IT SEEMS THAT MISS VIOLET'S UNCLE IS ENTIRELY ILLITERATE.
THUS, HE CANNOT EVEN WRITE A WILL.
DO WE KNOW WHAT LINE OF WORK SMITH PURSUED IN SOUTH AFRICA?
HRM. IF HE BUILT A FORTUNE AFTER MOVING THERE 25 YEARS AGO...
THE MOST OBVIOUS CHOICE WOULD BE MINING.
I WILL GO BY THE BROKERAGE FIRM TOMORROW, AND SEE IF THERE IS ANYTHING I CAN LEARN THERE.
THE BROKERAGE FIRM? CAN YOU POSSIBLY KNOW SOMEONE THERE?

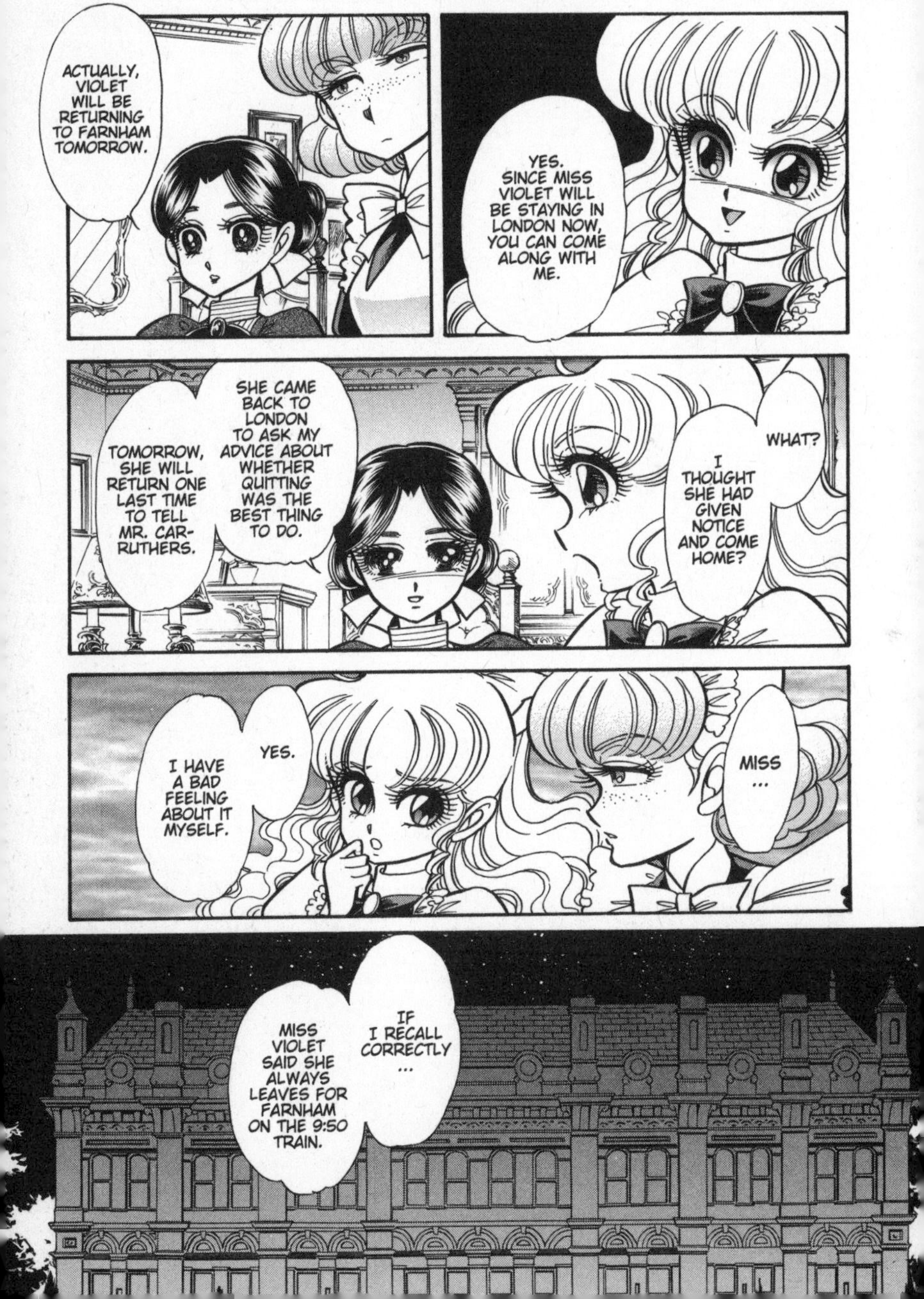
YES. SINCE MISS VIOLET WILL BE STAYING IN LONDON NOW, YOU CAN COME ALONG WITH ME.
ACTUALLY, VIOLET WILL BE RETURNING TO FARNHAM TOMORROW.
WHAT?
I THOUGHT SHE HAD GIVEN NOTICE AND COME HOME?
SHE CAME BACK TO LONDON TO ASK MY ADVICE ABOUT WHETHER QUITTING WAS THE BEST THING TO DO.
TOMORROW, SHE WILL RETURN ONE LAST TIME TO TELL MR. CAR-RUTHERS.
MISS ...
YES.
I HAVE A BAD FEELING ABOUT IT MYSELF.
IF I RECALL CORRECTLY ...
MISS VIOLET SAID SHE ALWAYS LEAVES FOR FARNHAM ON THE 9:50 TRAIN.

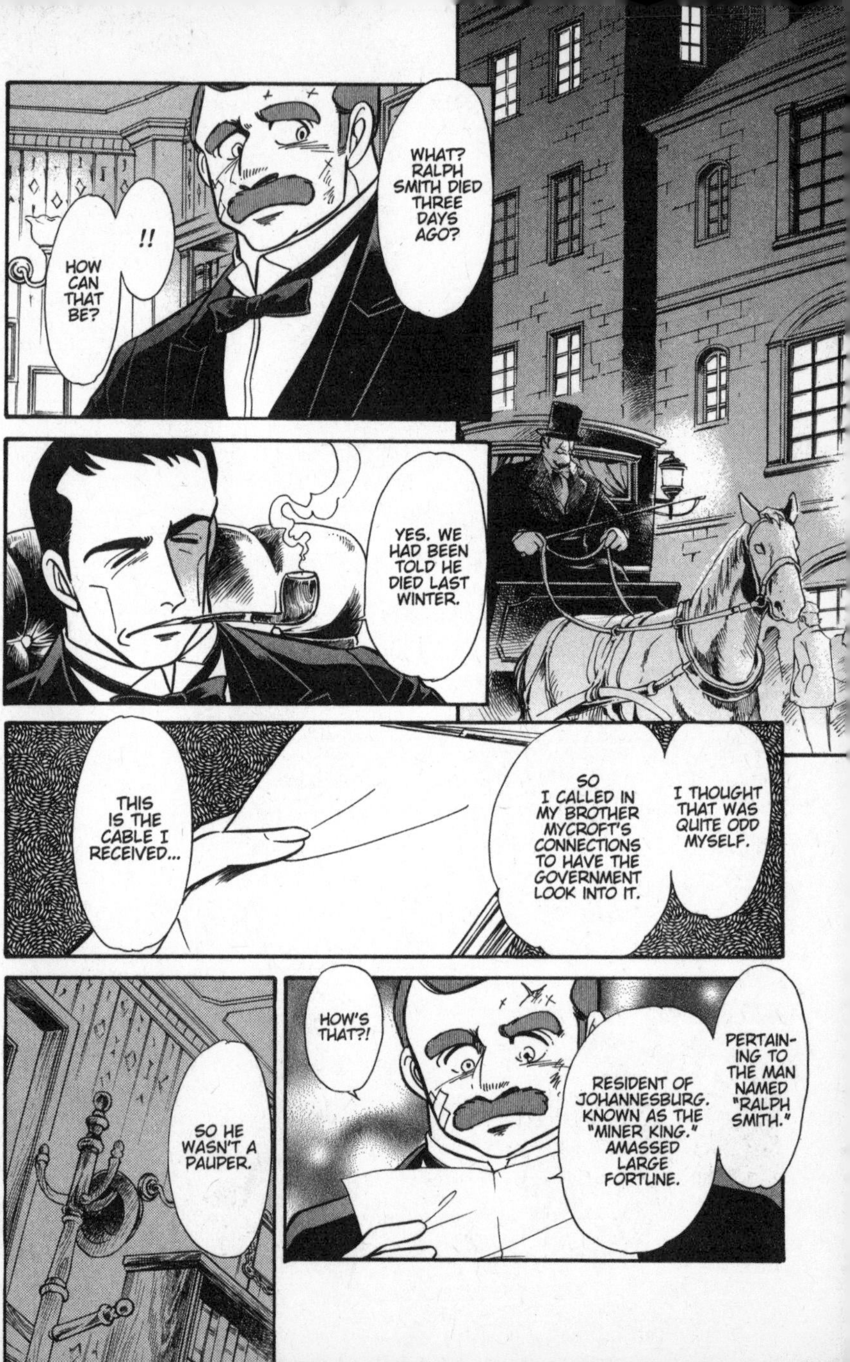
WHAT? RALPH SMITH DIED THREE DAYS AGO?
!!
HOW CAN THAT BE?
YES. WE HAD BEEN TOLD HE DIED LAST WINTER.
I THOUGHT THAT WAS QUITE ODD MYSELF.
SO I CALLED IN MY BROTHER MYCROFT'S CONNECTIONS TO HAVE THE GOVERNMENT LOOK INTO IT.
THIS IS THE CABLE I RECEIVED...
PERTAIN-ING TO THE MAN NAMED "RALPH SMITH."
RESIDENT OF JOHANNESBURG. KNOWN AS THE "MINER KING." AMASSED LARGE FORTUNE.
HOW'S THAT?!
SO HE WASN'T A PAUPER.

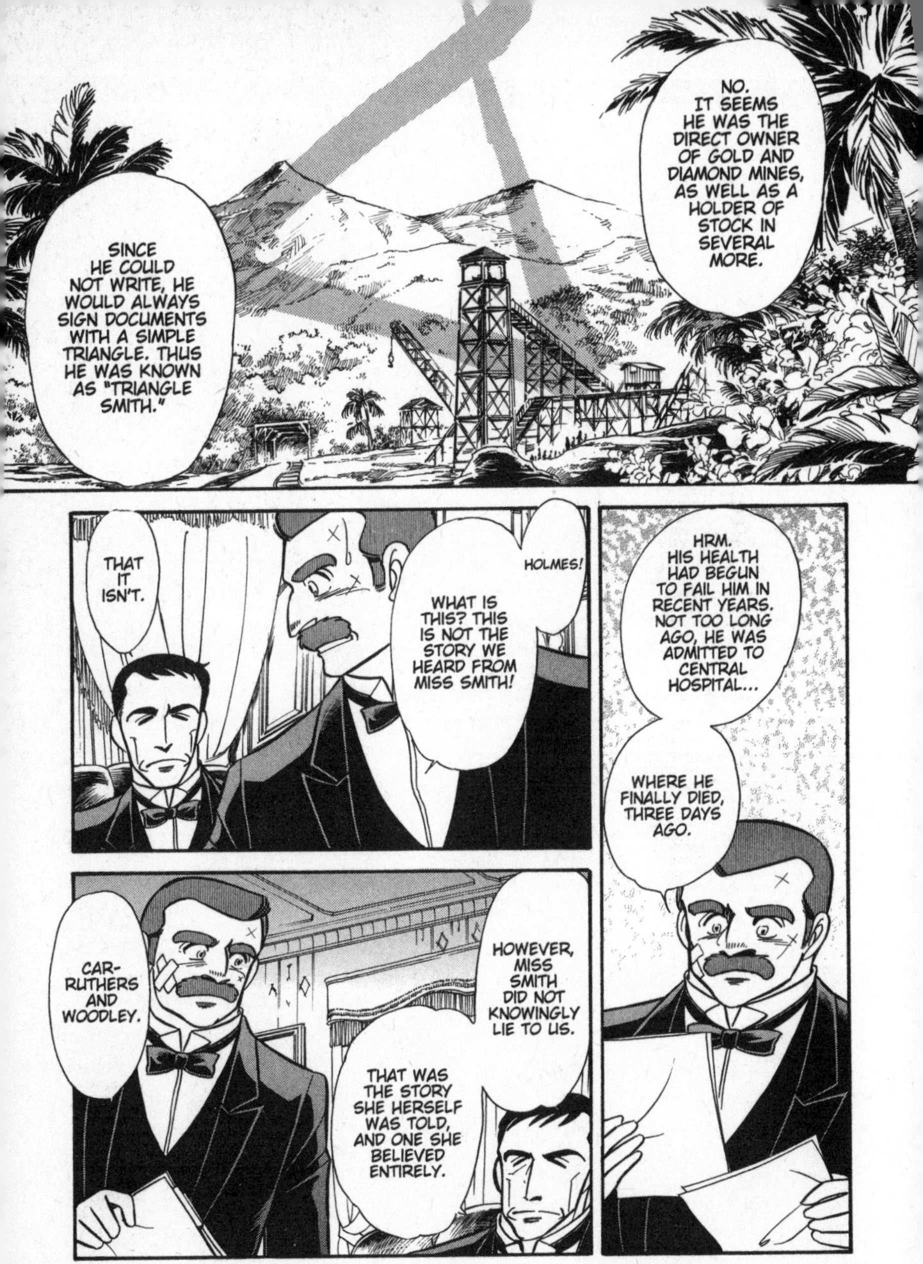
NO. IT SEEMS HE WAS THE DIRECT OWNER OF GOLD AND DIAMOND MINES, AS WELL AS A HOLDER OF STOCK IN SEVERAL MORE.
SINCE HE COULD NOT WRITE, HE WOULD ALWAYS SIGN DOCUMENTS WITH A SIMPLE TRIANGLE. THUS HE WAS KNOWN AS "TRIANGLE SMITH."
HRM. HIS HEALTH HAD BEGUN TO FAIL HIM IN RECENT YEARS. NOT TOO LONG AGO, HE WAS ADMITTED TO CENTRAL HOSPITAL...
WHERE HE FINALLY DIED, THREE DAYS AGO.
HOLMES!
WHAT IS THIS? THIS IS NOT THE STORY WE HEARD FROM MISS SMITH!
THAT IT ISN'T.
HOWEVER, MISS SMITH DID NOT KNOWINGLY LIE TO US.
THAT WAS THE STORY SHE HERSELF WAS TOLD, AND ONE SHE BELIEVED ENTIRELY.
CAR-RUTHERS AND WOODLEY.

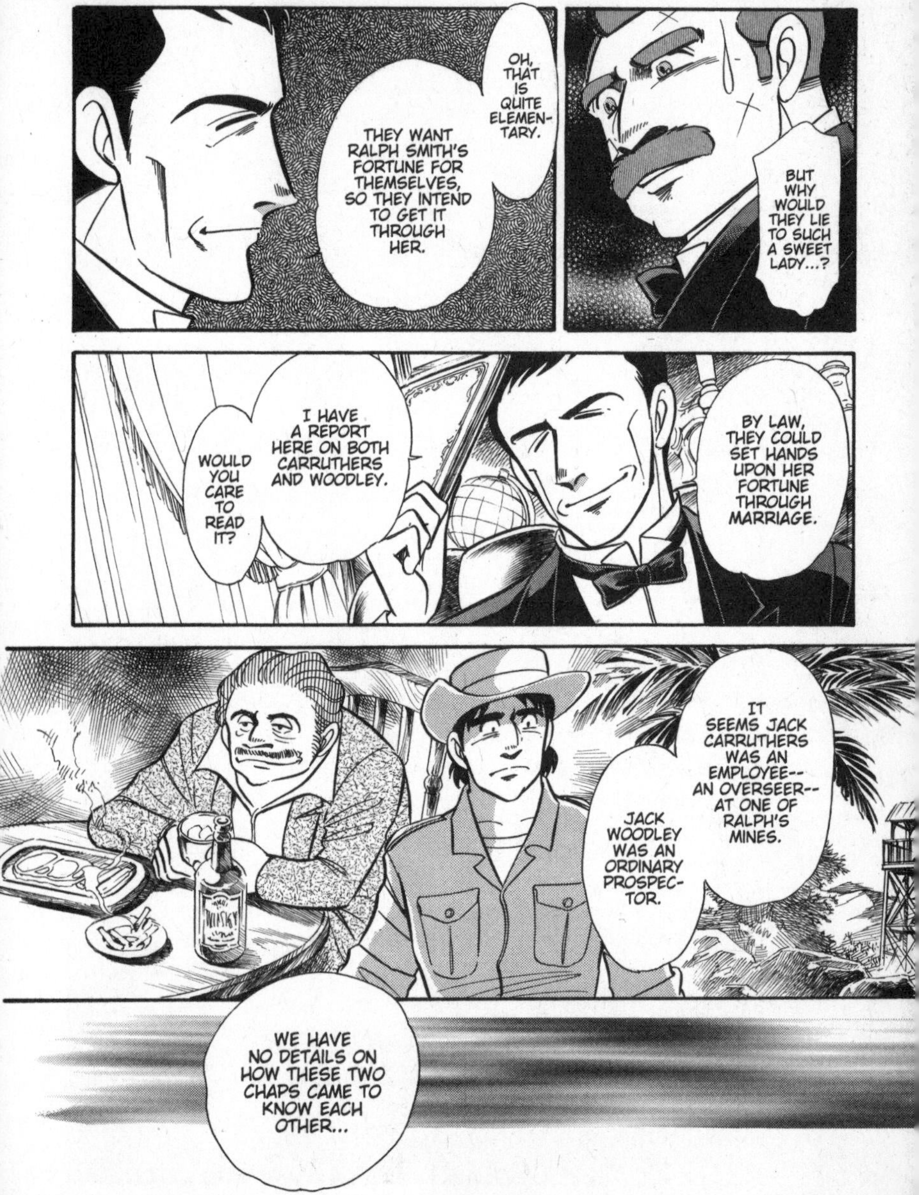
BUT WHY WOULD THEY LIE TO SUCH A SWEET LADY...?
OH, THAT IS QUITE ELEMENTARY.
THEY WANT RALPH SMITH'S FORTUNE FOR THEMSELVES, SO THEY INTEND TO GET IT THROUGH HER.
BY LAW, THEY COULD SET HANDS UPON HER FORTUNE THROUGH MARRIAGE.
I HAVE A REPORT HERE ON BOTH CARRUTHERS AND WOODLEY.
WOULD YOU CARE TO READ IT?
IT SEEMS JACK CARRUTHERS WAS AN EMPLOYEE--AN OVERSEER--AT ONE OF RALPH'S MINES.
JACK WOODLEY WAS AN ORDINARY PROSPECTOR.
WE HAVE NO DETAILS ON HOW THESE TWO CHAPS CAME TO KNOW EACH OTHER...

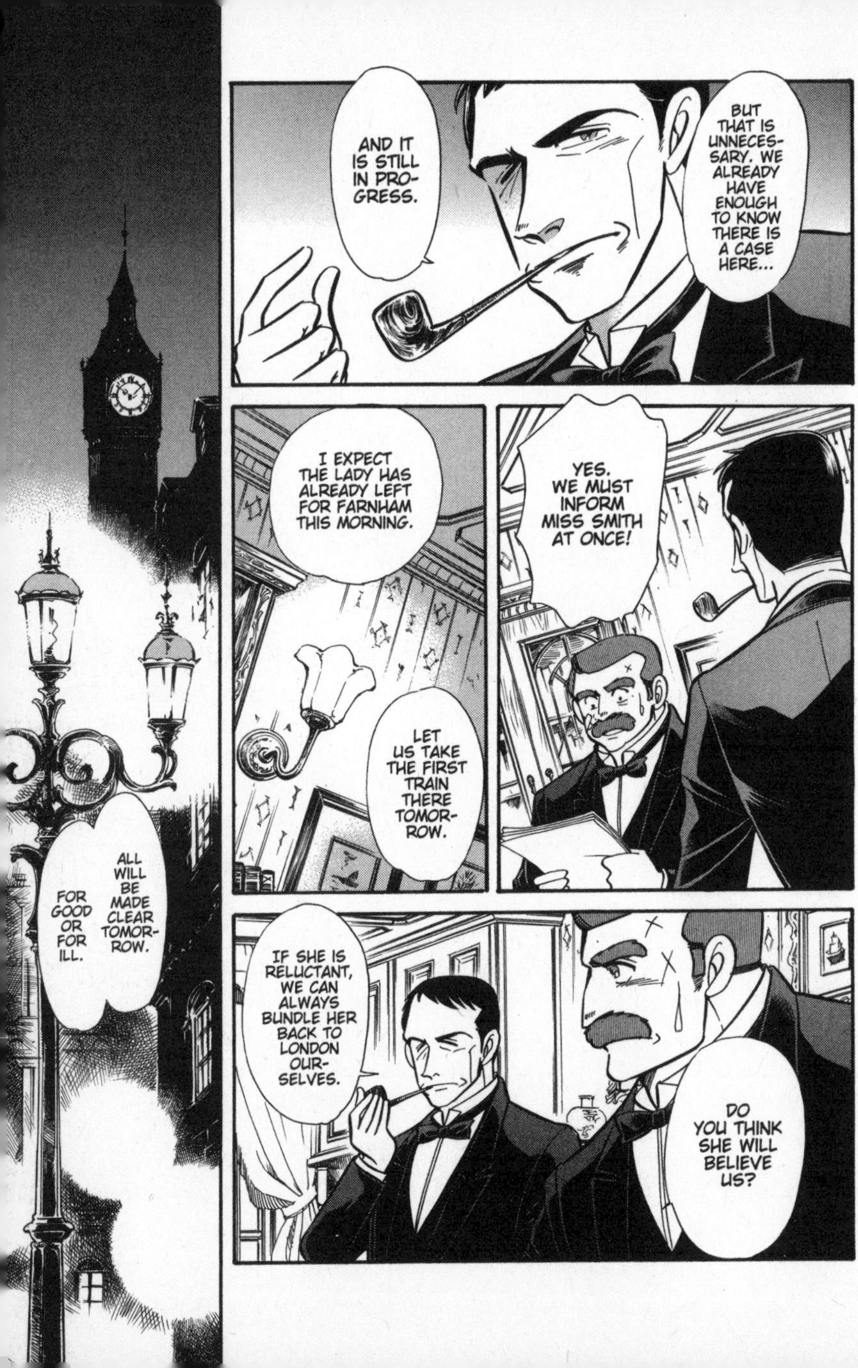
BUT THAT IS UNNECESSARY. WE ALREADY HAVE ENOUGH TO KNOW THERE IS A CASE HERE...
AND IT IS STILL IN PROGRESS.
YES. WE MUST INFORM MISS SMITH AT ONCE!
I EXPECT THE LADY HAS ALREADY LEFT FOR FARNHAM THIS MORNING.
LET US TAKE THE FIRST TRAIN THERE TOMORROW.
DO YOU THINK SHE WILL BELIEVE US?
IF SHE IS RELUCTANT, WE CAN ALWAYS BUNDLE HER BACK TO LONDON OURSELVES.
ALL WILL BE MADE CLEAR TOMORROW.
FOR GOOD OR FOR ILL.

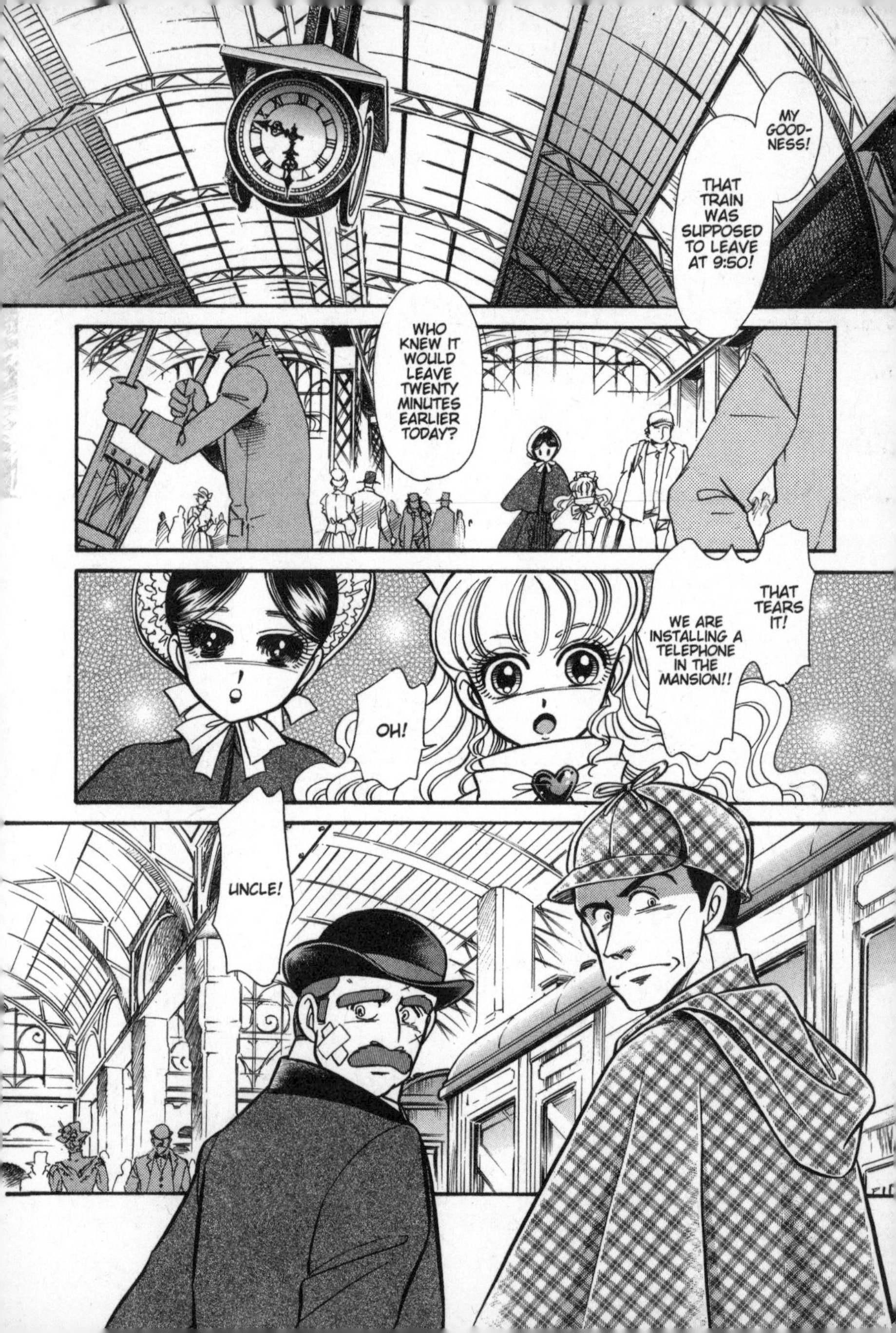
MY GOODNESS!
THAT TRAIN WAS SUPPOSED TO LEAVE AT 9:50!
WHO KNEW IT WOULD LEAVE TWENTY MINUTES EARLIER TODAY?
THAT TEARS IT!
WE ARE INSTALLING A TELEPHONE IN THE MANSION!!
OH!
UNCLE!

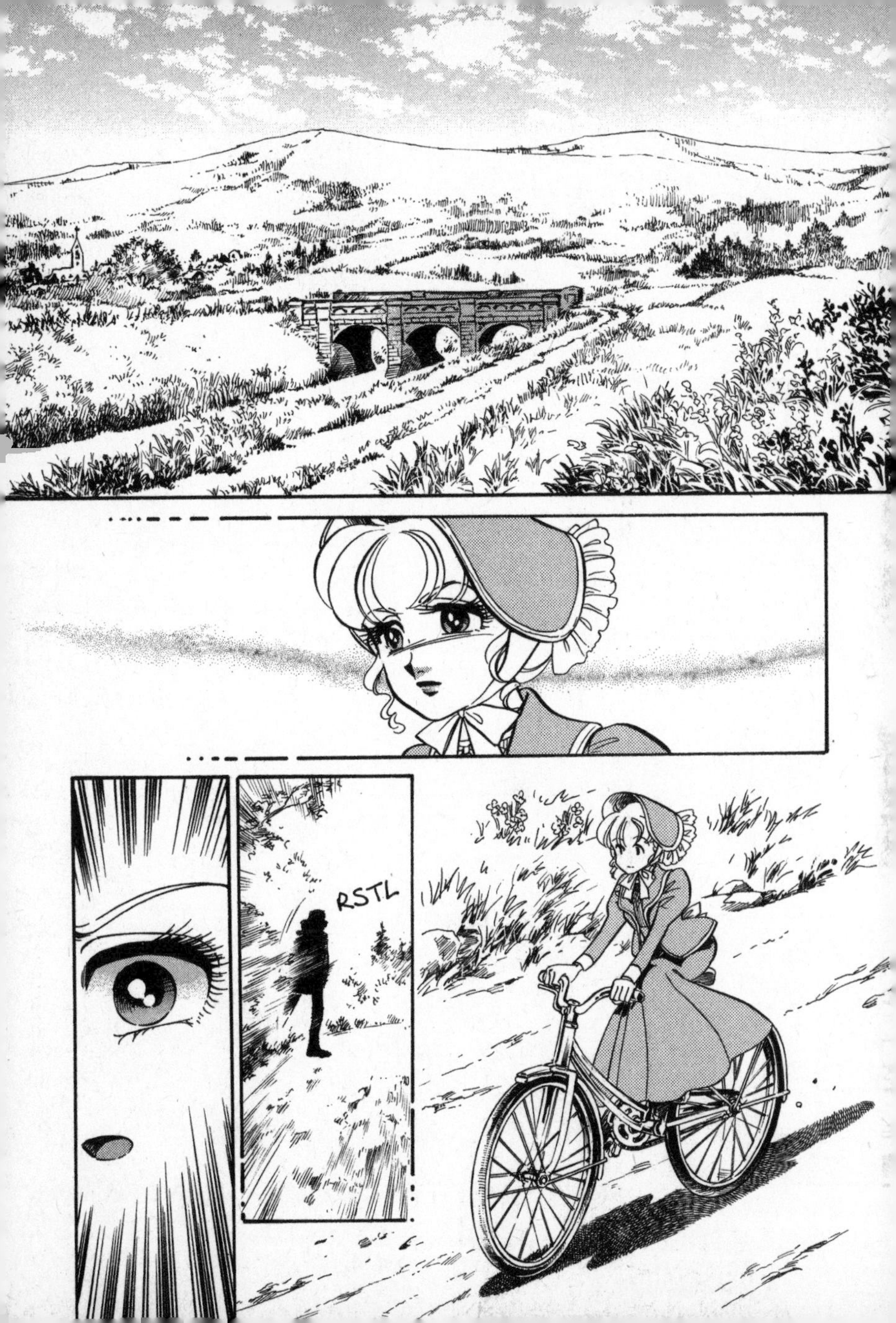
RSTL

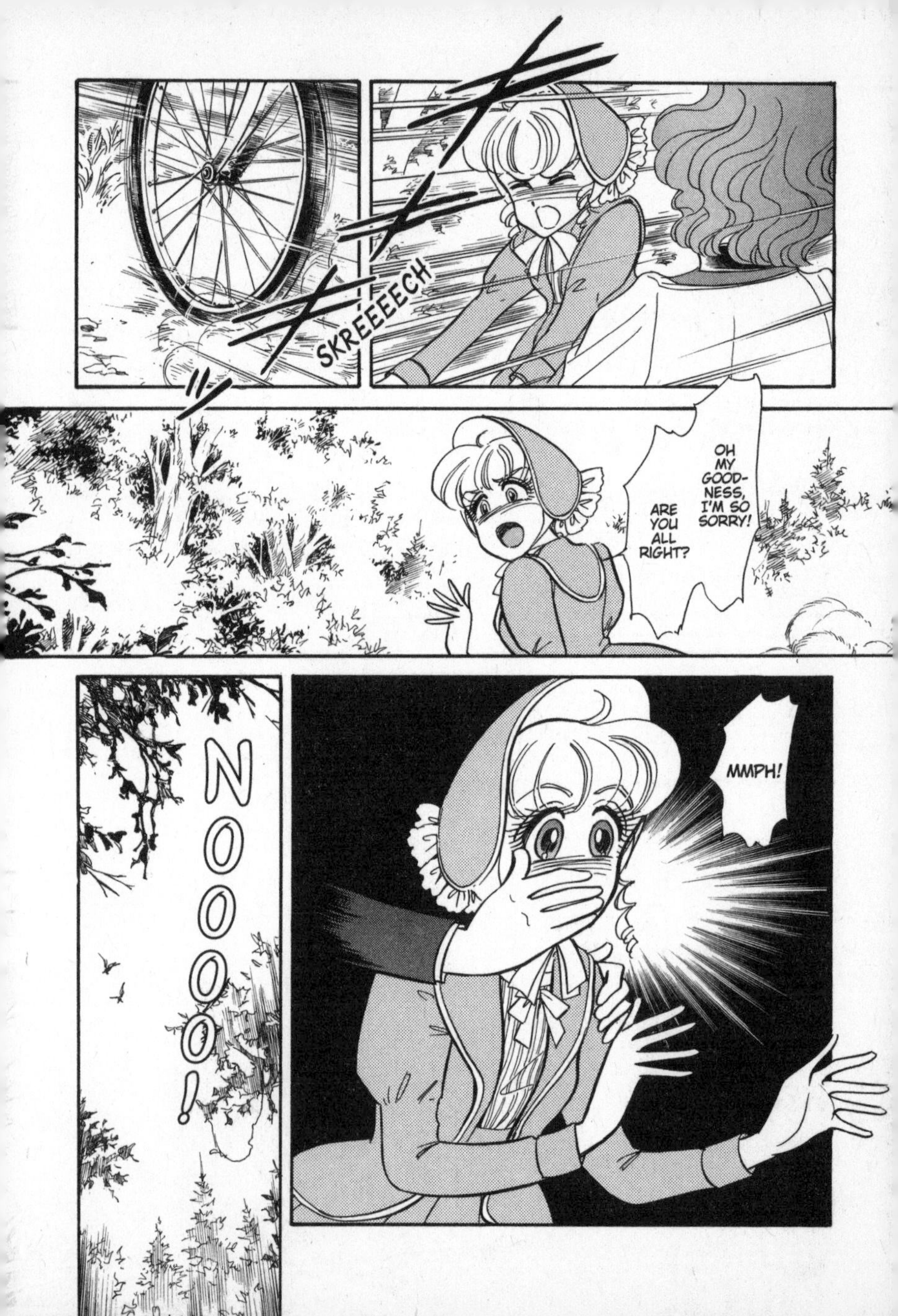
SKREEEECH
OH MY GOODNESS, I'M SO SORRY!
ARE YOU ALL RIGHT?
MMPH!
NOOOOO!

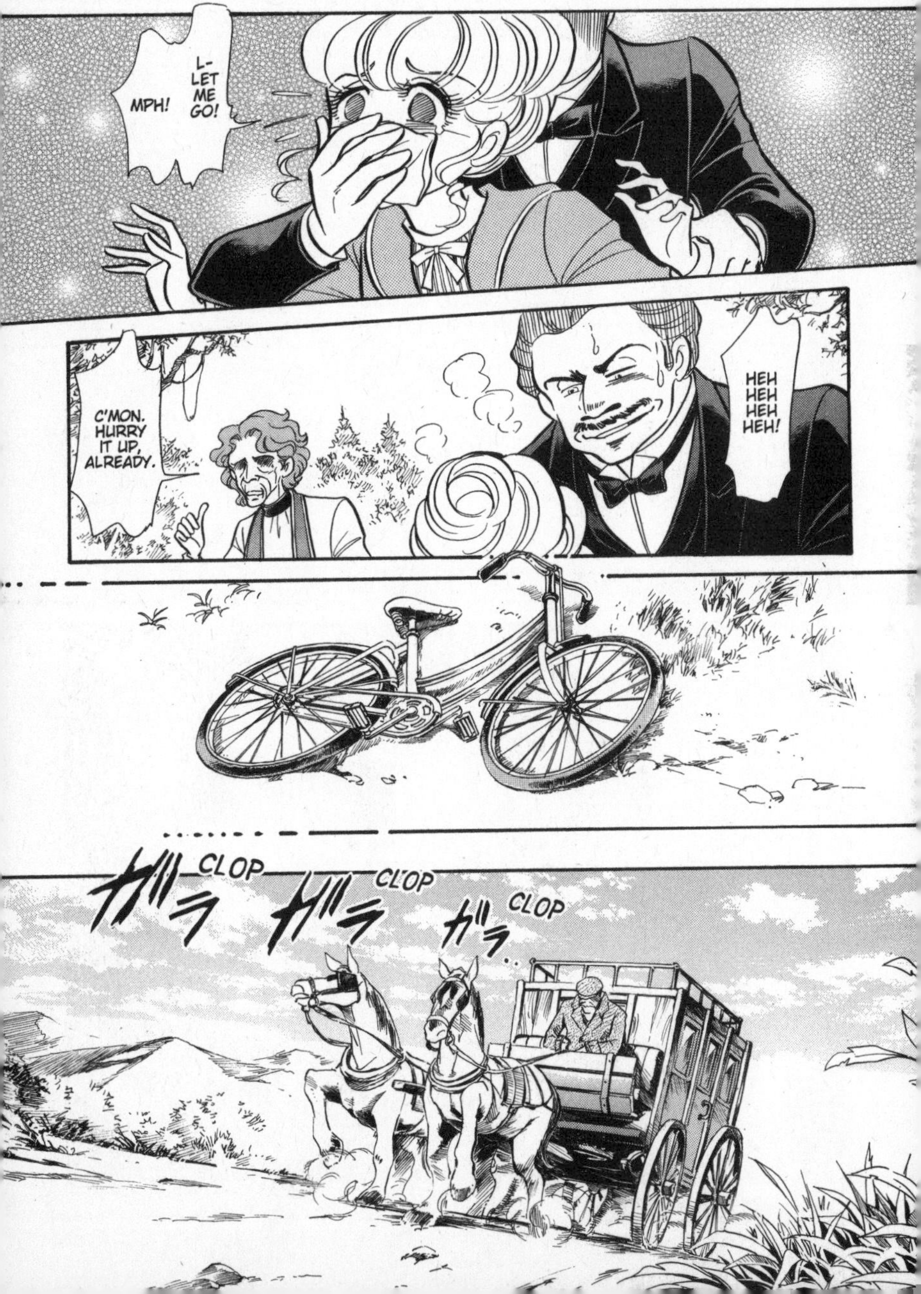
L-LET ME GO!
MPH!
HEH HEH HEH HEH!
C'MON. HURRY IT UP, ALREADY.
ガラ CLOP
ガラ CLOP
ガラ CLOP

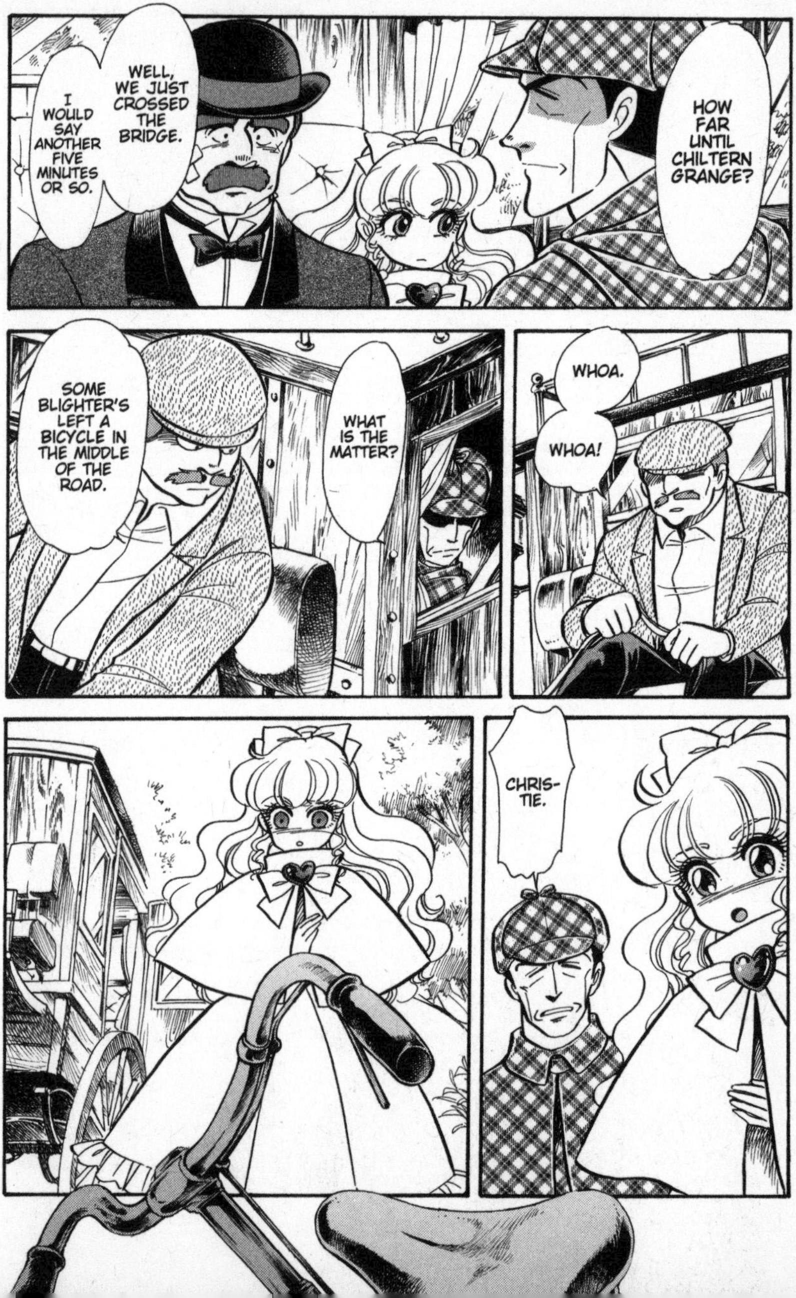
HOW FAR UNTIL CHILTERN GRANGE?
WELL, WE JUST CROSSED THE BRIDGE.
I WOULD SAY ANOTHER FIVE MINUTES OR SO.
WHOA.
WHOA!
WHAT IS THE MATTER?
SOME BLIGHTER'S LEFT A BICYCLE IN THE MIDDLE OF THE ROAD.
CHRIS-TIE.

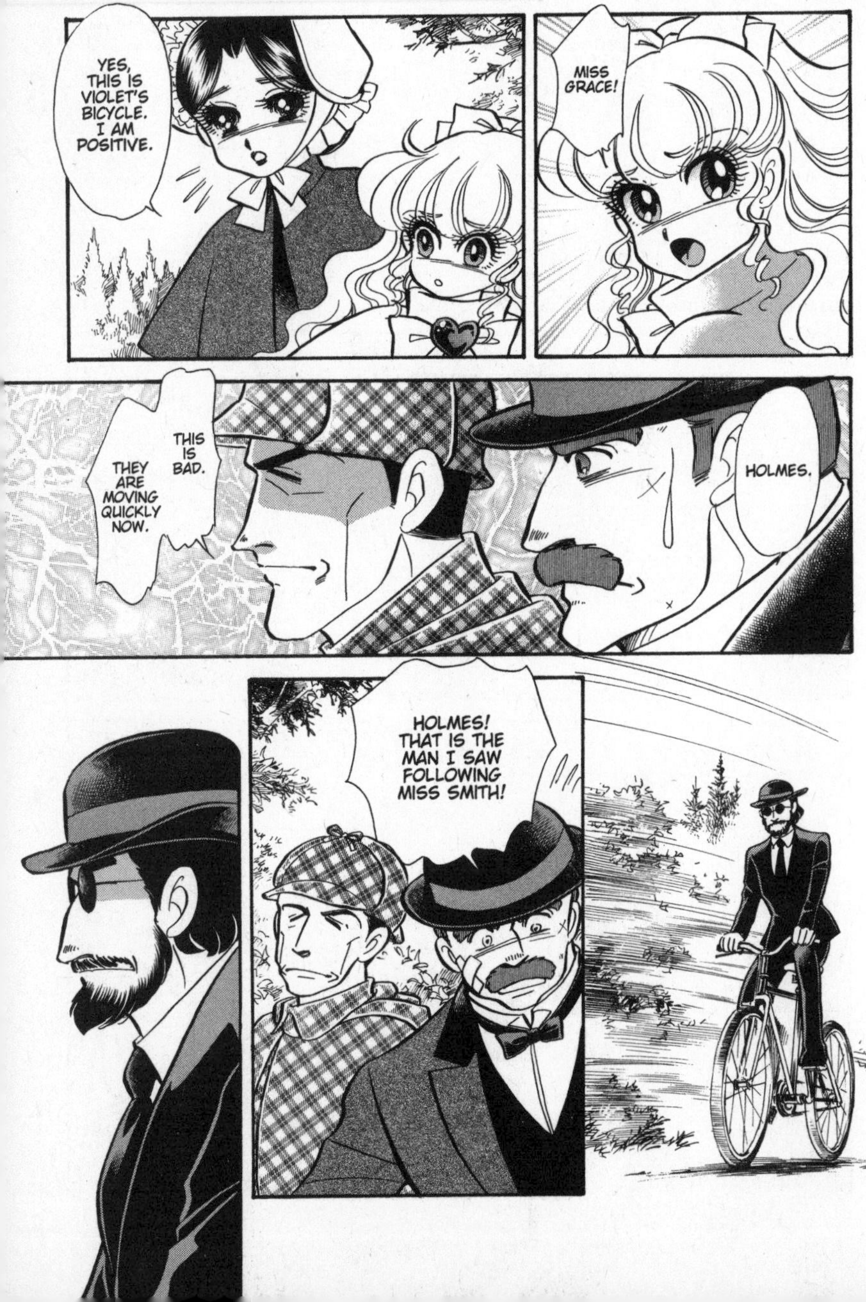
MISS GRACE!
YES, THIS IS VIOLET'S BICYCLE. I AM POSITIVE.
HOLMES.
THIS IS BAD.
THEY ARE MOVING QUICKLY NOW.
HOLMES! THAT IS THE MAN I SAW FOLLOWING MISS SMITH!

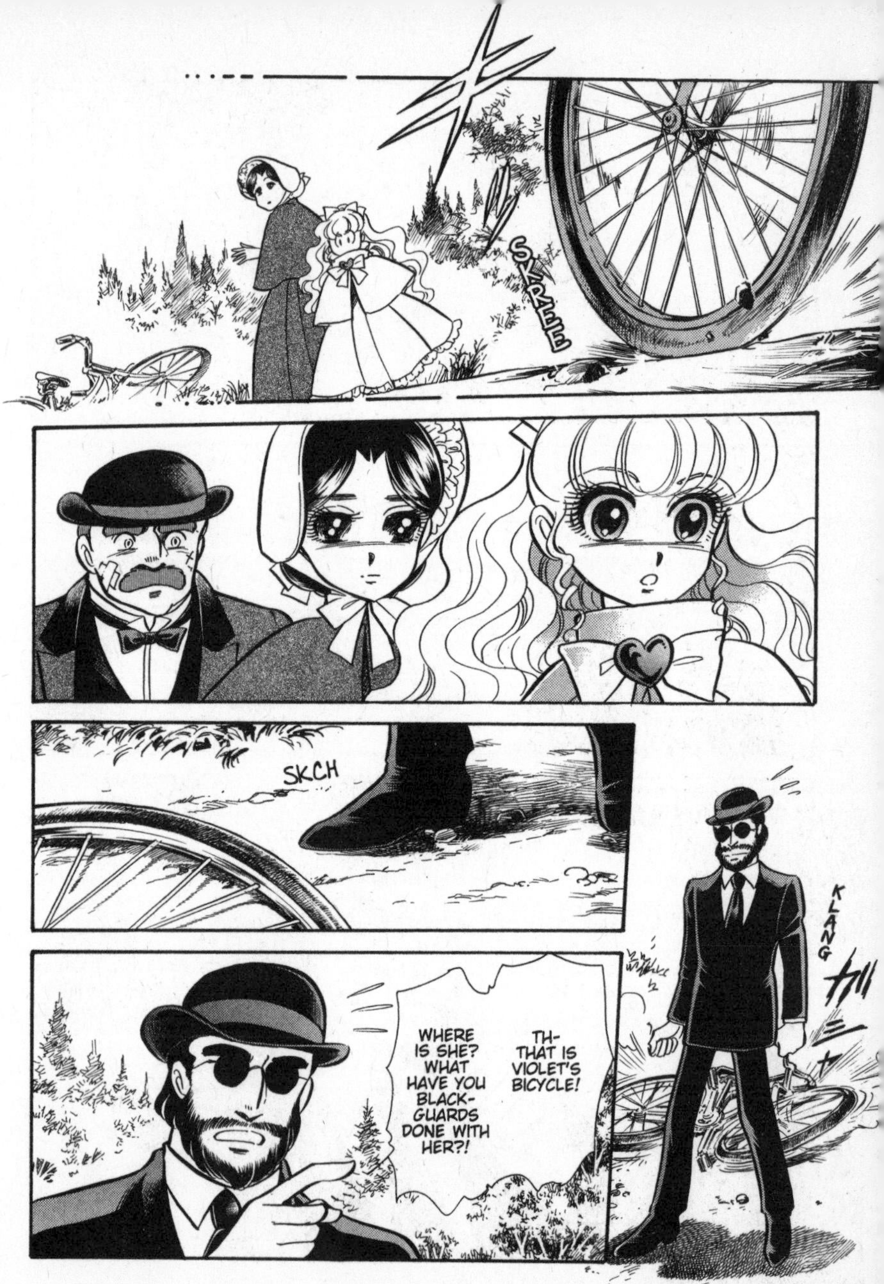
SKREEE
KLANG
SKCH
TH-
THAT IS
VIOLET'S
BICYCLE!
WHERE
IS SHE?
WHAT
HAVE YOU
BLACK-
GUARDS
DONE WITH
HER?!

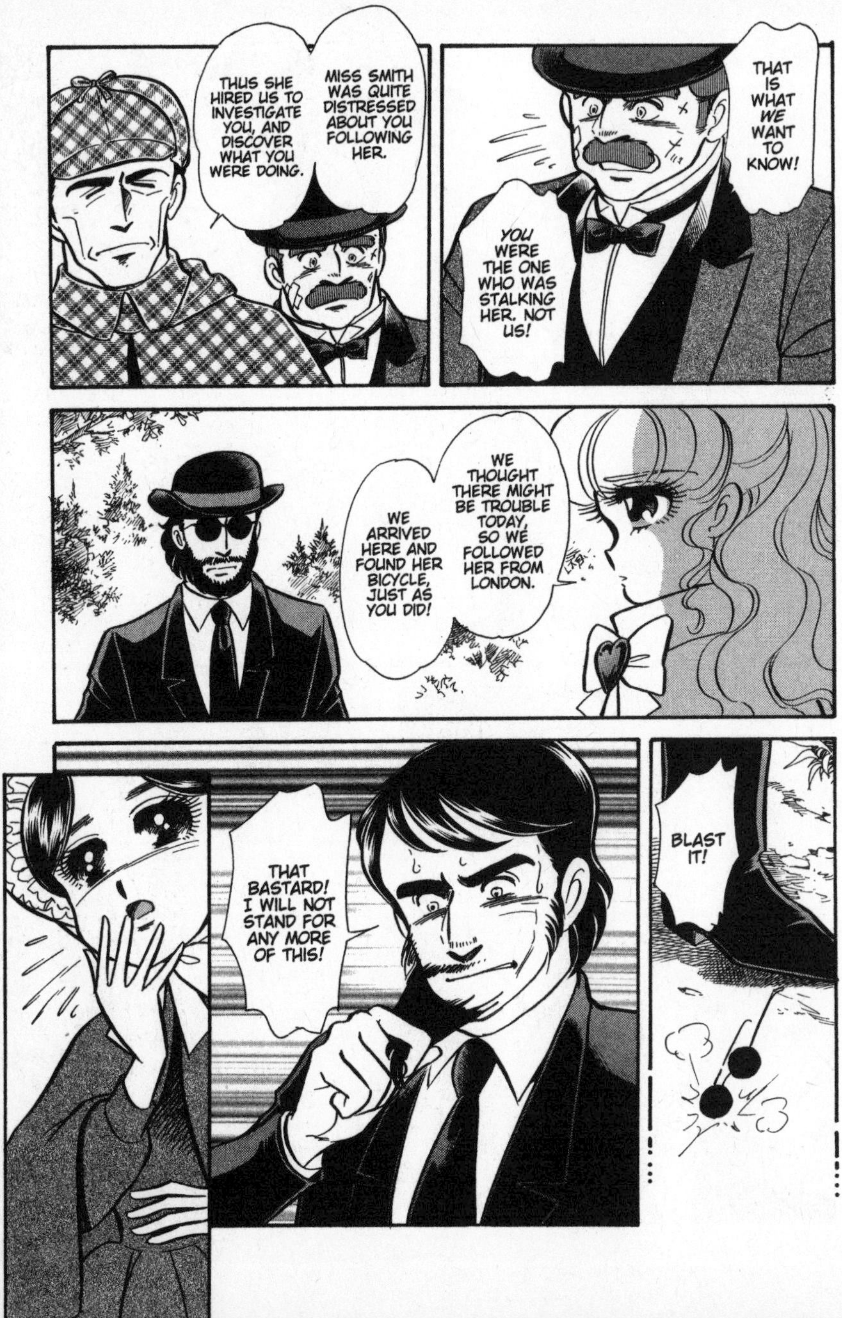
THAT IS WHAT WE WANT TO KNOW!
YOU WERE THE ONE WHO WAS STALKING HER. NOT US!
MISS SMITH WAS QUITE DISTRESSED ABOUT YOU FOLLOWING HER.
THUS SHE HIRED US TO INVESTIGATE YOU, AND DISCOVER WHAT YOU WERE DOING.
WE THOUGHT THERE MIGHT BE TROUBLE TODAY, SO WE FOLLOWED HER FROM LONDON.
WE ARRIVED HERE AND FOUND HER BICYCLE, JUST AS YOU DID!
BLAST IT!
THAT BASTARD! I WILL NOT STAND FOR ANY MORE OF THIS!

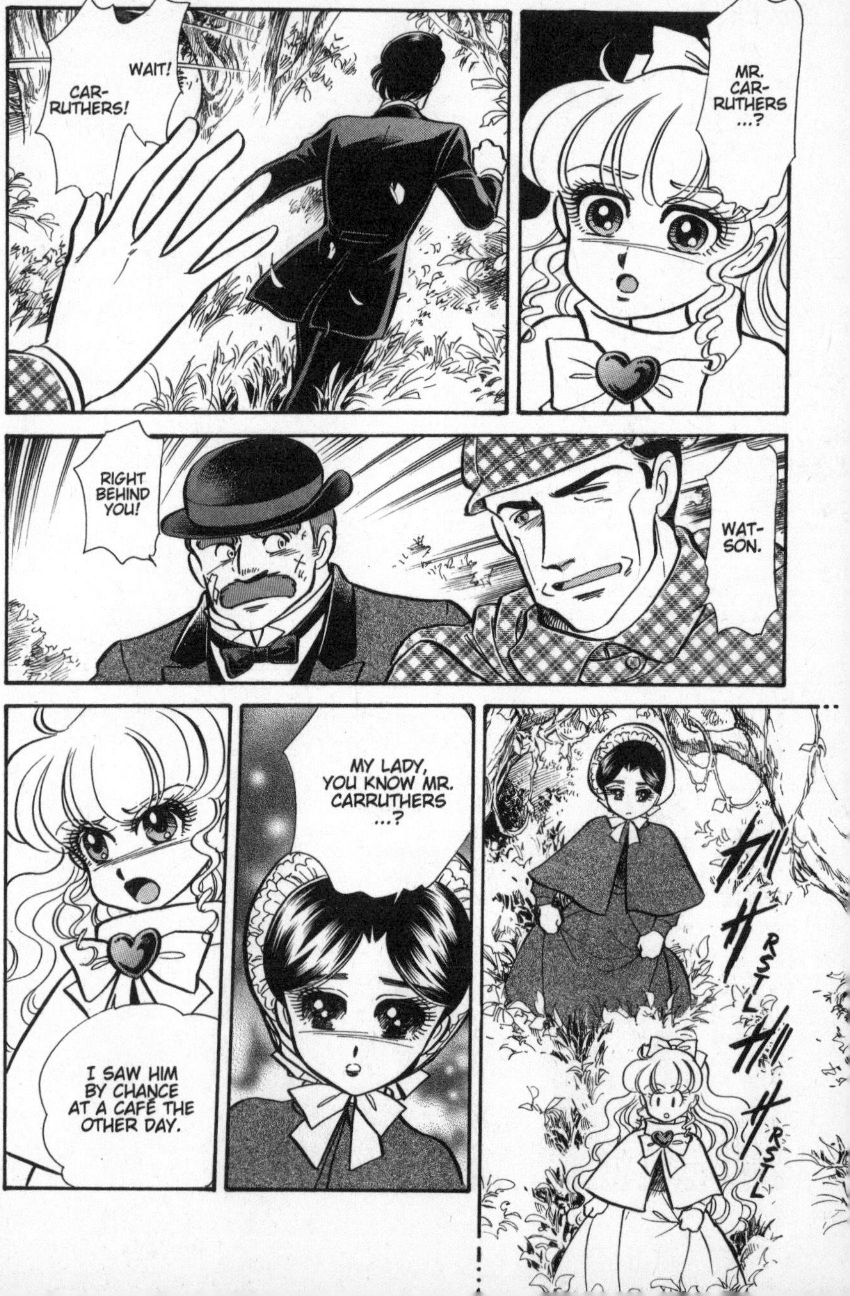
MR. CAR-RUTHERS ...?
WAIT! CAR-RUTHERS!
WAT-SON.
RIGHT BEHIND YOU!
RSTL
RSTL
MY LADY, YOU KNOW MR. CARRUTHERS ...?
I SAW HIM BY CHANCE AT A CAFÉ THE OTHER DAY.

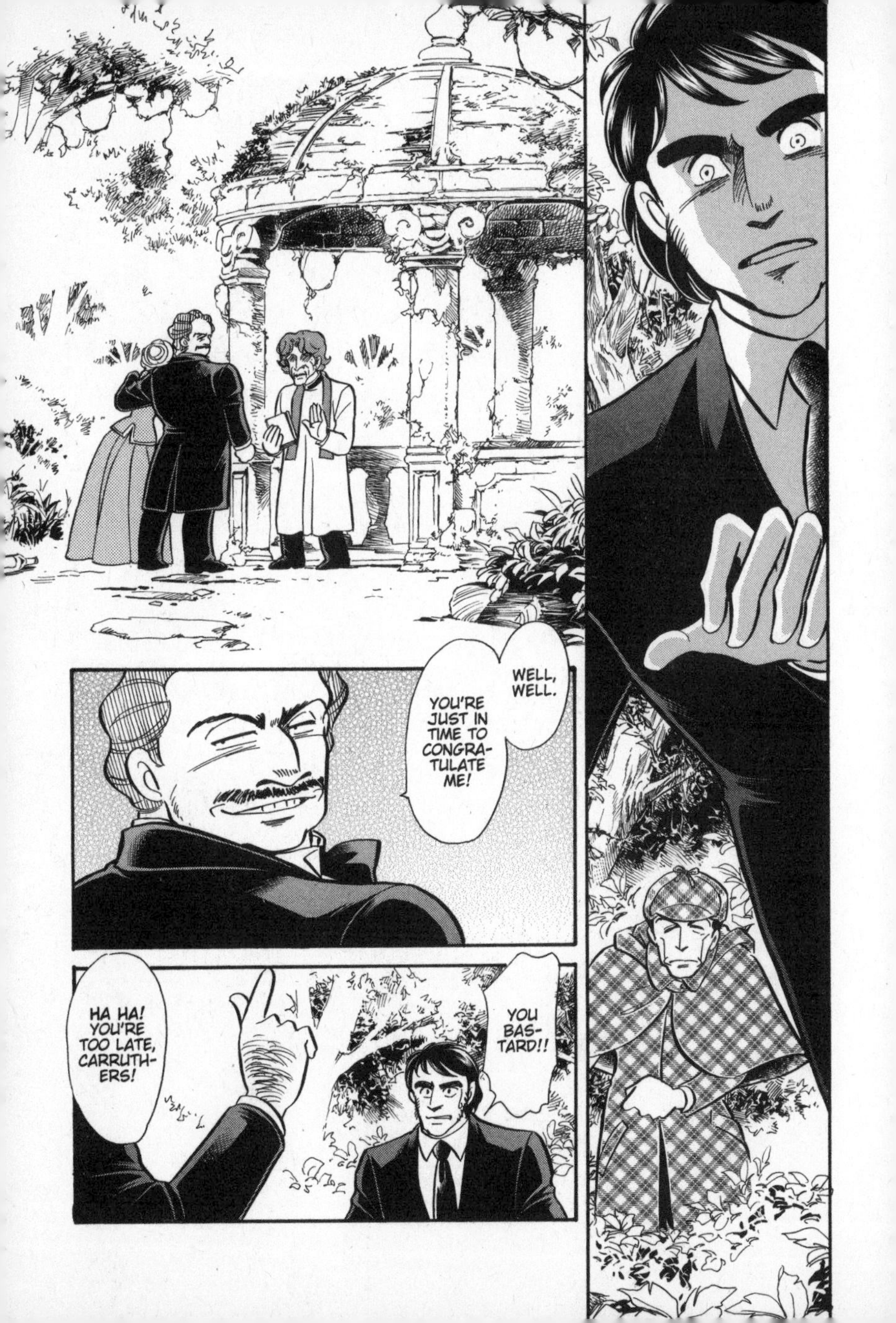
WELL, WELL.
YOU'RE JUST IN TIME TO CONGRATULATE ME!
YOU BASTARD!!
HA HA! YOU'RE TOO LATE, CARRUTHERS!

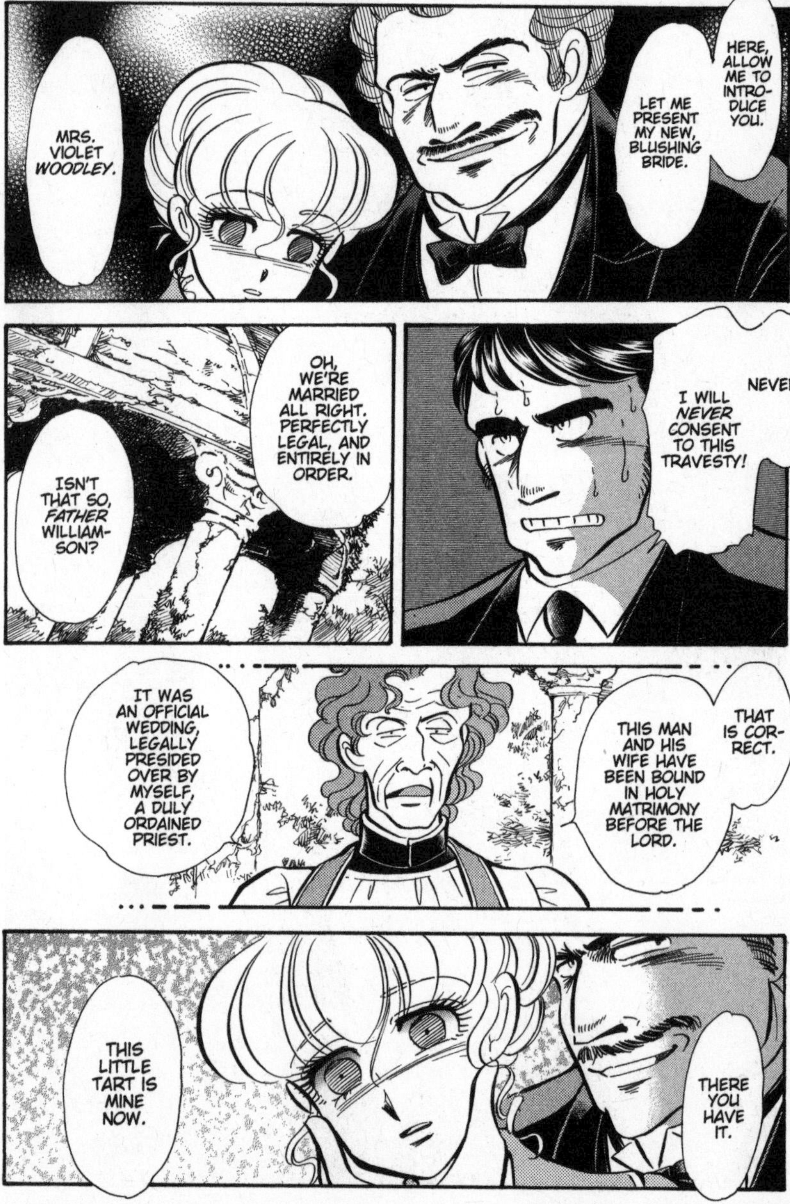
HERE, ALLOW ME TO INTRODUCE YOU.
LET ME PRESENT MY NEW, BLUSHING BRIDE.
MRS. VIOLET *WOODLEY*.
NEVER!
I WILL *NEVER* CONSENT TO THIS TRAVESTY!
OH, WE'RE MARRIED ALL RIGHT. PERFECTLY LEGAL, AND ENTIRELY IN ORDER.
ISN'T THAT SO, *FATHER* WILLIAMSON?
THAT IS CORRECT.
THIS MAN AND HIS WIFE HAVE BEEN BOUND IN HOLY MATRIMONY BEFORE THE LORD.
IT WAS AN OFFICIAL WEDDING, LEGALLY PRESIDED OVER BY MYSELF, A DULY ORDAINED PRIEST.
THERE YOU HAVE IT.
THIS LITTLE TART IS MINE NOW.

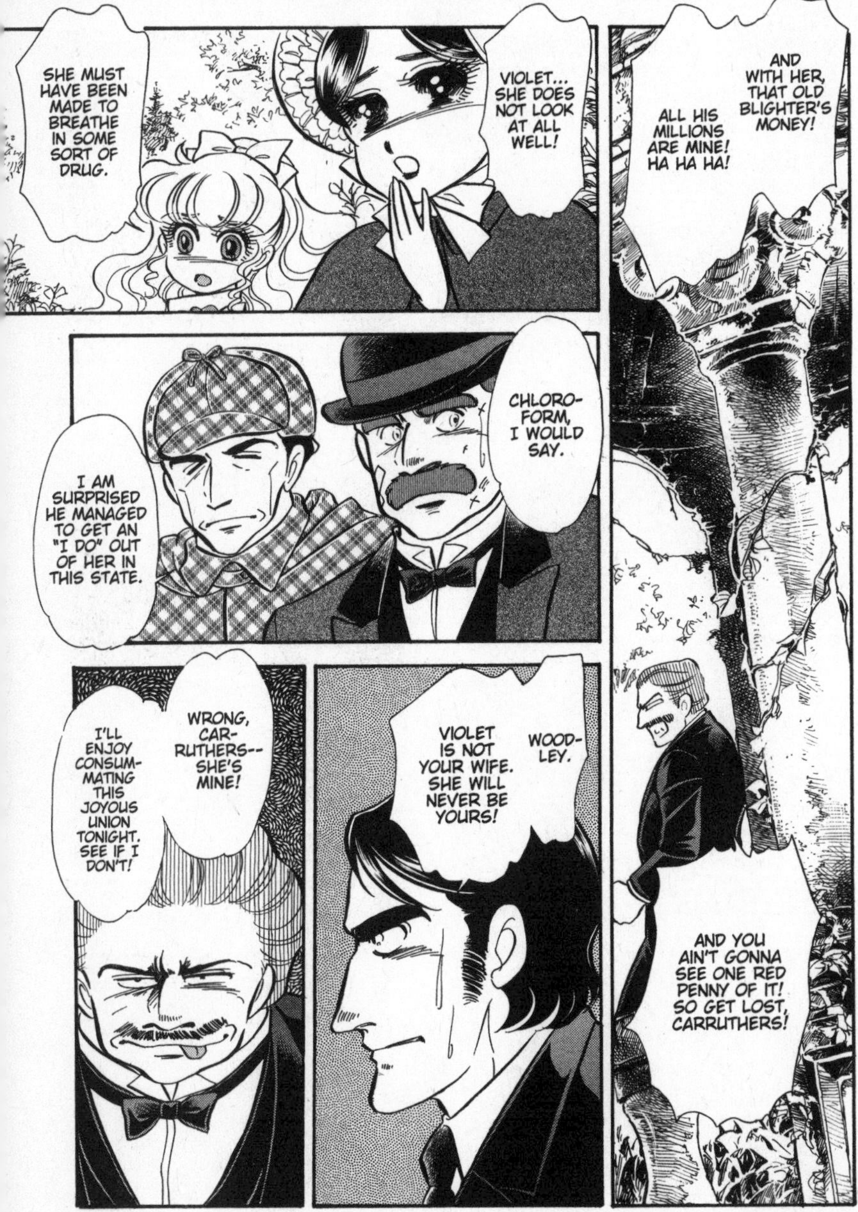
AND WITH HER, THAT OLD BLIGHTER'S MONEY!
ALL HIS MILLIONS ARE MINE! HA HA HA!
AND YOU AIN'T GONNA SEE ONE RED PENNY OF IT! SO GET LOST, CARRUTHERS!
VIOLET... SHE DOES NOT LOOK AT ALL WELL!
SHE MUST HAVE BEEN MADE TO BREATHE IN SOME SORT OF DRUG.
CHLORO-FORM, I WOULD SAY.
I AM SURPRISED HE MANAGED TO GET AN "I DO" OUT OF HER IN THIS STATE.
WOOD-LEY.
VIOLET IS NOT YOUR WIFE. SHE WILL NEVER BE YOURS!
WRONG, CAR-RUTHERS-- SHE'S MINE!
I'LL ENJOY CONSUM-MATING THIS JOYOUS UNION TONIGHT. SEE IF I DON'T!

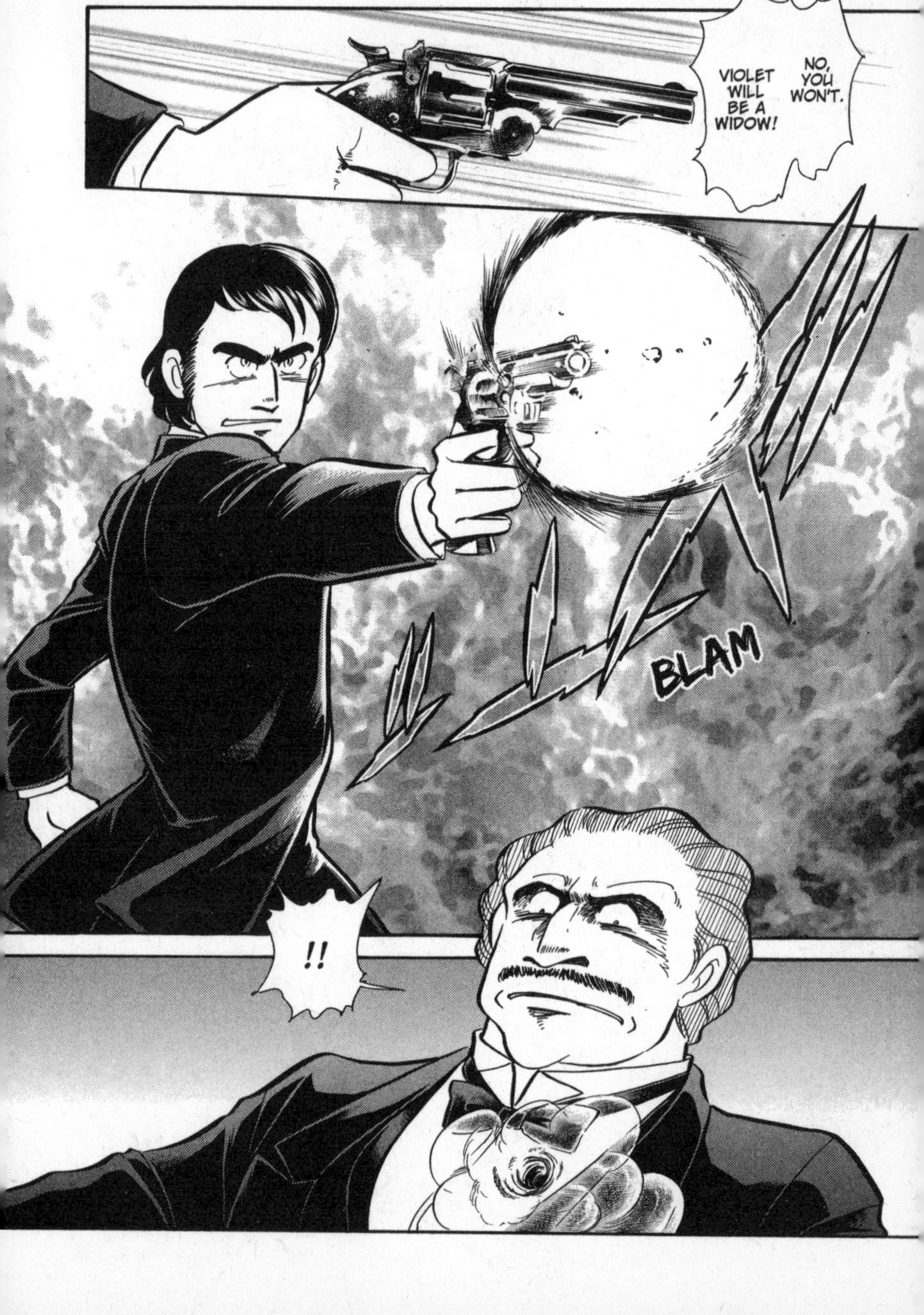
NO, YOU WON'T.
VIOLET WILL BE A WIDOW!
BLAM
!!

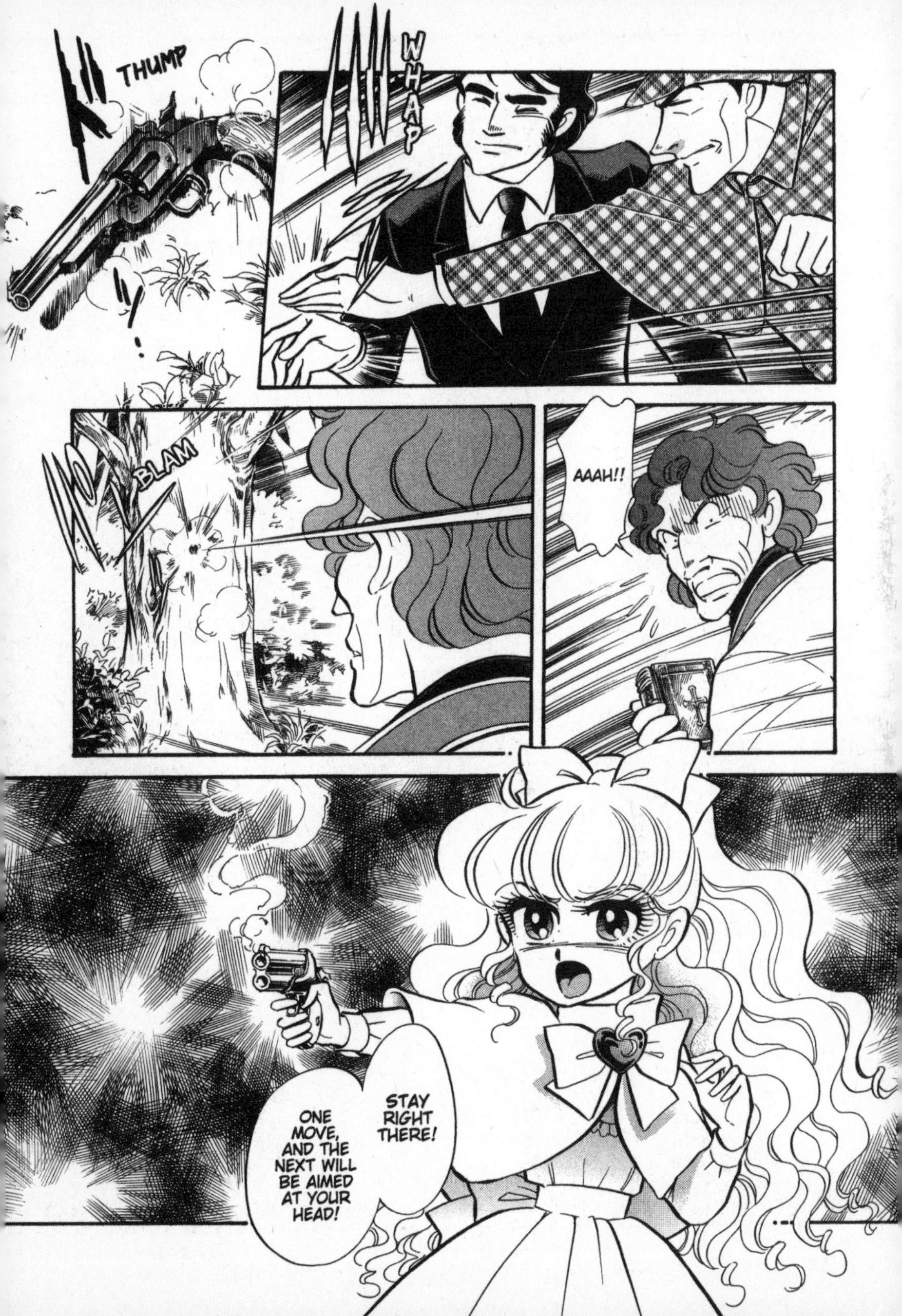
WHAP
THUMP
AAAH!!
BLAM
STAY RIGHT THERE!
ONE MOVE, AND THE NEXT WILL BE AIMED AT YOUR HEAD!

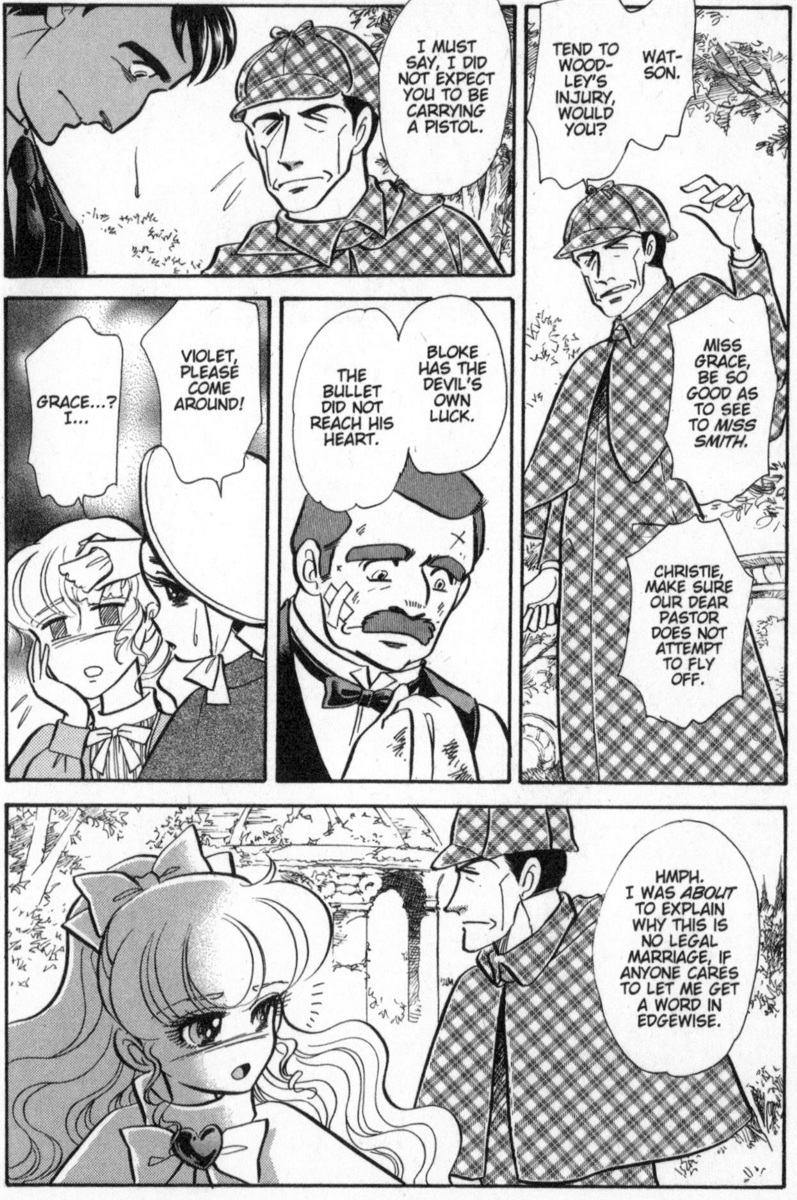
WAT-SON.
TEND TO WOODLEY'S INJURY, WOULD YOU?
MISS GRACE, BE SO GOOD AS TO SEE TO *MISS SMITH.*
CHRISTIE, MAKE SURE OUR DEAR PASTOR DOES NOT ATTEMPT TO FLY OFF.
I MUST SAY, I DID NOT EXPECT YOU TO BE CARRYING A PISTOL.
BLOKE HAS THE DEVIL'S OWN LUCK.
THE BULLET DID NOT REACH HIS HEART.
VIOLET, PLEASE COME AROUND!
GRACE...? I...
HMPH. I WAS *ABOUT* TO EXPLAIN WHY THIS IS NO LEGAL MARRIAGE, IF ANYONE CARES TO LET ME GET A WORD IN EDGEWISE.

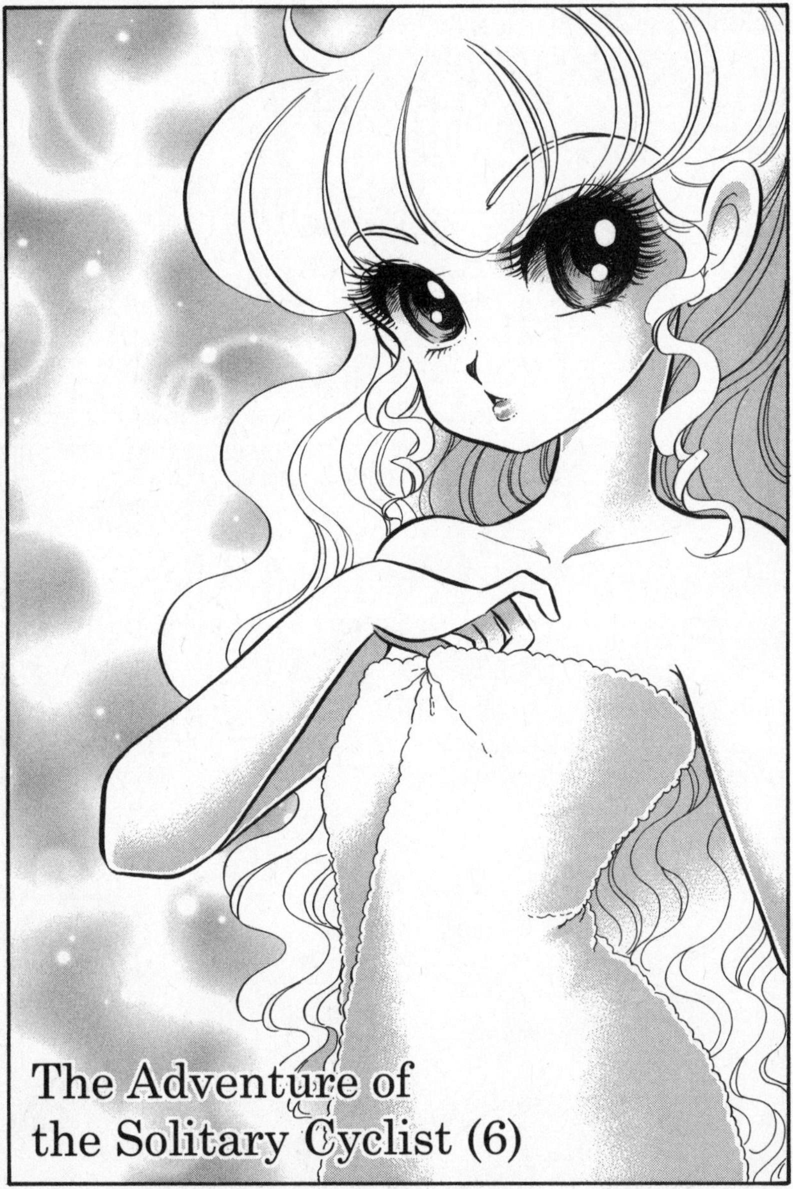

The Adventure of the Solitary Cyclist (6)

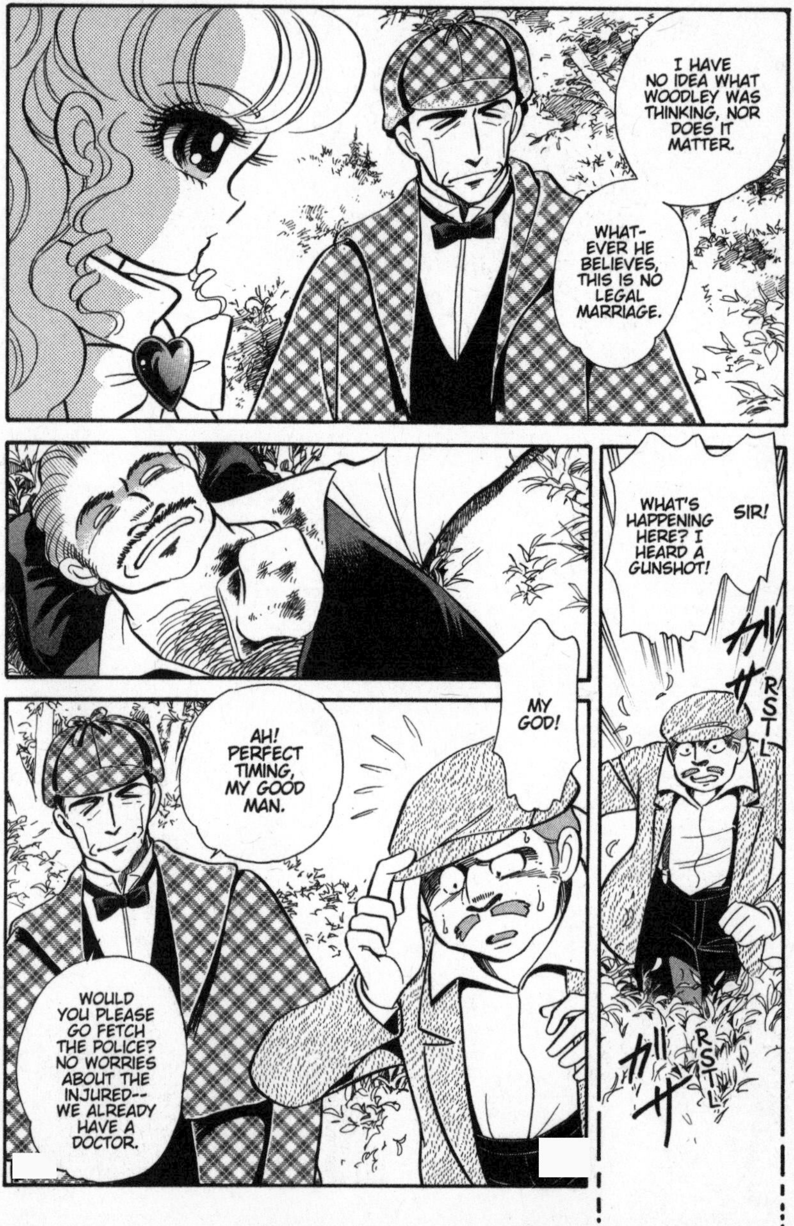
I HAVE NO IDEA WHAT WOODLEY WAS THINKING, NOR DOES IT MATTER.
WHAT-EVER HE BELIEVES, THIS IS NO LEGAL MARRIAGE.
SIR!
WHAT'S HAPPENING HERE? I HEARD A GUNSHOT!
RSTL
RSTL
MY GOD!
AH! PERFECT TIMING, MY GOOD MAN.
WOULD YOU PLEASE GO FETCH THE POLICE? NO WORRIES ABOUT THE INJURED--WE ALREADY HAVE A DOCTOR.

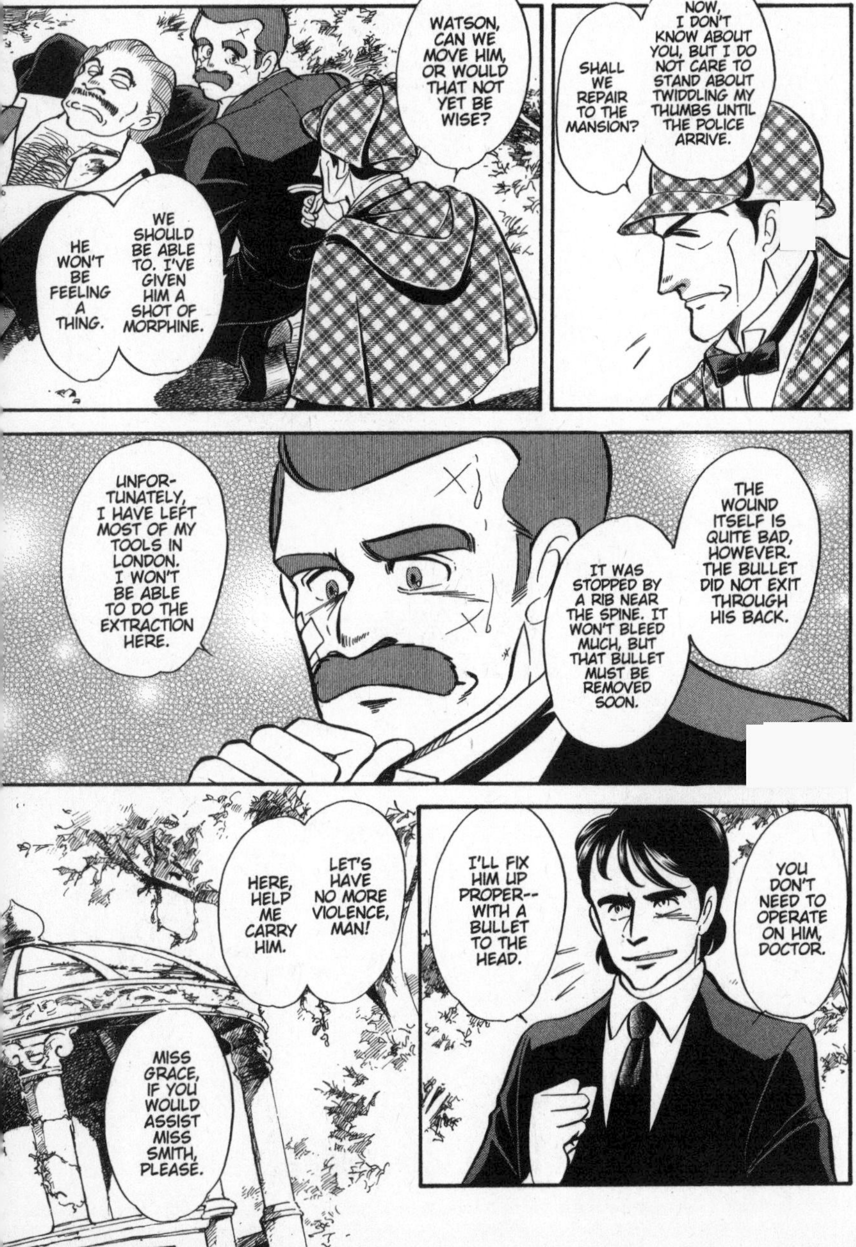
NOW, I DON'T KNOW ABOUT YOU, BUT I DO NOT CARE TO STAND ABOUT TWIDDLING MY THUMBS UNTIL THE POLICE ARRIVE.
SHALL WE REPAIR TO THE MANSION?
WATSON, CAN WE MOVE HIM, OR WOULD THAT NOT YET BE WISE?
WE SHOULD BE ABLE TO. I'VE GIVEN HIM A SHOT OF MORPHINE.
HE WON'T BE FEELING A THING.
THE WOUND ITSELF IS QUITE BAD, HOWEVER. THE BULLET DID NOT EXIT THROUGH HIS BACK.
IT WAS STOPPED BY A RIB NEAR THE SPINE. IT WON'T BLEED MUCH, BUT THAT BULLET MUST BE REMOVED SOON.
UNFOR-TUNATELY, I HAVE LEFT MOST OF MY TOOLS IN LONDON. I WON'T BE ABLE TO DO THE EXTRACTION HERE.
YOU DON'T NEED TO OPERATE ON HIM, DOCTOR.
I'LL FIX HIM UP PROPER--WITH A BULLET TO THE HEAD.
LET'S HAVE NO MORE VIOLENCE, MAN!
HERE, HELP ME CARRY HIM.
MISS GRACE, IF YOU WOULD ASSIST MISS SMITH, PLEASE.

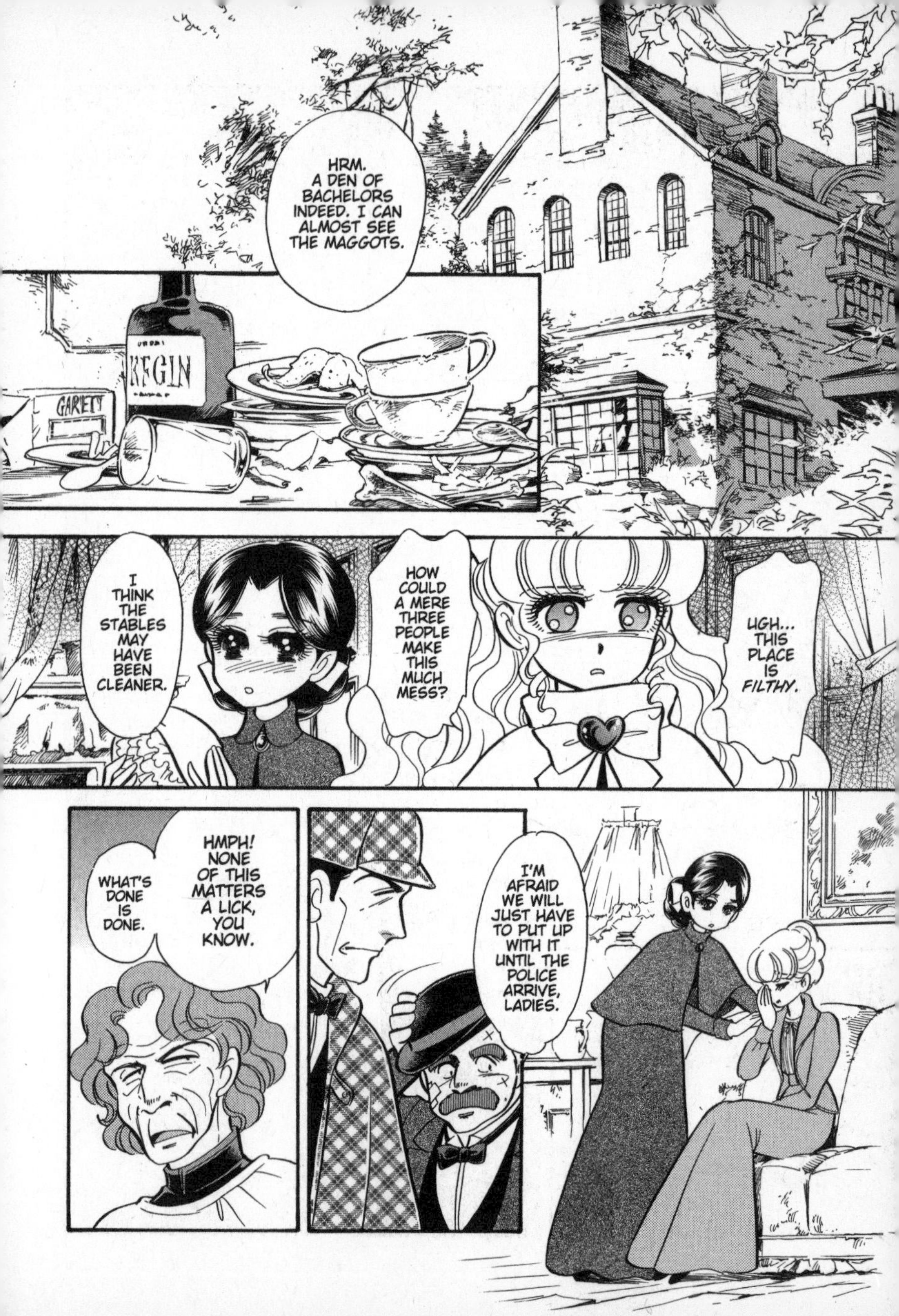
HRM. A DEN OF BACHELORS INDEED. I CAN ALMOST SEE THE MAGGOTS.
UGH... THIS PLACE IS *FILTHY.*
HOW COULD A MERE THREE PEOPLE MAKE THIS MUCH MESS?
I THINK THE STABLES MAY HAVE BEEN CLEANER.
I'M AFRAID WE WILL JUST HAVE TO PUT UP WITH IT UNTIL THE POLICE ARRIVE, LADIES.
HMPH! NONE OF THIS MATTERS A LICK, YOU KNOW.
WHAT'S DONE IS DONE.

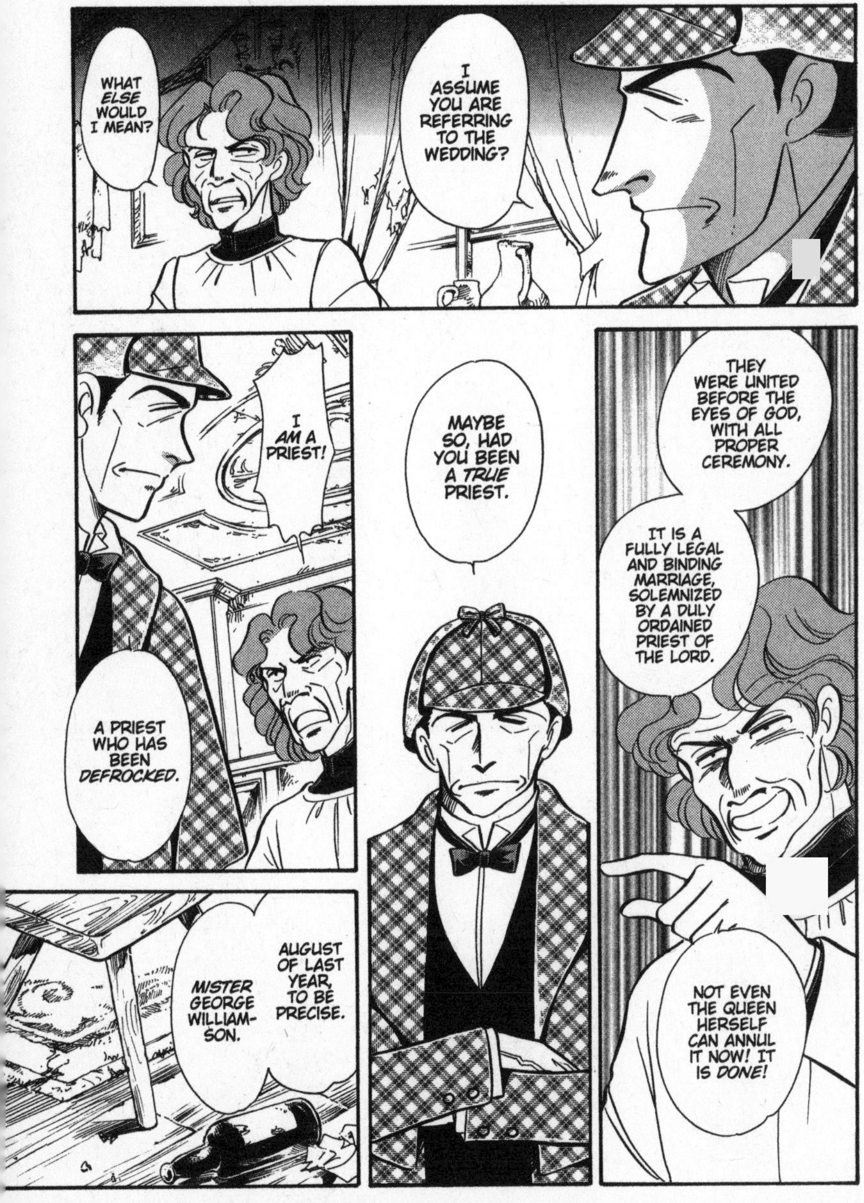
I ASSUME YOU ARE REFERRING TO THE WEDDING?
WHAT *ELSE* WOULD I MEAN?
THEY WERE UNITED BEFORE THE EYES OF GOD, WITH ALL PROPER CEREMONY.
IT IS A FULLY LEGAL AND BINDING MARRIAGE, SOLEMNIZED BY A DULY ORDAINED PRIEST OF THE LORD.
NOT EVEN THE QUEEN HERSELF CAN ANNUL IT NOW! IT IS *DONE*!
MAYBE SO, HAD YOU BEEN A *TRUE* PRIEST.
I *AM* A PRIEST!
A PRIEST WHO HAS BEEN *DEFROCKED*.
AUGUST OF LAST YEAR, TO BE PRECISE.
MISTER GEORGE WILLIAM-SON.

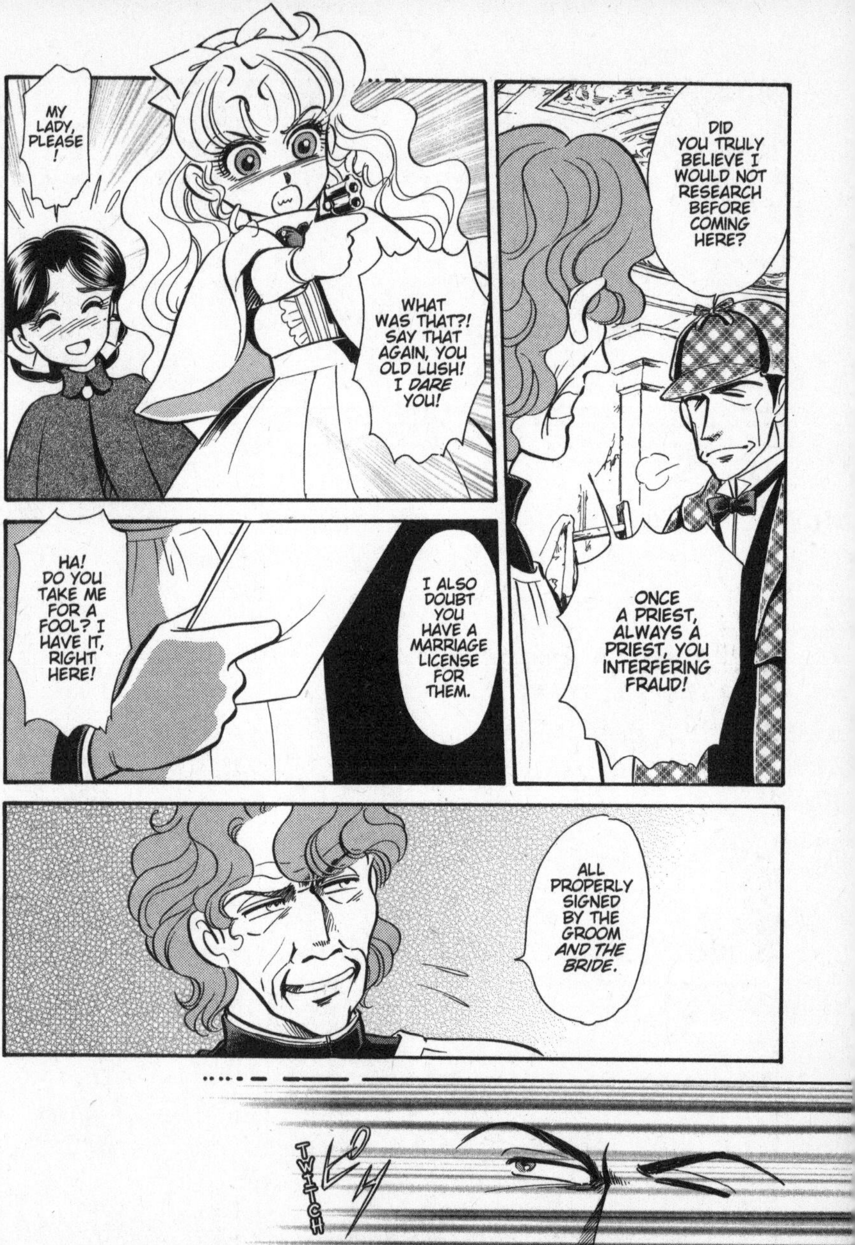
DID YOU TRULY BELIEVE I WOULD NOT RESEARCH BEFORE COMING HERE?
ONCE A PRIEST, ALWAYS A PRIEST, YOU INTERFERING FRAUD!
WHAT WAS THAT?! SAY THAT AGAIN, YOU OLD LUSH! I *DARE* YOU!
MY LADY, PLEASE!
I ALSO DOUBT YOU HAVE A MARRIAGE LICENSE FOR THEM.
HA! DO YOU TAKE ME FOR A FOOL? I HAVE IT, RIGHT HERE!
ALL PROPERLY SIGNED BY THE GROOM *AND THE BRIDE.*
TWITCH

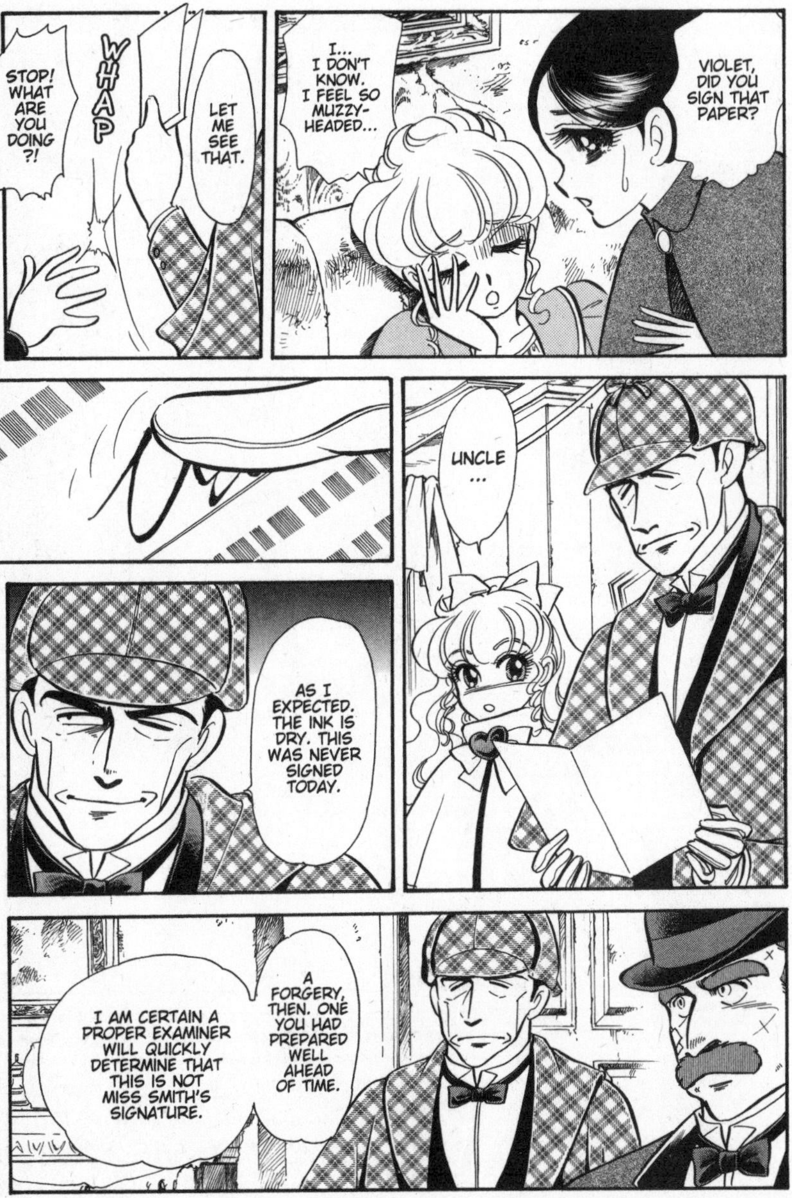
VIOLET, DID YOU SIGN THAT PAPER?
I... I DON'T KNOW. I FEEL SO MUZZY-HEADED...
LET ME SEE THAT.
WHAP
STOP! WHAT ARE YOU DOING?!
UNCLE...
AS I EXPECTED. THE INK IS DRY. THIS WAS NEVER SIGNED TODAY.
A FORGERY, THEN. ONE YOU HAD PREPARED WELL AHEAD OF TIME.
I AM CERTAIN A PROPER EXAMINER WILL QUICKLY DETERMINE THAT THIS IS NOT MISS SMITH'S SIGNATURE.

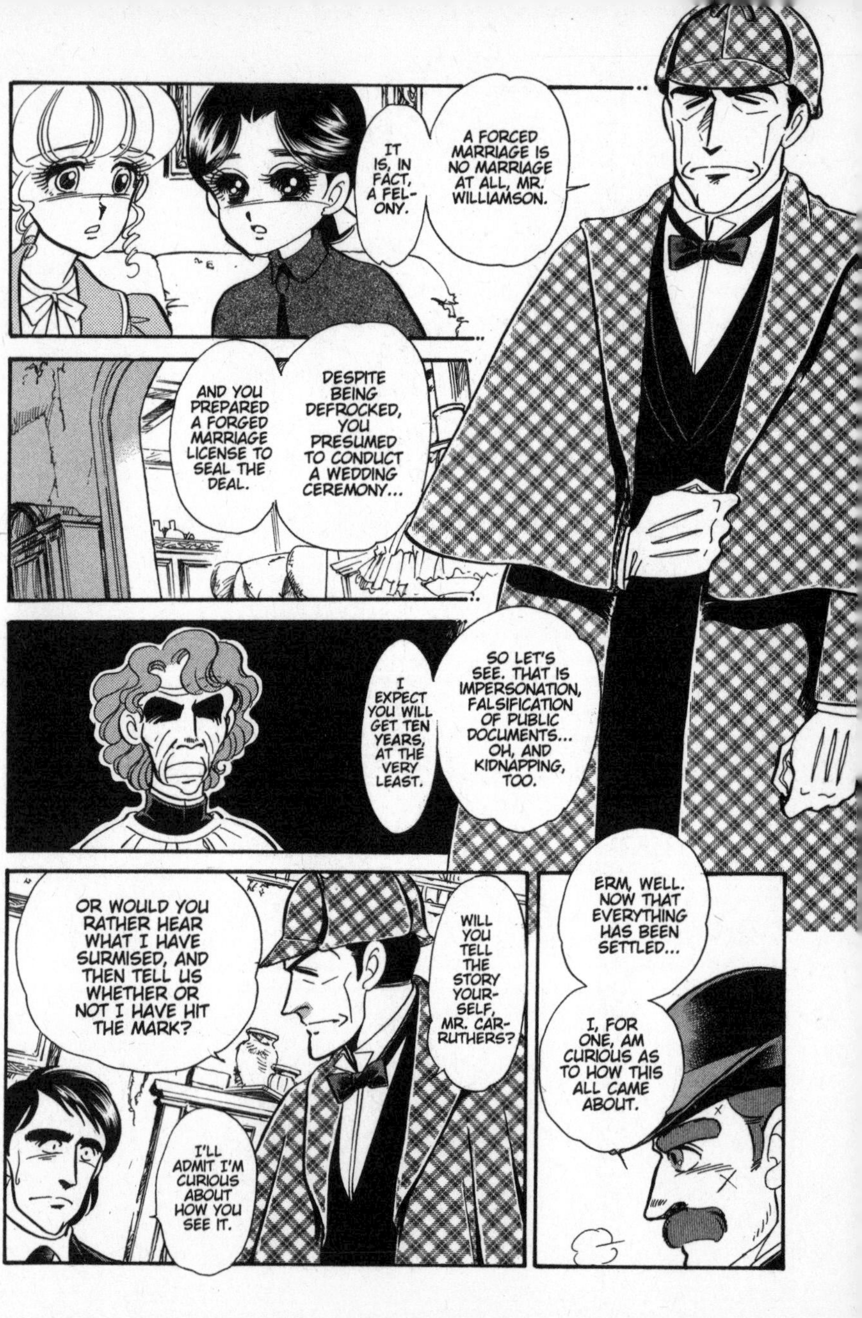
A FORCED MARRIAGE IS NO MARRIAGE AT ALL, MR. WILLIAMSON.
IT IS, IN FACT, A FEL-ONY.
DESPITE BEING DEFROCKED, YOU PRESUMED TO CONDUCT A WEDDING CEREMONY...
AND YOU PREPARED A FORGED MARRIAGE LICENSE TO SEAL THE DEAL.
SO LET'S SEE. THAT IS IMPERSONATION, FALSIFICATION OF PUBLIC DOCUMENTS... OH, AND KIDNAPPING, TOO.
I EXPECT YOU WILL GET TEN YEARS, AT THE VERY LEAST.
ERM, WELL. NOW THAT EVERYTHING HAS BEEN SETTLED...
I, FOR ONE, AM CURIOUS AS TO HOW THIS ALL CAME ABOUT.
WILL YOU TELL THE STORY YOUR-SELF, MR. CAR-RUTHERS?
OR WOULD YOU RATHER HEAR WHAT I HAVE SURMISED, AND THEN TELL US WHETHER OR NOT I HAVE HIT THE MARK?
I'LL ADMIT I'M CURIOUS ABOUT HOW YOU SEE IT.

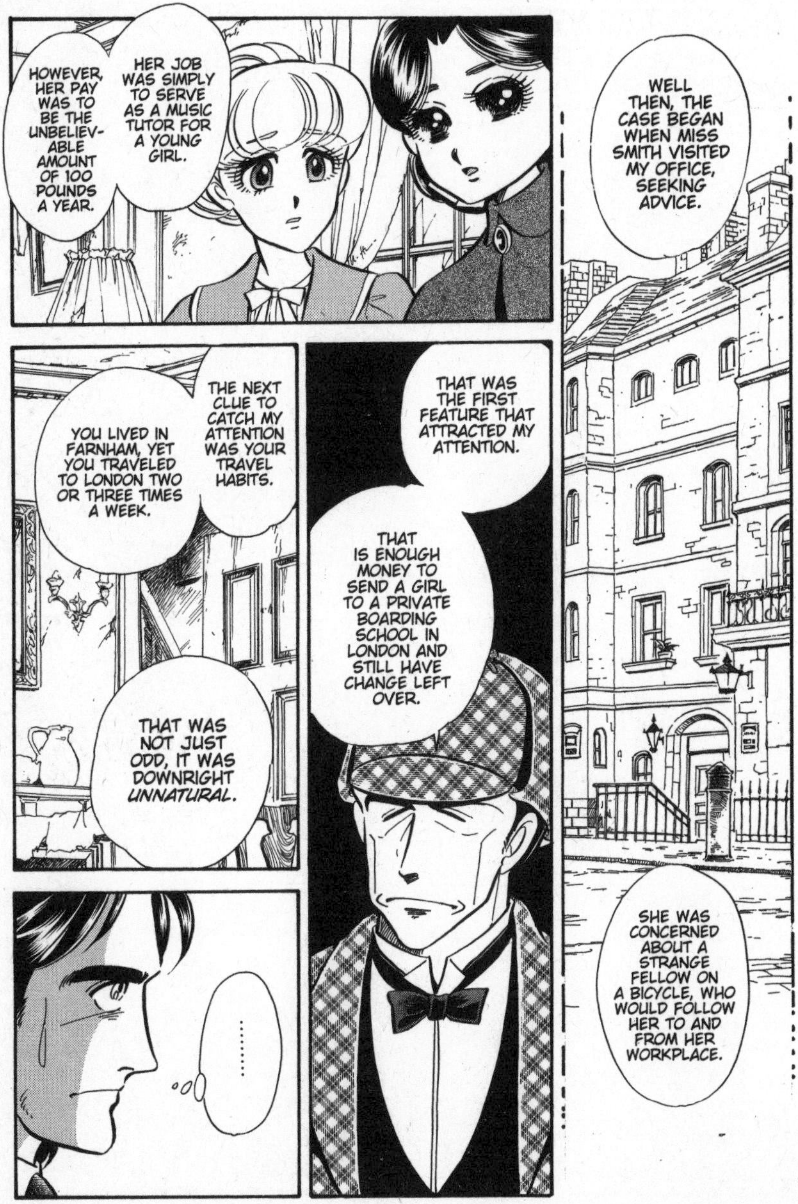

WELL THEN, THE CASE BEGAN WHEN MISS SMITH VISITED MY OFFICE, SEEKING ADVICE.
SHE WAS CONCERNED ABOUT A STRANGE FELLOW ON A BICYCLE, WHO WOULD FOLLOW HER TO AND FROM HER WORKPLACE.
HER JOB WAS SIMPLY TO SERVE AS A MUSIC TUTOR FOR A YOUNG GIRL.
HOWEVER, HER PAY WAS TO BE THE UNBELIEV-ABLE AMOUNT OF 100 POUNDS A YEAR.
THAT WAS THE FIRST FEATURE THAT ATTRACTED MY ATTENTION.
THAT IS ENOUGH MONEY TO SEND A GIRL TO A PRIVATE BOARDING SCHOOL IN LONDON AND STILL HAVE CHANGE LEFT OVER.
THE NEXT CLUE TO CATCH MY ATTENTION WAS YOUR TRAVEL HABITS.
YOU LIVED IN FARNHAM, YET YOU TRAVELED TO LONDON TWO OR THREE TIMES A WEEK.
THAT WAS NOT JUST ODD, IT WAS DOWNRIGHT *UNNATURAL*.
……

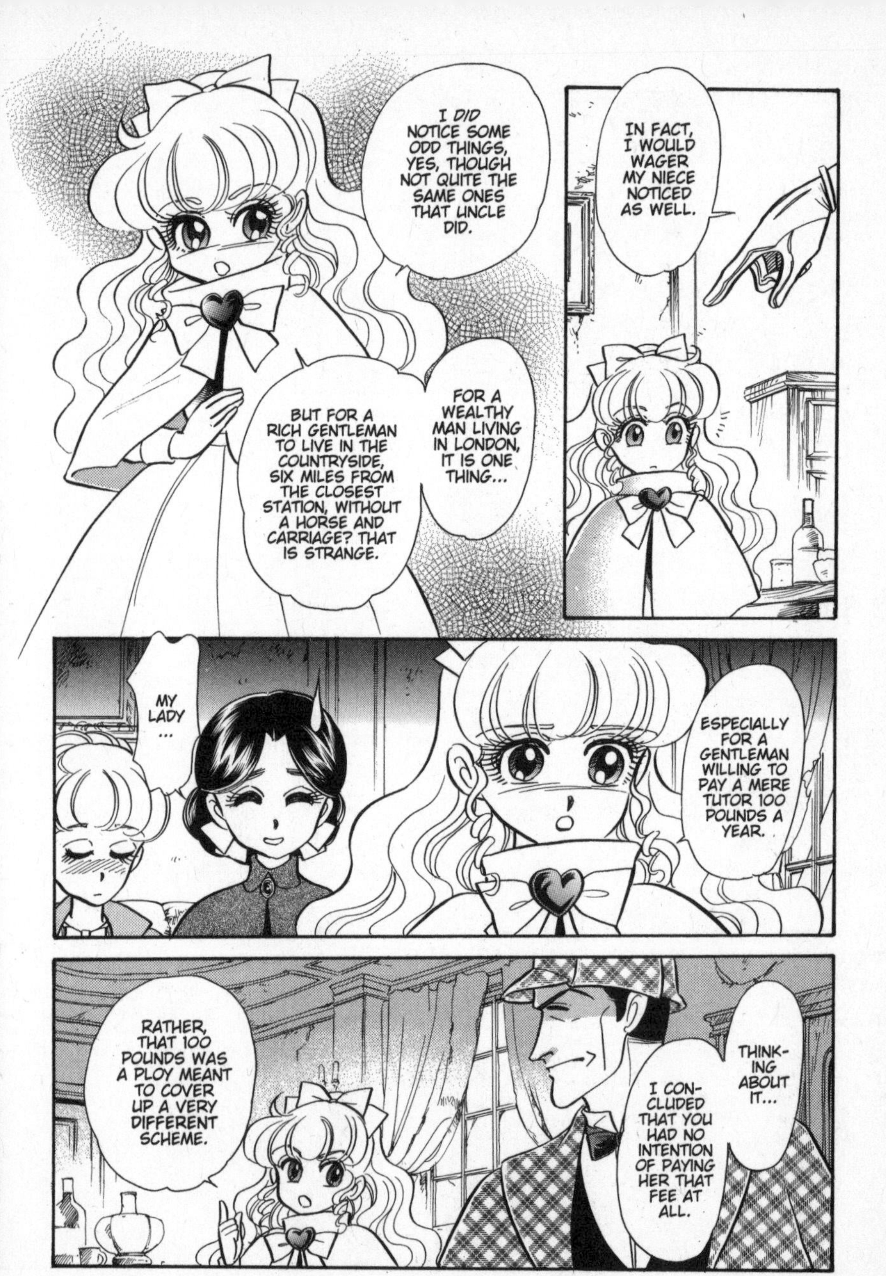
IN FACT, I WOULD WAGER MY NIECE NOTICED AS WELL.
I *DID* NOTICE SOME ODD THINGS, YES, THOUGH NOT QUITE THE SAME ONES THAT UNCLE DID.
FOR A WEALTHY MAN LIVING IN LONDON, IT IS ONE THING...
BUT FOR A RICH GENTLEMAN TO LIVE IN THE COUNTRYSIDE, SIX MILES FROM THE CLOSEST STATION, WITHOUT A HORSE AND CARRIAGE? THAT IS STRANGE.
ESPECIALLY FOR A GENTLEMAN WILLING TO PAY A MERE TUTOR 100 POUNDS A YEAR.
MY LADY ...
THINKING ABOUT IT...
I CONCLUDED THAT YOU HAD NO INTENTION OF PAYING HER THAT FEE AT ALL.
RATHER, THAT 100 POUNDS WAS A PLOY MEANT TO COVER UP A VERY DIFFERENT SCHEME.

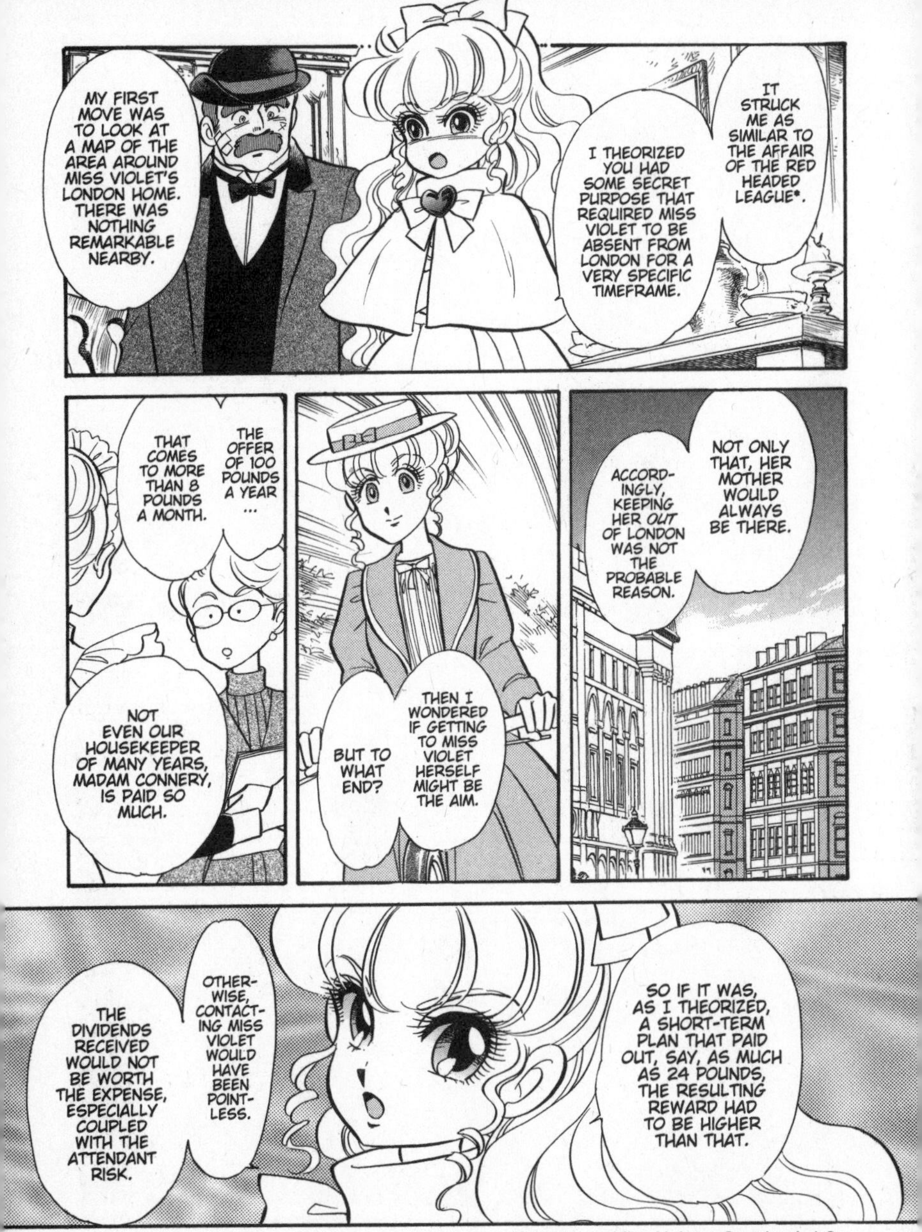
IT STRUCK ME AS SIMILAR TO THE AFFAIR OF THE RED HEADED LEAGUE*.
I THEORIZED YOU HAD SOME SECRET PURPOSE THAT REQUIRED MISS VIOLET TO BE ABSENT FROM LONDON FOR A VERY SPECIFIC TIMEFRAME.
MY FIRST MOVE WAS TO LOOK AT A MAP OF THE AREA AROUND MISS VIOLET'S LONDON HOME. THERE WAS NOTHING REMARKABLE NEARBY.
NOT ONLY THAT, HER MOTHER WOULD ALWAYS BE THERE.
ACCORD-INGLY, KEEPING HER *OUT* OF LONDON WAS NOT THE PROBABLE REASON.
THEN I WONDERED IF GETTING TO MISS VIOLET HERSELF MIGHT BE THE AIM.
BUT TO WHAT END?
THE OFFER OF 100 POUNDS A YEAR ...
THAT COMES TO MORE THAN 8 POUNDS A MONTH.
NOT EVEN OUR HOUSEKEEPER OF MANY YEARS, MADAM CONNERY, IS PAID SO MUCH.
SO IF IT WAS, AS I THEORIZED, A SHORT-TERM PLAN THAT PAID OUT, SAY, AS MUCH AS 24 POUNDS, THE RESULTING REWARD HAD TO BE HIGHER THAN THAT.
OTHER-WISE, CONTACT-ING MISS VIOLET WOULD HAVE BEEN POINT-LESS.
THE DIVIDENDS RECEIVED WOULD NOT BE WORTH THE EXPENSE, ESPECIALLY COUPLED WITH THE ATTENDANT RISK.

**See Young Miss Holmes Casebook 1-2.*

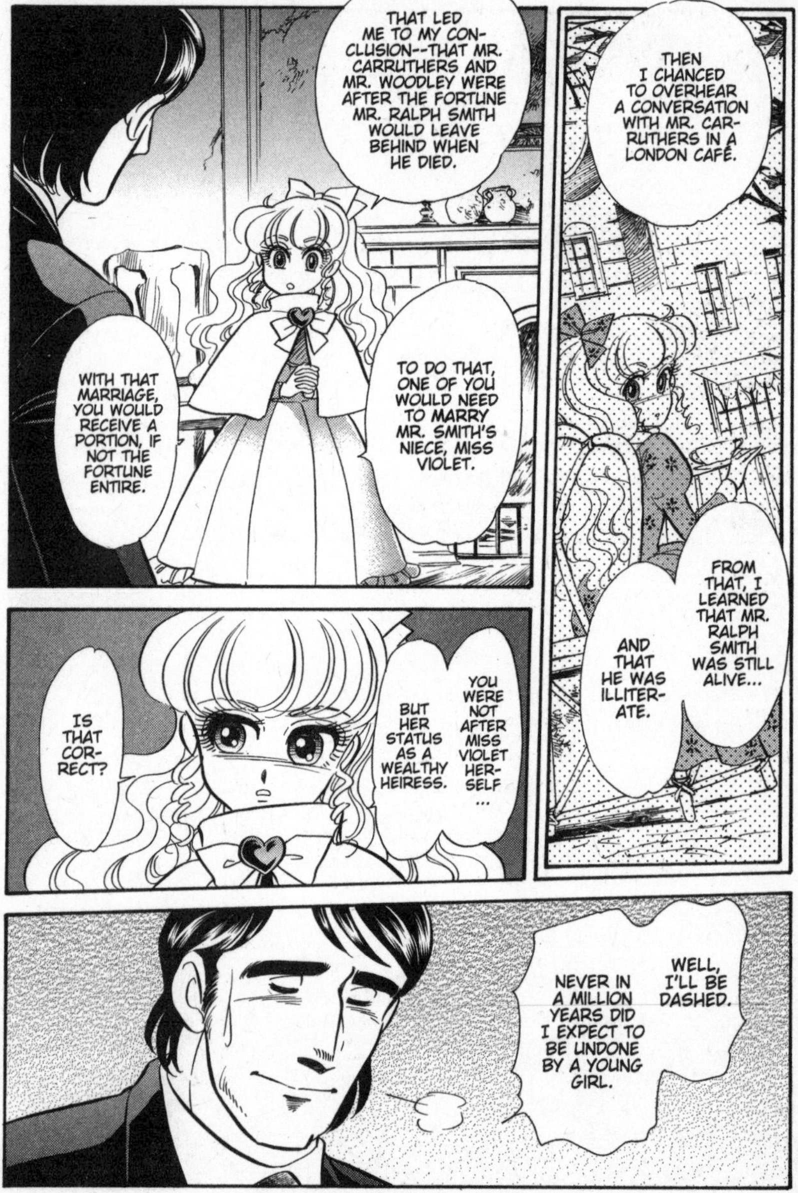
THEN I CHANCED TO OVERHEAR A CONVERSATION WITH MR. CARRUTHERS IN A LONDON CAFÉ.
FROM THAT, I LEARNED THAT MR. RALPH SMITH WAS STILL ALIVE...
AND THAT HE WAS ILLITERATE.
THAT LED ME TO MY CONCLUSION--THAT MR. CARRUTHERS AND MR. WOODLEY WERE AFTER THE FORTUNE MR. RALPH SMITH WOULD LEAVE BEHIND WHEN HE DIED.
TO DO THAT, ONE OF YOU WOULD NEED TO MARRY MR. SMITH'S NIECE, MISS VIOLET.
WITH THAT MARRIAGE, YOU WOULD RECEIVE A PORTION, IF NOT THE FORTUNE ENTIRE.
YOU WERE NOT AFTER MISS VIOLET HERSELF...
BUT HER STATUS AS A WEALTHY HEIRESS.
IS THAT CORRECT?
WELL, I'LL BE DASHED.
NEVER IN A MILLION YEARS DID I EXPECT TO BE UNDONE BY A YOUNG GIRL.

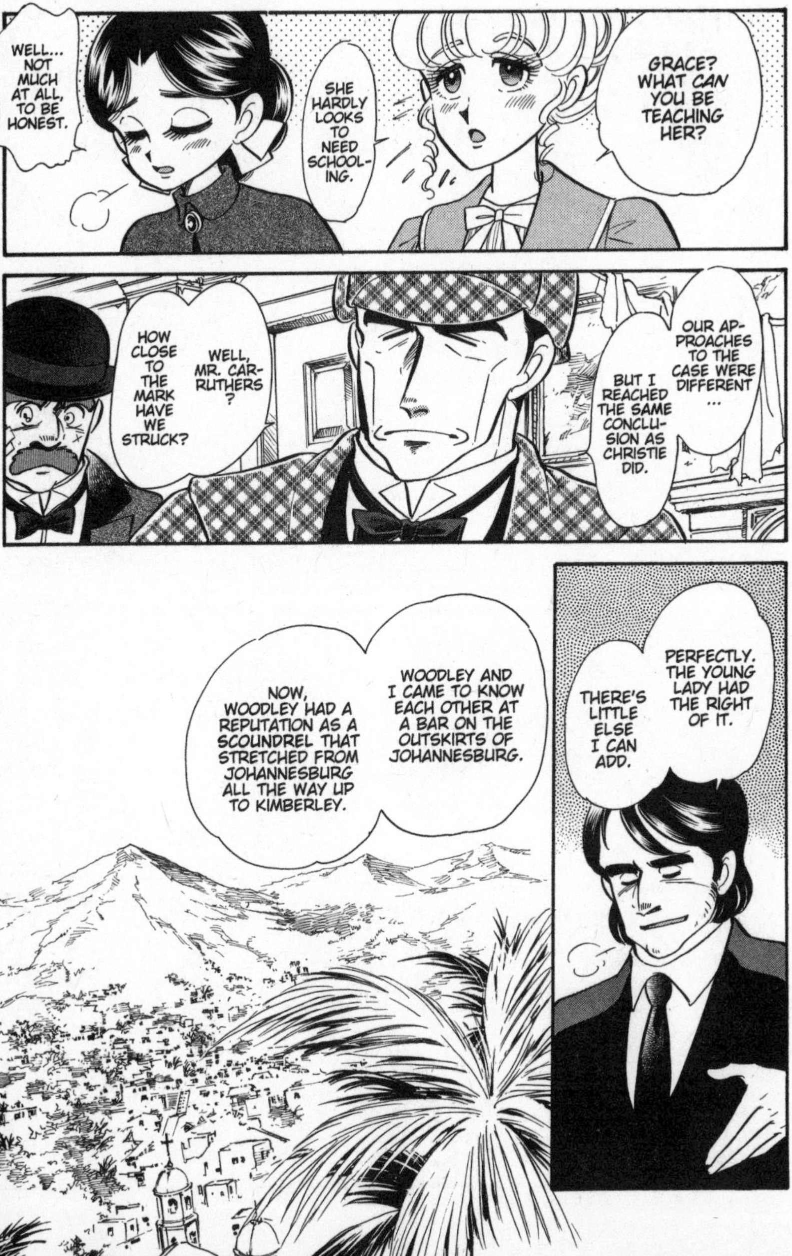
GRACE? WHAT CAN YOU BE TEACHING HER?
SHE HARDLY LOOKS TO NEED SCHOOLING.
WELL... NOT MUCH AT ALL, TO BE HONEST.
OUR APPROACHES TO THE CASE WERE DIFFERENT...
BUT I REACHED THE SAME CONCLUSION AS CHRISTIE DID.
WELL, MR. CARRUTHERS?
HOW CLOSE TO THE MARK HAVE WE STRUCK?
PERFECTLY. THE YOUNG LADY HAD THE RIGHT OF IT.
THERE'S LITTLE ELSE I CAN ADD.
WOODLEY AND I CAME TO KNOW EACH OTHER AT A BAR ON THE OUTSKIRTS OF JOHANNESBURG.
NOW, WOODLEY HAD A REPUTATION AS A SCOUNDREL THAT STRETCHED FROM JOHANNESBURG ALL THE WAY UP TO KIMBERLEY.

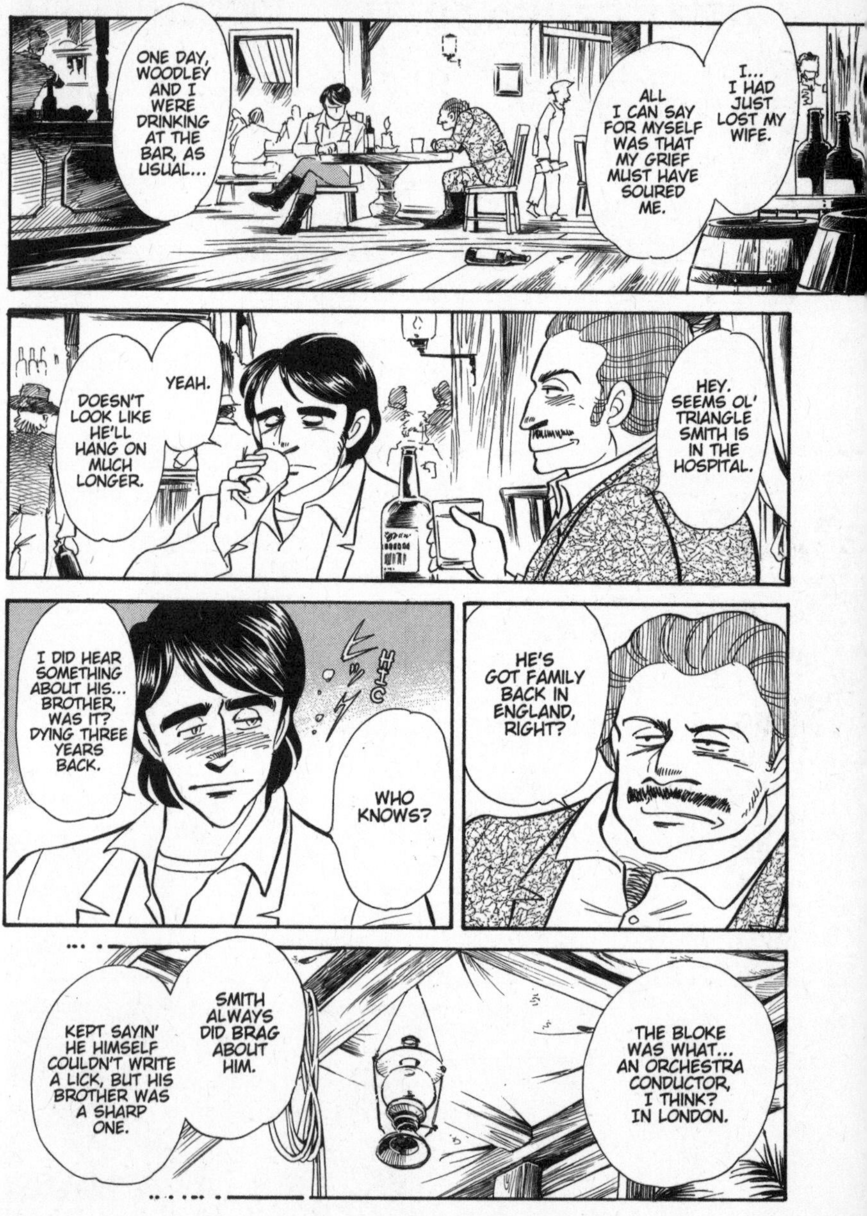

I... I HAD JUST LOST MY WIFE.
ALL I CAN SAY FOR MYSELF WAS THAT MY GRIEF MUST HAVE SOURED ME.
ONE DAY, WOODLEY AND I WERE DRINKING AT THE BAR, AS USUAL...
HEY. SEEMS OL' TRIANGLE SMITH IS IN THE HOSPITAL.
YEAH.
DOESN'T LOOK LIKE HE'LL HANG ON MUCH LONGER.
HE'S GOT FAMILY BACK IN ENGLAND, RIGHT?
HIC
WHO KNOWS?
I DID HEAR SOMETHING ABOUT HIS... BROTHER, WAS IT? DYING THREE YEARS BACK.
THE BLOKE WAS WHAT... AN ORCHESTRA CONDUCTOR, I THINK? IN LONDON.
SMITH ALWAYS DID BRAG ABOUT HIM.
KEPT SAYIN' HE HIMSELF COULDN'T WRITE A LICK, BUT HIS BROTHER WAS A SHARP ONE.

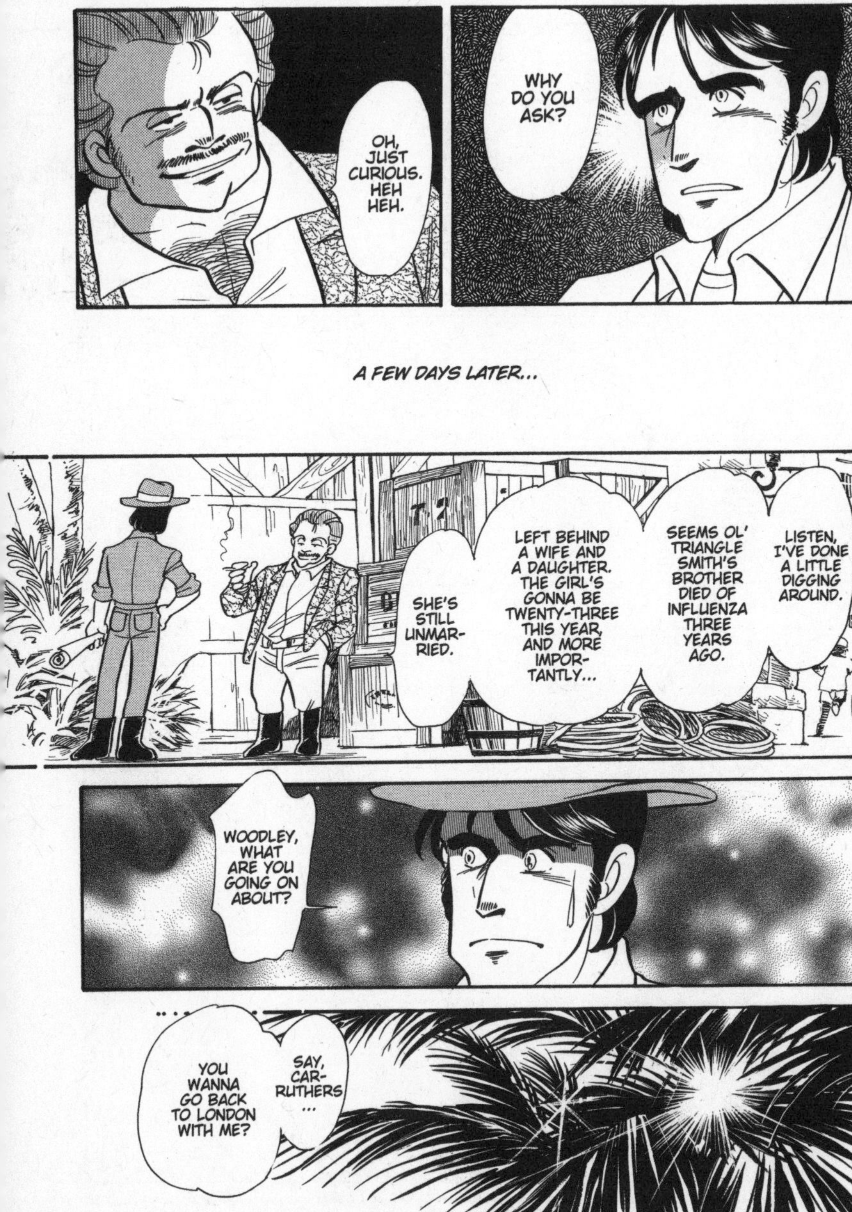
WHY DO YOU ASK?
OH, JUST CURIOUS. HEH HEH.
A FEW DAYS LATER...
LISTEN, I'VE DONE A LITTLE DIGGING AROUND.
SEEMS OL' TRIANGLE SMITH'S BROTHER DIED OF INFLUENZA THREE YEARS AGO.
LEFT BEHIND A WIFE AND A DAUGHTER. THE GIRL'S GONNA BE TWENTY-THREE THIS YEAR, AND MORE IMPOR-TANTLY...
SHE'S STILL UNMAR-RIED.
WOODLEY, WHAT ARE YOU GOING ON ABOUT?
SAY, CAR-RUTHERS ...
YOU WANNA GO BACK TO LONDON WITH ME?

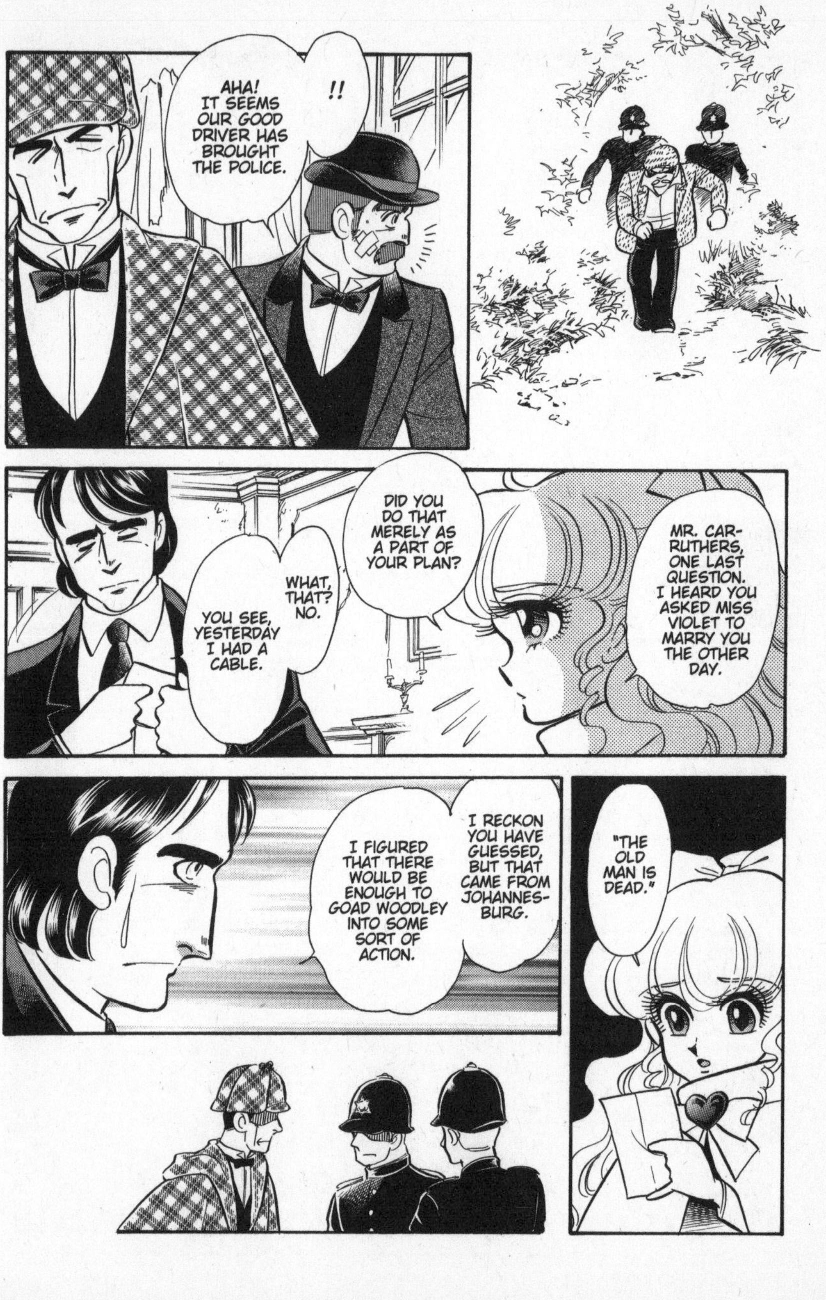
!!
AHA! IT SEEMS OUR GOOD DRIVER HAS BROUGHT THE POLICE.
MR. CAR-RUTHERS, ONE LAST QUESTION. I HEARD YOU ASKED MISS VIOLET TO MARRY YOU THE OTHER DAY.
DID YOU DO THAT MERELY AS A PART OF YOUR PLAN?
WHAT, THAT? NO.
YOU SEE, YESTERDAY I HAD A CABLE.
"THE OLD MAN IS DEAD."
I RECKON YOU HAVE GUESSED, BUT THAT CAME FROM JOHANNES-BURG.
I FIGURED THAT THERE WOULD BE ENOUGH TO GOAD WOODLEY INTO SOME SORT OF ACTION.

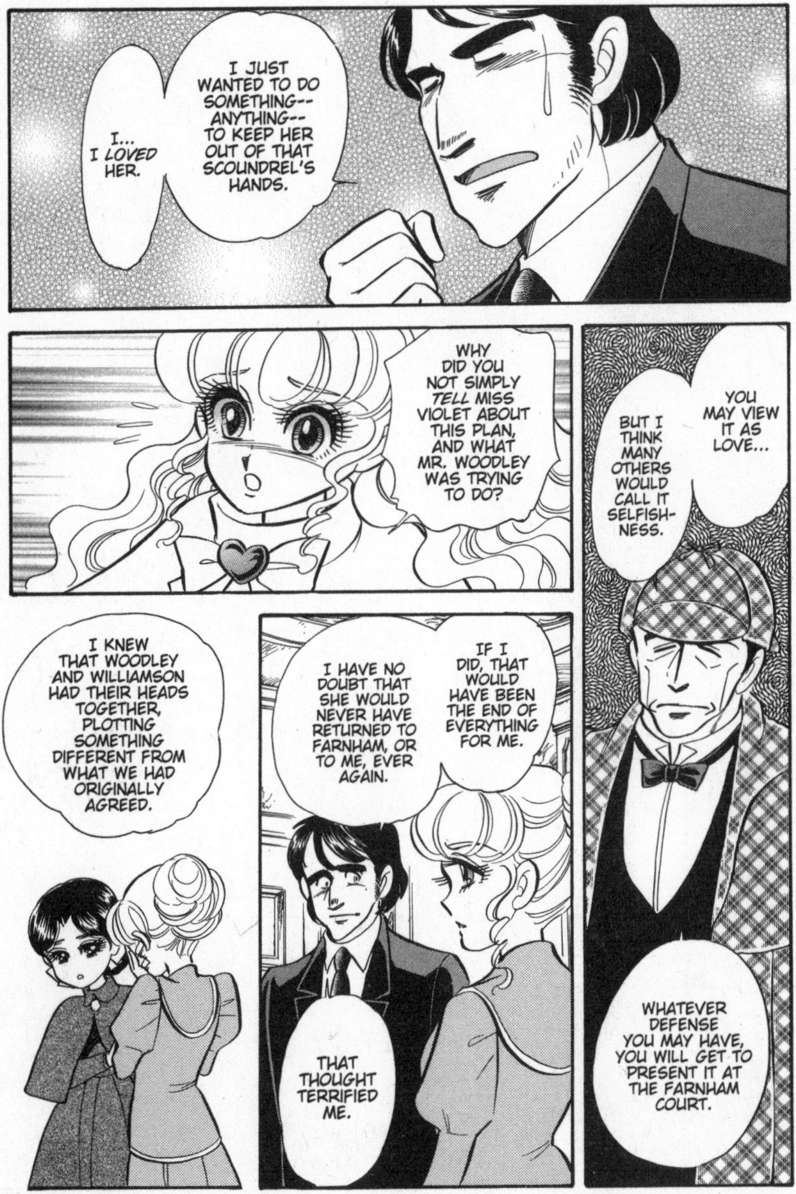
I JUST WANTED TO DO SOMETHING-- ANYTHING-- TO KEEP HER OUT OF THAT SCOUNDREL'S HANDS.
I... I *LOVED* HER.
YOU MAY VIEW IT AS LOVE...
BUT I THINK MANY OTHERS WOULD CALL IT SELFISH-NESS.
WHATEVER DEFENSE YOU MAY HAVE, YOU WILL GET TO PRESENT IT AT THE FARNHAM COURT.
WHY DID YOU NOT SIMPLY *TELL* MISS VIOLET ABOUT THIS PLAN, AND WHAT MR. WOODLEY WAS TRYING TO DO?
IF I DID, THAT WOULD HAVE BEEN THE END OF EVERYTHING FOR ME.
I HAVE NO DOUBT THAT SHE WOULD NEVER HAVE RETURNED TO FARNHAM, OR TO ME, EVER AGAIN.
THAT THOUGHT TERRIFIED ME.
I KNEW THAT WOODLEY AND WILLIAMSON HAD THEIR HEADS TOGETHER, PLOTTING SOMETHING DIFFERENT FROM WHAT WE HAD ORIGINALLY AGREED.

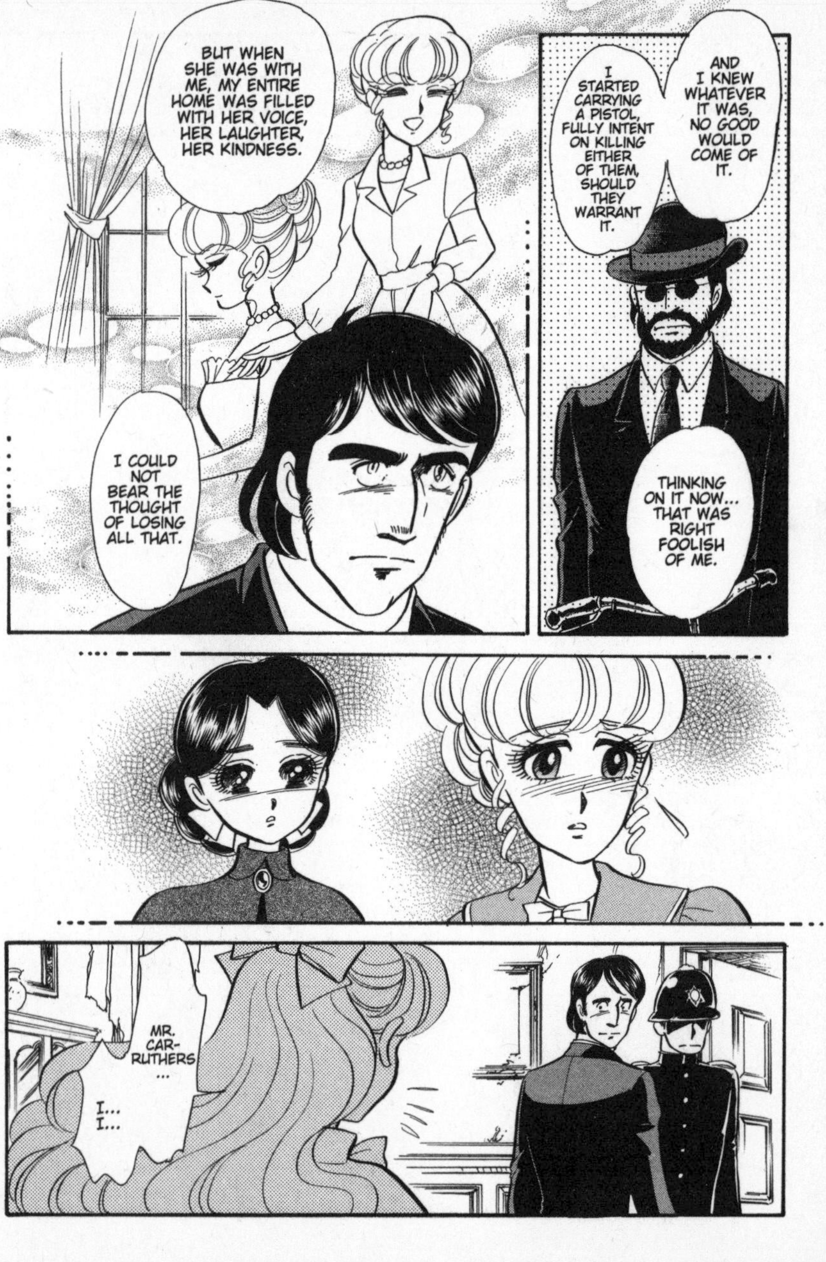
AND I KNEW WHATEVER IT WAS, NO GOOD WOULD COME OF IT.
I STARTED CARRYING A PISTOL, FULLY INTENT ON KILLING EITHER OF THEM, SHOULD THEY WARRANT IT.
THINKING ON IT NOW... THAT WAS RIGHT FOOLISH OF ME.
BUT WHEN SHE WAS WITH ME, MY ENTIRE HOME WAS FILLED WITH HER VOICE, HER LAUGHTER, HER KINDNESS.
I COULD NOT BEAR THE THOUGHT OF LOSING ALL THAT.
MR. CAR-RUTHERS ...
I... I...

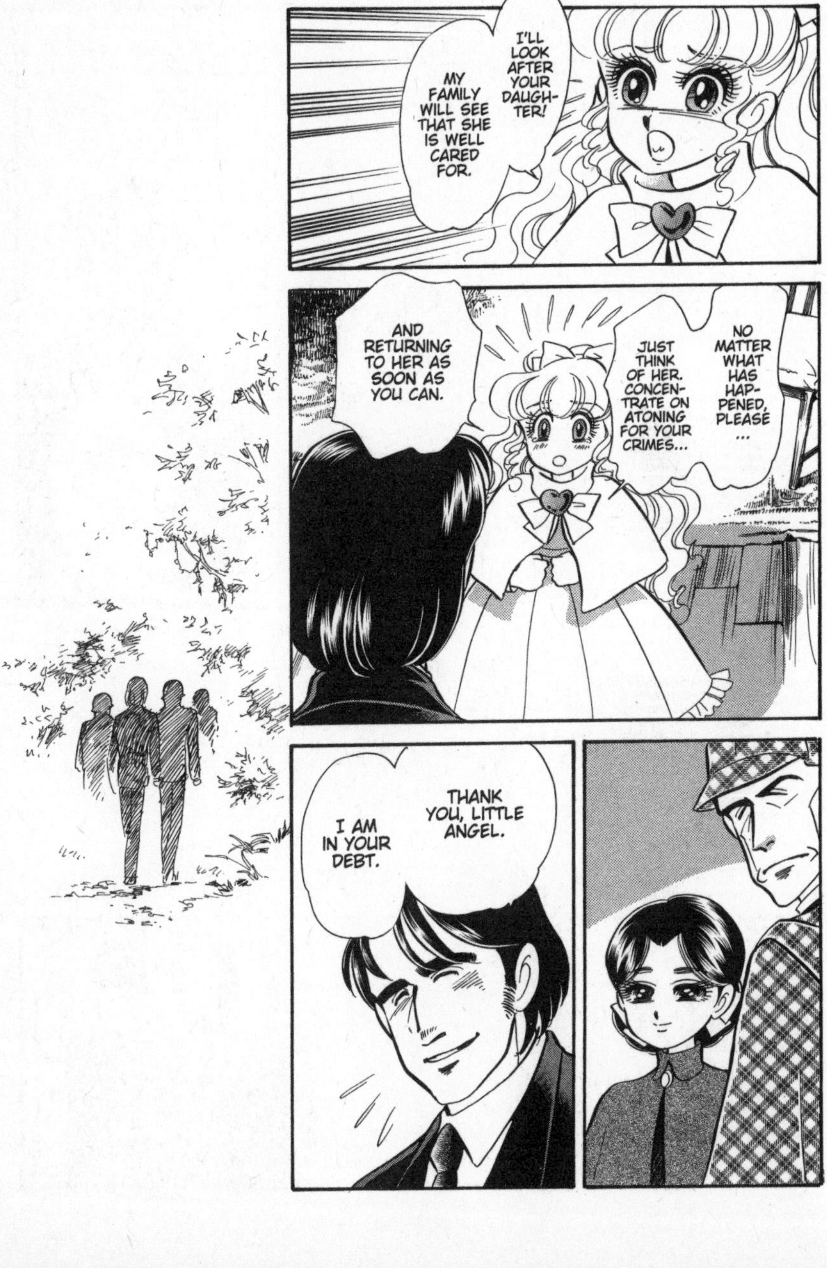
I'LL LOOK AFTER YOUR DAUGH-TER!
MY FAMILY WILL SEE THAT SHE IS WELL CARED FOR.
NO MATTER WHAT HAS HAP-PENED, PLEASE ...
JUST THINK OF HER. CONCEN-TRATE ON ATONING FOR YOUR CRIMES...
AND RETURNING TO HER AS SOON AS YOU CAN.
THANK YOU, LITTLE ANGEL.
I AM IN YOUR DEBT.

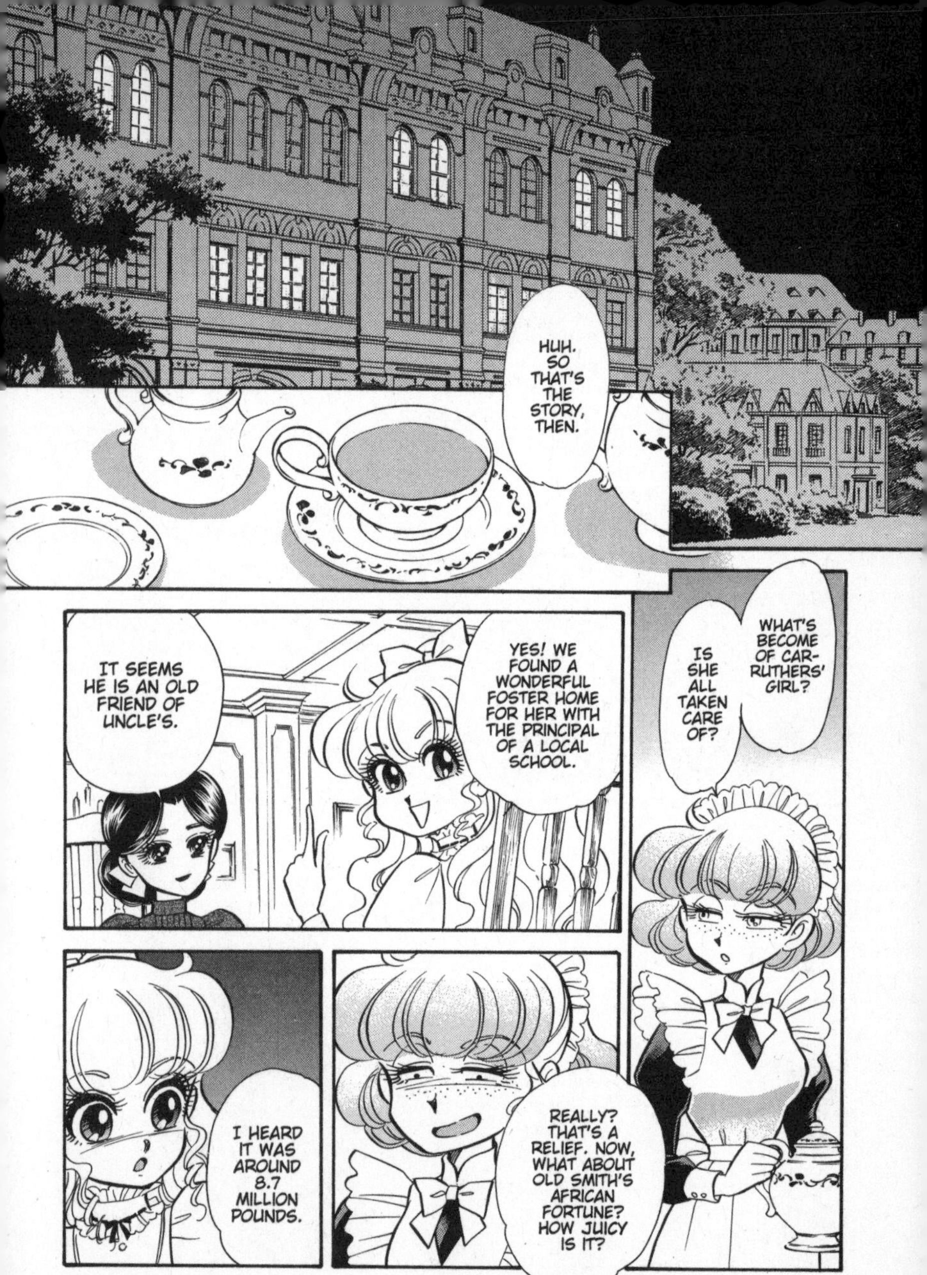
HUH. SO THAT'S THE STORY, THEN.
WHAT'S BECOME OF CAR-RUTHERS' GIRL?
IS SHE ALL TAKEN CARE OF?
YES! WE FOUND A WONDERFUL FOSTER HOME FOR HER WITH THE PRINCIPAL OF A LOCAL SCHOOL.
IT SEEMS HE IS AN OLD FRIEND OF UNCLE'S.
REALLY? THAT'S A RELIEF. NOW, WHAT ABOUT OLD SMITH'S AFRICAN FORTUNE? HOW JUICY IS IT?
I HEARD IT WAS AROUND 8.7 MILLION POUNDS.

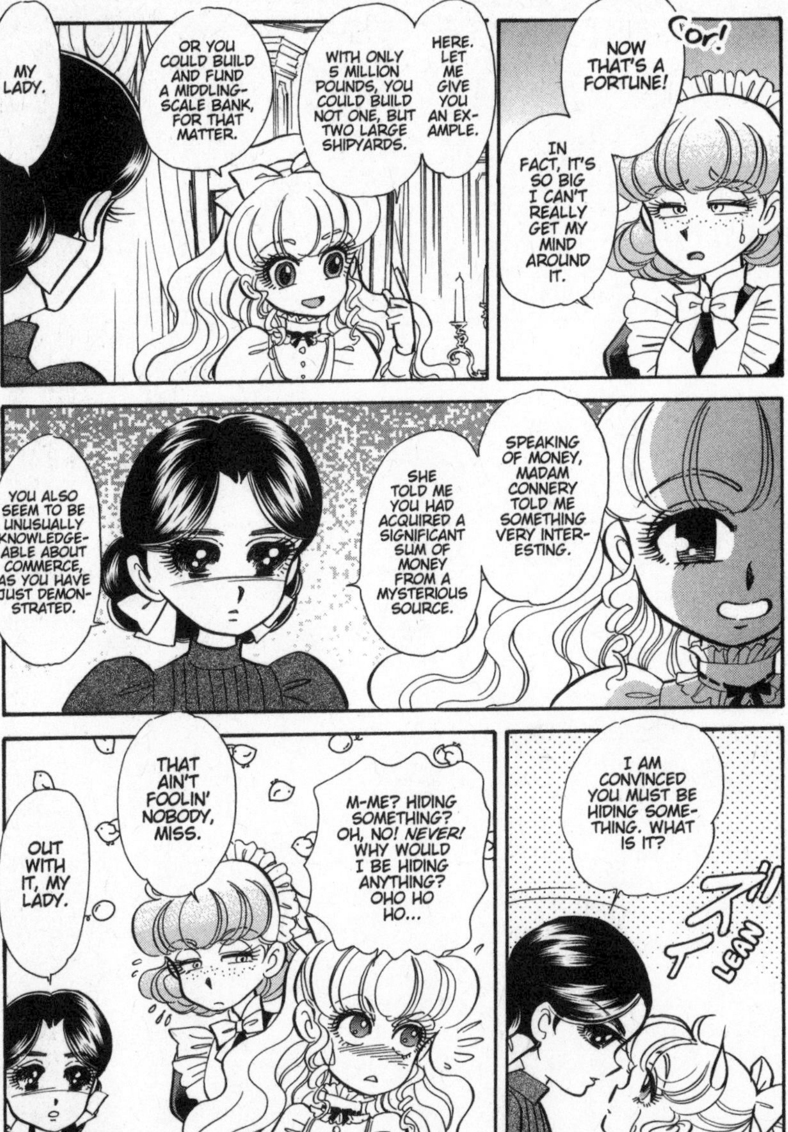
Cor!
NOW THAT'S A FORTUNE!
IN FACT, IT'S SO BIG I CAN'T REALLY GET MY MIND AROUND IT.
HERE. LET ME GIVE YOU AN EX-AMPLE.
WITH ONLY 5 MILLION POUNDS, YOU COULD BUILD NOT ONE, BUT TWO LARGE SHIPYARDS.
OR YOU COULD BUILD AND FUND A MIDDLING-SCALE BANK, FOR THAT MATTER.
MY LADY.
SPEAKING OF MONEY, MADAM CONNERY TOLD ME SOMETHING VERY INTER-ESTING.
SHE TOLD ME YOU HAD ACQUIRED A SIGNIFICANT SUM OF MONEY FROM A MYSTERIOUS SOURCE.
YOU ALSO SEEM TO BE UNUSUALLY KNOWLEDGE-ABLE ABOUT COMMERCE, AS YOU HAVE JUST DEMON-STRATED.
I AM CONVINCED YOU MUST BE HIDING SOME-THING. WHAT IS IT?
LEAN
M-ME? HIDING SOMETHING? OH, NO! *NEVER!* WHY WOULD I BE HIDING ANYTHING? OHO HO HO...
THAT AIN'T FOOLIN' NOBODY, MISS.
OUT WITH IT, MY LADY.

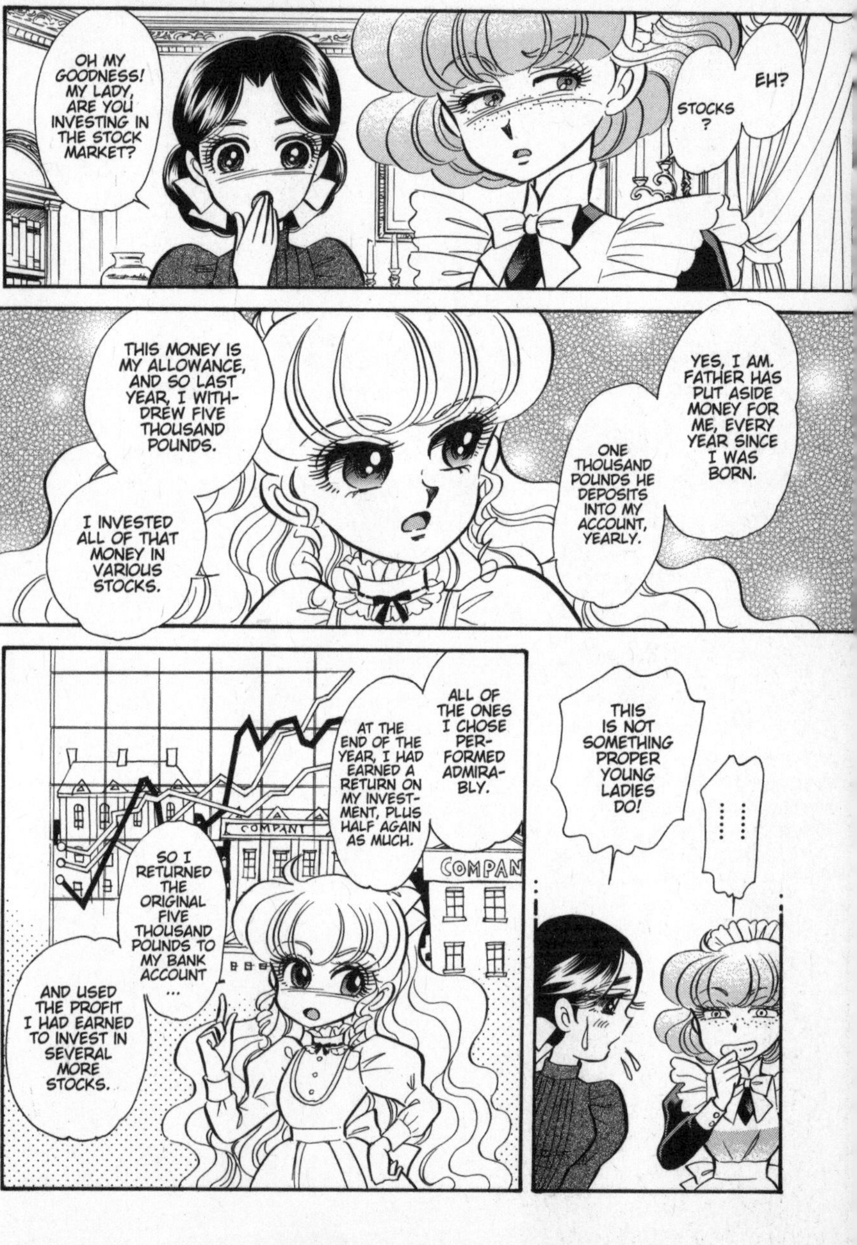
EH?
STOCKS ?
OH MY GOODNESS! MY LADY, ARE YOU INVESTING IN THE STOCK MARKET?
YES, I AM. FATHER HAS PUT ASIDE MONEY FOR ME, EVERY YEAR SINCE I WAS BORN.
ONE THOUSAND POUNDS HE DEPOSITS INTO MY ACCOUNT, YEARLY.
THIS MONEY IS MY ALLOWANCE, AND SO LAST YEAR, I WITH-DREW FIVE THOUSAND POUNDS.
I INVESTED ALL OF THAT MONEY IN VARIOUS STOCKS.
THIS IS NOT SOMETHING PROPER YOUNG LADIES DO!
......
ALL OF THE ONES I CHOSE PER-FORMED ADMIRA-BLY.
AT THE END OF THE YEAR, I HAD EARNED A RETURN ON MY INVEST-MENT, PLUS HALF AGAIN AS MUCH.
COMPANY
COMPAN
SO I RETURNED THE ORIGINAL FIVE THOUSAND POUNDS TO MY BANK ACCOUNT ...
AND USED THE PROFIT I HAD EARNED TO INVEST IN SEVERAL MORE STOCKS.

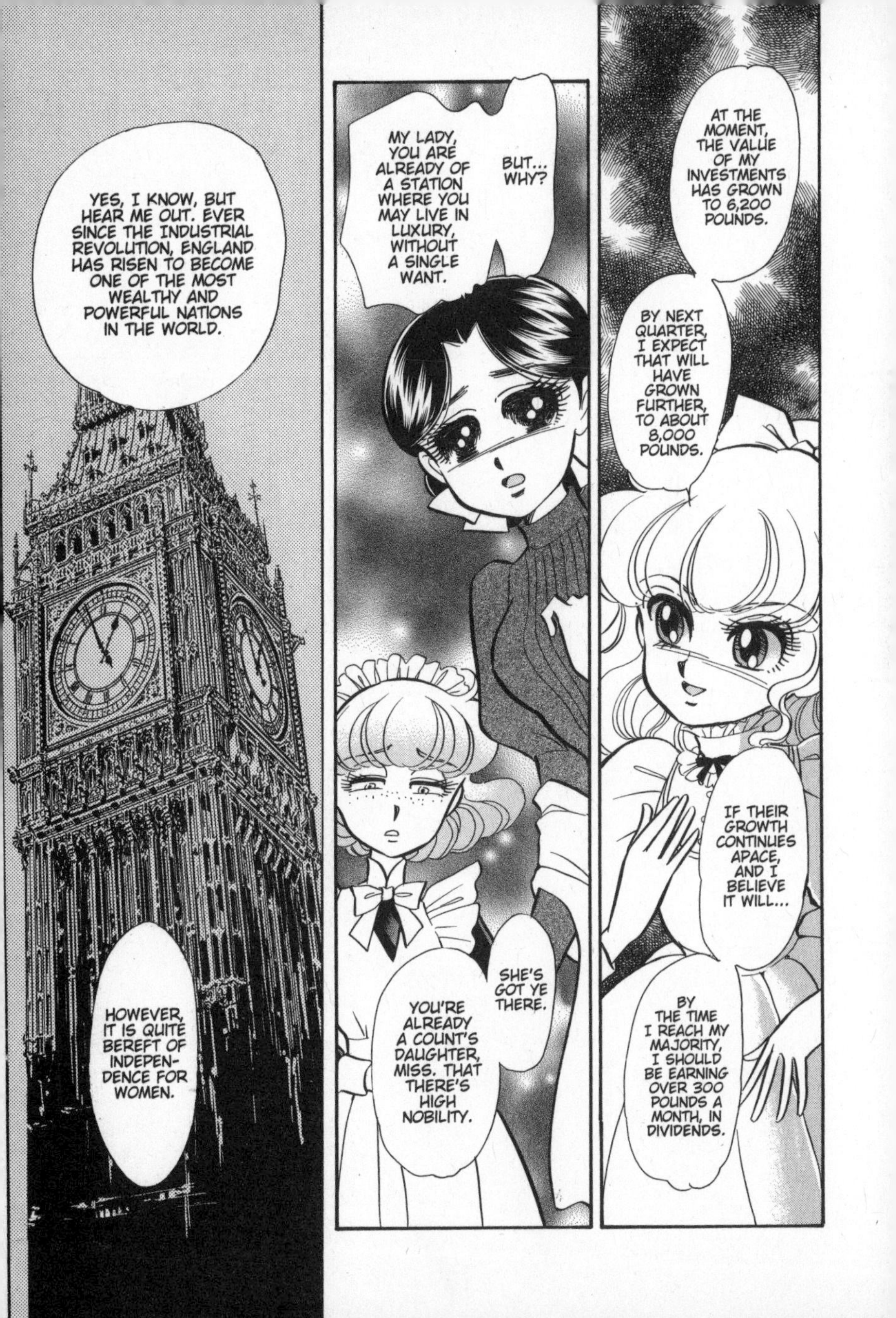
AT THE MOMENT, THE VALUE OF MY INVESTMENTS HAS GROWN TO 6,200 POUNDS.
BY NEXT QUARTER, I EXPECT THAT WILL HAVE GROWN FURTHER, TO ABOUT 8,000 POUNDS.
IF THEIR GROWTH CONTINUES APACE, AND I BELIEVE IT WILL...
BY THE TIME I REACH MY MAJORITY, I SHOULD BE EARNING OVER 300 POUNDS A MONTH, IN DIVIDENDS.
BUT... WHY?
MY LADY, YOU ARE ALREADY OF A STATION WHERE YOU MAY LIVE IN LUXURY, WITHOUT A SINGLE WANT.
SHE'S GOT YE THERE.
YOU'RE ALREADY A COUNT'S DAUGHTER, MISS. THAT THERE'S HIGH NOBILITY.
YES, I KNOW, BUT HEAR ME OUT. EVER SINCE THE INDUSTRIAL REVOLUTION, ENGLAND HAS RISEN TO BECOME ONE OF THE MOST WEALTHY AND POWERFUL NATIONS IN THE WORLD.
HOWEVER, IT IS QUITE BEREFT OF INDEPENDENCE FOR WOMEN.

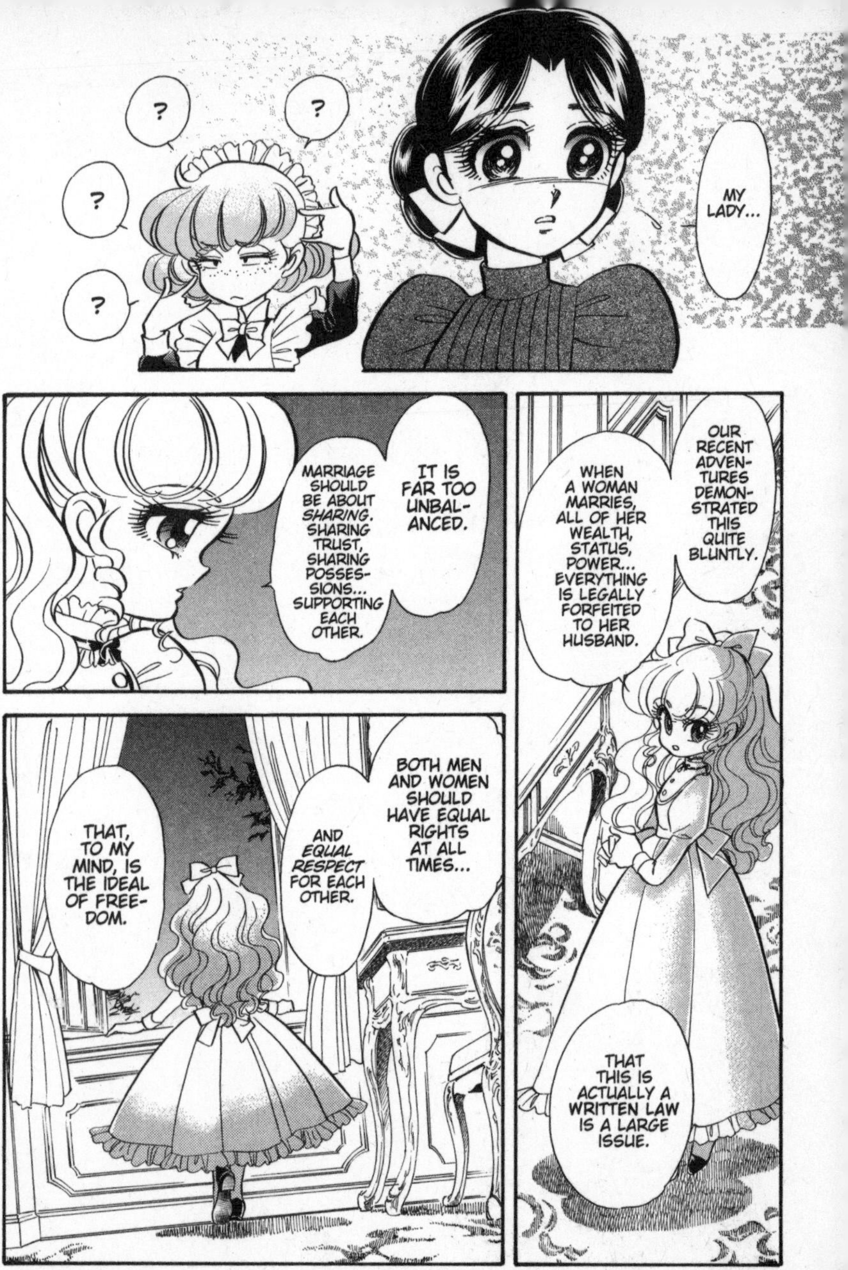
MY LADY...
?
?
?
?
OUR RECENT ADVENTURES DEMONSTRATED THIS QUITE BLUNTLY.
WHEN A WOMAN MARRIES, ALL OF HER WEALTH, STATUS, POWER... EVERYTHING IS LEGALLY FORFEITED TO HER HUSBAND.
THAT THIS IS ACTUALLY A WRITTEN LAW IS A LARGE ISSUE.
IT IS FAR TOO UNBALANCED.
MARRIAGE SHOULD BE ABOUT *SHARING*. SHARING TRUST, SHARING POSSESSIONS... SUPPORTING EACH OTHER.
BOTH MEN AND WOMEN SHOULD HAVE EQUAL RIGHTS AT ALL TIMES...
AND *EQUAL RESPECT* FOR EACH OTHER.
THAT, TO MY MIND, IS THE IDEAL OF FREEDOM.

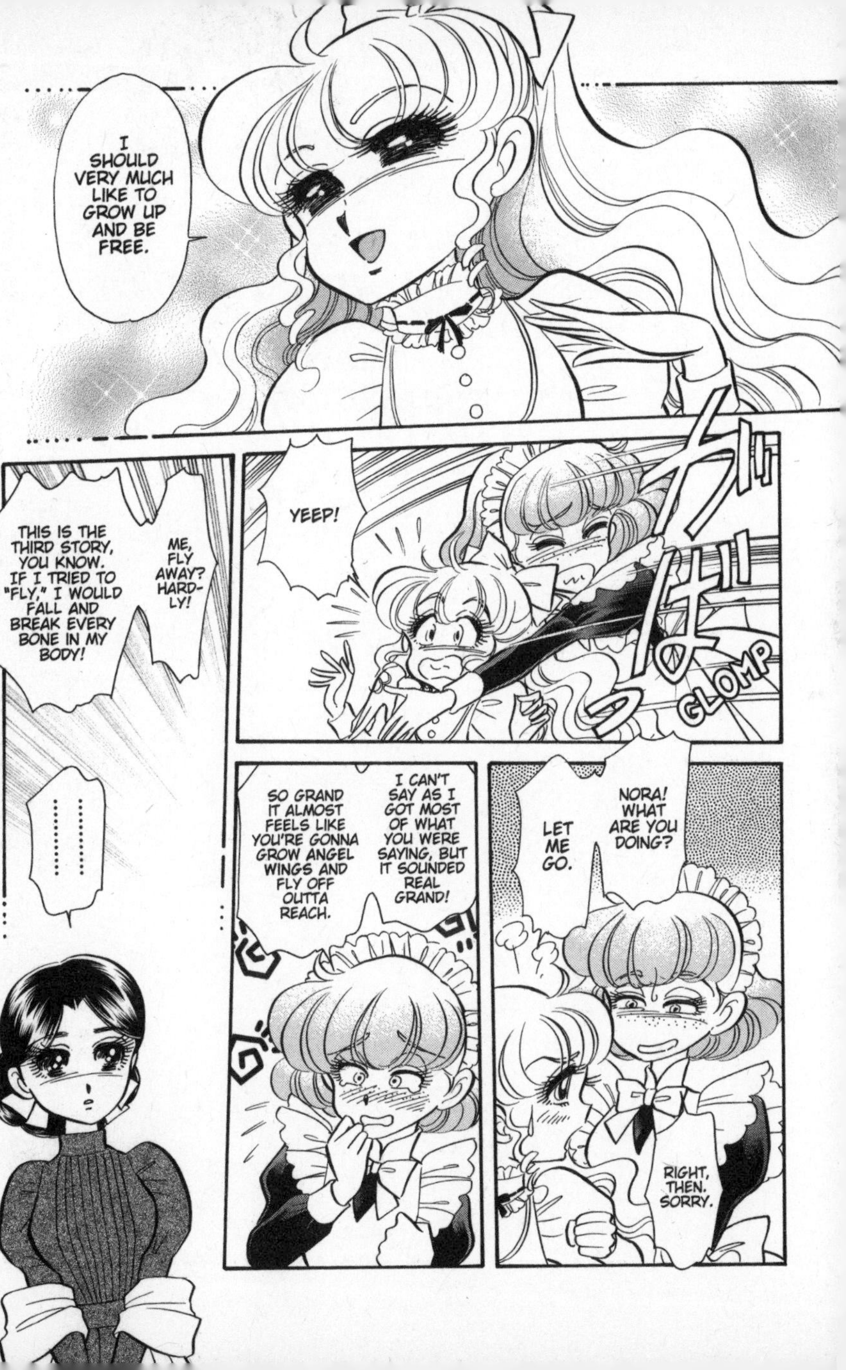

I SHOULD VERY MUCH LIKE TO GROW UP AND BE FREE.
YEEP!
GLOMP
NORA! WHAT ARE YOU DOING?
LET ME GO.
RIGHT, THEN. SORRY.
I CAN'T SAY AS I GOT MOST OF WHAT YOU WERE SAYING, BUT IT SOUNDED REAL GRAND!
SO GRAND IT ALMOST FEELS LIKE YOU'RE GONNA GROW ANGEL WINGS AND FLY OFF OUTTA REACH.
ME, FLY AWAY? HARDLY!
THIS IS THE THIRD STORY, YOU KNOW. IF I TRIED TO "FLY," I WOULD FALL AND BREAK EVERY BONE IN MY BODY!
......

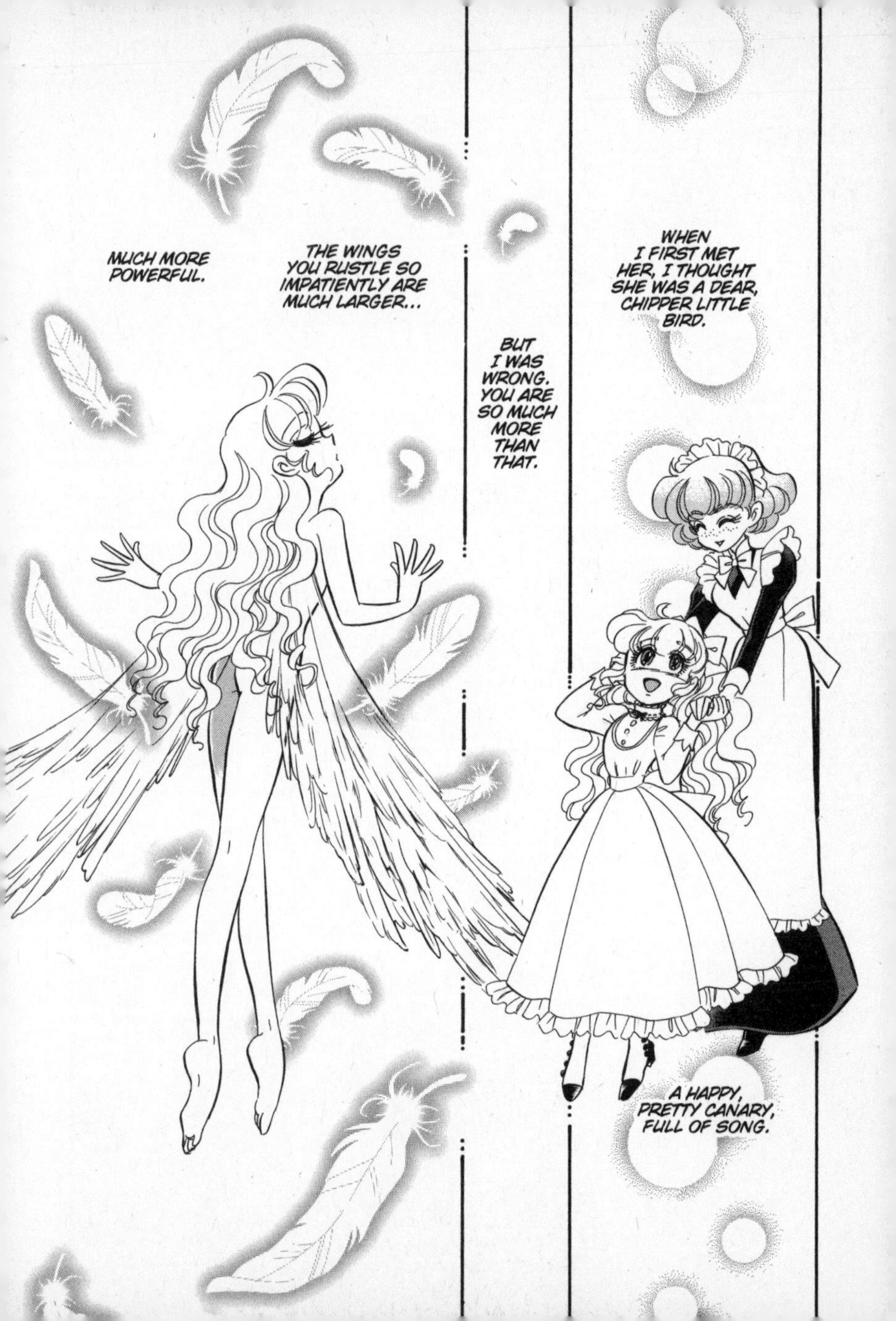
WHEN I FIRST MET HER, I THOUGHT SHE WAS A DEAR, CHIPPER LITTLE BIRD.
A HAPPY, PRETTY CANARY, FULL OF SONG.
BUT I WAS WRONG. YOU ARE SO MUCH MORE THAN THAT.
THE WINGS YOU RUSTLE SO IMPATIENTLY ARE MUCH LARGER...
MUCH MORE POWERFUL.

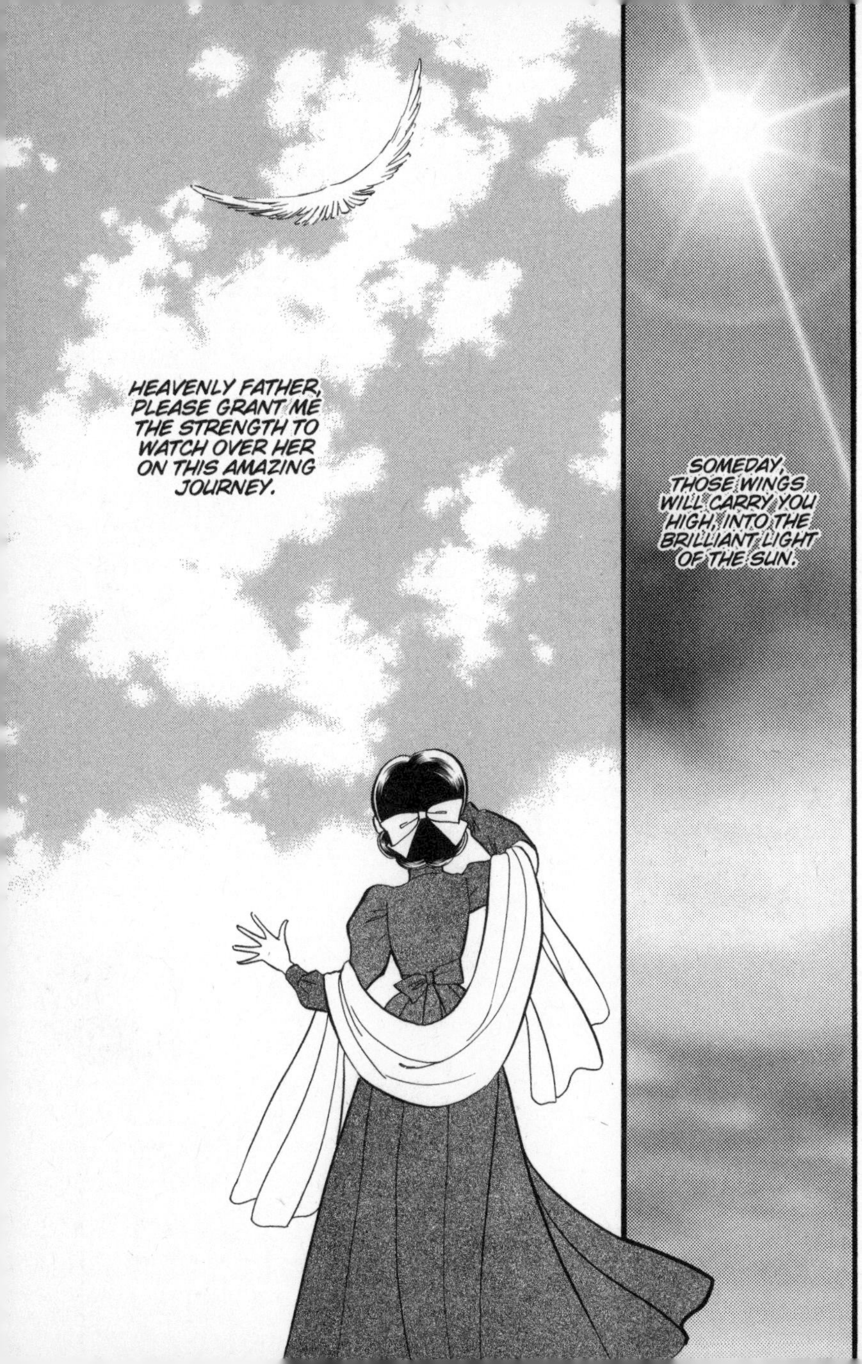
SOMEDAY, THOSE WINGS WILL CARRY YOU HIGH, INTO THE BRILLIANT LIGHT OF THE SUN.
HEAVENLY FATHER, PLEASE GRANT ME THE STRENGTH TO WATCH OVER HER ON THIS AMAZING JOURNEY.

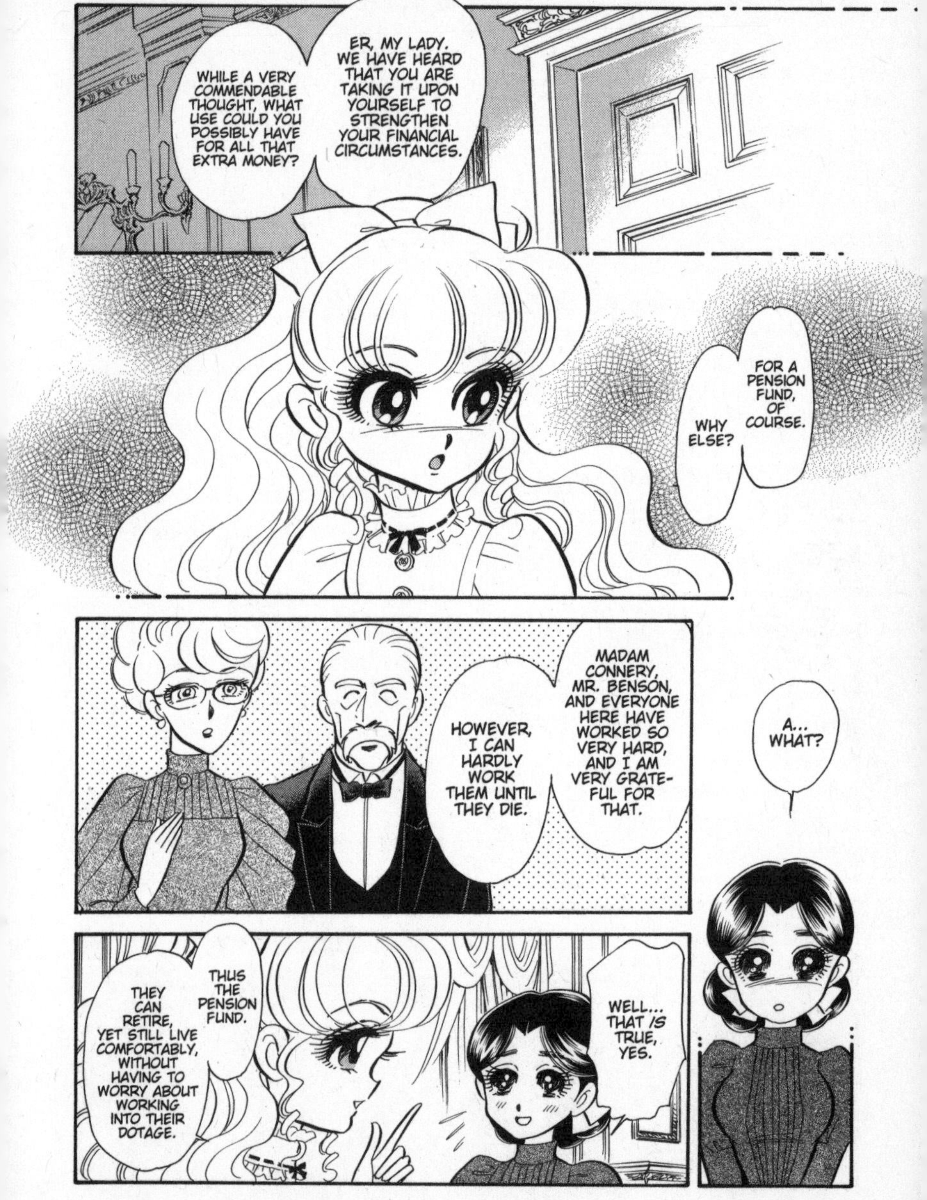
ER, MY LADY. WE HAVE HEARD THAT YOU ARE TAKING IT UPON YOURSELF TO STRENGTHEN YOUR FINANCIAL CIRCUMSTANCES.
WHILE A VERY COMMENDABLE THOUGHT, WHAT USE COULD YOU POSSIBLY HAVE FOR ALL THAT EXTRA MONEY?
FOR A PENSION FUND, OF COURSE.
WHY ELSE?
A... WHAT?
MADAM CONNERY, MR. BENSON, AND EVERYONE HERE HAVE WORKED SO VERY HARD, AND I AM VERY GRATE-FUL FOR THAT.
HOWEVER, I CAN HARDLY WORK THEM UNTIL THEY DIE.
WELL... THAT IS TRUE, YES.
THUS THE PENSION FUND.
THEY CAN RETIRE, YET STILL LIVE COMFORTABLY, WITHOUT HAVING TO WORRY ABOUT WORKING INTO THEIR DOTAGE.

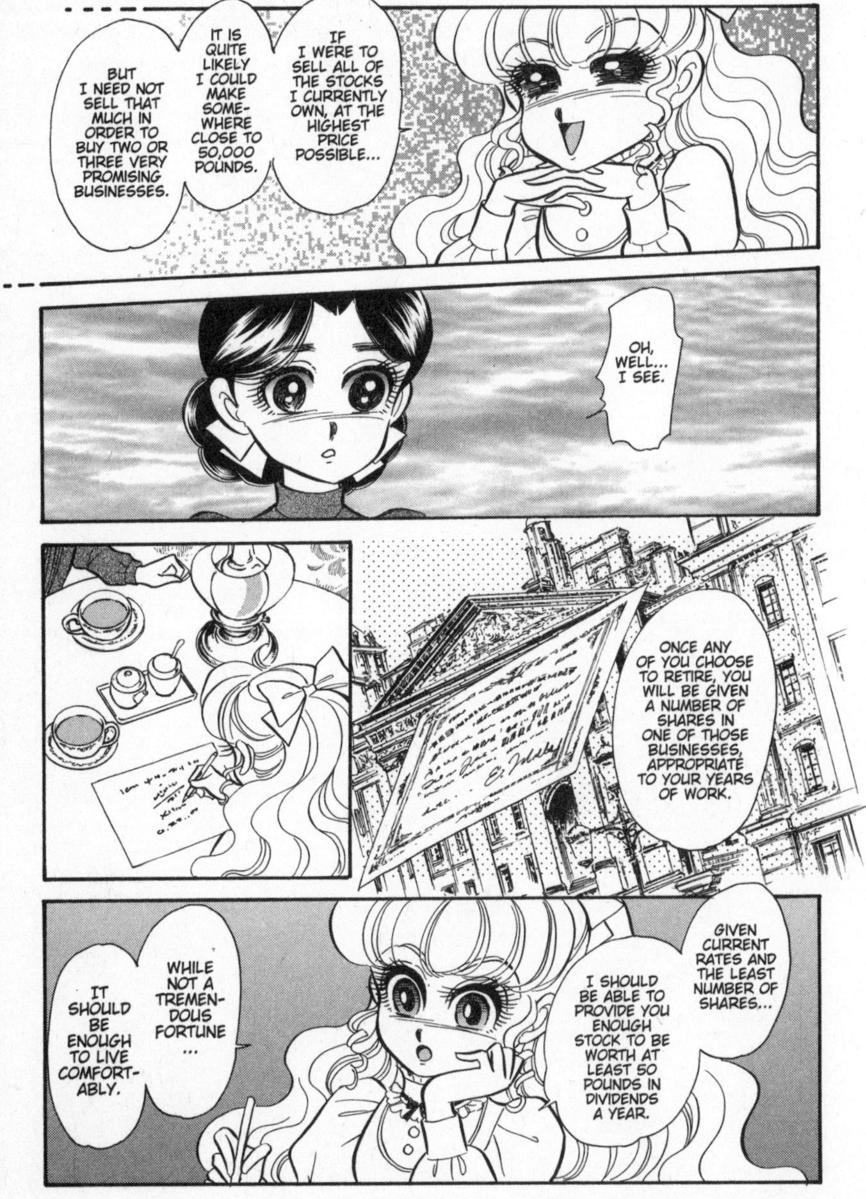
IF I WERE TO SELL ALL OF THE STOCKS I CURRENTLY OWN, AT THE HIGHEST PRICE POSSIBLE...
IT IS QUITE LIKELY I COULD MAKE SOME-WHERE CLOSE TO 50,000 POUNDS.
BUT I NEED NOT SELL THAT MUCH IN ORDER TO BUY TWO OR THREE VERY PROMISING BUSINESSES.
OH, WELL... I SEE.
ONCE ANY OF YOU CHOOSE TO RETIRE, YOU WILL BE GIVEN A NUMBER OF SHARES IN ONE OF THOSE BUSINESSES, APPROPRIATE TO YOUR YEARS OF WORK.
GIVEN CURRENT RATES AND THE LEAST NUMBER OF SHARES...
I SHOULD BE ABLE TO PROVIDE YOU ENOUGH STOCK TO BE WORTH AT LEAST 50 POUNDS IN DIVIDENDS A YEAR.
WHILE NOT A TREMEN-DOUS FORTUNE...
IT SHOULD BE ENOUGH TO LIVE COMFORT-ABLY.

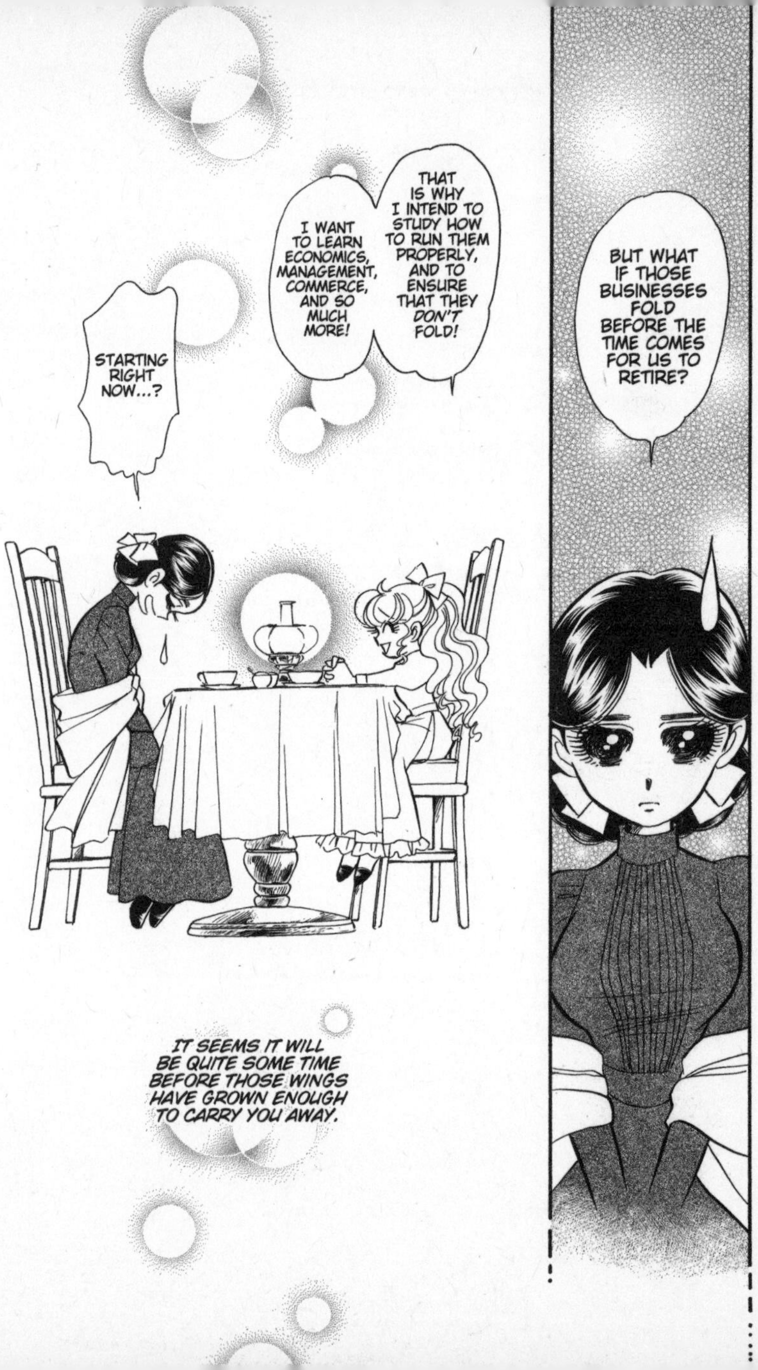
BUT WHAT IF THOSE BUSINESSES FOLD BEFORE THE TIME COMES FOR US TO RETIRE?
THAT IS WHY I INTEND TO STUDY HOW TO RUN THEM PROPERLY, AND TO ENSURE THAT THEY DON'T FOLD!
I WANT TO LEARN ECONOMICS, MANAGEMENT, COMMERCE, AND SO MUCH MORE!
STARTING RIGHT NOW...?
IT SEEMS IT WILL BE QUITE SOME TIME BEFORE THOSE WINGS HAVE GROWN ENOUGH TO CARRY YOU AWAY.

The Adventure of the Dying Message

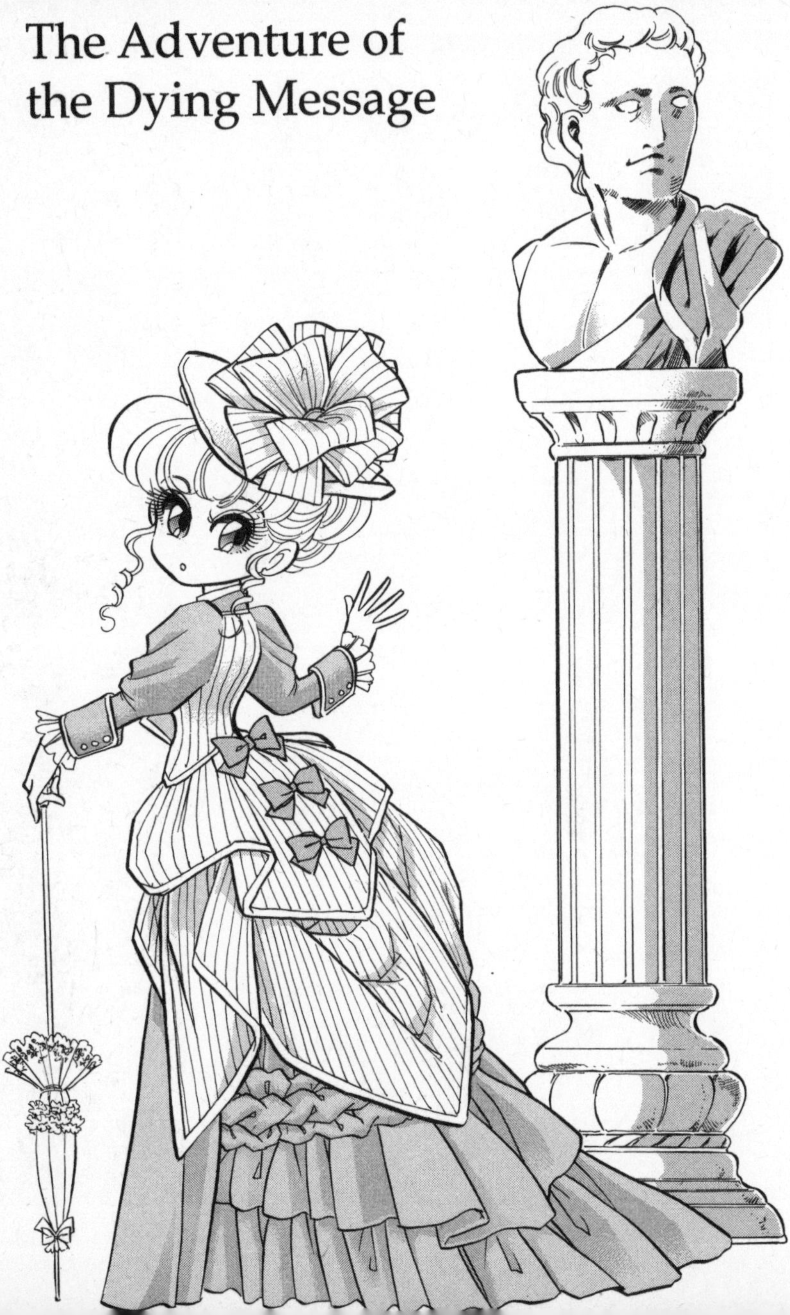

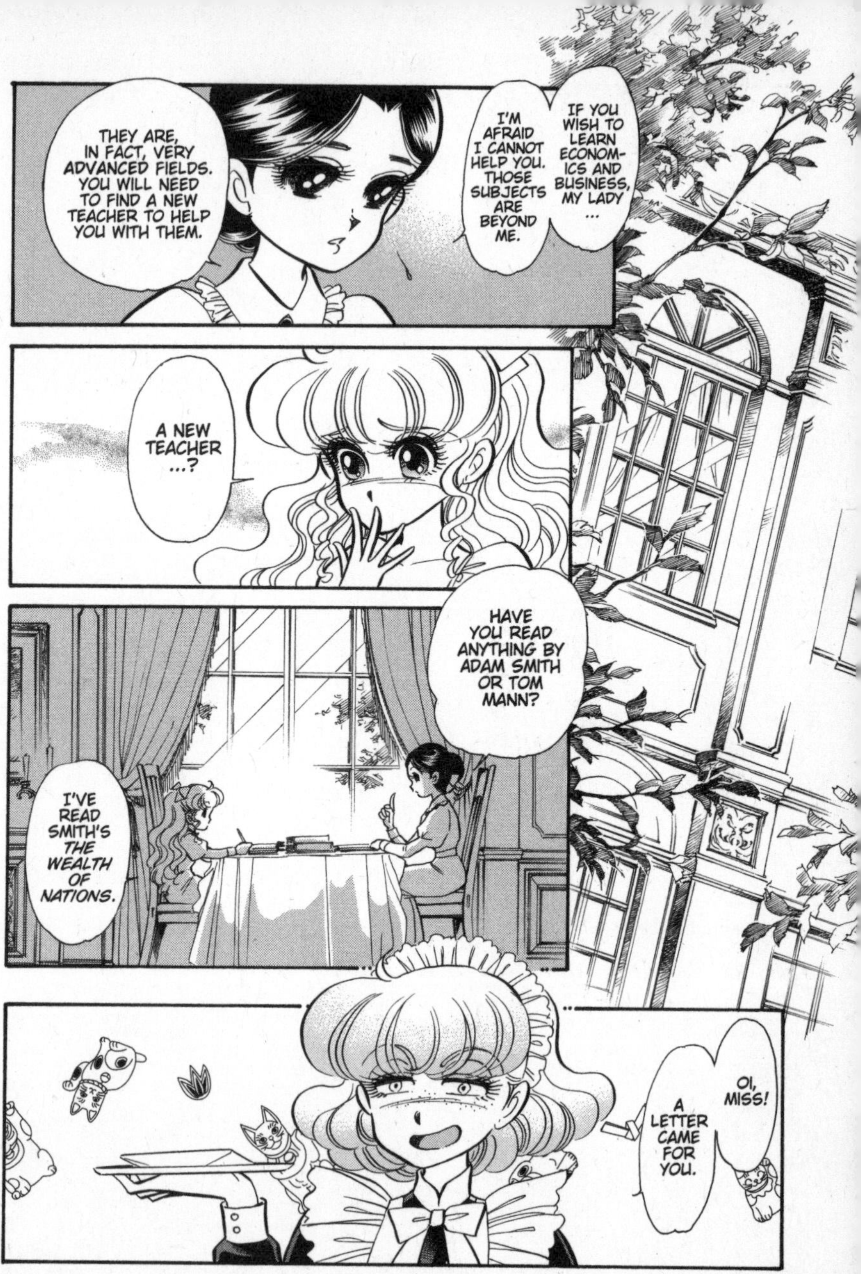
IF YOU WISH TO LEARN ECONOMICS AND BUSINESS, MY LADY ...
I'M AFRAID I CANNOT HELP YOU. THOSE SUBJECTS ARE BEYOND ME.
THEY ARE, IN FACT, VERY ADVANCED FIELDS. YOU WILL NEED TO FIND A NEW TEACHER TO HELP YOU WITH THEM.
A NEW TEACHER ...?
HAVE YOU READ ANYTHING BY ADAM SMITH OR TOM MANN?
I'VE READ SMITH'S *THE WEALTH OF NATIONS.*
OI, MISS!
A LETTER CAME FOR YOU.

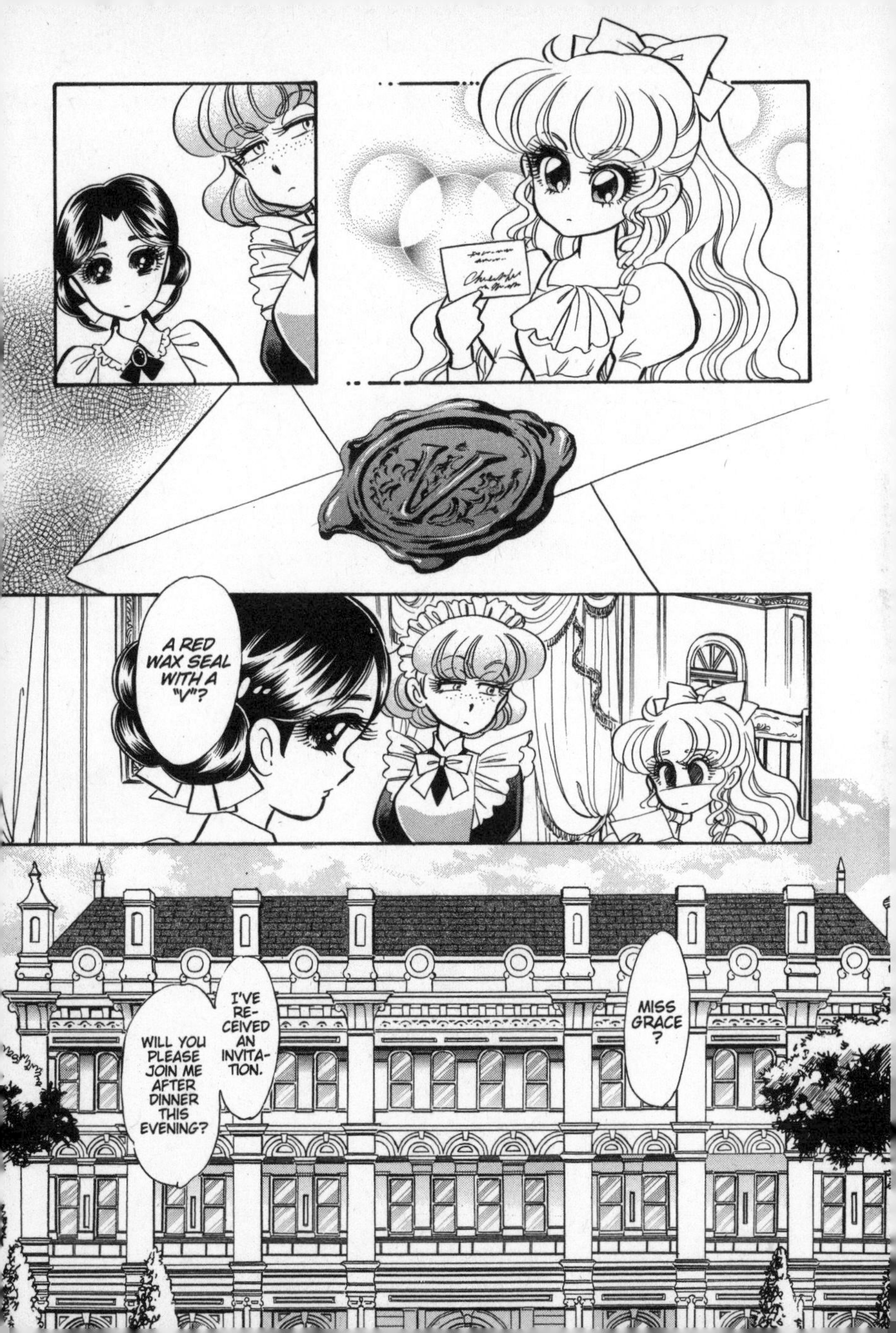
A RED WAX SEAL WITH A "V"?
MISS GRACE?
I'VE RECEIVED AN INVITATION.
WILL YOU PLEASE JOIN ME AFTER DINNER THIS EVENING?

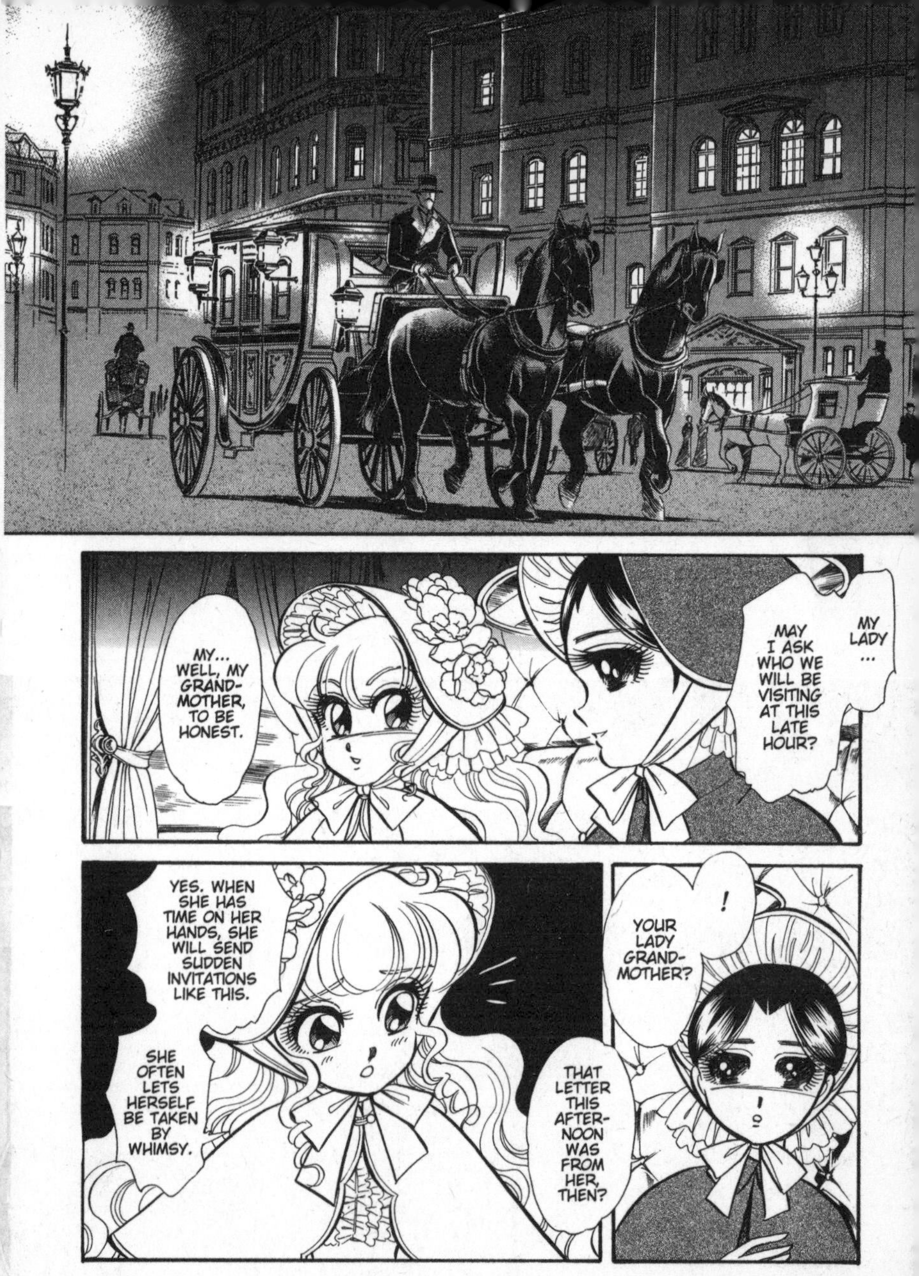
MY LADY ...
MAY I ASK WHO WE WILL BE VISITING AT THIS LATE HOUR?
MY... WELL, MY GRAND-MOTHER, TO BE HONEST.
!
YOUR LADY GRAND-MOTHER?
THAT LETTER THIS AFTER-NOON WAS FROM HER, THEN?
YES. WHEN SHE HAS TIME ON HER HANDS, SHE WILL SEND SUDDEN INVITATIONS LIKE THIS.
SHE OFTEN LETS HERSELF BE TAKEN BY WHIMSY.

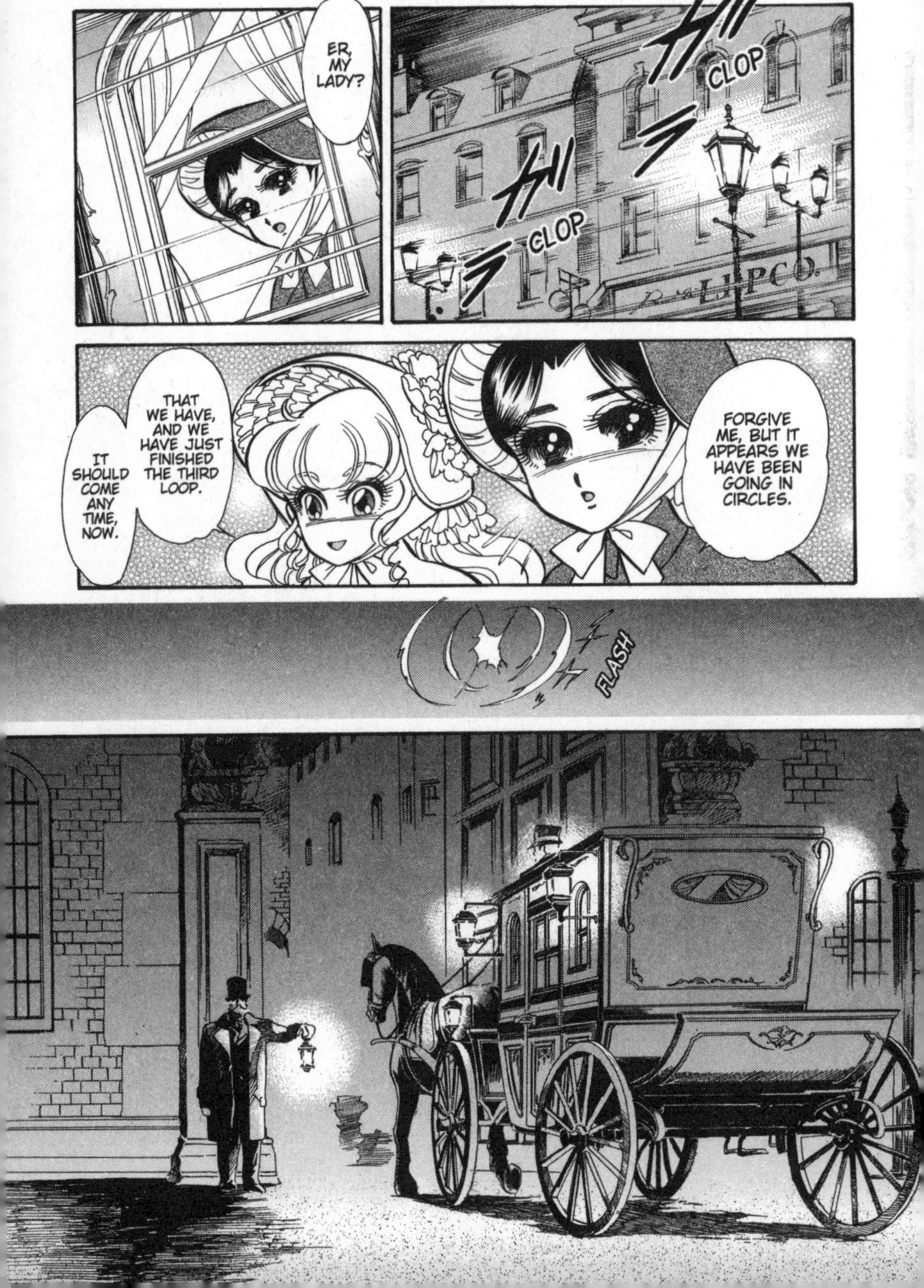

ガラ
CLOP
ガラ
CLOP
ER, MY LADY?
FORGIVE ME, BUT IT APPEARS WE HAVE BEEN GOING IN CIRCLES.
THAT WE HAVE, AND WE HAVE JUST FINISHED THE THIRD LOOP.
IT SHOULD COME ANY TIME, NOW.
FLASH

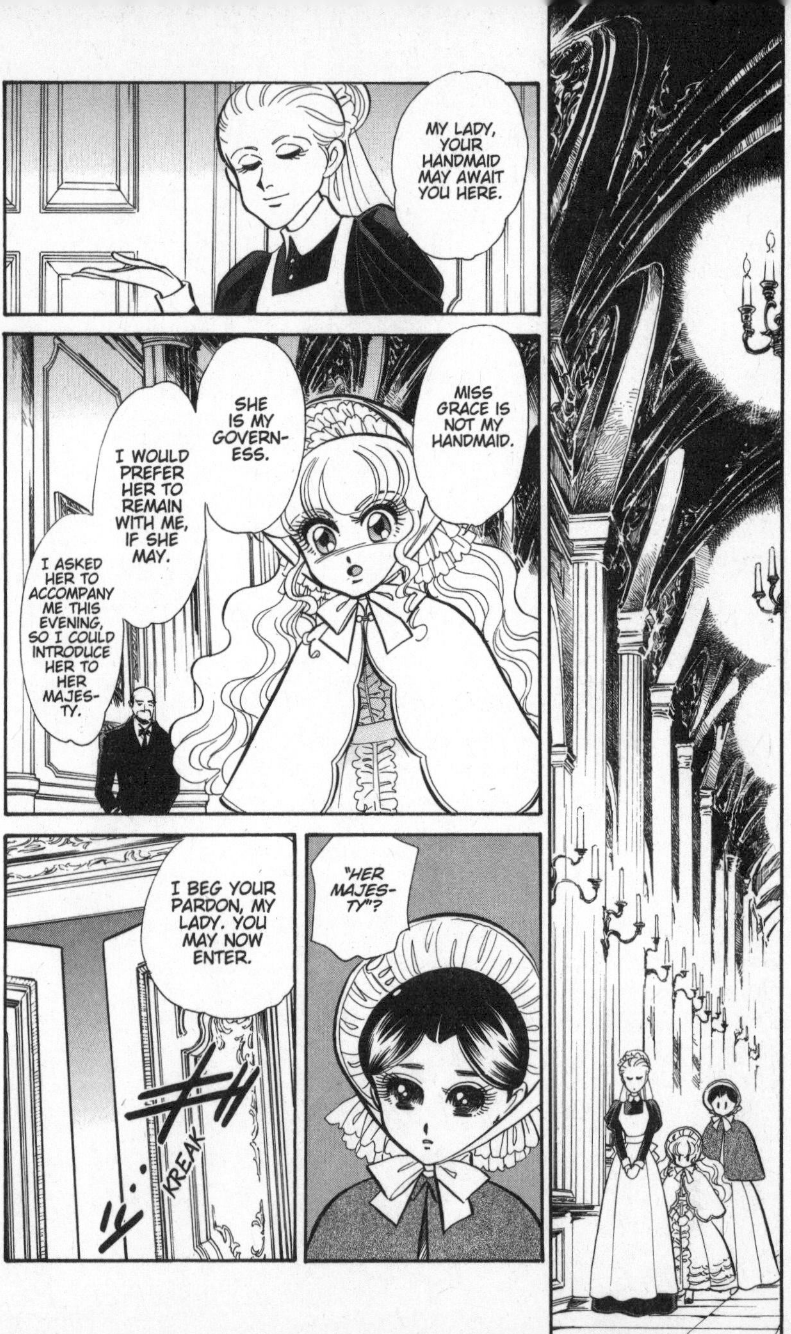
MY LADY, YOUR HANDMAID MAY AWAIT YOU HERE.
MISS GRACE IS NOT MY HANDMAID.
SHE IS MY GOVERN-ESS.
I WOULD PREFER HER TO REMAIN WITH ME, IF SHE MAY.
I ASKED HER TO ACCOMPANY ME THIS EVENING, SO I COULD INTRODUCE HER TO HER MAJES-TY.
"HER MAJES-TY"?
I BEG YOUR PARDON, MY LADY. YOU MAY NOW ENTER.
KREAK

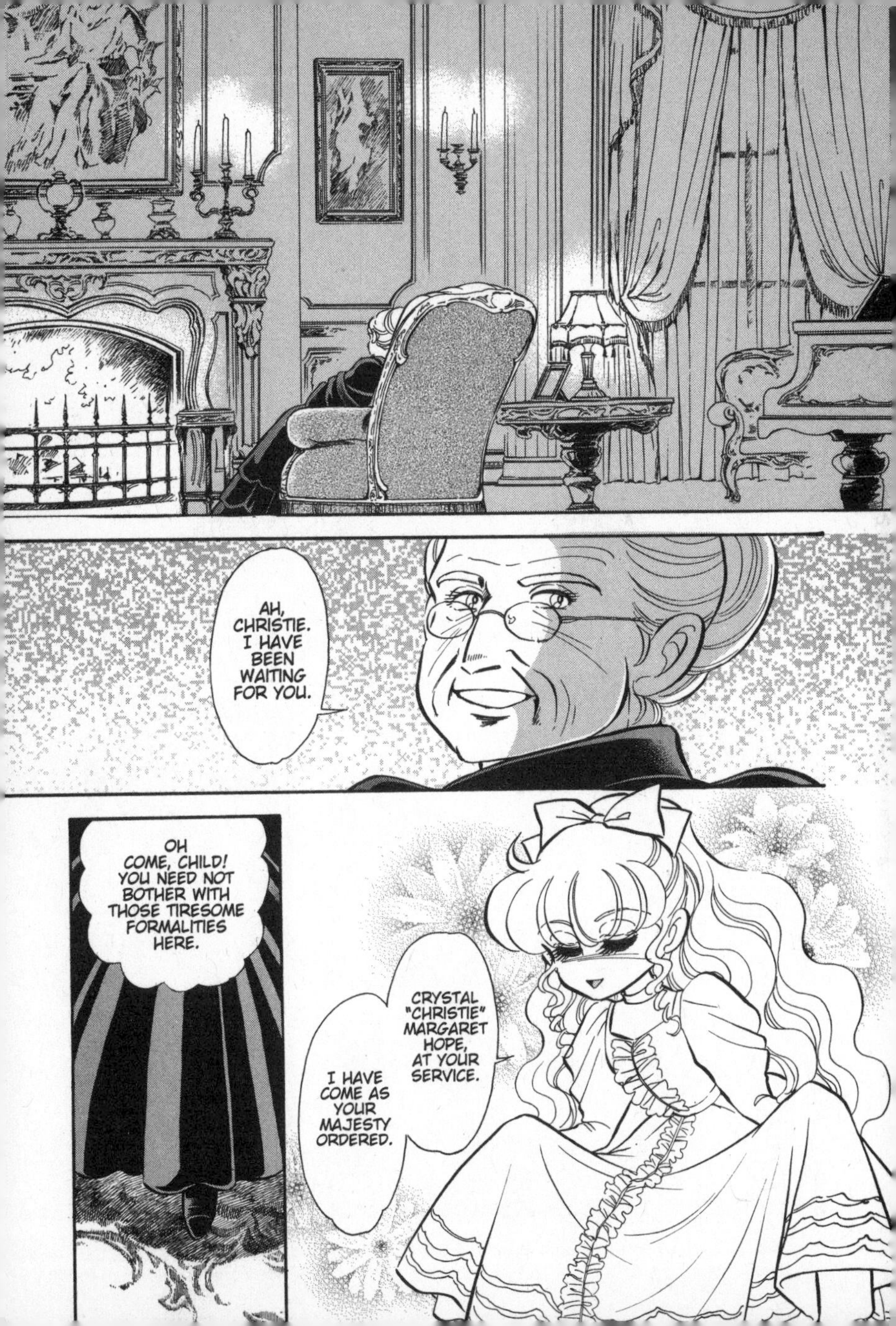
AH, CHRISTIE. I HAVE BEEN WAITING FOR YOU.
CRYSTAL "CHRISTIE" MARGARET HOPE, AT YOUR SERVICE.
I HAVE COME AS YOUR MAJESTY ORDERED.
OH COME, CHILD! YOU NEED NOT BOTHER WITH THOSE TIRESOME FORMALITIES HERE.

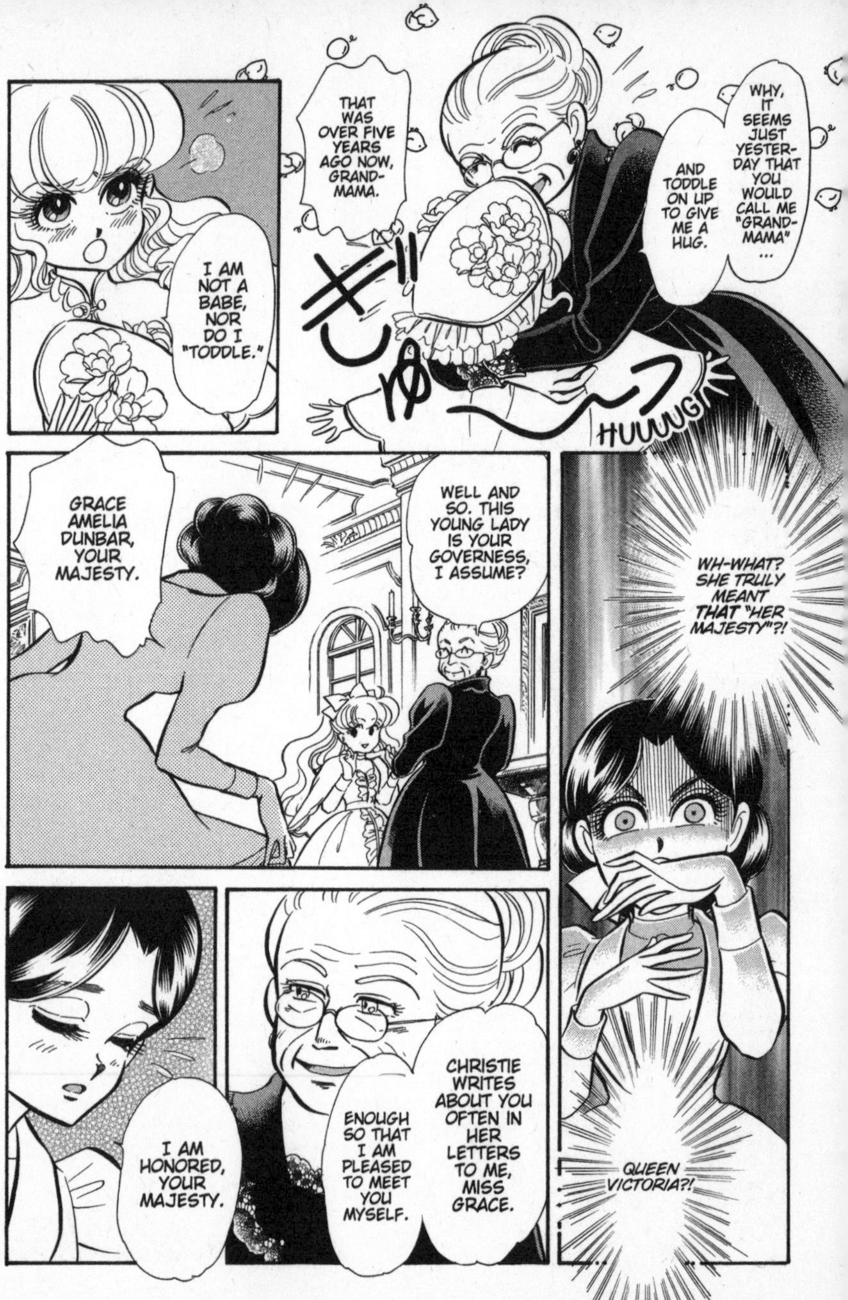
WHY, IT SEEMS JUST YESTERDAY THAT YOU WOULD CALL ME "GRAND-MAMA"...
AND TODDLE ON UP TO GIVE ME A HUG.
THAT WAS OVER FIVE YEARS AGO NOW, GRAND-MAMA.
HUUUUG
I AM NOT A BABE, NOR DO I "TODDLE."
WH-WHAT? SHE TRULY MEANT THAT "HER MAJESTY"?!
QUEEN VICTORIA?!
WELL AND SO. THIS YOUNG LADY IS YOUR GOVERNESS, I ASSUME?
GRACE AMELIA DUNBAR, YOUR MAJESTY.
CHRISTIE WRITES ABOUT YOU OFTEN IN HER LETTERS TO ME, MISS GRACE.
ENOUGH SO THAT I AM PLEASED TO MEET YOU MYSELF.
I AM HONORED, YOUR MAJESTY.

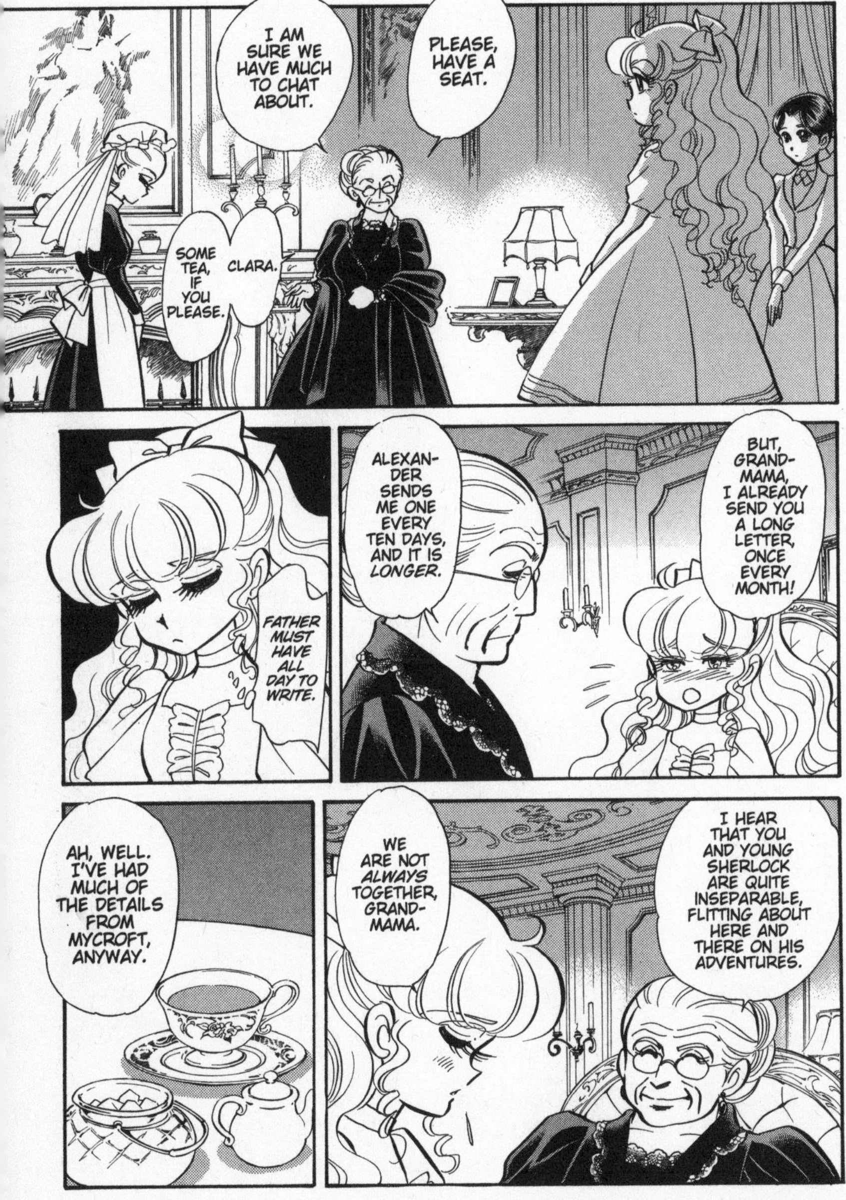
PLEASE, HAVE A SEAT.
I AM SURE WE HAVE MUCH TO CHAT ABOUT.
CLARA.
SOME TEA, IF YOU PLEASE.
BUT, GRANDMAMA, I ALREADY SEND YOU A LONG LETTER, ONCE EVERY MONTH!
ALEXANDER SENDS ME ONE EVERY TEN DAYS, AND IT IS *LONGER*.
FATHER MUST HAVE ALL DAY TO WRITE.
I HEAR THAT YOU AND YOUNG SHERLOCK ARE QUITE INSEPARABLE, FLITTING ABOUT HERE AND THERE ON HIS ADVENTURES.
WE ARE NOT *ALWAYS* TOGETHER, GRANDMAMA.
AH, WELL. I'VE HAD MUCH OF THE DETAILS FROM MYCROFT, ANYWAY.

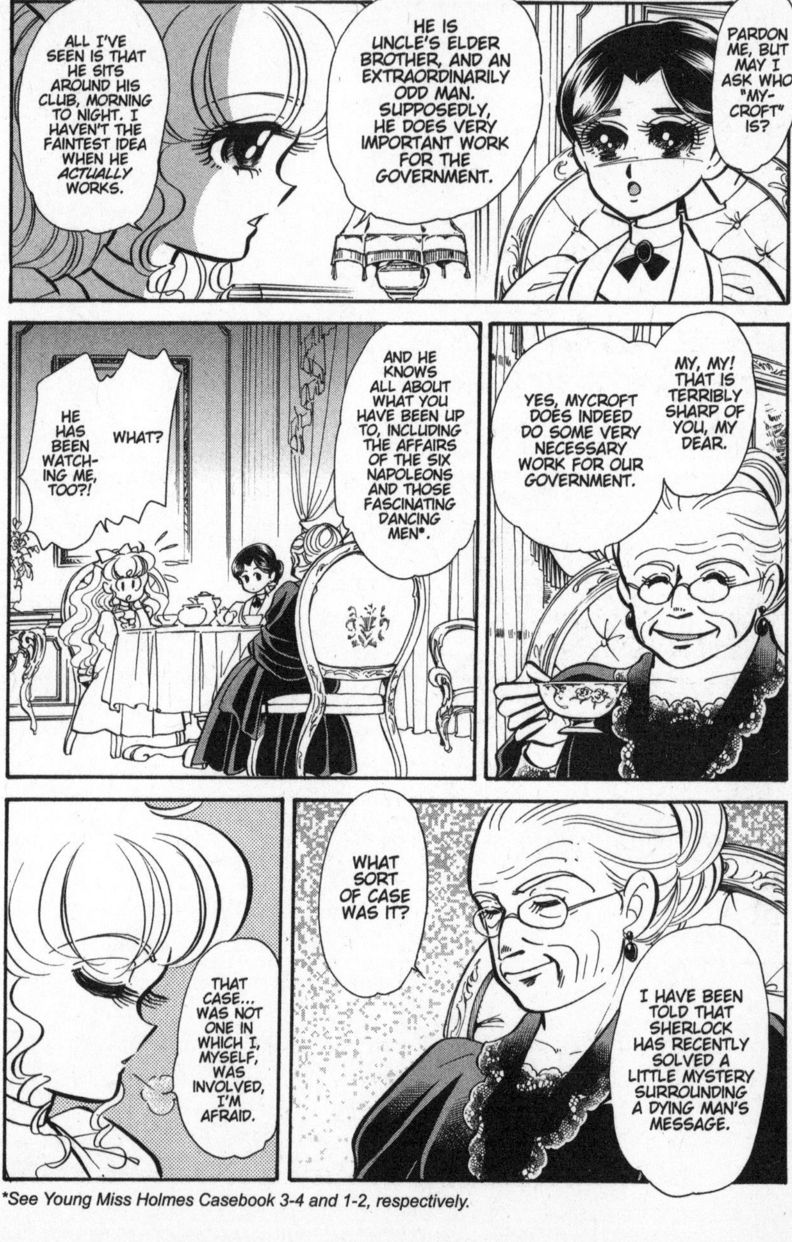
PARDON ME, BUT MAY I ASK WHO "MY-CROFT" IS?
HE IS UNCLE'S ELDER BROTHER, AND AN EXTRAORDINARILY ODD MAN. SUPPOSEDLY, HE DOES VERY IMPORTANT WORK FOR THE GOVERNMENT.
ALL I'VE SEEN IS THAT HE SITS AROUND HIS CLUB, MORNING TO NIGHT. I HAVEN'T THE FAINTEST IDEA WHEN HE *ACTUALLY* WORKS.
MY, MY! THAT IS TERRIBLY SHARP OF YOU, MY DEAR.
YES, MYCROFT DOES INDEED DO SOME VERY NECESSARY WORK FOR OUR GOVERNMENT.
AND HE KNOWS ALL ABOUT WHAT YOU HAVE BEEN UP TO, INCLUDING THE AFFAIRS OF THE SIX NAPOLEONS AND THOSE FASCINATING DANCING MEN*.
WHAT?
HE HAS BEEN WATCHING ME, TOO?!
I HAVE BEEN TOLD THAT SHERLOCK HAS RECENTLY SOLVED A LITTLE MYSTERY SURROUNDING A DYING MAN'S MESSAGE.
WHAT SORT OF CASE WAS IT?
THAT CASE... WAS NOT ONE IN WHICH I, MYSELF, WAS INVOLVED, I'M AFRAID.

**See Young Miss Holmes Casebook 3-4 and 1-2, respectively.*

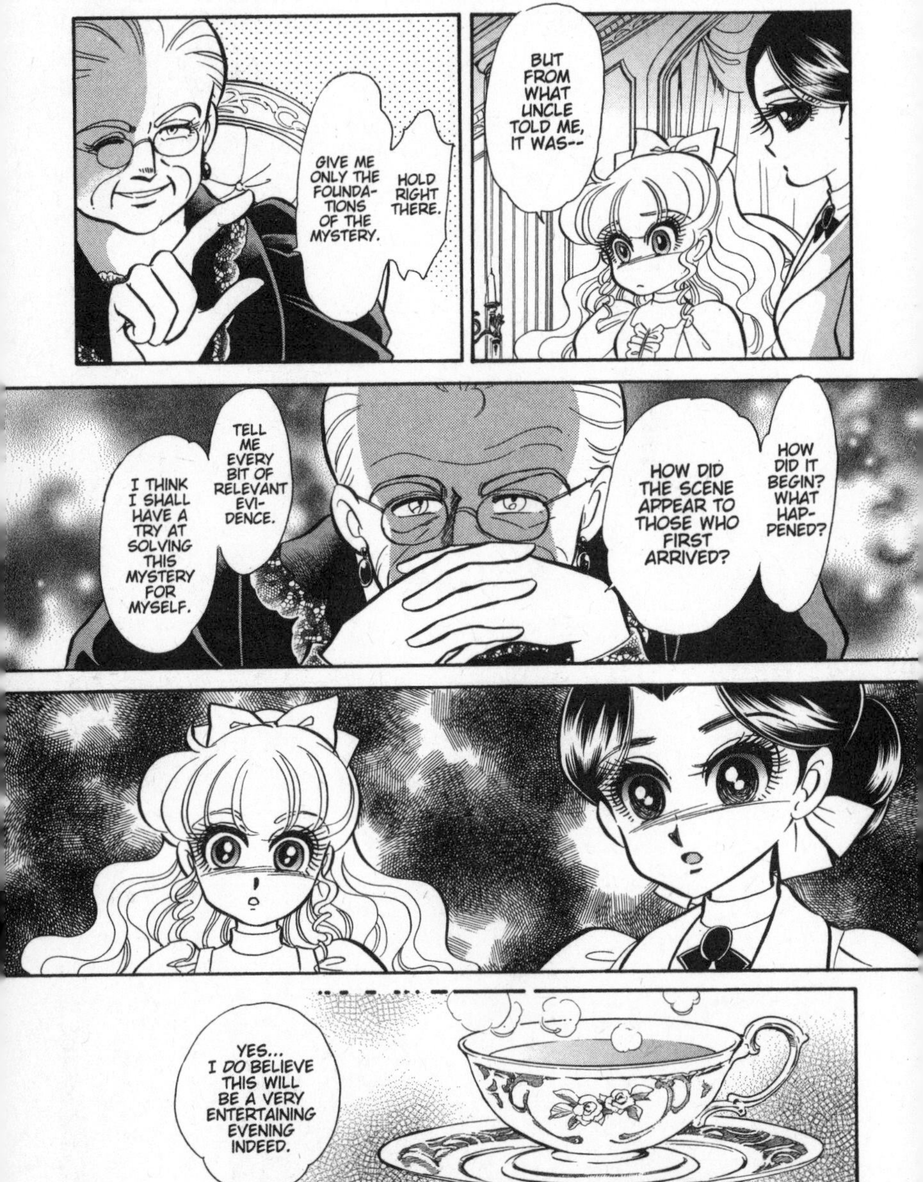
BUT FROM WHAT UNCLE TOLD ME, IT WAS--
HOLD RIGHT THERE.
GIVE ME ONLY THE FOUNDATIONS OF THE MYSTERY.
HOW DID IT BEGIN? WHAT HAPPENED?
HOW DID THE SCENE APPEAR TO THOSE WHO FIRST ARRIVED?
TELL ME EVERY BIT OF RELEVANT EVIDENCE.
I THINK I SHALL HAVE A TRY AT SOLVING THIS MYSTERY FOR MYSELF.
YES... I *DO* BELIEVE THIS WILL BE A VERY ENTERTAINING EVENING INDEED.

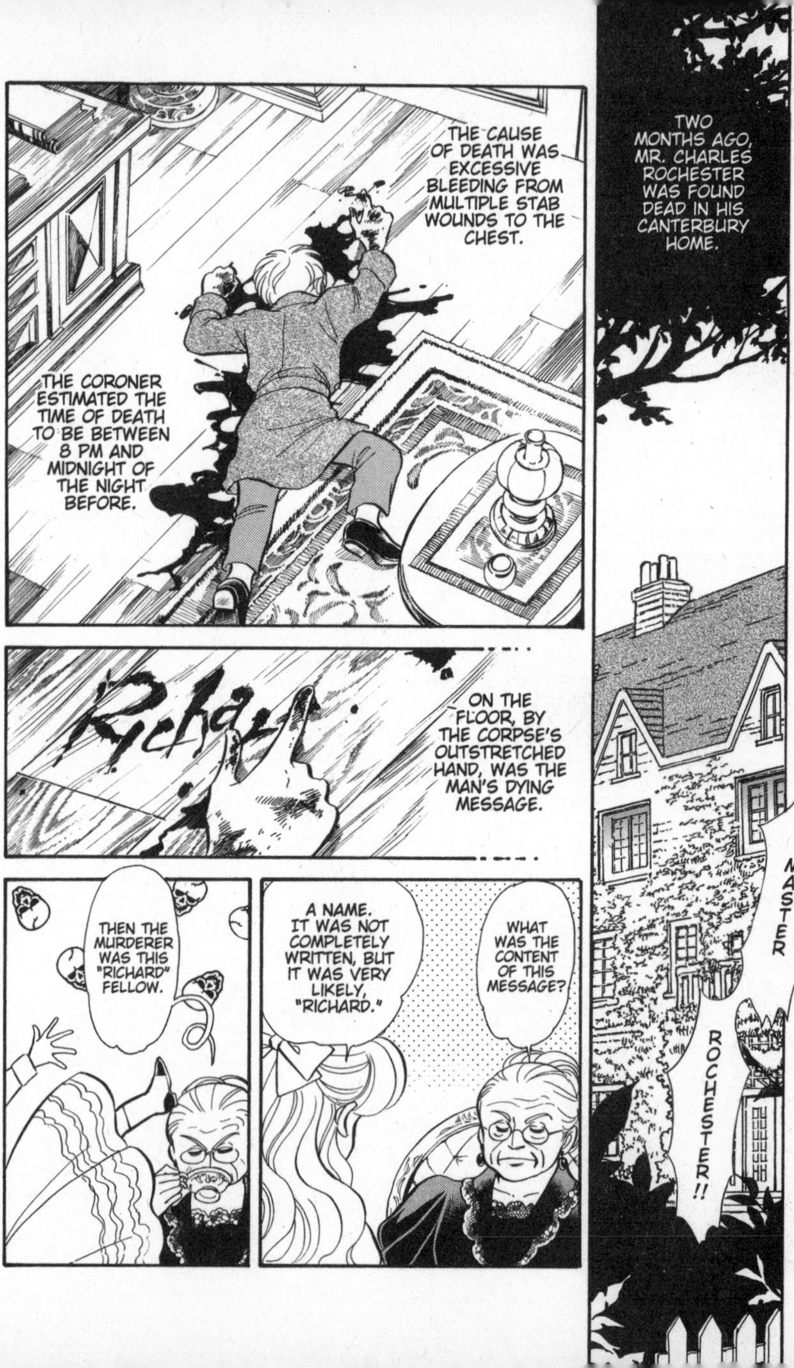
TWO MONTHS AGO, MR. CHARLES ROCHESTER WAS FOUND DEAD IN HIS CANTERBURY HOME.
MASTER ROCHESTER!!
THE CAUSE OF DEATH WAS EXCESSIVE BLEEDING FROM MULTIPLE STAB WOUNDS TO THE CHEST.
THE CORONER ESTIMATED THE TIME OF DEATH TO BE BETWEEN 8 PM AND MIDNIGHT OF THE NIGHT BEFORE.
ON THE FLOOR, BY THE CORPSE'S OUTSTRETCHED HAND, WAS THE MAN'S DYING MESSAGE.
Richa
WHAT WAS THE CONTENT OF THIS MESSAGE?
A NAME. IT WAS NOT COMPLETELY WRITTEN, BUT IT WAS VERY LIKELY, "RICHARD."
THEN THE MURDERER WAS THIS "RICHARD" FELLOW.

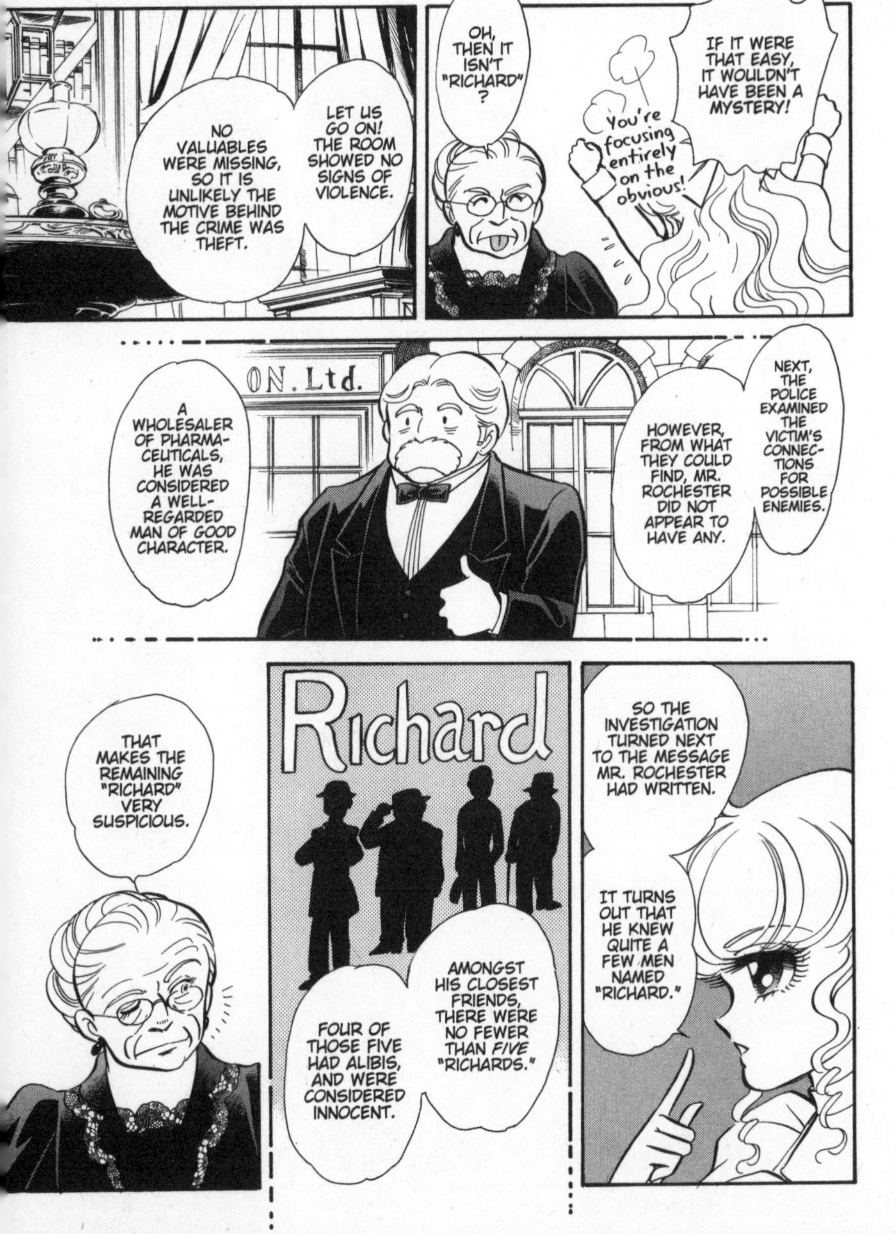
IF IT WERE THAT EASY, IT WOULDN'T HAVE BEEN A MYSTERY!
You're focusing entirely on the obvious!
OH, THEN IT ISN'T "RICHARD"?
LET US GO ON! THE ROOM SHOWED NO SIGNS OF VIOLENCE.
NO VALUABLES WERE MISSING, SO IT IS UNLIKELY THE MOTIVE BEHIND THE CRIME WAS THEFT.
NEXT, THE POLICE EXAMINED THE VICTIM'S CONNECTIONS FOR POSSIBLE ENEMIES.
HOWEVER, FROM WHAT THEY COULD FIND, MR. ROCHESTER DID NOT APPEAR TO HAVE ANY.
ON. Ltd.
A WHOLESALER OF PHARMACEUTICALS, HE WAS CONSIDERED A WELL-REGARDED MAN OF GOOD CHARACTER.
SO THE INVESTIGATION TURNED NEXT TO THE MESSAGE MR. ROCHESTER HAD WRITTEN.
IT TURNS OUT THAT HE KNEW QUITE A FEW MEN NAMED "RICHARD."
Richard
AMONGST HIS CLOSEST FRIENDS, THERE WERE NO FEWER THAN *FIVE* "RICHARDS."
FOUR OF THOSE FIVE HAD ALIBIS, AND WERE CONSIDERED INNOCENT.
THAT MAKES THE REMAINING "RICHARD" VERY SUSPICIOUS.

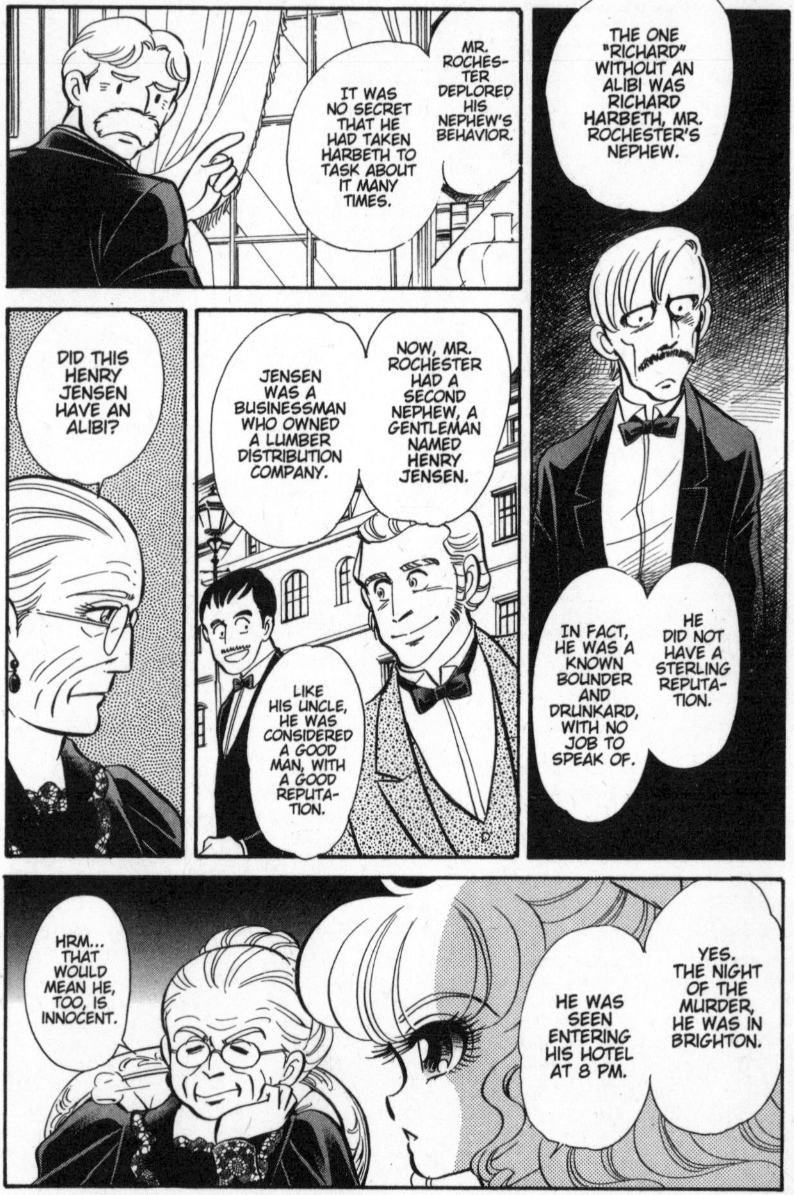
THE ONE "RICHARD" WITHOUT AN ALIBI WAS RICHARD HARBETH, MR. ROCHESTER'S NEPHEW.
HE DID NOT HAVE A STERLING REPUTATION.
IN FACT, HE WAS A KNOWN BOUNDER AND DRUNKARD, WITH NO JOB TO SPEAK OF.
MR. ROCHESTER DEPLORED HIS NEPHEW'S BEHAVIOR.
IT WAS NO SECRET THAT HE HAD TAKEN HARBETH TO TASK ABOUT IT MANY TIMES.
NOW, MR. ROCHESTER HAD A SECOND NEPHEW, A GENTLEMAN NAMED HENRY JENSEN.
JENSEN WAS A BUSINESSMAN WHO OWNED A LUMBER DISTRIBUTION COMPANY.
LIKE HIS UNCLE, HE WAS CONSIDERED A GOOD MAN, WITH A GOOD REPUTATION.
DID THIS HENRY JENSEN HAVE AN ALIBI?
YES. THE NIGHT OF THE MURDER, HE WAS IN BRIGHTON.
HE WAS SEEN ENTERING HIS HOTEL AT 8 PM.
HRM... THAT WOULD MEAN HE, TOO, IS INNOCENT.

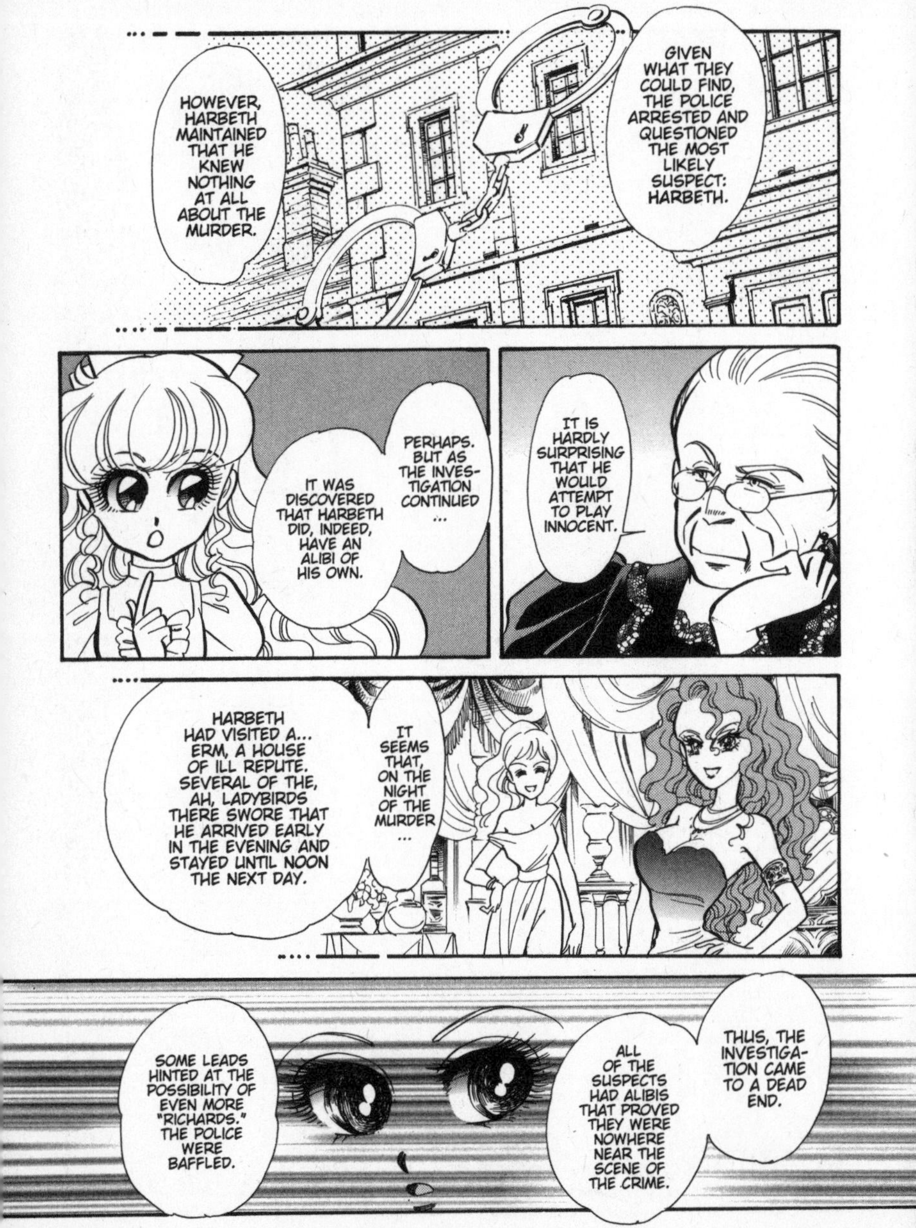
GIVEN WHAT THEY COULD FIND, THE POLICE ARRESTED AND QUESTIONED THE MOST LIKELY SUSPECT: HARBETH.
HOWEVER, HARBETH MAINTAINED THAT HE KNEW NOTHING AT ALL ABOUT THE MURDER.
IT IS HARDLY SURPRISING THAT HE WOULD ATTEMPT TO PLAY INNOCENT.
PERHAPS. BUT AS THE INVESTIGATION CONTINUED ...
IT WAS DISCOVERED THAT HARBETH DID, INDEED, HAVE AN ALIBI OF HIS OWN.
IT SEEMS THAT, ON THE NIGHT OF THE MURDER ...
HARBETH HAD VISITED A... ERM, A HOUSE OF ILL REPUTE. SEVERAL OF THE, AH, LADYBIRDS THERE SWORE THAT HE ARRIVED EARLY IN THE EVENING AND STAYED UNTIL NOON THE NEXT DAY.
THUS, THE INVESTIGATION CAME TO A DEAD END.
ALL OF THE SUSPECTS HAD ALIBIS THAT PROVED THEY WERE NOWHERE NEAR THE SCENE OF THE CRIME.
SOME LEADS HINTED AT THE POSSIBILITY OF EVEN MORE "RICHARDS." THE POLICE WERE BAFFLED.

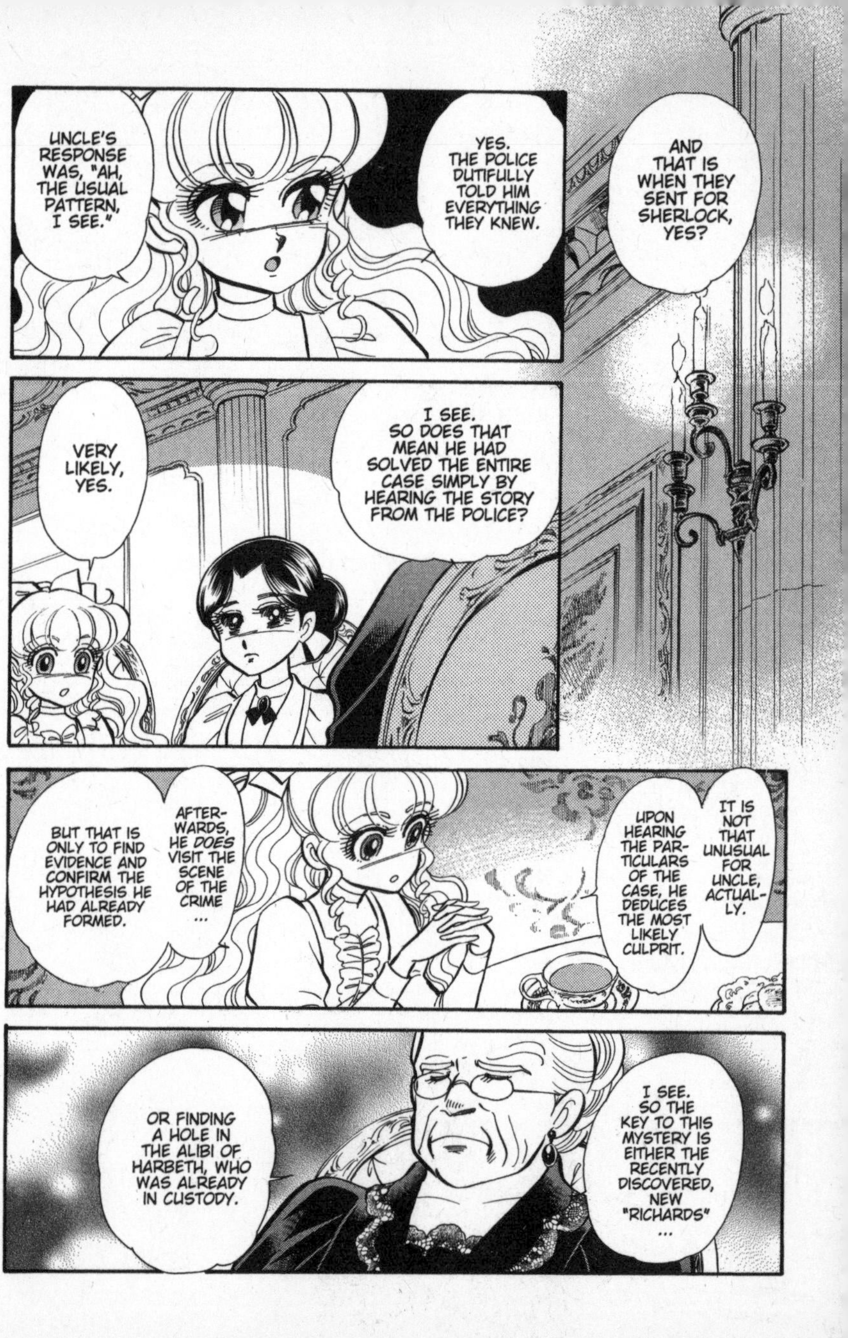
AND THAT IS WHEN THEY SENT FOR SHERLOCK, YES?
YES. THE POLICE DUTIFULLY TOLD HIM EVERYTHING THEY KNEW.
UNCLE'S RESPONSE WAS, "AH, THE USUAL PATTERN, I SEE."
I SEE. SO DOES THAT MEAN HE HAD SOLVED THE ENTIRE CASE SIMPLY BY HEARING THE STORY FROM THE POLICE?
VERY LIKELY, YES.
IT IS NOT THAT UNUSUAL FOR UNCLE, ACTUALLY.
UPON HEARING THE PARTICULARS OF THE CASE, HE DEDUCES THE MOST LIKELY CULPRIT.
AFTERWARDS, HE *DOES* VISIT THE SCENE OF THE CRIME ...
BUT THAT IS ONLY TO FIND EVIDENCE AND CONFIRM THE HYPOTHESIS HE HAD ALREADY FORMED.
I SEE. SO THE KEY TO THIS MYSTERY IS EITHER THE RECENTLY DISCOVERED, NEW "RICHARDS" ...
OR FINDING A HOLE IN THE ALIBI OF HARBETH, WHO WAS ALREADY IN CUSTODY.

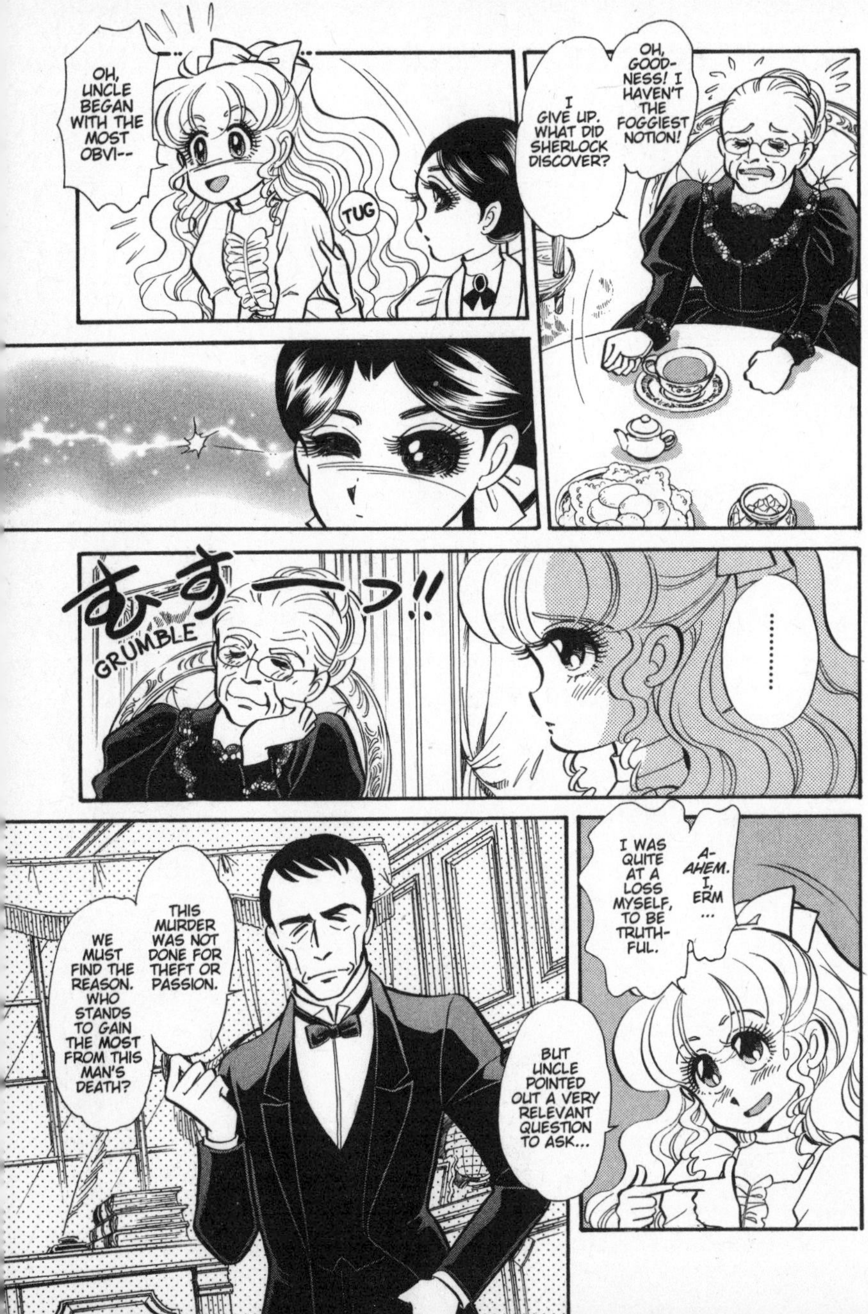
OH, GOODNESS! I HAVEN'T THE FOGGIEST NOTION!
I GIVE UP. WHAT DID SHERLOCK DISCOVER?
OH, UNCLE BEGAN WITH THE MOST OBVI--
TUG
......
むすーっ!!
GRUMBLE
A-AHEM. I, ERM ...
I WAS QUITE AT A LOSS MYSELF, TO BE TRUTHFUL.
BUT UNCLE POINTED OUT A VERY RELEVANT QUESTION TO ASK...
THIS MURDER WAS NOT DONE FOR THEFT OR PASSION.
WE MUST FIND THE REASON. WHO STANDS TO GAIN THE MOST FROM THIS MAN'S DEATH?

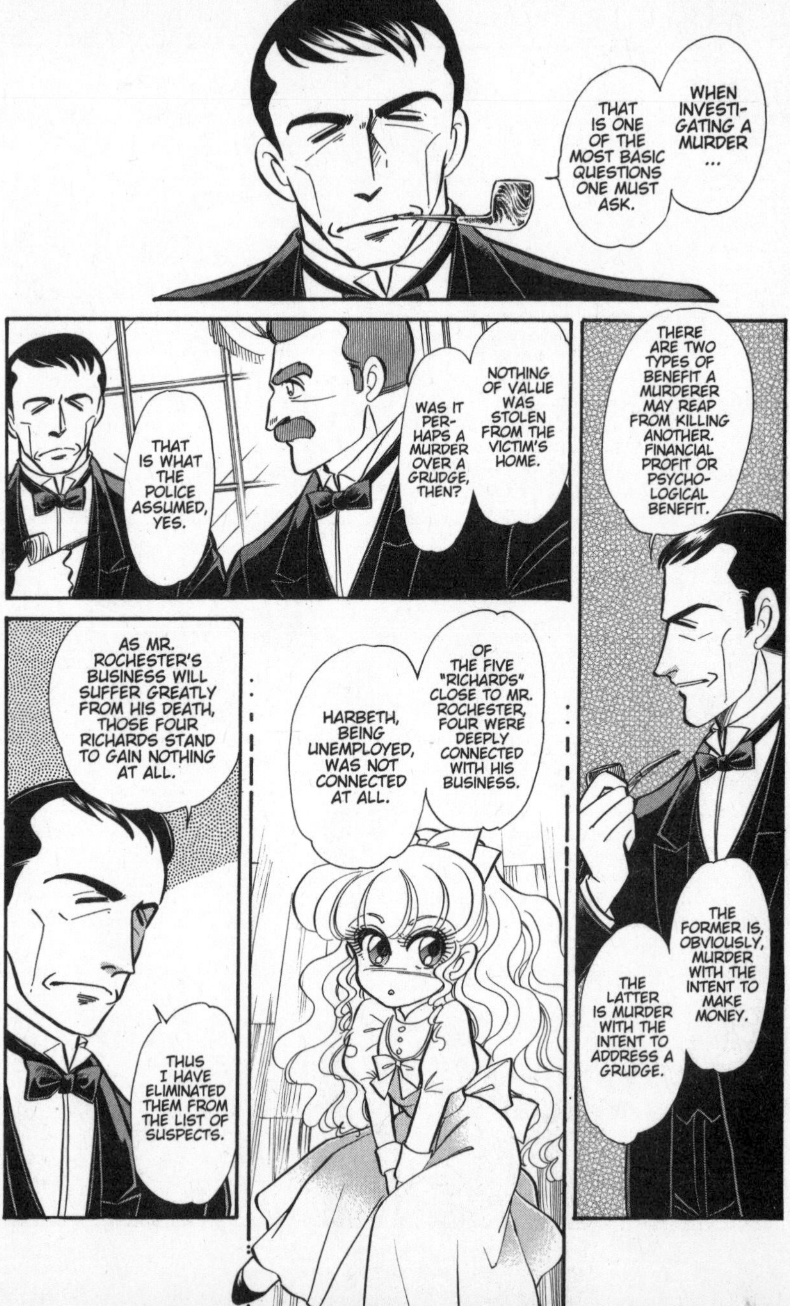
WHEN INVESTIGATING A MURDER ...
THAT IS ONE OF THE MOST BASIC QUESTIONS ONE MUST ASK.
THERE ARE TWO TYPES OF BENEFIT A MURDERER MAY REAP FROM KILLING ANOTHER. FINANCIAL PROFIT OR PSYCHOLOGICAL BENEFIT.
THE FORMER IS, OBVIOUSLY, MURDER WITH THE INTENT TO MAKE MONEY.
THE LATTER IS MURDER WITH THE INTENT TO ADDRESS A GRUDGE.
NOTHING OF VALUE WAS STOLEN FROM THE VICTIM'S HOME.
WAS IT PERHAPS A MURDER OVER A GRUDGE, THEN?
THAT IS WHAT THE POLICE ASSUMED, YES.
OF THE FIVE "RICHARDS" CLOSE TO MR. ROCHESTER, FOUR WERE DEEPLY CONNECTED WITH HIS BUSINESS.
HARBETH, BEING UNEMPLOYED, WAS NOT CONNECTED AT ALL.
AS MR. ROCHESTER'S BUSINESS WILL SUFFER GREATLY FROM HIS DEATH, THOSE FOUR RICHARDS STAND TO GAIN NOTHING AT ALL.
THUS I HAVE ELIMINATED THEM FROM THE LIST OF SUSPECTS.

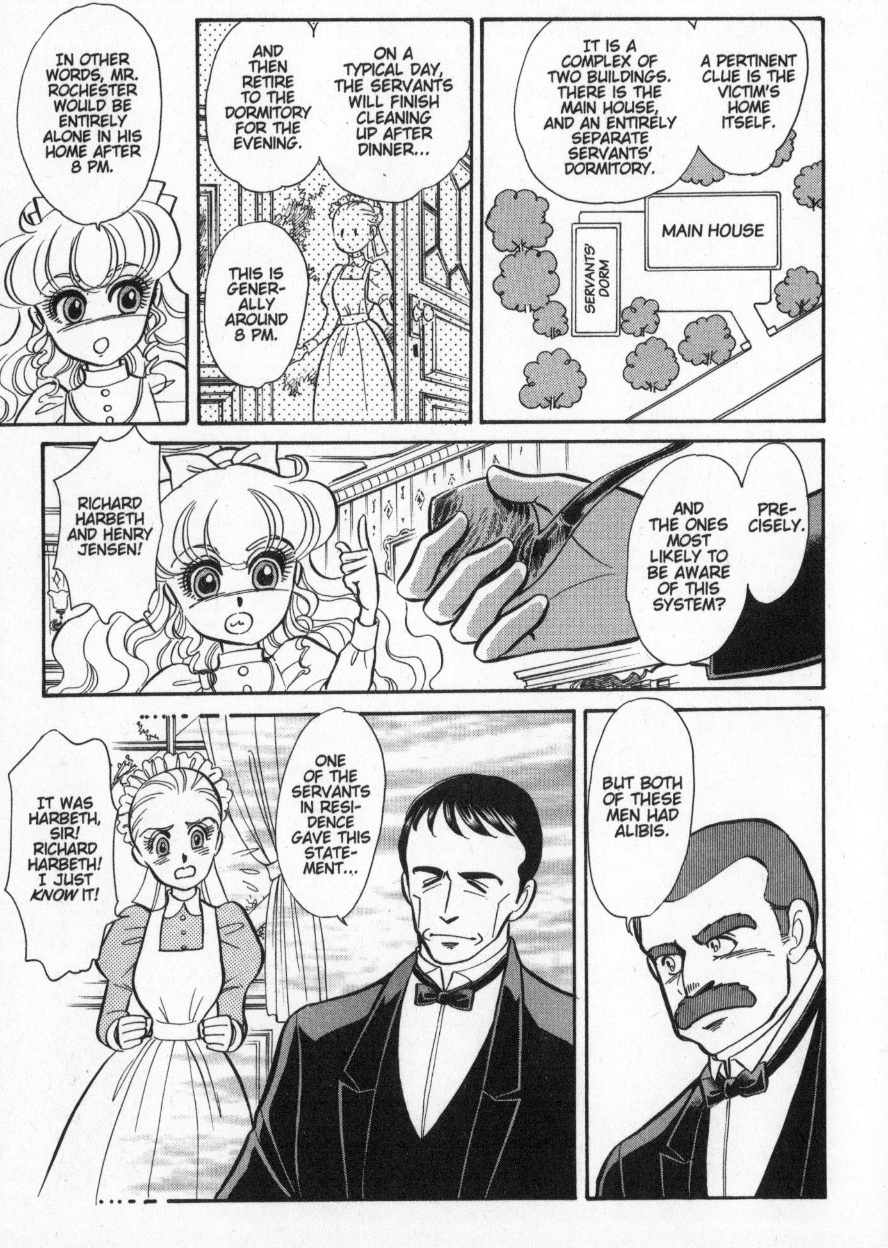
A PERTINENT CLUE IS THE VICTIM'S HOME ITSELF.
IT IS A COMPLEX OF TWO BUILDINGS. THERE IS THE MAIN HOUSE, AND AN ENTIRELY SEPARATE SERVANTS' DORMITORY.
MAIN HOUSE
SERVANTS' DORM
ON A TYPICAL DAY, THE SERVANTS WILL FINISH CLEANING UP AFTER DINNER...
AND THEN RETIRE TO THE DORMITORY FOR THE EVENING.
THIS IS GENERALLY AROUND 8 PM.
IN OTHER WORDS, MR. ROCHESTER WOULD BE ENTIRELY ALONE IN HIS HOME AFTER 8 PM.
PRECISELY.
AND THE ONES MOST LIKELY TO BE AWARE OF THIS SYSTEM?
RICHARD HARBETH AND HENRY JENSEN!
BUT BOTH OF THESE MEN HAD ALIBIS.
ONE OF THE SERVANTS IN RESIDENCE GAVE THIS STATEMENT...
IT WAS HARBETH, SIR! RICHARD HARBETH! I JUST *KNOW* IT!

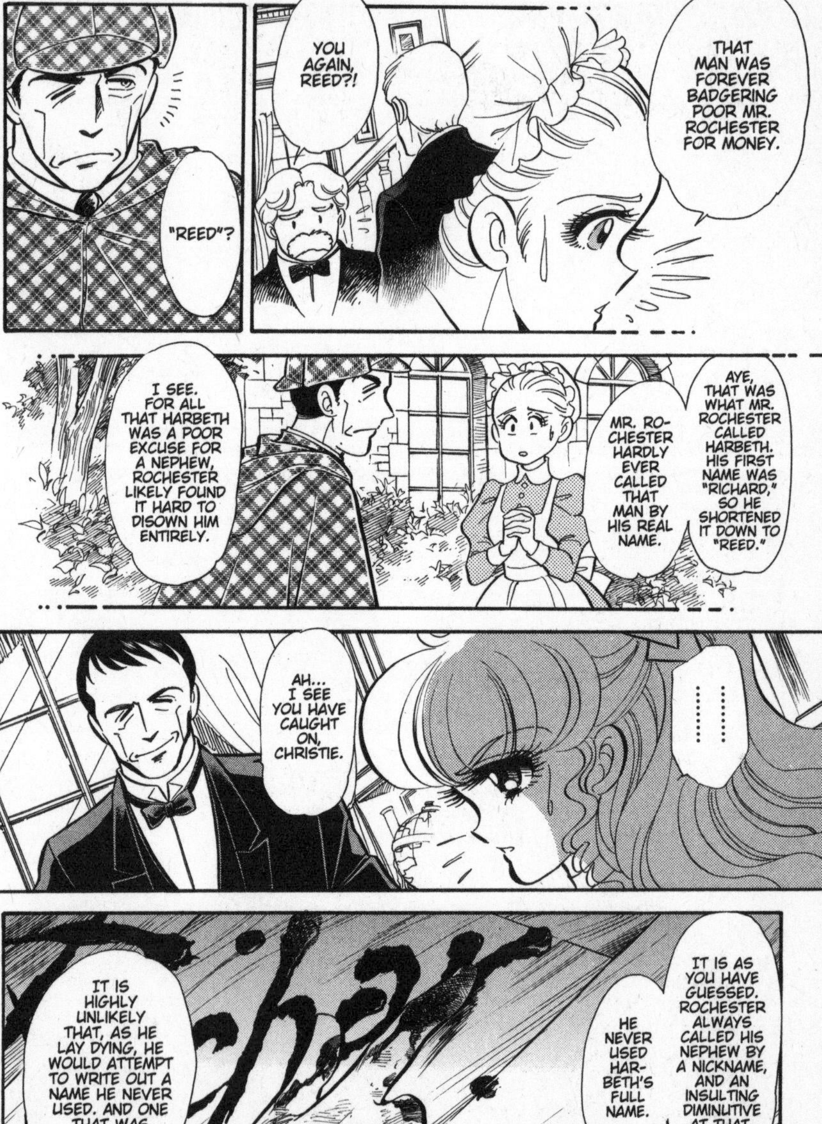
THAT MAN WAS FOREVER BADGERING POOR MR. ROCHESTER FOR MONEY.
YOU AGAIN, REED?!
"REED"?
AYE, THAT WAS WHAT MR. ROCHESTER CALLED HARBETH. HIS FIRST NAME WAS "RICHARD," SO HE SHORTENED IT DOWN TO "REED."
MR. ROCHESTER HARDLY EVER CALLED THAT MAN BY HIS REAL NAME.
I SEE. FOR ALL THAT HARBETH WAS A POOR EXCUSE FOR A NEPHEW, ROCHESTER LIKELY FOUND IT HARD TO DISOWN HIM ENTIRELY.
......
AH... I SEE YOU HAVE CAUGHT ON, CHRISTIE.
IT IS AS YOU HAVE GUESSED. ROCHESTER ALWAYS CALLED HIS NEPHEW BY A NICKNAME, AND AN INSULTING DIMINUTIVE AT THAT.
HE NEVER USED HARBETH'S FULL NAME.
IT IS HIGHLY UNLIKELY THAT, AS HE LAY DYING, HE WOULD ATTEMPT TO WRITE OUT A NAME HE NEVER USED. AND ONE THAT WAS LONGER, TO BOOT.

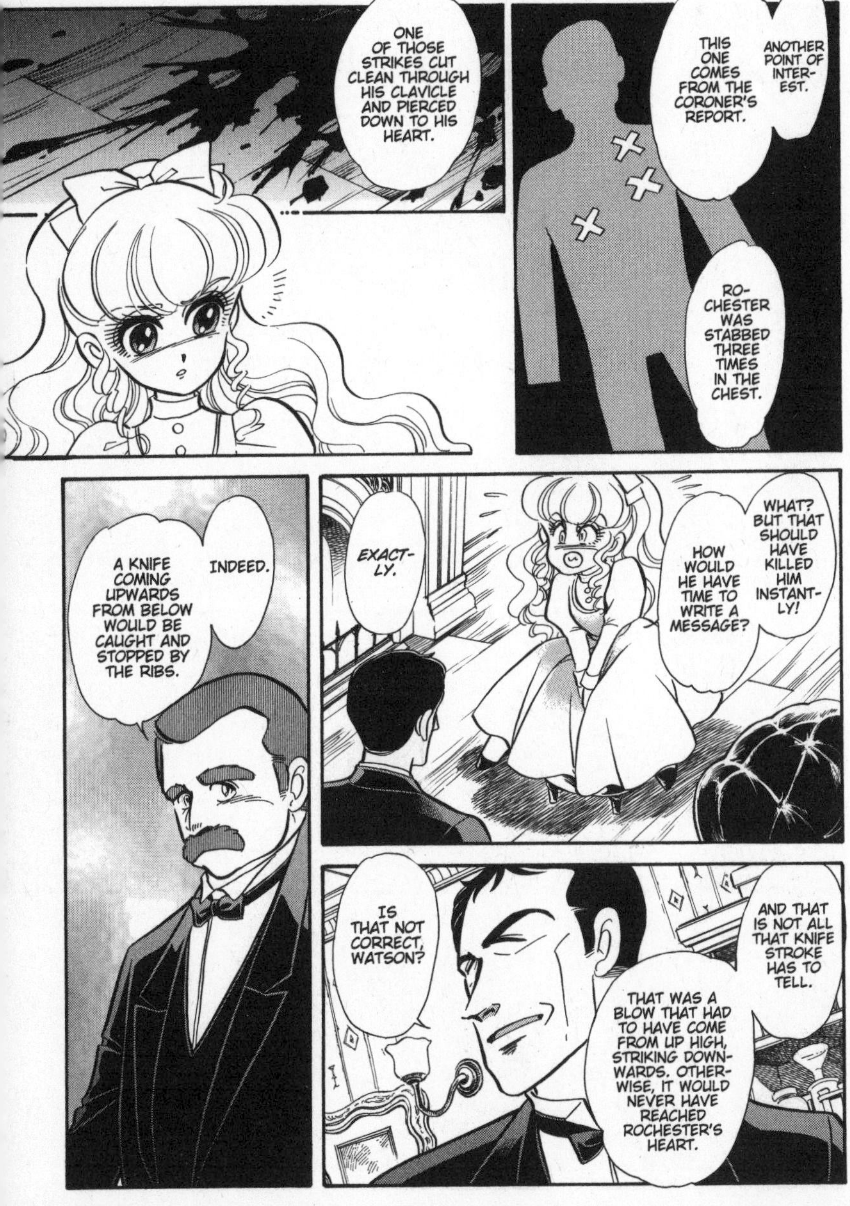
ANOTHER POINT OF INTEREST.
THIS ONE COMES FROM THE CORONER'S REPORT.
ROCHESTER WAS STABBED THREE TIMES IN THE CHEST.
ONE OF THOSE STRIKES CUT CLEAN THROUGH HIS CLAVICLE AND PIERCED DOWN TO HIS HEART.
WHAT? BUT THAT SHOULD HAVE KILLED HIM INSTANTLY!
HOW WOULD HE HAVE TIME TO WRITE A MESSAGE?
EXACTLY.
AND THAT IS NOT ALL THAT KNIFE STROKE HAS TO TELL.
THAT WAS A BLOW THAT HAD TO HAVE COME FROM UP HIGH, STRIKING DOWNWARDS. OTHERWISE, IT WOULD NEVER HAVE REACHED ROCHESTER'S HEART.
IS THAT NOT CORRECT, WATSON?
INDEED.
A KNIFE COMING UPWARDS FROM BELOW WOULD BE CAUGHT AND STOPPED BY THE RIBS.

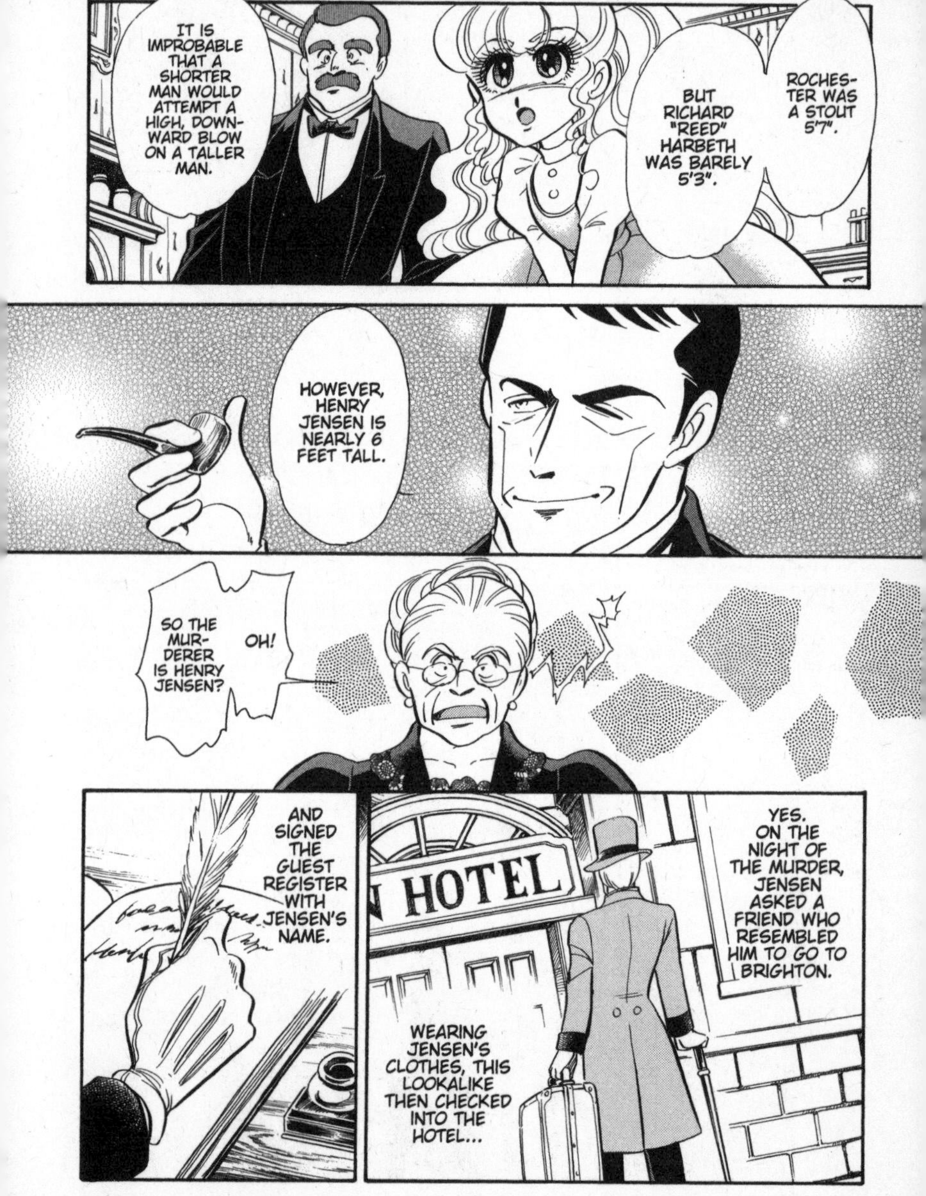
ROCHESTER WAS A STOUT 5'7".
BUT RICHARD "REED" HARBETH WAS BARELY 5'3".
IT IS IMPROBABLE THAT A SHORTER MAN WOULD ATTEMPT A HIGH, DOWNWARD BLOW ON A TALLER MAN.
HOWEVER, HENRY JENSEN IS NEARLY 6 FEET TALL.
OH!
SO THE MURDERER IS HENRY JENSEN?
YES. ON THE NIGHT OF THE MURDER, JENSEN ASKED A FRIEND WHO RESEMBLED HIM TO GO TO BRIGHTON.
HOTEL
WEARING JENSEN'S CLOTHES, THIS LOOKALIKE THEN CHECKED INTO THE HOTEL...
AND SIGNED THE GUEST REGISTER WITH JENSEN'S NAME.

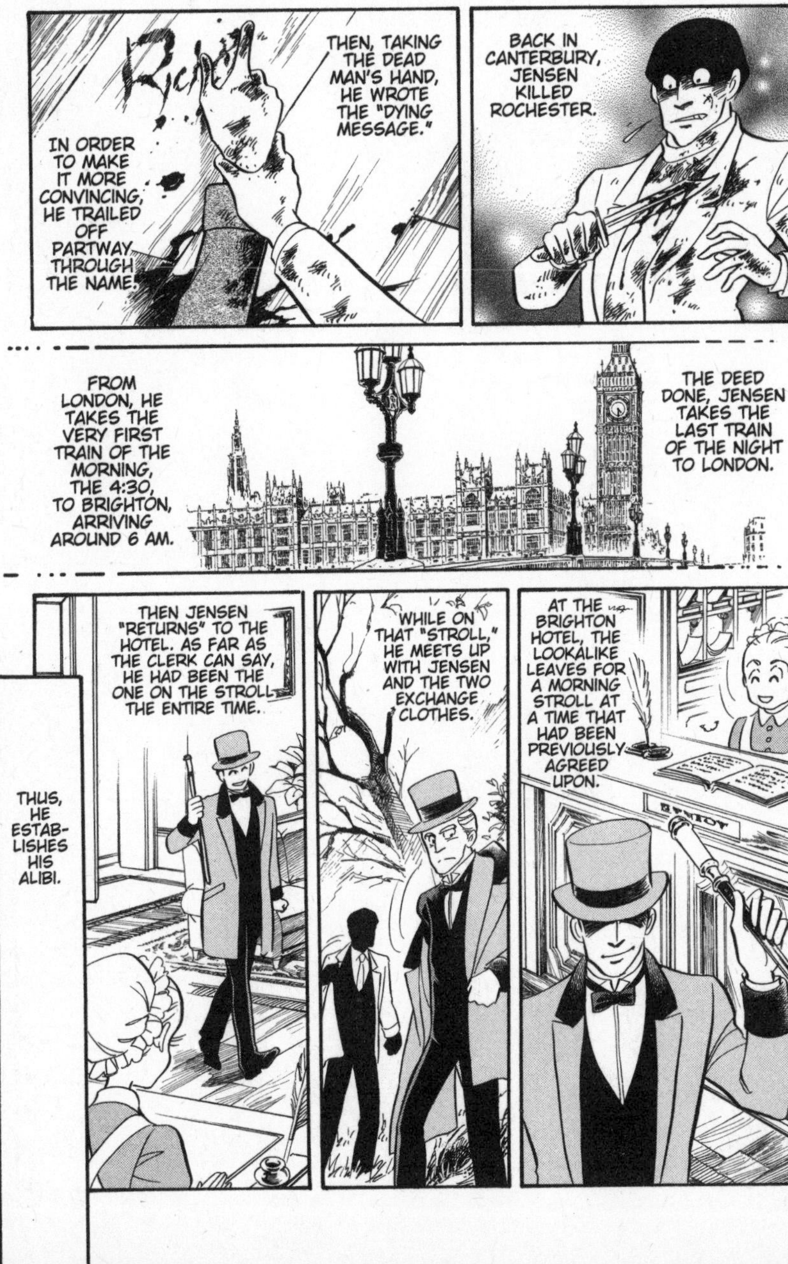
BACK IN CANTERBURY, JENSEN KILLED ROCHESTER.
THEN, TAKING THE DEAD MAN'S HAND, HE WROTE THE "DYING MESSAGE."
IN ORDER TO MAKE IT MORE CONVINCING, HE TRAILED OFF PARTWAY THROUGH THE NAME.
THE DEED DONE, JENSEN TAKES THE LAST TRAIN OF THE NIGHT TO LONDON.
FROM LONDON, HE TAKES THE VERY FIRST TRAIN OF THE MORNING, THE 4:30, TO BRIGHTON, ARRIVING AROUND 6 AM.
AT THE BRIGHTON HOTEL, THE LOOKALIKE LEAVES FOR A MORNING STROLL AT A TIME THAT HAD BEEN PREVIOUSLY AGREED UPON.
WHILE ON THAT "STROLL," HE MEETS UP WITH JENSEN AND THE TWO EXCHANGE CLOTHES.
THEN JENSEN "RETURNS" TO THE HOTEL. AS FAR AS THE CLERK CAN SAY, HE HAD BEEN THE ONE ON THE STROLL THE ENTIRE TIME.
THUS, HE ESTAB-LISHES HIS ALIBI.

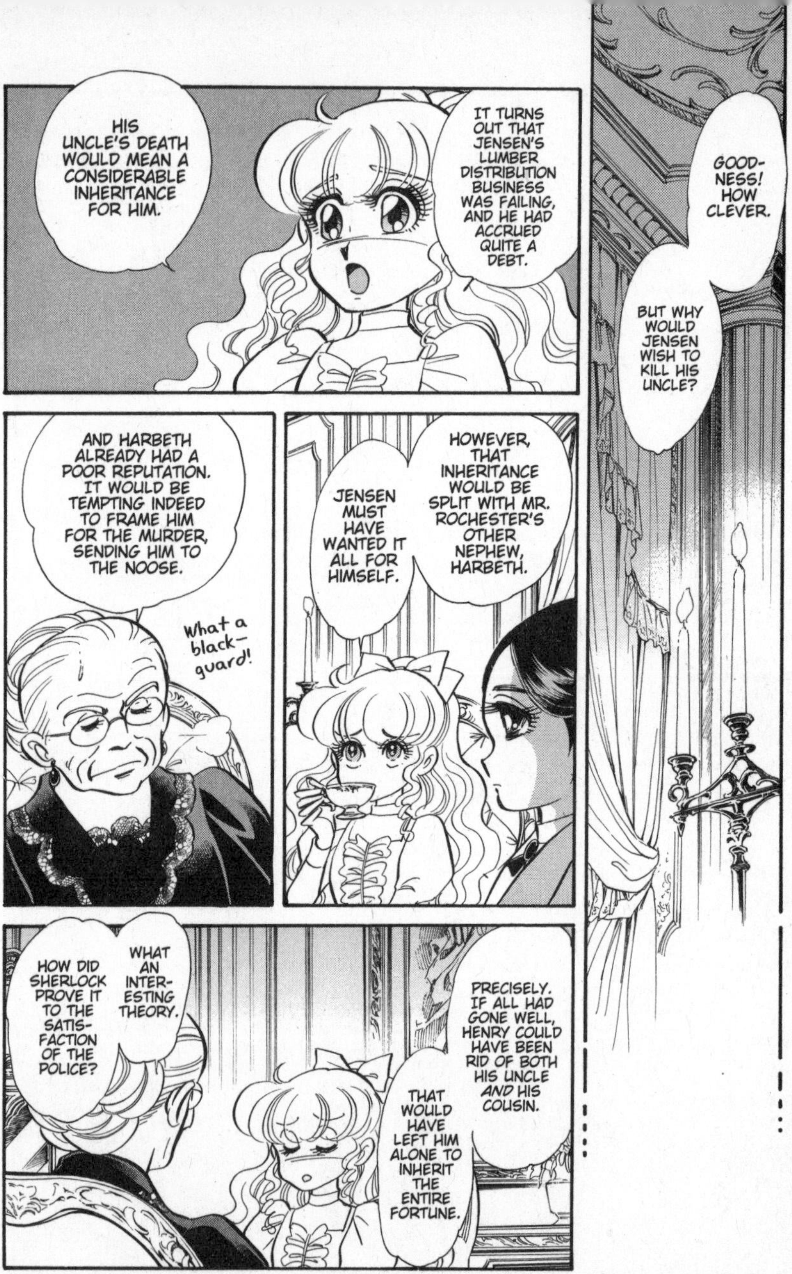
GOOD-NESS! HOW CLEVER.
BUT WHY WOULD JENSEN WISH TO KILL HIS UNCLE?
IT TURNS OUT THAT JENSEN'S LUMBER DISTRIBUTION BUSINESS WAS FAILING, AND HE HAD ACCRUED QUITE A DEBT.
HIS UNCLE'S DEATH WOULD MEAN A CONSIDERABLE INHERITANCE FOR HIM.
HOWEVER, THAT INHERITANCE WOULD BE SPLIT WITH MR. ROCHESTER'S OTHER NEPHEW, HARBETH.
JENSEN MUST HAVE WANTED IT ALL FOR HIMSELF.
AND HARBETH ALREADY HAD A POOR REPUTATION. IT WOULD BE TEMPTING INDEED TO FRAME HIM FOR THE MURDER, SENDING HIM TO THE NOOSE.
What a black-guard!
PRECISELY. IF ALL HAD GONE WELL, HENRY COULD HAVE BEEN RID OF BOTH HIS UNCLE *AND* HIS COUSIN.
THAT WOULD HAVE LEFT HIM ALONE TO INHERIT THE ENTIRE FORTUNE.
WHAT AN INTER-ESTING THEORY.
HOW DID SHERLOCK PROVE IT TO THE SATIS-FACTION OF THE POLICE?

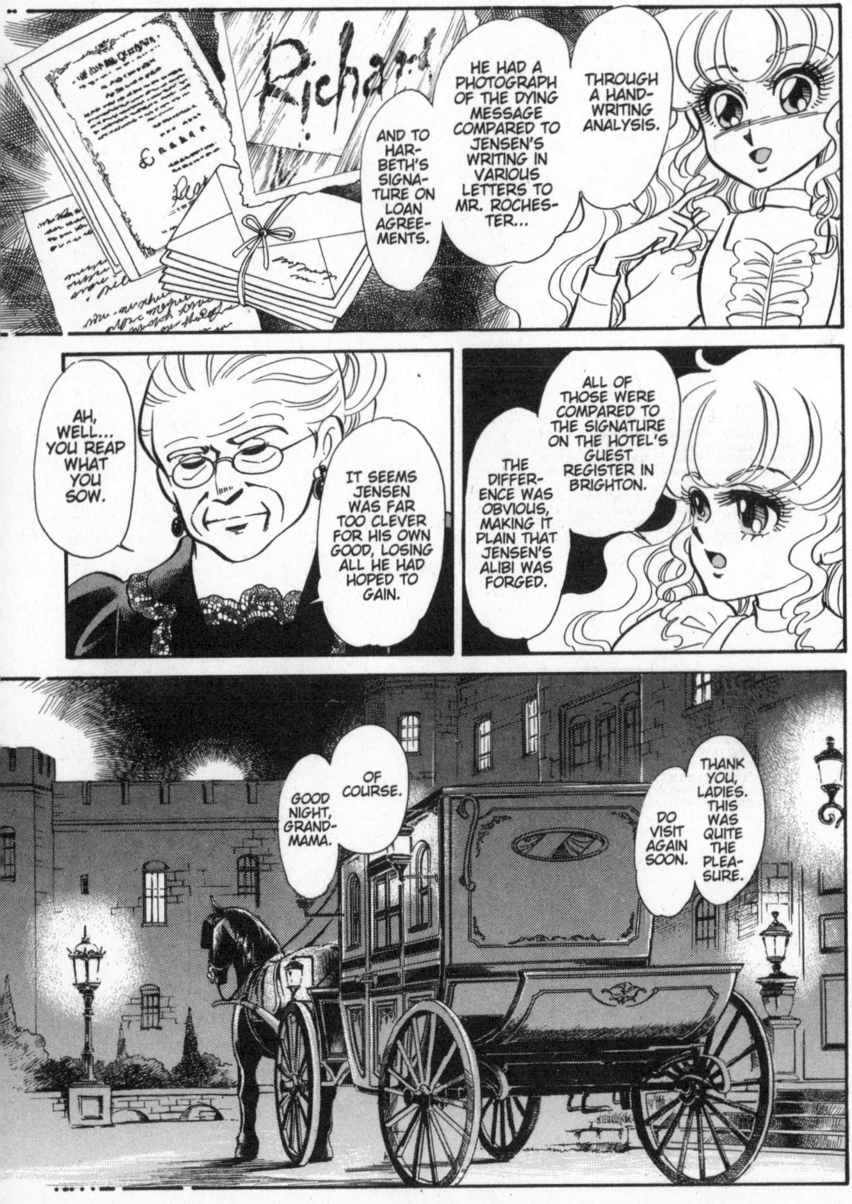
THROUGH A HAND-WRITING ANALYSIS.
HE HAD A PHOTOGRAPH OF THE DYING MESSAGE COMPARED TO JENSEN'S WRITING IN VARIOUS LETTERS TO MR. ROCHESTER...
Richard
AND TO HARBETH'S SIGNATURE ON LOAN AGREEMENTS.
ALL OF THOSE WERE COMPARED TO THE SIGNATURE ON THE HOTEL'S GUEST REGISTER IN BRIGHTON.
THE DIFFERENCE WAS OBVIOUS, MAKING IT PLAIN THAT JENSEN'S ALIBI WAS FORGED.
IT SEEMS JENSEN WAS FAR TOO CLEVER FOR HIS OWN GOOD, LOSING ALL HE HAD HOPED TO GAIN.
AH, WELL... YOU REAP WHAT YOU SOW.
THANK YOU, LADIES. THIS WAS QUITE THE PLEASURE.
DO VISIT AGAIN SOON.
OF COURSE.
GOOD NIGHT, GRANDMAMA.

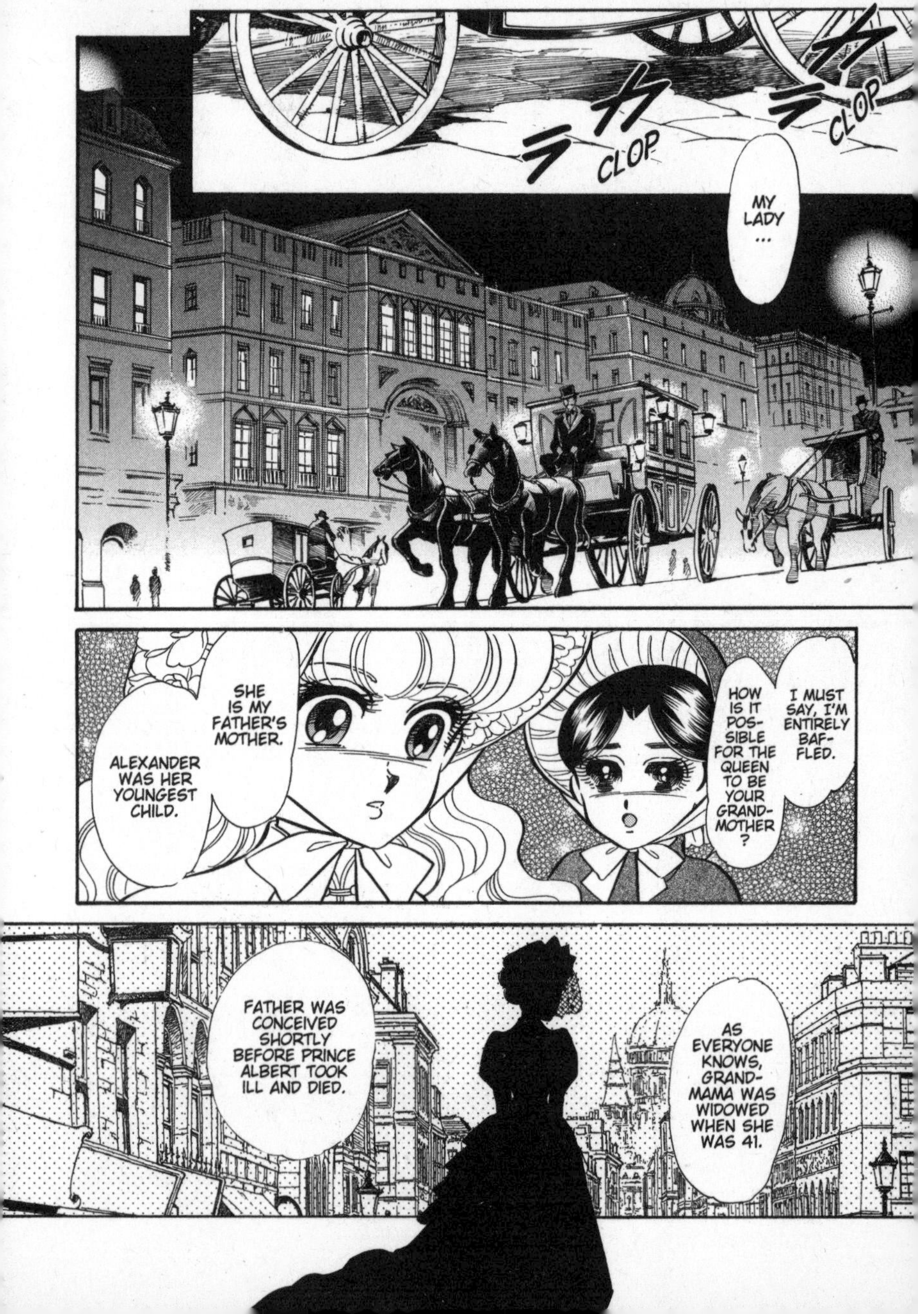

カラ
CLOP
カラ
CLOP
MY LADY ...
I MUST SAY, I'M ENTIRELY BAF-FLED.
HOW IS IT POS-SIBLE FOR THE QUEEN TO BE YOUR GRAND-MOTHER?
SHE IS MY FATHER'S MOTHER.
ALEXANDER WAS HER YOUNGEST CHILD.
AS EVERYONE KNOWS, GRAND-MAMA WAS WIDOWED WHEN SHE WAS 41.
FATHER WAS CONCEIVED SHORTLY BEFORE PRINCE ALBERT TOOK ILL AND DIED.

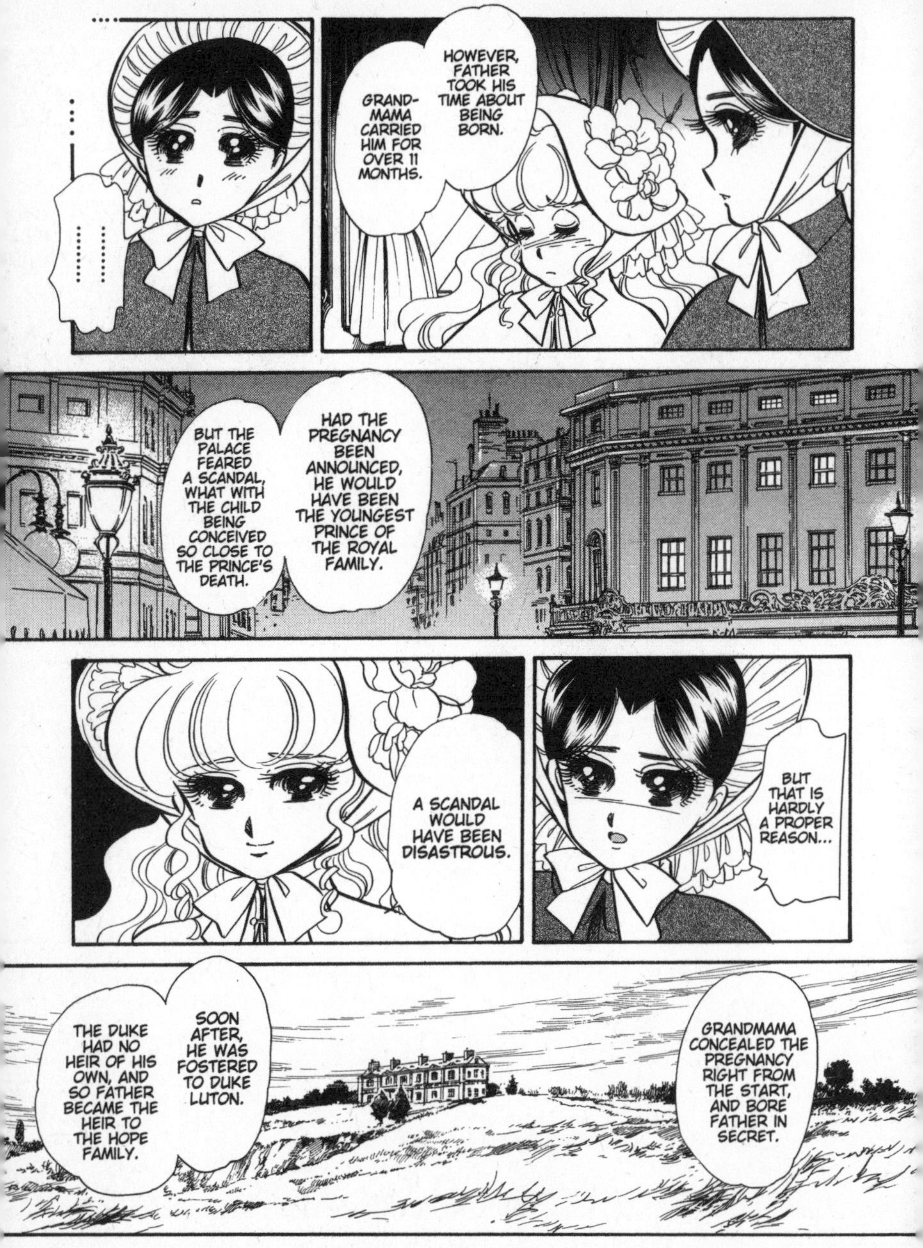
HOWEVER, FATHER TOOK HIS TIME ABOUT BEING BORN.
GRAND-MAMA CARRIED HIM FOR OVER 11 MONTHS.
.....
.....
......
HAD THE PREGNANCY BEEN ANNOUNCED, HE WOULD HAVE BEEN THE YOUNGEST PRINCE OF THE ROYAL FAMILY.
BUT THE PALACE FEARED A SCANDAL, WHAT WITH THE CHILD BEING CONCEIVED SO CLOSE TO THE PRINCE'S DEATH.
BUT THAT IS HARDLY A PROPER REASON...
A SCANDAL WOULD HAVE BEEN DISASTROUS.
GRANDMAMA CONCEALED THE PREGNANCY RIGHT FROM THE START, AND BORE FATHER IN SECRET.
SOON AFTER, HE WAS FOSTERED TO DUKE LUTON.
THE DUKE HAD NO HEIR OF HIS OWN, AND SO FATHER BECAME THE HEIR TO THE HOPE FAMILY.

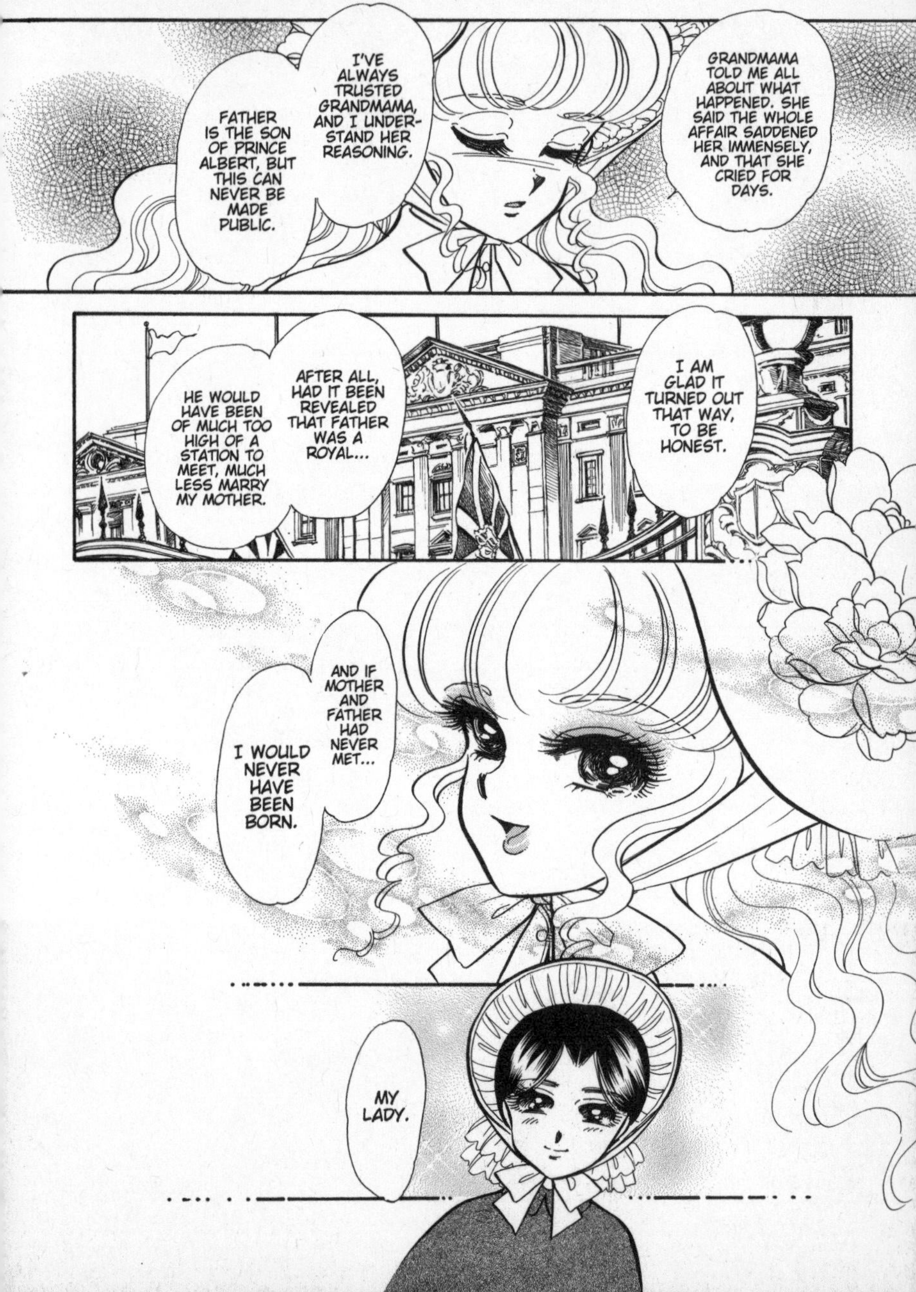
GRANDMAMA TOLD ME ALL ABOUT WHAT HAPPENED. SHE SAID THE WHOLE AFFAIR SADDENED HER IMMENSELY, AND THAT SHE CRIED FOR DAYS.
I'VE ALWAYS TRUSTED GRANDMAMA, AND I UNDER-STAND HER REASONING.
FATHER IS THE SON OF PRINCE ALBERT, BUT THIS CAN NEVER BE MADE PUBLIC.
I AM GLAD IT TURNED OUT THAT WAY, TO BE HONEST.
AFTER ALL, HAD IT BEEN REVEALED THAT FATHER WAS A ROYAL...
HE WOULD HAVE BEEN OF MUCH TOO HIGH OF A STATION TO MEET, MUCH LESS MARRY MY MOTHER.
AND IF MOTHER AND FATHER HAD NEVER MET...
I WOULD NEVER HAVE BEEN BORN.
MY LADY.

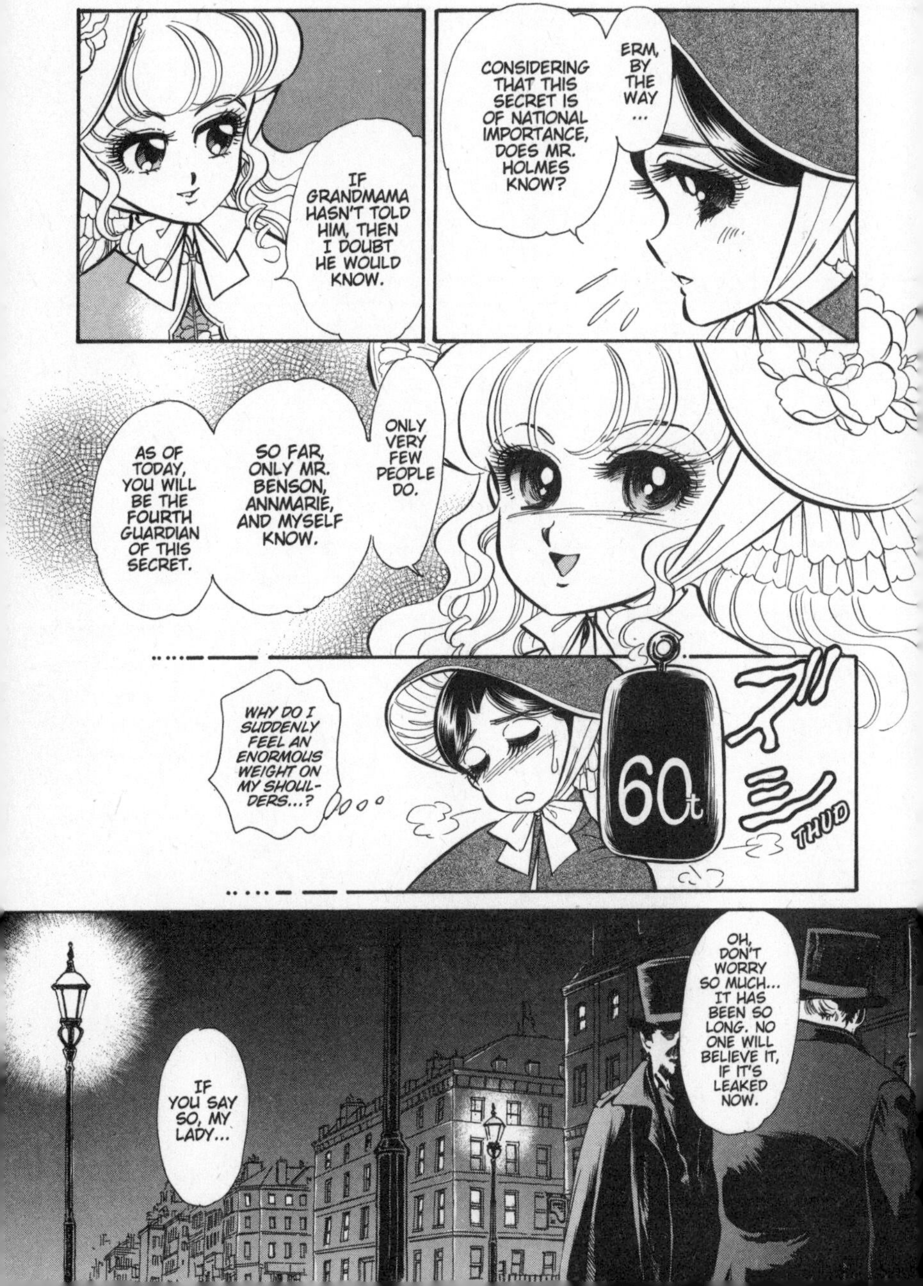
ERM, BY THE WAY...
CONSIDERING THAT THIS SECRET IS OF NATIONAL IMPORTANCE, DOES MR. HOLMES KNOW?
IF GRANDMAMA HASN'T TOLD HIM, THEN I DOUBT HE WOULD KNOW.
ONLY VERY FEW PEOPLE DO.
SO FAR, ONLY MR. BENSON, ANNMARIE, AND MYSELF KNOW.
AS OF TODAY, YOU WILL BE THE FOURTH GUARDIAN OF THIS SECRET.
60t
THUD
WHY DO I SUDDENLY FEEL AN ENORMOUS WEIGHT ON MY SHOULDERS...?
OH, DON'T WORRY SO MUCH... IT HAS BEEN SO LONG. NO ONE WILL BELIEVE IT, IF IT'S LEAKED NOW.
IF YOU SAY SO, MY LADY...

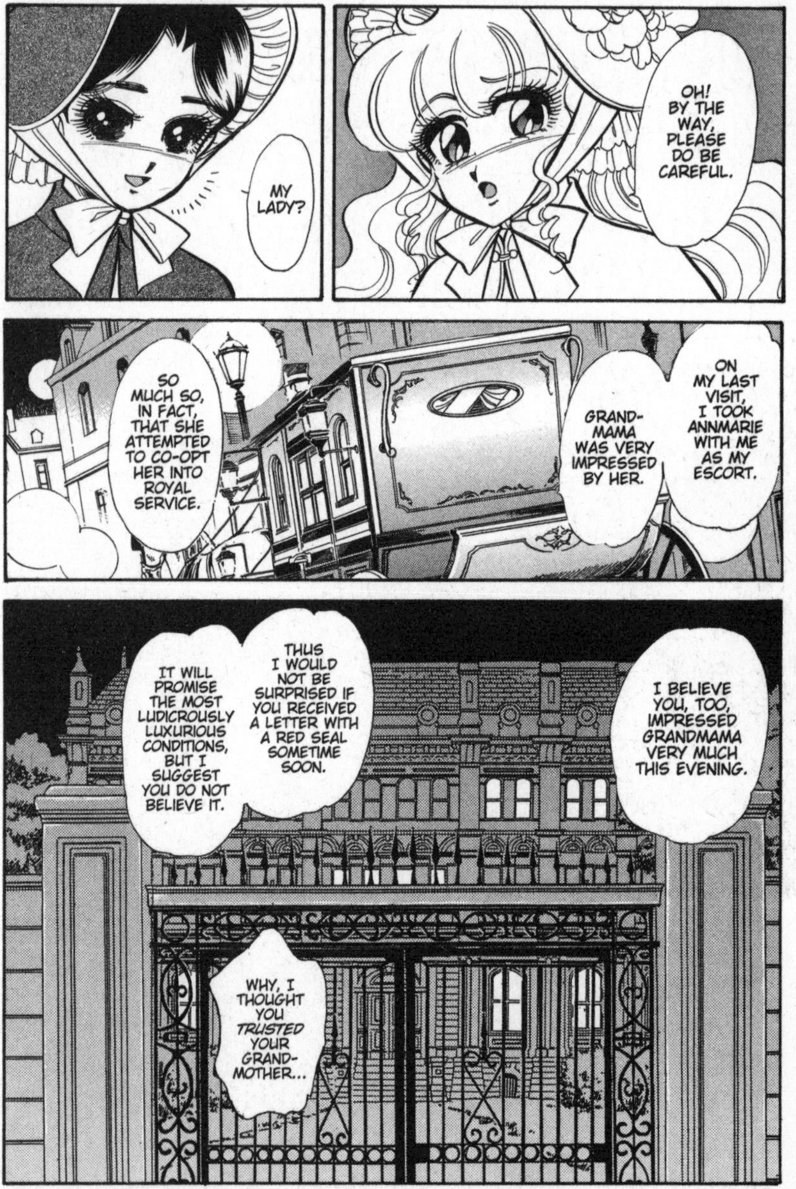
OH! BY THE WAY, PLEASE DO BE CAREFUL.
MY LADY?
ON MY LAST VISIT, I TOOK ANNMARIE WITH ME AS MY ESCORT.
GRANDMAMA WAS VERY IMPRESSED BY HER.
SO MUCH SO, IN FACT, THAT SHE ATTEMPTED TO CO-OPT HER INTO ROYAL SERVICE.
I BELIEVE YOU, TOO, IMPRESSED GRANDMAMA VERY MUCH THIS EVENING.
THUS I WOULD NOT BE SURPRISED IF YOU RECEIVED A LETTER WITH A RED SEAL SOMETIME SOON.
IT WILL PROMISE THE MOST LUDICROUSLY LUXURIOUS CONDITIONS, BUT I SUGGEST YOU DO NOT BELIEVE IT.
WHY, I THOUGHT YOU *TRUSTED* YOUR GRANDMOTHER...

The Adventure of the Flying Dancer (1)

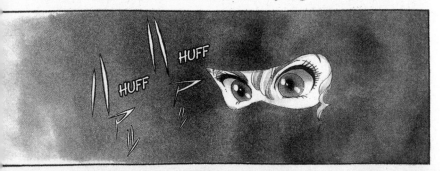

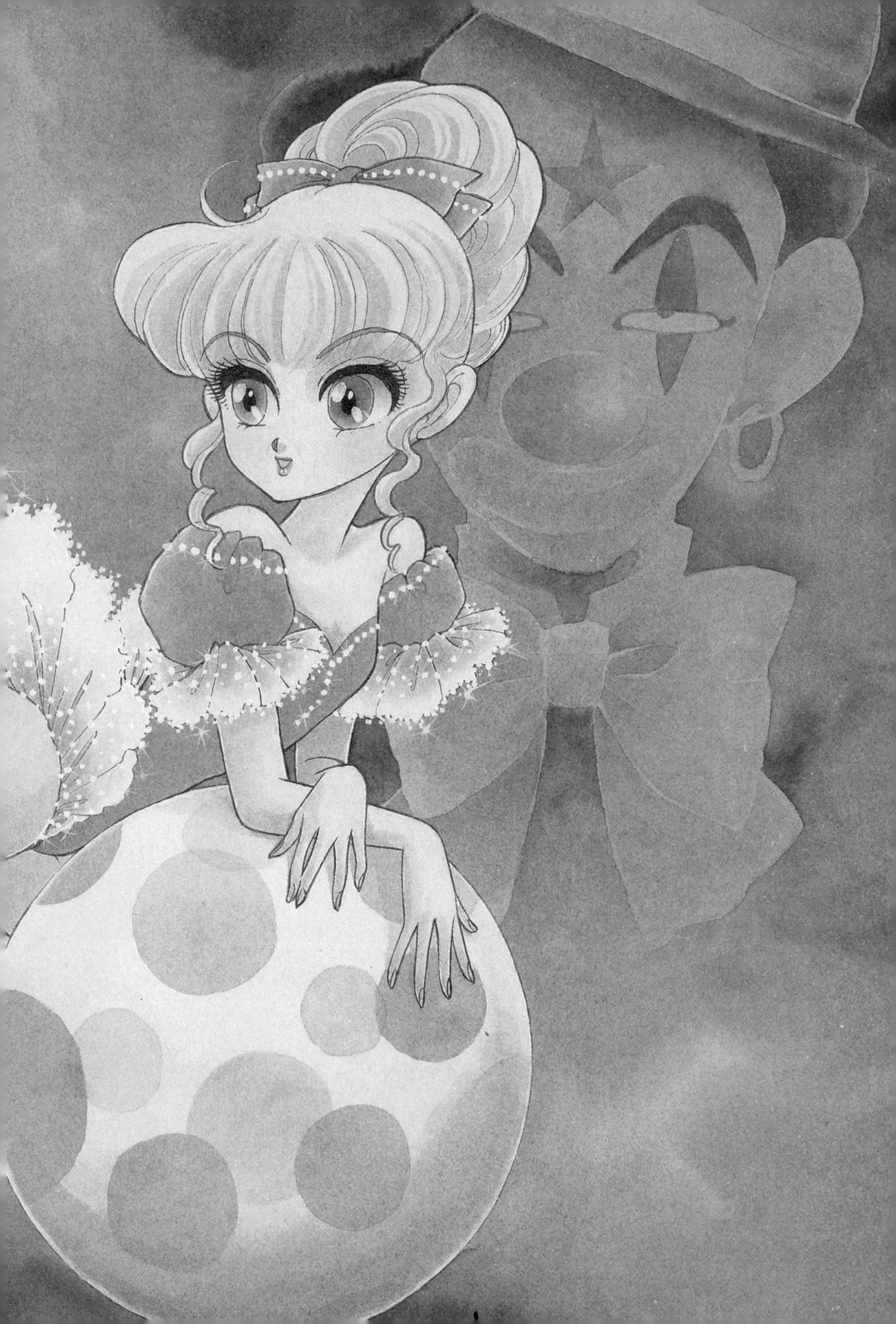

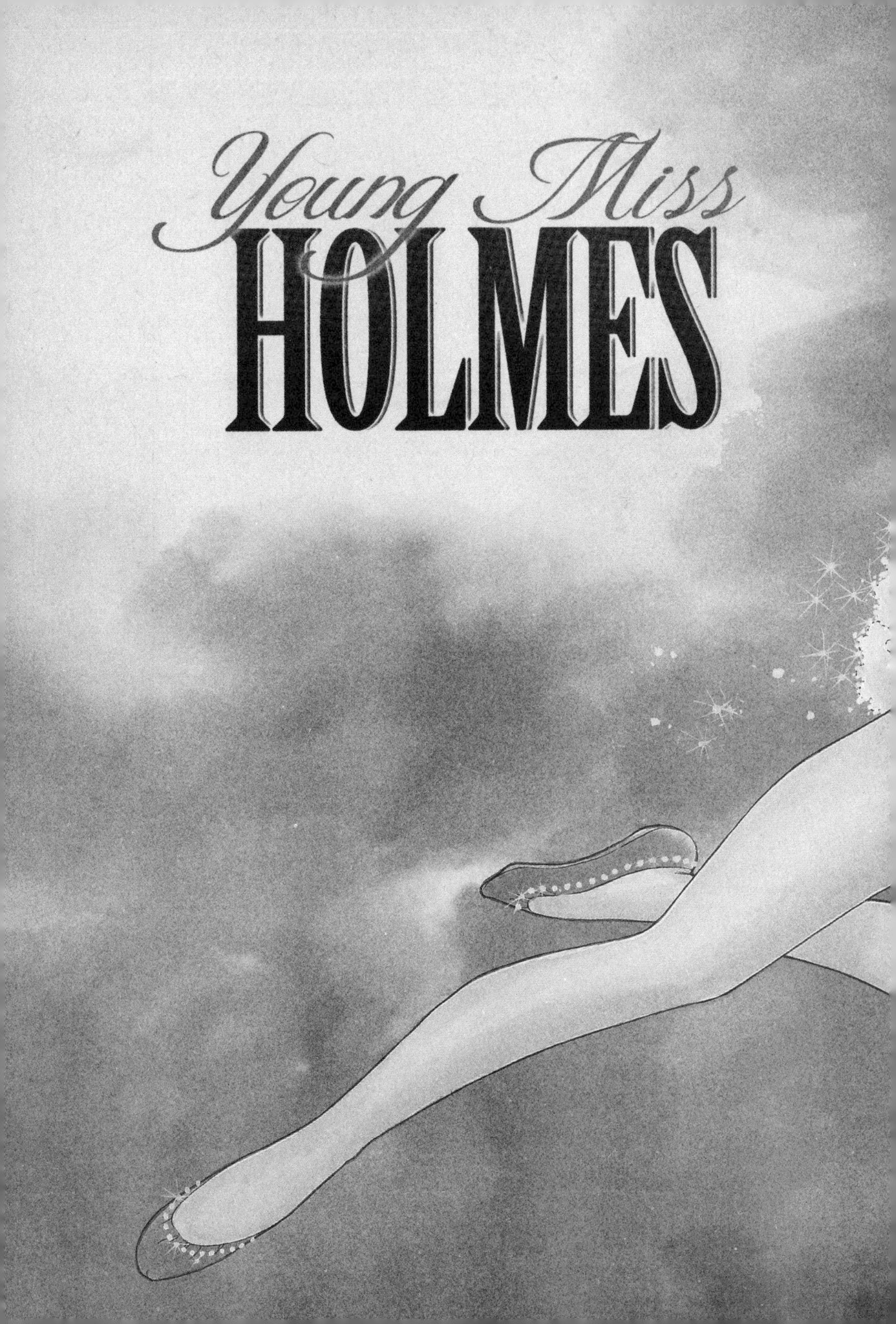
Young Miss
HOLMES

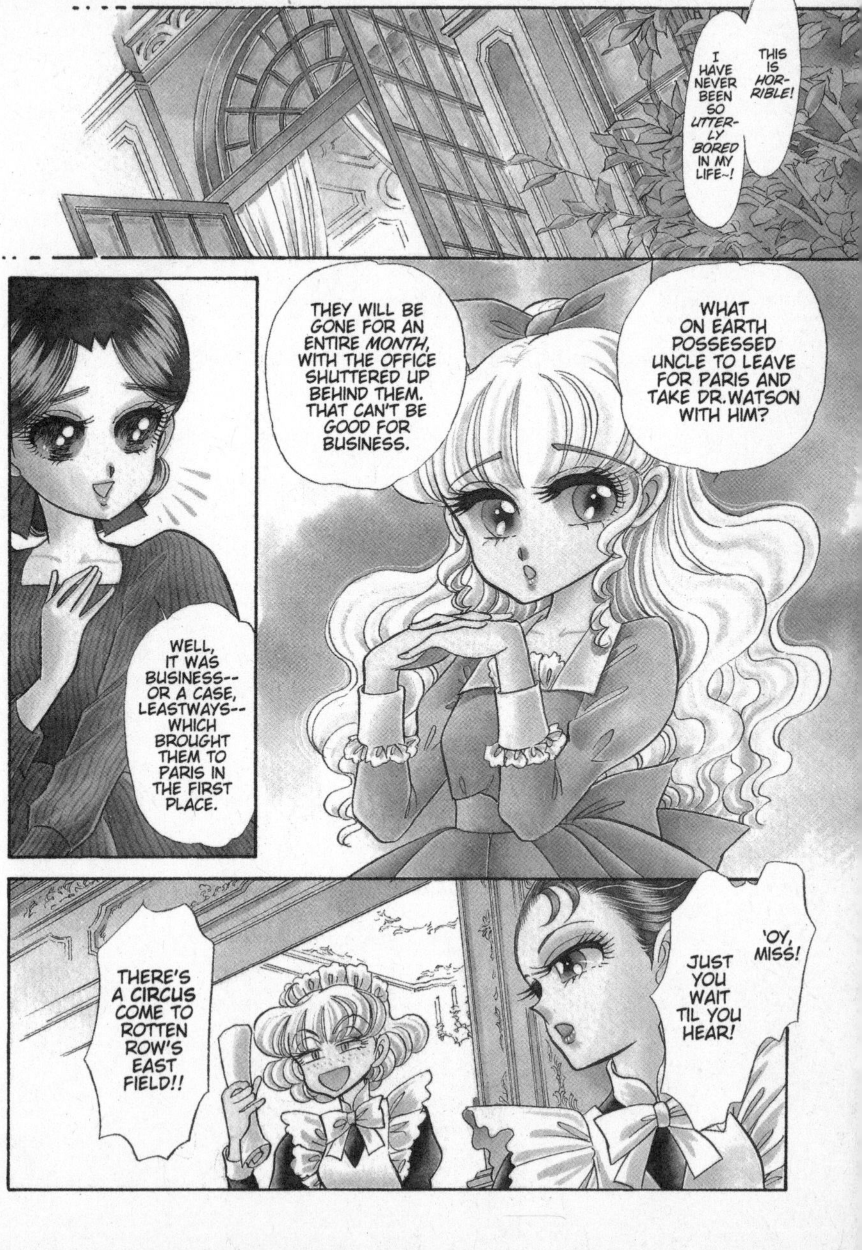
THIS IS HOR-RIBLE!
I HAVE NEVER BEEN SO UTTER-LY BORED IN MY LIFE~!
WHAT ON EARTH POSSESSED UNCLE TO LEAVE FOR PARIS AND TAKE DR.WATSON WITH HIM?
THEY WILL BE GONE FOR AN ENTIRE MONTH, WITH THE OFFICE SHUTTERED UP BEHIND THEM. THAT CAN'T BE GOOD FOR BUSINESS.
WELL, IT WAS BUSINESS-- OR A CASE, LEASTWAYS-- WHICH BROUGHT THEM TO PARIS IN THE FIRST PLACE.
'OY, MISS!
JUST YOU WAIT TIL YOU HEAR!
THERE'S A CIRCUS COME TO ROTTEN ROW'S EAST FIELD!!

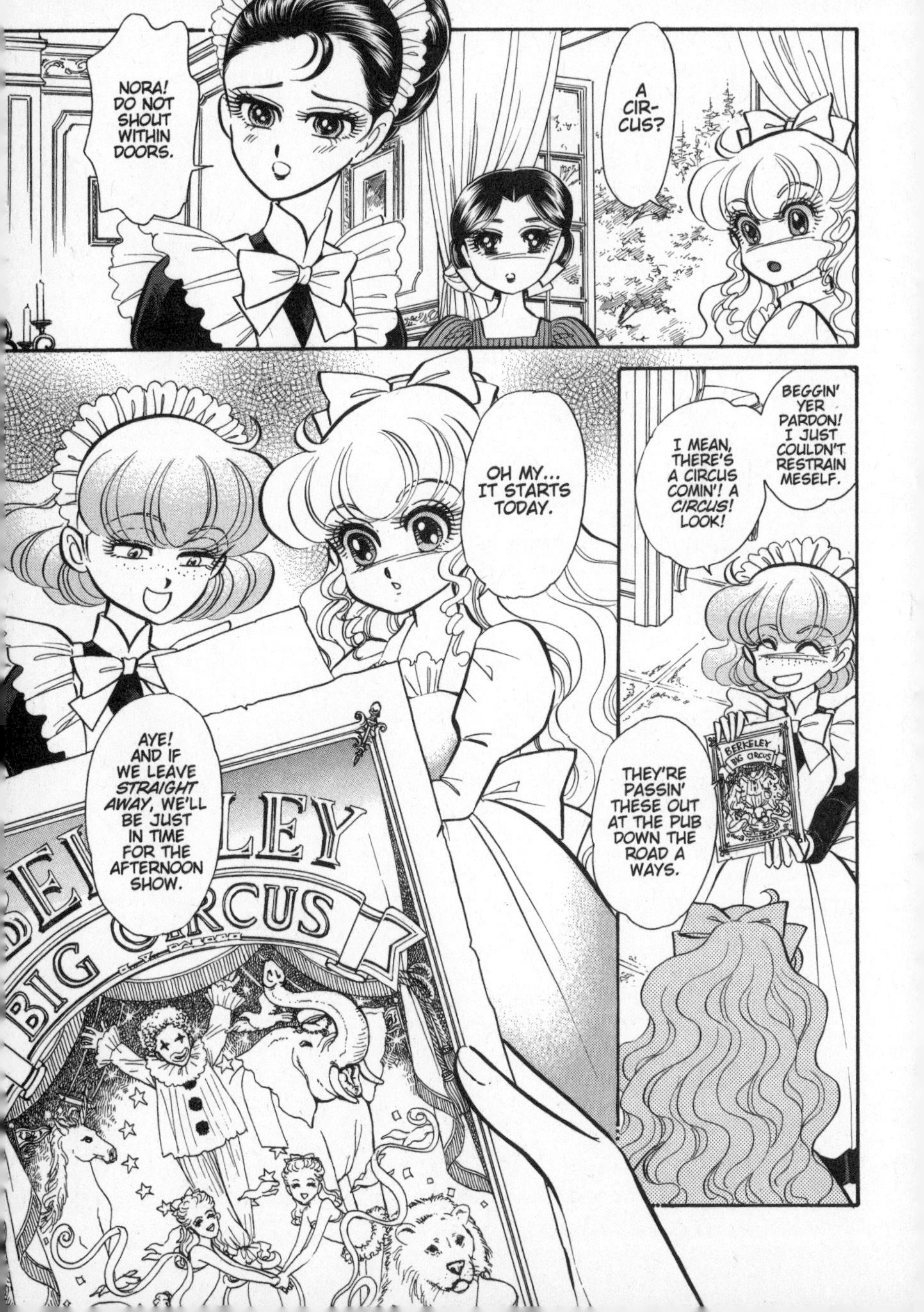
A CIR-CUS?
NORA! DO NOT SHOUT WITHIN DOORS.
BEGGIN' YER PARDON! I JUST COULDN'T RESTRAIN MESELF.
I MEAN, THERE'S A CIRCUS COMIN'! A *CIRCUS*! LOOK!
BERKELEY BIG CIRCUS
THEY'RE PASSIN' THESE OUT AT THE PUB DOWN THE ROAD A WAYS.
OH MY... IT STARTS TODAY.
AYE! AND IF WE LEAVE *STRAIGHT AWAY*, WE'LL BE JUST IN TIME FOR THE AFTERNOON SHOW.

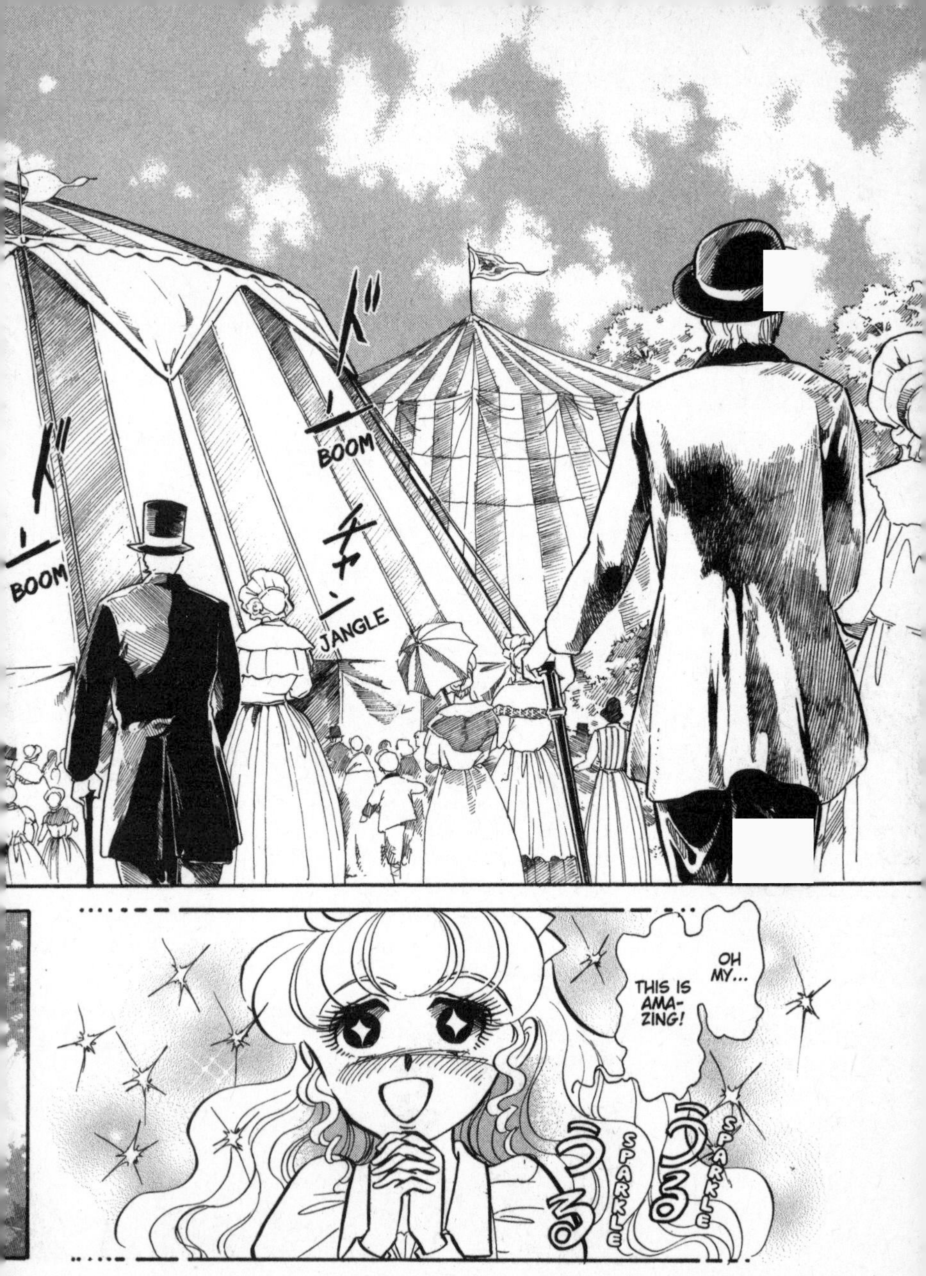
BOOM
JANGLE
BOOM
OH MY... THIS IS AMA-ZING!
SPARKLE
SPARKLE

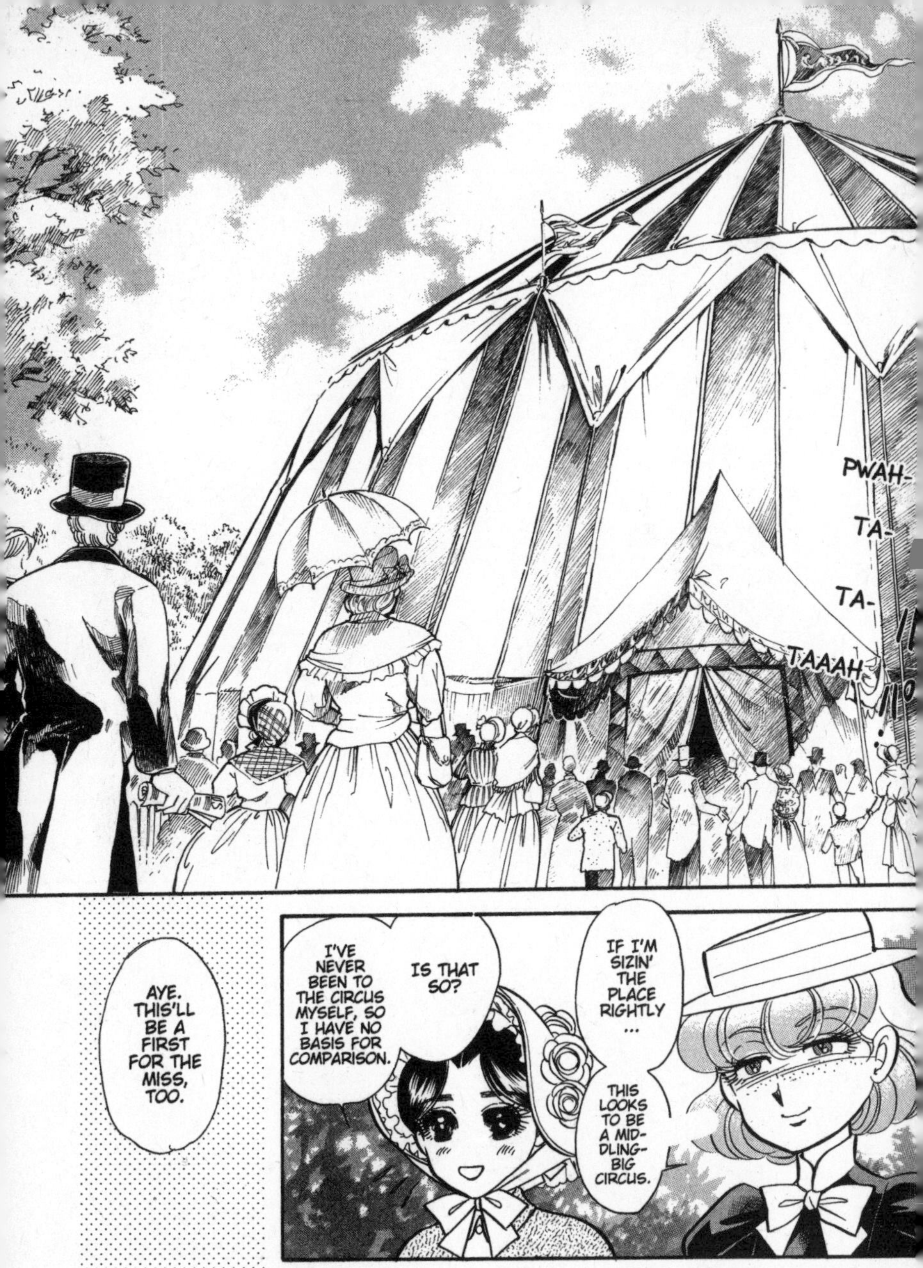
PWAH- TA- TA- TAAAH
IF I'M SIZIN' THE PLACE RIGHTLY ...
THIS LOOKS TO BE A MID-DLING-BIG CIRCUS.
IS THAT SO?
I'VE NEVER BEEN TO THE CIRCUS MYSELF, SO I HAVE NO BASIS FOR COMPARISON.
AYE. THIS'LL BE A FIRST FOR THE MISS, TOO.

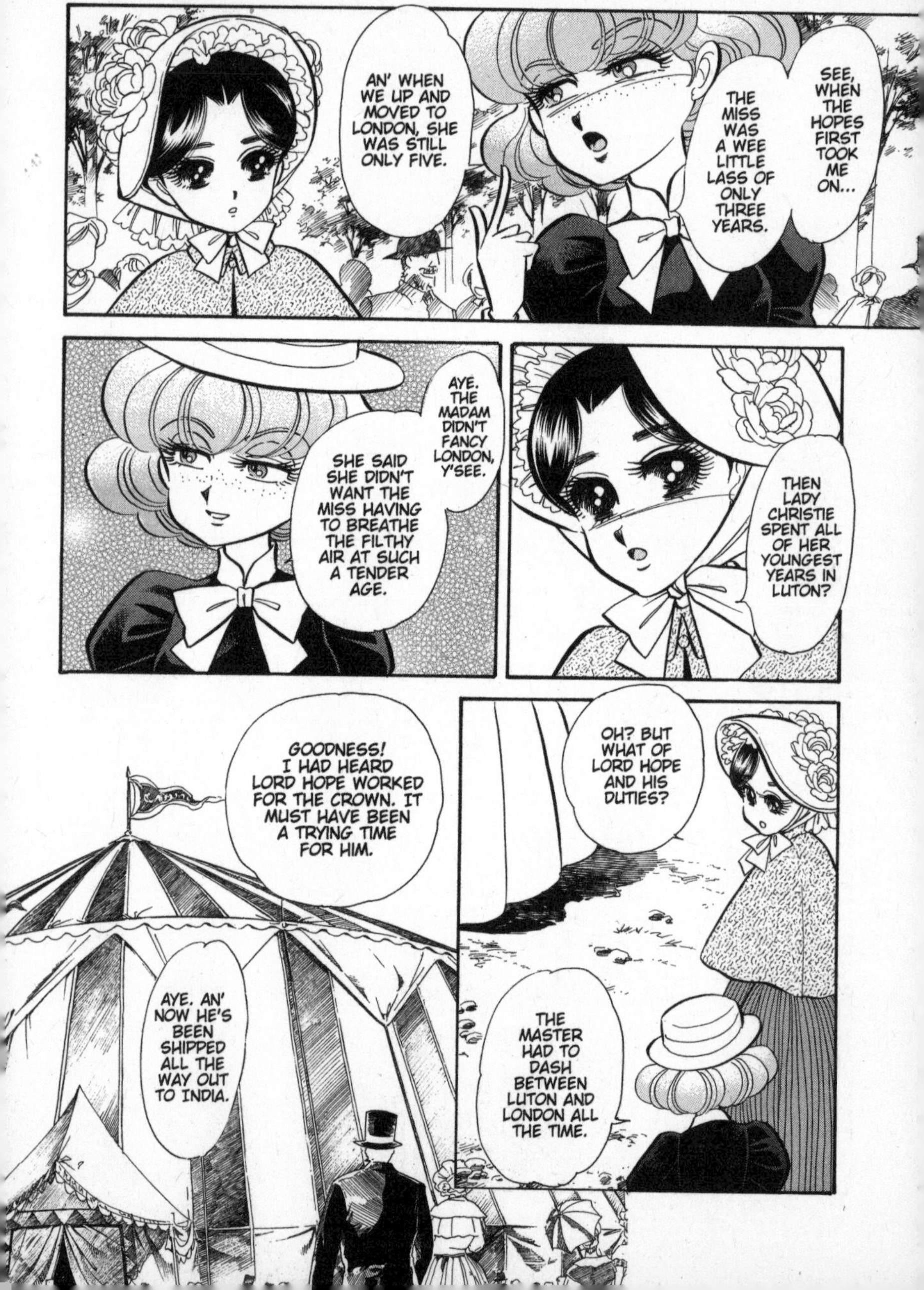
SEE, WHEN THE HOPES FIRST TOOK ME ON...
THE MISS WAS A WEE LITTLE LASS OF ONLY THREE YEARS.
AN' WHEN WE UP AND MOVED TO LONDON, SHE WAS STILL ONLY FIVE.
THEN LADY CHRISTIE SPENT ALL OF HER YOUNGEST YEARS IN LUTON?
AYE. THE MADAM DIDN'T FANCY LONDON, Y'SEE.
SHE SAID SHE DIDN'T WANT THE MISS HAVING TO BREATHE THE FILTHY AIR AT SUCH A TENDER AGE.
OH? BUT WHAT OF LORD HOPE AND HIS DUTIES?
THE MASTER HAD TO DASH BETWEEN LUTON AND LONDON ALL THE TIME.
GOODNESS! I HAD HEARD LORD HOPE WORKED FOR THE CROWN. IT MUST HAVE BEEN A TRYING TIME FOR HIM.
AYE. AN' NOW HE'S BEEN SHIPPED ALL THE WAY OUT TO INDIA.

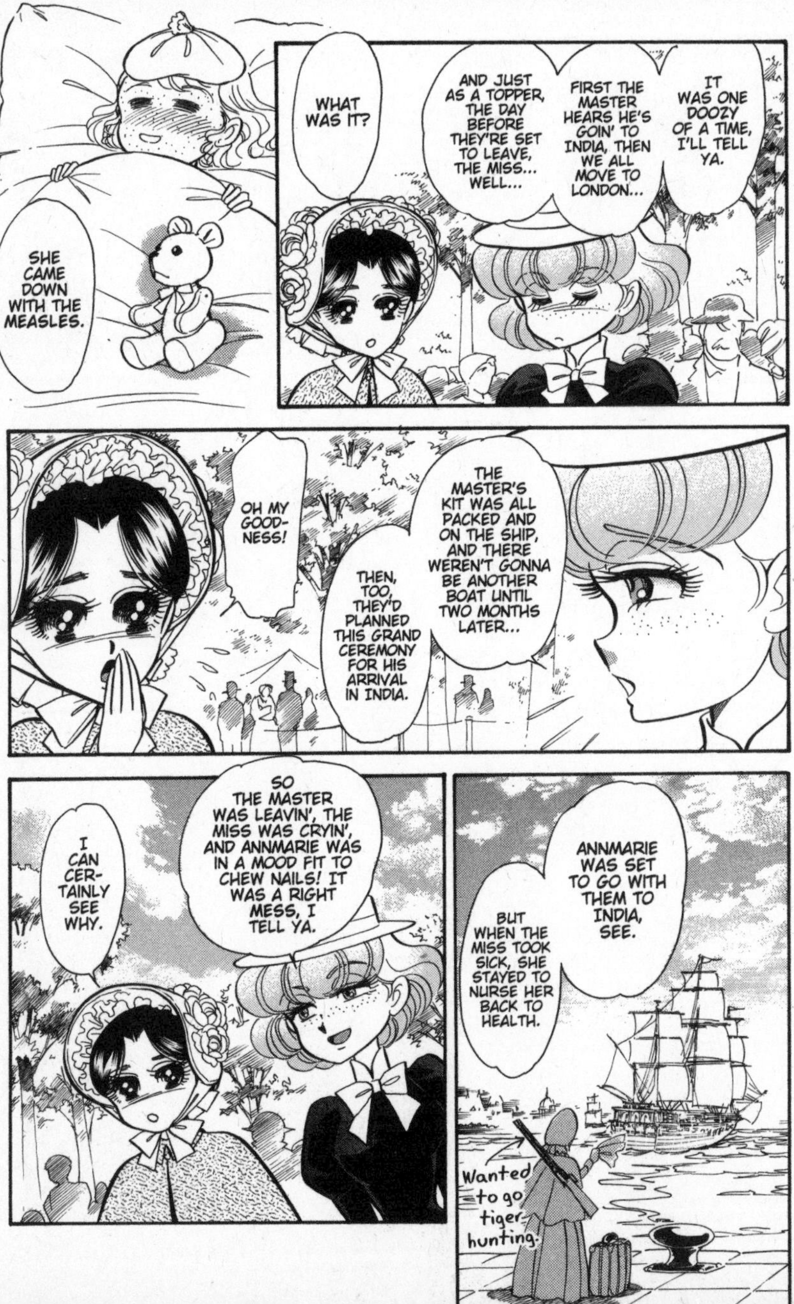
IT WAS ONE DOOZY OF A TIME, I'LL TELL YA.
FIRST THE MASTER HEARS HE'S GOIN' TO INDIA, THEN WE ALL MOVE TO LONDON...
AND JUST AS A TOPPER, THE DAY BEFORE THEY'RE SET TO LEAVE, THE MISS... WELL...
WHAT WAS IT?
SHE CAME DOWN WITH THE MEASLES.
THE MASTER'S KIT WAS ALL PACKED AND ON THE SHIP, AND THERE WEREN'T GONNA BE ANOTHER BOAT UNTIL TWO MONTHS LATER...
THEN, TOO, THEY'D PLANNED THIS GRAND CEREMONY FOR HIS ARRIVAL IN INDIA.
OH MY GOOD-NESS!
ANNMARIE WAS SET TO GO WITH THEM TO INDIA, SEE.
BUT WHEN THE MISS TOOK SICK, SHE STAYED TO NURSE HER BACK TO HEALTH.
Wanted to go tiger-hunting.
SO THE MASTER WAS LEAVIN', THE MISS WAS CRYIN', AND ANNMARIE WAS IN A MOOD FIT TO CHEW NAILS! IT WAS A RIGHT MESS, I TELL YA.
I CAN CER-TAINLY SEE WHY.

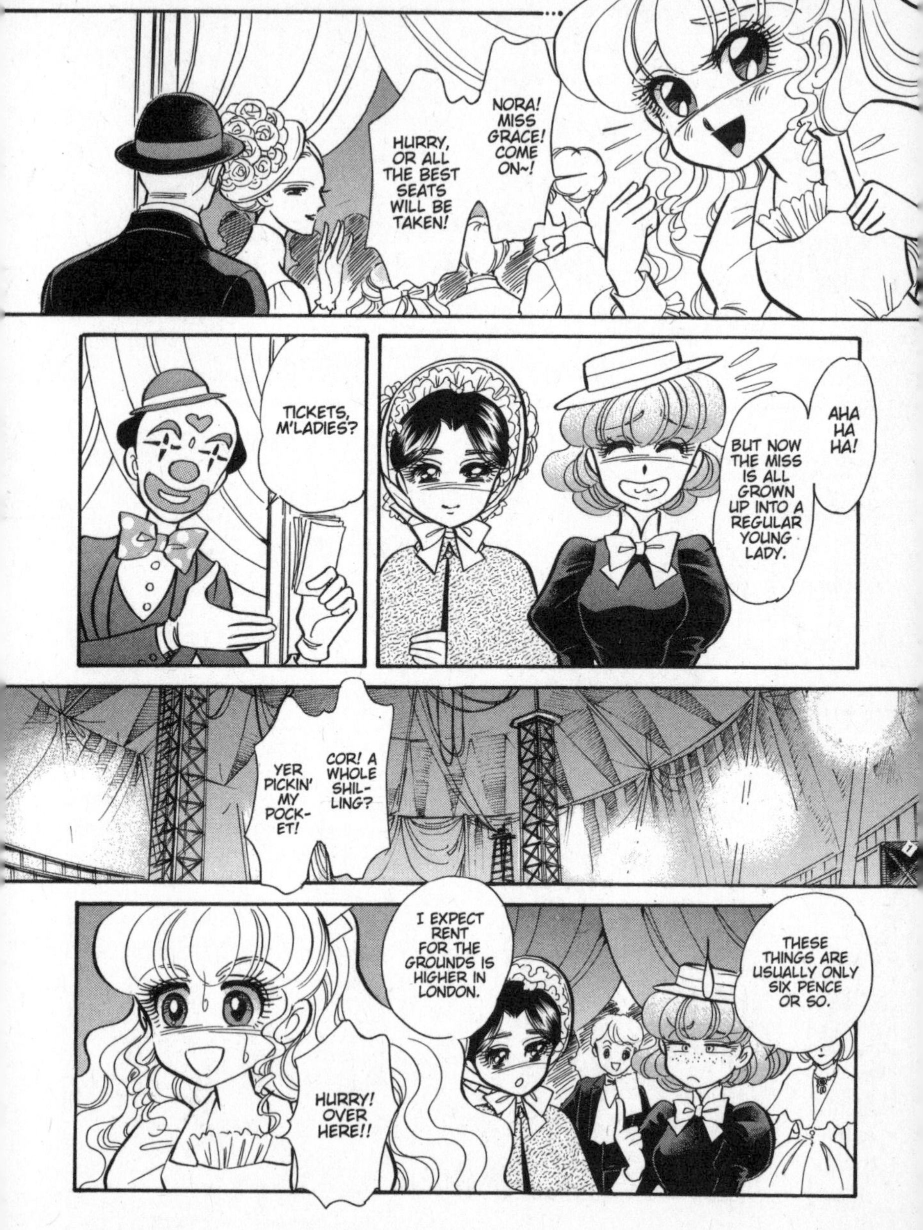
NORA! MISS GRACE! COME ON~!
HURRY, OR ALL THE BEST SEATS WILL BE TAKEN!
AHA HA HA!
BUT NOW THE MISS IS ALL GROWN UP INTO A REGULAR YOUNG LADY.
TICKETS, M'LADIES?
COR! A WHOLE SHIL-LING?
YER PICKIN' MY POCK-ET!
THESE THINGS ARE USUALLY ONLY SIX PENCE OR SO.
I EXPECT RENT FOR THE GROUNDS IS HIGHER IN LONDON.
HURRY! OVER HERE!!

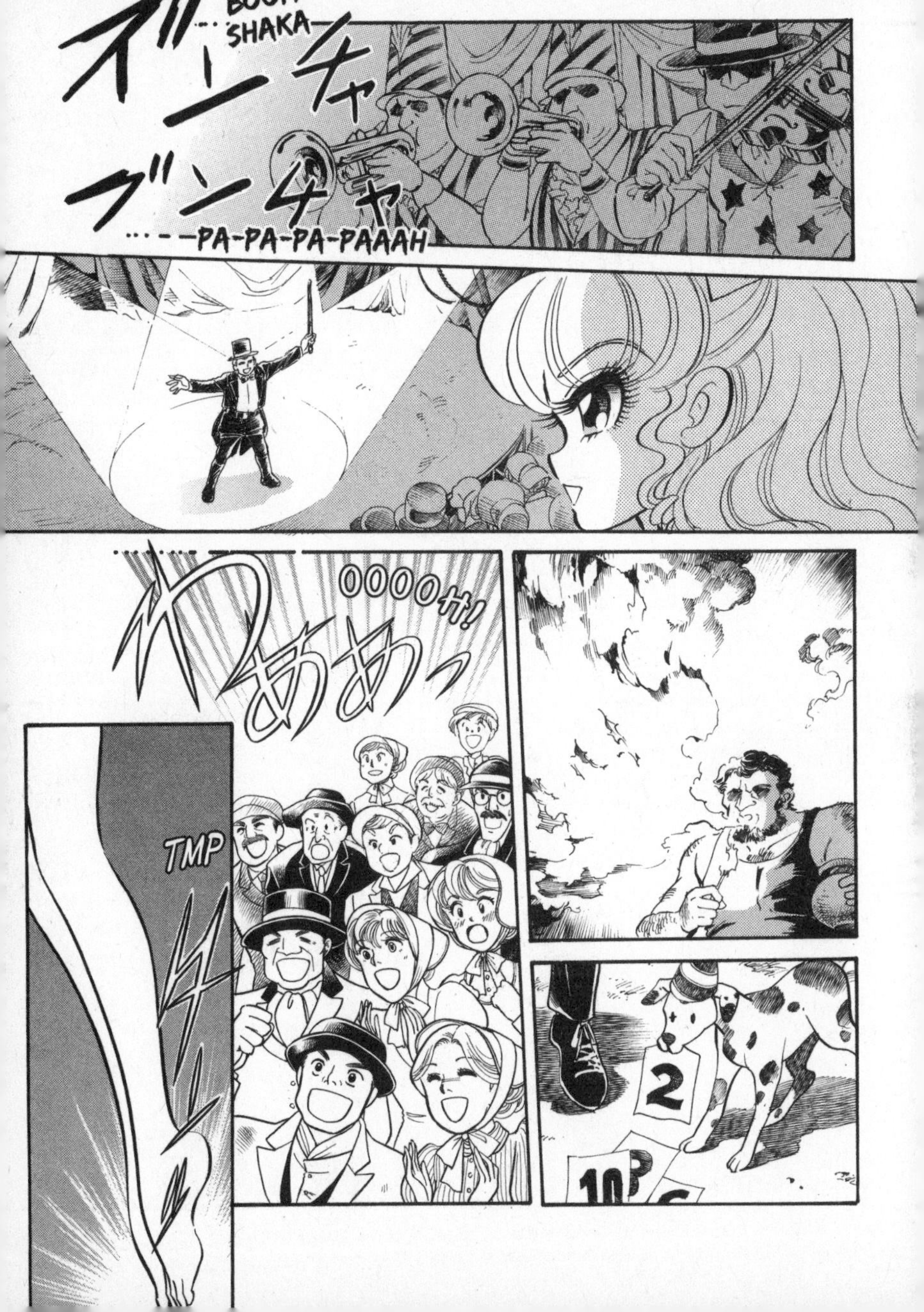
BOOM SHAKA
PA-PA-PA-PAAAH
わあああっ
OOOOH!
TMP

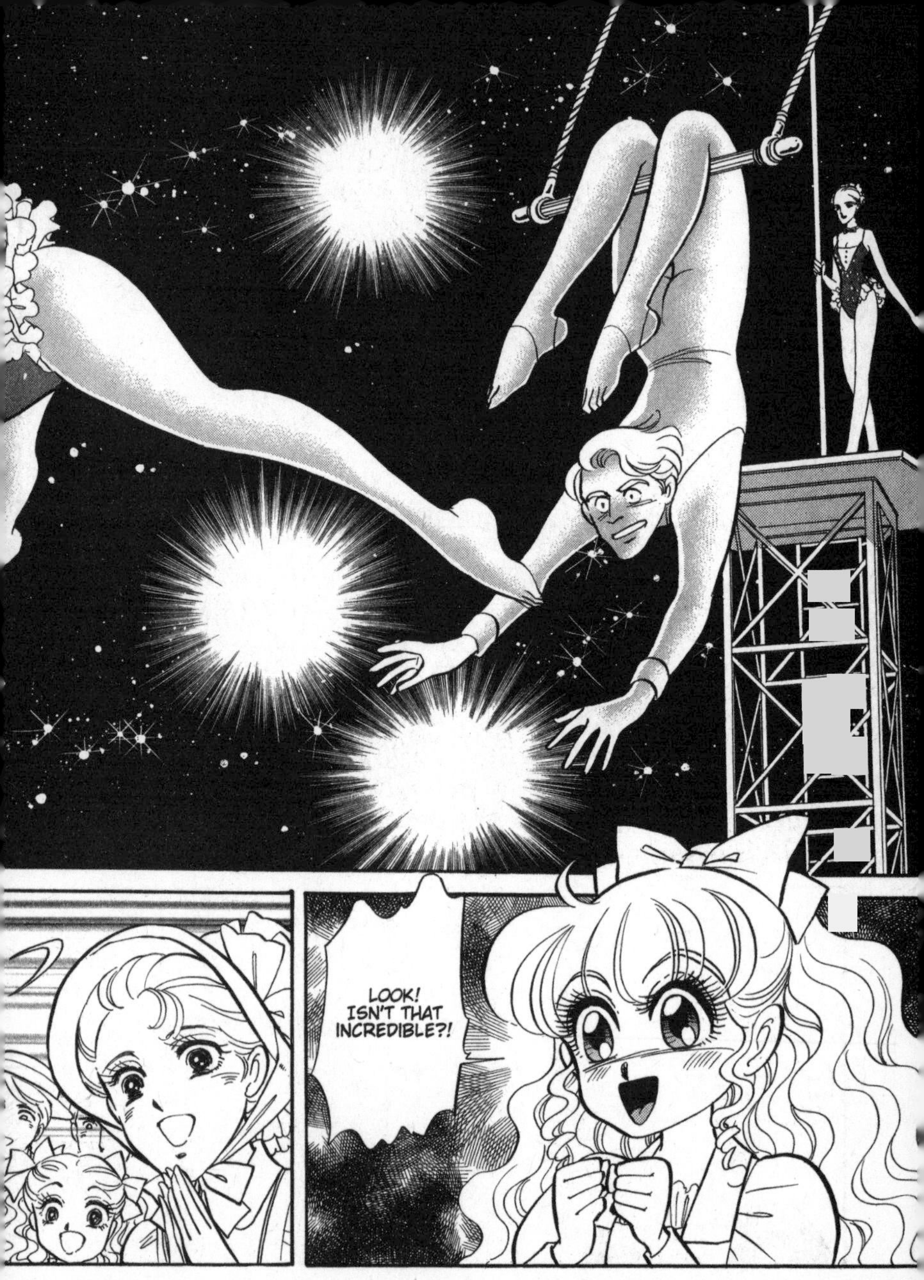
LOOK! ISN'T THAT INCREDIBLE?!

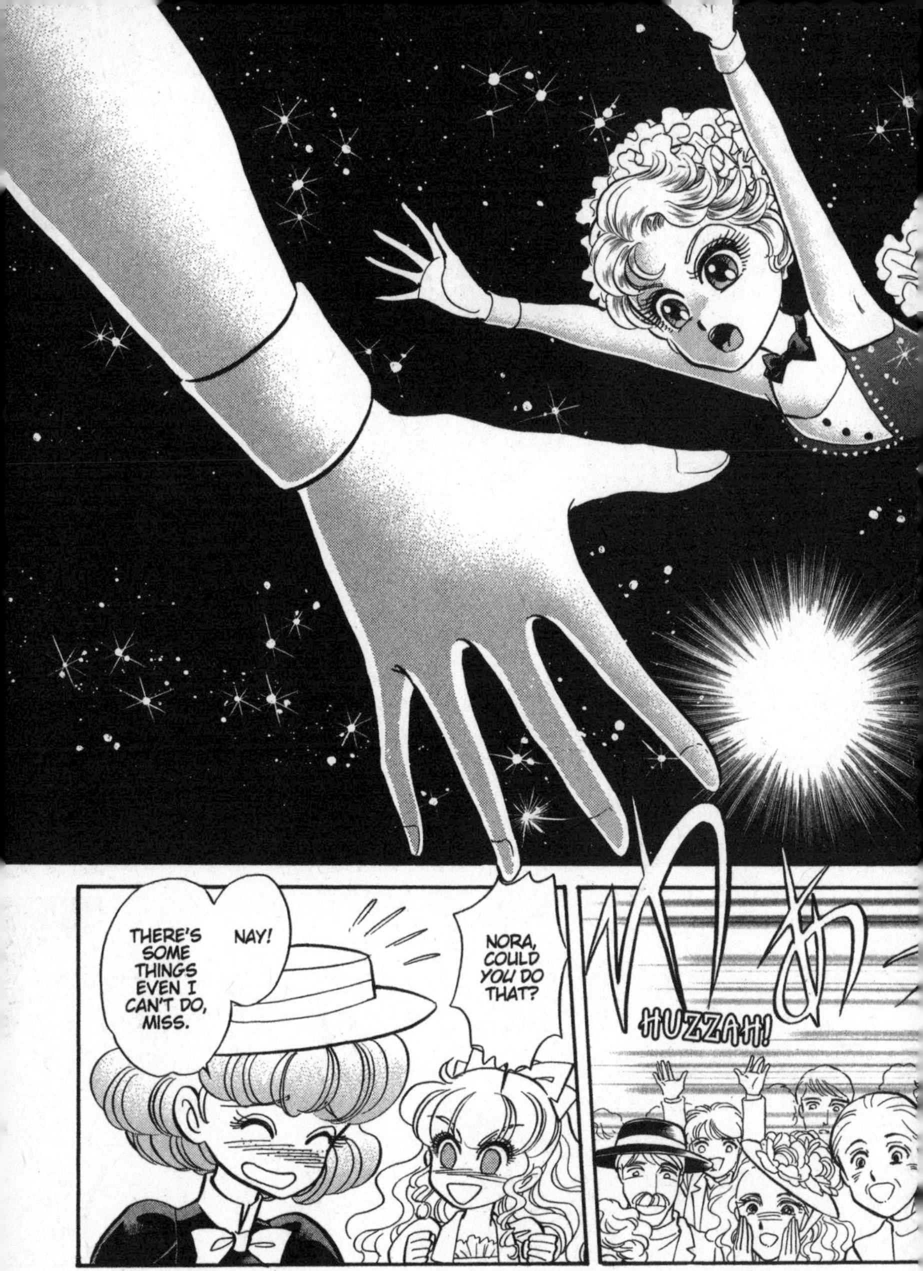
HUZZAH!
NORA, COULD YOU DO THAT?
NAY!
THERE'S SOME THINGS EVEN I CAN'T DO, MISS.

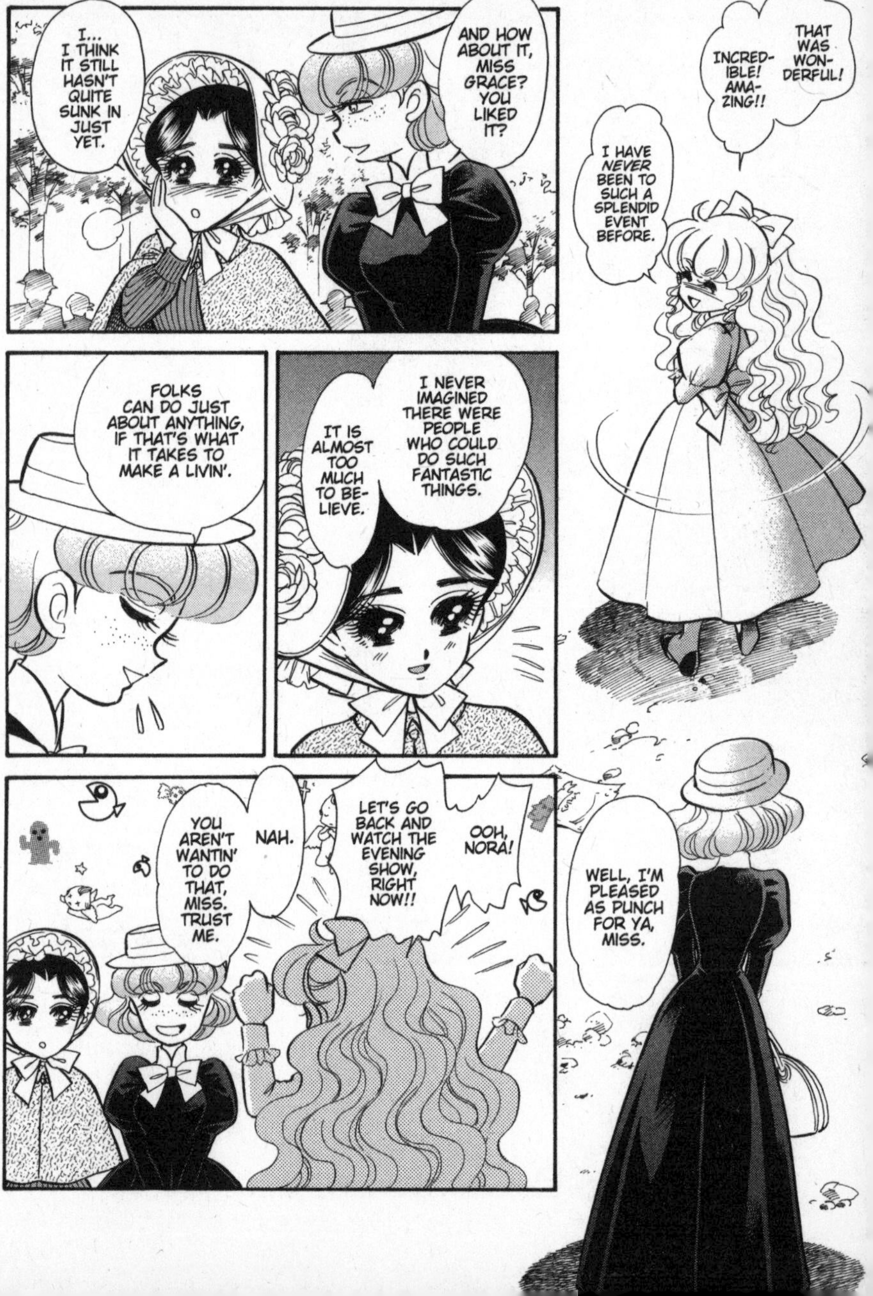
THAT WAS WONDERFUL!
INCREDIBLE! AMAZING!!
I HAVE *NEVER* BEEN TO SUCH A SPLENDID EVENT BEFORE.
WELL, I'M PLEASED AS PUNCH FOR YA, MISS.
AND HOW ABOUT IT, MISS GRACE? YOU LIKED IT?
I... I THINK IT STILL HASN'T QUITE SUNK IN JUST YET.
I NEVER IMAGINED THERE WERE PEOPLE WHO COULD DO SUCH FANTASTIC THINGS.
IT IS ALMOST TOO MUCH TO BELIEVE.
FOLKS CAN DO JUST ABOUT ANYTHING, IF THAT'S WHAT IT TAKES TO MAKE A LIVIN'.
OOH, NORA!
LET'S GO BACK AND WATCH THE EVENING SHOW, RIGHT NOW!!
NAH.
YOU AREN'T WANTIN' TO DO THAT, MISS. TRUST ME.

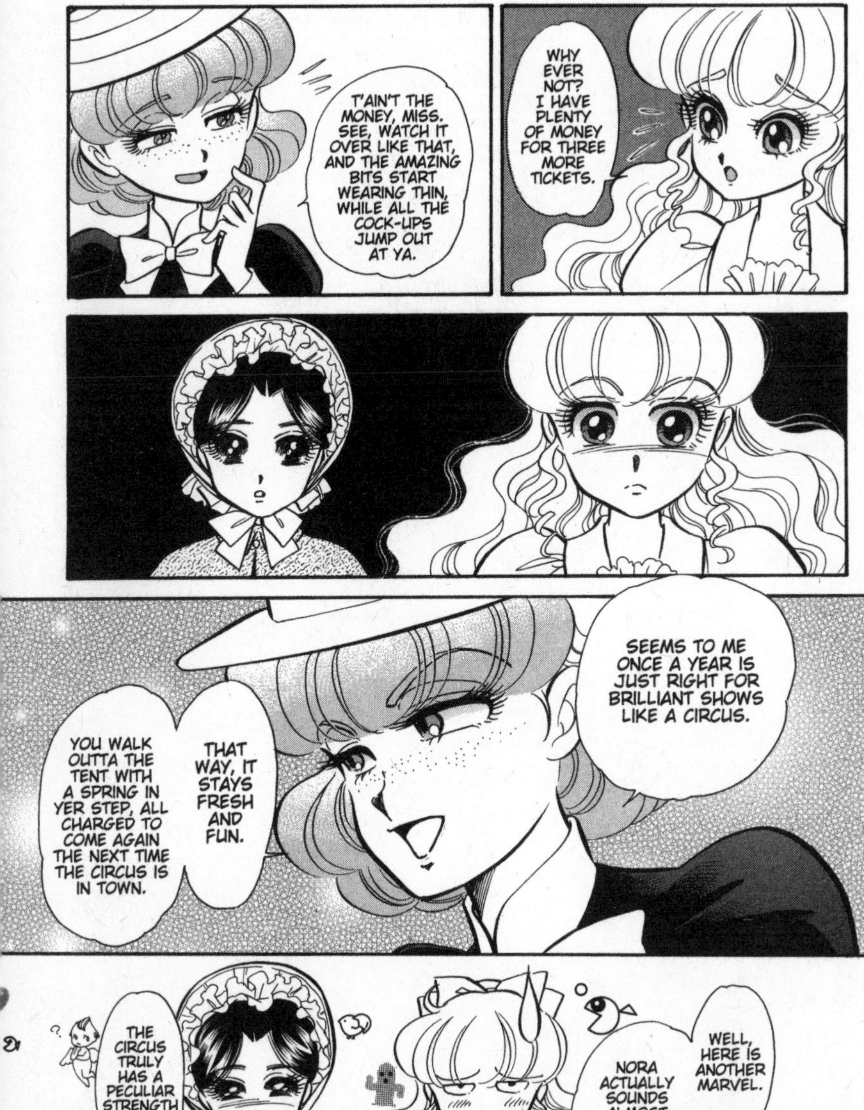
WHY EVER NOT? I HAVE PLENTY OF MONEY FOR THREE MORE TICKETS.
T'AIN'T THE MONEY, MISS. SEE, WATCH IT OVER LIKE THAT, AND THE AMAZING BITS START WEARING THIN, WHILE ALL THE COCK-UPS JUMP OUT AT YA.
SEEMS TO ME ONCE A YEAR IS JUST RIGHT FOR BRILLIANT SHOWS LIKE A CIRCUS.
THAT WAY, IT STAYS FRESH AND FUN.
YOU WALK OUTTA THE TENT WITH A SPRING IN YER STEP, ALL CHARGED TO COME AGAIN THE NEXT TIME THE CIRCUS IS IN TOWN.
WELL, HERE IS ANOTHER MARVEL.
NORA ACTUALLY SOUNDS ALMOST PHILOSO-PHICAL.
THE CIRCUS TRULY HAS A PECULIAR STRENGTH TO IT.

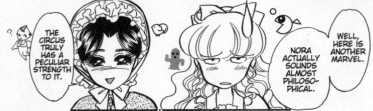

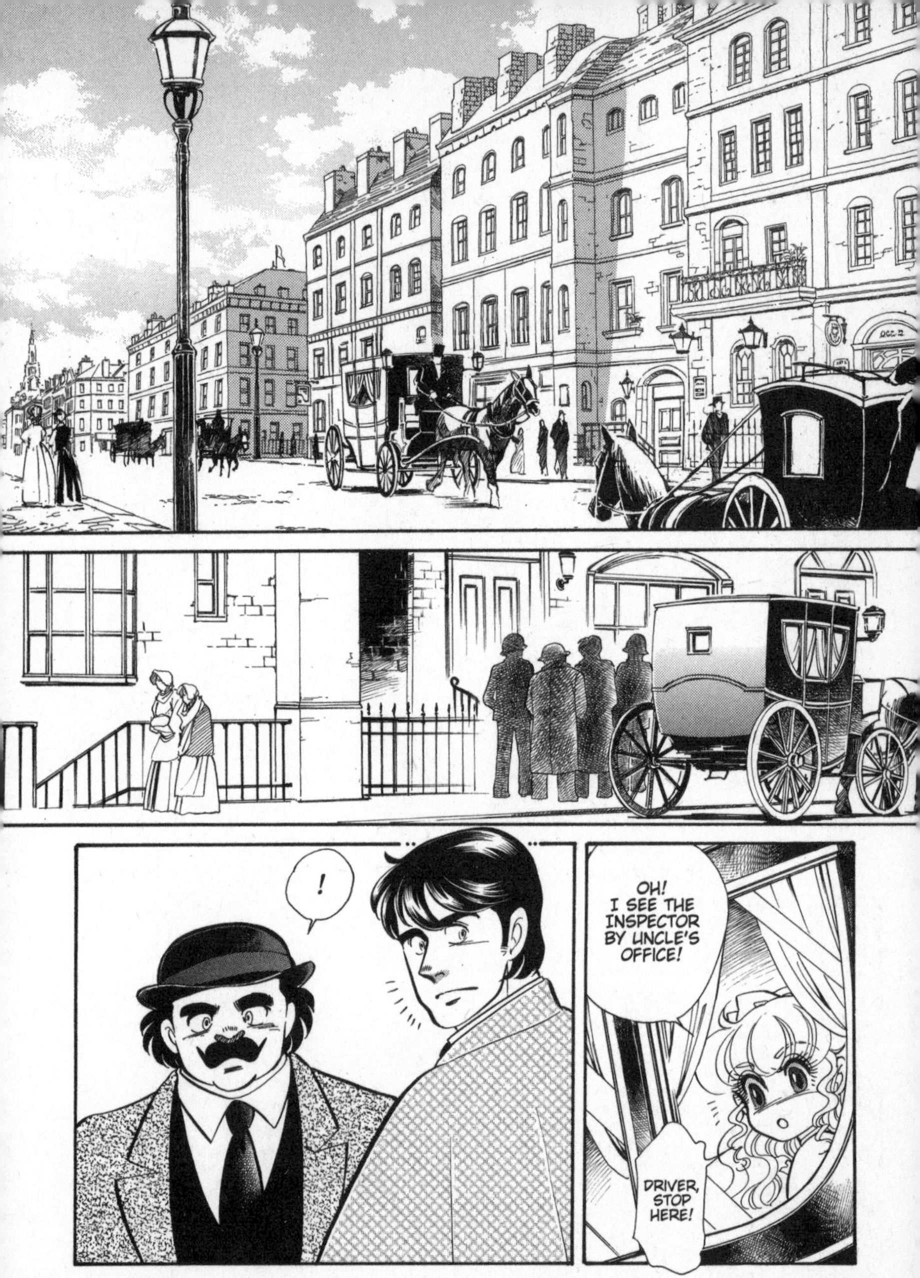
OH! I SEE THE INSPECTOR BY UNCLE'S OFFICE!
DRIVER, STOP HERE!
!

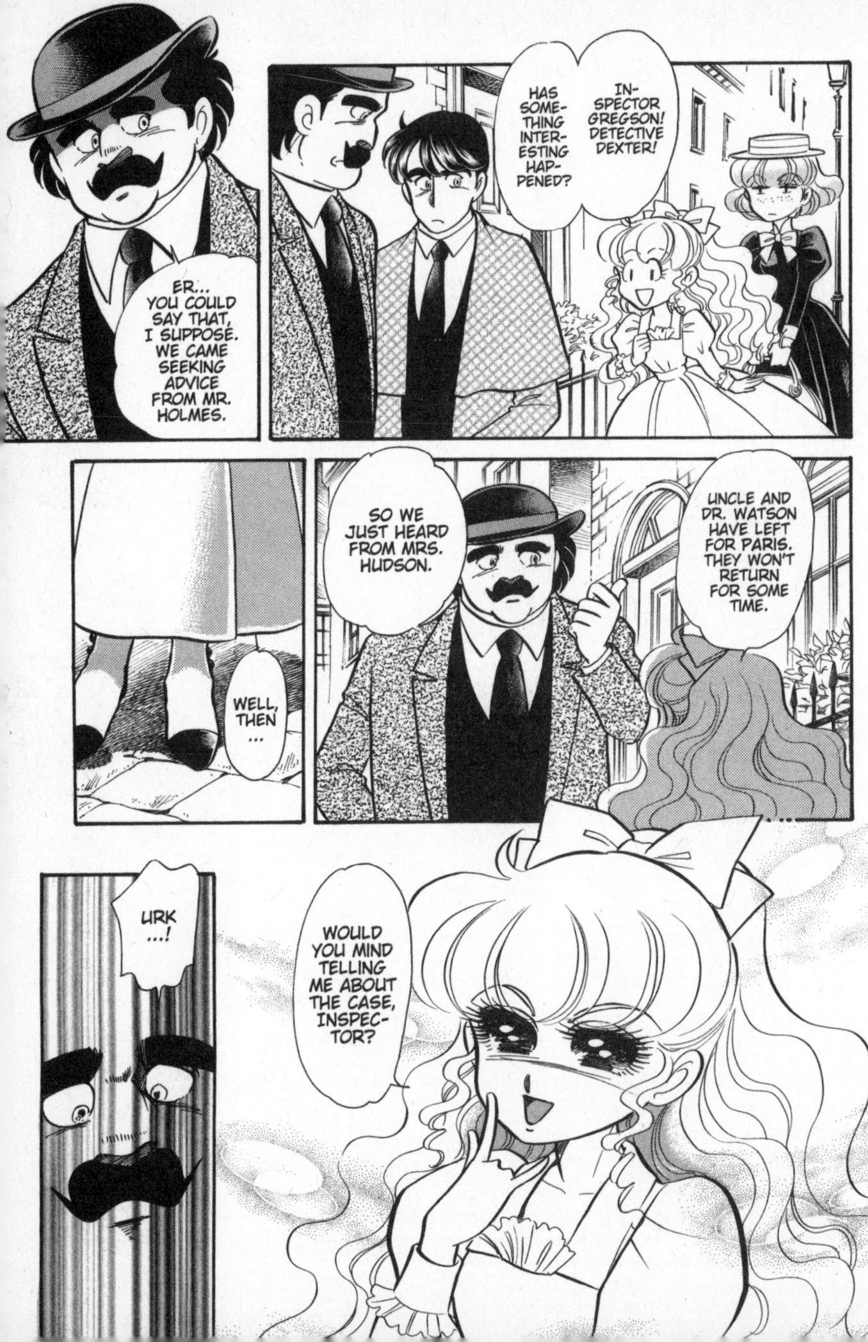
INSPECTOR GREGSON! DETECTIVE DEXTER!
HAS SOMETHING INTERESTING HAPPENED?
ER... YOU COULD SAY THAT, I SUPPOSE. WE CAME SEEKING ADVICE FROM MR. HOLMES.
UNCLE AND DR. WATSON HAVE LEFT FOR PARIS. THEY WON'T RETURN FOR SOME TIME.
SO WE JUST HEARD FROM MRS. HUDSON.
WELL, THEN ...
...
WOULD YOU MIND TELLING ME ABOUT THE CASE, INSPECTOR?
URK ...!

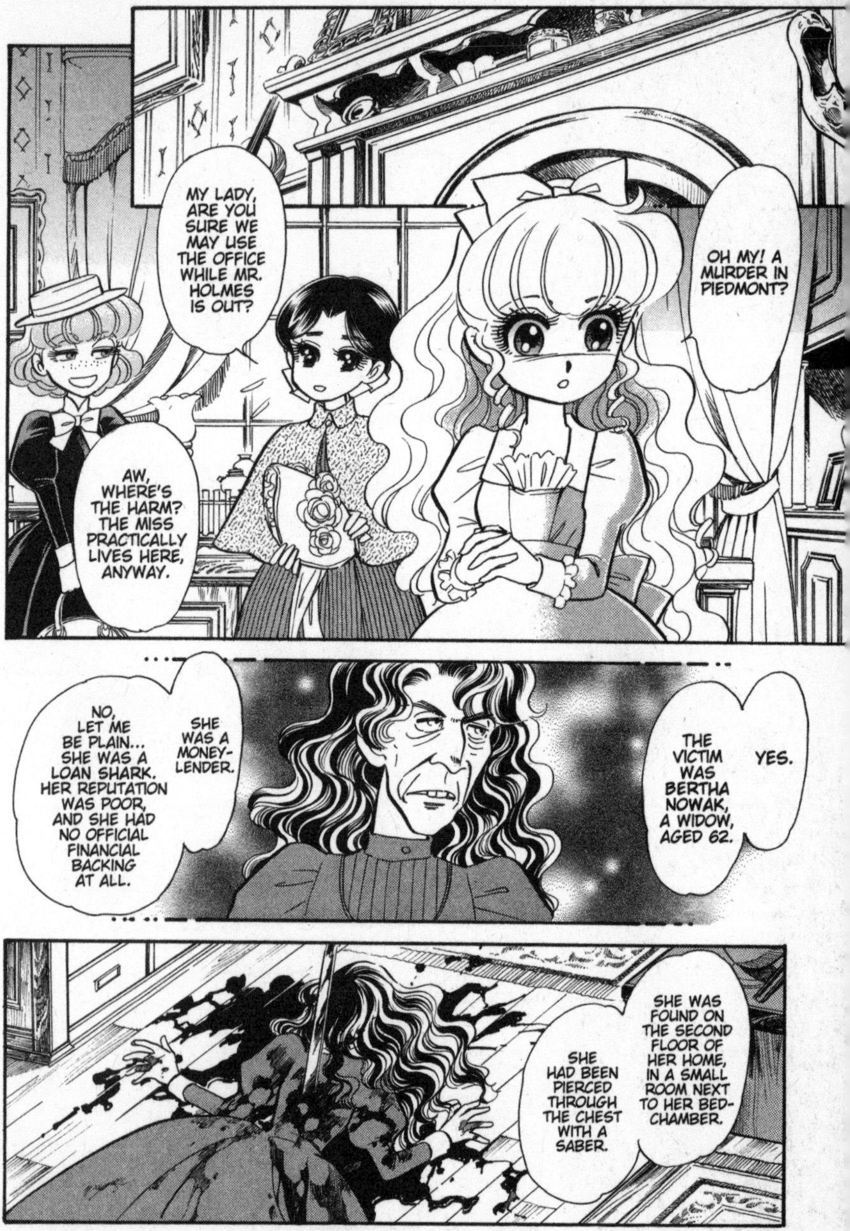
OH MY! A MURDER IN PIEDMONT?
MY LADY, ARE YOU SURE WE MAY USE THE OFFICE WHILE MR. HOLMES IS OUT?
AW, WHERE'S THE HARM? THE MISS PRACTICALLY LIVES HERE, ANYWAY.
YES.
THE VICTIM WAS BERTHA NOWAK, A WIDOW, AGED 62.
SHE WAS A MONEY-LENDER.
NO, LET ME BE PLAIN... SHE WAS A LOAN SHARK. HER REPUTATION WAS POOR, AND SHE HAD NO OFFICIAL FINANCIAL BACKING AT ALL.
SHE WAS FOUND ON THE SECOND FLOOR OF HER HOME, IN A SMALL ROOM NEXT TO HER BED-CHAMBER.
SHE HAD BEEN PIERCED THROUGH THE CHEST WITH A SABER.

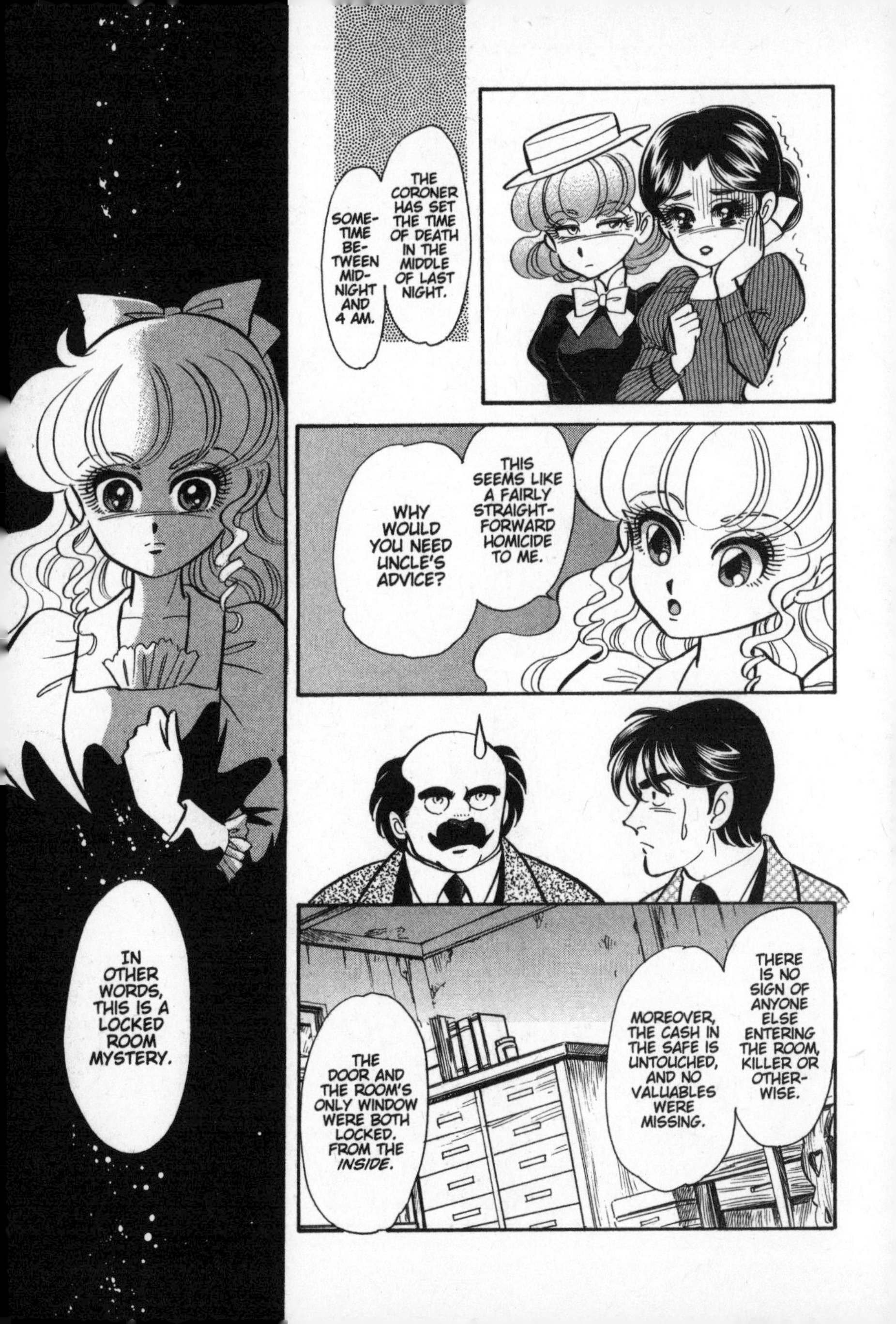
THE CORONER HAS SET THE TIME OF DEATH IN THE MIDDLE OF LAST NIGHT.
SOME-TIME BE-TWEEN MID-NIGHT AND 4 AM.
THIS SEEMS LIKE A FAIRLY STRAIGHT-FORWARD HOMICIDE TO ME.
WHY WOULD YOU NEED UNCLE'S ADVICE?
THERE IS NO SIGN OF ANYONE ELSE ENTERING THE ROOM, KILLER OR OTHER-WISE.
MOREOVER, THE CASH IN THE SAFE IS UNTOUCHED, AND NO VALUABLES WERE MISSING.
THE DOOR AND THE ROOM'S ONLY WINDOW WERE BOTH LOCKED. FROM THE *INSIDE*.
IN OTHER WORDS, THIS IS A LOCKED ROOM MYSTERY.

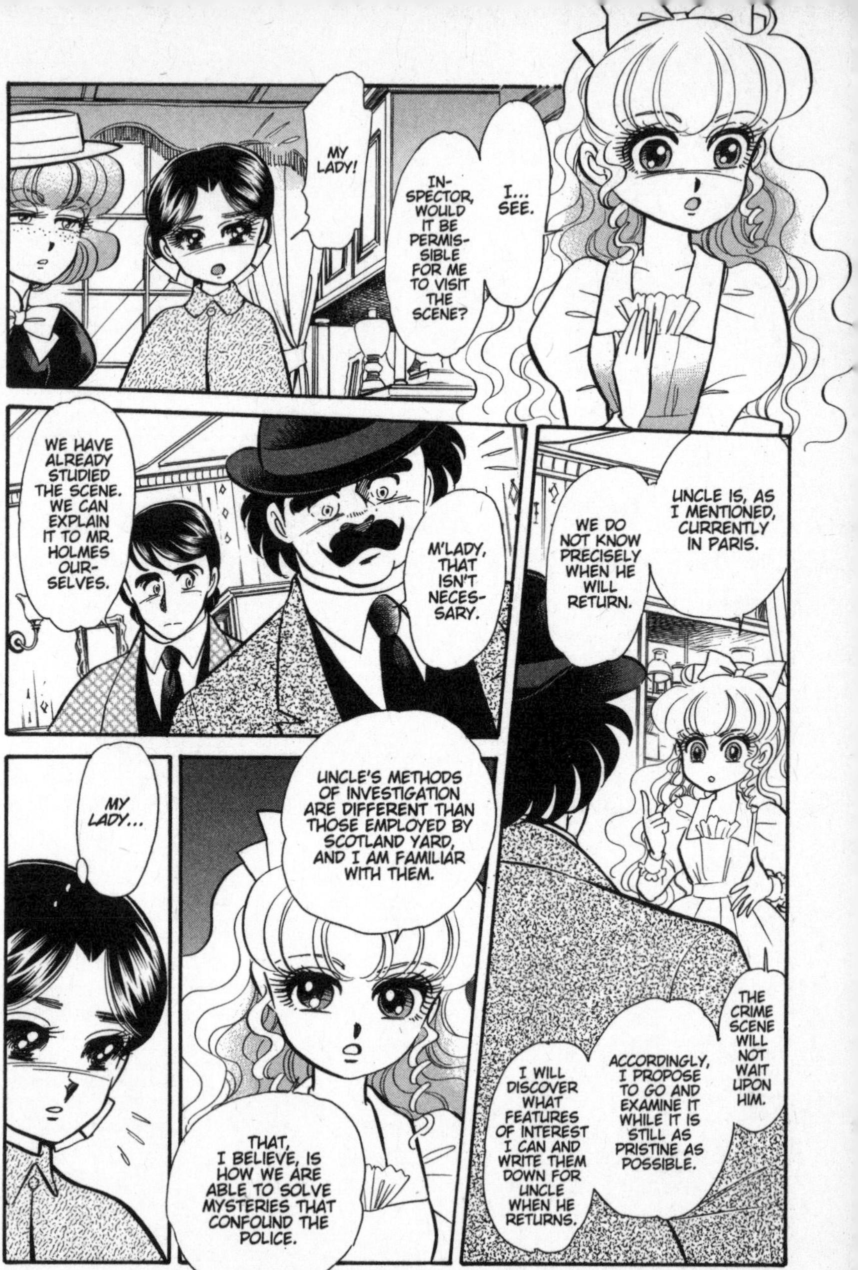
I... SEE.
INSPECTOR, WOULD IT BE PERMISSIBLE FOR ME TO VISIT THE SCENE?
MY LADY!
UNCLE IS, AS I MENTIONED, CURRENTLY IN PARIS.
WE DO NOT KNOW PRECISELY WHEN HE WILL RETURN.
THE CRIME SCENE WILL NOT WAIT UPON HIM.
ACCORDINGLY, I PROPOSE TO GO AND EXAMINE IT WHILE IT IS STILL AS PRISTINE AS POSSIBLE.
I WILL DISCOVER WHAT FEATURES OF INTEREST I CAN AND WRITE THEM DOWN FOR UNCLE WHEN HE RETURNS.
M'LADY, THAT ISN'T NECESSARY.
WE HAVE ALREADY STUDIED THE SCENE. WE CAN EXPLAIN IT TO MR. HOLMES OURSELVES.
UNCLE'S METHODS OF INVESTIGATION ARE DIFFERENT THAN THOSE EMPLOYED BY SCOTLAND YARD, AND I AM FAMILIAR WITH THEM.
THAT, I BELIEVE, IS HOW WE ARE ABLE TO SOLVE MYSTERIES THAT CONFOUND THE POLICE.
MY LADY...

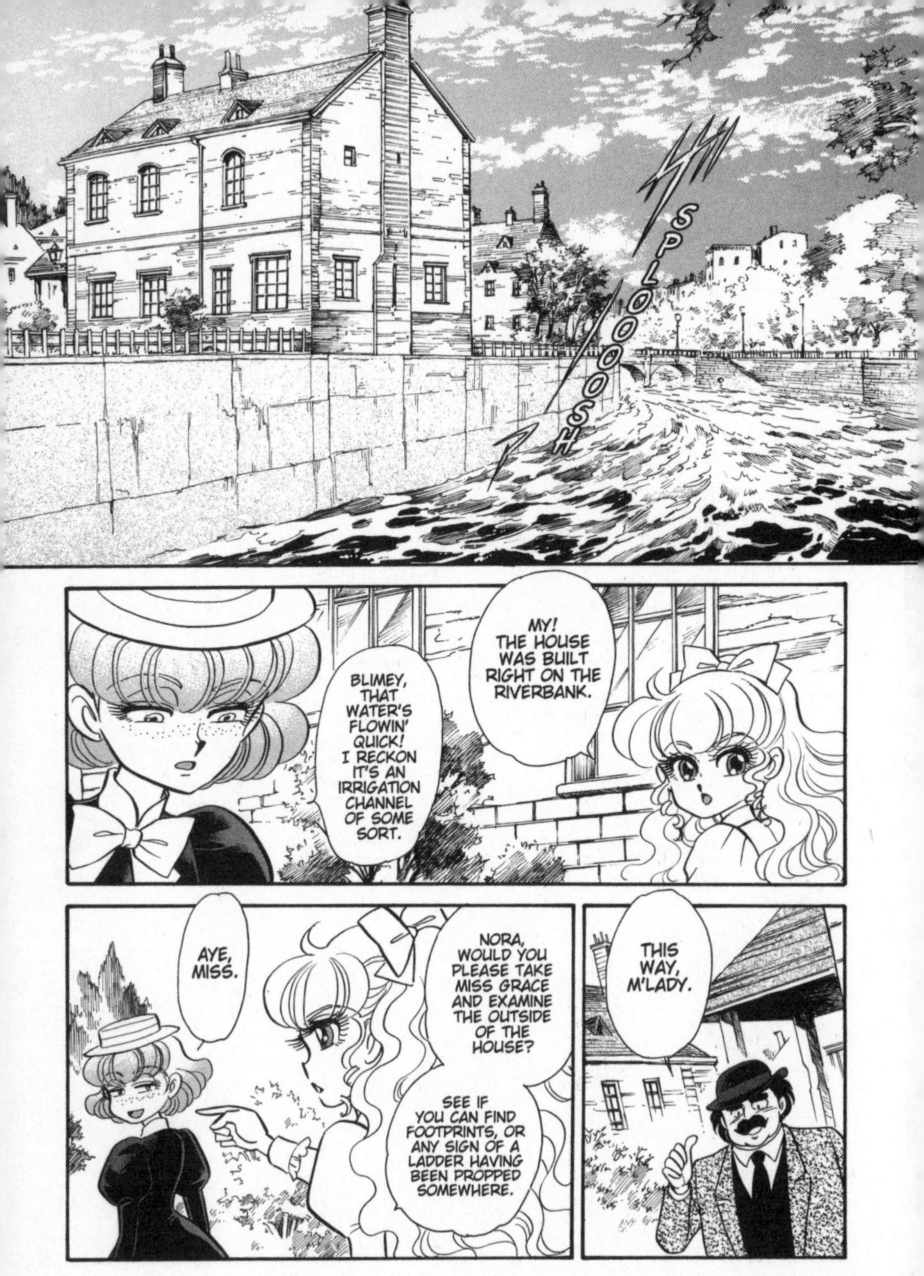
SPLOOOOOOSH
MY! THE HOUSE WAS BUILT RIGHT ON THE RIVERBANK.
BLIMEY, THAT WATER'S FLOWIN' QUICK! I RECKON IT'S AN IRRIGATION CHANNEL OF SOME SORT.
THIS WAY, M'LADY.
NORA, WOULD YOU PLEASE TAKE MISS GRACE AND EXAMINE THE OUTSIDE OF THE HOUSE?
SEE IF YOU CAN FIND FOOTPRINTS, OR ANY SIGN OF A LADDER HAVING BEEN PROPPED SOMEWHERE.
AYE, MISS.

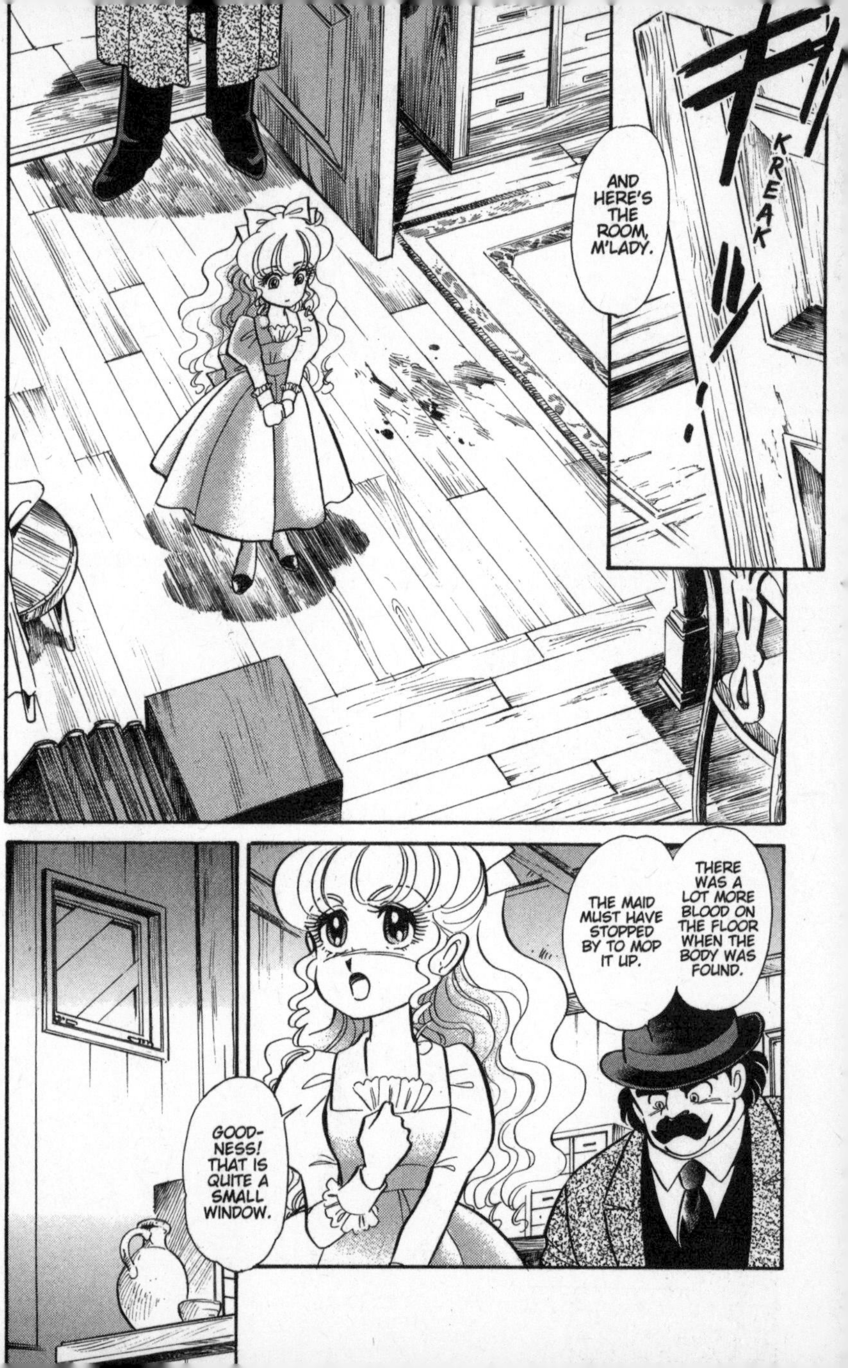
KREAK
AND HERE'S THE ROOM, M'LADY.
THERE WAS A LOT MORE BLOOD ON THE FLOOR WHEN THE BODY WAS FOUND.
THE MAID MUST HAVE STOPPED BY TO MOP IT UP.
GOOD-NESS! THAT IS QUITE A SMALL WINDOW.

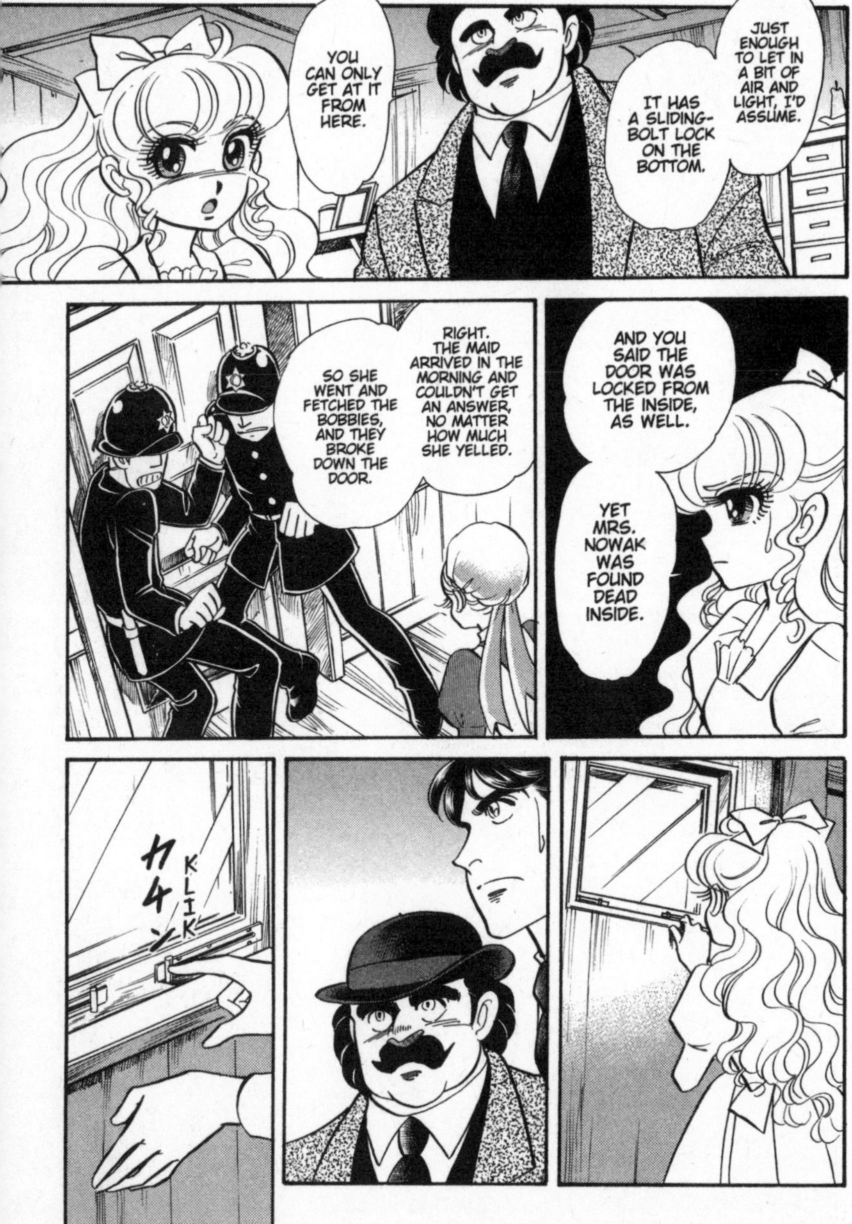
JUST ENOUGH TO LET IN A BIT OF AIR AND LIGHT, I'D ASSUME.
IT HAS A SLIDING-BOLT LOCK ON THE BOTTOM.
YOU CAN ONLY GET AT IT FROM HERE.
AND YOU SAID THE DOOR WAS LOCKED FROM THE INSIDE, AS WELL.
YET MRS. NOWAK WAS FOUND DEAD INSIDE.
RIGHT. THE MAID ARRIVED IN THE MORNING AND COULDN'T GET AN ANSWER, NO MATTER HOW MUCH SHE YELLED.
SO SHE WENT AND FETCHED THE BOBBIES, AND THEY BROKE DOWN THE DOOR.
カチン
KLIK

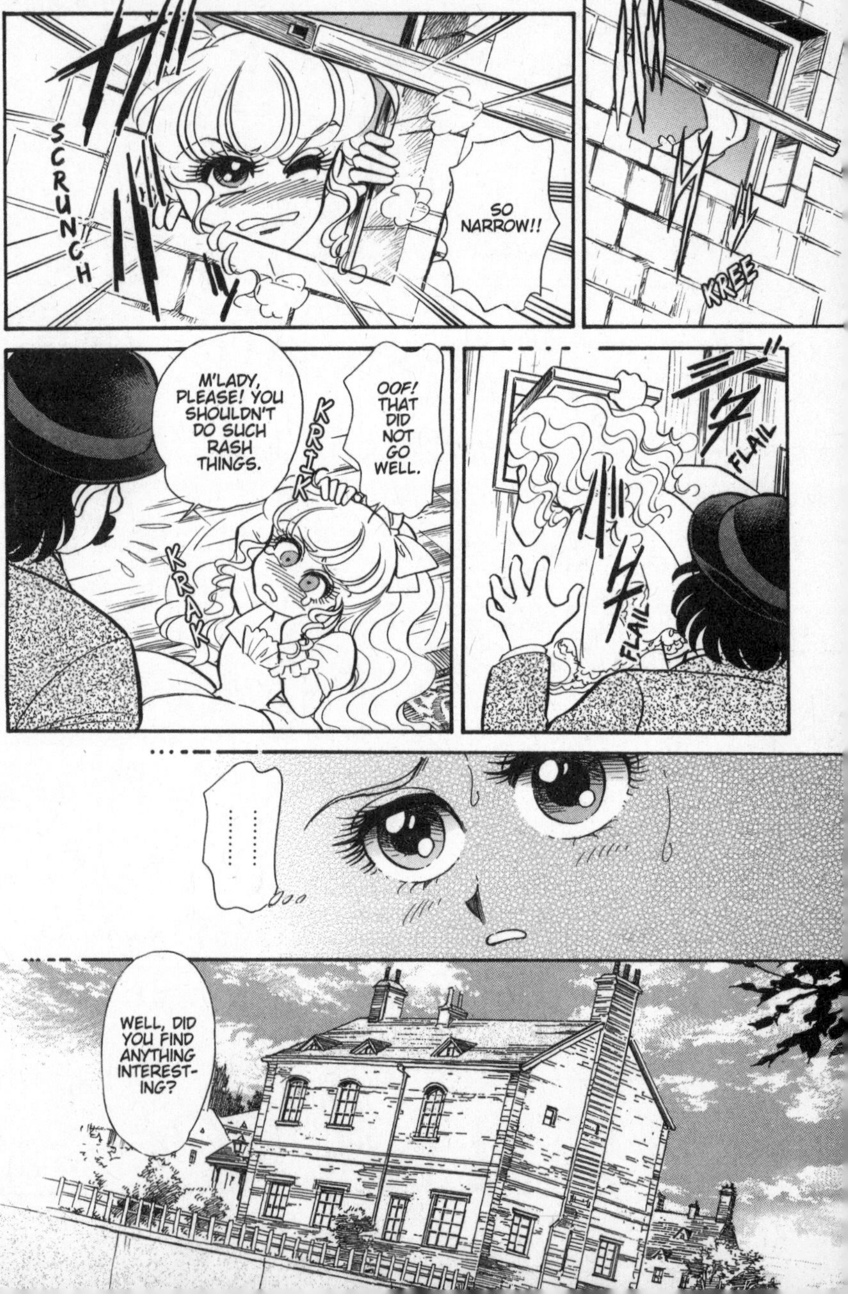
KREE
SO NARROW!!
SCRUNCH
FLAIL
FLAIL
OOF! THAT DID NOT GO WELL.
M'LADY, PLEASE! YOU SHOULDN'T DO SUCH RASH THINGS.
KRIK
KRAK
......
WELL, DID YOU FIND ANYTHING INTEREST-ING?

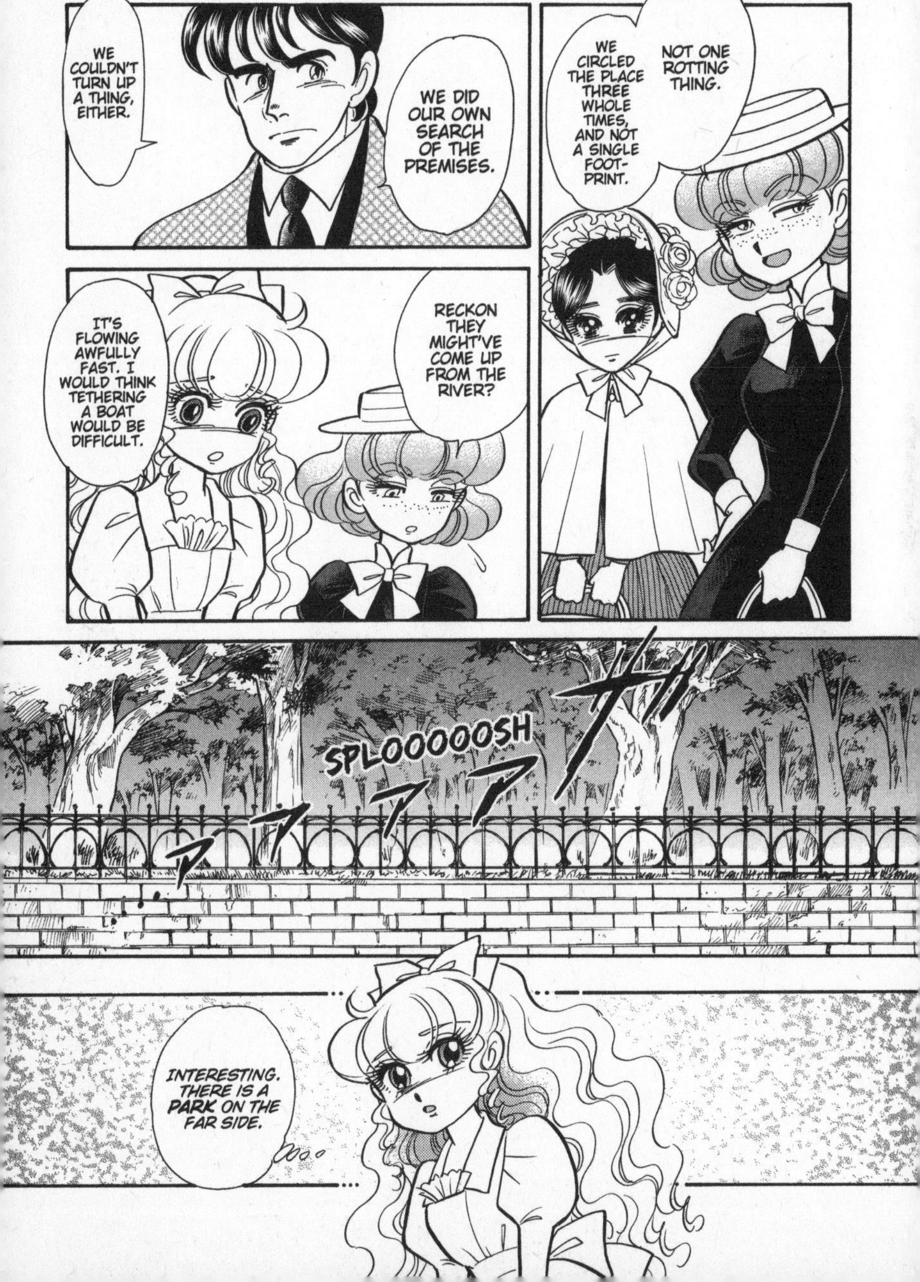
NOT ONE ROTTING THING.
WE CIRCLED THE PLACE THREE WHOLE TIMES, AND NOT A SINGLE FOOT-PRINT.
WE DID OUR OWN SEARCH OF THE PREMISES.
WE COULDN'T TURN UP A THING, EITHER.
RECKON THEY MIGHT'VE COME UP FROM THE RIVER?
IT'S FLOWING AWFULLY FAST. I WOULD THINK TETHERING A BOAT WOULD BE DIFFICULT.
SPLOOOOOSH
INTERESTING. THERE IS A **PARK** ON THE FAR SIDE.

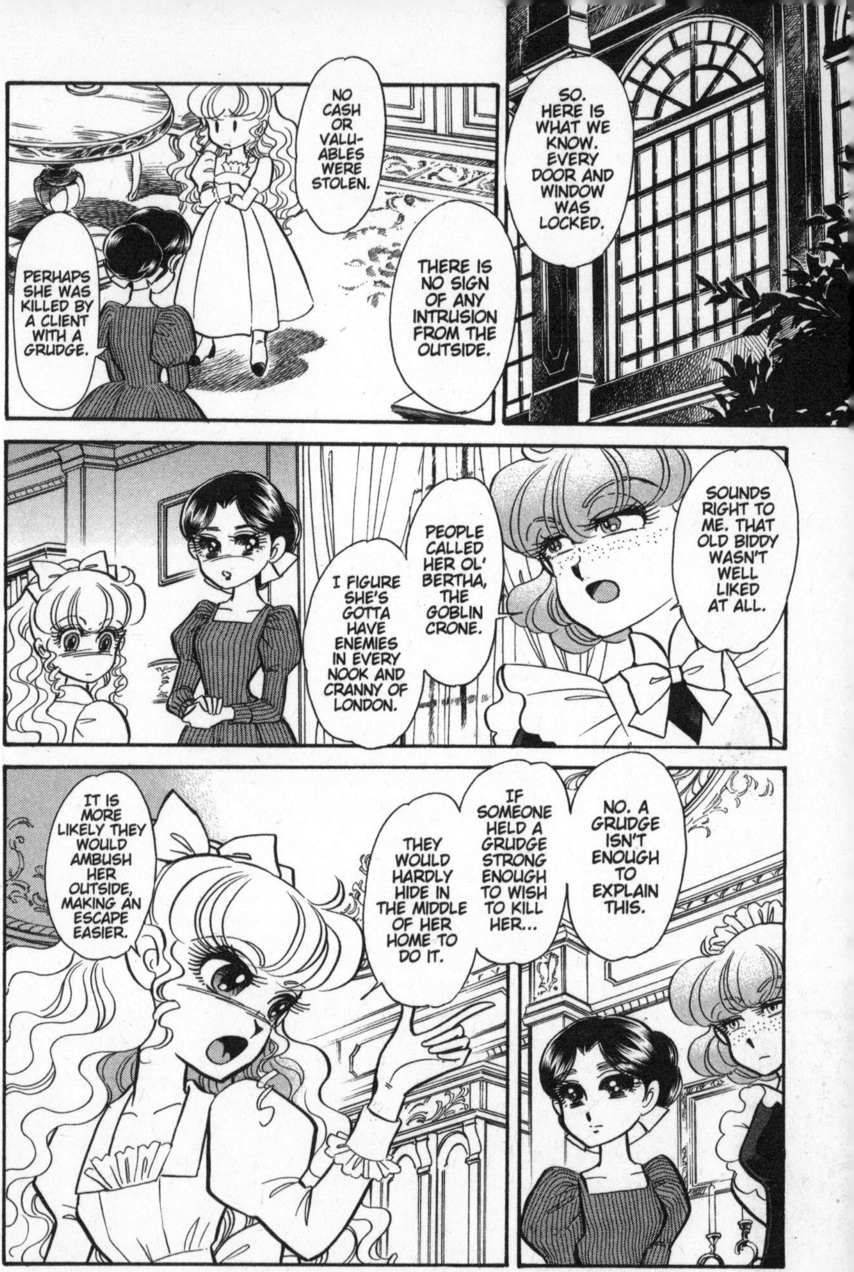
SO. HERE IS WHAT WE KNOW. EVERY DOOR AND WINDOW WAS LOCKED.
THERE IS NO SIGN OF ANY INTRUSION FROM THE OUTSIDE.
NO CASH OR VALU-ABLES WERE STOLEN.
PERHAPS SHE WAS KILLED BY A CLIENT WITH A GRUDGE.
SOUNDS RIGHT TO ME. THAT OLD BIDDY WASN'T WELL LIKED AT ALL.
PEOPLE CALLED HER OL' BERTHA, THE GOBLIN CRONE.
I FIGURE SHE'S GOTTA HAVE ENEMIES IN EVERY NOOK AND CRANNY OF LONDON.
NO. A GRUDGE ISN'T ENOUGH TO EXPLAIN THIS.
IF SOMEONE HELD A GRUDGE STRONG ENOUGH TO WISH TO KILL HER...
THEY WOULD HARDLY HIDE IN THE MIDDLE OF HER HOME TO DO IT.
IT IS MORE LIKELY THEY WOULD AMBUSH HER OUTSIDE, MAKING AN ESCAPE EASIER.

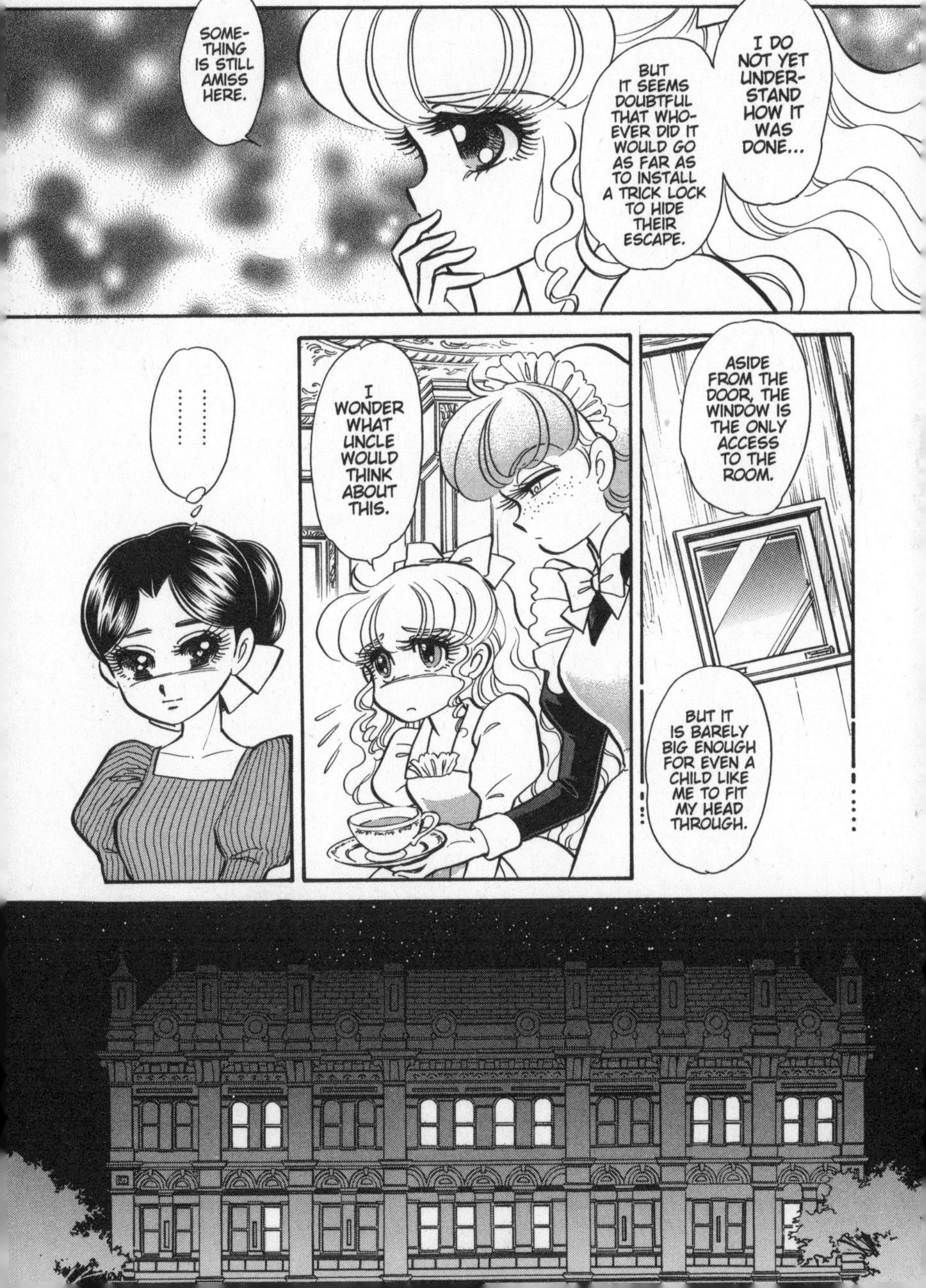
I DO NOT YET UNDERSTAND HOW IT WAS DONE...
BUT IT SEEMS DOUBTFUL THAT WHOEVER DID IT WOULD GO AS FAR AS TO INSTALL A TRICK LOCK TO HIDE THEIR ESCAPE.
SOMETHING IS STILL AMISS HERE.
ASIDE FROM THE DOOR, THE WINDOW IS THE ONLY ACCESS TO THE ROOM.
BUT IT IS BARELY BIG ENOUGH FOR EVEN A CHILD LIKE ME TO FIT MY HEAD THROUGH.
I WONDER WHAT UNCLE WOULD THINK ABOUT THIS.
......

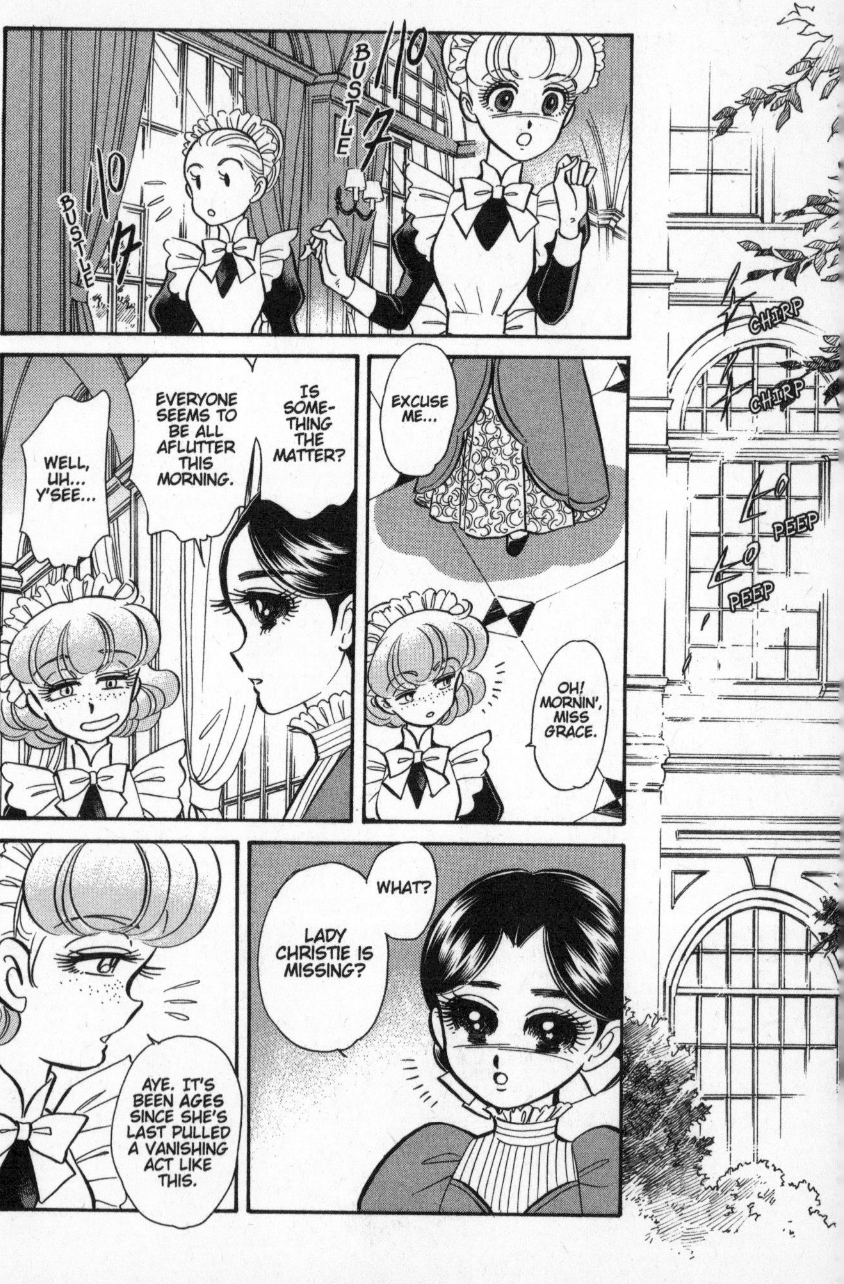
CHIRP
CHIRP
PEEP
PEEP
BUSTLE
BUSTLE
EXCUSE ME...
OH! MORNIN', MISS GRACE.
IS SOME-THING THE MATTER?
EVERYONE SEEMS TO BE ALL AFLUTTER THIS MORNING.
WELL, UH... Y'SEE...
WHAT?
LADY CHRISTIE IS MISSING?
AYE. IT'S BEEN AGES SINCE SHE'S LAST PULLED A VANISHING ACT LIKE THIS.

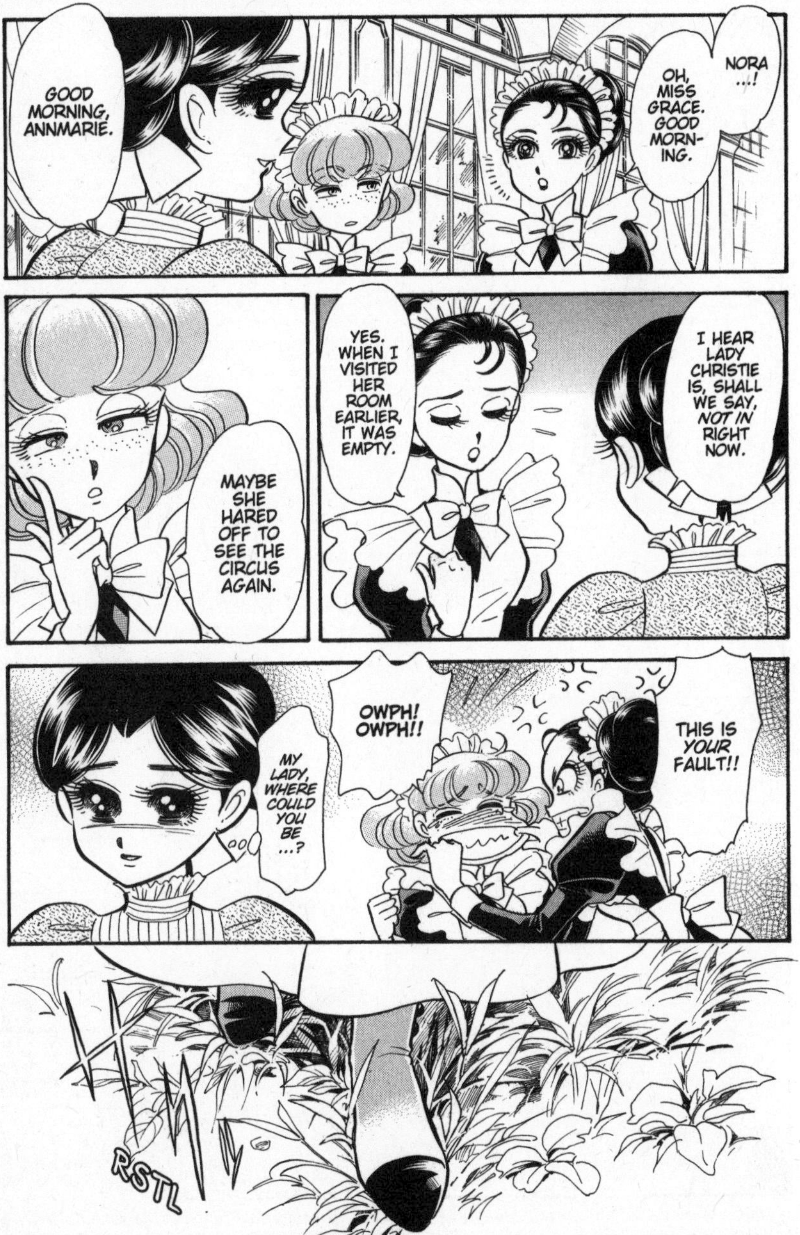
NORA ...!
OH, MISS GRACE. GOOD MORNING.
GOOD MORNING, ANNMARIE.
I HEAR LADY CHRISTIE IS, SHALL WE SAY, *NOT IN* RIGHT NOW.
YES. WHEN I VISITED HER ROOM EARLIER, IT WAS EMPTY.
MAYBE SHE HARED OFF TO SEE THE CIRCUS AGAIN.
THIS IS *YOUR* FAULT!!
OWPH! OWPH!!
MY LADY, WHERE COULD YOU BE ...?
RSTL

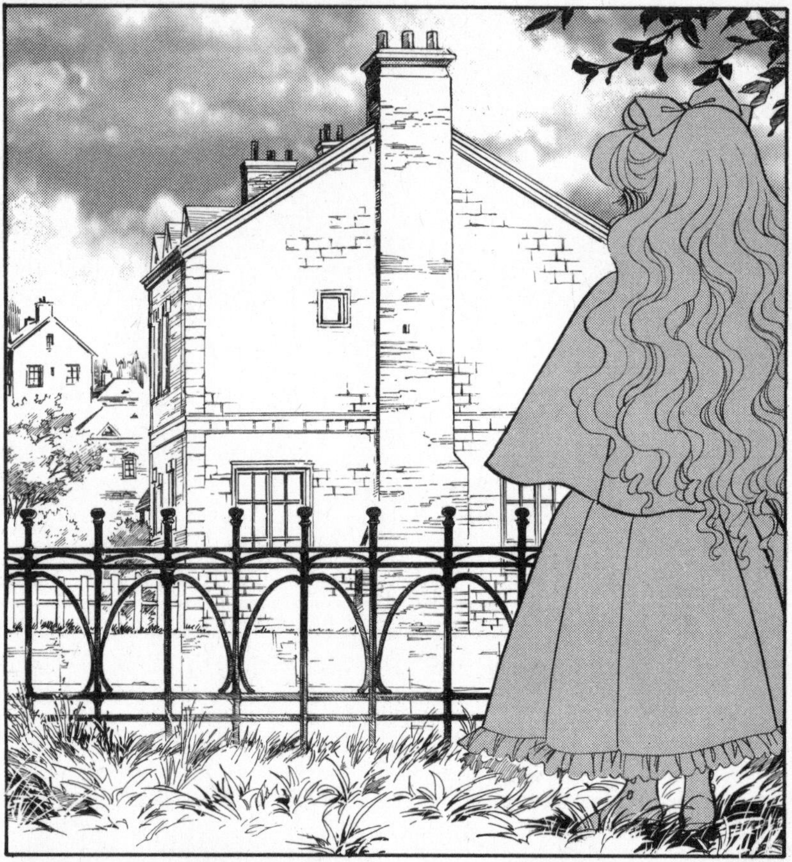

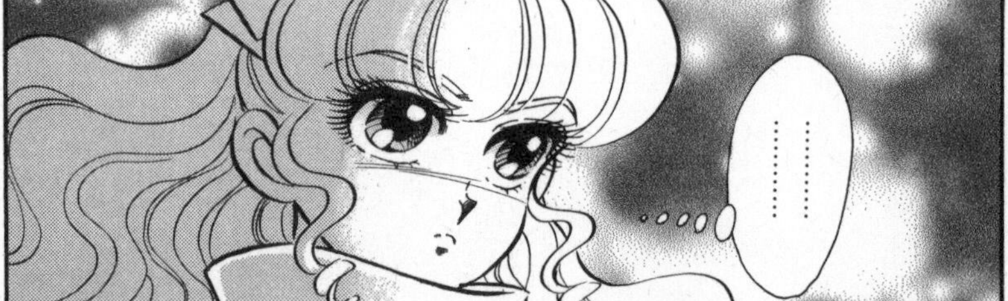
……

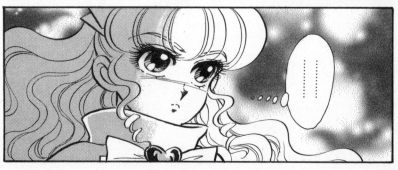

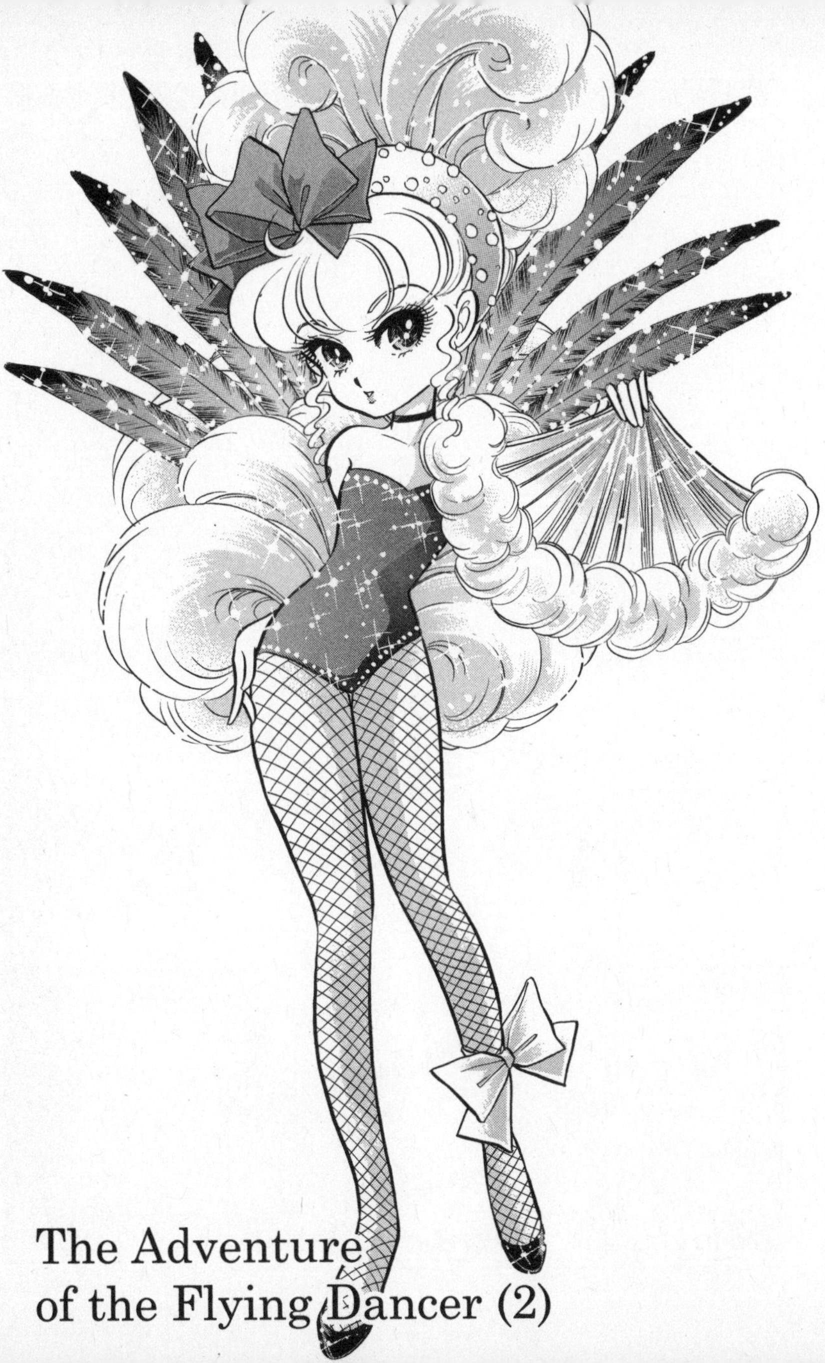

The Adventure of the Flying Dancer (2)

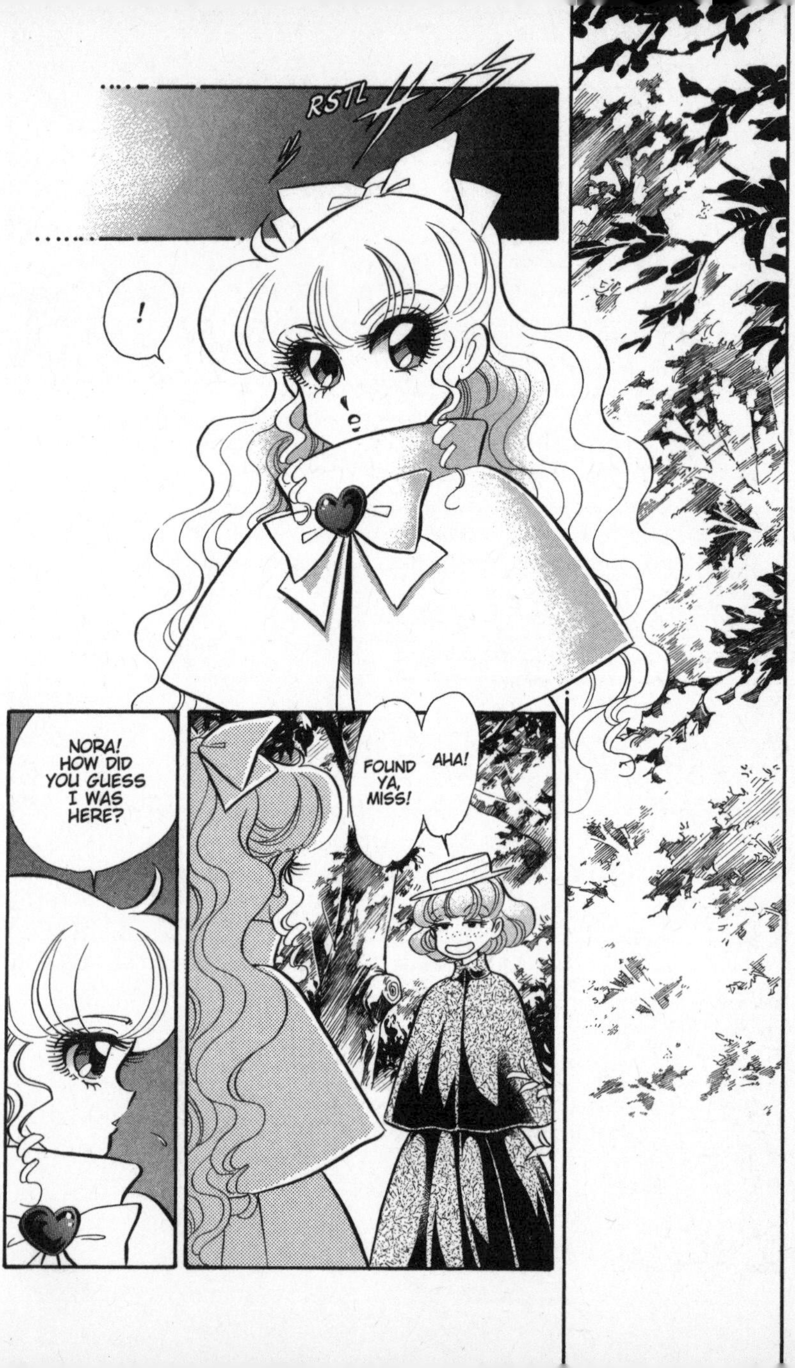
RSTL
!
AHA!
FOUND YA, MISS!
NORA! HOW DID YOU GUESS I WAS HERE?

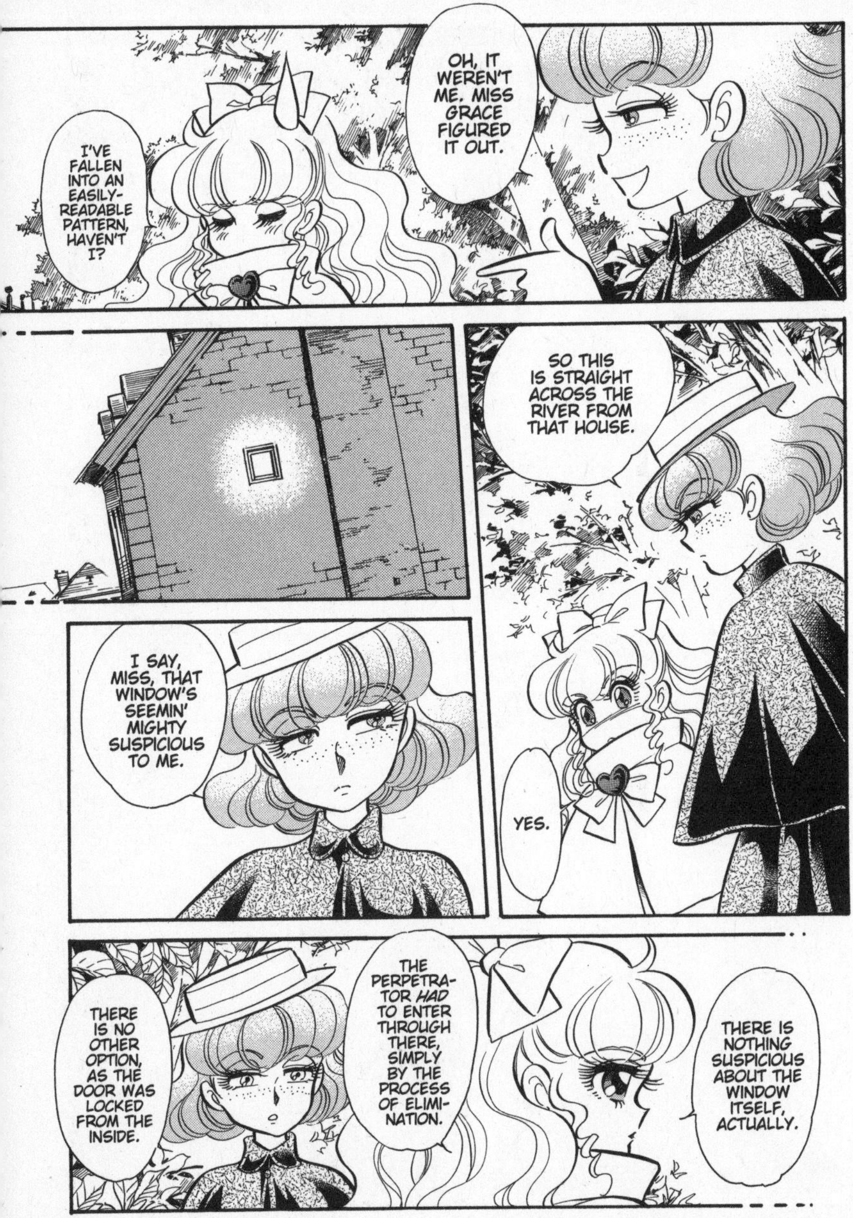
OH, IT WEREN'T ME. MISS GRACE FIGURED IT OUT.
I'VE FALLEN INTO AN EASILY-READABLE PATTERN, HAVEN'T I?
SO THIS IS STRAIGHT ACROSS THE RIVER FROM THAT HOUSE.
YES.
I SAY, MISS, THAT WINDOW'S SEEMIN' MIGHTY SUSPICIOUS TO ME.
THERE IS NOTHING SUSPICIOUS ABOUT THE WINDOW ITSELF, ACTUALLY.
THE PERPETRATOR *HAD* TO ENTER THROUGH THERE, SIMPLY BY THE PROCESS OF ELIMINATION.
THERE IS NO OTHER OPTION, AS THE DOOR WAS LOCKED FROM THE INSIDE.

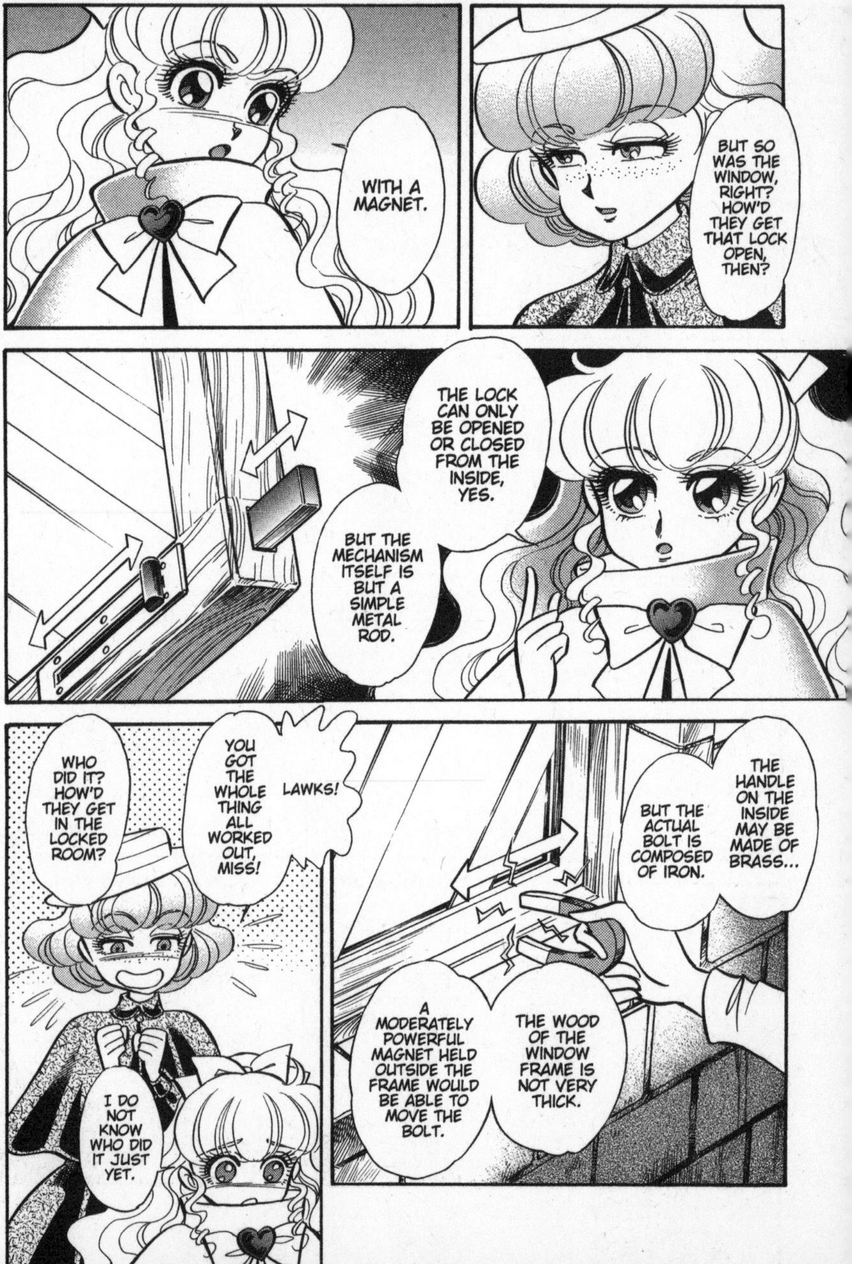
BUT SO WAS THE WINDOW, RIGHT? HOW'D THEY GET THAT LOCK OPEN, THEN?
WITH A MAGNET.
THE LOCK CAN ONLY BE OPENED OR CLOSED FROM THE INSIDE, YES.
BUT THE MECHANISM ITSELF IS BUT A SIMPLE METAL ROD.
THE HANDLE ON THE INSIDE MAY BE MADE OF BRASS...
BUT THE ACTUAL BOLT IS COMPOSED OF IRON.
THE WOOD OF THE WINDOW FRAME IS NOT VERY THICK.
A MODERATELY POWERFUL MAGNET HELD OUTSIDE THE FRAME WOULD BE ABLE TO MOVE THE BOLT.
LAWKS!
YOU GOT THE WHOLE THING ALL WORKED OUT, MISS!
WHO DID IT? HOW'D THEY GET IN THE LOCKED ROOM?
I DO NOT KNOW WHO DID IT JUST YET.

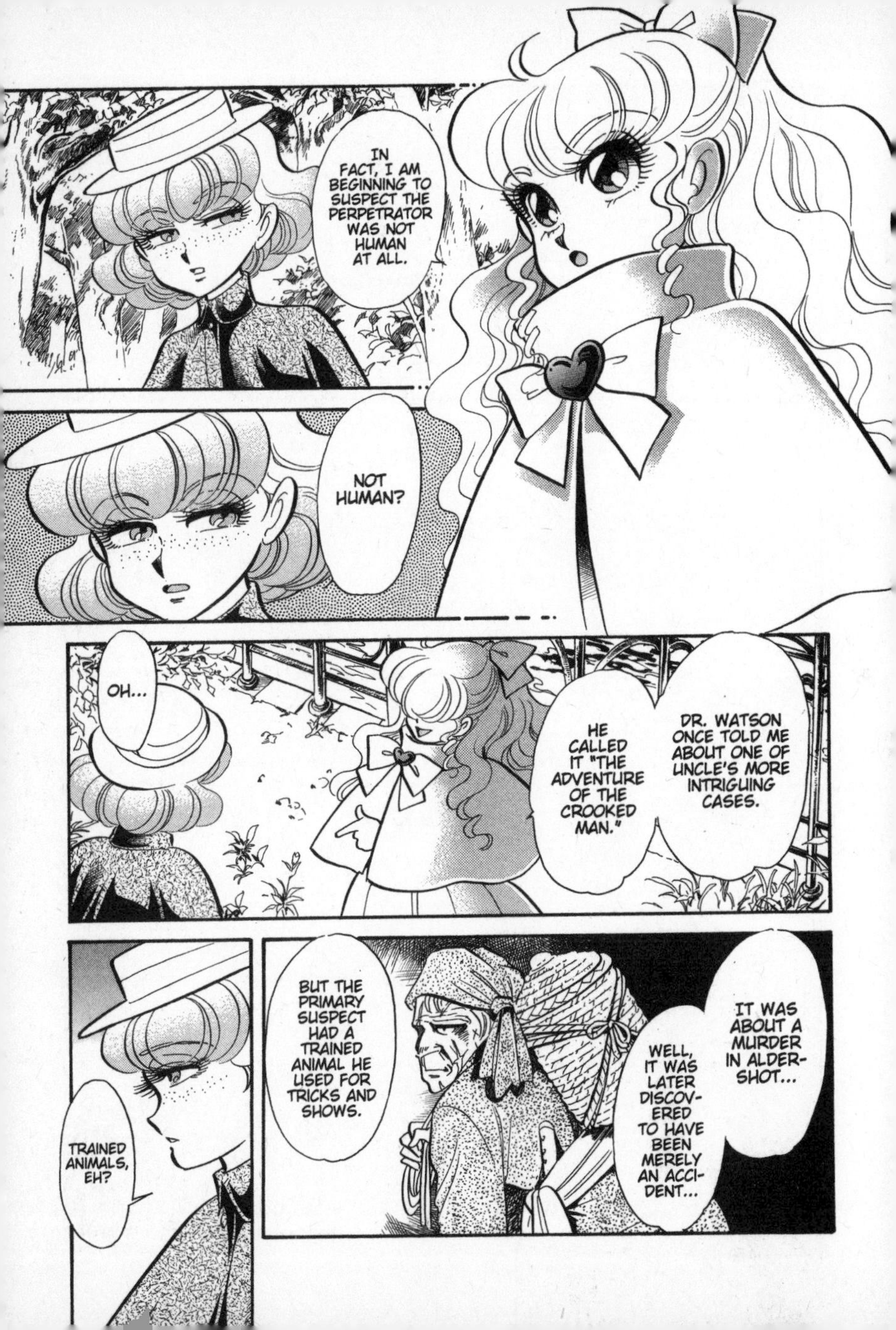
IN FACT, I AM BEGINNING TO SUSPECT THE PERPETRATOR WAS NOT HUMAN AT ALL.
NOT HUMAN?
DR. WATSON ONCE TOLD ME ABOUT ONE OF UNCLE'S MORE INTRIGUING CASES.
HE CALLED IT "THE ADVENTURE OF THE CROOKED MAN."
OH...
IT WAS ABOUT A MURDER IN ALDER-SHOT...
WELL, IT WAS LATER DISCOV-ERED TO HAVE BEEN MERELY AN ACCI-DENT...
BUT THE PRIMARY SUSPECT HAD A TRAINED ANIMAL HE USED FOR TRICKS AND SHOWS.
TRAINED ANIMALS, EH?

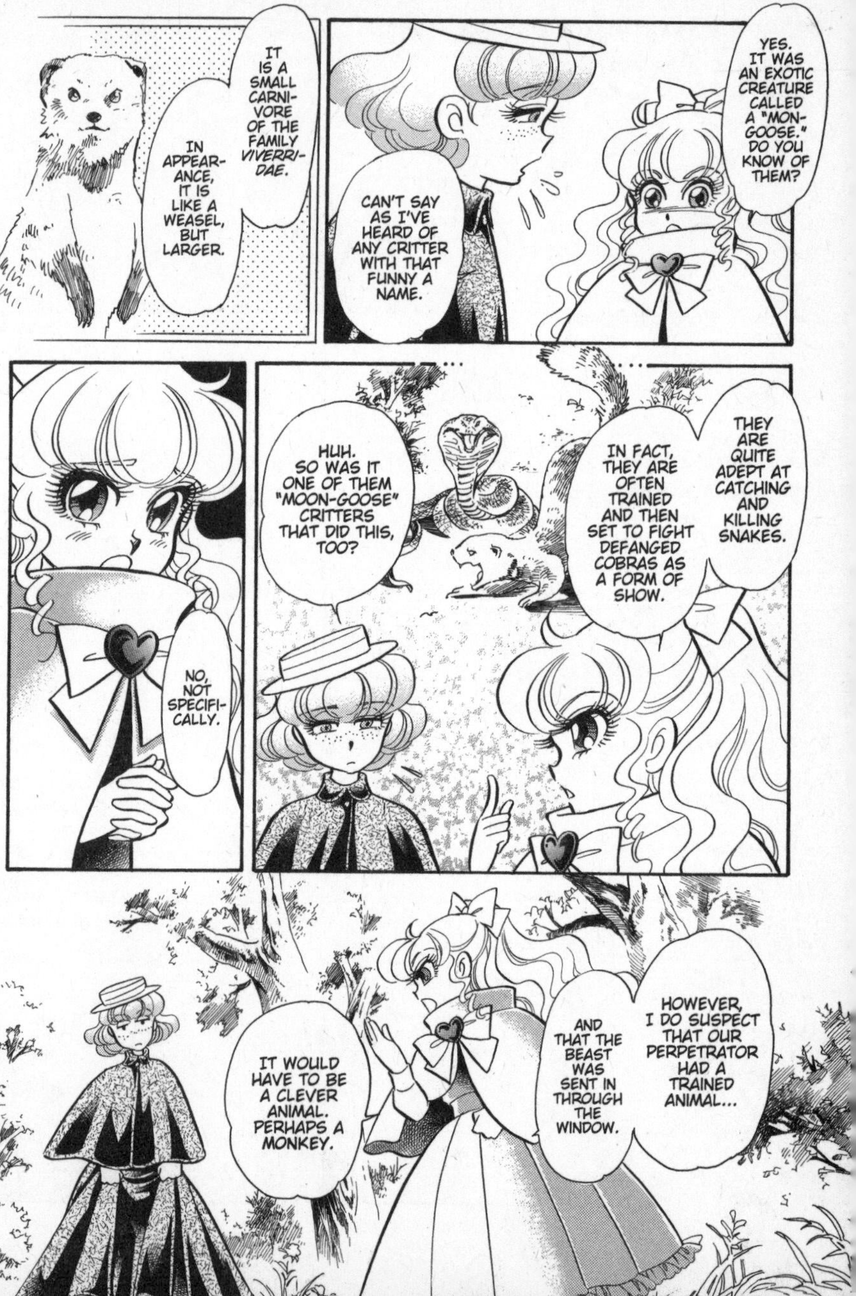
YES. IT WAS AN EXOTIC CREATURE CALLED A "MON-GOOSE." DO YOU KNOW OF THEM?
CAN'T SAY AS I'VE HEARD OF ANY CRITTER WITH THAT FUNNY A NAME.
IT IS A SMALL CARNI-VORE OF THE FAMILY VIVERRI-DAE.
IN APPEAR-ANCE, IT IS LIKE A WEASEL, BUT LARGER.
THEY ARE QUITE ADEPT AT CATCHING AND KILLING SNAKES.
IN FACT, THEY ARE OFTEN TRAINED AND THEN SET TO FIGHT DEFANGED COBRAS AS A FORM OF SHOW.
HUH. SO WAS IT ONE OF THEM "MOON-GOOSE" CRITTERS THAT DID THIS, TOO?
NO, NOT SPECIFI-CALLY.
HOWEVER, I DO SUSPECT THAT OUR PERPETRATOR HAD A TRAINED ANIMAL...
AND THAT THE BEAST WAS SENT IN THROUGH THE WINDOW.
IT WOULD HAVE TO BE A CLEVER ANIMAL. PERHAPS A MONKEY.

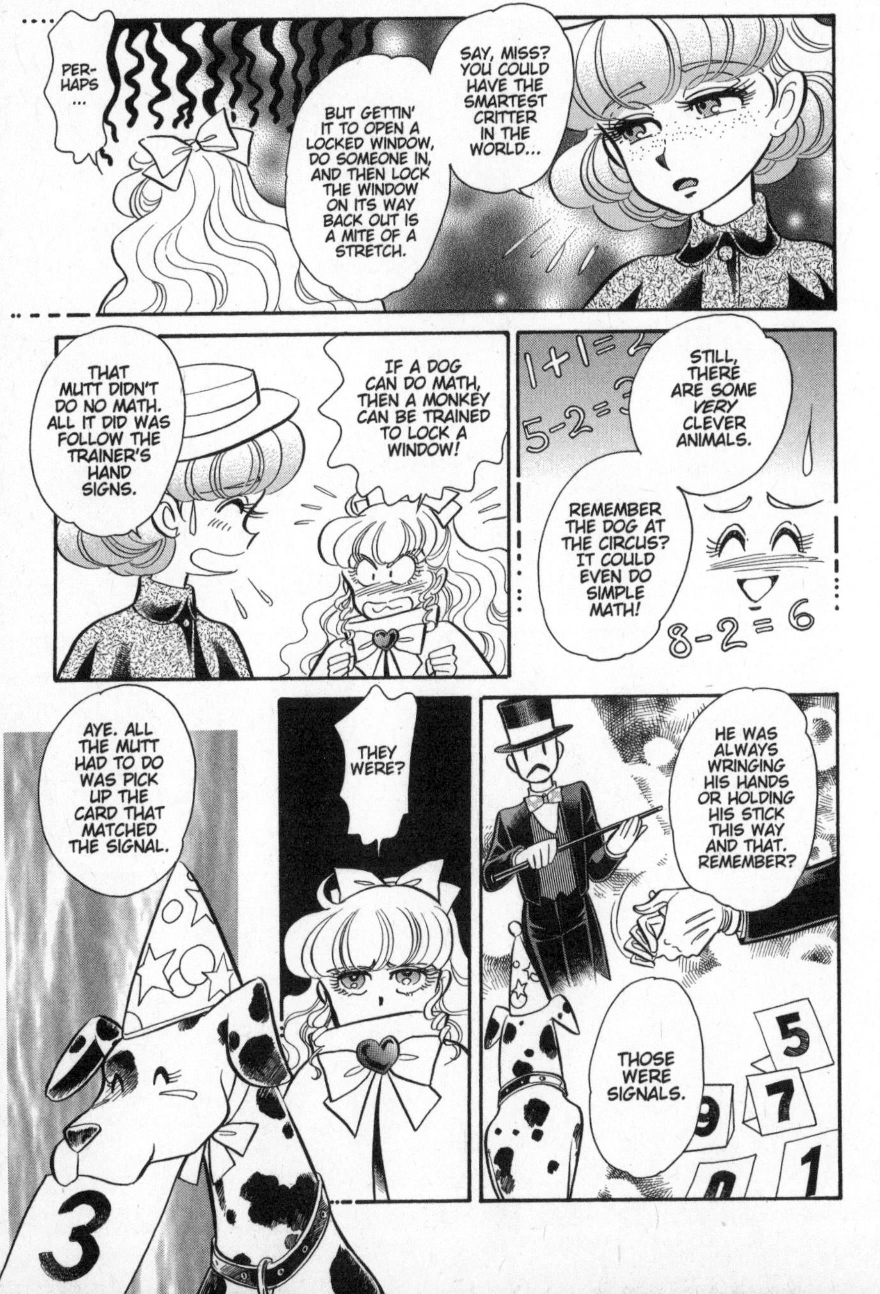
SAY, MISS? YOU COULD HAVE THE SMARTEST CRITTER IN THE WORLD...
BUT GETTIN' IT TO OPEN A LOCKED WINDOW, DO SOMEONE IN, AND THEN LOCK THE WINDOW ON ITS WAY BACK OUT IS A MITE OF A STRETCH.
PER-HAPS ...
STILL, THERE ARE SOME *VERY* CLEVER ANIMALS.
REMEMBER THE DOG AT THE CIRCUS? IT COULD EVEN DO SIMPLE MATH!
8-2=6
IF A DOG CAN DO MATH, THEN A MONKEY CAN BE TRAINED TO LOCK A WINDOW!
THAT MUTT DIDN'T DO NO MATH. ALL IT DID WAS FOLLOW THE TRAINER'S HAND SIGNS.
HE WAS ALWAYS WRINGING HIS HANDS OR HOLDING HIS STICK THIS WAY AND THAT. REMEMBER?
THOSE WERE SIGNALS.
THEY WERE?
AYE. ALL THE MUTT HAD TO DO WAS PICK UP THE CARD THAT MATCHED THE SIGNAL.

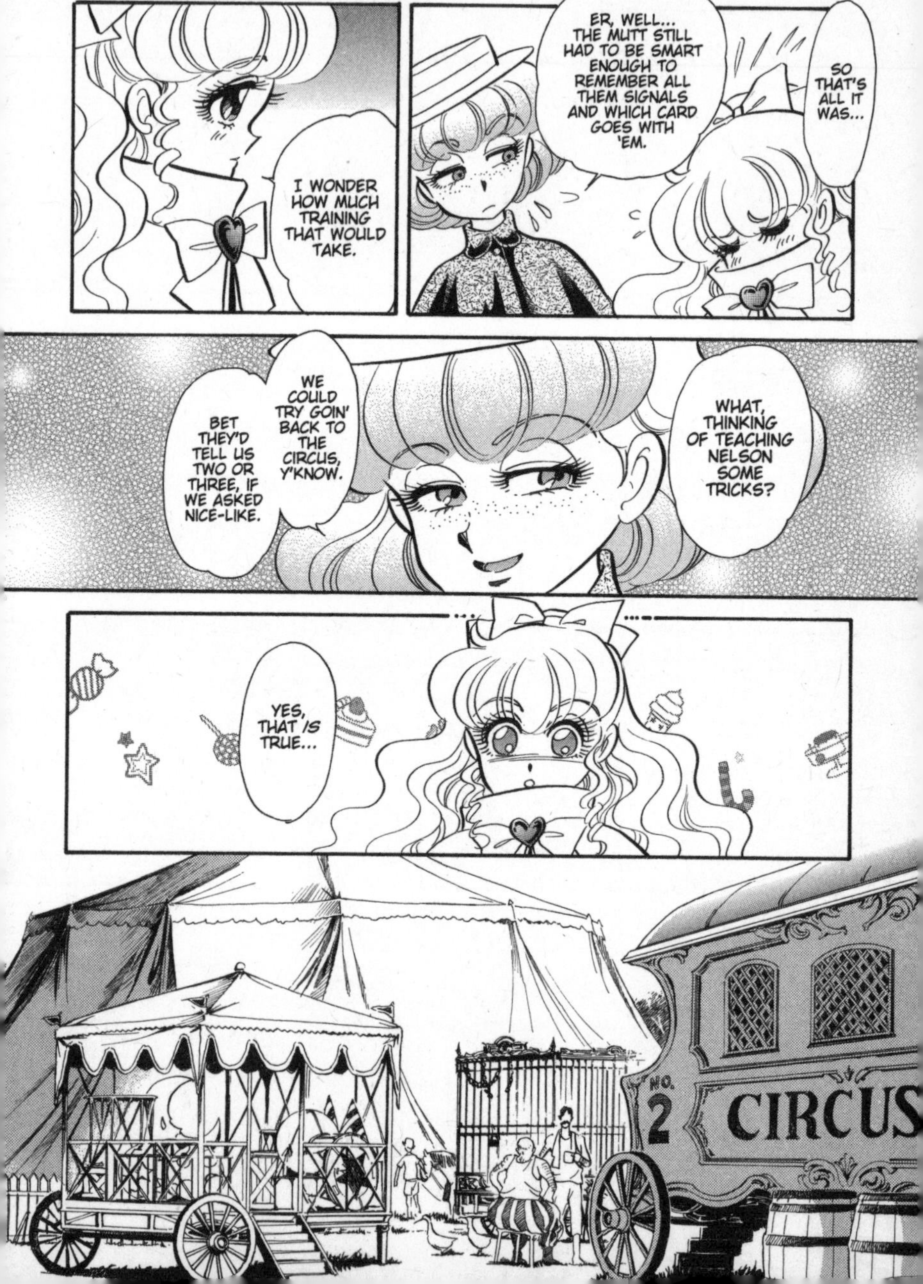
SO THAT'S ALL IT WAS...
ER, WELL... THE MUTT STILL HAD TO BE SMART ENOUGH TO REMEMBER ALL THEM SIGNALS AND WHICH CARD GOES WITH 'EM.
I WONDER HOW MUCH TRAINING THAT WOULD TAKE.
WHAT, THINKING OF TEACHING NELSON SOME TRICKS?
WE COULD TRY GOIN' BACK TO THE CIRCUS, Y'KNOW.
BET THEY'D TELL US TWO OR THREE, IF WE ASKED NICE-LIKE.
YES, THAT *IS* TRUE...
NO. 2
CIRCUS

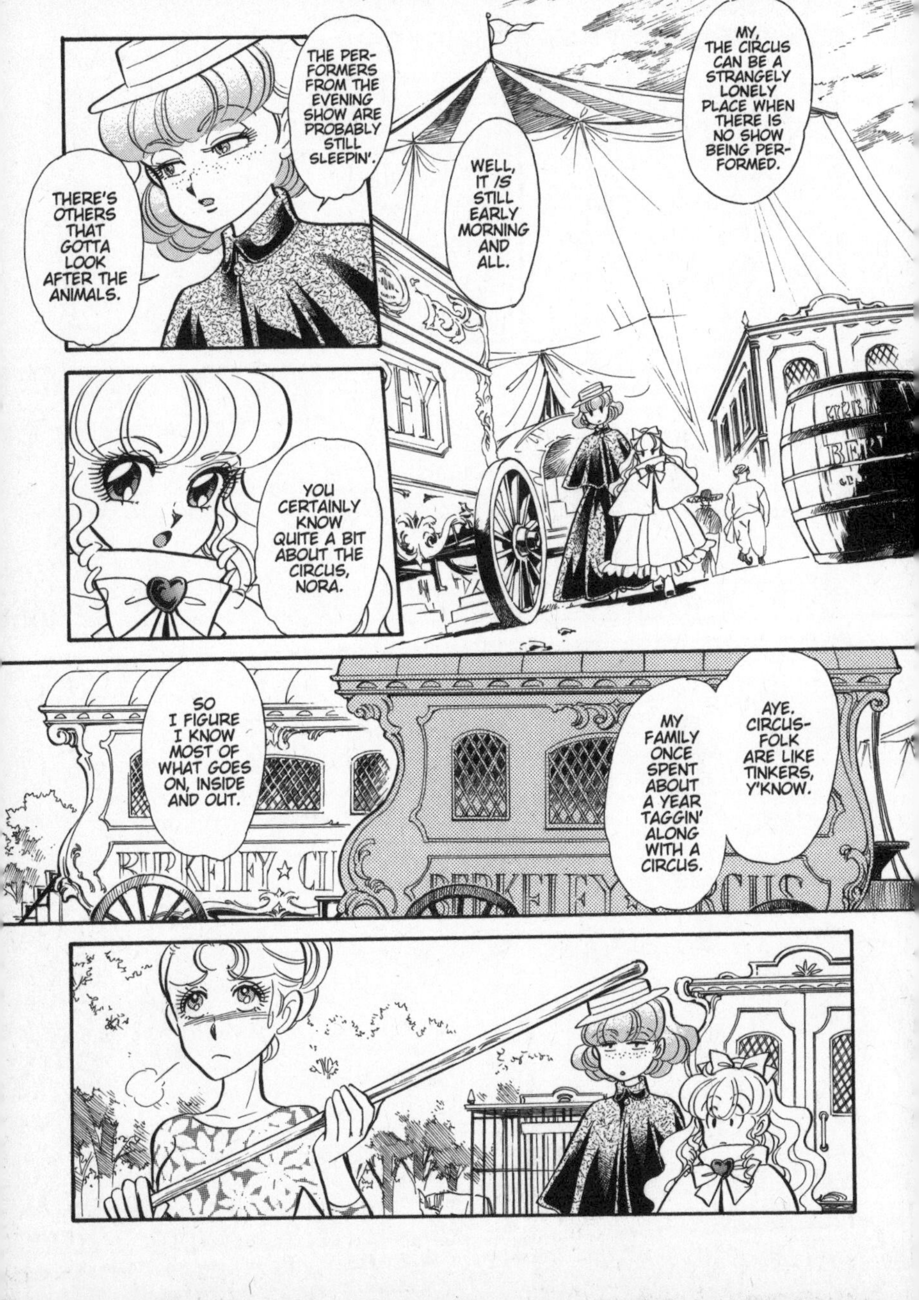
MY, THE CIRCUS CAN BE A STRANGELY LONELY PLACE WHEN THERE IS NO SHOW BEING PERFORMED.
WELL, IT *IS* STILL EARLY MORNING AND ALL.
THE PERFORMERS FROM THE EVENING SHOW ARE PROBABLY STILL SLEEPIN'.
THERE'S OTHERS THAT GOTTA LOOK AFTER THE ANIMALS.
YOU CERTAINLY KNOW QUITE A BIT ABOUT THE CIRCUS, NORA.
AYE. CIRCUS-FOLK ARE LIKE TINKERS, Y'KNOW.
MY FAMILY ONCE SPENT ABOUT A YEAR TAGGIN' ALONG WITH A CIRCUS.
SO I FIGURE I KNOW MOST OF WHAT GOES ON, INSIDE AND OUT.

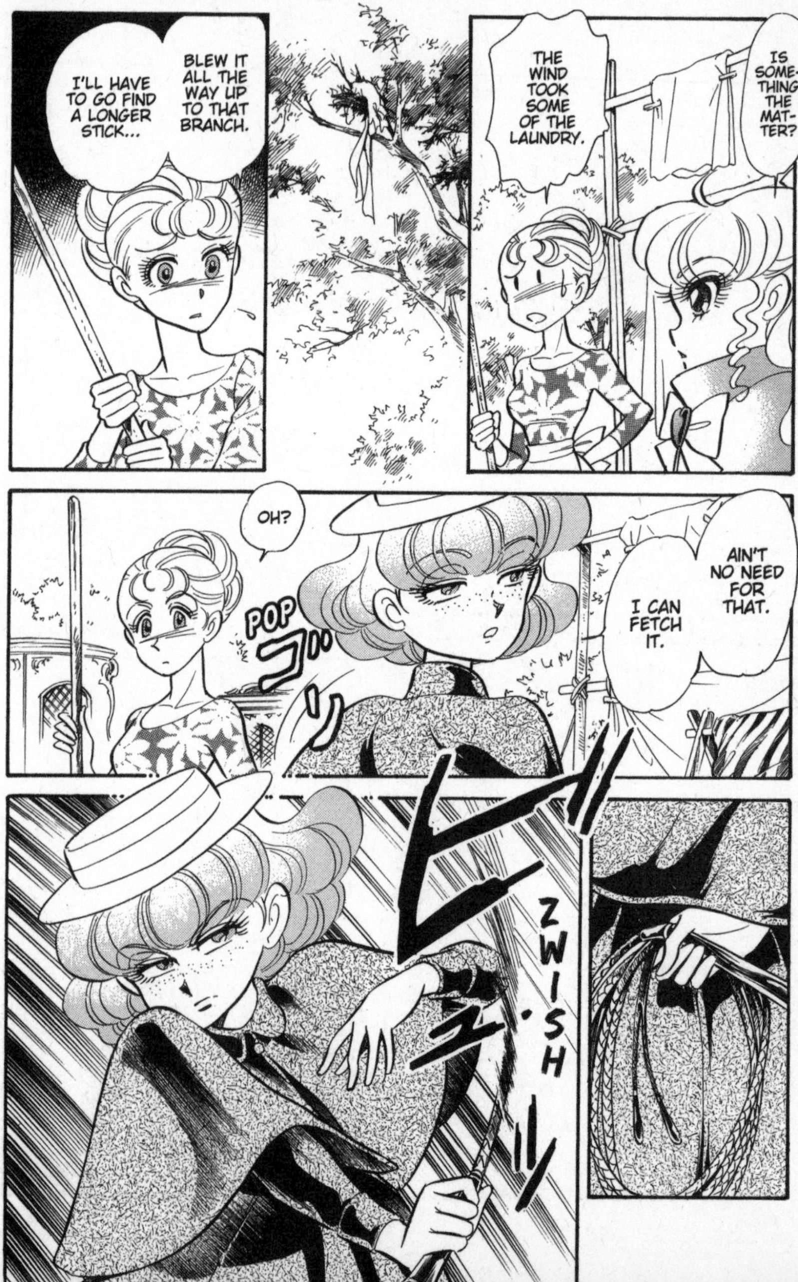
IS SOMETHING THE MATTER?
THE WIND TOOK SOME OF THE LAUNDRY.
BLEW IT ALL THE WAY UP TO THAT BRANCH.
I'LL HAVE TO GO FIND A LONGER STICK...
AIN'T NO NEED FOR THAT.
I CAN FETCH IT.
POP
OH?
ZWISH

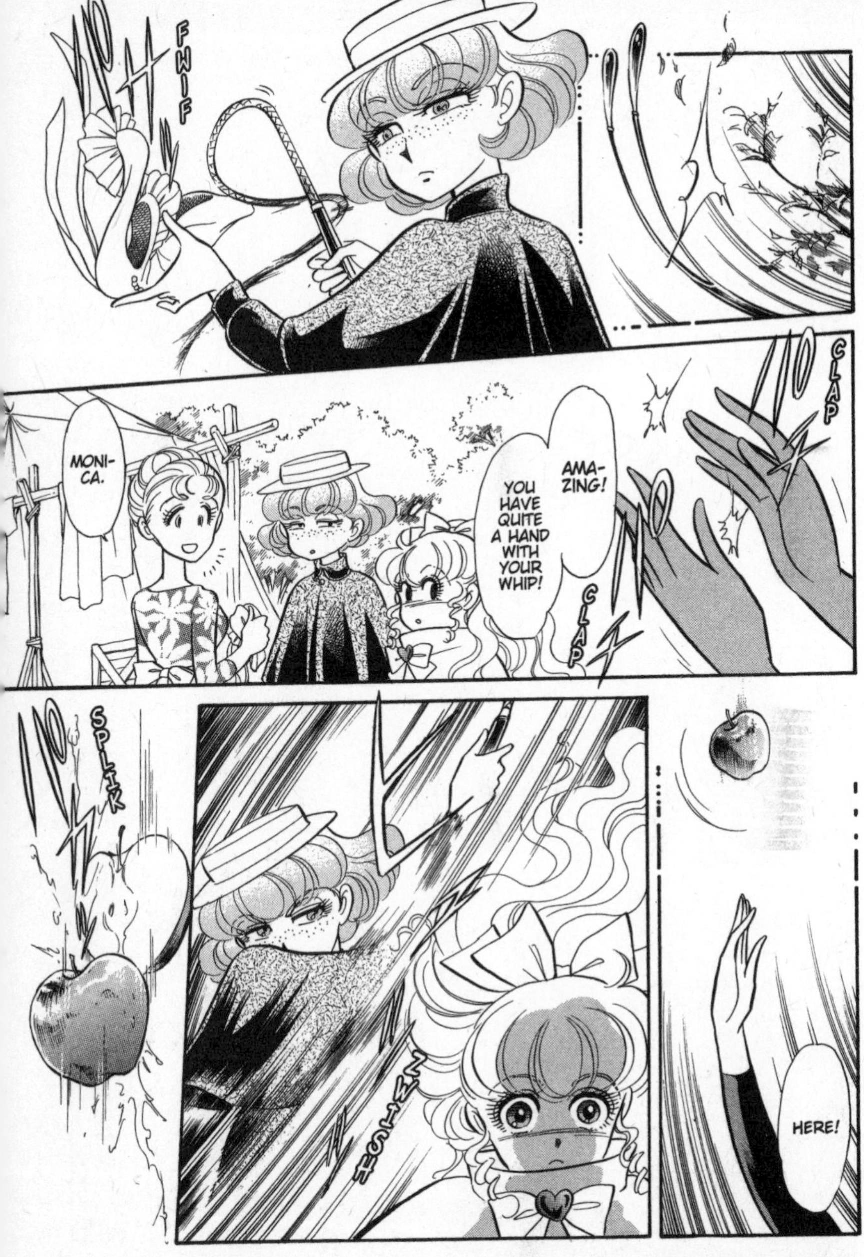
FWIF
CLAP
AMA-ZING!
YOU HAVE QUITE A HAND WITH YOUR WHIP!
CLAP
MONICA.
HERE!
ZWISH
SPLIK

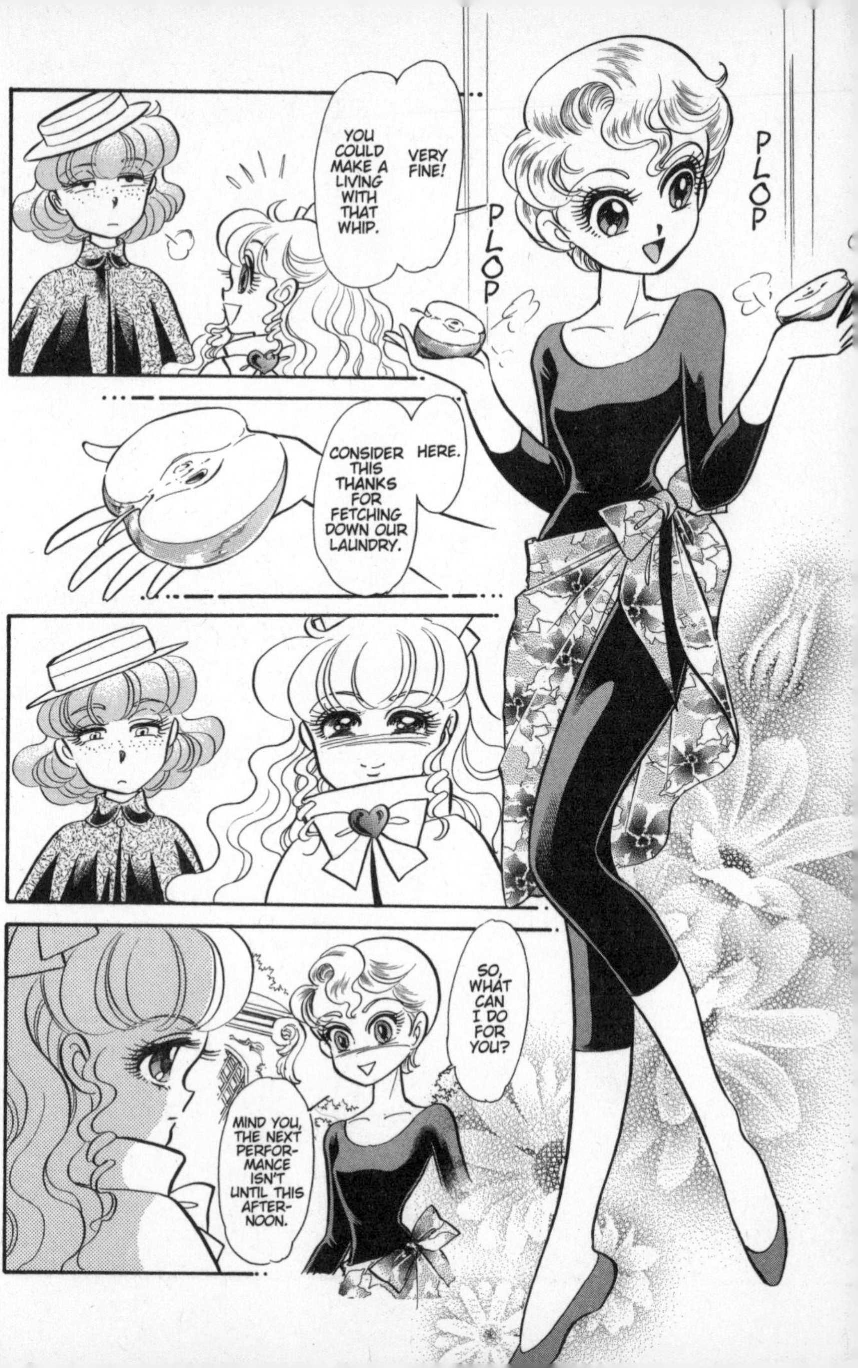
PLOP
PLOP
VERY FINE!
YOU COULD MAKE A LIVING WITH THAT WHIP.
HERE.
CONSIDER THIS THANKS FOR FETCHING DOWN OUR LAUNDRY.
SO, WHAT CAN I DO FOR YOU?
MIND YOU, THE NEXT PERFORMANCE ISN'T UNTIL THIS AFTERNOON.

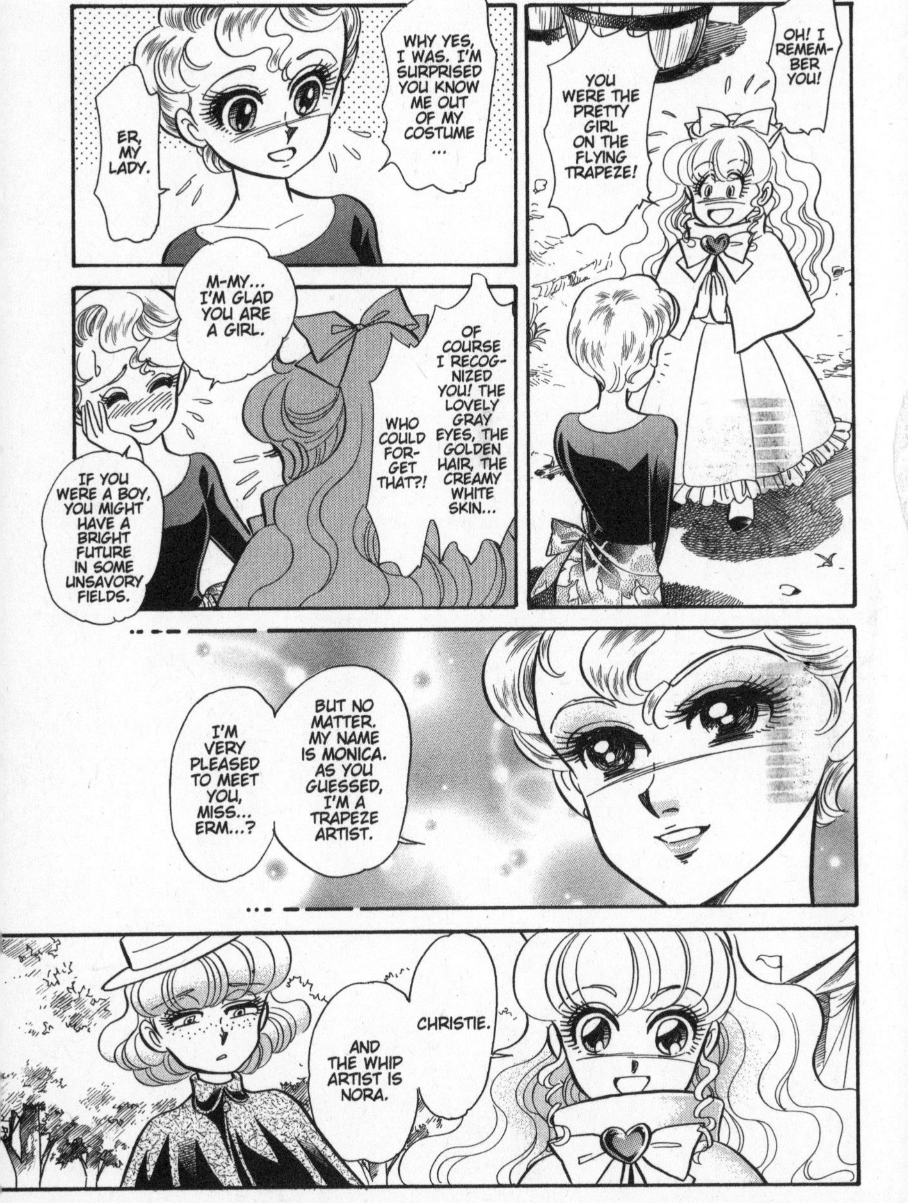
OH! I REMEMBER YOU!
YOU WERE THE PRETTY GIRL ON THE FLYING TRAPEZE!
WHY YES, I WAS. I'M SURPRISED YOU KNOW ME OUT OF MY COSTUME ...
ER, MY LADY.
OF COURSE I RECOGNIZED YOU! THE LOVELY GRAY EYES, THE GOLDEN HAIR, THE CREAMY WHITE SKIN...
WHO COULD FORGET THAT?!
M-MY... I'M GLAD YOU ARE A GIRL.
IF YOU WERE A BOY, YOU MIGHT HAVE A BRIGHT FUTURE IN SOME UNSAVORY FIELDS.
BUT NO MATTER. MY NAME IS MONICA. AS YOU GUESSED, I'M A TRAPEZE ARTIST.
I'M VERY PLEASED TO MEET YOU, MISS... ERM...?
CHRISTIE.
AND THE WHIP ARTIST IS NORA.

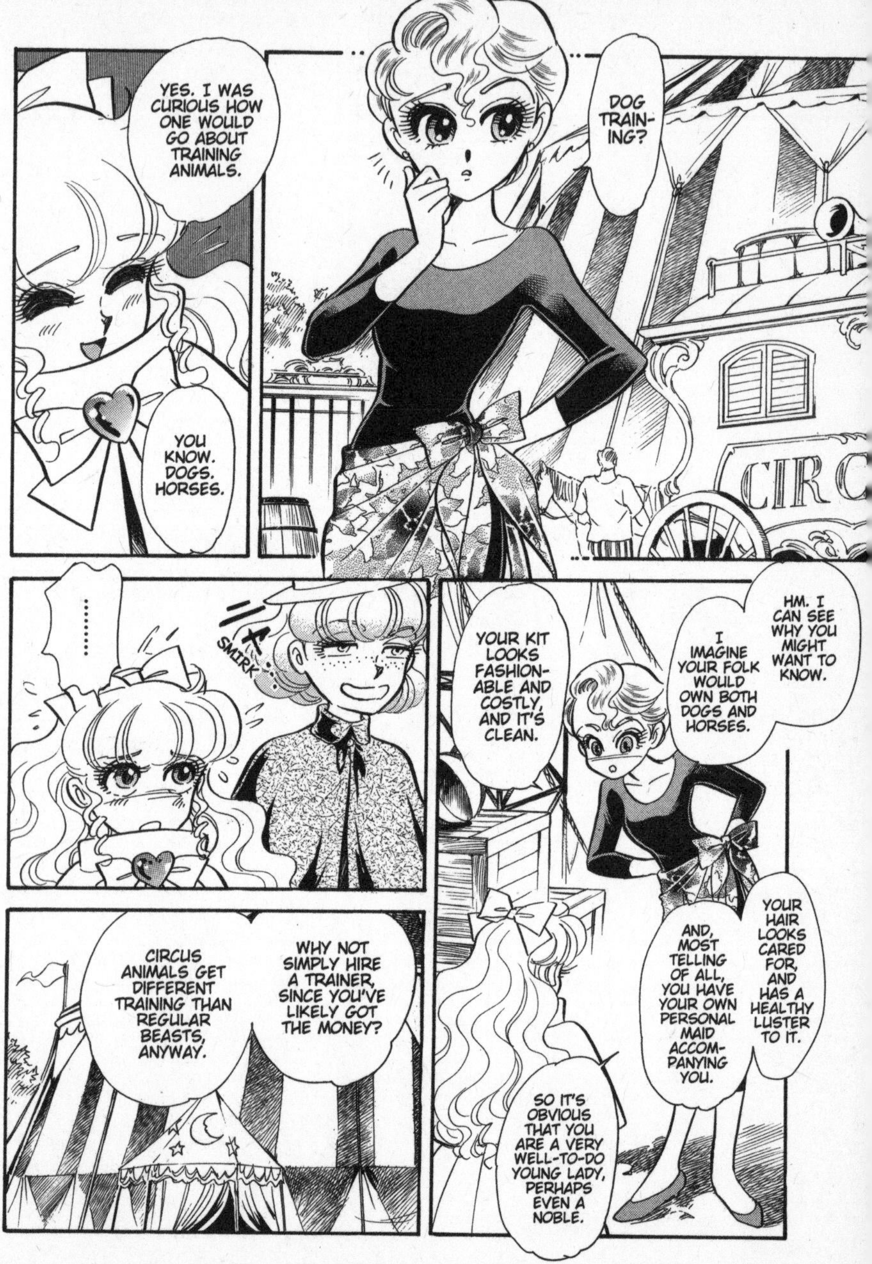
...
...
DOG TRAINING?
CIRC
YES. I WAS CURIOUS HOW ONE WOULD GO ABOUT TRAINING ANIMALS.
YOU KNOW. DOGS. HORSES.
HM. I CAN SEE WHY YOU MIGHT WANT TO KNOW.
I IMAGINE YOUR FOLK WOULD OWN BOTH DOGS AND HORSES.
YOUR KIT LOOKS FASHIONABLE AND COSTLY, AND IT'S CLEAN.
YOUR HAIR LOOKS CARED FOR, AND HAS A HEALTHY LUSTER TO IT.
AND, MOST TELLING OF ALL, YOU HAVE YOUR OWN PERSONAL MAID ACCOMPANYING YOU.
SO IT'S OBVIOUS THAT YOU ARE A VERY WELL-TO-DO YOUNG LADY, PERHAPS EVEN A NOBLE.
SMIRK
......
WHY NOT SIMPLY HIRE A TRAINER, SINCE YOU'VE LIKELY GOT THE MONEY?
CIRCUS ANIMALS GET DIFFERENT TRAINING THAN REGULAR BEASTS, ANYWAY.

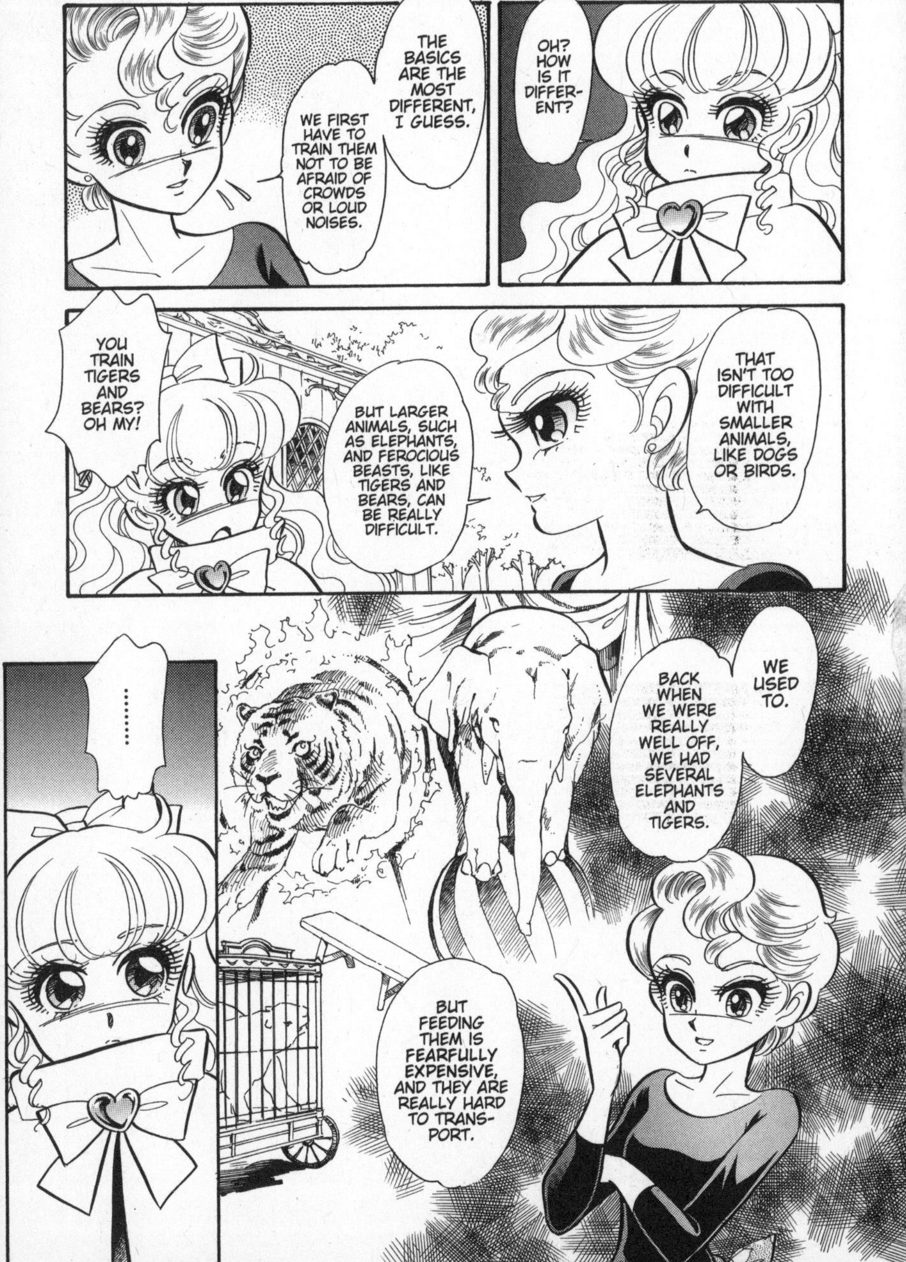
OH? HOW IS IT DIFFER-ENT?
THE BASICS ARE THE MOST DIFFERENT, I GUESS.
WE FIRST HAVE TO TRAIN THEM NOT TO BE AFRAID OF CROWDS OR LOUD NOISES.
THAT ISN'T TOO DIFFICULT WITH SMALLER ANIMALS, LIKE DOGS OR BIRDS.
BUT LARGER ANIMALS, SUCH AS ELEPHANTS, AND FEROCIOUS BEASTS, LIKE TIGERS AND BEARS, CAN BE REALLY DIFFICULT.
YOU TRAIN TIGERS AND BEARS? OH MY!
WE USED TO.
BACK WHEN WE WERE REALLY WELL OFF, WE HAD SEVERAL ELEPHANTS AND TIGERS.
BUT FEEDING THEM IS FEARFULLY EXPENSIVE, AND THEY ARE REALLY HARD TO TRANS-PORT.
......

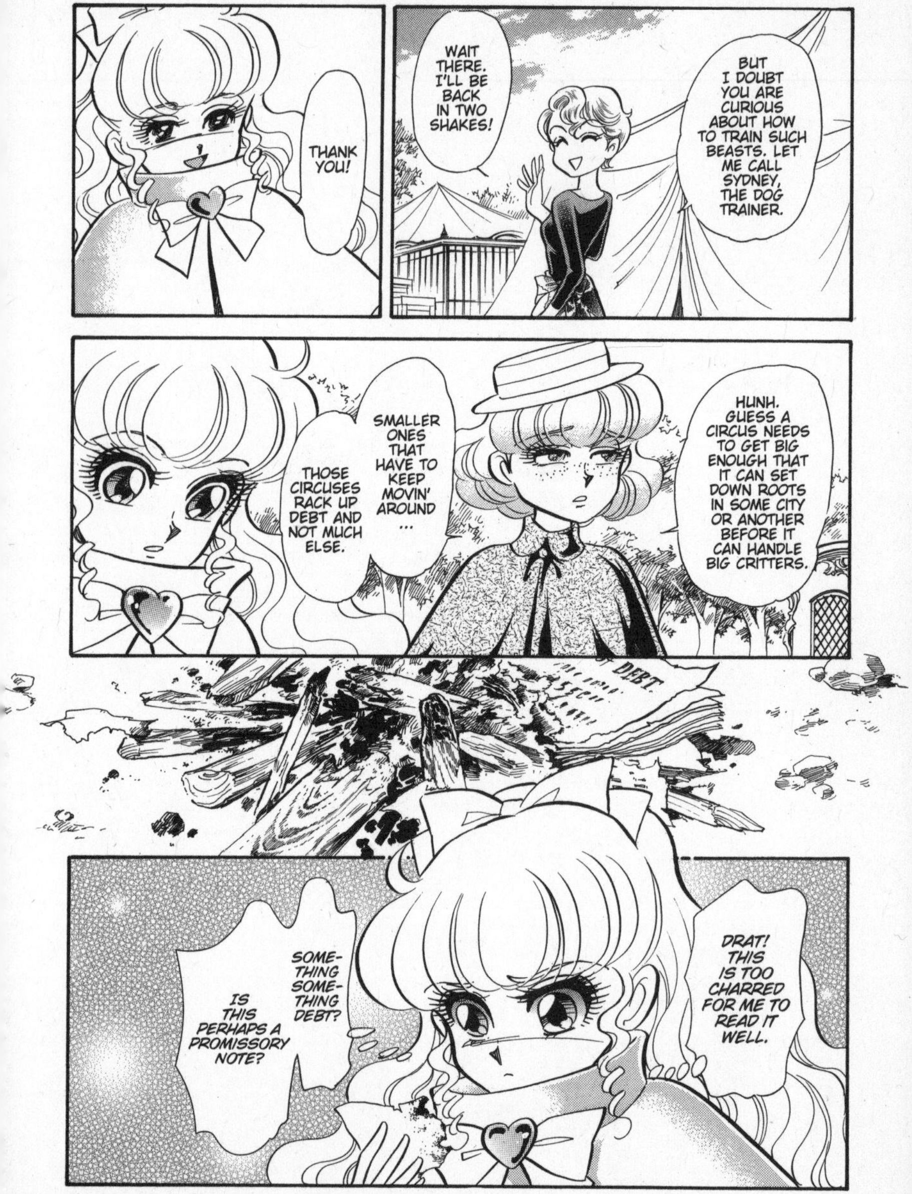
BUT I DOUBT YOU ARE CURIOUS ABOUT HOW TO TRAIN SUCH BEASTS. LET ME CALL SYDNEY, THE DOG TRAINER.
WAIT THERE. I'LL BE BACK IN TWO SHAKES!
THANK YOU!
HUNH. GUESS A CIRCUS NEEDS TO GET BIG ENOUGH THAT IT CAN SET DOWN ROOTS IN SOME CITY OR ANOTHER BEFORE IT CAN HANDLE BIG CRITTERS.
SMALLER ONES THAT HAVE TO KEEP MOVIN' AROUND ...
THOSE CIRCUSES RACK UP DEBT AND NOT MUCH ELSE.
DEBT
DRAT! THIS IS TOO CHARRED FOR ME TO READ IT WELL.
SOME-THING SOME-THING DEBT?
IS THIS PERHAPS A PROMISSORY NOTE?

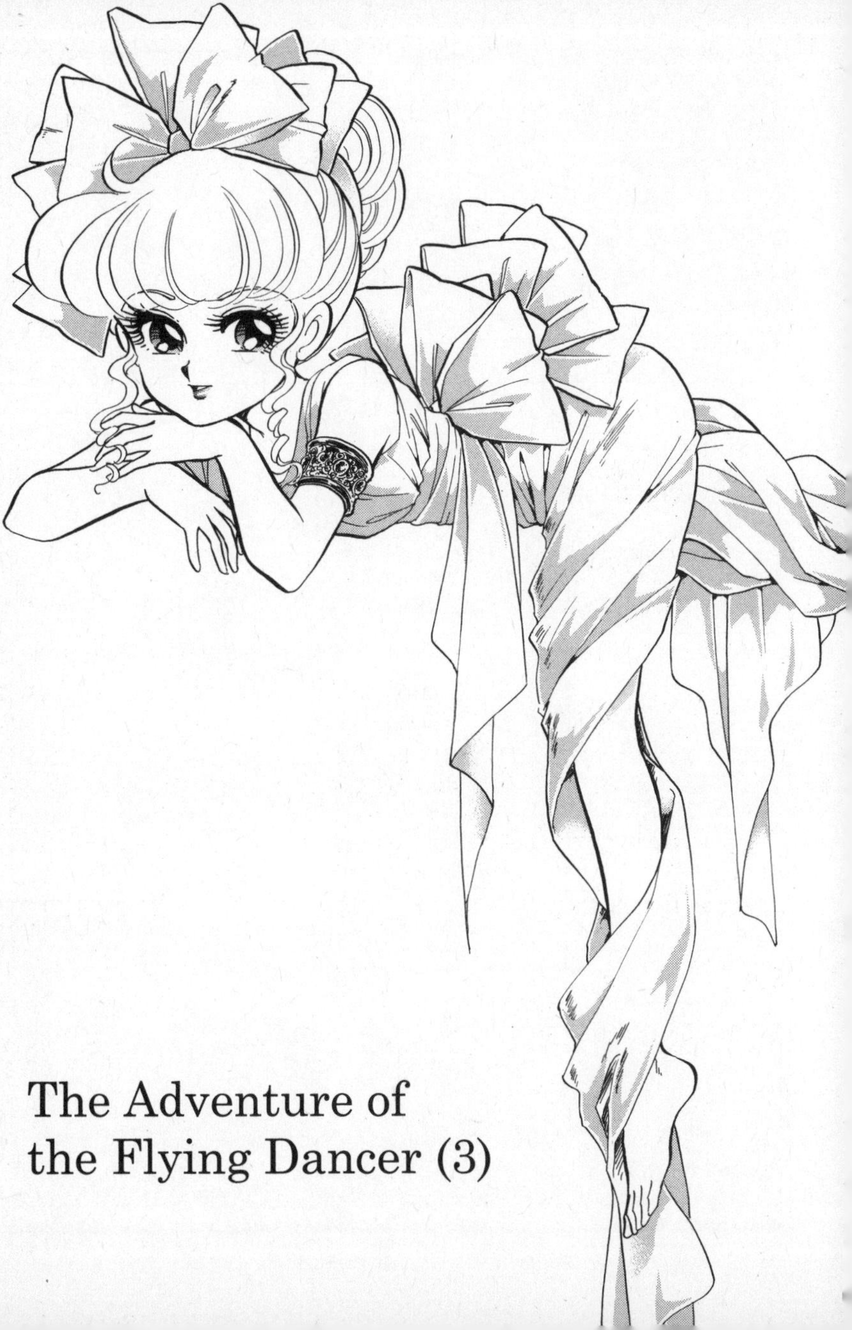

The Adventure of the Flying Dancer (3)

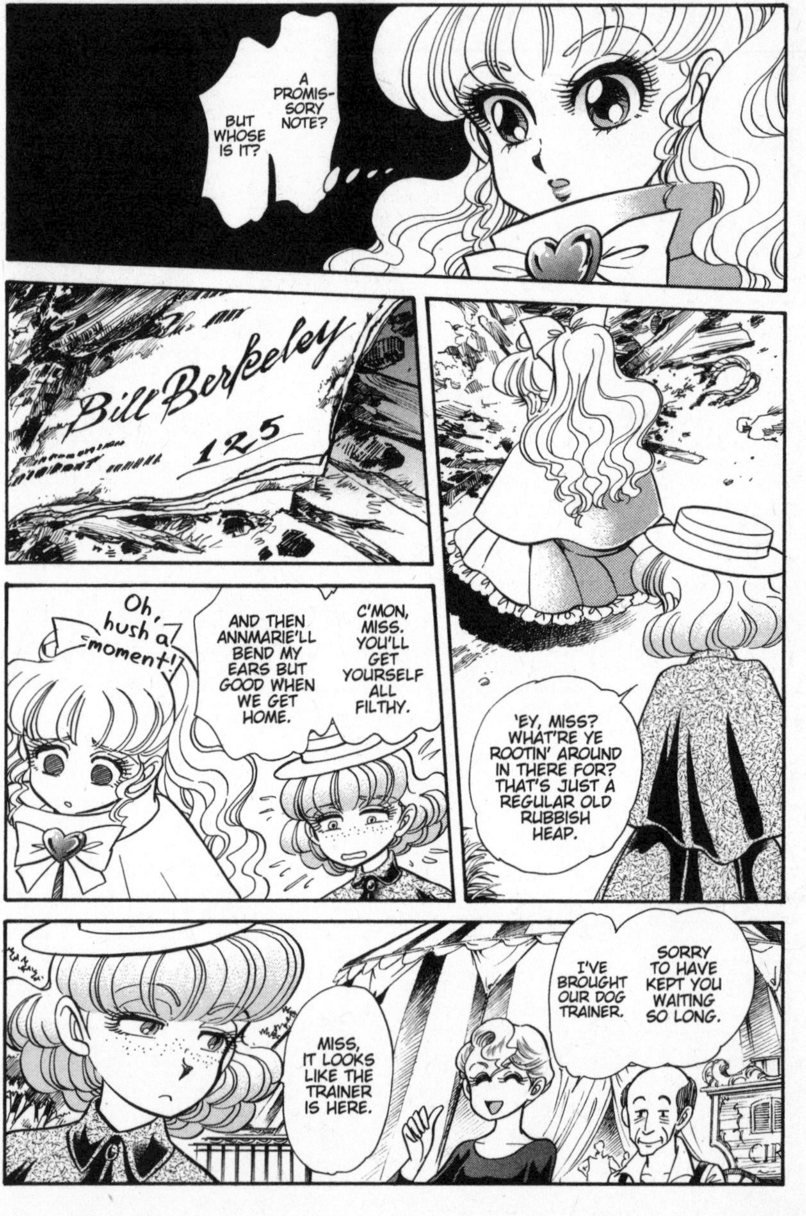
A PROMISSORY NOTE?
BUT WHOSE IS IT?
....
'EY, MISS? WHAT'RE YE ROOTIN' AROUND IN THERE FOR? THAT'S JUST A REGULAR OLD RUBBISH HEAP.
Bill Berkeley
125
C'MON, MISS. YOU'LL GET YOURSELF ALL FILTHY.
AND THEN ANNMARIE'LL BEND MY EARS BUT GOOD WHEN WE GET HOME.
Oh, hush a moment!
SORRY TO HAVE KEPT YOU WAITING SO LONG.
I'VE BROUGHT OUR DOG TRAINER.
MISS, IT LOOKS LIKE THE TRAINER IS HERE.

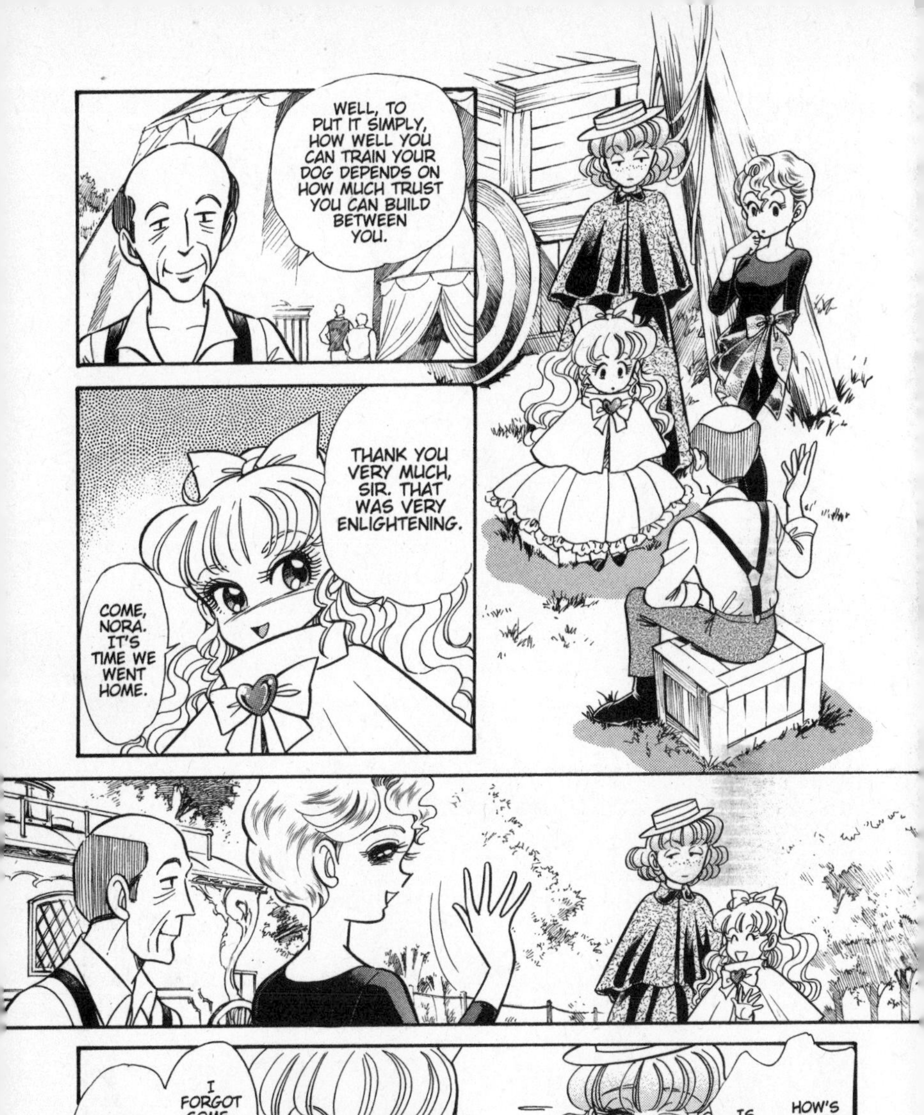
WELL, TO PUT IT SIMPLY, HOW WELL YOU CAN TRAIN YOUR DOG DEPENDS ON HOW MUCH TRUST YOU CAN BUILD BETWEEN YOU.
THANK YOU VERY MUCH, SIR. THAT WAS VERY ENLIGHTENING.
COME, NORA. IT'S TIME WE WENT HOME.
HOW'S THAT? ALREADY, MISS?
IS SOMETHIN' WRONG?
I FORGOT SOMETHING VERY IMPORTANT.
WE NEED TO VISIT SCOTLAND YARD.

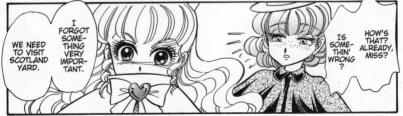

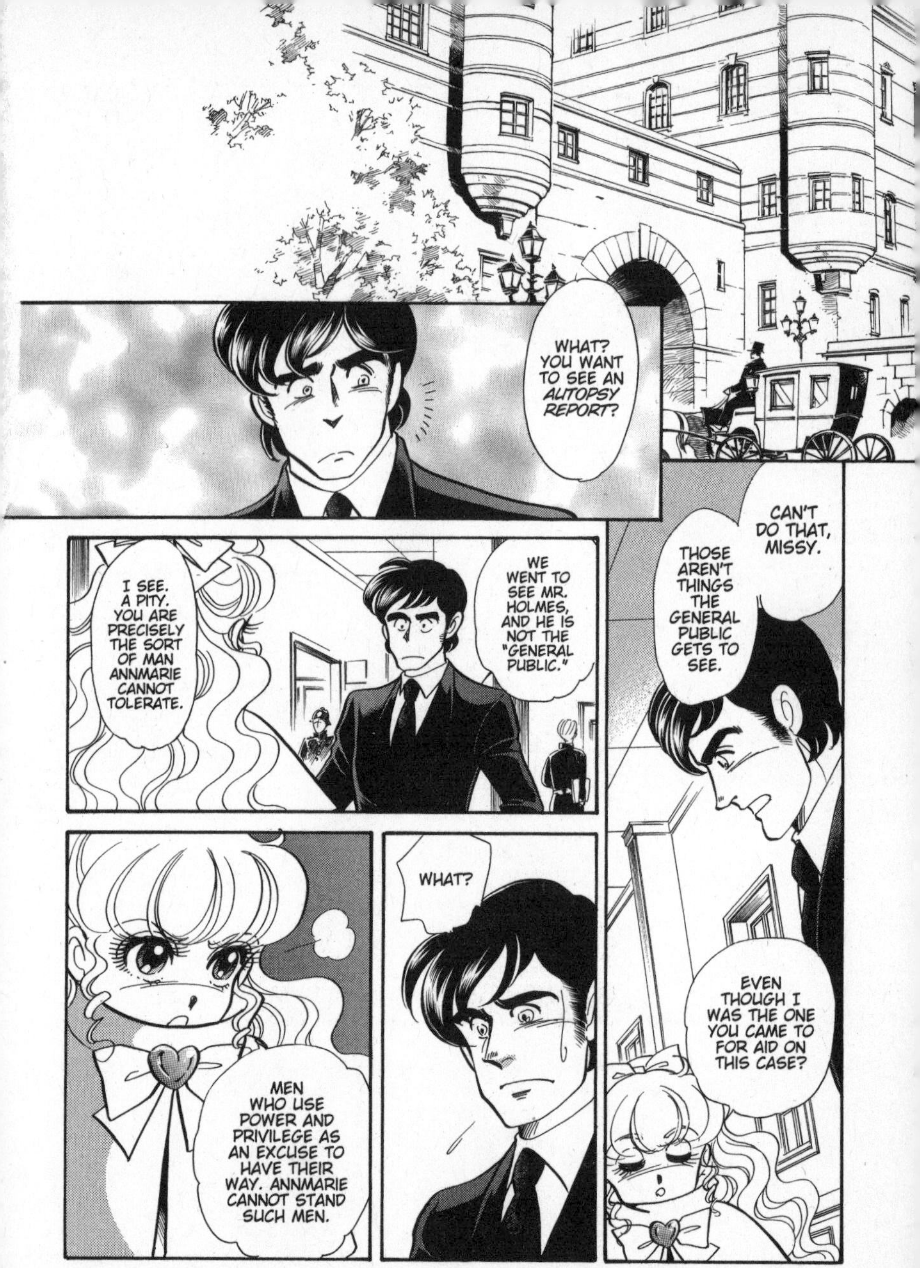
WHAT? YOU WANT TO SEE AN *AUTOPSY REPORT?*
CAN'T DO THAT, MISSY.
THOSE AREN'T THINGS THE GENERAL PUBLIC GETS TO SEE.
EVEN THOUGH I WAS THE ONE YOU CAME TO FOR AID ON THIS CASE?
WE WENT TO SEE MR. HOLMES, AND HE IS NOT THE "GENERAL PUBLIC."
I SEE. A PITY. YOU ARE PRECISELY THE SORT OF MAN ANNMARIE CANNOT TOLERATE.
WHAT?
MEN WHO USE POWER AND PRIVILEGE AS AN EXCUSE TO HAVE THEIR WAY. ANNMARIE CANNOT STAND SUCH MEN.

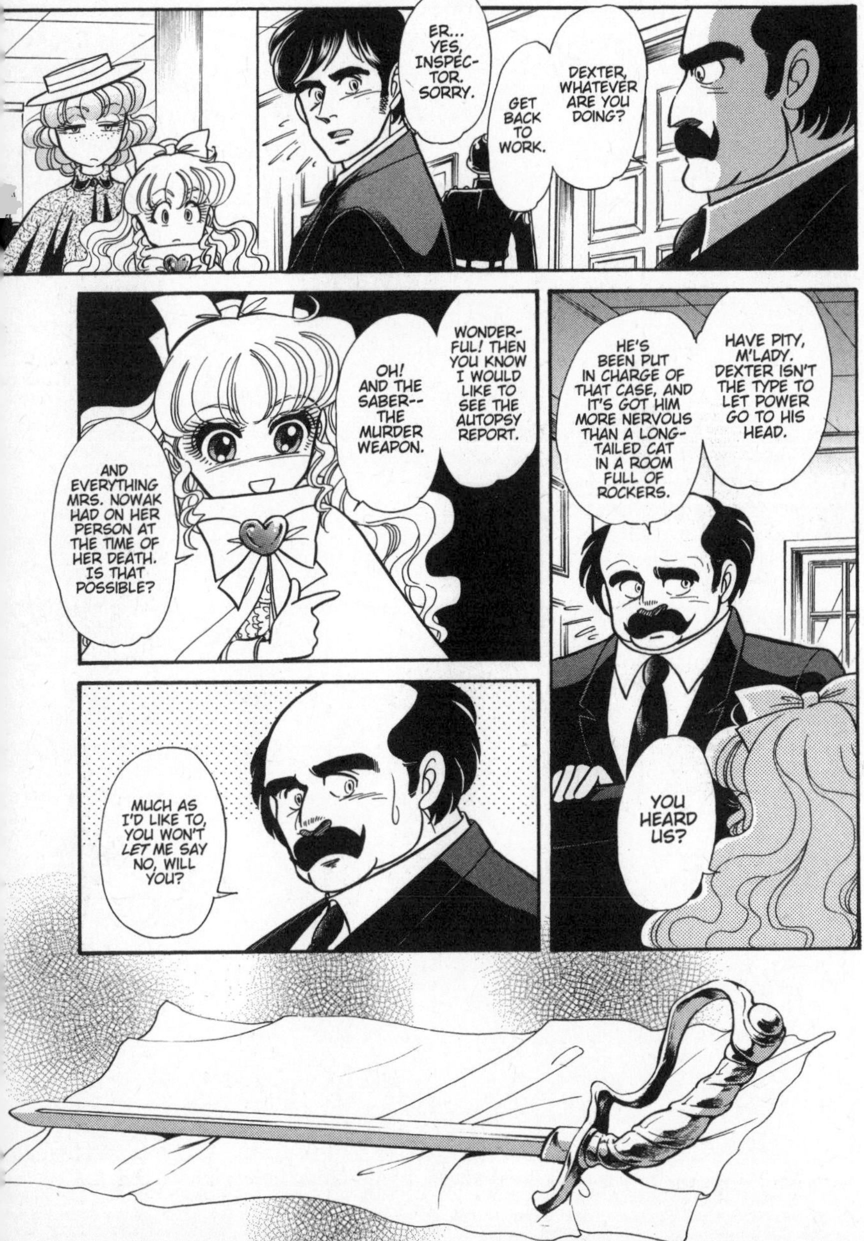
DEXTER, WHATEVER ARE YOU DOING?
GET BACK TO WORK.
ER... YES, INSPECTOR. SORRY.
HAVE PITY, M'LADY. DEXTER ISN'T THE TYPE TO LET POWER GO TO HIS HEAD.
HE'S BEEN PUT IN CHARGE OF THAT CASE, AND IT'S GOT HIM MORE NERVOUS THAN A LONG-TAILED CAT IN A ROOM FULL OF ROCKERS.
YOU HEARD US?
WONDERFUL! THEN YOU KNOW I WOULD LIKE TO SEE THE AUTOPSY REPORT.
OH! AND THE SABER--THE MURDER WEAPON.
AND EVERYTHING MRS. NOWAK HAD ON HER PERSON AT THE TIME OF HER DEATH. IS THAT POSSIBLE?
MUCH AS I'D LIKE TO, YOU WON'T *LET* ME SAY NO, WILL YOU?

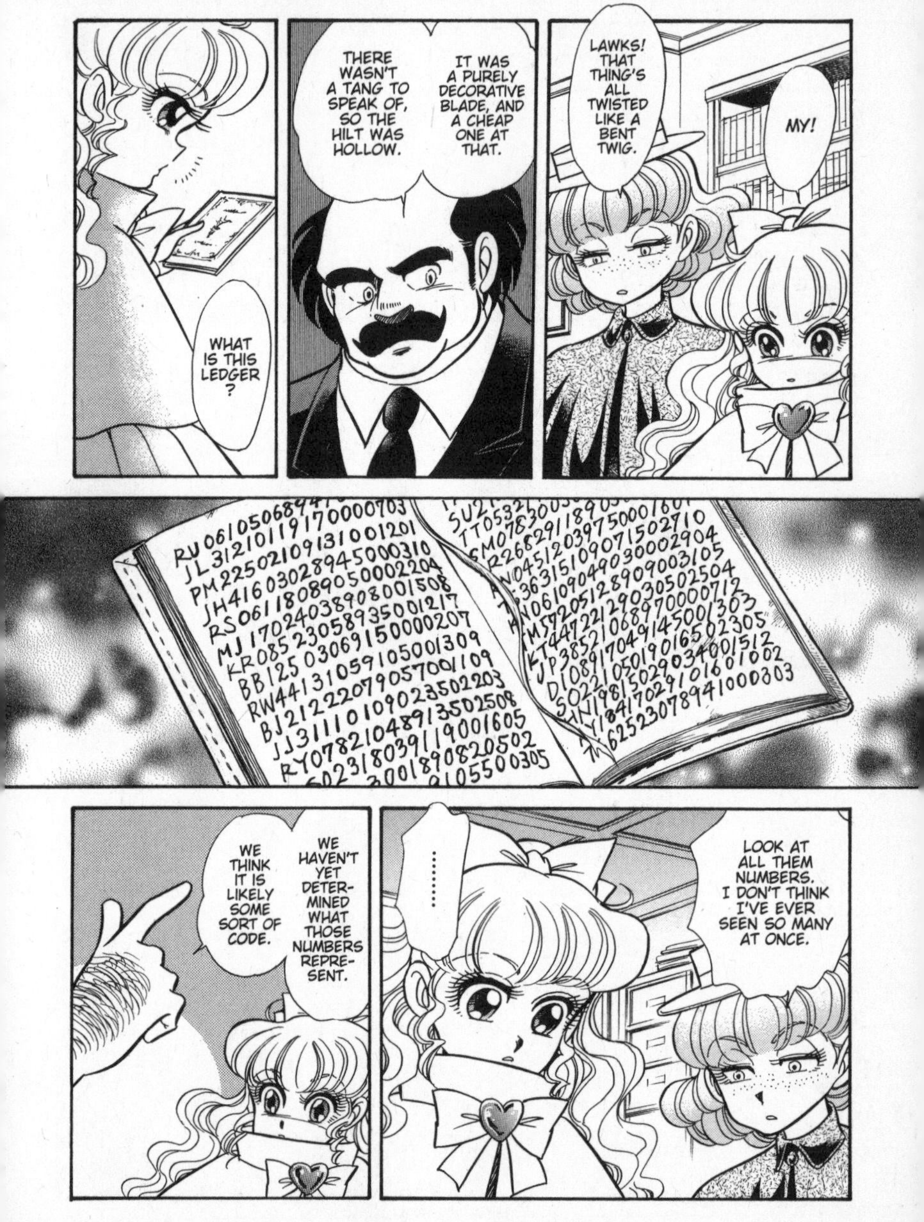
MY!
LAWKS! THAT THING'S ALL TWISTED LIKE A BENT TWIG.
THERE WASN'T A TANG TO SPEAK OF, SO THE HILT WAS HOLLOW. IT WAS A PURELY DECORATIVE BLADE, AND A CHEAP ONE AT THAT.
WHAT IS THIS LEDGER?
LOOK AT ALL THEM NUMBERS. I DON'T THINK I'VE EVER SEEN SO MANY AT ONCE.
......
WE HAVEN'T YET DETERMINED WHAT THOSE NUMBERS REPRESENT.
WE THINK IT IS LIKELY SOME SORT OF CODE.

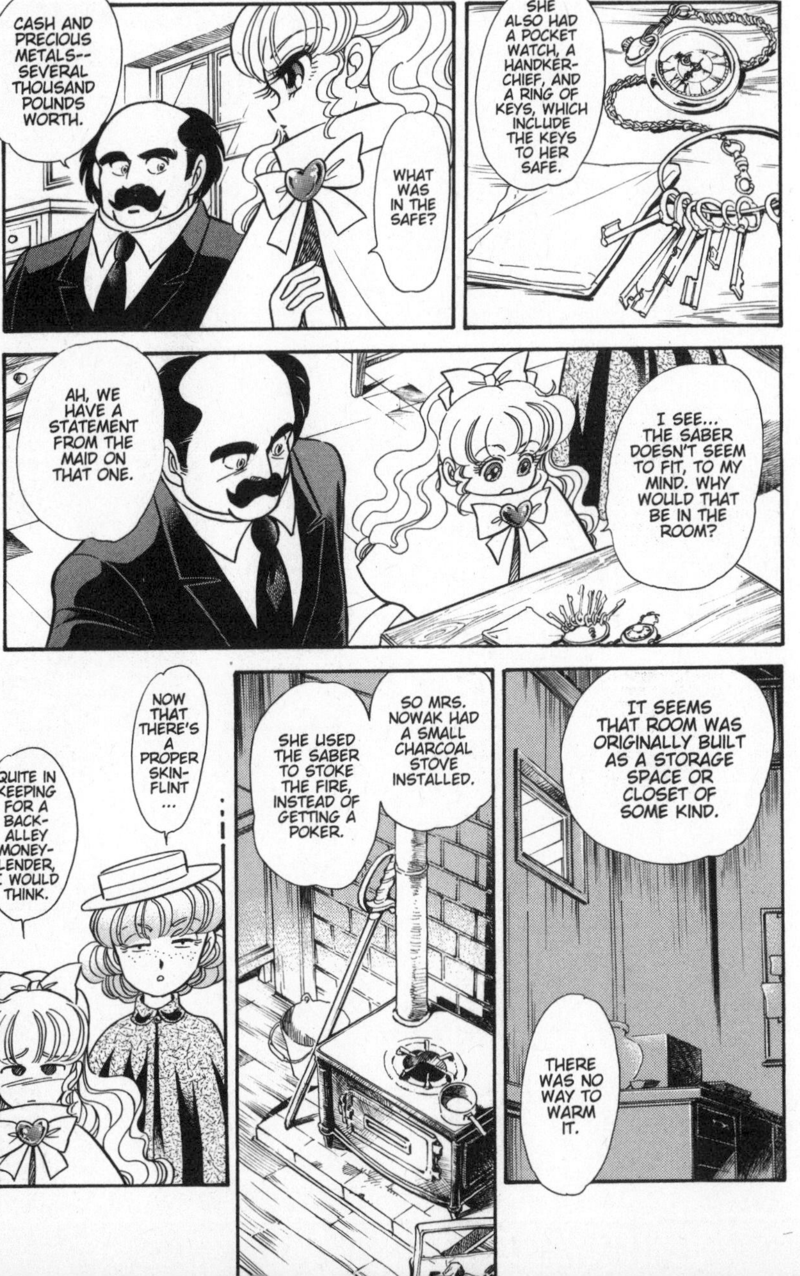
SHE ALSO HAD A POCKET WATCH, A HANDKER-CHIEF, AND A RING OF KEYS, WHICH INCLUDE THE KEYS TO HER SAFE.
WHAT WAS IN THE SAFE?
CASH AND PRECIOUS METALS-- SEVERAL THOUSAND POUNDS WORTH.
I SEE... THE SABER DOESN'T SEEM TO FIT, TO MY MIND. WHY WOULD THAT BE IN THE ROOM?
AH, WE HAVE A STATEMENT FROM THE MAID ON THAT ONE.
IT SEEMS THAT ROOM WAS ORIGINALLY BUILT AS A STORAGE SPACE OR CLOSET OF SOME KIND.
THERE WAS NO WAY TO WARM IT.
SO MRS. NOWAK HAD A SMALL CHARCOAL STOVE INSTALLED.
SHE USED THE SABER TO STOKE THE FIRE, INSTEAD OF GETTING A POKER.
NOW THAT THERE'S A PROPER SKIN-FLINT ...
QUITE IN KEEPING FOR A BACK-ALLEY MONEY-LENDER, I WOULD THINK.

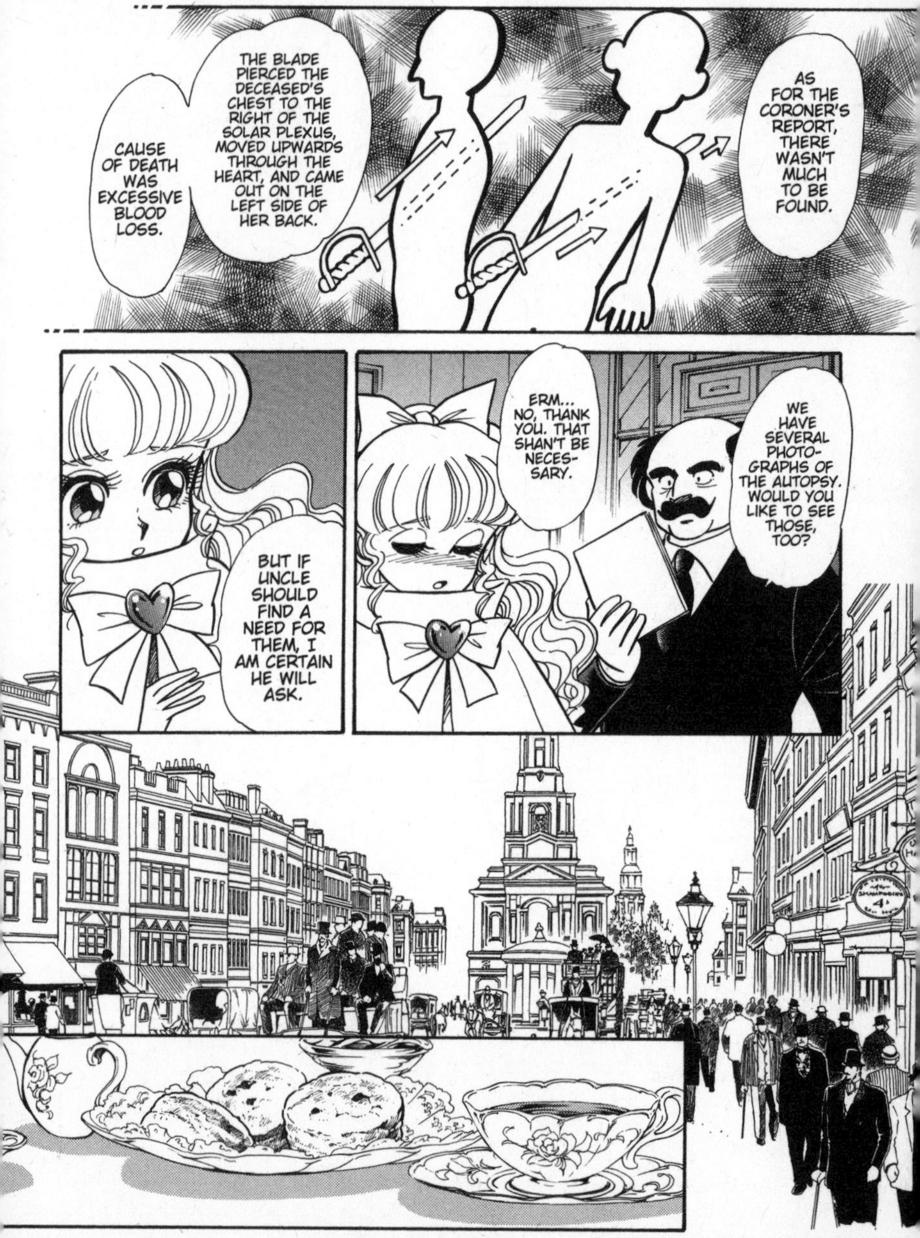
AS FOR THE CORONER'S REPORT, THERE WASN'T MUCH TO BE FOUND.
THE BLADE PIERCED THE DECEASED'S CHEST TO THE RIGHT OF THE SOLAR PLEXUS, MOVED UPWARDS THROUGH THE HEART, AND CAME OUT ON THE LEFT SIDE OF HER BACK.
CAUSE OF DEATH WAS EXCESSIVE BLOOD LOSS.
WE HAVE SEVERAL PHOTOGRAPHS OF THE AUTOPSY. WOULD YOU LIKE TO SEE THOSE, TOO?
ERM... NO, THANK YOU. THAT SHAN'T BE NECESSARY.
BUT IF UNCLE SHOULD FIND A NEED FOR THEM, I AM CERTAIN HE WILL ASK.

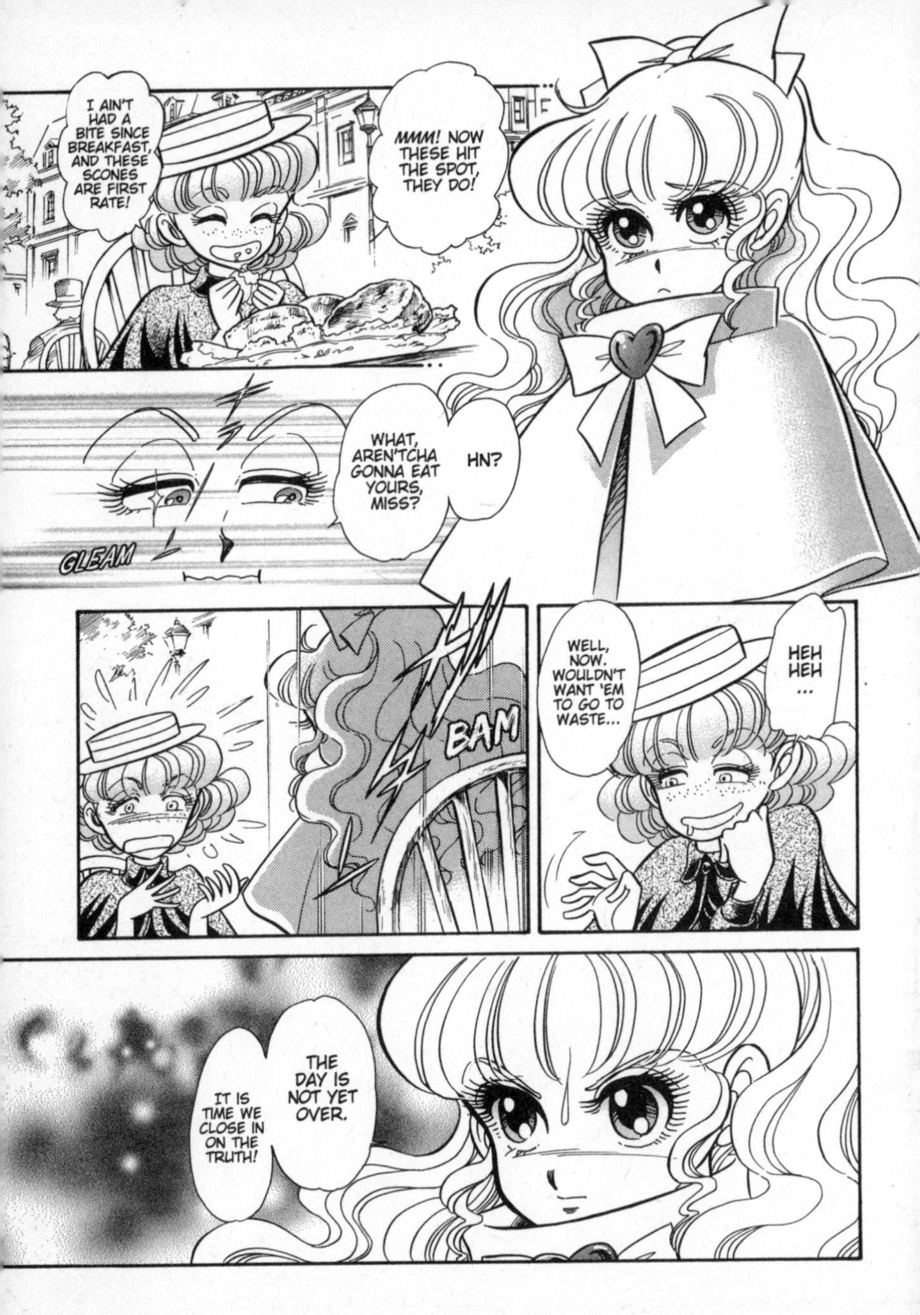
MMM! NOW THESE HIT THE SPOT, THEY DO!
I AIN'T HAD A BITE SINCE BREAKFAST, AND THESE SCONES ARE FIRST RATE!
HN?
WHAT, AREN'TCHA GONNA EAT YOURS, MISS?
GLEAM
HEH HEH ...
WELL, NOW. WOULDN'T WANT 'EM TO GO TO WASTE...
BAM
THE DAY IS NOT YET OVER.
IT IS TIME WE CLOSE IN ON THE TRUTH!

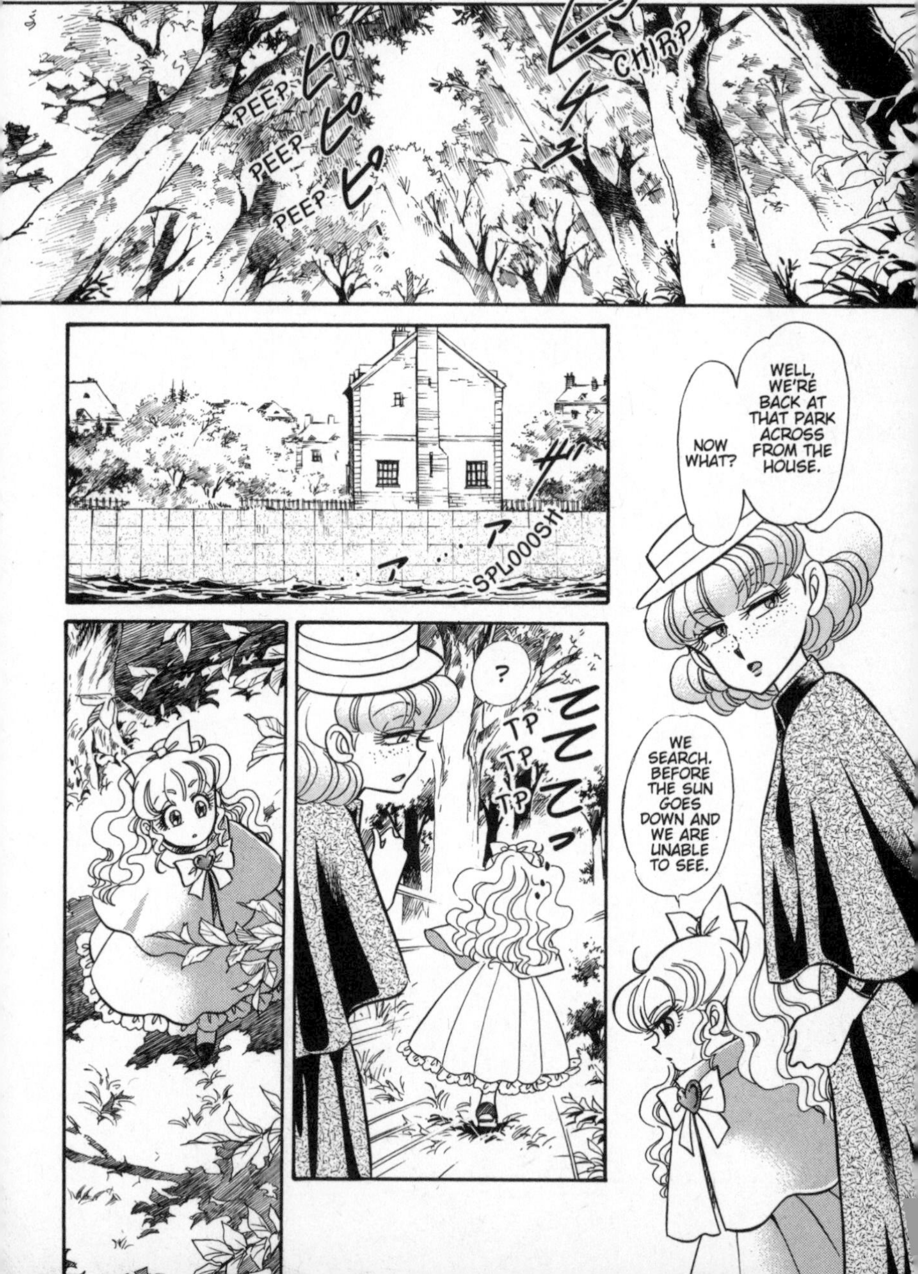
CHIRP
PEEP
PEEP
PEEP
WELL, WE'RE BACK AT THAT PARK ACROSS FROM THE HOUSE.
NOW WHAT?
WE SEARCH. BEFORE THE SUN GOES DOWN AND WE ARE UNABLE TO SEE.
SPLOOOSH
?
TP
TP
TP

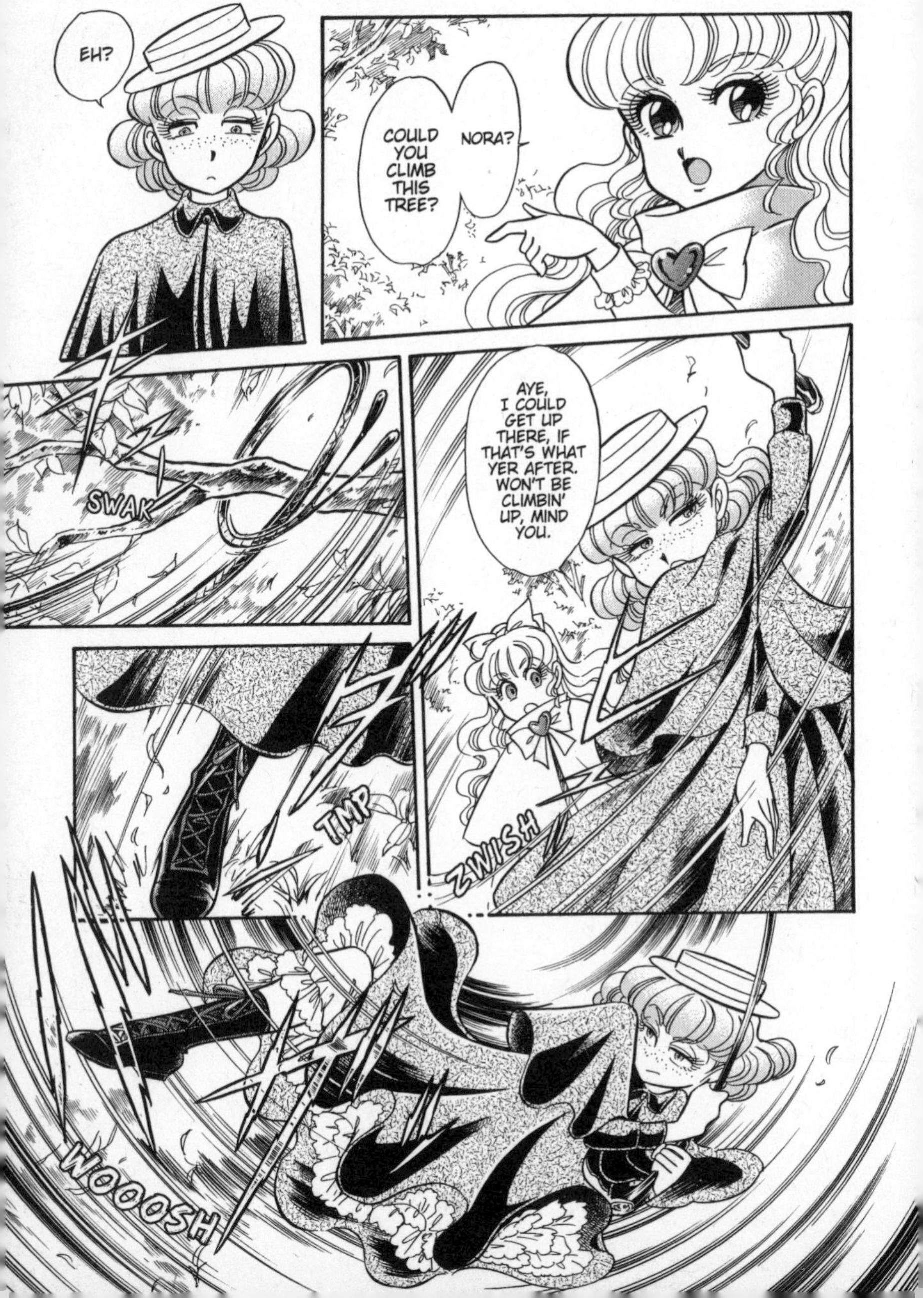
NORA?
COULD YOU CLIMB THIS TREE?
EH?
AYE, I COULD GET UP THERE, IF THAT'S WHAT YER AFTER. WON'T BE CLIMBIN' UP, MIND YOU.
ZWISH
SWAK
TMP
WOOOSH

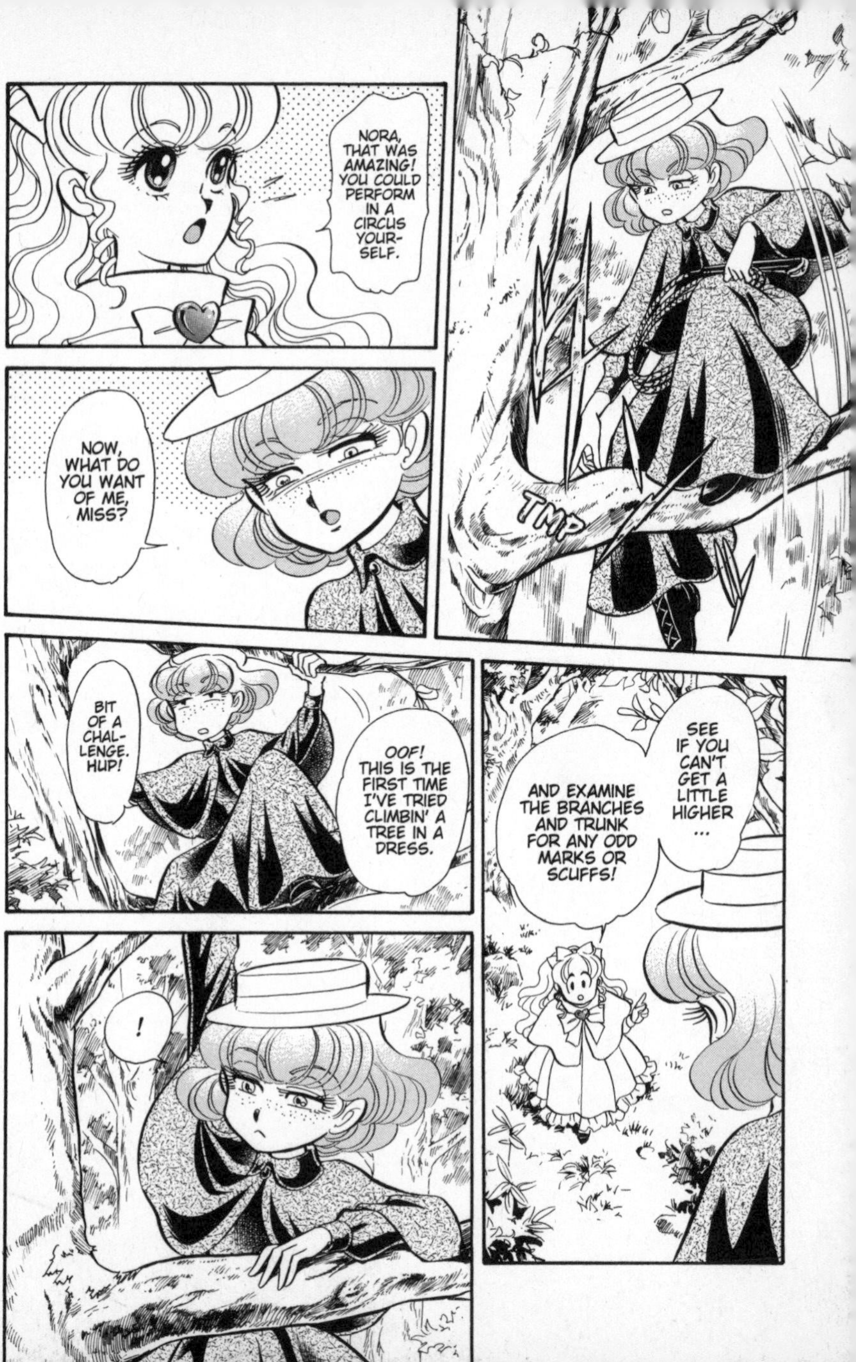
TMP
NORA, THAT WAS AMAZING! YOU COULD PERFORM IN A CIRCUS YOURSELF.
NOW, WHAT DO YOU WANT OF ME, MISS?
SEE IF YOU CAN'T GET A LITTLE HIGHER ...
AND EXAMINE THE BRANCHES AND TRUNK FOR ANY ODD MARKS OR SCUFFS!
BIT OF A CHAL-LENGE. HUP!
OOF! THIS IS THE FIRST TIME I'VE TRIED CLIMBIN' A TREE IN A DRESS.
!

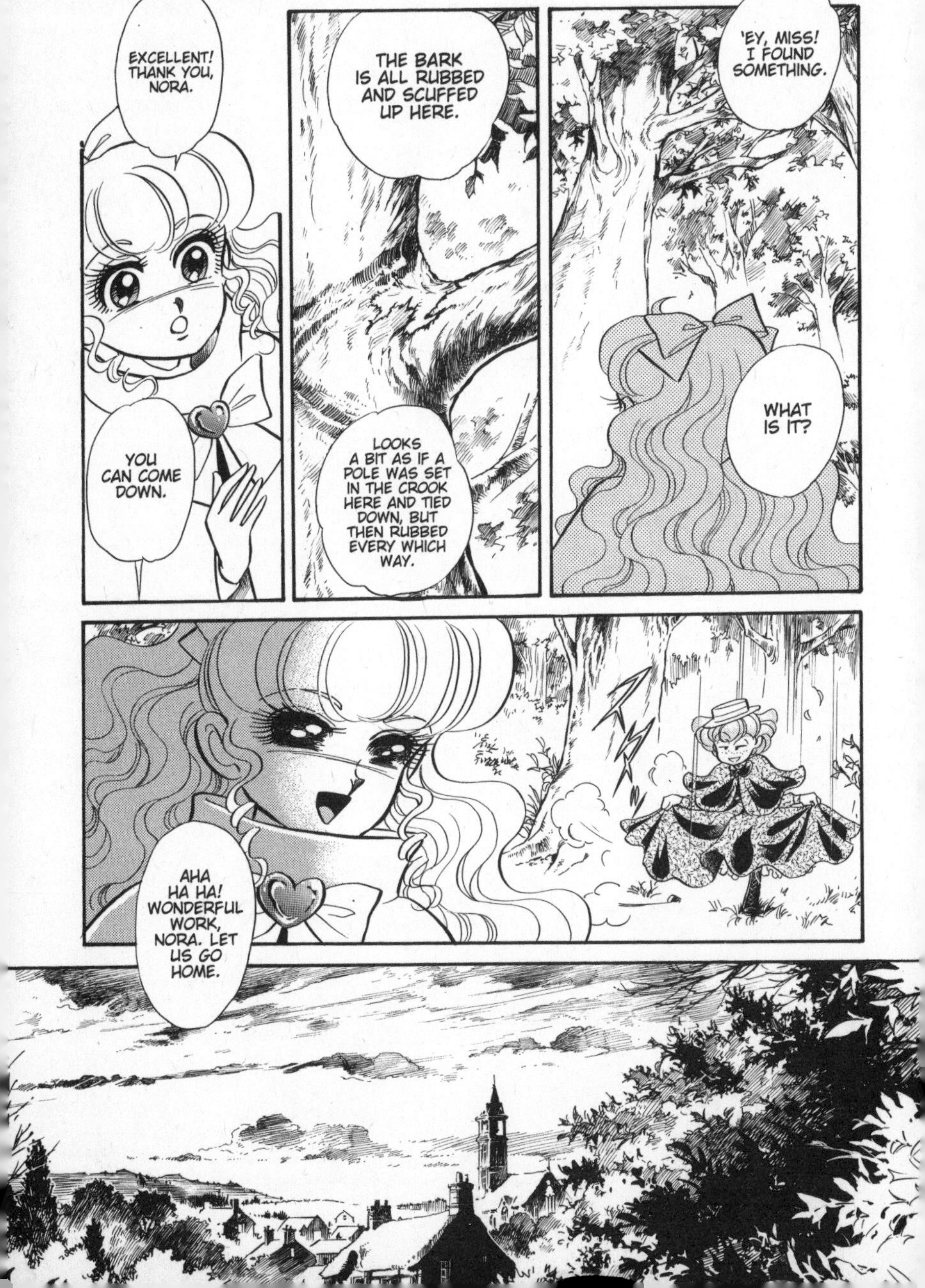
'EY, MISS! I FOUND SOMETHING.
WHAT IS IT?
THE BARK IS ALL RUBBED AND SCUFFED UP HERE.
LOOKS A BIT AS IF A POLE WAS SET IN THE CROOK HERE AND TIED DOWN, BUT THEN RUBBED EVERY WHICH WAY.
EXCELLENT! THANK YOU, NORA.
YOU CAN COME DOWN.
AHA HA HA! WONDERFUL WORK, NORA. LET US GO HOME.

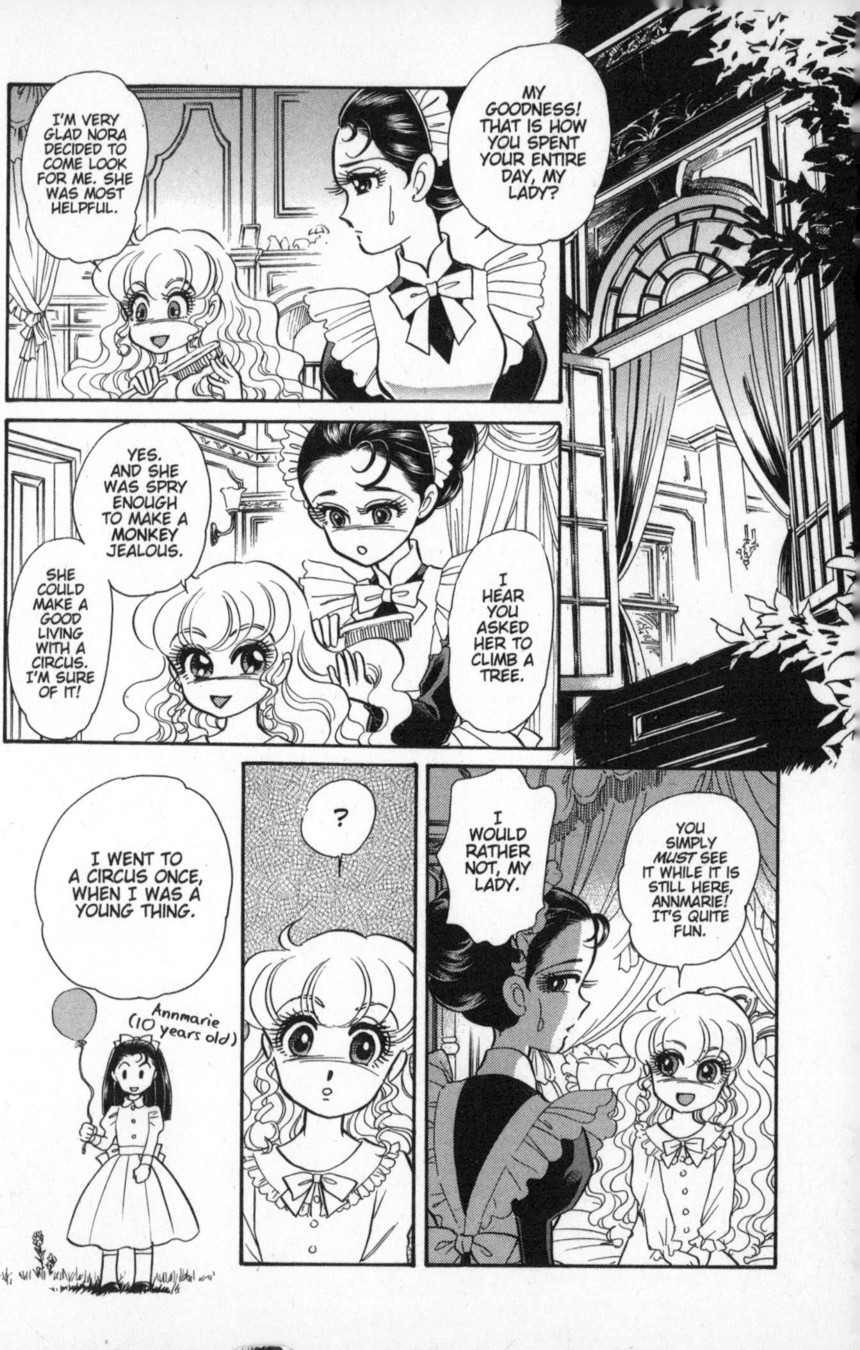
MY GOODNESS! THAT IS HOW YOU SPENT YOUR ENTIRE DAY, MY LADY?
I'M VERY GLAD NORA DECIDED TO COME LOOK FOR ME. SHE WAS MOST HELPFUL.
I HEAR YOU ASKED HER TO CLIMB A TREE.
YES. AND SHE WAS SPRY ENOUGH TO MAKE A MONKEY JEALOUS.
SHE COULD MAKE A GOOD LIVING WITH A CIRCUS. I'M SURE OF IT!
YOU SIMPLY *MUST* SEE IT WHILE IT IS STILL HERE, ANNMARIE! IT'S QUITE FUN.
I WOULD RATHER NOT, MY LADY.
?
I WENT TO A CIRCUS ONCE, WHEN I WAS A YOUNG THING.
Annmarie (10 years old)

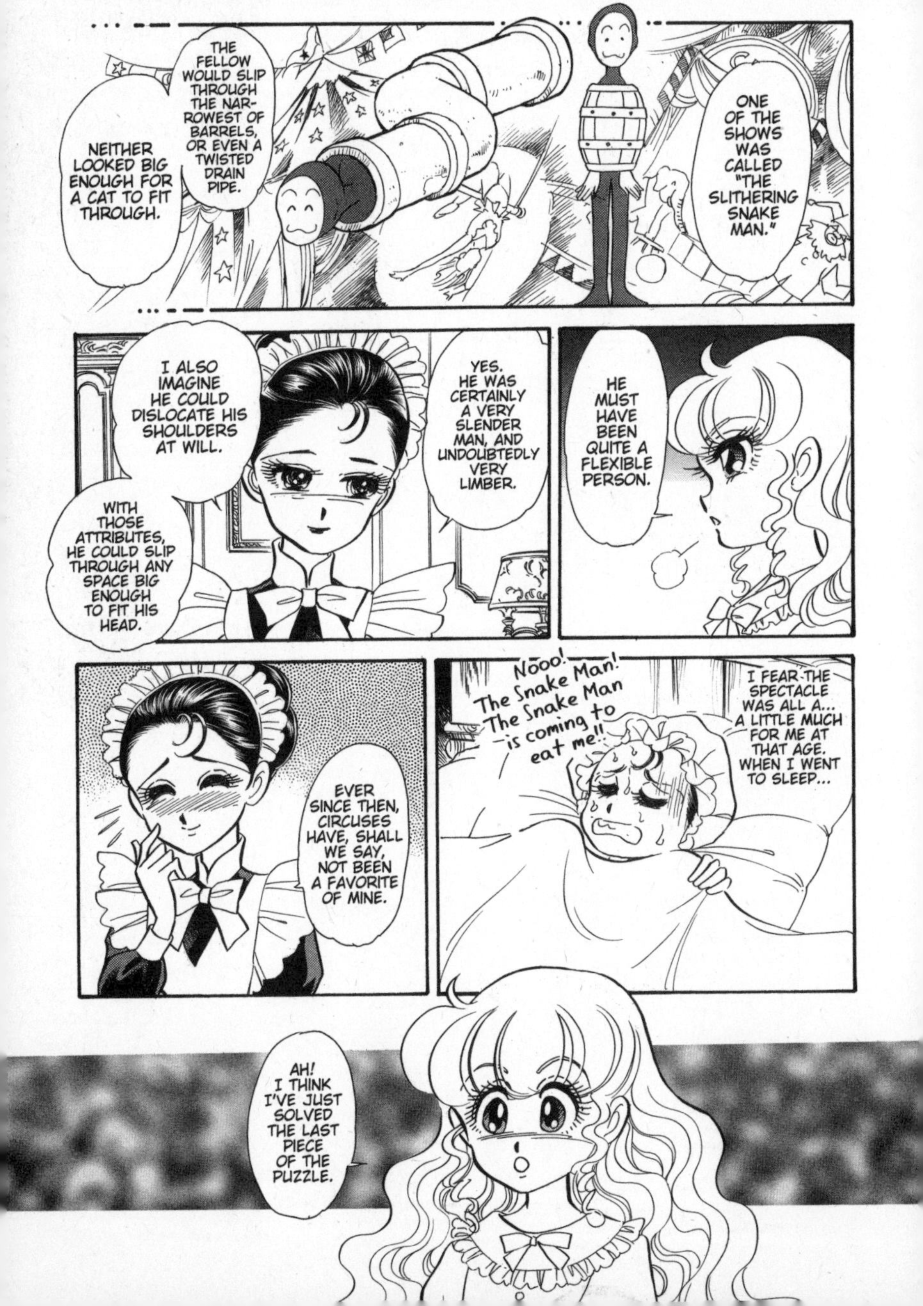
ONE OF THE SHOWS WAS CALLED "THE SLITHERING SNAKE MAN."
THE FELLOW WOULD SLIP THROUGH THE NAR-ROWEST OF BARRELS, OR EVEN A TWISTED DRAIN PIPE.
NEITHER LOOKED BIG ENOUGH FOR A CAT TO FIT THROUGH.
HE MUST HAVE BEEN QUITE A FLEXIBLE PERSON.
YES. HE WAS CERTAINLY A VERY SLENDER MAN, AND UNDOUBTEDLY VERY LIMBER.
I ALSO IMAGINE HE COULD DISLOCATE HIS SHOULDERS AT WILL.
WITH THOSE ATTRIBUTES, HE COULD SLIP THROUGH ANY SPACE BIG ENOUGH TO FIT HIS HEAD.
I FEAR THE SPECTACLE WAS ALL A... A LITTLE MUCH FOR ME AT THAT AGE. WHEN I WENT TO SLEEP...
Nooo! The Snake Man! The Snake Man is coming to eat me!!
EVER SINCE THEN, CIRCUSES HAVE, SHALL WE SAY, NOT BEEN A FAVORITE OF MINE.
AH! I THINK I'VE JUST SOLVED THE LAST PIECE OF THE PUZZLE.

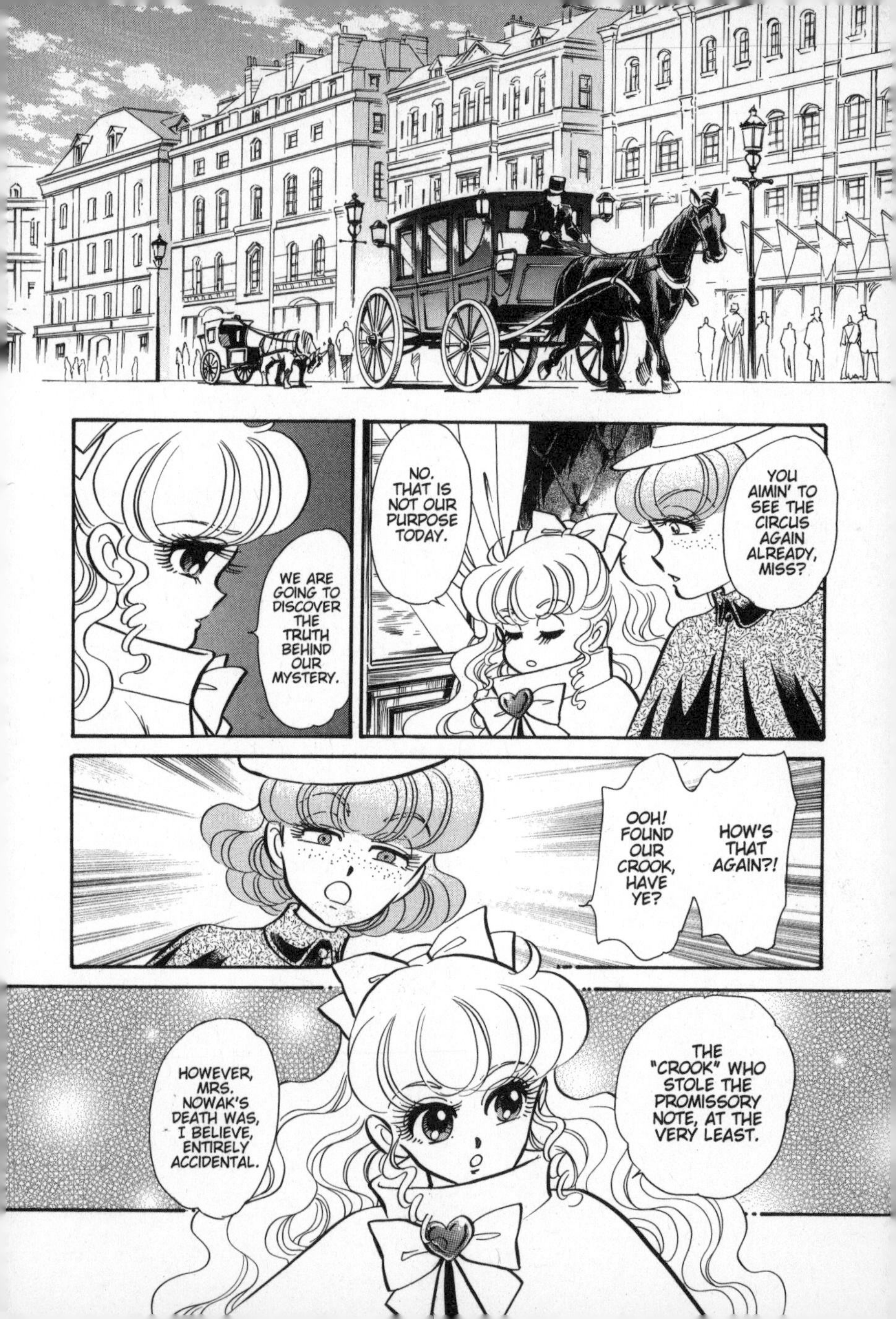
YOU AIMIN' TO SEE THE CIRCUS AGAIN ALREADY, MISS?
NO. THAT IS NOT OUR PURPOSE TODAY.
WE ARE GOING TO DISCOVER THE TRUTH BEHIND OUR MYSTERY.
HOW'S THAT AGAIN?!
OOH! FOUND OUR CROOK, HAVE YE?
THE "CROOK" WHO STOLE THE PROMISSORY NOTE, AT THE VERY LEAST.
HOWEVER, MRS. NOWAK'S DEATH WAS, I BELIEVE, ENTIRELY ACCIDENTAL.

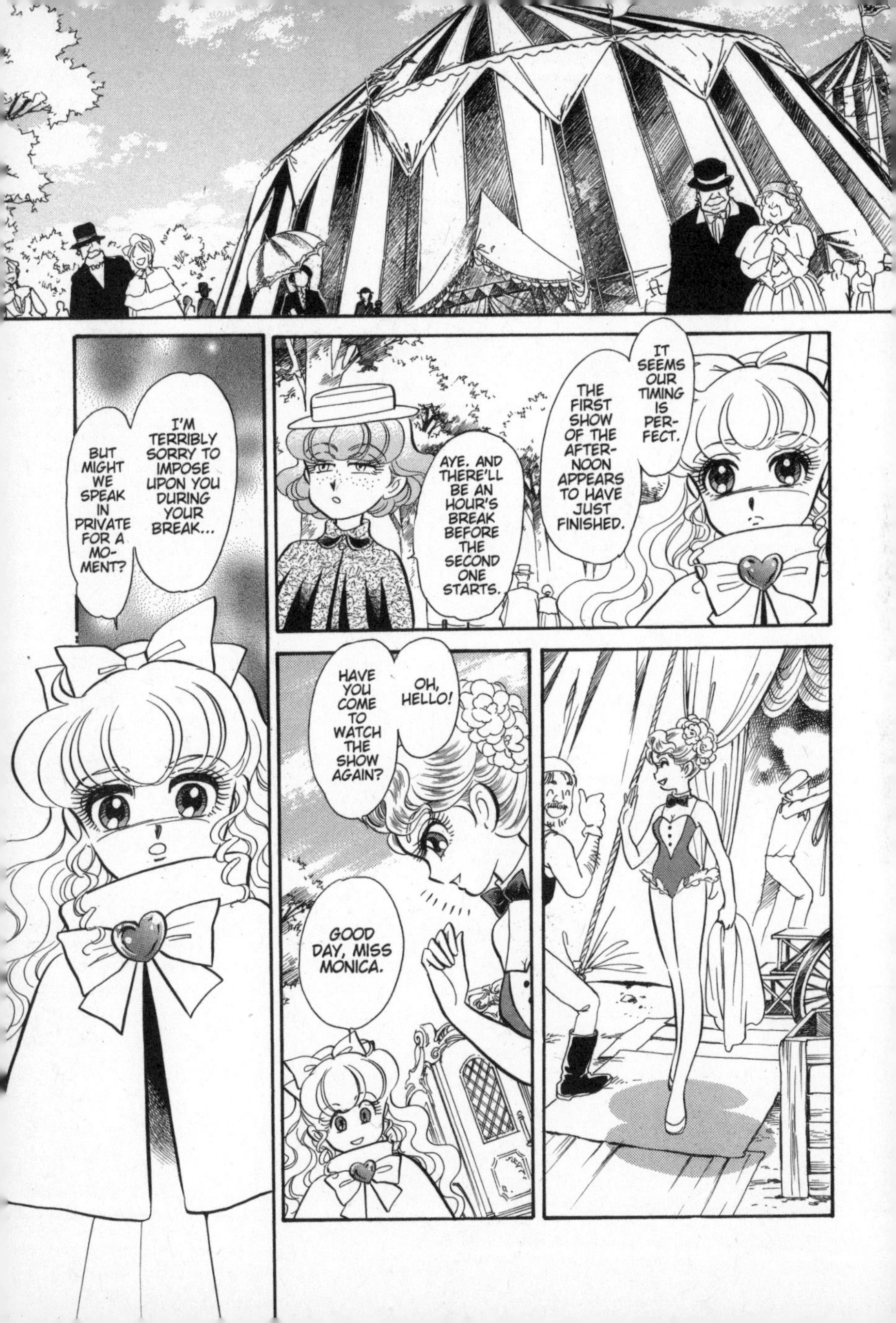
IT SEEMS OUR TIMING IS PERFECT.
THE FIRST SHOW OF THE AFTERNOON APPEARS TO HAVE JUST FINISHED.
AYE. AND THERE'LL BE AN HOUR'S BREAK BEFORE THE SECOND ONE STARTS.
OH, HELLO!
HAVE YOU COME TO WATCH THE SHOW AGAIN?
GOOD DAY, MISS MONICA.
I'M TERRIBLY SORRY TO IMPOSE UPON YOU DURING YOUR BREAK...
BUT MIGHT WE SPEAK IN PRIVATE FOR A MOMENT?

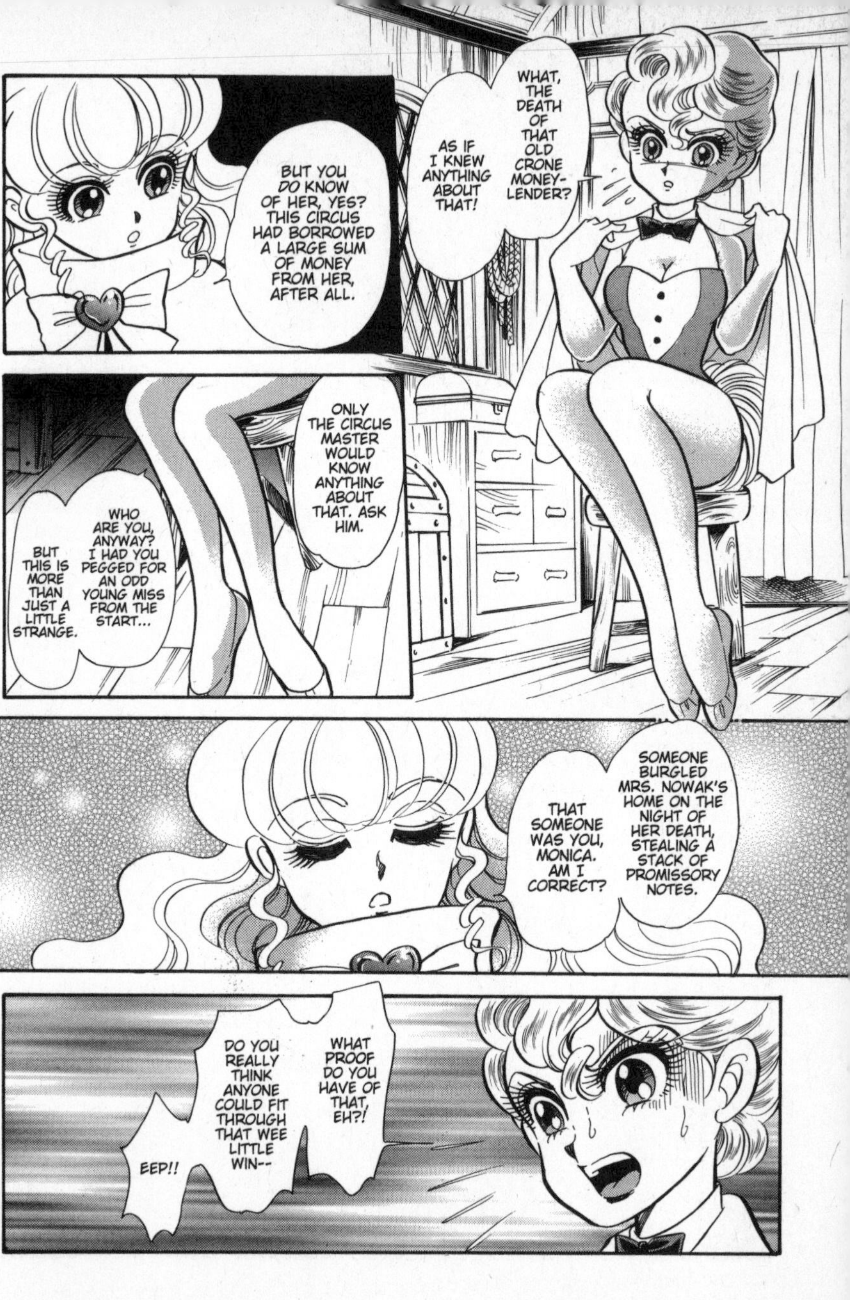

WHAT, THE DEATH OF THAT OLD CRONE MONEY-LENDER?
AS IF I KNEW ANYTHING ABOUT THAT!
BUT YOU DO KNOW OF HER, YES? THIS CIRCUS HAD BORROWED A LARGE SUM OF MONEY FROM HER, AFTER ALL.
ONLY THE CIRCUS MASTER WOULD KNOW ANYTHING ABOUT THAT. ASK HIM.
WHO ARE YOU, ANYWAY? I HAD YOU PEGGED FOR AN ODD YOUNG MISS FROM THE START...
BUT THIS IS MORE THAN JUST A LITTLE STRANGE.
SOMEONE BURGLED MRS. NOWAK'S HOME ON THE NIGHT OF HER DEATH, STEALING A STACK OF PROMISSORY NOTES.
THAT SOMEONE WAS YOU, MONICA. AM I CORRECT?
WHAT PROOF DO YOU HAVE OF THAT, EH?!
DO YOU REALLY THINK ANYONE COULD FIT THROUGH THAT WEE LITTLE WIN--
EEP!!

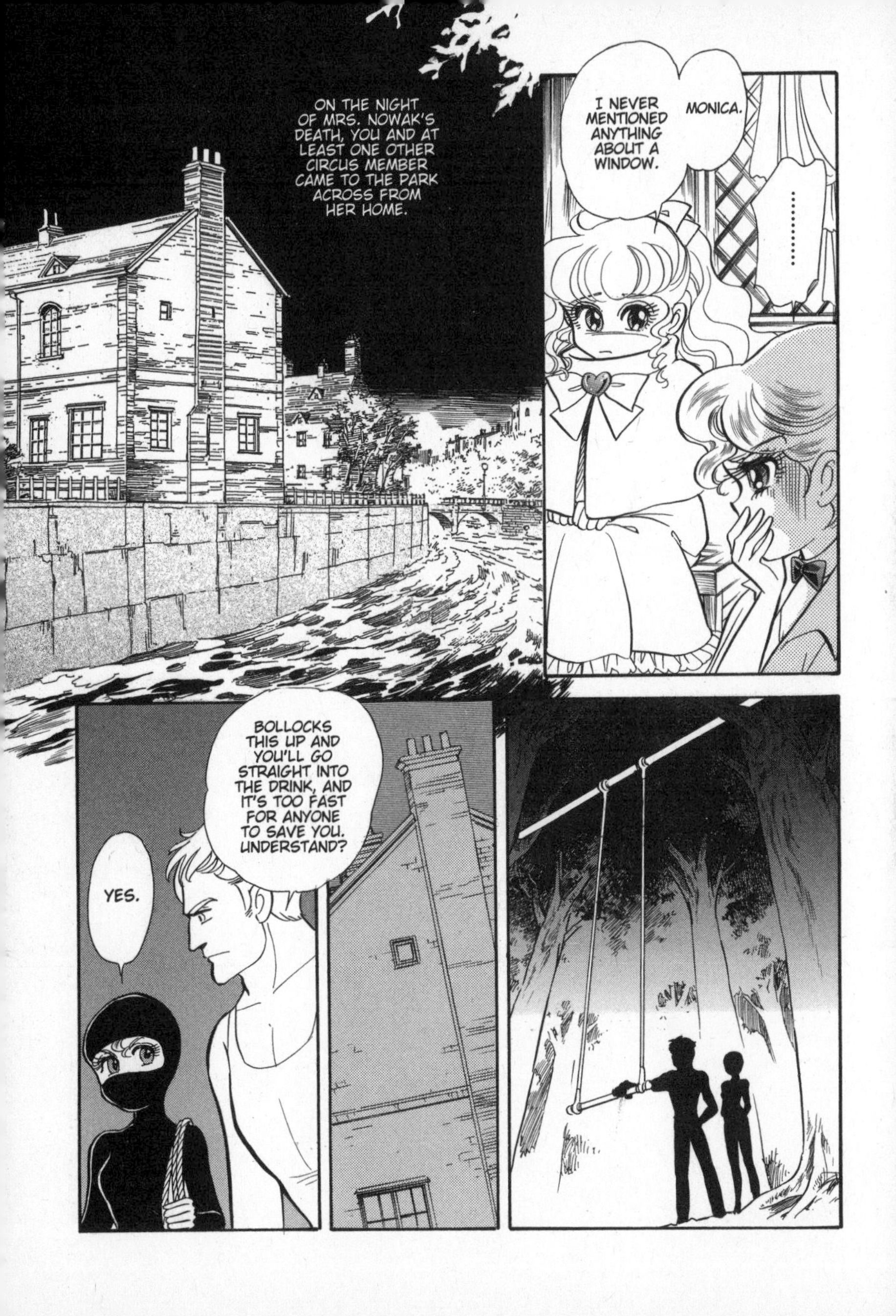
MONICA.
I NEVER MENTIONED ANYTHING ABOUT A WINDOW.
……
ON THE NIGHT OF MRS. NOWAK'S DEATH, YOU AND AT LEAST ONE OTHER CIRCUS MEMBER CAME TO THE PARK ACROSS FROM HER HOME.
BOLLOCKS THIS UP AND YOU'LL GO STRAIGHT INTO THE DRINK, AND IT'S TOO FAST FOR ANYONE TO SAVE YOU. UNDERSTAND?
YES.

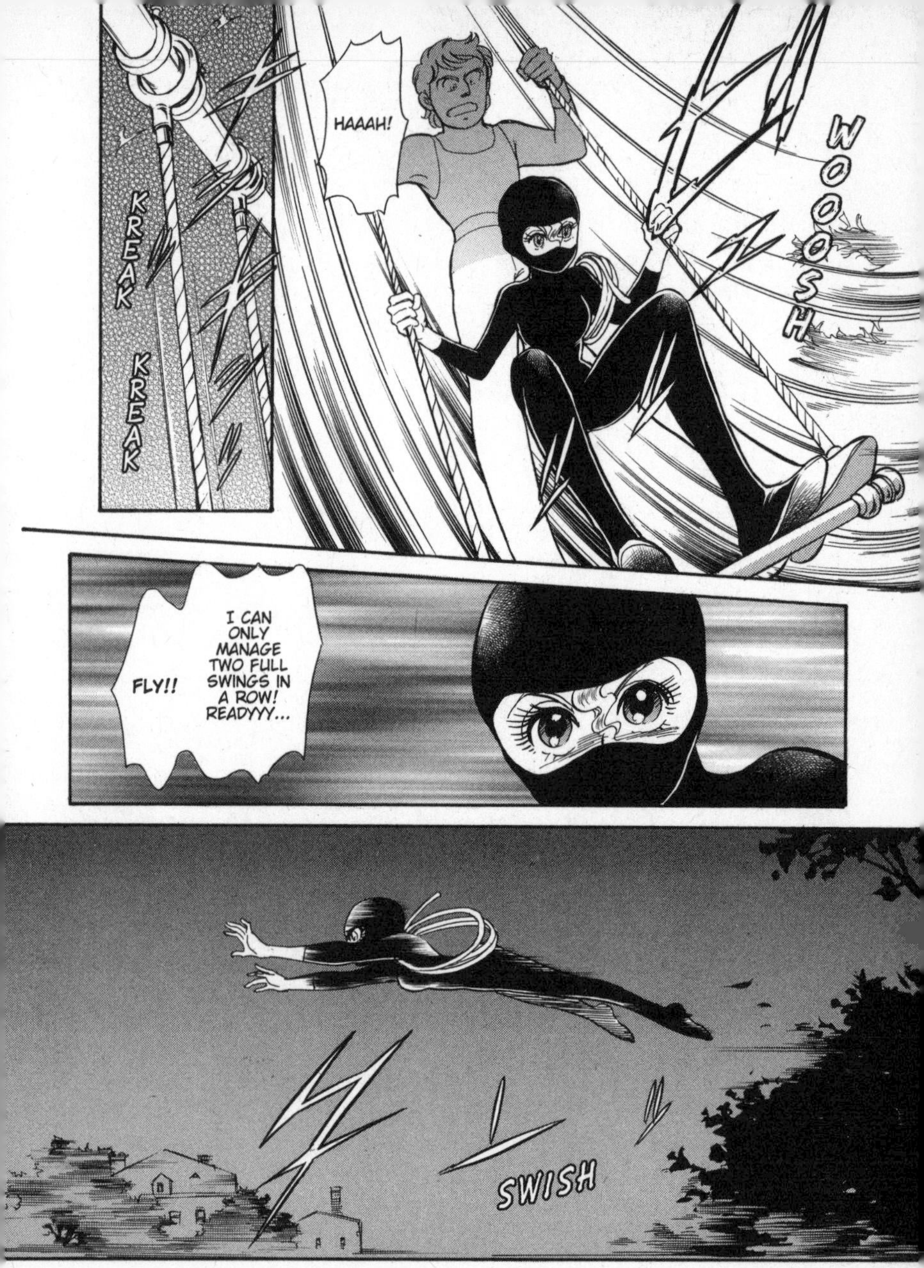
HAAAH!
WOOOSH
KREAK KREAK
I CAN ONLY MANAGE TWO FULL SWINGS IN A ROW! READYYY...
FLY!!
SWISH

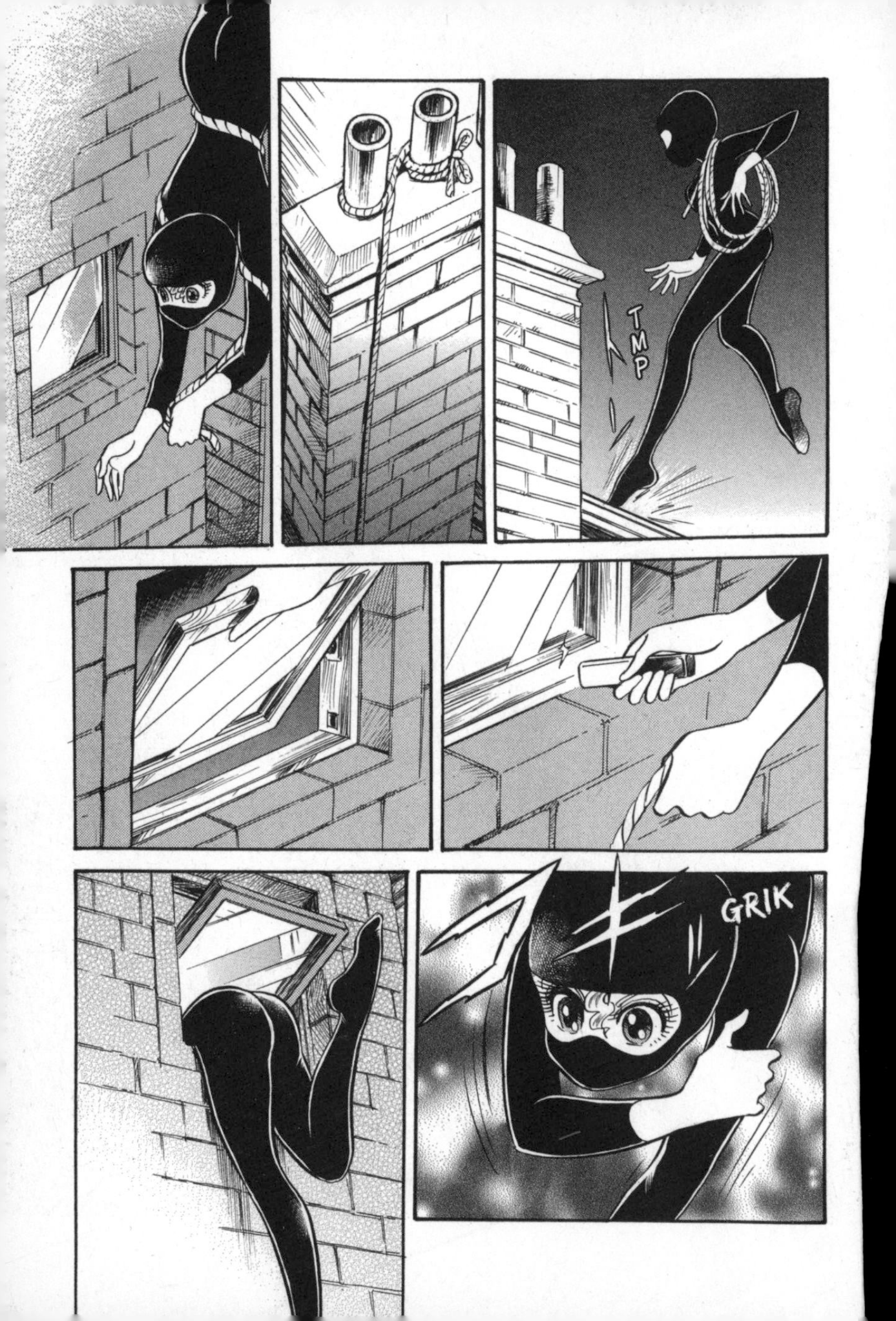
TMP
GRIK

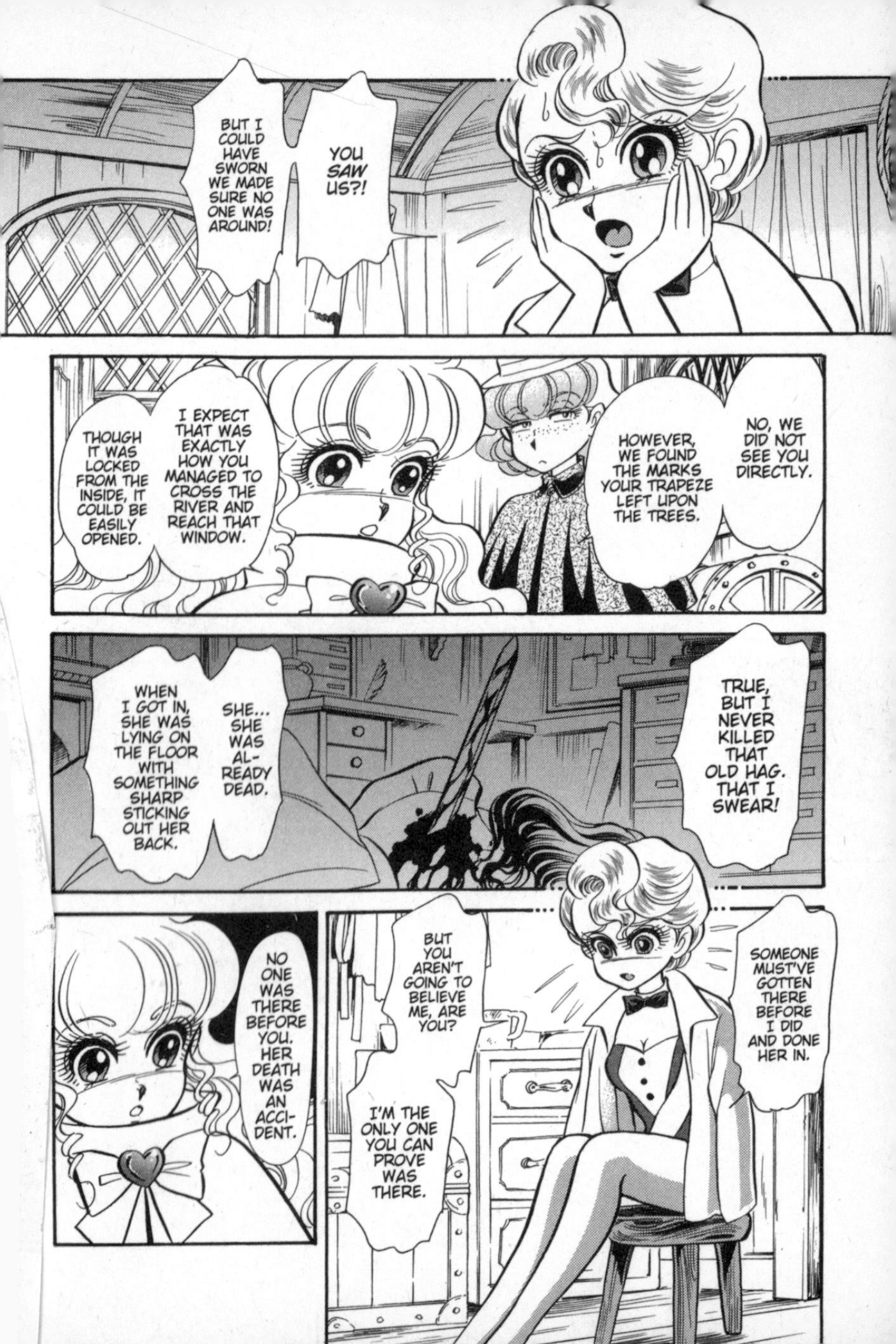
YOU SAW US?!
BUT I COULD HAVE SWORN WE MADE SURE NO ONE WAS AROUND!
NO, WE DID NOT SEE YOU DIRECTLY.
HOWEVER, WE FOUND THE MARKS YOUR TRAPEZE LEFT UPON THE TREES.
I EXPECT THAT WAS EXACTLY HOW YOU MANAGED TO CROSS THE RIVER AND REACH THAT WINDOW.
THOUGH IT WAS LOCKED FROM THE INSIDE, IT COULD BE EASILY OPENED.
TRUE, BUT I NEVER KILLED THAT OLD HAG. THAT I SWEAR!
SHE... SHE WAS ALREADY DEAD.
WHEN I GOT IN, SHE WAS LYING ON THE FLOOR WITH SOMETHING SHARP STICKING OUT HER BACK.
SOMEONE MUST'VE GOTTEN THERE BEFORE I DID AND DONE HER IN.
BUT YOU AREN'T GOING TO BELIEVE ME, ARE YOU?
I'M THE ONLY ONE YOU CAN PROVE WAS THERE.
NO ONE WAS THERE BEFORE YOU. HER DEATH WAS AN ACCIDENT.

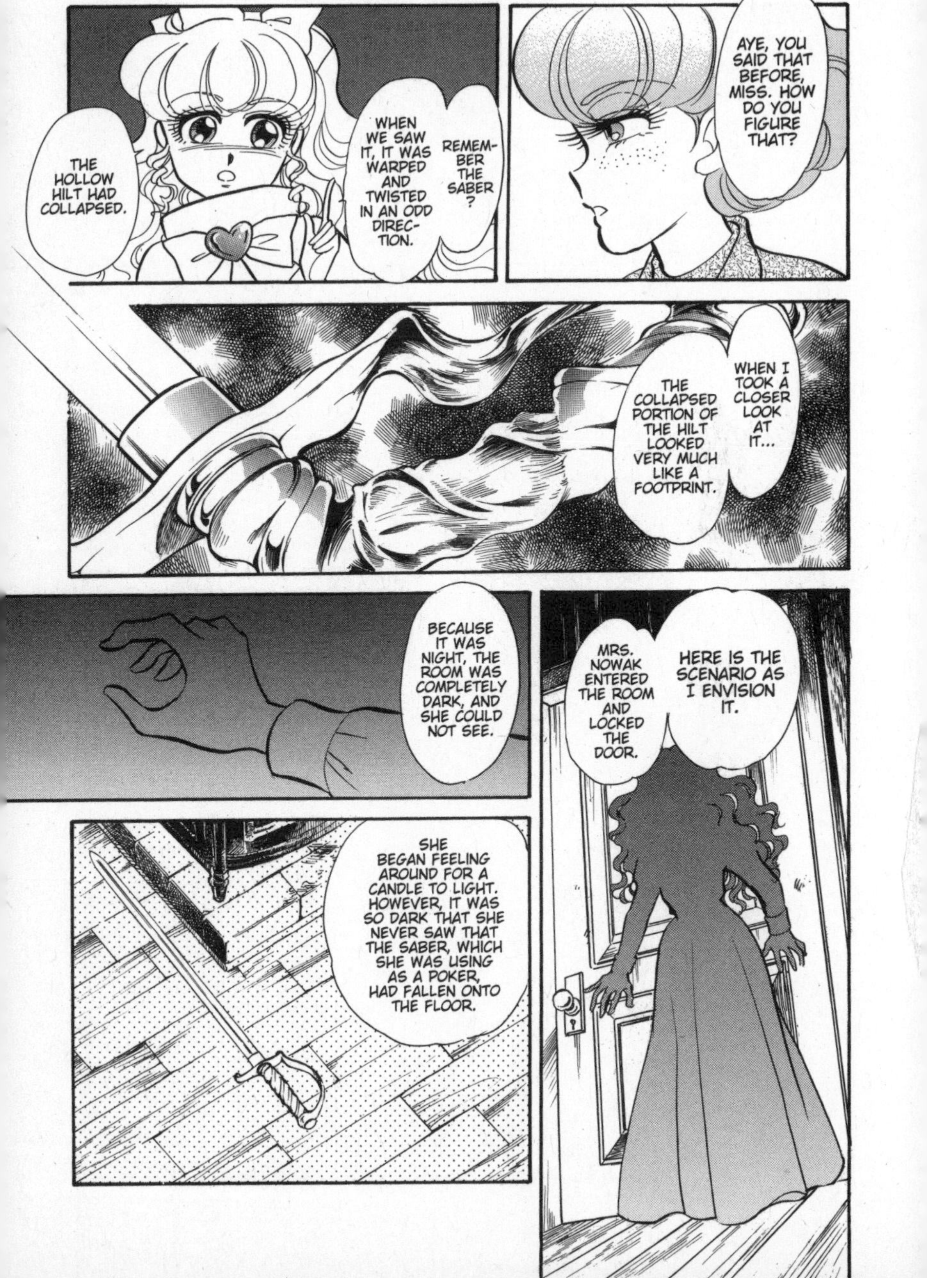
AYE, YOU SAID THAT BEFORE, MISS. HOW DO YOU FIGURE THAT?
REMEMBER THE SABER?
WHEN WE SAW IT, IT WAS WARPED AND TWISTED IN AN ODD DIRECTION.
THE HOLLOW HILT HAD COLLAPSED.
WHEN I TOOK A CLOSER LOOK AT IT...
THE COLLAPSED PORTION OF THE HILT LOOKED VERY MUCH LIKE A FOOTPRINT.
HERE IS THE SCENARIO AS I ENVISION IT.
MRS. NOWAK ENTERED THE ROOM AND LOCKED THE DOOR.
BECAUSE IT WAS NIGHT, THE ROOM WAS COMPLETELY DARK, AND SHE COULD NOT SEE.
SHE BEGAN FEELING AROUND FOR A CANDLE TO LIGHT. HOWEVER, IT WAS SO DARK THAT SHE NEVER SAW THAT THE SABER, WHICH SHE WAS USING AS A POKER, HAD FALLEN ONTO THE FLOOR.

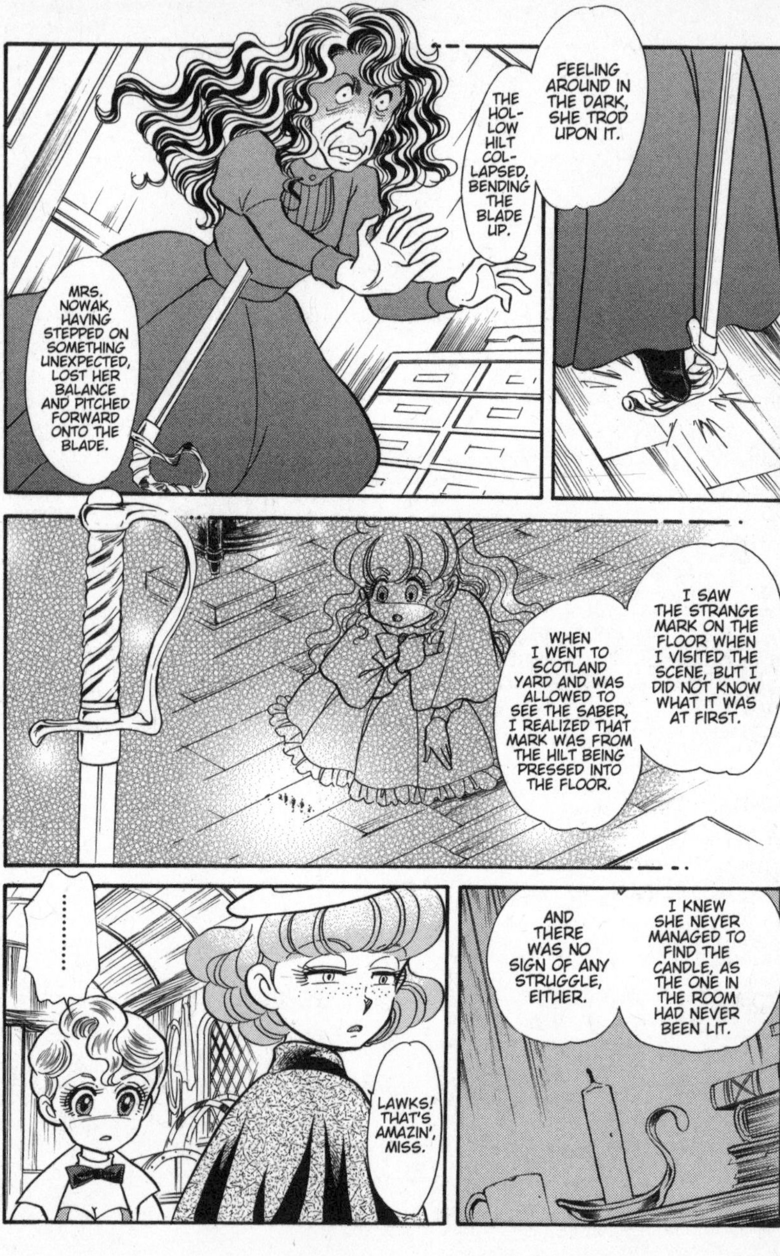
FEELING AROUND IN THE DARK, SHE TROD UPON IT.
THE HOLLOW HILT COLLAPSED, BENDING THE BLADE UP.
MRS. NOWAK, HAVING STEPPED ON SOMETHING UNEXPECTED, LOST HER BALANCE AND PITCHED FORWARD ONTO THE BLADE.
I SAW THE STRANGE MARK ON THE FLOOR WHEN I VISITED THE SCENE, BUT I DID NOT KNOW WHAT IT WAS AT FIRST.
WHEN I WENT TO SCOTLAND YARD AND WAS ALLOWED TO SEE THE SABER, I REALIZED THAT MARK WAS FROM THE HILT BEING PRESSED INTO THE FLOOR.
I KNEW SHE NEVER MANAGED TO FIND THE CANDLE, AS THE ONE IN THE ROOM HAD NEVER BEEN LIT.
AND THERE WAS NO SIGN OF ANY STRUGGLE, EITHER.
......
LAWKS! THAT'S AMAZIN', MISS.

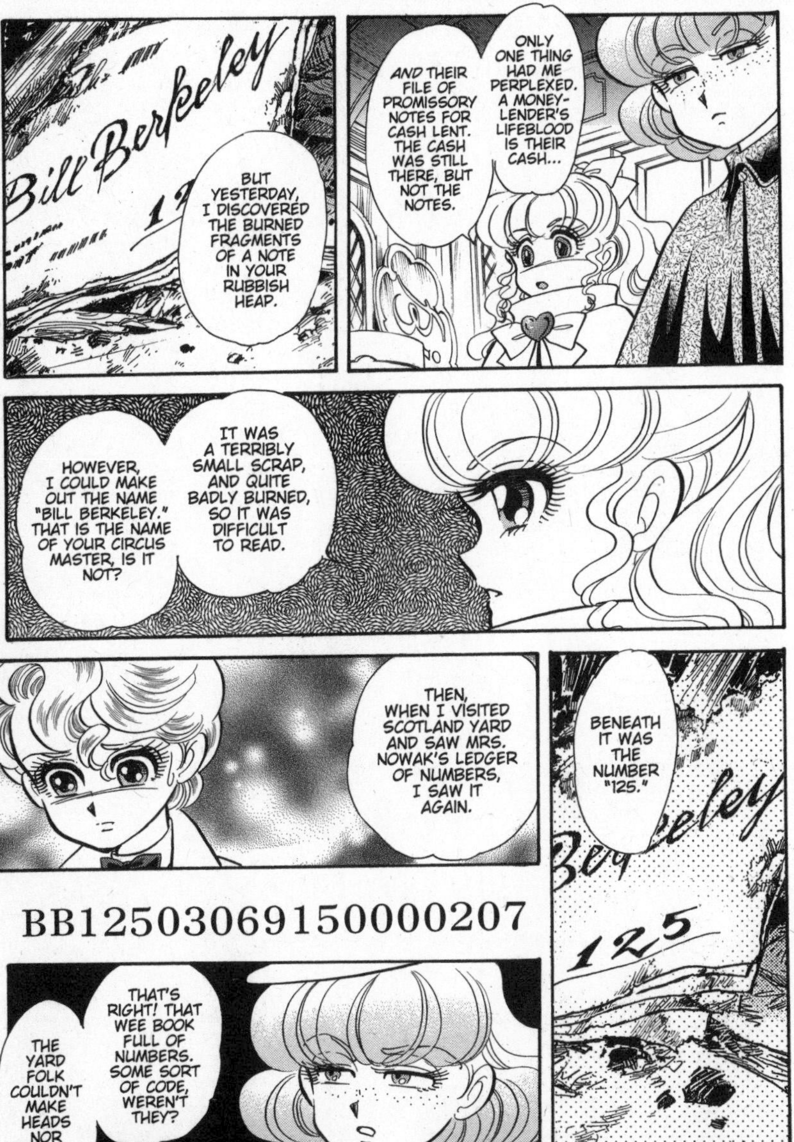
ONLY ONE THING HAD ME PERPLEXED. A MONEY-LENDER'S LIFEBLOOD IS THEIR CASH...
AND THEIR FILE OF PROMISSORY NOTES FOR CASH LENT. THE CASH WAS STILL THERE, BUT NOT THE NOTES.
Bill Berkeley
BUT YESTERDAY, I DISCOVERED THE BURNED FRAGMENTS OF A NOTE IN YOUR RUBBISH HEAP.
IT WAS A TERRIBLY SMALL SCRAP, AND QUITE BADLY BURNED, SO IT WAS DIFFICULT TO READ.
HOWEVER, I COULD MAKE OUT THE NAME "BILL BERKELEY." THAT IS THE NAME OF YOUR CIRCUS MASTER, IS IT NOT?
BENEATH IT WAS THE NUMBER "125."
125
THEN, WHEN I VISITED SCOTLAND YARD AND SAW MRS. NOWAK'S LEDGER OF NUMBERS, I SAW IT AGAIN.
BB1250306915000207
THAT'S RIGHT! THAT WEE BOOK FULL OF NUMBERS. SOME SORT OF CODE, WEREN'T THEY?
THE YARD FOLK COULDN'T MAKE HEADS NOR TAILS OF IT.

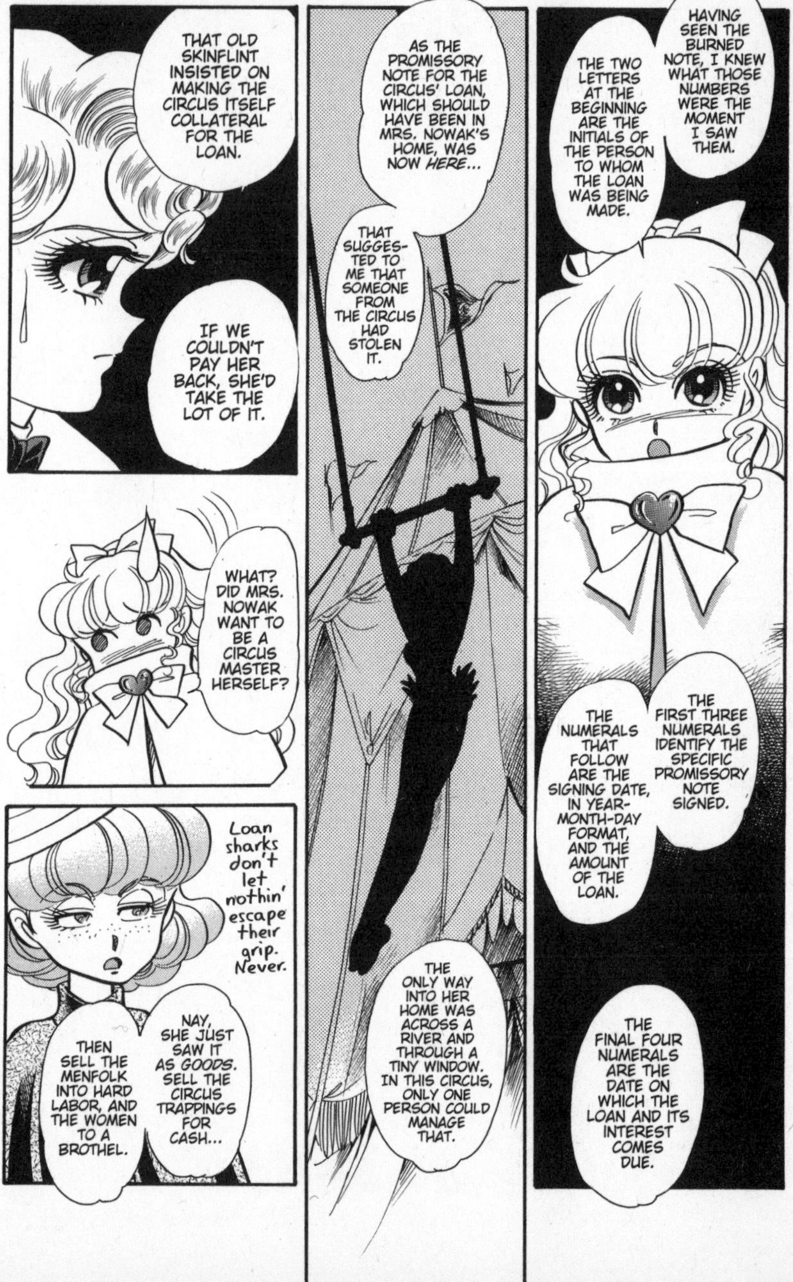
HAVING SEEN THE BURNED NOTE, I KNEW WHAT THOSE NUMBERS WERE THE MOMENT I SAW THEM.
THE TWO LETTERS AT THE BEGINNING ARE THE INITIALS OF THE PERSON TO WHOM THE LOAN WAS BEING MADE.
THE FIRST THREE NUMERALS IDENTIFY THE SPECIFIC PROMISSORY NOTE SIGNED.
THE NUMERALS THAT FOLLOW ARE THE SIGNING DATE, IN YEAR-MONTH-DAY FORMAT, AND THE AMOUNT OF THE LOAN.
THE FINAL FOUR NUMERALS ARE THE DATE ON WHICH THE LOAN AND ITS INTEREST COMES DUE.
AS THE PROMISSORY NOTE FOR THE CIRCUS' LOAN, WHICH SHOULD HAVE BEEN IN MRS. NOWAK'S HOME, WAS NOW *HERE*...
THAT SUGGES-TED TO ME THAT SOMEONE FROM THE CIRCUS HAD STOLEN IT.
THE ONLY WAY INTO HER HOME WAS ACROSS A RIVER AND THROUGH A TINY WINDOW. IN THIS CIRCUS, ONLY ONE PERSON COULD MANAGE THAT.
THAT OLD SKINFLINT INSISTED ON MAKING THE CIRCUS ITSELF COLLATERAL FOR THE LOAN.
IF WE COULDN'T PAY HER BACK, SHE'D TAKE THE LOT OF IT.
WHAT? DID MRS. NOWAK WANT TO BE A CIRCUS MASTER HERSELF?
Loan sharks don't let nothin' escape their grip. Never.
NAY, SHE JUST SAW IT AS *GOODS*. SELL THE CIRCUS TRAPPINGS FOR CASH...
THEN SELL THE MENFOLK INTO HARD LABOR, AND THE WOMEN TO A BROTHEL.

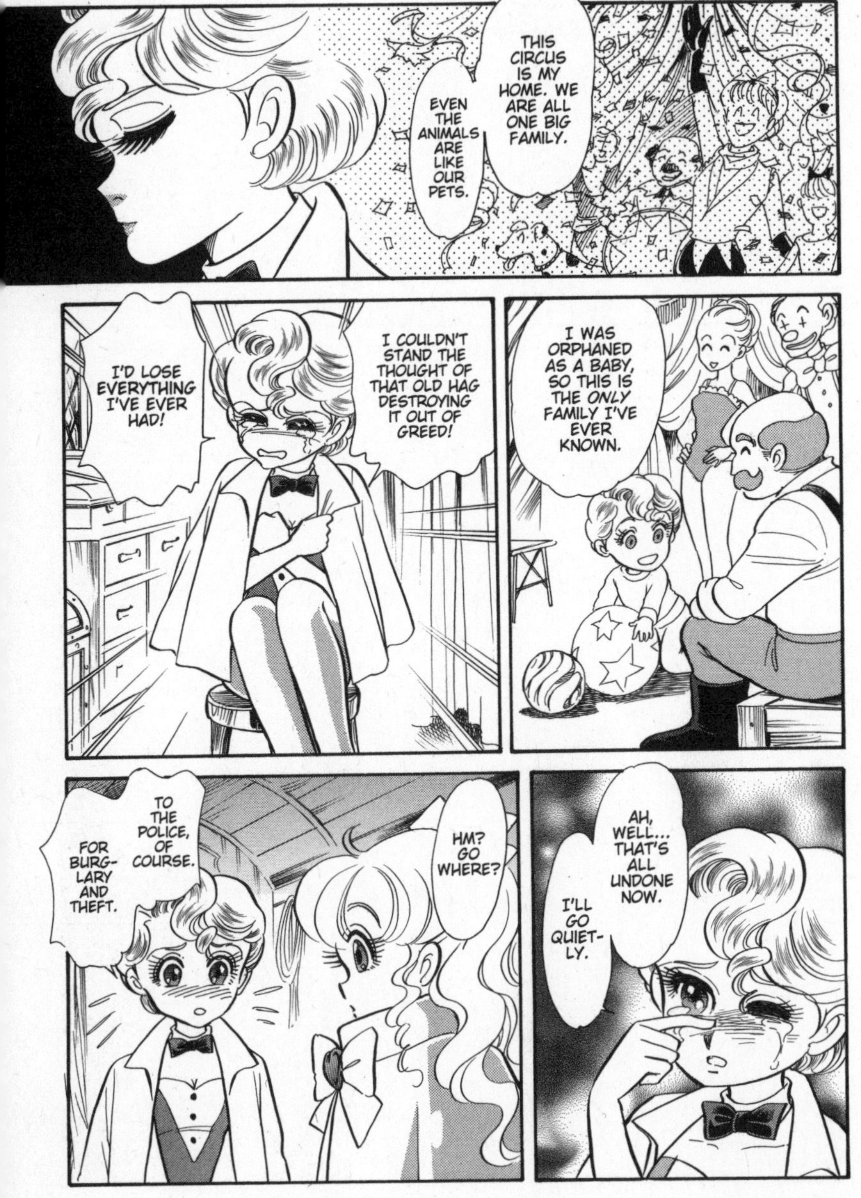
THIS CIRCUS IS MY HOME. WE ARE ALL ONE BIG FAMILY.
EVEN THE ANIMALS ARE LIKE OUR PETS.
I WAS ORPHANED AS A BABY, SO THIS IS THE *ONLY* FAMILY I'VE EVER KNOWN.
I COULDN'T STAND THE THOUGHT OF THAT OLD HAG DESTROYING IT OUT OF GREED!
I'D LOSE EVERYTHING I'VE EVER HAD!
AH, WELL... THAT'S ALL UNDONE NOW.
I'LL GO QUIET-LY.
HM? GO WHERE?
TO THE POLICE, OF COURSE.
FOR BURGLARY AND THEFT.

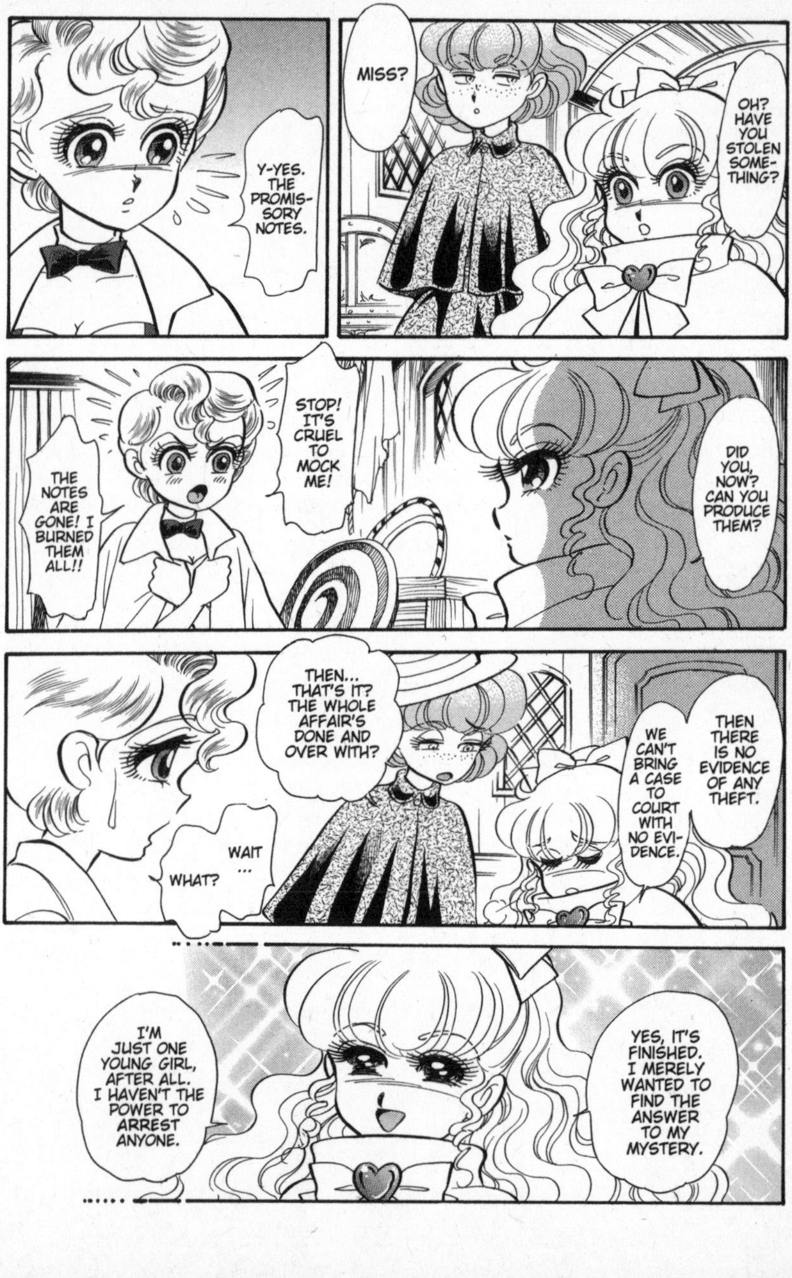
MISS?
OH? HAVE YOU STOLEN SOMETHING?
Y-YES. THE PROMISSORY NOTES.
DID YOU, NOW? CAN YOU PRODUCE THEM?
STOP! IT'S CRUEL TO MOCK ME!
THE NOTES ARE GONE! I BURNED THEM ALL!!
THEN THERE IS NO EVIDENCE OF ANY THEFT.
WE CAN'T BRING A CASE TO COURT WITH NO EVIDENCE.
THEN... THAT'S IT? THE WHOLE AFFAIR'S DONE AND OVER WITH?
WAIT ...
WHAT?
YES, IT'S FINISHED. I MERELY WANTED TO FIND THE ANSWER TO MY MYSTERY.
I'M JUST ONE YOUNG GIRL, AFTER ALL. I HAVEN'T THE POWER TO ARREST ANYONE.

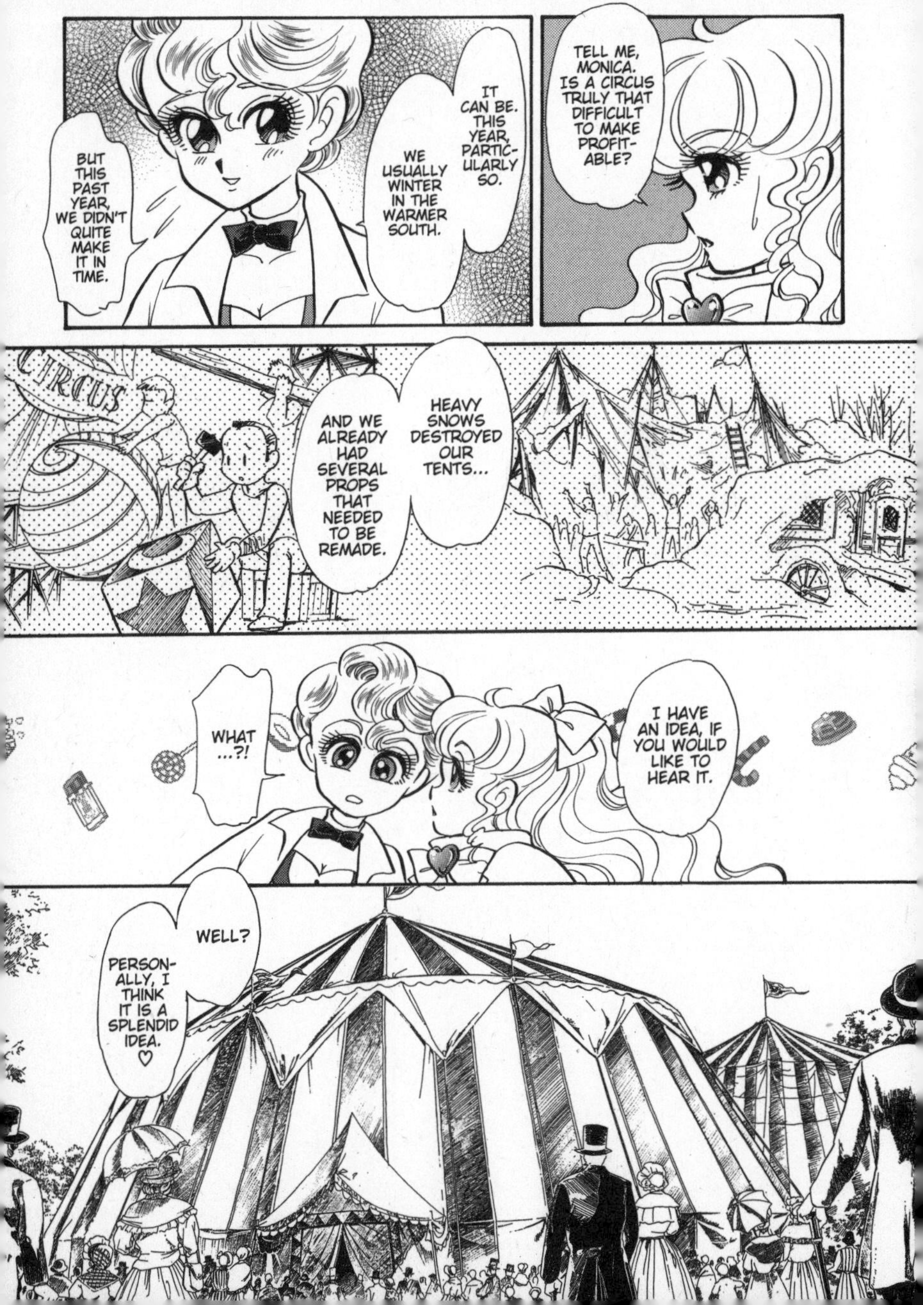
TELL ME, MONICA. IS A CIRCUS TRULY THAT DIFFICULT TO MAKE PROFIT-ABLE?
IT CAN BE. THIS YEAR, PARTIC-ULARLY SO.
WE USUALLY WINTER IN THE WARMER SOUTH.
BUT THIS PAST YEAR, WE DIDN'T QUITE MAKE IT IN TIME.
HEAVY SNOWS DESTROYED OUR TENTS...
AND WE ALREADY HAD SEVERAL PROPS THAT NEEDED TO BE REMADE.
CIRCUS
I HAVE AN IDEA, IF YOU WOULD LIKE TO HEAR IT.
WHAT ...?!
WELL?
PERSON-ALLY, I THINK IT IS A SPLENDID IDEA. ♡

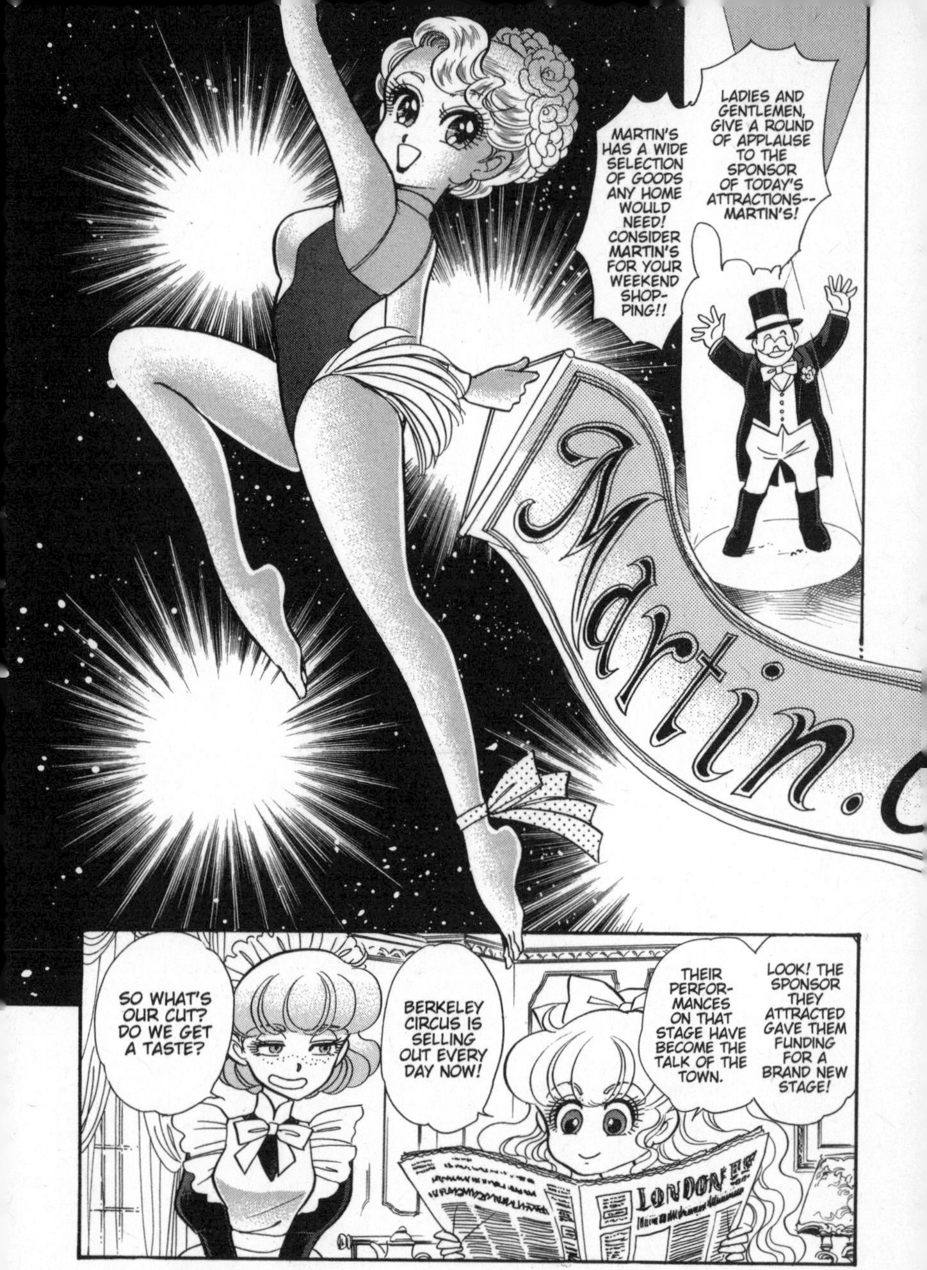
LADIES AND GENTLEMEN, GIVE A ROUND OF APPLAUSE TO THE SPONSOR OF TODAY'S ATTRACTIONS-- MARTIN'S!
MARTIN'S HAS A WIDE SELECTION OF GOODS ANY HOME WOULD NEED! CONSIDER MARTIN'S FOR YOUR WEEKEND SHOP-PING!!
Martin.
LOOK! THE SPONSOR THEY ATTRACTED GAVE THEM FUNDING FOR A BRAND NEW STAGE!
THEIR PERFOR-MANCES ON THAT STAGE HAVE BECOME THE TALK OF THE TOWN.
BERKELEY CIRCUS IS SELLING OUT EVERY DAY NOW!
SO WHAT'S OUR CUT? DO WE GET A TASTE?
LONDON

The Adventure of the Famous Trainer (1)

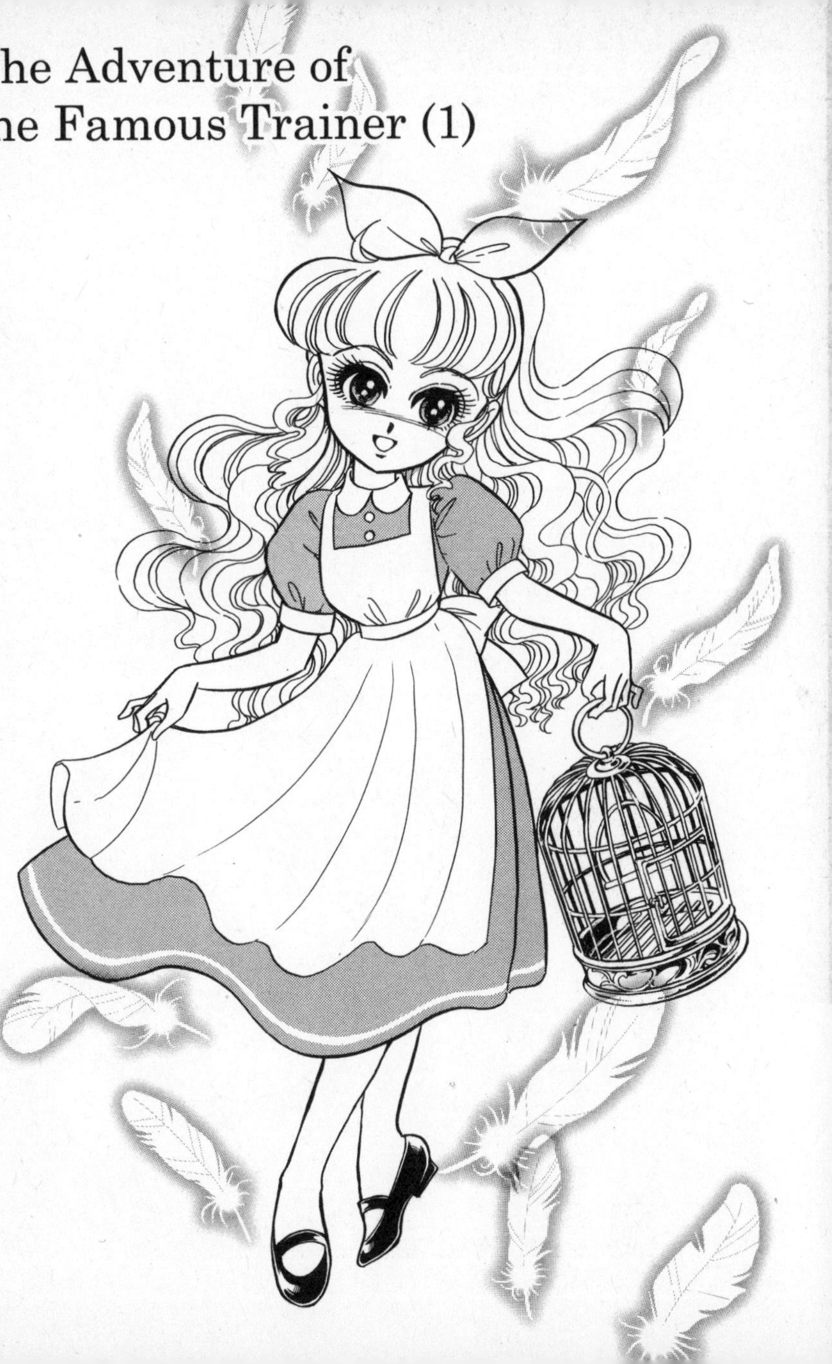

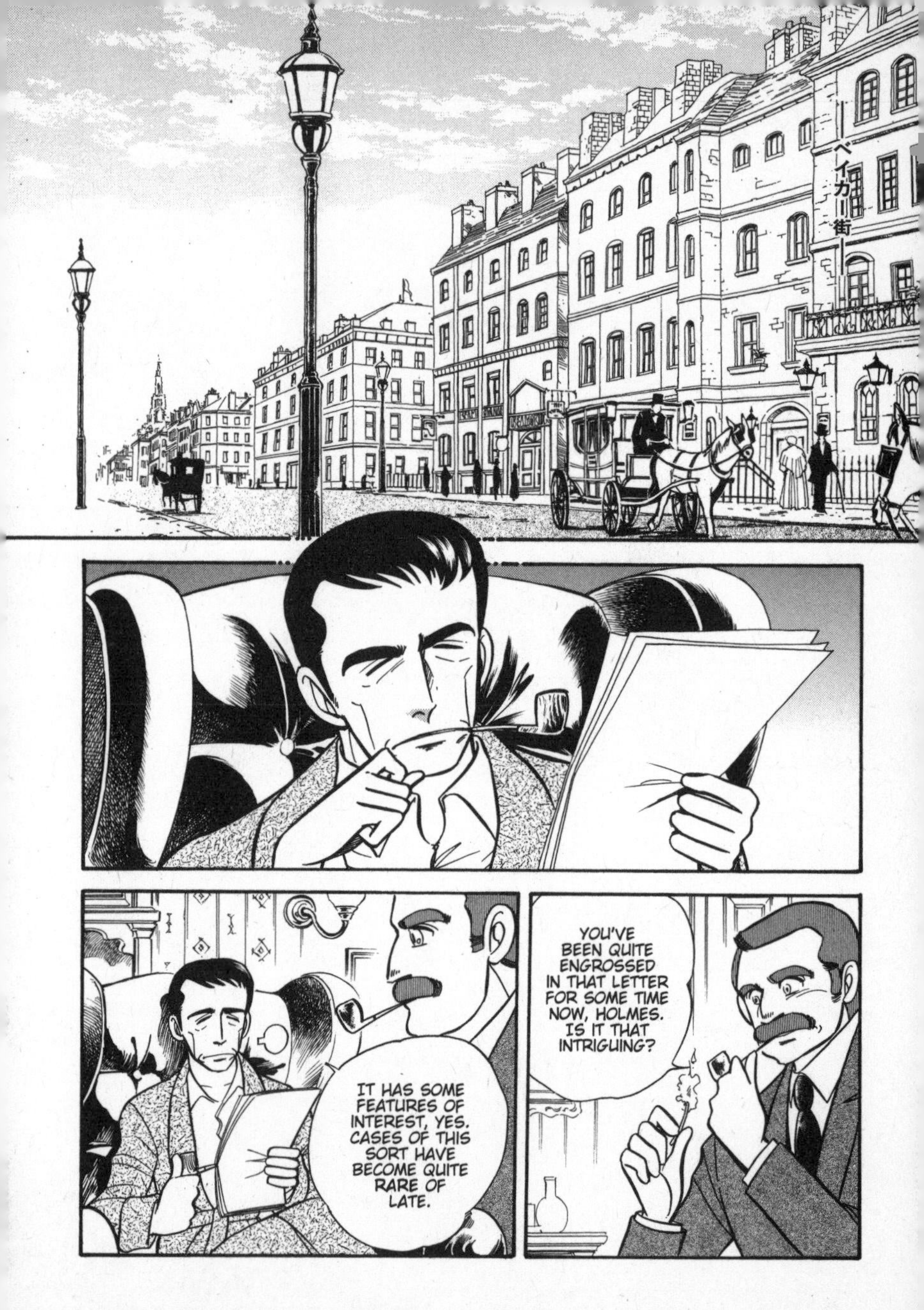
ベイカー街
YOU'VE BEEN QUITE ENGROSSED IN THAT LETTER FOR SOME TIME NOW, HOLMES. IS IT THAT INTRIGUING?
IT HAS SOME FEATURES OF INTEREST, YES. CASES OF THIS SORT HAVE BECOME QUITE RARE OF LATE.

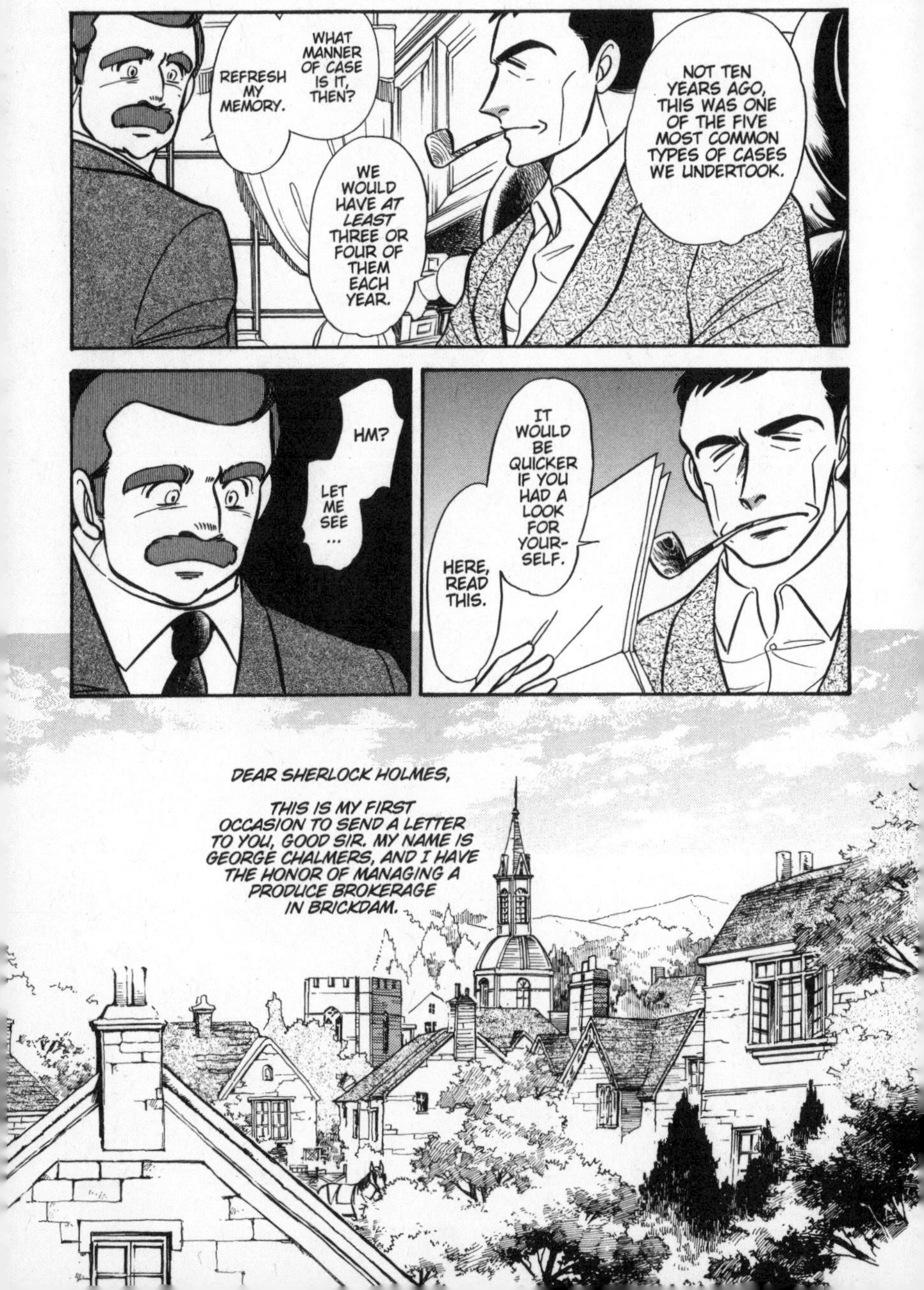
NOT TEN YEARS AGO, THIS WAS ONE OF THE FIVE MOST COMMON TYPES OF CASES WE UNDERTOOK.
WHAT MANNER OF CASE IS IT, THEN?
WE WOULD HAVE AT *LEAST* THREE OR FOUR OF THEM EACH YEAR.
REFRESH MY MEMORY.
IT WOULD BE QUICKER IF YOU HAD A LOOK FOR YOUR-SELF.
HERE, READ THIS.
HM?
LET ME SEE ...
DEAR SHERLOCK HOLMES,
THIS IS MY FIRST OCCASION TO SEND A LETTER TO YOU, GOOD SIR. MY NAME IS GEORGE CHALMERS, AND I HAVE THE HONOR OF MANAGING A PRODUCE BROKERAGE IN BRICKDAM.

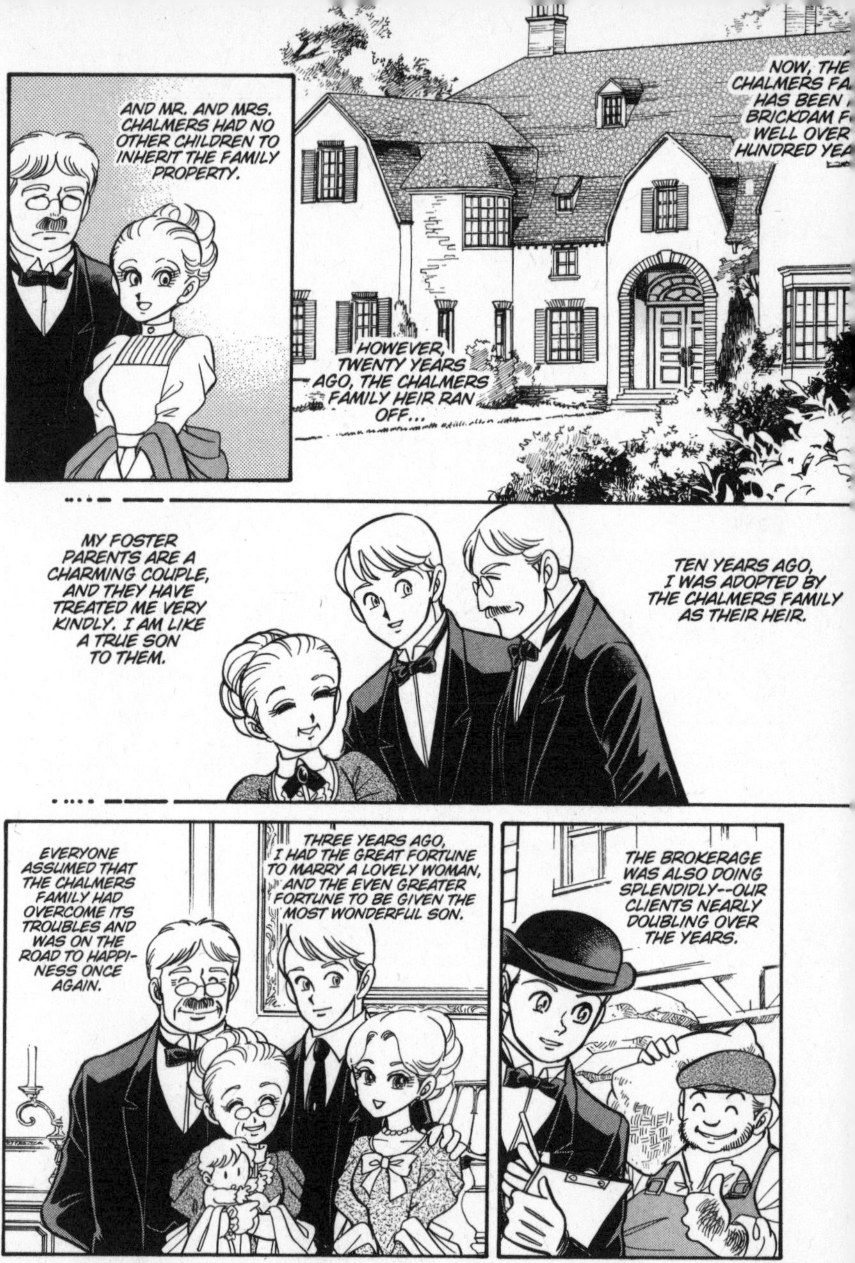
NOW, THE CHALMERS FA HAS BEEN BRICKDAM F WELL OVER HUNDRED YEA
HOWEVER, TWENTY YEARS AGO, THE CHALMERS FAMILY HEIR RAN OFF...
AND MR. AND MRS. CHALMERS HAD NO OTHER CHILDREN TO INHERIT THE FAMILY PROPERTY.
TEN YEARS AGO, I WAS ADOPTED BY THE CHALMERS FAMILY AS THEIR HEIR.
MY FOSTER PARENTS ARE A CHARMING COUPLE, AND THEY HAVE TREATED ME VERY KINDLY. I AM LIKE A TRUE SON TO THEM.
THE BROKERAGE WAS ALSO DOING SPLENDIDLY--OUR CLIENTS NEARLY DOUBLING OVER THE YEARS.
THREE YEARS AGO, I HAD THE GREAT FORTUNE TO MARRY A LOVELY WOMAN, AND THE EVEN GREATER FORTUNE TO BE GIVEN THE MOST WONDERFUL SON.
EVERYONE ASSUMED THAT THE CHALMERS FAMILY HAD OVERCOME ITS TROUBLES AND WAS ON THE ROAD TO HAPPINESS ONCE AGAIN.

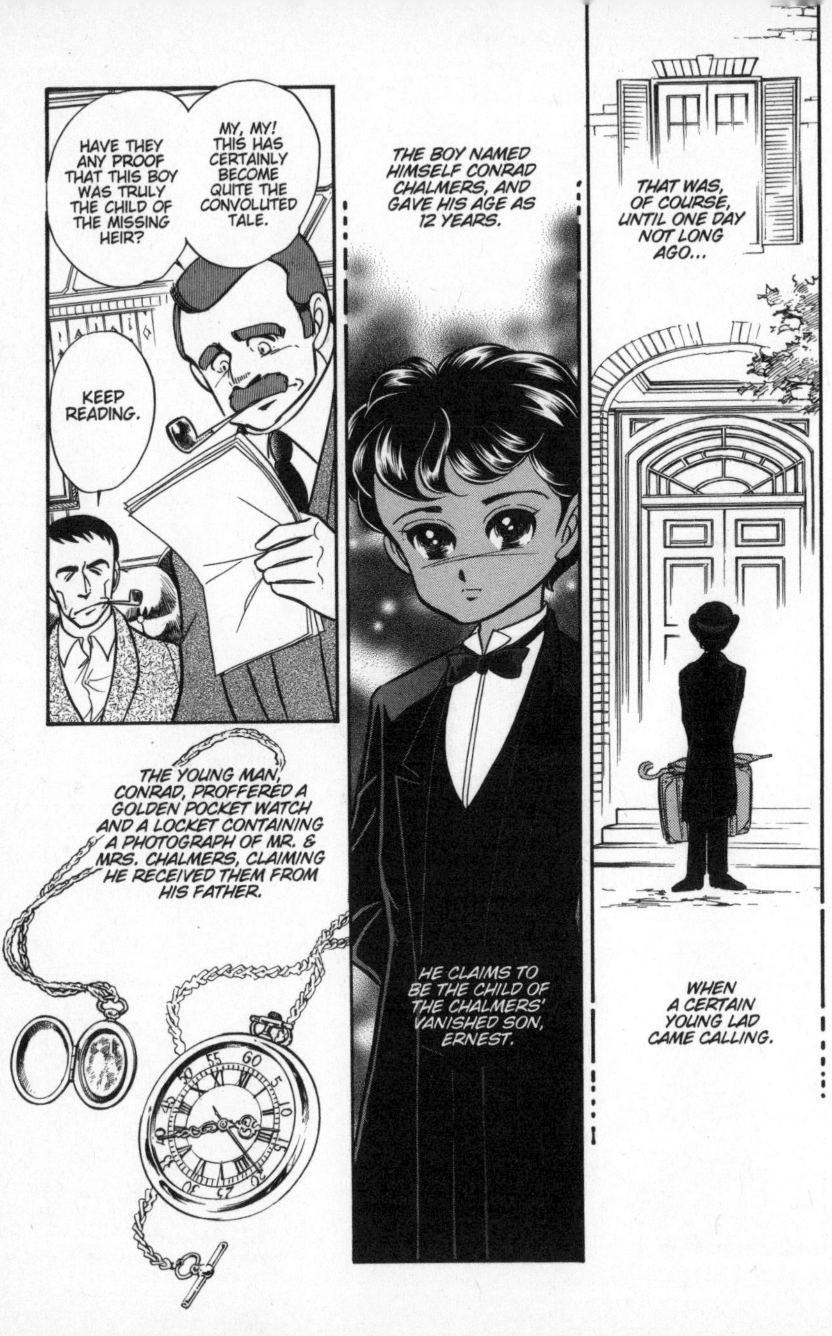
THAT WAS, OF COURSE, UNTIL ONE DAY NOT LONG AGO...
WHEN A CERTAIN YOUNG LAD CAME CALLING.
THE BOY NAMED HIMSELF CONRAD CHALMERS, AND GAVE HIS AGE AS 12 YEARS.
HE CLAIMS TO BE THE CHILD OF THE CHALMERS' VANISHED SON, ERNEST.
MY, MY! THIS HAS CERTAINLY BECOME QUITE THE CONVOLUTED TALE.
HAVE THEY ANY PROOF THAT THIS BOY WAS TRULY THE CHILD OF THE MISSING HEIR?
KEEP READING.
THE YOUNG MAN, CONRAD, PROFFERED A GOLDEN POCKET WATCH AND A LOCKET CONTAINING A PHOTOGRAPH OF MR. & MRS. CHALMERS, CLAIMING HE RECEIVED THEM FROM HIS FATHER.

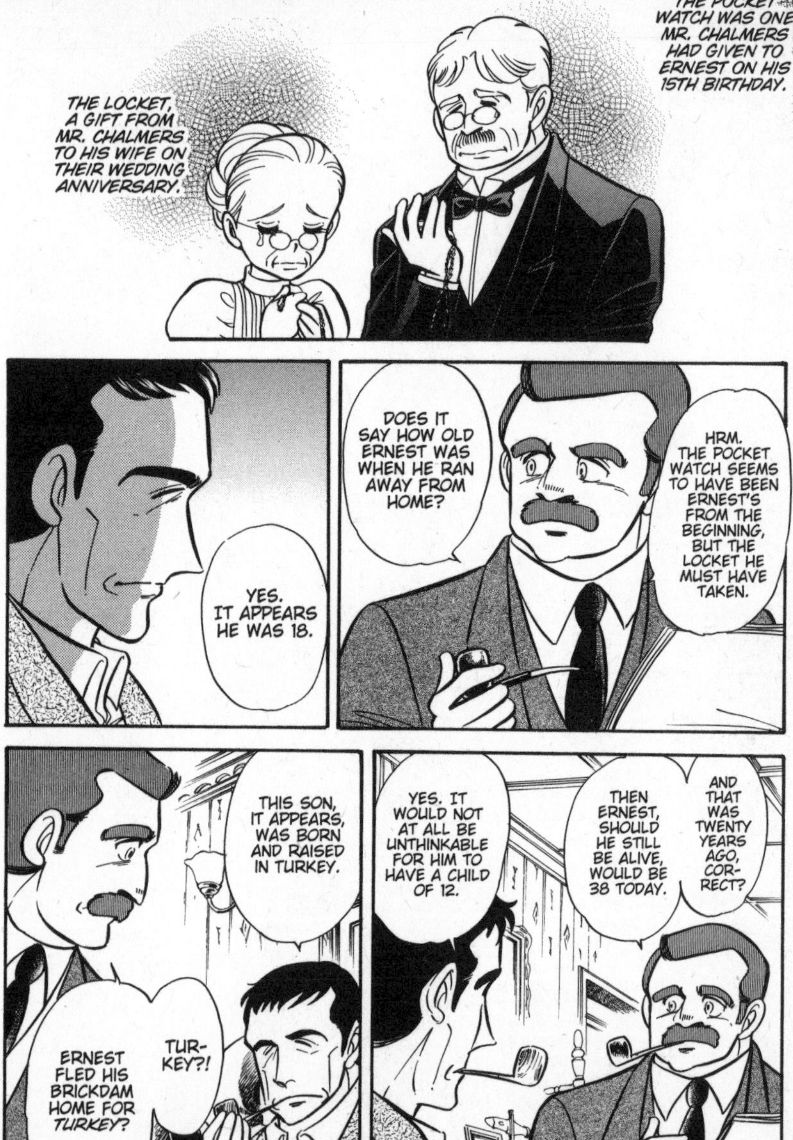
THE POCKET WATCH WAS ONE MR. CHALMERS HAD GIVEN TO ERNEST ON HIS 15TH BIRTHDAY.
THE LOCKET, A GIFT FROM MR. CHALMERS TO HIS WIFE ON THEIR WEDDING ANNIVERSARY.
HRM. THE POCKET WATCH SEEMS TO HAVE BEEN ERNEST'S FROM THE BEGINNING, BUT THE LOCKET HE MUST HAVE TAKEN.
DOES IT SAY HOW OLD ERNEST WAS WHEN HE RAN AWAY FROM HOME?
YES. IT APPEARS HE WAS 18.
AND THAT WAS TWENTY YEARS AGO, COR-RECT?
THEN ERNEST, SHOULD HE STILL BE ALIVE, WOULD BE 38 TODAY.
YES. IT WOULD NOT AT ALL BE UNTHINKABLE FOR HIM TO HAVE A CHILD OF 12.
THIS SON, IT APPEARS, WAS BORN AND RAISED IN TURKEY.
TUR-KEY?!
ERNEST FLED HIS BRICKDAM HOME FOR *TURKEY?*

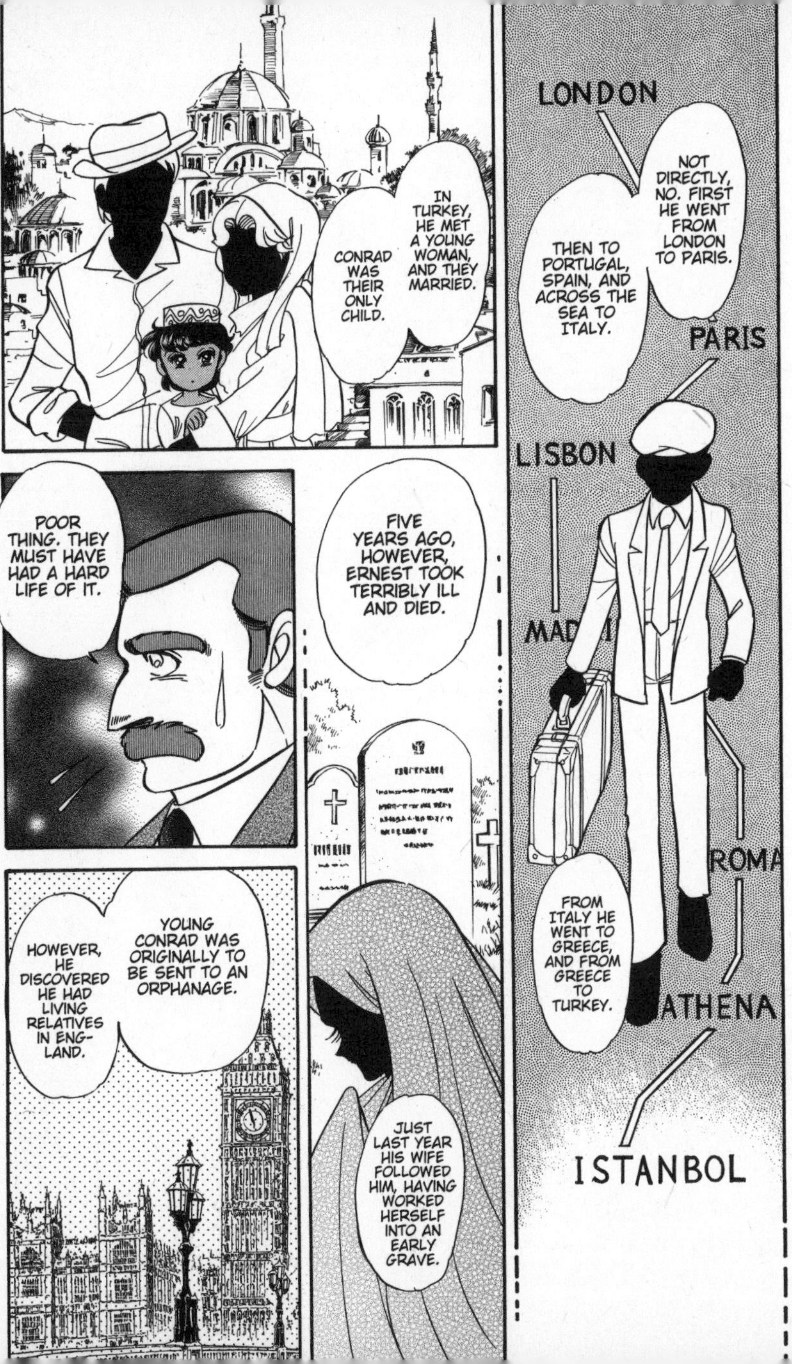
NOT DIRECTLY, NO. FIRST HE WENT FROM LONDON TO PARIS.
THEN TO PORTUGAL, SPAIN, AND ACROSS THE SEA TO ITALY.
LONDON
PARIS
LISBON
ROMA
FROM ITALY HE WENT TO GREECE, AND FROM GREECE TO TURKEY.
ATHENA
ISTANBOL
IN TURKEY, HE MET A YOUNG WOMAN, AND THEY MARRIED.
CONRAD WAS THEIR ONLY CHILD.
FIVE YEARS AGO, HOWEVER, ERNEST TOOK TERRIBLY ILL AND DIED.
JUST LAST YEAR HIS WIFE FOLLOWED HIM, HAVING WORKED HERSELF INTO AN EARLY GRAVE.
POOR THING. THEY MUST HAVE HAD A HARD LIFE OF IT.
YOUNG CONRAD WAS ORIGINALLY TO BE SENT TO AN ORPHANAGE.
HOWEVER, HE DISCOVERED HE HAD LIVING RELATIVES IN ENG-LAND.

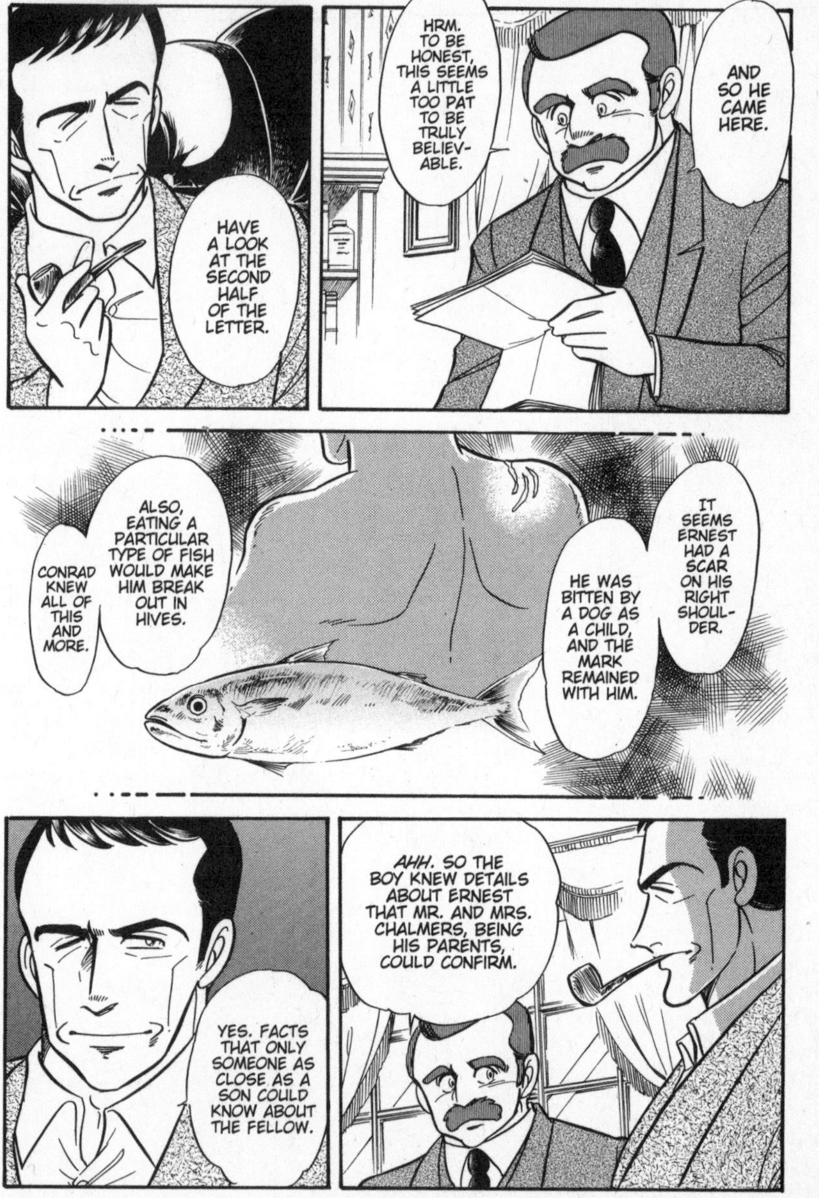
AND SO HE CAME HERE.
HRM. TO BE HONEST, THIS SEEMS A LITTLE TOO PAT TO BE TRULY BELIEVABLE.
HAVE A LOOK AT THE SECOND HALF OF THE LETTER.
IT SEEMS ERNEST HAD A SCAR ON HIS RIGHT SHOULDER.
HE WAS BITTEN BY A DOG AS A CHILD, AND THE MARK REMAINED WITH HIM.
ALSO, EATING A PARTICULAR TYPE OF FISH WOULD MAKE HIM BREAK OUT IN HIVES.
CONRAD KNEW ALL OF THIS AND MORE.
AHH. SO THE BOY KNEW DETAILS ABOUT ERNEST THAT MR. AND MRS. CHALMERS, BEING HIS PARENTS, COULD CONFIRM.
YES. FACTS THAT ONLY SOMEONE AS CLOSE AS A SON COULD KNOW ABOUT THE FELLOW.

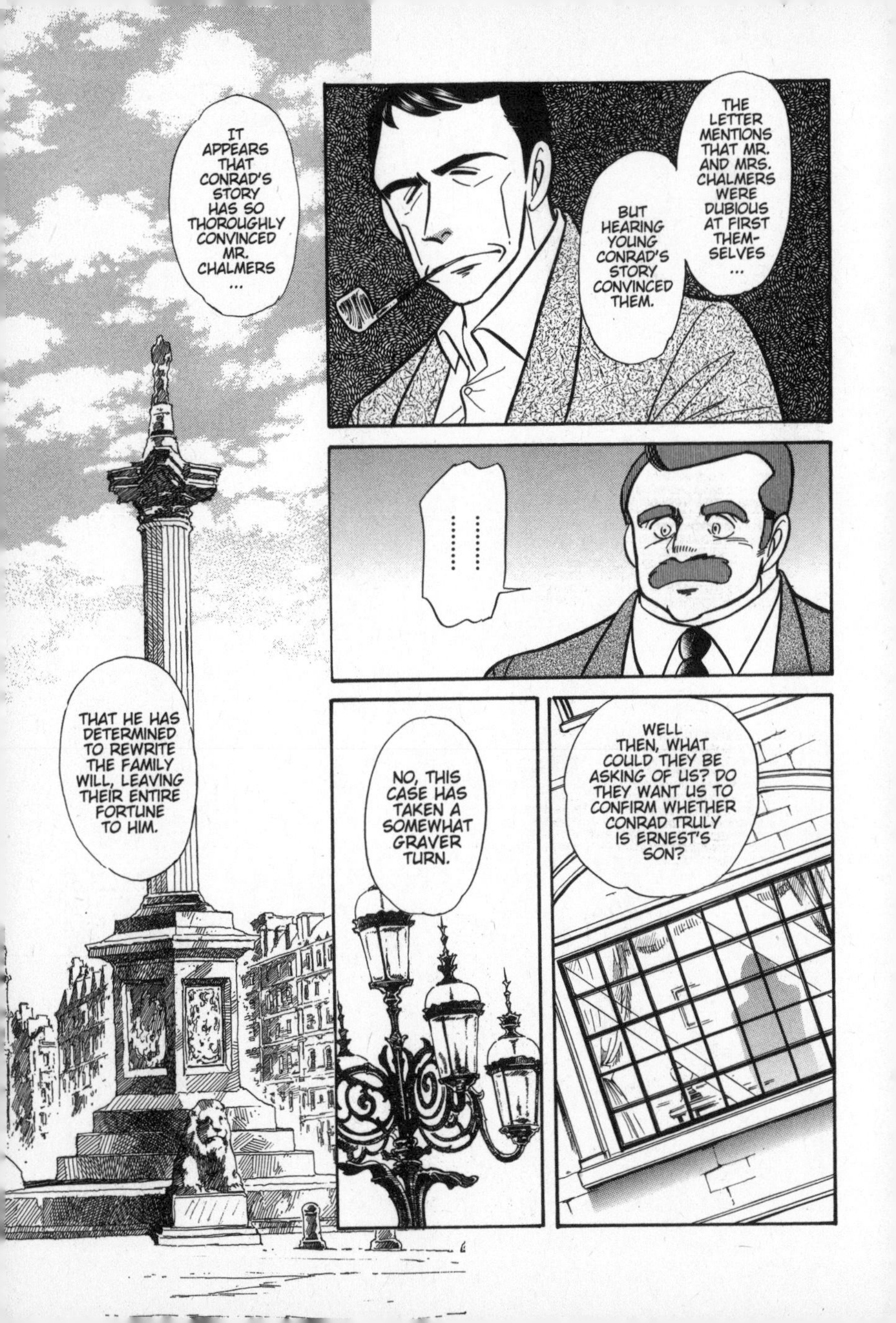
THE LETTER MENTIONS THAT MR. AND MRS. CHALMERS WERE DUBIOUS AT FIRST THEM-SELVES ...
BUT HEARING YOUNG CONRAD'S STORY CONVINCED THEM.
......
WELL THEN, WHAT COULD THEY BE ASKING OF US? DO THEY WANT US TO CONFIRM WHETHER CONRAD TRULY IS ERNEST'S SON?
NO, THIS CASE HAS TAKEN A SOMEWHAT GRAVER TURN.
IT APPEARS THAT CONRAD'S STORY HAS SO THOROUGHLY CONVINCED MR. CHALMERS ...
THAT HE HAS DETERMINED TO REWRITE THE FAMILY WILL, LEAVING THEIR ENTIRE FORTUNE TO HIM.

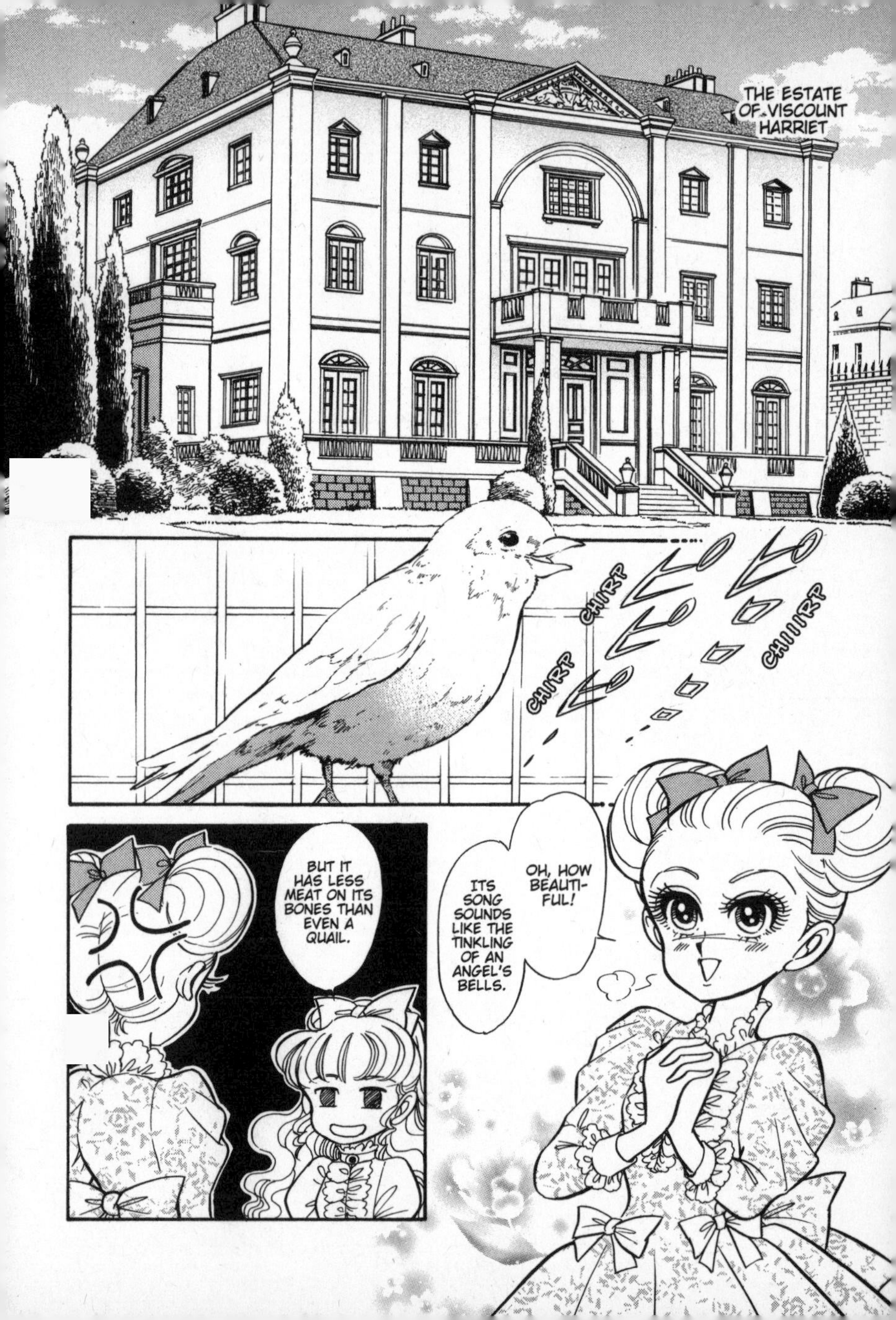
THE ESTATE OF VISCOUNT HARRIET
CHIIIRP
CHIRP
CHIRP
CHIRP
OH, HOW BEAUTI-FUL!
ITS SONG SOUNDS LIKE THE TINKLING OF AN ANGEL'S BELLS.
BUT IT HAS LESS MEAT ON ITS BONES THAN EVEN A QUAIL.

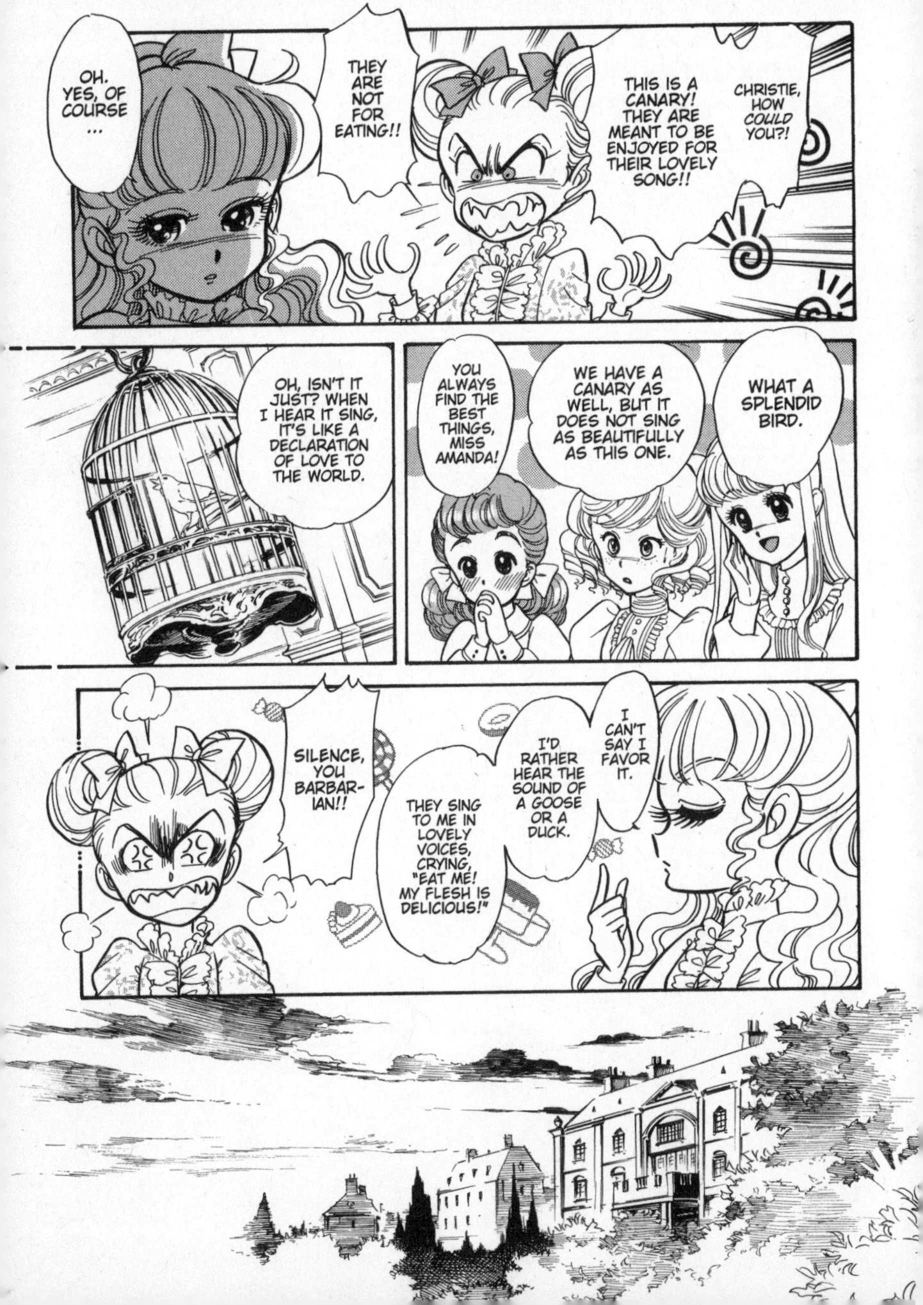
CHRISTIE, HOW COULD YOU?!
THIS IS A CANARY! THEY ARE MEANT TO BE ENJOYED FOR THEIR LOVELY SONG!!
THEY ARE NOT FOR EATING!!
OH. YES, OF COURSE ...
WHAT A SPLENDID BIRD.
WE HAVE A CANARY AS WELL, BUT IT DOES NOT SING AS BEAUTIFULLY AS THIS ONE.
YOU ALWAYS FIND THE BEST THINGS, MISS AMANDA!
OH, ISN'T IT JUST? WHEN I HEAR IT SING, IT'S LIKE A DECLARATION OF LOVE TO THE WORLD.
I CAN'T SAY I FAVOR IT.
I'D RATHER HEAR THE SOUND OF A GOOSE OR A DUCK.
THEY SING TO ME IN LOVELY VOICES, CRYING, "EAT ME! MY FLESH IS DELICIOUS!"
SILENCE, YOU BARBARIAN!!

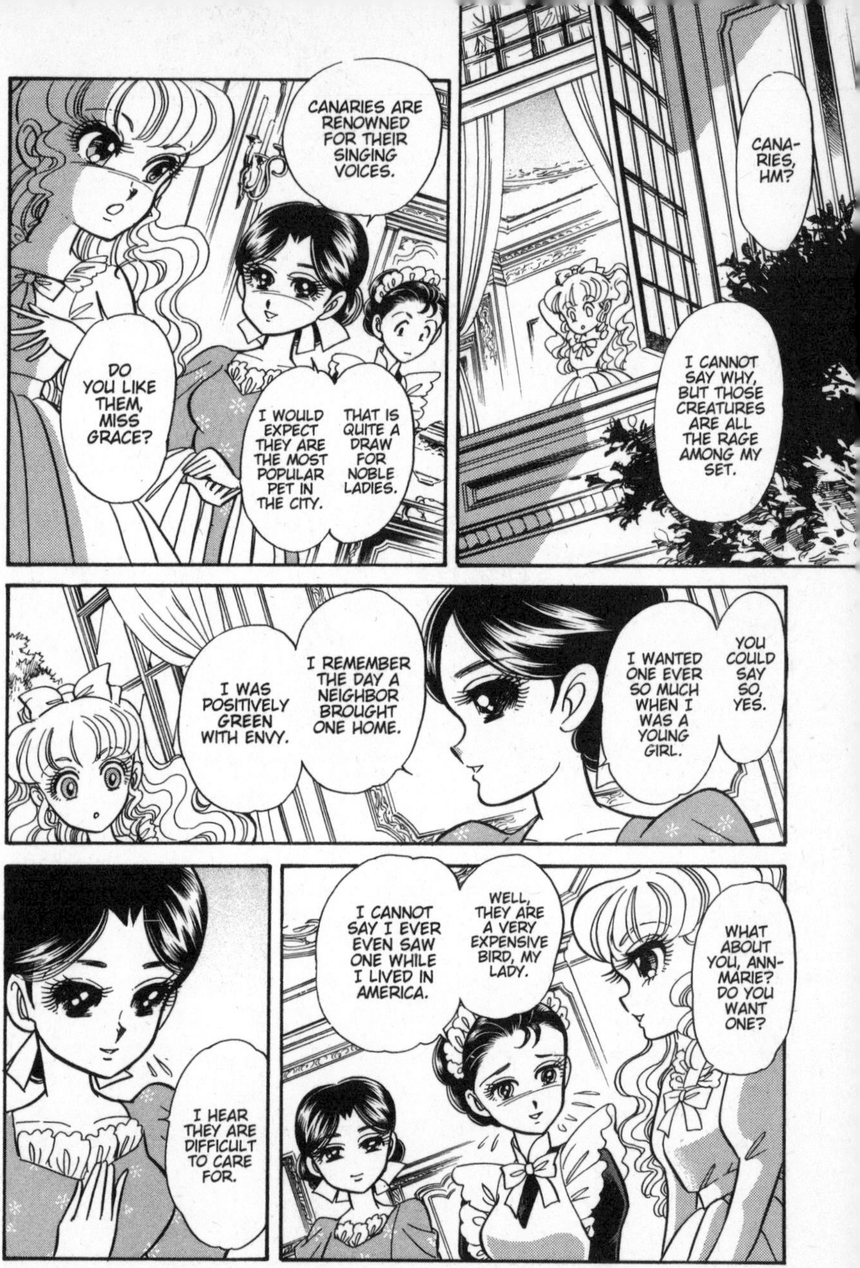
CANA-RIES, HM?
I CANNOT SAY WHY, BUT THOSE CREATURES ARE ALL THE RAGE AMONG MY SET.
CANARIES ARE RENOWNED FOR THEIR SINGING VOICES.
THAT IS QUITE A DRAW FOR NOBLE LADIES.
I WOULD EXPECT THEY ARE THE MOST POPULAR PET IN THE CITY.
DO YOU LIKE THEM, MISS GRACE?
YOU COULD SAY SO, YES.
I WANTED ONE EVER SO MUCH WHEN I WAS A YOUNG GIRL.
I REMEMBER THE DAY A NEIGHBOR BROUGHT ONE HOME.
I WAS POSITIVELY GREEN WITH ENVY.
WHAT ABOUT YOU, ANN-MARIE? DO YOU WANT ONE?
WELL, THEY ARE A VERY EXPENSIVE BIRD, MY LADY.
I CANNOT SAY I EVER EVEN SAW ONE WHILE I LIVED IN AMERICA.
I HEAR THEY ARE DIFFICULT TO CARE FOR.

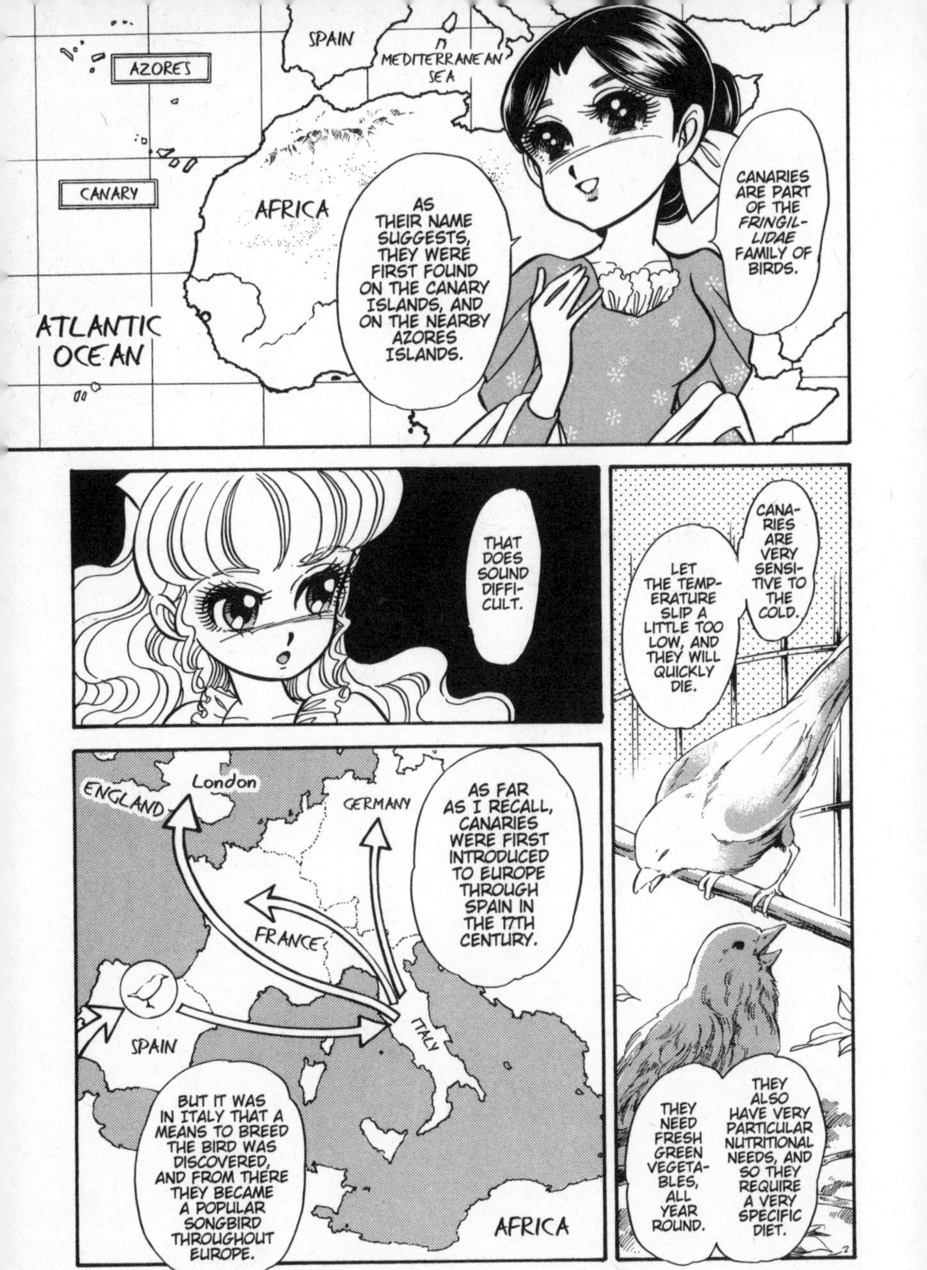

CANARIES ARE PART OF THE *FRINGILLIDAE* FAMILY OF BIRDS.
MEDITERRANEAN SEA
SPAIN
AZORES
AS THEIR NAME SUGGESTS, THEY WERE FIRST FOUND ON THE CANARY ISLANDS, AND ON THE NEARBY AZORES ISLANDS.
CANARY
AFRICA
ATLANTIC OCEAN
CANARIES ARE VERY SENSITIVE TO THE COLD.
LET THE TEMPERATURE SLIP A LITTLE TOO LOW, AND THEY WILL QUICKLY DIE.
THEY ALSO HAVE VERY PARTICULAR NUTRITIONAL NEEDS, AND SO THEY REQUIRE A VERY SPECIFIC DIET.
THEY NEED FRESH GREEN VEGETABLES, ALL YEAR ROUND.
THAT DOES SOUND DIFFICULT.
AS FAR AS I RECALL, CANARIES WERE FIRST INTRODUCED TO EUROPE THROUGH SPAIN IN THE 17TH CENTURY.
GERMANY
London
ENGLAND
FRANCE
ITALY
SPAIN
BUT IT WAS IN ITALY THAT A MEANS TO BREED THE BIRD WAS DISCOVERED, AND FROM THERE THEY BECAME A POPULAR SONGBIRD THROUGHOUT EUROPE.
AFRICA

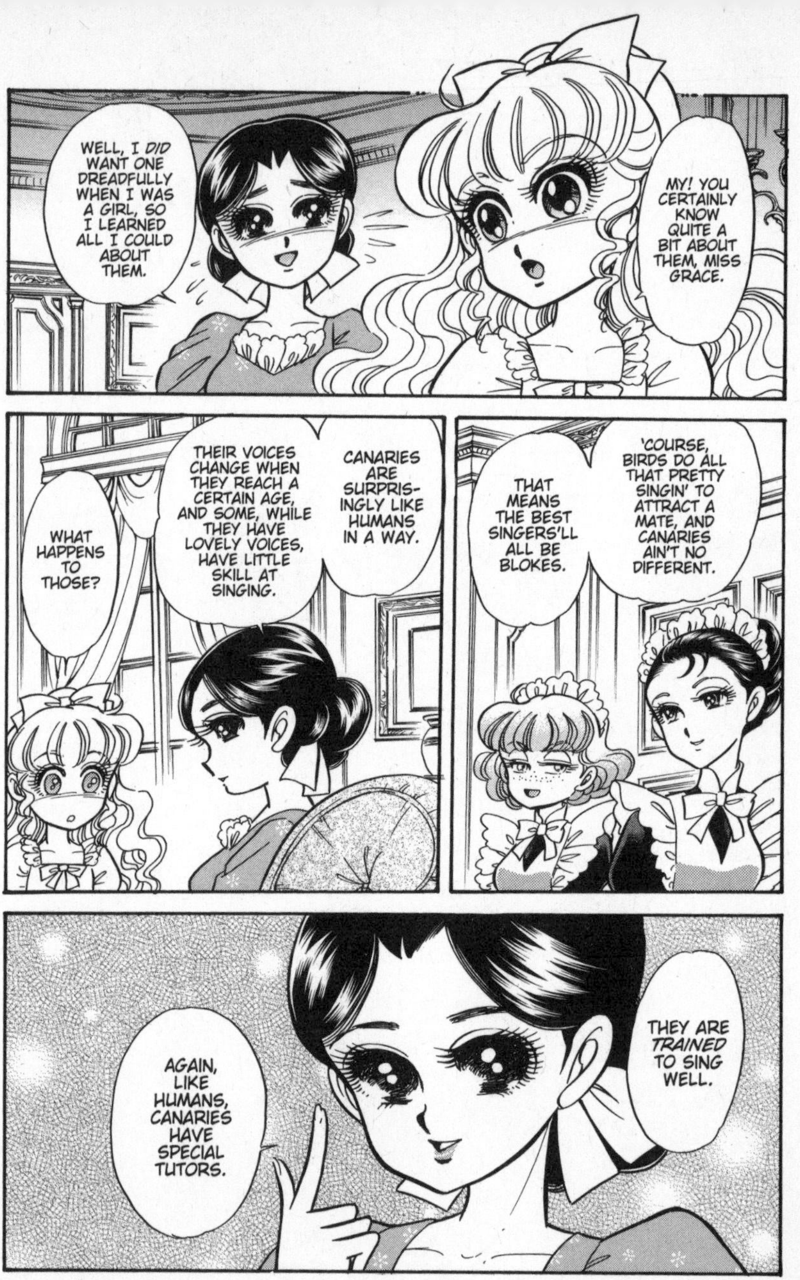
MY! YOU CERTAINLY KNOW QUITE A BIT ABOUT THEM, MISS GRACE.
WELL, I *DID* WANT ONE DREADFULLY WHEN I WAS A GIRL, SO I LEARNED ALL I COULD ABOUT THEM.
'COURSE, BIRDS DO ALL THAT PRETTY SINGIN' TO ATTRACT A MATE, AND CANARIES AIN'T NO DIFFERENT.
THAT MEANS THE BEST SINGERS'LL ALL BE BLOKES.
CANARIES ARE SURPRISINGLY LIKE HUMANS IN A WAY.
THEIR VOICES CHANGE WHEN THEY REACH A CERTAIN AGE, AND SOME, WHILE THEY HAVE LOVELY VOICES, HAVE LITTLE SKILL AT SINGING.
WHAT HAPPENS TO THOSE?
THEY ARE *TRAINED* TO SING WELL.
AGAIN, LIKE HUMANS, CANARIES HAVE SPECIAL TUTORS.

The Adventure of the Famous Trainer (2)

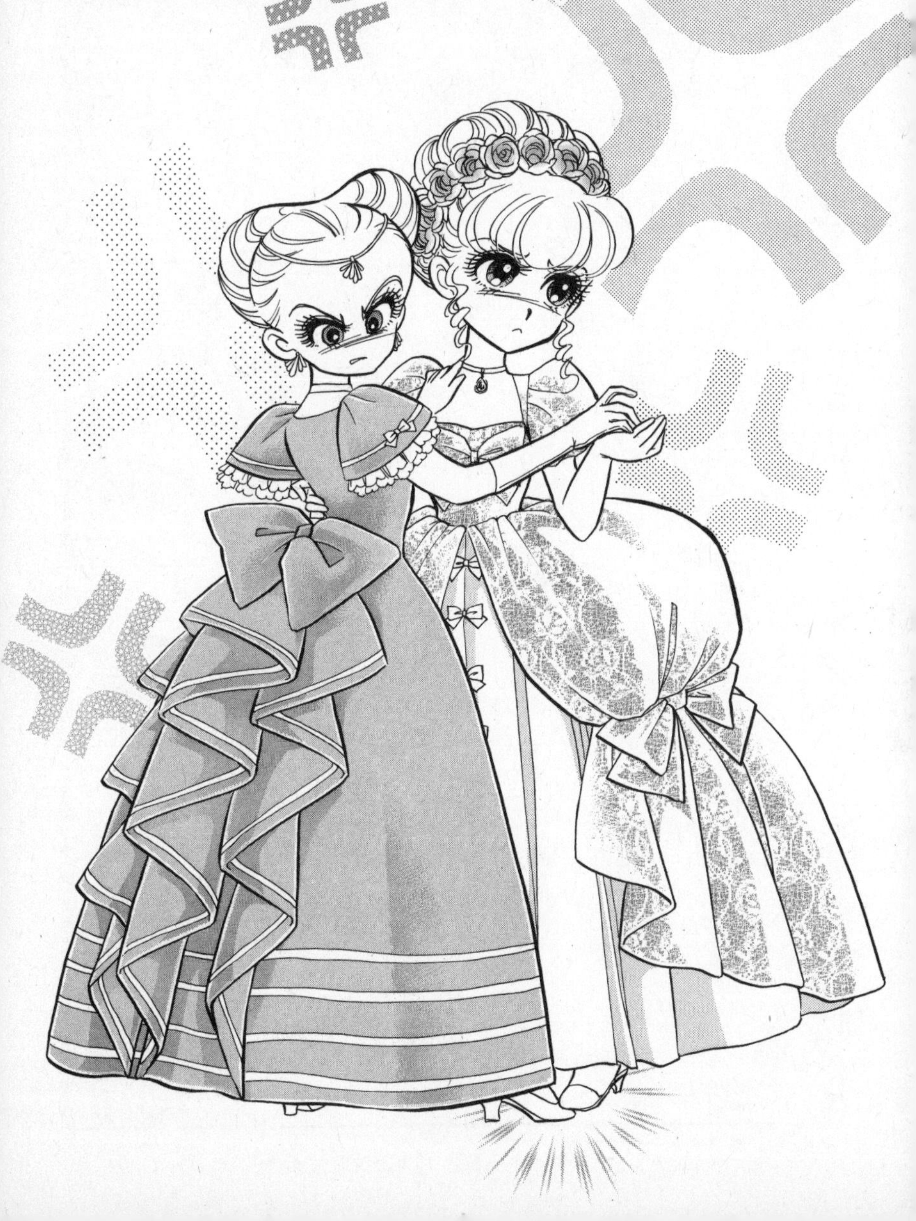

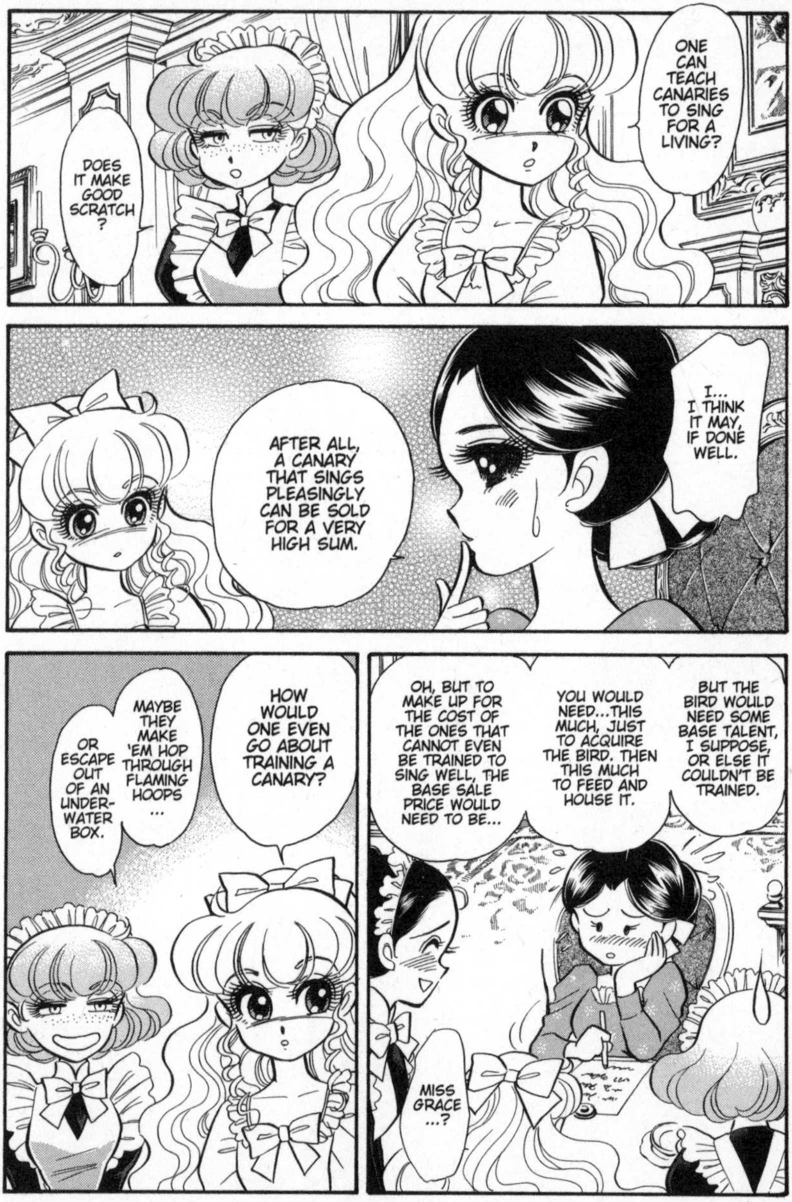
ONE CAN TEACH CANARIES TO SING FOR A LIVING?
DOES IT MAKE GOOD SCRATCH ?
I... I THINK IT MAY, IF DONE WELL.
AFTER ALL, A CANARY THAT SINGS PLEASINGLY CAN BE SOLD FOR A VERY HIGH SUM.
BUT THE BIRD WOULD NEED SOME BASE TALENT, I SUPPOSE, OR ELSE IT COULDN'T BE TRAINED.
YOU WOULD NEED...THIS MUCH, JUST TO ACQUIRE THE BIRD. THEN THIS MUCH TO FEED AND HOUSE IT.
OH, BUT TO MAKE UP FOR THE COST OF THE ONES THAT CANNOT EVEN BE TRAINED TO SING WELL, THE BASE SALE PRICE WOULD NEED TO BE...
MISS GRACE ...?
HOW WOULD ONE EVEN GO ABOUT TRAINING A CANARY?
MAYBE THEY MAKE 'EM HOP THROUGH FLAMING HOOPS ...
OR ESCAPE OUT OF AN UNDER-WATER BOX.

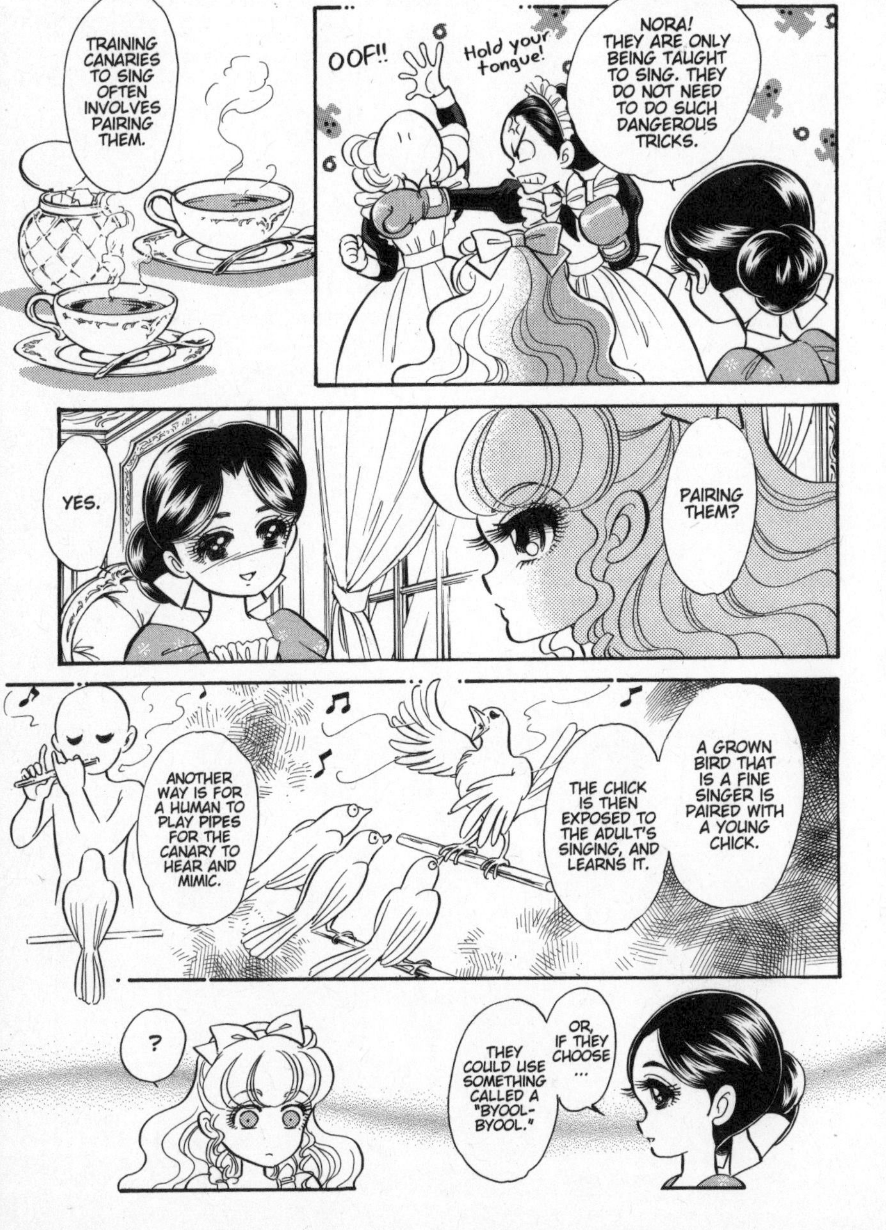
NORA! THEY ARE ONLY BEING TAUGHT TO SING. THEY DO NOT NEED TO DO SUCH DANGEROUS TRICKS.
Hold your tongue!
OOF!!
TRAINING CANARIES TO SING OFTEN INVOLVES PAIRING THEM.
PAIRING THEM?
YES.
A GROWN BIRD THAT IS A FINE SINGER IS PAIRED WITH A YOUNG CHICK.
THE CHICK IS THEN EXPOSED TO THE ADULT'S SINGING, AND LEARNS IT.
ANOTHER WAY IS FOR A HUMAN TO PLAY PIPES FOR THE CANARY TO HEAR AND MIMIC.
OR, IF THEY CHOOSE ...
THEY COULD USE SOMETHING CALLED A "BYOOL-BYOOL."
?

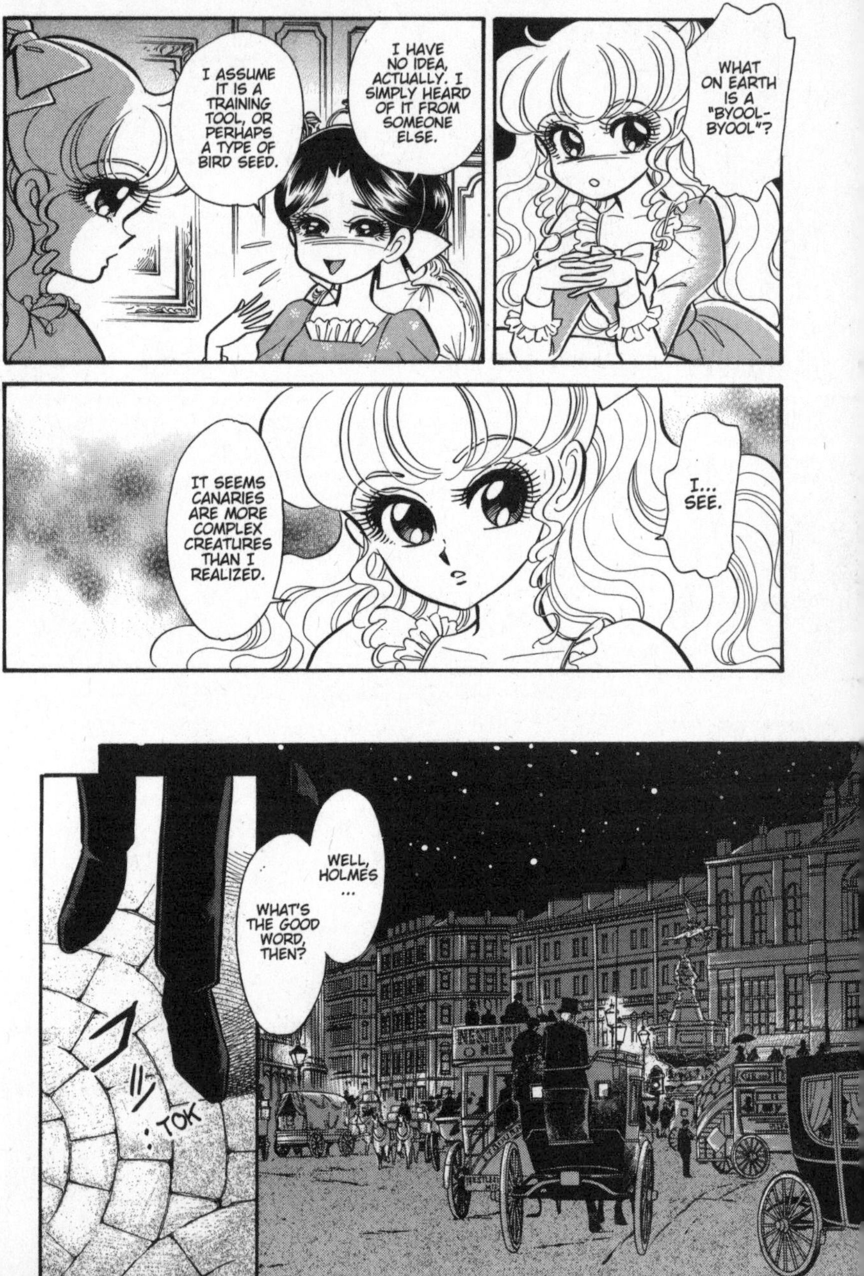
WHAT ON EARTH IS A "BYOOL-BYOOL"?
I HAVE NO IDEA, ACTUALLY. I SIMPLY HEARD OF IT FROM SOMEONE ELSE.
I ASSUME IT IS A TRAINING TOOL, OR PERHAPS A TYPE OF BIRD SEED.
I... SEE.
IT SEEMS CANARIES ARE MORE COMPLEX CREATURES THAN I REALIZED.
WELL, HOLMES ...
WHAT'S THE GOOD WORD, THEN?
TOK

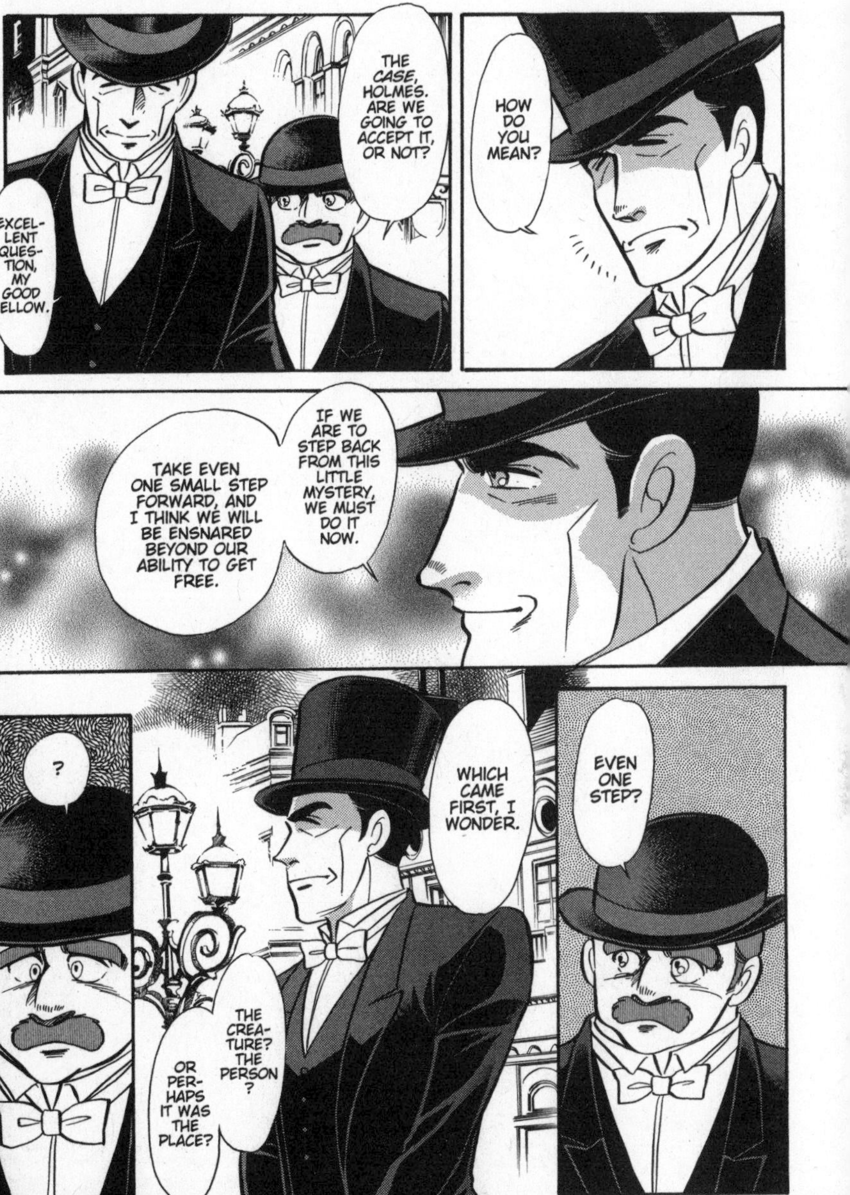
HOW DO YOU MEAN?
THE CASE, HOLMES. ARE WE GOING TO ACCEPT IT, OR NOT?
EXCEL-LENT QUES-TION, MY GOOD FELLOW.
IF WE ARE TO STEP BACK FROM THIS LITTLE MYSTERY, WE MUST DO IT NOW.
TAKE EVEN ONE SMALL STEP FORWARD, AND I THINK WE WILL BE ENSNARED BEYOND OUR ABILITY TO GET FREE.
EVEN ONE STEP?
WHICH CAME FIRST, I WONDER.
THE CREA-TURE? THE PERSON?
OR PER-HAPS IT WAS THE PLACE?
?

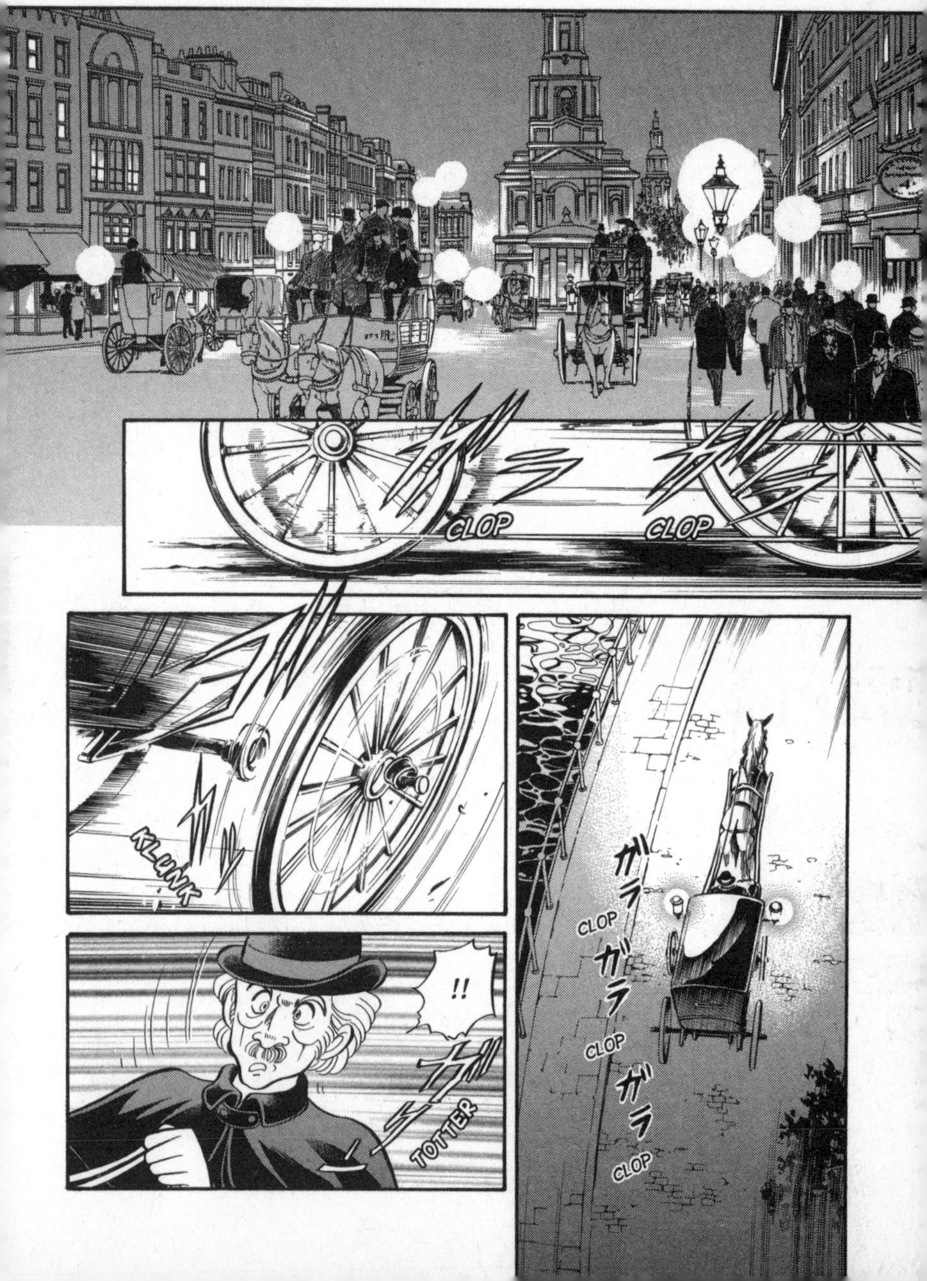
CLOP
CLOP
ガラ
CLOP
ガラ
CLOP
ガラ
CLOP
KLUNK
!!
TOTTER

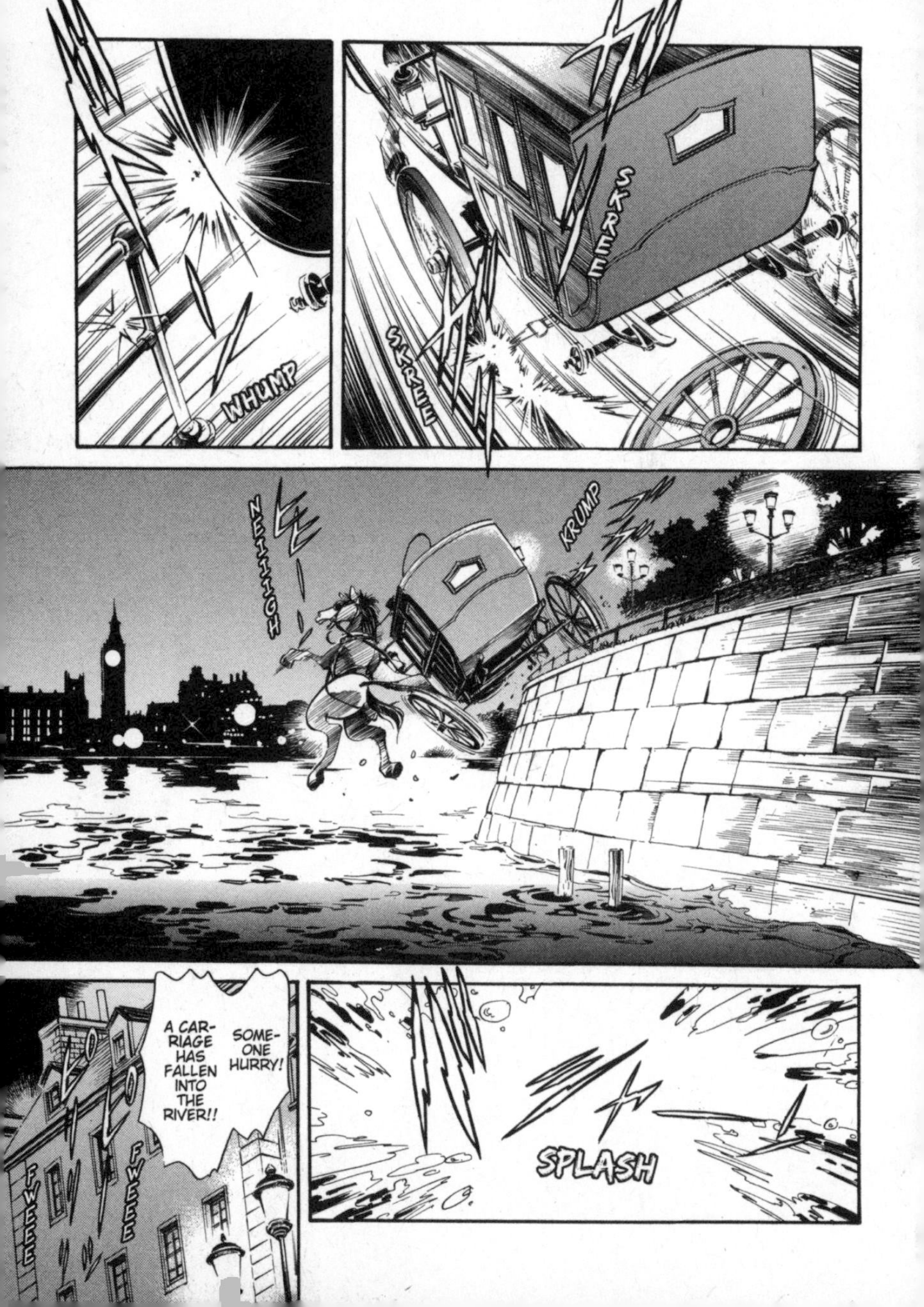
SKREE
SKREE
WHUMP
KRUMP
NEIIIGH
SPLASH
A CARRIAGE HAS FALLEN INTO THE RIVER!! SOMEONE HURRY!
FWEEE
FWEEE

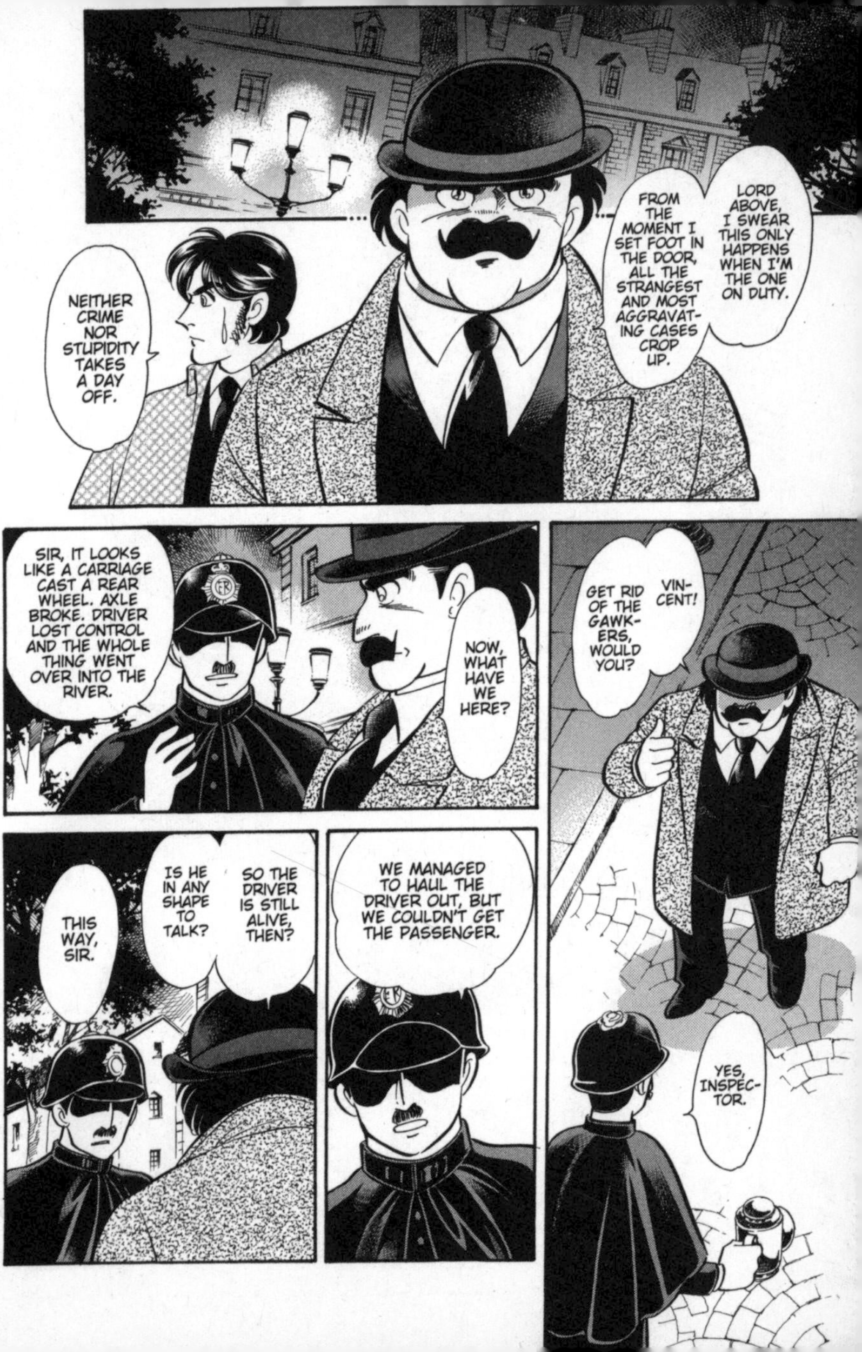
LORD ABOVE, I SWEAR THIS ONLY HAPPENS WHEN I'M THE ONE ON DUTY.
FROM THE MOMENT I SET FOOT IN THE DOOR, ALL THE STRANGEST AND MOST AGGRAVATING CASES CROP UP.
NEITHER CRIME NOR STUPIDITY TAKES A DAY OFF.
VINCENT!
GET RID OF THE GAWKERS, WOULD YOU?
YES, INSPECTOR.
NOW, WHAT HAVE WE HERE?
SIR, IT LOOKS LIKE A CARRIAGE CAST A REAR WHEEL. AXLE BROKE. DRIVER LOST CONTROL AND THE WHOLE THING WENT OVER INTO THE RIVER.
WE MANAGED TO HAUL THE DRIVER OUT, BUT WE COULDN'T GET THE PASSENGER.
SO THE DRIVER IS STILL ALIVE, THEN?
IS HE IN ANY SHAPE TO TALK?
THIS WAY, SIR.

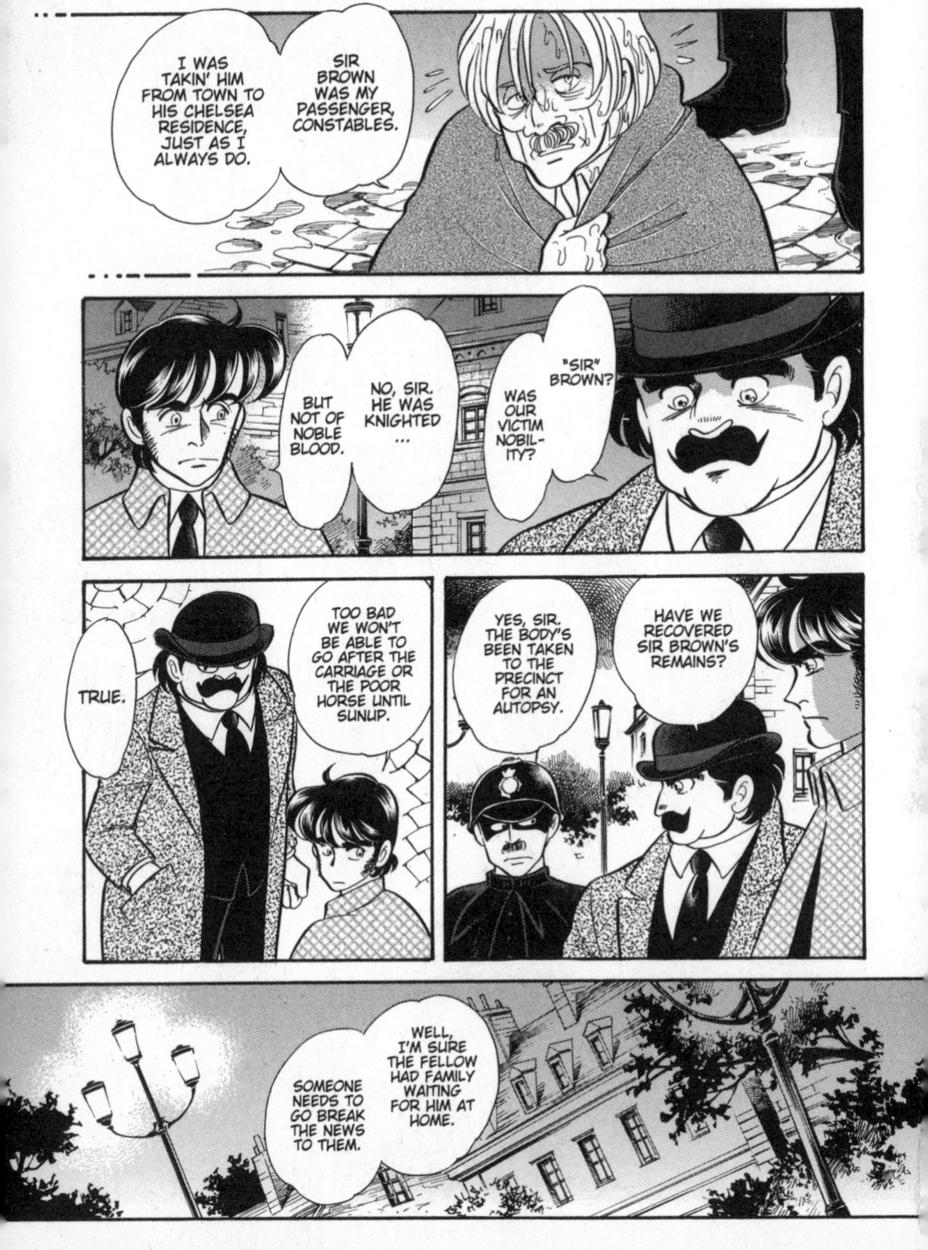
SIR BROWN WAS MY PASSENGER, CONSTABLES.
I WAS TAKIN' HIM FROM TOWN TO HIS CHELSEA RESIDENCE, JUST AS I ALWAYS DO.
"SIR" BROWN?
WAS OUR VICTIM NOBILITY?
NO, SIR. HE WAS KNIGHTED ...
BUT NOT OF NOBLE BLOOD.
HAVE WE RECOVERED SIR BROWN'S REMAINS?
YES, SIR. THE BODY'S BEEN TAKEN TO THE PRECINCT FOR AN AUTOPSY.
TOO BAD WE WON'T BE ABLE TO GO AFTER THE CARRIAGE OR THE POOR HORSE UNTIL SUNUP.
TRUE.
WELL, I'M SURE THE FELLOW HAD FAMILY WAITING FOR HIM AT HOME.
SOMEONE NEEDS TO GO BREAK THE NEWS TO THEM.

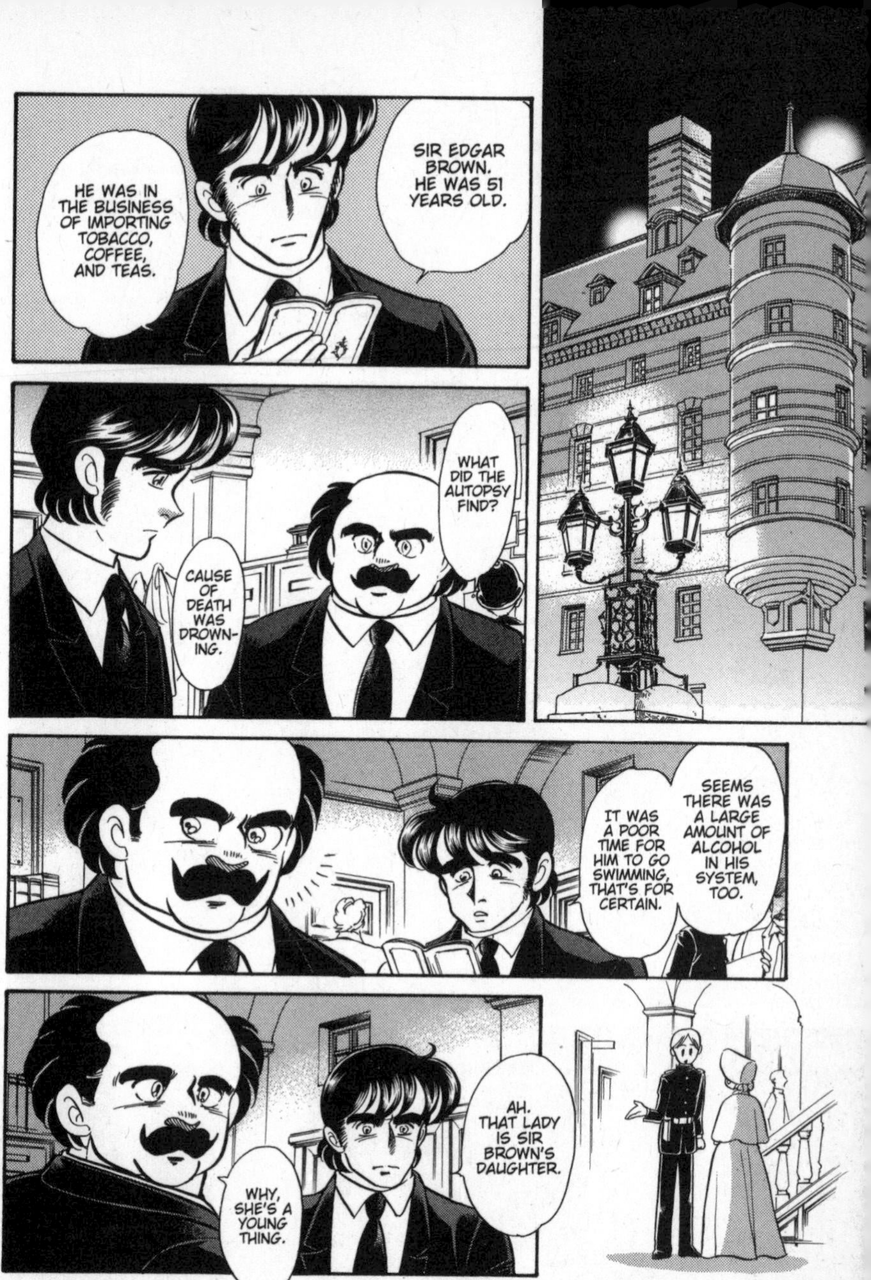
SIR EDGAR BROWN. HE WAS 51 YEARS OLD.
HE WAS IN THE BUSINESS OF IMPORTING TOBACCO, COFFEE, AND TEAS.
WHAT DID THE AUTOPSY FIND?
CAUSE OF DEATH WAS DROWN-ING.
SEEMS THERE WAS A LARGE AMOUNT OF ALCOHOL IN HIS SYSTEM, TOO.
IT WAS A POOR TIME FOR HIM TO GO SWIMMING, THAT'S FOR CERTAIN.
AH. THAT LADY IS SIR BROWN'S DAUGHTER.
WHY, SHE'S A YOUNG THING.

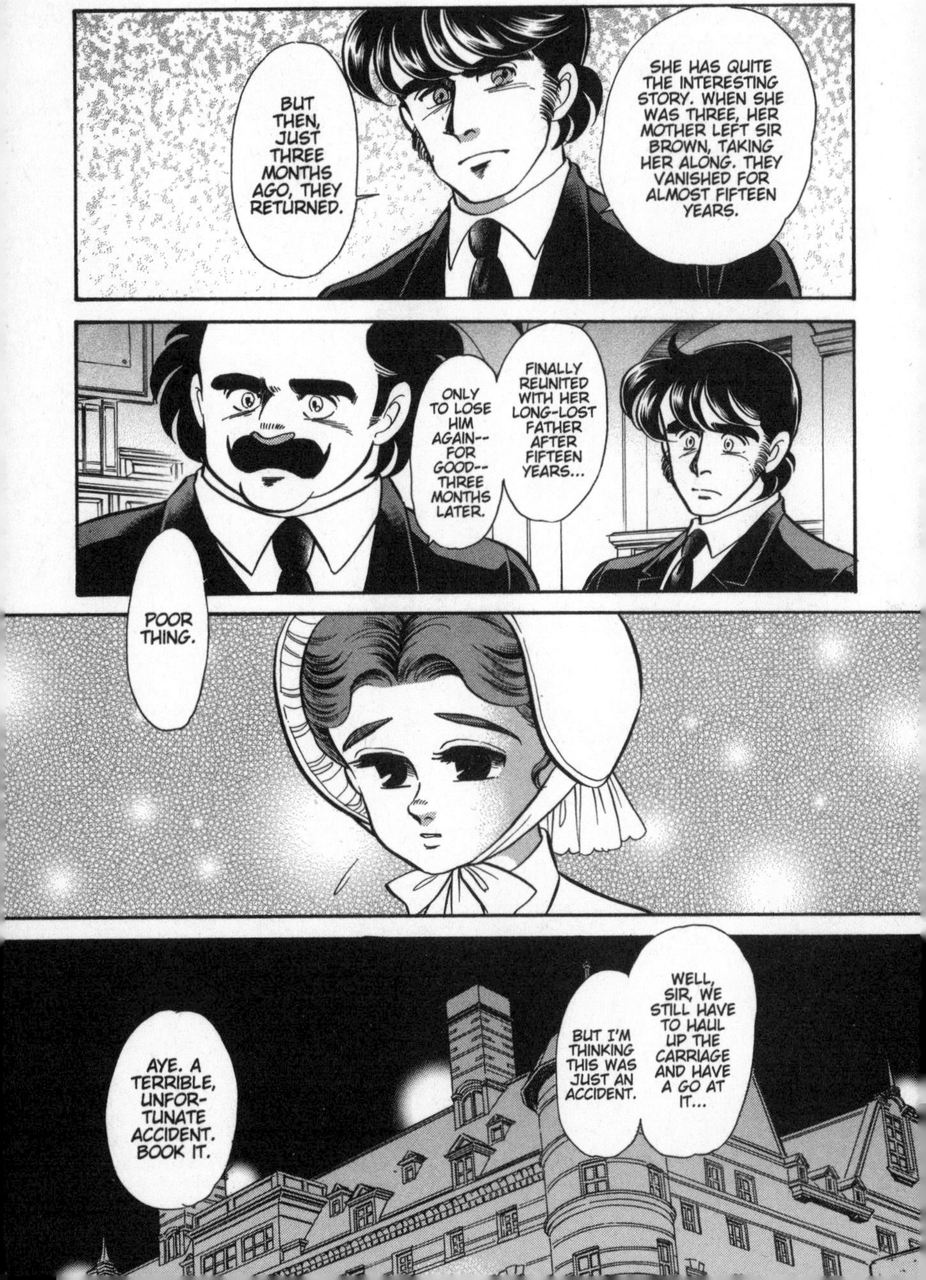
SHE HAS QUITE THE INTERESTING STORY. WHEN SHE WAS THREE, HER MOTHER LEFT SIR BROWN, TAKING HER ALONG. THEY VANISHED FOR ALMOST FIFTEEN YEARS.
BUT THEN, JUST THREE MONTHS AGO, THEY RETURNED.
FINALLY REUNITED WITH HER LONG-LOST FATHER AFTER FIFTEEN YEARS...
ONLY TO LOSE HIM AGAIN-- FOR GOOD-- THREE MONTHS LATER.
POOR THING.
WELL, SIR, WE STILL HAVE TO HAUL UP THE CARRIAGE AND HAVE A GO AT IT...
BUT I'M THINKING THIS WAS JUST AN ACCIDENT.
AYE. A TERRIBLE, UNFORTUNATE ACCIDENT. BOOK IT.

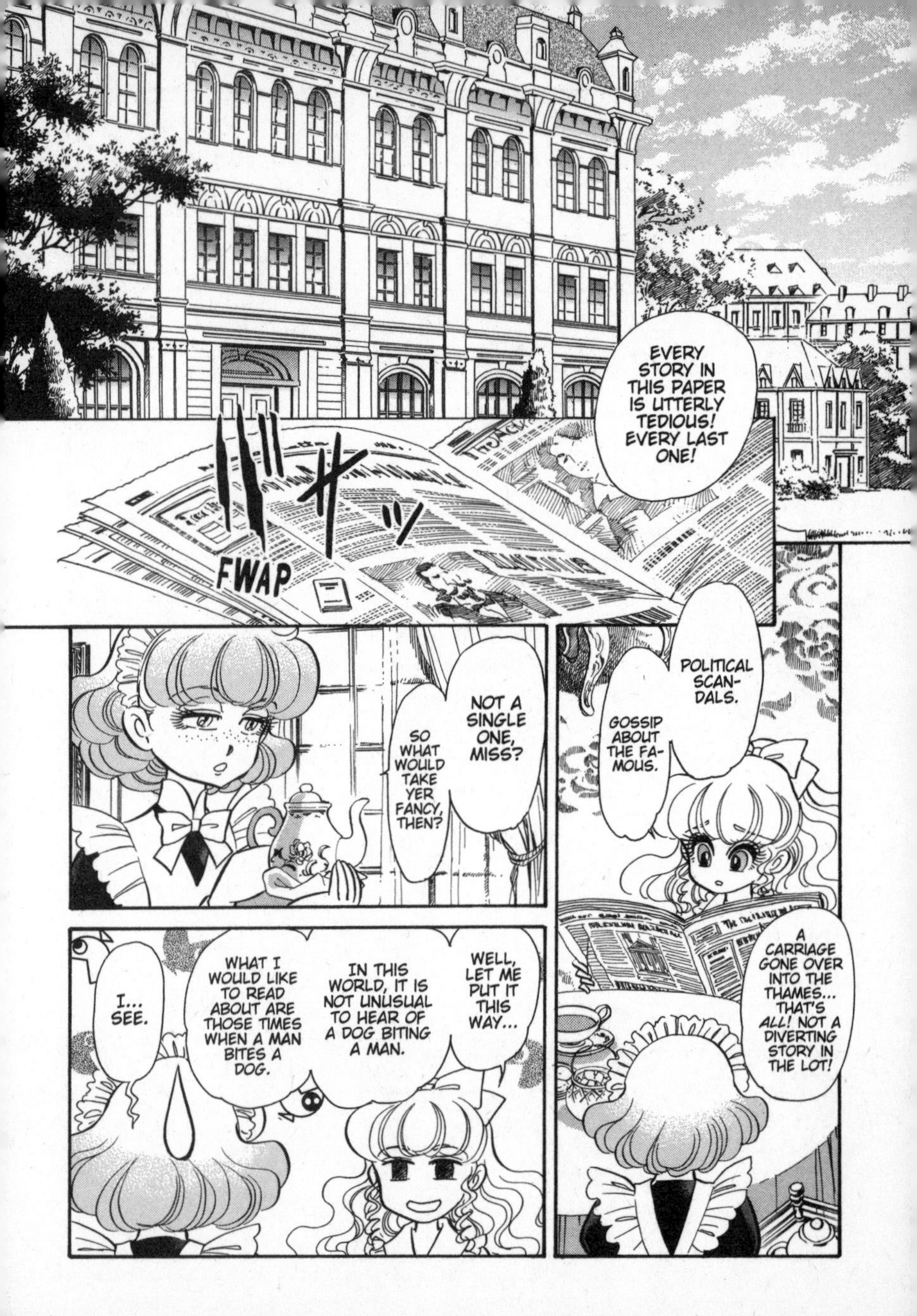
EVERY STORY IN THIS PAPER IS UTTERLY TEDIOUS! EVERY LAST ONE!
バサッ
FWAP
POLITICAL SCANDALS.
GOSSIP ABOUT THE FAMOUS.
A CARRIAGE GONE OVER INTO THE THAMES... THAT'S *ALL*! NOT A DIVERTING STORY IN THE LOT!
NOT A SINGLE ONE, MISS?
SO WHAT WOULD TAKE YER FANCY, THEN?
WELL, LET ME PUT IT THIS WAY...
IN THIS WORLD, IT IS NOT UNUSUAL TO HEAR OF A DOG BITING A MAN.
WHAT I WOULD LIKE TO READ ABOUT ARE THOSE TIMES WHEN A MAN BITES A DOG.
I... SEE.

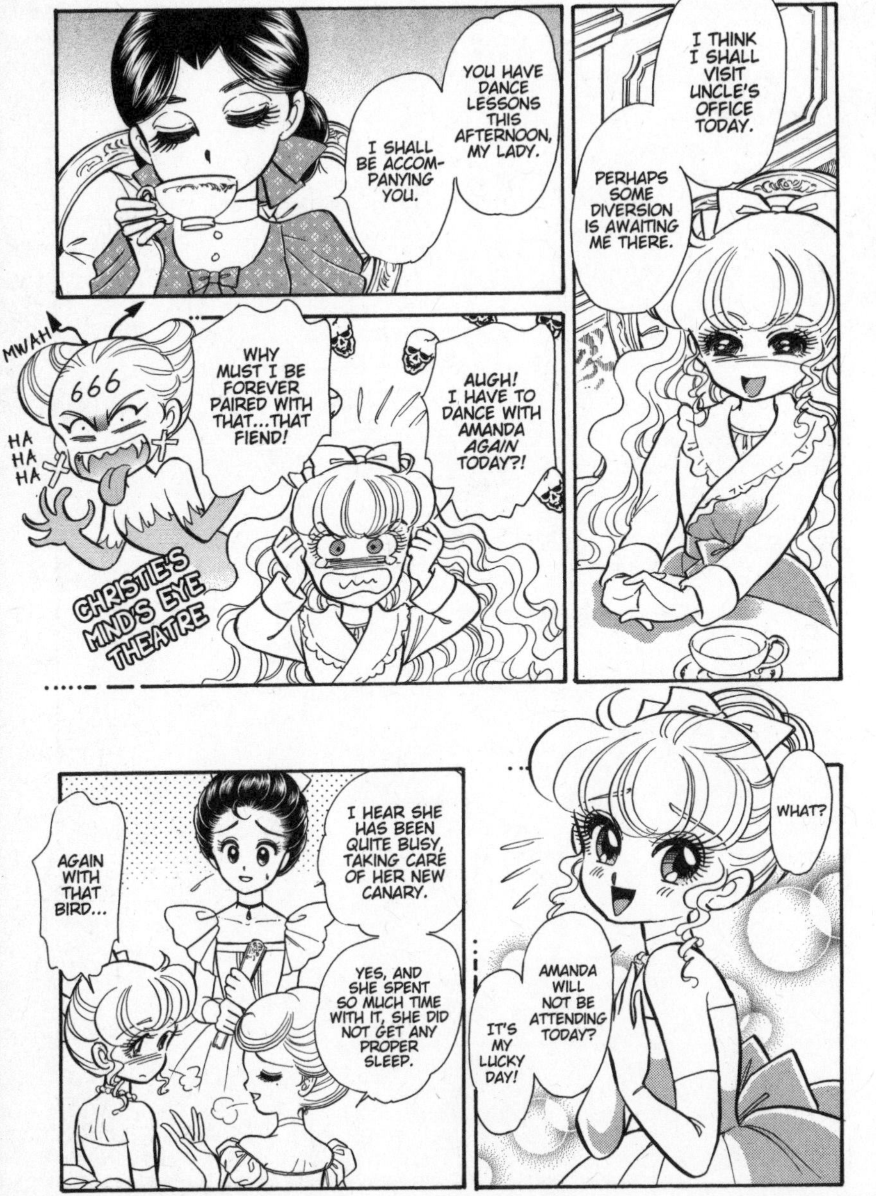
I THINK I SHALL VISIT UNCLE'S OFFICE TODAY.
PERHAPS SOME DIVERSION IS AWAITING ME THERE.
YOU HAVE DANCE LESSONS THIS AFTERNOON, MY LADY.
I SHALL BE ACCOMPANYING YOU.
AUGH! I HAVE TO DANCE WITH AMANDA AGAIN TODAY?!
WHY MUST I BE FOREVER PAIRED WITH THAT...THAT FIEND!
MWAH
666
HA HA HA
CHRISTIE'S MIND'S EYE THEATRE
WHAT?
AMANDA WILL NOT BE ATTENDING TODAY?
IT'S MY LUCKY DAY!
I HEAR SHE HAS BEEN QUITE BUSY, TAKING CARE OF HER NEW CANARY.
YES, AND SHE SPENT SO MUCH TIME WITH IT, SHE DID NOT GET ANY PROPER SLEEP.
AGAIN WITH THAT BIRD...

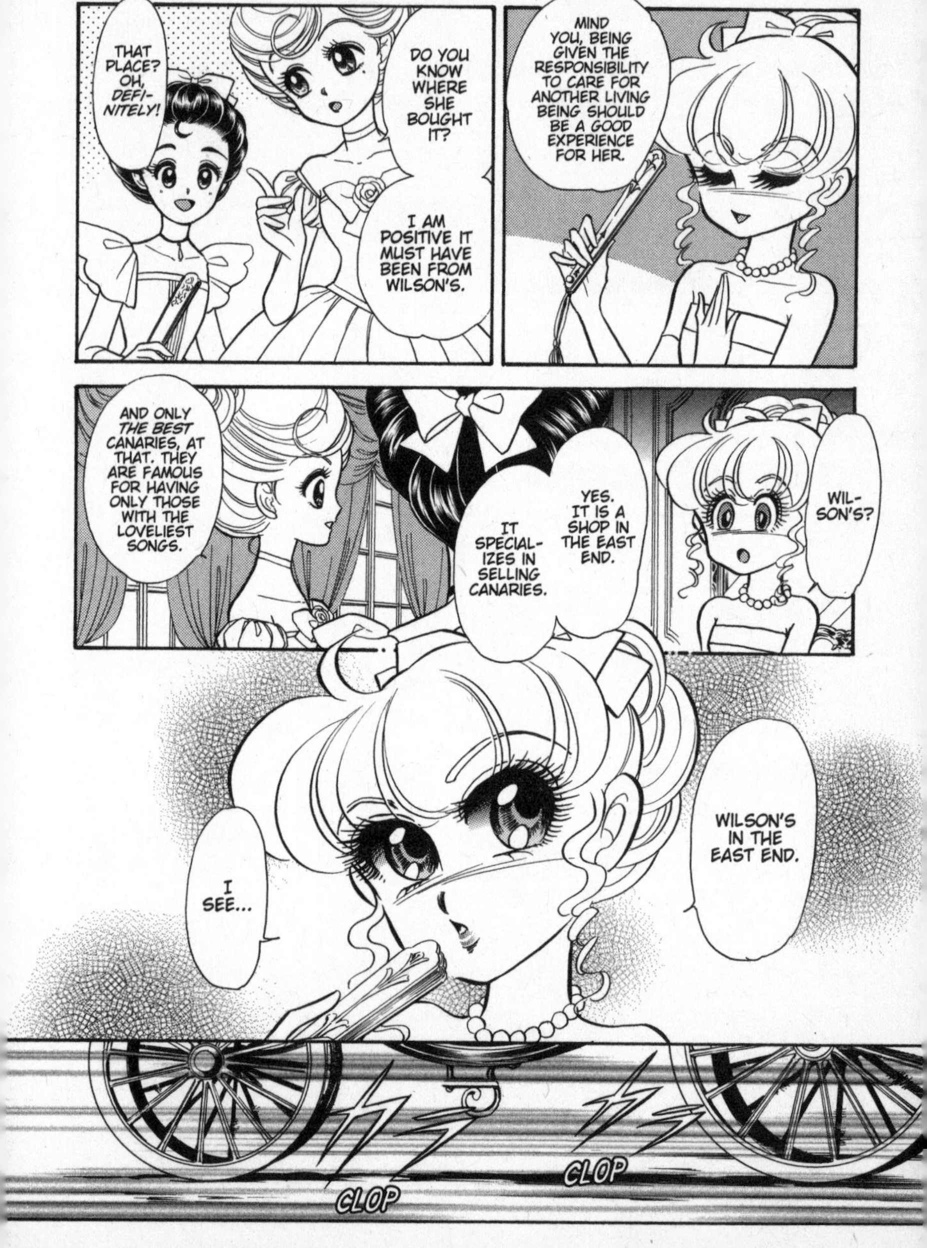
MIND YOU, BEING GIVEN THE RESPONSIBILITY TO CARE FOR ANOTHER LIVING BEING SHOULD BE A GOOD EXPERIENCE FOR HER.
DO YOU KNOW WHERE SHE BOUGHT IT?
THAT PLACE? OH, *DEFINITELY!*
I AM POSITIVE IT MUST HAVE BEEN FROM WILSON'S.
WIL-SON'S?
YES. IT IS A SHOP IN THE EAST END.
IT SPECIALIZES IN SELLING CANARIES.
AND ONLY *THE BEST* CANARIES, AT THAT. THEY ARE FAMOUS FOR HAVING ONLY THOSE WITH THE LOVELIEST SONGS.
WILSON'S IN THE EAST END.
I SEE...
CLOP
CLOP

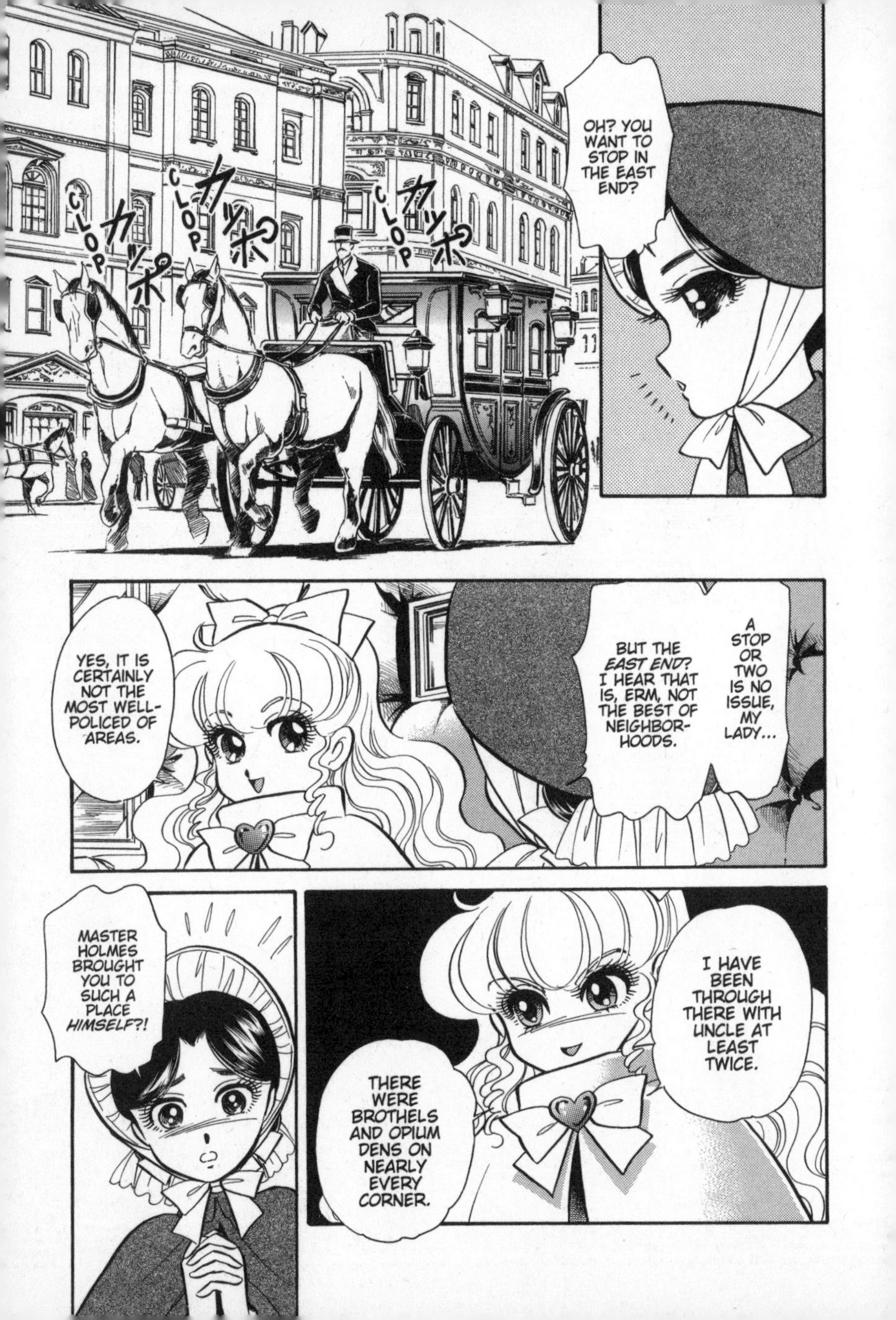
OH? YOU WANT TO STOP IN THE EAST END?
CLOP カッポ
CLOP カッポ
CLOP カッポ
A STOP OR TWO IS NO ISSUE, MY LADY...
BUT THE *EAST END?* I HEAR THAT IS, ERM, NOT THE BEST OF NEIGHBOR-HOODS.
YES, IT IS CERTAINLY NOT THE MOST WELL-POLICED OF AREAS.
I HAVE BEEN THROUGH THERE WITH UNCLE AT LEAST TWICE.
THERE WERE BROTHELS AND OPIUM DENS ON NEARLY EVERY CORNER.
MASTER HOLMES BROUGHT YOU TO SUCH A PLACE *HIMSELF?!*

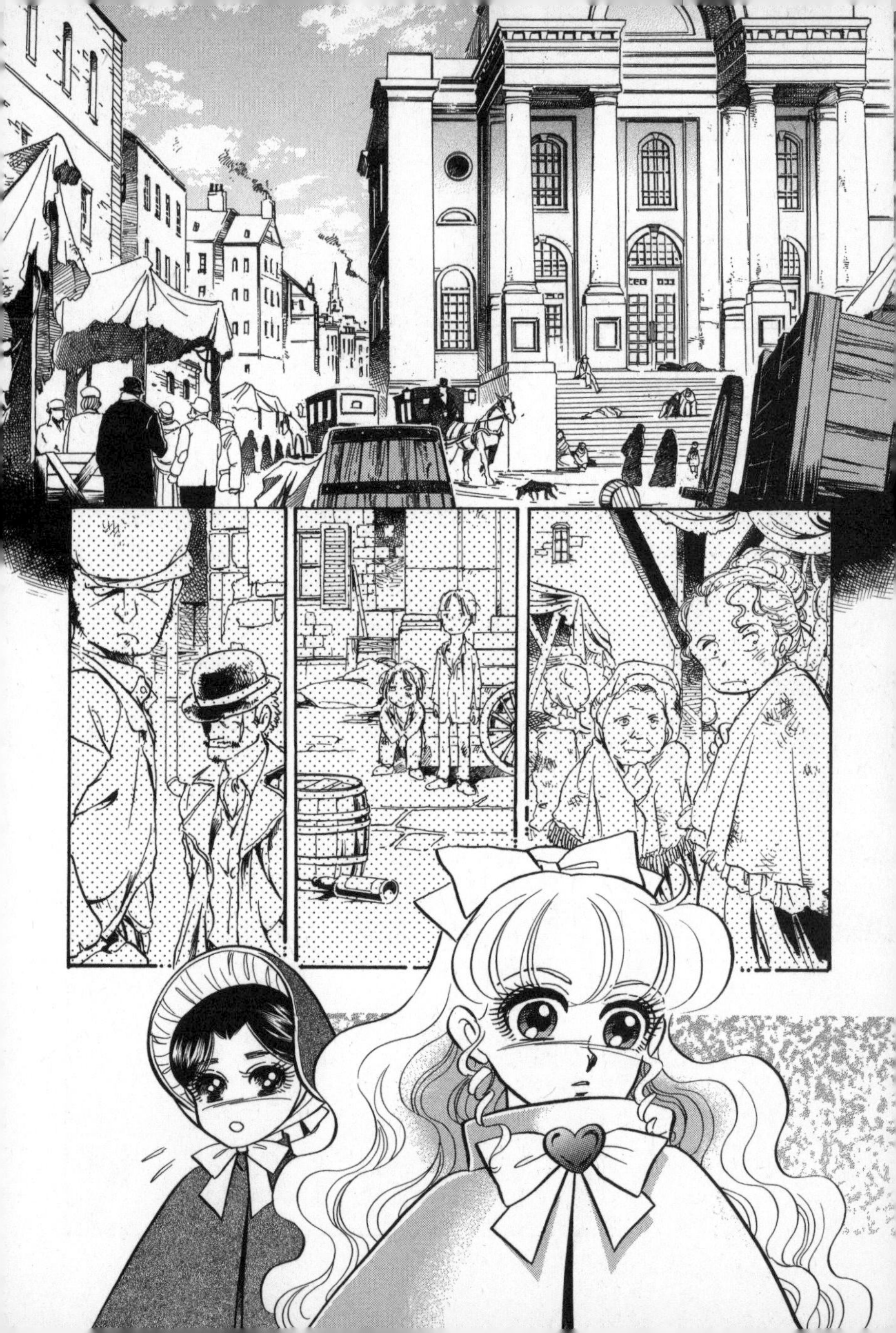

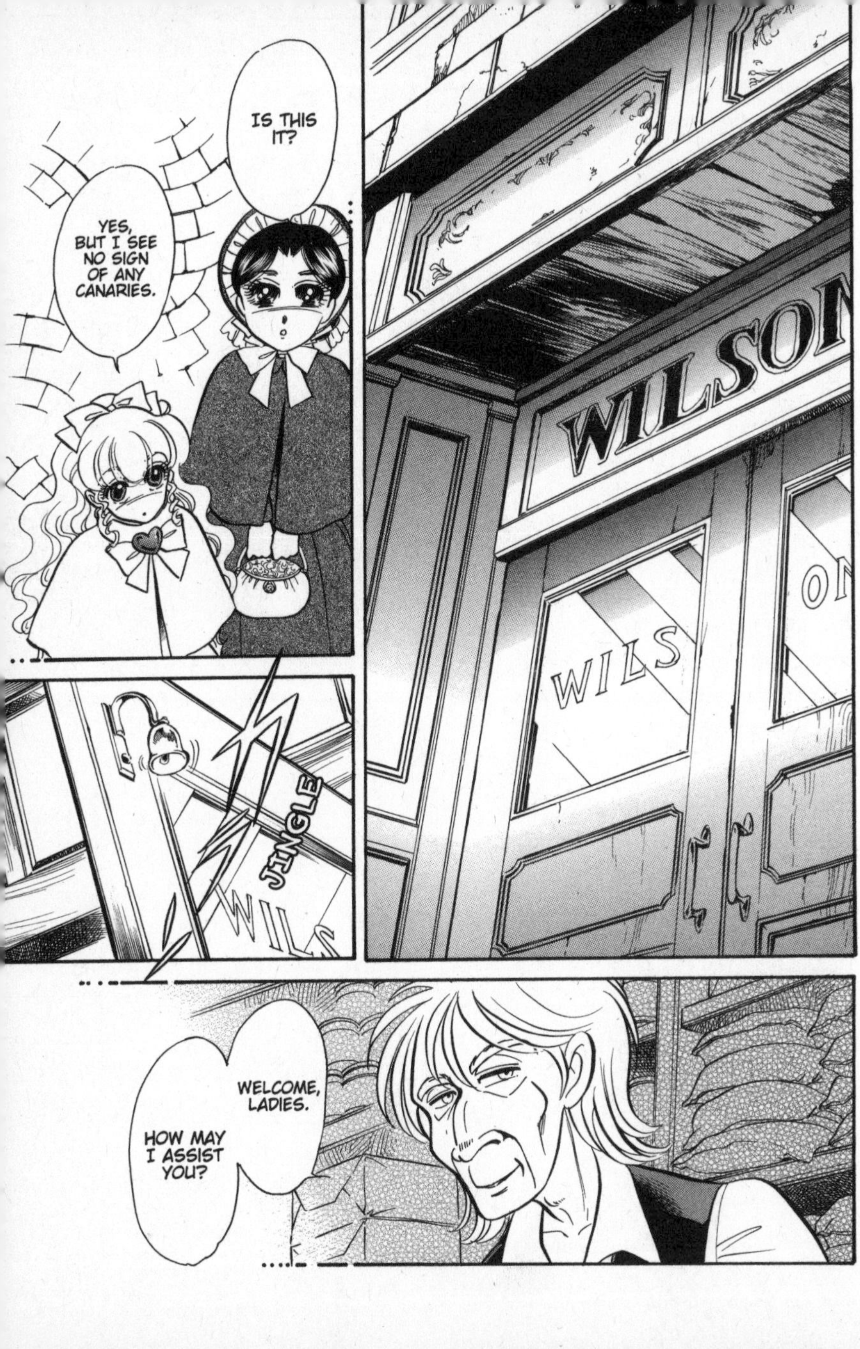
WILSO
WILSON
WILS
ON
IS THIS IT?
YES, BUT I SEE NO SIGN OF ANY CANARIES.
JINGLE
WILS
WELCOME, LADIES.
HOW MAY I ASSIST YOU?

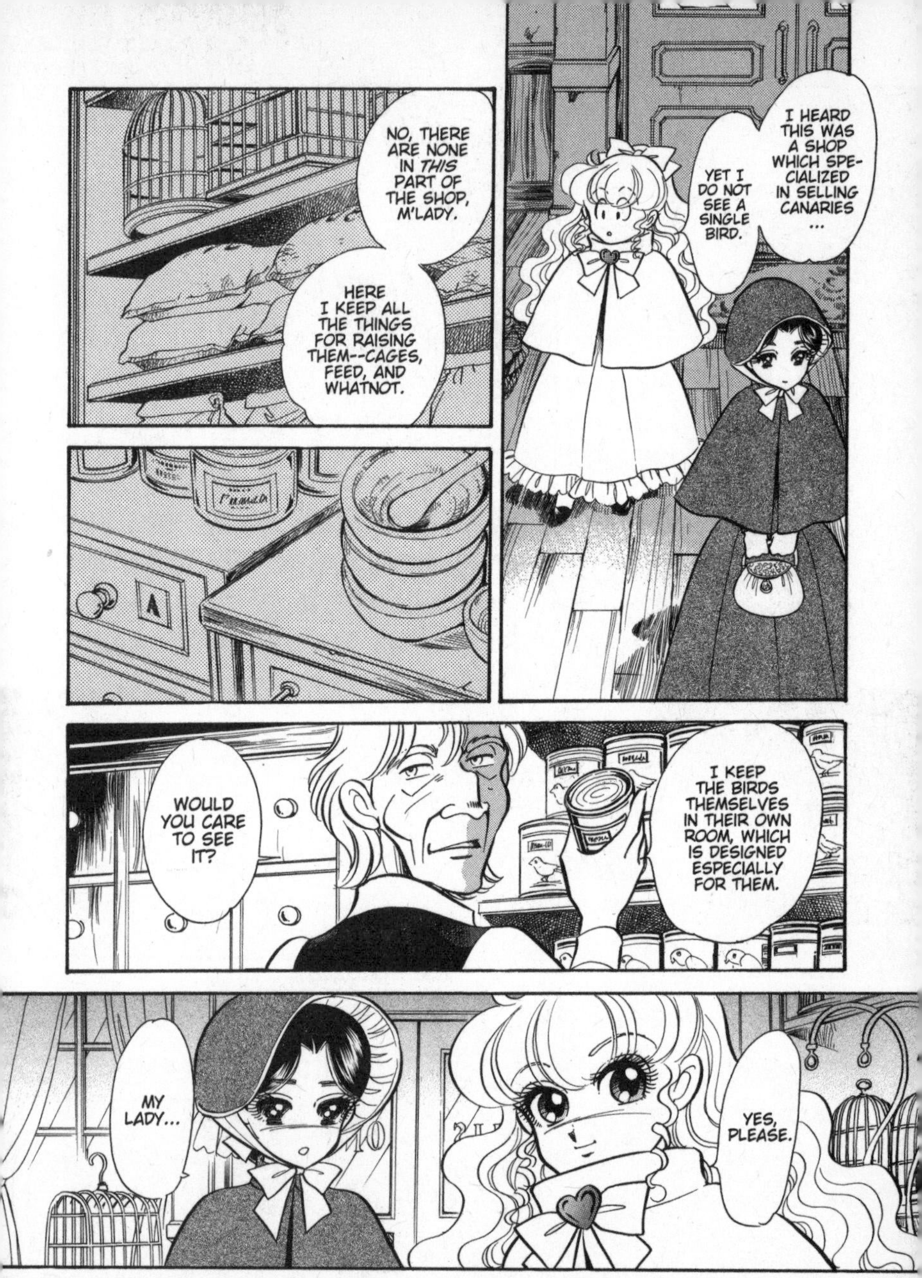
I HEARD THIS WAS A SHOP WHICH SPECIALIZED IN SELLING CANARIES...
YET I DO NOT SEE A SINGLE BIRD.
NO, THERE ARE NONE IN *THIS* PART OF THE SHOP, M'LADY.
HERE I KEEP ALL THE THINGS FOR RAISING THEM--CAGES, FEED, AND WHATNOT.
I KEEP THE BIRDS THEMSELVES IN THEIR OWN ROOM, WHICH IS DESIGNED ESPECIALLY FOR THEM.
WOULD YOU CARE TO SEE IT?
YES, PLEASE.
MY LADY...

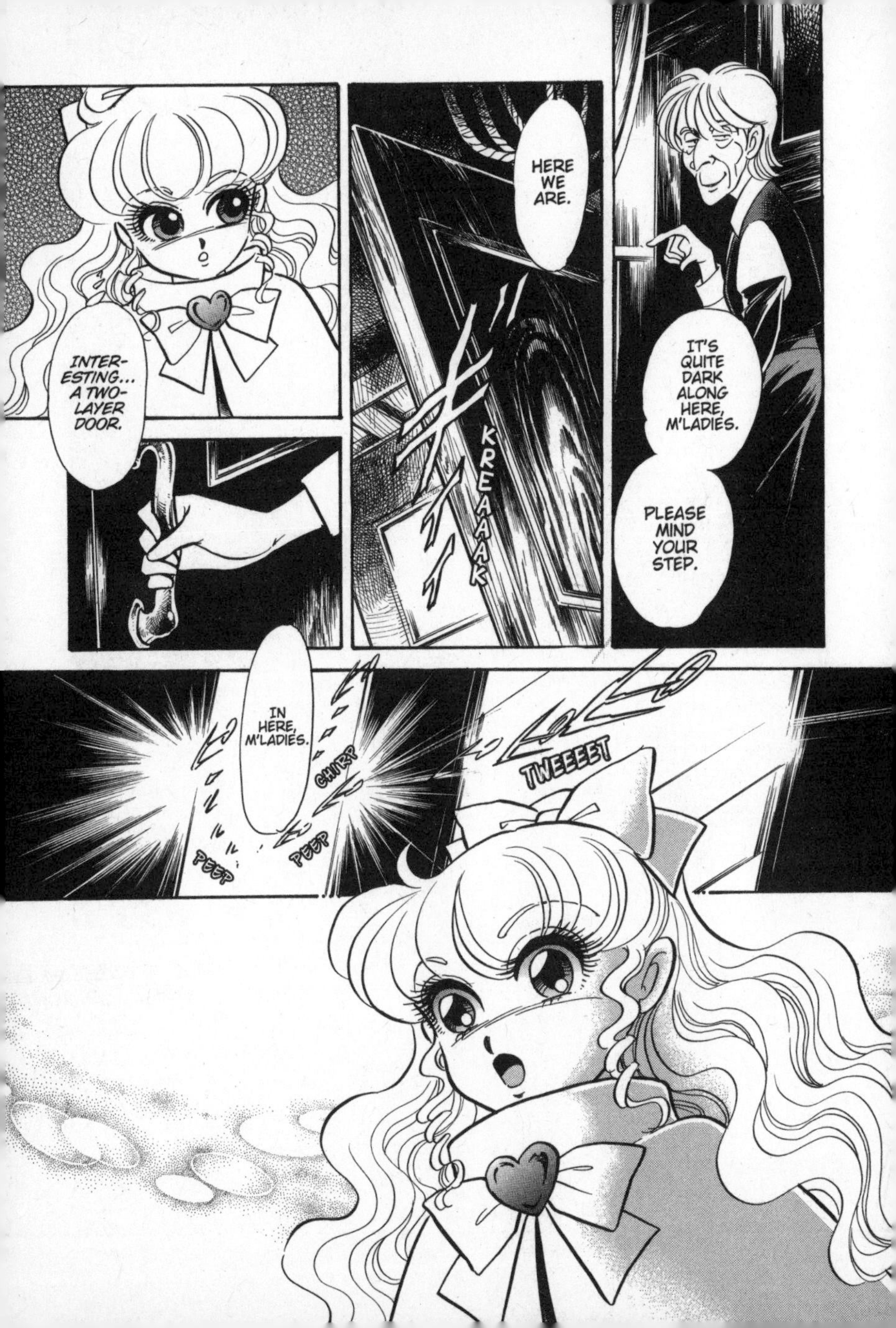
IT'S QUITE DARK ALONG HERE, M'LADIES.
PLEASE MIND YOUR STEP.
HERE WE ARE.
KREAAAAK
INTER-ESTING... A TWO-LAYER DOOR.
TWEEEET
CHIRP
PEEP
IN HERE, M'LADIES.
PEEP

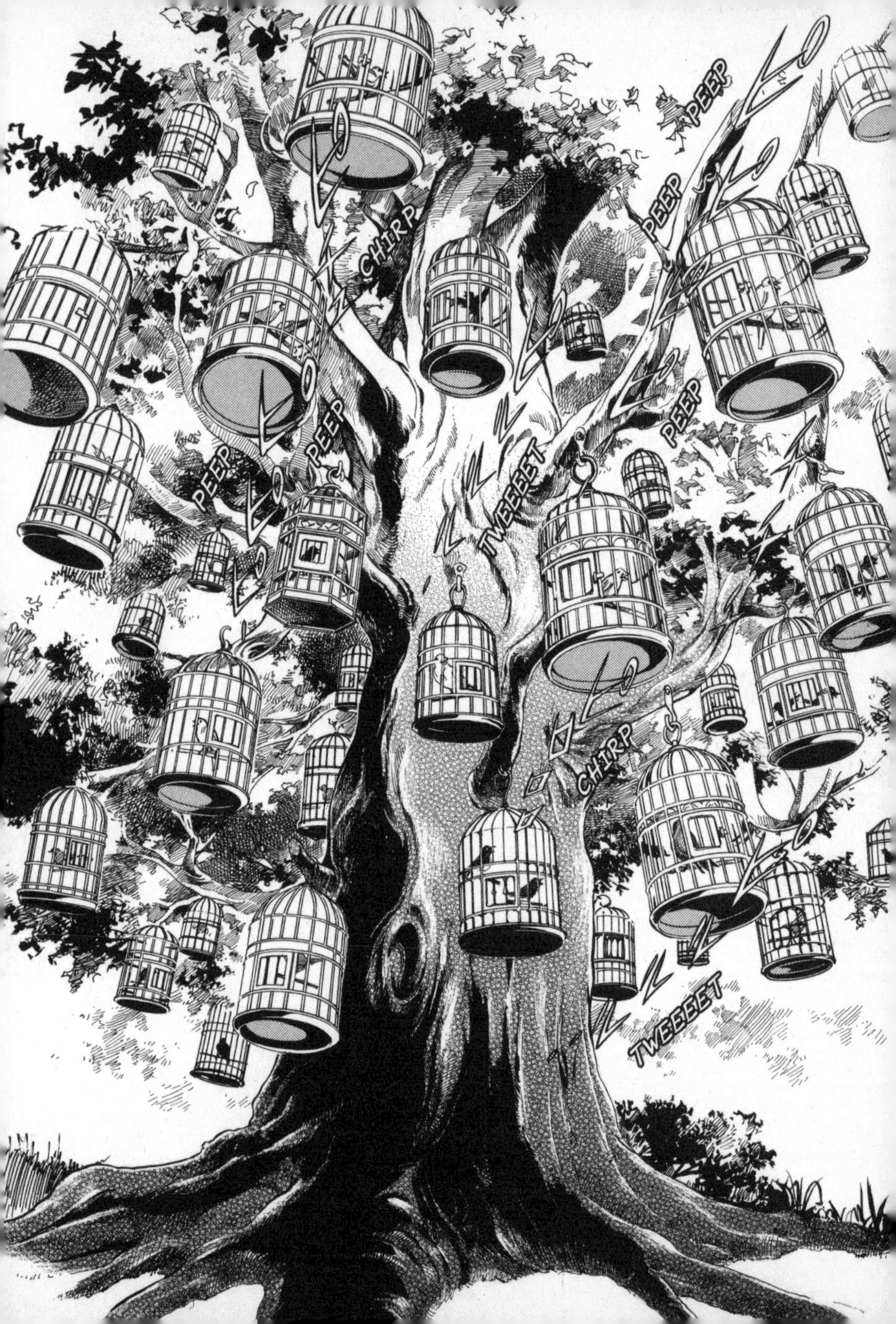
PEEP
PEEP
PEEP
PEEP
CHIRP
TWEEEET
PEEP
PEEP
CHIRP
TWEEEET

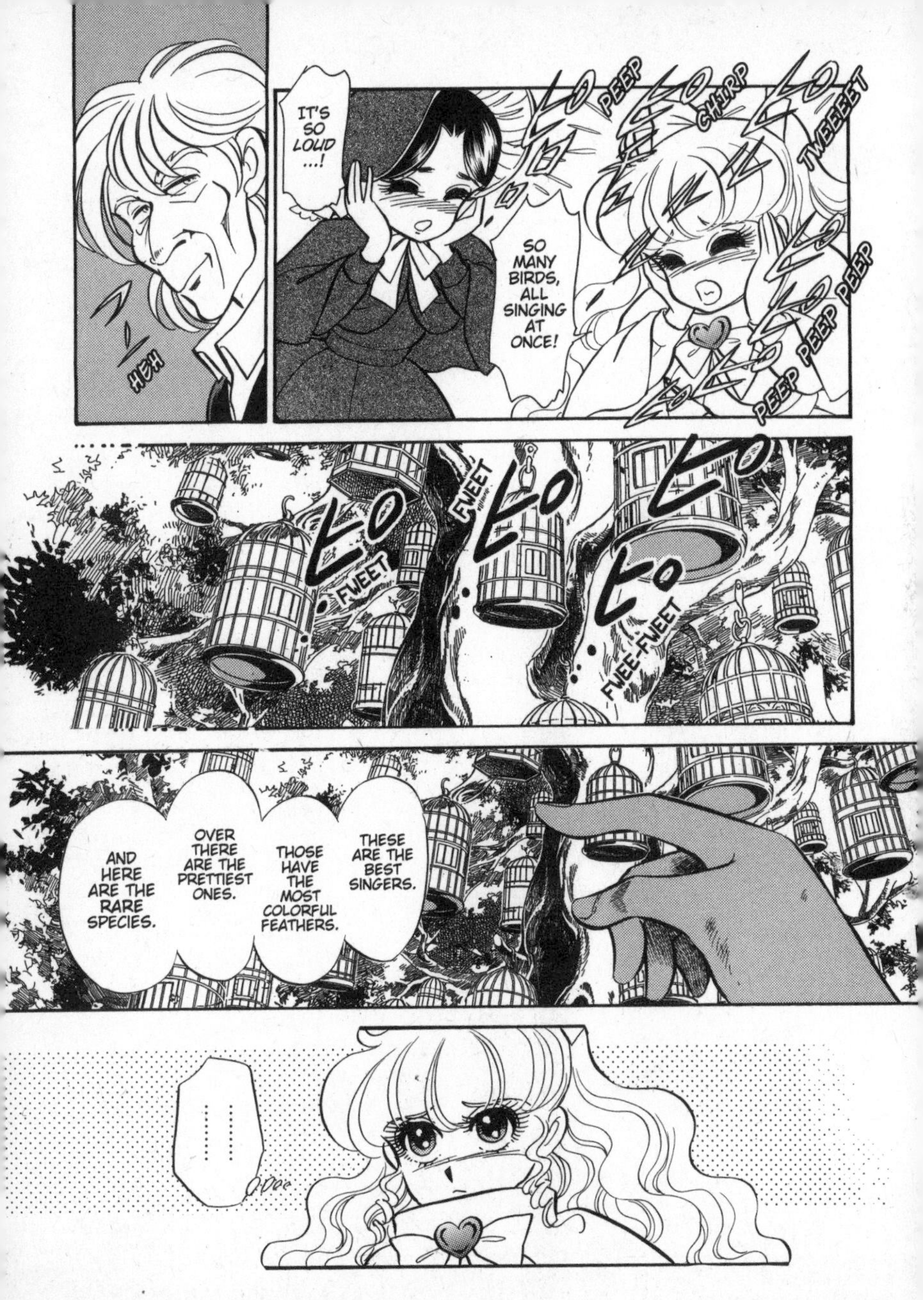
PEEP
CHIRP
TWEEEET
PEEP PEEP PEEP
SO MANY BIRDS, ALL SINGING AT ONCE!
IT'S SO LOUD ...!
HEH
FWEET
FWEET
FWEE-FWEET
THESE ARE THE BEST SINGERS.
THOSE HAVE THE MOST COLORFUL FEATHERS.
OVER THERE ARE THE PRETTIEST ONES.
AND HERE ARE THE RARE SPECIES.
......

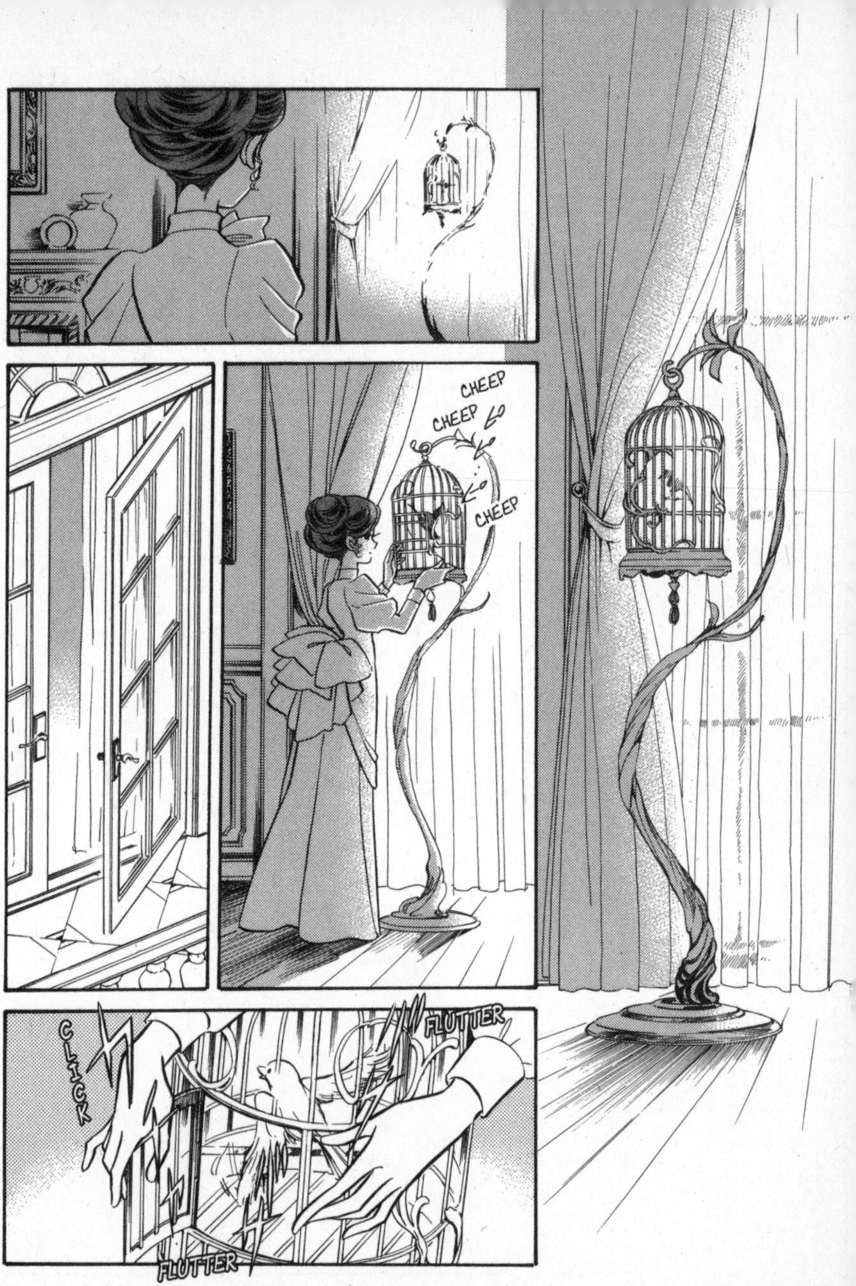
CHEEP
CHEEP
CHEEP
FLUTTER
CLICK
FLUTTER

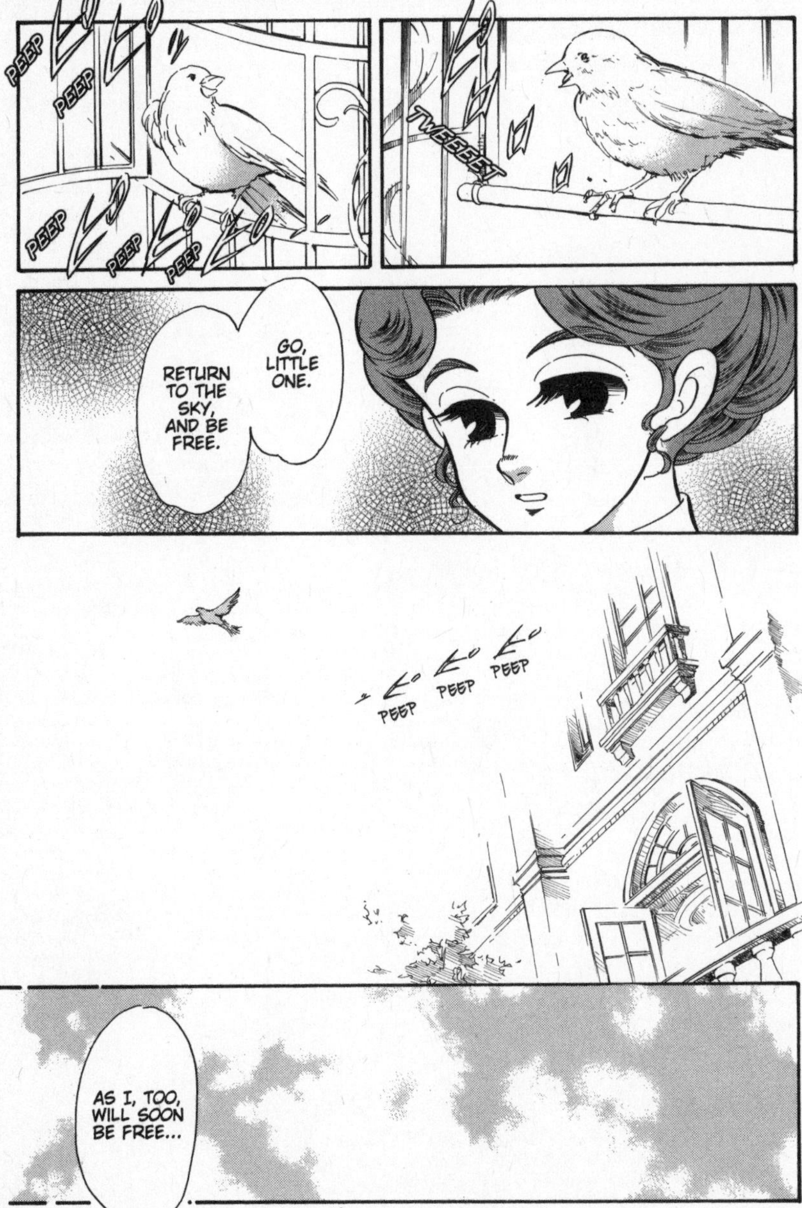
TWEEEET
PEEP
PEEP
PEEP
PEEP
PEEP
GO, LITTLE ONE.
RETURN TO THE SKY, AND BE FREE.
PEEP
PEEP
PEEP
AS I, TOO, WILL SOON BE FREE...

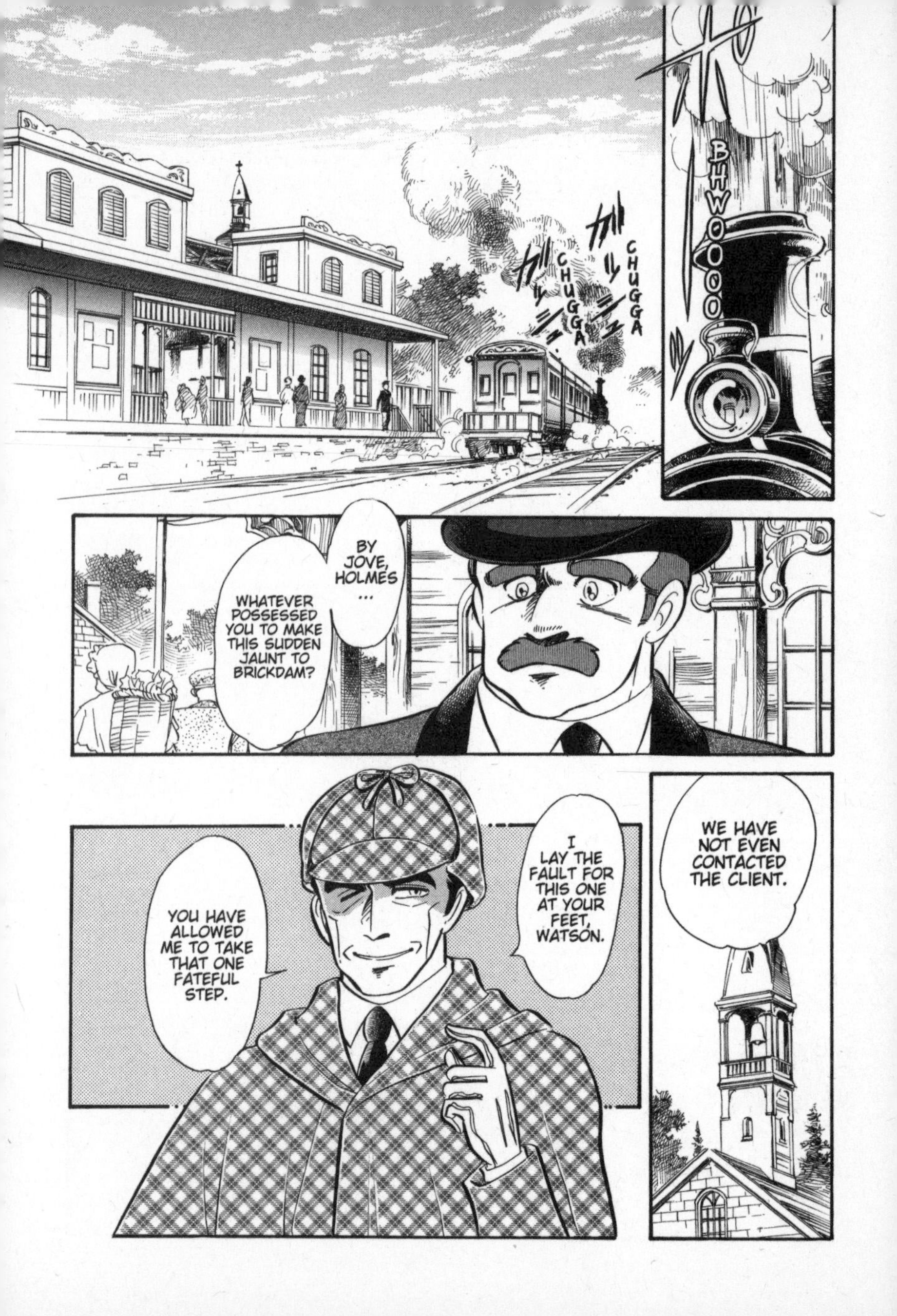
BHWOOOO
CHUGGA
CHUGGA
BY JOVE, HOLMES...
WHATEVER POSSESSED YOU TO MAKE THIS SUDDEN JAUNT TO BRICKDAM?
WE HAVE NOT EVEN CONTACTED THE CLIENT.
I LAY THE FAULT FOR THIS ONE AT YOUR FEET, WATSON.
YOU HAVE ALLOWED ME TO TAKE THAT ONE FATEFUL STEP.

The Adventure of the Famous Trainer (3)

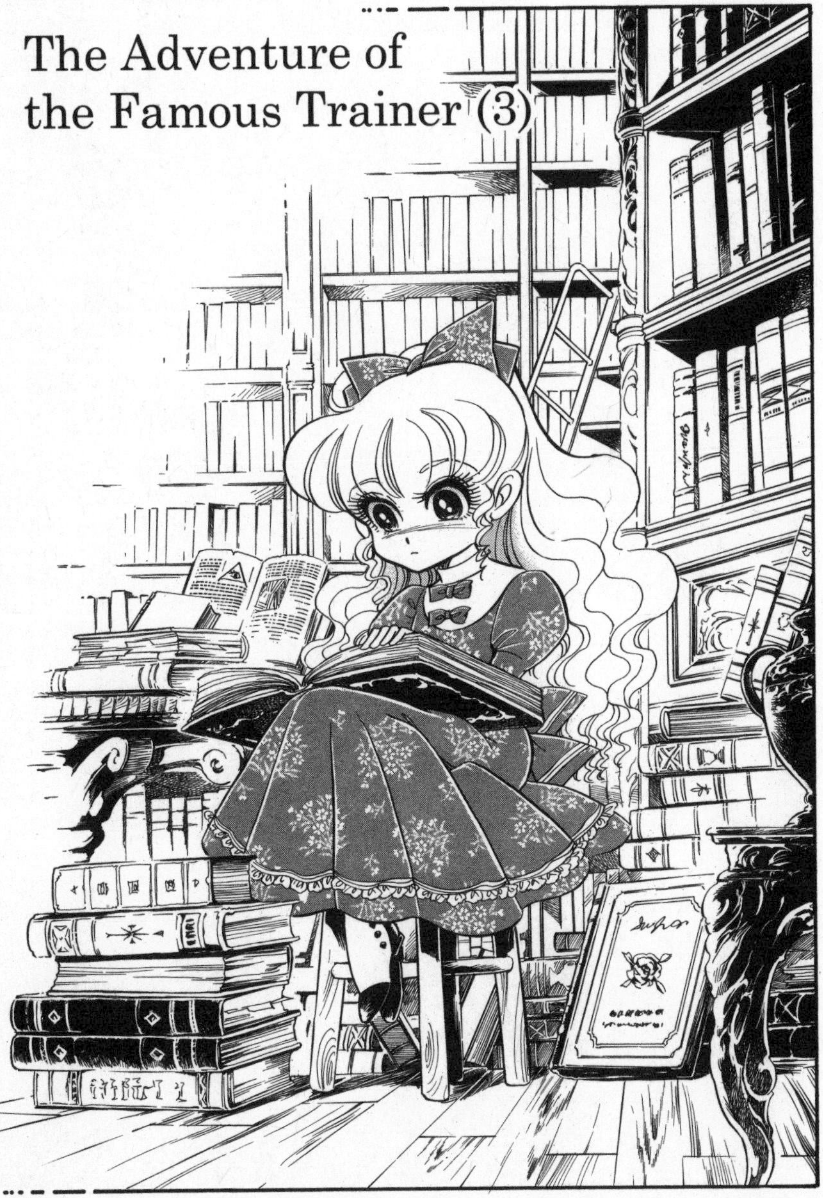

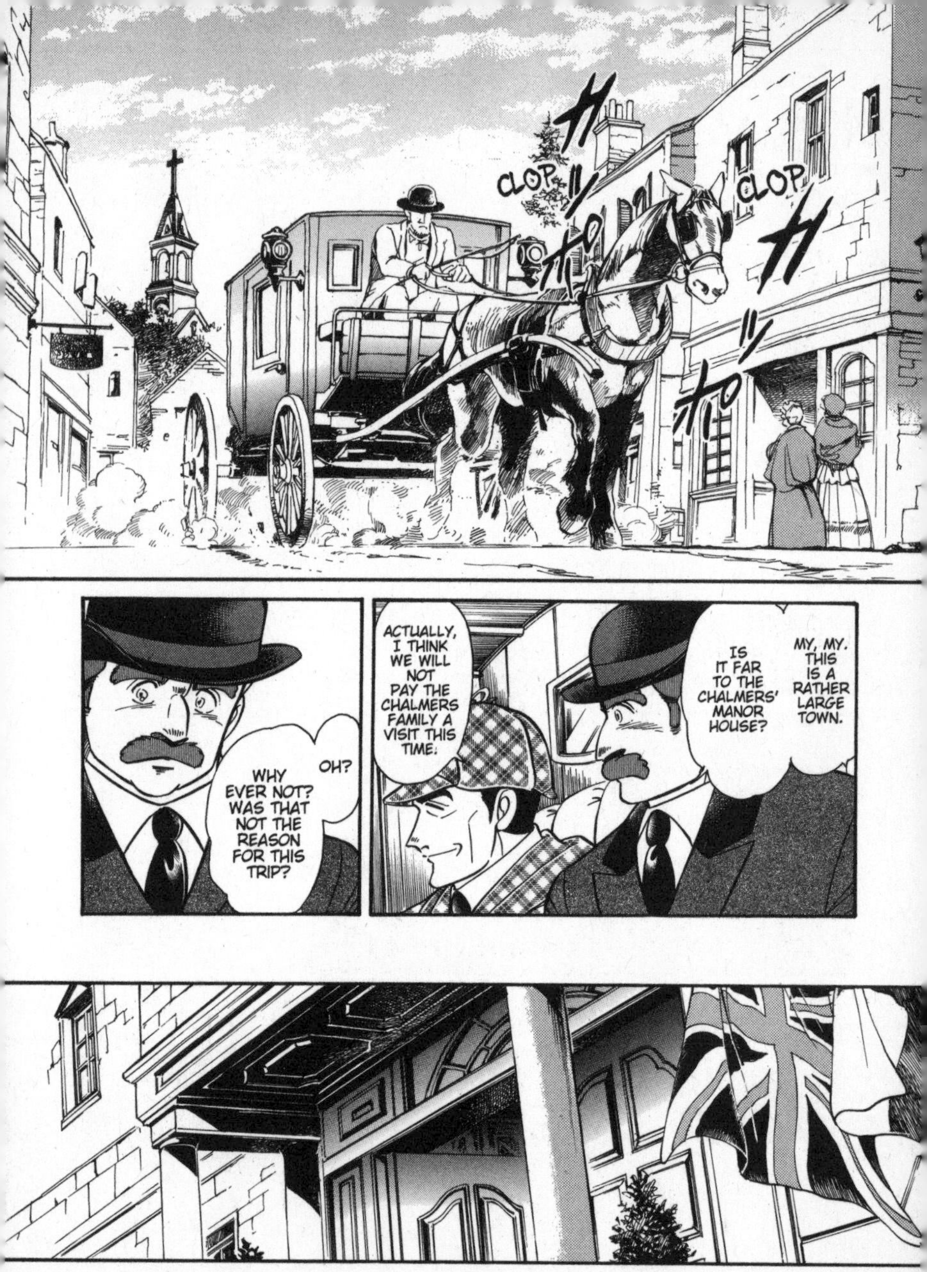
CLOP
CLOP
MY, MY. THIS IS A RATHER LARGE TOWN.
IS IT FAR TO THE CHALMERS' MANOR HOUSE?
ACTUALLY, I THINK WE WILL NOT PAY THE CHALMERS FAMILY A VISIT THIS TIME.
OH?
WHY EVER NOT? WAS THAT NOT THE REASON FOR THIS TRIP?

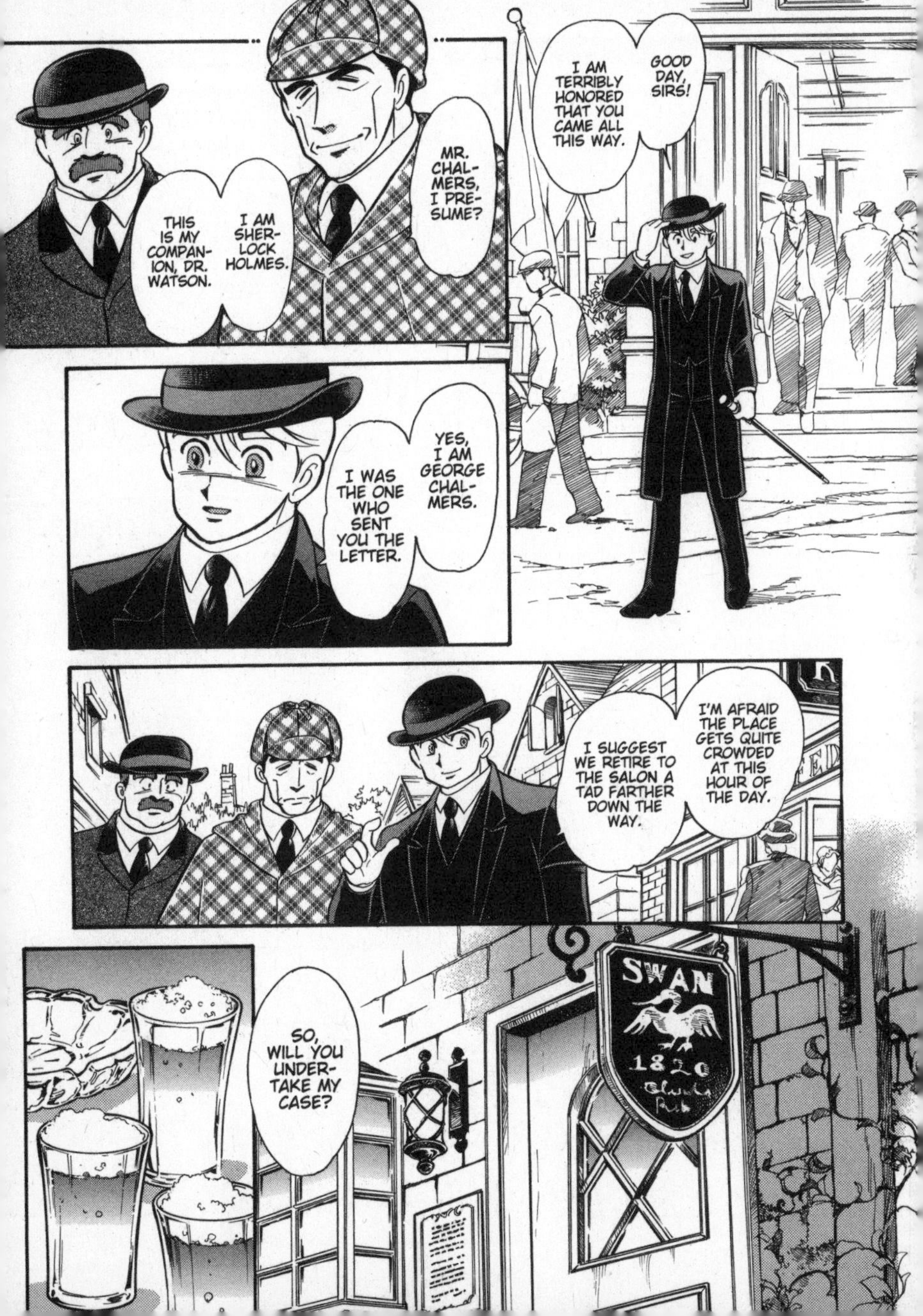
GOOD DAY, SIRS!
I AM TERRIBLY HONORED THAT YOU CAME ALL THIS WAY.
MR. CHALMERS, I PRESUME?
I AM SHERLOCK HOLMES.
THIS IS MY COMPANION, DR. WATSON.
YES, I AM GEORGE CHALMERS.
I WAS THE ONE WHO SENT YOU THE LETTER.
I'M AFRAID THE PLACE GETS QUITE CROWDED AT THIS HOUR OF THE DAY.
I SUGGEST WE RETIRE TO THE SALON A TAD FARTHER DOWN THE WAY.
SWAN
1820
SO, WILL YOU UNDERTAKE MY CASE?

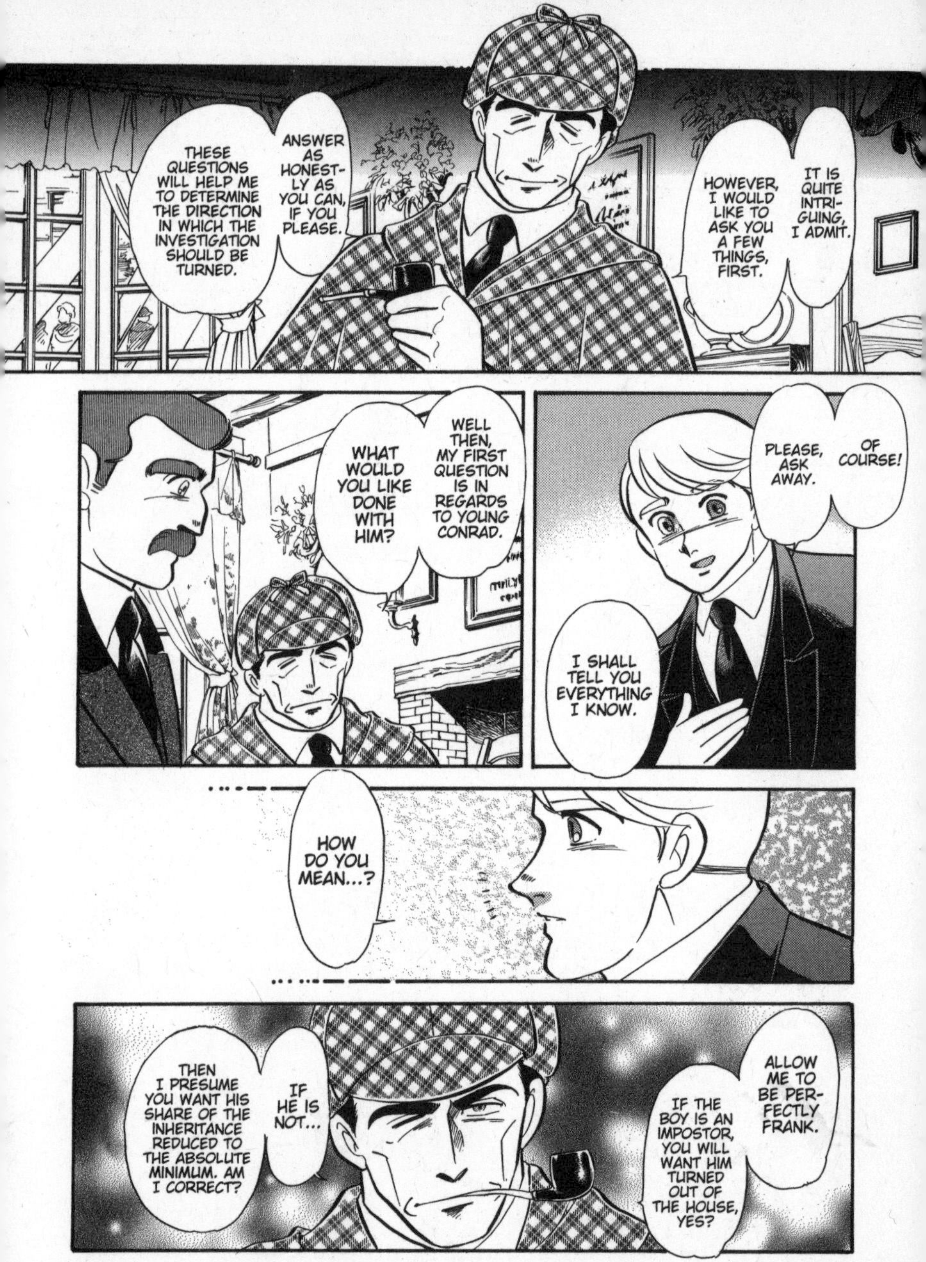
IT IS QUITE INTRIGUING, I ADMIT.
HOWEVER, I WOULD LIKE TO ASK YOU A FEW THINGS, FIRST.
ANSWER AS HONESTLY AS YOU CAN, IF YOU PLEASE.
THESE QUESTIONS WILL HELP ME TO DETERMINE THE DIRECTION IN WHICH THE INVESTIGATION SHOULD BE TURNED.
OF COURSE!
PLEASE, ASK AWAY.
I SHALL TELL YOU EVERYTHING I KNOW.
WELL THEN, MY FIRST QUESTION IS IN REGARDS TO YOUNG CONRAD.
WHAT WOULD YOU LIKE DONE WITH HIM?
HOW DO YOU MEAN...?
ALLOW ME TO BE PERFECTLY FRANK.
IF THE BOY IS AN IMPOSTOR, YOU WILL WANT HIM TURNED OUT OF THE HOUSE, YES?
IF HE IS NOT...
THEN I PRESUME YOU WANT HIS SHARE OF THE INHERITANCE REDUCED TO THE ABSOLUTE MINIMUM. AM I CORRECT?

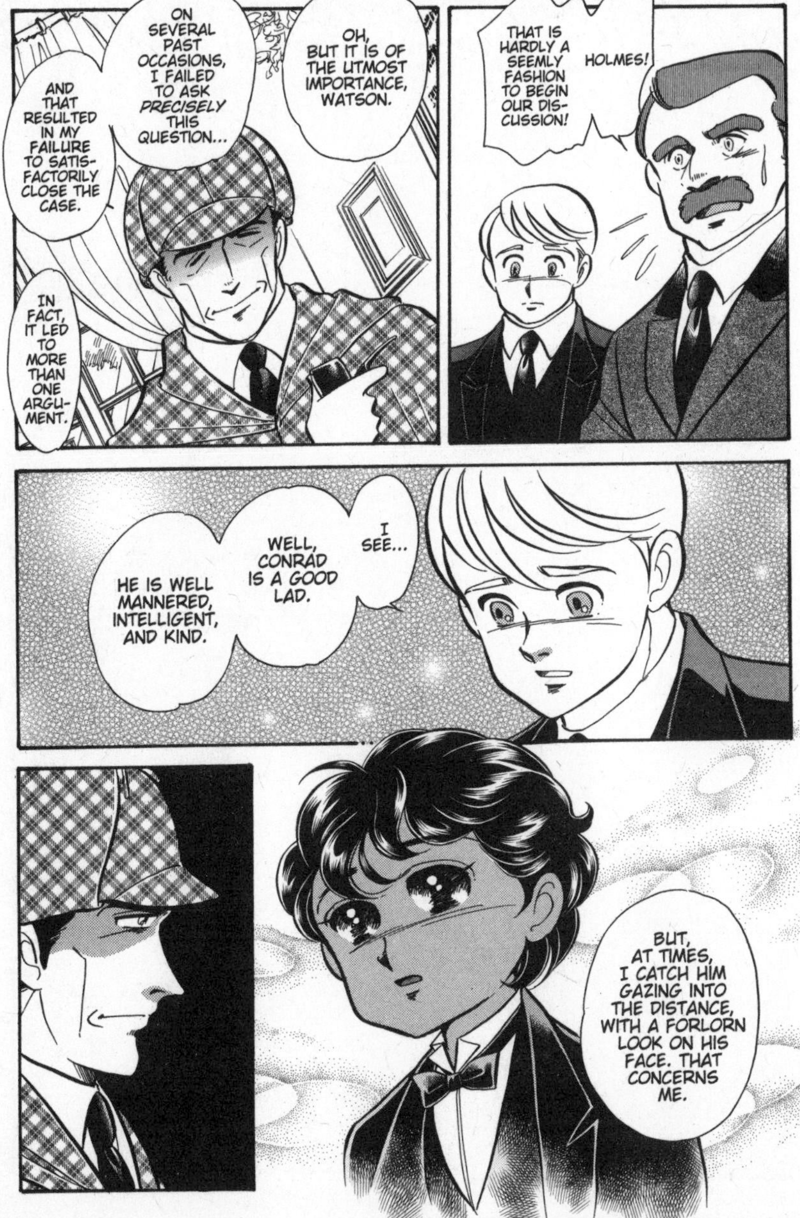

HOLMES!
THAT IS HARDLY A SEEMLY FASHION TO BEGIN OUR DISCUSSION!
OH, BUT IT IS OF THE UTMOST IMPORTANCE, WATSON.
ON SEVERAL PAST OCCASIONS, I FAILED TO ASK *PRECISELY* THIS QUESTION...
AND THAT RESULTED IN MY FAILURE TO SATISFACTORILY CLOSE THE CASE.
IN FACT, IT LED TO MORE THAN ONE ARGUMENT.
I SEE...
WELL, CONRAD IS A GOOD LAD.
HE IS WELL MANNERED, INTELLIGENT, AND KIND.
...
BUT, AT TIMES, I CATCH HIM GAZING INTO THE DISTANCE, WITH A FORLORN LOOK ON HIS FACE. THAT CONCERNS ME.

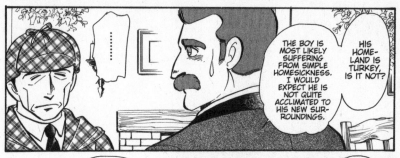

HIS HOME-LAND IS TURKEY, IS IT NOT?
THE BOY IS MOST LIKELY SUFFERING FROM SIMPLE HOMESICKNESS. I WOULD EXPECT HE IS NOT QUITE ACCLIMATED TO HIS NEW SUR-ROUNDINGS.
......
BOTH OF MY STEP-PARENTS ARE CONVINCED THAT CONRAD IS TRULY THEIR GRANDSON.
BUT IF THEY PROVE TO BE MIS-TAKEN ...
YES, THEN EVERYTHING YOUR FAMILY HAS WORKED SO HARD TO BUILD WILL BE STOLEN BY A COMPLETE STRANGER.
WELL, ASSUM-ING THAT HE IS, IN FACT, AN IMPOS-TOR...
IT WOULD BE QUITE A FEAT FOR A 12-YEAR-OLD BOY TO CONCOCT SUCH AN ELABORATE HOAX.
THERE *MUST* BE ANOTHER PLAYER BEHIND HIM, PULLING HIS STRINGS, AS IT WERE.

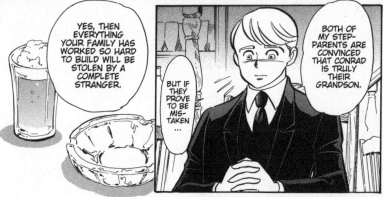

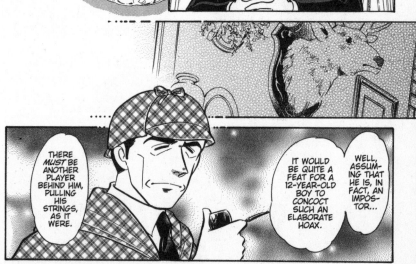

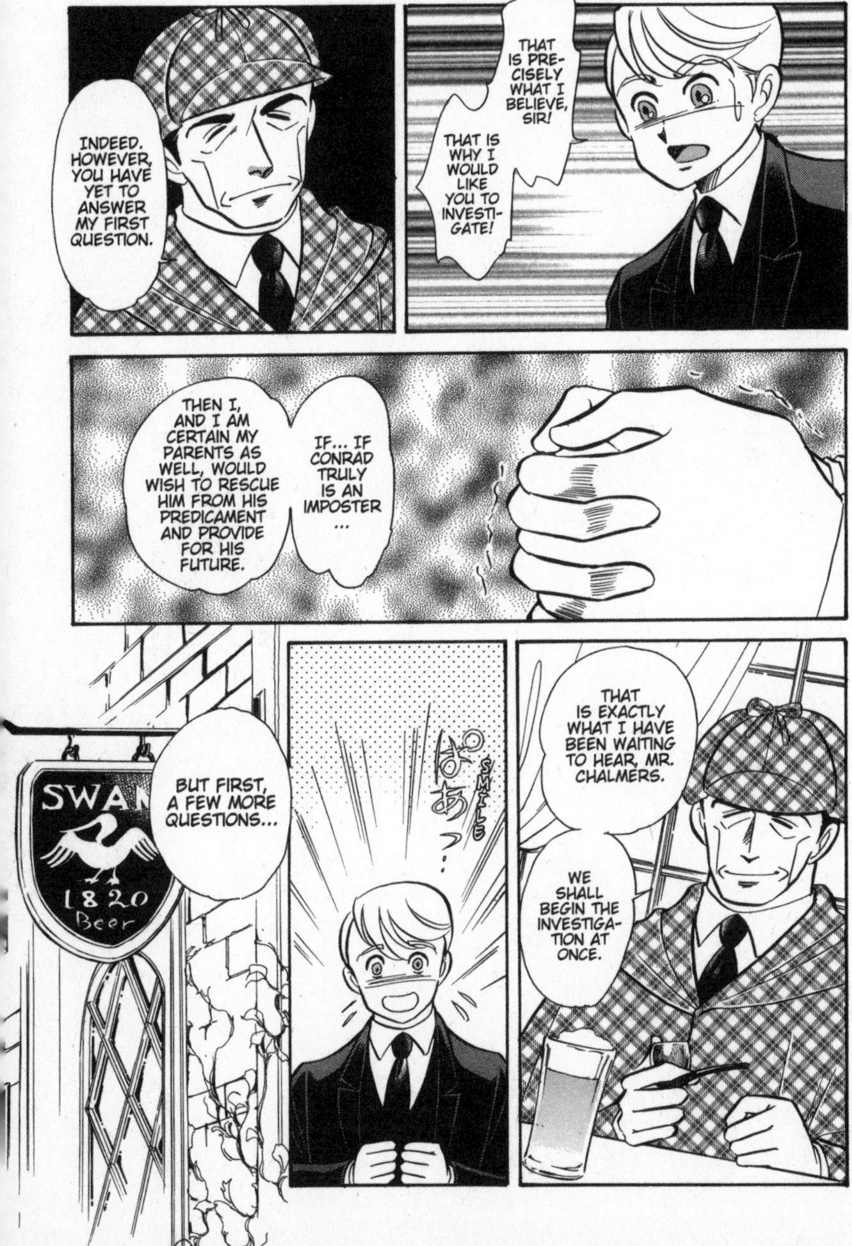
THAT IS PRECISELY WHAT I BELIEVE, SIR!
THAT IS WHY I WOULD LIKE YOU TO INVESTIGATE!
INDEED. HOWEVER, YOU HAVE YET TO ANSWER MY FIRST QUESTION.
IF... IF CONRAD TRULY IS AN IMPOSTER ...
THEN I, AND I AM CERTAIN MY PARENTS AS WELL, WOULD WISH TO RESCUE HIM FROM HIS PREDICAMENT AND PROVIDE FOR HIS FUTURE.
THAT IS EXACTLY WHAT I HAVE BEEN WAITING TO HEAR, MR. CHALMERS.
WE SHALL BEGIN THE INVESTIGATION AT ONCE.
はあっ
SMILE
SWAN
1820
Beer
BUT FIRST, A FEW MORE QUESTIONS...

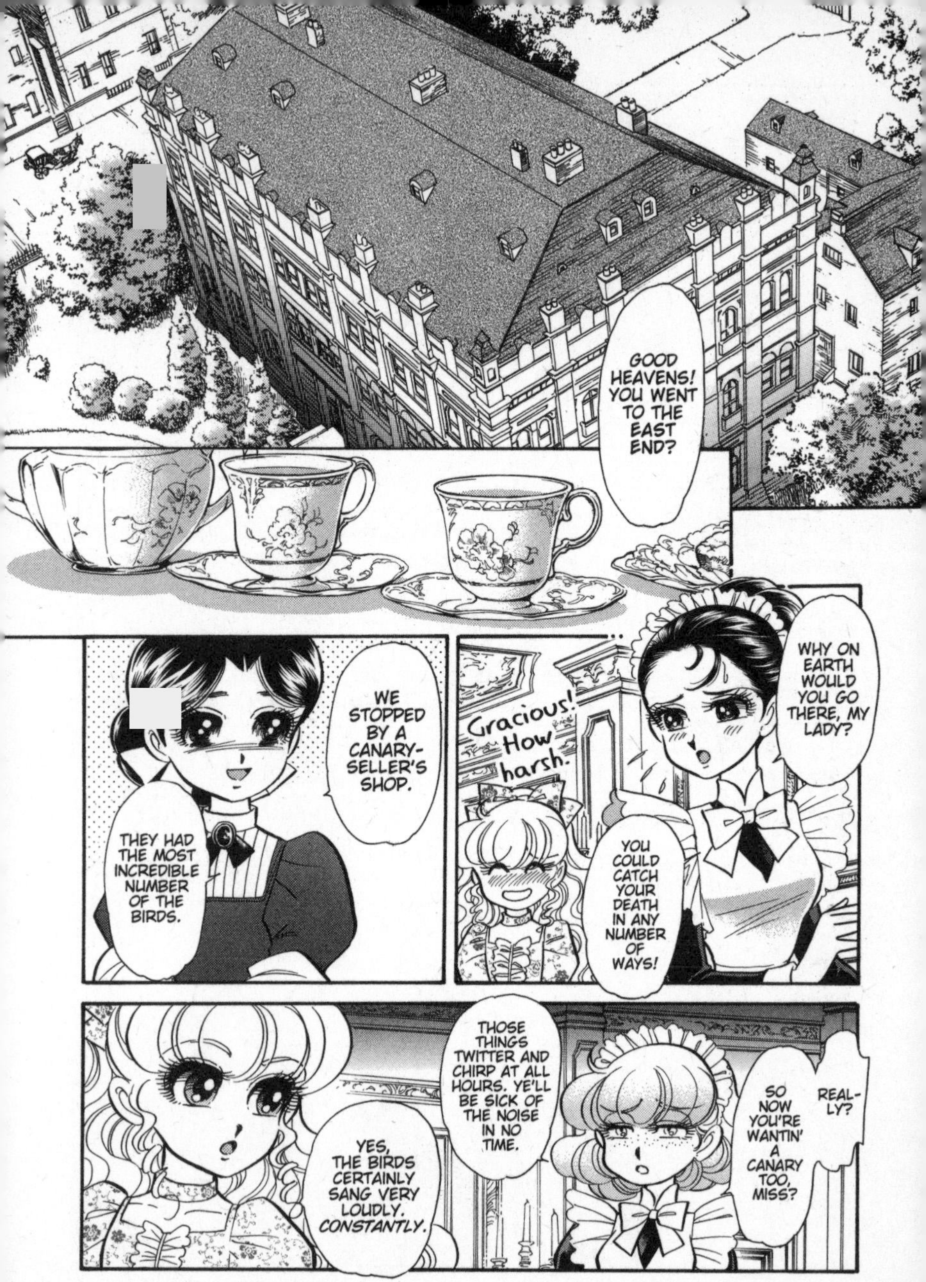
GOOD HEAVENS! YOU WENT TO THE EAST END?
...
WHY ON EARTH WOULD YOU GO THERE, MY LADY?
Gracious! How harsh.
YOU COULD CATCH YOUR DEATH IN ANY NUMBER OF WAYS!
WE STOPPED BY A CANARY-SELLER'S SHOP.
THEY HAD THE MOST INCREDIBLE NUMBER OF THE BIRDS.
REAL-LY?
SO NOW YOU'RE WANTIN' A CANARY TOO, MISS?
THOSE THINGS TWITTER AND CHIRP AT ALL HOURS. YE'LL BE SICK OF THE NOISE IN NO TIME.
YES, THE BIRDS CERTAINLY SANG VERY LOUDLY. *CONSTANTLY*.

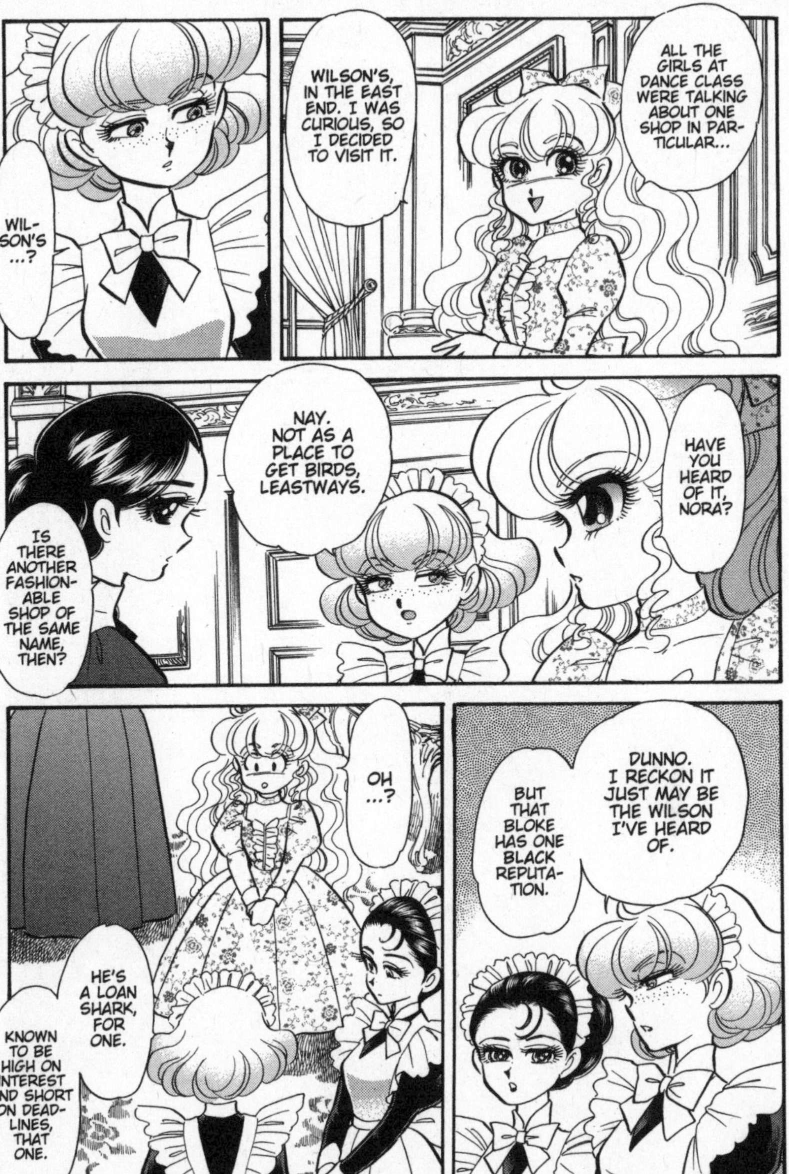
ALL THE GIRLS AT DANCE CLASS WERE TALKING ABOUT ONE SHOP IN PAR-TICULAR...
WILSON'S, IN THE EAST END. I WAS CURIOUS, SO I DECIDED TO VISIT IT.
WIL-SON'S ...?
HAVE YOU HEARD OF IT, NORA?
NAY. NOT AS A PLACE TO GET BIRDS, LEASTWAYS.
IS THERE ANOTHER FASHION-ABLE SHOP OF THE SAME NAME, THEN?
DUNNO. I RECKON IT JUST MAY BE THE WILSON I'VE HEARD OF.
BUT THAT BLOKE HAS ONE BLACK REPUTA-TION.
OH ...?
HE'S A LOAN SHARK, FOR ONE.
KNOWN TO BE HIGH ON INTEREST AND SHORT ON DEAD-LINES, THAT ONE.

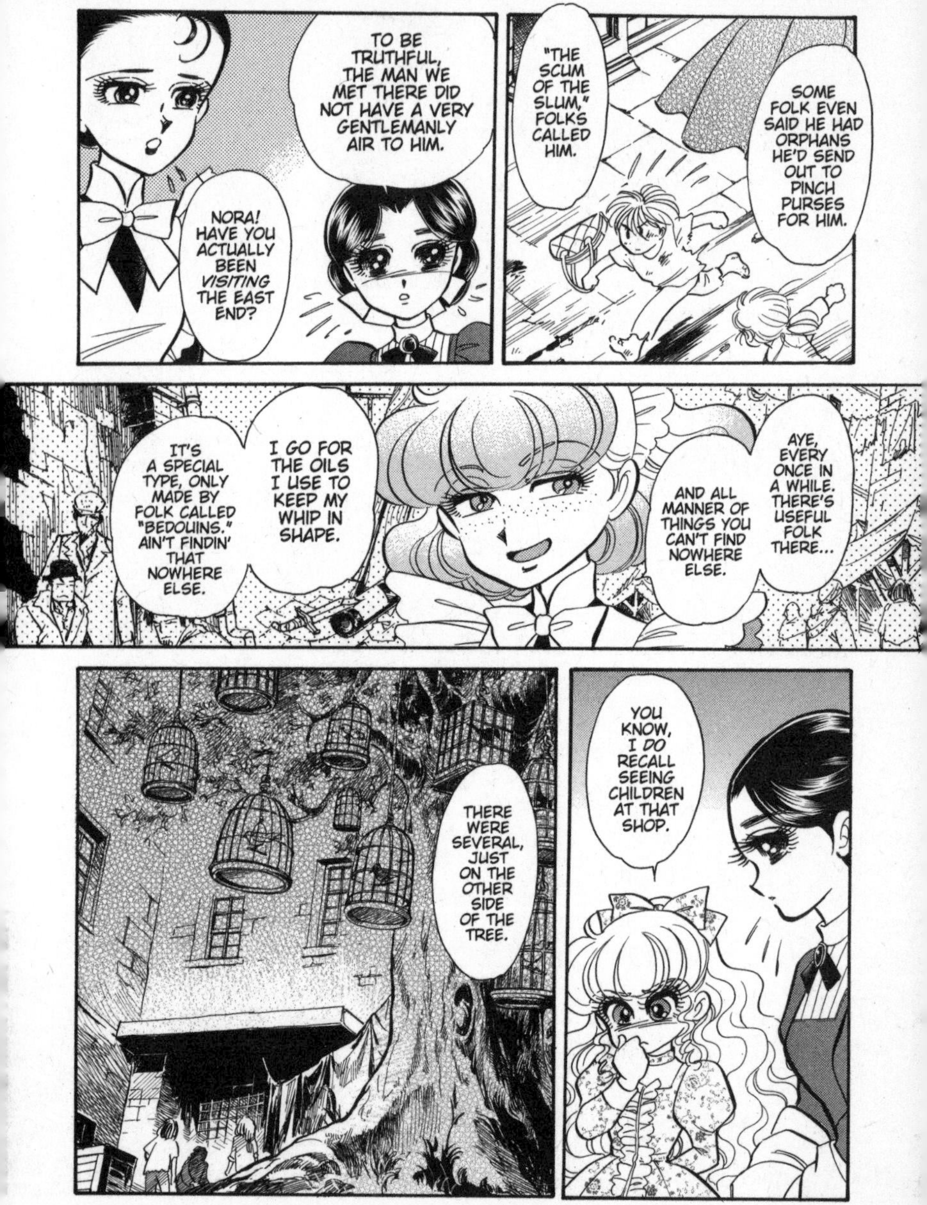
"THE SCUM OF THE SLUM," FOLKS CALLED HIM.
SOME FOLK EVEN SAID HE HAD ORPHANS HE'D SEND OUT TO PINCH PURSES FOR HIM.
TO BE TRUTHFUL, THE MAN WE MET THERE DID NOT HAVE A VERY GENTLEMANLY AIR TO HIM.
NORA! HAVE YOU ACTUALLY BEEN *VISITING* THE EAST END?
AYE, EVERY ONCE IN A WHILE. THERE'S USEFUL FOLK THERE...
AND ALL MANNER OF THINGS YOU CAN'T FIND NOWHERE ELSE.
I GO FOR THE OILS I USE TO KEEP MY WHIP IN SHAPE.
IT'S A SPECIAL TYPE, ONLY MADE BY FOLK CALLED "BEDOUINS." AIN'T FINDIN' THAT NOWHERE ELSE.
YOU KNOW, I *DO* RECALL SEEING CHILDREN AT THAT SHOP.
THERE WERE SEVERAL, JUST ON THE OTHER SIDE OF THE TREE.

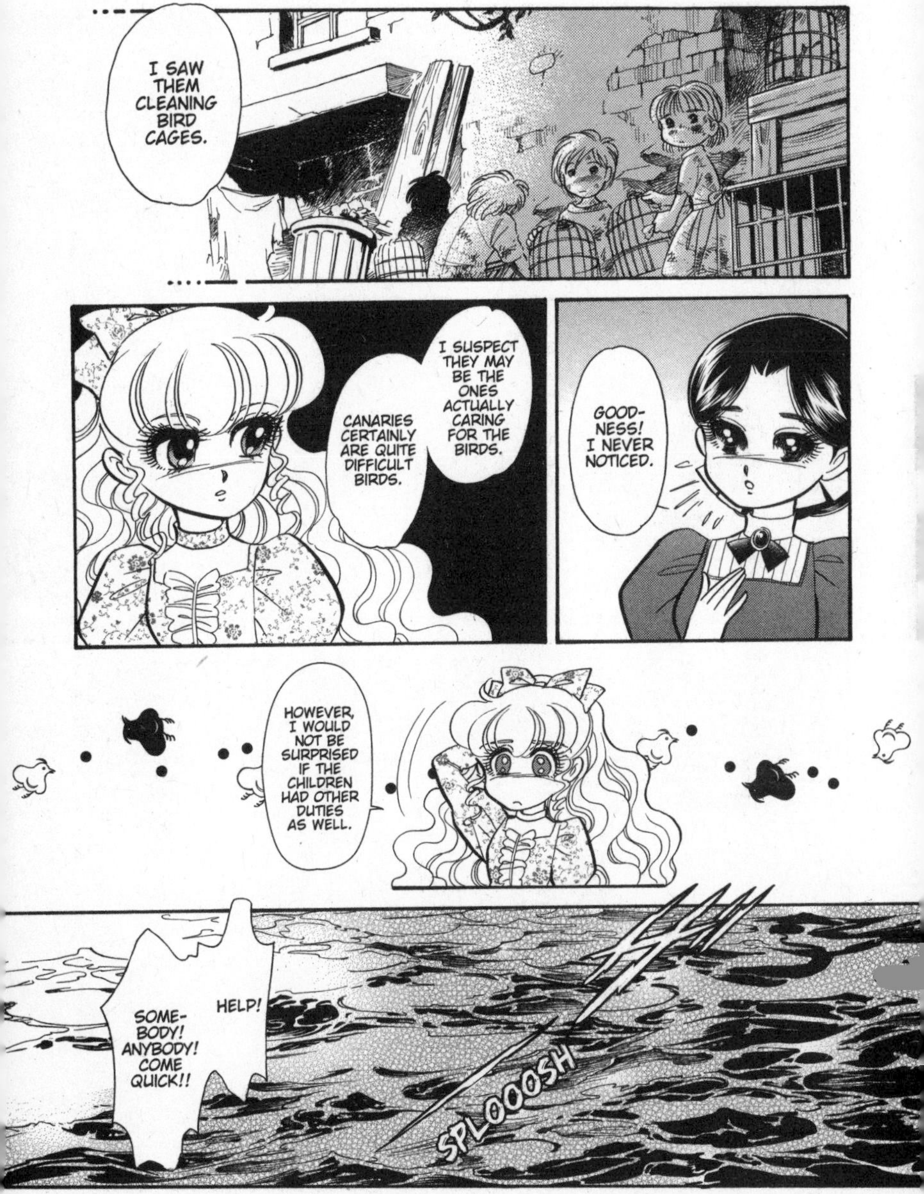
I SAW THEM CLEANING BIRD CAGES.
GOOD-NESS! I NEVER NOTICED.
I SUSPECT THEY MAY BE THE ONES ACTUALLY CARING FOR THE BIRDS.
CANARIES CERTAINLY ARE QUITE DIFFICULT BIRDS.
HOWEVER, I WOULD NOT BE SURPRISED IF THE CHILDREN HAD OTHER DUTIES AS WELL.
SPLOOOSH
HELP!
SOME-BODY! ANYBODY! COME QUICK!!

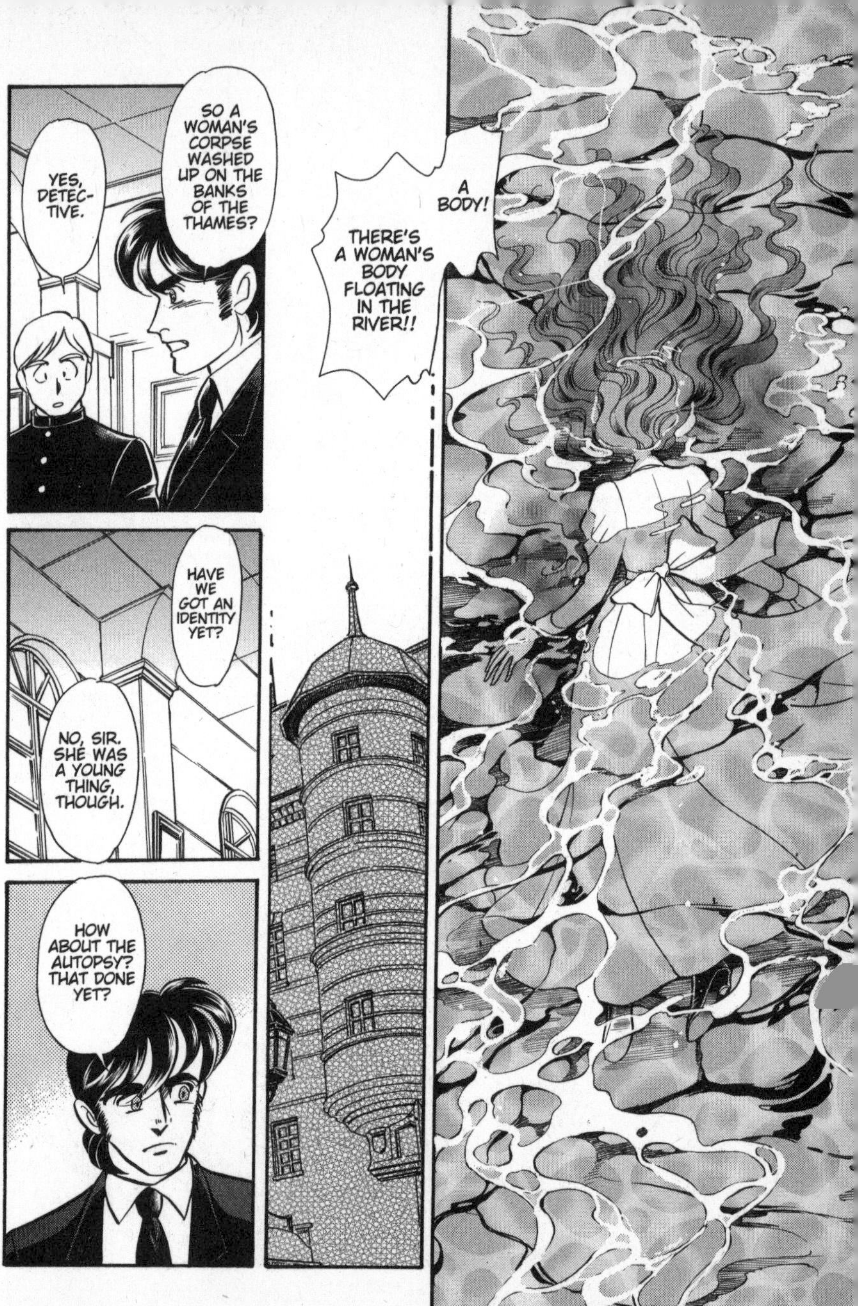
A BODY!
THERE'S A WOMAN'S BODY FLOATING IN THE RIVER!!
SO A WOMAN'S CORPSE WASHED UP ON THE BANKS OF THE THAMES?
YES, DETECTIVE.
HAVE WE GOT AN IDENTITY YET?
NO, SIR. SHE WAS A YOUNG THING, THOUGH.
HOW ABOUT THE AUTOPSY? THAT DONE YET?

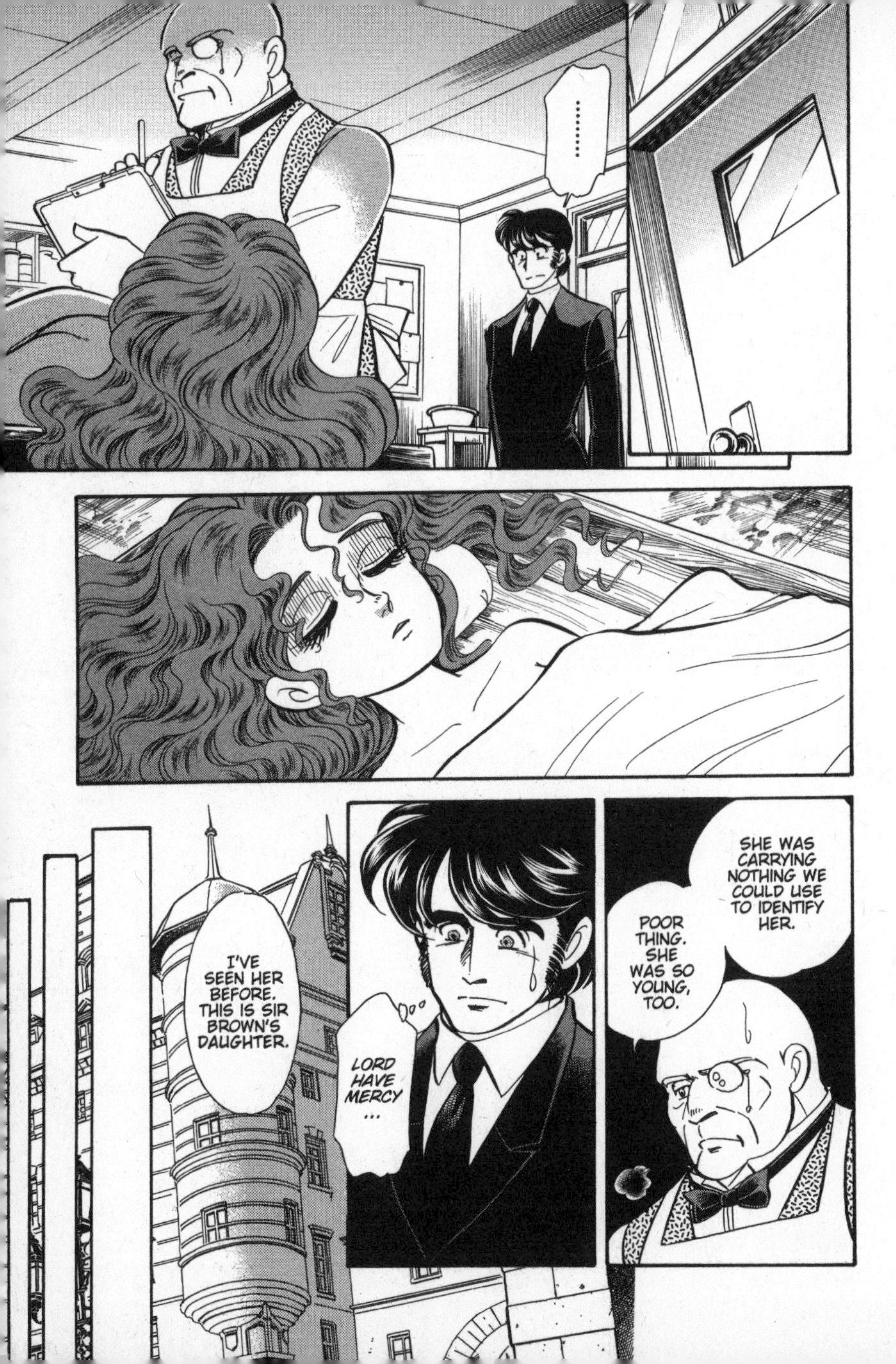

......
SHE WAS CARRYING NOTHING WE COULD USE TO IDENTIFY HER.
POOR THING. SHE WAS SO YOUNG, TOO.
LORD HAVE MERCY ...
I'VE SEEN HER BEFORE. THIS IS SIR BROWN'S DAUGHTER.

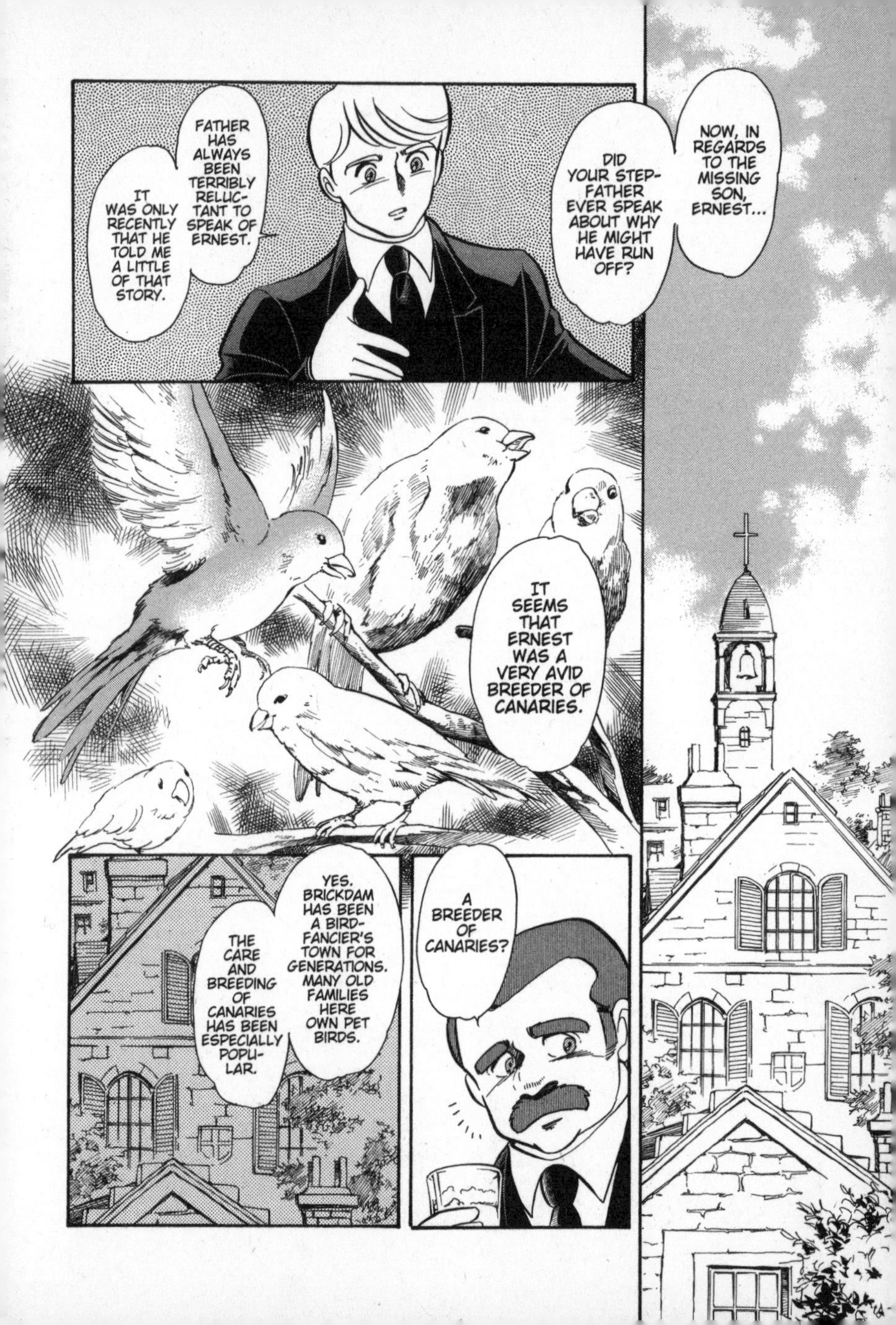
NOW, IN REGARDS TO THE MISSING SON, ERNEST...
DID YOUR STEP-FATHER EVER SPEAK ABOUT WHY HE MIGHT HAVE RUN OFF?
FATHER HAS ALWAYS BEEN TERRIBLY RELUC-TANT TO SPEAK OF ERNEST.
IT WAS ONLY RECENTLY THAT HE TOLD ME A LITTLE OF THAT STORY.
IT SEEMS THAT ERNEST WAS A VERY AVID BREEDER OF CANARIES.
A BREEDER OF CANARIES?
YES. BRICKDAM HAS BEEN A BIRD-FANCIER'S TOWN FOR GENERATIONS. MANY OLD FAMILIES HERE OWN PET BIRDS.
THE CARE AND BREEDING OF CANARIES HAS BEEN ESPECIALLY POPU-LAR.

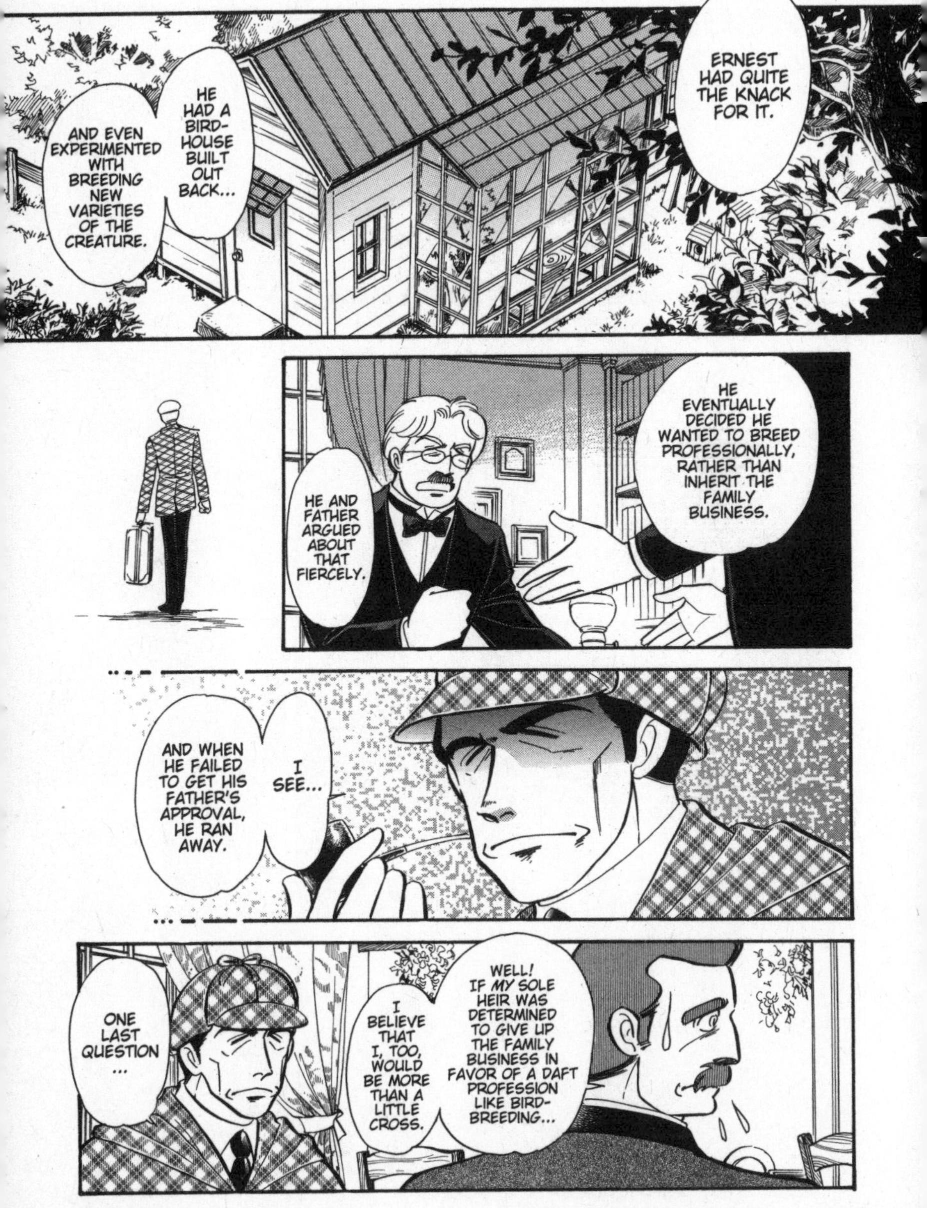

ERNEST HAD QUITE THE KNACK FOR IT.
HE HAD A BIRD-HOUSE BUILT OUT BACK...
AND EVEN EXPERIMENTED WITH BREEDING NEW VARIETIES OF THE CREATURE.
HE EVENTUALLY DECIDED HE WANTED TO BREED PROFESSIONALLY, RATHER THAN INHERIT THE FAMILY BUSINESS.
HE AND FATHER ARGUED ABOUT THAT FIERCELY.
I SEE...
AND WHEN HE FAILED TO GET HIS FATHER'S APPROVAL, HE RAN AWAY.
WELL! IF MY SOLE HEIR WAS DETERMINED TO GIVE UP THE FAMILY BUSINESS IN FAVOR OF A DAFT PROFESSION LIKE BIRD-BREEDING...
I BELIEVE THAT I, TOO, WOULD BE MORE THAN A LITTLE CROSS.
ONE LAST QUESTION ...

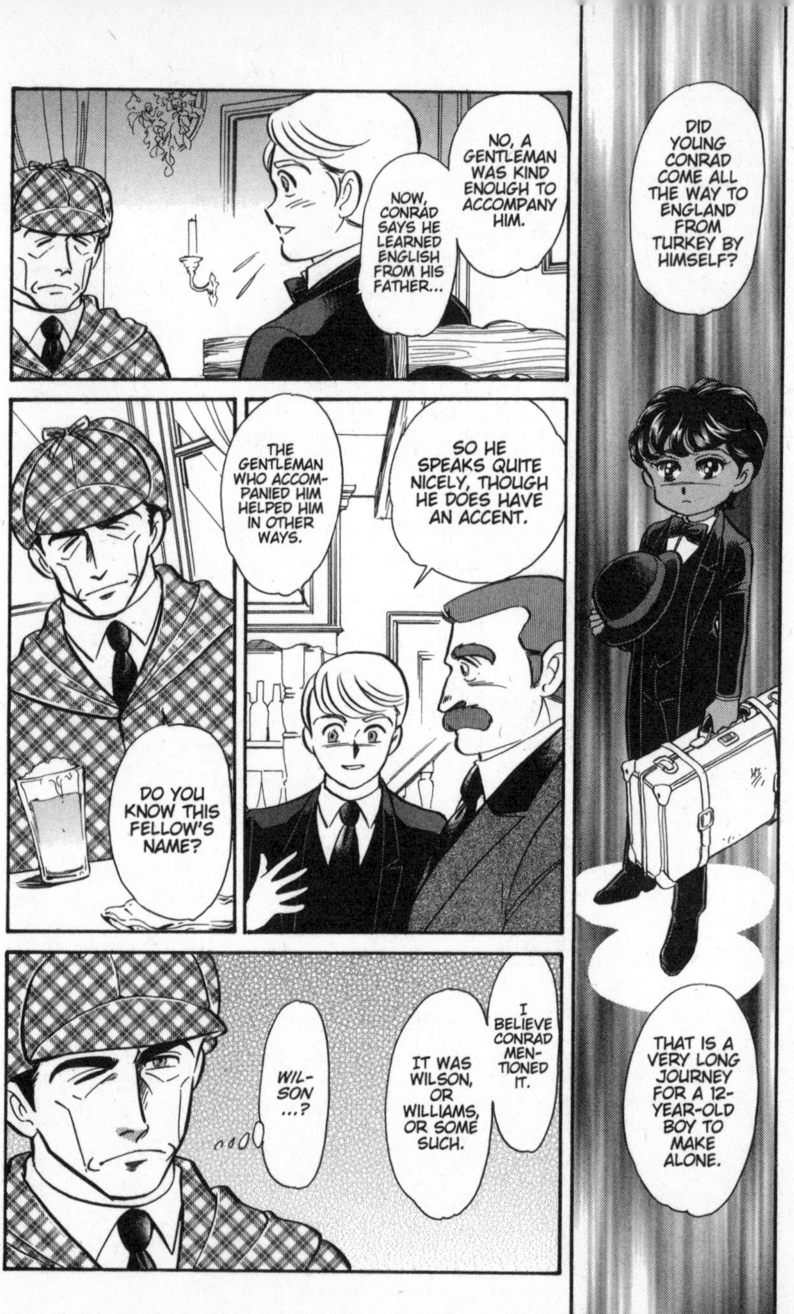
DID YOUNG CONRAD COME ALL THE WAY TO ENGLAND FROM TURKEY BY HIMSELF?
THAT IS A VERY LONG JOURNEY FOR A 12-YEAR-OLD BOY TO MAKE ALONE.
NO, A GENTLEMAN WAS KIND ENOUGH TO ACCOMPANY HIM.
NOW, CONRAD SAYS HE LEARNED ENGLISH FROM HIS FATHER...
SO HE SPEAKS QUITE NICELY, THOUGH HE DOES HAVE AN ACCENT.
THE GENTLEMAN WHO ACCOMPANIED HIM HELPED HIM IN OTHER WAYS.
DO YOU KNOW THIS FELLOW'S NAME?
I BELIEVE CONRAD MENTIONED IT.
IT WAS WILSON, OR WILLIAMS, OR SOME SUCH.
WIL-SON ...?

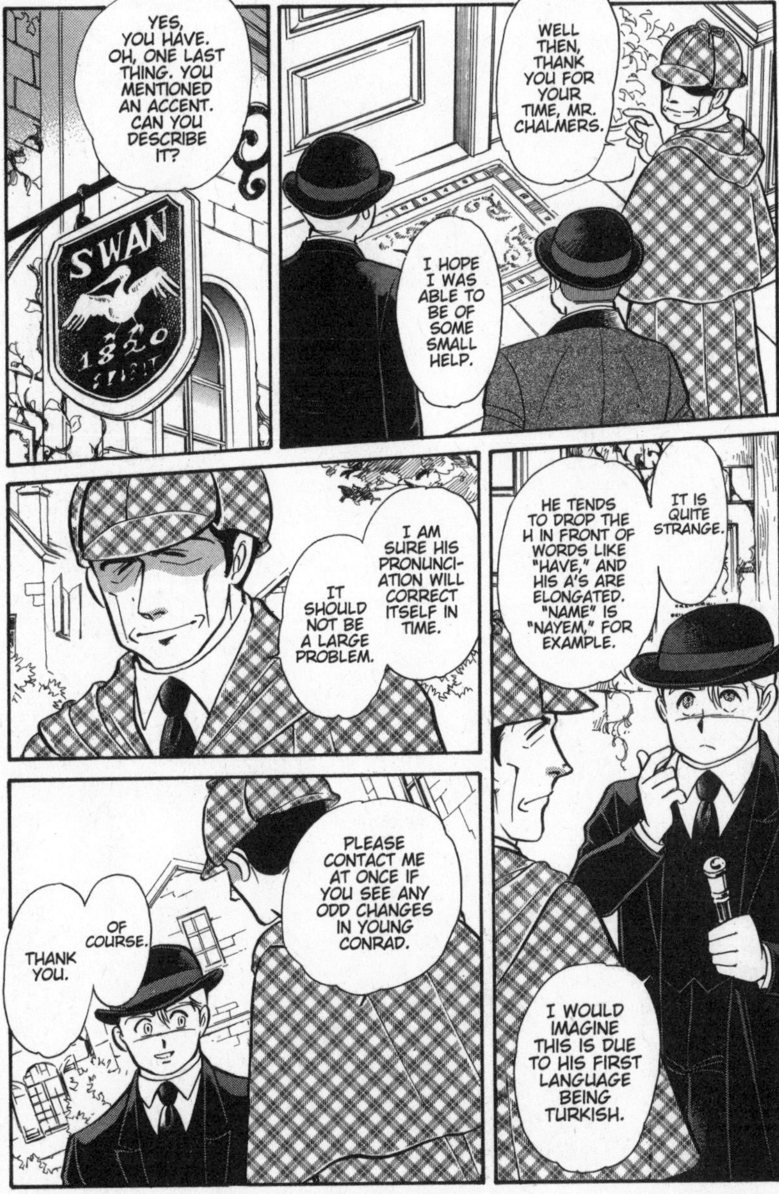
WELL THEN, THANK YOU FOR YOUR TIME, MR. CHALMERS.
I HOPE I WAS ABLE TO BE OF SOME SMALL HELP.
YES, YOU HAVE. OH, ONE LAST THING. YOU MENTIONED AN ACCENT. CAN YOU DESCRIBE IT?
SWAN
1820
IT IS QUITE STRANGE.
HE TENDS TO DROP THE H IN FRONT OF WORDS LIKE "HAVE," AND HIS A'S ARE ELONGATED. "NAME" IS "NAYEM," FOR EXAMPLE.
I WOULD IMAGINE THIS IS DUE TO HIS FIRST LANGUAGE BEING TURKISH.
I AM SURE HIS PRONUNCIATION WILL CORRECT ITSELF IN TIME.
IT SHOULD NOT BE A LARGE PROBLEM.
PLEASE CONTACT ME AT ONCE IF YOU SEE ANY ODD CHANGES IN YOUNG CONRAD.
OF COURSE.
THANK YOU.

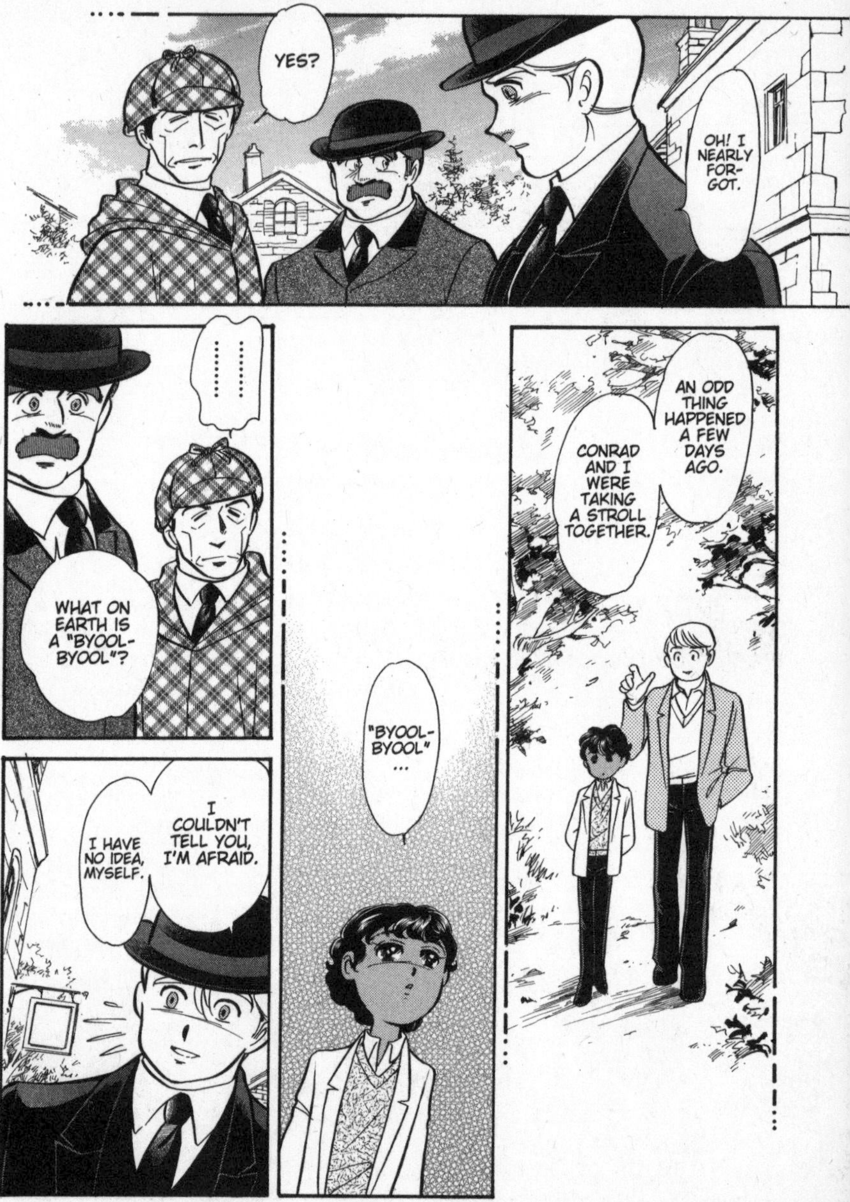
OH! I NEARLY FOR-GOT.
YES?
AN ODD THING HAPPENED A FEW DAYS AGO.
CONRAD AND I WERE TAKING A STROLL TOGETHER.
"BYOOL-BYOOL" ...
......
WHAT ON EARTH IS A "BYOOL-BYOOL"?
I COULDN'T TELL YOU, I'M AFRAID.
I HAVE NO IDEA, MYSELF.

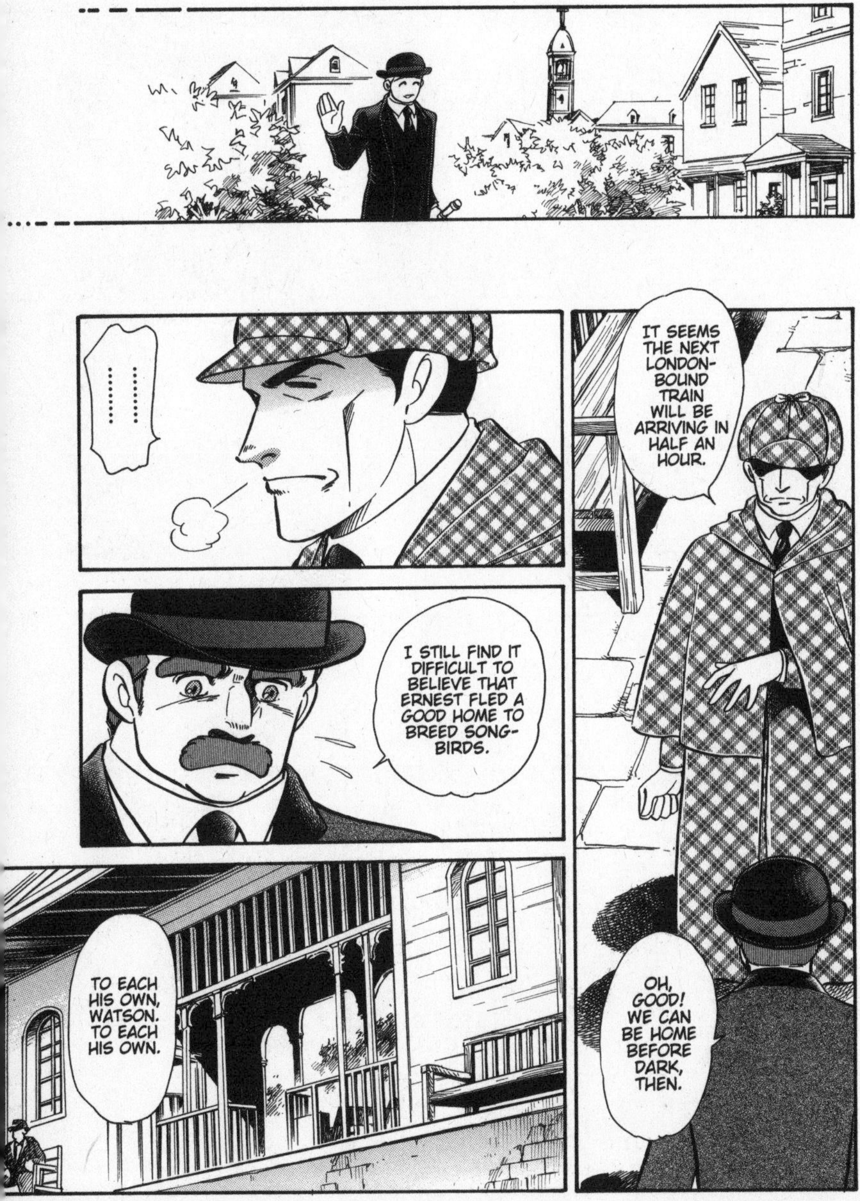
IT SEEMS THE NEXT LONDON-BOUND TRAIN WILL BE ARRIVING IN HALF AN HOUR.
OH, GOOD! WE CAN BE HOME BEFORE DARK, THEN.
......
I STILL FIND IT DIFFICULT TO BELIEVE THAT ERNEST FLED A GOOD HOME TO BREED SONG-BIRDS.
TO EACH HIS OWN, WATSON. TO EACH HIS OWN.

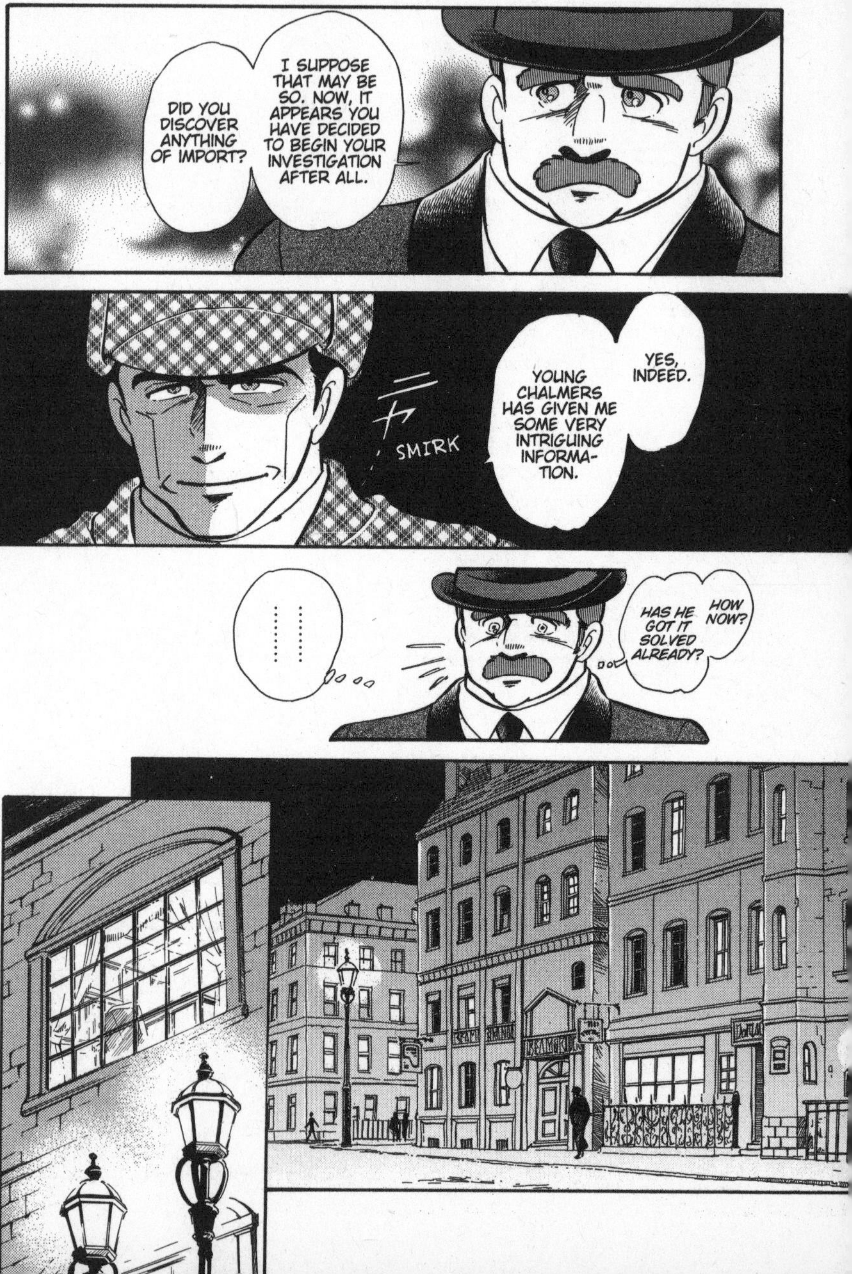
I SUPPOSE THAT MAY BE SO. NOW, IT APPEARS YOU HAVE DECIDED TO BEGIN YOUR INVESTIGATION AFTER ALL.
DID YOU DISCOVER ANYTHING OF IMPORT?
YES, INDEED.
YOUNG CHALMERS HAS GIVEN ME SOME VERY INTRIGUING INFORMATION.
ニヤ
SMIRK
HOW NOW?
HAS HE GOT IT SOLVED ALREADY?
......

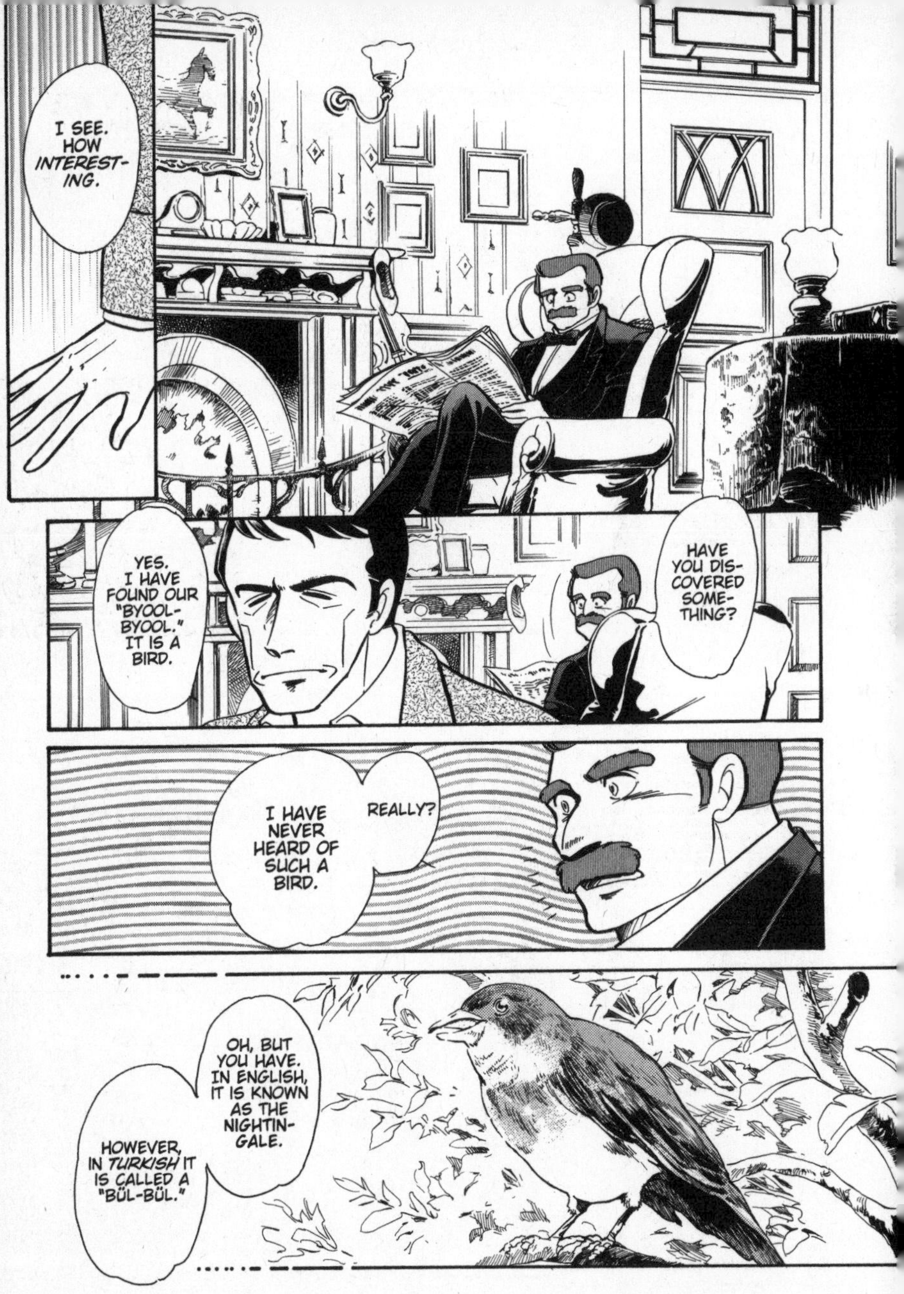
I SEE. HOW INTEREST-ING.
HAVE YOU DIS-COVERED SOME-THING?
YES. I HAVE FOUND OUR "BYOOL-BYOOL." IT IS A BIRD.
REALLY?
I HAVE NEVER HEARD OF SUCH A BIRD.
OH, BUT YOU HAVE. IN ENGLISH, IT IS KNOWN AS THE NIGHTIN-GALE.
HOWEVER, IN *TURKISH* IT IS CALLED A "BÜL-BÜL."

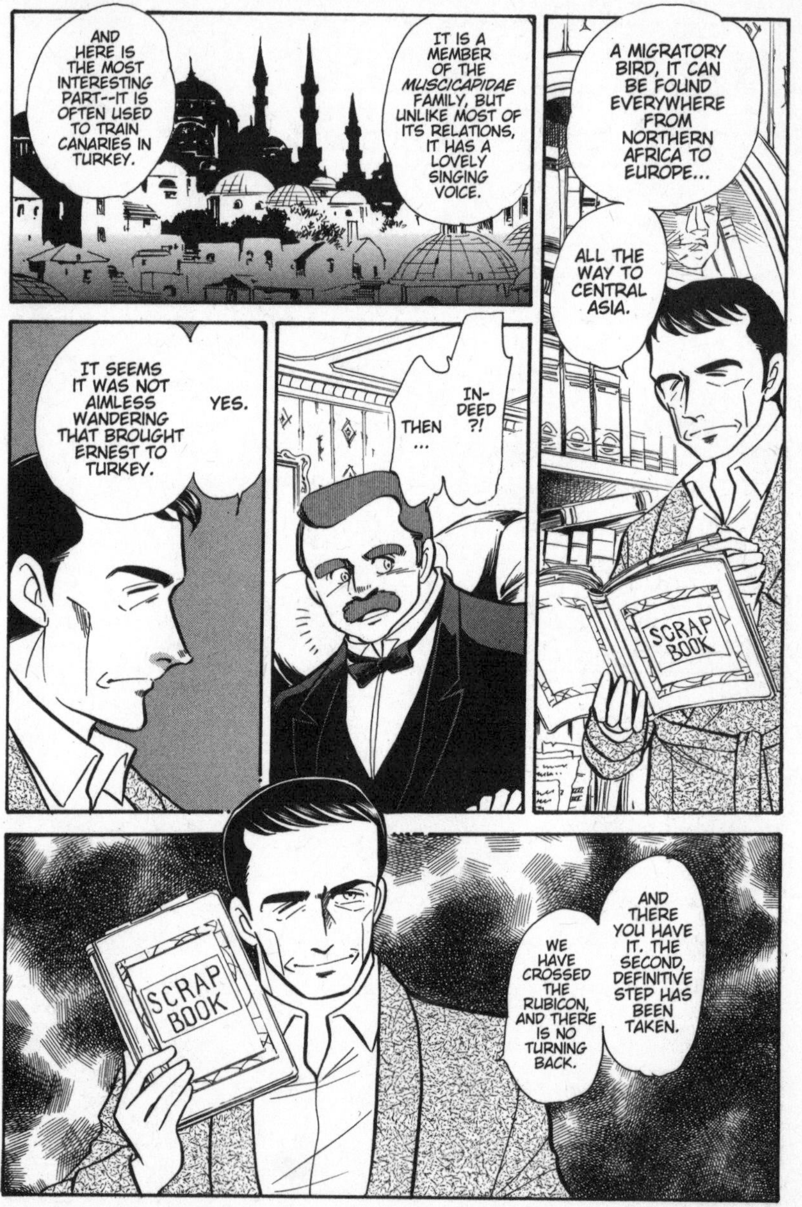
A MIGRATORY BIRD, IT CAN BE FOUND EVERYWHERE FROM NORTHERN AFRICA TO EUROPE...
ALL THE WAY TO CENTRAL ASIA.
SCRAP BOOK
IT IS A MEMBER OF THE *MUSCICAPIDAE* FAMILY, BUT UNLIKE MOST OF ITS RELATIONS, IT HAS A LOVELY SINGING VOICE.
AND HERE IS THE MOST INTERESTING PART--IT IS OFTEN USED TO TRAIN CANARIES IN TURKEY.
INDEED?!
THEN...
YES.
IT SEEMS IT WAS NOT AIMLESS WANDERING THAT BROUGHT ERNEST TO TURKEY.
AND THERE YOU HAVE IT. THE SECOND, DEFINITIVE STEP HAS BEEN TAKEN.
WE HAVE CROSSED THE RUBICON, AND THERE IS NO TURNING BACK.
SCRAP BOOK

The Adventure of the Famous Trainer (4)

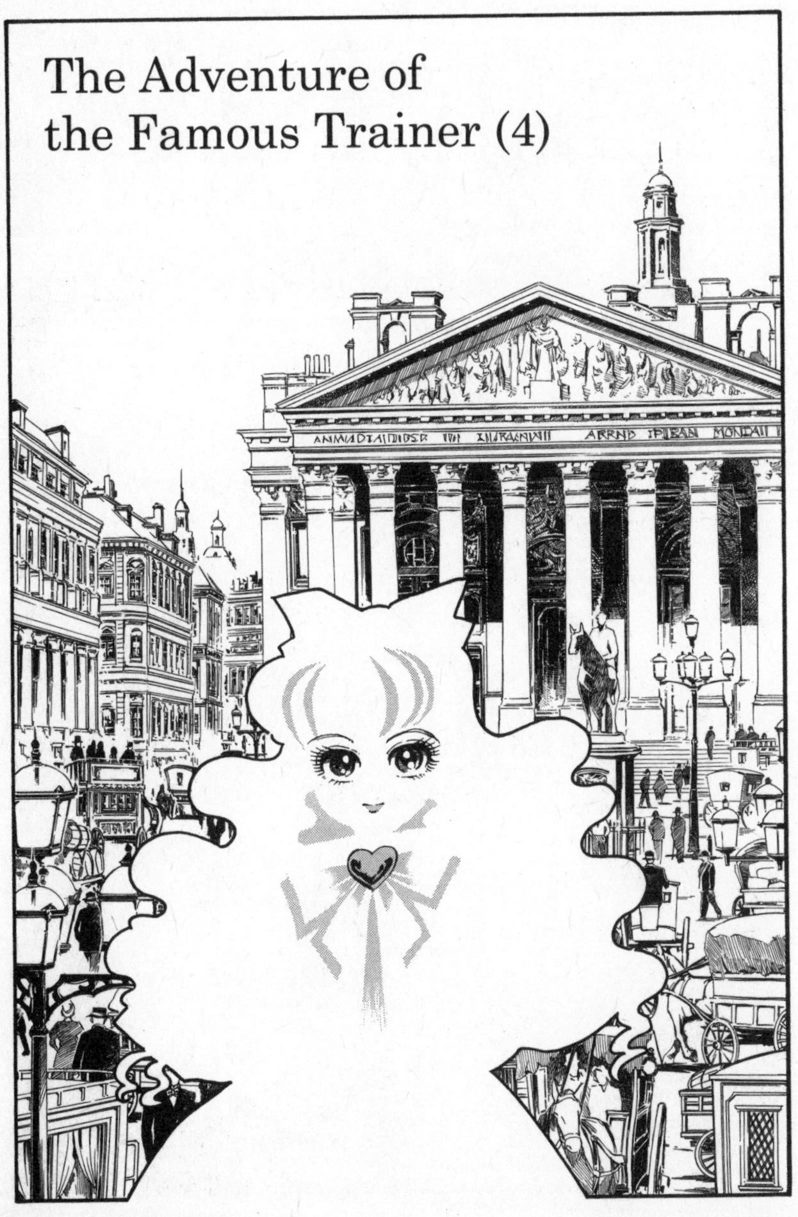

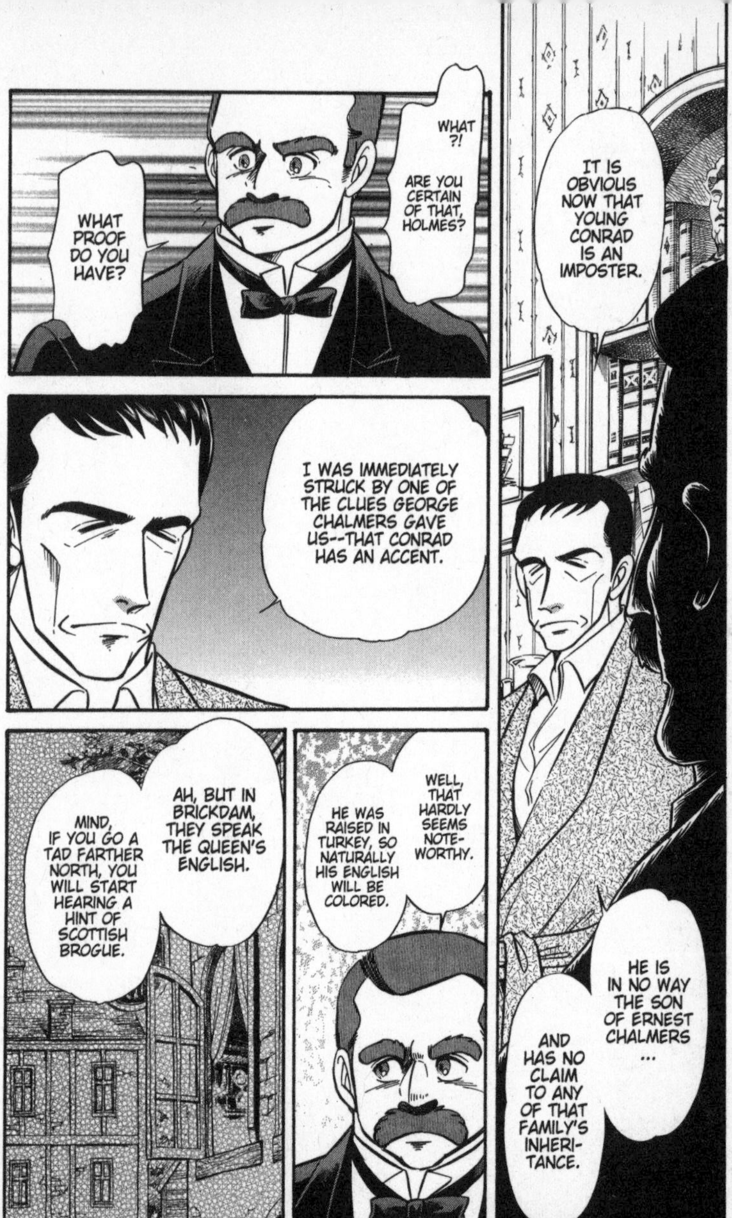
IT IS OBVIOUS NOW THAT YOUNG CONRAD IS AN IMPOSTER.
WHAT?!
ARE YOU CERTAIN OF THAT, HOLMES?
WHAT PROOF DO YOU HAVE?
I WAS IMMEDIATELY STRUCK BY ONE OF THE CLUES GEORGE CHALMERS GAVE US--THAT CONRAD HAS AN ACCENT.
WELL, THAT HARDLY SEEMS NOTE-WORTHY.
HE WAS RAISED IN TURKEY, SO NATURALLY HIS ENGLISH WILL BE COLORED.
AH, BUT IN BRICKDAM, THEY SPEAK THE QUEEN'S ENGLISH.
MIND, IF YOU GO A TAD FARTHER NORTH, YOU WILL START HEARING A HINT OF SCOTTISH BROGUE.
HE IS IN NO WAY THE SON OF ERNEST CHALMERS ...
AND HAS NO CLAIM TO ANY OF THAT FAMILY'S INHERI-TANCE.

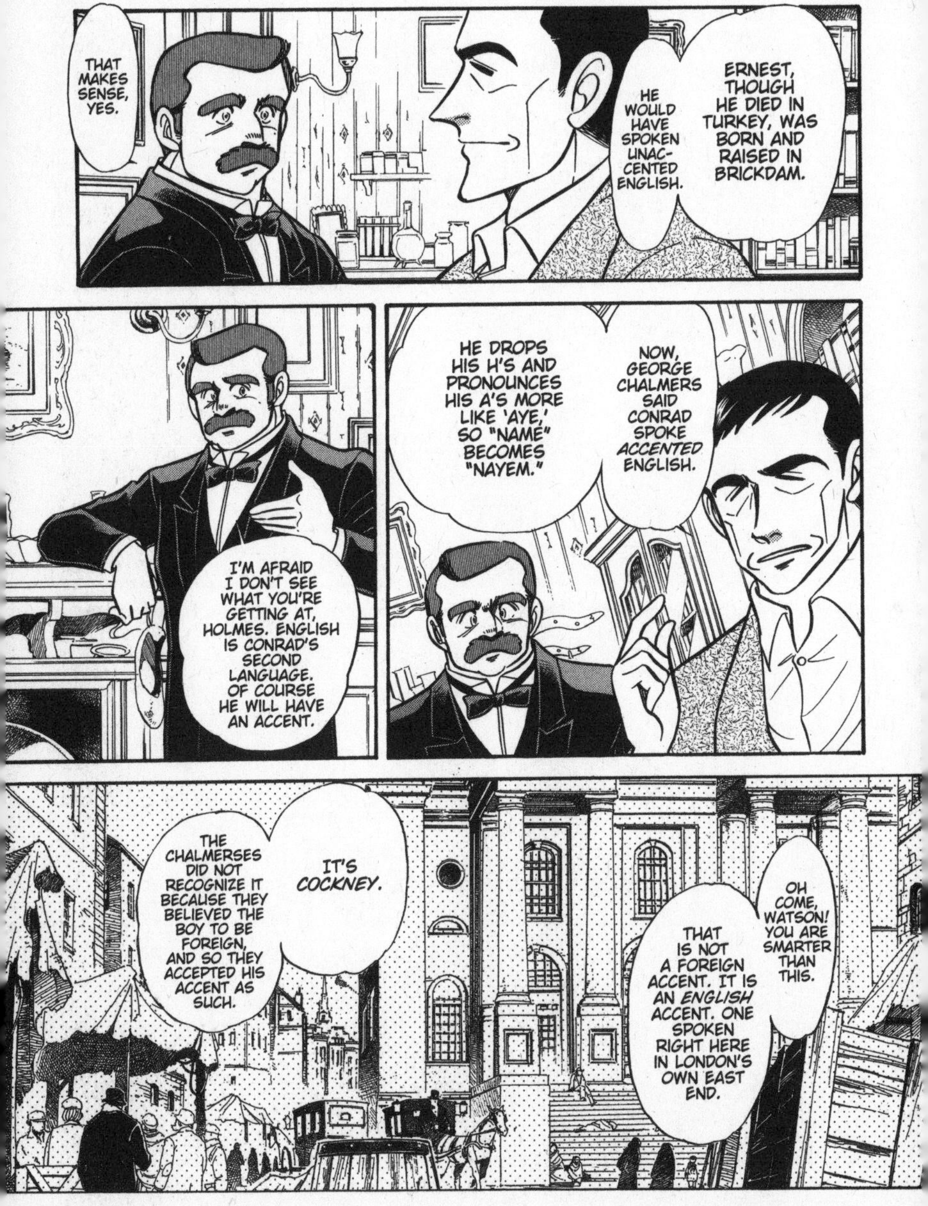
ERNEST, THOUGH HE DIED IN TURKEY, WAS BORN AND RAISED IN BRICKDAM.
HE WOULD HAVE SPOKEN UNACCENTED ENGLISH.
THAT MAKES SENSE, YES.
NOW, GEORGE CHALMERS SAID CONRAD SPOKE *ACCENTED* ENGLISH.
HE DROPS HIS H'S AND PRONOUNCES HIS A'S MORE LIKE 'AYE,' SO "NAME" BECOMES "NAYEM."
I'M AFRAID I DON'T SEE WHAT YOU'RE GETTING AT, HOLMES. ENGLISH IS CONRAD'S SECOND LANGUAGE. OF COURSE HE WILL HAVE AN ACCENT.
OH COME, WATSON! YOU ARE SMARTER THAN THIS.
THAT IS NOT A FOREIGN ACCENT. IT IS AN *ENGLISH* ACCENT. ONE SPOKEN RIGHT HERE IN LONDON'S OWN EAST END.
IT'S *COCKNEY*.
THE CHALMERSES DID NOT RECOGNIZE IT BECAUSE THEY BELIEVED THE BOY TO BE FOREIGN, AND SO THEY ACCEPTED HIS ACCENT AS SUCH.

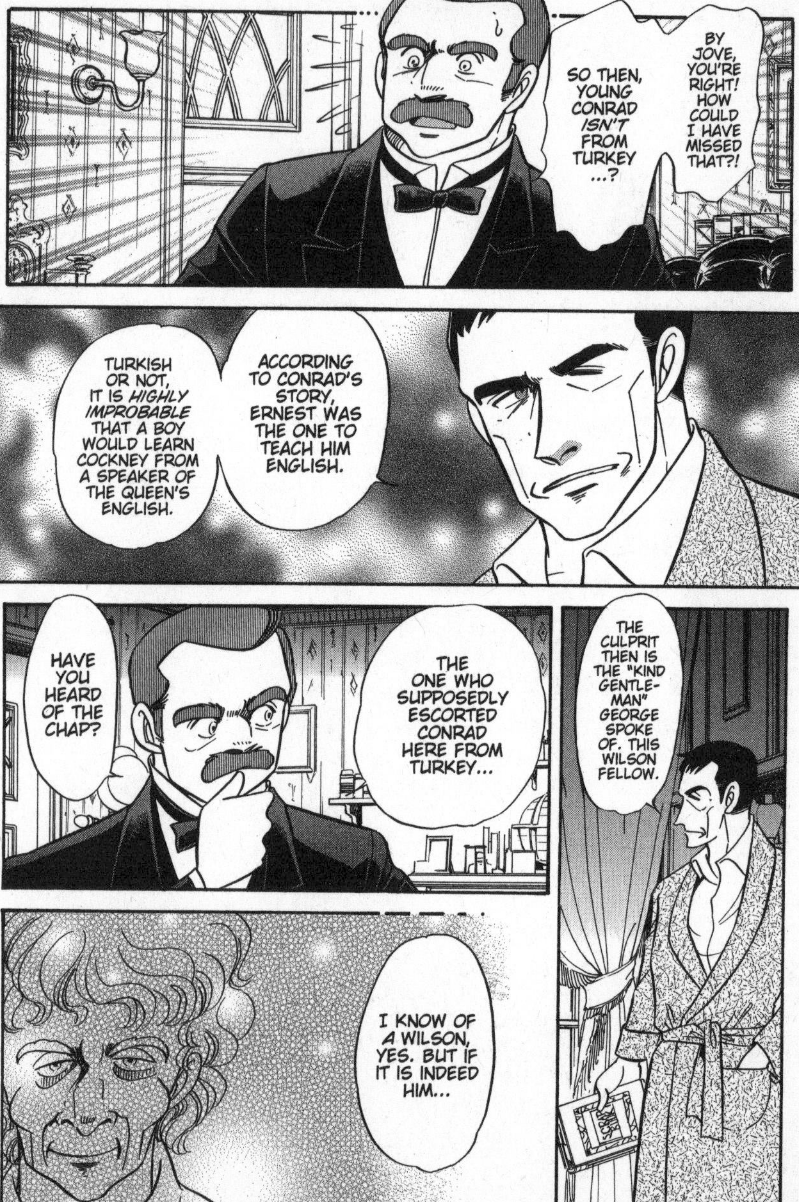
BY JOVE, YOU'RE RIGHT! HOW COULD I HAVE MISSED THAT?!
SO THEN, YOUNG CONRAD *ISN'T* FROM TURKEY ...?
ACCORDING TO CONRAD'S STORY, ERNEST WAS THE ONE TO TEACH HIM ENGLISH.
TURKISH OR NOT, IT IS *HIGHLY IMPROBABLE* THAT A BOY WOULD LEARN COCKNEY FROM A SPEAKER OF THE QUEEN'S ENGLISH.
THE CULPRIT THEN IS THE "KIND GENTLE-MAN" GEORGE SPOKE OF. THIS WILSON FELLOW.
THE ONE WHO SUPPOSEDLY ESCORTED CONRAD HERE FROM TURKEY...
HAVE YOU HEARD OF THE CHAP?
I KNOW OF A WILSON, YES. BUT IF IT IS INDEED HIM...

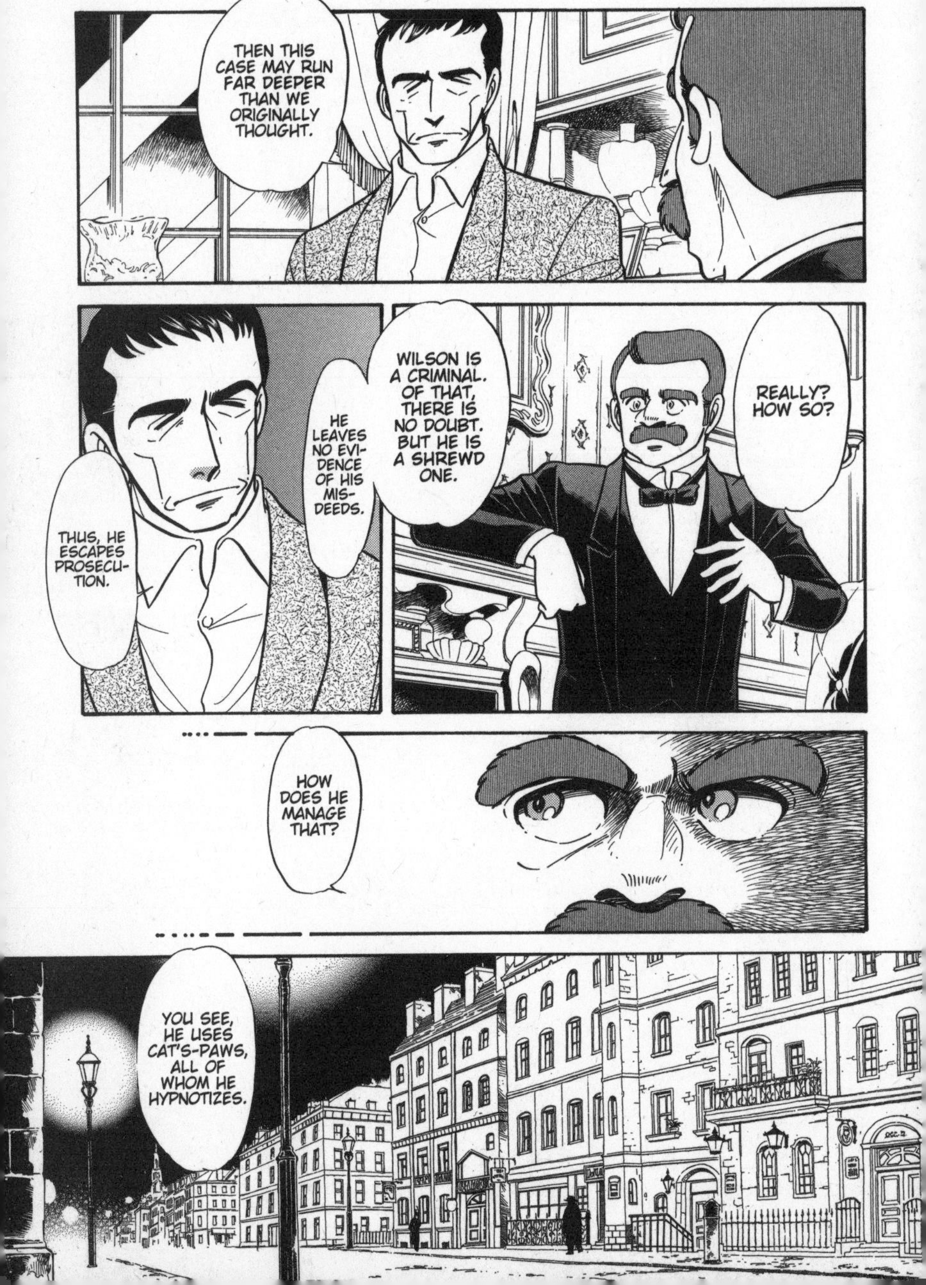
THEN THIS CASE MAY RUN FAR DEEPER THAN WE ORIGINALLY THOUGHT.
REALLY? HOW SO?
WILSON IS A CRIMINAL. OF THAT, THERE IS NO DOUBT. BUT HE IS A SHREWD ONE.
HE LEAVES NO EVI-DENCE OF HIS MIS-DEEDS.
THUS, HE ESCAPES PROSECU-TION.
HOW DOES HE MANAGE THAT?
YOU SEE, HE USES CAT'S-PAWS, ALL OF WHOM HE HYPNOTIZES.

NO MATTER. I WAS SIMPLY DOING A LITTLE RE-SEARCH.

I'M SORRY. I WAS NOT AWARE ANYONE WAS USING THE LIBRARY.

MY LADY.

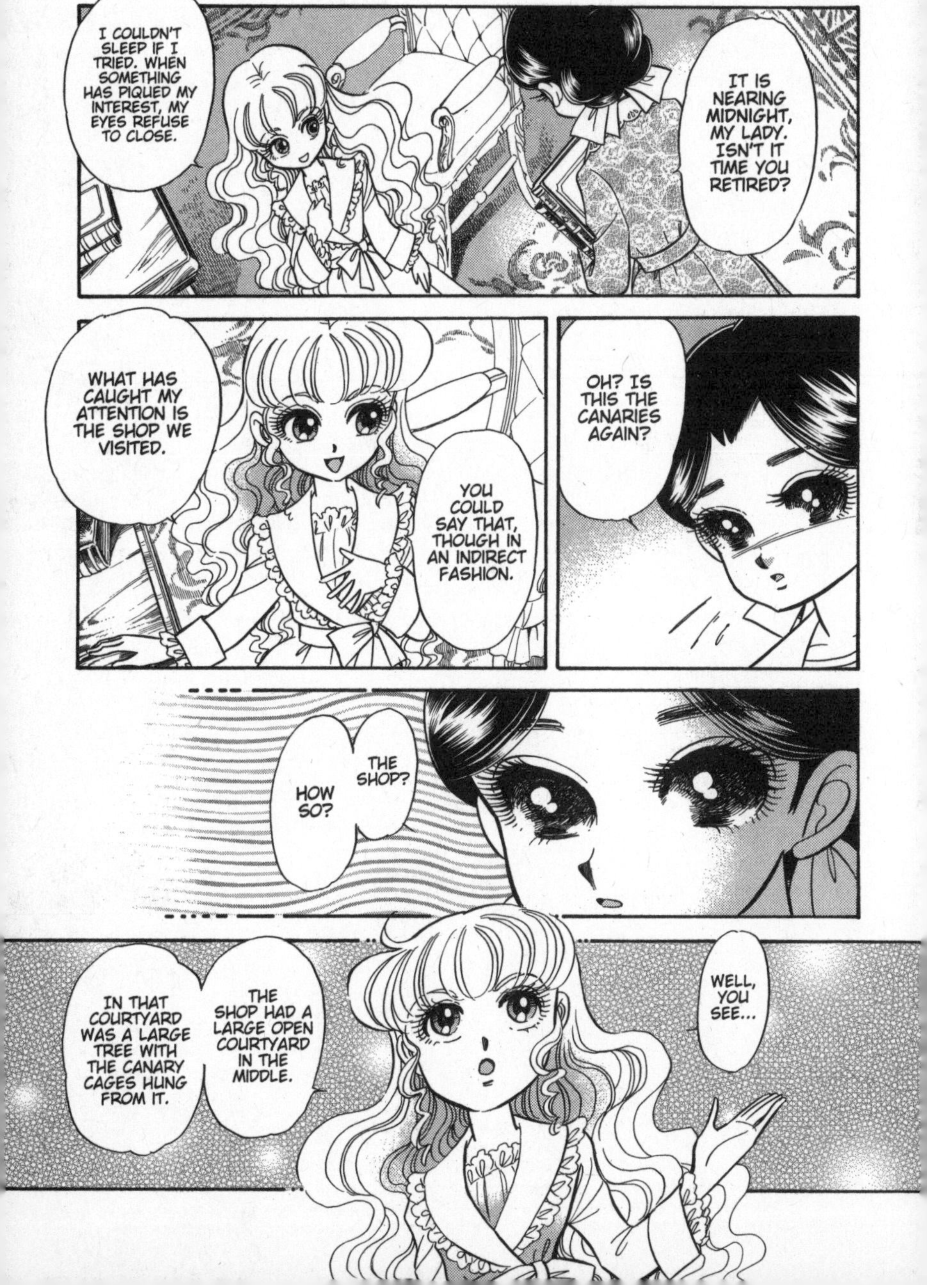
IT IS NEARING MIDNIGHT, MY LADY. ISN'T IT TIME YOU RETIRED?
I COULDN'T SLEEP IF I TRIED. WHEN SOMETHING HAS PIQUED MY INTEREST, MY EYES REFUSE TO CLOSE.
OH? IS THIS THE CANARIES AGAIN?
YOU COULD SAY THAT, THOUGH IN AN INDIRECT FASHION.
WHAT HAS CAUGHT MY ATTENTION IS THE SHOP WE VISITED.
THE SHOP?
HOW SO?
WELL, YOU SEE...
THE SHOP HAD A LARGE OPEN COURTYARD IN THE MIDDLE.
IN THAT COURTYARD WAS A LARGE TREE WITH THE CANARY CAGES HUNG FROM IT.

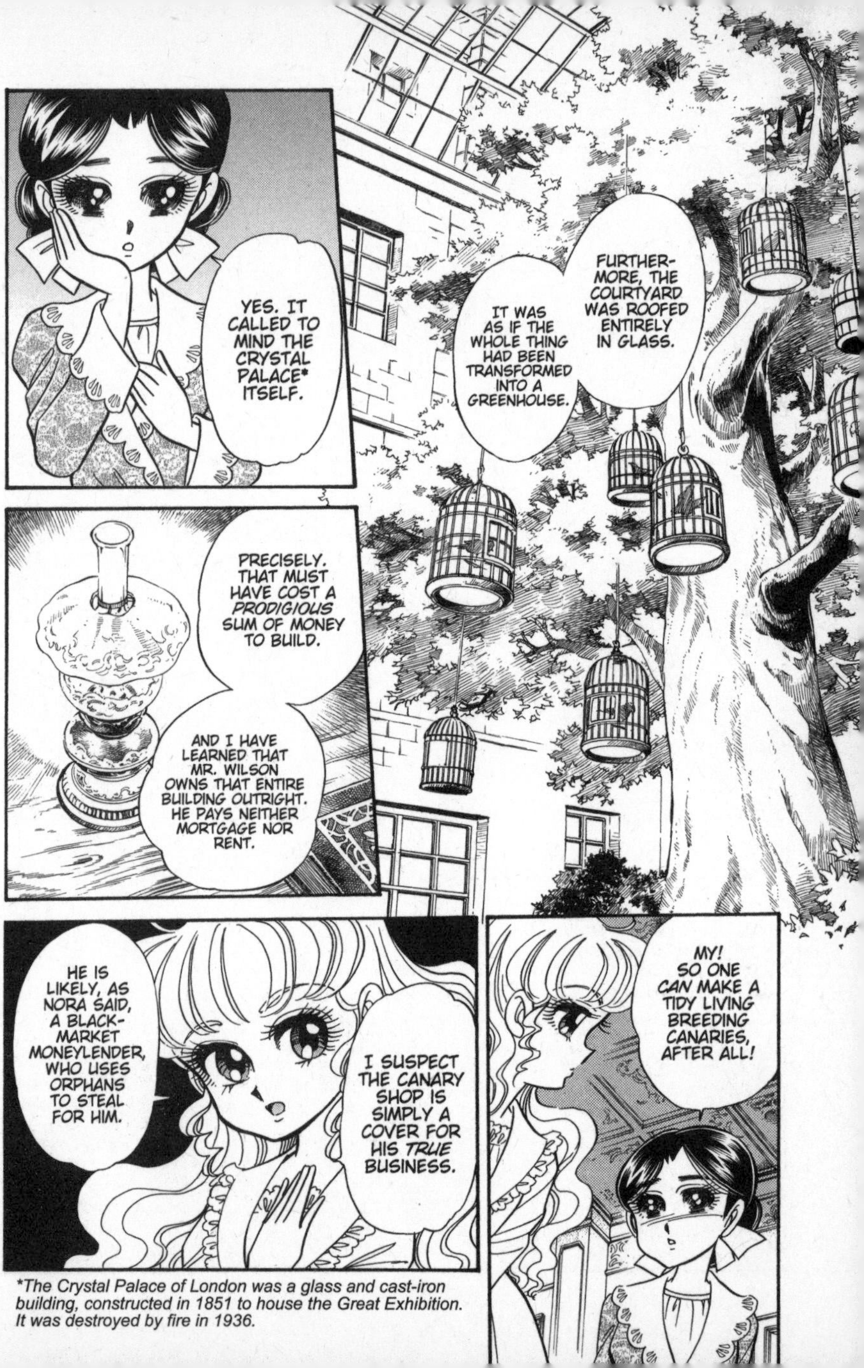
FURTHER-MORE, THE COURTYARD WAS ROOFED ENTIRELY IN GLASS.
IT WAS AS IF THE WHOLE THING HAD BEEN TRANSFORMED INTO A GREENHOUSE.
YES. IT CALLED TO MIND THE CRYSTAL PALACE* ITSELF.
PRECISELY. THAT MUST HAVE COST A *PRODIGIOUS* SUM OF MONEY TO BUILD.
AND I HAVE LEARNED THAT MR. WILSON OWNS THAT ENTIRE BUILDING OUTRIGHT. HE PAYS NEITHER MORTGAGE NOR RENT.
MY! SO ONE *CAN* MAKE A TIDY LIVING BREEDING CANARIES, AFTER ALL!
I SUSPECT THE CANARY SHOP IS SIMPLY A COVER FOR HIS *TRUE* BUSINESS.
HE IS LIKELY, AS NORA SAID, A BLACK-MARKET MONEYLENDER, WHO USES ORPHANS TO STEAL FOR HIM.

**The Crystal Palace of London was a glass and cast-iron building, constructed in 1851 to house the Great Exhibition. It was destroyed by fire in 1936.*

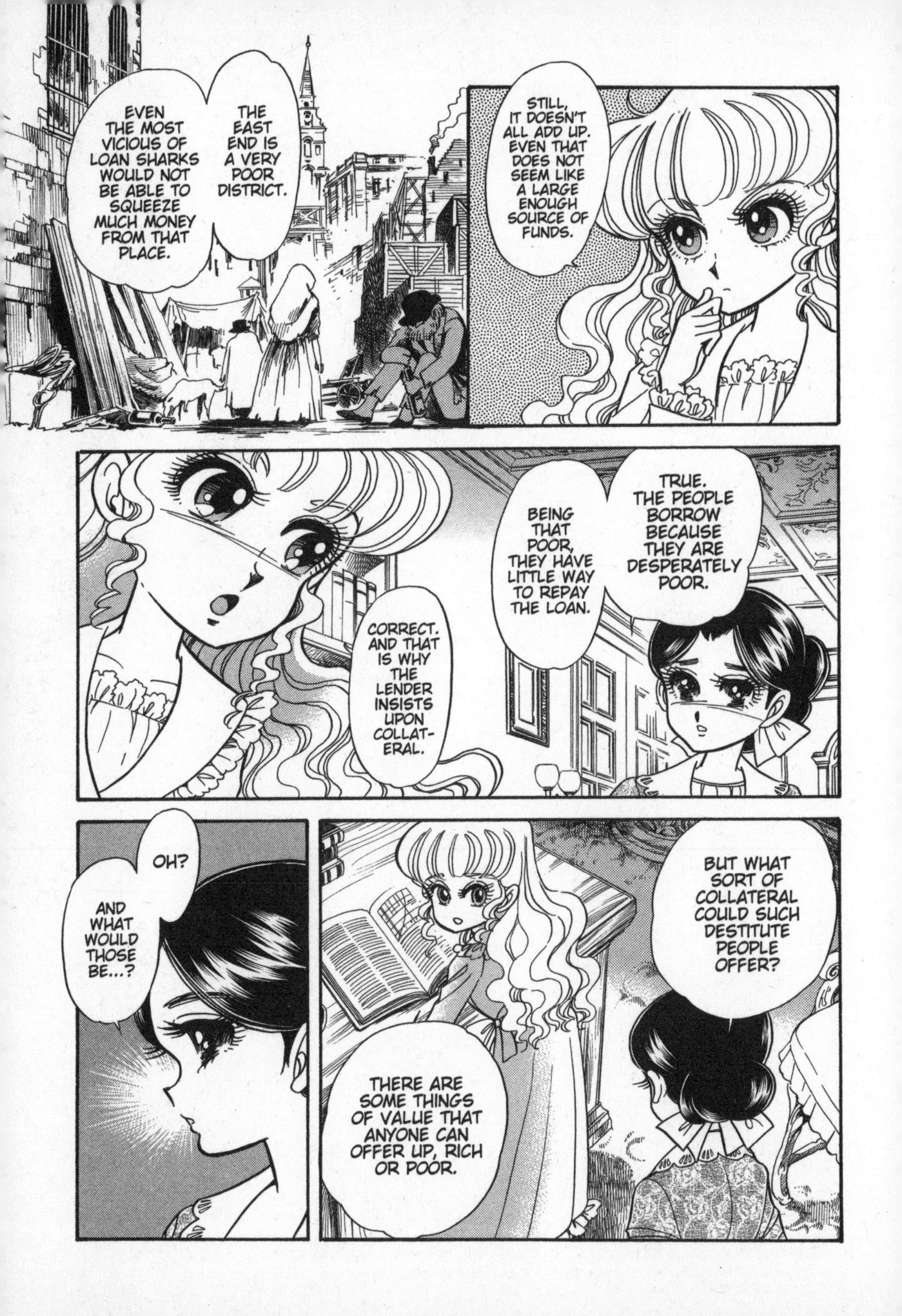
STILL, IT DOESN'T ALL ADD UP. EVEN THAT DOES NOT SEEM LIKE A LARGE ENOUGH SOURCE OF FUNDS.
THE EAST END IS A VERY POOR DISTRICT.
EVEN THE MOST VICIOUS OF LOAN SHARKS WOULD NOT BE ABLE TO SQUEEZE MUCH MONEY FROM THAT PLACE.
TRUE. THE PEOPLE BORROW BECAUSE THEY ARE DESPERATELY POOR.
BEING THAT POOR, THEY HAVE LITTLE WAY TO REPAY THE LOAN.
CORRECT. AND THAT IS WHY THE LENDER INSISTS UPON COLLATERAL.
BUT WHAT SORT OF COLLATERAL COULD SUCH DESTITUTE PEOPLE OFFER?
THERE ARE SOME THINGS OF VALUE THAT ANYONE CAN OFFER UP, RICH OR POOR.
OH?
AND WHAT WOULD THOSE BE...?

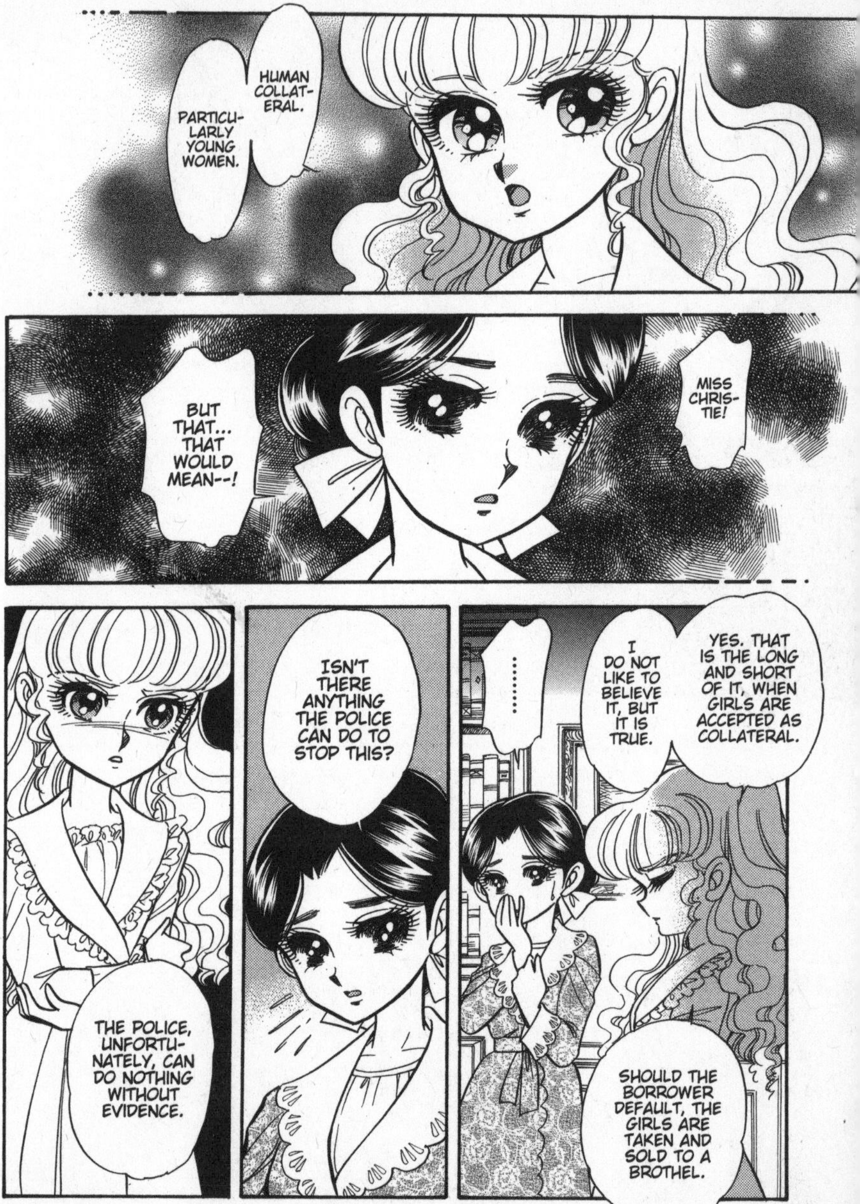
HUMAN COLLATERAL.
PARTICULARLY YOUNG WOMEN.
MISS CHRISTIE!
BUT THAT... THAT WOULD MEAN--!
YES. THAT IS THE LONG AND SHORT OF IT, WHEN GIRLS ARE ACCEPTED AS COLLATERAL.
I DO NOT LIKE TO BELIEVE IT, BUT IT IS TRUE.
....
SHOULD THE BORROWER DEFAULT, THE GIRLS ARE TAKEN AND SOLD TO A BROTHEL.
ISN'T THERE ANYTHING THE POLICE CAN DO TO STOP THIS?
THE POLICE, UNFORTUNATELY, CAN DO NOTHING WITHOUT EVIDENCE.

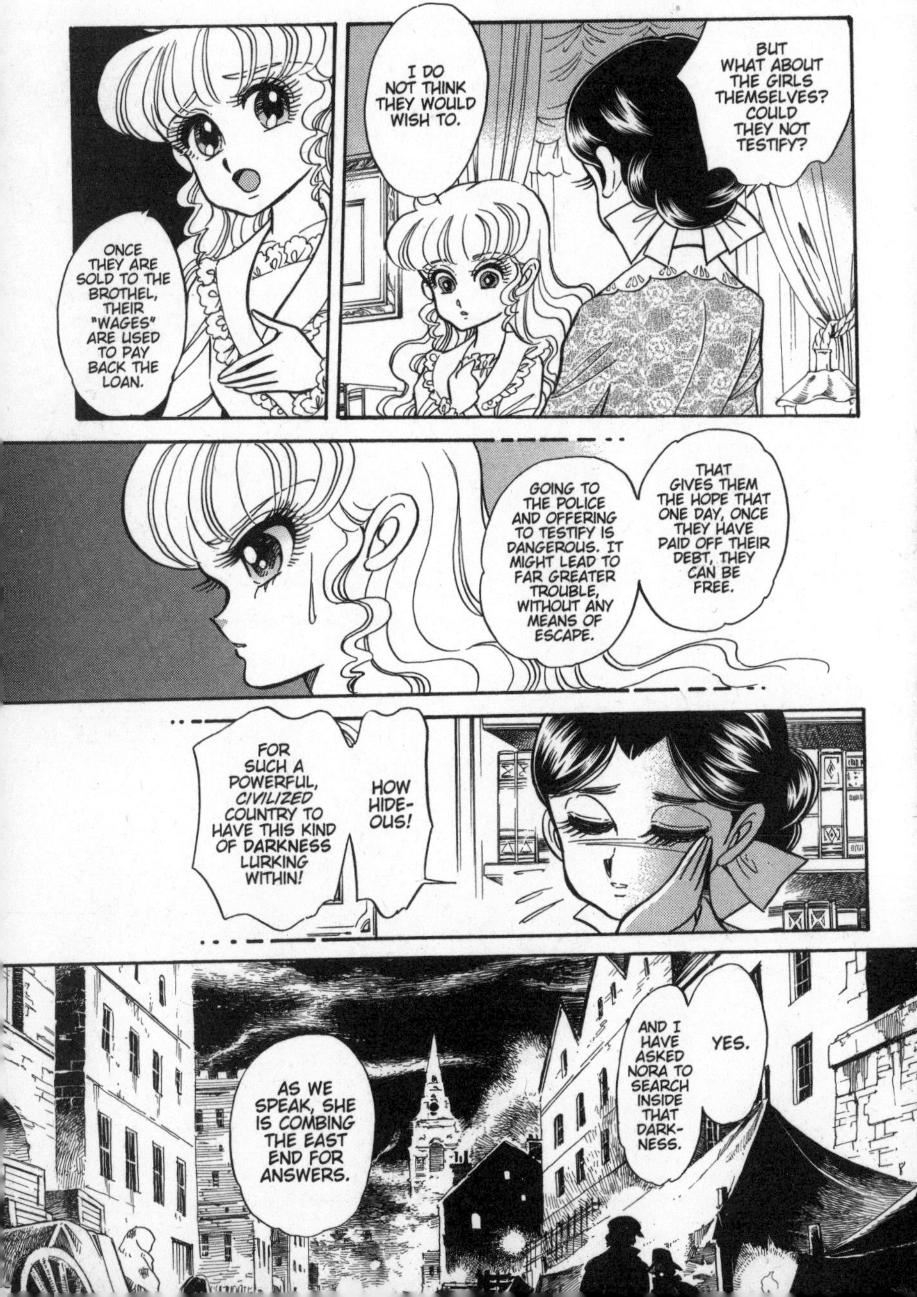
BUT WHAT ABOUT THE GIRLS THEMSELVES? COULD THEY NOT TESTIFY?
I DO NOT THINK THEY WOULD WISH TO.
ONCE THEY ARE SOLD TO THE BROTHEL, THEIR "WAGES" ARE USED TO PAY BACK THE LOAN.
THAT GIVES THEM THE HOPE THAT ONE DAY, ONCE THEY HAVE PAID OFF THEIR DEBT, THEY CAN BE FREE.
GOING TO THE POLICE AND OFFERING TO TESTIFY IS DANGEROUS. IT MIGHT LEAD TO FAR GREATER TROUBLE, WITHOUT ANY MEANS OF ESCAPE.
HOW HIDE-OUS!
FOR SUCH A POWERFUL, *CIVILIZED* COUNTRY TO HAVE THIS KIND OF DARKNESS LURKING WITHIN!
YES.
AND I HAVE ASKED NORA TO SEARCH INSIDE THAT DARK-NESS.
AS WE SPEAK, SHE IS COMBING THE EAST END FOR ANSWERS.

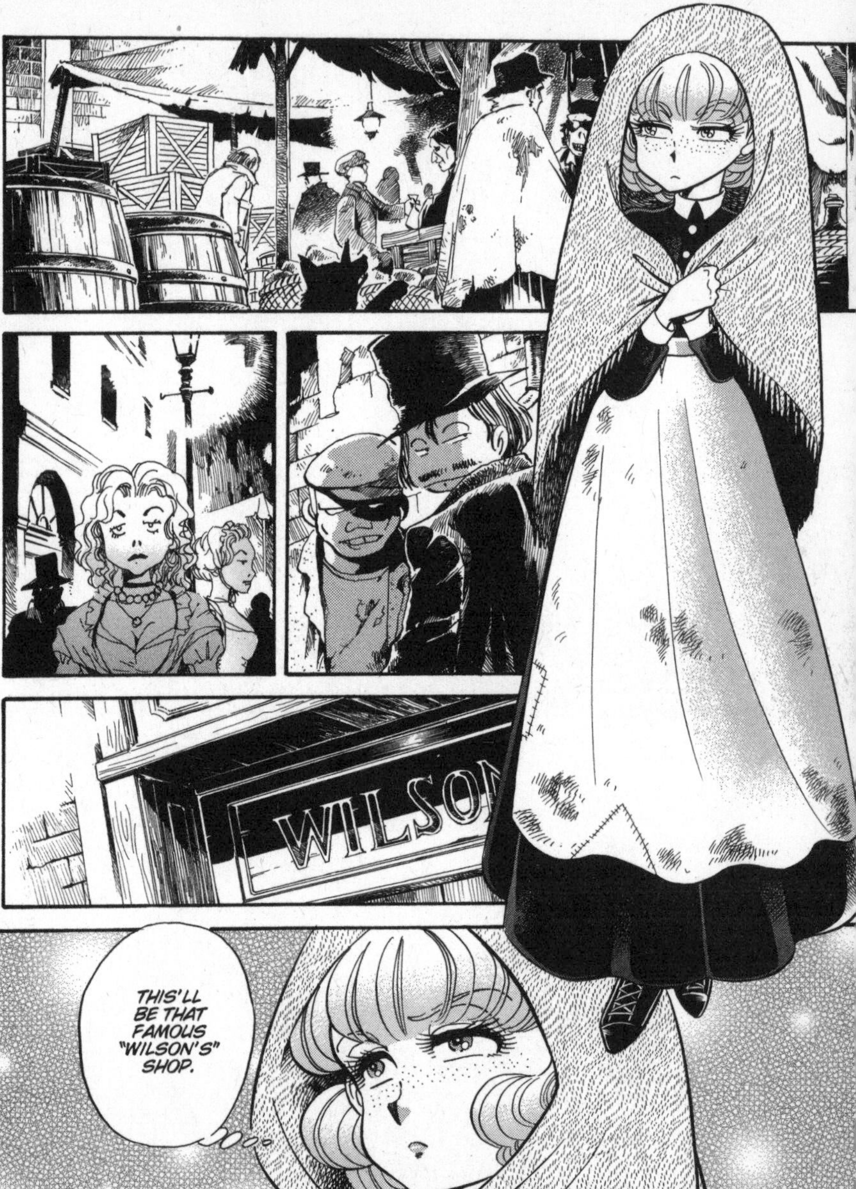
WILSON
THIS'LL BE THAT FAMOUS "WILSON'S" SHOP.

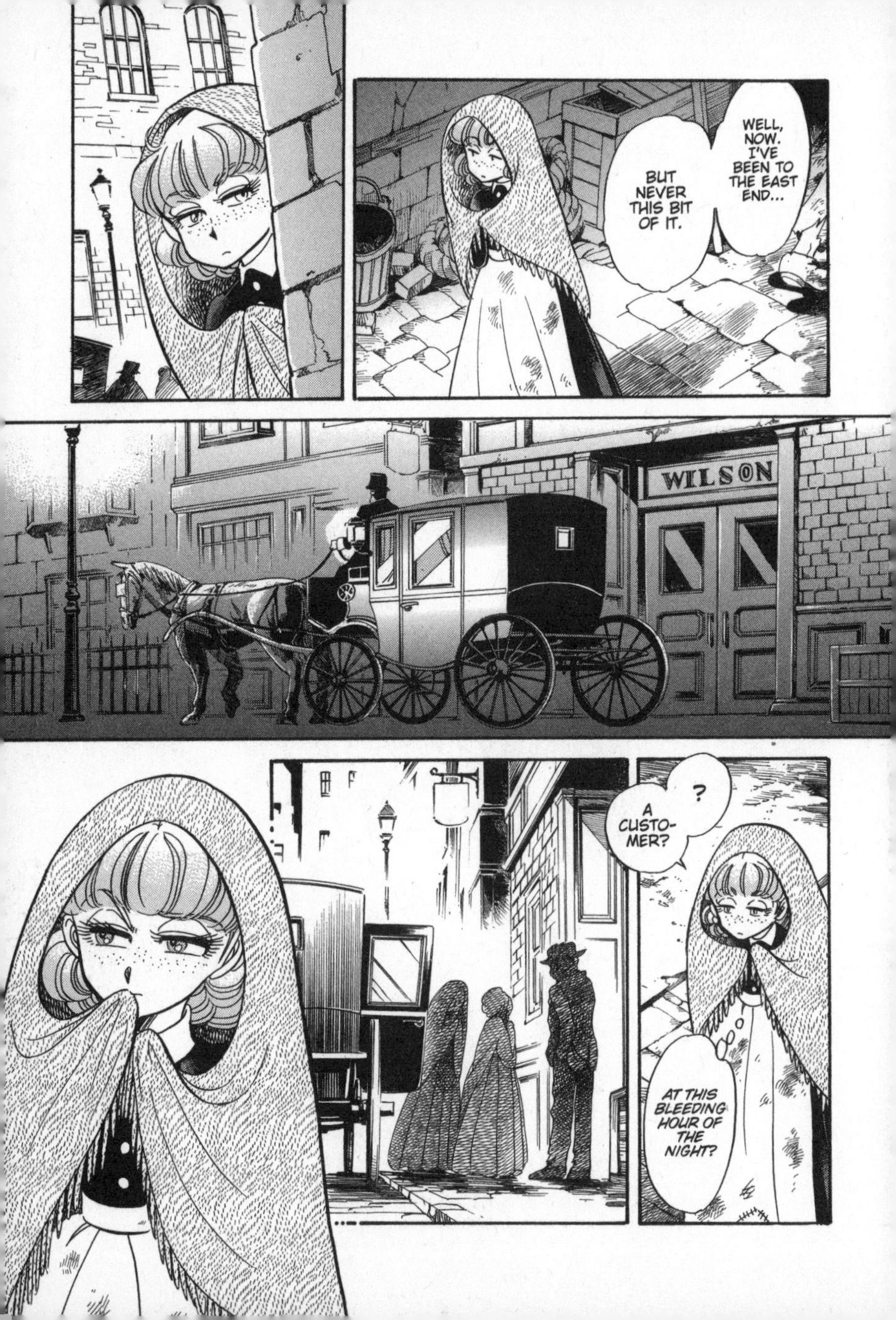
WELL, NOW. I'VE BEEN TO THE EAST END...
BUT NEVER THIS BIT OF IT.
WILSON
?
A CUSTO- MER?
AT THIS BLEEDING HOUR OF THE NIGHT?

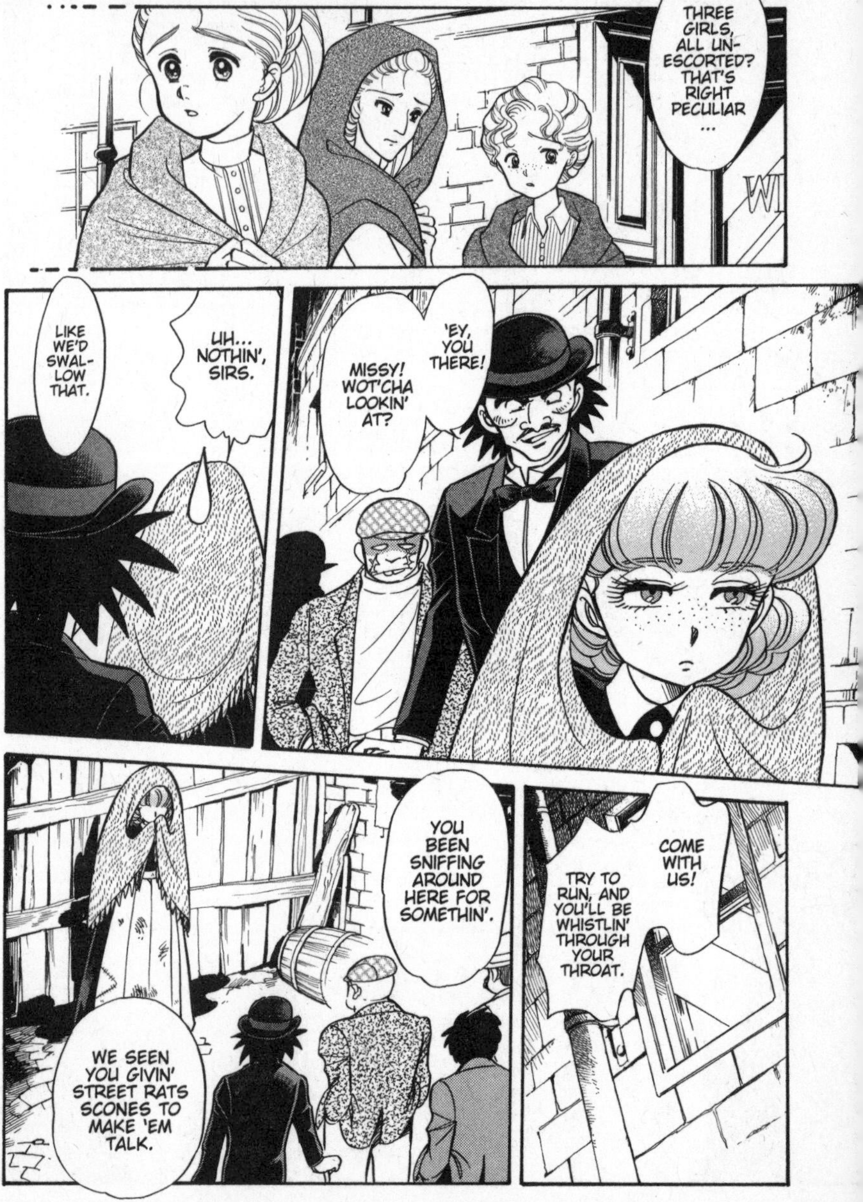
THREE GIRLS, ALL UN-ESCORTED? THAT'S RIGHT PECULIAR ...
'EY, YOU THERE!
MISSY! WOT'CHA LOOKIN' AT?
UH... NOTHIN', SIRS.
LIKE WE'D SWAL-LOW THAT.
COME WITH US!
TRY TO RUN, AND YOU'LL BE WHISTLIN' THROUGH YOUR THROAT.
YOU BEEN SNIFFING AROUND HERE FOR SOMETHIN'.
WE SEEN YOU GIVIN' STREET RATS SCONES TO MAKE 'EM TALK.

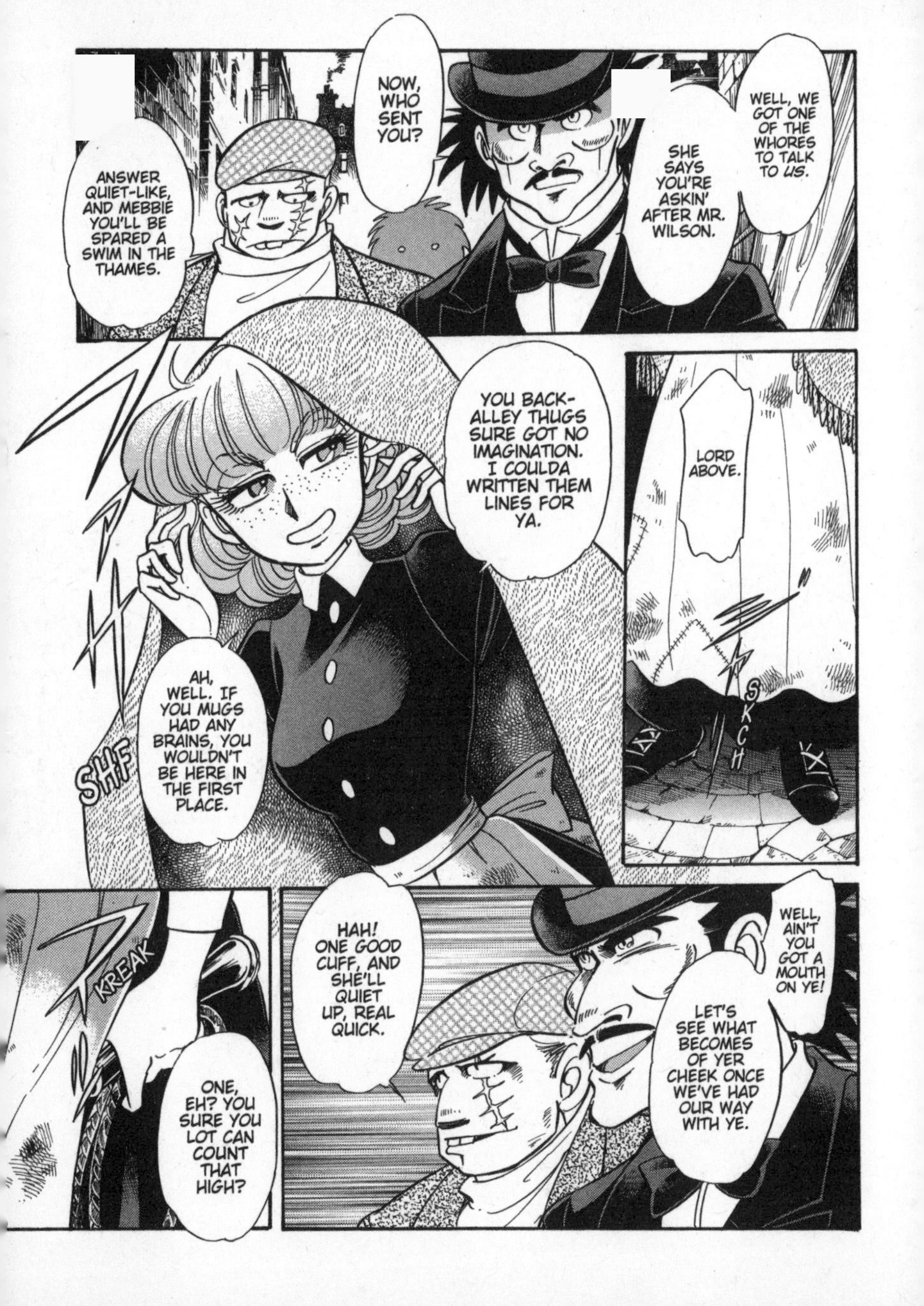
WELL, WE GOT ONE OF THE WHORES TO TALK TO US.
SHE SAYS YOU'RE ASKIN' AFTER MR. WILSON.
NOW, WHO SENT YOU?
ANSWER QUIET-LIKE, AND MEBBIE YOU'LL BE SPARED A SWIM IN THE THAMES.
LORD ABOVE.
SKCH
YOU BACK-ALLEY THUGS SURE GOT NO IMAGINATION. I COULDA WRITTEN THEM LINES FOR YA.
AH, WELL. IF YOU MUGS HAD ANY BRAINS, YOU WOULDN'T BE HERE IN THE FIRST PLACE.
SHF
WELL, AIN'T YOU GOT A MOUTH ON YE!
LET'S SEE WHAT BECOMES OF YER CHEEK ONCE WE'VE HAD OUR WAY WITH YE.
HAH! ONE GOOD CUFF, AND SHE'LL QUIET UP, REAL QUICK.
KREAK
ONE, EH? YOU SURE YOU LOT CAN COUNT THAT HIGH?

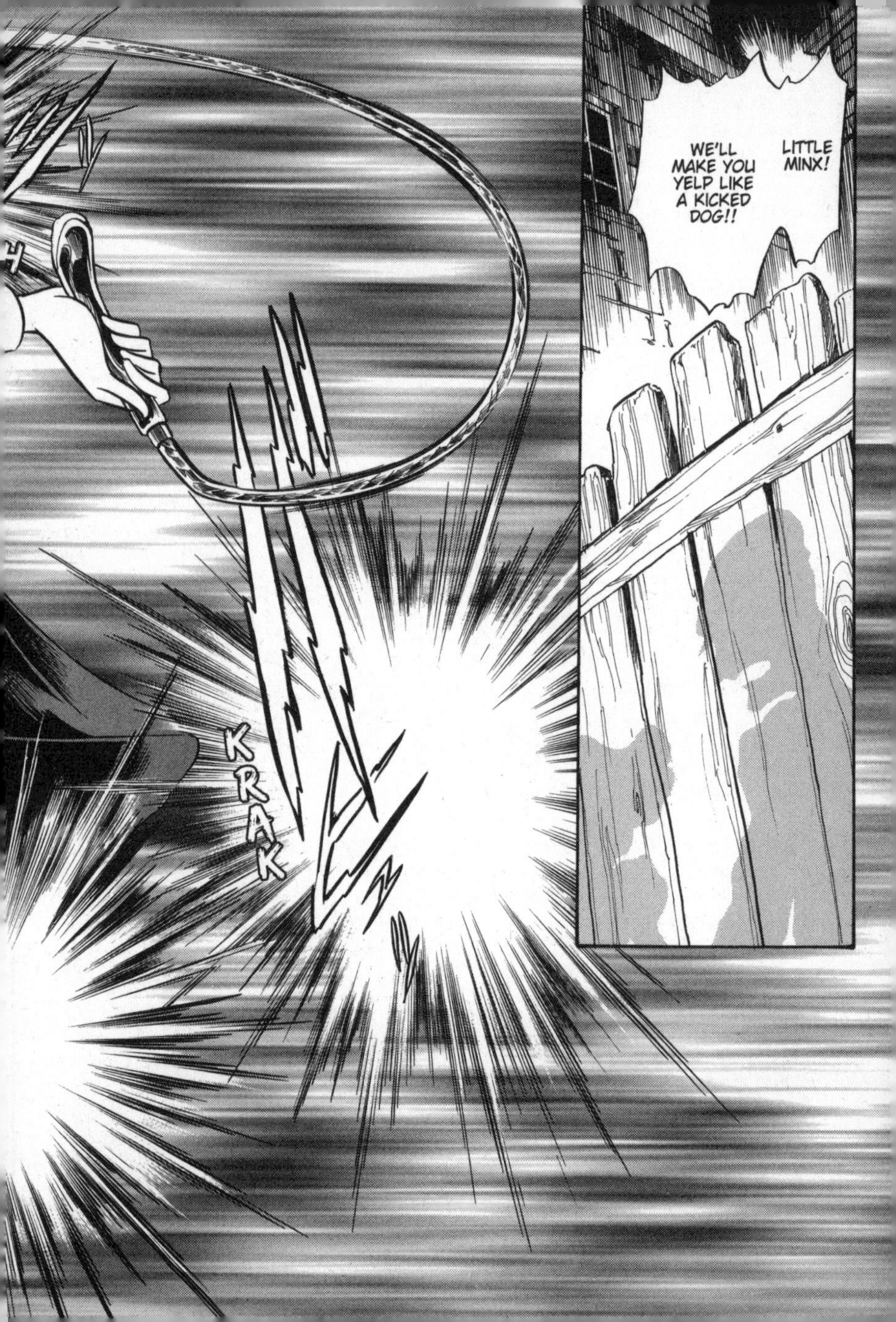
LITTLE MINX!
WE'LL MAKE YOU YELP LIKE A KICKED DOG!!
KRAK

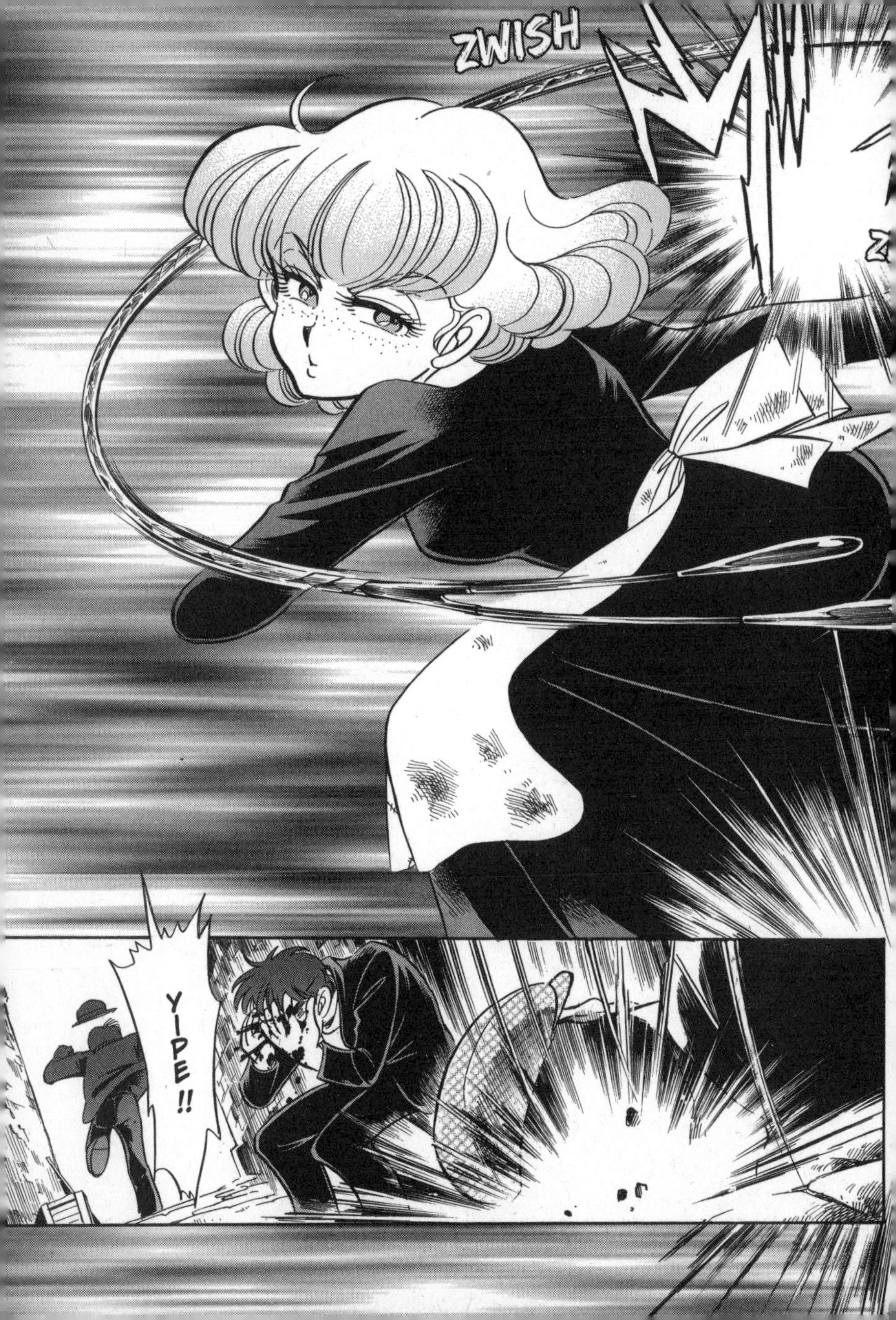
ZWISH
YIPE !!

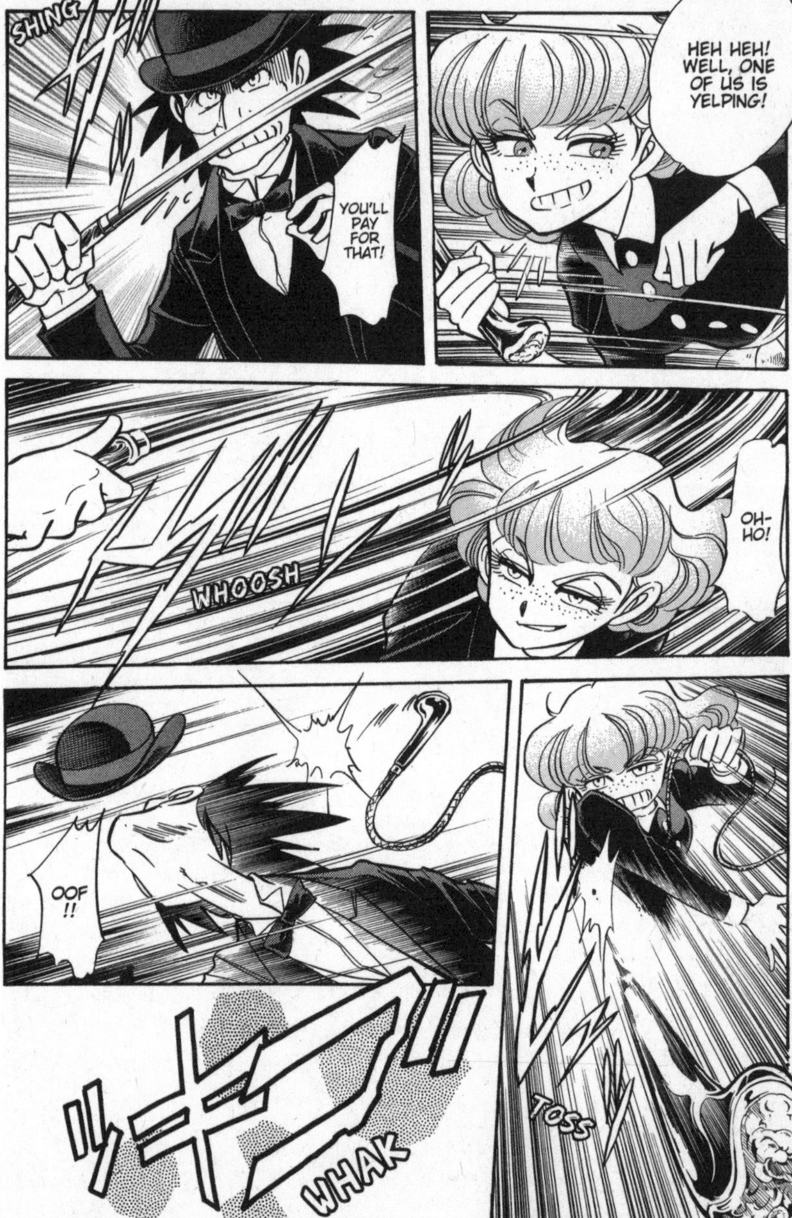
HEH HEH! WELL, ONE OF US IS YELPING!
SHING
YOU'LL PAY FOR THAT!
OH-HO!
WHOOSH
TOSS
OOF !!
WHAK

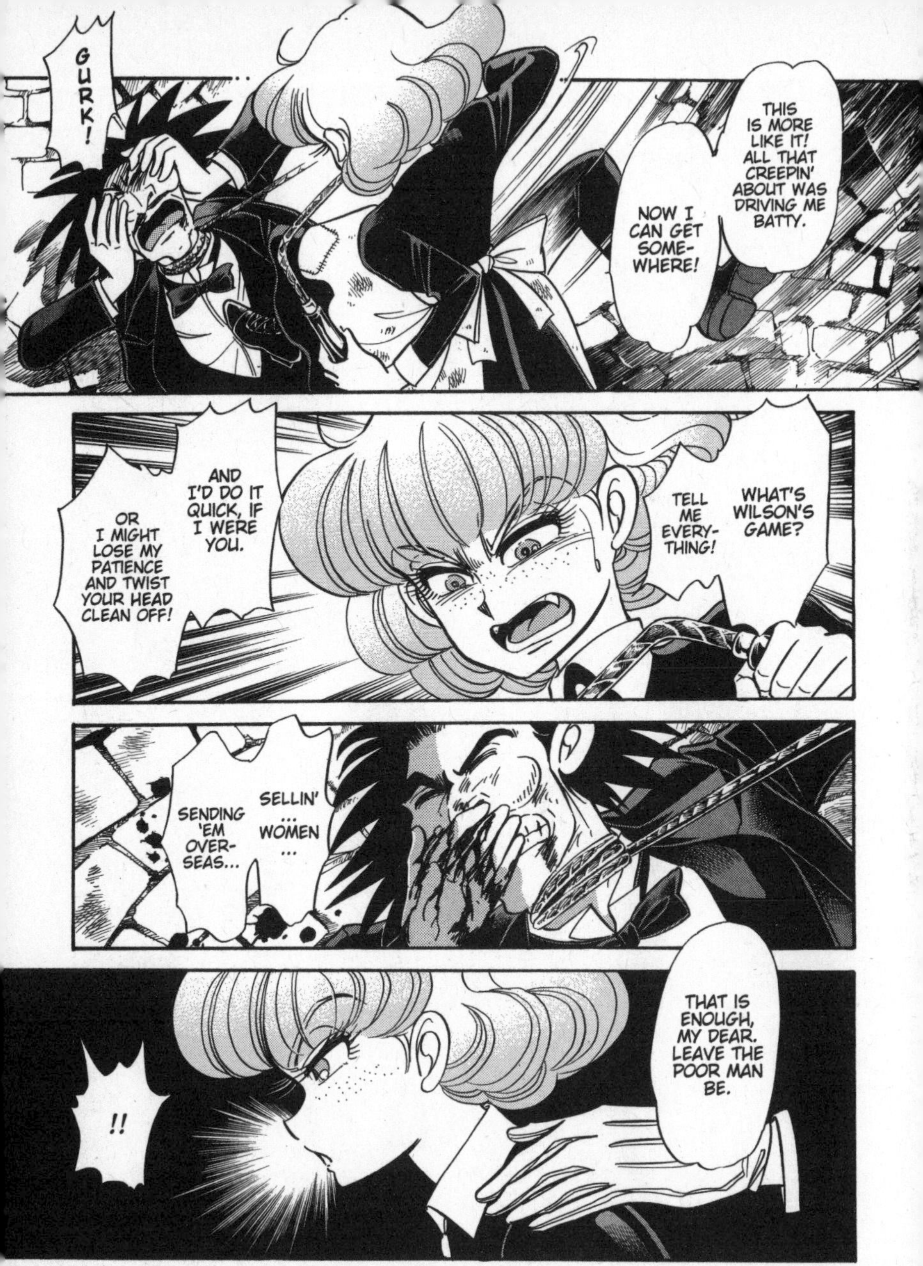
THIS IS MORE LIKE IT! ALL THAT CREEPIN' ABOUT WAS DRIVING ME BATTY.
NOW I CAN GET SOME-WHERE!
GURK! ...
WHAT'S WILSON'S GAME?
TELL ME EVERY-THING!
AND I'D DO IT QUICK, IF I WERE YOU.
OR I MIGHT LOSE MY PATIENCE AND TWIST YOUR HEAD CLEAN OFF!
SELLIN' ... WOMEN ...
SENDING 'EM OVER-SEAS...
THAT IS ENOUGH, MY DEAR. LEAVE THE POOR MAN BE.
!!

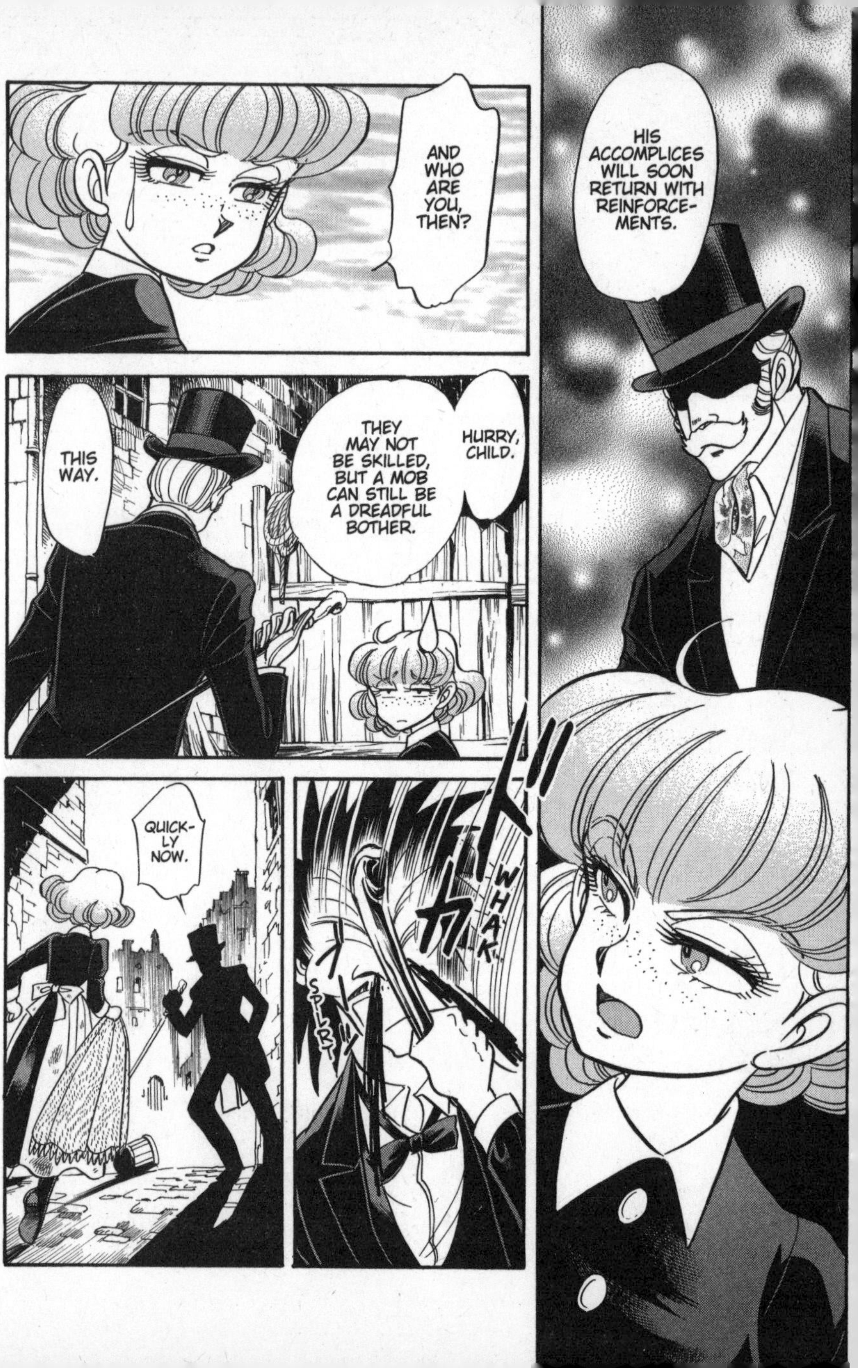
HIS ACCOMPLICES WILL SOON RETURN WITH REINFORCEMENTS.
AND WHO ARE YOU, THEN?
HURRY, CHILD.
THEY MAY NOT BE SKILLED, BUT A MOB CAN STILL BE A DREADFUL BOTHER.
THIS WAY.
WHAK
SPLRT
QUICKLY NOW.

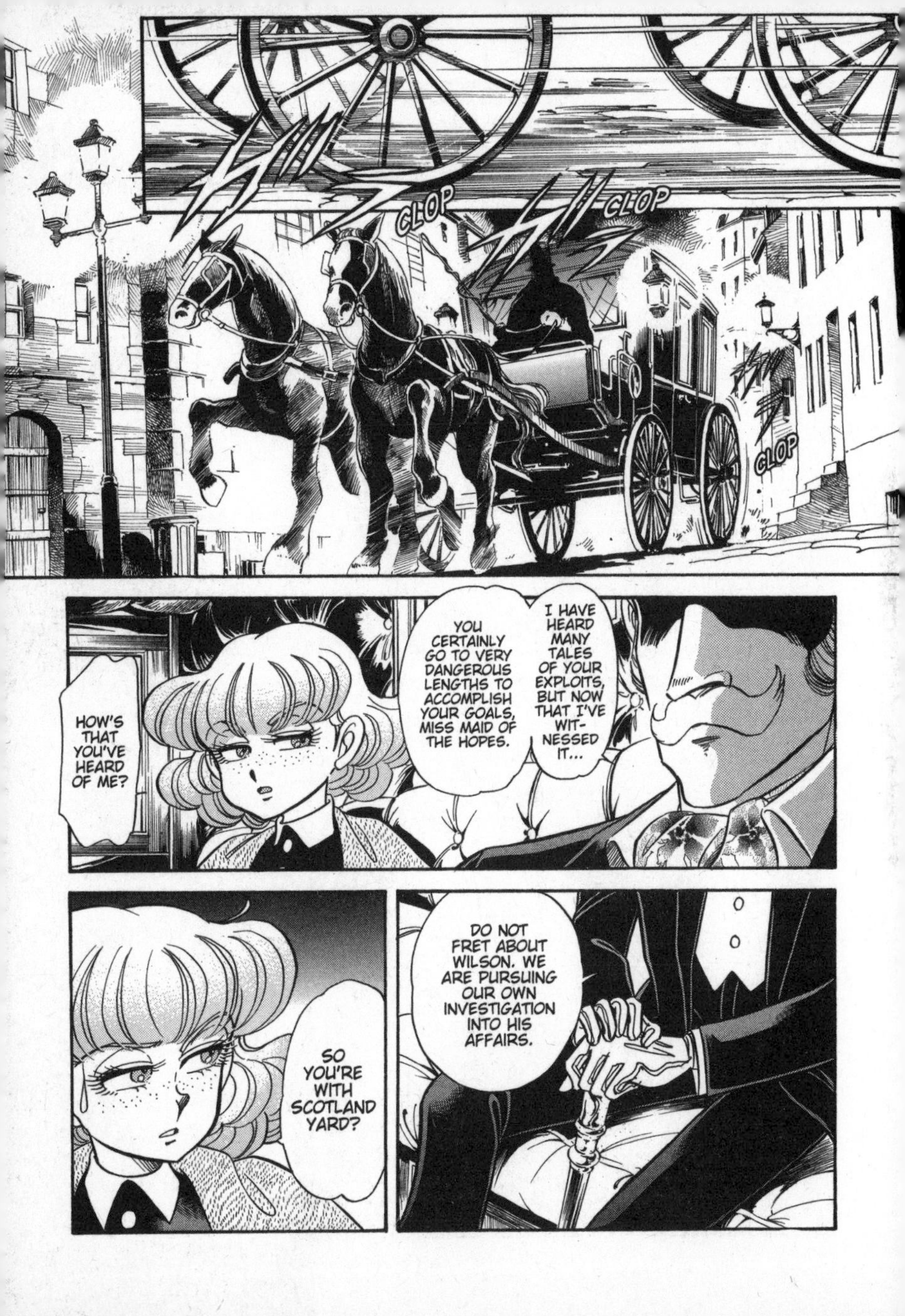
CLOP
CLOP
CLOP
I HAVE HEARD MANY TALES OF YOUR EXPLOITS, BUT NOW THAT I'VE WIT-NESSED IT...
YOU CERTAINLY GO TO VERY DANGEROUS LENGTHS TO ACCOMPLISH YOUR GOALS, MISS MAID OF THE HOPES.
HOW'S THAT YOU'VE HEARD OF ME?
DO NOT FRET ABOUT WILSON. WE ARE PURSUING OUR OWN INVESTIGATION INTO HIS AFFAIRS.
SO YOU'RE WITH SCOTLAND YARD?

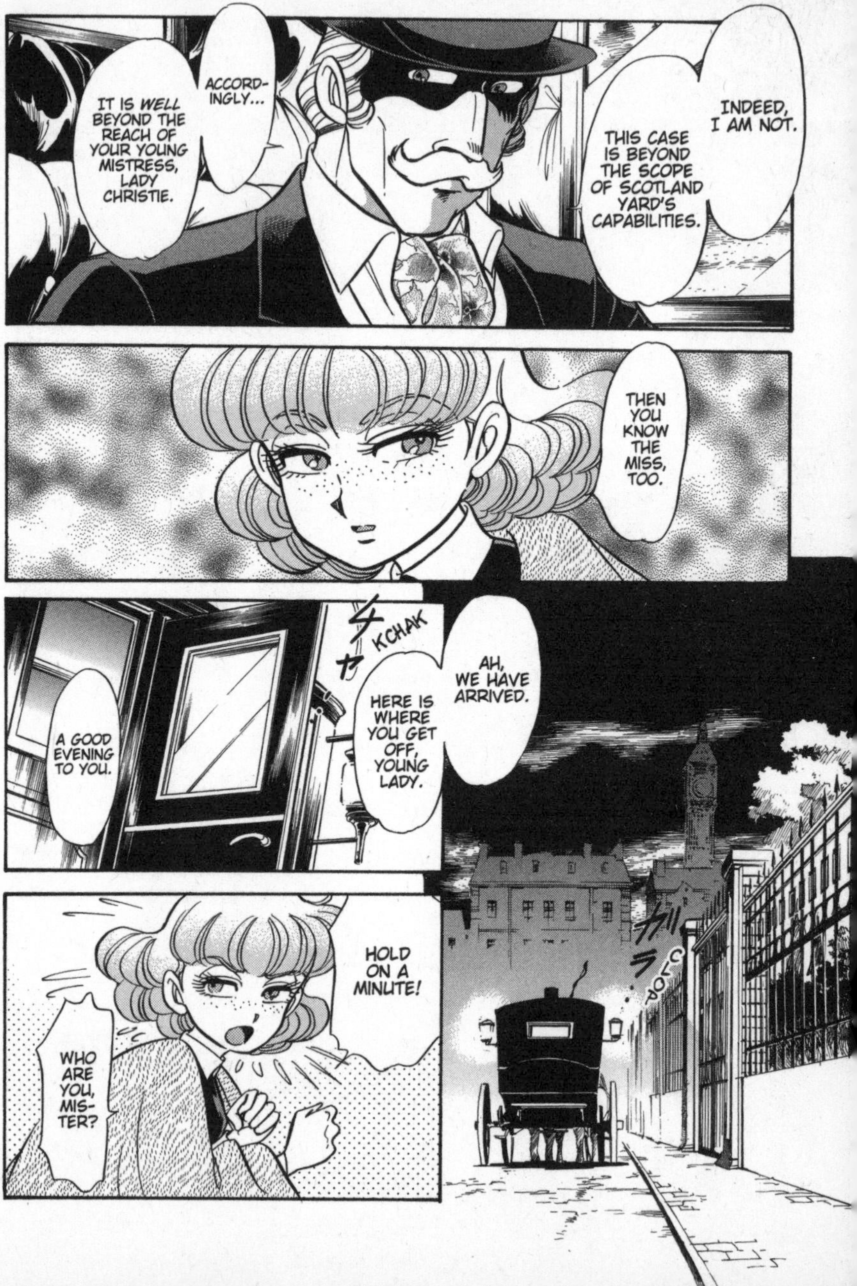
INDEED, I AM NOT.
THIS CASE IS BEYOND THE SCOPE OF SCOTLAND YARD'S CAPABILITIES.
ACCORDINGLY...
IT IS *WELL* BEYOND THE REACH OF YOUR YOUNG MISTRESS, LADY CHRISTIE.
THEN YOU KNOW THE MISS, TOO.
CLOP
KCHAK
AH, WE HAVE ARRIVED.
HERE IS WHERE YOU GET OFF, YOUNG LADY.
A GOOD EVENING TO YOU.
HOLD ON A MINUTE!
WHO ARE YOU, MISTER?

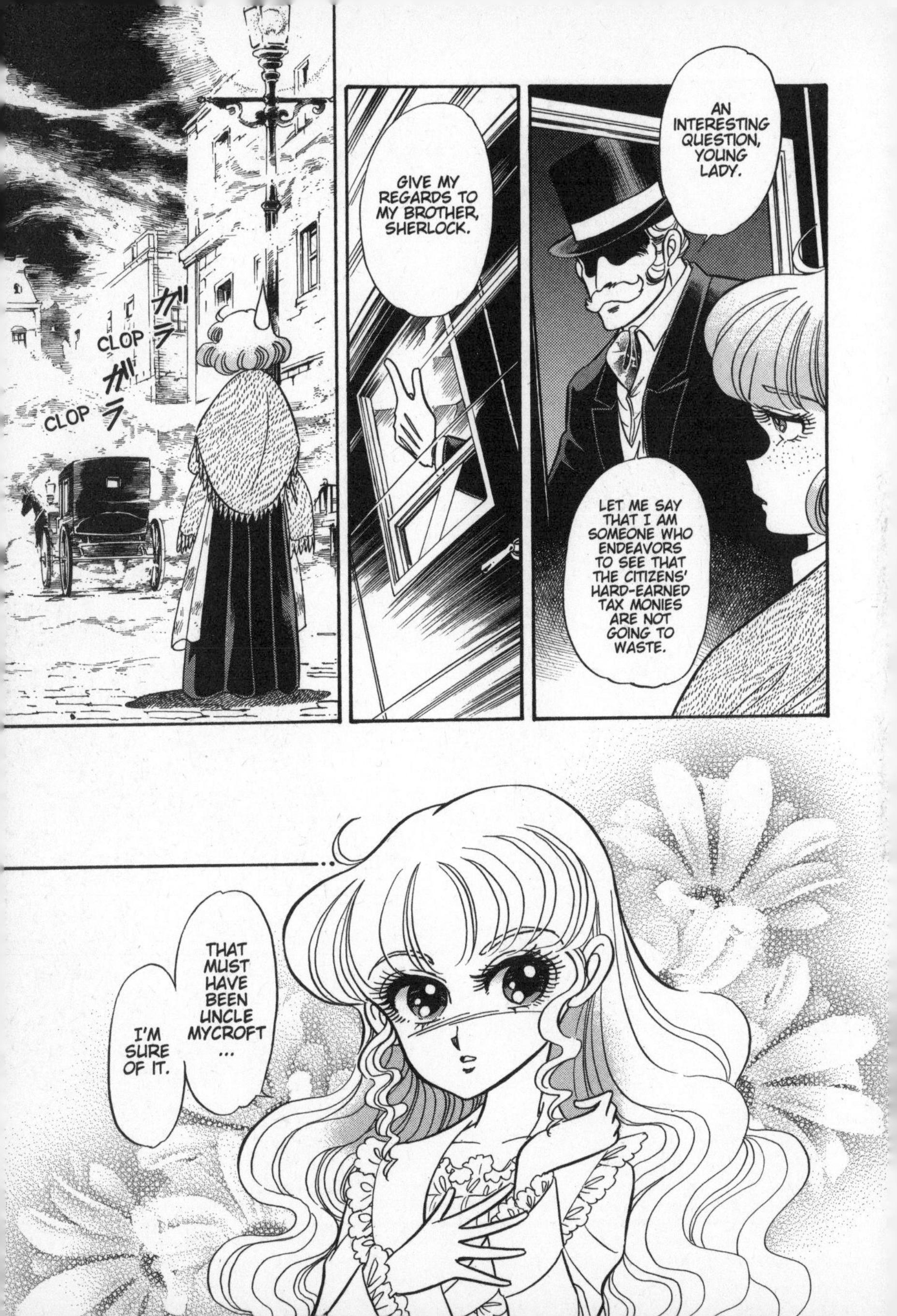
AN INTERESTING QUESTION, YOUNG LADY.
LET ME SAY THAT I AM SOMEONE WHO ENDEAVORS TO SEE THAT THE CITIZENS' HARD-EARNED TAX MONIES ARE NOT GOING TO WASTE.
GIVE MY REGARDS TO MY BROTHER, SHERLOCK.
CLOP
ガラ
CLOP
ガラ
THAT MUST HAVE BEEN UNCLE MYCROFT ...
I'M SURE OF IT.

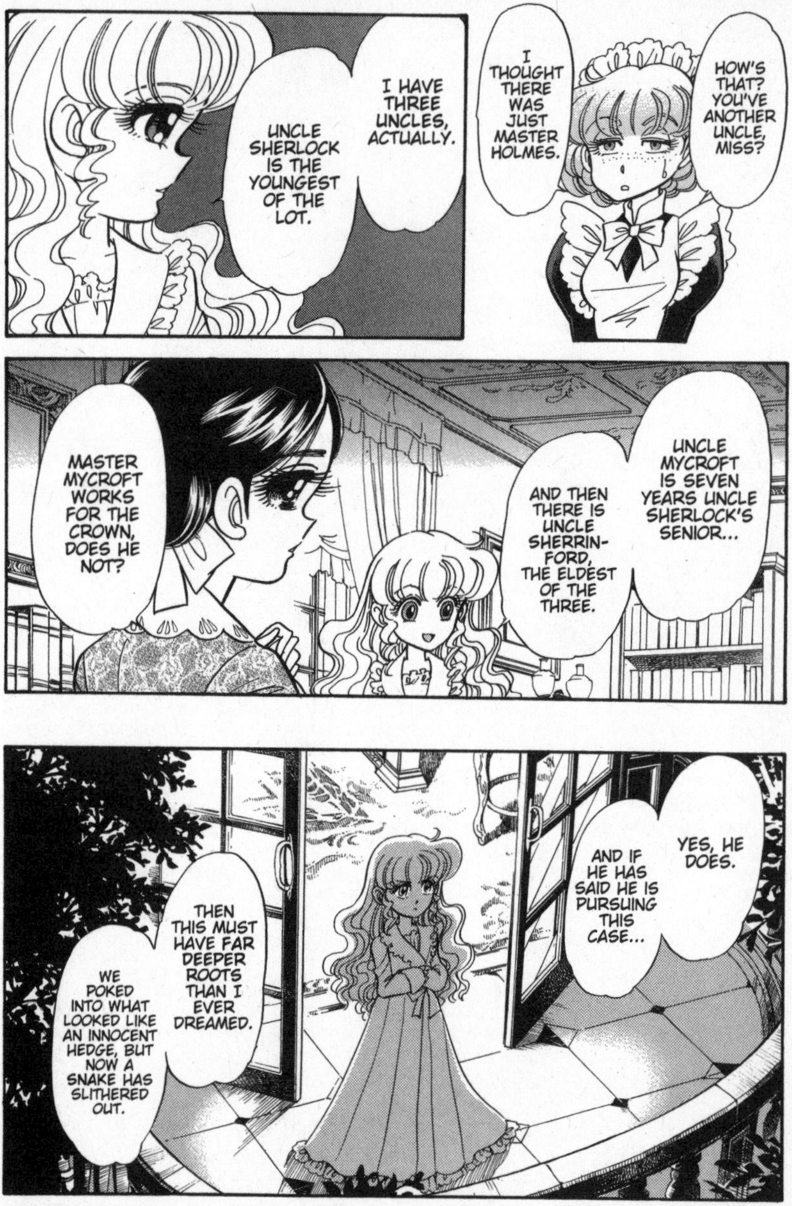
HOW'S THAT? YOU'VE ANOTHER UNCLE, MISS?
I THOUGHT THERE WAS JUST MASTER HOLMES.
I HAVE THREE UNCLES, ACTUALLY.
UNCLE SHERLOCK IS THE YOUNGEST OF THE LOT.
UNCLE MYCROFT IS SEVEN YEARS UNCLE SHERLOCK'S SENIOR...
AND THEN THERE IS UNCLE SHERRIN-FORD, THE ELDEST OF THE THREE.
MASTER MYCROFT WORKS FOR THE CROWN, DOES HE NOT?
YES, HE DOES.
AND IF HE HAS SAID HE IS PURSUING THIS CASE...
THEN THIS MUST HAVE FAR DEEPER ROOTS THAN I EVER DREAMED.
WE POKED INTO WHAT LOOKED LIKE AN INNOCENT HEDGE, BUT NOW A SNAKE HAS SLITHERED OUT.

The Adventure of the Famous Trainer (5)

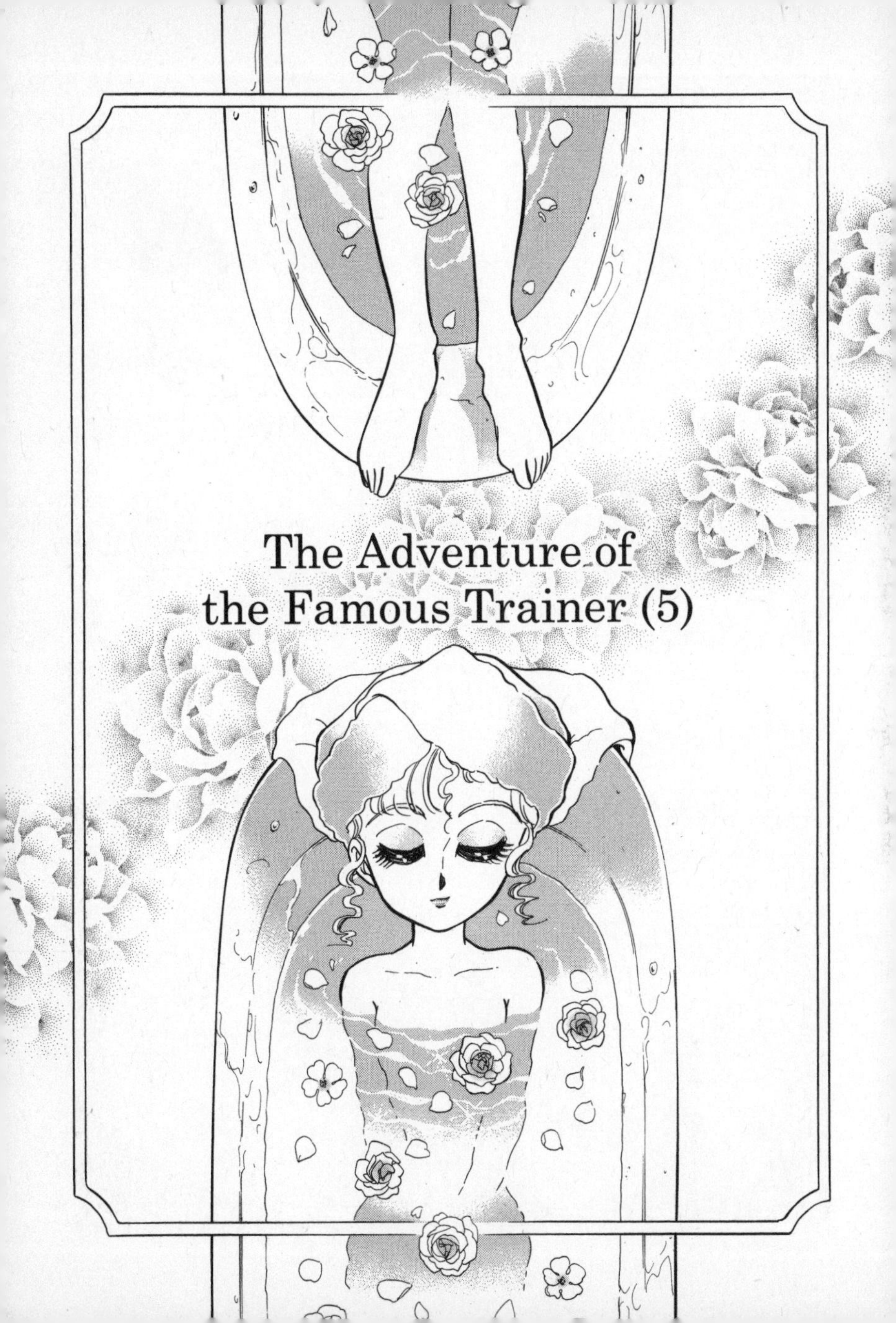

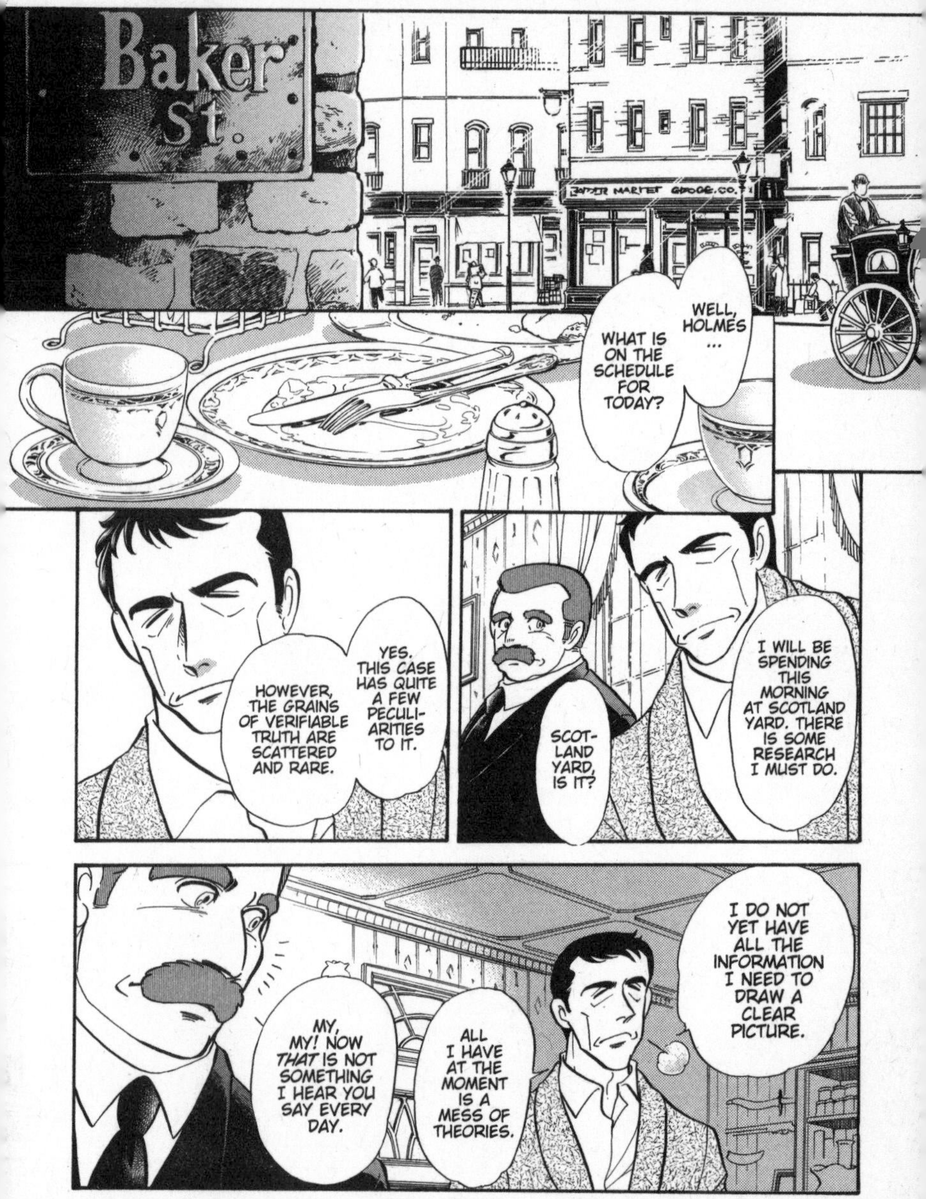
Baker St.
WELL, HOLMES ...
WHAT IS ON THE SCHEDULE FOR TODAY?
I WILL BE SPENDING THIS MORNING AT SCOTLAND YARD. THERE IS SOME RESEARCH I MUST DO.
SCOTLAND YARD, IS IT?
YES. THIS CASE HAS QUITE A FEW PECULIARITIES TO IT.
HOWEVER, THE GRAINS OF VERIFIABLE TRUTH ARE SCATTERED AND RARE.
I DO NOT YET HAVE ALL THE INFORMATION I NEED TO DRAW A CLEAR PICTURE.
ALL I HAVE AT THE MOMENT IS A MESS OF THEORIES.
MY, MY! NOW *THAT* IS NOT SOMETHING I HEAR YOU SAY EVERY DAY.

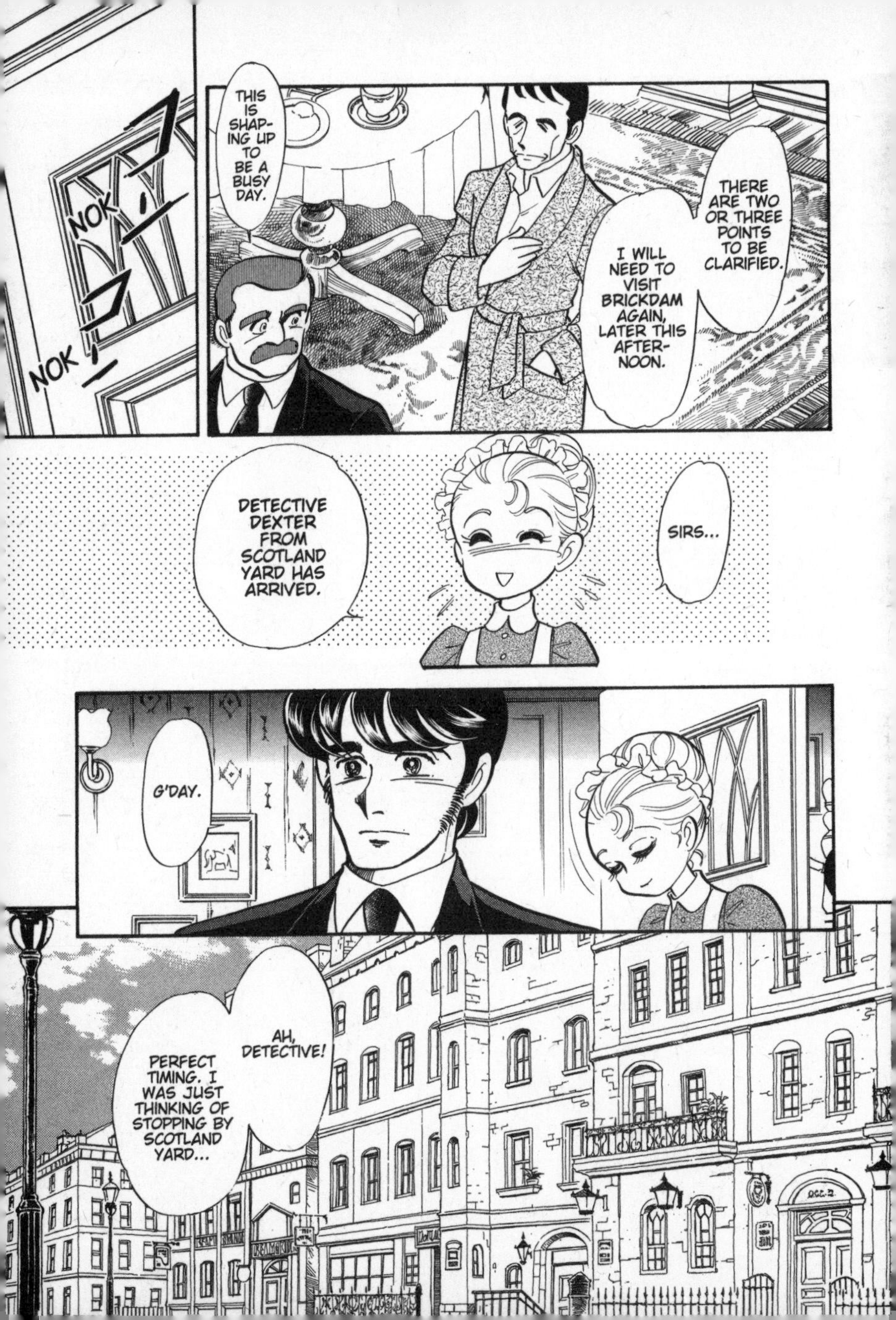
THERE ARE TWO OR THREE POINTS TO BE CLARIFIED.
I WILL NEED TO VISIT BRICKDAM AGAIN, LATER THIS AFTER-NOON.
THIS IS SHAP-ING UP TO BE A BUSY DAY.
NOK
NOK
SIRS...
DETECTIVE DEXTER FROM SCOTLAND YARD HAS ARRIVED.
G'DAY.
AH, DETECTIVE!
PERFECT TIMING. I WAS JUST THINKING OF STOPPING BY SCOTLAND YARD...

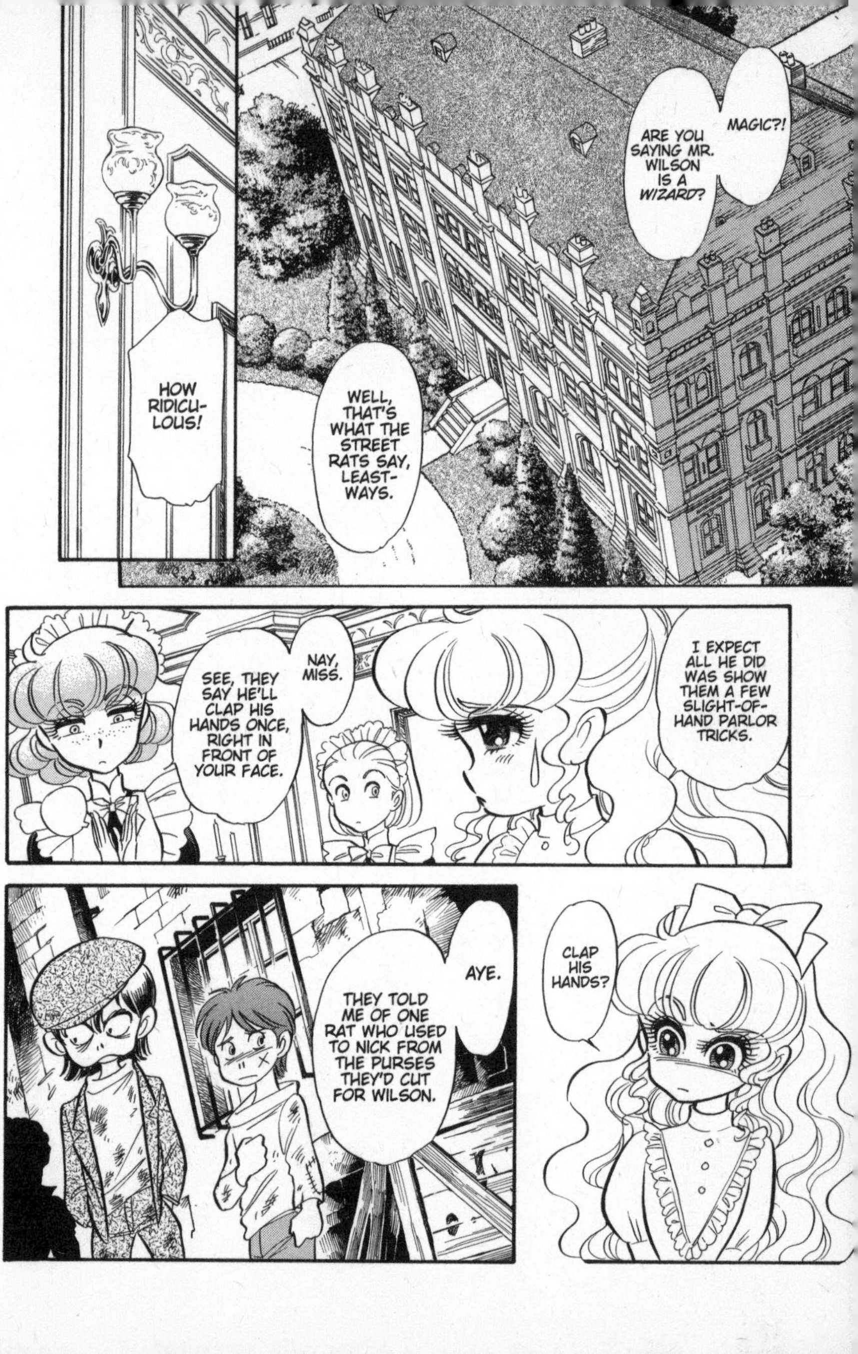
MAGIC?!
ARE YOU SAYING MR. WILSON IS A WIZARD?
WELL, THAT'S WHAT THE STREET RATS SAY, LEASTWAYS.
HOW RIDICULOUS!
I EXPECT ALL HE DID WAS SHOW THEM A FEW SLIGHT-OF-HAND PARLOR TRICKS.
NAY, MISS.
SEE, THEY SAY HE'LL CLAP HIS HANDS ONCE, RIGHT IN FRONT OF YOUR FACE.
CLAP HIS HANDS?
AYE.
THEY TOLD ME OF ONE RAT WHO USED TO NICK FROM THE PURSES THEY'D CUT FOR WILSON.

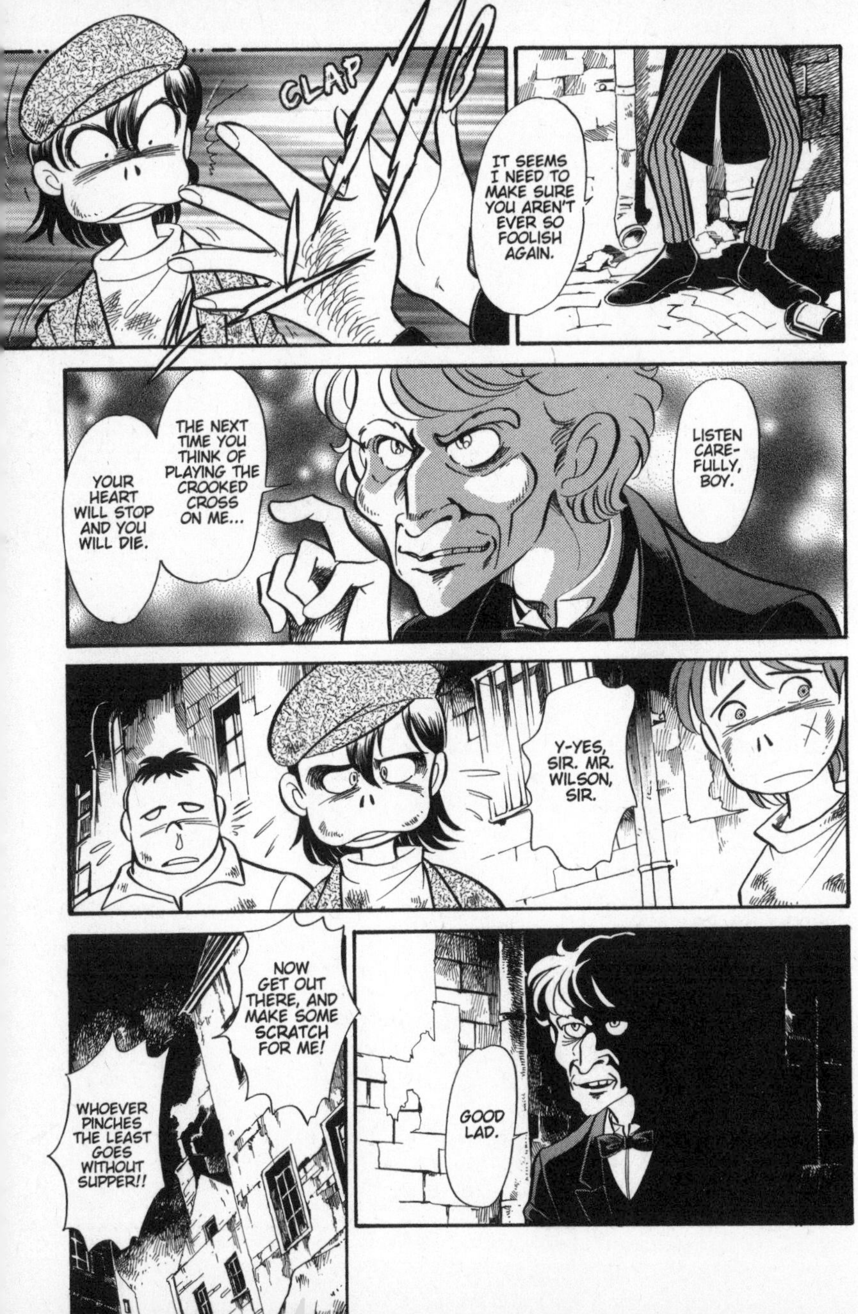
IT SEEMS I NEED TO MAKE SURE YOU AREN'T EVER SO FOOLISH AGAIN.
CLAP
LISTEN CARE-FULLY, BOY.
THE NEXT TIME YOU THINK OF PLAYING THE CROOKED CROSS ON ME...
YOUR HEART WILL STOP AND YOU WILL DIE.
Y-YES, SIR. MR. WILSON, SIR.
GOOD LAD.
NOW GET OUT THERE, AND MAKE SOME SCRATCH FOR ME!
WHOEVER PINCHES THE LEAST GOES WITHOUT SUPPER!!

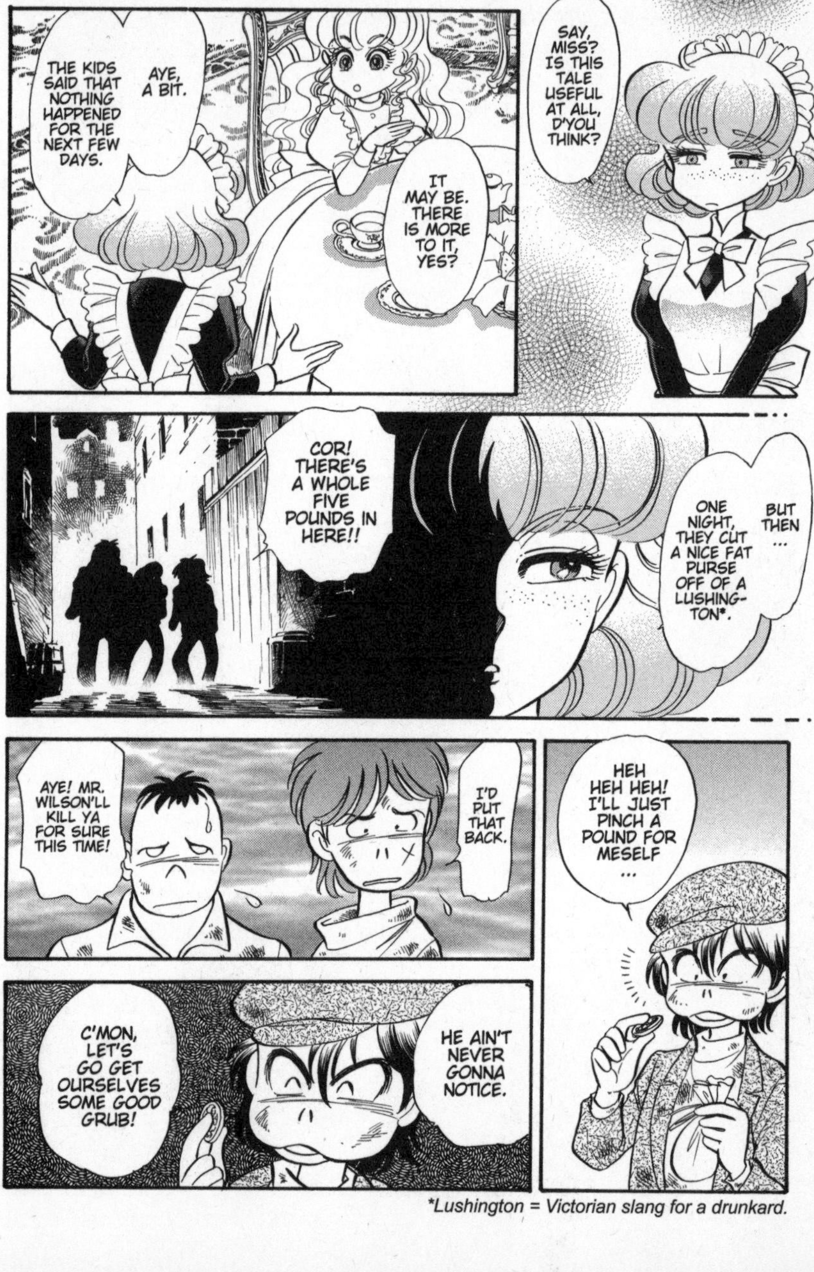
SAY, MISS? IS THIS TALE USEFUL AT ALL, D'YOU THINK?
IT MAY BE. THERE IS MORE TO IT, YES?
AYE, A BIT.
THE KIDS SAID THAT NOTHING HAPPENED FOR THE NEXT FEW DAYS.
BUT THEN ...
ONE NIGHT, THEY CUT A NICE FAT PURSE OFF OF A LUSHINGTON*.
COR! THERE'S A WHOLE FIVE POUNDS IN HERE!!
HEH HEH HEH! I'LL JUST PINCH A POUND FOR MESELF ...
I'D PUT THAT BACK.
AYE! MR. WILSON'LL KILL YA FOR SURE THIS TIME!
HE AIN'T NEVER GONNA NOTICE.
C'MON, LET'S GO GET OURSELVES SOME GOOD GRUB!

**Lushington = Victorian slang for a drunkard.*

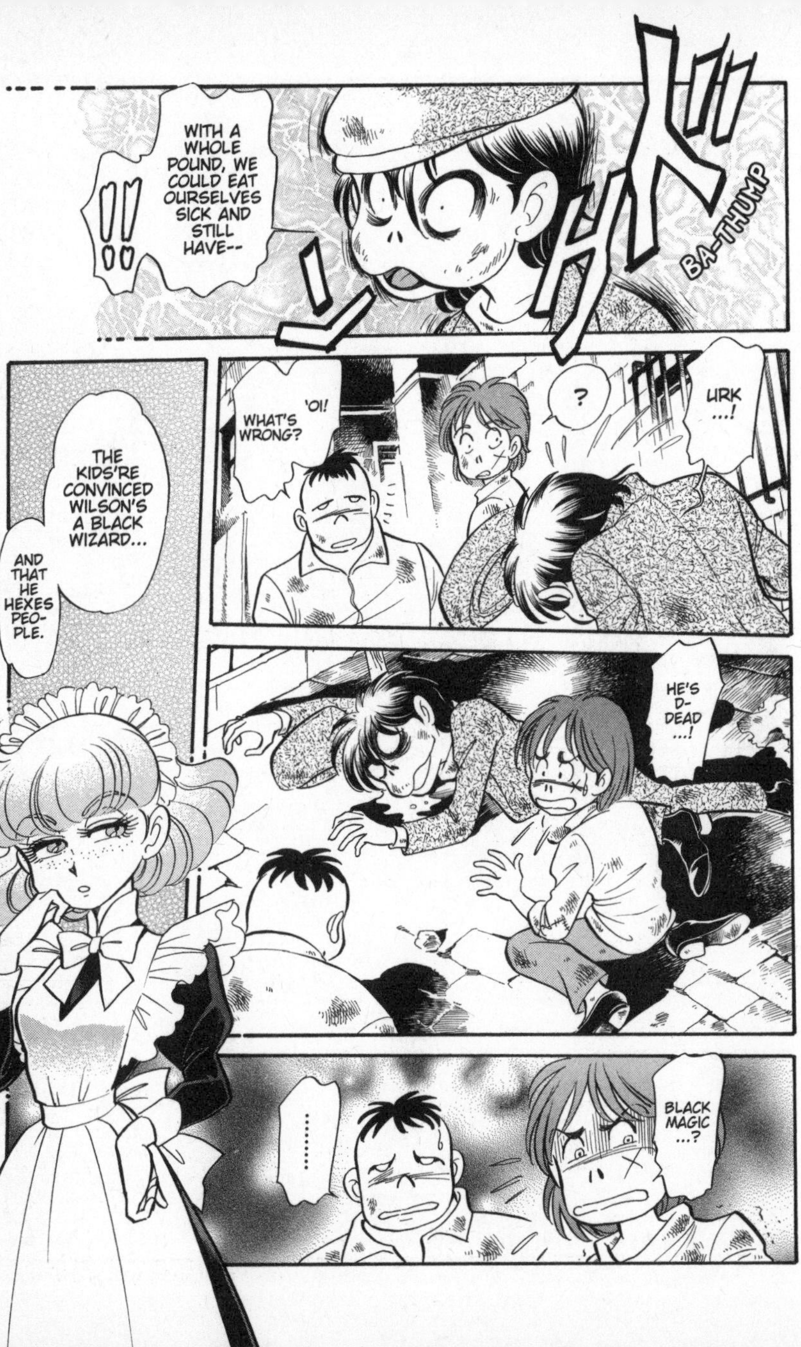
BA-THUMP
WITH A WHOLE POUND, WE COULD EAT OURSELVES SICK AND STILL HAVE--
!!
URK ...!
?
'OI! WHAT'S WRONG?
HE'S D-DEAD ...!
BLACK MAGIC ...?
....
THE KIDS'RE CONVINCED WILSON'S A BLACK WIZARD...
AND THAT HE HEXES PEO-PLE.

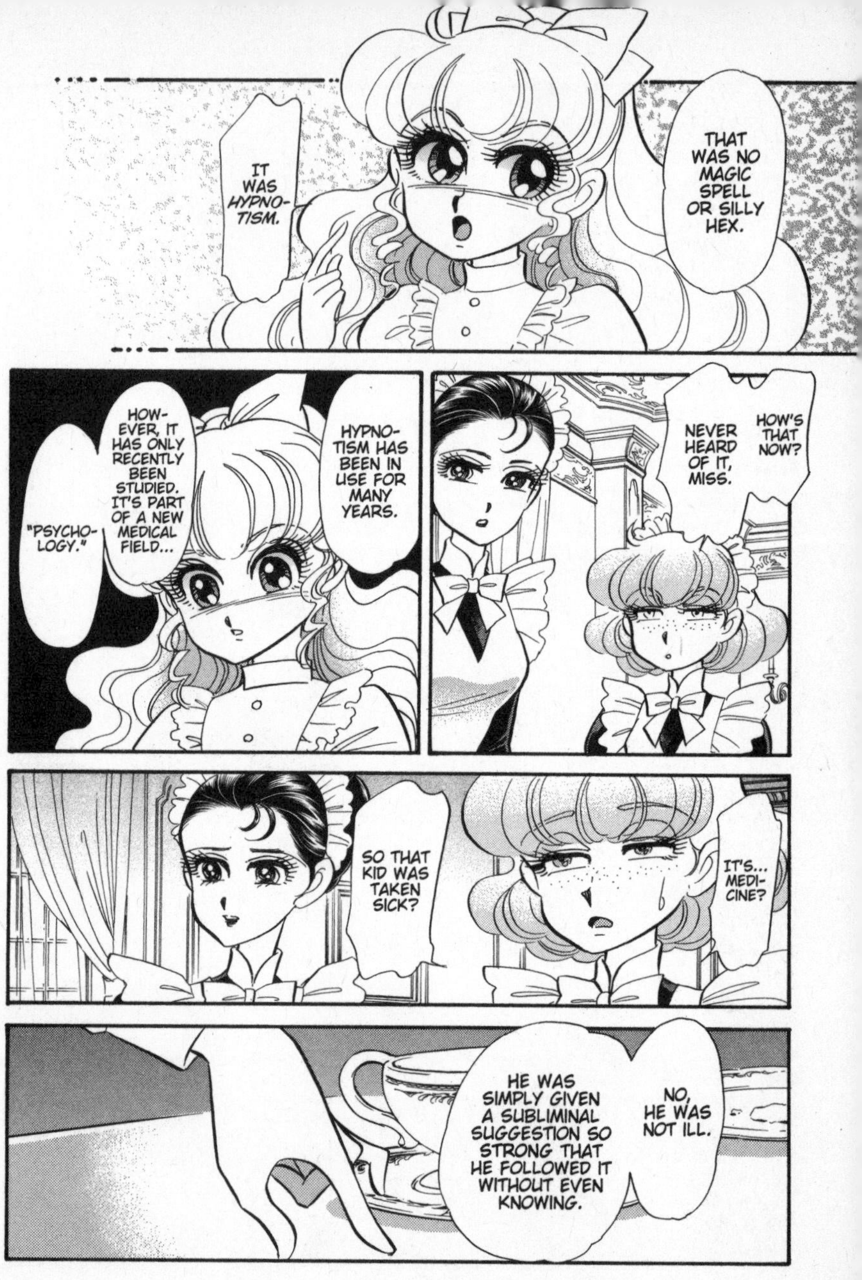
THAT WAS NO MAGIC SPELL OR SILLY HEX.
IT WAS HYPNOTISM.
HOW'S THAT NOW?
NEVER HEARD OF IT, MISS.
HYPNOTISM HAS BEEN IN USE FOR MANY YEARS.
HOWEVER, IT HAS ONLY RECENTLY BEEN STUDIED. IT'S PART OF A NEW MEDICAL FIELD...
"PSYCHOLOGY."
IT'S... MEDICINE?
SO THAT KID WAS TAKEN SICK?
NO, HE WAS NOT ILL.
HE WAS SIMPLY GIVEN A SUBLIMINAL SUGGESTION SO STRONG THAT HE FOLLOWED IT WITHOUT EVEN KNOWING.

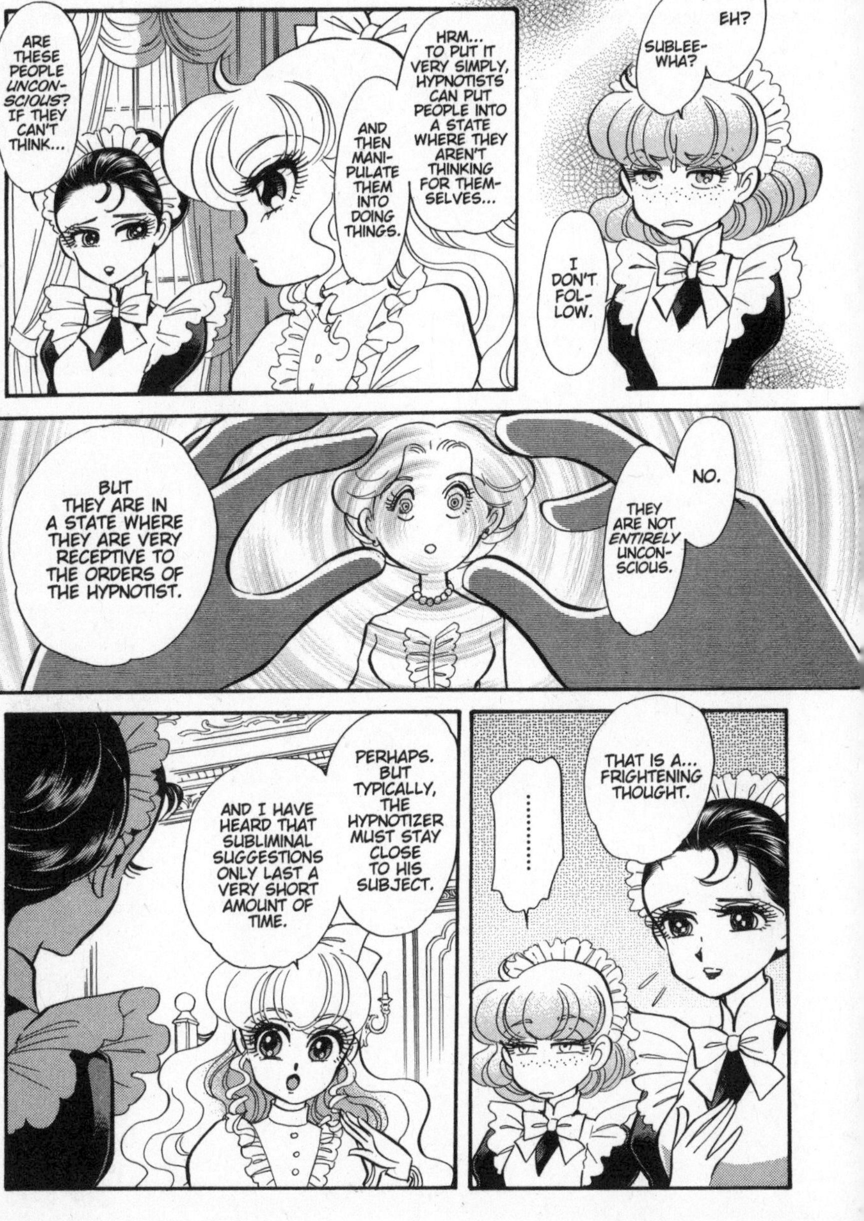
EH? SUBLEE-WHA?
I DON'T FOL-LOW.
HRM... TO PUT IT VERY SIMPLY, HYPNOTISTS CAN PUT PEOPLE INTO A STATE WHERE THEY AREN'T THINKING FOR THEM-SELVES...
AND THEN MANI-PULATE THEM INTO DOING THINGS.
ARE THESE PEOPLE *UNCON-SCIOUS?* IF THEY CAN'T THINK...
NO.
THEY ARE NOT *ENTIRELY* UNCON-SCIOUS.
BUT THEY ARE IN A STATE WHERE THEY ARE VERY RECEPTIVE TO THE ORDERS OF THE HYPNOTIST.
THAT IS A... FRIGHTENING THOUGHT.
....
PERHAPS. BUT TYPICALLY, THE HYPNOTIZER MUST STAY CLOSE TO HIS SUBJECT.
AND I HAVE HEARD THAT SUBLIMINAL SUGGESTIONS ONLY LAST A VERY SHORT AMOUNT OF TIME.

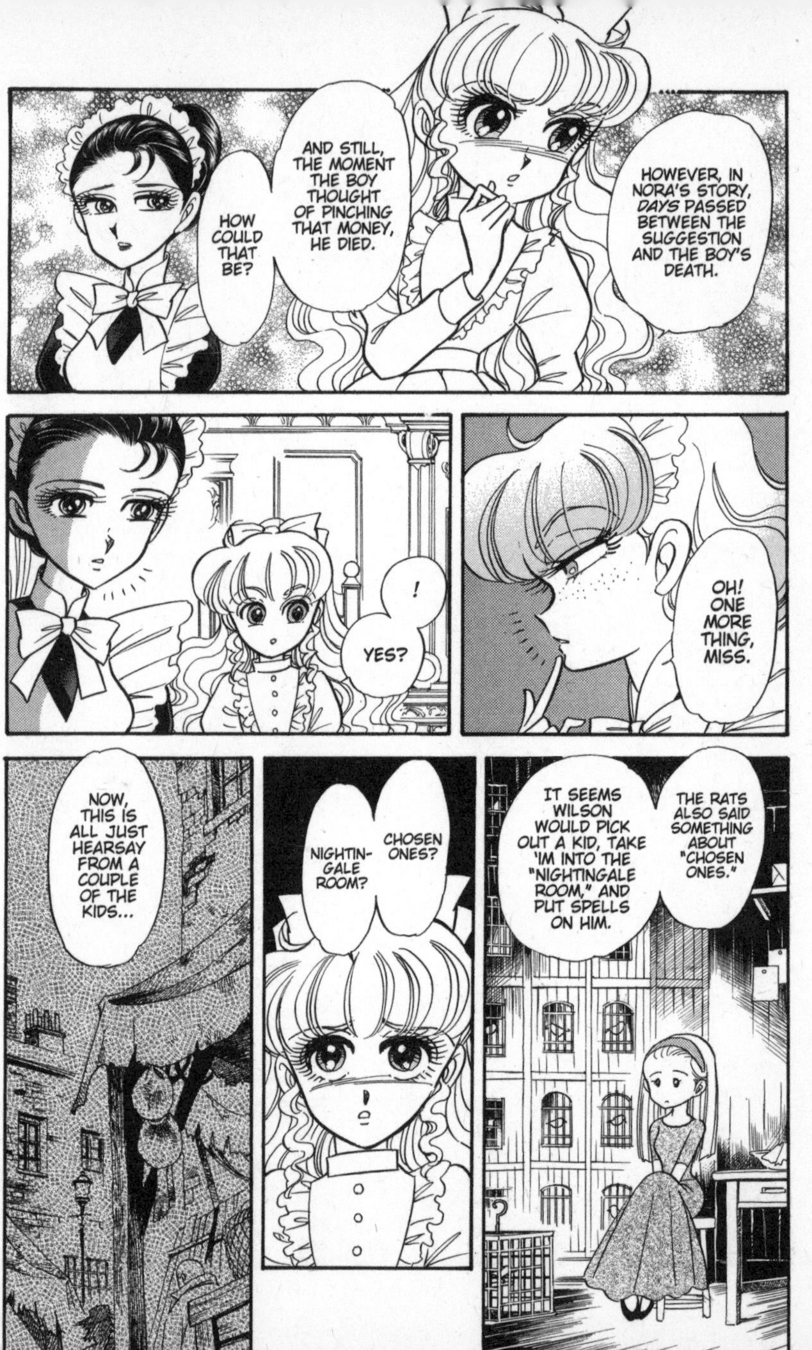
HOWEVER, IN NORA'S STORY, *DAYS* PASSED BETWEEN THE SUGGESTION AND THE BOY'S DEATH.
AND STILL, THE MOMENT THE BOY THOUGHT OF PINCHING THAT MONEY, HE DIED.
HOW COULD THAT BE?
OH! ONE MORE THING, MISS.
!
YES?
THE RATS ALSO SAID SOMETHING ABOUT "CHOSEN ONES."
IT SEEMS WILSON WOULD PICK OUT A KID, TAKE 'IM INTO THE "NIGHTINGALE ROOM," AND PUT SPELLS ON HIM.
CHOSEN ONES?
NIGHTIN-GALE ROOM?
NOW, THIS IS ALL JUST HEARSAY FROM A COUPLE OF THE KIDS...

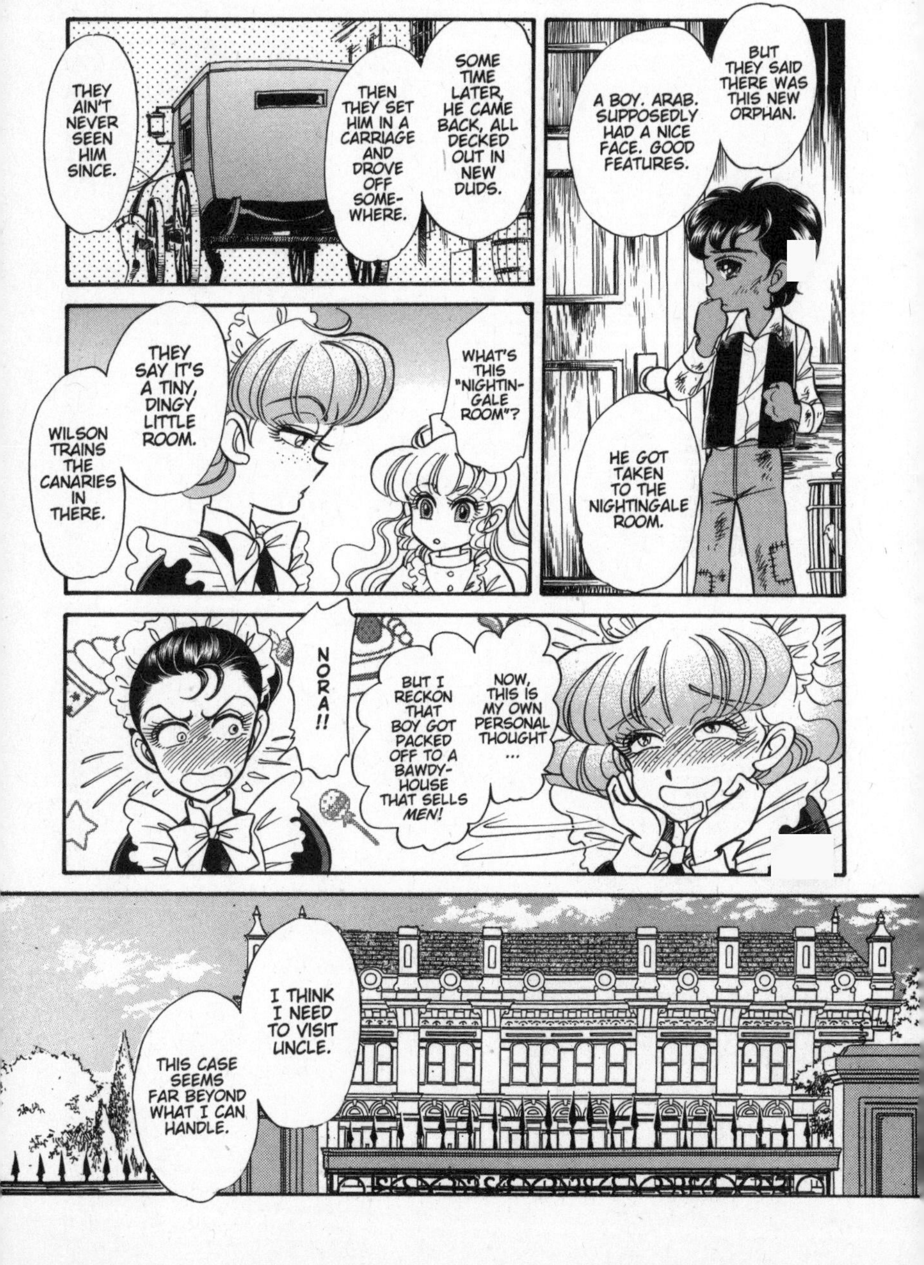
BUT THEY SAID THERE WAS THIS NEW ORPHAN.
A BOY. ARAB. SUPPOSEDLY HAD A NICE FACE. GOOD FEATURES.
HE GOT TAKEN TO THE NIGHTINGALE ROOM.
SOME TIME LATER, HE CAME BACK, ALL DECKED OUT IN NEW DUDS.
THEN THEY SET HIM IN A CARRIAGE AND DROVE OFF SOME-WHERE.
THEY AIN'T NEVER SEEN HIM SINCE.
WHAT'S THIS "NIGHTIN-GALE ROOM"?
THEY SAY IT'S A TINY, DINGY LITTLE ROOM.
WILSON TRAINS THE CANARIES IN THERE.
NOW, THIS IS MY OWN PERSONAL THOUGHT ...
BUT I RECKON THAT BOY GOT PACKED OFF TO A BAWDY-HOUSE THAT SELLS *MEN!*
NORA!!
I THINK I NEED TO VISIT UNCLE.
THIS CASE SEEMS FAR BEYOND WHAT I CAN HANDLE.

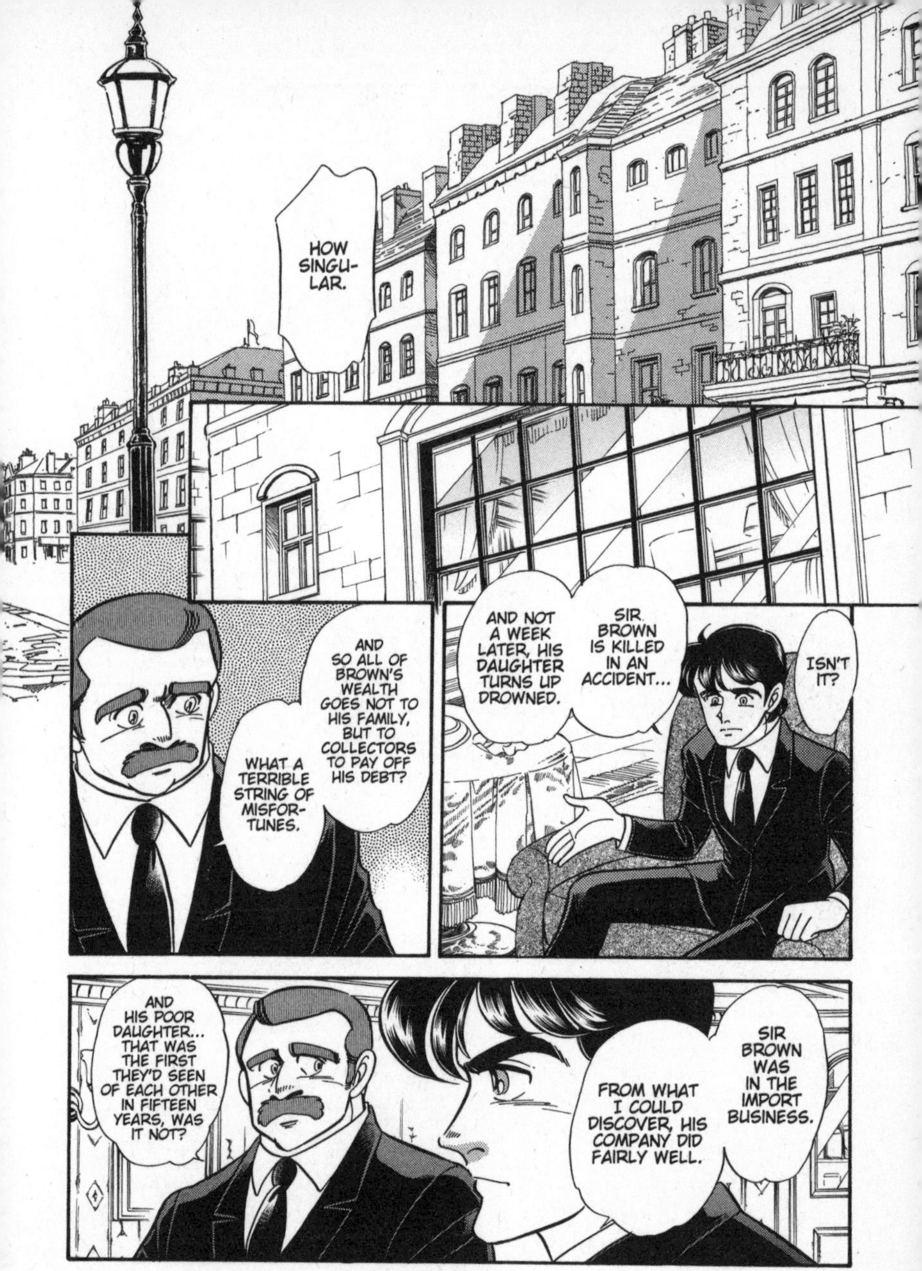
HOW SINGU-LAR.
ISN'T IT?
SIR BROWN IS KILLED IN AN ACCIDENT...
AND NOT A WEEK LATER, HIS DAUGHTER TURNS UP DROWNED.
AND SO ALL OF BROWN'S WEALTH GOES NOT TO HIS FAMILY, BUT TO COLLECTORS TO PAY OFF HIS DEBT?
WHAT A TERRIBLE STRING OF MISFOR-TUNES.
SIR BROWN WAS IN THE IMPORT BUSINESS.
FROM WHAT I COULD DISCOVER, HIS COMPANY DID FAIRLY WELL.
AND HIS POOR DAUGHTER... THAT WAS THE FIRST THEY'D SEEN OF EACH OTHER IN FIFTEEN YEARS, WAS IT NOT?

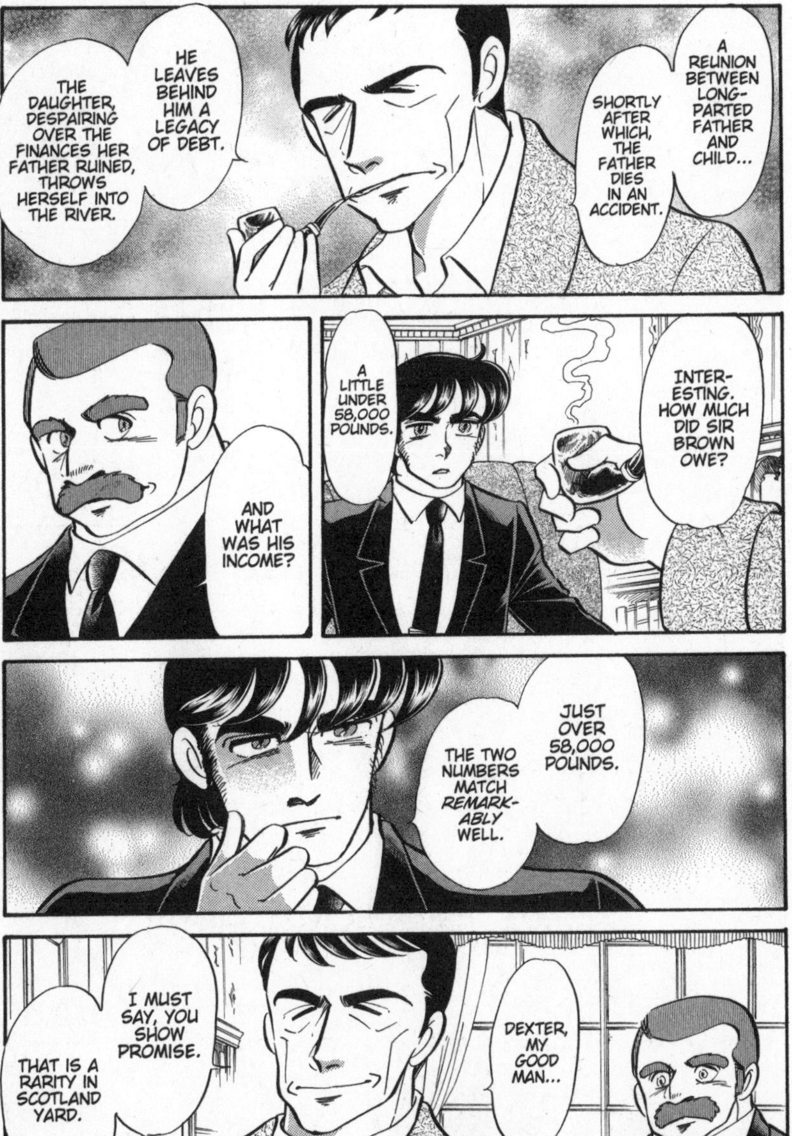
A REUNION BETWEEN LONG-PARTED FATHER AND CHILD...
SHORTLY AFTER WHICH, THE FATHER DIES IN AN ACCIDENT.
HE LEAVES BEHIND HIM A LEGACY OF DEBT.
THE DAUGHTER, DESPAIRING OVER THE FINANCES HER FATHER RUINED, THROWS HERSELF INTO THE RIVER.
INTERESTING. HOW MUCH DID SIR BROWN OWE?
A LITTLE UNDER 58,000 POUNDS.
AND WHAT WAS HIS INCOME?
JUST OVER 58,000 POUNDS.
THE TWO NUMBERS MATCH *REMARKABLY* WELL.
DEXTER, MY GOOD MAN...
I MUST SAY, YOU SHOW PROMISE.
THAT IS A RARITY IN SCOTLAND YARD.

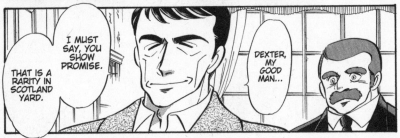

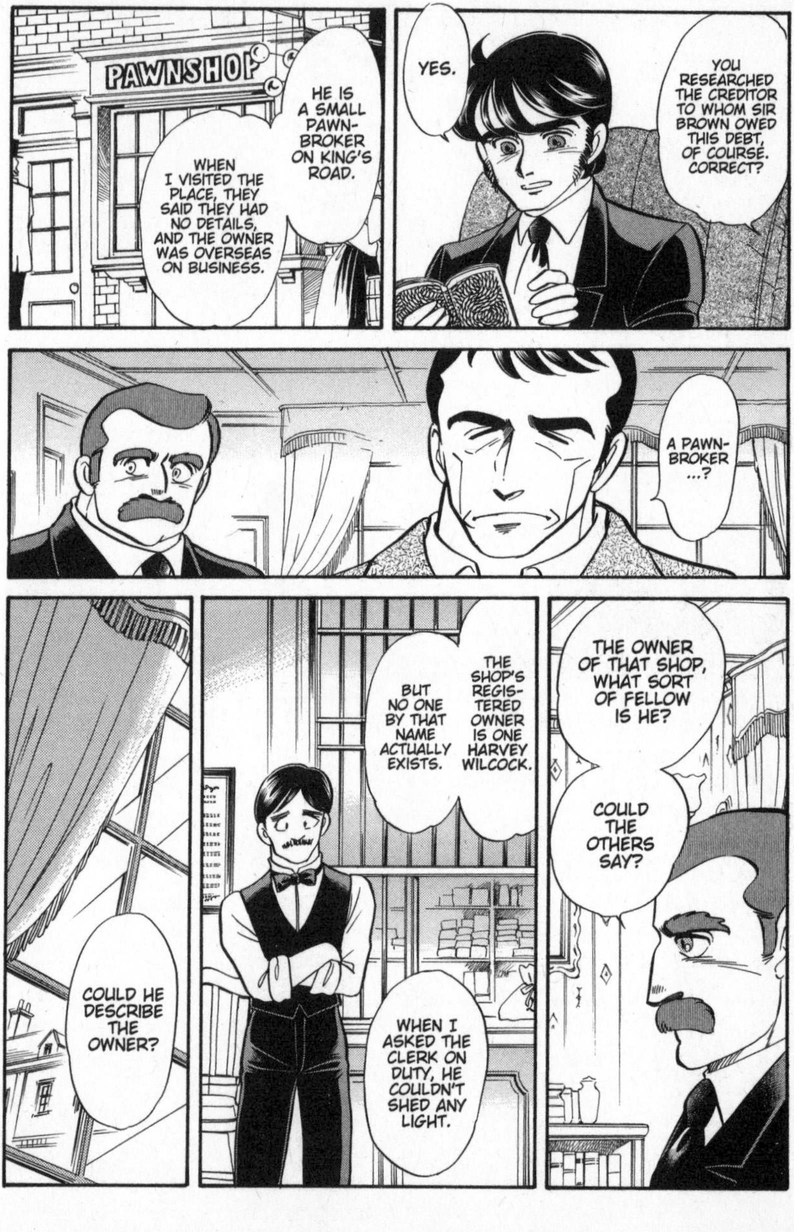
YOU RESEARCHED THE CREDITOR TO WHOM SIR BROWN OWED THIS DEBT, OF COURSE. CORRECT?
YES.
PAWNSHOP
HE IS A SMALL PAWN-BROKER ON KING'S ROAD.
WHEN I VISITED THE PLACE, THEY SAID THEY HAD NO DETAILS, AND THE OWNER WAS OVERSEAS ON BUSINESS.
A PAWN-BROKER ...?
THE OWNER OF THAT SHOP, WHAT SORT OF FELLOW IS HE?
COULD THE OTHERS SAY?
THE SHOP'S REGIS-TERED OWNER IS ONE HARVEY WILCOCK.
BUT NO ONE BY THAT NAME ACTUALLY EXISTS.
WHEN I ASKED THE CLERK ON DUTY, HE COULDN'T SHED ANY LIGHT.
COULD HE DESCRIBE THE OWNER?

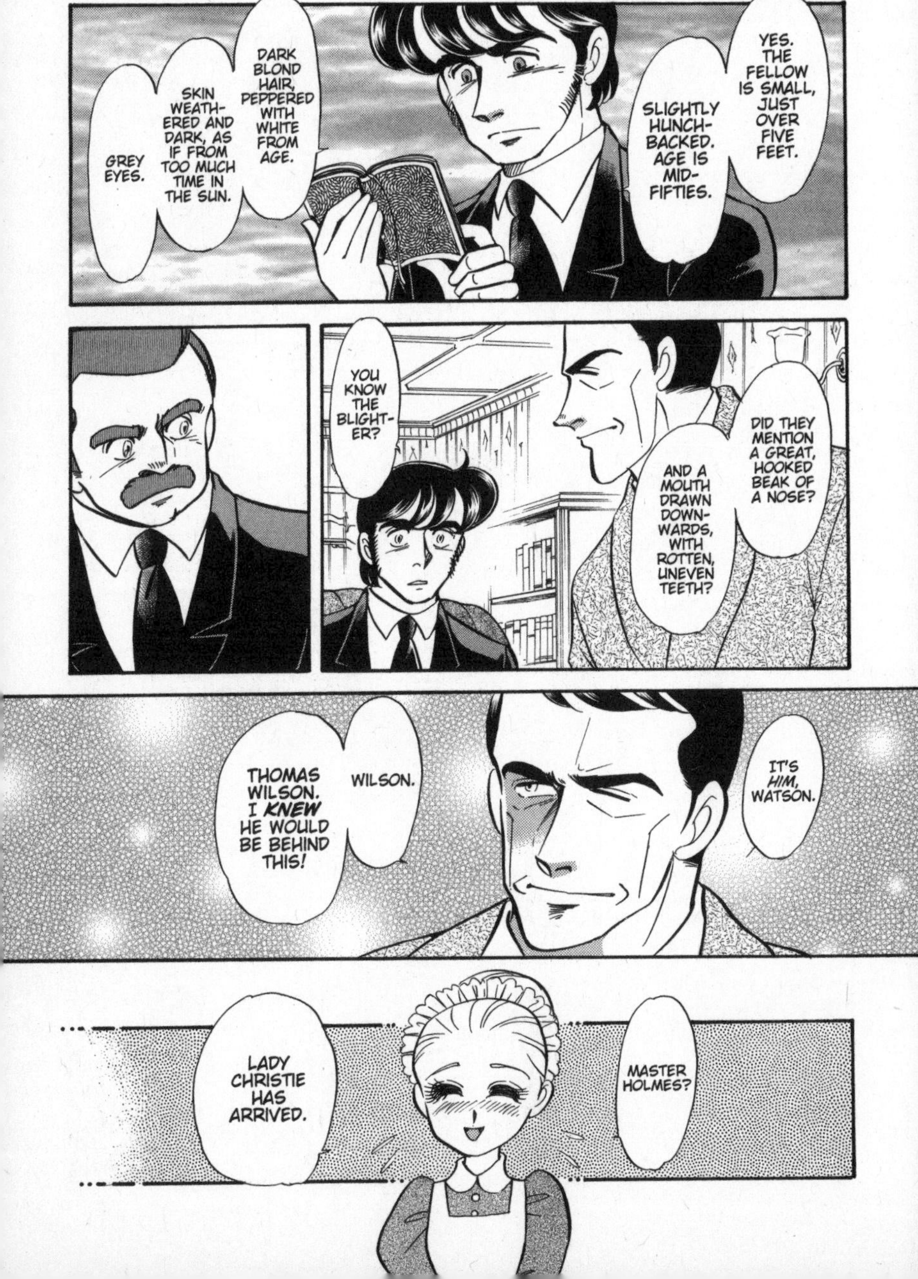
YES. THE FELLOW IS SMALL, JUST OVER FIVE FEET.
SLIGHTLY HUNCH-BACKED. AGE IS MID-FIFTIES.
DARK BLOND HAIR, PEPPERED WITH WHITE FROM AGE.
SKIN WEATH-ERED AND DARK, AS IF FROM TOO MUCH TIME IN THE SUN.
GREY EYES.
DID THEY MENTION A GREAT, HOOKED BEAK OF A NOSE?
AND A MOUTH DRAWN DOWN-WARDS, WITH ROTTEN, UNEVEN TEETH?
YOU KNOW THE BLIGHT-ER?
IT'S *HIM*, WATSON.
WILSON.
THOMAS WILSON. I ***KNEW*** HE WOULD BE BEHIND THIS!
MASTER HOLMES?
LADY CHRISTIE HAS ARRIVED.

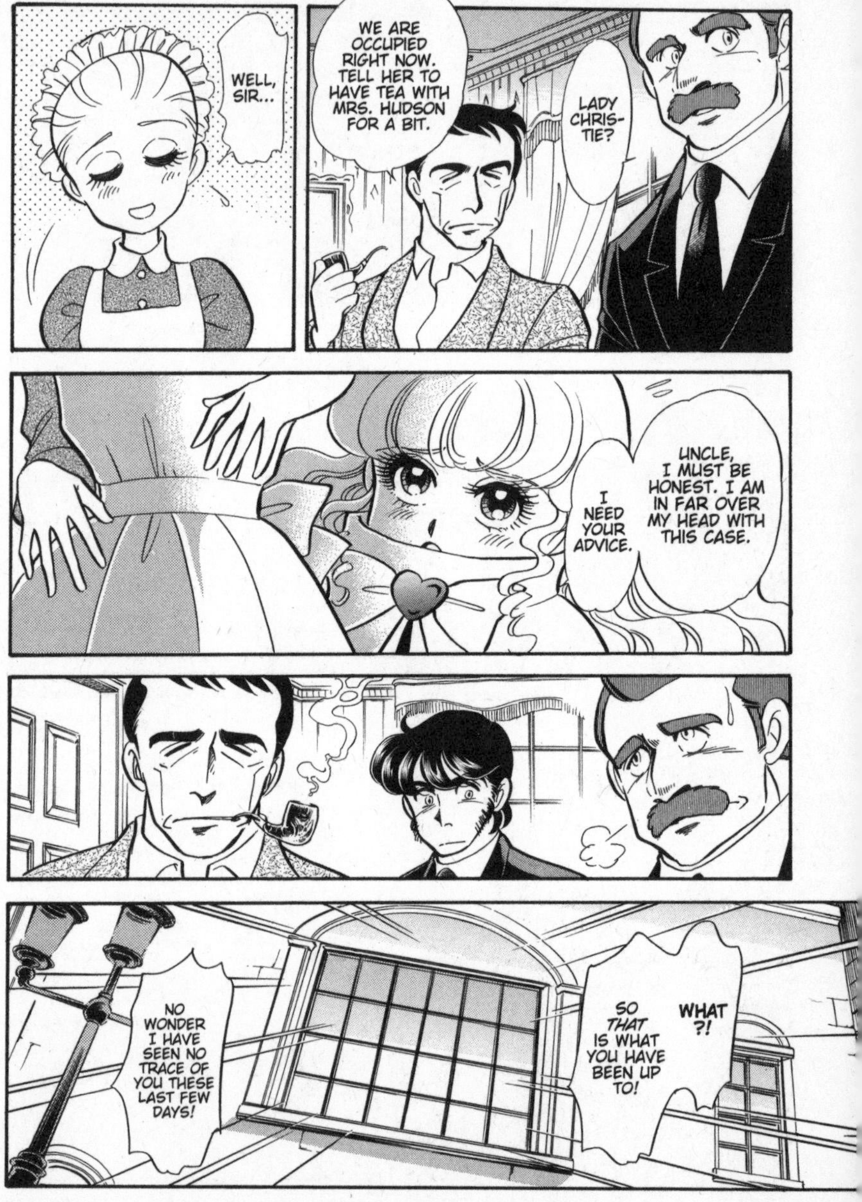
LADY CHRISTIE?
WE ARE OCCUPIED RIGHT NOW. TELL HER TO HAVE TEA WITH MRS. HUDSON FOR A BIT.
WELL, SIR...
UNCLE, I MUST BE HONEST. I AM IN FAR OVER MY HEAD WITH THIS CASE.
I NEED YOUR ADVICE.
WHAT?!
SO *THAT* IS WHAT YOU HAVE BEEN UP TO!
NO WONDER I HAVE SEEN NO TRACE OF YOU THESE LAST FEW DAYS!

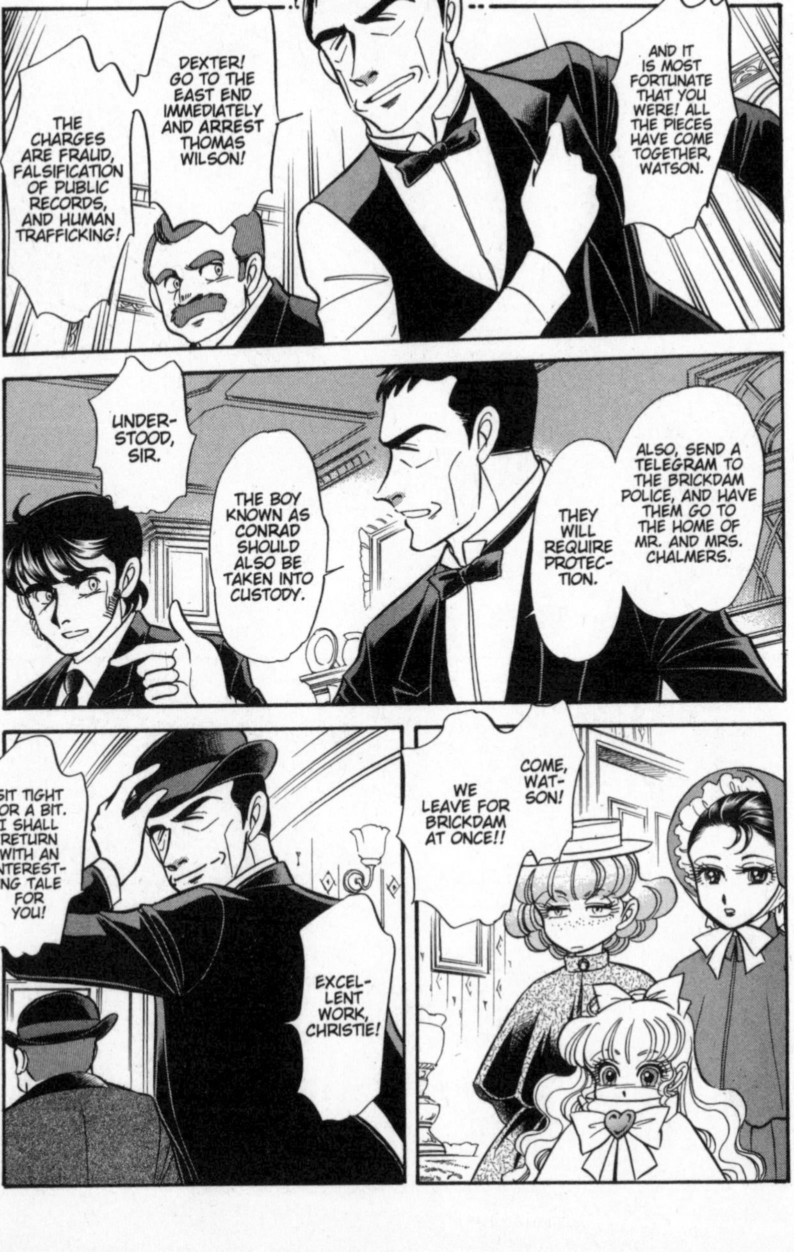
AND IT IS MOST FORTUNATE THAT YOU WERE! ALL THE PIECES HAVE COME TOGETHER, WATSON.
DEXTER! GO TO THE EAST END IMMEDIATELY AND ARREST THOMAS WILSON!
THE CHARGES ARE FRAUD, FALSIFICATION OF PUBLIC RECORDS, AND HUMAN TRAFFICKING!
ALSO, SEND A TELEGRAM TO THE BRICKDAM POLICE, AND HAVE THEM GO TO THE HOME OF MR. AND MRS. CHALMERS.
THEY WILL REQUIRE PROTEC-TION.
THE BOY KNOWN AS CONRAD SHOULD ALSO BE TAKEN INTO CUSTODY.
UNDER-STOOD, SIR.
COME, WAT-SON!
WE LEAVE FOR BRICKDAM AT ONCE!!
SIT TIGHT FOR A BIT. I SHALL RETURN WITH AN INTEREST-ING TALE FOR YOU!
EXCEL-LENT WORK, CHRISTIE!

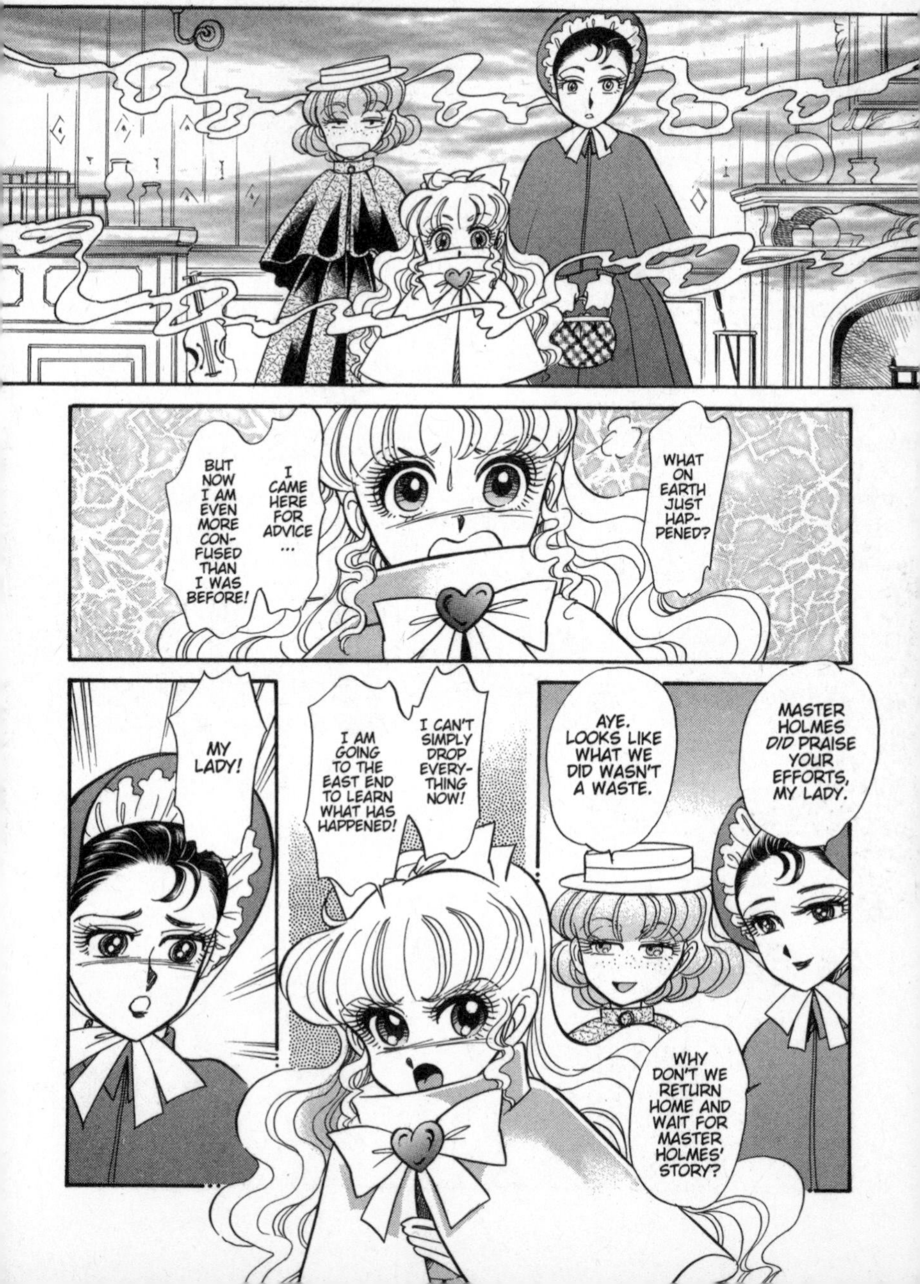
WHAT ON EARTH JUST HAPPENED?
I CAME HERE FOR ADVICE...
BUT NOW I AM EVEN MORE CONFUSED THAN I WAS BEFORE!
MASTER HOLMES *DID* PRAISE YOUR EFFORTS, MY LADY.
AYE. LOOKS LIKE WHAT WE DID WASN'T A WASTE.
WHY DON'T WE RETURN HOME AND WAIT FOR MASTER HOLMES' STORY?
I CAN'T SIMPLY DROP EVERYTHING NOW!
I AM GOING TO THE EAST END TO LEARN WHAT HAS HAPPENED!
MY LADY!

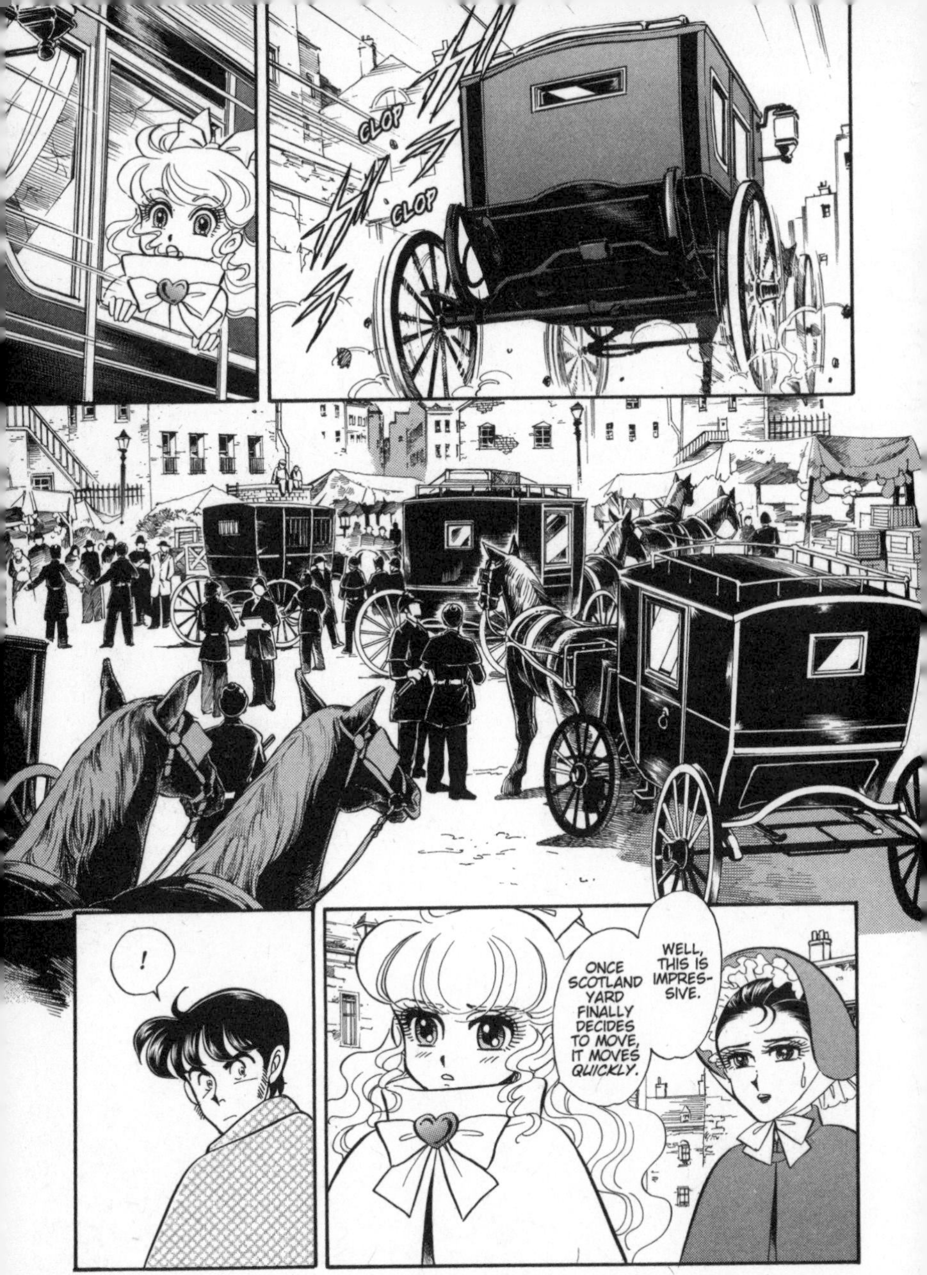
CLOP
CLOP
WELL, THIS IS IMPRESSIVE.
ONCE SCOTLAND YARD FINALLY DECIDES TO MOVE, IT MOVES *QUICKLY*.
!

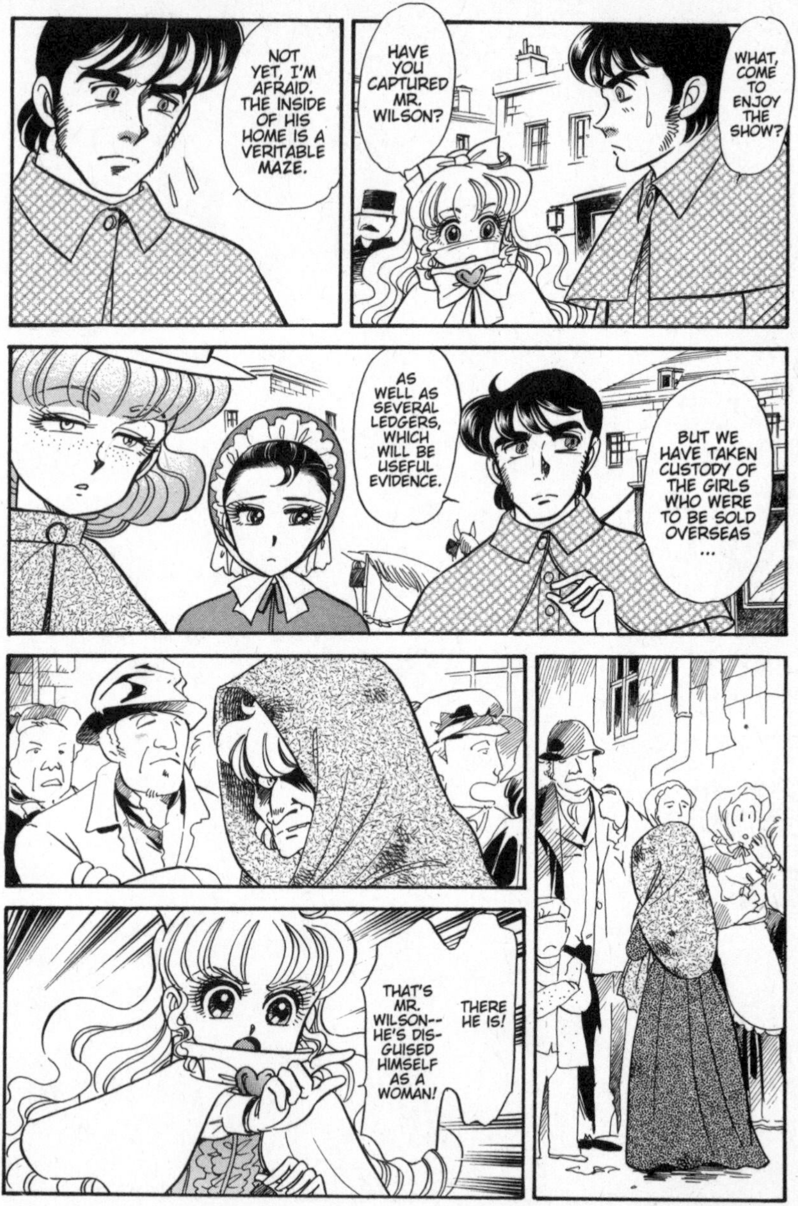
WHAT, COME TO ENJOY THE SHOW?
HAVE YOU CAPTURED MR. WILSON?
NOT YET, I'M AFRAID. THE INSIDE OF HIS HOME IS A VERITABLE MAZE.
BUT WE HAVE TAKEN CUSTODY OF THE GIRLS WHO WERE TO BE SOLD OVERSEAS ...
AS WELL AS SEVERAL LEDGERS, WHICH WILL BE USEFUL EVIDENCE.
THERE HE IS!
THAT'S MR. WILSON-- HE'S DISGUISED HIMSELF AS A WOMAN!

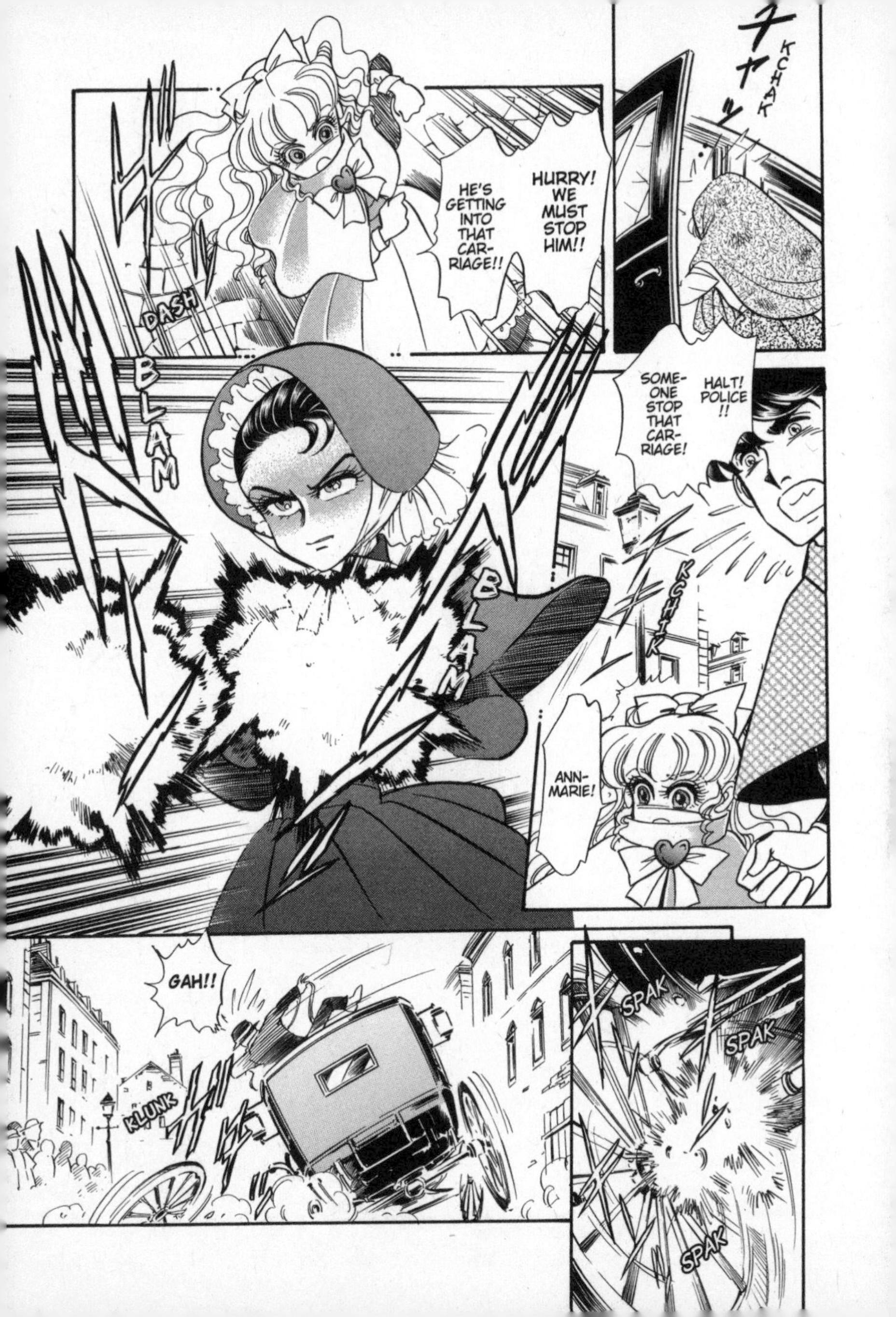
チャッ
KCHAK
HURRY! WE MUST STOP HIM!!
HE'S GETTING INTO THAT CAR-RIAGE!!
DASH
HALT! POLICE!!
SOME-ONE STOP THAT CAR-RIAGE!
KSHIK
ANN-MARIE!
BLAM
BLAM
SPAK
SPAK
SPAK
GAH!!
KLUNK

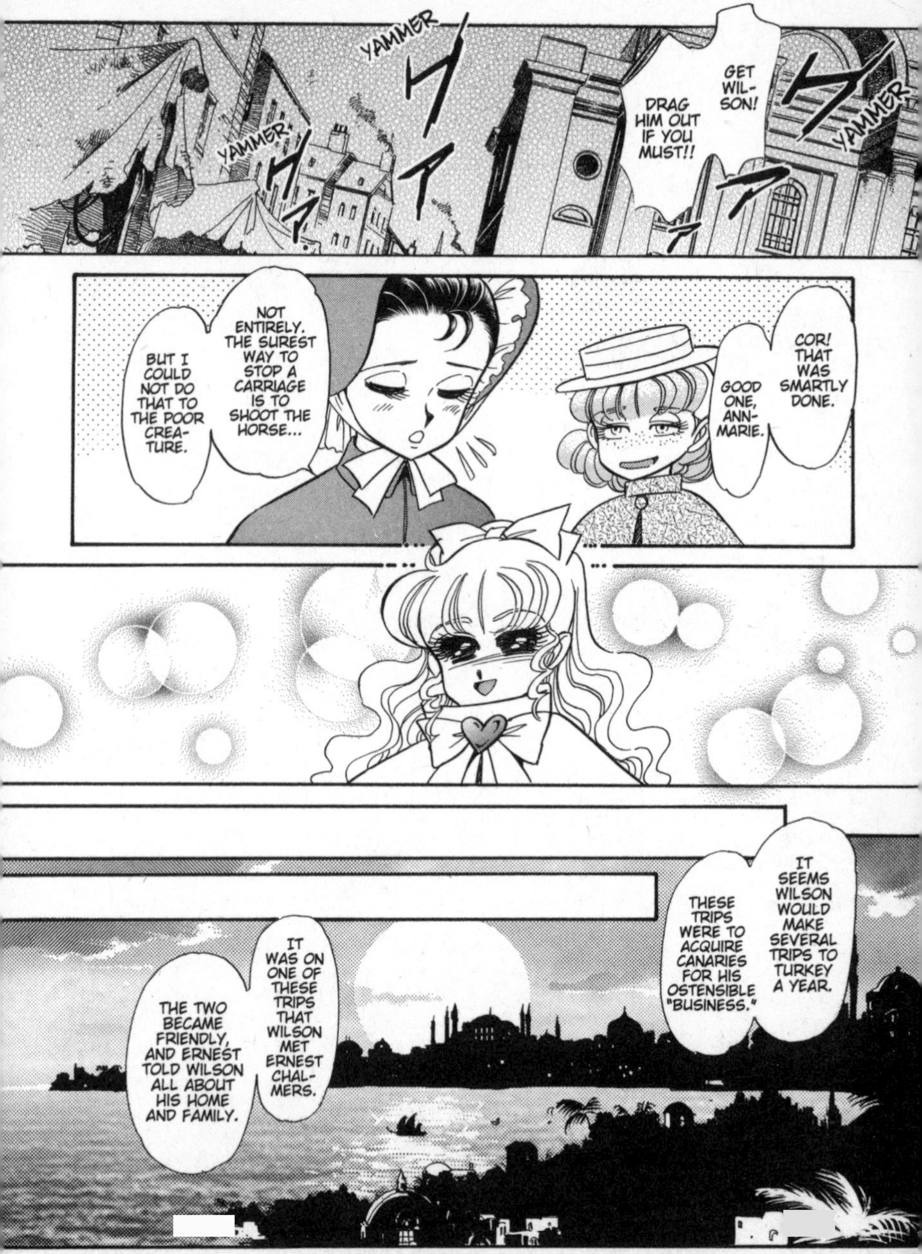
YAMMER
GET WIL-SON!
DRAG HIM OUT IF YOU MUST!!
YAMMER
YAMMER
COR! THAT WAS SMARTLY DONE.
GOOD ONE, ANN-MARIE.
NOT ENTIRELY. THE SUREST WAY TO STOP A CARRIAGE IS TO SHOOT THE HORSE...
BUT I COULD NOT DO THAT TO THE POOR CREA-TURE.
IT SEEMS WILSON WOULD MAKE SEVERAL TRIPS TO TURKEY A YEAR.
THESE TRIPS WERE TO ACQUIRE CANARIES FOR HIS OSTENSIBLE "BUSINESS."
IT WAS ON ONE OF THESE TRIPS THAT WILSON MET ERNEST CHAL-MERS.
THE TWO BECAME FRIENDLY, AND ERNEST TOLD WILSON ALL ABOUT HIS HOME AND FAMILY.

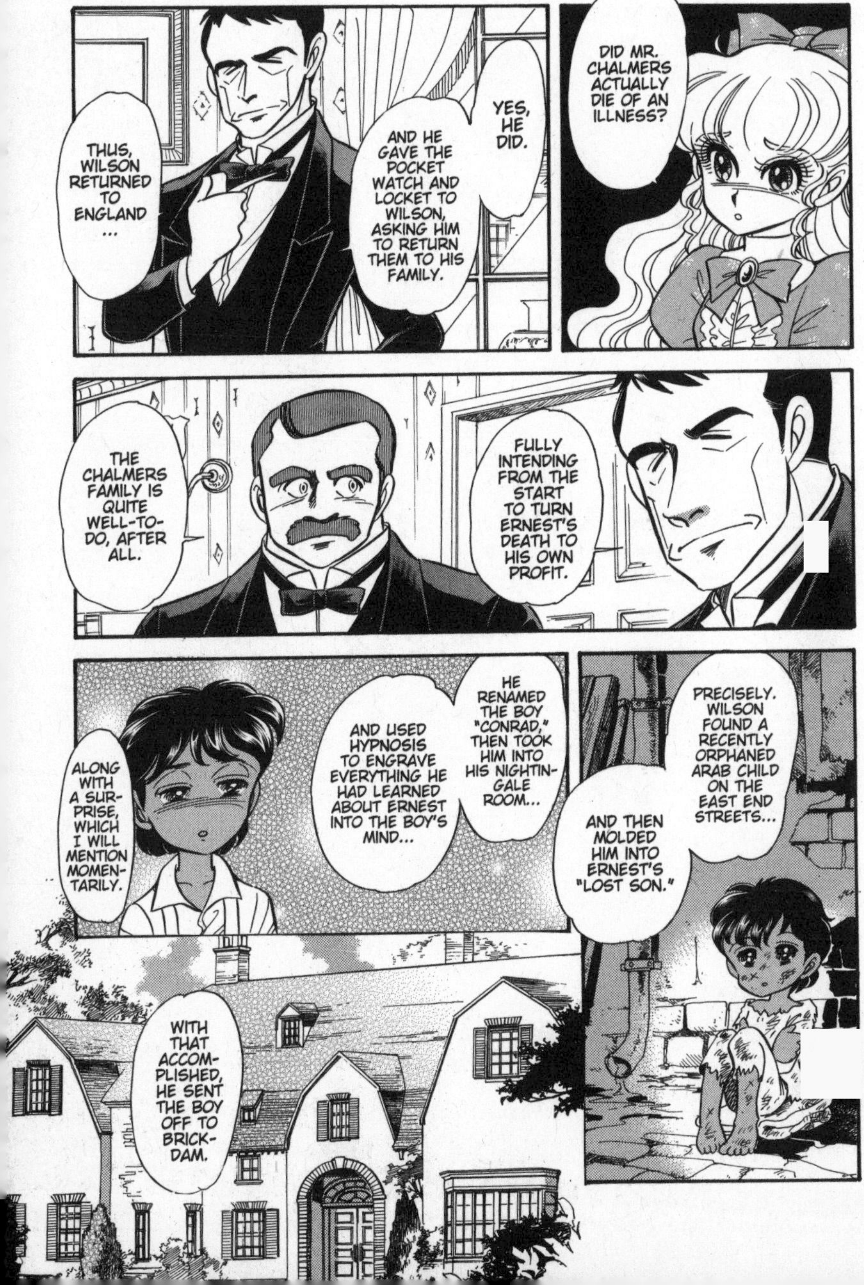
DID MR. CHALMERS ACTUALLY DIE OF AN ILLNESS?
YES, HE DID.
AND HE GAVE THE POCKET WATCH AND LOCKET TO WILSON, ASKING HIM TO RETURN THEM TO HIS FAMILY.
THUS, WILSON RETURNED TO ENGLAND ...
FULLY INTENDING FROM THE START TO TURN ERNEST'S DEATH TO HIS OWN PROFIT.
THE CHALMERS FAMILY IS QUITE WELL-TO-DO, AFTER ALL.
PRECISELY. WILSON FOUND A RECENTLY ORPHANED ARAB CHILD ON THE EAST END STREETS...
AND THEN MOLDED HIM INTO ERNEST'S "LOST SON."
HE RENAMED THE BOY "CONRAD," THEN TOOK HIM INTO HIS NIGHTINGALE ROOM...
AND USED HYPNOSIS TO ENGRAVE EVERYTHING HE HAD LEARNED ABOUT ERNEST INTO THE BOY'S MIND...
ALONG WITH A SURPRISE, WHICH I WILL MENTION MOMENTARILY.
WITH THAT ACCOMPLISHED, HE SENT THE BOY OFF TO BRICKDAM.

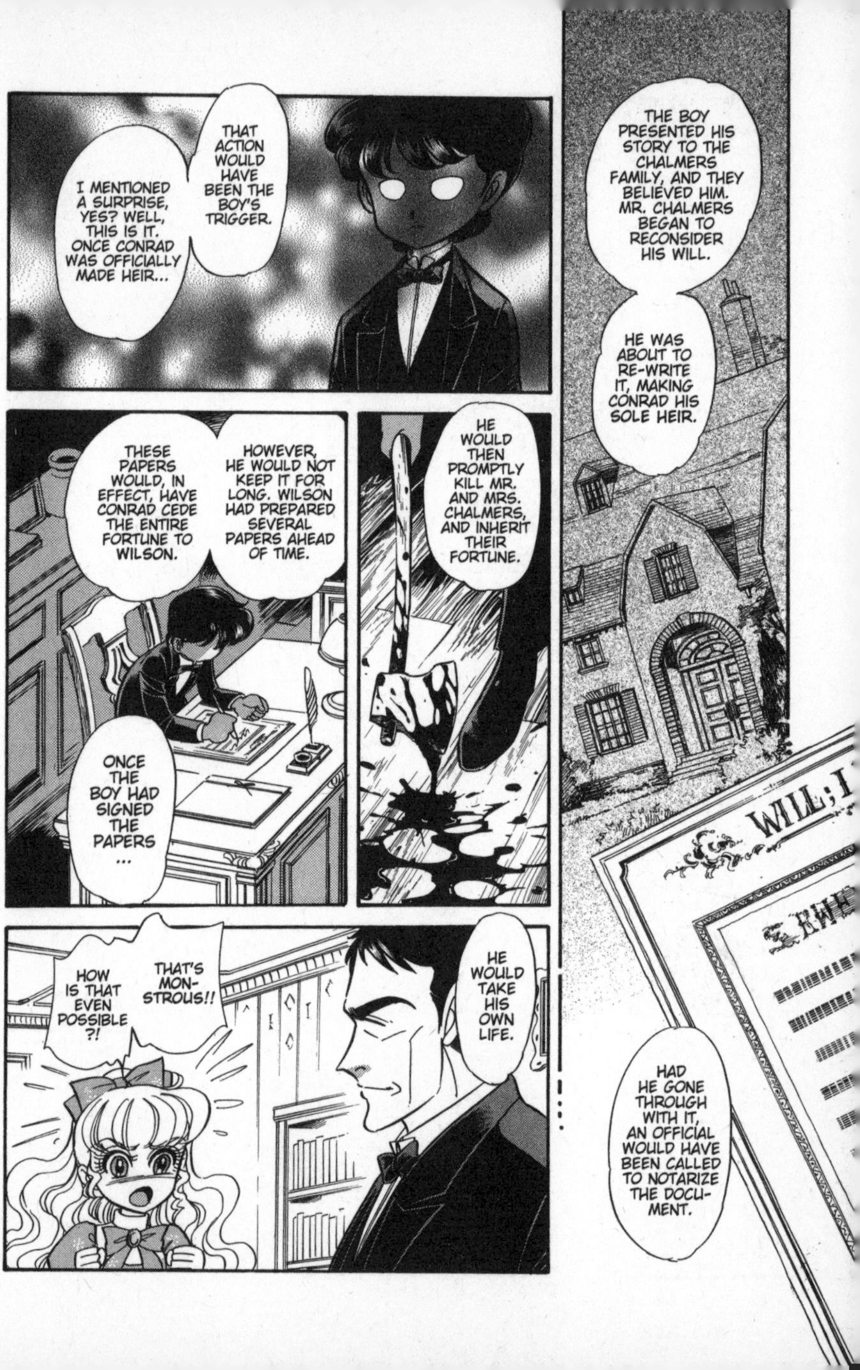
THE BOY PRESENTED HIS STORY TO THE CHALMERS FAMILY, AND THEY BELIEVED HIM. MR. CHALMERS BEGAN TO RECONSIDER HIS WILL.
HE WAS ABOUT TO RE-WRITE IT, MAKING CONRAD HIS SOLE HEIR.
HAD HE GONE THROUGH WITH IT, AN OFFICIAL WOULD HAVE BEEN CALLED TO NOTARIZE THE DOCU-MENT.
THAT ACTION WOULD HAVE BEEN THE BOY'S TRIGGER.
I MENTIONED A SURPRISE, YES? WELL, THIS IS IT. ONCE CONRAD WAS OFFICIALLY MADE HEIR...
HE WOULD THEN PROMPTLY KILL MR. AND MRS. CHALMERS, AND INHERIT THEIR FORTUNE.
HOWEVER, HE WOULD NOT KEEP IT FOR LONG. WILSON HAD PREPARED SEVERAL PAPERS AHEAD OF TIME.
THESE PAPERS WOULD, IN EFFECT, HAVE CONRAD CEDE THE ENTIRE FORTUNE TO WILSON.
ONCE THE BOY HAD SIGNED THE PAPERS ...
HE WOULD TAKE HIS OWN LIFE.
THAT'S MON-STROUS!!
HOW IS THAT EVEN POSSIBLE ?!

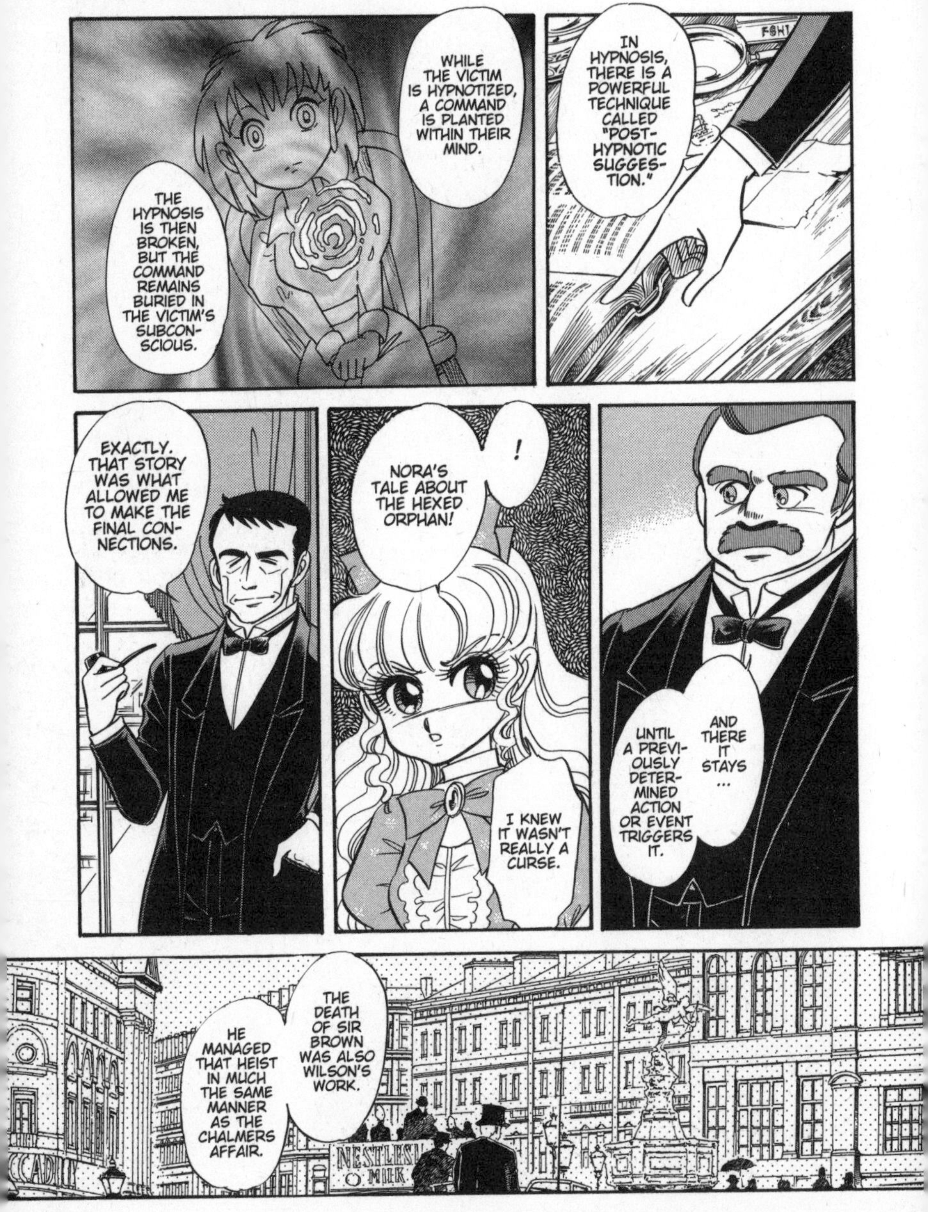

IN HYPNOSIS, THERE IS A POWERFUL TECHNIQUE CALLED "POST-HYPNOTIC SUGGES-TION."
WHILE THE VICTIM IS HYPNOTIZED, A COMMAND IS PLANTED WITHIN THEIR MIND.
THE HYPNOSIS IS THEN BROKEN, BUT THE COMMAND REMAINS BURIED IN THE VICTIM'S SUBCON-SCIOUS.
AND THERE IT STAYS ...
UNTIL A PREVI-OUSLY DETER-MINED ACTION OR EVENT TRIGGERS IT.
!
NORA'S TALE ABOUT THE HEXED ORPHAN!
I KNEW IT WASN'T REALLY A CURSE.
EXACTLY. THAT STORY WAS WHAT ALLOWED ME TO MAKE THE FINAL CON-NECTIONS.
THE DEATH OF SIR BROWN WAS ALSO WILSON'S WORK.
HE MANAGED THAT HEIST IN MUCH THE SAME MANNER AS THE CHALMERS AFFAIR.

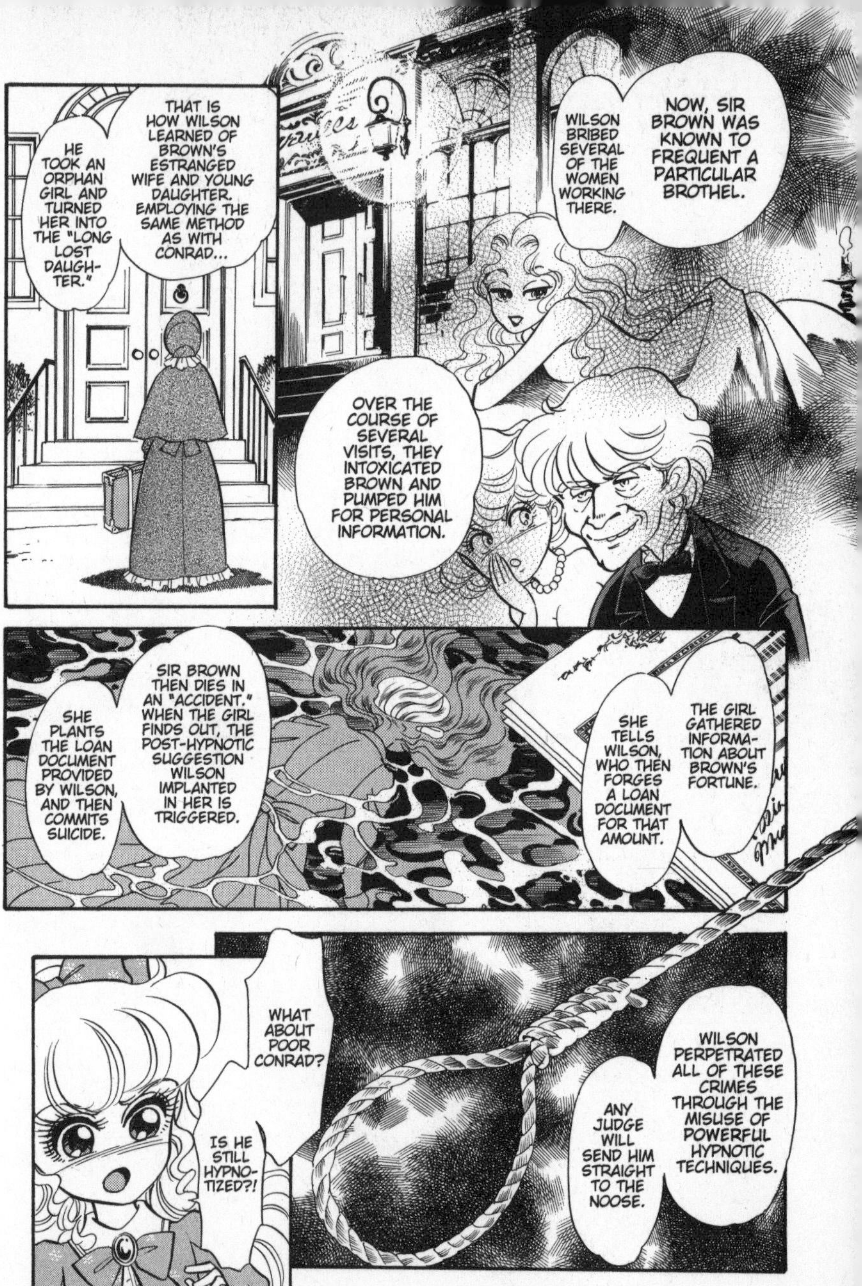
NOW, SIR BROWN WAS KNOWN TO FREQUENT A PARTICULAR BROTHEL.
WILSON BRIBED SEVERAL OF THE WOMEN WORKING THERE.
OVER THE COURSE OF SEVERAL VISITS, THEY INTOXICATED BROWN AND PUMPED HIM FOR PERSONAL INFORMATION.
THAT IS HOW WILSON LEARNED OF BROWN'S ESTRANGED WIFE AND YOUNG DAUGHTER. EMPLOYING THE SAME METHOD AS WITH CONRAD...
HE TOOK AN ORPHAN GIRL AND TURNED HER INTO THE "LONG LOST DAUGHTER."
THE GIRL GATHERED INFORMATION ABOUT BROWN'S FORTUNE.
SHE TELLS WILSON, WHO THEN FORGES A LOAN DOCUMENT FOR THAT AMOUNT.
SIR BROWN THEN DIES IN AN "ACCIDENT." WHEN THE GIRL FINDS OUT, THE POST-HYPNOTIC SUGGESTION WILSON IMPLANTED IN HER IS TRIGGERED.
SHE PLANTS THE LOAN DOCUMENT PROVIDED BY WILSON, AND THEN COMMITS SUICIDE.
WILSON PERPETRATED ALL OF THESE CRIMES THROUGH THE MISUSE OF POWERFUL HYPNOTIC TECHNIQUES.
ANY JUDGE WILL SEND HIM STRAIGHT TO THE NOOSE.
WHAT ABOUT POOR CONRAD?
IS HE STILL HYPNOTIZED?!

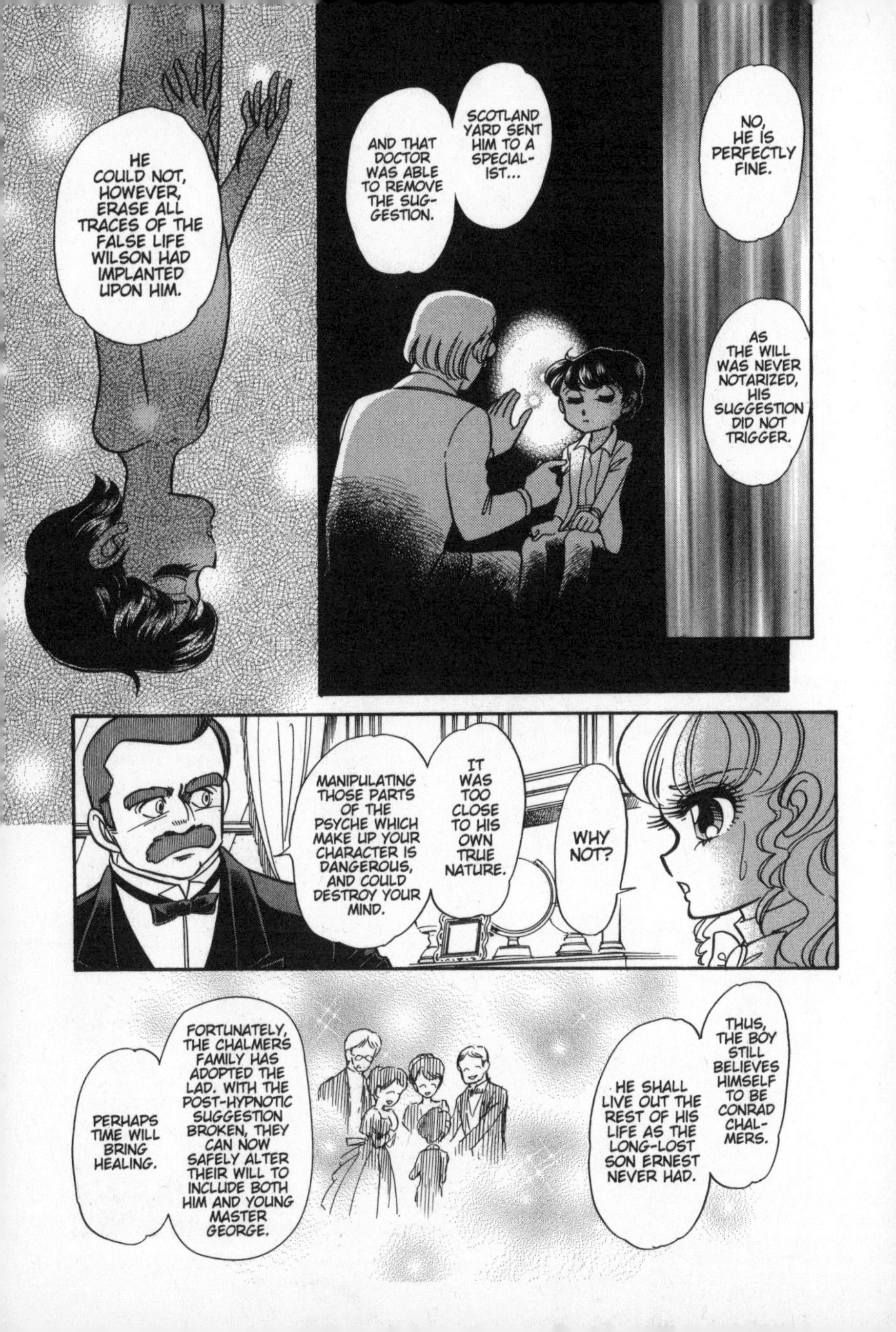

NO, HE IS PERFECTLY FINE.
AS THE WILL WAS NEVER NOTARIZED, HIS SUGGESTION DID NOT TRIGGER.
SCOTLAND YARD SENT HIM TO A SPECIALIST...
AND THAT DOCTOR WAS ABLE TO REMOVE THE SUGGESTION.
HE COULD NOT, HOWEVER, ERASE ALL TRACES OF THE FALSE LIFE WILSON HAD IMPLANTED UPON HIM.
WHY NOT?
IT WAS TOO CLOSE TO HIS OWN TRUE NATURE.
MANIPULATING THOSE PARTS OF THE PSYCHE WHICH MAKE UP YOUR CHARACTER IS DANGEROUS, AND COULD DESTROY YOUR MIND.
THUS, THE BOY STILL BELIEVES HIMSELF TO BE CONRAD CHALMERS.
HE SHALL LIVE OUT THE REST OF HIS LIFE AS THE LONG-LOST SON ERNEST NEVER HAD.
FORTUNATELY, THE CHALMERS FAMILY HAS ADOPTED THE LAD. WITH THE POST-HYPNOTIC SUGGESTION BROKEN, THEY CAN NOW SAFELY ALTER THEIR WILL TO INCLUDE BOTH HIM AND YOUNG MASTER GEORGE.
PERHAPS TIME WILL BRING HEALING.

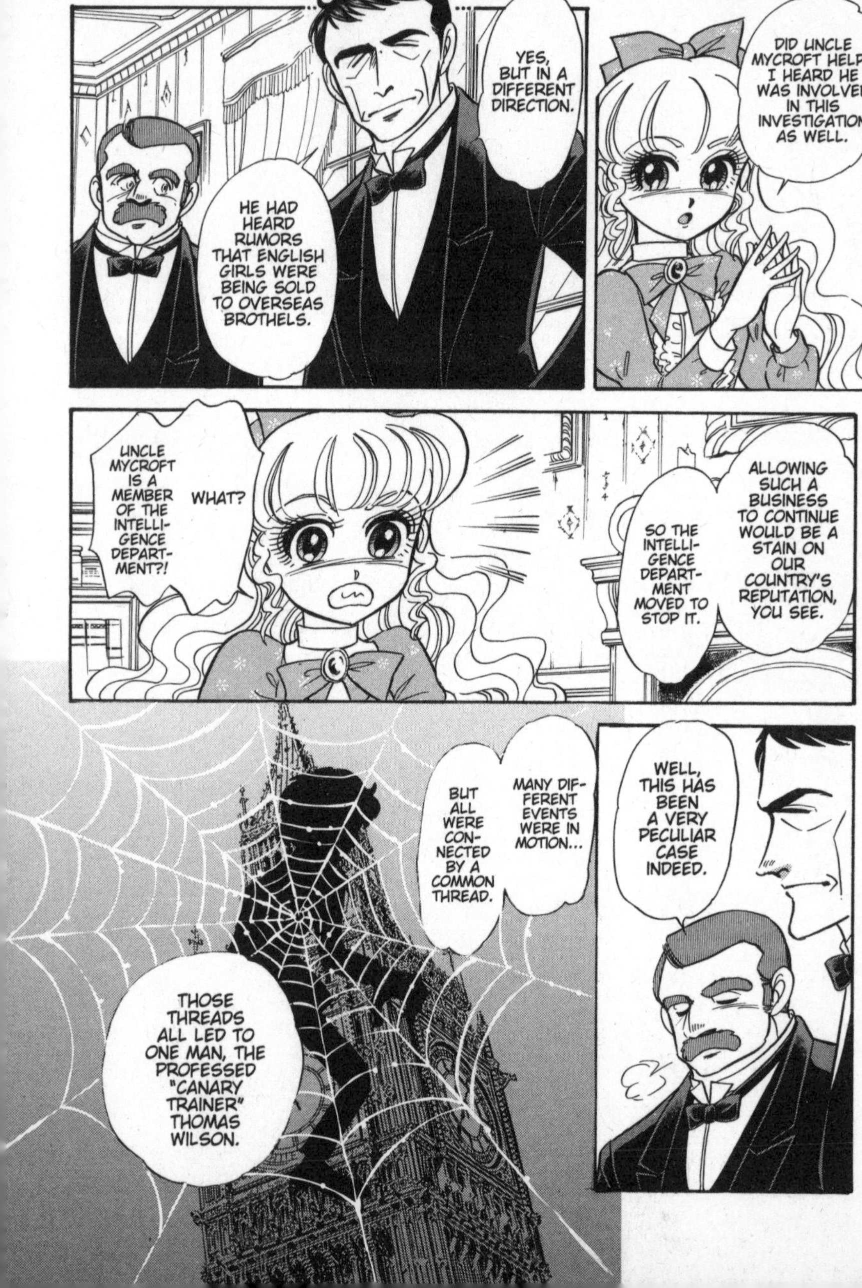
DID UNCLE MYCROFT HELP? I HEARD HE WAS INVOLVED IN THIS INVESTIGATION AS WELL.
YES, BUT IN A DIFFERENT DIRECTION.
HE HAD HEARD RUMORS THAT ENGLISH GIRLS WERE BEING SOLD TO OVERSEAS BROTHELS.
ALLOWING SUCH A BUSINESS TO CONTINUE WOULD BE A STAIN ON OUR COUNTRY'S REPUTATION, YOU SEE.
SO THE INTELLIGENCE DEPARTMENT MOVED TO STOP IT.
WHAT?
UNCLE MYCROFT IS A MEMBER OF THE INTELLIGENCE DEPARTMENT?!
WELL, THIS HAS BEEN A VERY PECULIAR CASE INDEED.
MANY DIFFERENT EVENTS WERE IN MOTION...
BUT ALL WERE CONNECTED BY A COMMON THREAD.
THOSE THREADS ALL LED TO ONE MAN, THE PROFESSED "CANARY TRAINER" THOMAS WILSON.

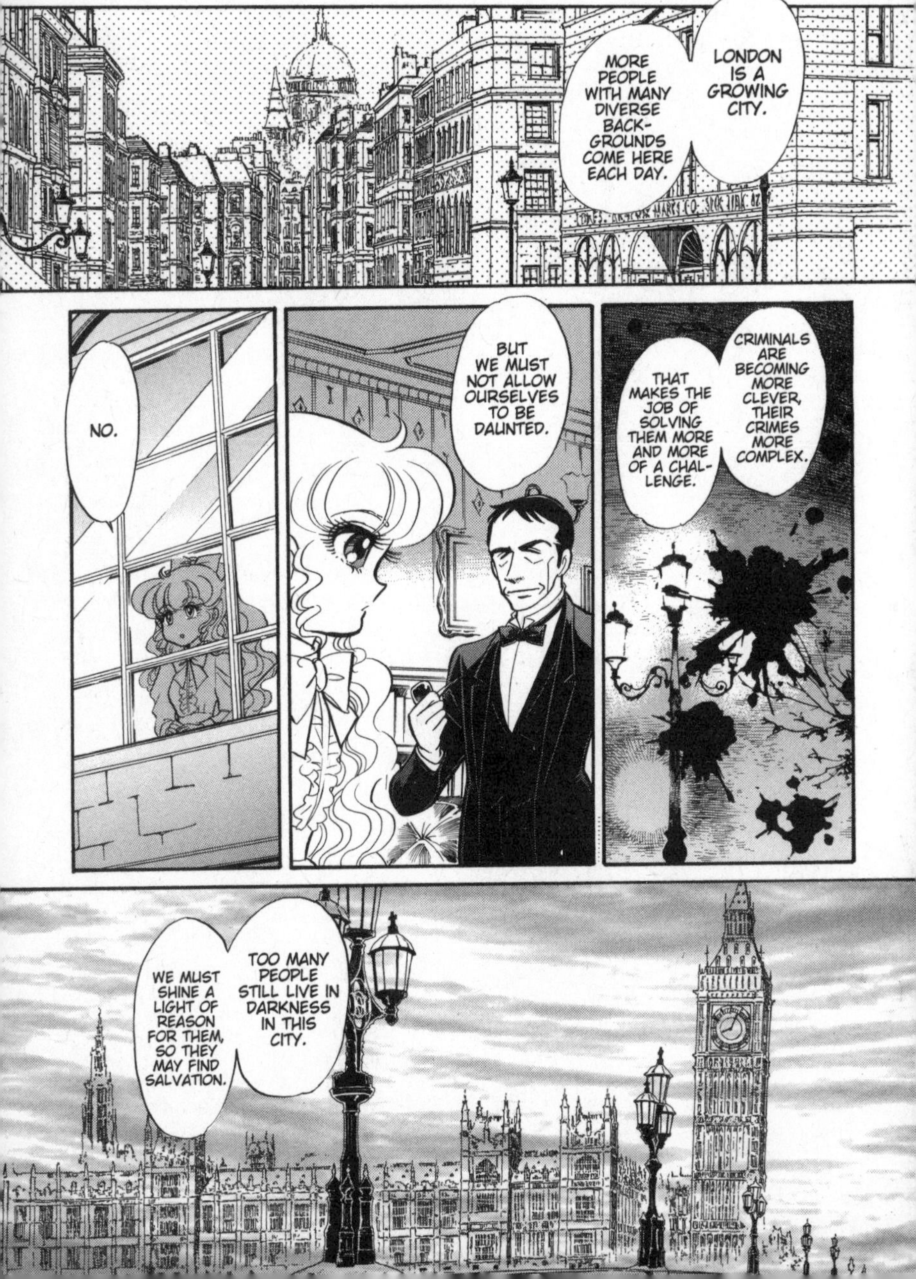
LONDON IS A GROWING CITY.
MORE PEOPLE WITH MANY DIVERSE BACKGROUNDS COME HERE EACH DAY.
CRIMINALS ARE BECOMING MORE CLEVER, THEIR CRIMES MORE COMPLEX.
THAT MAKES THE JOB OF SOLVING THEM MORE AND MORE OF A CHALLENGE.
BUT WE MUST NOT ALLOW OURSELVES TO BE DAUNTED.
NO.
TOO MANY PEOPLE STILL LIVE IN DARKNESS IN THIS CITY.
WE MUST SHINE A LIGHT OF REASON FOR THEM, SO THEY MAY FIND SALVATION.

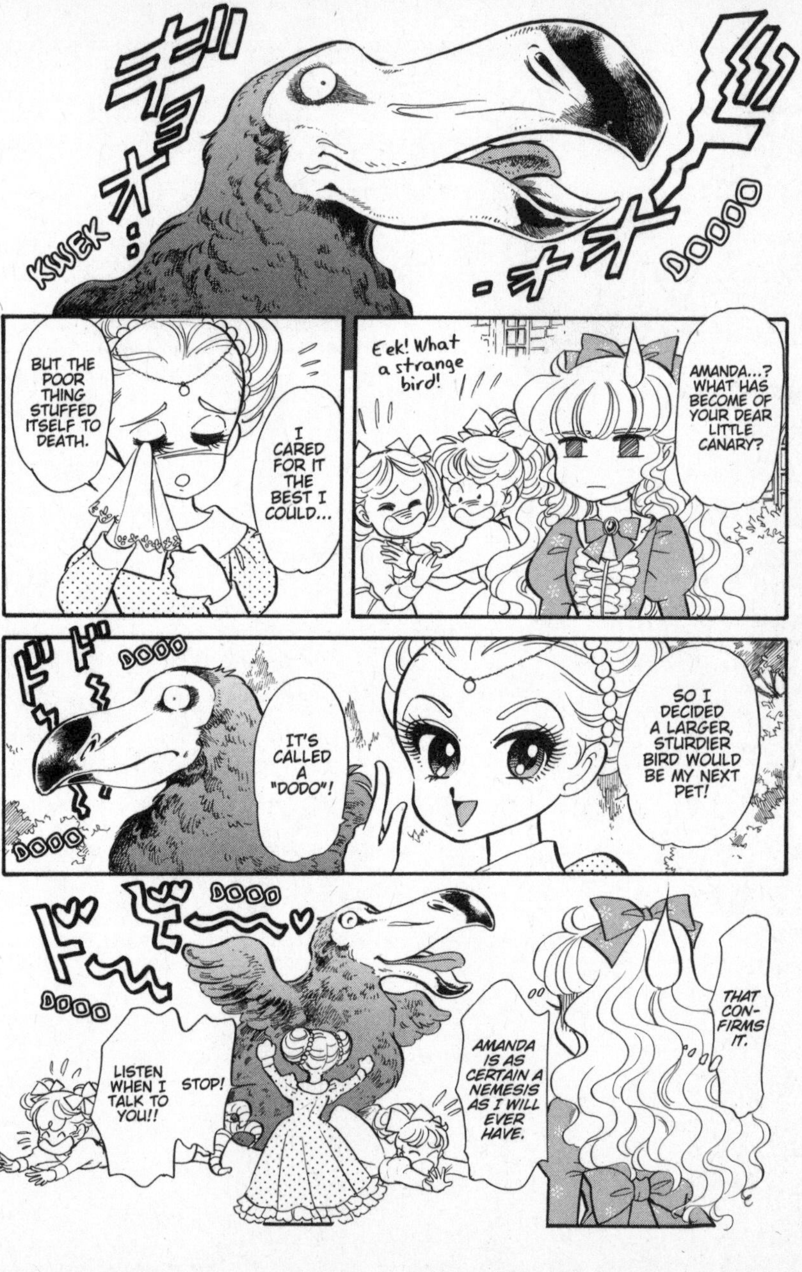
DOOOOO
KWEEK
AMANDA...? WHAT HAS BECOME OF YOUR DEAR LITTLE CANARY?
Eek! What a strange bird!
I CARED FOR IT THE BEST I COULD...
BUT THE POOR THING STUFFED ITSELF TO DEATH.
SO I DECIDED A LARGER, STURDIER BIRD WOULD BE MY NEXT PET!
IT'S CALLED A "DODO"!
DOOO
DOOO
THAT CON-FIRMS IT.
AMANDA IS AS CERTAIN A NEMESIS AS I WILL EVER HAVE.
DOOO
DOOO
STOP!
LISTEN WHEN I TALK TO YOU!!

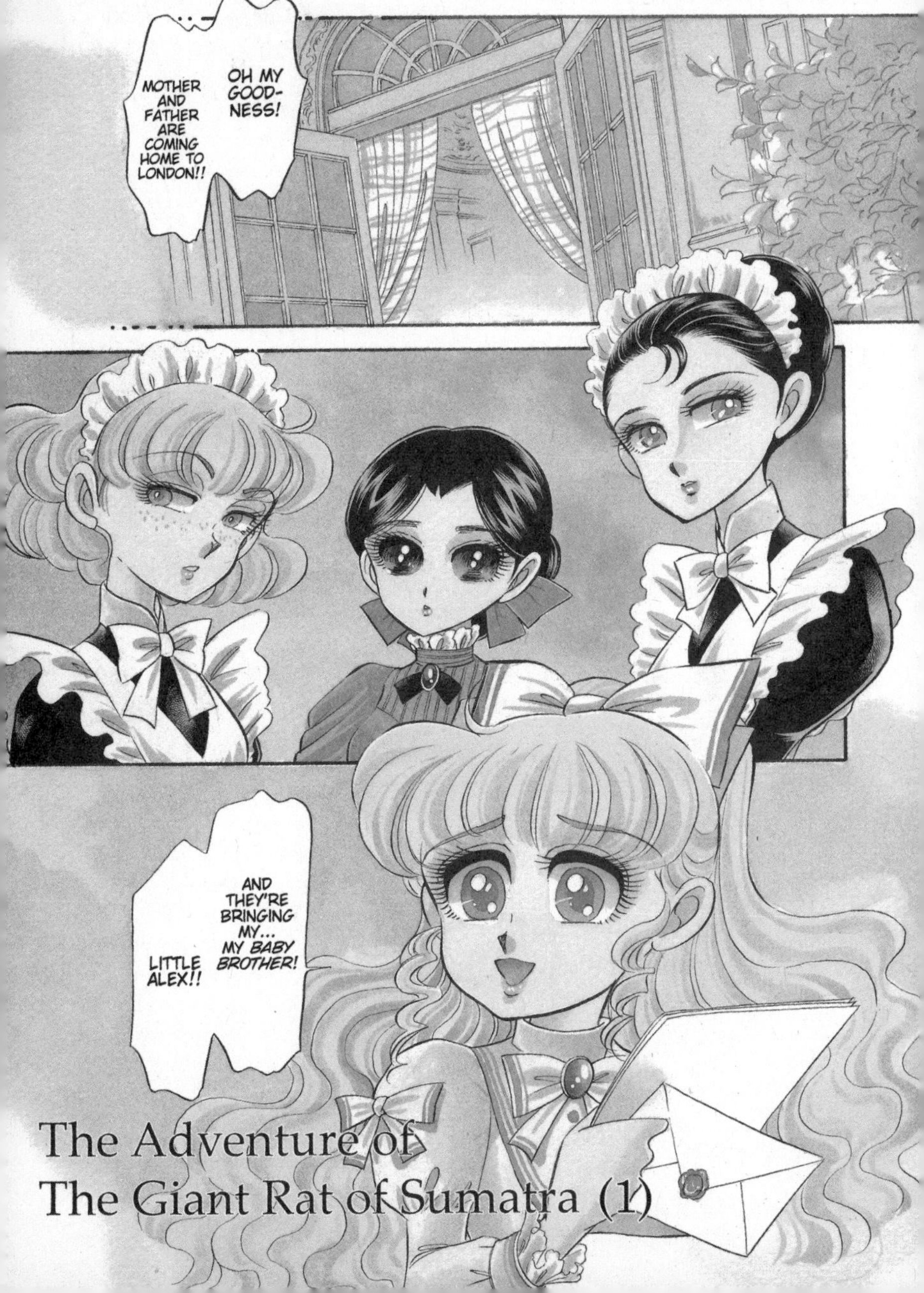
OH MY GOODNESS!
MOTHER AND FATHER ARE COMING HOME TO LONDON!!
AND THEY'RE BRINGING MY... MY *BABY BROTHER!*
LITTLE ALEX!!

The Adventure of The Giant Rat of Sumatra (1)

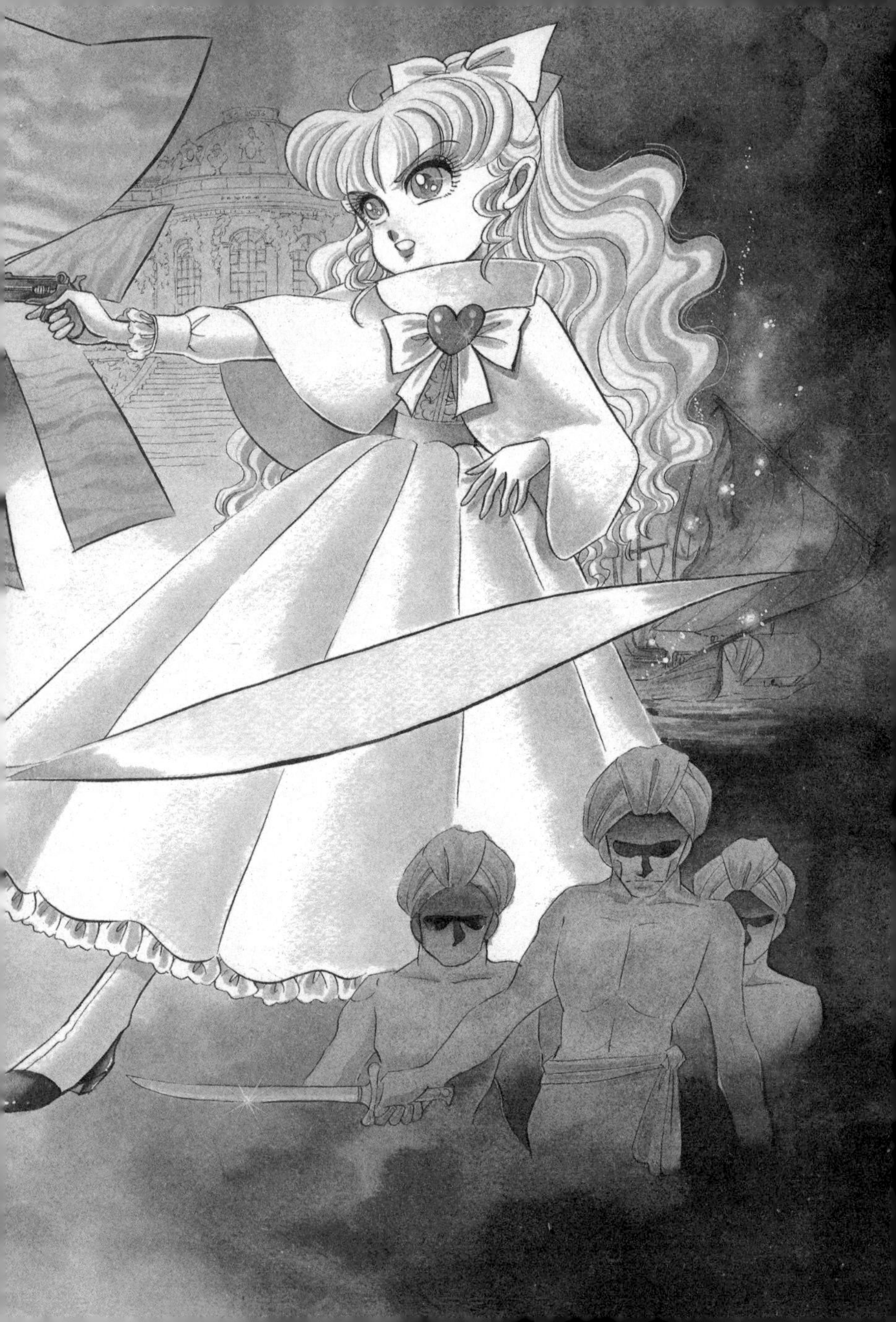

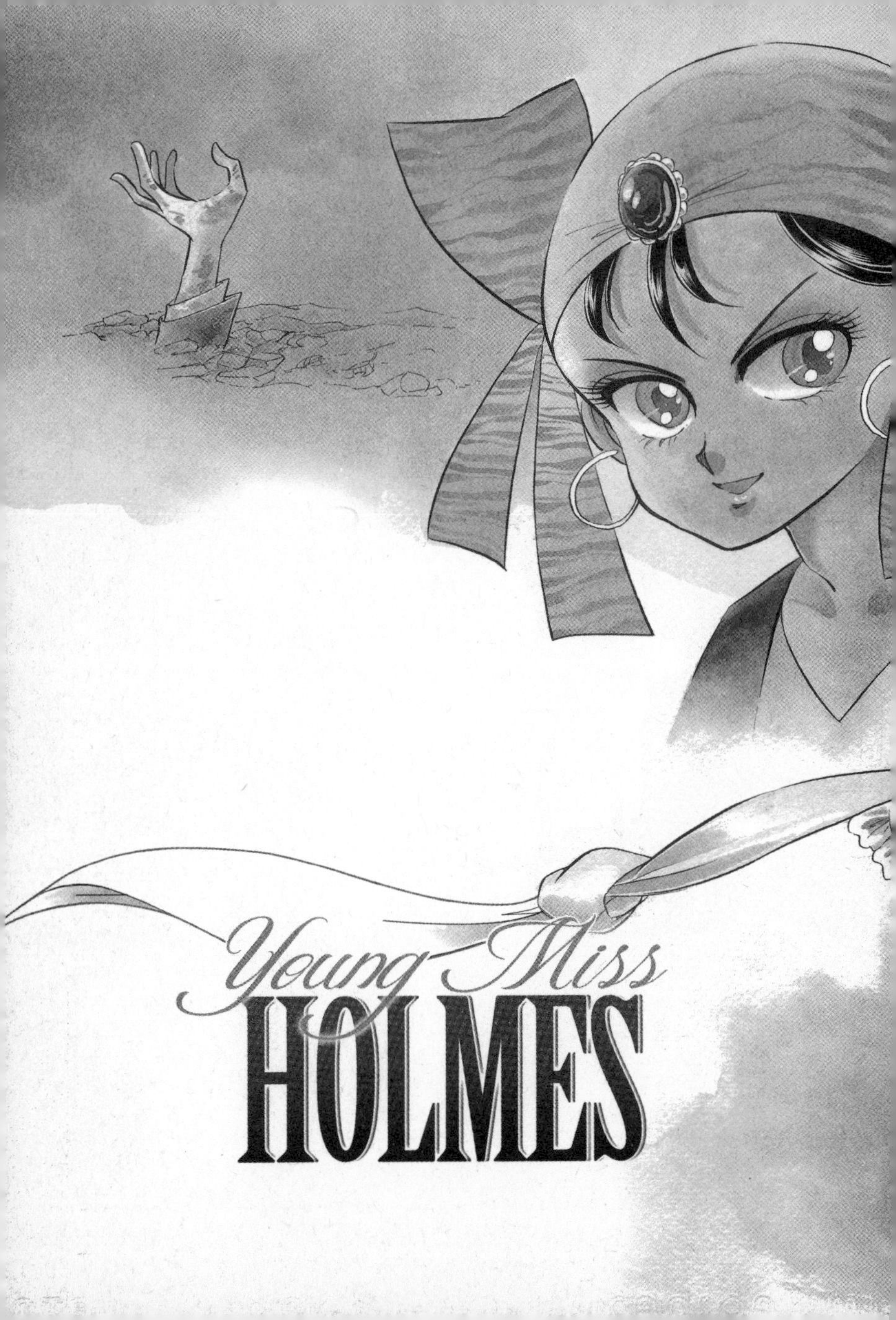
Young Miss
HOLMES

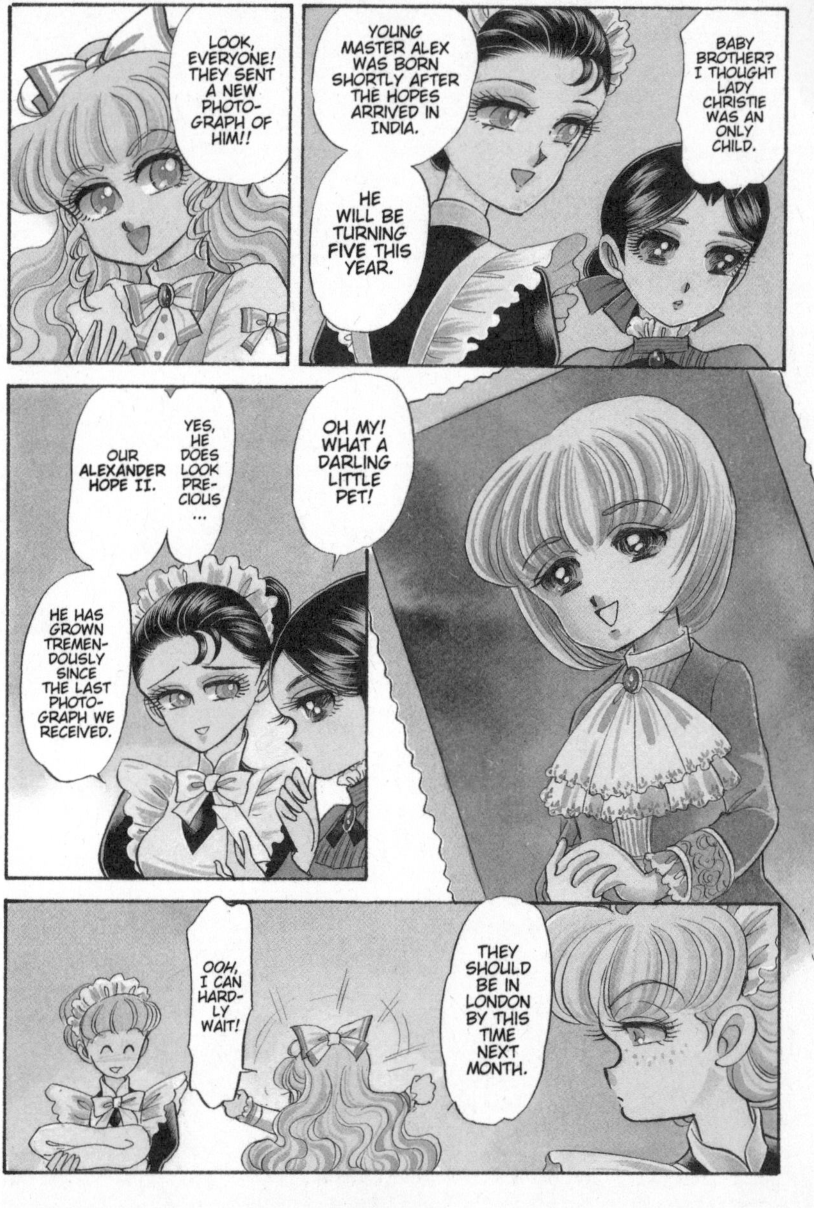
BABY BROTHER? I THOUGHT LADY CHRISTIE WAS AN ONLY CHILD.
YOUNG MASTER ALEX WAS BORN SHORTLY AFTER THE HOPES ARRIVED IN INDIA.
HE WILL BE TURNING FIVE THIS YEAR.
LOOK, EVERYONE! THEY SENT A NEW PHOTO-GRAPH OF HIM!!
OH MY! WHAT A DARLING LITTLE PET!
YES, HE DOES LOOK PRE-CIOUS...
OUR ALEXANDER HOPE II.
HE HAS GROWN TREMEN-DOUSLY SINCE THE LAST PHOTO-GRAPH WE RECEIVED.
THEY SHOULD BE IN LONDON BY THIS TIME NEXT MONTH.
OOH, I CAN HARD-LY WAIT!

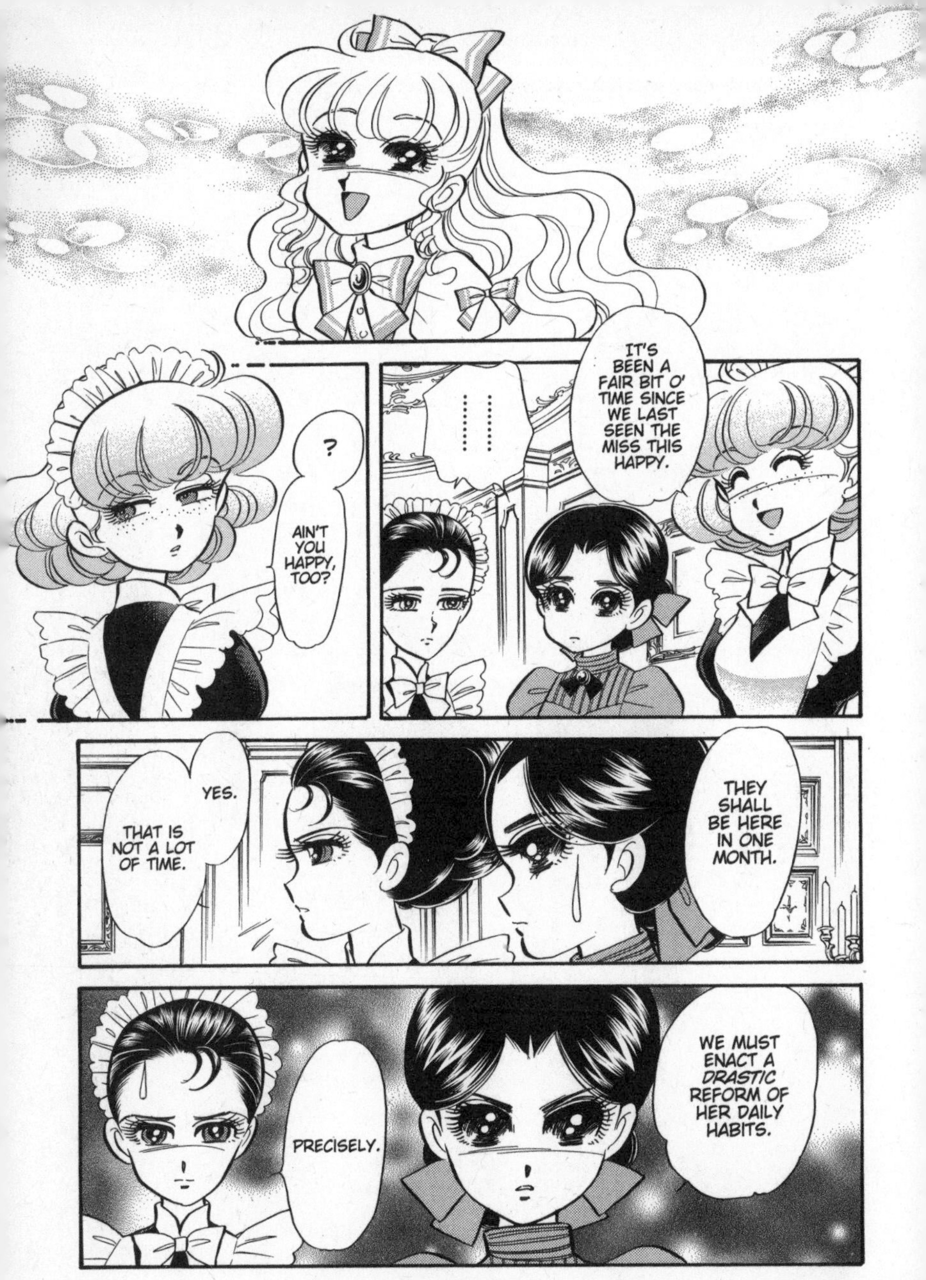
IT'S BEEN A FAIR BIT O' TIME SINCE WE LAST SEEN THE MISS THIS HAPPY.
......
?
AIN'T YOU HAPPY, TOO?
THEY SHALL BE HERE IN ONE MONTH.
YES.
THAT IS NOT A LOT OF TIME.
WE MUST ENACT A *DRASTIC* REFORM OF HER DAILY HABITS.
PRECISELY.

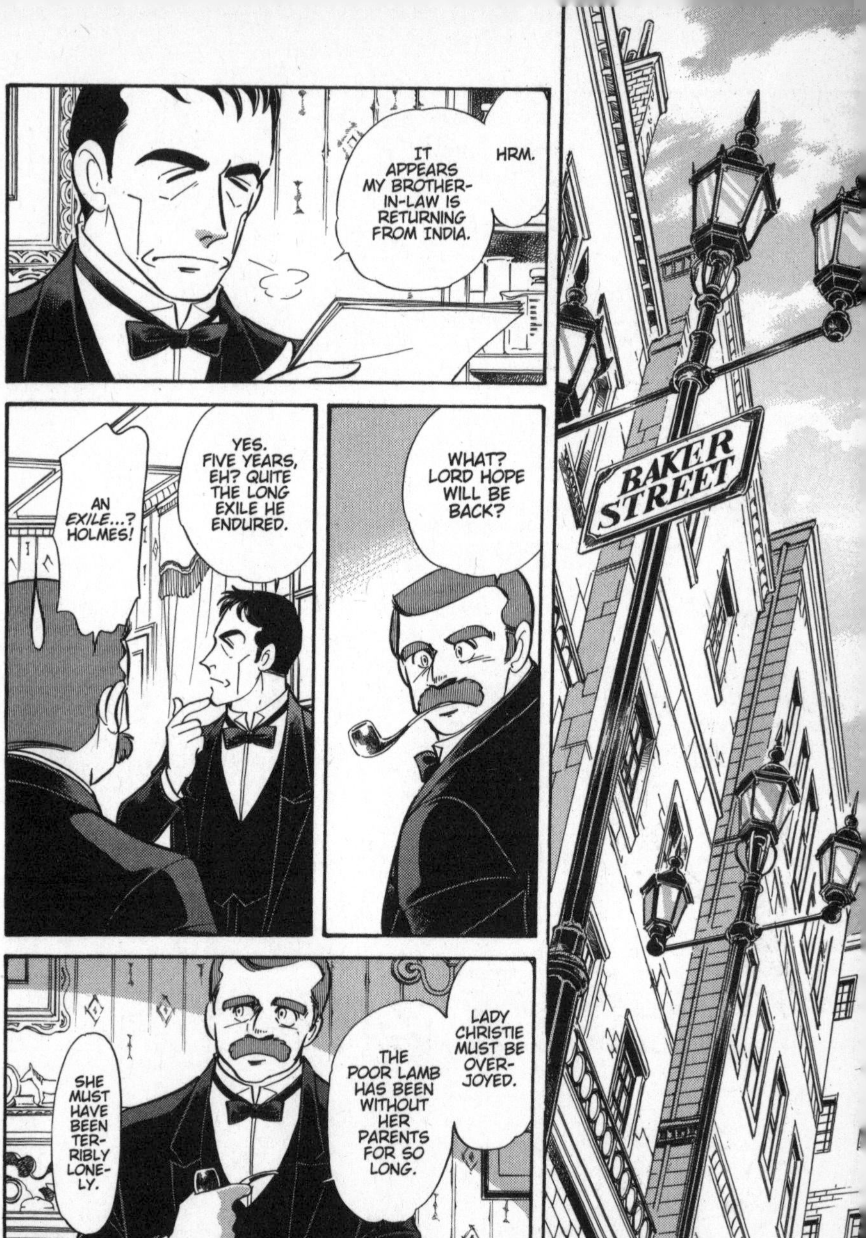
BAKER STREET
HRM.
IT APPEARS MY BROTHER-IN-LAW IS RETURNING FROM INDIA.
WHAT? LORD HOPE WILL BE BACK?
YES. FIVE YEARS, EH? QUITE THE LONG EXILE HE ENDURED.
AN *EXILE*...? HOLMES!
LADY CHRISTIE MUST BE OVER-JOYED.
THE POOR LAMB HAS BEEN WITHOUT HER PARENTS FOR SO LONG.
SHE MUST HAVE BEEN TER-RIBLY LONE-LY.

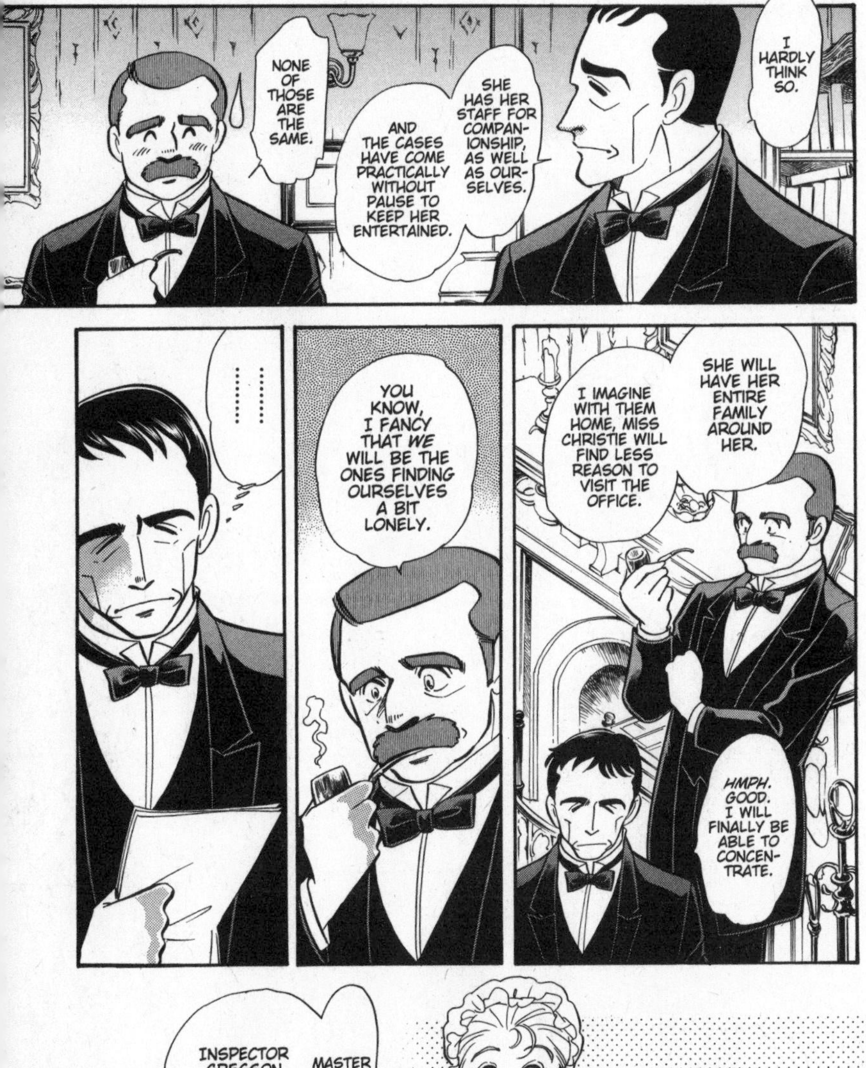
I HARDLY THINK SO.
SHE HAS HER STAFF FOR COMPANIONSHIP, AS WELL AS OURSELVES.
AND THE CASES HAVE COME PRACTICALLY WITHOUT PAUSE TO KEEP HER ENTERTAINED.
NONE OF THOSE ARE THE SAME.
SHE WILL HAVE HER ENTIRE FAMILY AROUND HER.
I IMAGINE WITH THEM HOME, MISS CHRISTIE WILL FIND LESS REASON TO VISIT THE OFFICE.
HMPH. GOOD. I WILL FINALLY BE ABLE TO CONCENTRATE.
YOU KNOW, I FANCY THAT *WE* WILL BE THE ONES FINDING OURSELVES A BIT LONELY.
......
MASTER HOLMES.
INSPECTOR GREGSON FROM SCOTLAND YARD HAS ARRIVED.

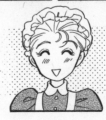

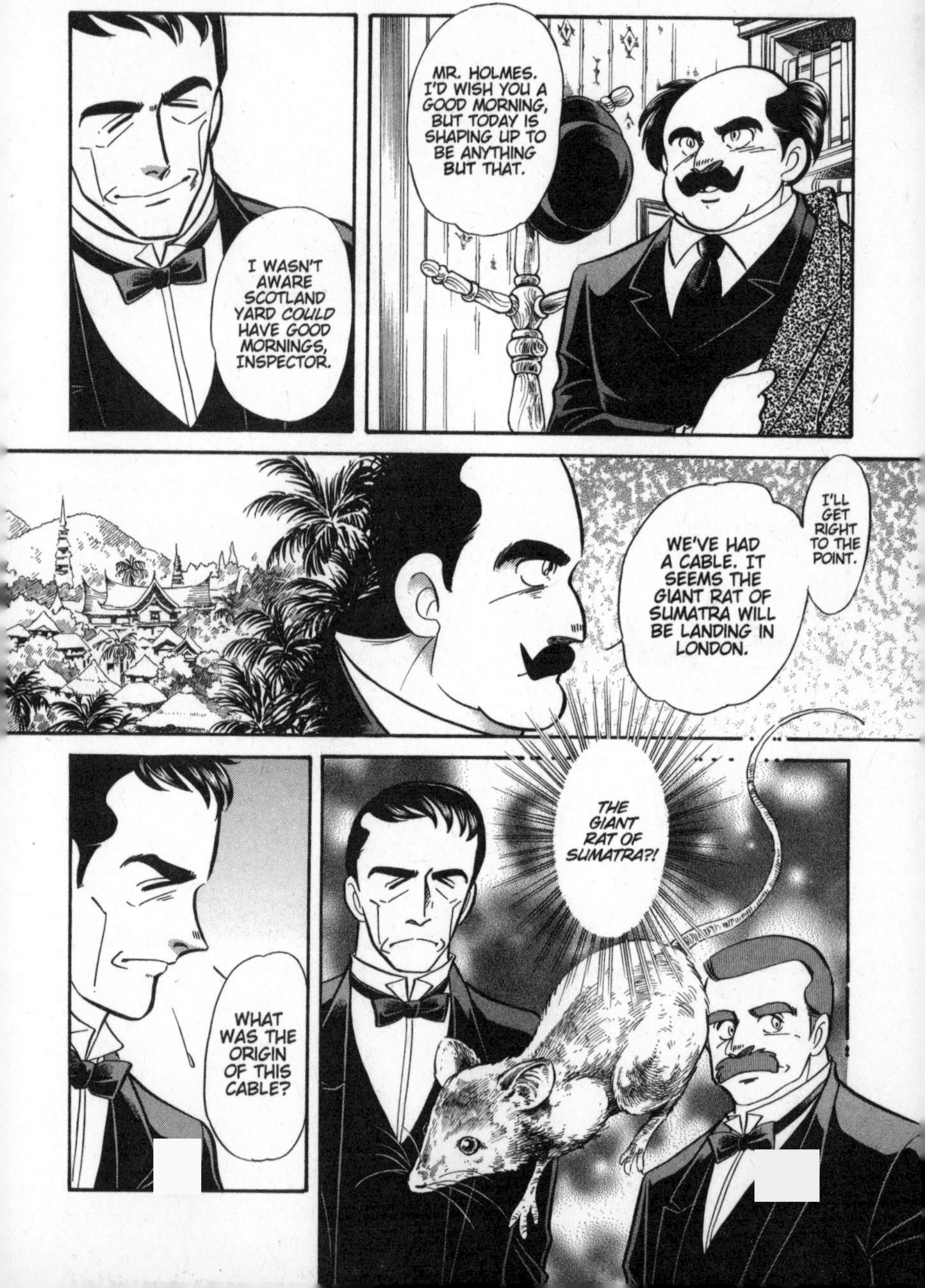
MR. HOLMES. I'D WISH YOU A GOOD MORNING, BUT TODAY IS SHAPING UP TO BE ANYTHING BUT THAT.
I WASN'T AWARE SCOTLAND YARD *COULD* HAVE GOOD MORNINGS, INSPECTOR.
I'LL GET RIGHT TO THE POINT.
WE'VE HAD A CABLE. IT SEEMS THE GIANT RAT OF SUMATRA WILL BE LANDING IN LONDON.
THE GIANT RAT OF SUMATRA?!
WHAT WAS THE ORIGIN OF THIS CABLE?

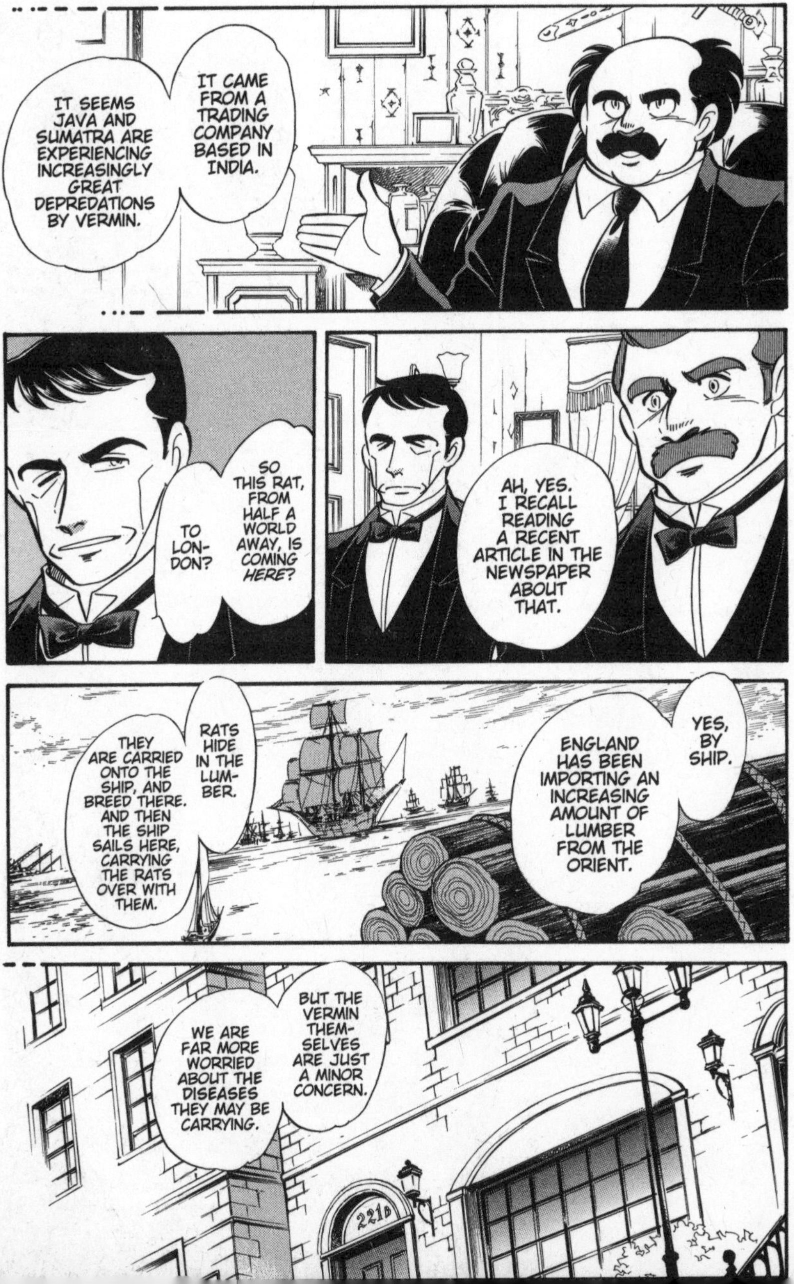
IT CAME FROM A TRADING COMPANY BASED IN INDIA.
IT SEEMS JAVA AND SUMATRA ARE EXPERIENCING INCREASINGLY GREAT DEPREDATIONS BY VERMIN.
AH, YES. I RECALL READING A RECENT ARTICLE IN THE NEWSPAPER ABOUT THAT.
SO THIS RAT, FROM HALF A WORLD AWAY, IS COMING *HERE*?
TO LON-DON?
YES, BY SHIP.
ENGLAND HAS BEEN IMPORTING AN INCREASING AMOUNT OF LUMBER FROM THE ORIENT.
RATS HIDE IN THE LUM-BER.
THEY ARE CARRIED ONTO THE SHIP, AND BREED THERE. AND THEN THE SHIP SAILS HERE, CARRYING THE RATS OVER WITH THEM.
BUT THE VERMIN THEM-SELVES ARE JUST A MINOR CONCERN.
WE ARE FAR MORE WORRIED ABOUT THE DISEASES THEY MAY BE CARRYING.
221b

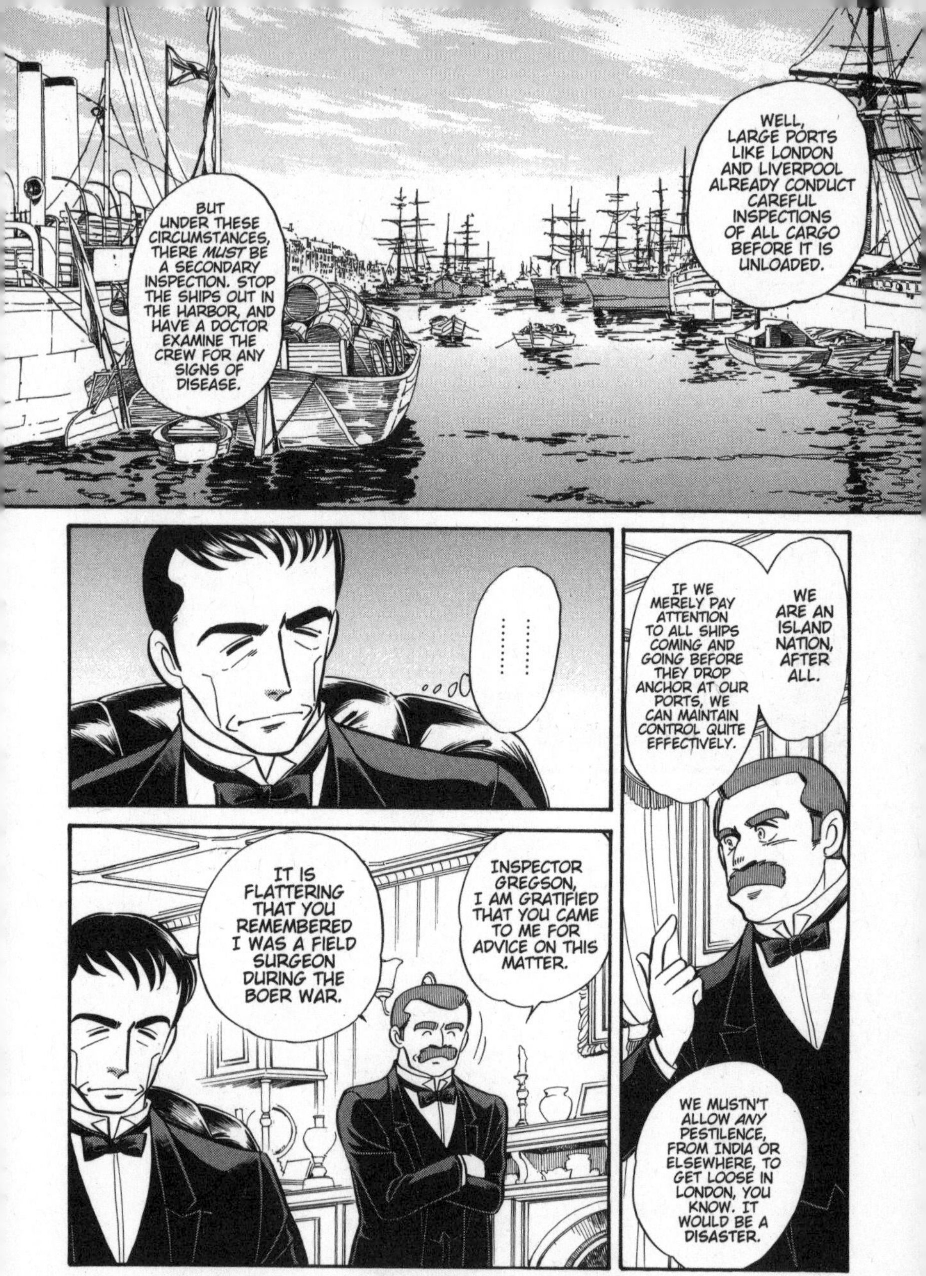

WELL, LARGE PORTS LIKE LONDON AND LIVERPOOL ALREADY CONDUCT CAREFUL INSPECTIONS OF ALL CARGO BEFORE IT IS UNLOADED.
BUT UNDER THESE CIRCUMSTANCES, THERE *MUST* BE A SECONDARY INSPECTION. STOP THE SHIPS OUT IN THE HARBOR, AND HAVE A DOCTOR EXAMINE THE CREW FOR ANY SIGNS OF DISEASE.
WE ARE AN ISLAND NATION, AFTER ALL.
IF WE MERELY PAY ATTENTION TO ALL SHIPS COMING AND GOING BEFORE THEY DROP ANCHOR AT OUR PORTS, WE CAN MAINTAIN CONTROL QUITE EFFECTIVELY.
WE MUSTN'T ALLOW *ANY* PESTILENCE, FROM INDIA OR ELSEWHERE, TO GET LOOSE IN LONDON, YOU KNOW. IT WOULD BE A DISASTER.
......
INSPECTOR GREGSON, I AM GRATIFIED THAT YOU CAME TO ME FOR ADVICE ON THIS MATTER.
IT IS FLATTERING THAT YOU REMEMBERED I WAS A FIELD SURGEON DURING THE BOER WAR.

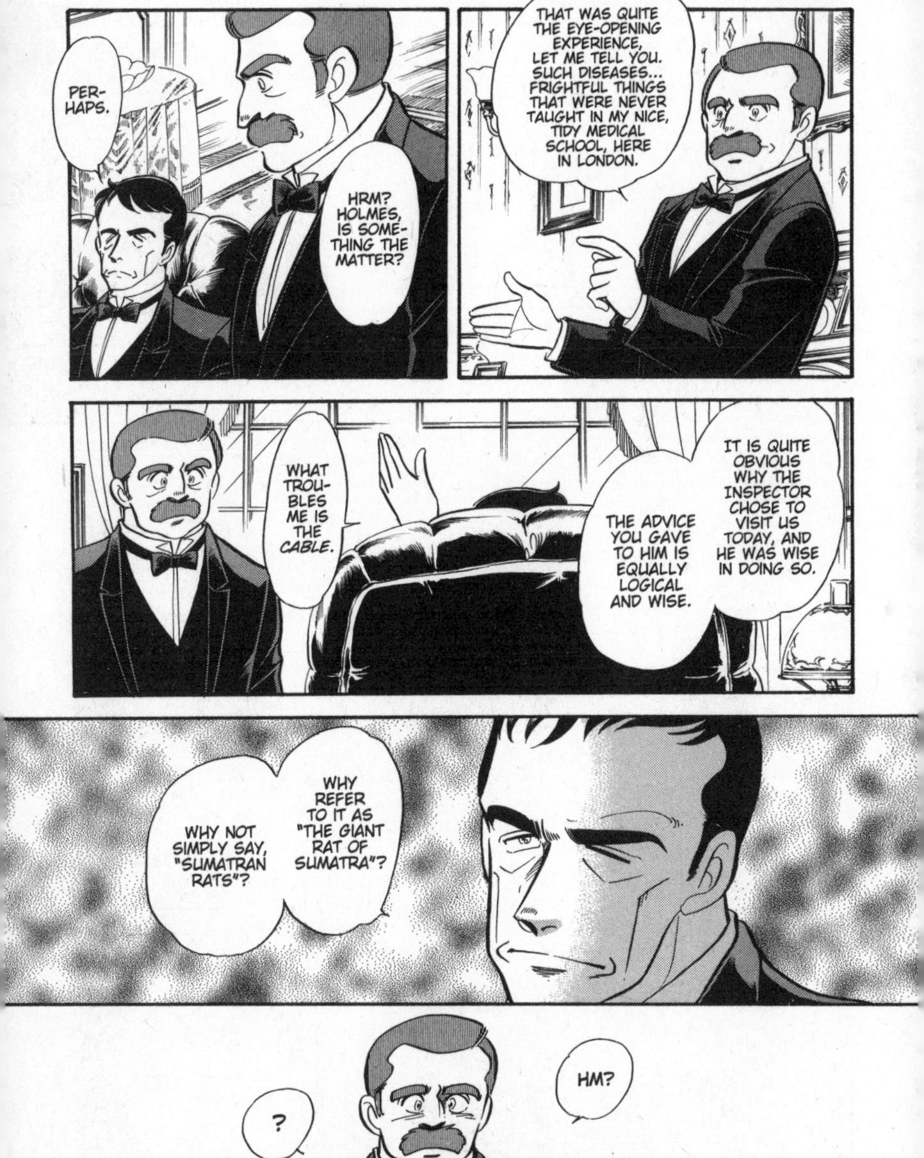
THAT WAS QUITE THE EYE-OPENING EXPERIENCE, LET ME TELL YOU. SUCH DISEASES... FRIGHTFUL THINGS THAT WERE NEVER TAUGHT IN MY NICE, TIDY MEDICAL SCHOOL, HERE IN LONDON.
HRM? HOLMES, IS SOMETHING THE MATTER?
PER-HAPS.
IT IS QUITE OBVIOUS WHY THE INSPECTOR CHOSE TO VISIT US TODAY, AND HE WAS WISE IN DOING SO.
THE ADVICE YOU GAVE TO HIM IS EQUALLY LOGICAL AND WISE.
WHAT TROU-BLES ME IS THE CABLE.
WHY REFER TO IT AS "THE GIANT RAT OF SUMATRA"?
WHY NOT SIMPLY SAY, "SUMATRAN RATS"?
HM?
?

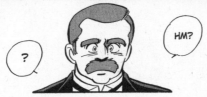

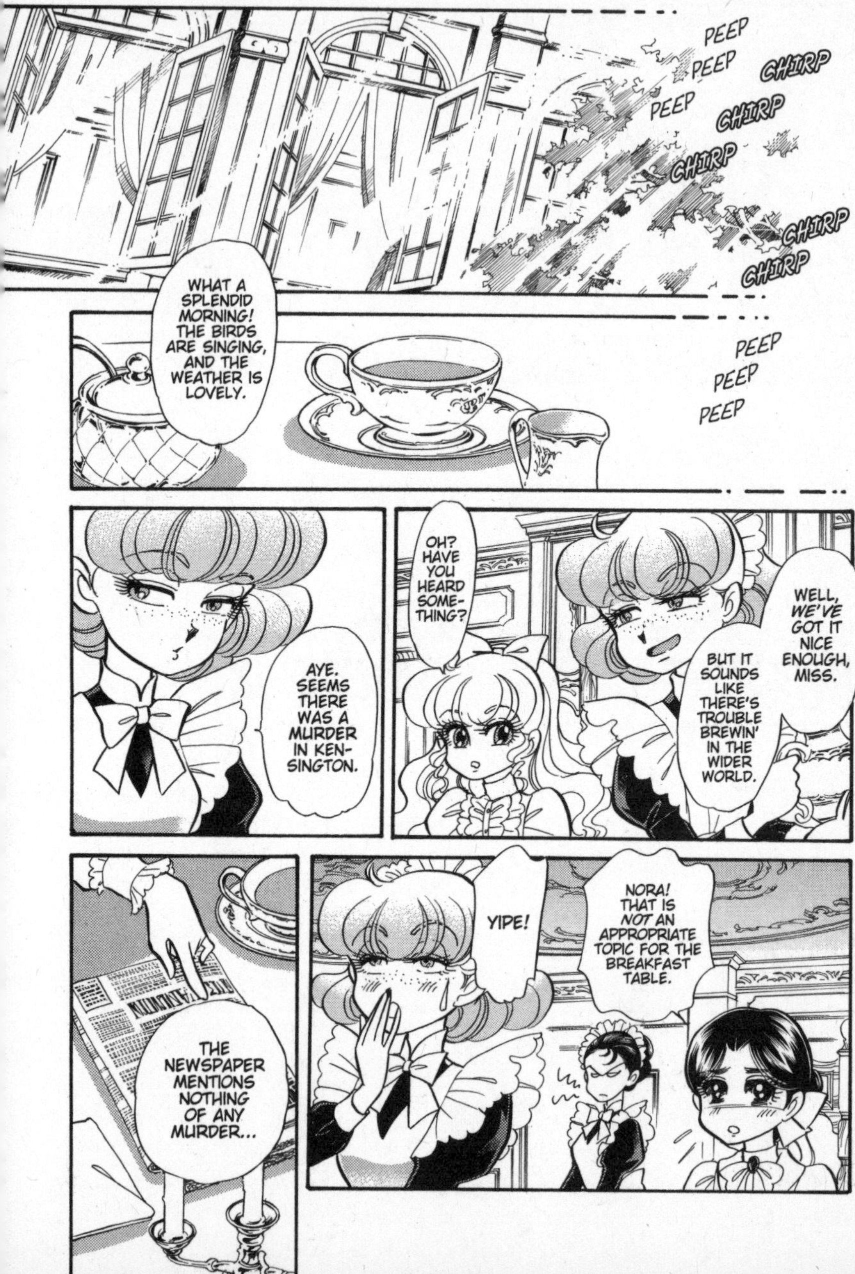
PEEP
PEEP
PEEP
CHIRP
CHIRP
CHIRP
CHIRP
CHIRP
WHAT A SPLENDID MORNING! THE BIRDS ARE SINGING, AND THE WEATHER IS LOVELY.
PEEP
PEEP
PEEP
WELL, *WE'VE* GOT IT NICE ENOUGH, MISS.
BUT IT SOUNDS LIKE THERE'S TROUBLE BREWIN' IN THE WIDER WORLD.
OH? HAVE YOU HEARD SOME-THING?
AYE. SEEMS THERE WAS A MURDER IN KEN-SINGTON.
NORA! THAT IS *NOT* AN APPROPRIATE TOPIC FOR THE BREAKFAST TABLE.
YIPE!
THE NEWSPAPER MENTIONS NOTHING OF ANY MURDER...

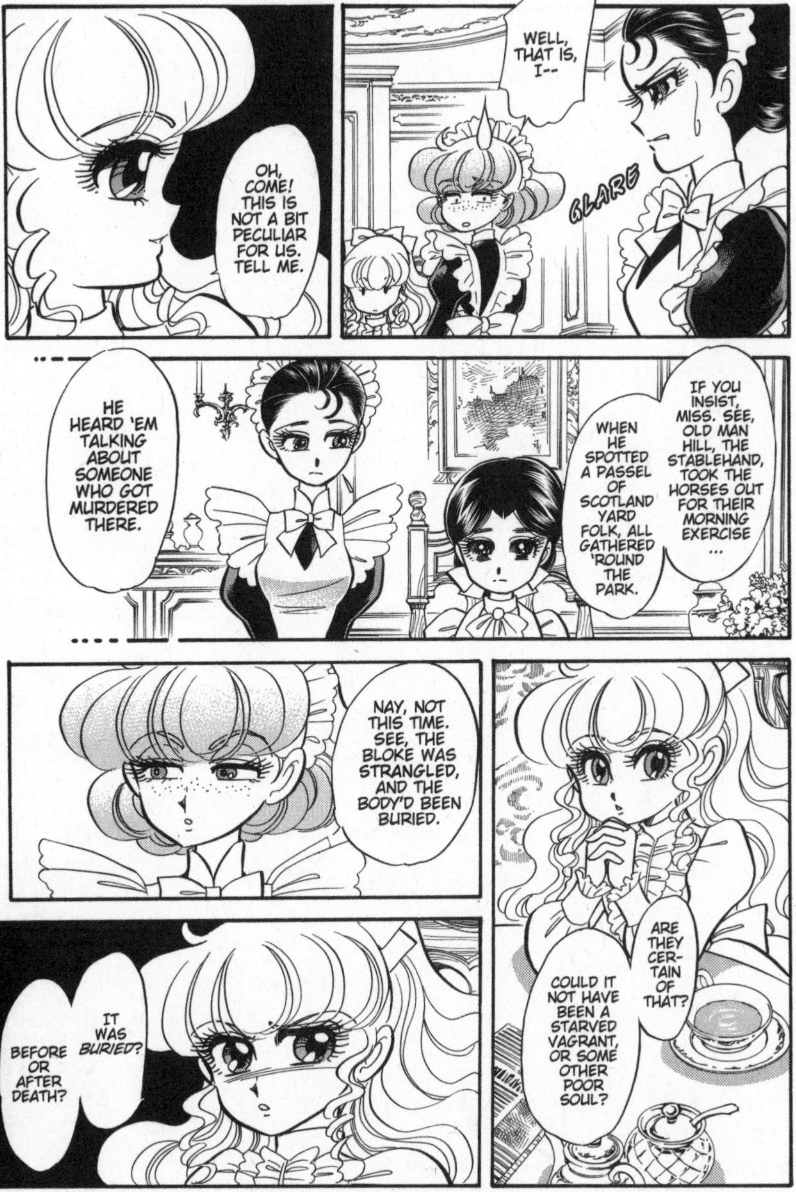
WELL, THAT IS, I--
GLARE
OH, COME! THIS IS NOT A BIT PECULIAR FOR US. TELL ME.
IF YOU INSIST, MISS. SEE, OLD MAN HILL, THE STABLEHAND, TOOK THE HORSES OUT FOR THEIR MORNING EXERCISE ...
WHEN HE SPOTTED A PASSEL OF SCOTLAND YARD FOLK, ALL GATHERED 'ROUND THE PARK.
HE HEARD 'EM TALKING ABOUT SOMEONE WHO GOT MURDERED THERE.
ARE THEY CER-TAIN OF THAT?
COULD IT NOT HAVE BEEN A STARVED VAGRANT, OR SOME OTHER POOR SOUL?
NAY, NOT THIS TIME. SEE, THE BLOKE WAS STRANGLED, AND THE BODY'D BEEN BURIED.
IT WAS *BURIED*?
BEFORE OR AFTER DEATH?

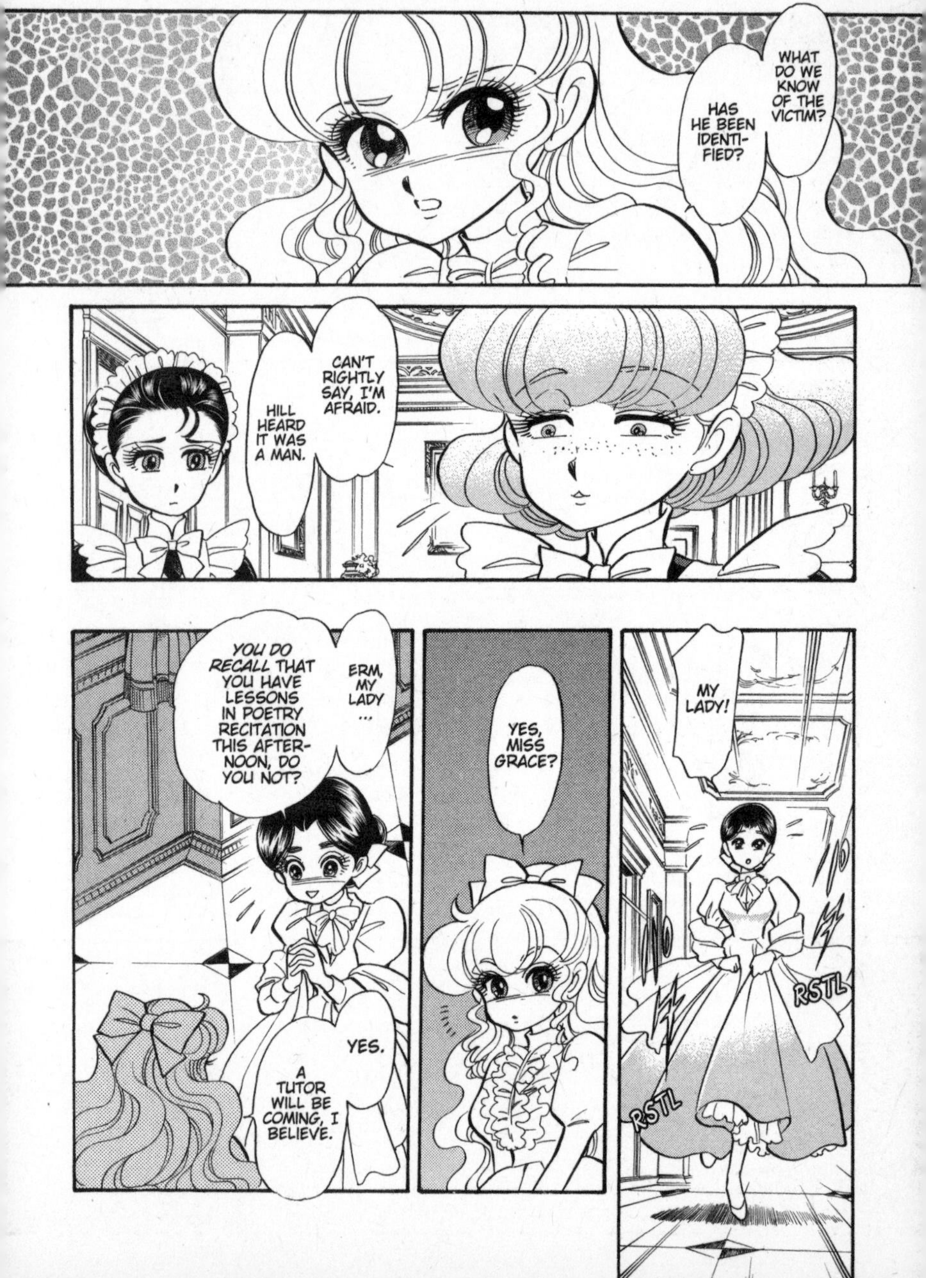
WHAT DO WE KNOW OF THE VICTIM?
HAS HE BEEN IDENTIFIED?
CAN'T RIGHTLY SAY, I'M AFRAID.
HILL HEARD IT WAS A MAN.
MY LADY!
RSTL
RSTL
YES, MISS GRACE?
ERM, MY LADY ...
YOU DO RECALL THAT YOU HAVE LESSONS IN POETRY RECITATION THIS AFTERNOON, DO YOU NOT?
YES.
A TUTOR WILL BE COMING, I BELIEVE.

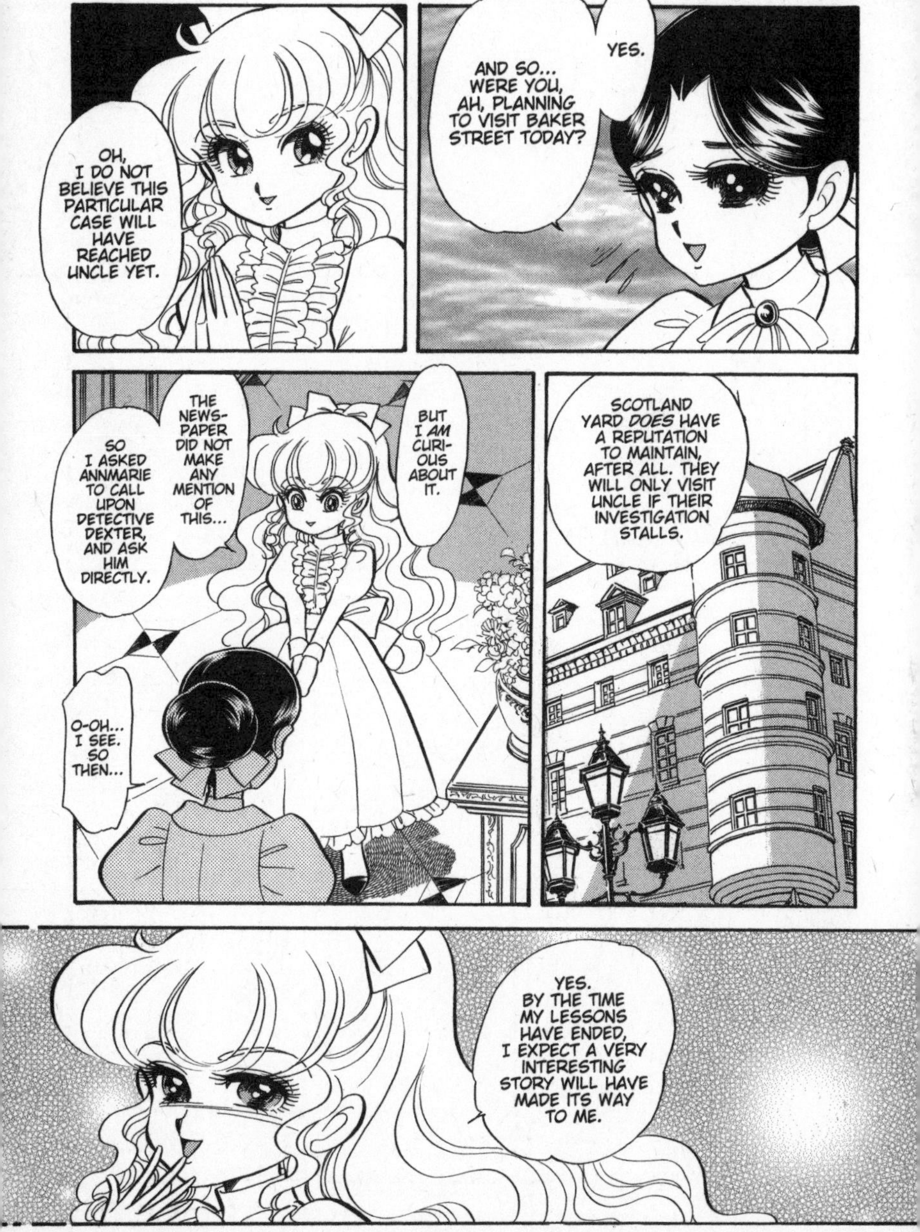
YES.
AND SO... WERE YOU, AH, PLANNING TO VISIT BAKER STREET TODAY?
OH, I DO NOT BELIEVE THIS PARTICULAR CASE WILL HAVE REACHED UNCLE YET.
SCOTLAND YARD *DOES* HAVE A REPUTATION TO MAINTAIN, AFTER ALL. THEY WILL ONLY VISIT UNCLE IF THEIR INVESTIGATION STALLS.
BUT I *AM* CURIOUS ABOUT IT.
THE NEWSPAPER DID NOT MAKE ANY MENTION OF THIS...
SO I ASKED ANNMARIE TO CALL UPON DETECTIVE DEXTER, AND ASK HIM DIRECTLY.
O-OH... I SEE. SO THEN...
YES. BY THE TIME MY LESSONS HAVE ENDED, I EXPECT A VERY INTERESTING STORY WILL HAVE MADE ITS WAY TO ME.

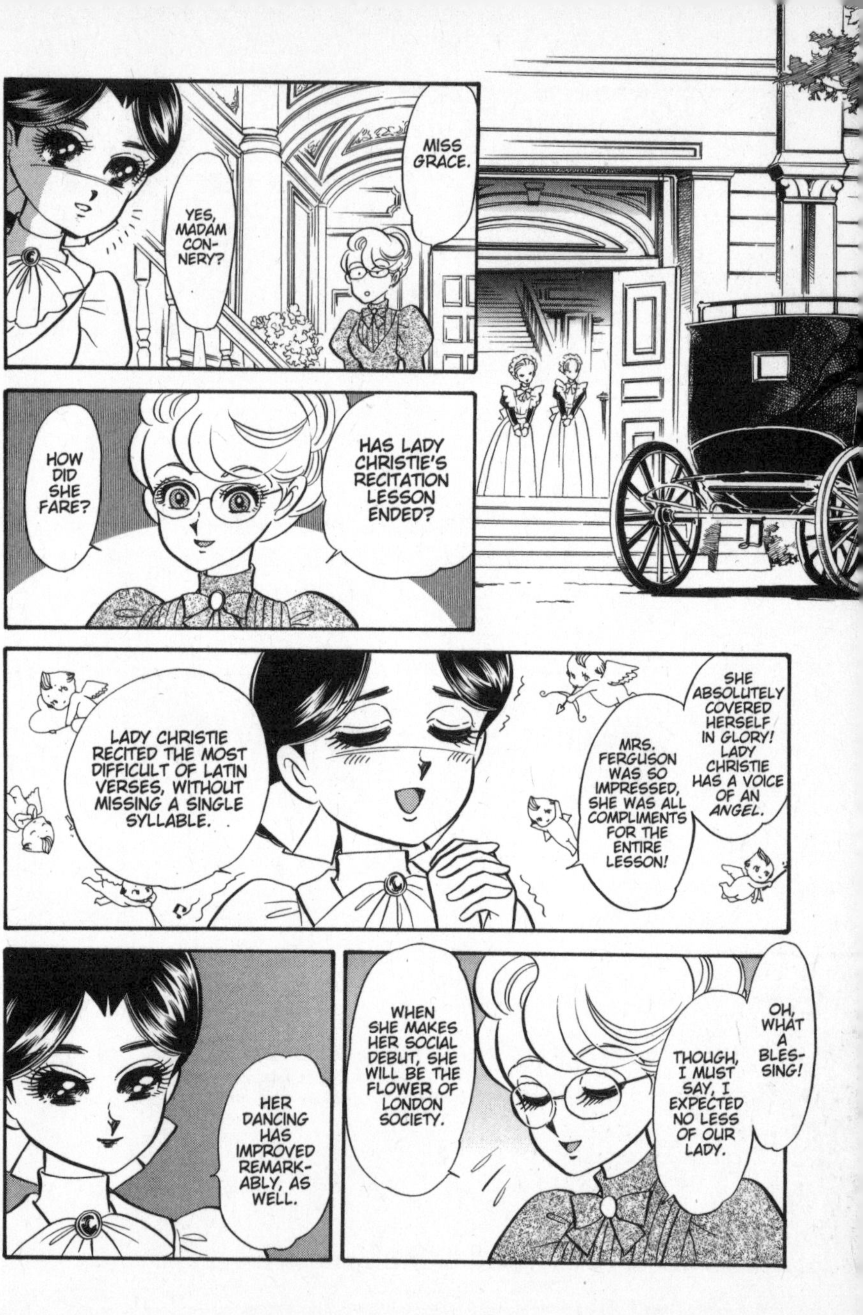
MISS GRACE.
YES, MADAM CONNERY?
HAS LADY CHRISTIE'S RECITATION LESSON ENDED?
HOW DID SHE FARE?
SHE ABSOLUTELY COVERED HERSELF IN GLORY! LADY CHRISTIE HAS A VOICE OF AN ANGEL.
MRS. FERGUSON WAS SO IMPRESSED, SHE WAS ALL COMPLIMENTS FOR THE ENTIRE LESSON!
LADY CHRISTIE RECITED THE MOST DIFFICULT OF LATIN VERSES, WITHOUT MISSING A SINGLE SYLLABLE.
OH, WHAT A BLESSING!
THOUGH, I MUST SAY, I EXPECTED NO LESS OF OUR LADY.
WHEN SHE MAKES HER SOCIAL DEBUT, SHE WILL BE THE FLOWER OF LONDON SOCIETY.
HER DANCING HAS IMPROVED REMARKABLY, AS WELL.

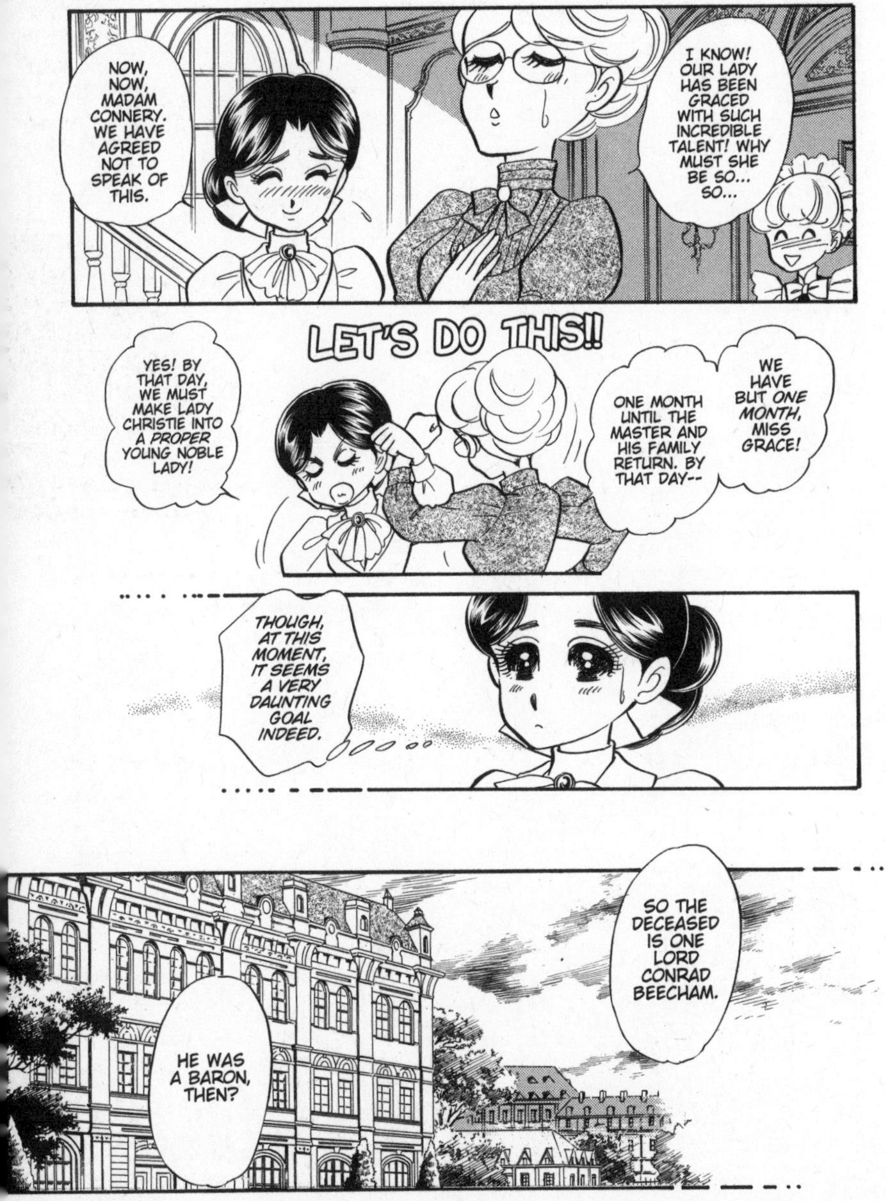
I KNOW! OUR LADY HAS BEEN GRACED WITH SUCH INCREDIBLE TALENT! WHY MUST SHE BE SO... SO...
NOW, NOW, MADAM CONNERY. WE HAVE AGREED NOT TO SPEAK OF THIS.
WE HAVE BUT *ONE MONTH*, MISS GRACE!
ONE MONTH UNTIL THE MASTER AND HIS FAMILY RETURN. BY THAT DAY--
YES! BY THAT DAY, WE MUST MAKE LADY CHRISTIE INTO A *PROPER* YOUNG NOBLE LADY!
LET'S DO THIS!!
THOUGH, AT THIS MOMENT, IT SEEMS A VERY DAUNTING GOAL INDEED.
SO THE DECEASED IS ONE LORD CONRAD BEECHAM.
HE WAS A BARON, THEN?

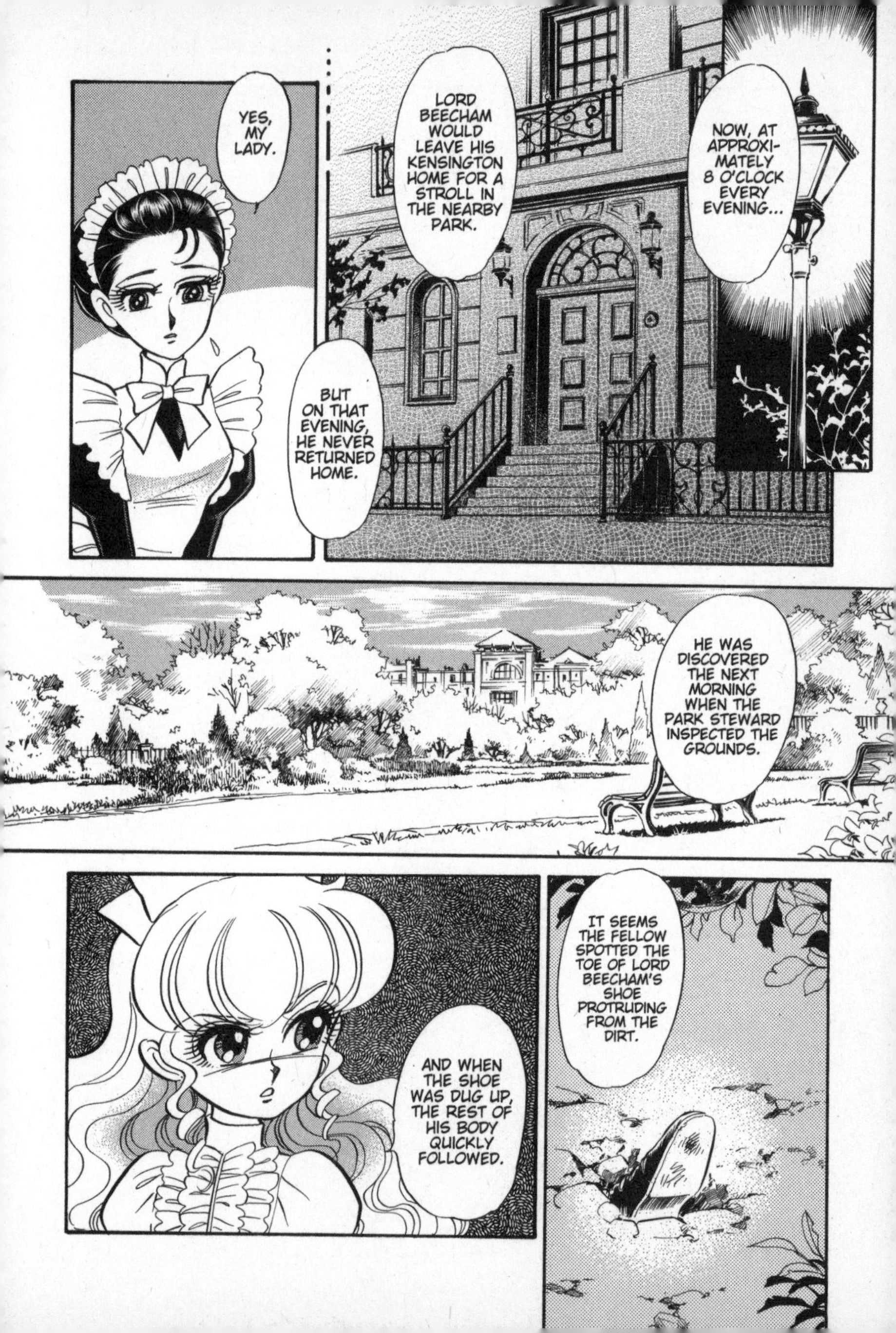
NOW, AT APPROXI-MATELY 8 O'CLOCK EVERY EVENING...
LORD BEECHAM WOULD LEAVE HIS KENSINGTON HOME FOR A STROLL IN THE NEARBY PARK.
BUT ON THAT EVENING, HE NEVER RETURNED HOME.
YES, MY LADY.
HE WAS DISCOVERED THE NEXT MORNING WHEN THE PARK STEWARD INSPECTED THE GROUNDS.
IT SEEMS THE FELLOW SPOTTED THE TOE OF LORD BEECHAM'S SHOE PROTRUDING FROM THE DIRT.
AND WHEN THE SHOE WAS DUG UP, THE REST OF HIS BODY QUICKLY FOLLOWED.

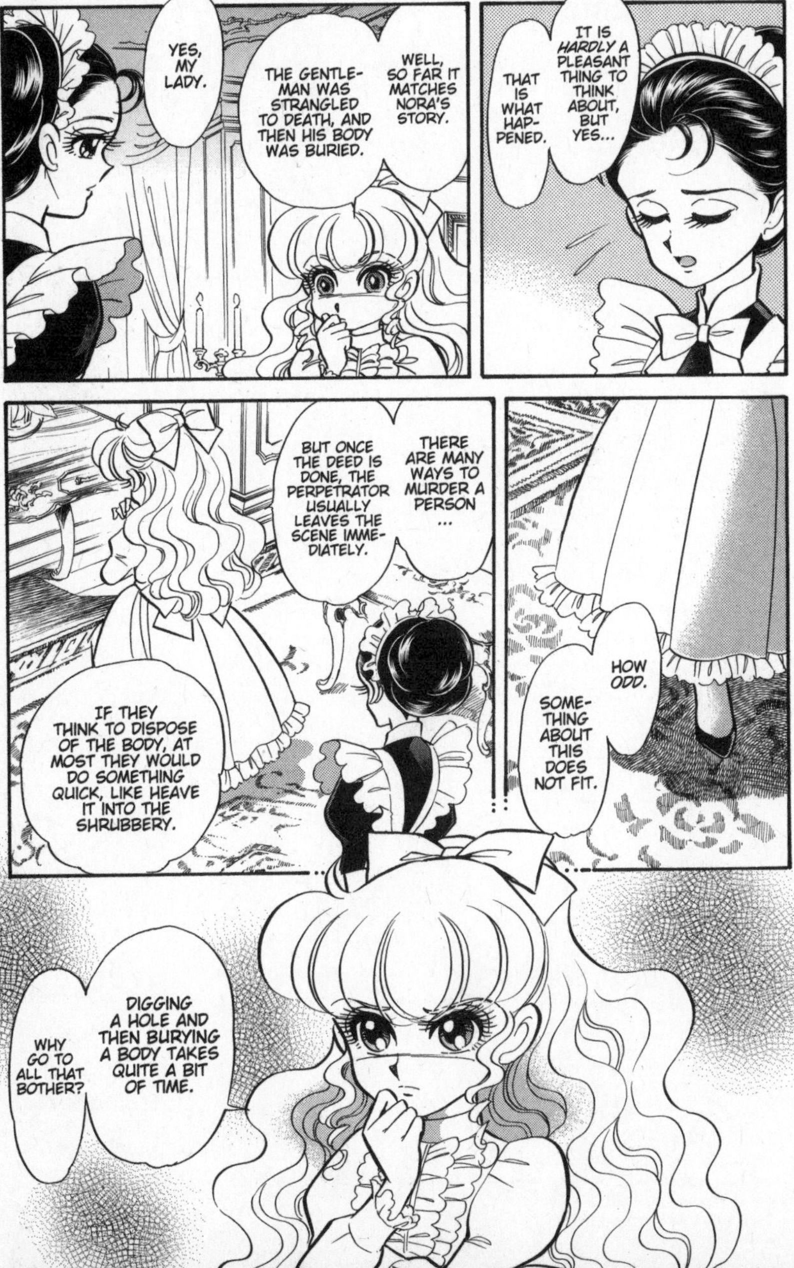
IT IS *HARDLY* A PLEASANT THING TO THINK ABOUT, BUT YES...
THAT IS WHAT HAPPENED.
WELL, SO FAR IT MATCHES NORA'S STORY.
THE GENTLEMAN WAS STRANGLED TO DEATH, AND THEN HIS BODY WAS BURIED.
YES, MY LADY.
HOW ODD.
SOMETHING ABOUT THIS DOES NOT FIT.
THERE ARE MANY WAYS TO MURDER A PERSON ...
BUT ONCE THE DEED IS DONE, THE PERPETRATOR USUALLY LEAVES THE SCENE IMMEDIATELY.
IF THEY THINK TO DISPOSE OF THE BODY, AT MOST THEY WOULD DO SOMETHING QUICK, LIKE HEAVE IT INTO THE SHRUBBERY.
DIGGING A HOLE AND THEN BURYING A BODY TAKES QUITE A BIT OF TIME.
WHY GO TO ALL THAT BOTHER?

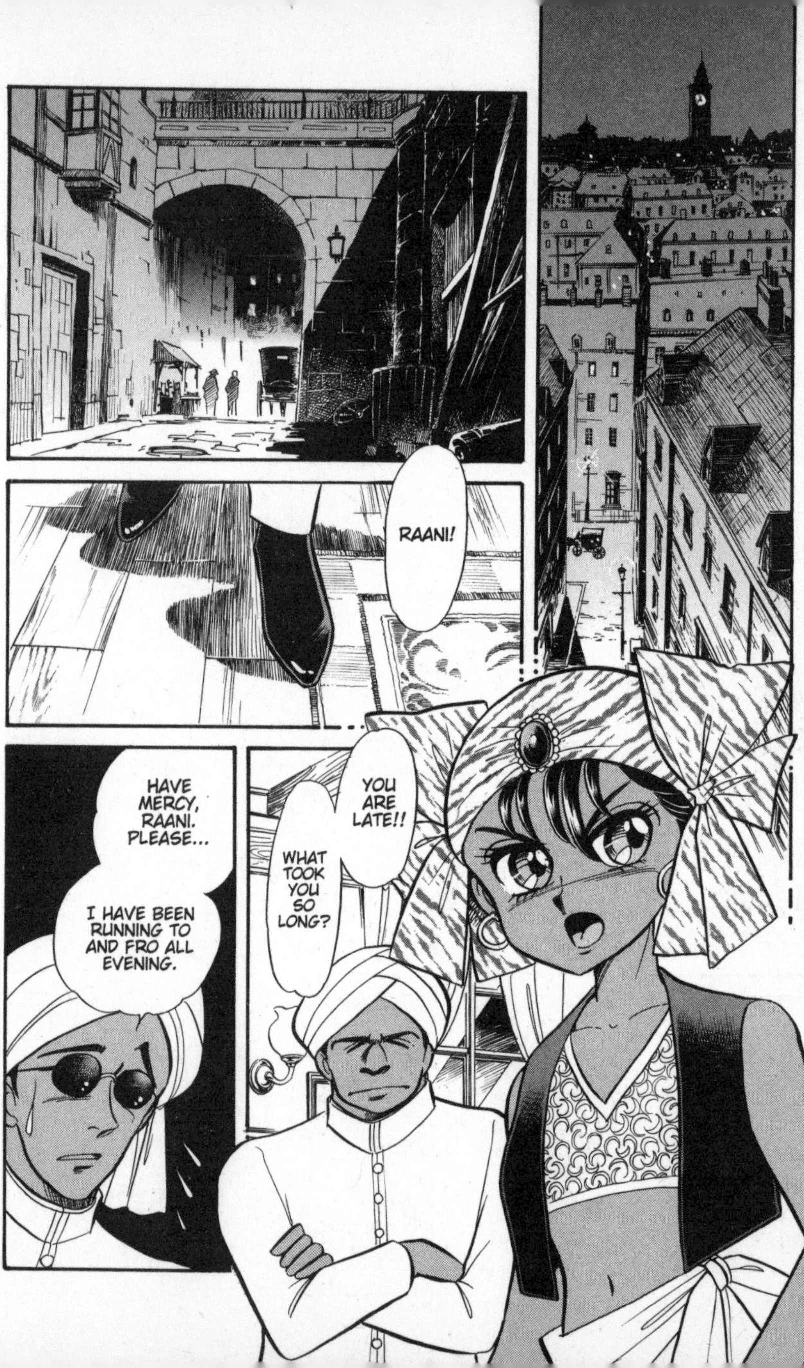
RAANI!
YOU ARE LATE!!
WHAT TOOK YOU SO LONG?
HAVE MERCY, RAANI. PLEASE...
I HAVE BEEN RUNNING TO AND FRO ALL EVENING.

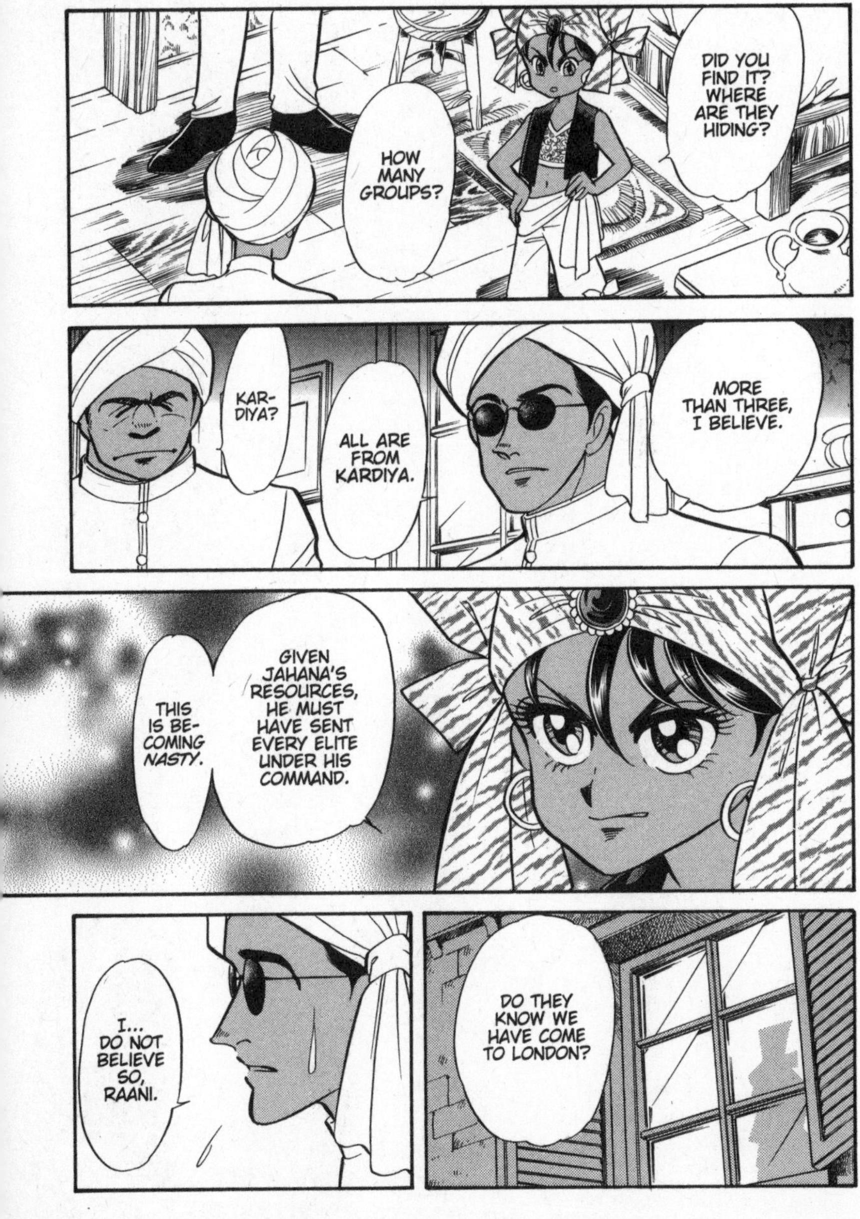
DID YOU FIND IT? WHERE ARE THEY HIDING?
HOW MANY GROUPS?
MORE THAN THREE, I BELIEVE.
ALL ARE FROM KARDIYA.
KARDIYA?
GIVEN JAHANA'S RESOURCES, HE MUST HAVE SENT EVERY ELITE UNDER HIS COMMAND.
THIS IS BECOMING *NASTY*.
DO THEY KNOW WE HAVE COME TO LONDON?
I... DO NOT BELIEVE SO, RAANI.

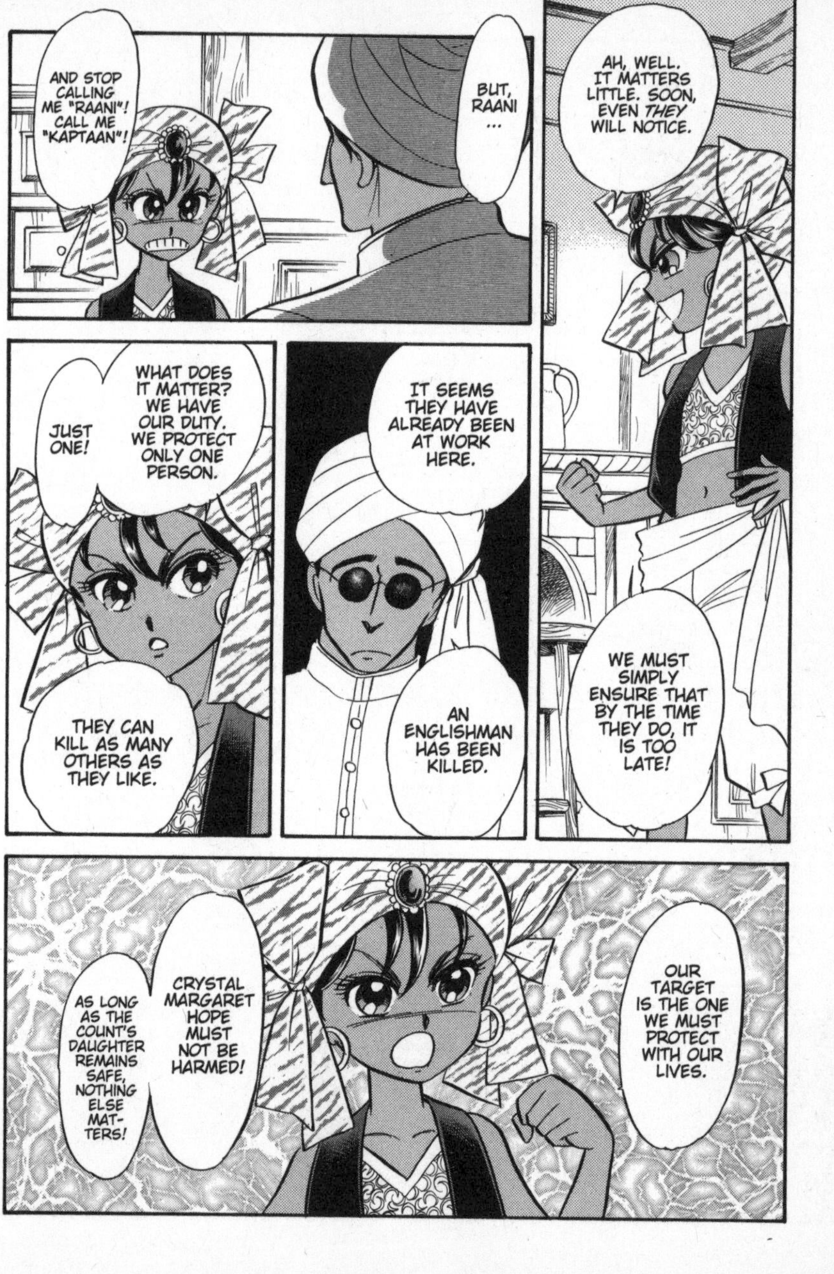
AH, WELL. IT MATTERS LITTLE. SOON, EVEN *THEY* WILL NOTICE.
WE MUST SIMPLY ENSURE THAT BY THE TIME THEY DO, IT IS TOO LATE!
BUT, RAANI ...
AND STOP CALLING ME "RAANI"! CALL ME "KAPTAAN"!
IT SEEMS THEY HAVE ALREADY BEEN AT WORK HERE.
AN ENGLISHMAN HAS BEEN KILLED.
WHAT DOES IT MATTER? WE HAVE OUR DUTY. WE PROTECT ONLY ONE PERSON.
JUST ONE!
THEY CAN KILL AS MANY OTHERS AS THEY LIKE.
OUR TARGET IS THE ONE WE MUST PROTECT WITH OUR LIVES.
CRYSTAL MARGARET HOPE MUST NOT BE HARMED!
AS LONG AS THE COUNT'S DAUGHTER REMAINS SAFE, NOTHING ELSE MAT-TERS!

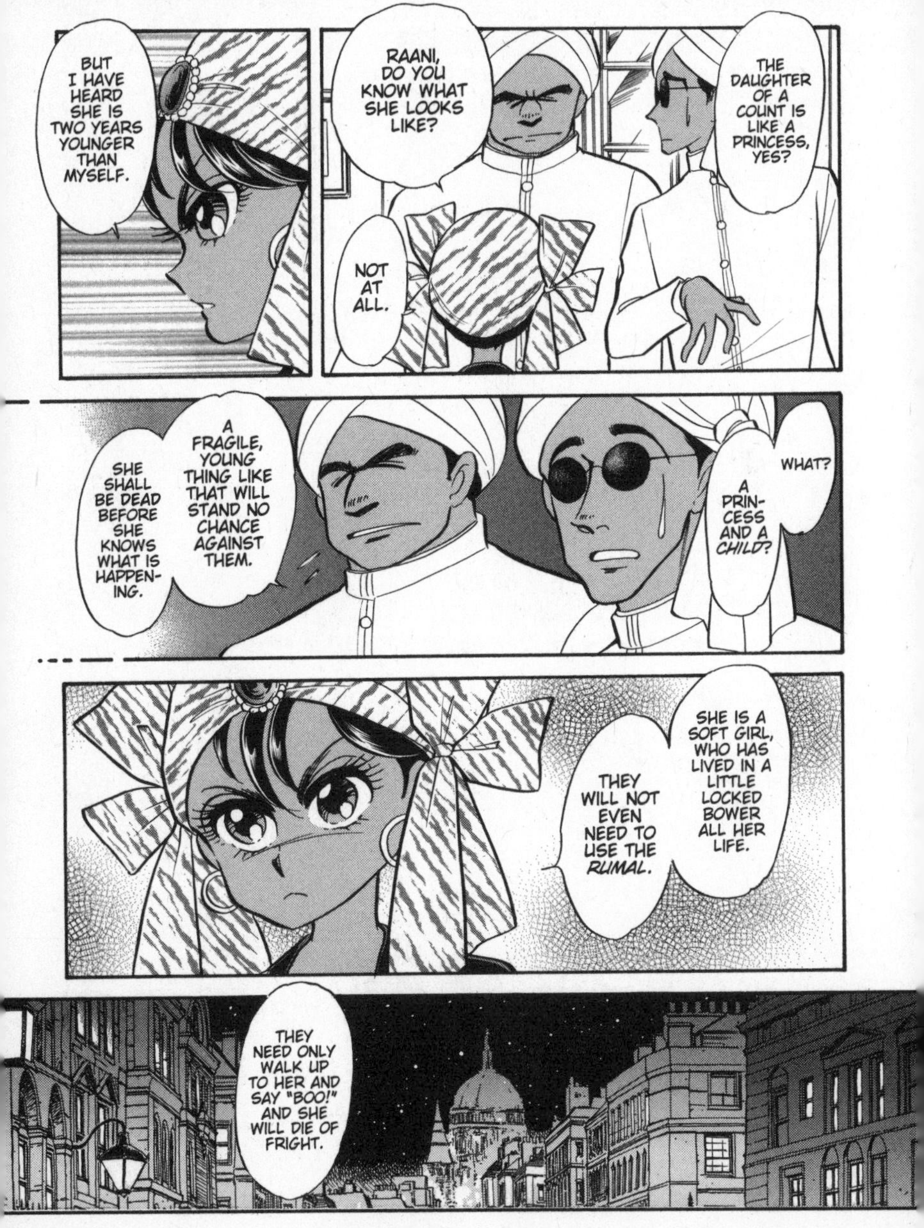
THE DAUGHTER OF A COUNT IS LIKE A PRINCESS, YES?
RAANI, DO YOU KNOW WHAT SHE LOOKS LIKE?
NOT AT ALL.
BUT I HAVE HEARD SHE IS TWO YEARS YOUNGER THAN MYSELF.
WHAT?
A PRIN-CESS AND A *CHILD*?
A FRAGILE, YOUNG THING LIKE THAT WILL STAND NO CHANCE AGAINST THEM.
SHE SHALL BE DEAD BEFORE SHE KNOWS WHAT IS HAPPEN-ING.
SHE IS A SOFT GIRL, WHO HAS LIVED IN A LITTLE LOCKED BOWER ALL HER LIFE.
THEY WILL NOT EVEN NEED TO USE THE *RUMAL*.
THEY NEED ONLY WALK UP TO HER AND SAY "BOO!" AND SHE WILL DIE OF FRIGHT.

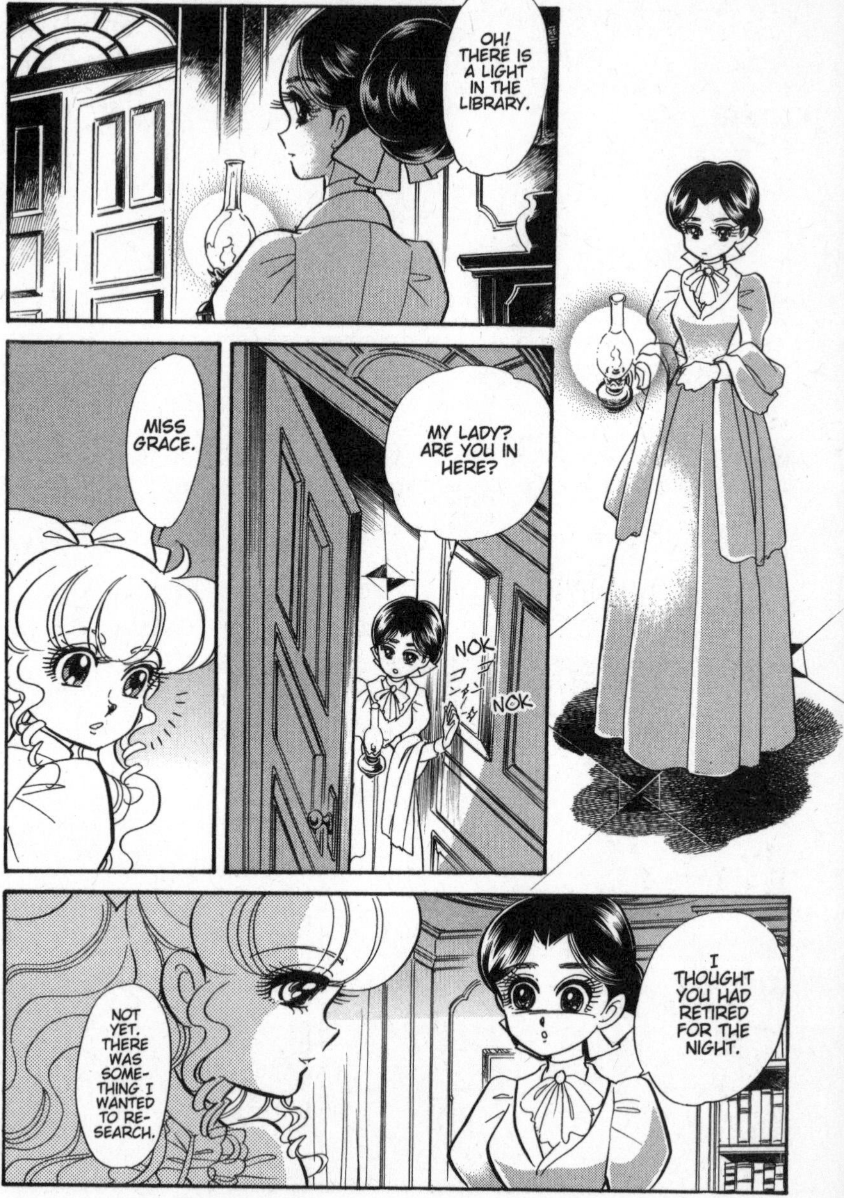
OH! THERE IS A LIGHT IN THE LIBRARY.
MY LADY? ARE YOU IN HERE?
NOK
NOK
MISS GRACE.
I THOUGHT YOU HAD RETIRED FOR THE NIGHT.
NOT YET. THERE WAS SOME-THING I WANTED TO RE-SEARCH.

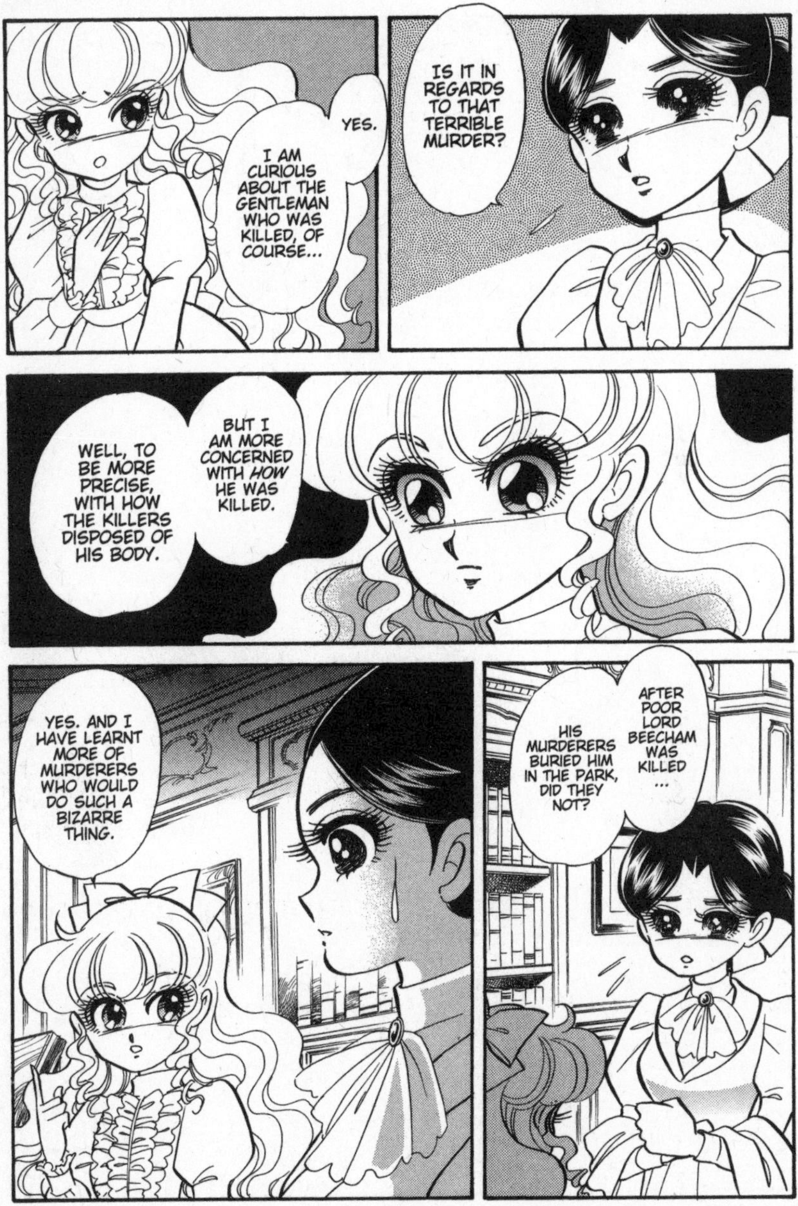
IS IT IN REGARDS TO THAT TERRIBLE MURDER?
YES.
I AM CURIOUS ABOUT THE GENTLEMAN WHO WAS KILLED, OF COURSE...
BUT I AM MORE CONCERNED WITH *HOW* HE WAS KILLED.
WELL, TO BE MORE PRECISE, WITH HOW THE KILLERS DISPOSED OF HIS BODY.
AFTER POOR LORD BEECHAM WAS KILLED ...
HIS MURDERERS BURIED HIM IN THE PARK, DID THEY NOT?
YES. AND I HAVE LEARNT MORE OF MURDERERS WHO WOULD DO SUCH A BIZARRE THING.

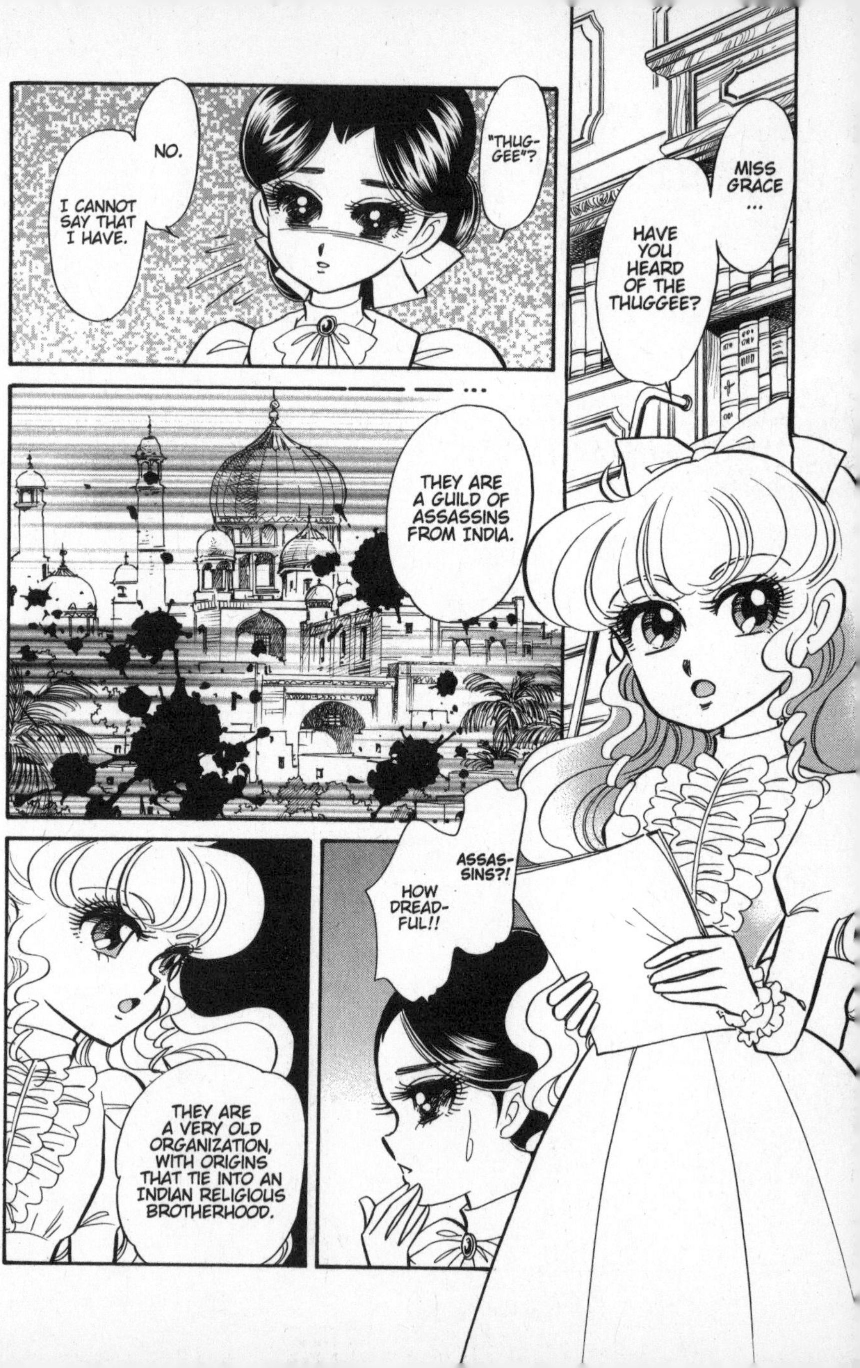
MISS GRACE ...
HAVE YOU HEARD OF THE THUGGEE?
"THUGGEE"?
NO.
I CANNOT SAY THAT I HAVE.
THEY ARE A GUILD OF ASSASSINS FROM INDIA.
ASSAS-SINS?!
HOW DREAD-FUL!!
THEY ARE A VERY OLD ORGANIZATION, WITH ORIGINS THAT TIE INTO AN INDIAN RELIGIOUS BROTHERHOOD.

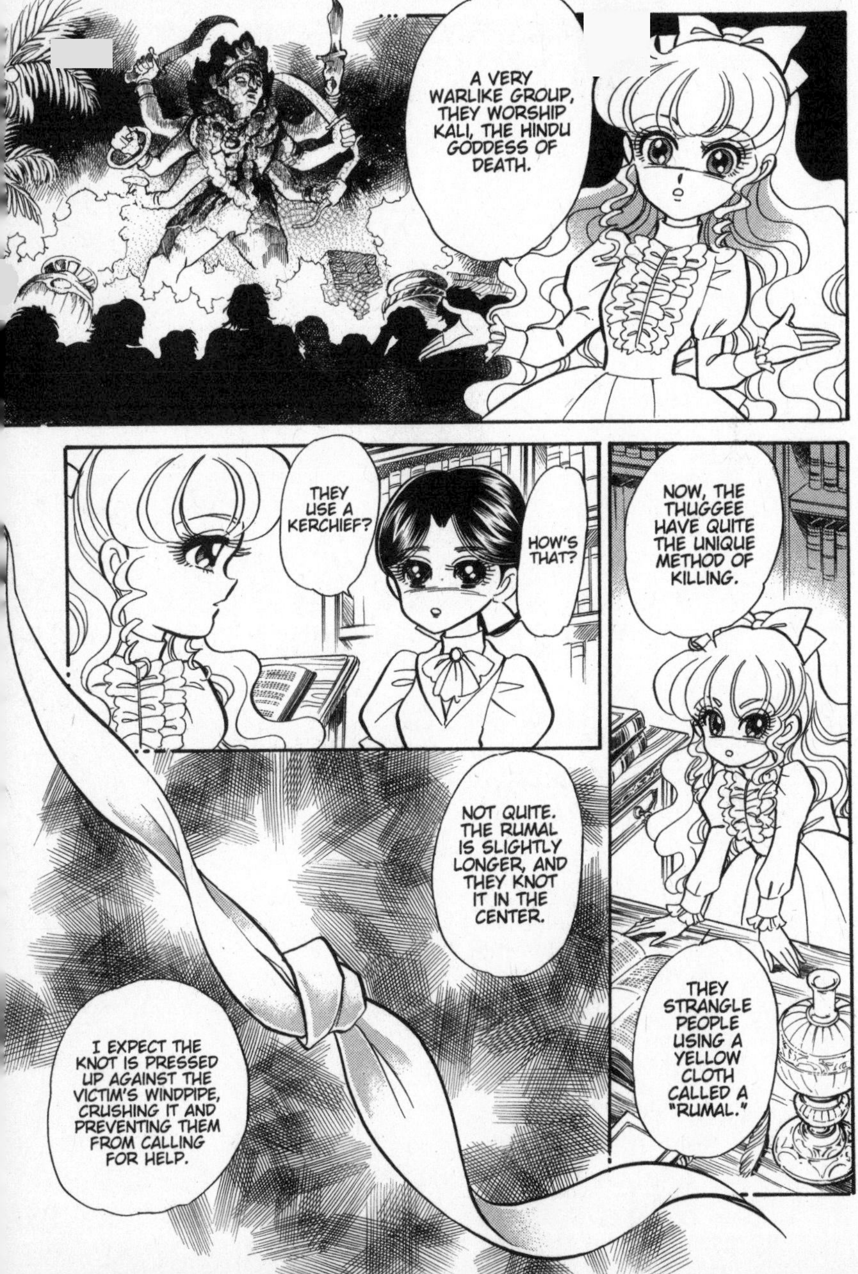
A VERY WARLIKE GROUP, THEY WORSHIP KALI, THE HINDU GODDESS OF DEATH.
NOW, THE THUGGEE HAVE QUITE THE UNIQUE METHOD OF KILLING.
THEY STRANGLE PEOPLE USING A YELLOW CLOTH CALLED A "RUMAL."
THEY USE A KERCHIEF?
HOW'S THAT?
NOT QUITE. THE RUMAL IS SLIGHTLY LONGER, AND THEY KNOT IT IN THE CENTER.
I EXPECT THE KNOT IS PRESSED UP AGAINST THE VICTIM'S WINDPIPE, CRUSHING IT AND PREVENTING THEM FROM CALLING FOR HELP.

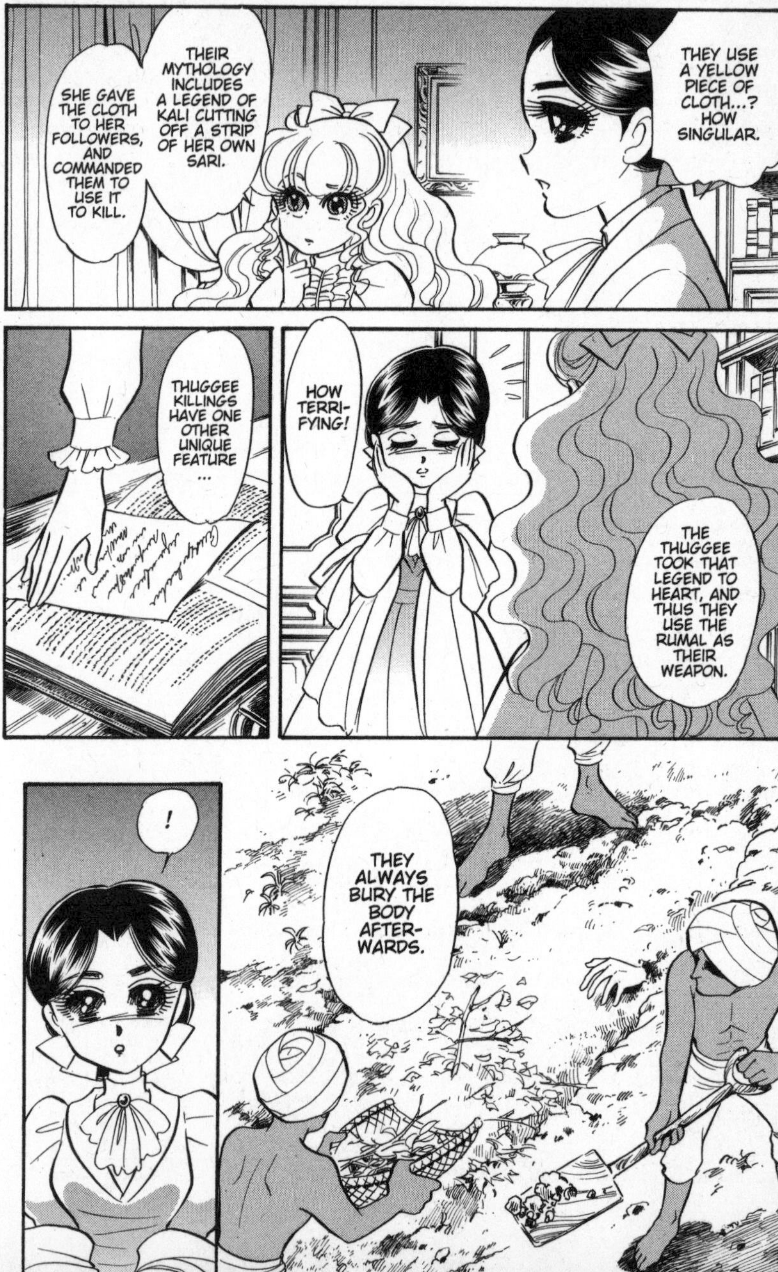
THEY USE A YELLOW PIECE OF CLOTH...? HOW SINGULAR.
THEIR MYTHOLOGY INCLUDES A LEGEND OF KALI CUTTING OFF A STRIP OF HER OWN SARI.
SHE GAVE THE CLOTH TO HER FOLLOWERS, AND COMMANDED THEM TO USE IT TO KILL.
THE THUGGEE TOOK THAT LEGEND TO HEART, AND THUS THEY USE THE RUMAL AS THEIR WEAPON.
HOW TERRI-FYING!
THUGGEE KILLINGS HAVE ONE OTHER UNIQUE FEATURE ...
THEY ALWAYS BURY THE BODY AFTER-WARDS.
!

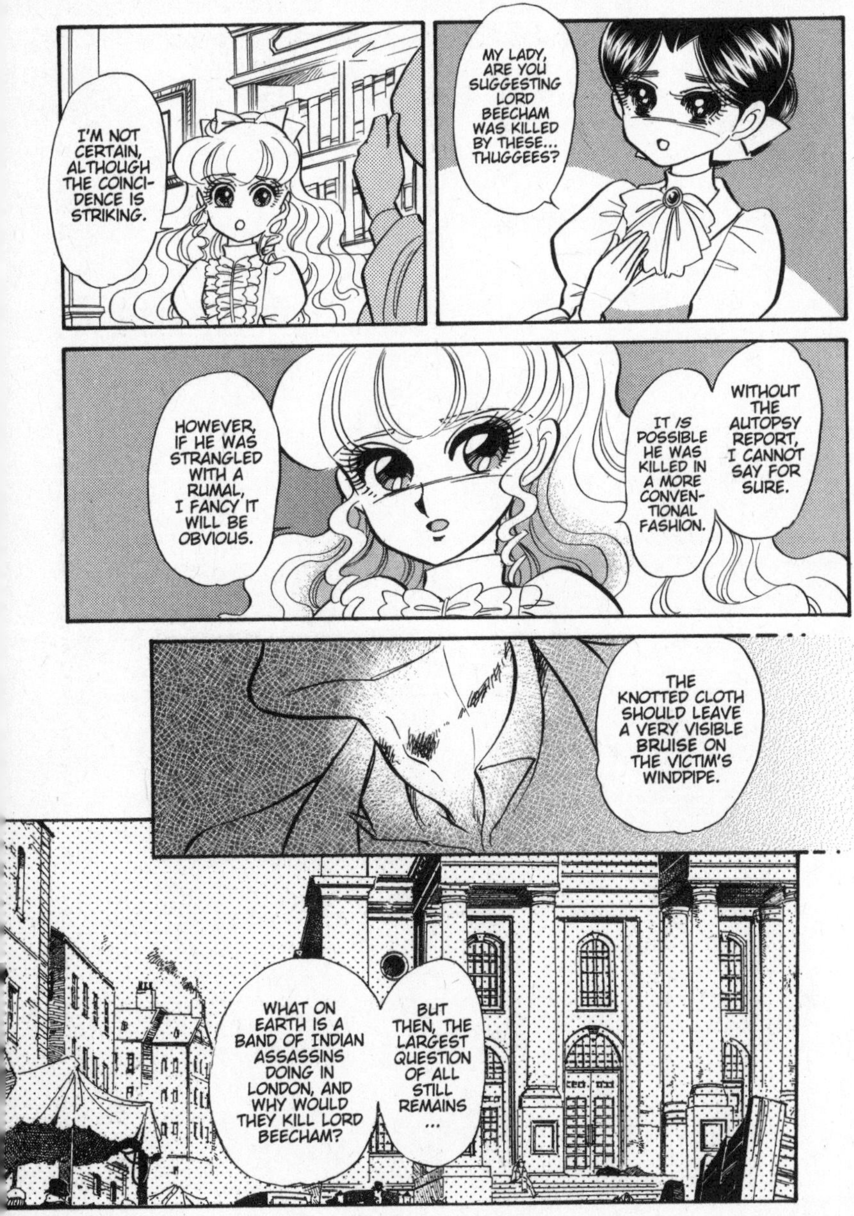
MY LADY, ARE YOU SUGGESTING LORD BEECHAM WAS KILLED BY THESE... THUGGEES?
I'M NOT CERTAIN, ALTHOUGH THE COINCIDENCE IS STRIKING.
WITHOUT THE AUTOPSY REPORT, I CANNOT SAY FOR SURE.
IT IS POSSIBLE HE WAS KILLED IN A MORE CONVENTIONAL FASHION.
HOWEVER, IF HE WAS STRANGLED WITH A RUMAL, I FANCY IT WILL BE OBVIOUS.
THE KNOTTED CLOTH SHOULD LEAVE A VERY VISIBLE BRUISE ON THE VICTIM'S WINDPIPE.
BUT THEN, THE LARGEST QUESTION OF ALL STILL REMAINS ...
WHAT ON EARTH IS A BAND OF INDIAN ASSASSINS DOING IN LONDON, AND WHY WOULD THEY KILL LORD BEECHAM?

I CANNOT HELP BUT WONDER IF THERE IS ANY CONNECTION TO FATHER'S RETURN.

MY LADY ...

The Adventure of The Giant Rat of Sumatra (2)

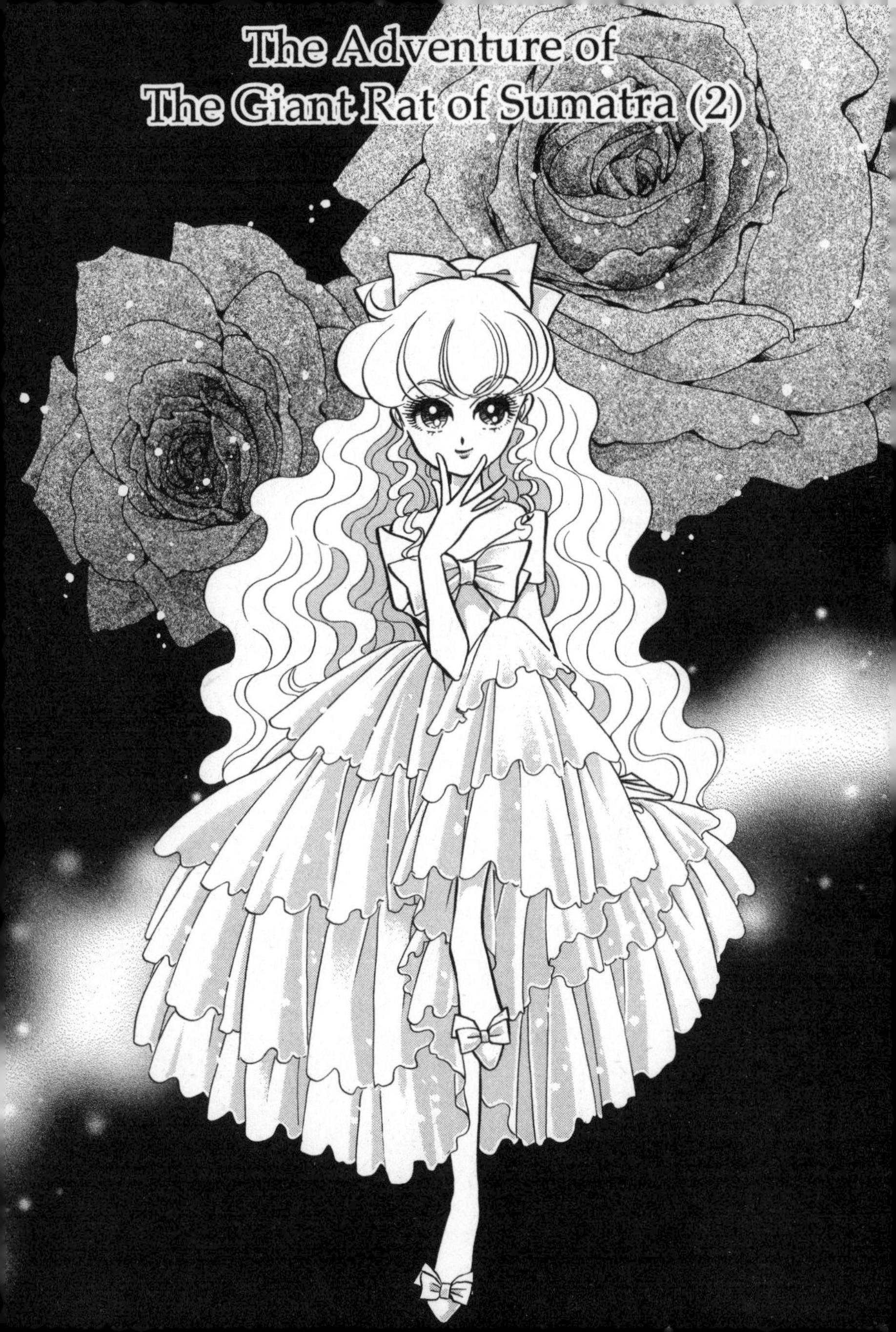

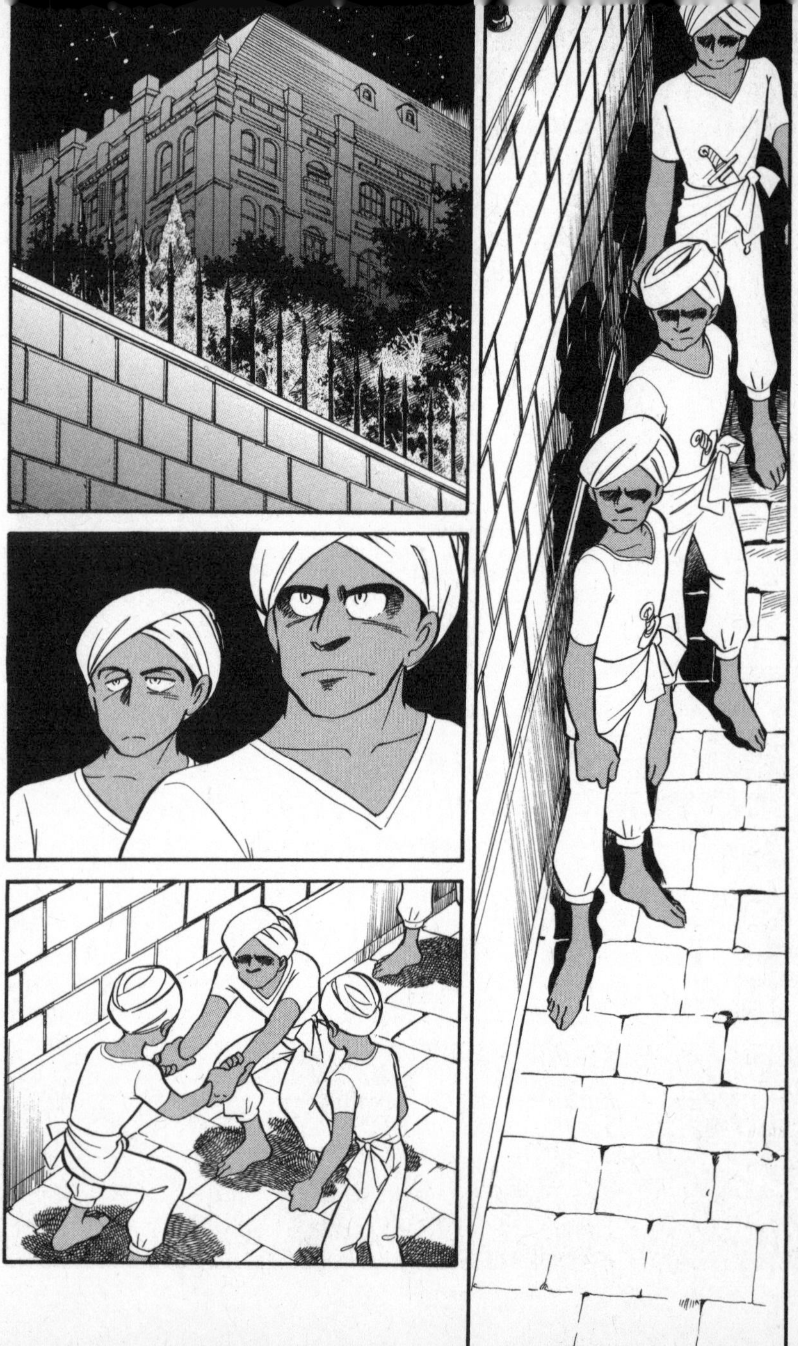

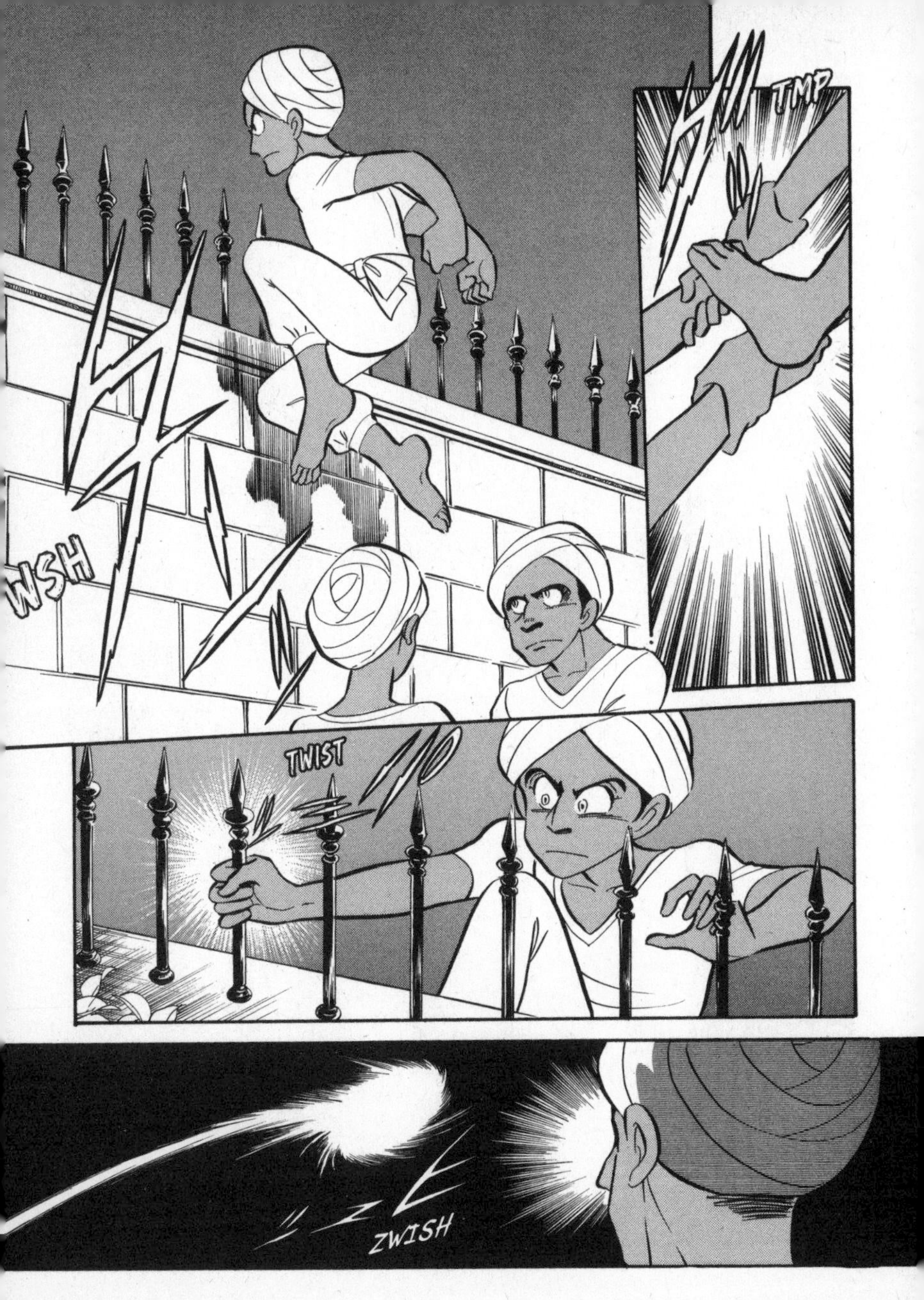
TMP
WSH
TWIST
ZWISH

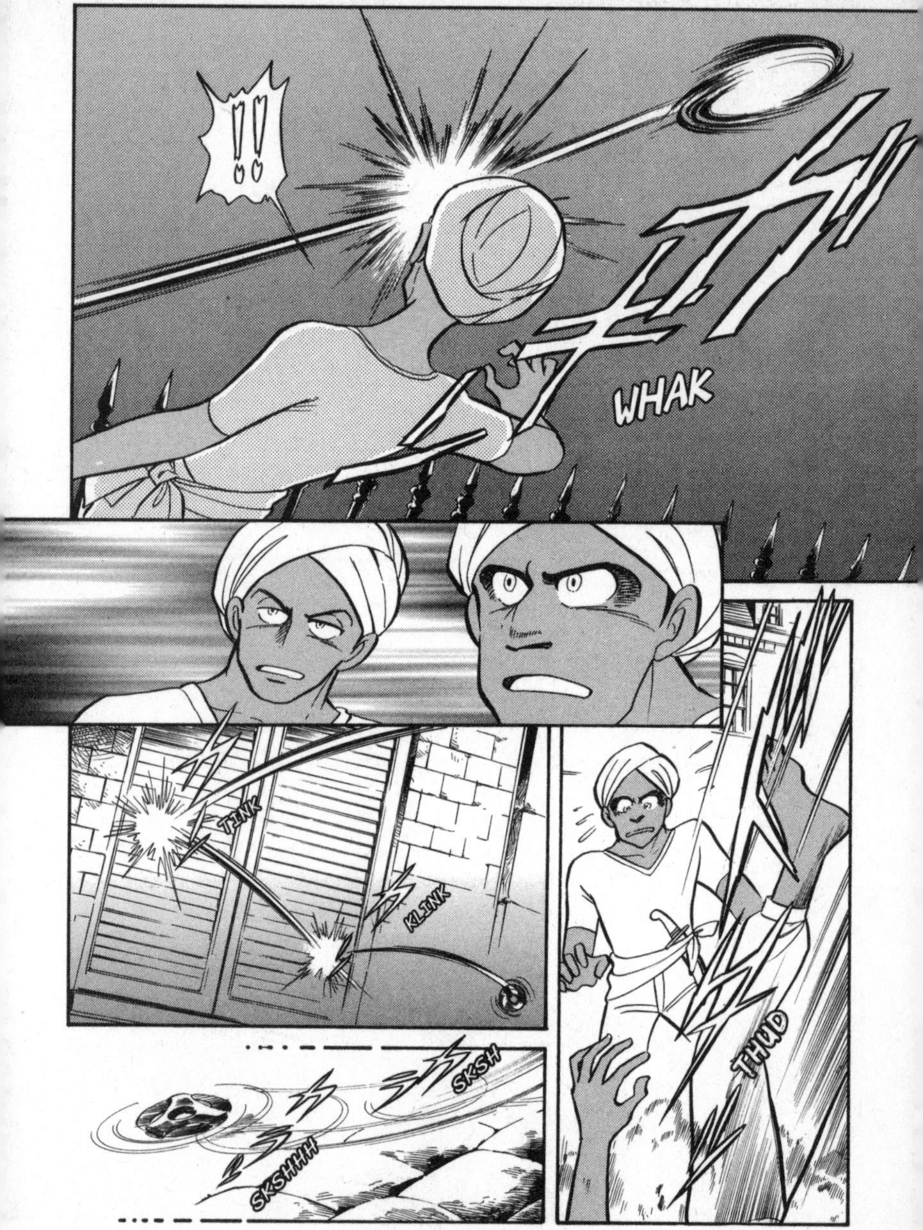
!!
WHAK
THUD
TINK
KLINK
SKSH
SKSHHH

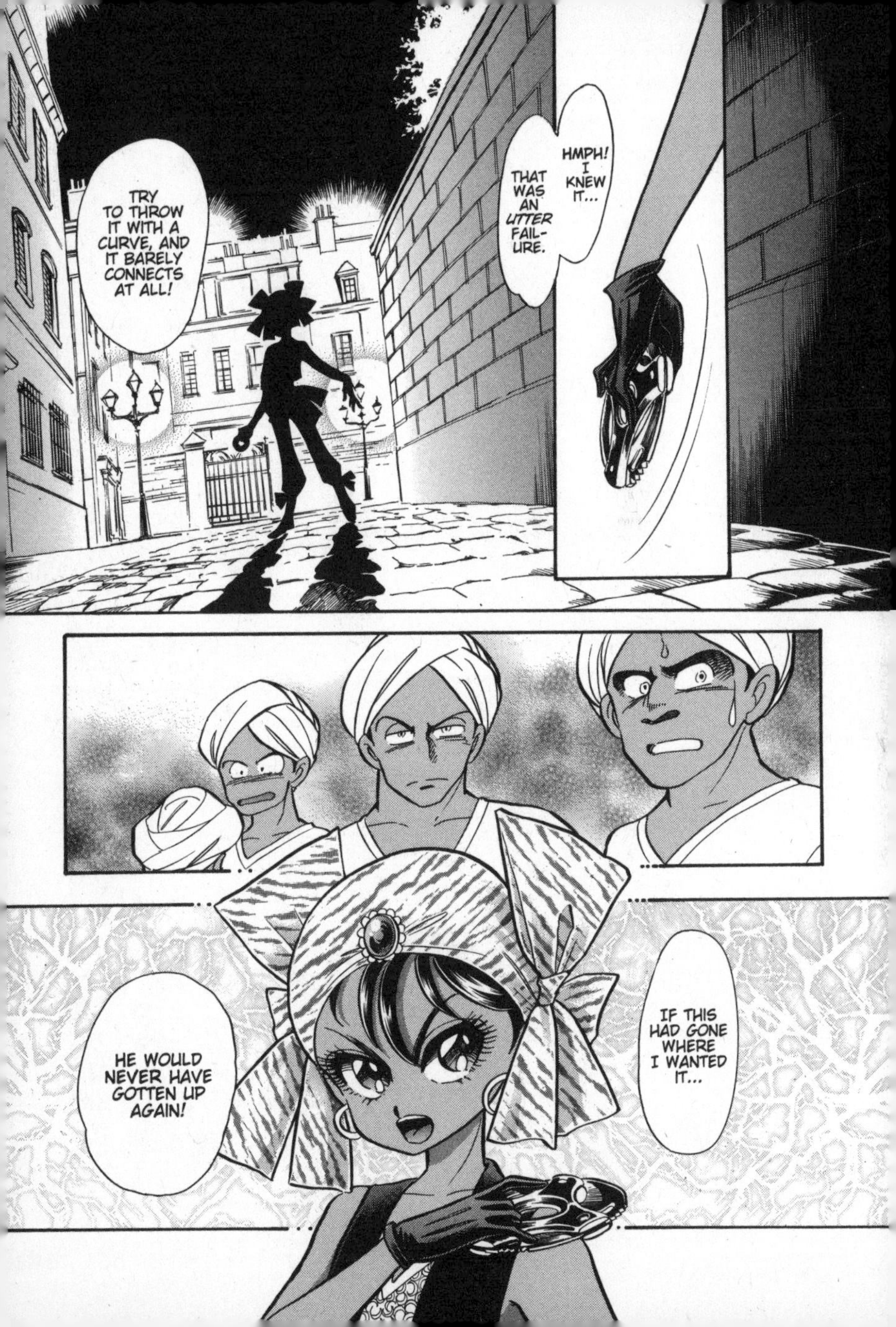
HMPH! I KNEW IT... THAT WAS AN UTTER FAILURE.
TRY TO THROW IT WITH A CURVE, AND IT BARELY CONNECTS AT ALL!
IF THIS HAD GONE WHERE I WANTED IT...
HE WOULD NEVER HAVE GOTTEN UP AGAIN!

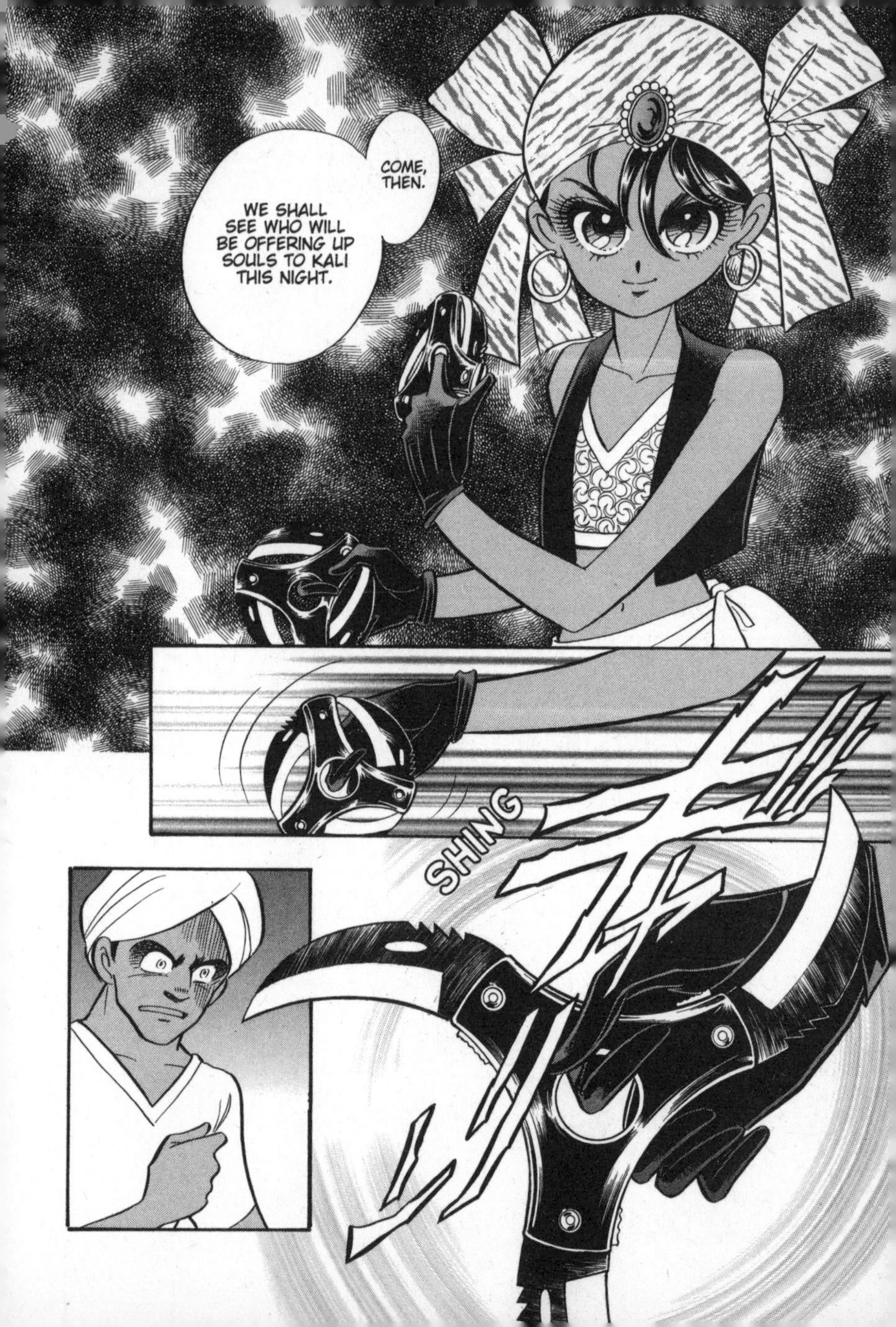
COME, THEN.
WE SHALL SEE WHO WILL BE OFFERING UP SOULS TO KALI THIS NIGHT.
SHING

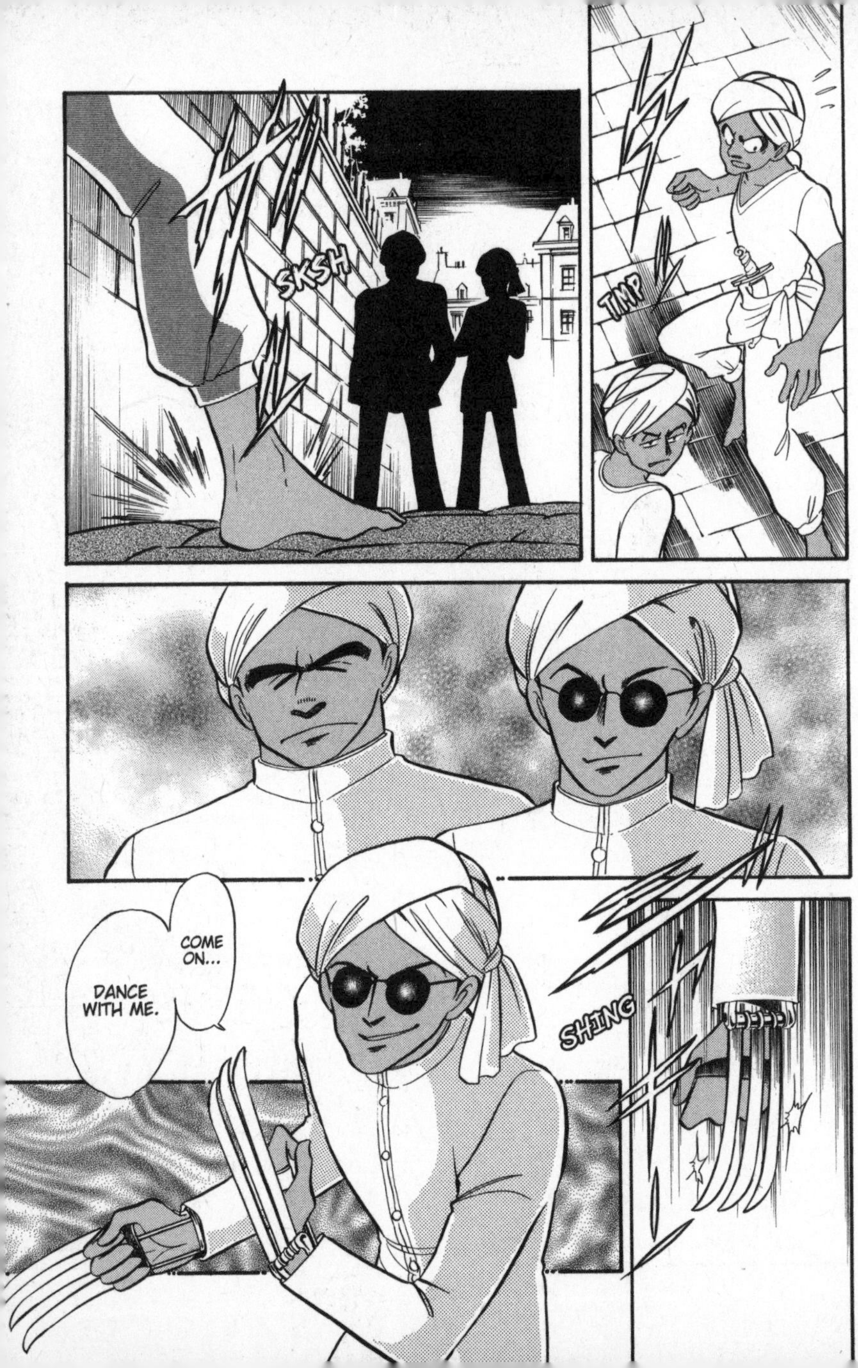
TMP
SKSH
SHING
COME ON...
DANCE WITH ME.

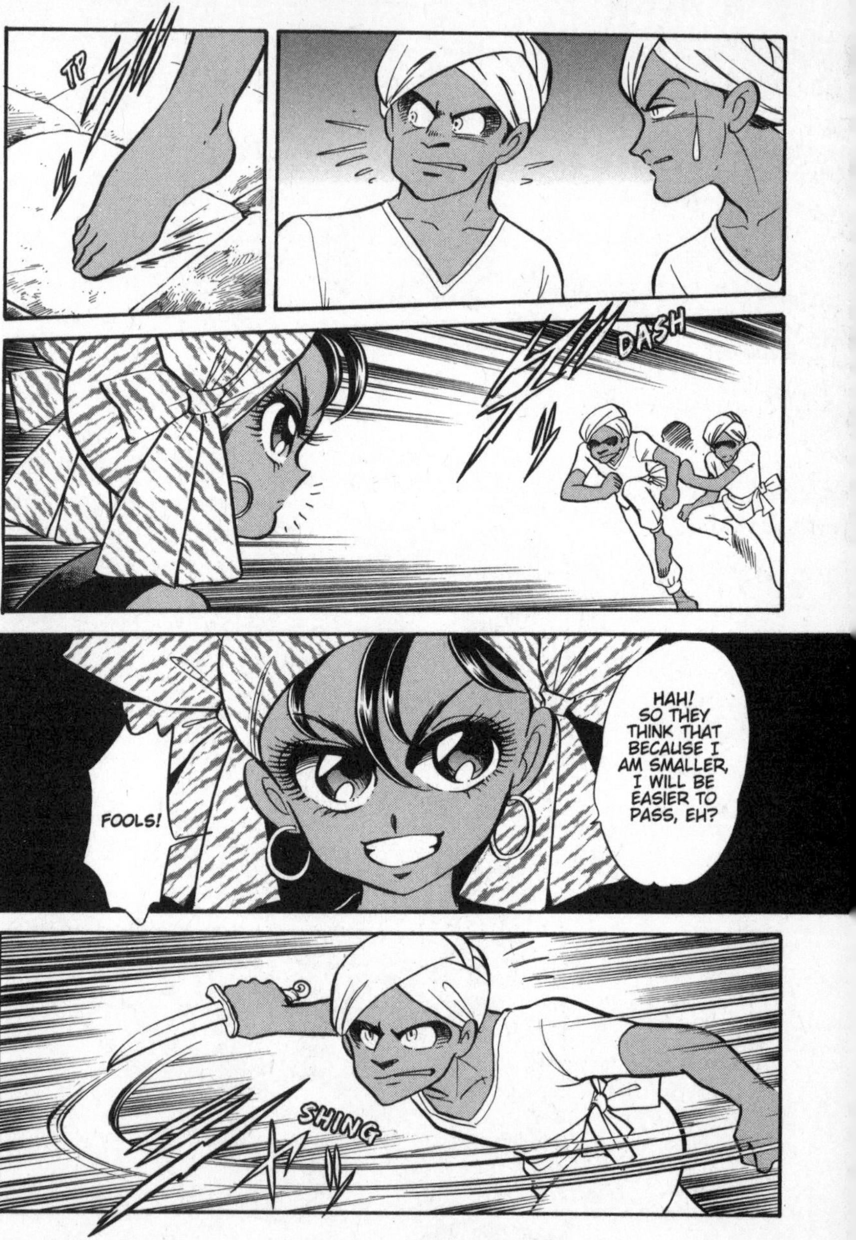
TP
DASH
HAH! SO THEY THINK THAT BECAUSE I AM SMALLER, I WILL BE EASIER TO PASS, EH?
FOOLS!
SHING

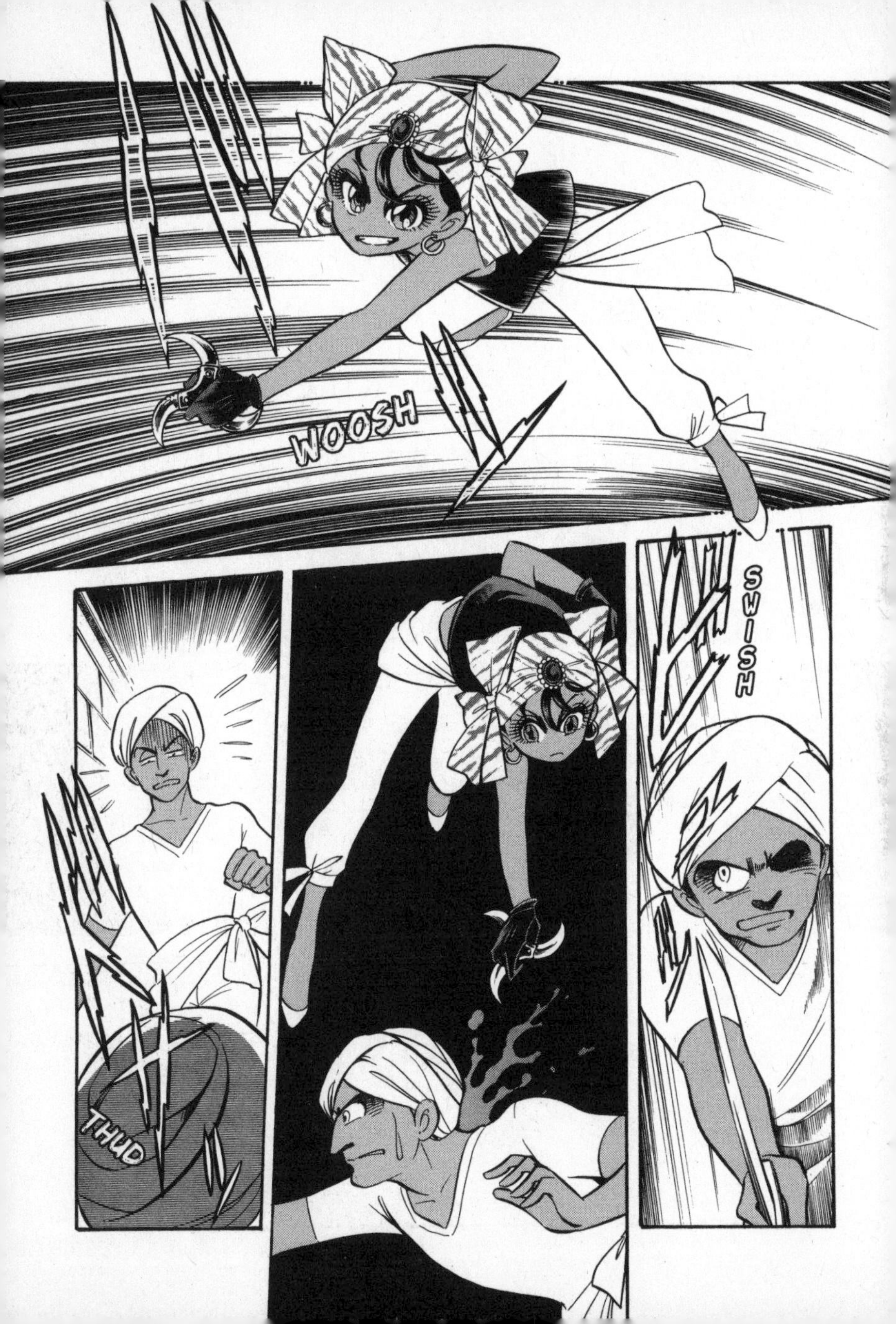
WOOSH
SWISH
THUD

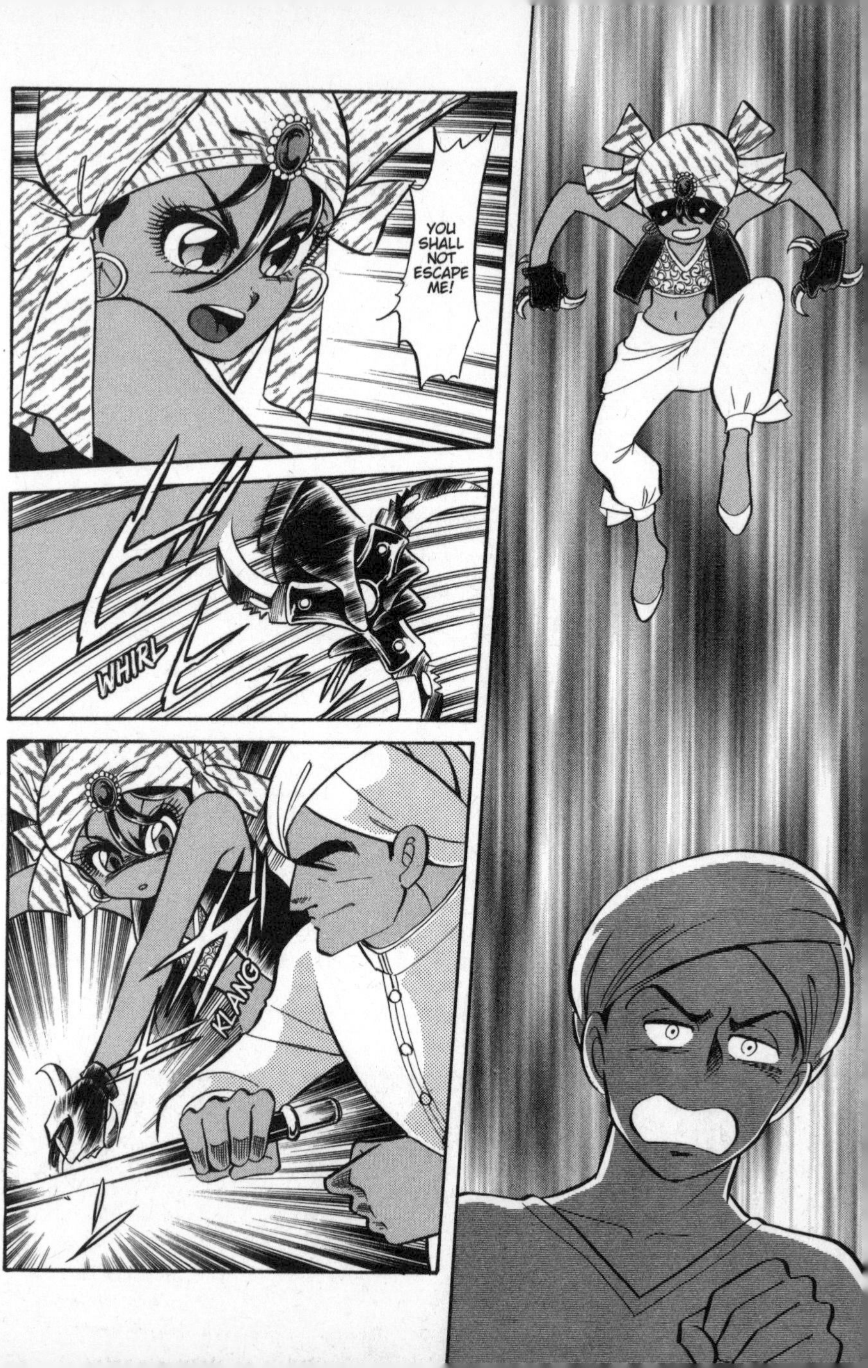
YOU SHALL NOT ESCAPE ME!
WHIRL
KLANG

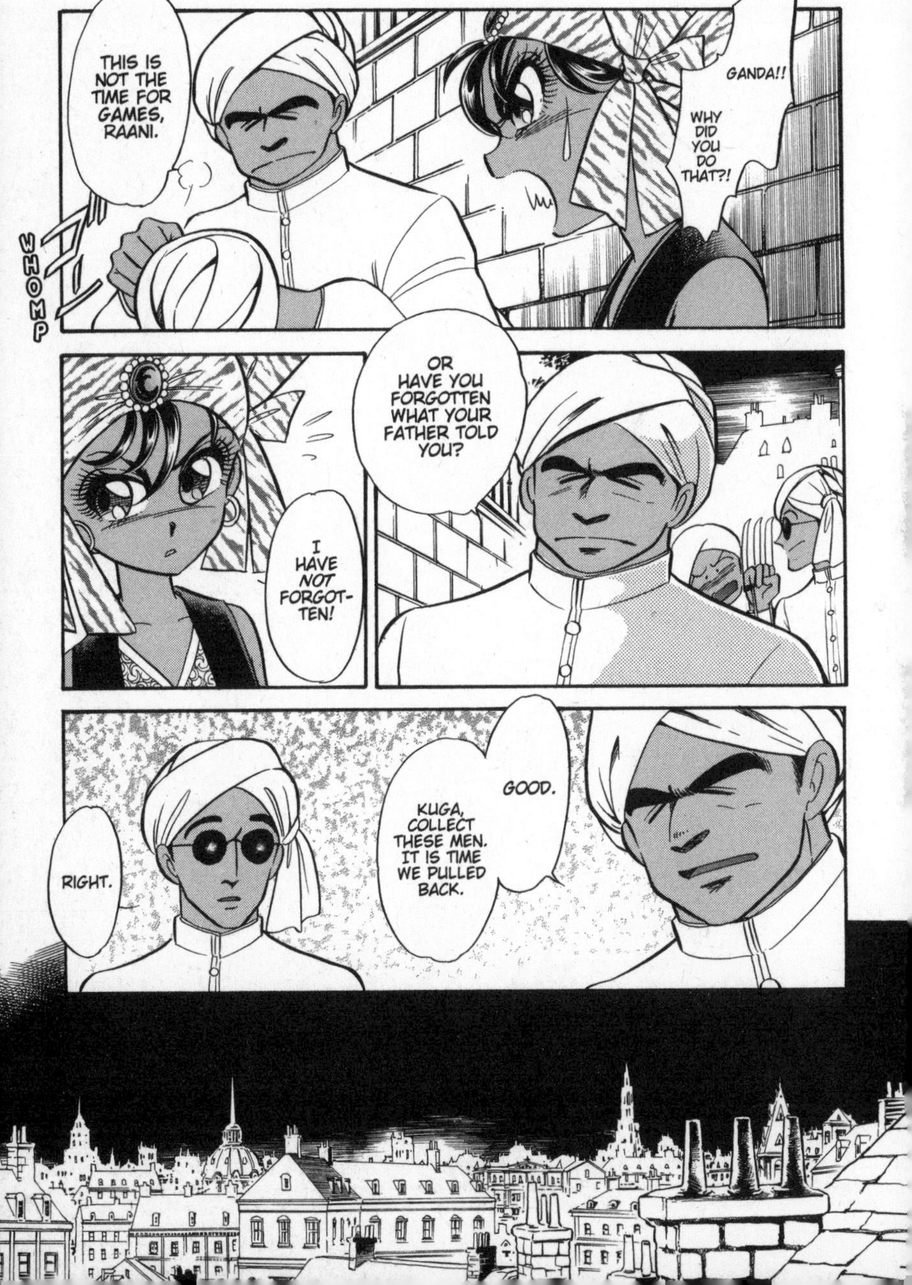
GANDA!!
WHY DID YOU DO THAT?!
THIS IS NOT THE TIME FOR GAMES, RAANI.
WHOMP
OR HAVE YOU FORGOTTEN WHAT YOUR FATHER TOLD YOU?
I HAVE *NOT* FORGOTTEN!
GOOD.
KUGA, COLLECT THESE MEN. IT IS TIME WE PULLED BACK.
RIGHT.

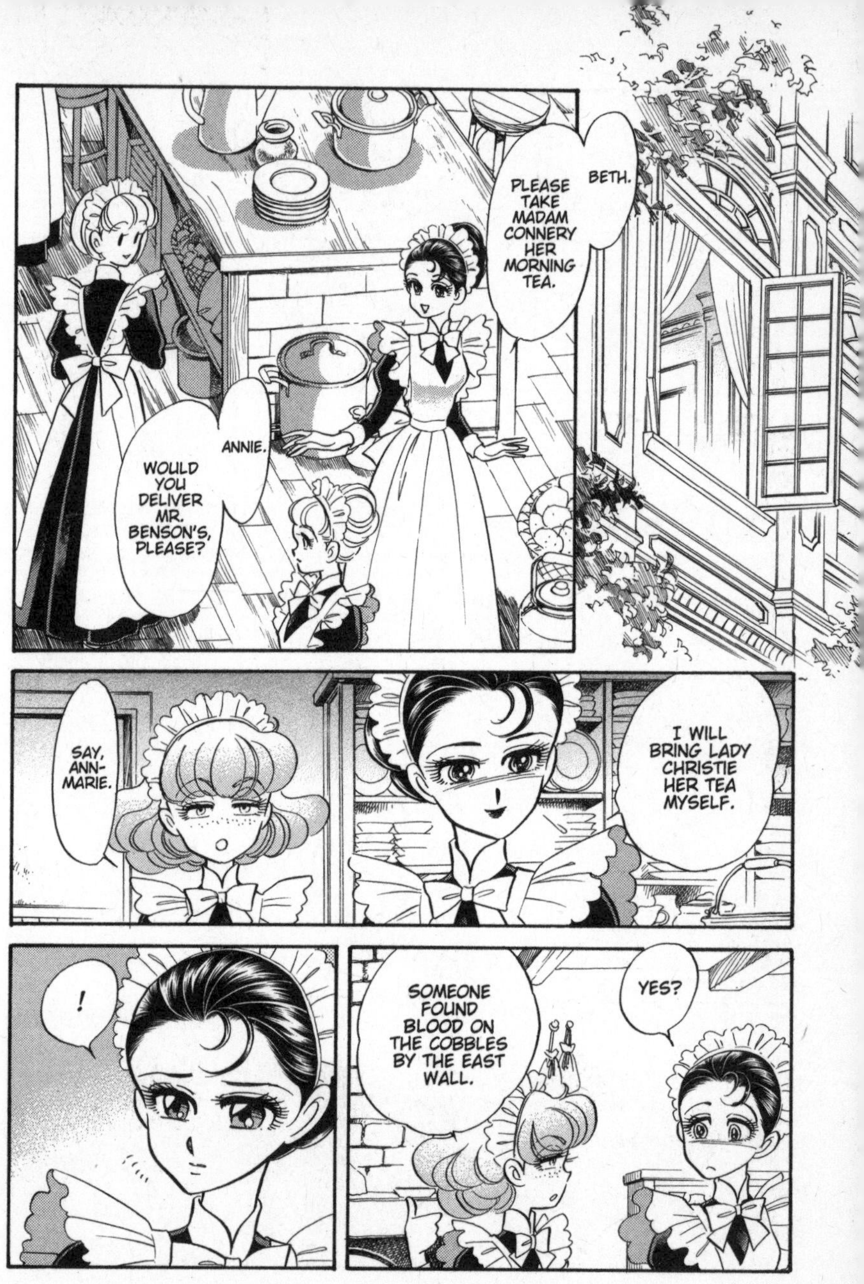
BETH.
PLEASE TAKE MADAM CONNERY HER MORNING TEA.
ANNIE.
WOULD YOU DELIVER MR. BENSON'S, PLEASE?
I WILL BRING LADY CHRISTIE HER TEA MYSELF.
SAY, ANN-MARIE.
YES?
SOMEONE FOUND BLOOD ON THE COBBLES BY THE EAST WALL.
!

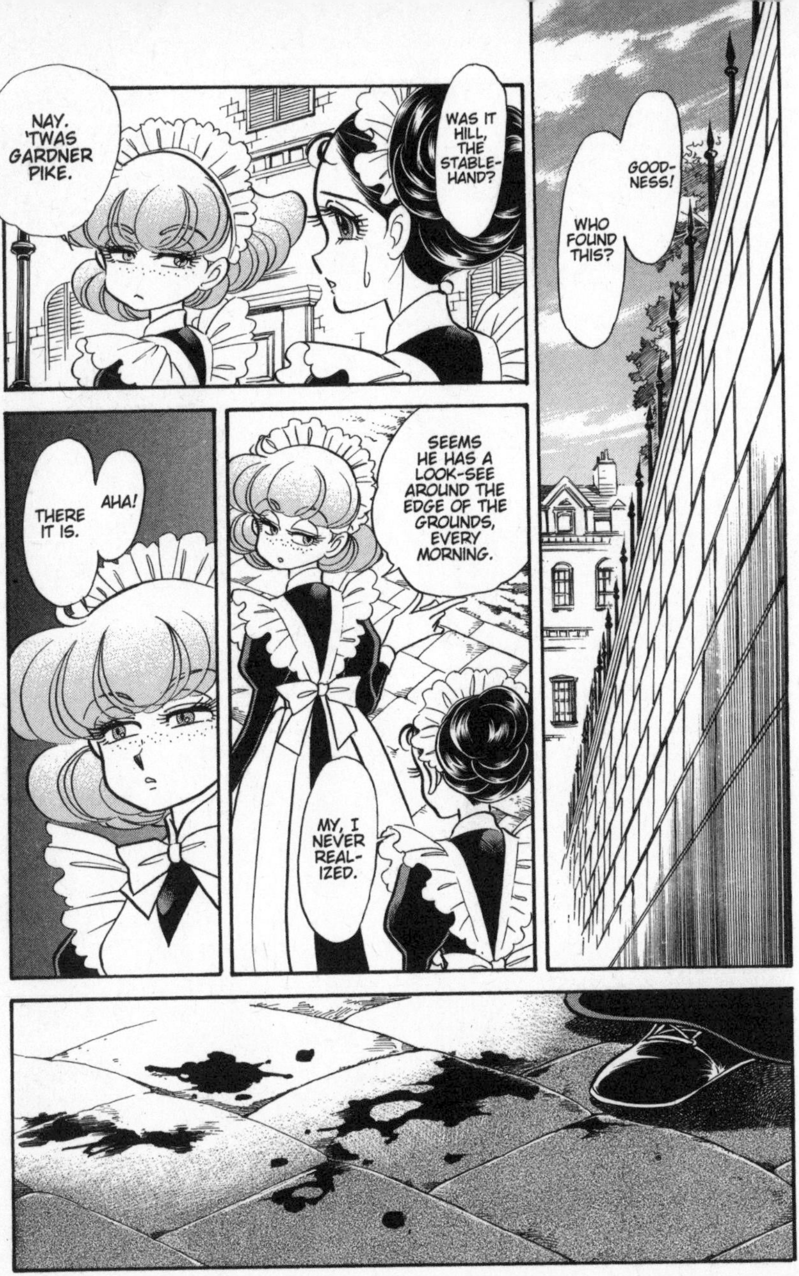
GOODNESS! WHO FOUND THIS?
WAS IT HILL, THE STABLEHAND?
NAY. 'TWAS GARDNER PIKE.
SEEMS HE HAS A LOOK-SEE AROUND THE EDGE OF THE GROUNDS, EVERY MORNING.
MY, I NEVER REALIZED.
AHA! THERE IT IS.

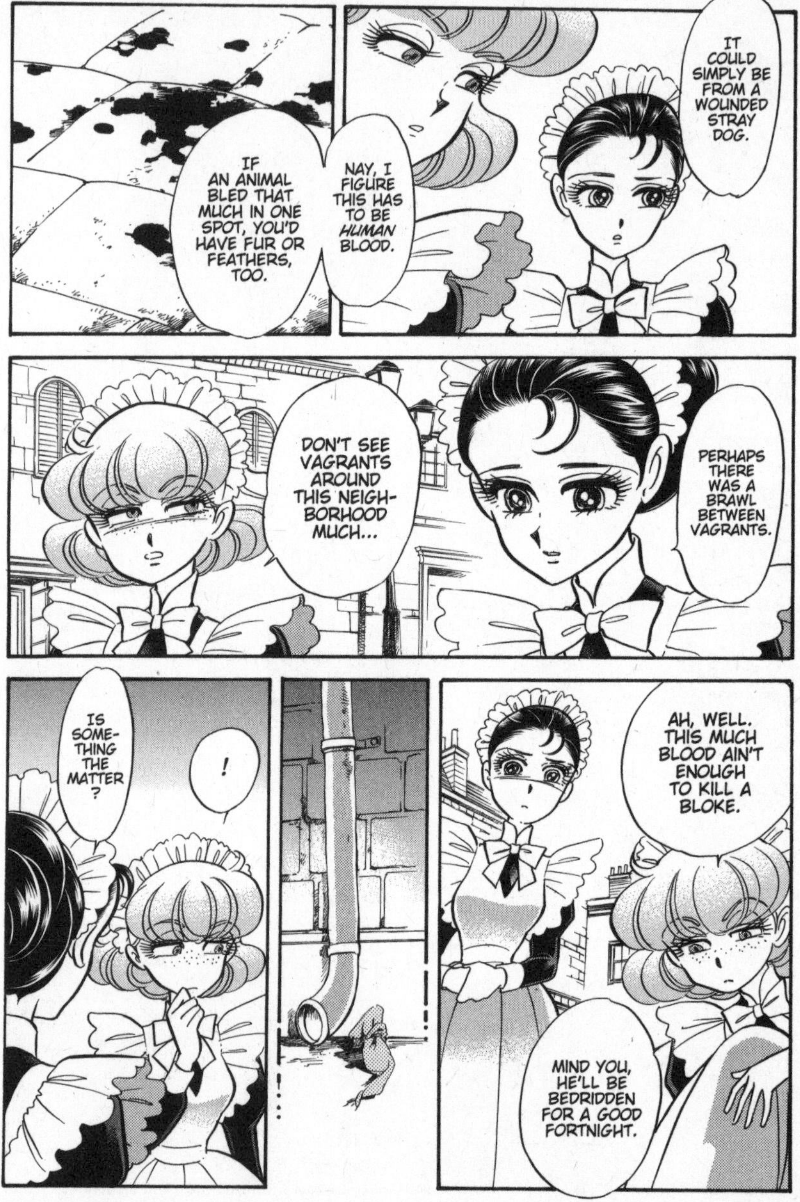
IT COULD SIMPLY BE FROM A WOUNDED STRAY DOG.
NAY, I FIGURE THIS HAS TO BE *HUMAN* BLOOD.
IF AN ANIMAL BLED THAT MUCH IN ONE SPOT, YOU'D HAVE FUR OR FEATHERS, TOO.
PERHAPS THERE WAS A BRAWL BETWEEN VAGRANTS.
DON'T SEE VAGRANTS AROUND THIS NEIGHBORHOOD MUCH...
AH, WELL. THIS MUCH BLOOD AIN'T ENOUGH TO KILL A BLOKE.
MIND YOU, HE'LL BE BEDRIDDEN FOR A GOOD FORTNIGHT.
!
IS SOMETHING THE MATTER?

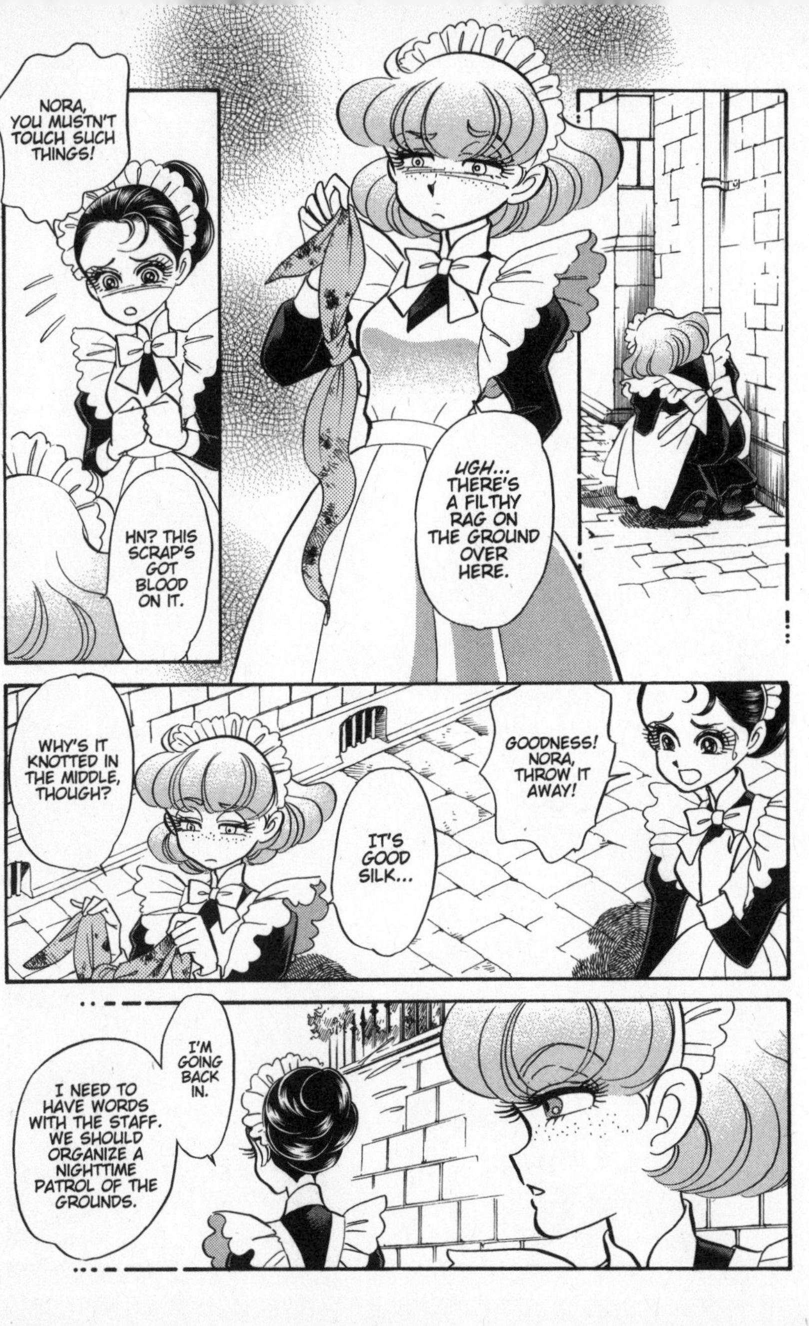
UGH... THERE'S A FILTHY RAG ON THE GROUND OVER HERE.
NORA, YOU MUSTN'T TOUCH SUCH THINGS!
HN? THIS SCRAP'S GOT BLOOD ON IT.
GOODNESS! NORA, THROW IT AWAY!
IT'S GOOD SILK...
WHY'S IT KNOTTED IN THE MIDDLE, THOUGH?
I'M GOING BACK IN.
I NEED TO HAVE WORDS WITH THE STAFF. WE SHOULD ORGANIZE A NIGHTTIME PATROL OF THE GROUNDS.

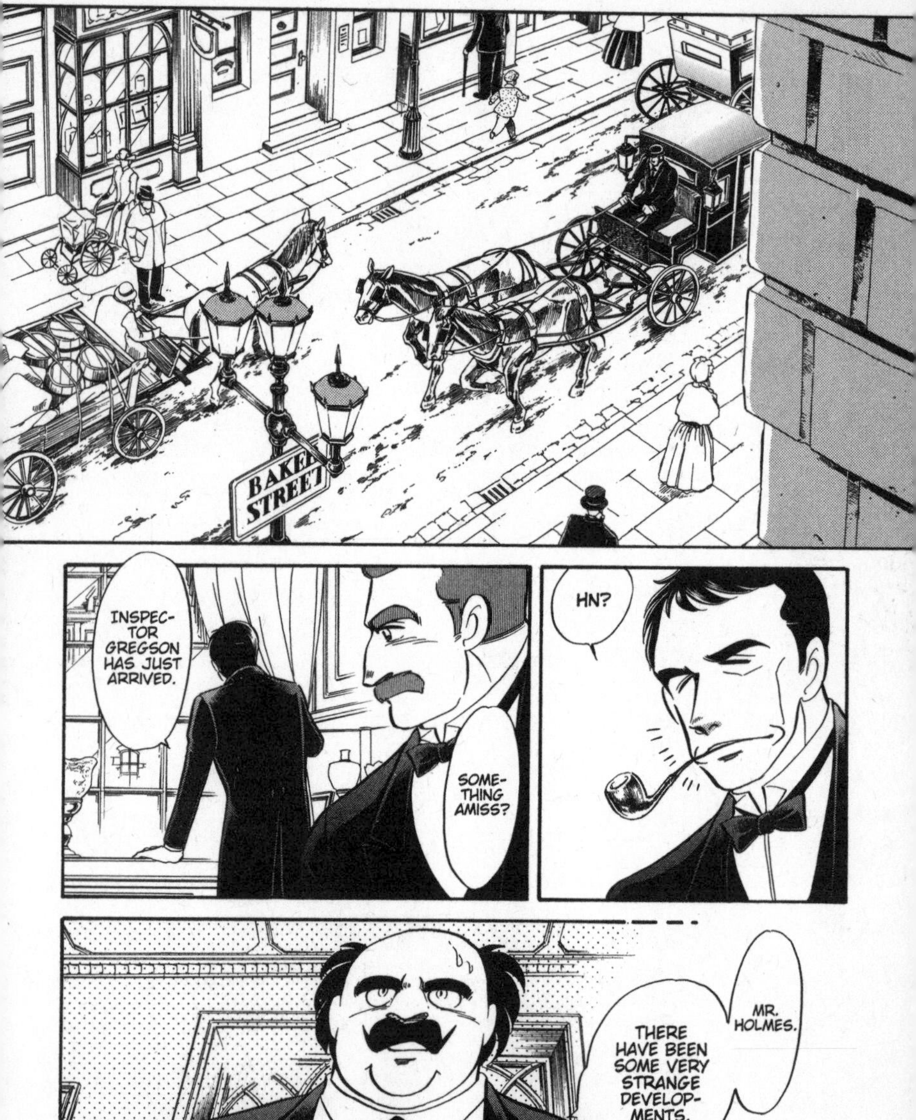

BAKE
STREET
HN?
SOME-THING AMISS?
INSPEC-TOR GREGSON HAS JUST ARRIVED.
MR. HOLMES.
THERE HAVE BEEN SOME VERY STRANGE DEVELOP-MENTS.

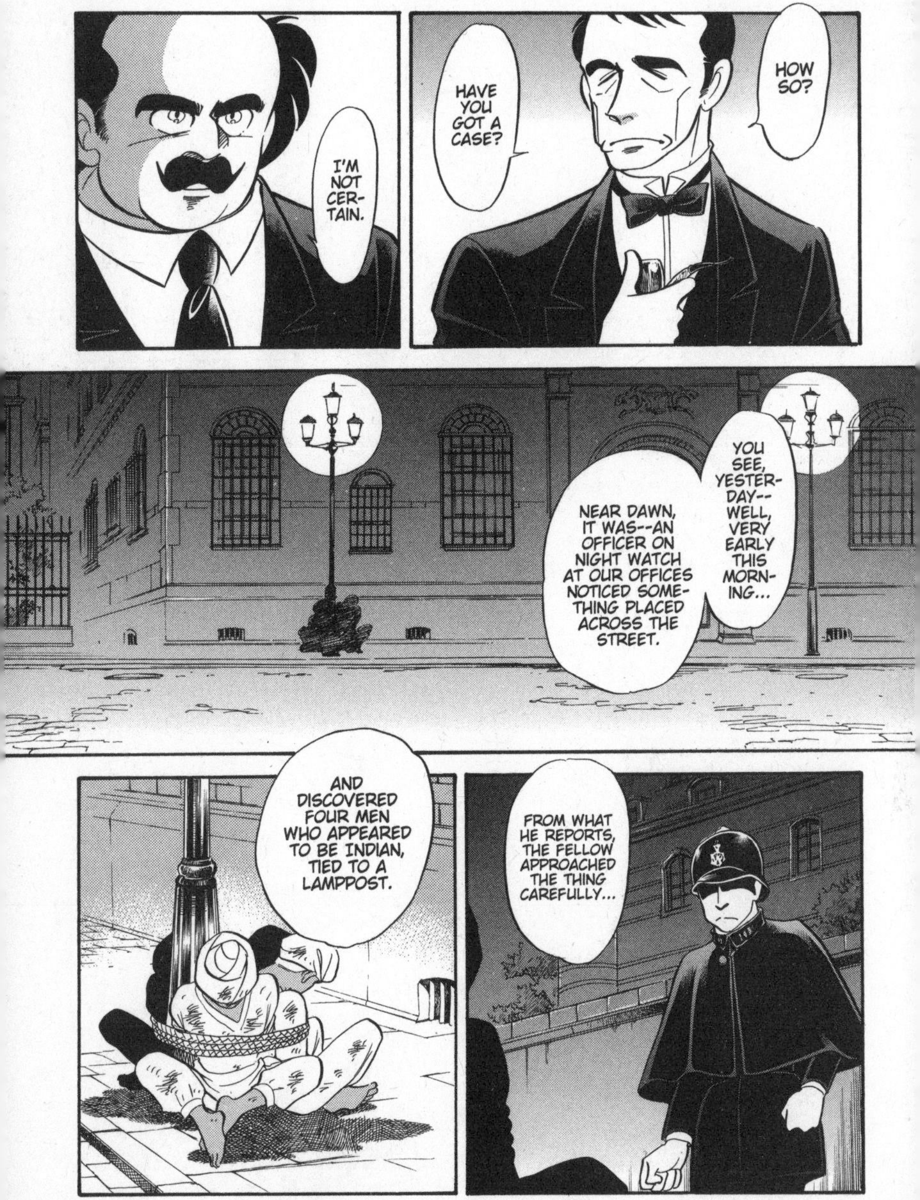
HOW SO?
HAVE YOU GOT A CASE?
I'M NOT CER-TAIN.
YOU SEE, YESTER-DAY--WELL, VERY EARLY THIS MORN-ING...
NEAR DAWN, IT WAS--AN OFFICER ON NIGHT WATCH AT OUR OFFICES NOTICED SOME-THING PLACED ACROSS THE STREET.
FROM WHAT HE REPORTS, THE FELLOW APPROACHED THE THING CAREFULLY...
AND DISCOVERED FOUR MEN WHO APPEARED TO BE INDIAN, TIED TO A LAMPPOST.

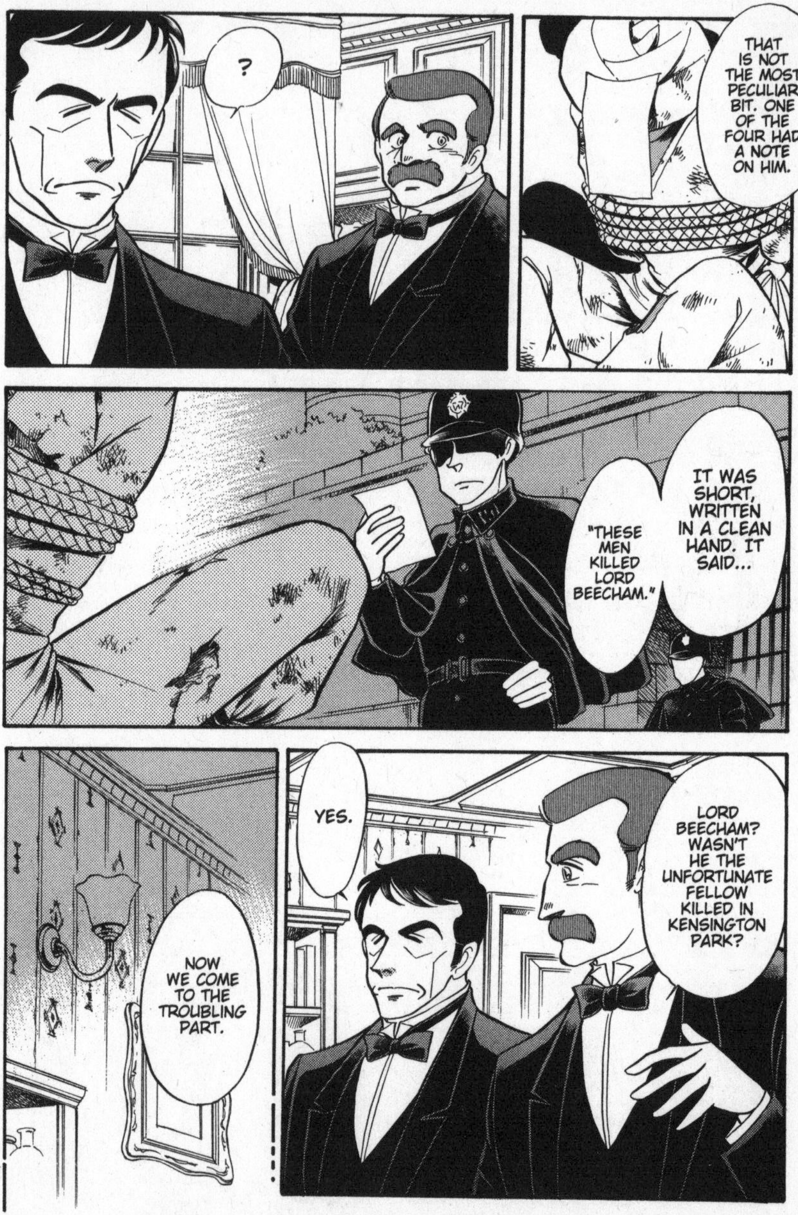
THAT IS NOT THE MOST PECULIAR BIT. ONE OF THE FOUR HAD A NOTE ON HIM.
?
IT WAS SHORT, WRITTEN IN A CLEAN HAND. IT SAID...
"THESE MEN KILLED LORD BEECHAM."
LORD BEECHAM? WASN'T HE THE UNFORTUNATE FELLOW KILLED IN KENSINGTON PARK?
YES.
NOW WE COME TO THE TROUBLING PART.

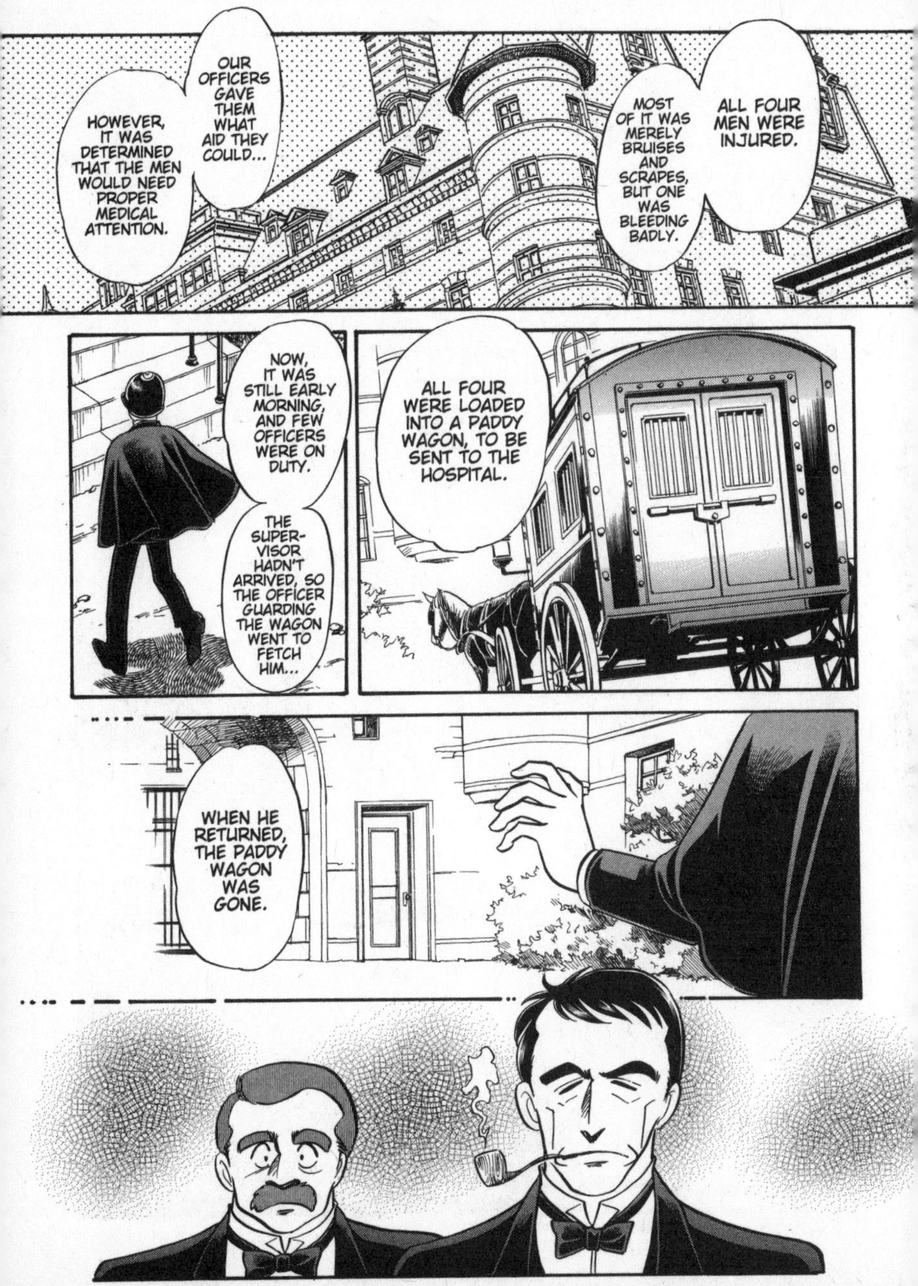
ALL FOUR MEN WERE INJURED.
MOST OF IT WAS MERELY BRUISES AND SCRAPES, BUT ONE WAS BLEEDING BADLY.
OUR OFFICERS GAVE THEM WHAT AID THEY COULD...
HOWEVER, IT WAS DETERMINED THAT THE MEN WOULD NEED PROPER MEDICAL ATTENTION.
ALL FOUR WERE LOADED INTO A PADDY WAGON, TO BE SENT TO THE HOSPITAL.
NOW, IT WAS STILL EARLY MORNING, AND FEW OFFICERS WERE ON DUTY.
THE SUPER-VISOR HADN'T ARRIVED, SO THE OFFICER GUARDING THE WAGON WENT TO FETCH HIM...
WHEN HE RETURNED, THE PADDY WAGON WAS GONE.

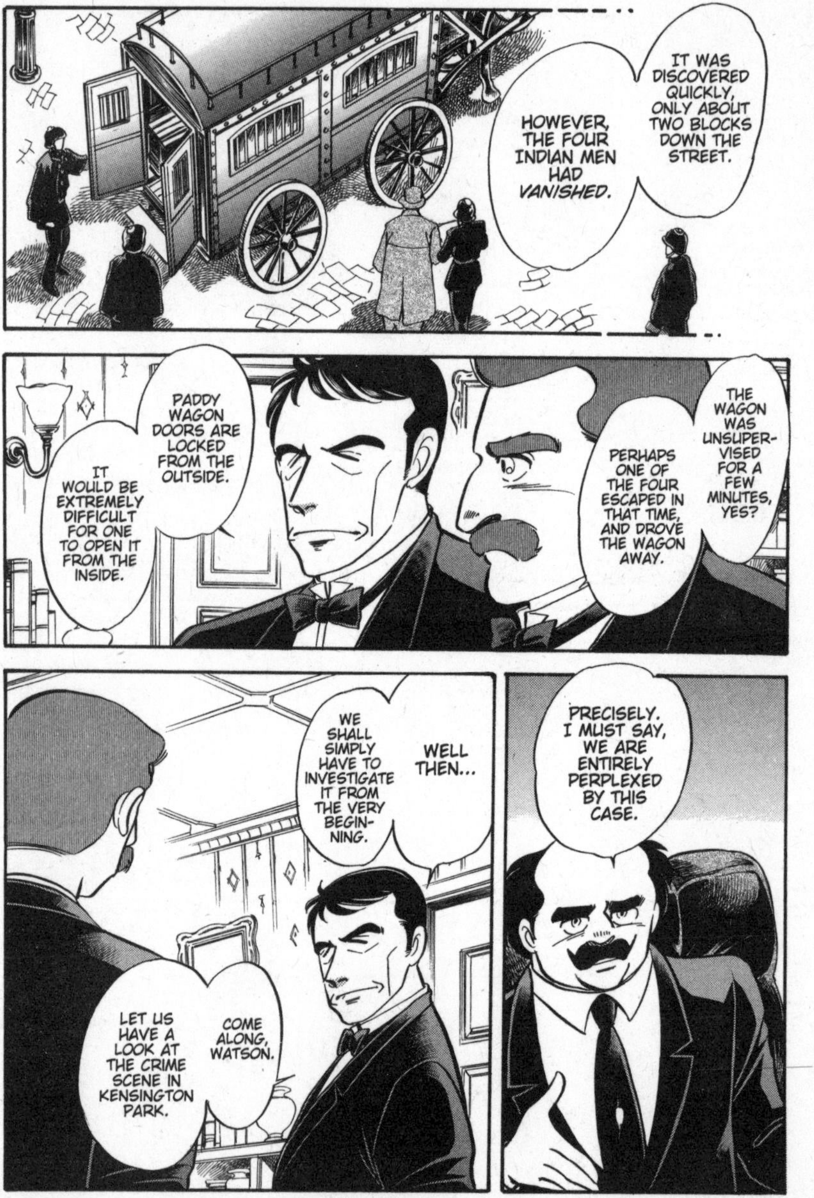
IT WAS DISCOVERED QUICKLY, ONLY ABOUT TWO BLOCKS DOWN THE STREET.
HOWEVER, THE FOUR INDIAN MEN HAD *VANISHED*.
THE WAGON WAS UNSUPERVISED FOR A FEW MINUTES, YES?
PERHAPS ONE OF THE FOUR ESCAPED IN THAT TIME, AND DROVE THE WAGON AWAY.
PADDY WAGON DOORS ARE LOCKED FROM THE OUTSIDE.
IT WOULD BE EXTREMELY DIFFICULT FOR ONE TO OPEN IT FROM THE INSIDE.
PRECISELY. I MUST SAY, WE ARE ENTIRELY PERPLEXED BY THIS CASE.
WELL THEN...
WE SHALL SIMPLY HAVE TO INVESTIGATE IT FROM THE VERY BEGINNING.
COME ALONG, WATSON.
LET US HAVE A LOOK AT THE CRIME SCENE IN KENSINGTON PARK.

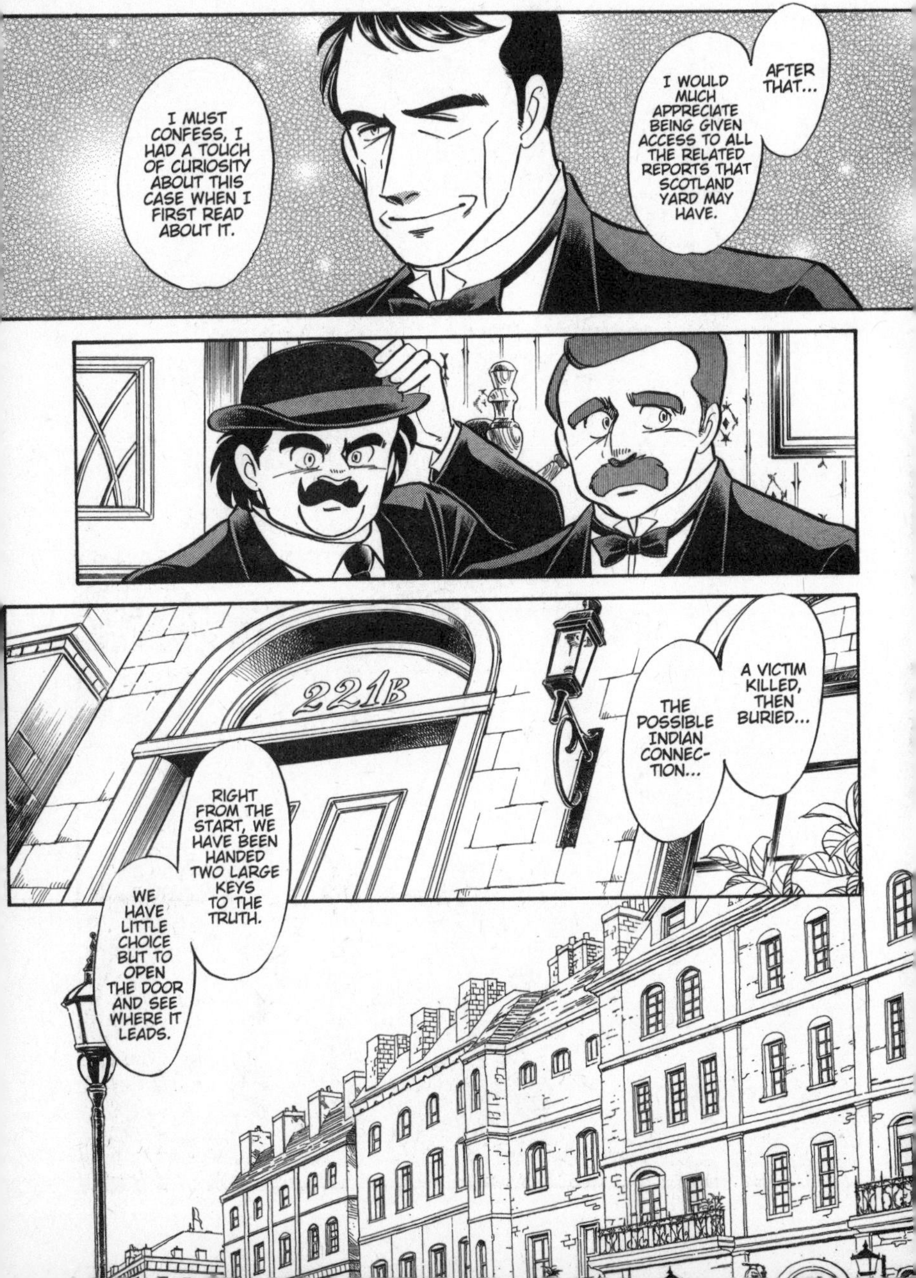
AFTER THAT...
I WOULD MUCH APPRECIATE BEING GIVEN ACCESS TO ALL THE RELATED REPORTS THAT SCOTLAND YARD MAY HAVE.
I MUST CONFESS, I HAD A TOUCH OF CURIOSITY ABOUT THIS CASE WHEN I FIRST READ ABOUT IT.
A VICTIM KILLED, THEN BURIED...
THE POSSIBLE INDIAN CONNECTION...
221B
RIGHT FROM THE START, WE HAVE BEEN HANDED TWO LARGE KEYS TO THE TRUTH.
WE HAVE LITTLE CHOICE BUT TO OPEN THE DOOR AND SEE WHERE IT LEADS.

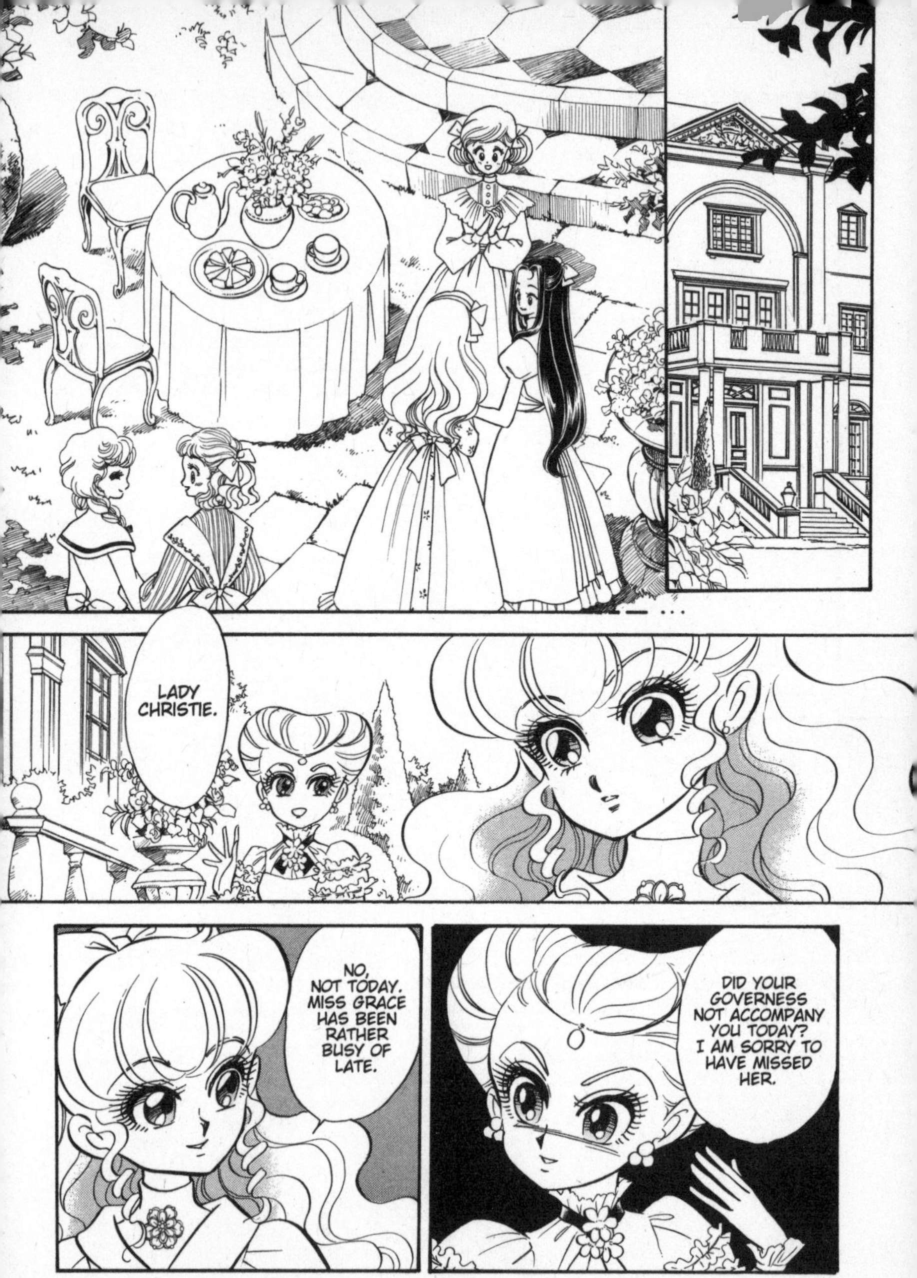
LADY CHRISTIE.
DID YOUR GOVERNESS NOT ACCOMPANY YOU TODAY? I AM SORRY TO HAVE MISSED HER.
NO, NOT TODAY. MISS GRACE HAS BEEN RATHER BUSY OF LATE.

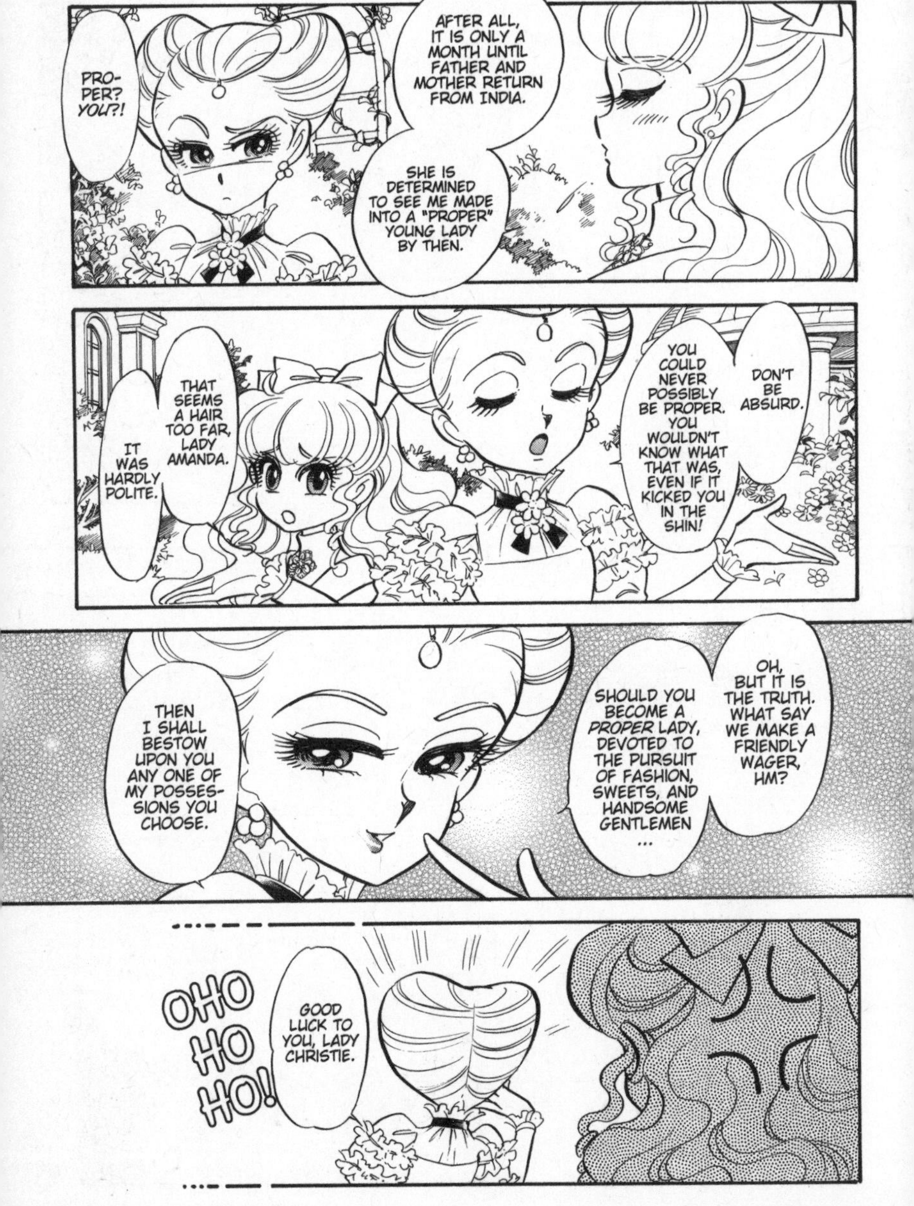
AFTER ALL, IT IS ONLY A MONTH UNTIL FATHER AND MOTHER RETURN FROM INDIA.
SHE IS DETERMINED TO SEE ME MADE INTO A "PROPER" YOUNG LADY BY THEN.
PROPER? YOU?!
DON'T BE ABSURD.
YOU COULD NEVER POSSIBLY BE PROPER. YOU WOULDN'T KNOW WHAT THAT WAS, EVEN IF IT KICKED YOU IN THE SHIN!
THAT SEEMS A HAIR TOO FAR, LADY AMANDA.
IT WAS HARDLY POLITE.
OH, BUT IT IS THE TRUTH. WHAT SAY WE MAKE A FRIENDLY WAGER, HM?
SHOULD YOU BECOME A *PROPER* LADY, DEVOTED TO THE PURSUIT OF FASHION, SWEETS, AND HANDSOME GENTLEMEN ...
THEN I SHALL BESTOW UPON YOU ANY ONE OF MY POSSESSIONS YOU CHOOSE.
GOOD LUCK TO YOU, LADY CHRISTIE.
OHO HO HO HO!

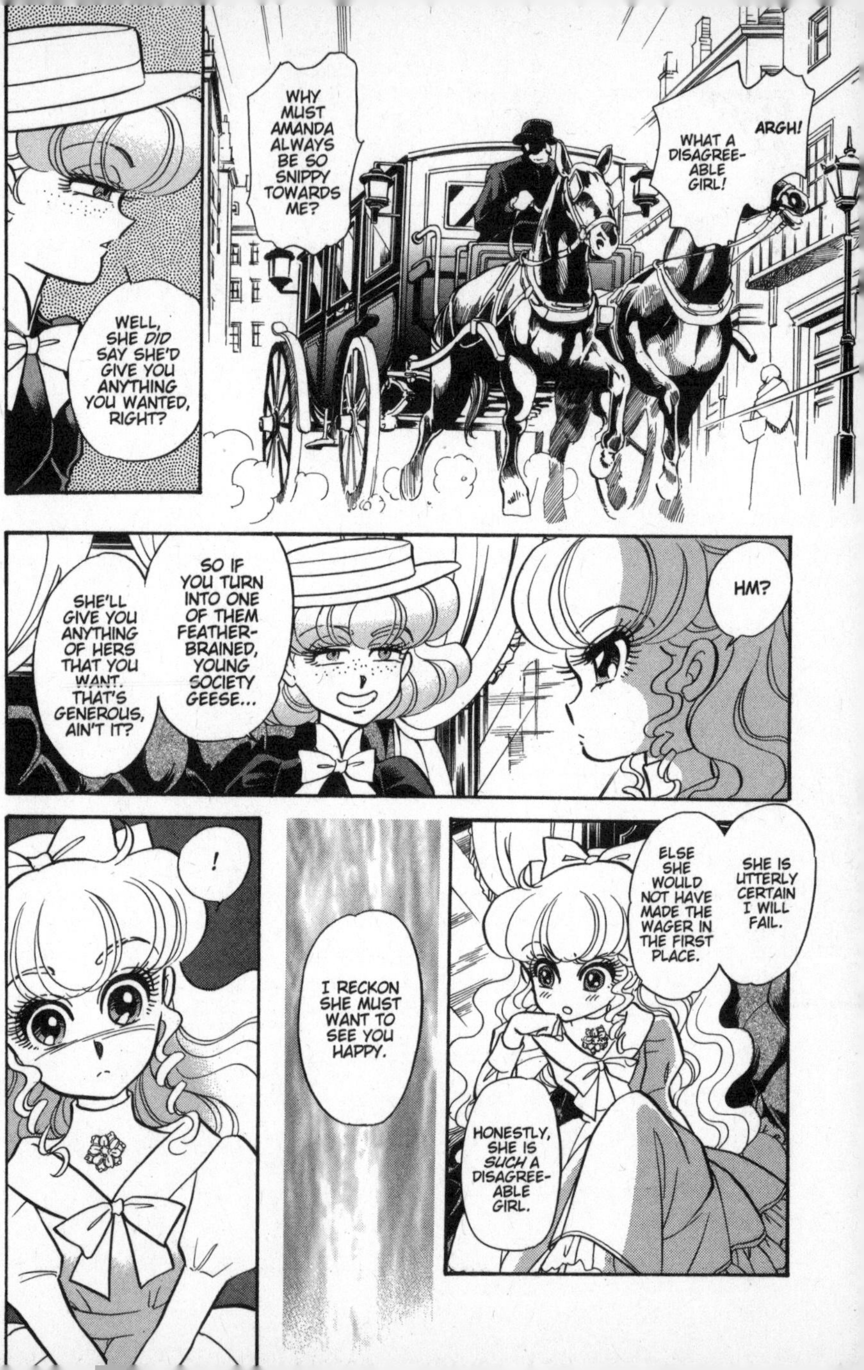
ARGH!
WHAT A DISAGREEABLE GIRL!
WHY MUST AMANDA ALWAYS BE SO SNIPPY TOWARDS ME?
WELL, SHE *DID* SAY SHE'D GIVE YOU ANYTHING YOU WANTED, RIGHT?
HM?
SO IF YOU TURN INTO ONE OF THEM FEATHER-BRAINED, YOUNG SOCIETY GEESE...
SHE'LL GIVE YOU ANYTHING OF HERS THAT YOU WANT. THAT'S GENEROUS, AIN'T IT?
SHE IS UTTERLY CERTAIN I WILL FAIL.
ELSE SHE WOULD NOT HAVE MADE THE WAGER IN THE FIRST PLACE.
HONESTLY, SHE IS *SUCH* A DISAGREEABLE GIRL.
I RECKON SHE MUST WANT TO SEE YOU HAPPY.
!

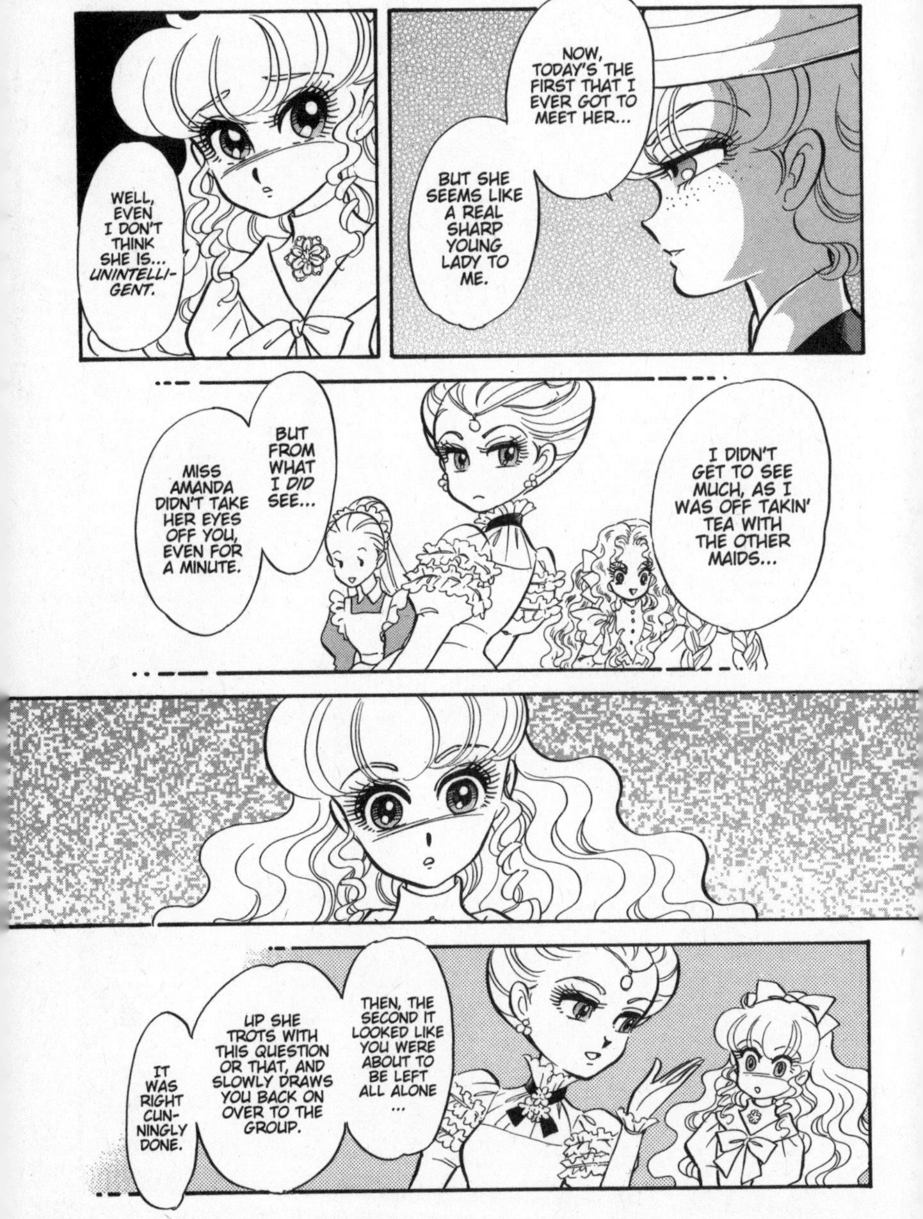
NOW, TODAY'S THE FIRST THAT I EVER GOT TO MEET HER...
BUT SHE SEEMS LIKE A REAL SHARP YOUNG LADY TO ME.
WELL, EVEN I DON'T THINK SHE IS... *UNINTELLIGENT.*
I DIDN'T GET TO SEE MUCH, AS I WAS OFF TAKIN' TEA WITH THE OTHER MAIDS...
BUT FROM WHAT I *DID* SEE...
MISS AMANDA DIDN'T TAKE HER EYES OFF YOU, EVEN FOR A MINUTE.
THEN, THE SECOND IT LOOKED LIKE YOU WERE ABOUT TO BE LEFT ALL ALONE ...
UP SHE TROTS WITH THIS QUESTION OR THAT, AND SLOWLY DRAWS YOU BACK ON OVER TO THE GROUP.
IT WAS RIGHT CUN-NINGLY DONE.

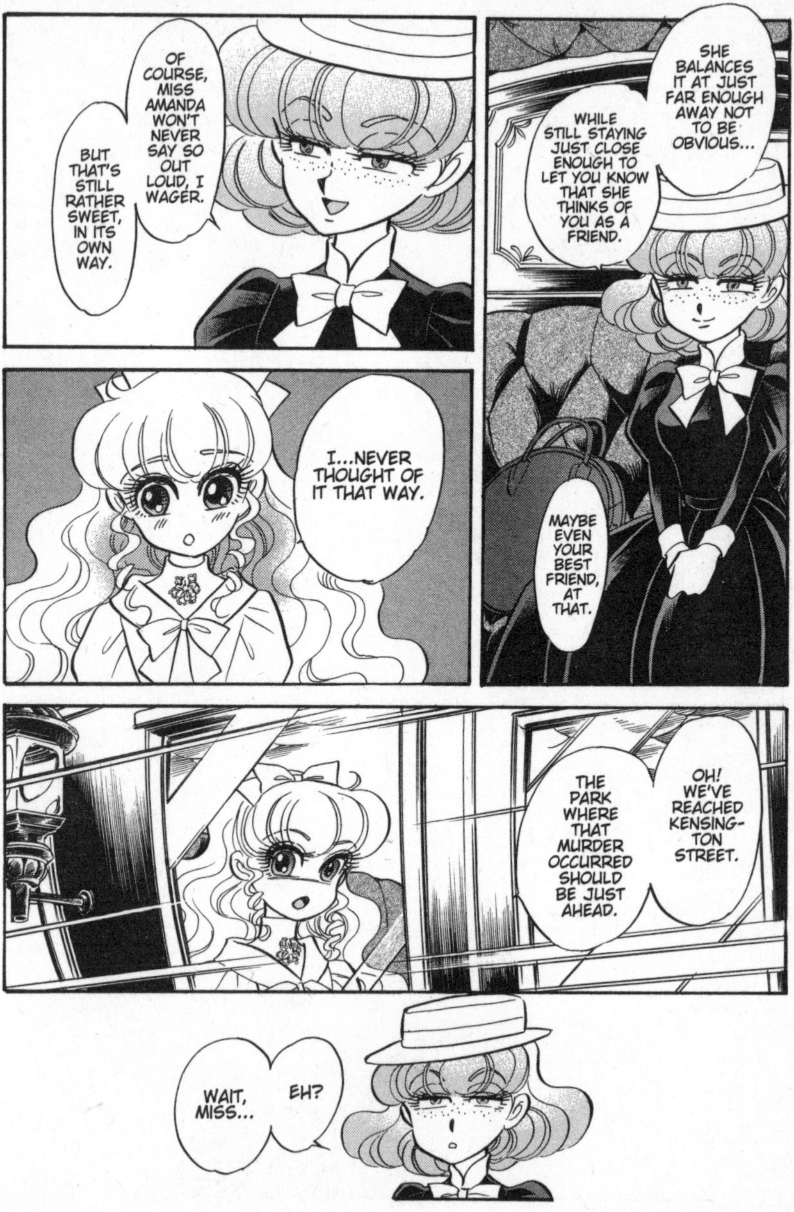
SHE BALANCES IT AT JUST FAR ENOUGH AWAY NOT TO BE OBVIOUS...
WHILE STILL STAYING JUST CLOSE ENOUGH TO LET YOU KNOW THAT SHE THINKS OF YOU AS A FRIEND.
MAYBE EVEN YOUR BEST FRIEND, AT THAT.
OF COURSE, MISS AMANDA WON'T NEVER SAY SO OUT LOUD, I WAGER.
BUT THAT'S STILL RATHER SWEET, IN ITS OWN WAY.
I...NEVER THOUGHT OF IT THAT WAY.
OH! WE'VE REACHED KENSING-TON STREET.
THE PARK WHERE THAT MURDER OCCURRED SHOULD BE JUST AHEAD.
EH?
WAIT, MISS...

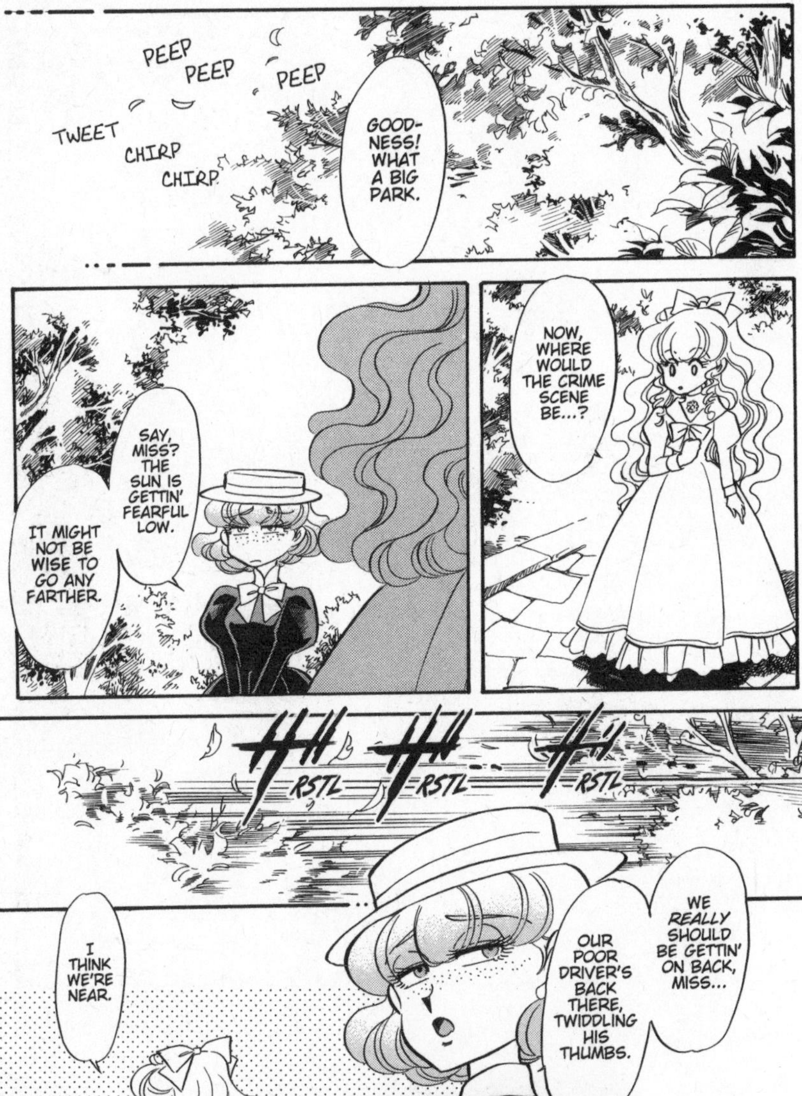
GOODNESS! WHAT A BIG PARK.
PEEP
PEEP
PEEP
TWEET
CHIRP
CHIRP
NOW, WHERE WOULD THE CRIME SCENE BE...?
SAY, MISS? THE SUN IS GETTIN' FEARFUL LOW.
IT MIGHT NOT BE WISE TO GO ANY FARTHER.
RSTL
RSTL
RSTL
WE *REALLY* SHOULD BE GETTIN' ON BACK, MISS...
OUR POOR DRIVER'S BACK THERE, TWIDDLING HIS THUMBS.
I THINK WE'RE NEAR.

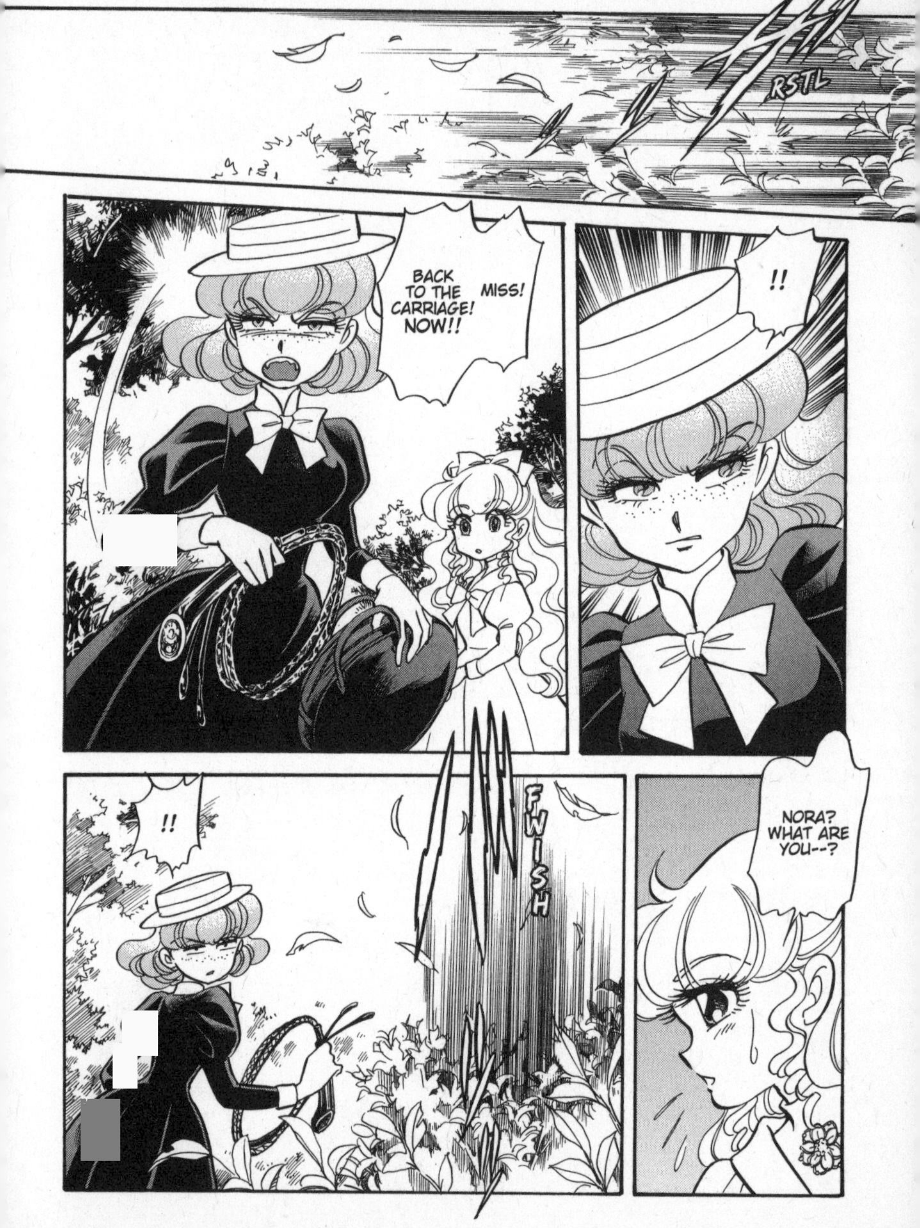
RSTL
!!
MISS!
BACK TO THE CARRIAGE! NOW!!
NORA? WHAT ARE YOU--?
FWISH
!!

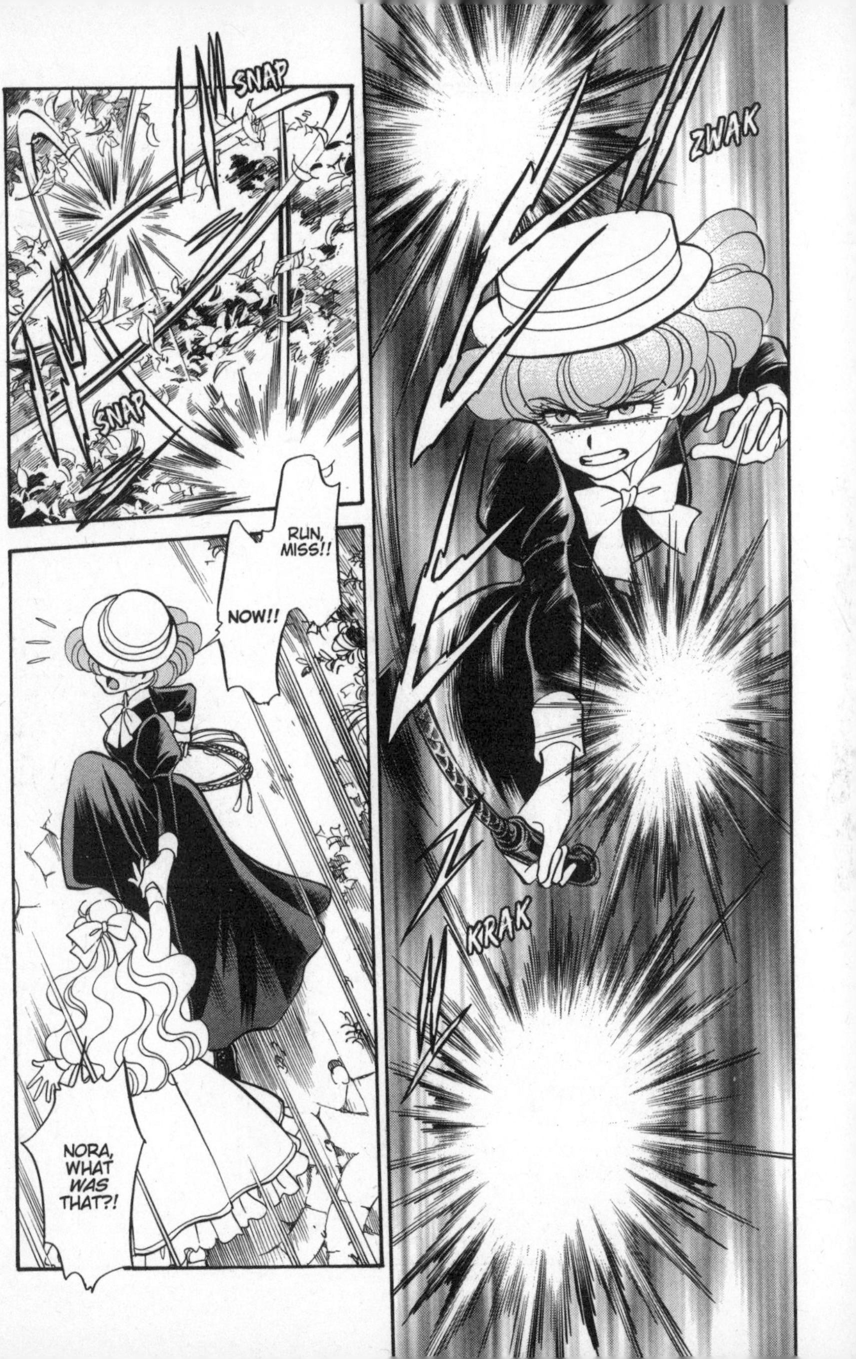
ZWAK
KRAK
SNAP
SNAP
RUN, MISS!!
NOW!!
NORA, WHAT *WAS* THAT?!

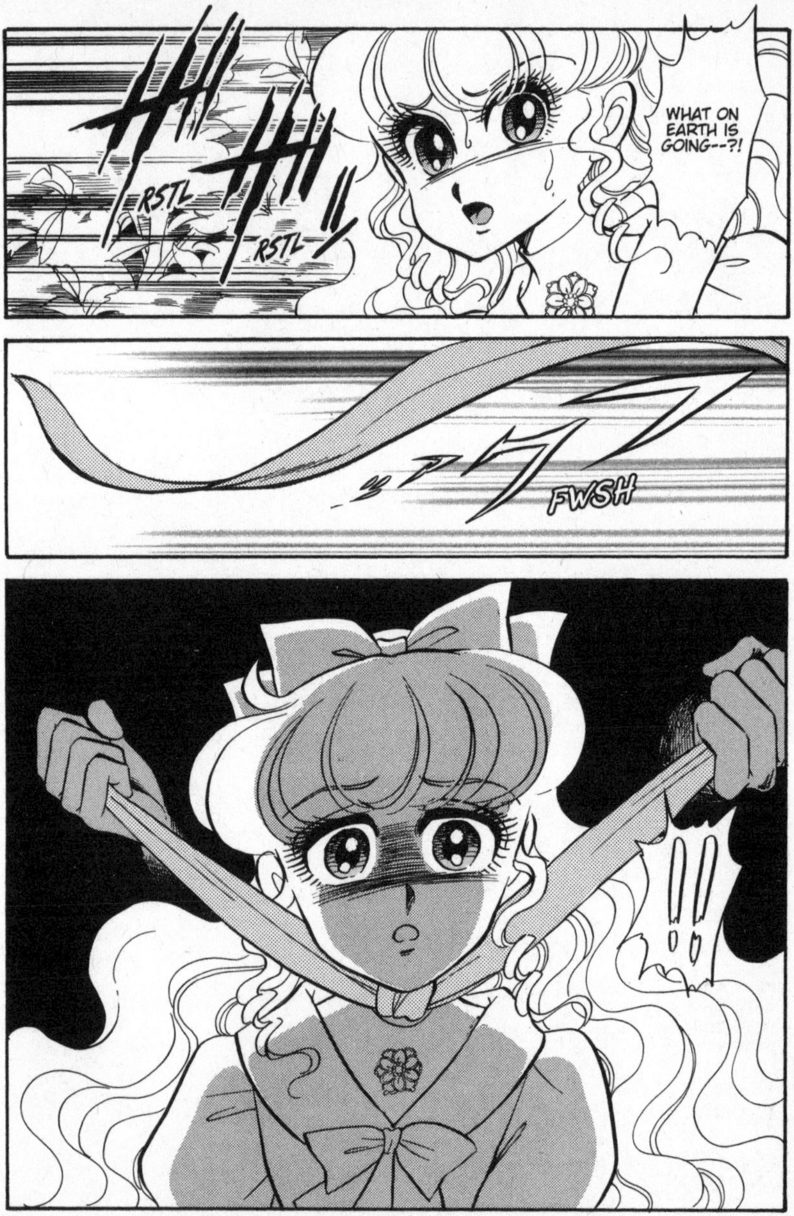
WHAT ON EARTH IS GOING--?!
RSTL
RSTL
FWSH
!!

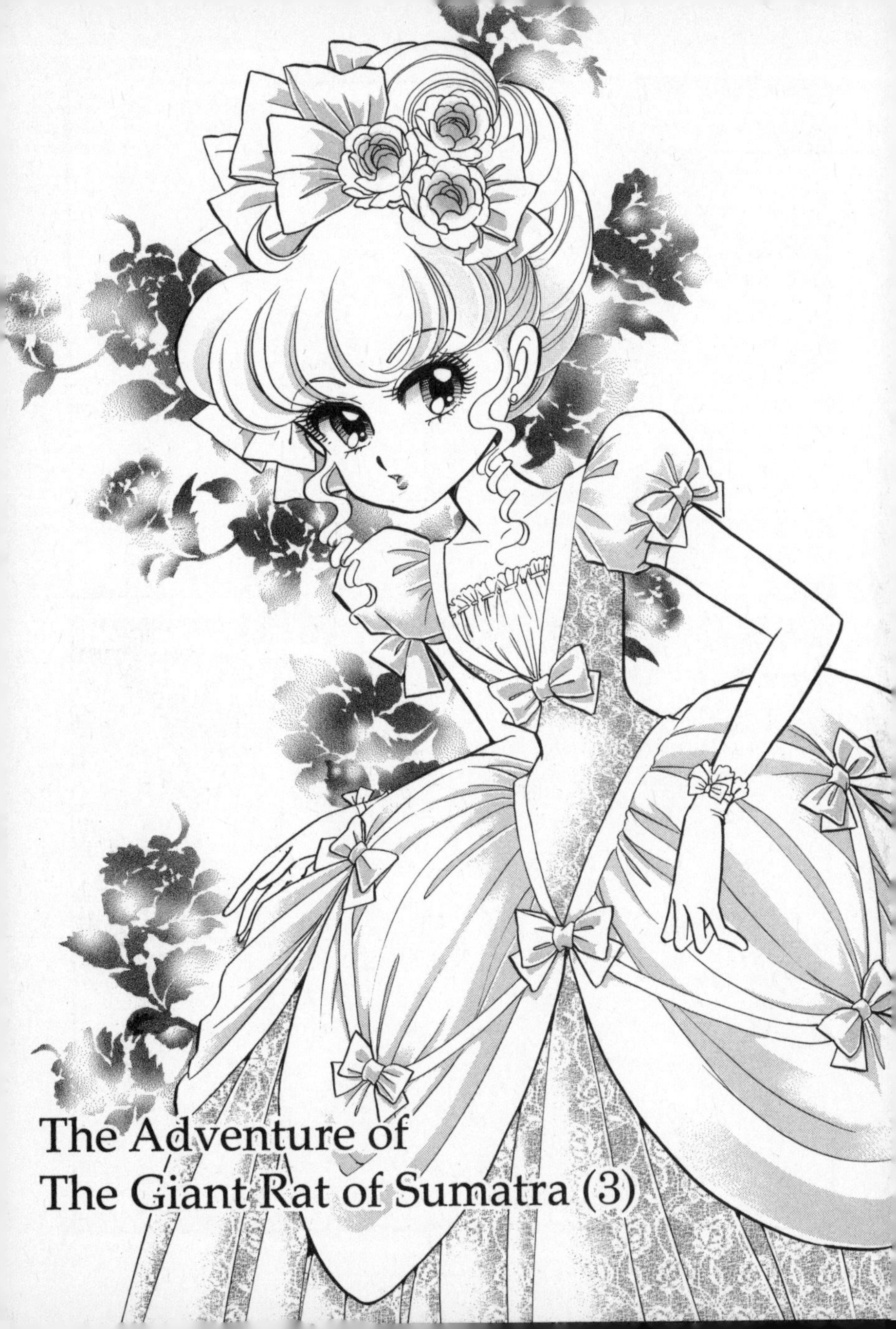

The Adventure of The Giant Rat of Sumatra (3)

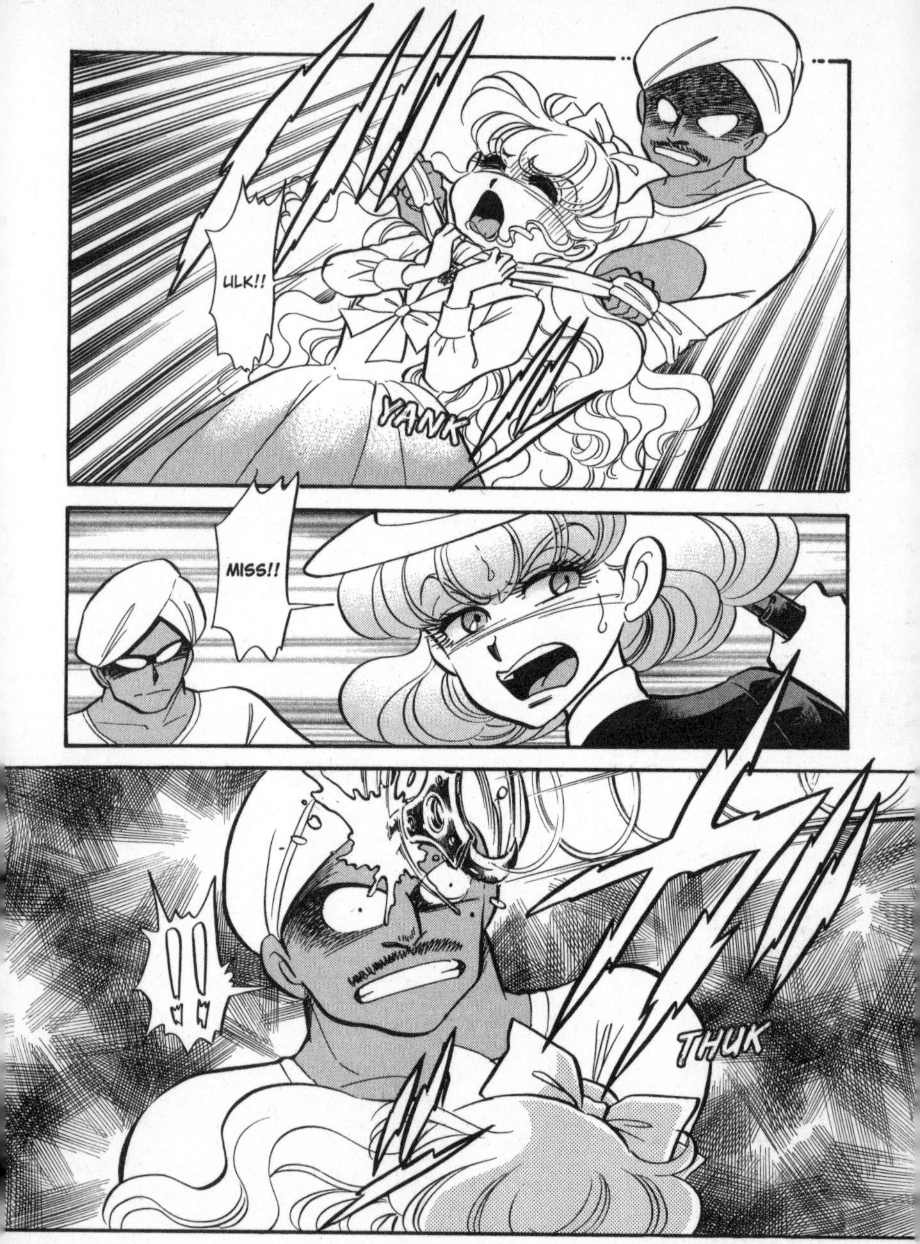
ULK!!
YANK
MISS!!
THUK
!!

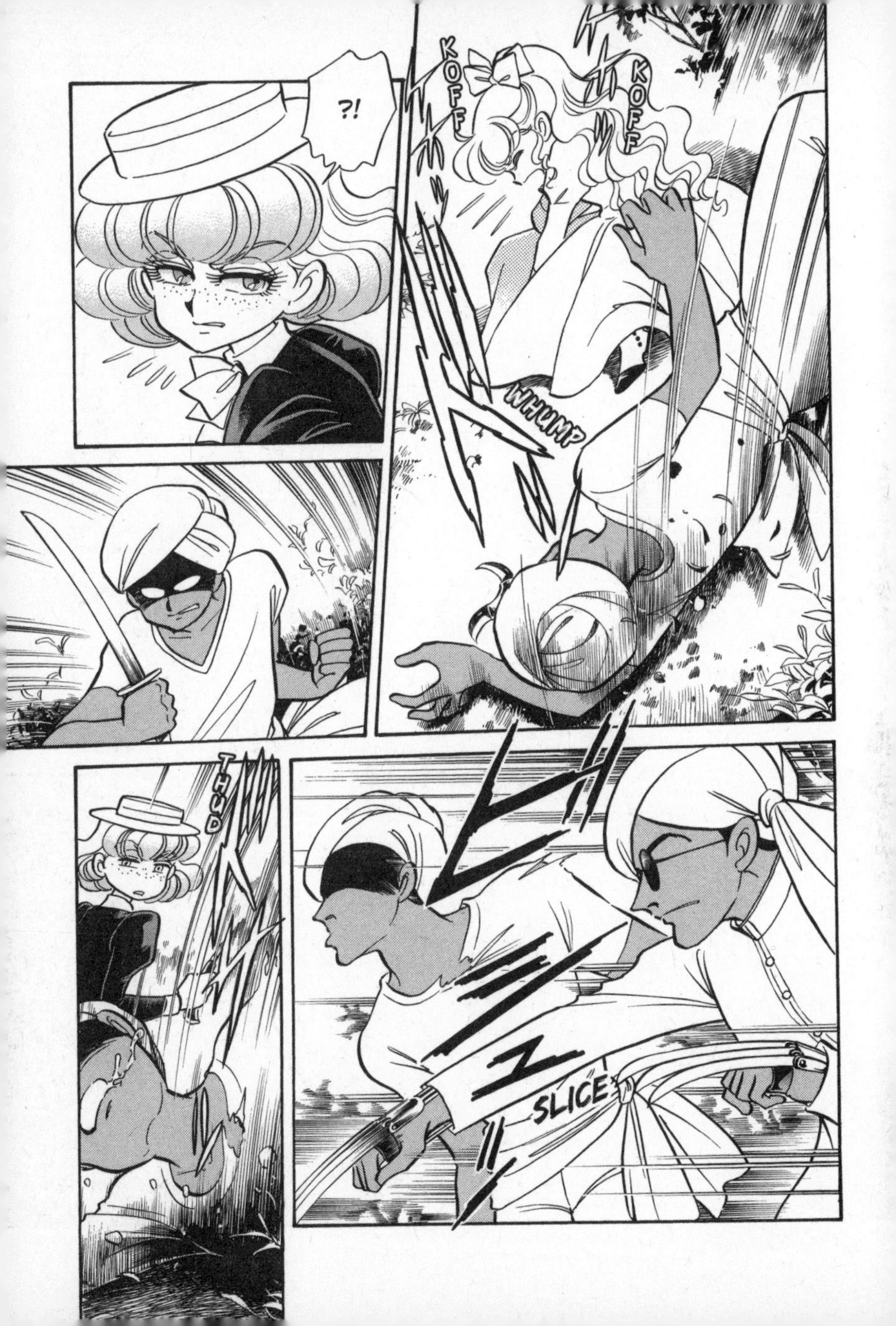
KOFF
KOFF
WHUMP
?!
SLICE
THUD

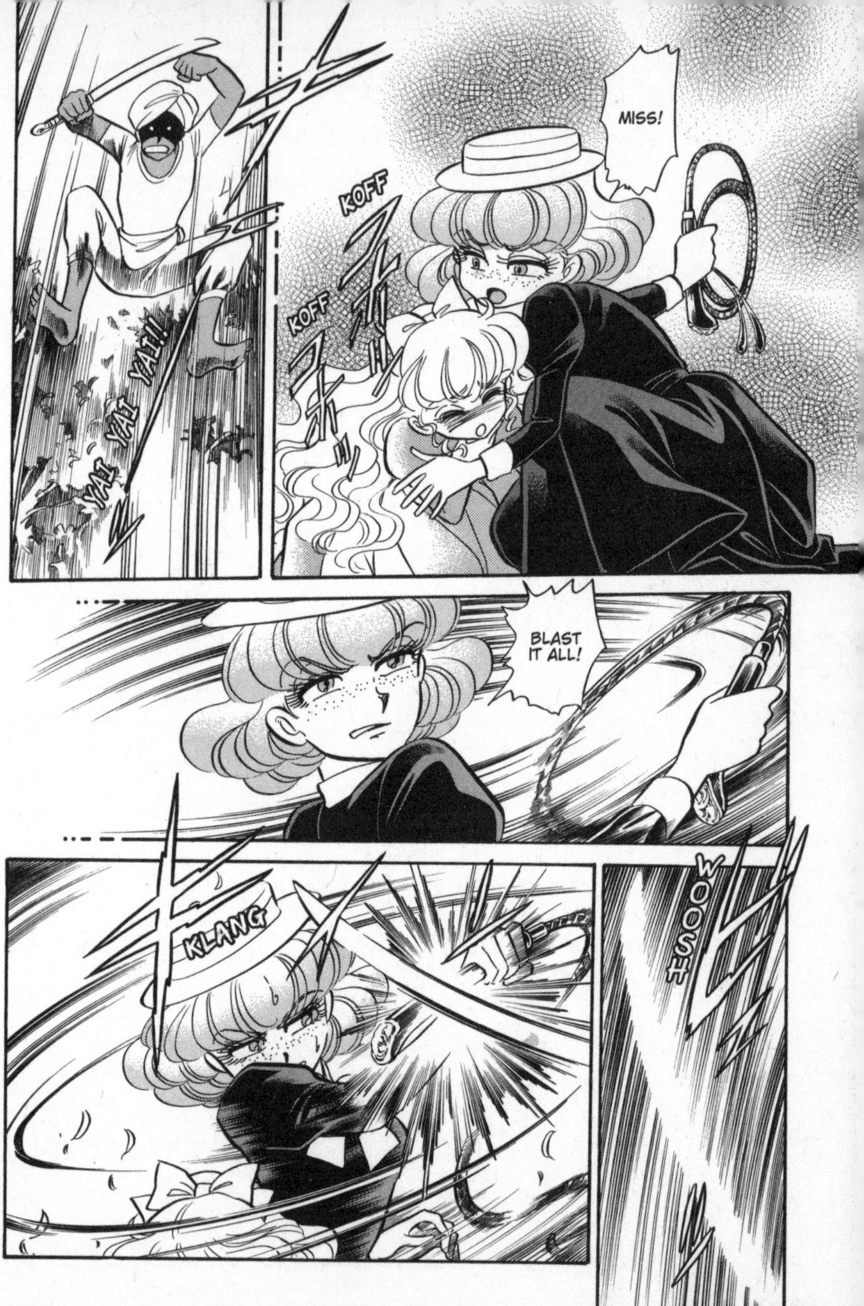
MISS!
KOFF
KOFF
YAI YAI YAI!!
BLAST IT ALL!
WOOSH
KLANG

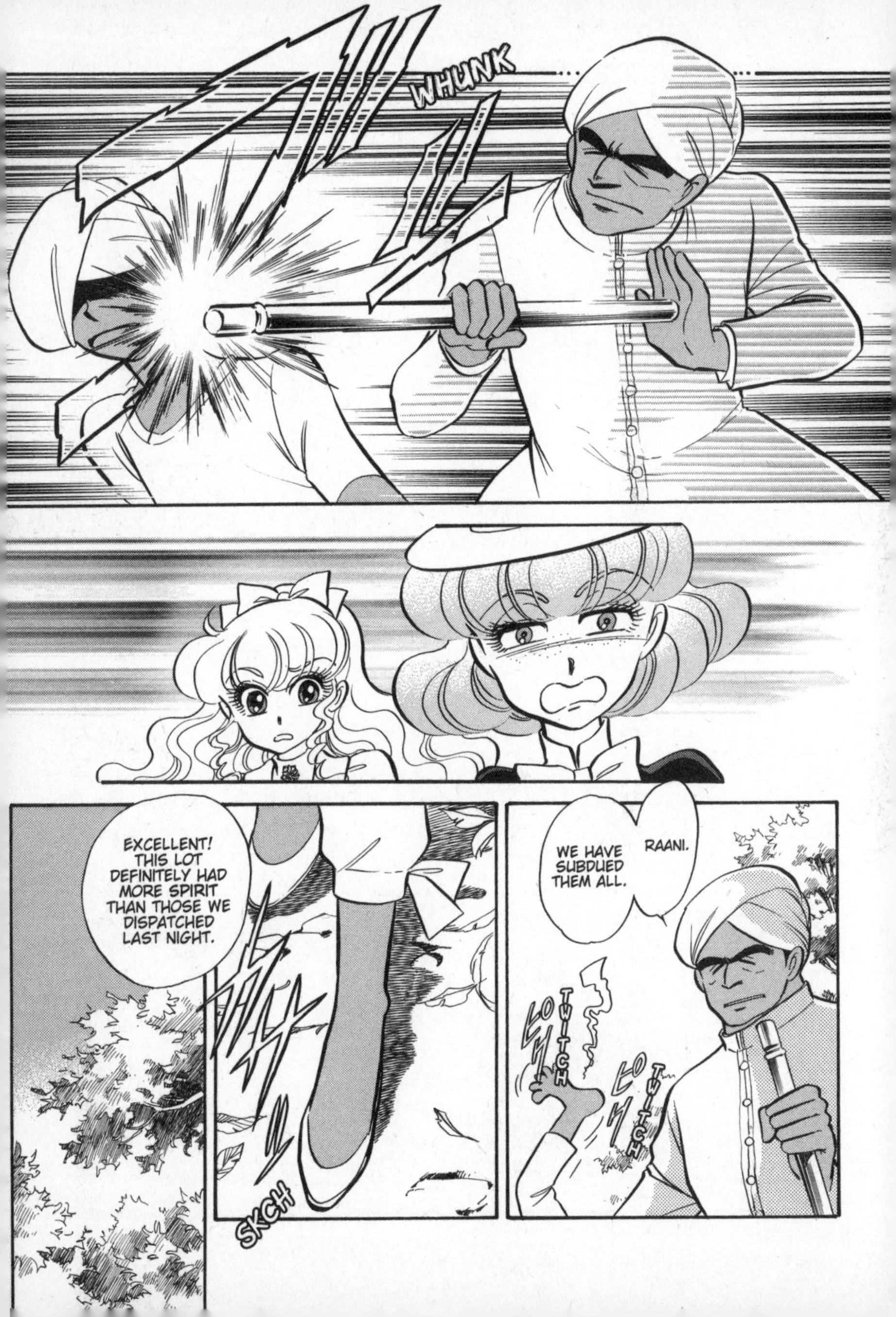
WHUNK
RAANI.
WE HAVE SUBDUED THEM ALL.
TWITCH
TWITCH
SKCH
EXCELLENT! THIS LOT DEFINITELY HAD MORE SPIRIT THAN THOSE WE DISPATCHED LAST NIGHT.

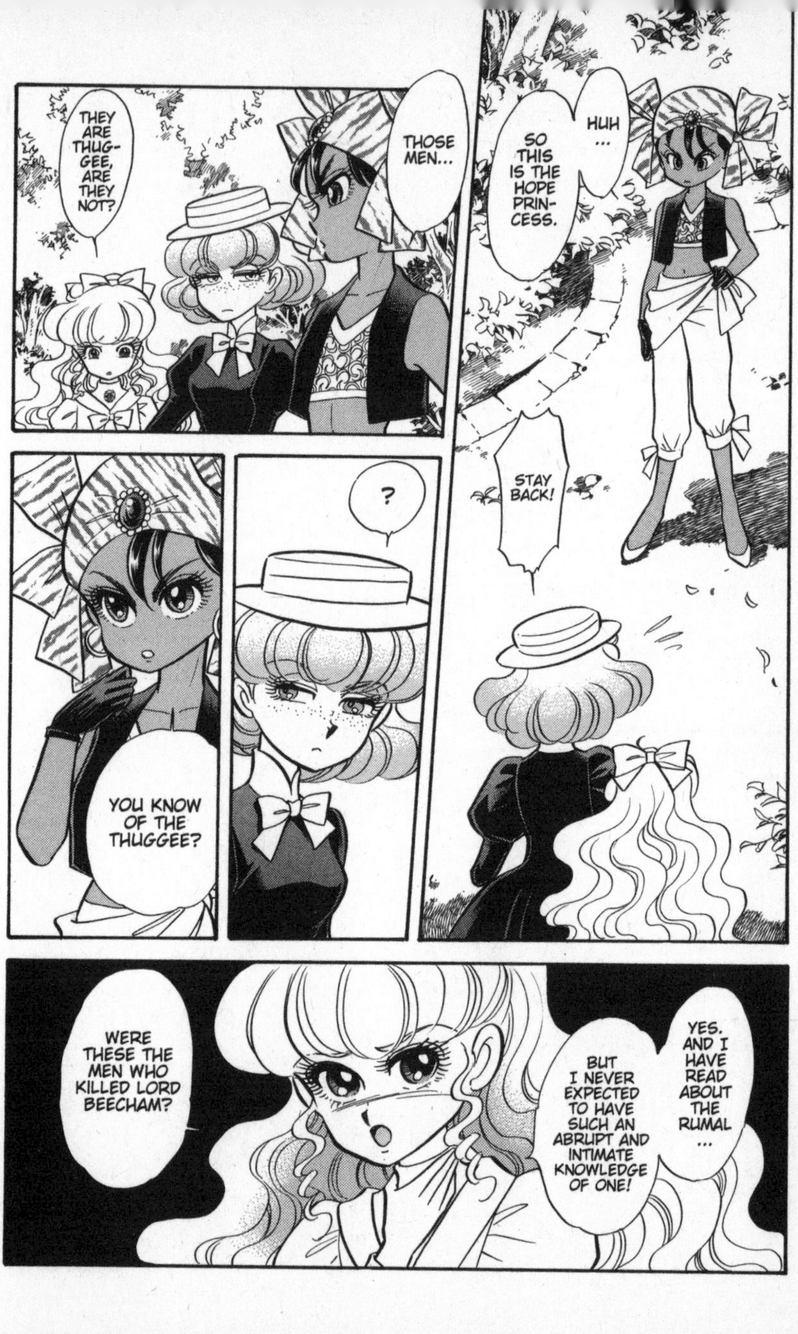
HUH ...
SO THIS IS THE HOPE PRINCESS.
STAY BACK!
THOSE MEN...
THEY ARE THUGGEE, ARE THEY NOT?
?
YOU KNOW OF THE THUGGEE?
YES. AND I HAVE READ ABOUT THE RUMAL ...
BUT I NEVER EXPECTED TO HAVE SUCH AN ABRUPT AND INTIMATE KNOWLEDGE OF ONE!
WERE THESE THE MEN WHO KILLED LORD BEECHAM?

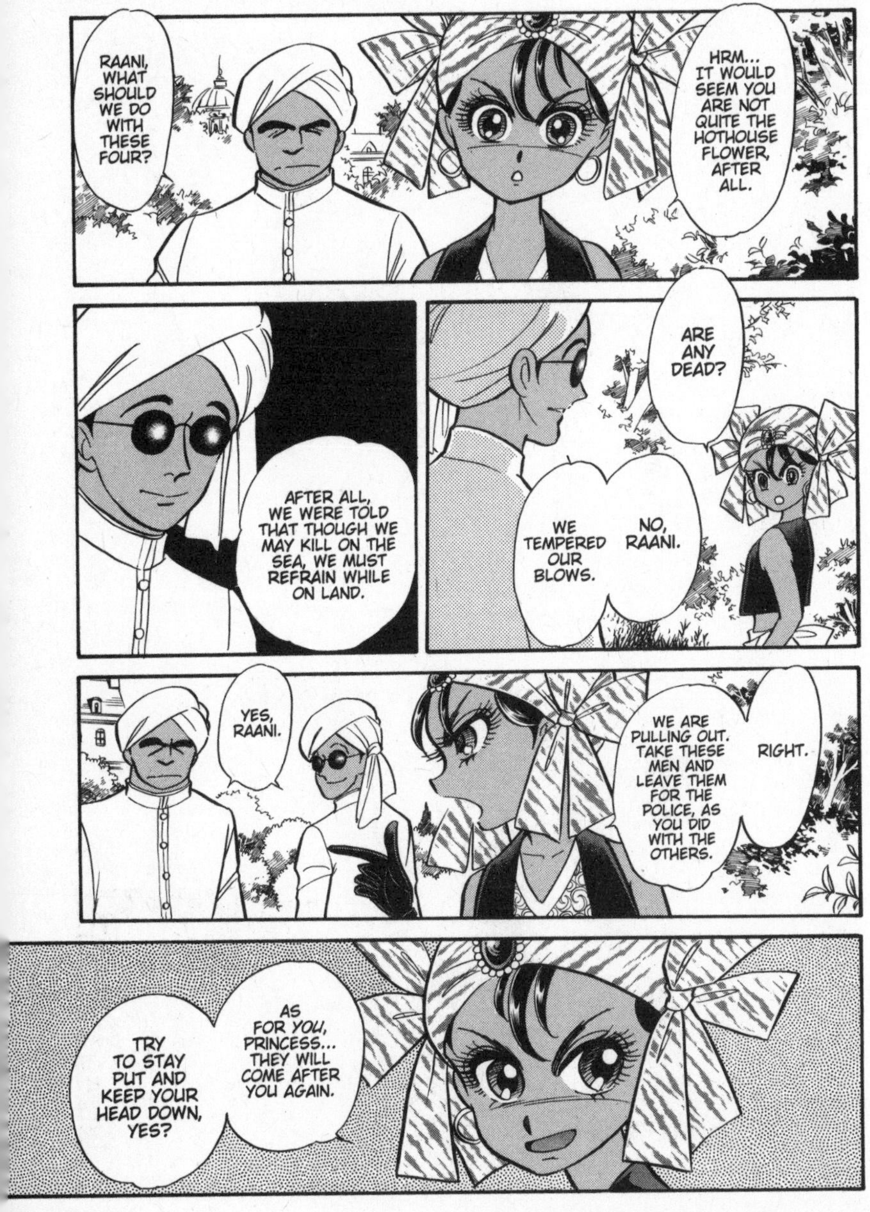
HRM... IT WOULD SEEM YOU ARE NOT QUITE THE HOTHOUSE FLOWER, AFTER ALL.
RAANI, WHAT SHOULD WE DO WITH THESE FOUR?
ARE ANY DEAD?
NO, RAANI.
WE TEMPERED OUR BLOWS.
AFTER ALL, WE WERE TOLD THAT THOUGH WE MAY KILL ON THE SEA, WE MUST REFRAIN WHILE ON LAND.
RIGHT.
WE ARE PULLING OUT. TAKE THESE MEN AND LEAVE THEM FOR THE POLICE, AS YOU DID WITH THE OTHERS.
YES, RAANI.
AS FOR *YOU*, PRINCESS... THEY WILL COME AFTER YOU AGAIN.
TRY TO STAY PUT AND KEEP YOUR HEAD DOWN, YES?

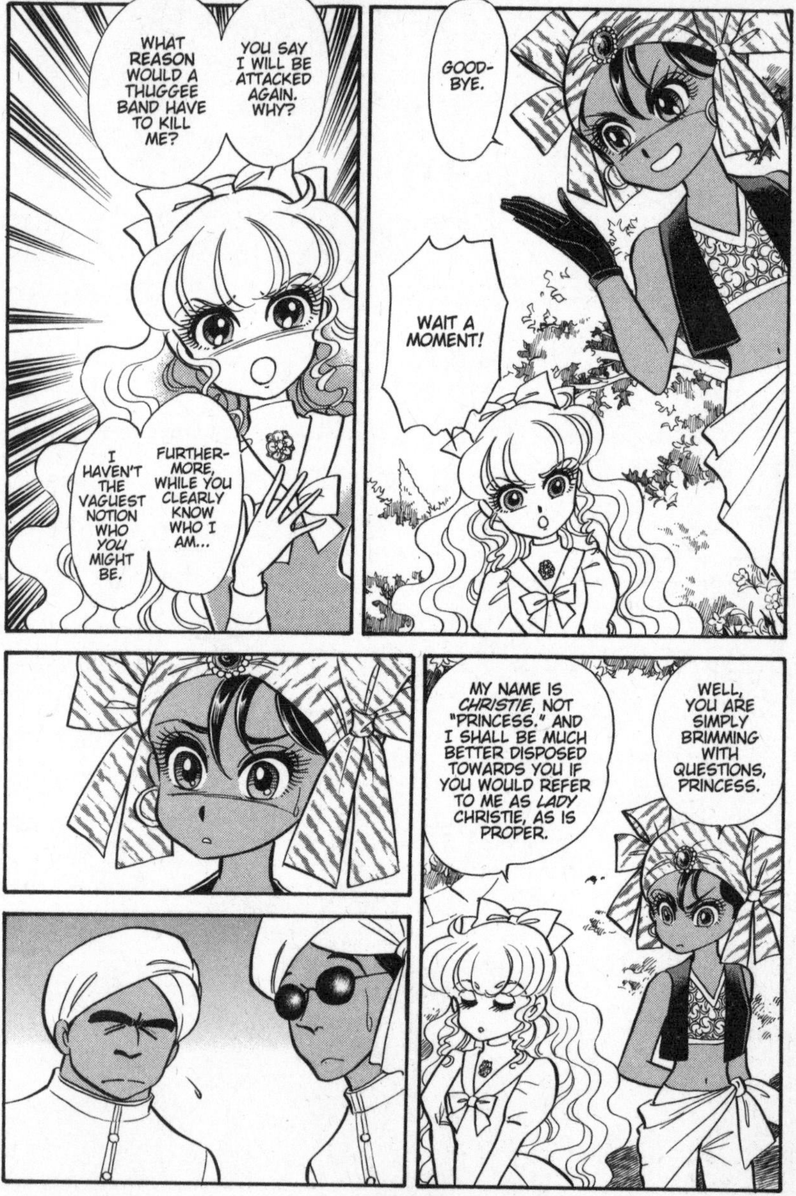
GOOD-BYE.
WAIT A MOMENT!
YOU SAY I WILL BE ATTACKED AGAIN. WHY?
WHAT REASON WOULD A THUGGEE BAND HAVE TO KILL ME?
FURTHERMORE, WHILE YOU CLEARLY KNOW WHO I AM...
I HAVEN'T THE VAGUEST NOTION WHO *YOU* MIGHT BE.
WELL, YOU ARE SIMPLY BRIMMING WITH QUESTIONS, PRINCESS.
MY NAME IS *CHRISTIE*, NOT "PRINCESS." AND I SHALL BE MUCH BETTER DISPOSED TOWARDS YOU IF YOU WOULD REFER TO ME AS *LADY* CHRISTIE, AS IS PROPER.

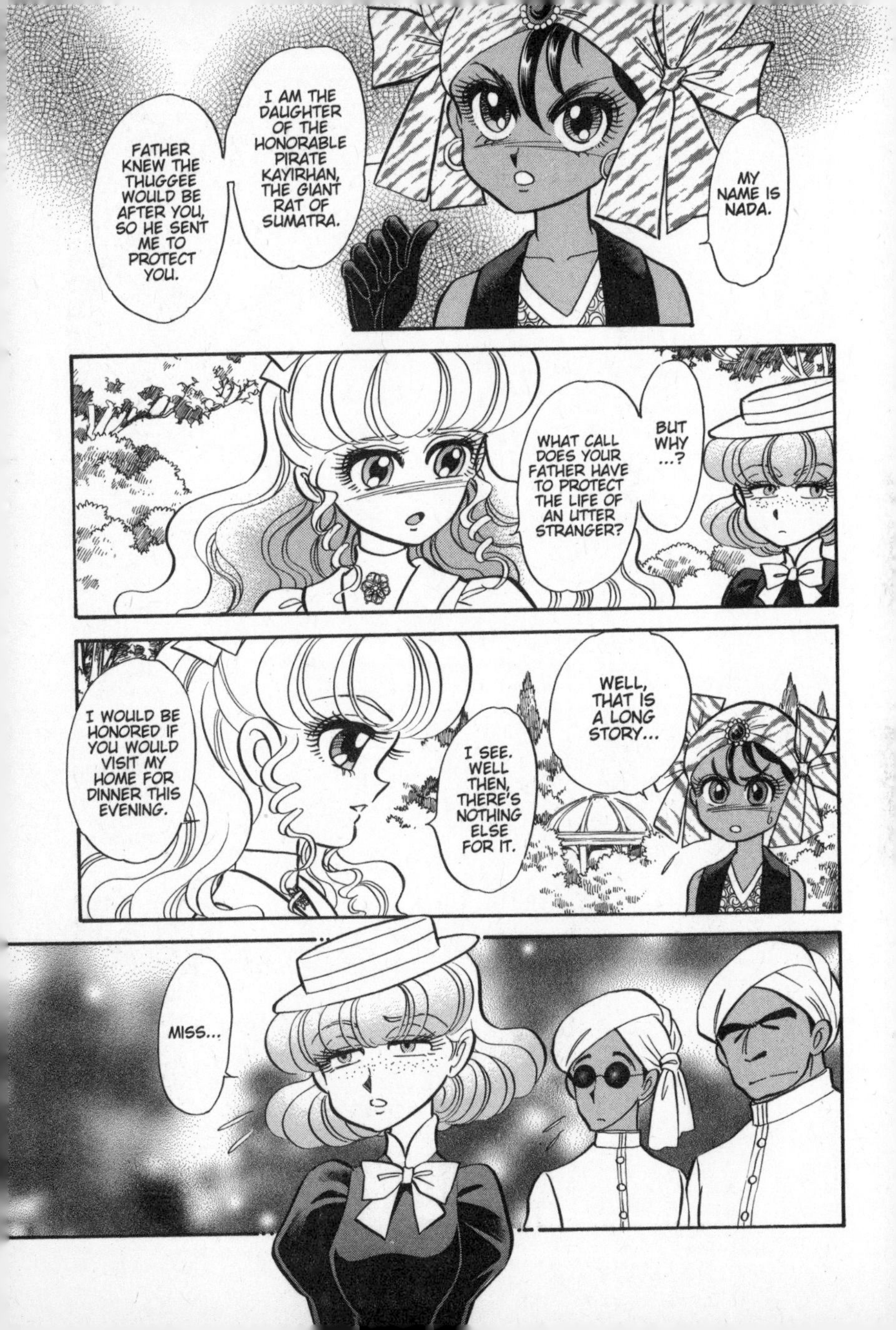
MY NAME IS NADA.
I AM THE DAUGHTER OF THE HONORABLE PIRATE KAYIRHAN, THE GIANT RAT OF SUMATRA.
FATHER KNEW THE THUGGEE WOULD BE AFTER YOU, SO HE SENT ME TO PROTECT YOU.
BUT WHY ...?
WHAT CALL DOES YOUR FATHER HAVE TO PROTECT THE LIFE OF AN UTTER STRANGER?
WELL, THAT IS A LONG STORY...
I SEE. WELL THEN, THERE'S NOTHING ELSE FOR IT.
I WOULD BE HONORED IF YOU WOULD VISIT MY HOME FOR DINNER THIS EVENING.
MISS...

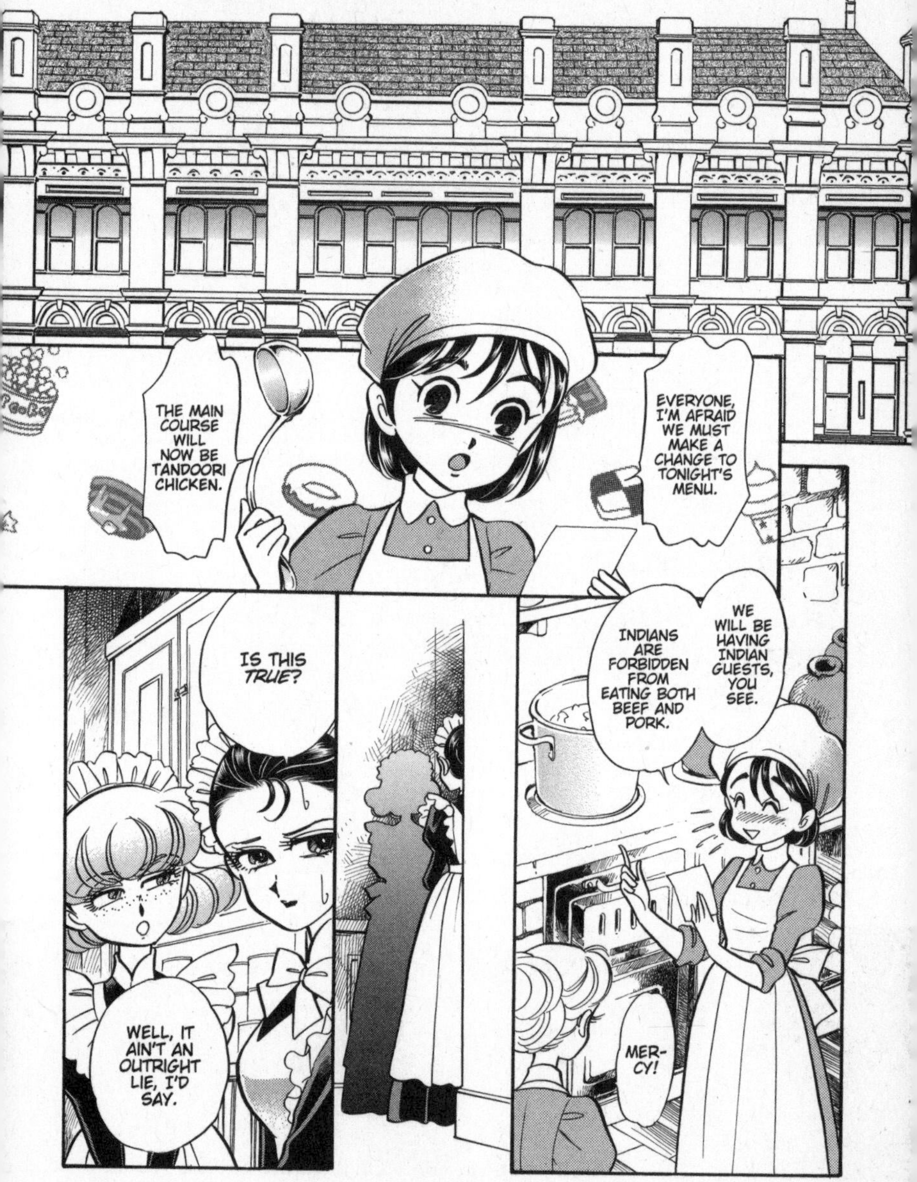
EVERYONE, I'M AFRAID WE MUST MAKE A CHANGE TO TONIGHT'S MENU.
THE MAIN COURSE WILL NOW BE TANDOORI CHICKEN.
WE WILL BE HAVING INDIAN GUESTS, YOU SEE.
INDIANS ARE FORBIDDEN FROM EATING BOTH BEEF AND PORK.
MERCY!
IS THIS *TRUE?*
WELL, IT AIN'T AN OUTRIGHT LIE, I'D SAY.

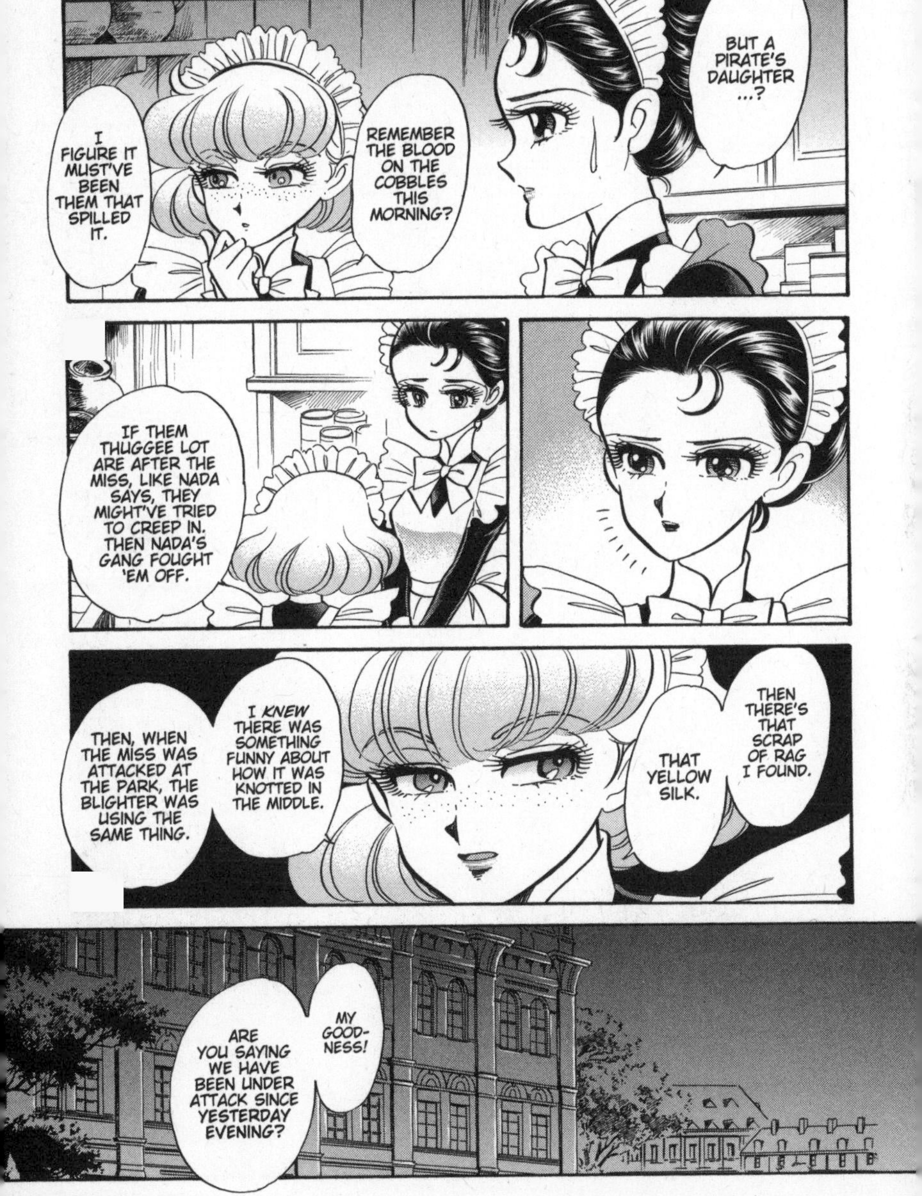
BUT A PIRATE'S DAUGHTER ...?
REMEMBER THE BLOOD ON THE COBBLES THIS MORNING?
I FIGURE IT MUST'VE BEEN THEM THAT SPILLED IT.
IF THEM THUGGEE LOT ARE AFTER THE MISS, LIKE NADA SAYS, THEY MIGHT'VE TRIED TO CREEP IN. THEN NADA'S GANG FOUGHT 'EM OFF.
THEN THERE'S THAT SCRAP OF RAG I FOUND.
THAT YELLOW SILK.
I *KNEW* THERE WAS SOMETHING FUNNY ABOUT HOW IT WAS KNOTTED IN THE MIDDLE.
THEN, WHEN THE MISS WAS ATTACKED AT THE PARK, THE BLIGHTER WAS USING THE SAME THING.
MY GOOD-NESS!
ARE YOU SAYING WE HAVE BEEN UNDER ATTACK SINCE YESTERDAY EVENING?

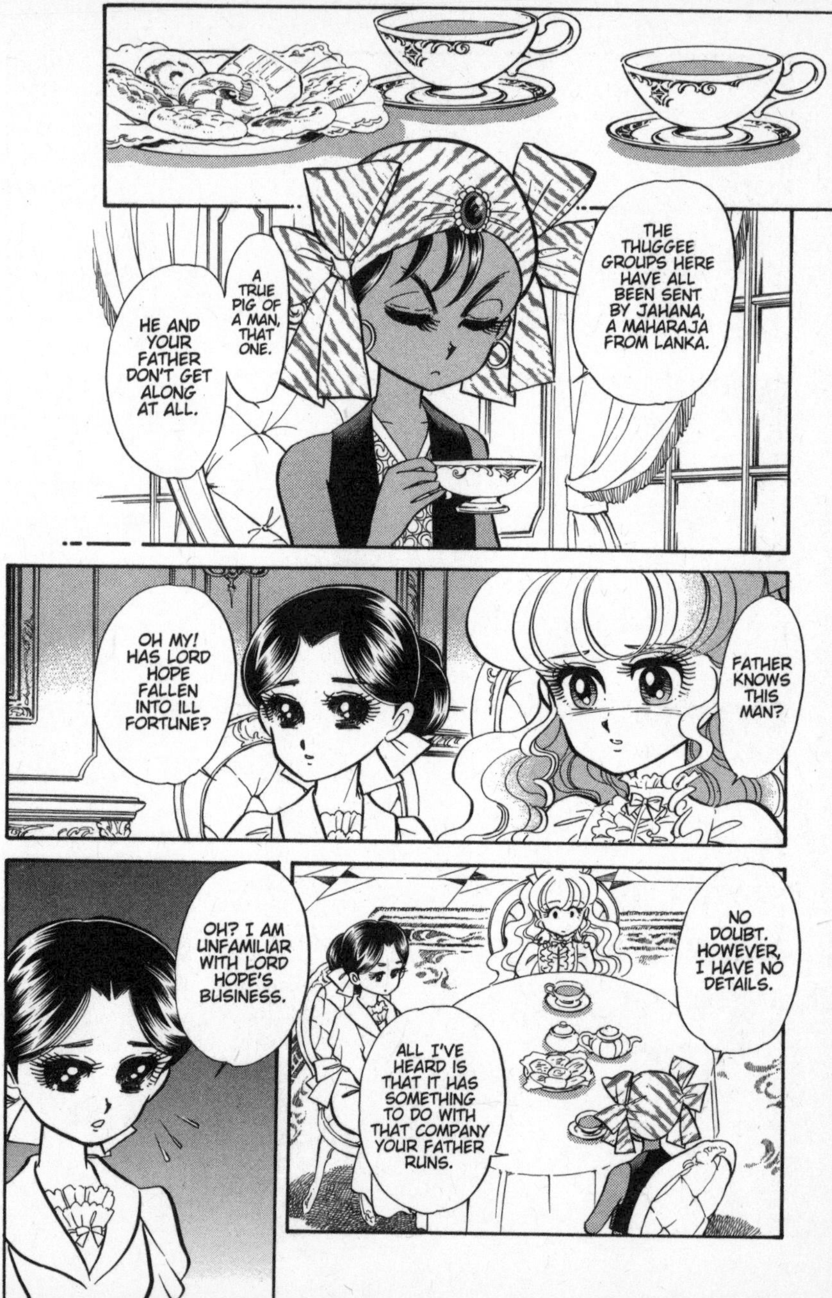
THE THUGGEE GROUPS HERE HAVE ALL BEEN SENT BY JAHANA, A MAHARAJA FROM LANKA.
A TRUE PIG OF A MAN, THAT ONE.
HE AND YOUR FATHER DON'T GET ALONG AT ALL.
FATHER KNOWS THIS MAN?
OH MY! HAS LORD HOPE FALLEN INTO ILL FORTUNE?
NO DOUBT. HOWEVER, I HAVE NO DETAILS.
ALL I'VE HEARD IS THAT IT HAS SOMETHING TO DO WITH THAT COMPANY YOUR FATHER RUNS.
OH? I AM UNFAMILIAR WITH LORD HOPE'S BUSINESS.

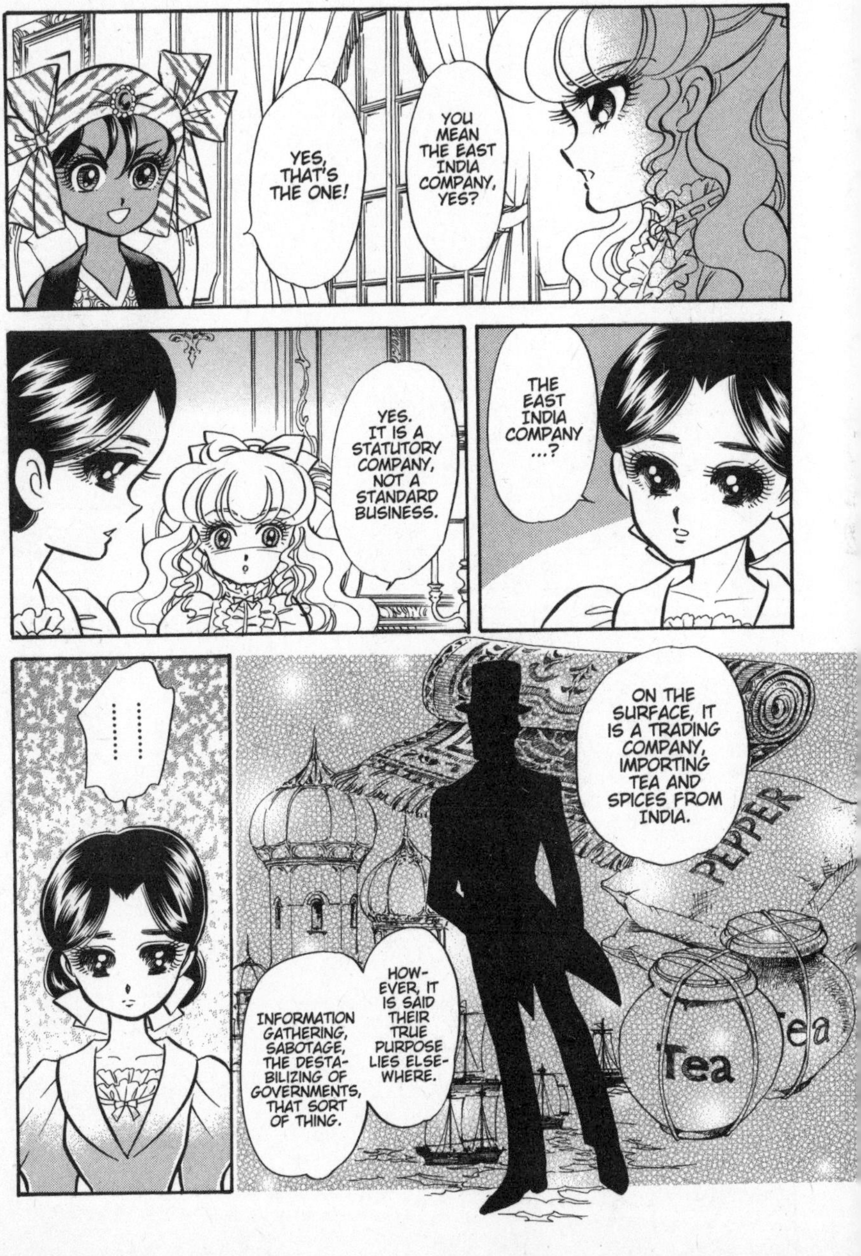
YOU MEAN THE EAST INDIA COMPANY, YES?
YES, THAT'S THE ONE!
THE EAST INDIA COMPANY ...?
YES. IT IS A STATUTORY COMPANY, NOT A STANDARD BUSINESS.
ON THE SURFACE, IT IS A TRADING COMPANY, IMPORTING TEA AND SPICES FROM INDIA.
PEPPER
Tea
HOW-EVER, IT IS SAID THEIR TRUE PURPOSE LIES ELSE-WHERE.
INFORMATION GATHERING, SABOTAGE, THE DESTA-BILIZING OF GOVERNMENTS, THAT SORT OF THING.
......

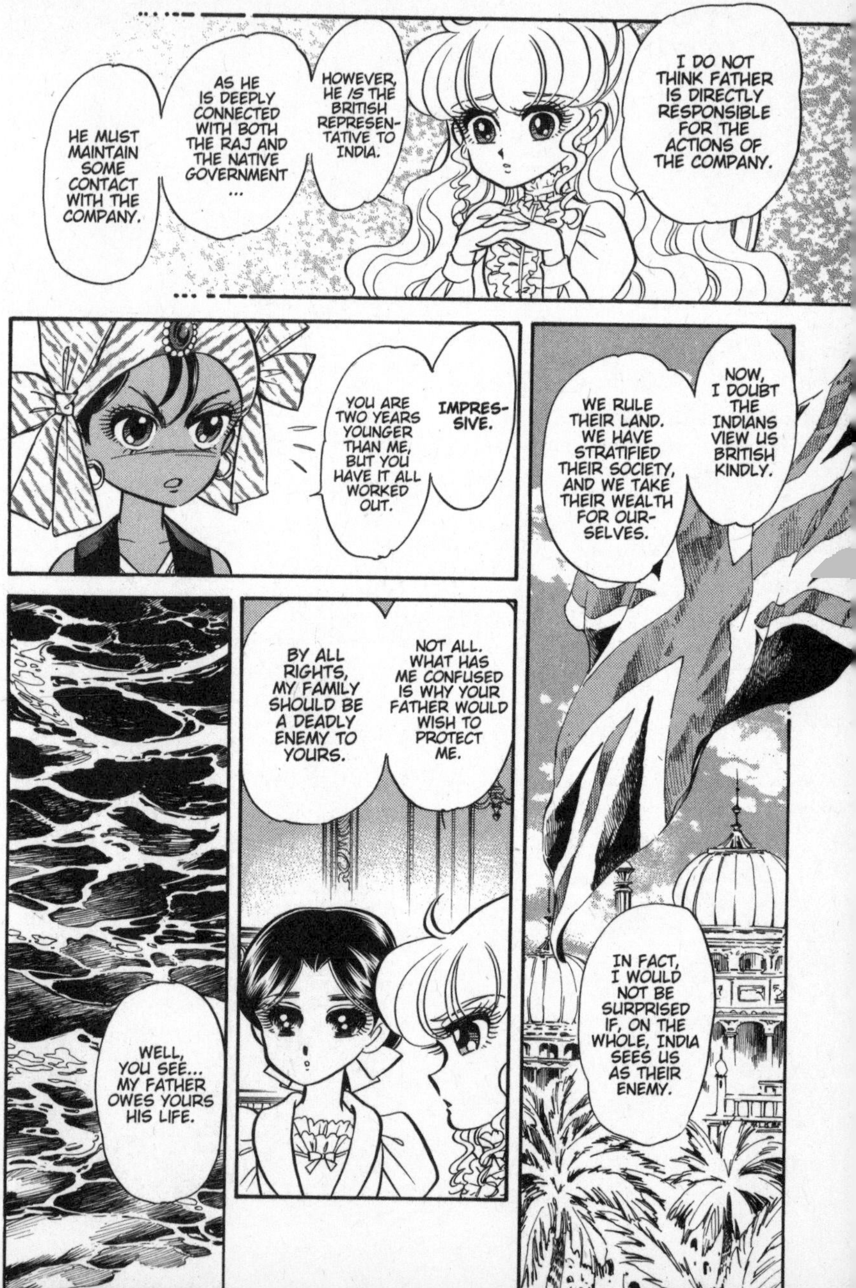
I DO NOT THINK FATHER IS DIRECTLY RESPONSIBLE FOR THE ACTIONS OF THE COMPANY.
HOWEVER, HE IS THE BRITISH REPRESENTATIVE TO INDIA.
AS HE IS DEEPLY CONNECTED WITH BOTH THE RAJ AND THE NATIVE GOVERNMENT ...
HE MUST MAINTAIN SOME CONTACT WITH THE COMPANY.
NOW, I DOUBT THE INDIANS VIEW US BRITISH KINDLY.
WE RULE THEIR LAND. WE HAVE STRATIFIED THEIR SOCIETY, AND WE TAKE THEIR WEALTH FOR OURSELVES.
IN FACT, I WOULD NOT BE SURPRISED IF, ON THE WHOLE, INDIA SEES US AS THEIR ENEMY.
IMPRESSIVE.
YOU ARE TWO YEARS YOUNGER THAN ME, BUT YOU HAVE IT ALL WORKED OUT.
NOT ALL. WHAT HAS ME CONFUSED IS WHY YOUR FATHER WOULD WISH TO PROTECT ME.
BY ALL RIGHTS, MY FAMILY SHOULD BE A DEADLY ENEMY TO YOURS.
WELL, YOU SEE... MY FATHER OWES YOURS HIS LIFE.

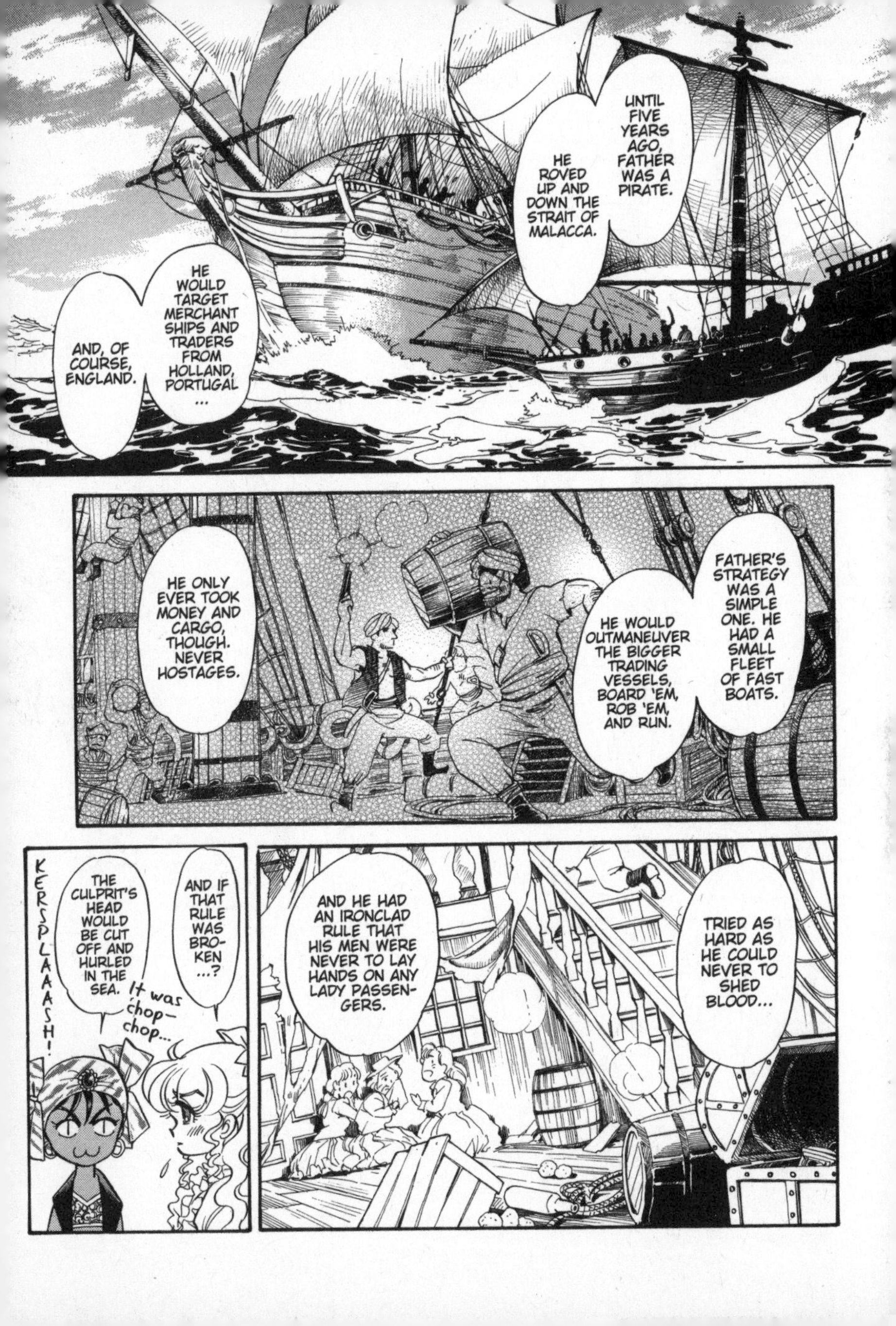
UNTIL FIVE YEARS AGO, FATHER WAS A PIRATE.
HE ROVED UP AND DOWN THE STRAIT OF MALACCA.
HE WOULD TARGET MERCHANT SHIPS AND TRADERS FROM HOLLAND, PORTUGAL ...
AND, OF COURSE, ENGLAND.
FATHER'S STRATEGY WAS A SIMPLE ONE. HE HAD A SMALL FLEET OF FAST BOATS.
HE WOULD OUTMANEUVER THE BIGGER TRADING VESSELS, BOARD 'EM, ROB 'EM, AND RUN.
HE ONLY EVER TOOK MONEY AND CARGO, THOUGH. NEVER HOSTAGES.
TRIED AS HARD AS HE COULD NEVER TO SHED BLOOD...
AND HE HAD AN IRONCLAD RULE THAT HIS MEN WERE NEVER TO LAY HANDS ON ANY LADY PASSENGERS.
AND IF THAT RULE WAS BROKEN ...?
THE CULPRIT'S HEAD WOULD BE CUT OFF AND HURLED IN THE SEA.
KERSPLAAAASH!
It was chop-chop...

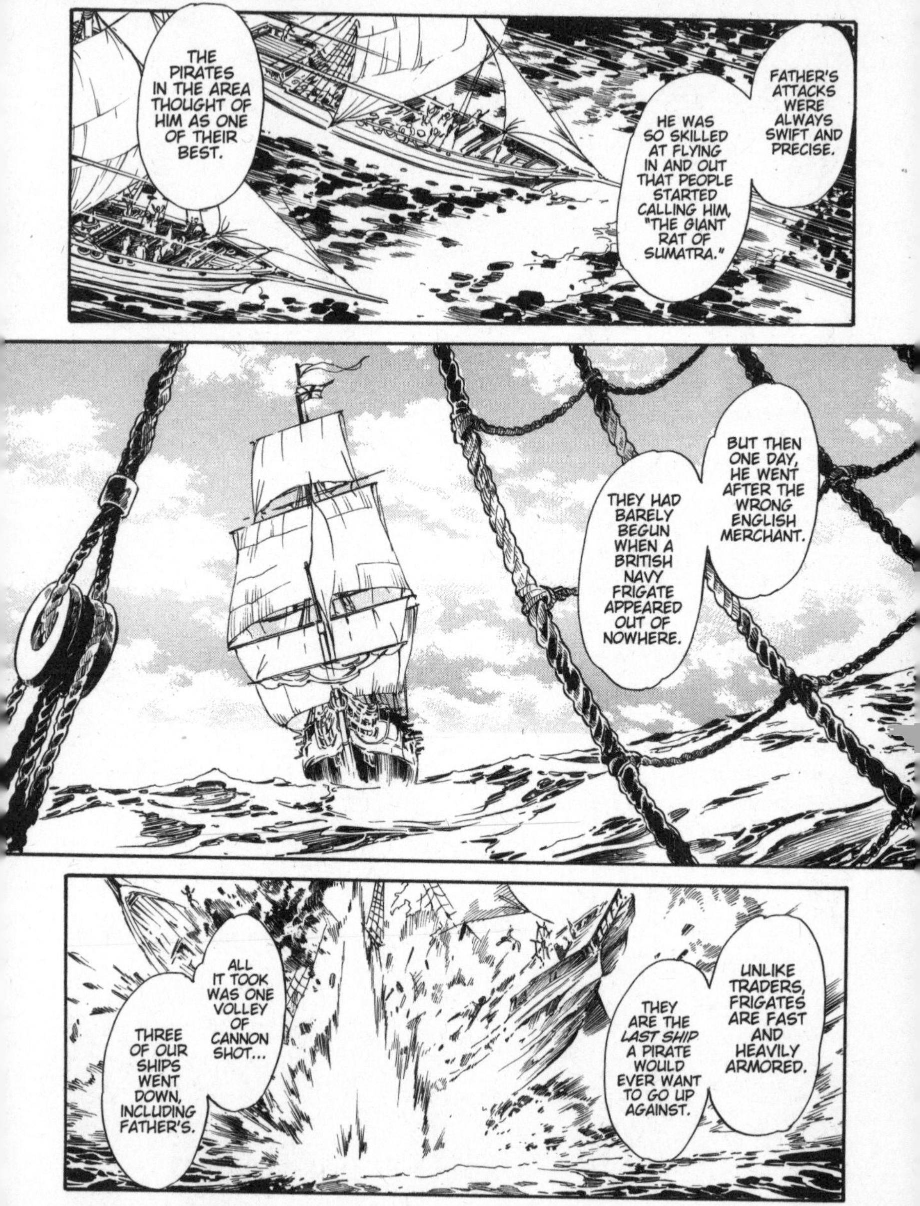
FATHER'S ATTACKS WERE ALWAYS SWIFT AND PRECISE.
HE WAS SO SKILLED AT FLYING IN AND OUT THAT PEOPLE STARTED CALLING HIM, "THE GIANT RAT OF SUMATRA."
THE PIRATES IN THE AREA THOUGHT OF HIM AS ONE OF THEIR BEST.
BUT THEN ONE DAY, HE WENT AFTER THE WRONG ENGLISH MERCHANT.
THEY HAD BARELY BEGUN WHEN A BRITISH NAVY FRIGATE APPEARED OUT OF NOWHERE.
UNLIKE TRADERS, FRIGATES ARE FAST AND HEAVILY ARMORED.
THEY ARE THE *LAST SHIP* A PIRATE WOULD EVER WANT TO GO UP AGAINST.
ALL IT TOOK WAS ONE VOLLEY OF CANNON SHOT...
THREE OF OUR SHIPS WENT DOWN, INCLUDING FATHER'S.

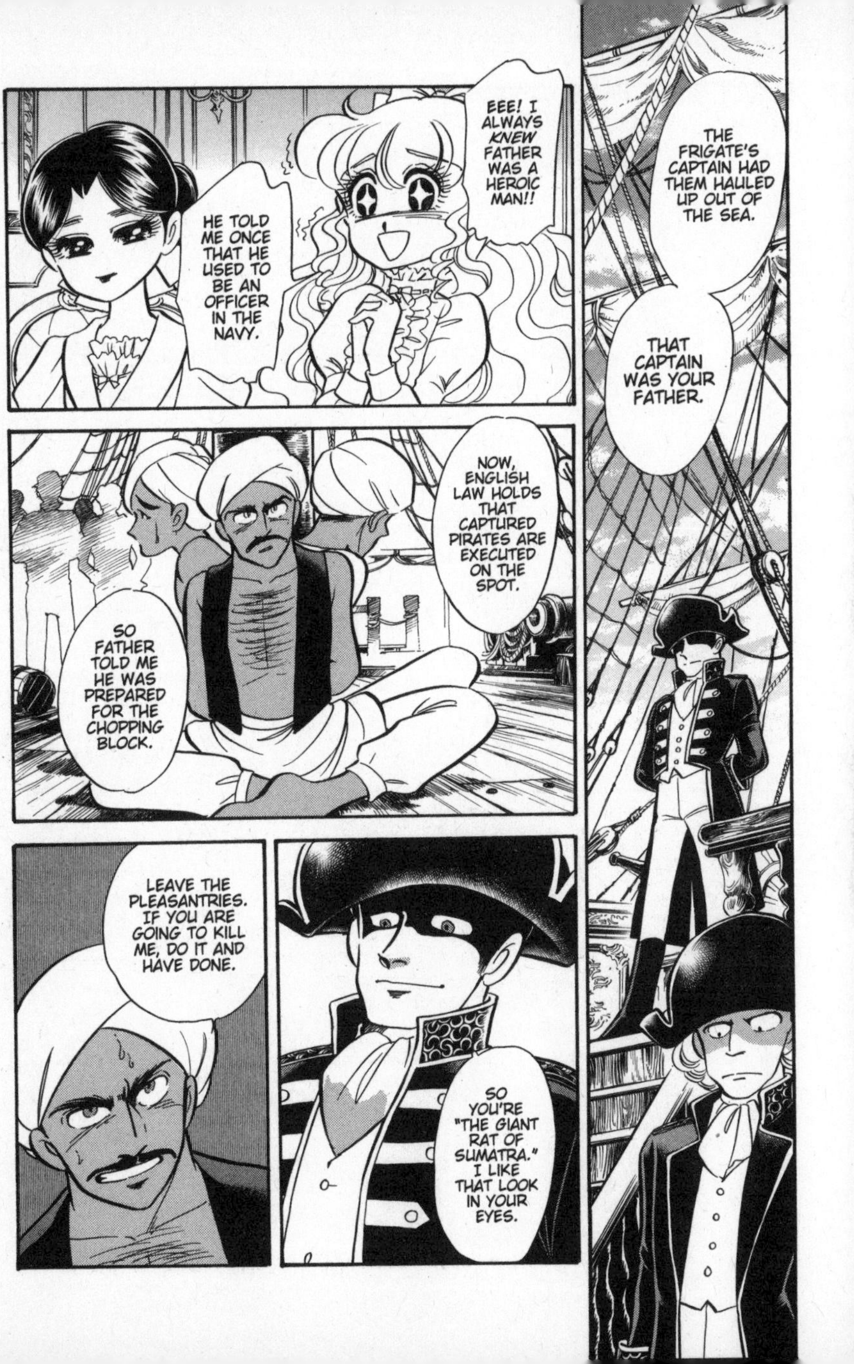
THE FRIGATE'S CAPTAIN HAD THEM HAULED UP OUT OF THE SEA.
THAT CAPTAIN WAS YOUR FATHER.
EEE! I ALWAYS *KNEW* FATHER WAS A HEROIC MAN!!
HE TOLD ME ONCE THAT HE USED TO BE AN OFFICER IN THE NAVY.
NOW, ENGLISH LAW HOLDS THAT CAPTURED PIRATES ARE EXECUTED ON THE SPOT.
SO FATHER TOLD ME HE WAS PREPARED FOR THE CHOPPING BLOCK.
SO YOU'RE "THE GIANT RAT OF SUMATRA." I LIKE THAT LOOK IN YOUR EYES.
LEAVE THE PLEASANTRIES. IF YOU ARE GOING TO KILL ME, DO IT AND HAVE DONE.

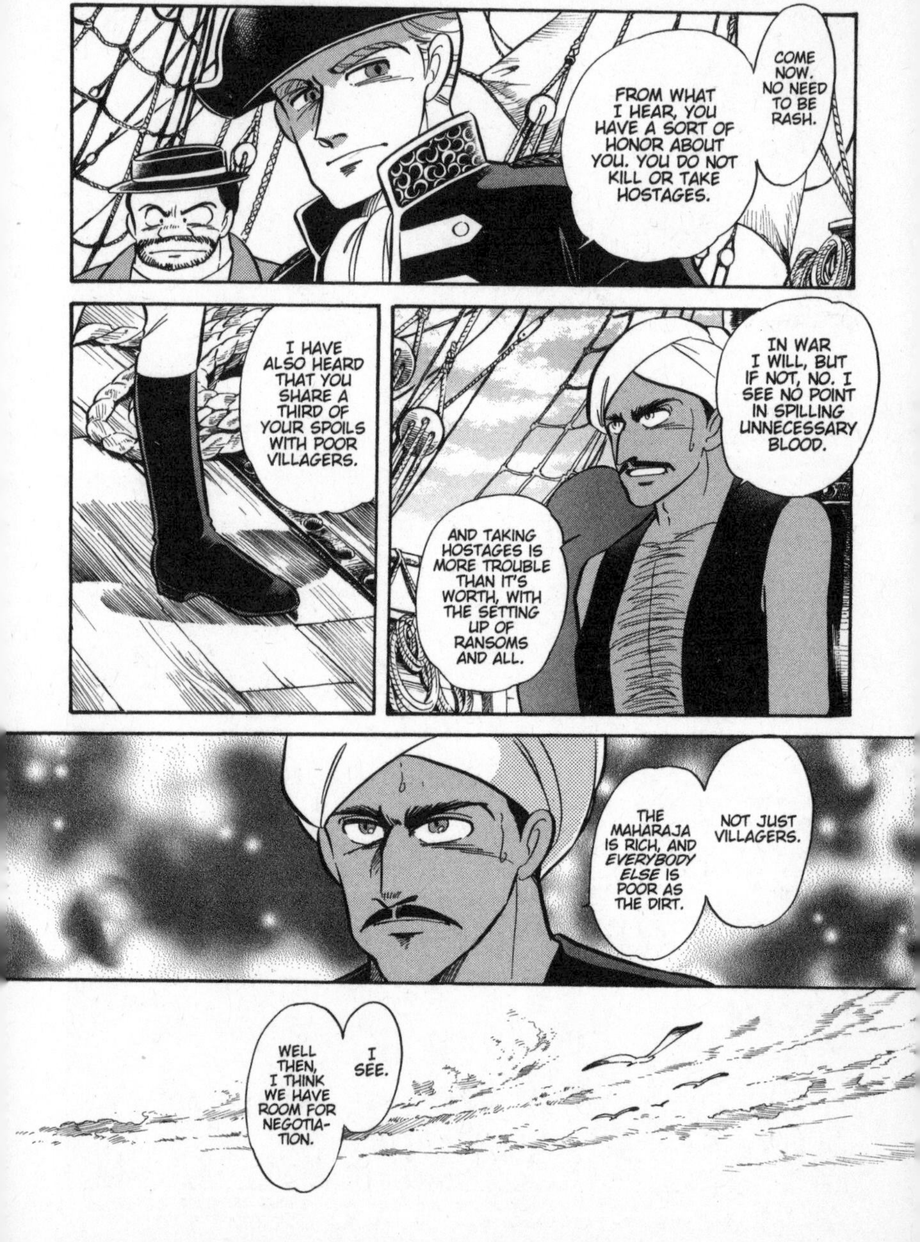
COME NOW. NO NEED TO BE RASH.
FROM WHAT I HEAR, YOU HAVE A SORT OF HONOR ABOUT YOU. YOU DO NOT KILL OR TAKE HOSTAGES.
IN WAR I WILL, BUT IF NOT, NO. I SEE NO POINT IN SPILLING UNNECESSARY BLOOD.
AND TAKING HOSTAGES IS MORE TROUBLE THAN IT'S WORTH, WITH THE SETTING UP OF RANSOMS AND ALL.
I HAVE ALSO HEARD THAT YOU SHARE A THIRD OF YOUR SPOILS WITH POOR VILLAGERS.
NOT JUST VILLAGERS.
THE MAHARAJA IS RICH, AND *EVERYBODY ELSE* IS POOR AS THE DIRT.
I SEE.
WELL THEN, I THINK WE HAVE ROOM FOR NEGOTIA-TION.

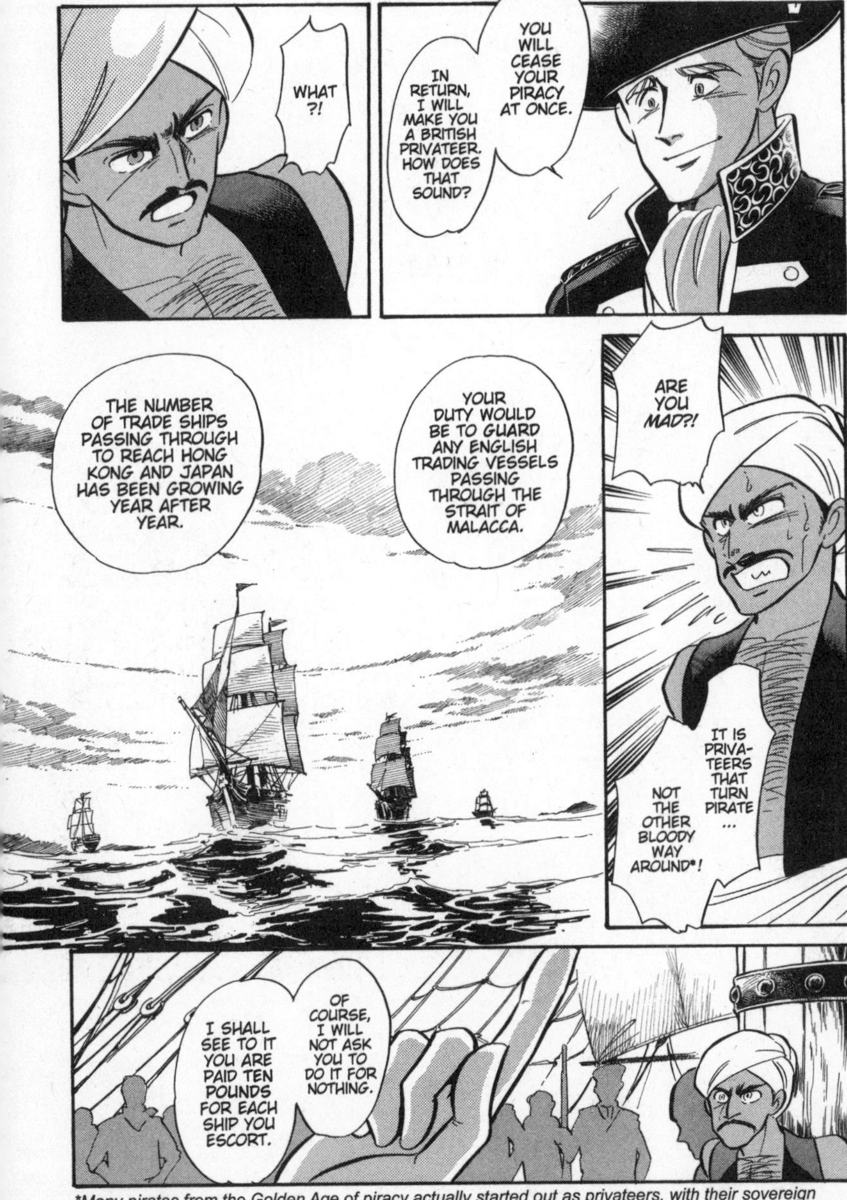
YOU WILL CEASE YOUR PIRACY AT ONCE.
IN RETURN, I WILL MAKE YOU A BRITISH PRIVATEER. HOW DOES THAT SOUND?
WHAT ?!
ARE YOU MAD?!
IT IS PRIVATEERS THAT TURN PIRATE ...
NOT THE OTHER BLOODY WAY AROUND*!
YOUR DUTY WOULD BE TO GUARD ANY ENGLISH TRADING VESSELS PASSING THROUGH THE STRAIT OF MALACCA.
THE NUMBER OF TRADE SHIPS PASSING THROUGH TO REACH HONG KONG AND JAPAN HAS BEEN GROWING YEAR AFTER YEAR.
OF COURSE, I WILL NOT ASK YOU TO DO IT FOR NOTHING.
I SHALL SEE TO IT YOU ARE PAID TEN POUNDS FOR EACH SHIP YOU ESCORT.

*Many pirates from the Golden Age of piracy actually started out as privateers, with their sovereign nation turning a blind eye to their activities, as long as they only robbed from that nation's enemies.

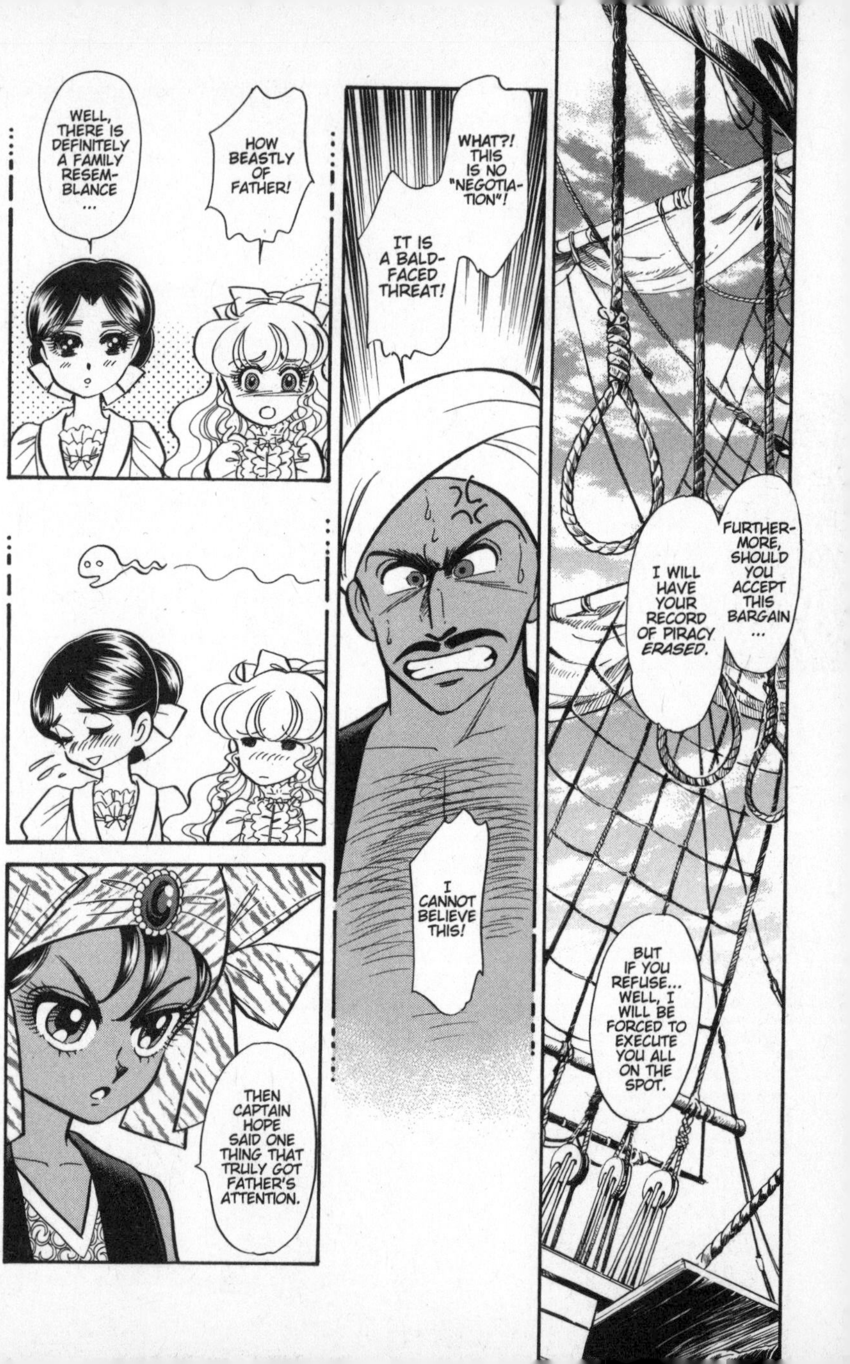
FURTHERMORE, SHOULD YOU ACCEPT THIS BARGAIN...
I WILL HAVE YOUR RECORD OF PIRACY ERASED.
BUT IF YOU REFUSE... WELL, I WILL BE FORCED TO EXECUTE YOU ALL ON THE SPOT.
WHAT?! THIS IS NO "NEGOTIATION"!
IT IS A BALD-FACED THREAT!
I CANNOT BELIEVE THIS!
HOW BEASTLY OF FATHER!
WELL, THERE IS DEFINITELY A FAMILY RESEMBLANCE...
THEN CAPTAIN HOPE SAID ONE THING THAT TRULY GOT FATHER'S ATTENTION.

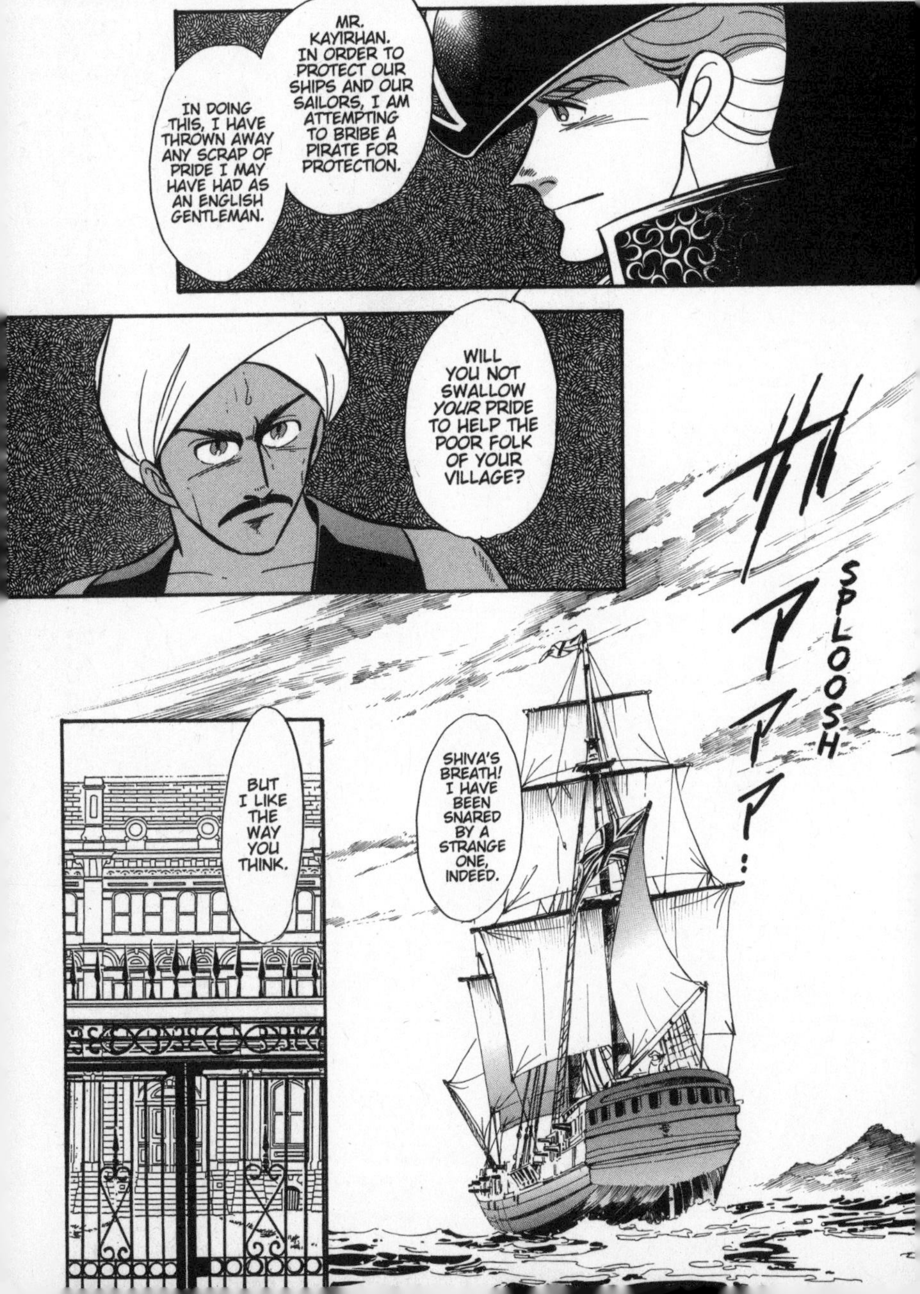
MR. KAYIRHAN. IN ORDER TO PROTECT OUR SHIPS AND OUR SAILORS, I AM ATTEMPTING TO BRIBE A PIRATE FOR PROTECTION.
IN DOING THIS, I HAVE THROWN AWAY ANY SCRAP OF PRIDE I MAY HAVE HAD AS AN ENGLISH GENTLEMAN.
WILL YOU NOT SWALLOW *YOUR* PRIDE TO HELP THE POOR FOLK OF YOUR VILLAGE?
SPLOOSH
SHIVA'S BREATH! I HAVE BEEN SNARED BY A STRANGE ONE, INDEED.
BUT I LIKE THE WAY YOU THINK.

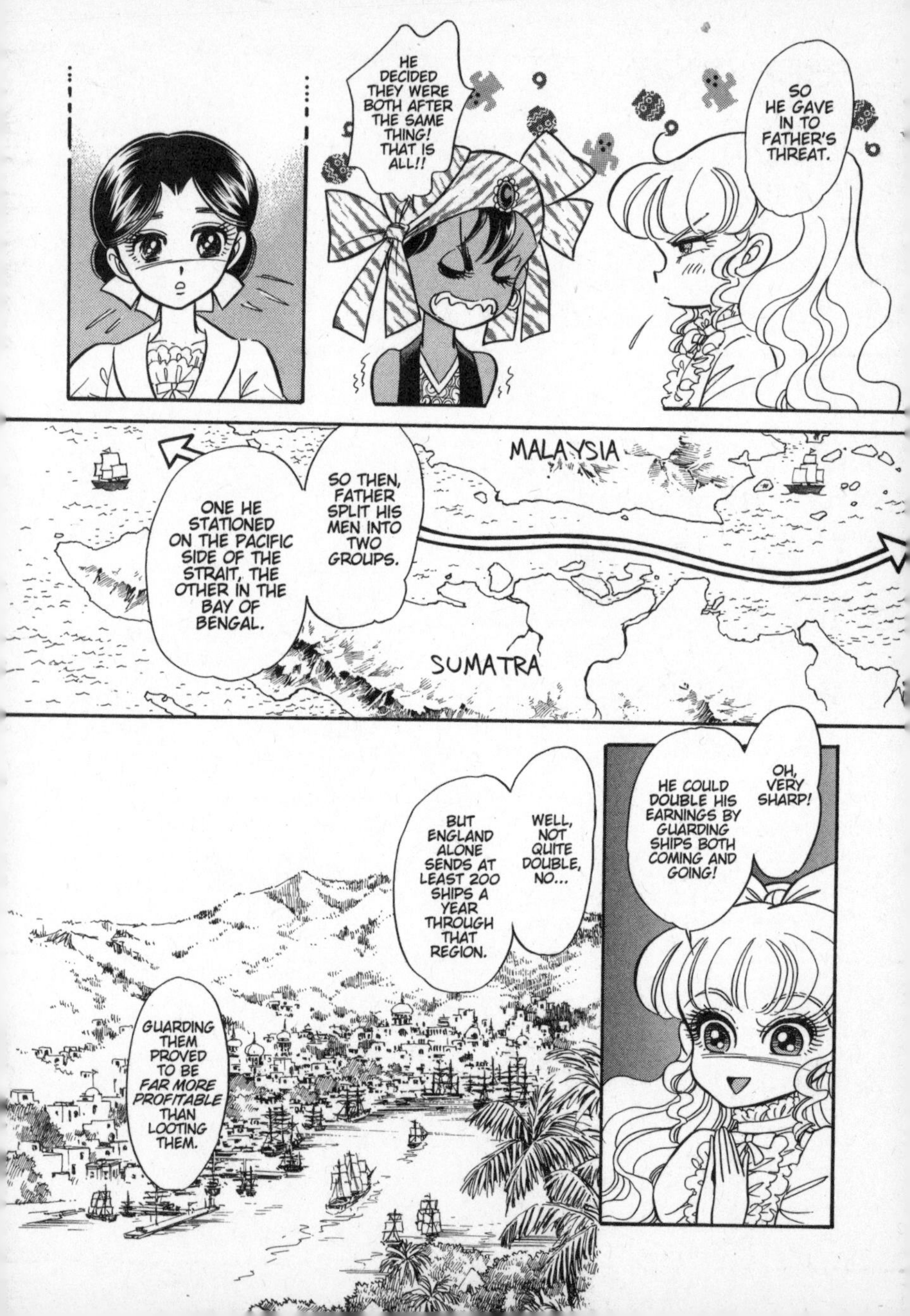
SO HE GAVE IN TO FATHER'S THREAT.
HE DECIDED THEY WERE BOTH AFTER THE SAME THING! THAT IS ALL!!
MALAYSIA
SO THEN, FATHER SPLIT HIS MEN INTO TWO GROUPS.
ONE HE STATIONED ON THE PACIFIC SIDE OF THE STRAIT, THE OTHER IN THE BAY OF BENGAL.
SUMATRA
OH, VERY SHARP!
HE COULD DOUBLE HIS EARNINGS BY GUARDING SHIPS BOTH COMING AND GOING!
WELL, NOT QUITE DOUBLE, NO...
BUT ENGLAND ALONE SENDS AT LEAST 200 SHIPS A YEAR THROUGH THAT REGION.
GUARDING THEM PROVED TO BE *FAR MORE PROFITABLE* THAN LOOTING THEM.

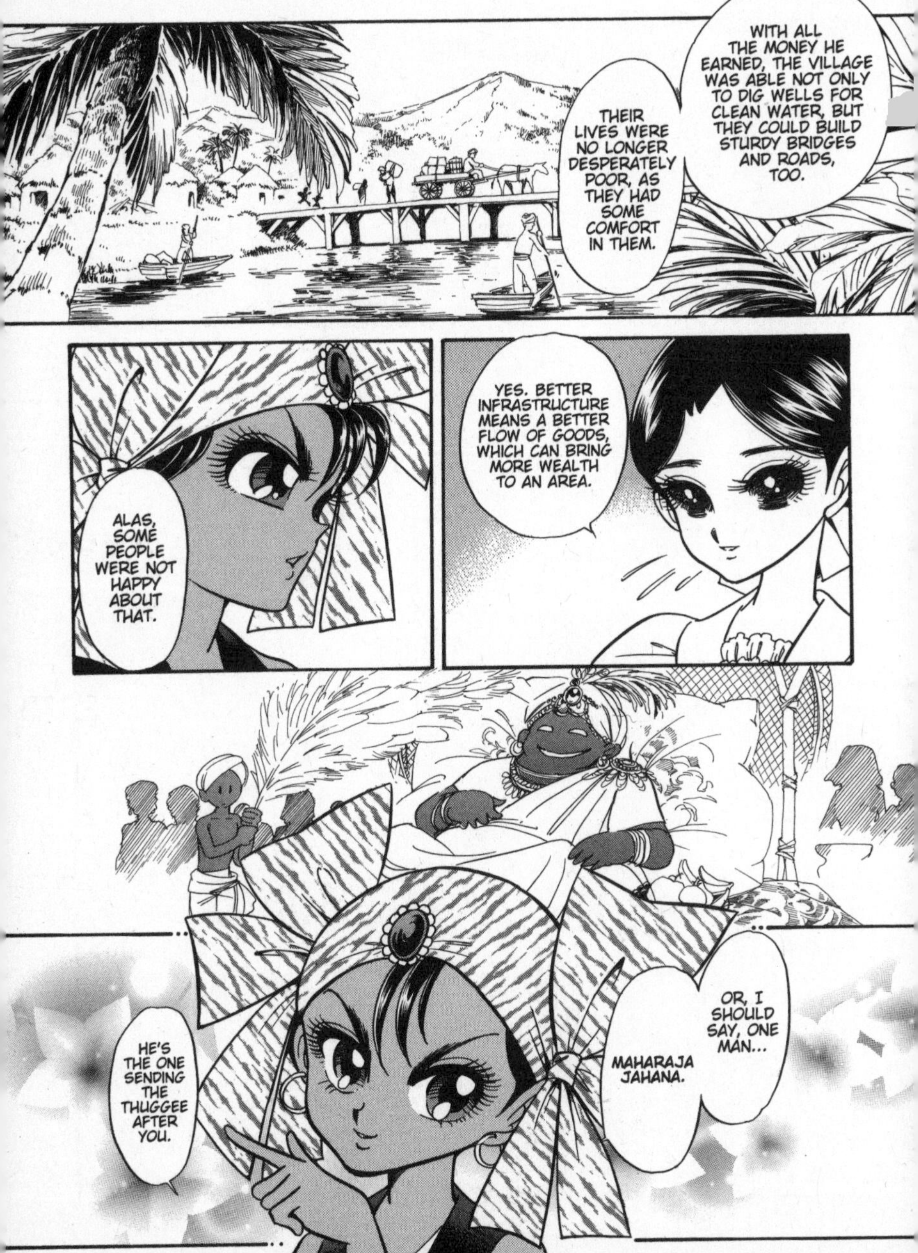
WITH ALL THE MONEY HE EARNED, THE VILLAGE WAS ABLE NOT ONLY TO DIG WELLS FOR CLEAN WATER, BUT THEY COULD BUILD STURDY BRIDGES AND ROADS, TOO.
THEIR LIVES WERE NO LONGER DESPERATELY POOR, AS THEY HAD SOME COMFORT IN THEM.
YES. BETTER INFRASTRUCTURE MEANS A BETTER FLOW OF GOODS, WHICH CAN BRING MORE WEALTH TO AN AREA.
ALAS, SOME PEOPLE WERE NOT HAPPY ABOUT THAT.
OR, I SHOULD SAY, ONE MAN...
MAHARAJA JAHANA.
HE'S THE ONE SENDING THE THUGGEE AFTER YOU.

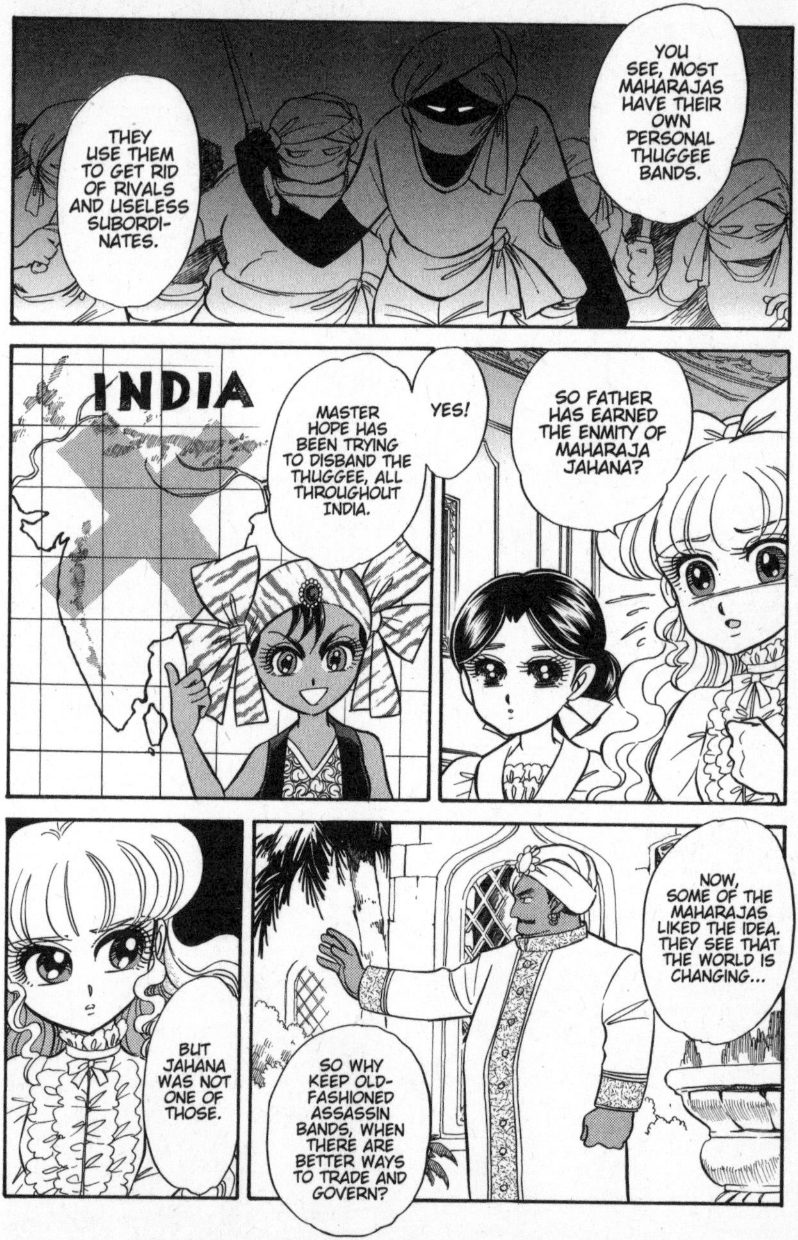
YOU SEE, MOST MAHARAJAS HAVE THEIR OWN PERSONAL THUGGEE BANDS.
THEY USE THEM TO GET RID OF RIVALS AND USELESS SUBORDI-NATES.
SO FATHER HAS EARNED THE ENMITY OF MAHARAJA JAHANA?
YES!
MASTER HOPE HAS BEEN TRYING TO DISBAND THE THUGGEE, ALL THROUGHOUT INDIA.
INDIA
NOW, SOME OF THE MAHARAJAS LIKED THE IDEA. THEY SEE THAT THE WORLD IS CHANGING...
SO WHY KEEP OLD-FASHIONED ASSASSIN BANDS, WHEN THERE ARE BETTER WAYS TO TRADE AND GOVERN?
BUT JAHANA WAS NOT ONE OF THOSE.

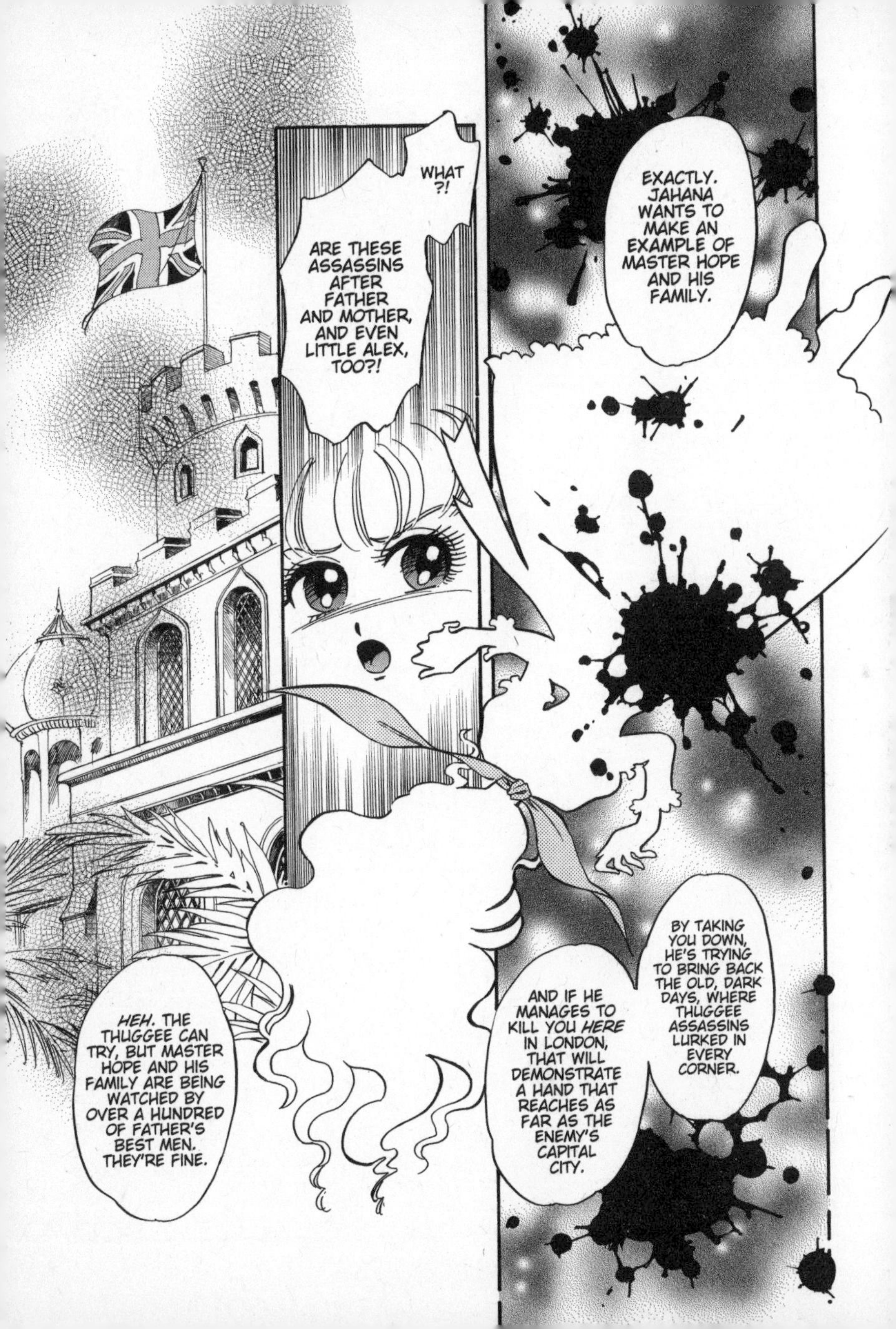
EXACTLY. JAHANA WANTS TO MAKE AN EXAMPLE OF MASTER HOPE AND HIS FAMILY.
BY TAKING YOU DOWN, HE'S TRYING TO BRING BACK THE OLD, DARK DAYS, WHERE THUGGEE ASSASSINS LURKED IN EVERY CORNER.
AND IF HE MANAGES TO KILL YOU *HERE* IN LONDON, THAT WILL DEMONSTRATE A HAND THAT REACHES AS FAR AS THE ENEMY'S CAPITAL CITY.
WHAT ?!
ARE THESE ASSASSINS AFTER FATHER AND MOTHER, AND EVEN LITTLE ALEX, TOO?!
HEH. THE THUGGEE CAN TRY, BUT MASTER HOPE AND HIS FAMILY ARE BEING WATCHED BY OVER A HUNDRED OF FATHER'S BEST MEN. THEY'RE FINE.

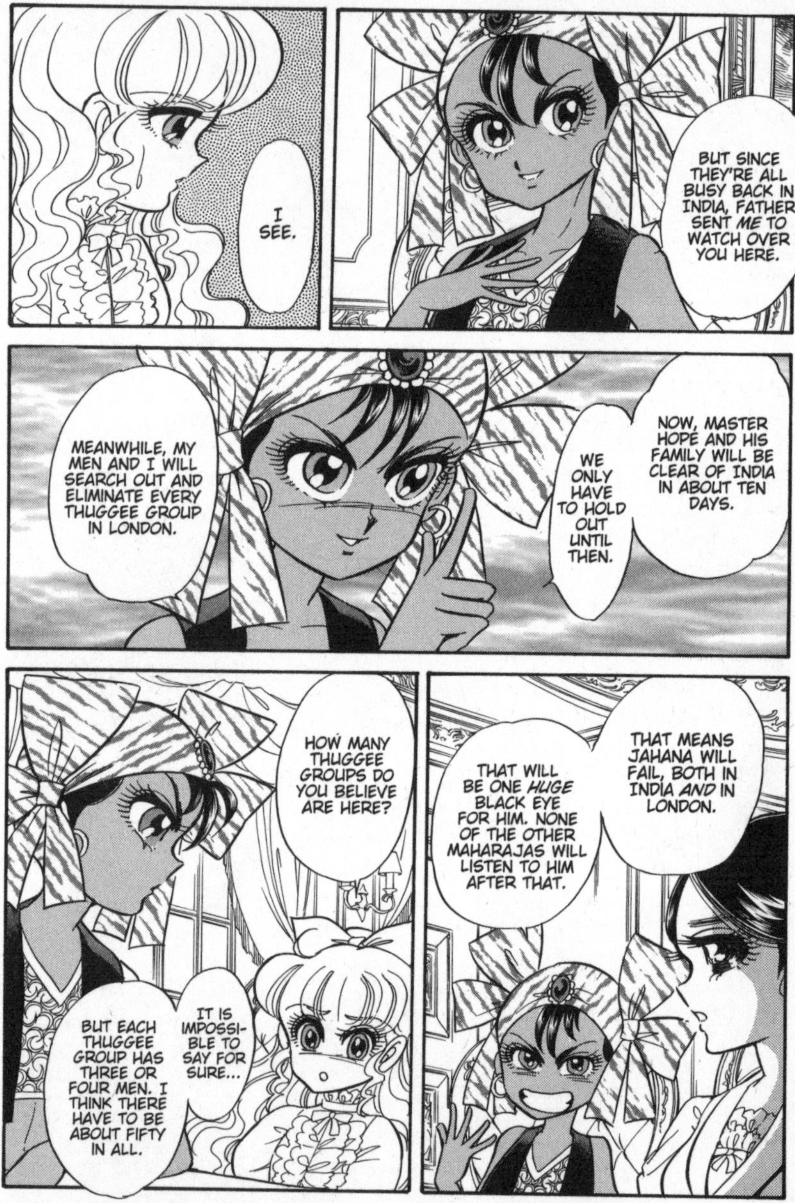
BUT SINCE THEY'RE ALL BUSY BACK IN INDIA, FATHER SENT *ME* TO WATCH OVER YOU HERE.
I SEE.
NOW, MASTER HOPE AND HIS FAMILY WILL BE CLEAR OF INDIA IN ABOUT TEN DAYS.
WE ONLY HAVE TO HOLD OUT UNTIL THEN.
MEANWHILE, MY MEN AND I WILL SEARCH OUT AND ELIMINATE EVERY THUGGEE GROUP IN LONDON.
THAT MEANS JAHANA WILL FAIL, BOTH IN INDIA *AND* IN LONDON.
THAT WILL BE ONE *HUGE* BLACK EYE FOR HIM. NONE OF THE OTHER MAHARAJAS WILL LISTEN TO HIM AFTER THAT.
HOW MANY THUGGEE GROUPS DO YOU BELIEVE ARE HERE?
IT IS IMPOSSI-BLE TO SAY FOR SURE...
BUT EACH THUGGEE GROUP HAS THREE OR FOUR MEN. I THINK THERE HAVE TO BE ABOUT FIFTY IN ALL.

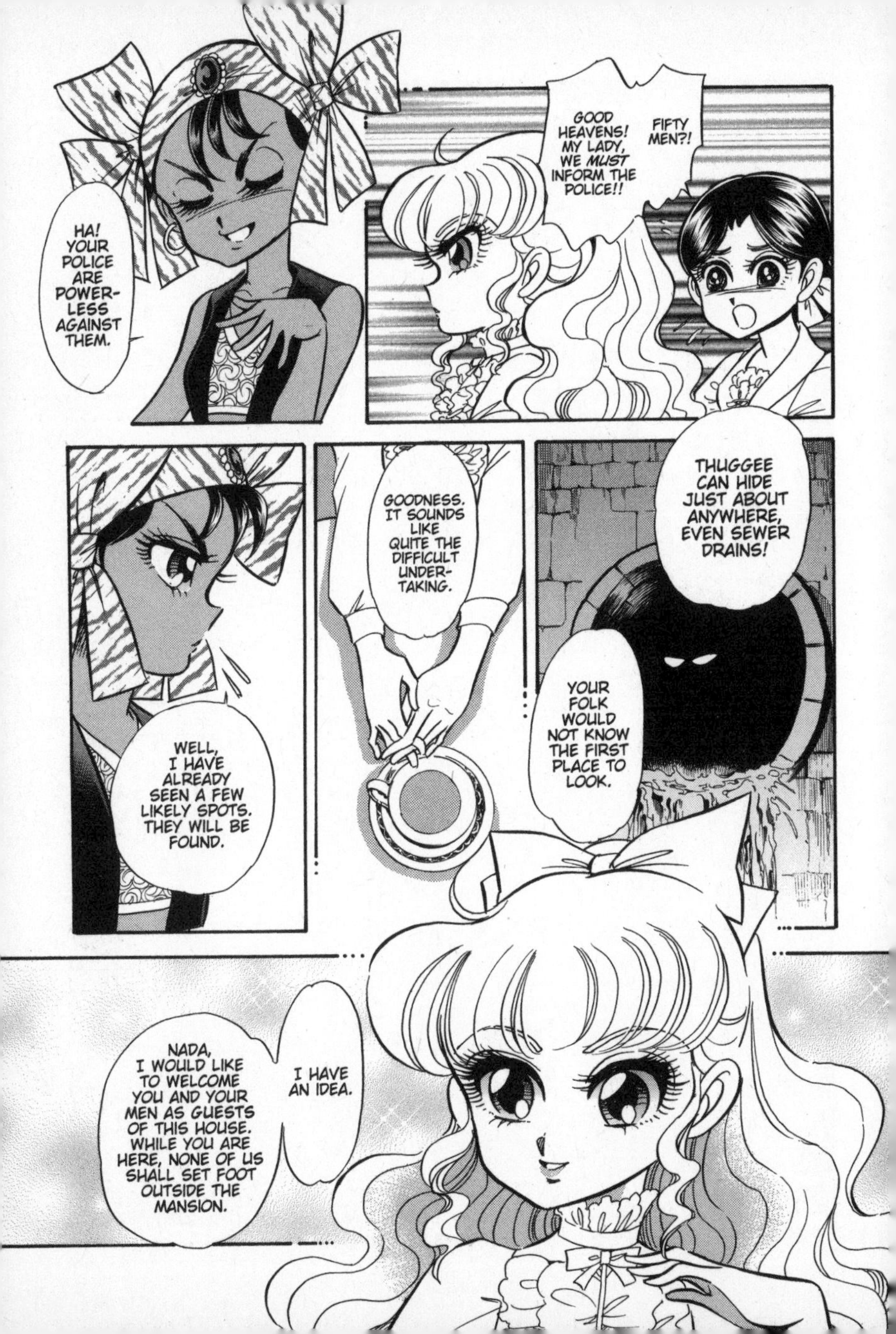
FIFTY MEN?!
GOOD HEAVENS! MY LADY, WE *MUST* INFORM THE POLICE!!
HA! YOUR POLICE ARE POWERLESS AGAINST THEM.
THUGGEE CAN HIDE JUST ABOUT ANYWHERE, EVEN SEWER DRAINS!
YOUR FOLK WOULD NOT KNOW THE FIRST PLACE TO LOOK.
GOODNESS. IT SOUNDS LIKE QUITE THE DIFFICULT UNDERTAKING.
WELL, I HAVE ALREADY SEEN A FEW LIKELY SPOTS. THEY WILL BE FOUND.
I HAVE AN IDEA.
NADA, I WOULD LIKE TO WELCOME YOU AND YOUR MEN AS GUESTS OF THIS HOUSE. WHILE YOU ARE HERE, NONE OF US SHALL SET FOOT OUTSIDE THE MANSION.

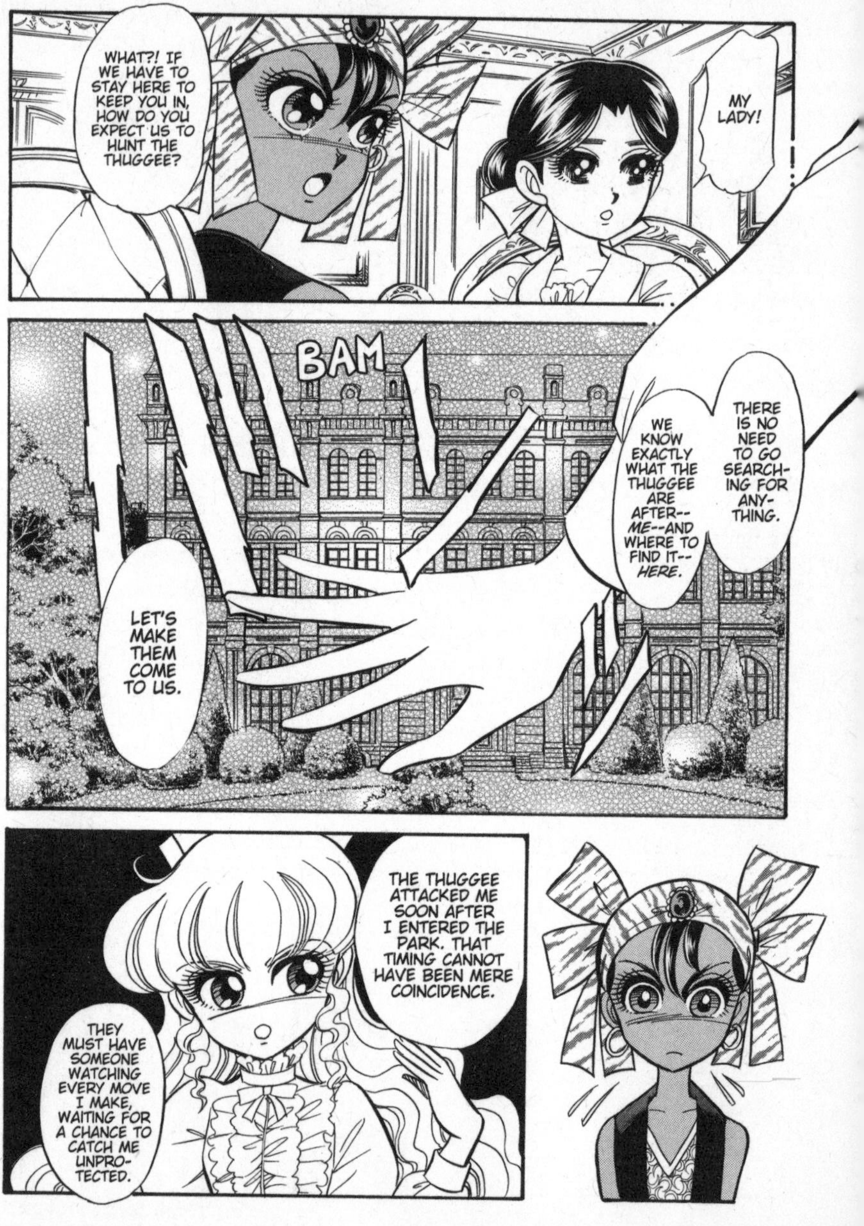
MY LADY!
WHAT?! IF WE HAVE TO STAY HERE TO KEEP YOU IN, HOW DO YOU EXPECT US TO HUNT THE THUGGEE?
THERE IS NO NEED TO GO SEARCHING FOR ANYTHING.
WE KNOW EXACTLY WHAT THE THUGGEE ARE AFTER--*ME*--AND WHERE TO FIND IT--*HERE*.
BAM
LET'S MAKE THEM COME TO US.
THE THUGGEE ATTACKED ME SOON AFTER I ENTERED THE PARK. THAT TIMING CANNOT HAVE BEEN MERE COINCIDENCE.
THEY MUST HAVE SOMEONE WATCHING EVERY MOVE I MAKE, WAITING FOR A CHANCE TO CATCH ME UNPROTECTED.

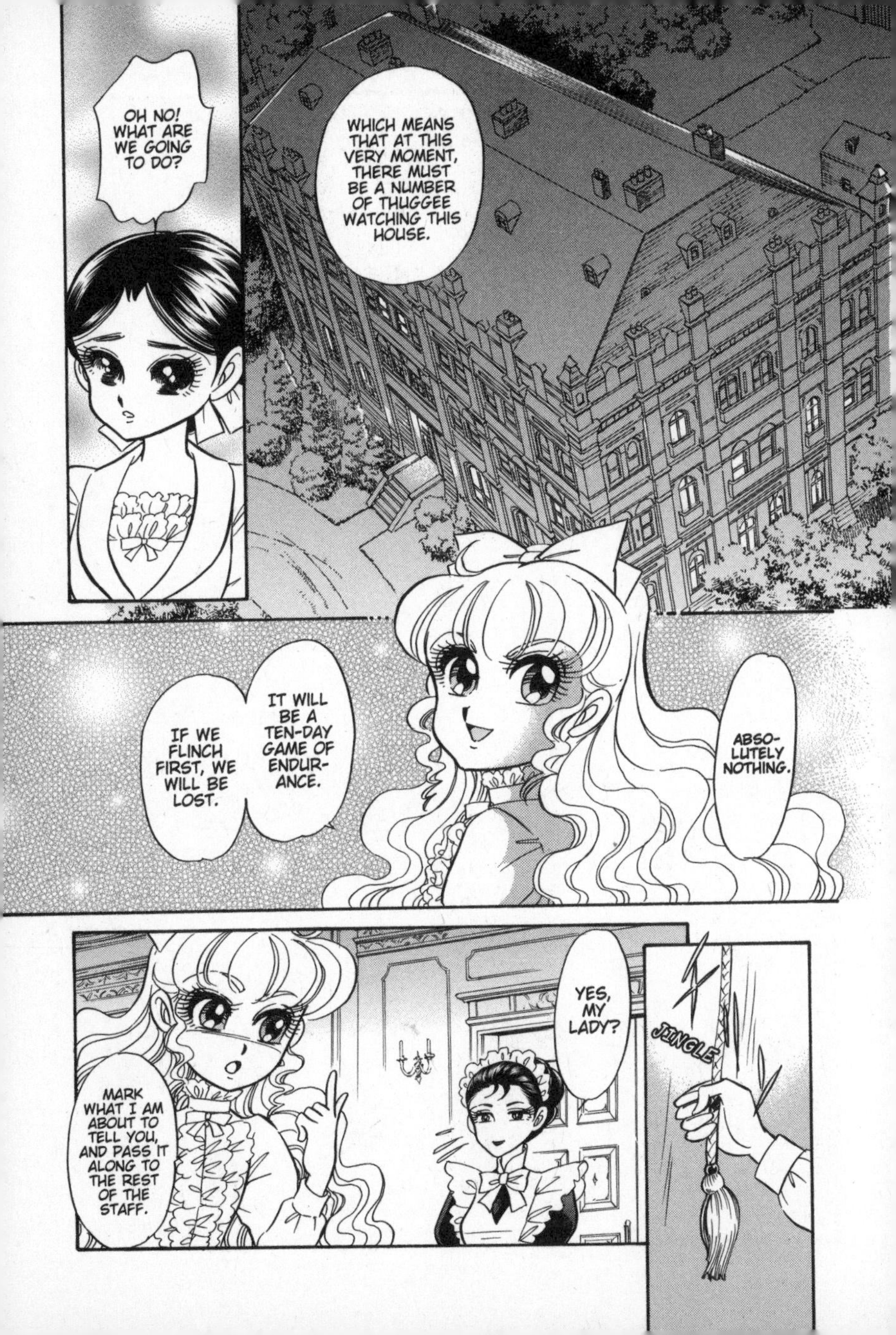
WHICH MEANS THAT AT THIS VERY MOMENT, THERE MUST BE A NUMBER OF THUGGEE WATCHING THIS HOUSE.
OH NO! WHAT ARE WE GOING TO DO?
ABSO-LUTELY NOTHING.
IT WILL BE A TEN-DAY GAME OF ENDUR-ANCE.
IF WE FLINCH FIRST, WE WILL BE LOST.
JINGLE
YES, MY LADY?
MARK WHAT I AM ABOUT TO TELL YOU, AND PASS IT ALONG TO THE REST OF THE STAFF.

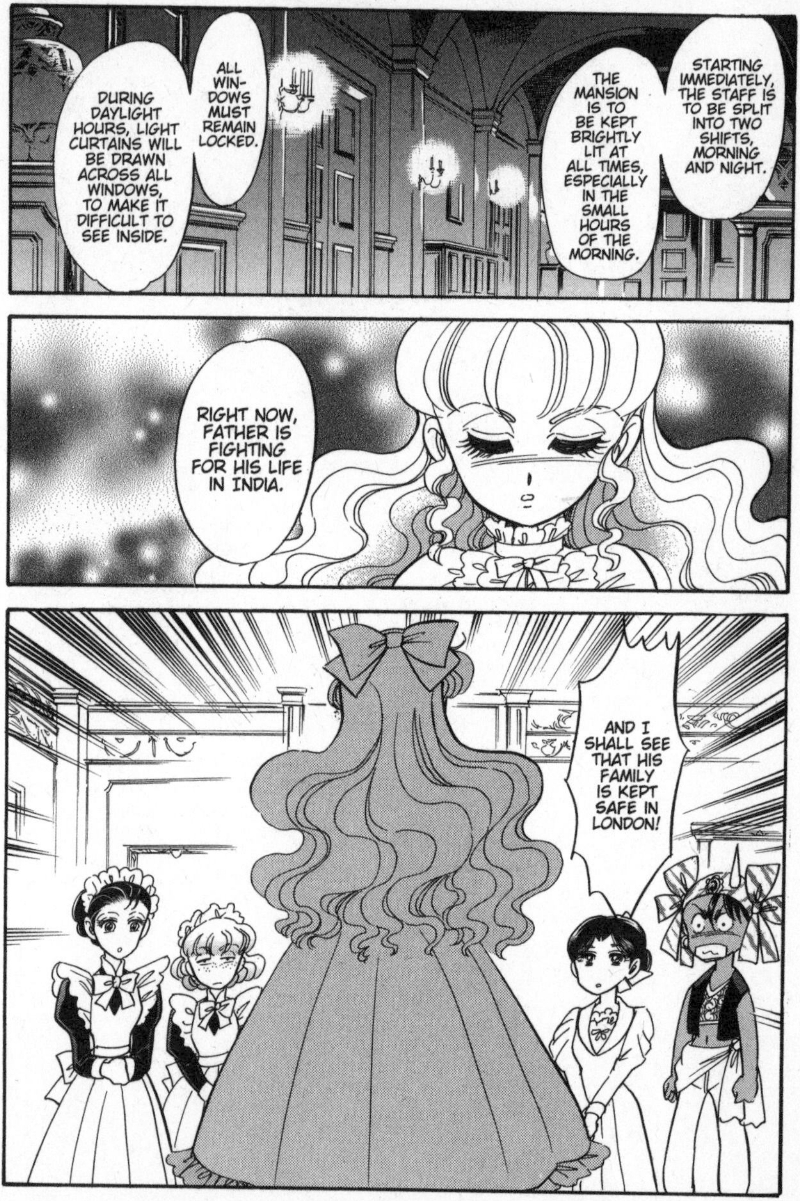
STARTING IMMEDIATELY, THE STAFF IS TO BE SPLIT INTO TWO SHIFTS, MORNING AND NIGHT.
THE MANSION IS TO BE KEPT BRIGHTLY LIT AT ALL TIMES, ESPECIALLY IN THE SMALL HOURS OF THE MORNING.
ALL WINDOWS MUST REMAIN LOCKED.
DURING DAYLIGHT HOURS, LIGHT CURTAINS WILL BE DRAWN ACROSS ALL WINDOWS, TO MAKE IT DIFFICULT TO SEE INSIDE.
RIGHT NOW, FATHER IS FIGHTING FOR HIS LIFE IN INDIA.
AND I SHALL SEE THAT HIS FAMILY IS KEPT SAFE IN LONDON!

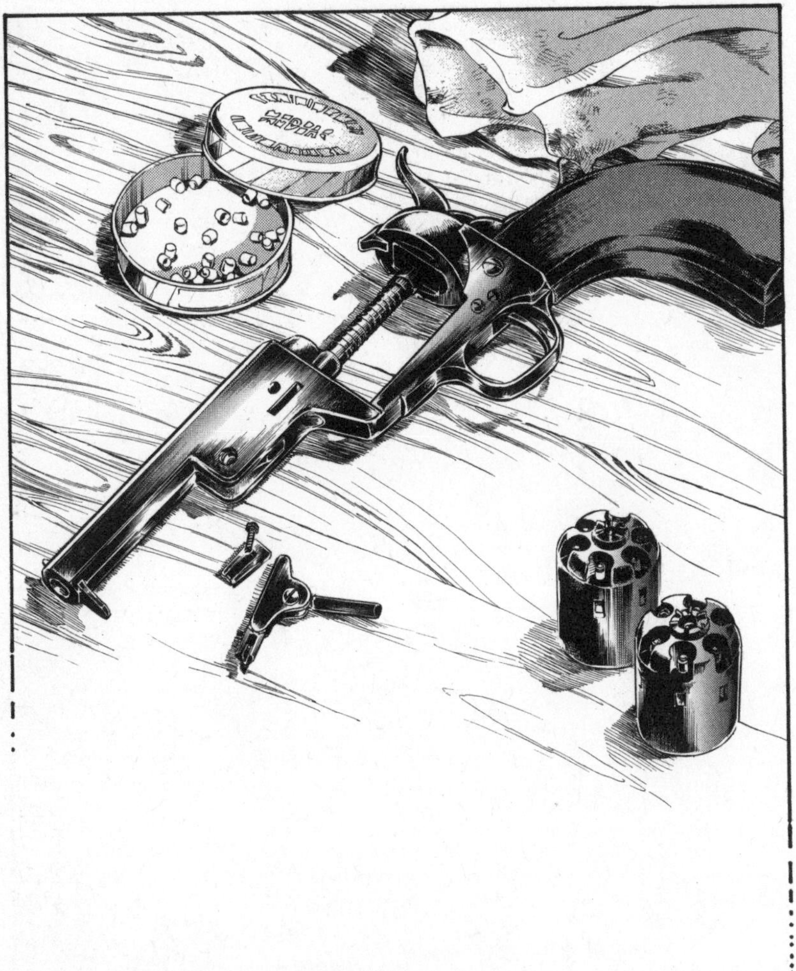

The Adventure of The Giant Rat of Sumatra (4)

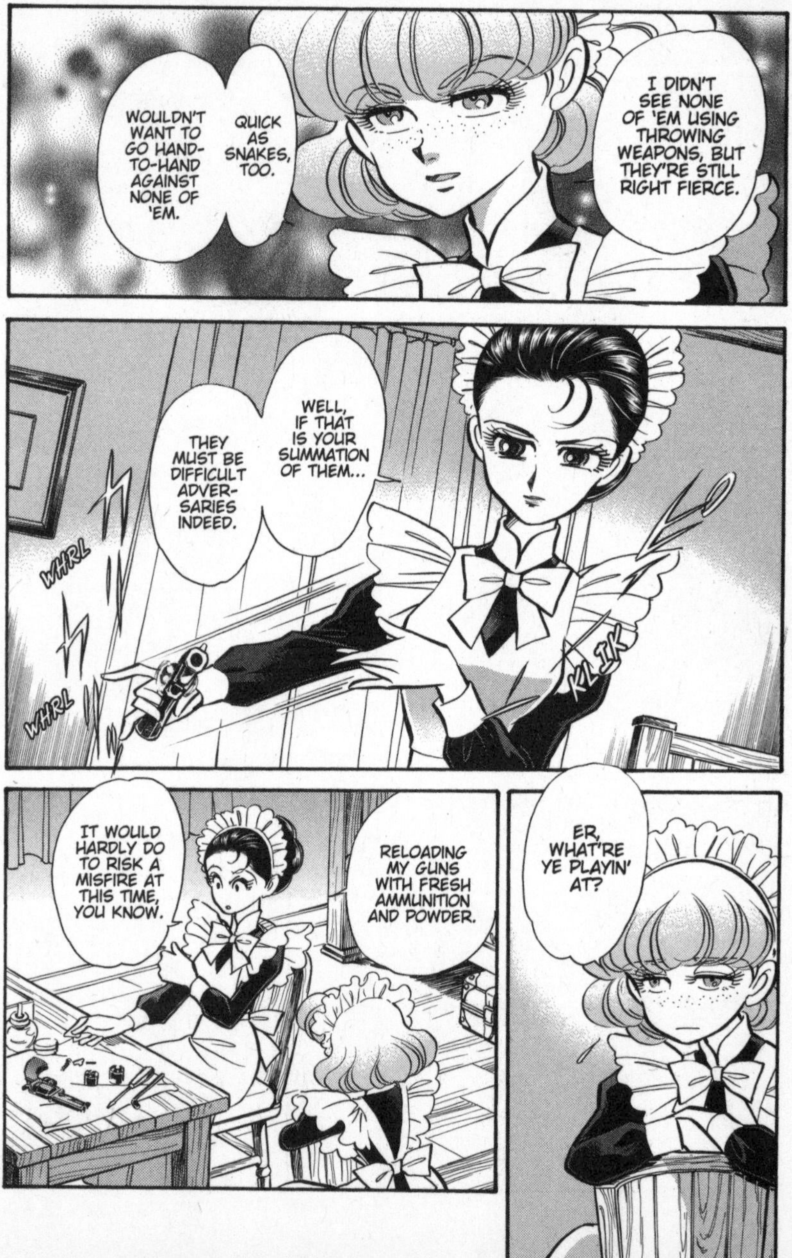
I DIDN'T SEE NONE OF 'EM USING THROWING WEAPONS, BUT THEY'RE STILL RIGHT FIERCE.
QUICK AS SNAKES, TOO.
WOULDN'T WANT TO GO HAND-TO-HAND AGAINST NONE OF 'EM.
KLIK
WELL, IF THAT IS YOUR SUMMATION OF THEM...
THEY MUST BE DIFFICULT ADVERSARIES INDEED.
WHRL
WHRL
ER, WHAT'RE YE PLAYIN' AT?
RELOADING MY GUNS WITH FRESH AMMUNITION AND POWDER.
IT WOULD HARDLY DO TO RISK A MISFIRE AT THIS TIME, YOU KNOW.

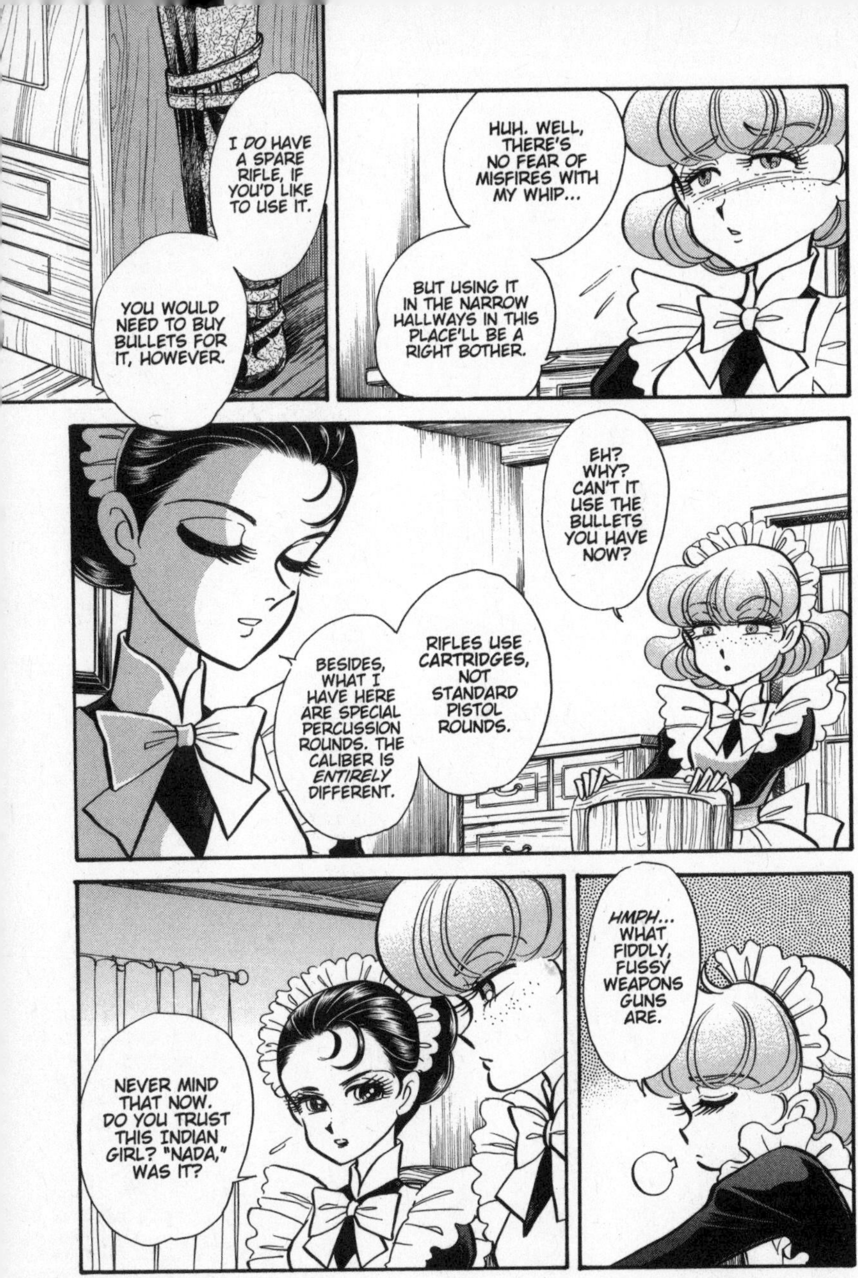
HUH. WELL, THERE'S NO FEAR OF MISFIRES WITH MY WHIP...
BUT USING IT IN THE NARROW HALLWAYS IN THIS PLACE'LL BE A RIGHT BOTHER.
I *DO* HAVE A SPARE RIFLE, IF YOU'D LIKE TO USE IT.
YOU WOULD NEED TO BUY BULLETS FOR IT, HOWEVER.
EH? WHY? CAN'T IT USE THE BULLETS YOU HAVE NOW?
RIFLES USE CARTRIDGES, NOT STANDARD PISTOL ROUNDS.
BESIDES, WHAT I HAVE HERE ARE SPECIAL PERCUSSION ROUNDS. THE CALIBER IS *ENTIRELY* DIFFERENT.
HMPH... WHAT FIDDLY, FUSSY WEAPONS GUNS ARE.
NEVER MIND THAT NOW. DO YOU TRUST THIS INDIAN GIRL? "NADA," WAS IT?

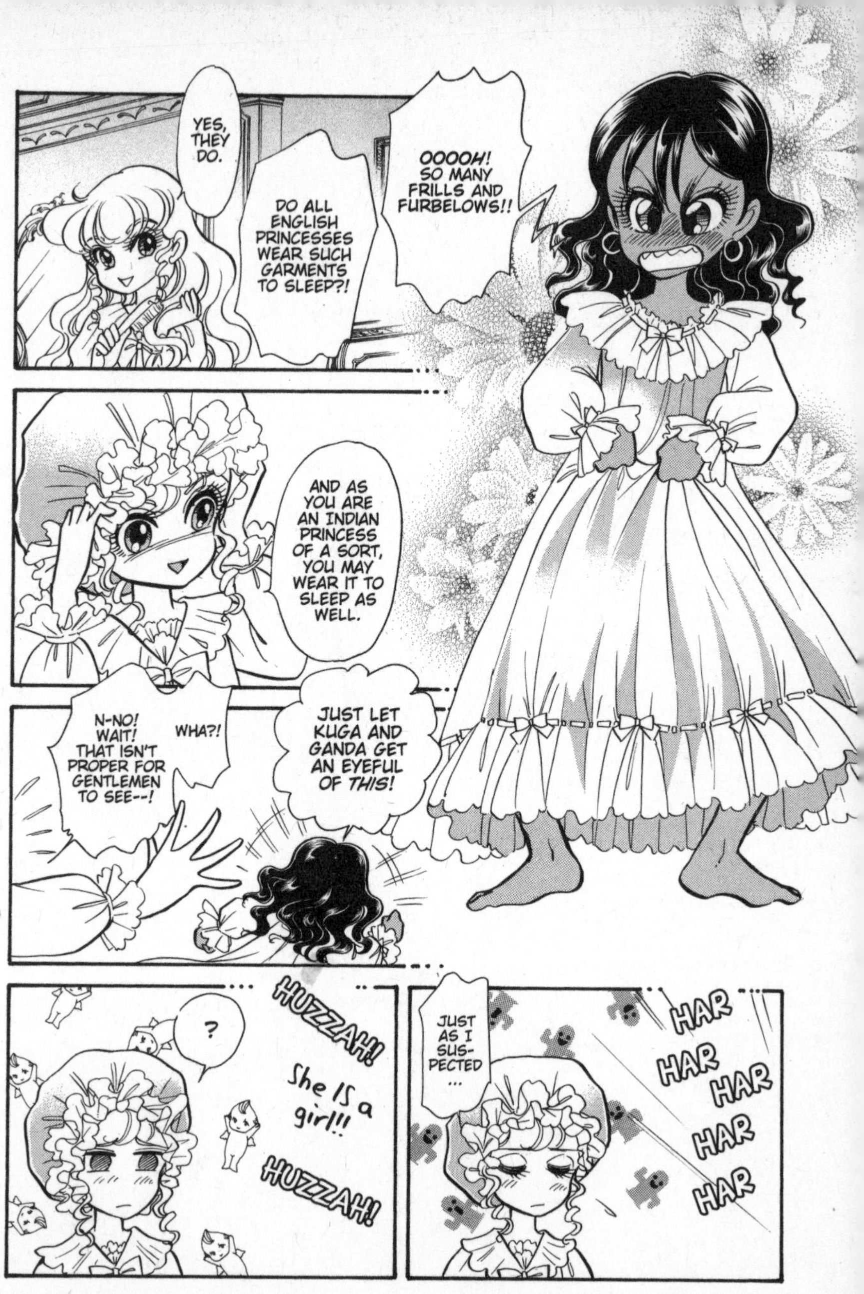
OOOOH! SO MANY FRILLS AND FURBELOWS!!
DO ALL ENGLISH PRINCESSES WEAR SUCH GARMENTS TO SLEEP?!
YES, THEY DO.
AND AS YOU ARE AN INDIAN PRINCESS OF A SORT, YOU MAY WEAR IT TO SLEEP AS WELL.
JUST LET KUGA AND GANDA GET AN EYEFUL OF THIS!
WHA?!
N-NO! WAIT! THAT ISN'T PROPER FOR GENTLEMEN TO SEE--!
HAR
HAR
HAR
HAR
HAR
JUST AS I SUSPECTED ...
HUZZAH!
?
She IS a girl!!!
HUZZAH!

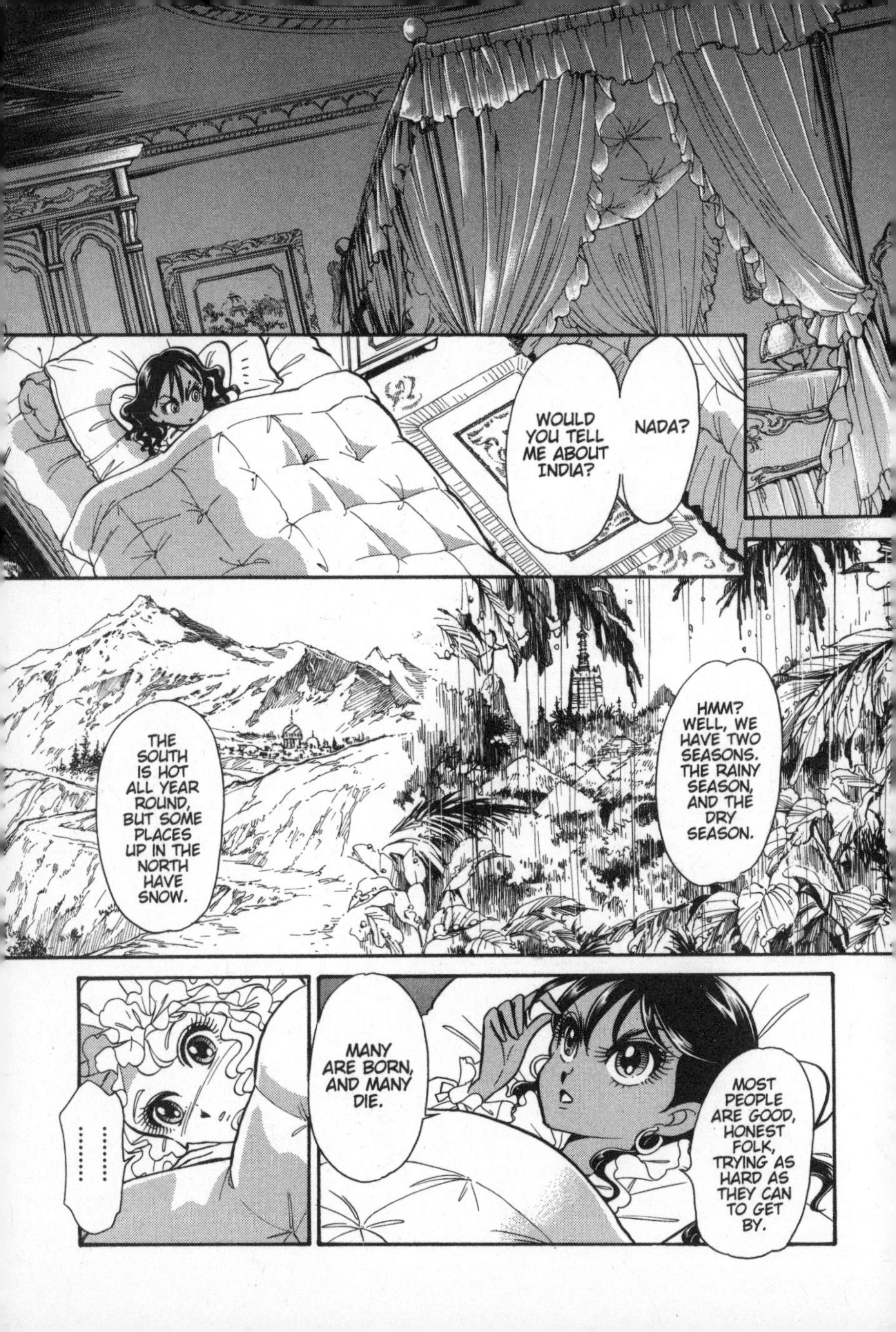
NADA?
WOULD YOU TELL ME ABOUT INDIA?
HMM? WELL, WE HAVE TWO SEASONS. THE RAINY SEASON, AND THE DRY SEASON.
THE SOUTH IS HOT ALL YEAR ROUND, BUT SOME PLACES UP IN THE NORTH HAVE SNOW.
MOST PEOPLE ARE GOOD, HONEST FOLK, TRYING AS HARD AS THEY CAN TO GET BY.
MANY ARE BORN, AND MANY DIE.
....

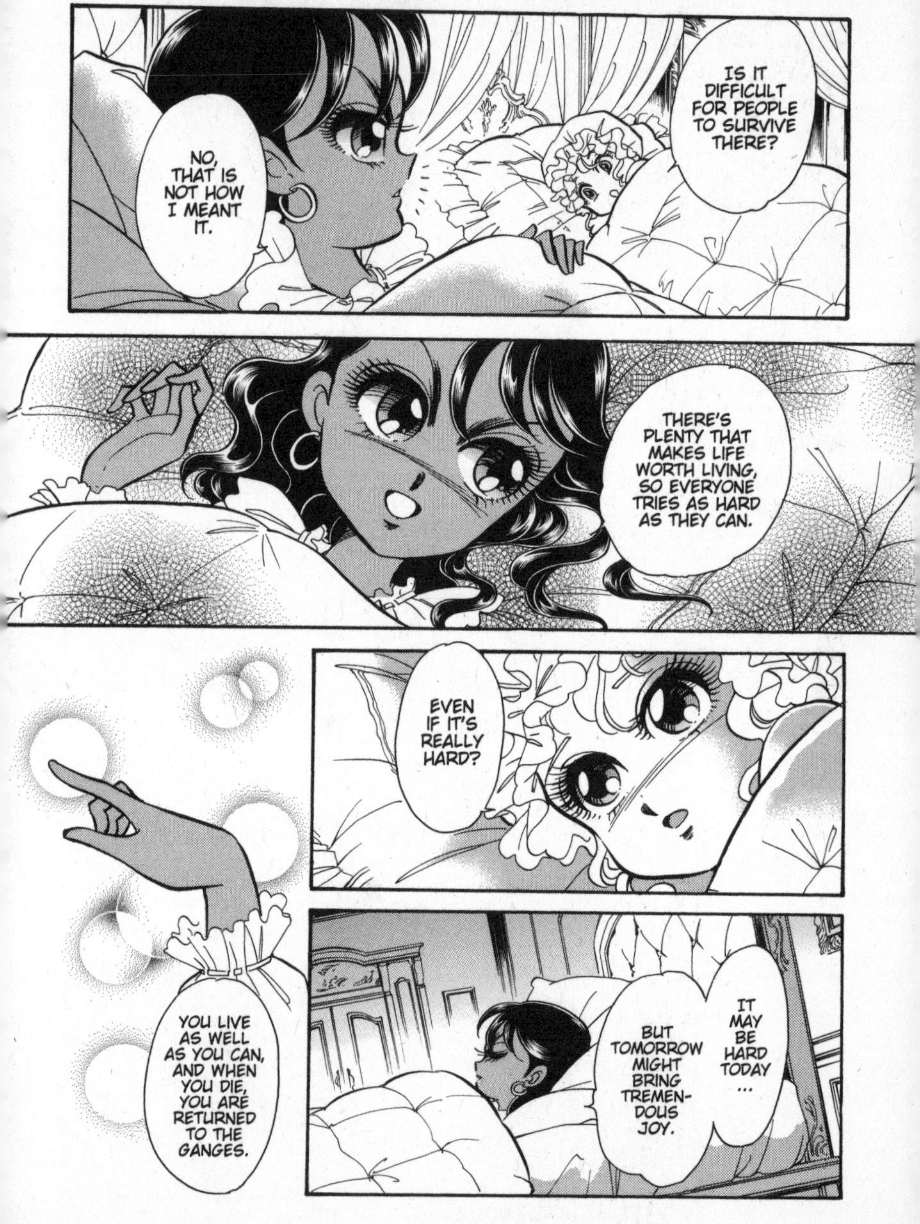
IS IT DIFFICULT FOR PEOPLE TO SURVIVE THERE?
NO, THAT IS NOT HOW I MEANT IT.
THERE'S PLENTY THAT MAKES LIFE WORTH LIVING, SO EVERYONE TRIES AS HARD AS THEY CAN.
EVEN IF IT'S REALLY HARD?
IT MAY BE HARD TODAY ...
BUT TOMORROW MIGHT BRING TREMEN-DOUS JOY.
YOU LIVE AS WELL AS YOU CAN, AND WHEN YOU DIE, YOU ARE RETURNED TO THE GANGES.

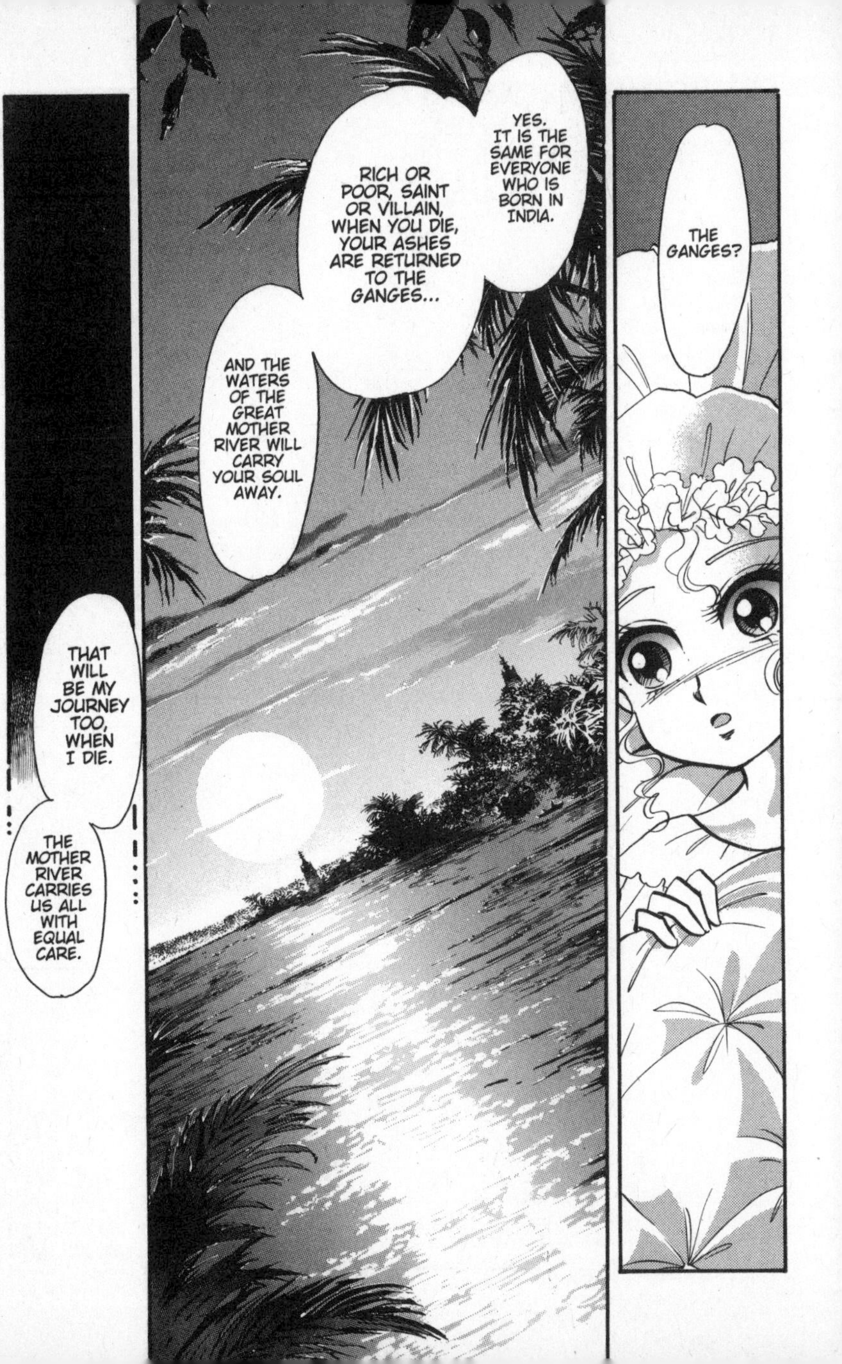
THE GANGES?
YES. IT IS THE SAME FOR EVERYONE WHO IS BORN IN INDIA.
RICH OR POOR, SAINT OR VILLAIN, WHEN YOU DIE, YOUR ASHES ARE RETURNED TO THE GANGES...
AND THE WATERS OF THE GREAT MOTHER RIVER WILL CARRY YOUR SOUL AWAY.
THAT WILL BE MY JOURNEY TOO, WHEN I DIE.
THE MOTHER RIVER CARRIES US ALL WITH EQUAL CARE.

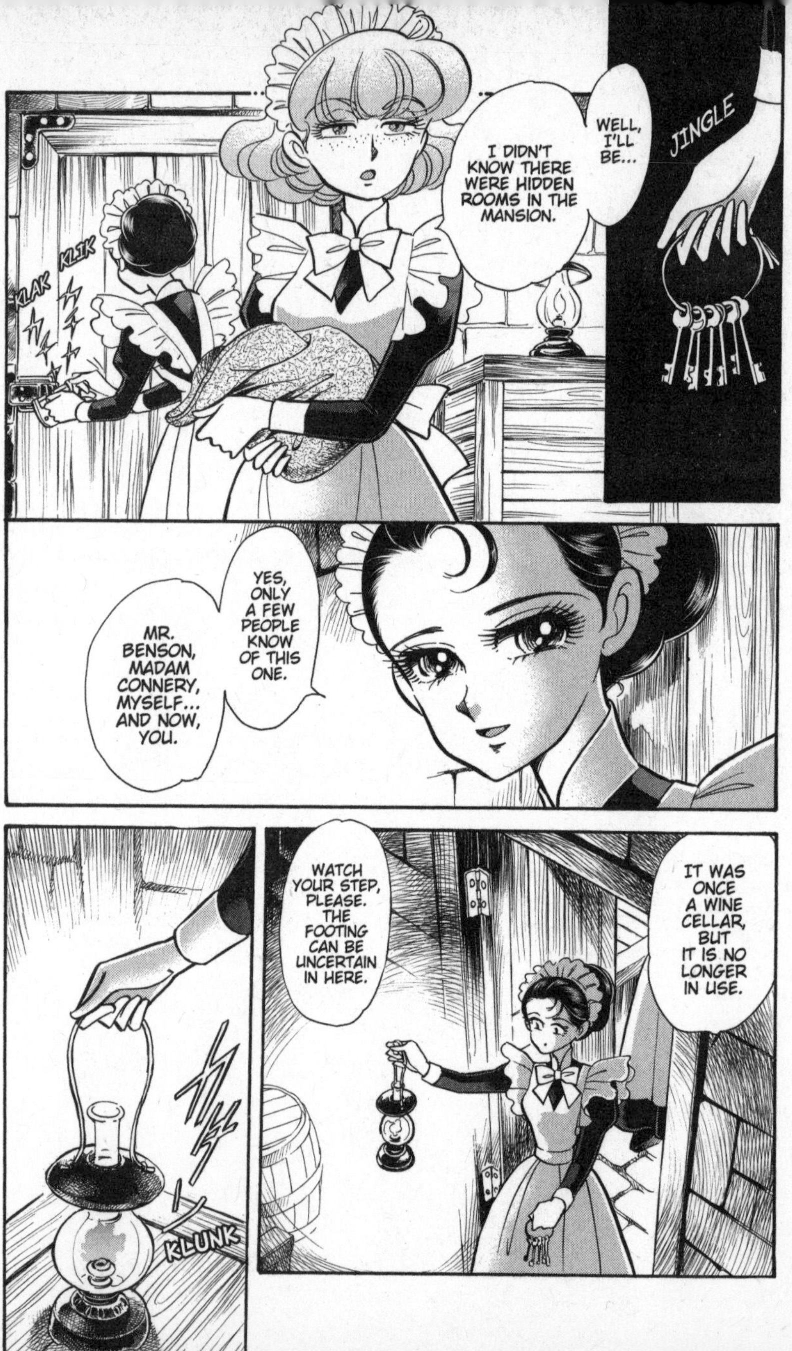
JINGLE
WELL, I'LL BE...
I DIDN'T KNOW THERE WERE HIDDEN ROOMS IN THE MANSION.
KLIK
KLAK
YES, ONLY A FEW PEOPLE KNOW OF THIS ONE.
MR. BENSON, MADAM CONNERY, MYSELF... AND NOW, YOU.
IT WAS ONCE A WINE CELLAR, BUT IT IS NO LONGER IN USE.
WATCH YOUR STEP, PLEASE. THE FOOTING CAN BE UNCERTAIN IN HERE.
KLUNK

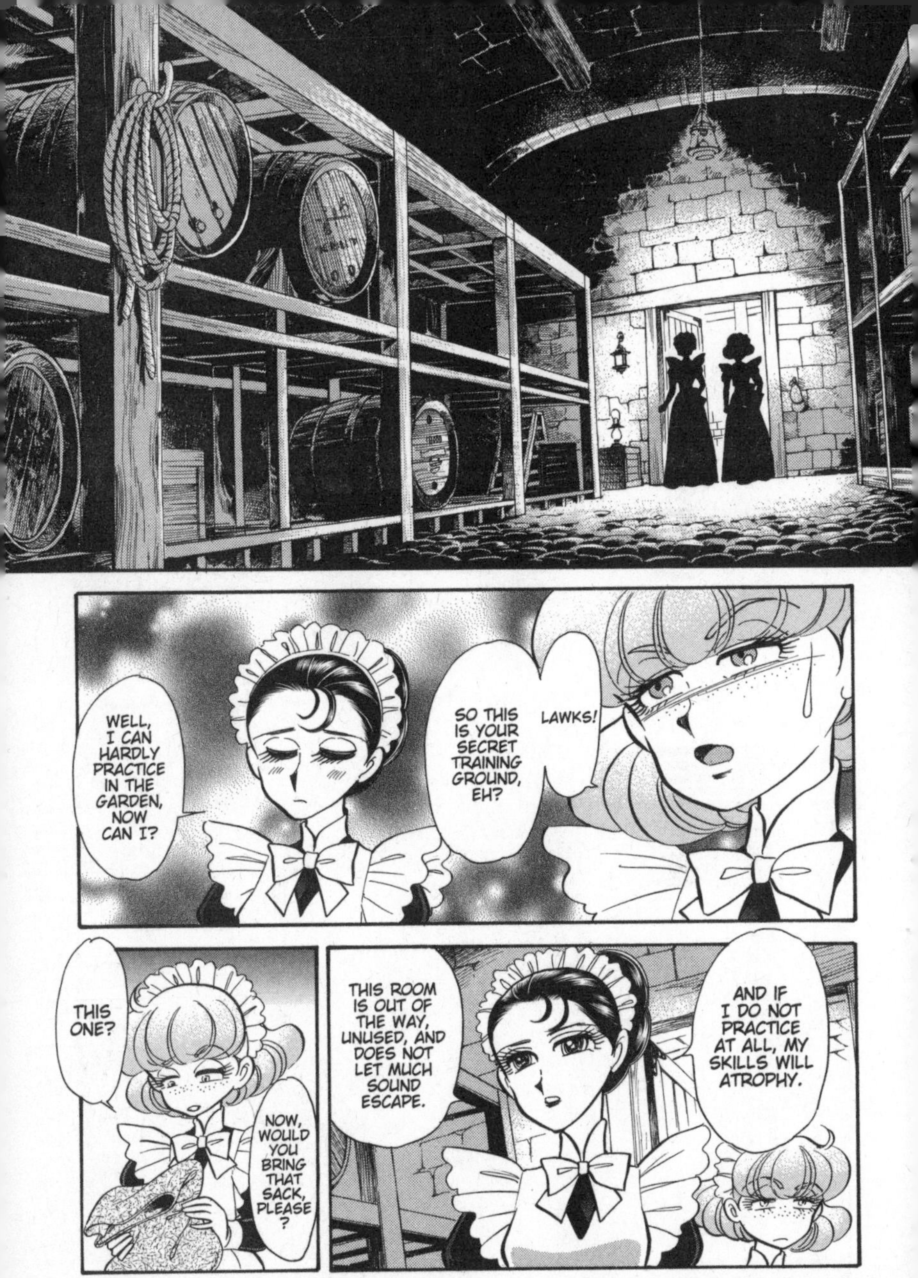
LAWKS!
SO THIS IS YOUR SECRET TRAINING GROUND, EH?
WELL, I CAN HARDLY PRACTICE IN THE GARDEN, NOW CAN I?
THIS ROOM IS OUT OF THE WAY, UNUSED, AND DOES NOT LET MUCH SOUND ESCAPE.
AND IF I DO NOT PRACTICE AT ALL, MY SKILLS WILL ATROPHY.
NOW, WOULD YOU BRING THAT SACK, PLEASE?
THIS ONE?

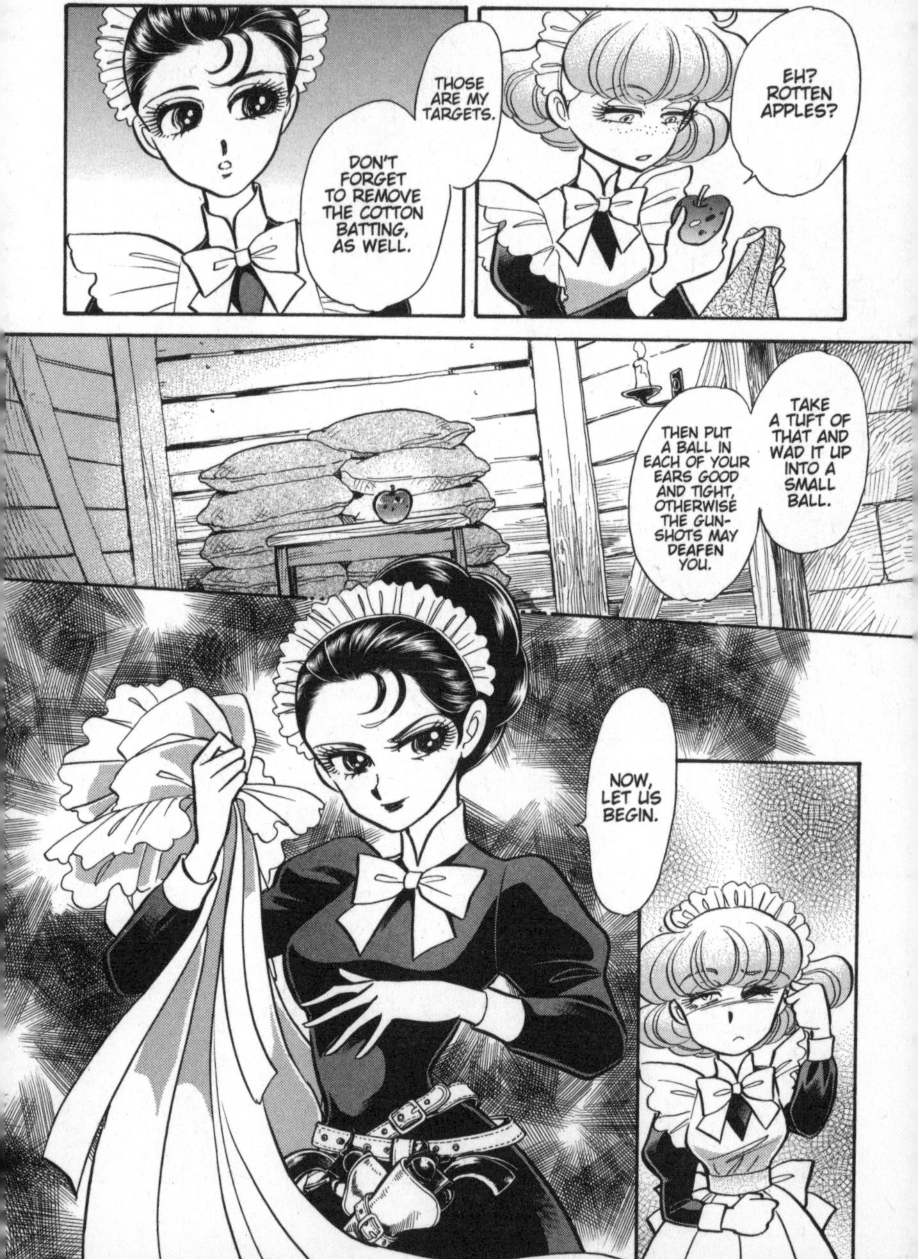
EH? ROTTEN APPLES?
THOSE ARE MY TARGETS.
DON'T FORGET TO REMOVE THE COTTON BATTING, AS WELL.
TAKE A TUFT OF THAT AND WAD IT UP INTO A SMALL BALL.
THEN PUT A BALL IN EACH OF YOUR EARS GOOD AND TIGHT, OTHERWISE THE GUN-SHOTS MAY DEAFEN YOU.
NOW, LET US BEGIN.

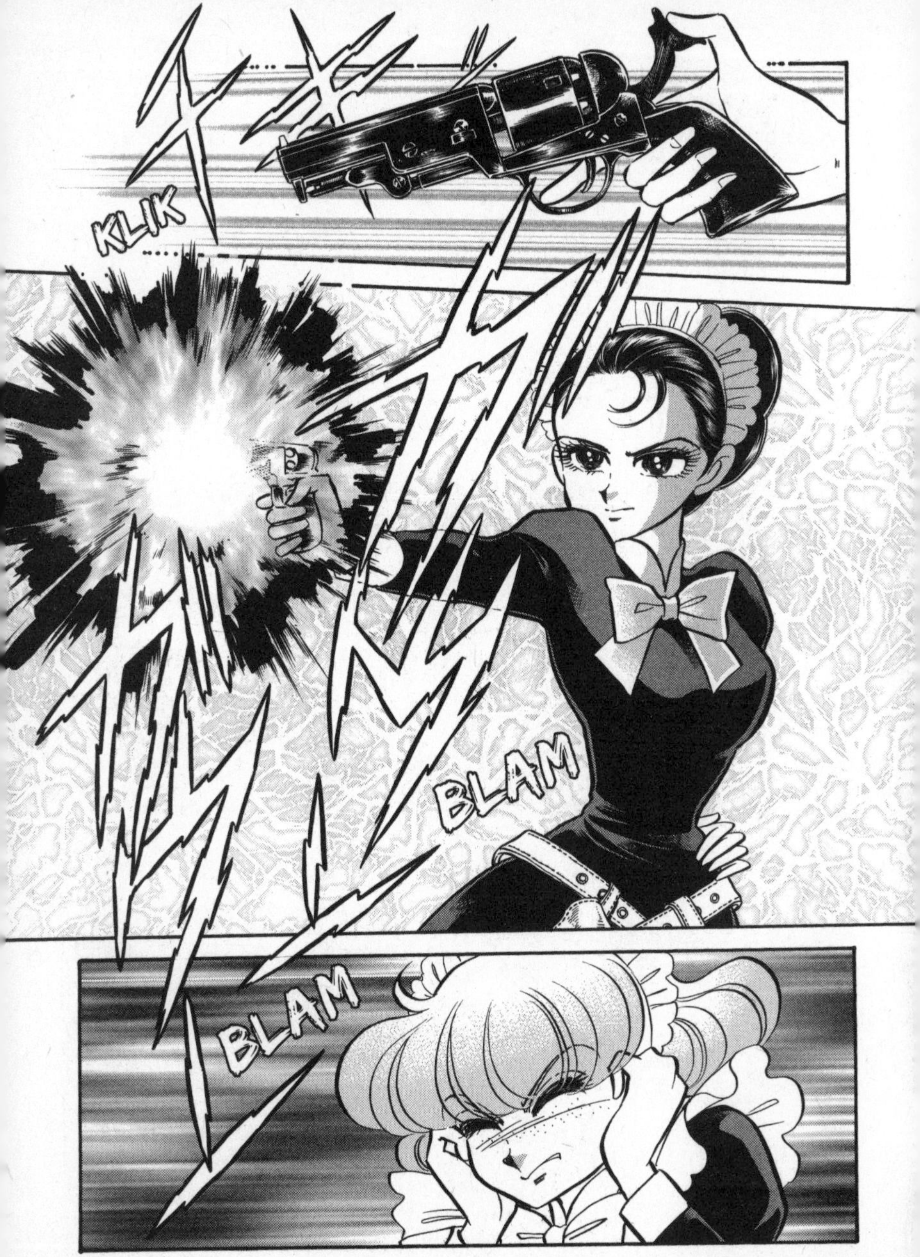
KLIK
BLAM
BLAM

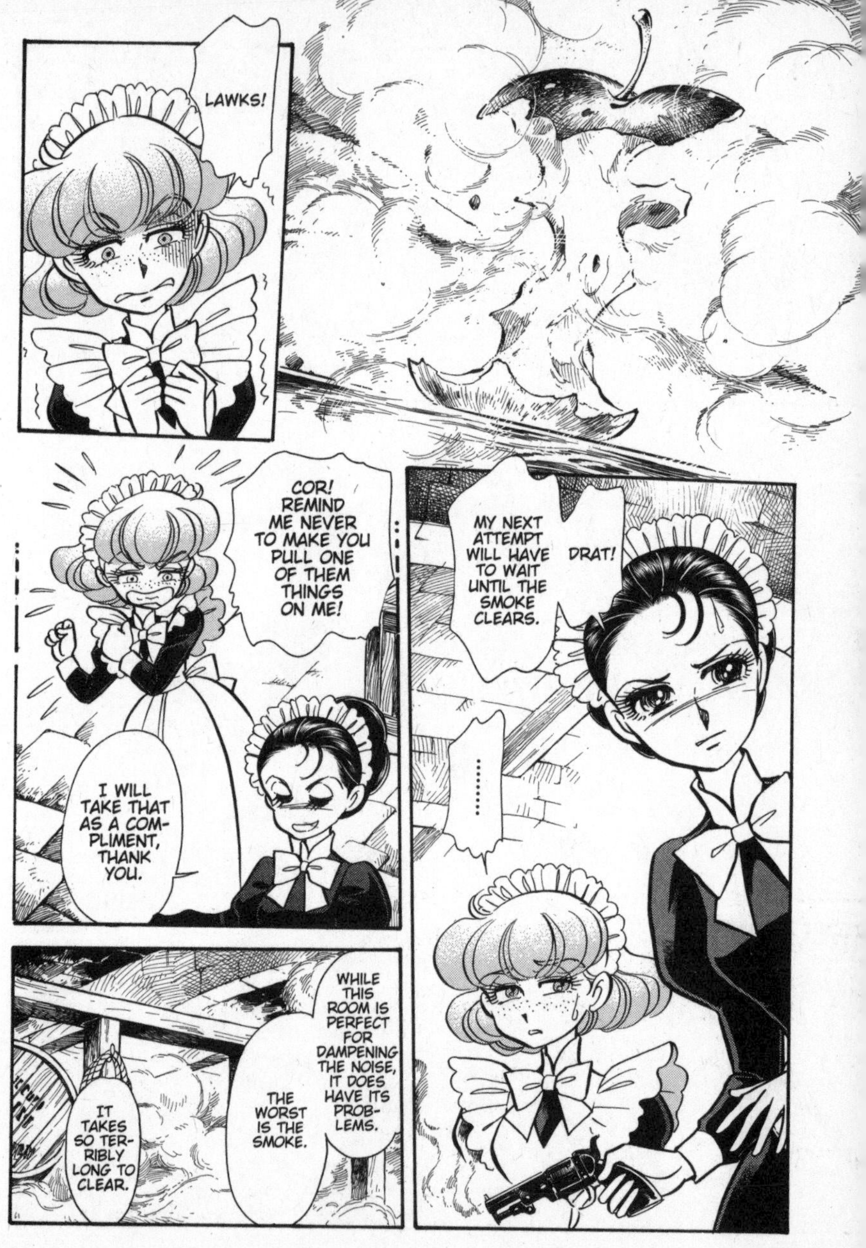
LAWKS!
DRAT!
MY NEXT ATTEMPT WILL HAVE TO WAIT UNTIL THE SMOKE CLEARS.
......
COR! REMIND ME NEVER TO MAKE YOU PULL ONE OF THEM THINGS ON ME!
I WILL TAKE THAT AS A COMPLIMENT, THANK YOU.
WHILE THIS ROOM IS PERFECT FOR DAMPENING THE NOISE, IT DOES HAVE ITS PROBLEMS.
THE WORST IS THE SMOKE.
IT TAKES SO TERRIBLY LONG TO CLEAR.

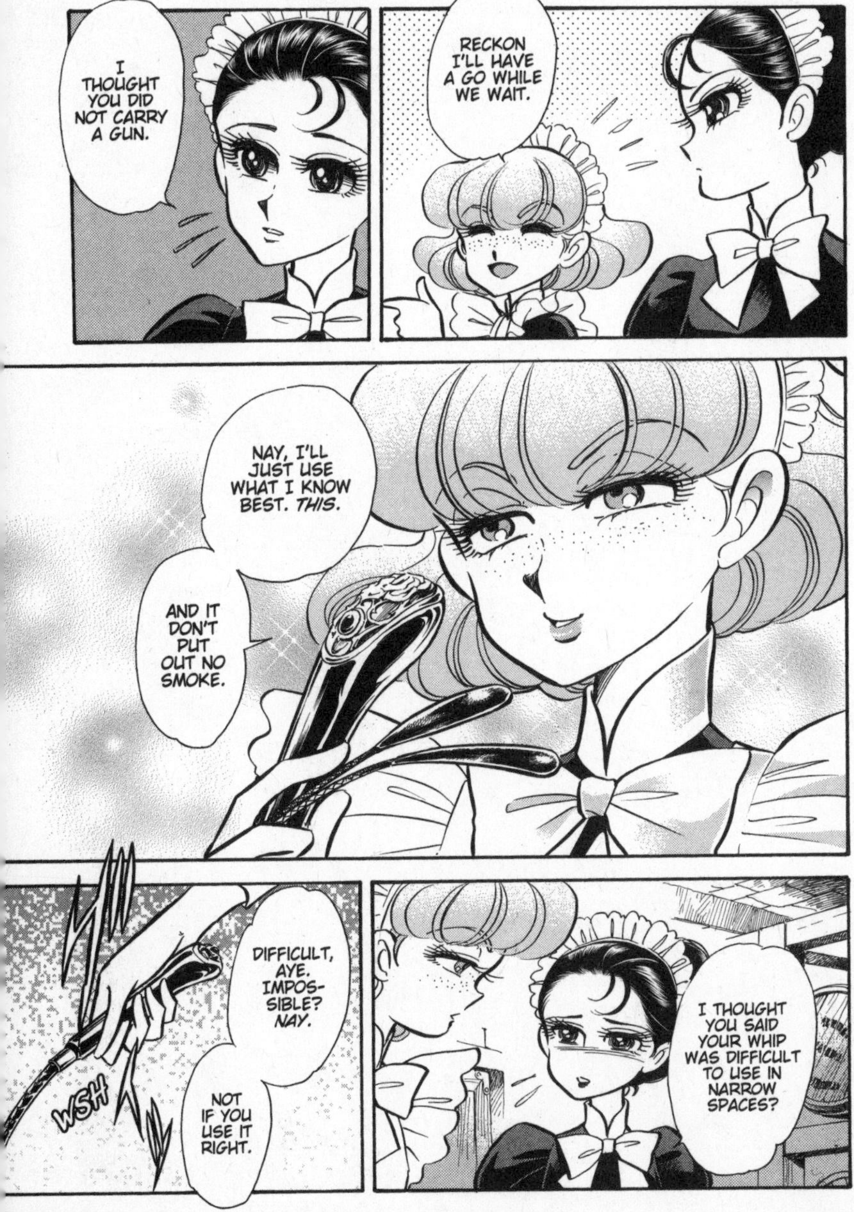
RECKON I'LL HAVE A GO WHILE WE WAIT.
I THOUGHT YOU DID NOT CARRY A GUN.
NAY, I'LL JUST USE WHAT I KNOW BEST. *THIS*.
AND IT DON'T PUT OUT NO SMOKE.
I THOUGHT YOU SAID YOUR WHIP WAS DIFFICULT TO USE IN NARROW SPACES?
DIFFICULT, AYE. IMPOSSIBLE? NAY.
NOT IF YOU USE IT RIGHT.
WSH

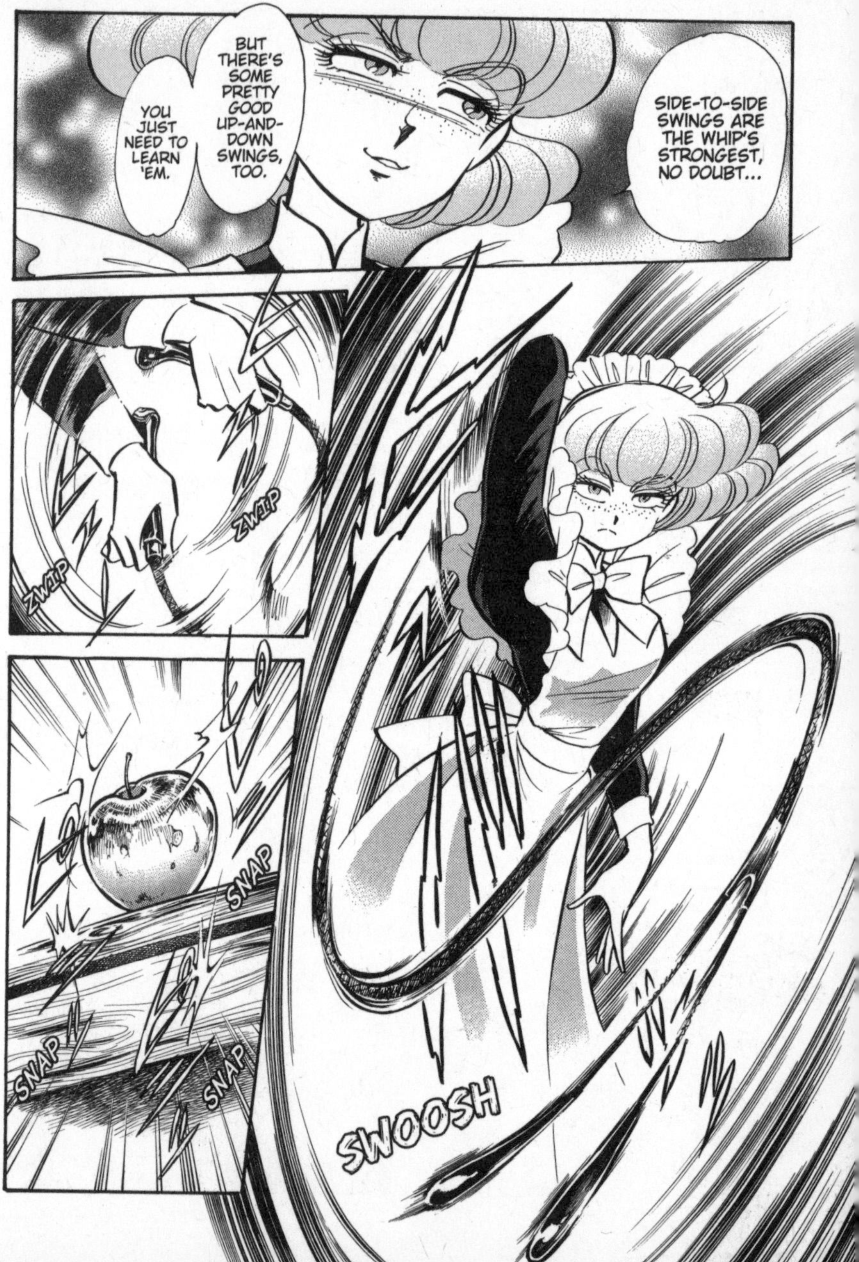
SIDE-TO-SIDE SWINGS ARE THE WHIP'S STRONGEST, NO DOUBT...
BUT THERE'S SOME PRETTY GOOD UP-AND-DOWN SWINGS, TOO.
YOU JUST NEED TO LEARN 'EM.
ZWIP
ZWIP
SWOOSH
SNAP
SNAP
SNAP

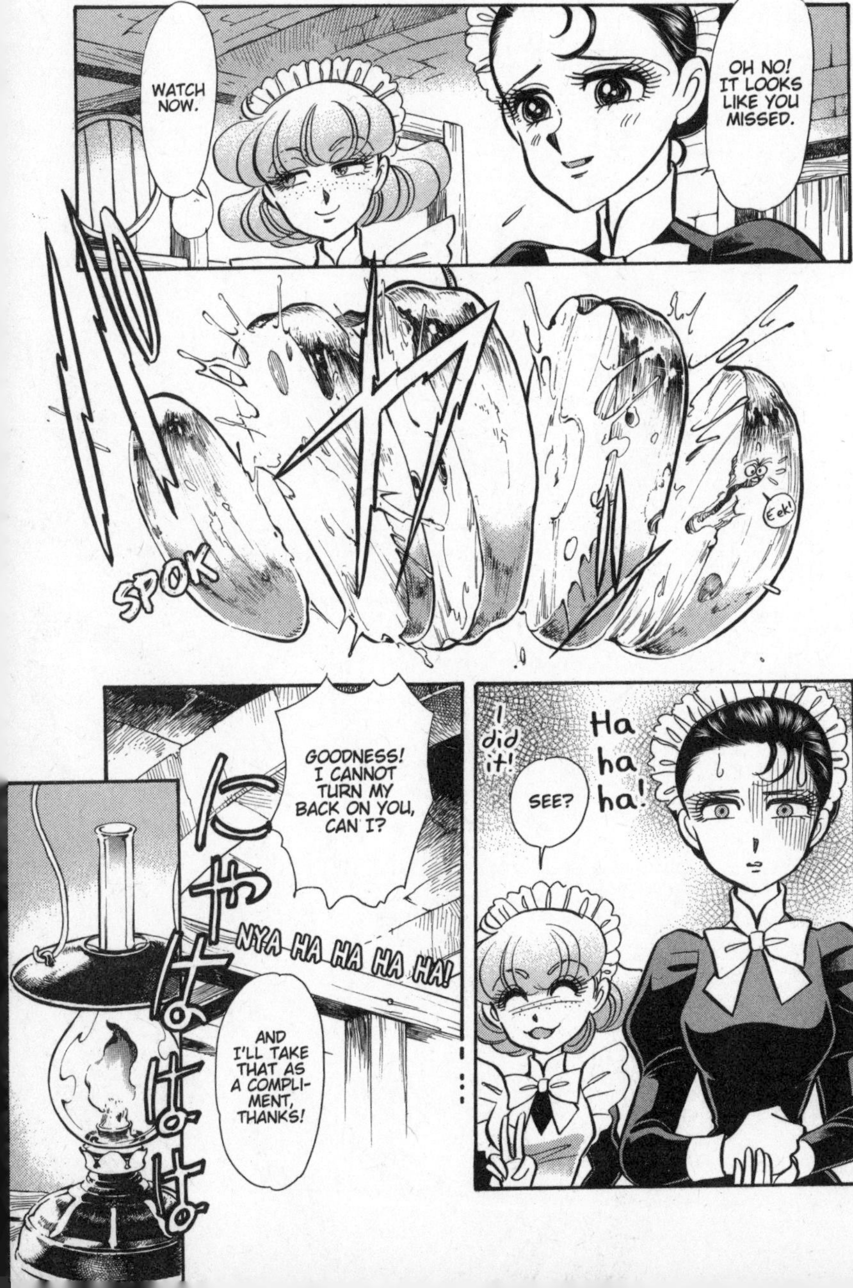

OH NO! IT LOOKS LIKE YOU MISSED.
WATCH NOW.
Eek!
SPOK
Ha ha ha!
I did it!
SEE?
GOODNESS! I CANNOT TURN MY BACK ON YOU, CAN I?
NYA HA HA HA HA!
AND I'LL TAKE THAT AS A COMPLIMENT, THANKS!

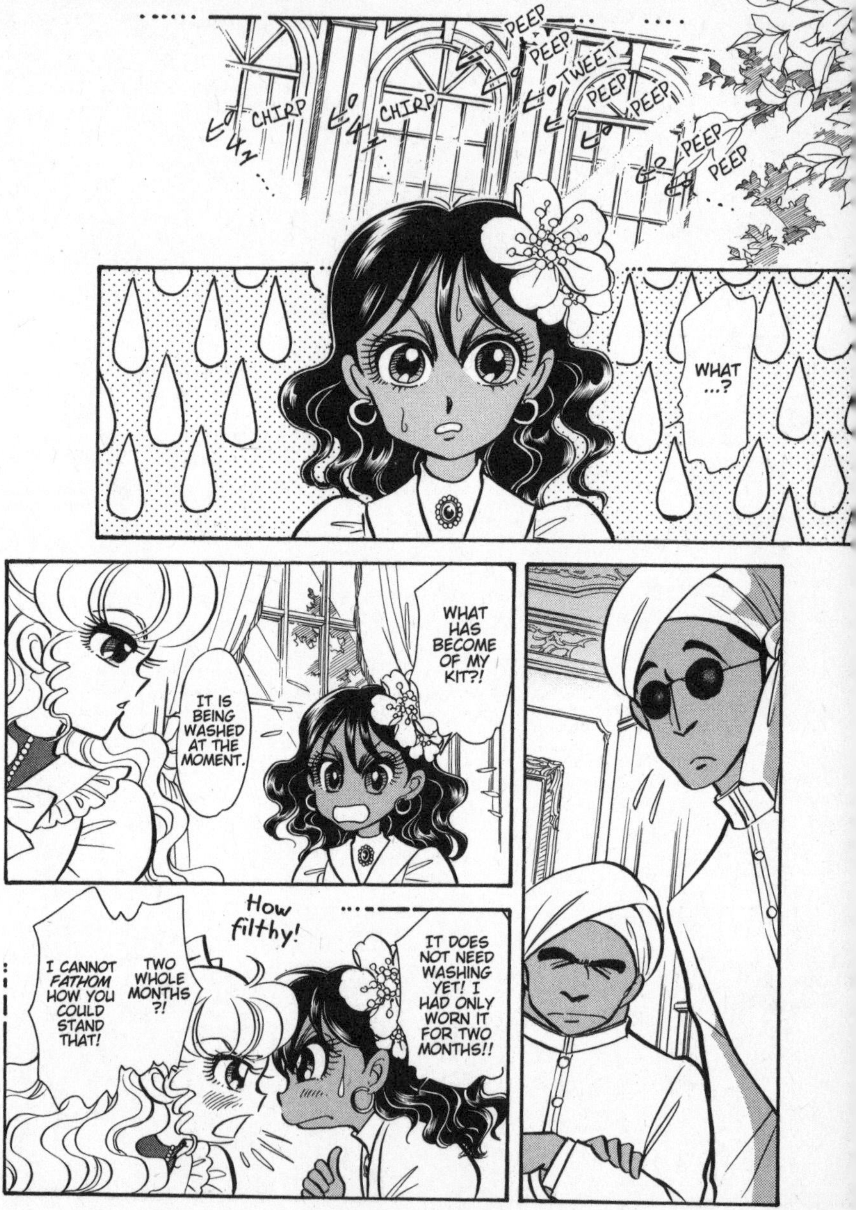
PEEP
PEEP
PEEP
PEEP
TWEET
PEEP
PEEP
CHIRP
CHIRP
WHAT ...?
WHAT HAS BECOME OF MY KIT?!
IT IS BEING WASHED AT THE MOMENT.
IT DOES NOT NEED WASHING YET! I HAD ONLY WORN IT FOR TWO MONTHS!!
How filthy!
TWO WHOLE MONTHS ?!
I CANNOT *FATHOM* HOW YOU COULD STAND THAT!

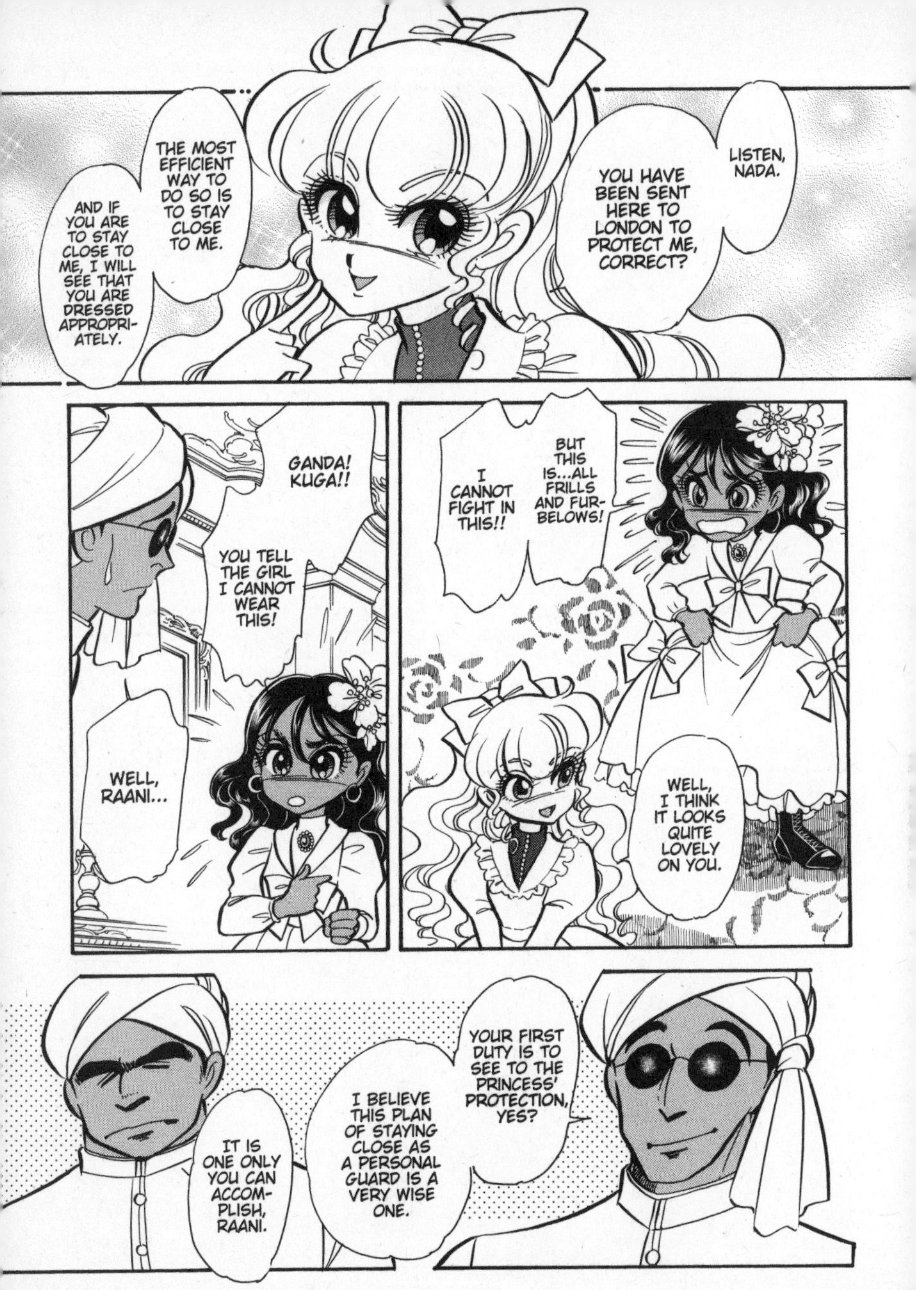
LISTEN, NADA.
YOU HAVE BEEN SENT HERE TO LONDON TO PROTECT ME, CORRECT?
THE MOST EFFICIENT WAY TO DO SO IS TO STAY CLOSE TO ME.
AND IF YOU ARE TO STAY CLOSE TO ME, I WILL SEE THAT YOU ARE DRESSED APPROPRIATELY.
BUT THIS IS...ALL FRILLS AND FURBELOWS!
I CANNOT FIGHT IN THIS!!
WELL, I THINK IT LOOKS QUITE LOVELY ON YOU.
GANDA! KUGA!!
YOU TELL THE GIRL I CANNOT WEAR THIS!
WELL, RAANI...
YOUR FIRST DUTY IS TO SEE TO THE PRINCESS' PROTECTION, YES?
I BELIEVE THIS PLAN OF STAYING CLOSE AS A PERSONAL GUARD IS A VERY WISE ONE.
IT IS ONE ONLY YOU CAN ACCOMPLISH, RAANI.

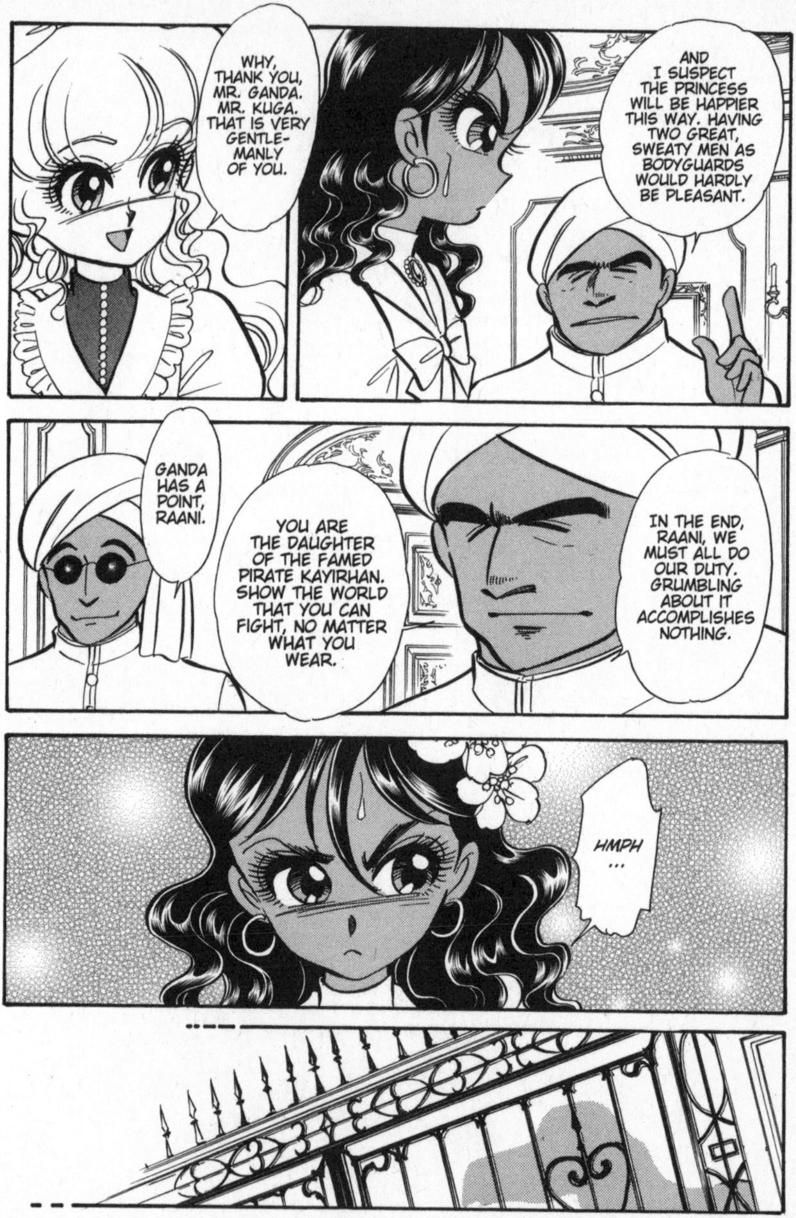
AND I SUSPECT THE PRINCESS WILL BE HAPPIER THIS WAY. HAVING TWO GREAT, SWEATY MEN AS BODYGUARDS WOULD HARDLY BE PLEASANT.
WHY, THANK YOU, MR. GANDA. MR. KUGA. THAT IS VERY GENTLEMANLY OF YOU.
IN THE END, RAANI, WE MUST ALL DO OUR DUTY. GRUMBLING ABOUT IT ACCOMPLISHES NOTHING.
YOU ARE THE DAUGHTER OF THE FAMED PIRATE KAYIRHAN. SHOW THE WORLD THAT YOU CAN FIGHT, NO MATTER WHAT YOU WEAR.
GANDA HAS A POINT, RAANI.
HMPH ...

The Adventure of The Giant Rat of Sumatra (5)

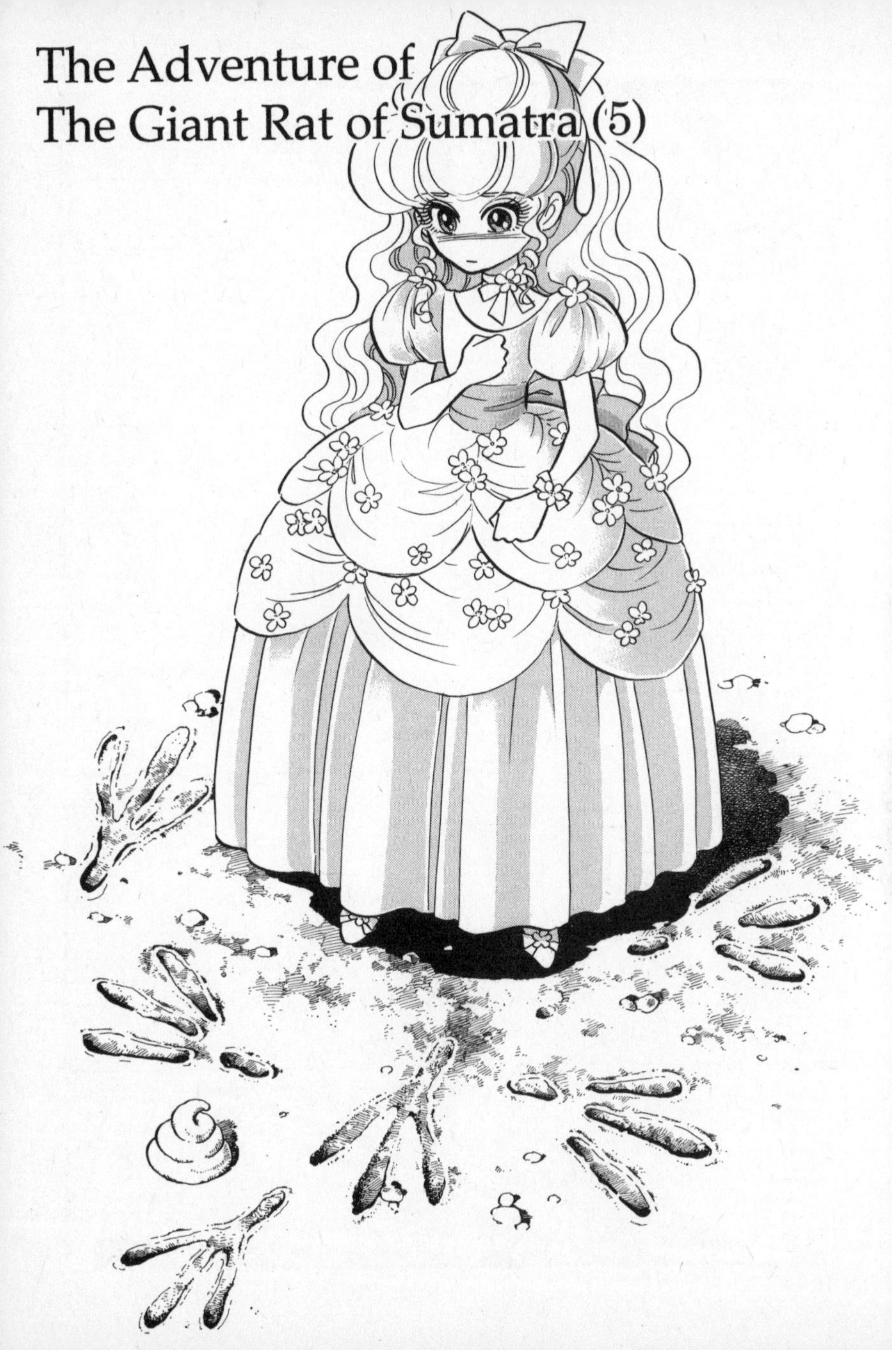

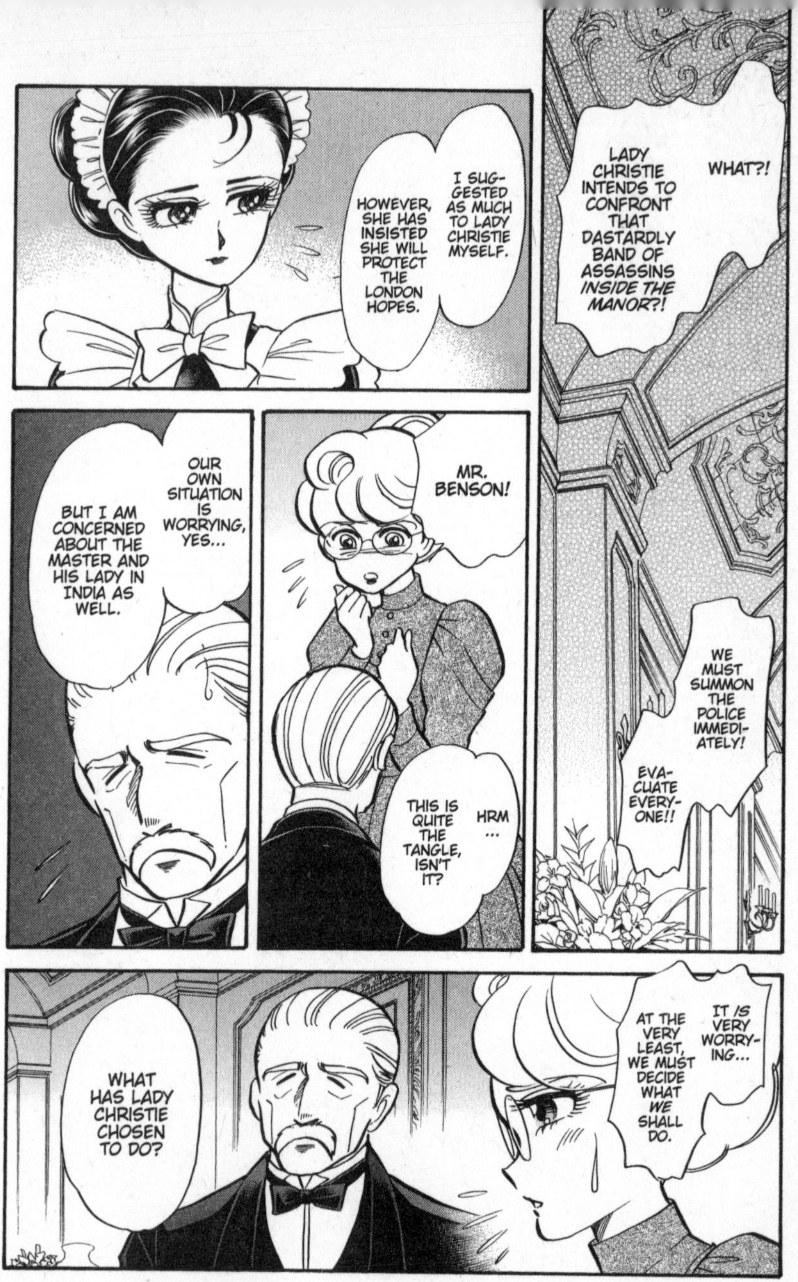
WHAT?!
LADY CHRISTIE INTENDS TO CONFRONT THAT DASTARDLY BAND OF ASSASSINS *INSIDE THE MANOR?!*
WE MUST SUMMON THE POLICE IMMEDIATELY!
EVACUATE EVERYONE!!
I SUGGESTED AS MUCH TO LADY CHRISTIE MYSELF.
HOWEVER, SHE HAS INSISTED SHE WILL PROTECT THE LONDON HOPES.
MR. BENSON!
HRM...
THIS IS QUITE THE TANGLE, ISN'T IT?
OUR OWN SITUATION IS WORRYING, YES...
BUT I AM CONCERNED ABOUT THE MASTER AND HIS LADY IN INDIA AS WELL.
IT *IS* VERY WORRYING...
AT THE VERY LEAST, WE MUST DECIDE WHAT *WE* SHALL DO.
WHAT HAS LADY CHRISTIE CHOSEN TO DO?

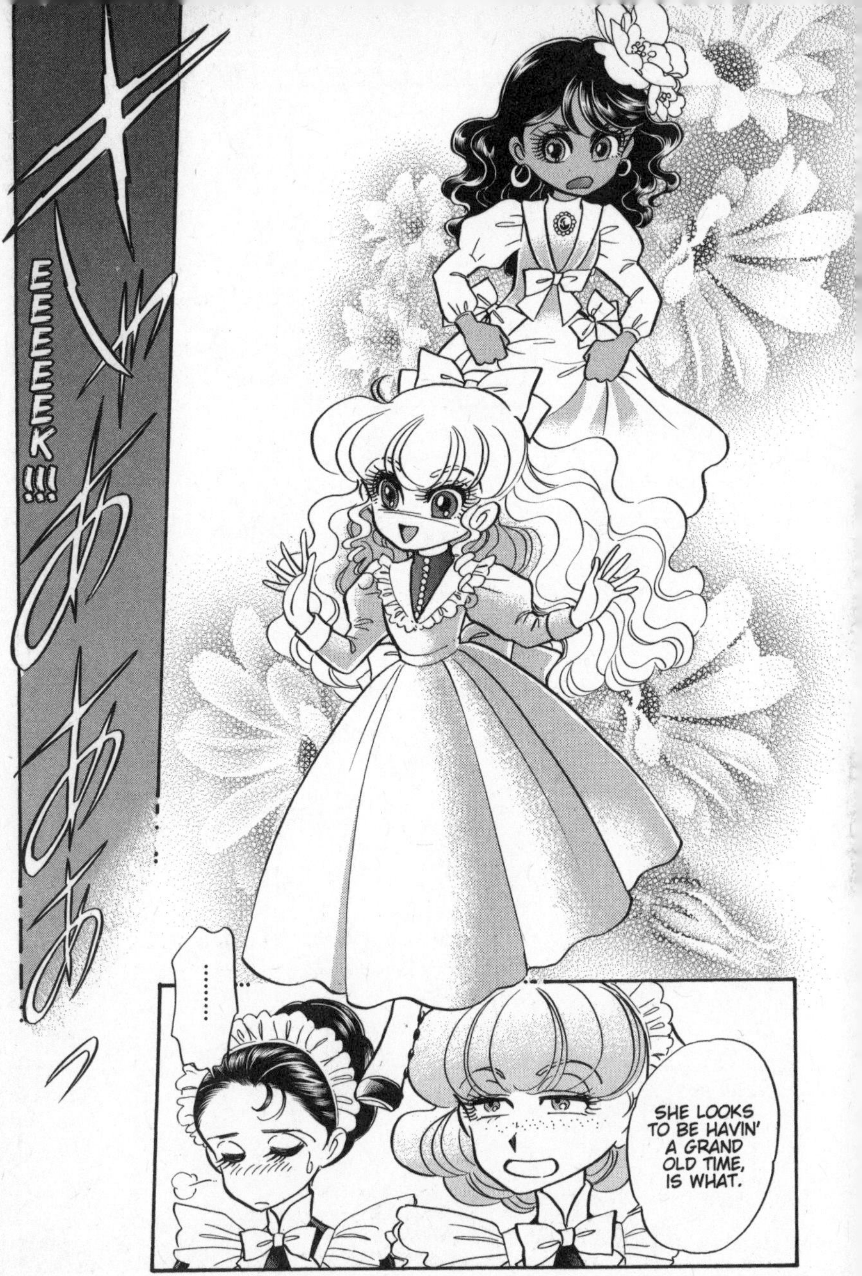
EEEEEEK!!!
……
SHE LOOKS TO BE HAVIN' A GRAND OLD TIME, IS WHAT.

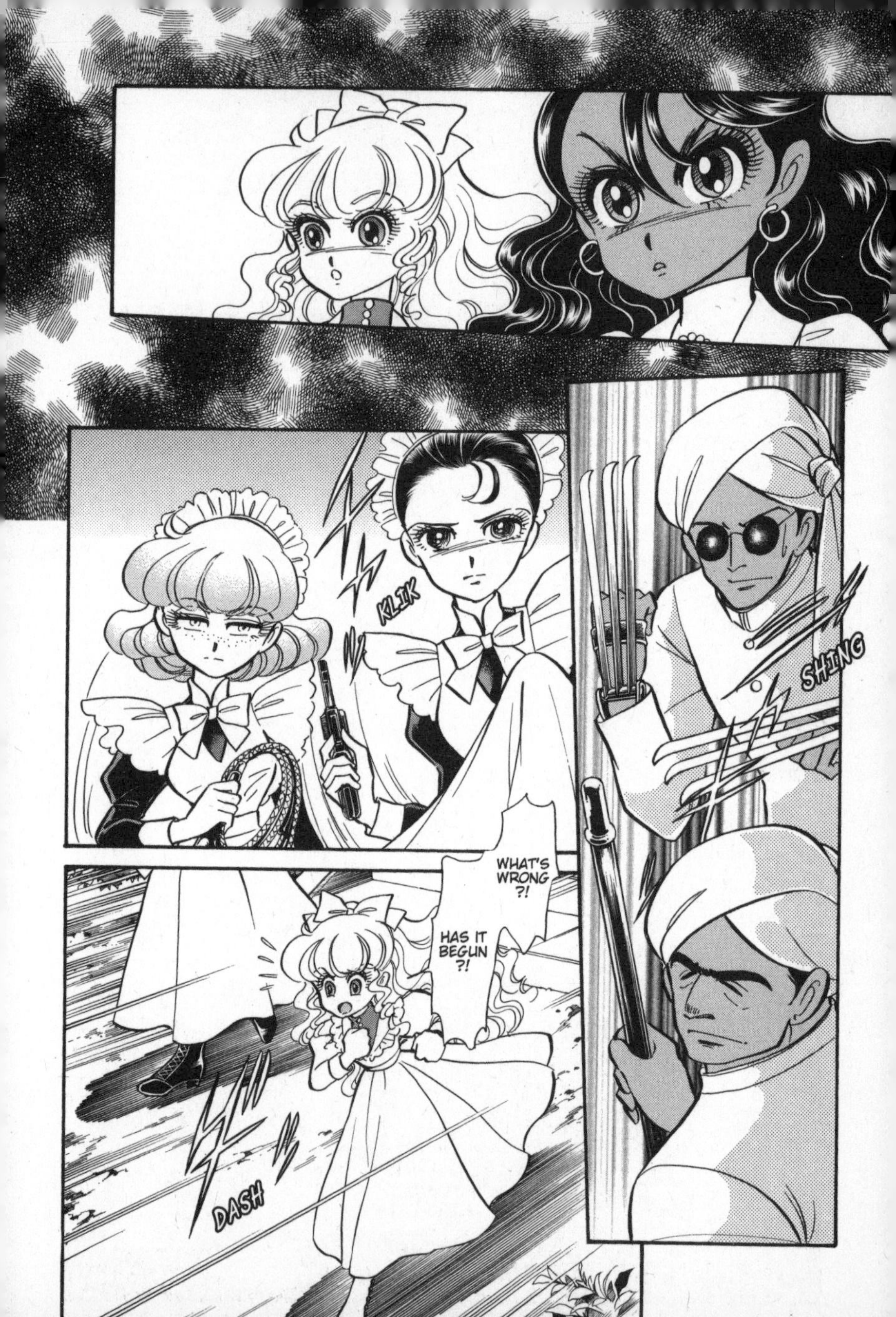
SHING
KLIK
WHAT'S WRONG ?!
HAS IT BEGUN ?!
DASH

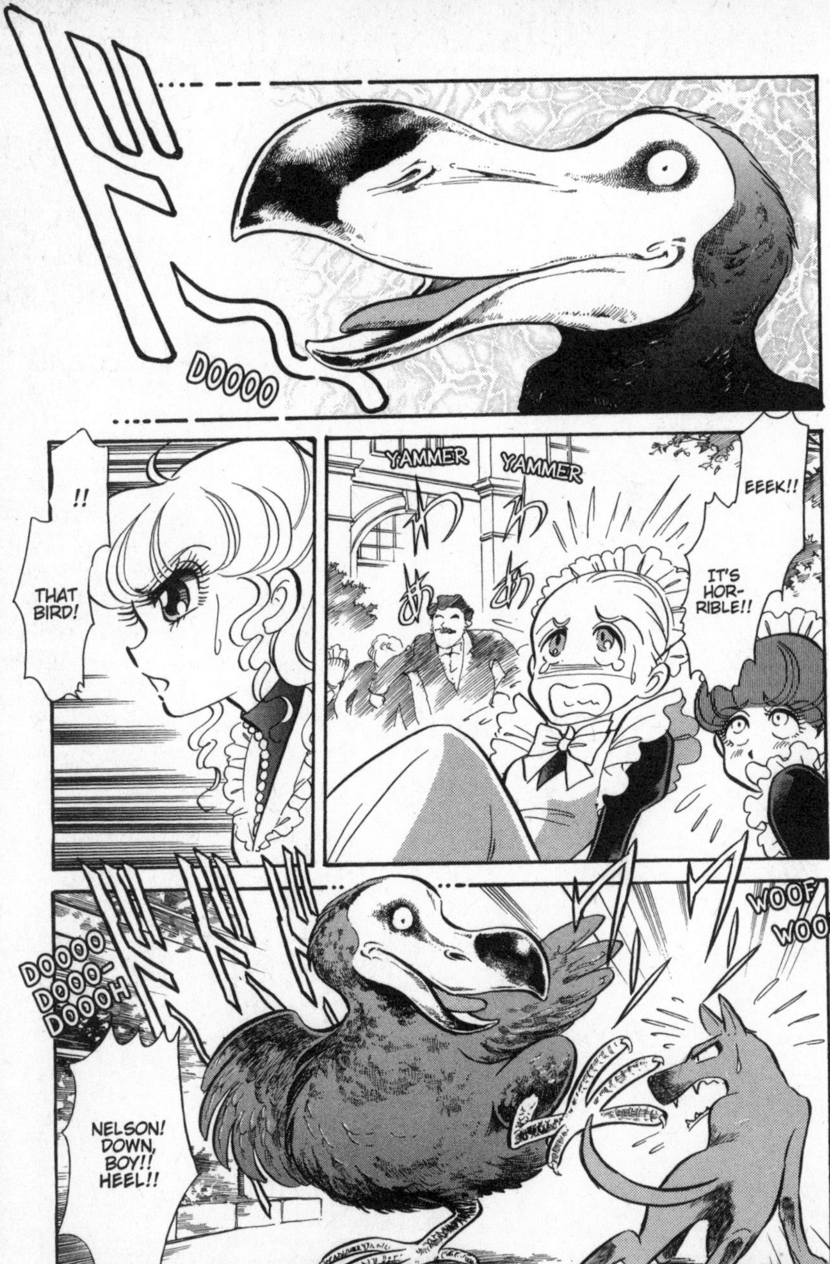
DOOOO
EEEK!!
YAMMER
YAMMER
IT'S HOR-RIBLE!!
!!
THAT BIRD!
WOOF WOOF
DOOOO-DOOO-DOOOH
NELSON! DOWN, BOY!! HEEL!!

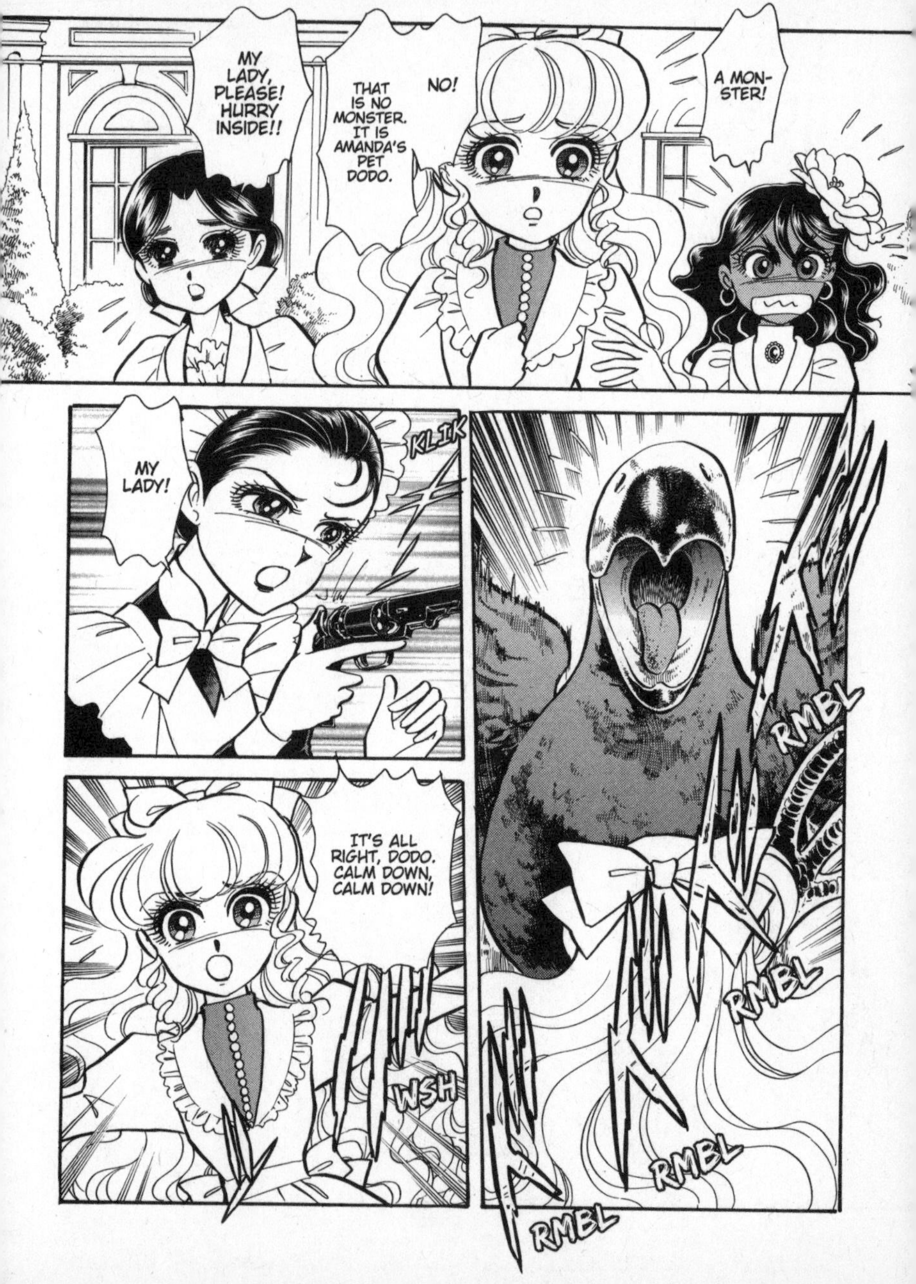
A MON-
STER!
NO!
THAT IS NO MONSTER. IT IS AMANDA'S PET DODO.
MY LADY, PLEASE! HURRY INSIDE!!
RMBL
RMBL
RMBL
RMBL
KLIK
MY LADY!
IT'S ALL RIGHT, DODO. CALM DOWN, CALM DOWN!
WSH

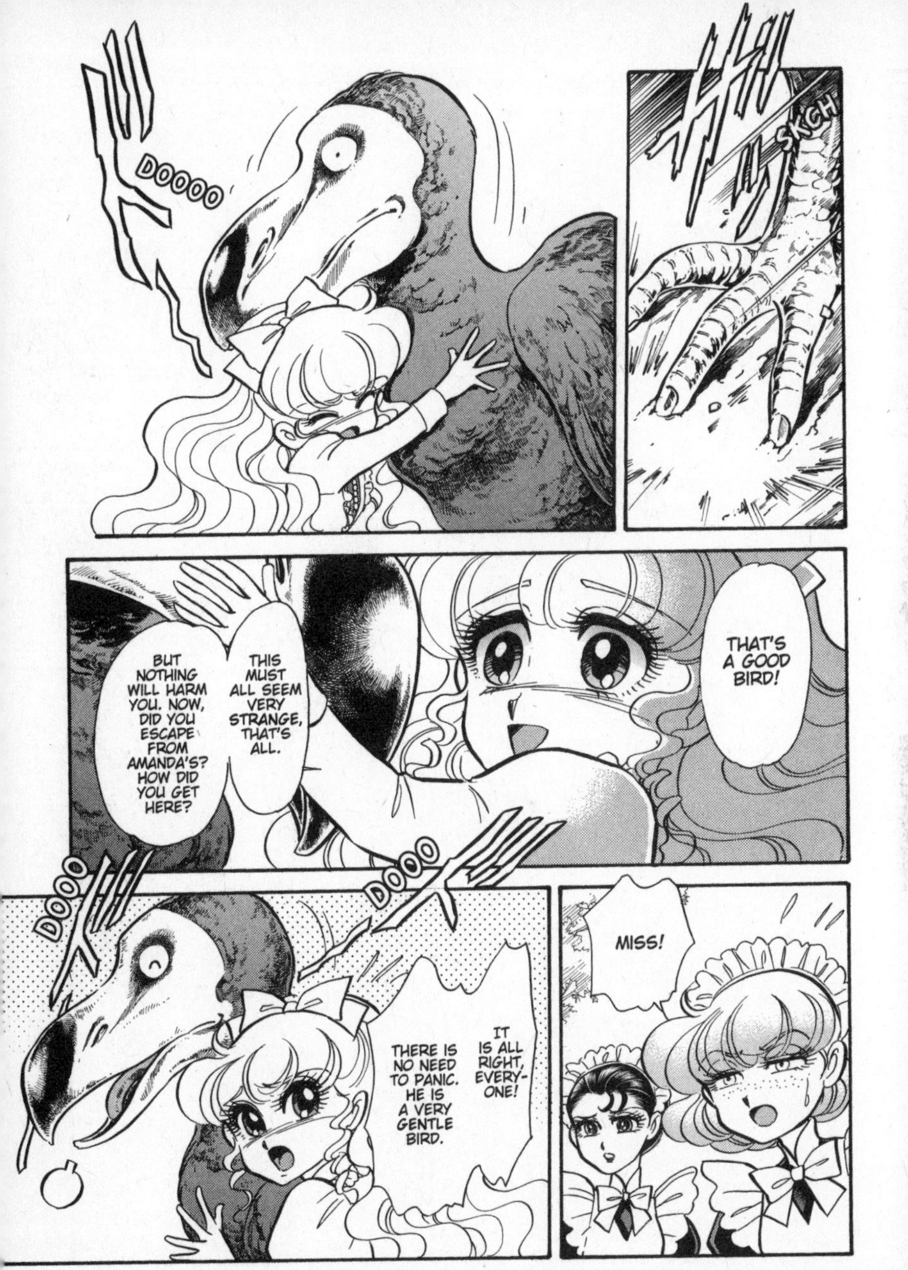
SKCH
DOOOO
THAT'S A GOOD BIRD!
THIS MUST ALL SEEM VERY STRANGE, THAT'S ALL.
BUT NOTHING WILL HARM YOU. NOW, DID YOU ESCAPE FROM AMANDA'S? HOW DID YOU GET HERE?
MISS!
DOOO
IT IS ALL RIGHT, EVERY-ONE!
THERE IS NO NEED TO PANIC. HE IS A VERY GENTLE BIRD.
DOOO

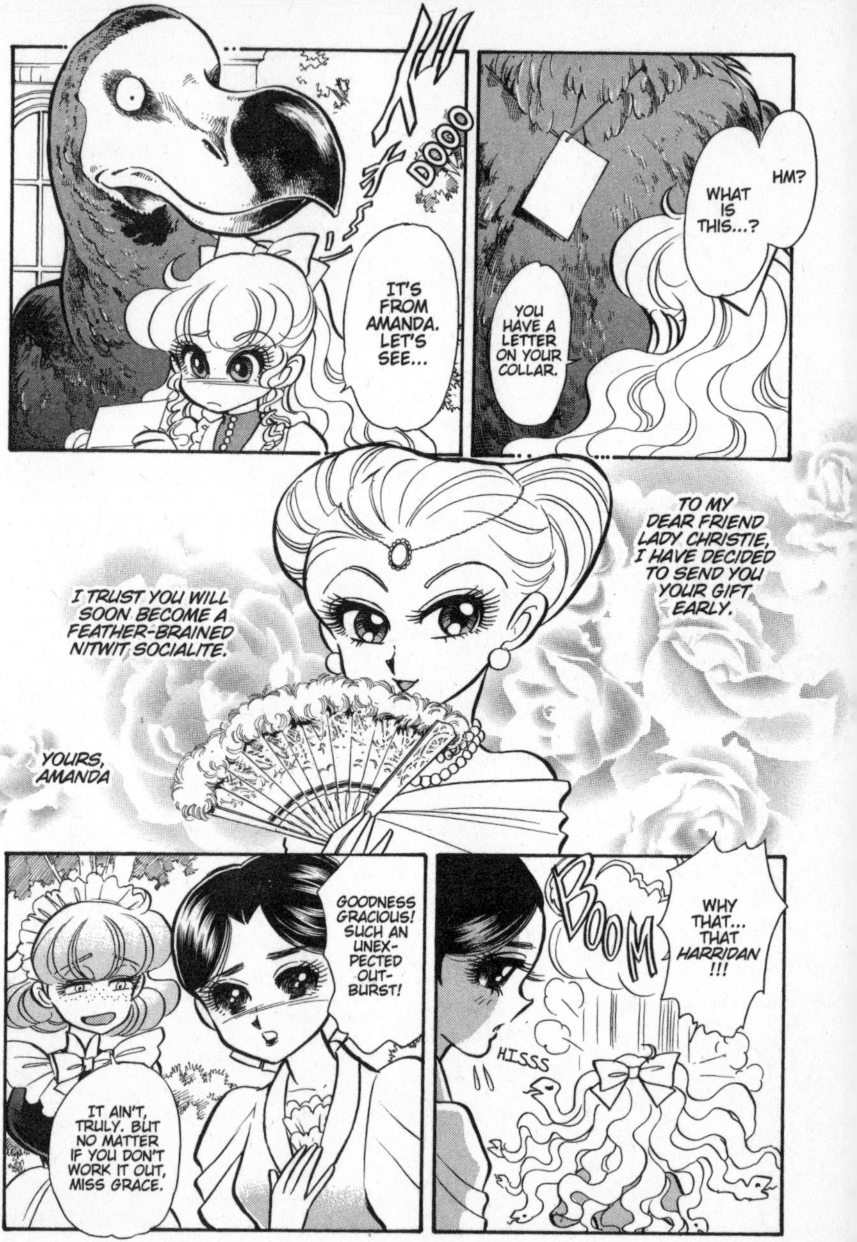
HM? WHAT IS THIS...?
YOU HAVE A LETTER ON YOUR COLLAR.
DOOO
IT'S FROM AMANDA. LET'S SEE...
TO MY DEAR FRIEND LADY CHRISTIE, I HAVE DECIDED TO SEND YOU YOUR GIFT EARLY.
I TRUST YOU WILL SOON BECOME A FEATHER-BRAINED NITWIT SOCIALITE.
YOURS, AMANDA
BOOM
WHY THAT... THAT HARRIDAN!!!
HISSS
GOODNESS GRACIOUS! SUCH AN UNEX-PECTED OUT-BURST!
IT AIN'T, TRULY. BUT NO MATTER IF YOU DON'T WORK IT OUT, MISS GRACE.

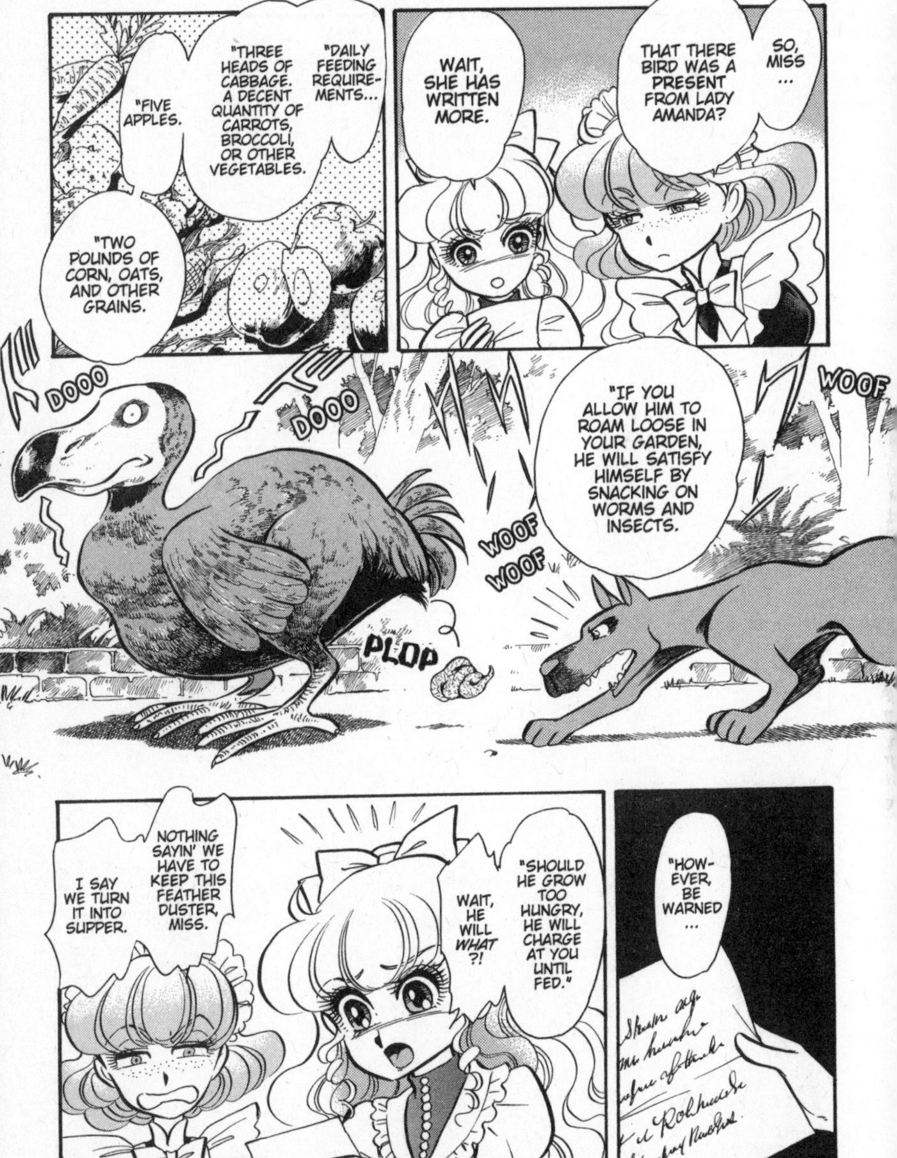
SO, MISS ...
THAT THERE BIRD WAS A PRESENT FROM LADY AMANDA?
WAIT, SHE HAS WRITTEN MORE.
"DAILY FEEDING REQUIRE-MENTS...
"THREE HEADS OF CABBAGE. A DECENT QUANTITY OF CARROTS, BROCCOLI, OR OTHER VEGETABLES.
"FIVE APPLES.
"TWO POUNDS OF CORN, OATS, AND OTHER GRAINS.
WOOF
"IF YOU ALLOW HIM TO ROAM LOOSE IN YOUR GARDEN, HE WILL SATISFY HIMSELF BY SNACKING ON WORMS AND INSECTS.
WOOF WOOF
DOOO
DOOO
PLOP
"HOW-EVER, BE WARNED ...
"SHOULD HE GROW TOO HUNGRY, HE WILL CHARGE AT YOU UNTIL FED."
WAIT, HE WILL *WHAT* ?!
NOTHING SAYIN' WE HAVE TO KEEP THIS FEATHER DUSTER, MISS.
I SAY WE TURN IT INTO SUPPER.

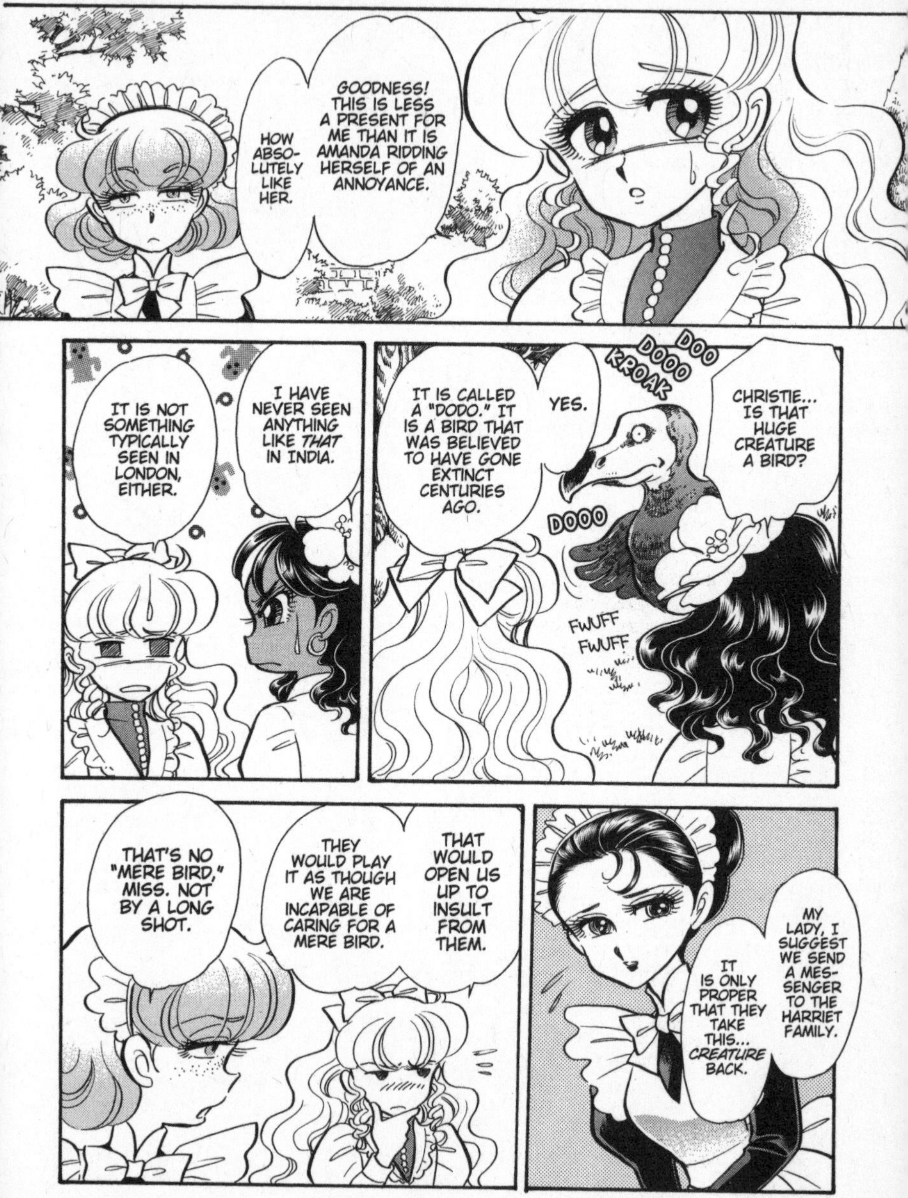
GOODNESS! THIS IS LESS A PRESENT FOR ME THAN IT IS AMANDA RIDDING HERSELF OF AN ANNOYANCE.
HOW ABSO-LUTELY LIKE HER.
CHRISTIE... IS THAT HUGE CREATURE A BIRD?
DOO DOOO KROAK
YES.
IT IS CALLED A "DODO." IT IS A BIRD THAT WAS BELIEVED TO HAVE GONE EXTINCT CENTURIES AGO.
DOOO
FWUFF FWUFF
I HAVE NEVER SEEN ANYTHING LIKE *THAT* IN INDIA.
IT IS NOT SOMETHING TYPICALLY SEEN IN LONDON, EITHER.
MY LADY, I SUGGEST WE SEND A MES-SENGER TO THE HARRIET FAMILY.
IT IS ONLY PROPER THAT THEY TAKE THIS... *CREATURE* BACK.
THAT WOULD OPEN US UP TO INSULT FROM THEM.
THEY WOULD PLAY IT AS THOUGH WE ARE INCAPABLE OF CARING FOR A MERE BIRD.
THAT'S NO "MERE BIRD," MISS. NOT BY A LONG SHOT.

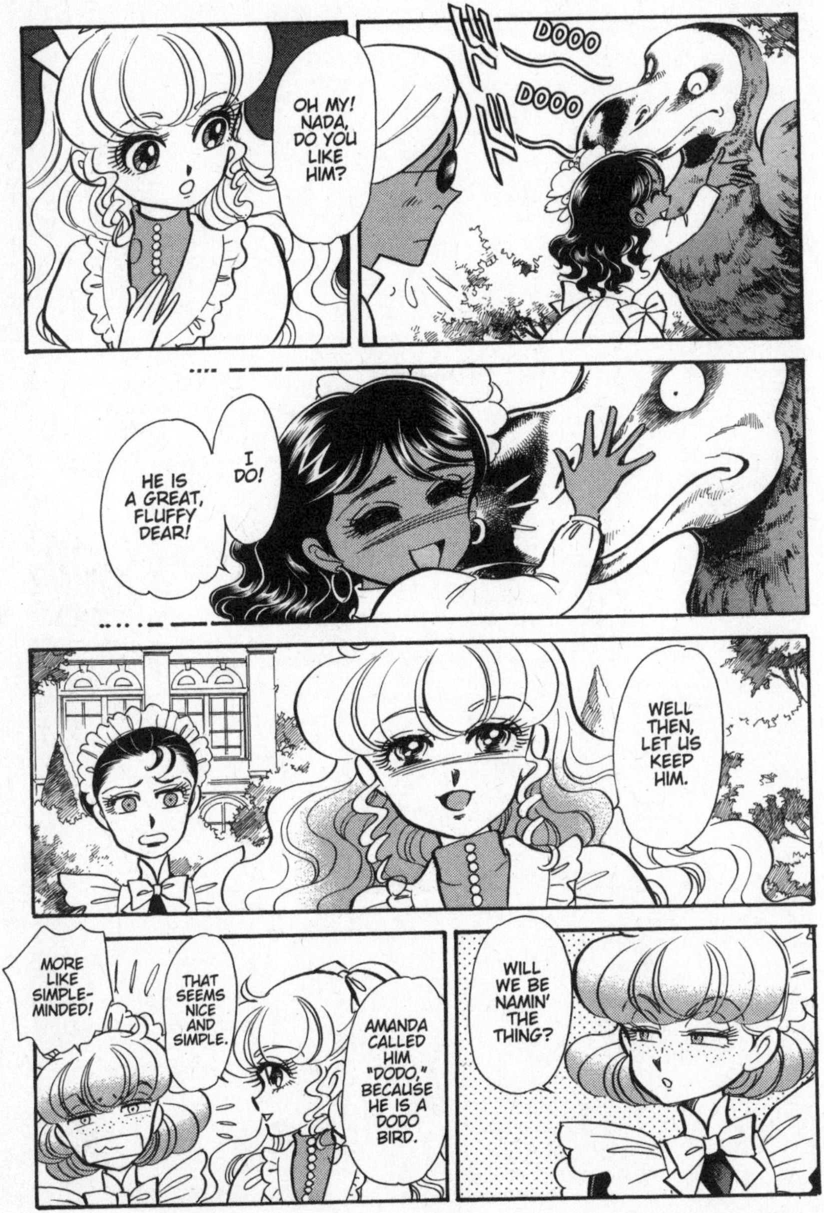
DOOO
DOOO
OH MY! NADA, DO YOU LIKE HIM?
I DO!
HE IS A GREAT, FLUFFY DEAR!
WELL THEN, LET US KEEP HIM.
WILL WE BE NAMIN' THE THING?
AMANDA CALLED HIM "DODO," BECAUSE HE IS A DODO BIRD.
THAT SEEMS NICE AND SIMPLE.
MORE LIKE SIMPLE-MINDED!

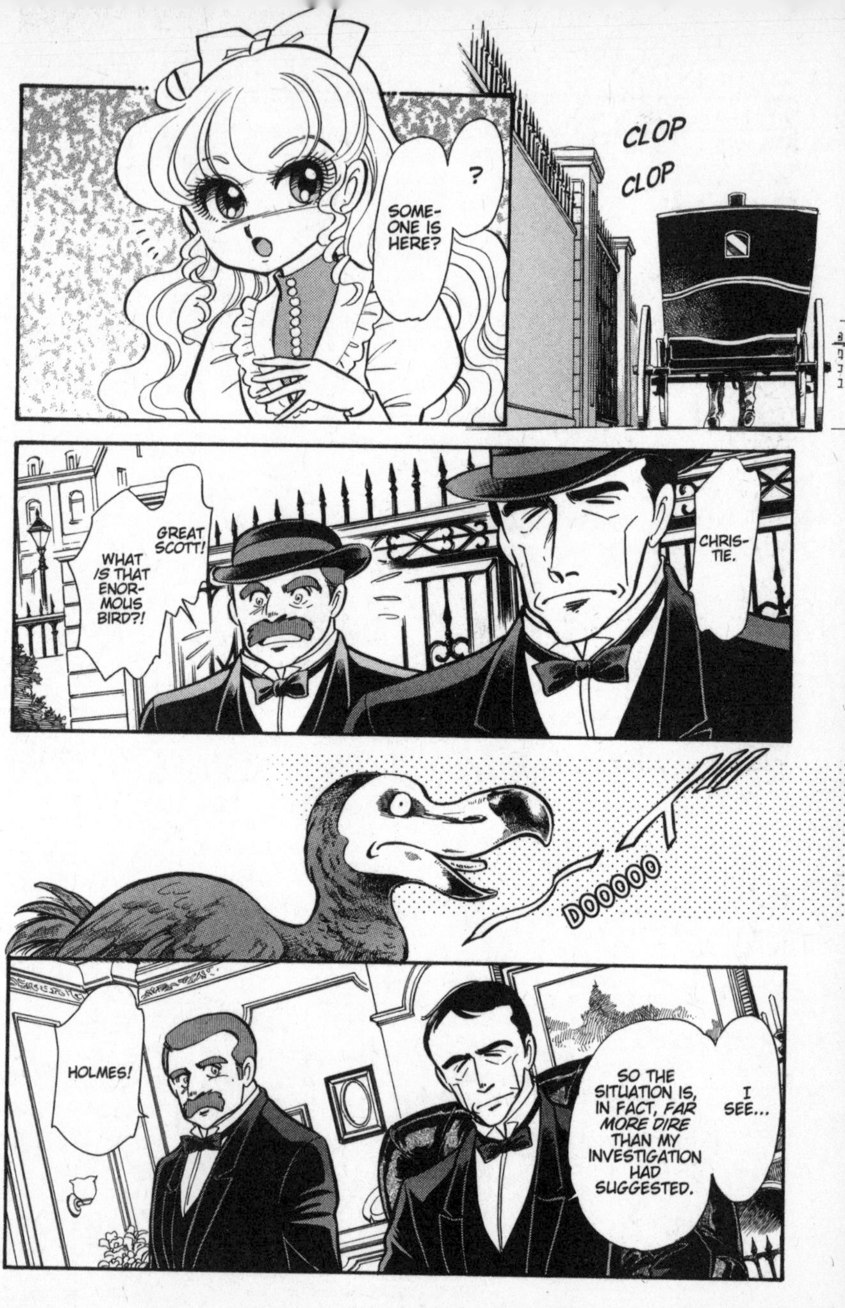
CLOP
CLOP
? SOME-ONE IS HERE?
CHRIS-TIE.
GREAT SCOTT! WHAT *IS* THAT ENOR-MOUS BIRD?!
DOOOOO
I SEE...
SO THE SITUATION IS, IN FACT, *FAR MORE DIRE* THAN MY INVESTIGATION HAD SUGGESTED.
HOLMES!

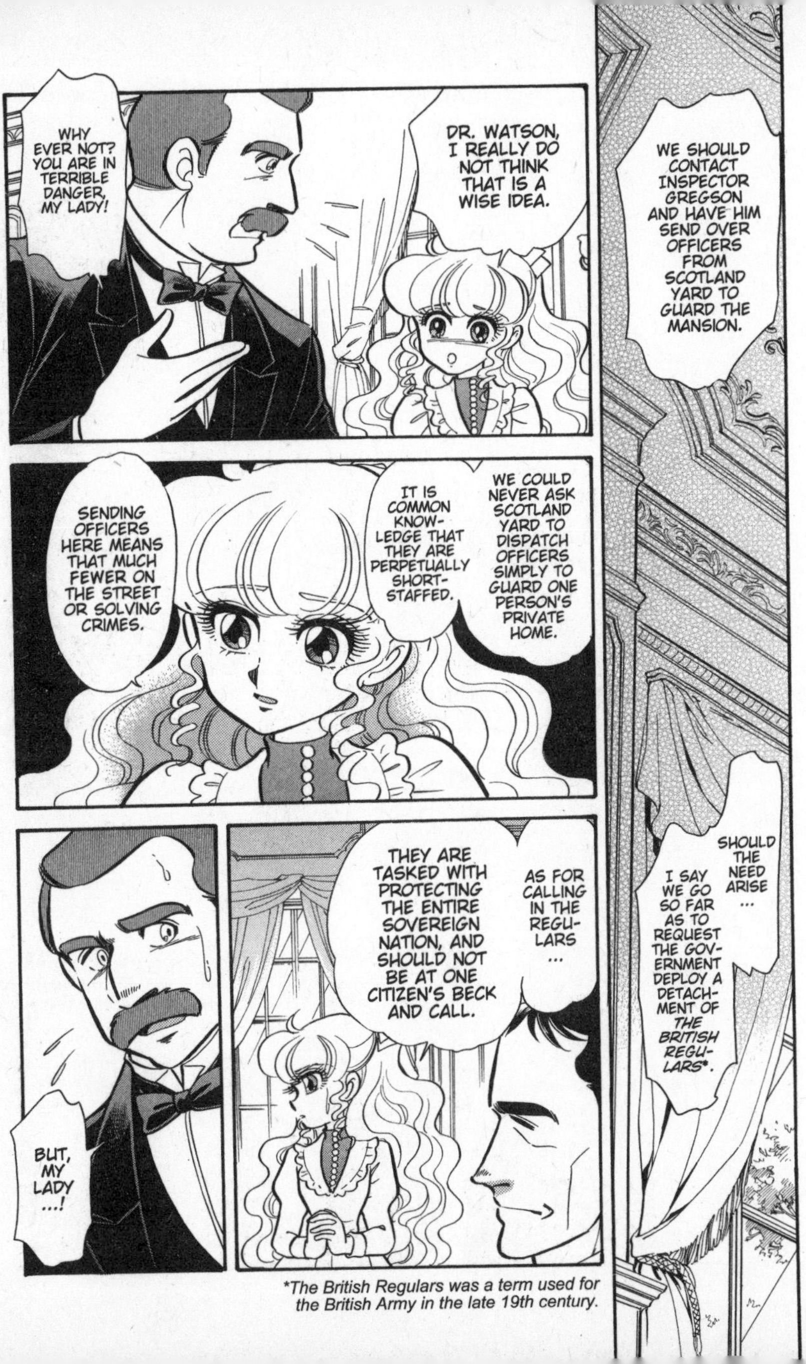
WE SHOULD CONTACT INSPECTOR GREGSON AND HAVE HIM SEND OVER OFFICERS FROM SCOTLAND YARD TO GUARD THE MANSION.
SHOULD THE NEED ARISE ...
I SAY WE GO SO FAR AS TO REQUEST THE GOVERNMENT DEPLOY A DETACHMENT OF *THE BRITISH REGULARS**.
DR. WATSON, I REALLY DO NOT THINK THAT IS A WISE IDEA.
WHY EVER NOT? YOU ARE IN TERRIBLE DANGER, MY LADY!
WE COULD NEVER ASK SCOTLAND YARD TO DISPATCH OFFICERS SIMPLY TO GUARD ONE PERSON'S PRIVATE HOME.
IT IS COMMON KNOWLEDGE THAT THEY ARE PERPETUALLY SHORT-STAFFED.
SENDING OFFICERS HERE MEANS THAT MUCH FEWER ON THE STREET OR SOLVING CRIMES.
AS FOR CALLING IN THE REGULARS ...
THEY ARE TASKED WITH PROTECTING THE ENTIRE SOVEREIGN NATION, AND SHOULD NOT BE AT ONE CITIZEN'S BECK AND CALL.
BUT, MY LADY ...!

**The British Regulars was a term used for the British Army in the late 19th century.*

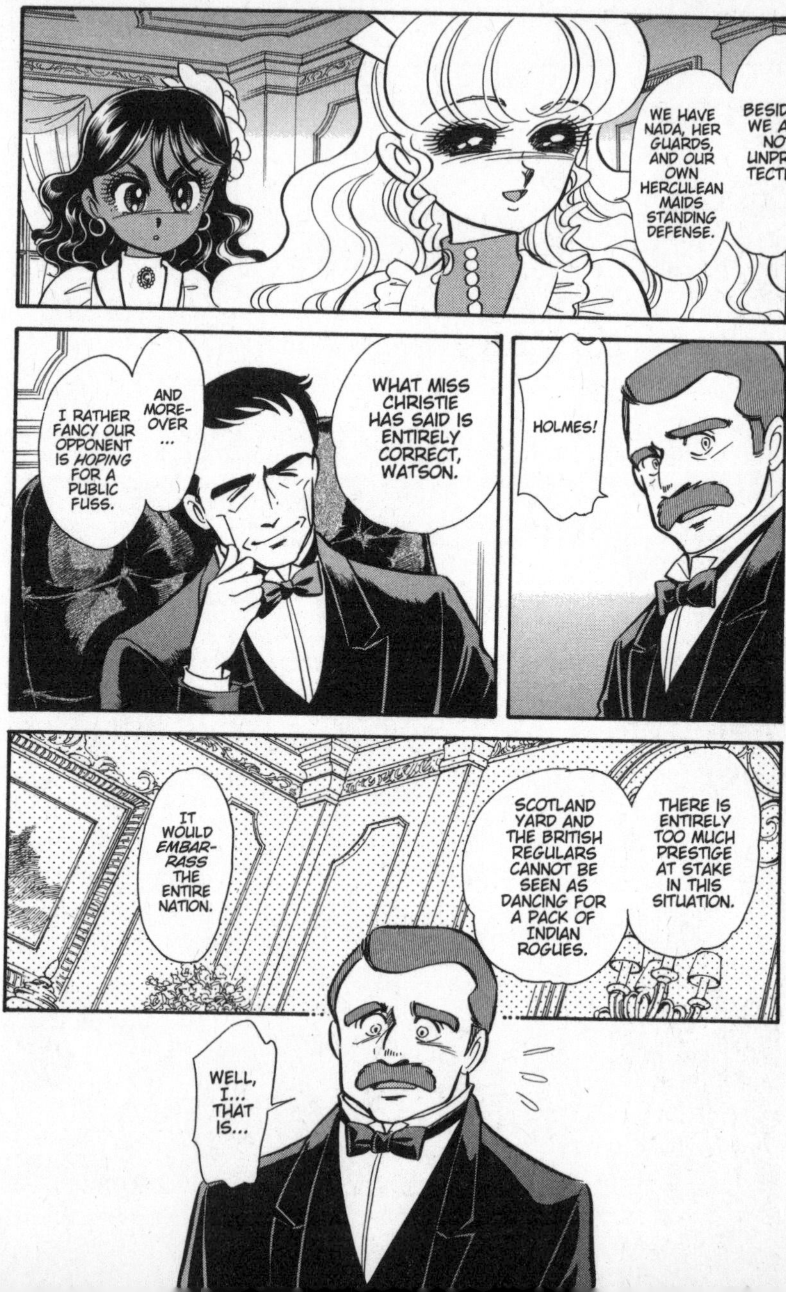
BESIDES, WE ARE NOT UNPROTECTED.
WE HAVE NADA, HER GUARDS, AND OUR OWN HERCULEAN MAIDS STANDING DEFENSE.
HOLMES!
WHAT MISS CHRISTIE HAS SAID IS ENTIRELY CORRECT, WATSON.
AND MOREOVER ...
I RATHER FANCY OUR OPPONENT IS *HOPING* FOR A PUBLIC FUSS.
THERE IS ENTIRELY TOO MUCH PRESTIGE AT STAKE IN THIS SITUATION.
SCOTLAND YARD AND THE BRITISH REGULARS CANNOT BE SEEN AS DANCING FOR A PACK OF INDIAN ROGUES.
IT WOULD EMBARRASS THE ENTIRE NATION.
WELL, I... THAT IS...

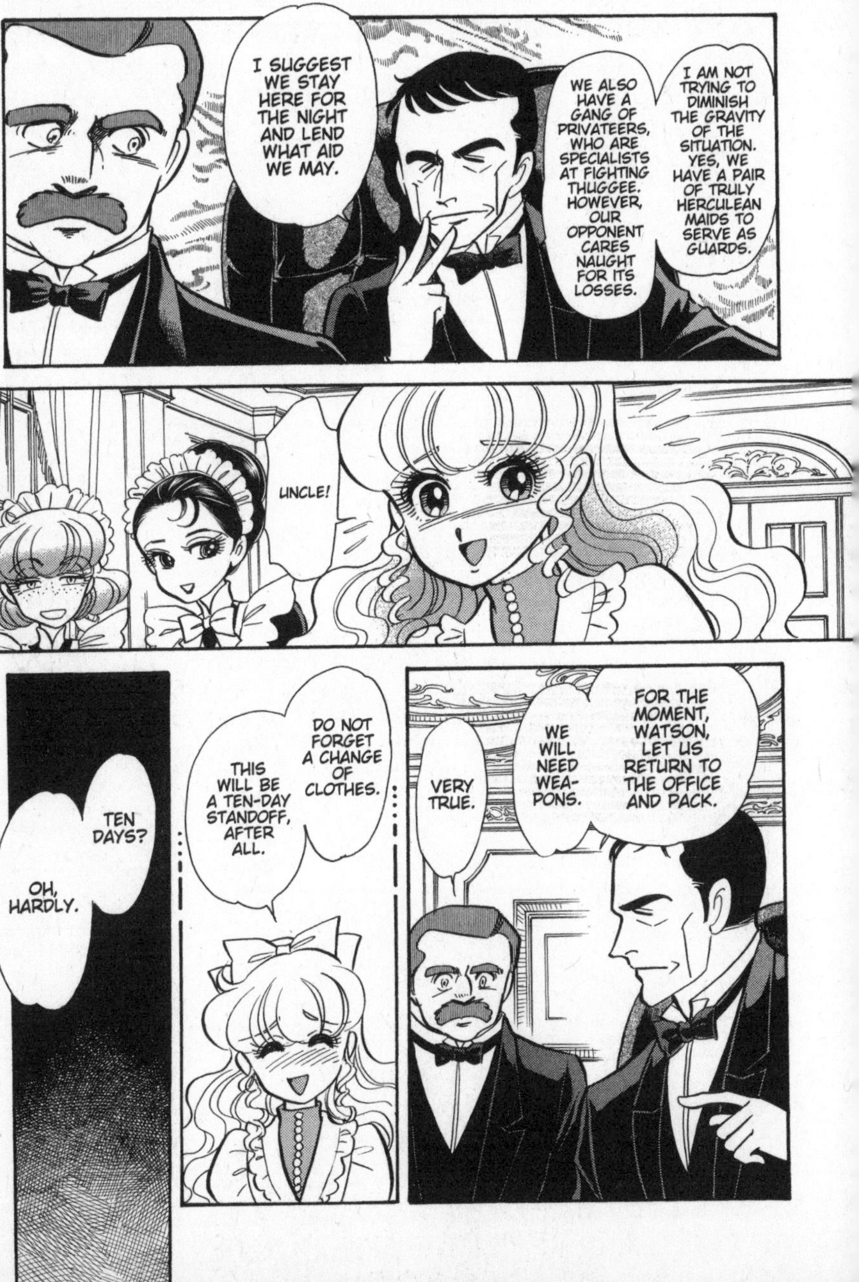
I AM NOT TRYING TO DIMINISH THE GRAVITY OF THE SITUATION. YES, WE HAVE A PAIR OF TRULY HERCULEAN MAIDS TO SERVE AS GUARDS.
WE ALSO HAVE A GANG OF PRIVATEERS, WHO ARE SPECIALISTS AT FIGHTING THUGGEE. HOWEVER, OUR OPPONENT CARES NAUGHT FOR ITS LOSSES.
I SUGGEST WE STAY HERE FOR THE NIGHT AND LEND WHAT AID WE MAY.
UNCLE!
FOR THE MOMENT, WATSON, LET US RETURN TO THE OFFICE AND PACK.
WE WILL NEED WEA-PONS.
VERY TRUE.
DO NOT FORGET A CHANGE OF CLOTHES.
THIS WILL BE A TEN-DAY STANDOFF, AFTER ALL.
TEN DAYS?
OH, HARDLY.

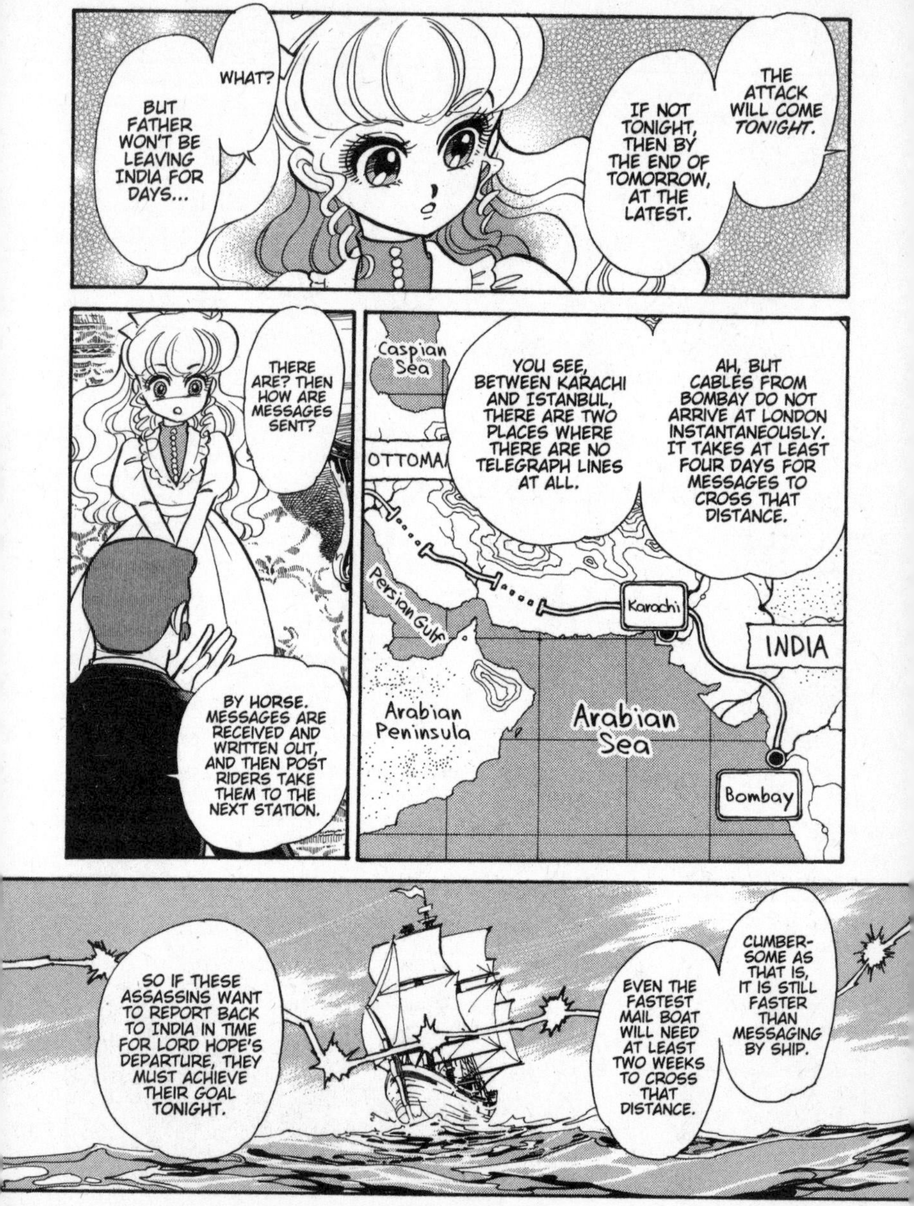
THE ATTACK WILL COME *TONIGHT*.
IF NOT TONIGHT, THEN BY THE END OF TOMORROW, AT THE LATEST.
WHAT?
BUT FATHER WON'T BE LEAVING INDIA FOR DAYS...
AH, BUT CABLES FROM BOMBAY DO NOT ARRIVE AT LONDON INSTANTANEOUSLY. IT TAKES AT LEAST FOUR DAYS FOR MESSAGES TO CROSS THAT DISTANCE.
YOU SEE, BETWEEN KARACHI AND ISTANBUL, THERE ARE TWO PLACES WHERE THERE ARE NO TELEGRAPH LINES AT ALL.
Caspian Sea
OTTOMA
Persian Gulf
Karachi
INDIA
Arabian Peninsula
Arabian Sea
Bombay
THERE ARE? THEN HOW ARE MESSAGES SENT?
BY HORSE. MESSAGES ARE RECEIVED AND WRITTEN OUT, AND THEN POST RIDERS TAKE THEM TO THE NEXT STATION.
CUMBER-SOME AS THAT IS, IT IS STILL FASTER THAN MESSAGING BY SHIP.
EVEN THE FASTEST MAIL BOAT WILL NEED AT LEAST TWO WEEKS TO CROSS THAT DISTANCE.
SO IF THESE ASSASSINS WANT TO REPORT BACK TO INDIA IN TIME FOR LORD HOPE'S DEPARTURE, THEY MUST ACHIEVE THEIR GOAL TONIGHT.

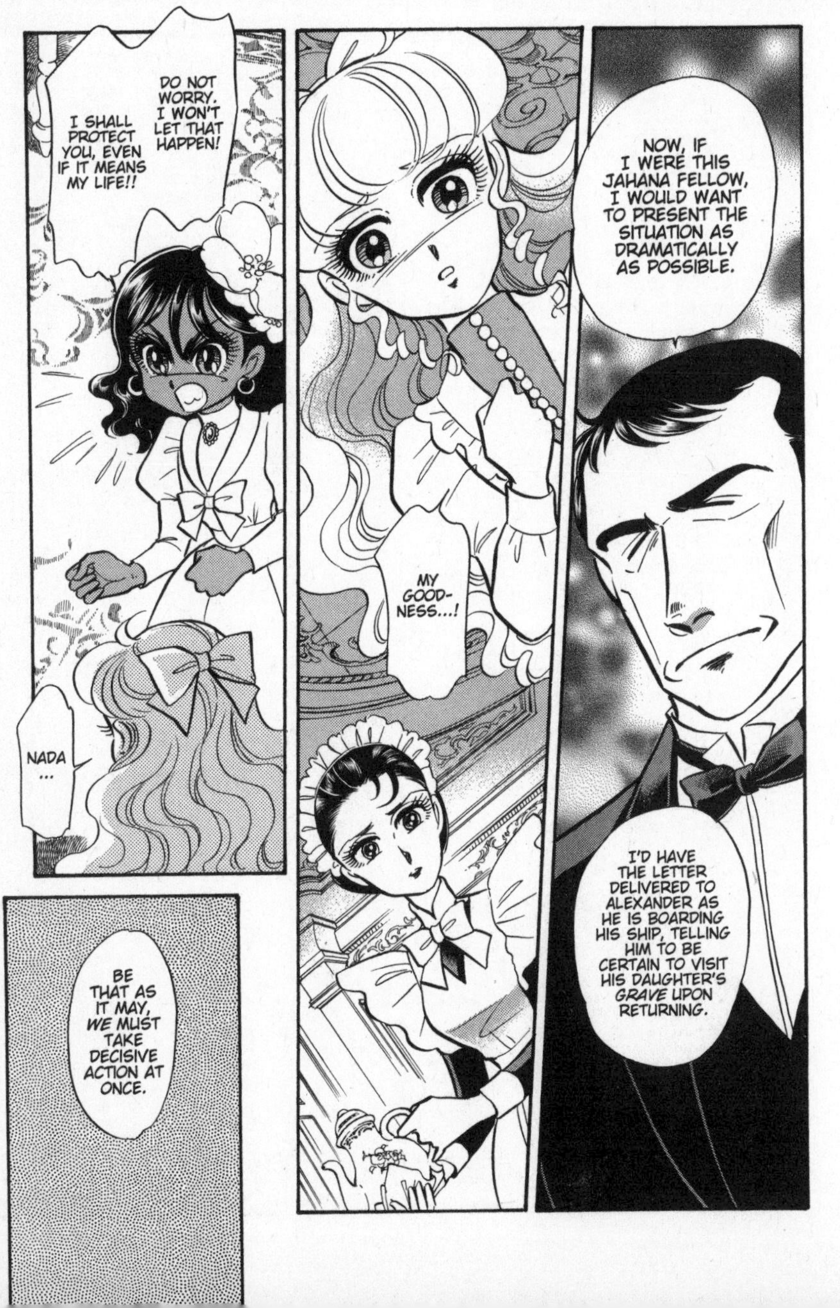
NOW, IF I WERE THIS JAHANA FELLOW, I WOULD WANT TO PRESENT THE SITUATION AS DRAMATICALLY AS POSSIBLE.
I'D HAVE THE LETTER DELIVERED TO ALEXANDER AS HE IS BOARDING HIS SHIP, TELLING HIM TO BE CERTAIN TO VISIT HIS DAUGHTER'S *GRAVE* UPON RETURNING.
MY GOODNESS...!
DO NOT WORRY. I WON'T LET THAT HAPPEN!
I SHALL PROTECT YOU, EVEN IF IT MEANS MY LIFE!!
NADA ...
BE THAT AS IT MAY, *WE* MUST TAKE DECISIVE ACTION AT ONCE.

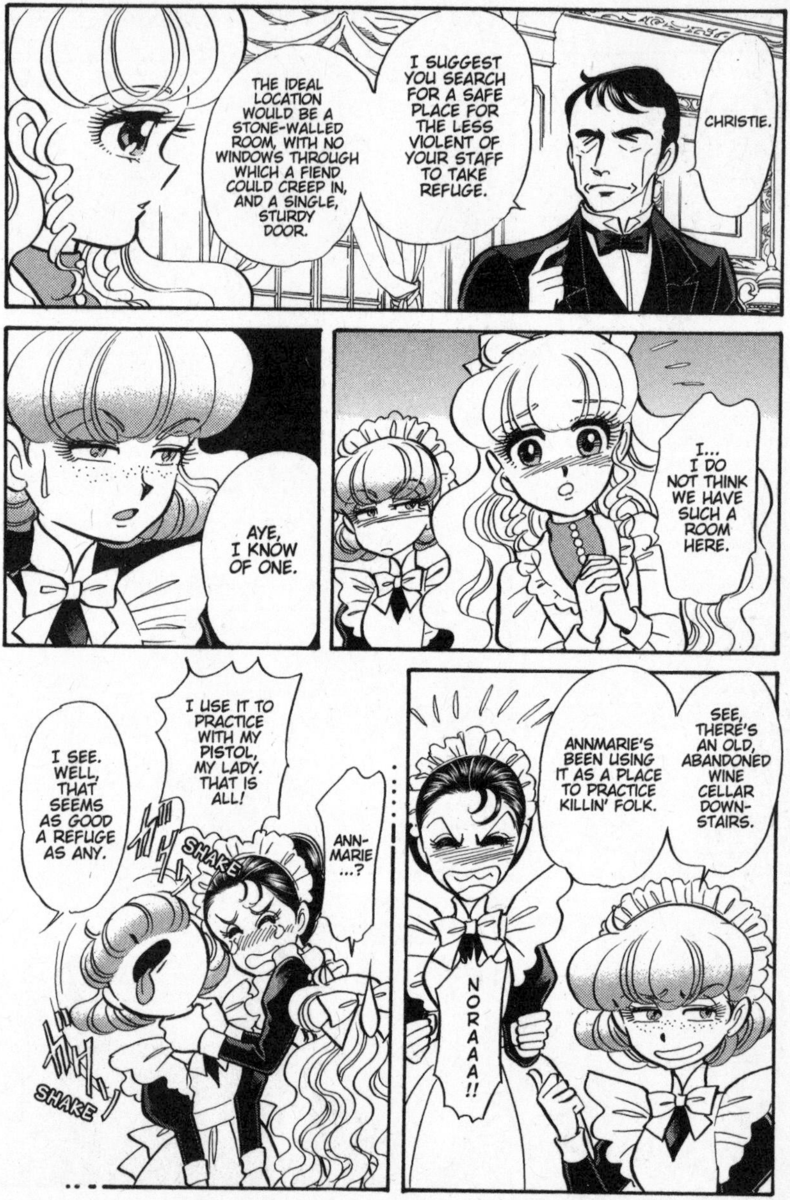
CHRISTIE.
I SUGGEST YOU SEARCH FOR A SAFE PLACE FOR THE LESS VIOLENT OF YOUR STAFF TO TAKE REFUGE.
THE IDEAL LOCATION WOULD BE A STONE-WALLED ROOM, WITH NO WINDOWS THROUGH WHICH A FIEND COULD CREEP IN, AND A SINGLE, STURDY DOOR.
I... I DO NOT THINK WE HAVE SUCH A ROOM HERE.
AYE, I KNOW OF ONE.
SEE, THERE'S AN OLD, ABANDONED WINE CELLAR DOWN-STAIRS.
ANNMARIE'S BEEN USING IT AS A PLACE TO PRACTICE KILLIN' FOLK.
NORAAA!!
ANN-MARIE ...?
I USE IT TO PRACTICE WITH MY PISTOL, MY LADY. THAT IS ALL!
SHAKE
SHAKE
I SEE. WELL, THAT SEEMS AS GOOD A REFUGE AS ANY.

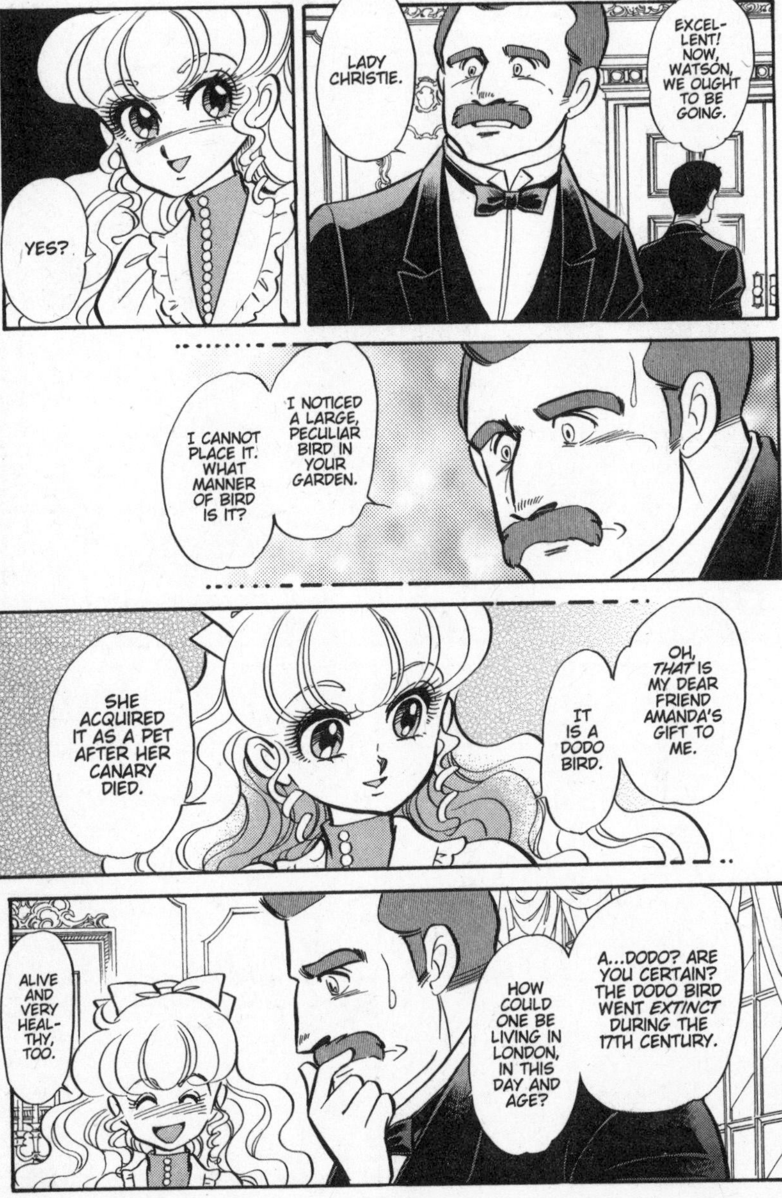
EXCEL-LENT! NOW, WATSON, WE OUGHT TO BE GOING.
LADY CHRISTIE.
YES?
I NOTICED A LARGE, PECULIAR BIRD IN YOUR GARDEN.
I CANNOT PLACE IT. WHAT MANNER OF BIRD IS IT?
OH, *THAT* IS MY DEAR FRIEND AMANDA'S GIFT TO ME.
IT IS A DODO BIRD.
SHE ACQUIRED IT AS A PET AFTER HER CANARY DIED.
A...DODO? ARE YOU CERTAIN? THE DODO BIRD WENT *EXTINCT* DURING THE 17TH CENTURY.
HOW COULD ONE BE LIVING IN LONDON, IN THIS DAY AND AGE?
ALIVE AND VERY HEAL-THY, TOO.

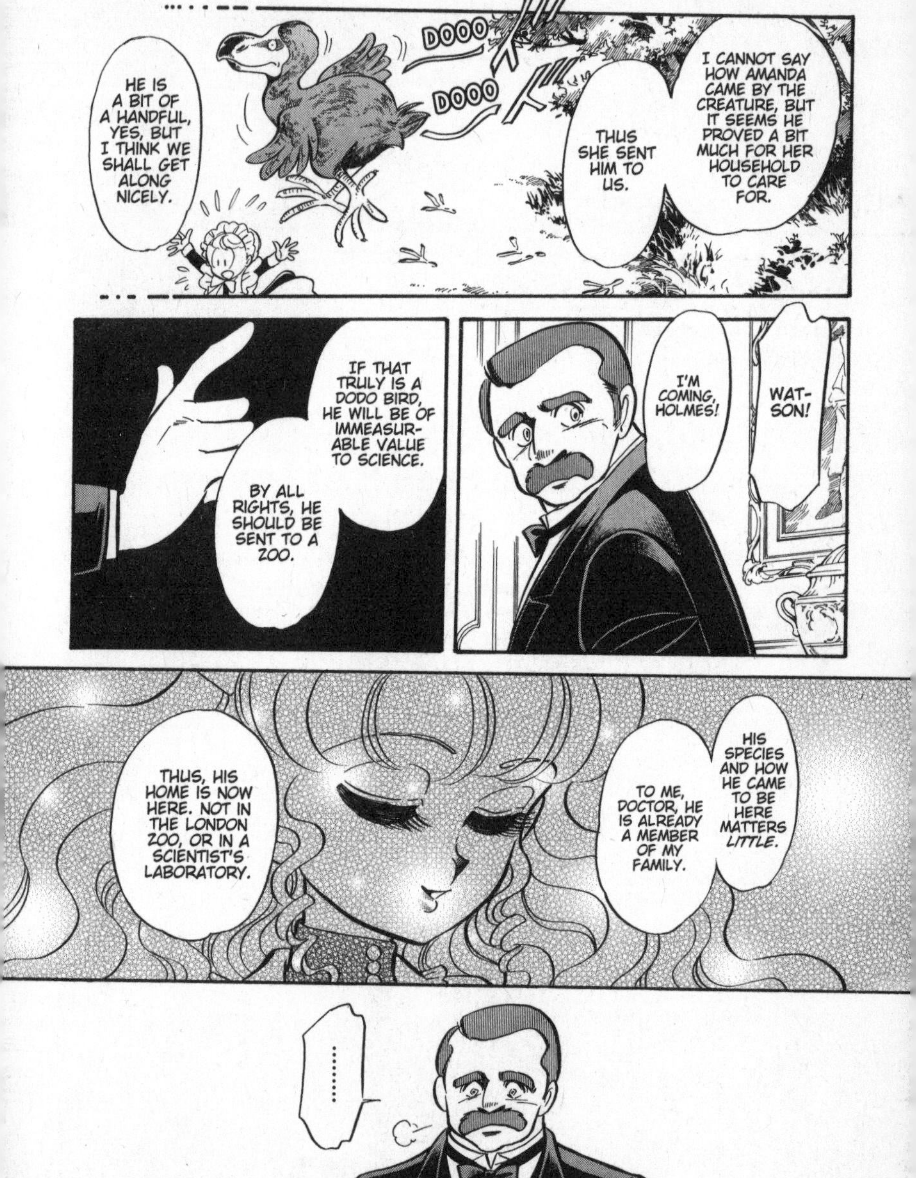
I CANNOT SAY HOW AMANDA CAME BY THE CREATURE, BUT IT SEEMS HE PROVED A BIT MUCH FOR HER HOUSEHOLD TO CARE FOR.
THUS SHE SENT HIM TO US.
DOOO
DOOO
HE IS A BIT OF A HANDFUL, YES, BUT I THINK WE SHALL GET ALONG NICELY.
WAT-SON!
I'M COMING, HOLMES!
IF THAT TRULY IS A DODO BIRD, HE WILL BE OF IMMEASURABLE VALUE TO SCIENCE.
BY ALL RIGHTS, HE SHOULD BE SENT TO A ZOO.
HIS SPECIES AND HOW HE CAME TO BE HERE MATTERS *LITTLE*.
TO ME, DOCTOR, HE IS ALREADY A MEMBER OF MY FAMILY.
THUS, HIS HOME IS NOW HERE. NOT IN THE LONDON ZOO, OR IN A SCIENTIST'S LABORATORY.
......

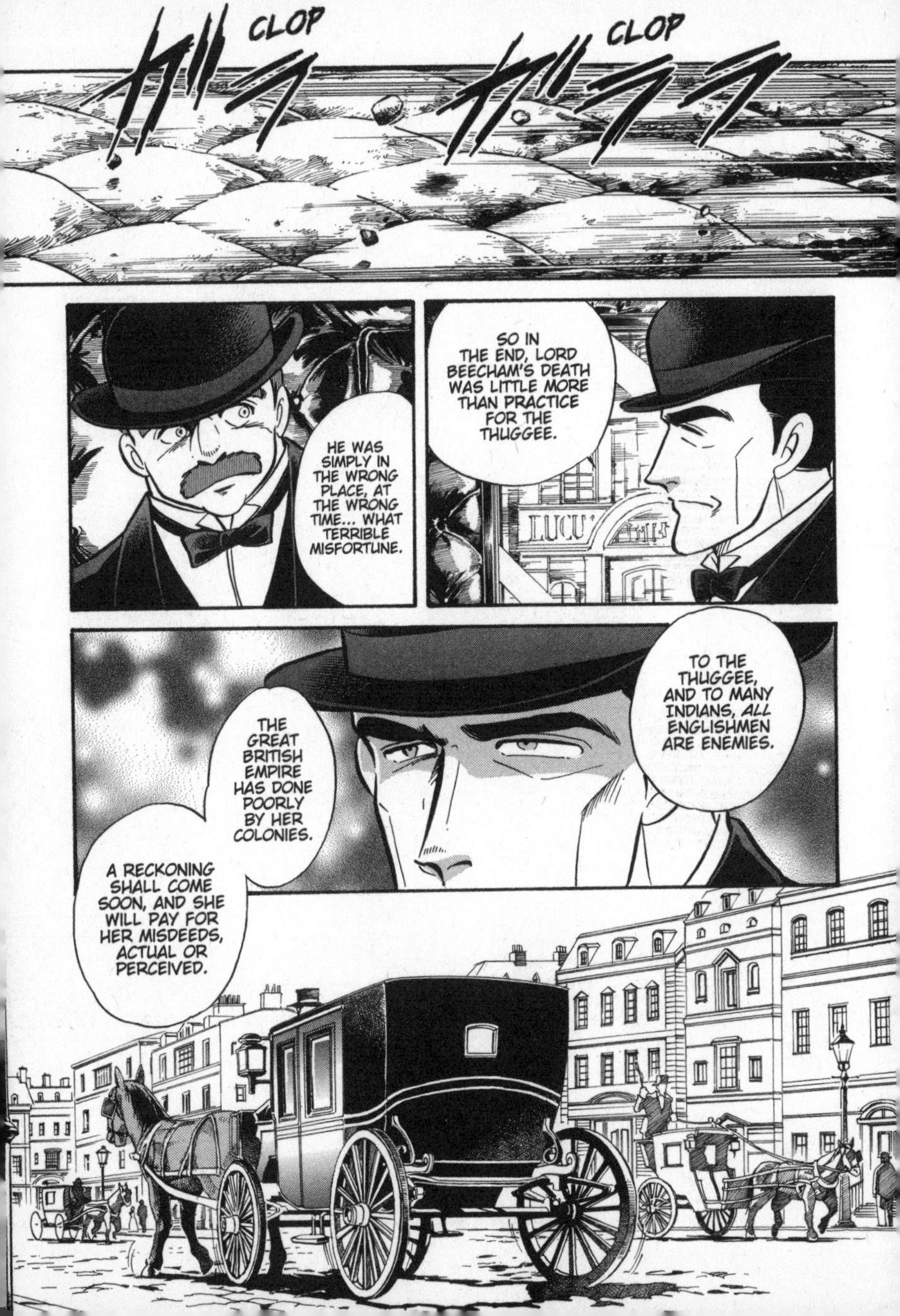
CLOP
CLOP
SO IN THE END, LORD BEECHAM'S DEATH WAS LITTLE MORE THAN PRACTICE FOR THE THUGGEE.
HE WAS SIMPLY IN THE WRONG PLACE, AT THE WRONG TIME... WHAT TERRIBLE MISFORTUNE.
TO THE THUGGEE, AND TO MANY INDIANS, *ALL* ENGLISHMEN ARE ENEMIES.
THE GREAT BRITISH EMPIRE HAS DONE POORLY BY HER COLONIES.
A RECKONING SHALL COME SOON, AND SHE WILL PAY FOR HER MISDEEDS, ACTUAL OR PERCEIVED.

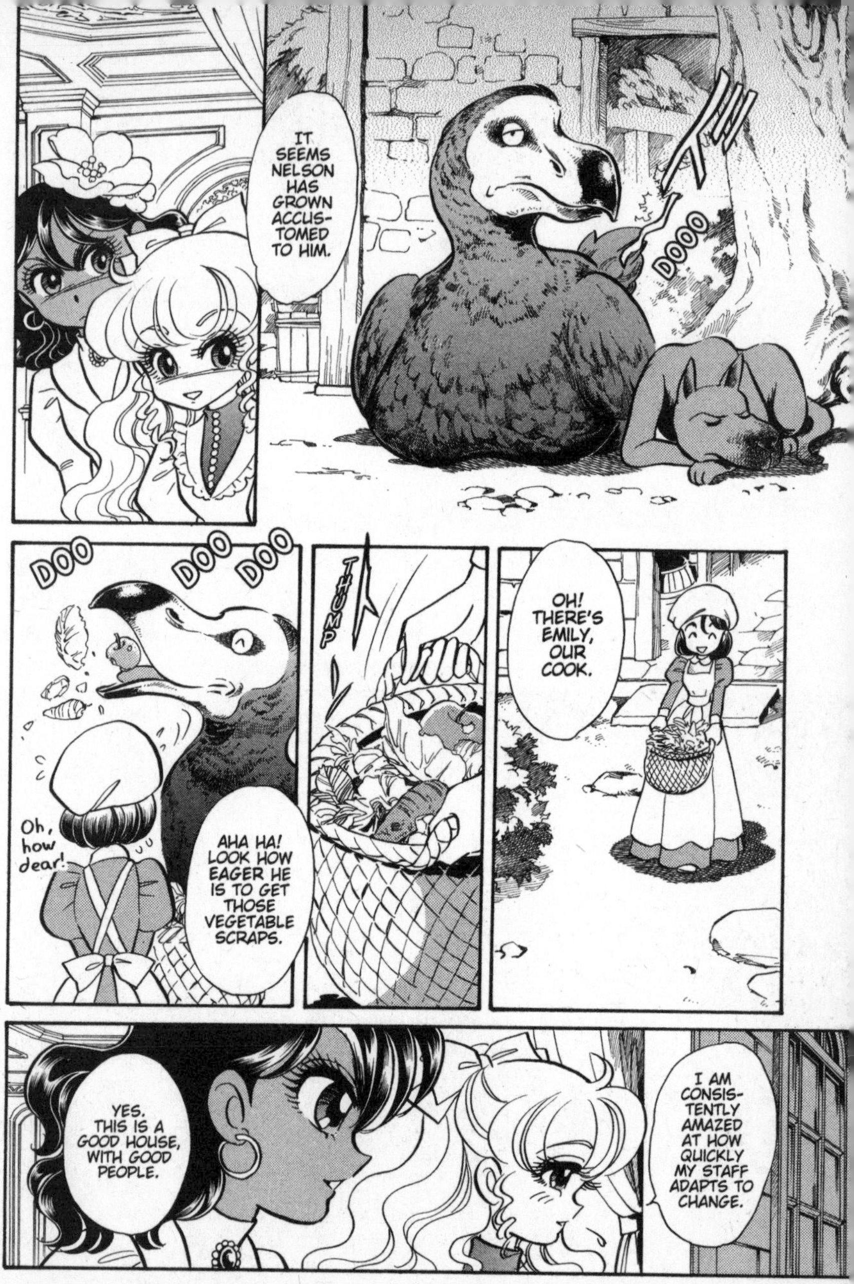
IT SEEMS NELSON HAS GROWN ACCUS-TOMED TO HIM.
DOOO
OH! THERE'S EMILY, OUR COOK.
THUMP
DOO DOO DOO
AHA HA! LOOK HOW EAGER HE IS TO GET THOSE VEGETABLE SCRAPS.
Oh, how dear!
I AM CONSIS-TENTLY AMAZED AT HOW QUICKLY MY STAFF ADAPTS TO CHANGE.
YES. THIS IS A GOOD HOUSE, WITH GOOD PEOPLE.

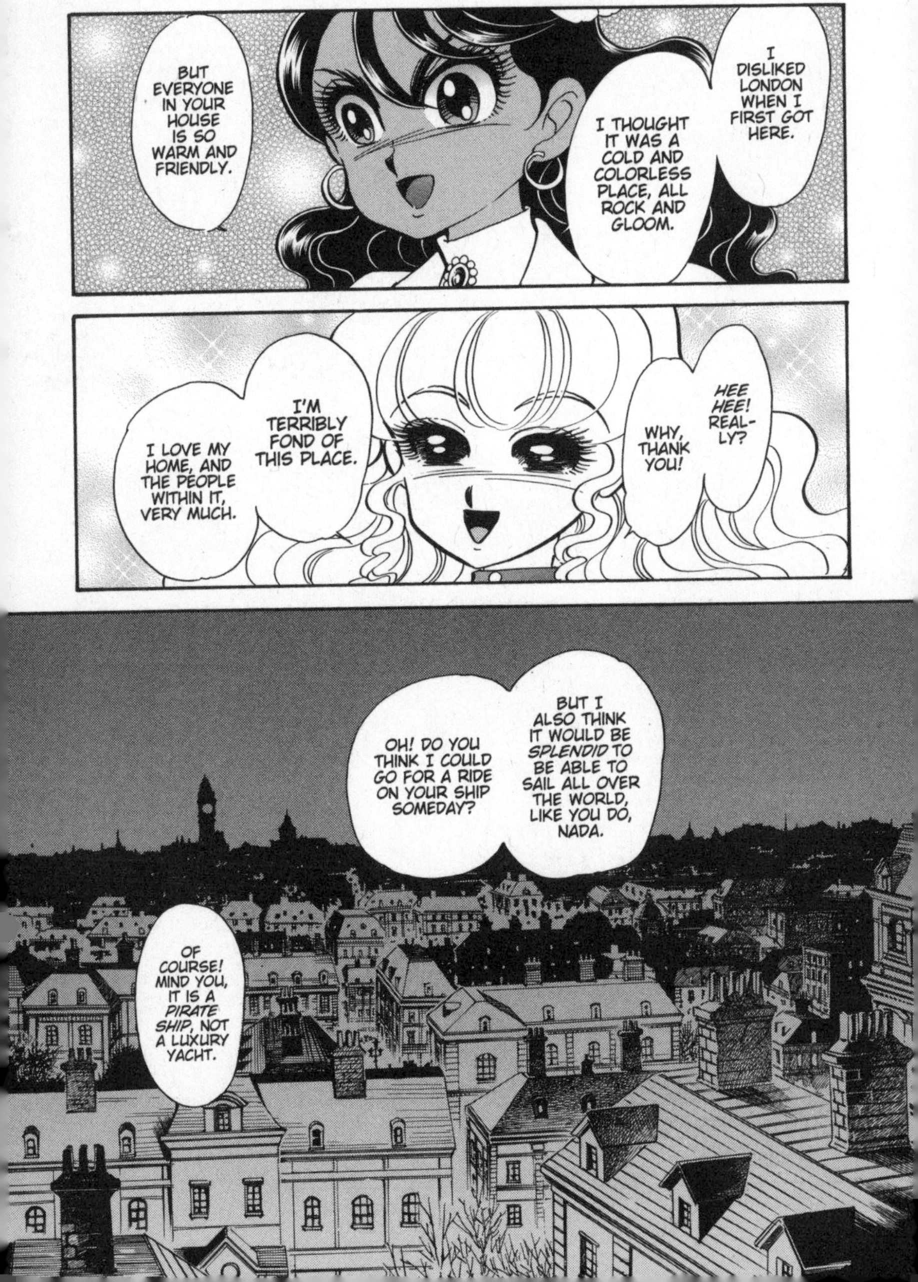
I DISLIKED LONDON WHEN I FIRST GOT HERE.
I THOUGHT IT WAS A COLD AND COLORLESS PLACE, ALL ROCK AND GLOOM.
BUT EVERYONE IN YOUR HOUSE IS SO WARM AND FRIENDLY.
HEE HEE! REAL-LY?
WHY, THANK YOU!
I'M TERRIBLY FOND OF THIS PLACE.
I LOVE MY HOME, AND THE PEOPLE WITHIN IT, VERY MUCH.
BUT I ALSO THINK IT WOULD BE *SPLENDID* TO BE ABLE TO SAIL ALL OVER THE WORLD, LIKE YOU DO, NADA.
OH! DO YOU THINK I COULD GO FOR A RIDE ON YOUR SHIP SOMEDAY?
OF COURSE! MIND YOU, IT IS A *PIRATE SHIP*, NOT A LUXURY YACHT.

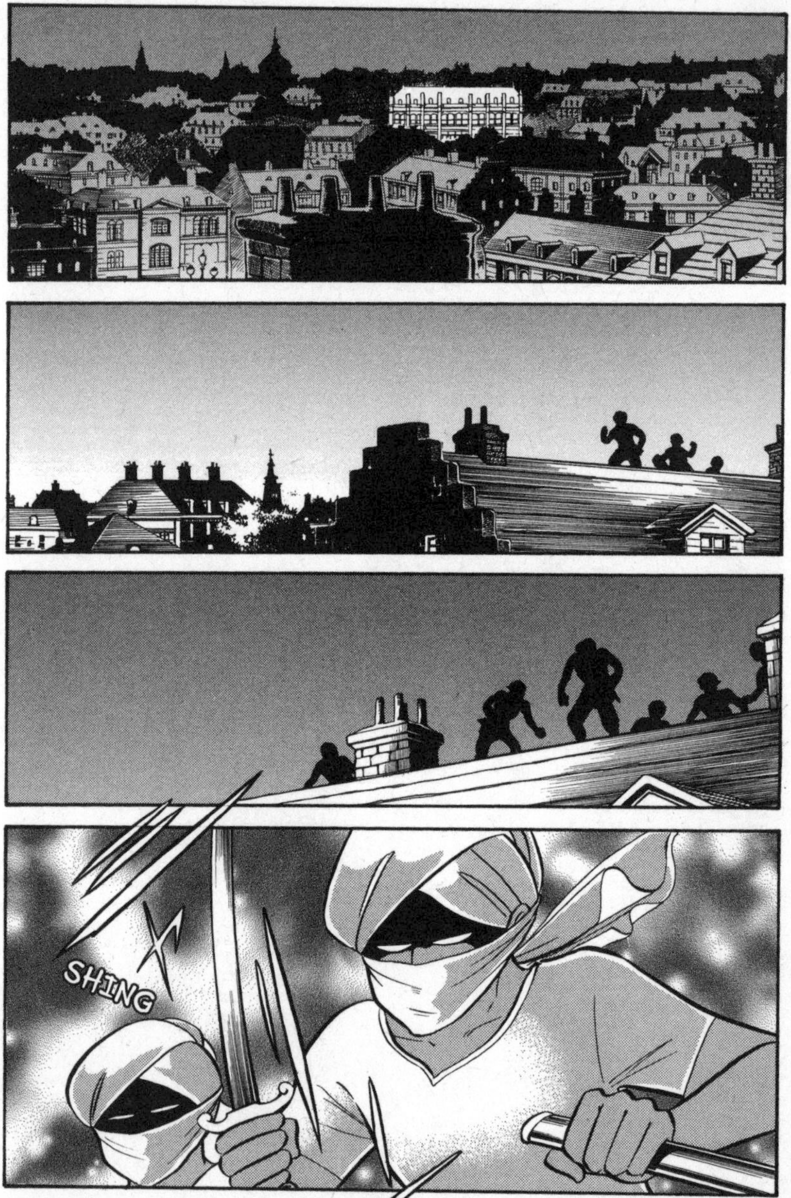
SHING

The Adventure of The Giant Rat of Sumatra (6)

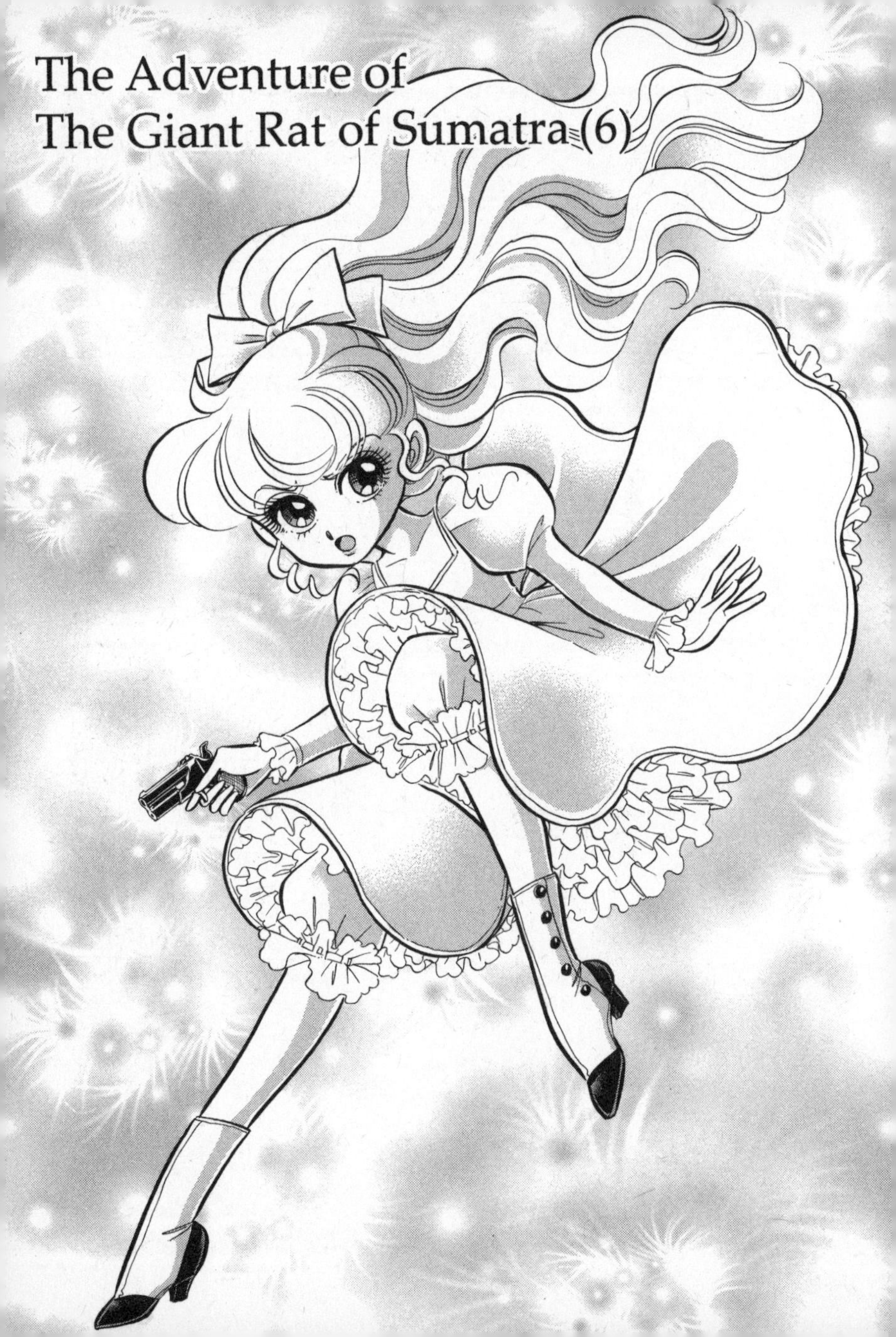

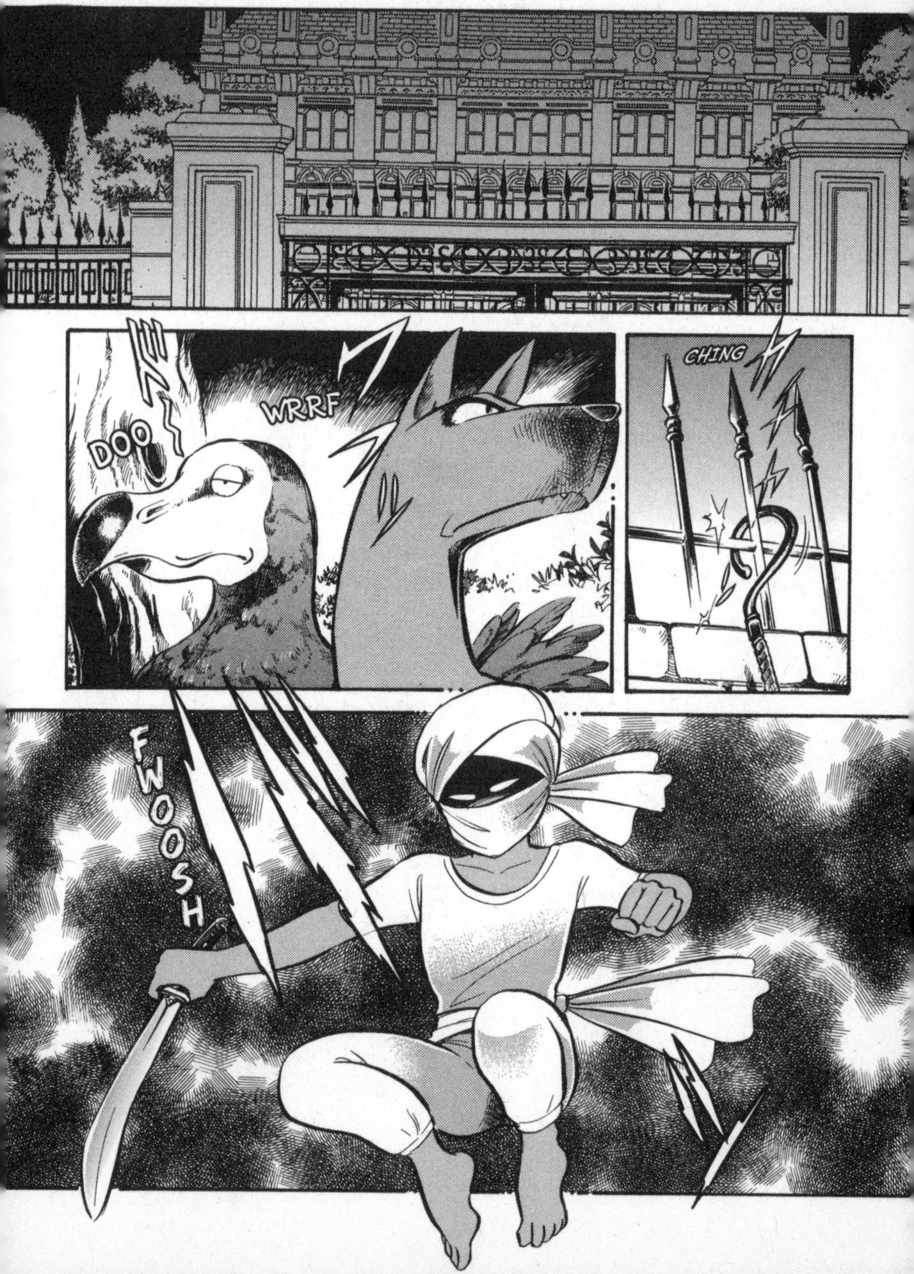
CHING
WRRF
DOO
FWOOSH

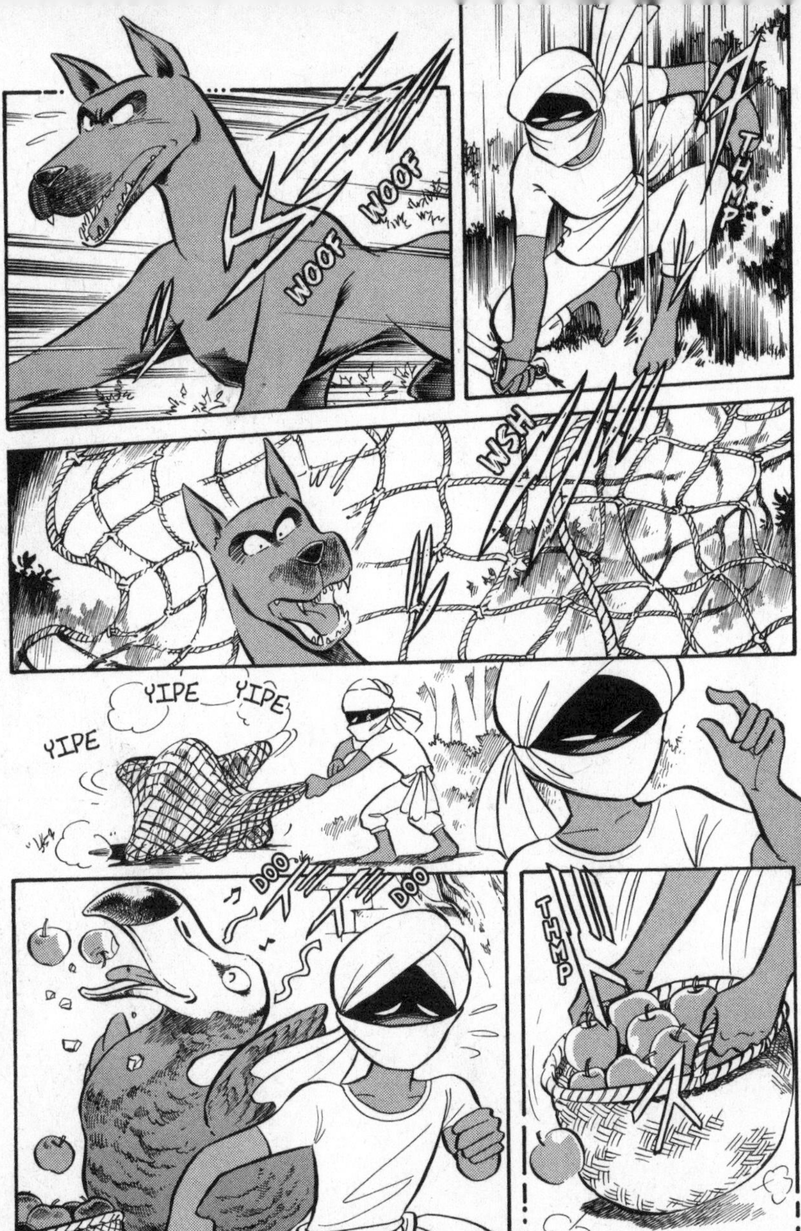
THMP
WOOF
WOOF
WOOF
WSH
YIPE
YIPE
YIPE
THMP
DOO
DOO

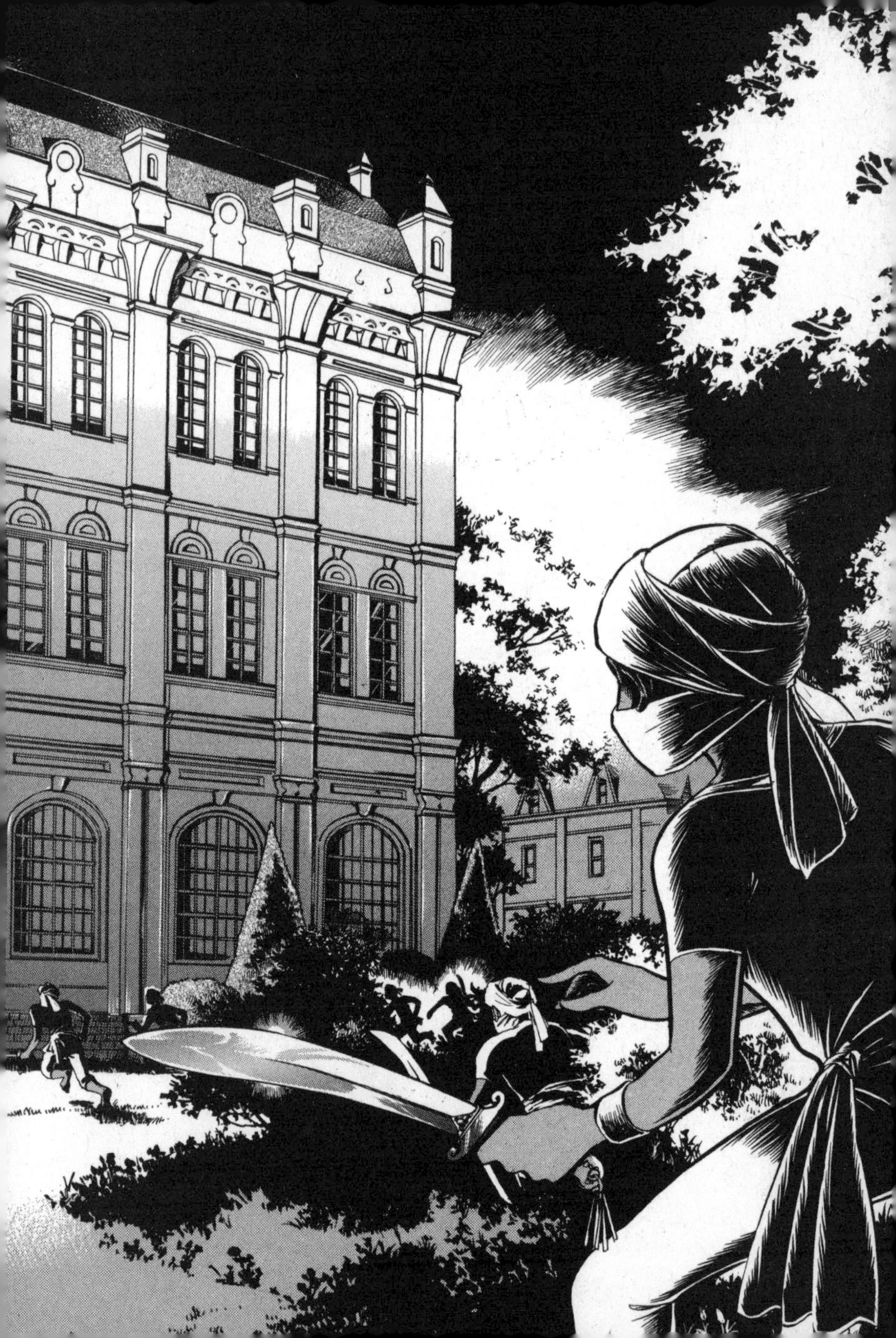

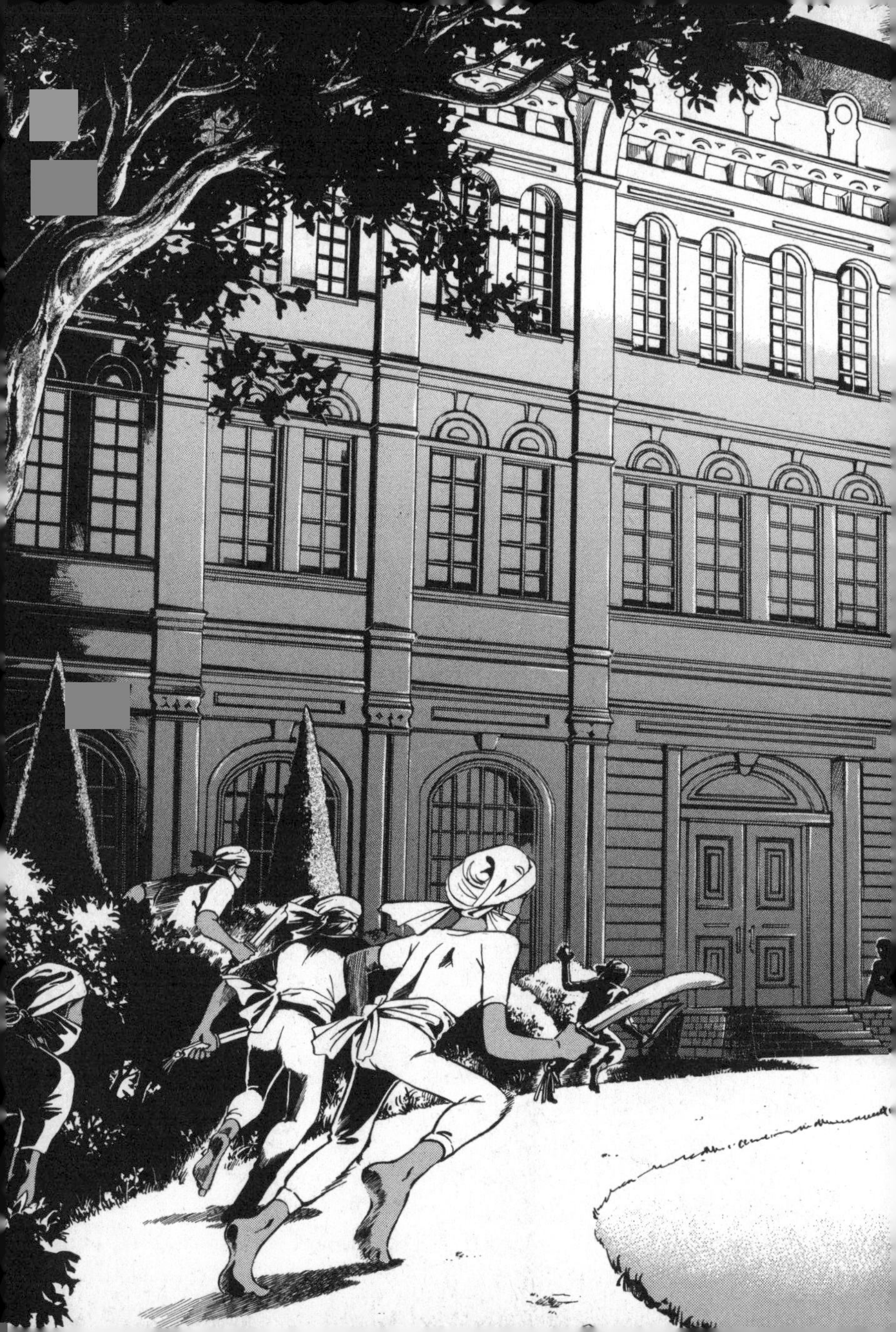

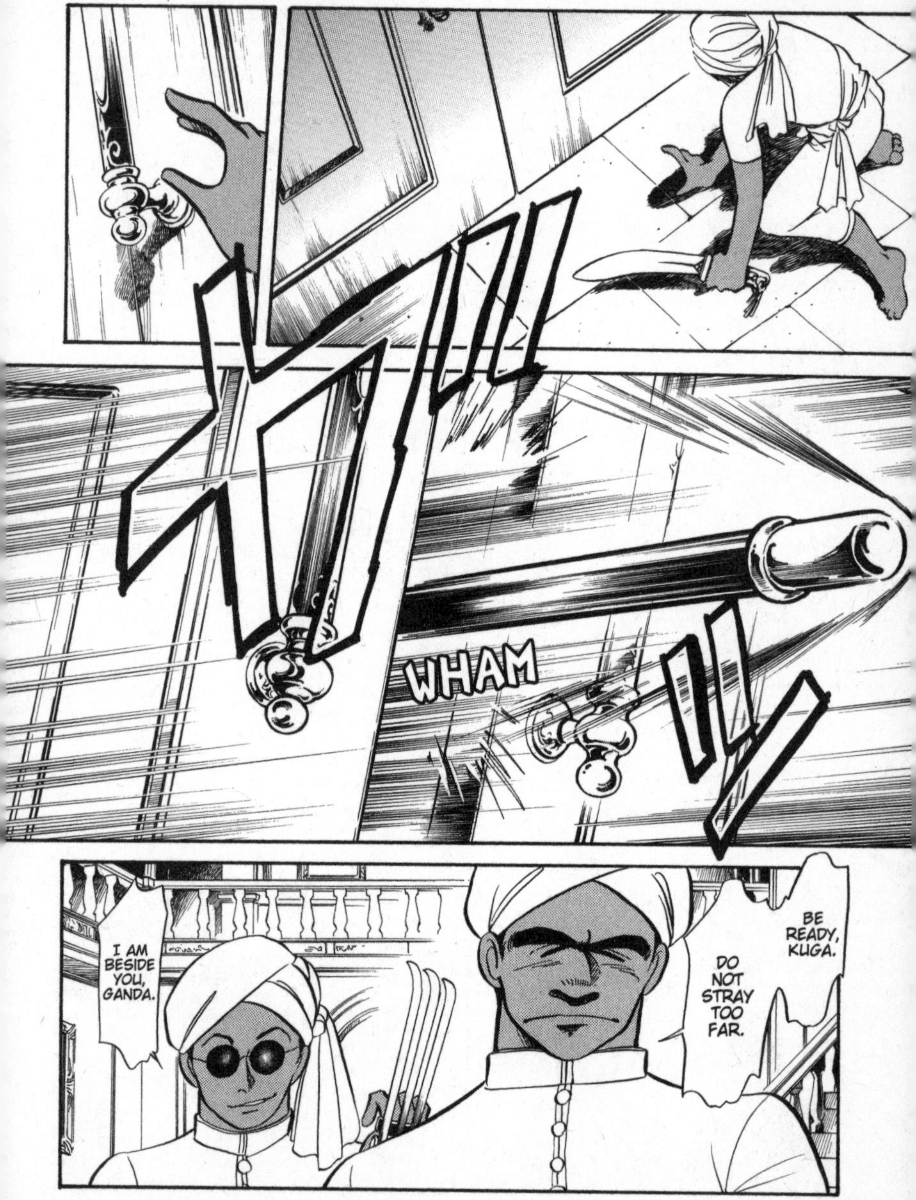
WHAM
BE READY, KUGA.
DO NOT STRAY TOO FAR.
I AM BESIDE YOU, GANDA.

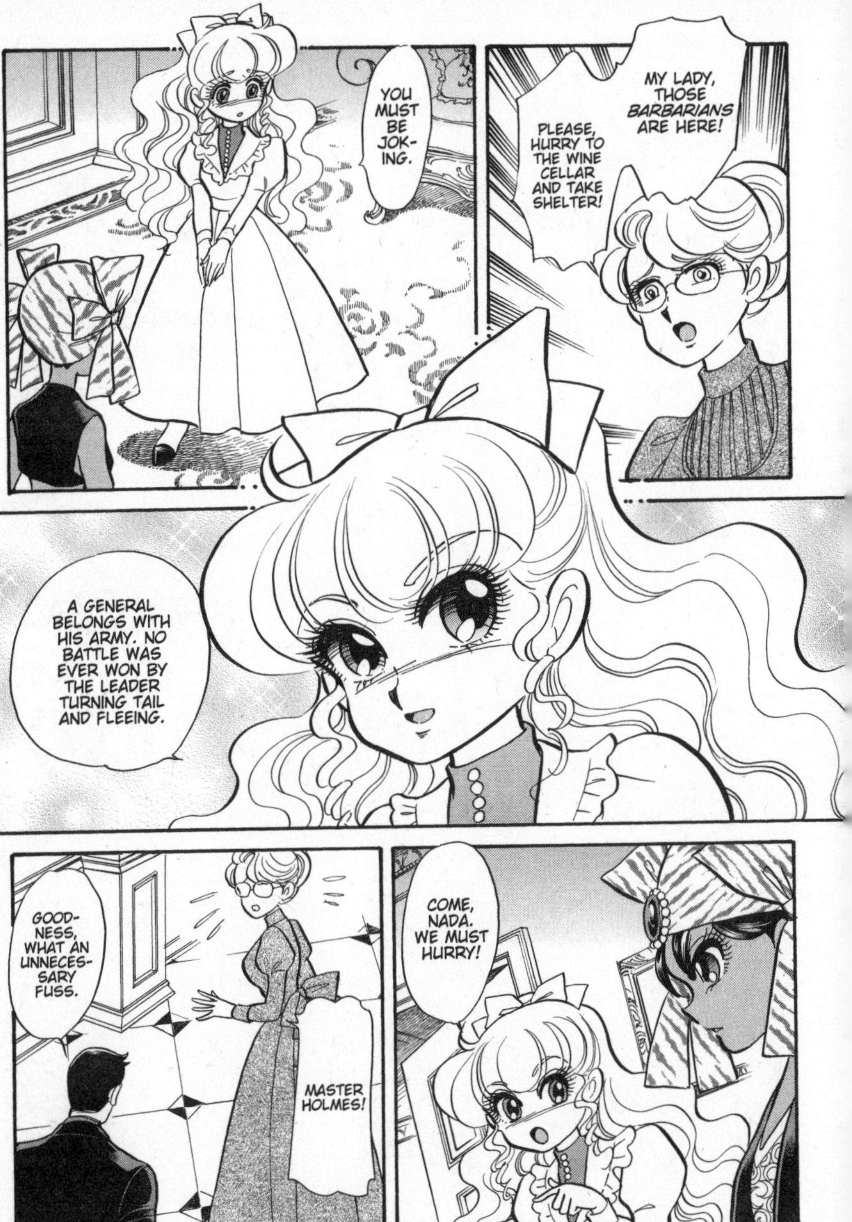
MY LADY, THOSE *BARBARIANS* ARE HERE!
PLEASE, HURRY TO THE WINE CELLAR AND TAKE SHELTER!
YOU MUST BE JOK-ING.
A GENERAL BELONGS WITH HIS ARMY. NO BATTLE WAS EVER WON BY THE LEADER TURNING TAIL AND FLEEING.
COME, NADA. WE MUST HURRY!
MASTER HOLMES!
GOODNESS, WHAT AN UNNECES-SARY FUSS.

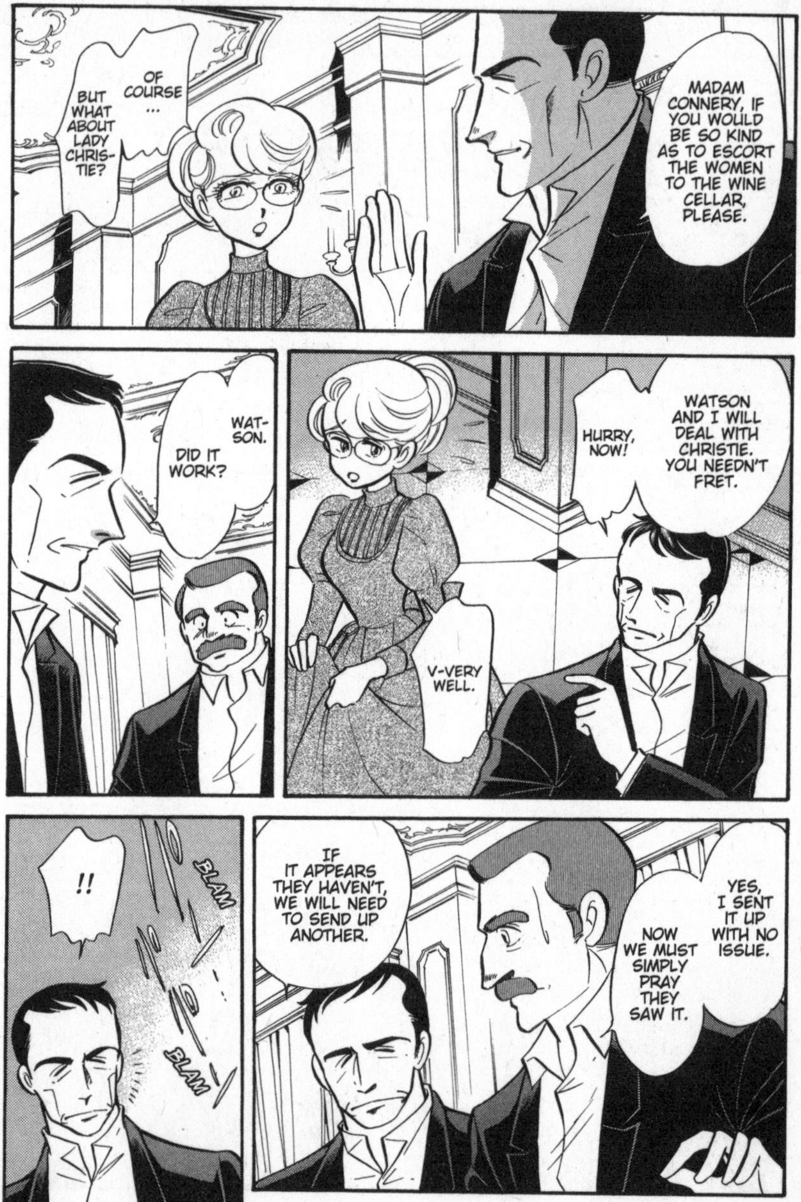
MADAM CONNERY, IF YOU WOULD BE SO KIND AS TO ESCORT THE WOMEN TO THE WINE CELLAR, PLEASE.
OF COURSE ...
BUT WHAT ABOUT LADY CHRIS-TIE?
WATSON AND I WILL DEAL WITH CHRISTIE. YOU NEEDN'T FRET.
HURRY, NOW!
V-VERY WELL.
WAT-SON.
DID IT WORK?
YES, I SENT IT UP WITH NO ISSUE.
NOW WE MUST SIMPLY PRAY THEY SAW IT.
IF IT APPEARS THEY HAVEN'T, WE WILL NEED TO SEND UP ANOTHER.
!!
BLAM
BLAM

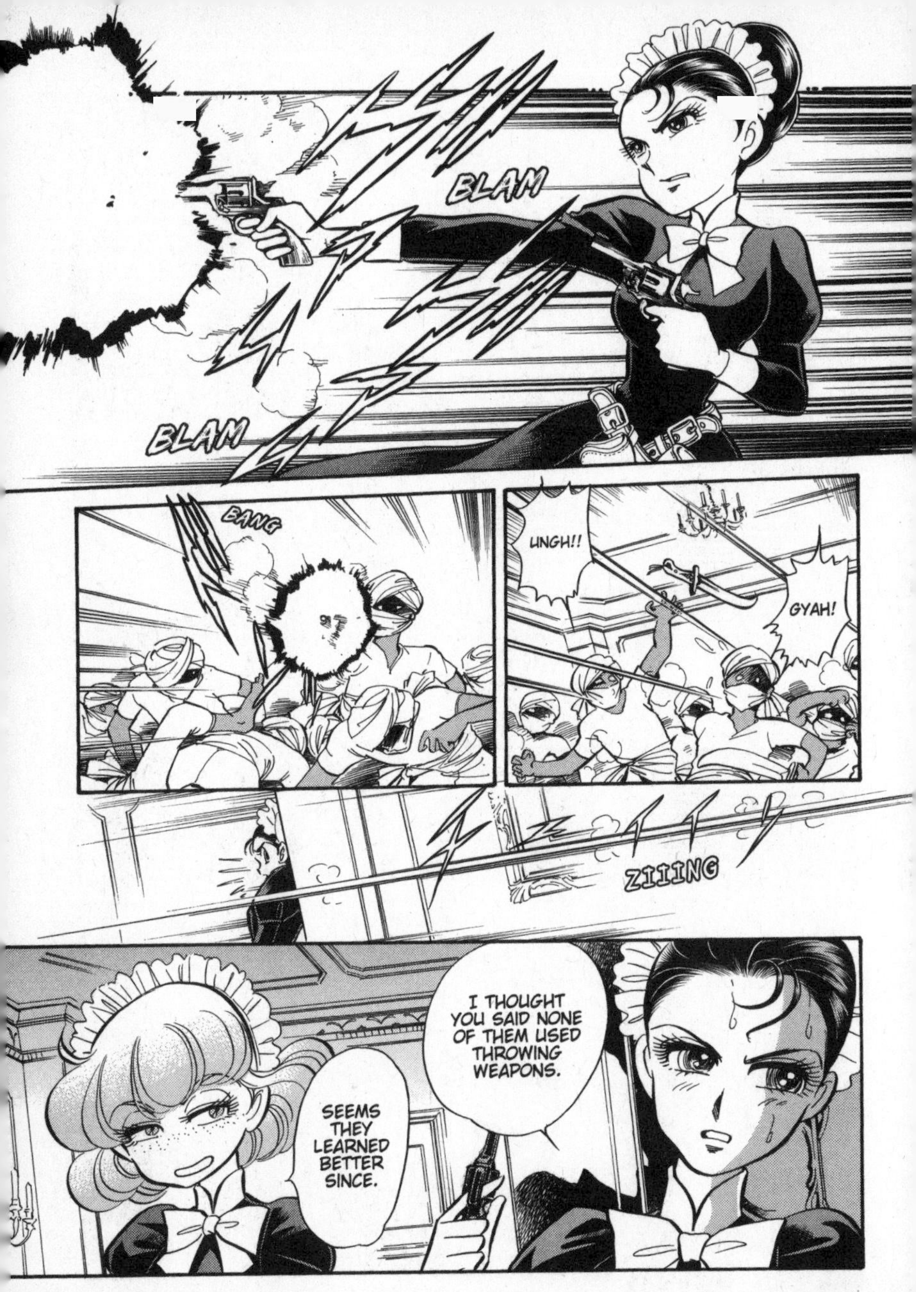
BLAM
BLAM
UNGH!!
GYAH!
BANG
ZIIING
I THOUGHT YOU SAID NONE OF THEM USED THROWING WEAPONS.
SEEMS THEY LEARNED BETTER SINCE.

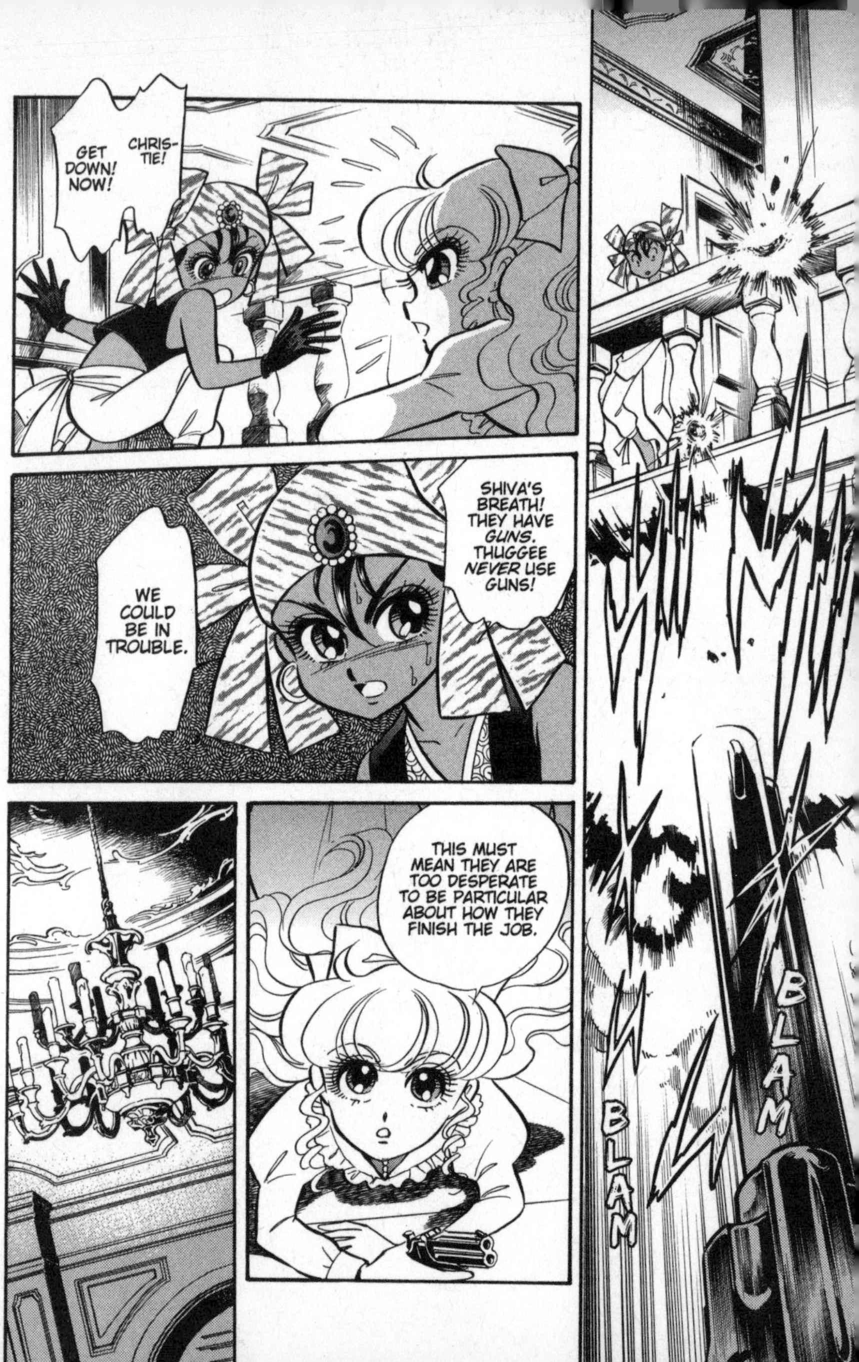
BLAM
BLAM
CHRIS-TIE!
GET DOWN! NOW!
SHIVA'S BREATH! THEY HAVE GUNS. THUGGEE NEVER USE GUNS!
WE COULD BE IN TROUBLE.
THIS MUST MEAN THEY ARE TOO DESPERATE TO BE PARTICULAR ABOUT HOW THEY FINISH THE JOB.

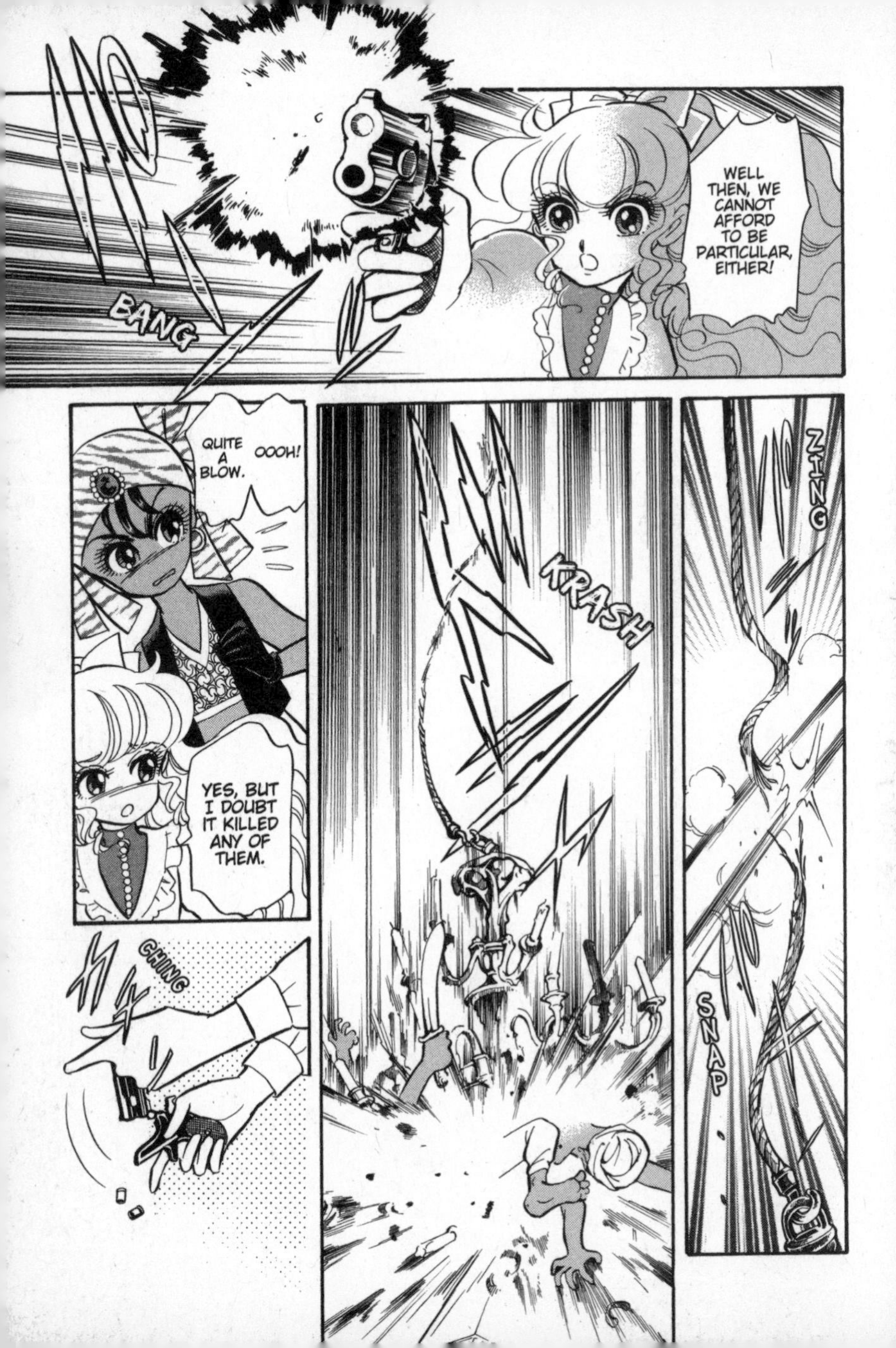
WELL THEN, WE CANNOT AFFORD TO BE PARTICULAR, EITHER!
BANG
ZING
SNAP
KRASH
OOOH!
QUITE A BLOW.
YES, BUT I DOUBT IT KILLED ANY OF THEM.
CHING

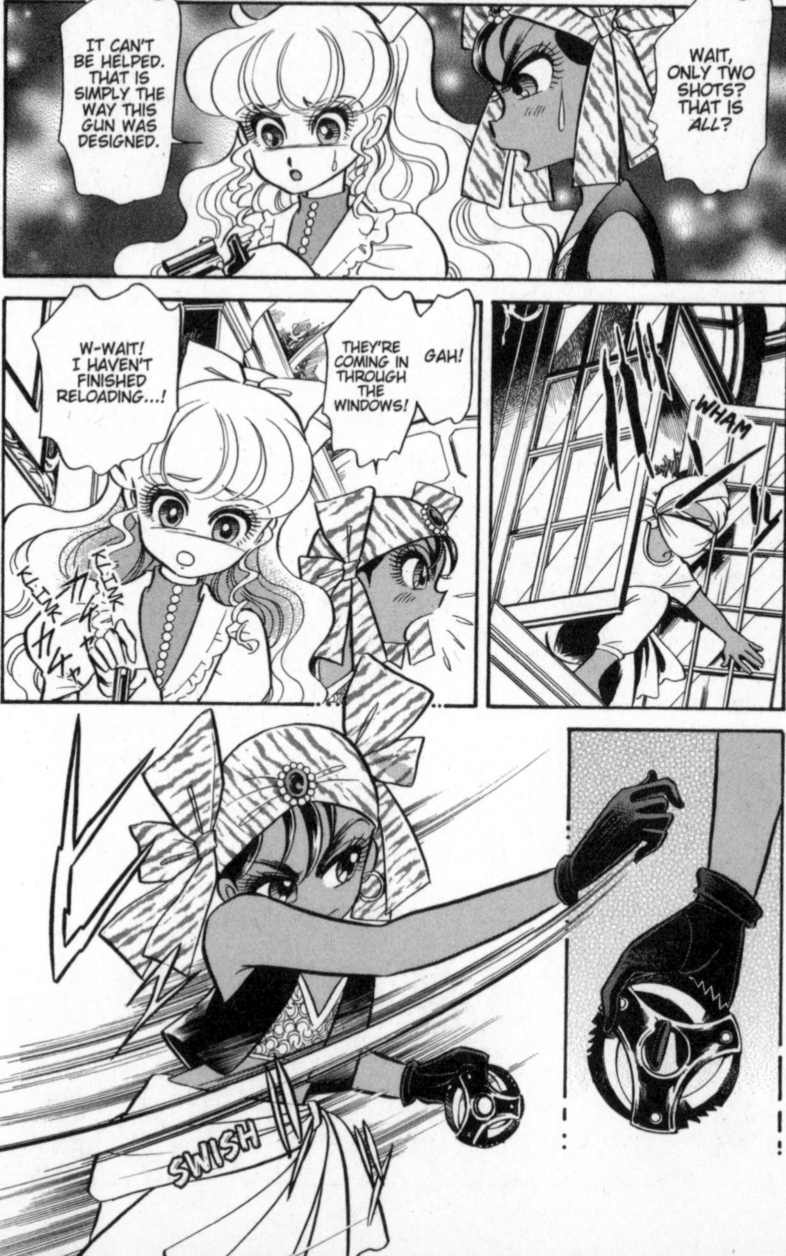
WAIT, ONLY TWO SHOTS? THAT IS ALL?
IT CAN'T BE HELPED. THAT IS SIMPLY THE WAY THIS GUN WAS DESIGNED.
WHAM
GAH!
THEY'RE COMING IN THROUGH THE WINDOWS!
W-WAIT! I HAVEN'T FINISHED RELOADING...!
KLINK
KLINK
SWISH

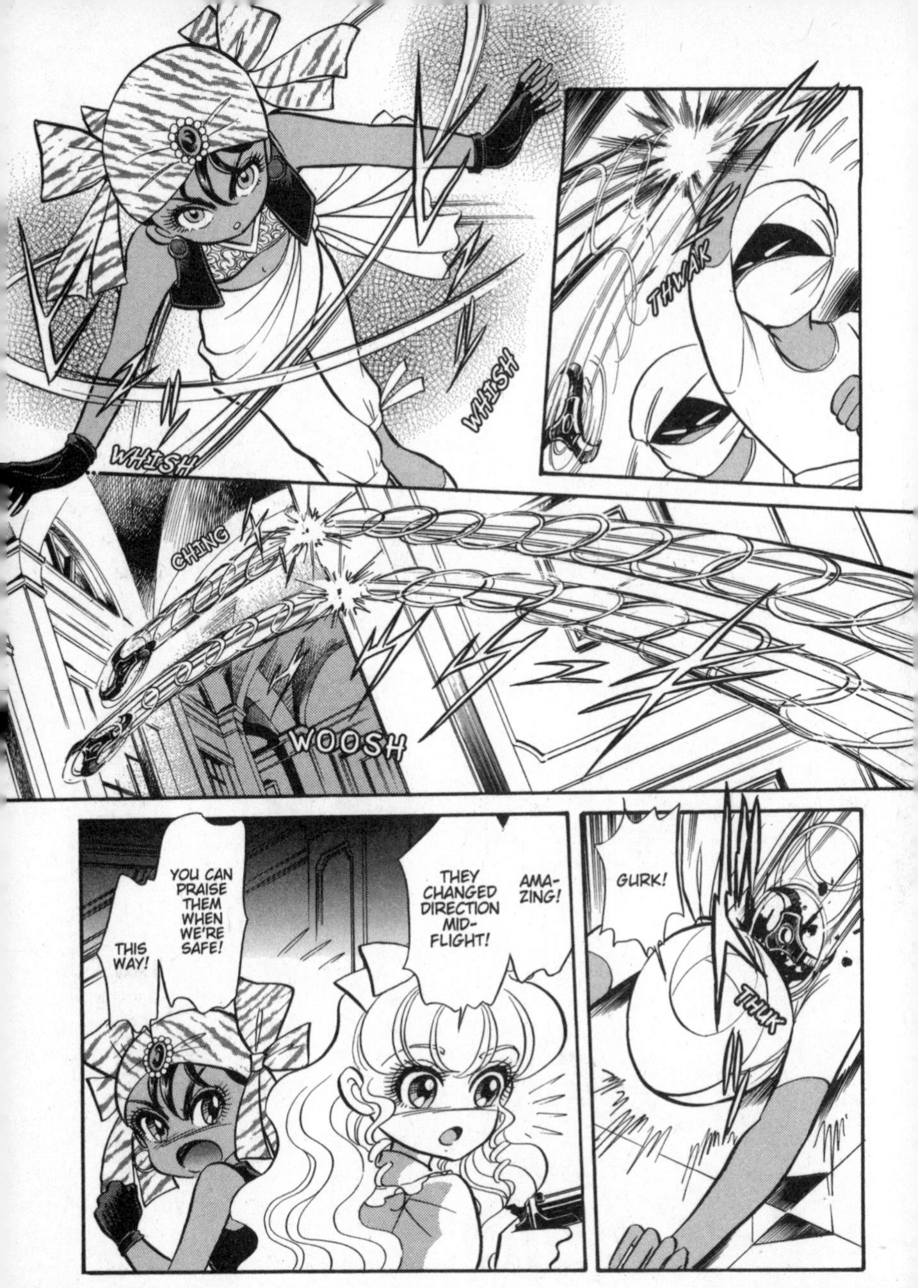
THWAK
WHISH
WHISH
CHING
WOOSH
GURK!
THUK
AMA-ZING!
THEY CHANGED DIRECTION MID-FLIGHT!
YOU CAN PRAISE THEM WHEN WE'RE SAFE!
THIS WAY!

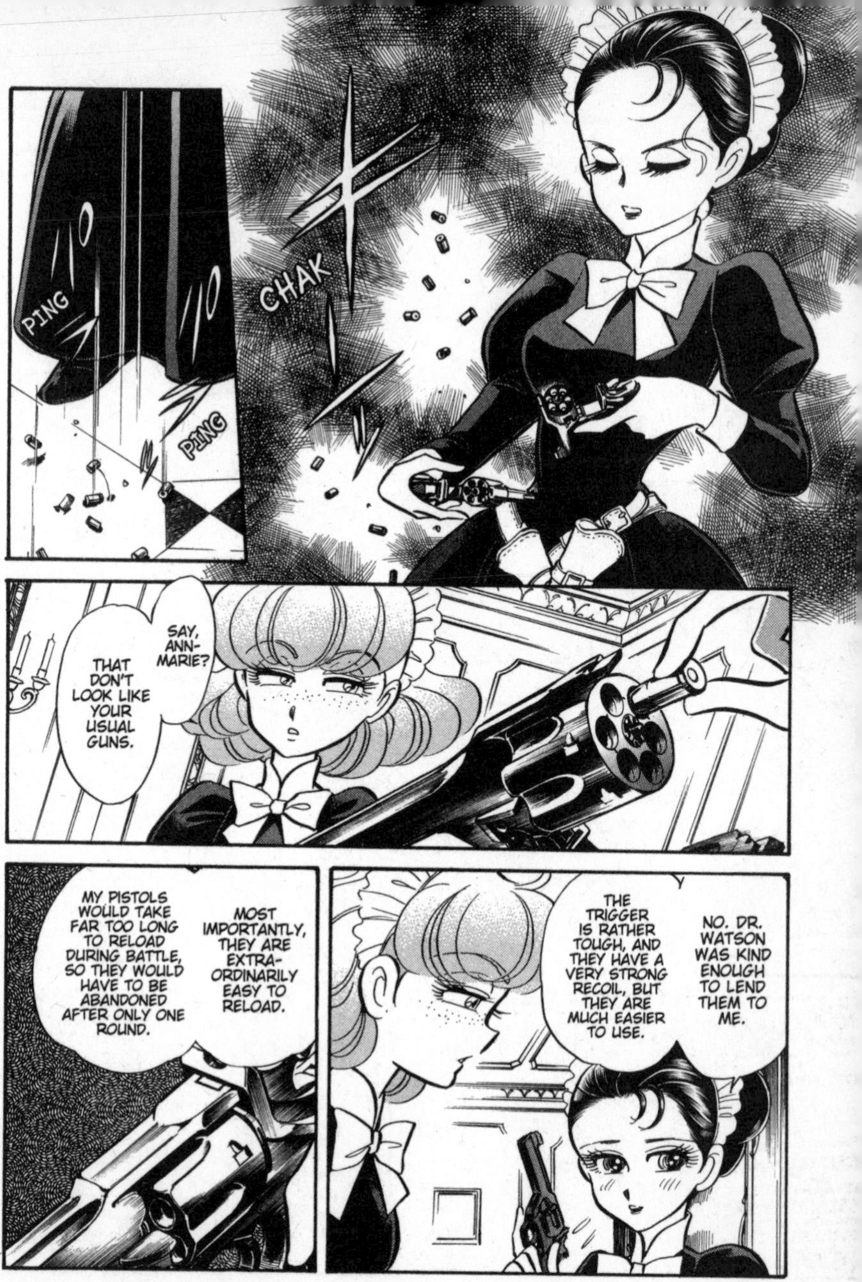
CHAK
PING
PING
SAY, ANN-MARIE?
THAT DON'T LOOK LIKE YOUR USUAL GUNS.
NO. DR. WATSON WAS KIND ENOUGH TO LEND THEM TO ME.
THE TRIGGER IS RATHER TOUGH, AND THEY HAVE A VERY STRONG RECOIL, BUT THEY ARE MUCH EASIER TO USE.
MOST IMPORTANTLY, THEY ARE EXTRA-ORDINARILY EASY TO RELOAD.
MY PISTOLS WOULD TAKE FAR TOO LONG TO RELOAD DURING BATTLE, SO THEY WOULD HAVE TO BE ABANDONED AFTER ONLY ONE ROUND.

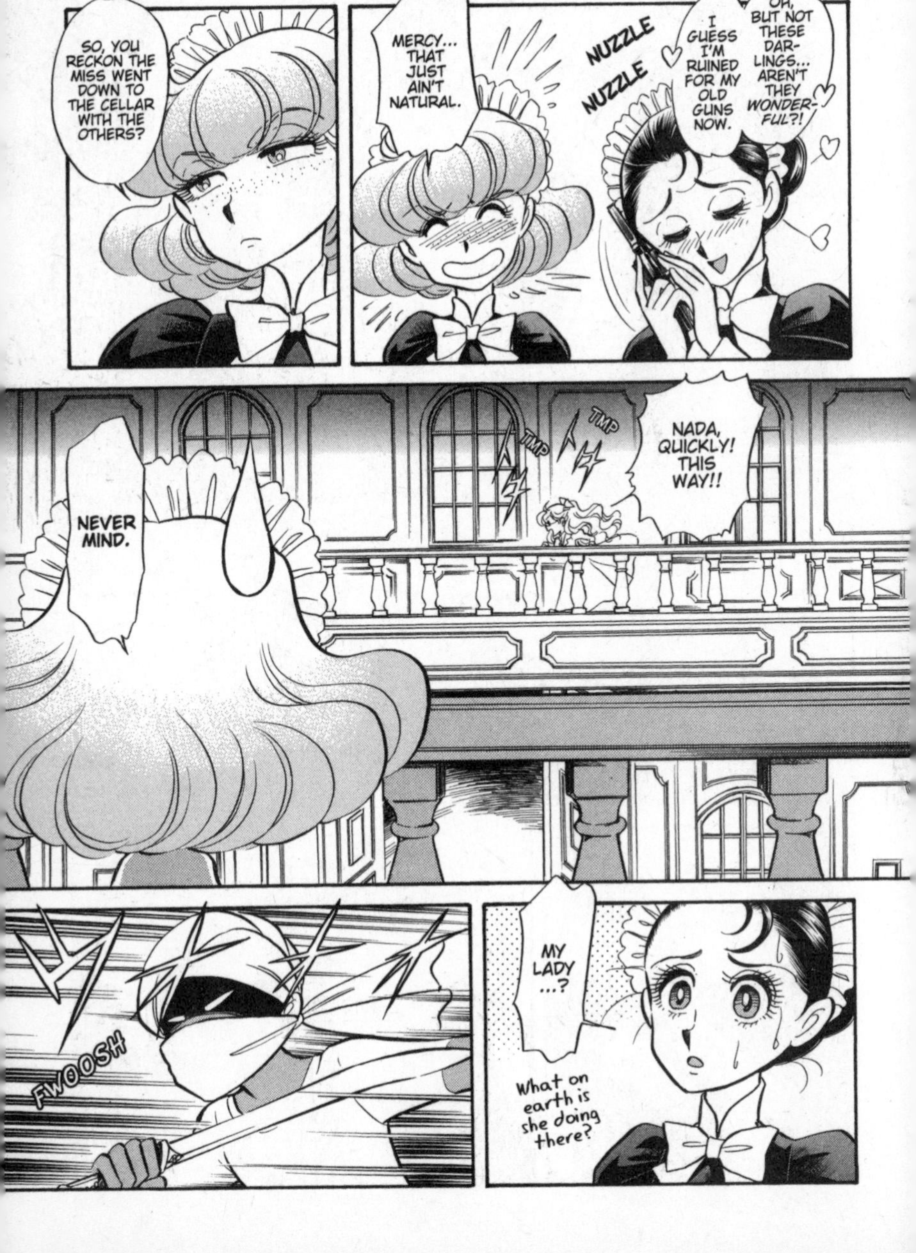
OH, BUT NOT THESE DARLINGS... AREN'T THEY WONDERFUL?!
I GUESS I'M RUINED FOR MY OLD GUNS NOW.
NUZZLE NUZZLE
MERCY... THAT JUST AIN'T NATURAL.
SO, YOU RECKON THE MISS WENT DOWN TO THE CELLAR WITH THE OTHERS?
NADA, QUICKLY! THIS WAY!!
TMP TMP
NEVER MIND.
MY LADY ...?
What on earth is she doing there?
FWOOSH

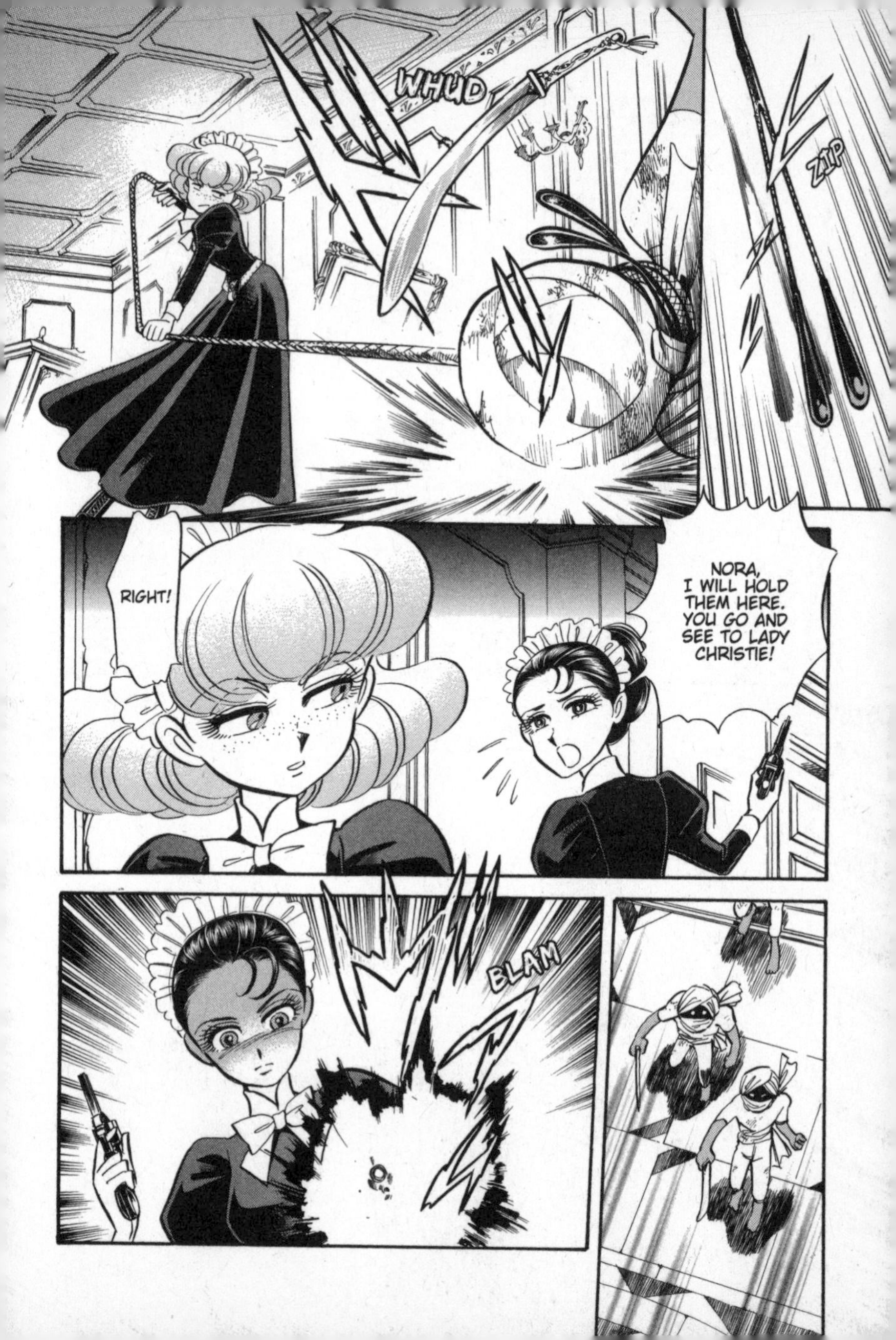
ZIP
WHUD
NORA, I WILL HOLD THEM HERE. YOU GO AND SEE TO LADY CHRISTIE!
RIGHT!
BLAM

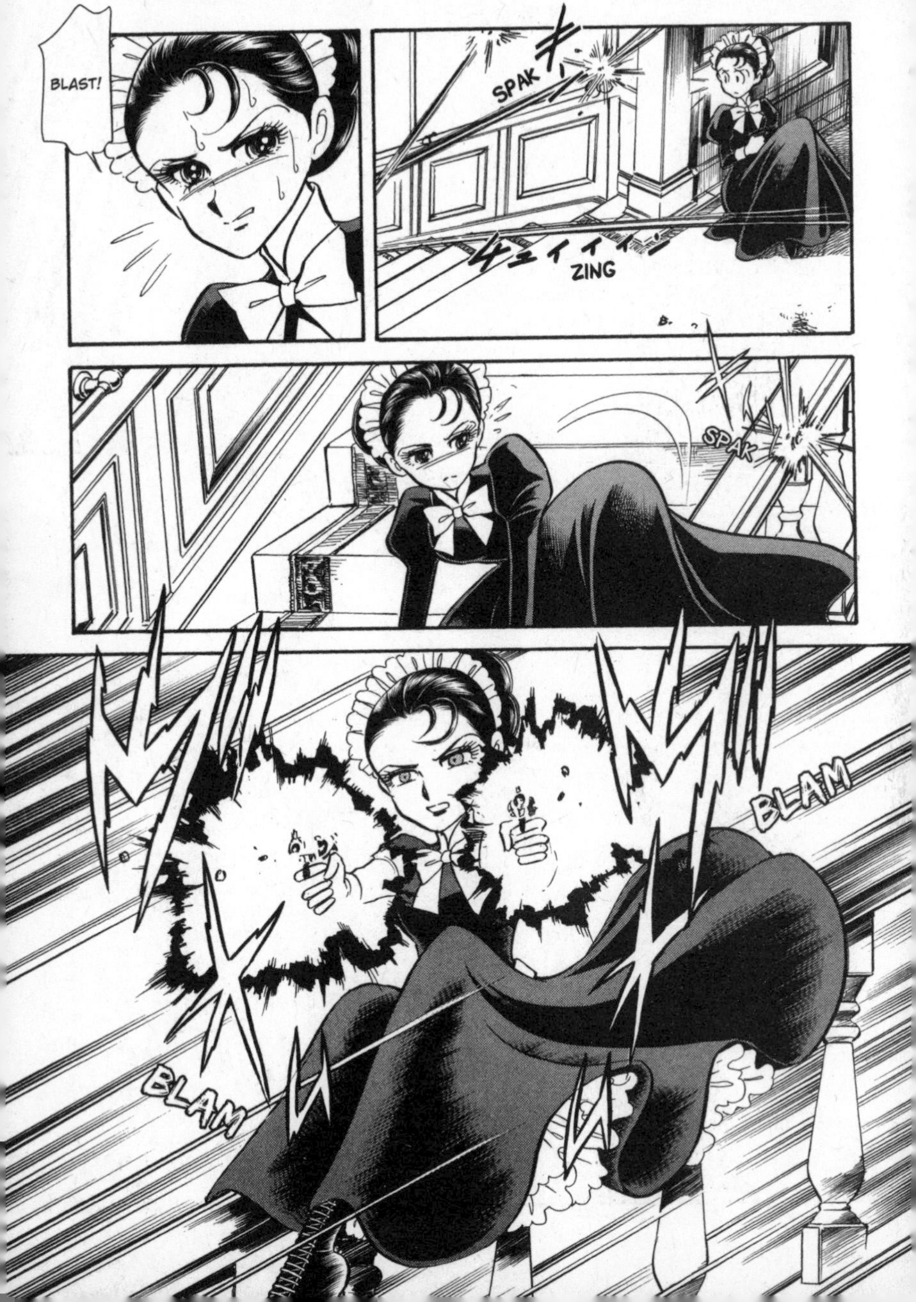
SPAK
ZING
BLAST!
SPAK
BLAM
BLAM

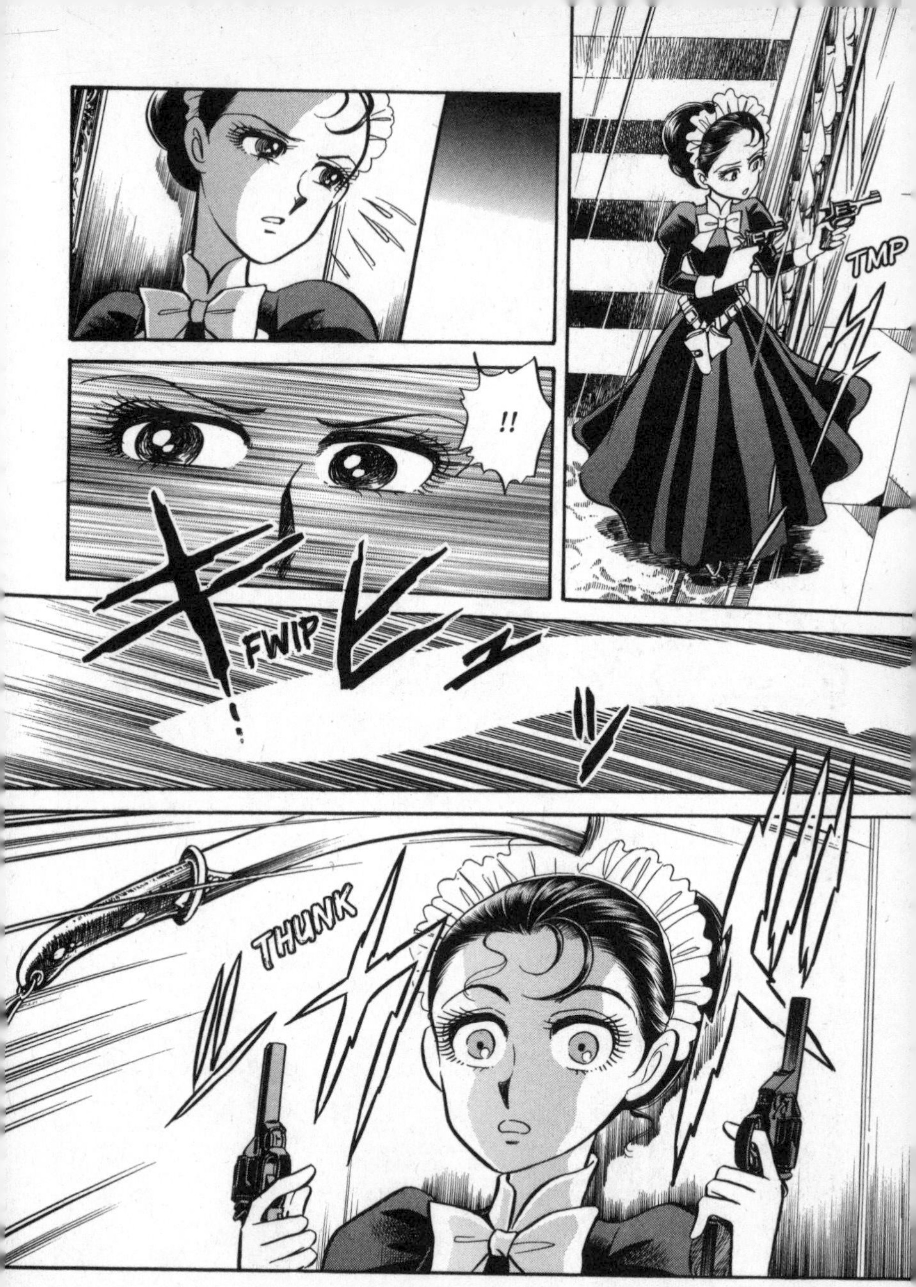
TMP
!!
FWIP
THUNK

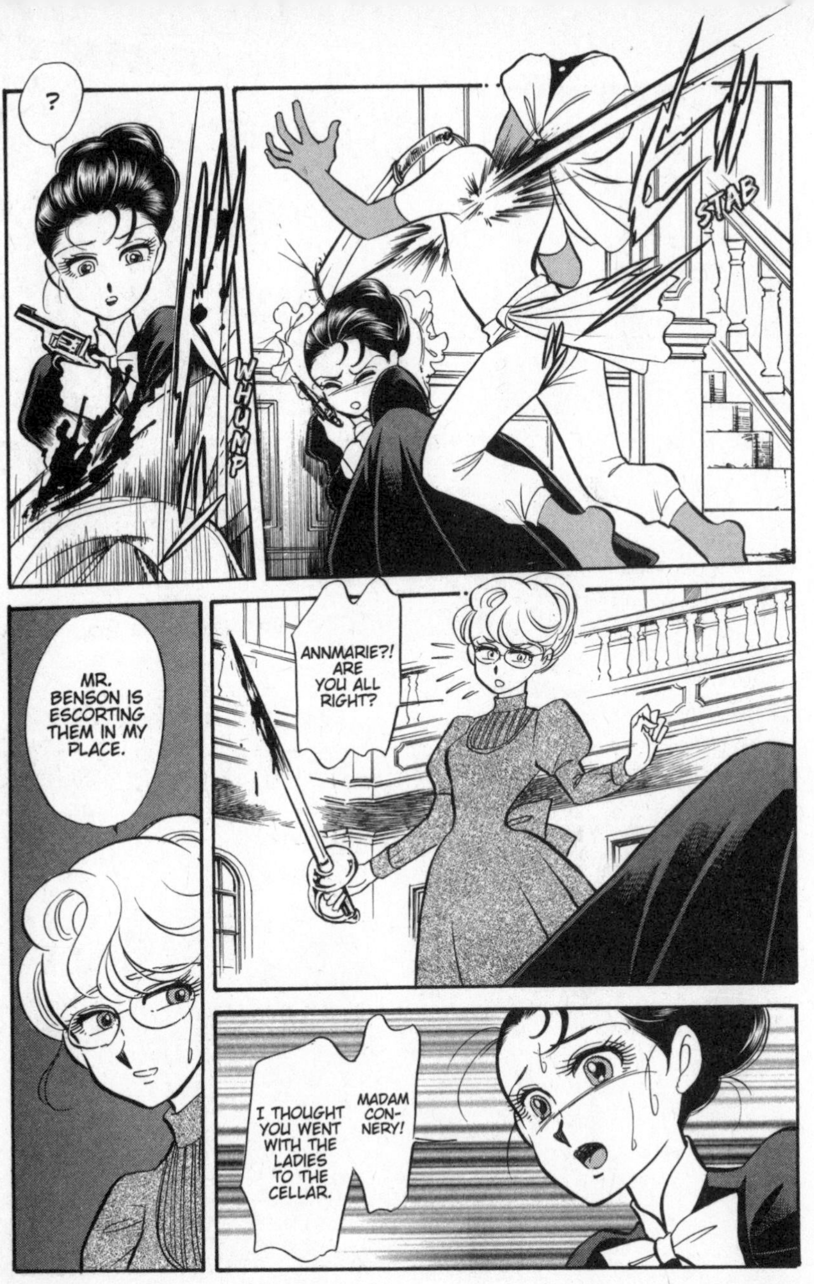
STAB
?
WHUMP
ANNMARIE?! ARE YOU ALL RIGHT?
MADAM CON-NERY!
I THOUGHT YOU WENT WITH THE LADIES TO THE CELLAR.
MR. BENSON IS ESCORTING THEM IN MY PLACE.

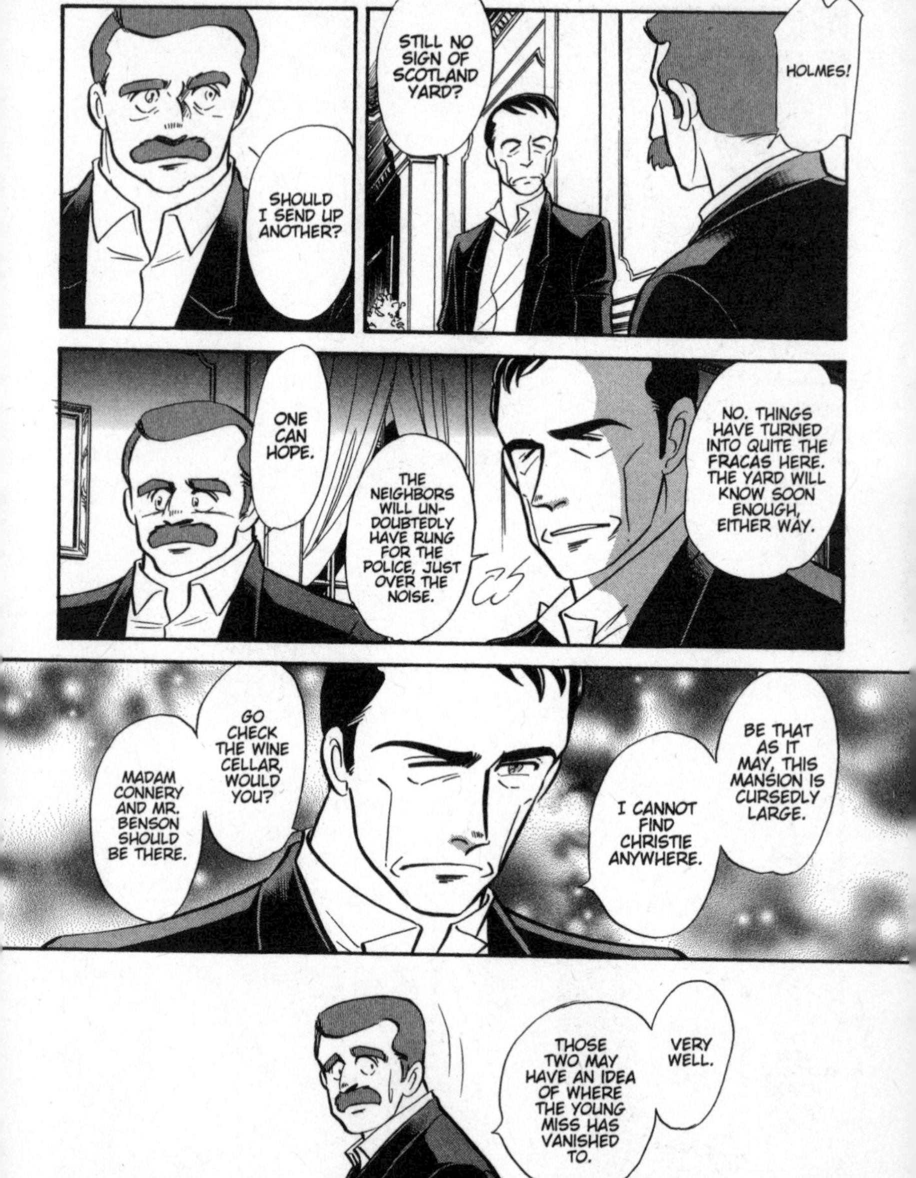
HOLMES!
STILL NO SIGN OF SCOTLAND YARD?
SHOULD I SEND UP ANOTHER?
NO. THINGS HAVE TURNED INTO QUITE THE FRACAS HERE. THE YARD WILL KNOW SOON ENOUGH, EITHER WAY.
THE NEIGHBORS WILL UN-DOUBTEDLY HAVE RUNG FOR THE POLICE, JUST OVER THE NOISE.
ONE CAN HOPE.
BE THAT AS IT MAY, THIS MANSION IS CURSEDLY LARGE.
I CANNOT FIND CHRISTIE ANYWHERE.
GO CHECK THE WINE CELLAR, WOULD YOU?
MADAM CONNERY AND MR. BENSON SHOULD BE THERE.
VERY WELL.
THOSE TWO MAY HAVE AN IDEA OF WHERE THE YOUNG MISS HAS VANISHED TO.

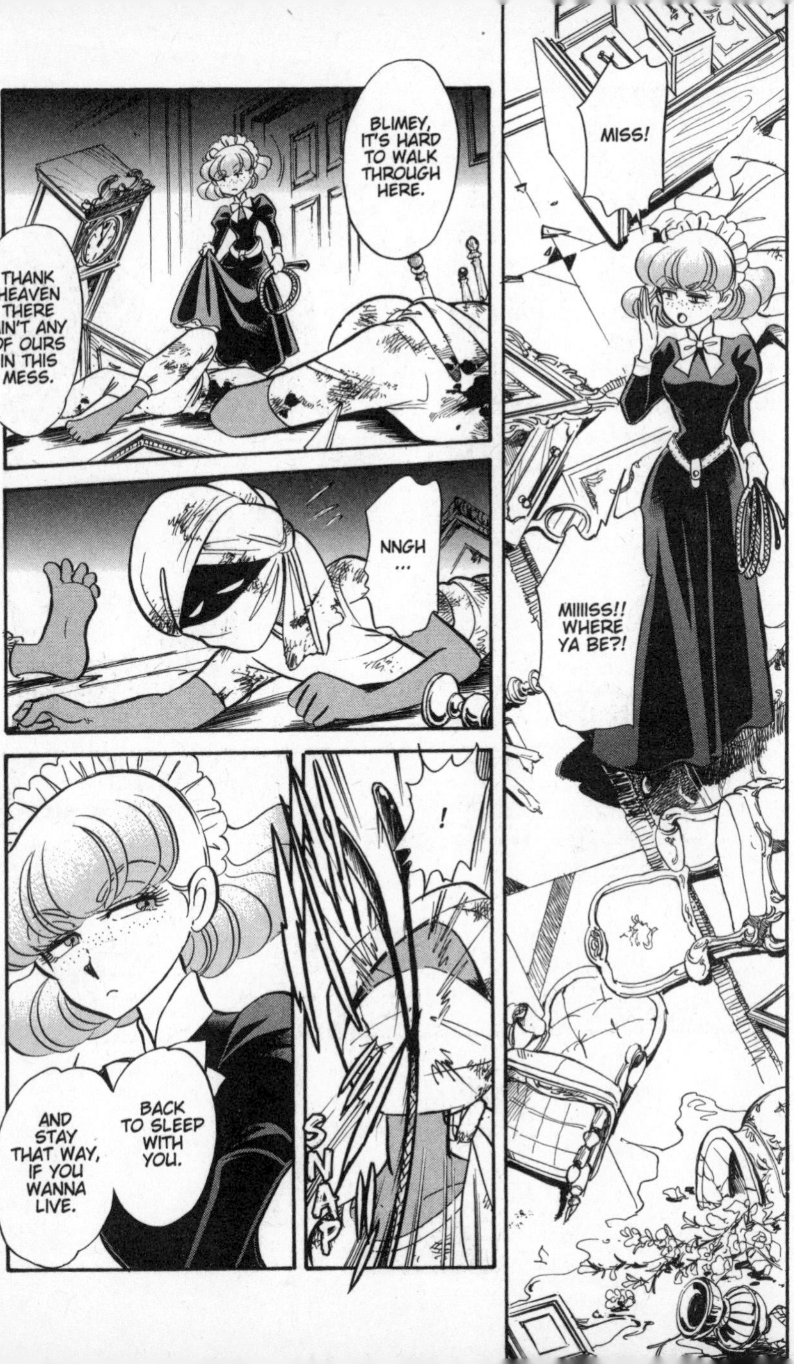
MISS!
MIIIISS!! WHERE YA BE?!
BLIMEY, IT'S HARD TO WALK THROUGH HERE.
THANK HEAVEN THERE AIN'T ANY OF OURS IN THIS MESS.
NNGH ...
!
SNAP
BACK TO SLEEP WITH YOU.
AND STAY THAT WAY, IF YOU WANNA LIVE.

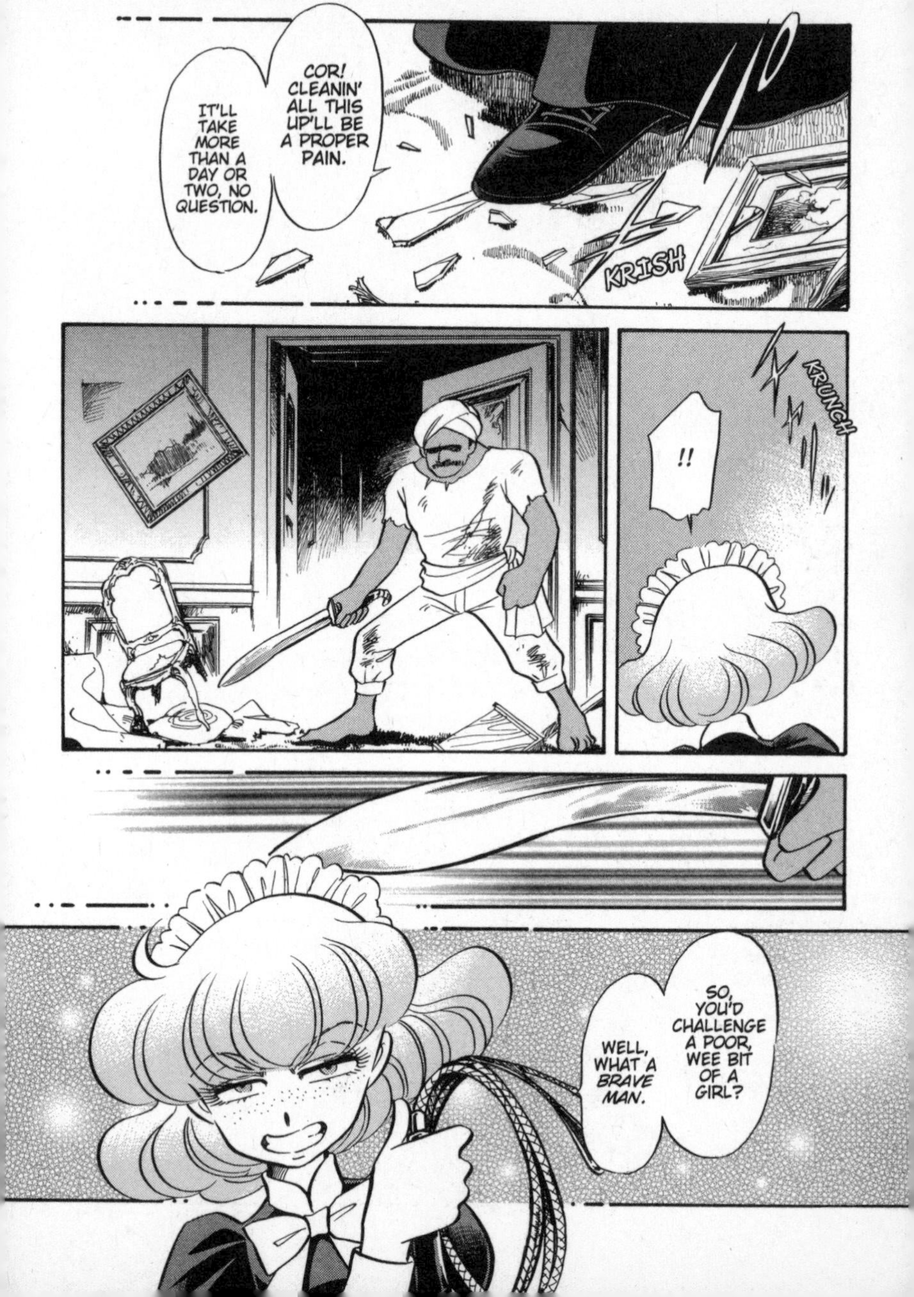
KRISH
COR! CLEANIN' ALL THIS UP'LL BE A PROPER PAIN.
IT'LL TAKE MORE THAN A DAY OR TWO, NO QUESTION.
KRUNCH
!!
SO, YOU'D CHALLENGE A POOR, WEE BIT OF A GIRL?
WELL, WHAT A *BRAVE* MAN.

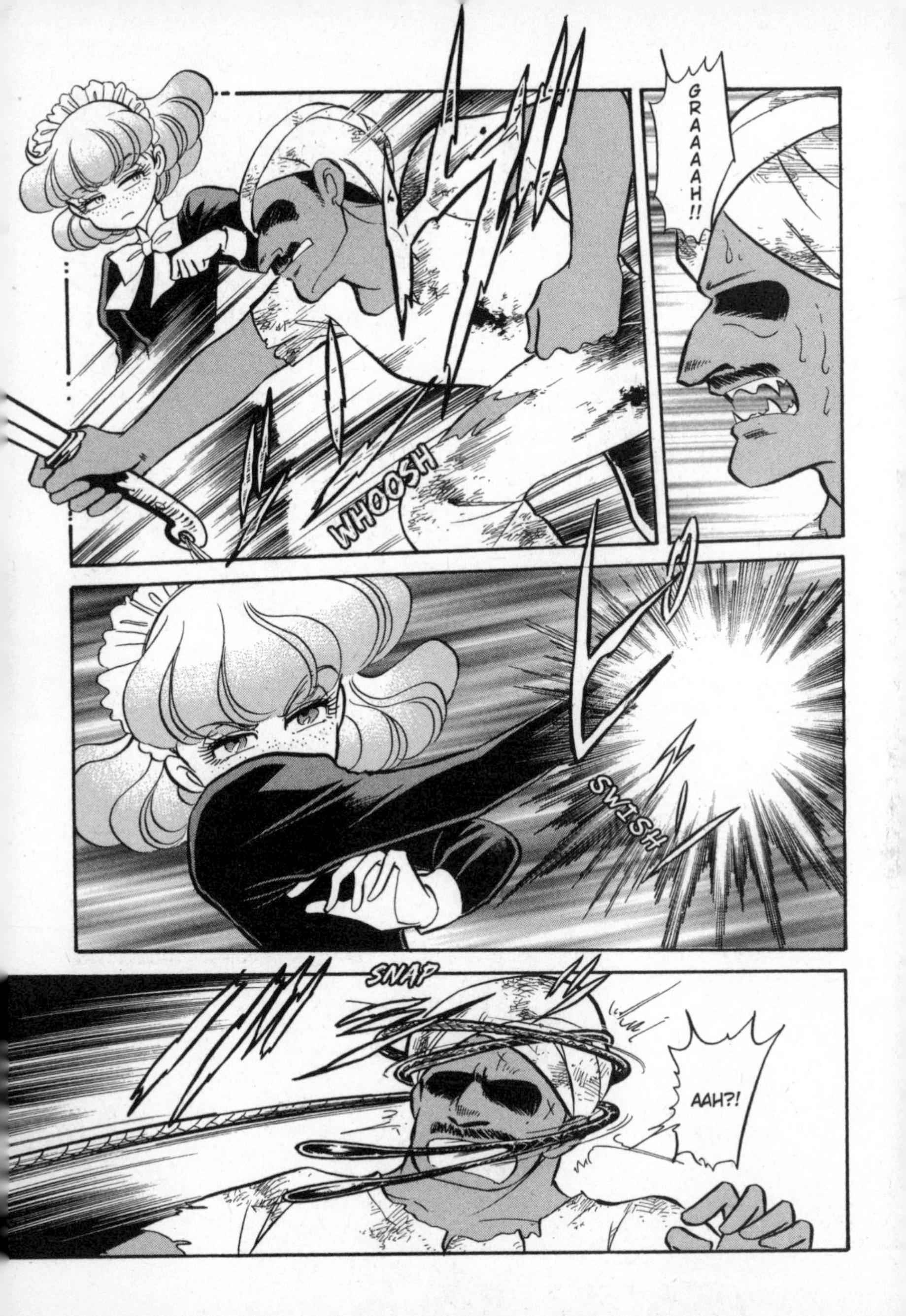
GRAAAAAH!!
WHOOSH
SWISH
SNAP
AAH?!

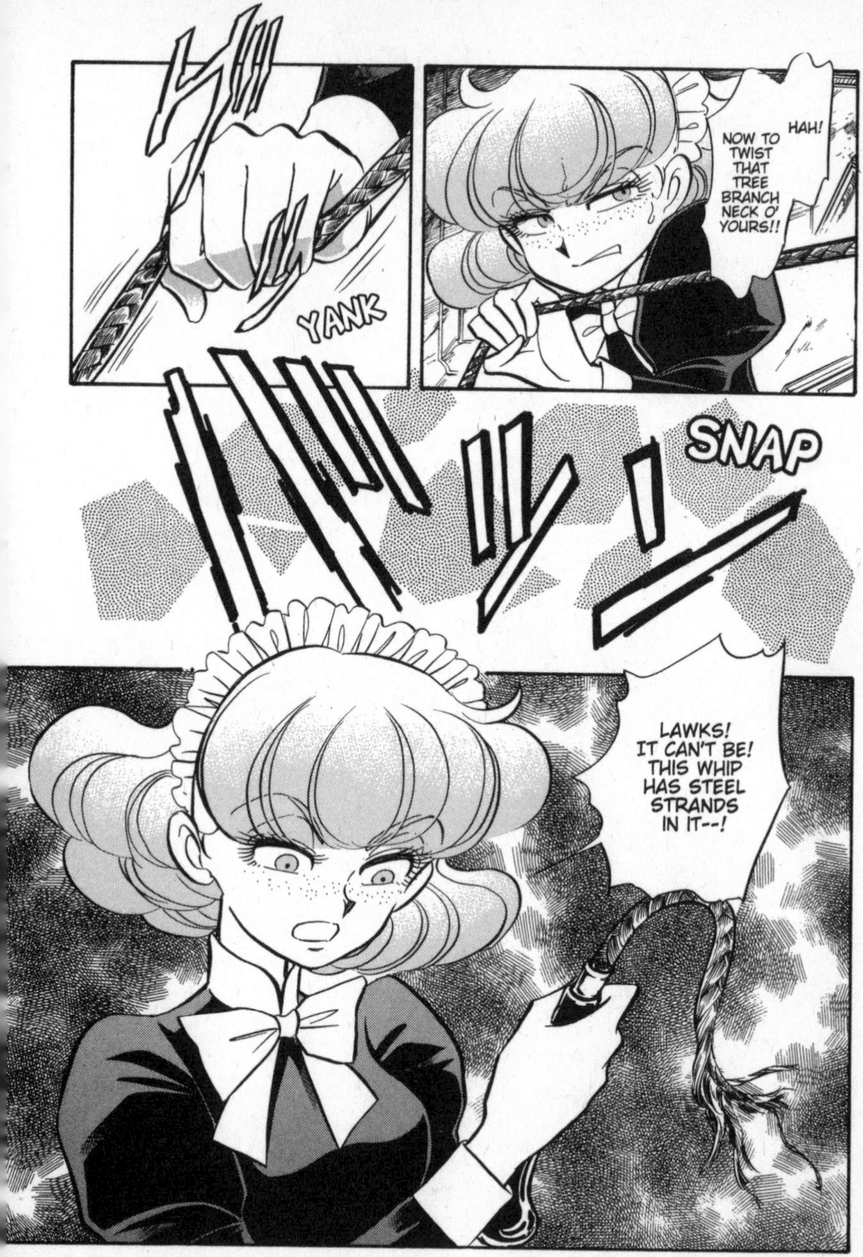
HAH!
NOW TO TWIST THAT TREE BRANCH NECK O' YOURS!!
YANK
SNAP
LAWKS! IT CAN'T BE! THIS WHIP HAS STEEL STRANDS IN IT--!

The Adventure of The Giant Rat of Sumatra (7)

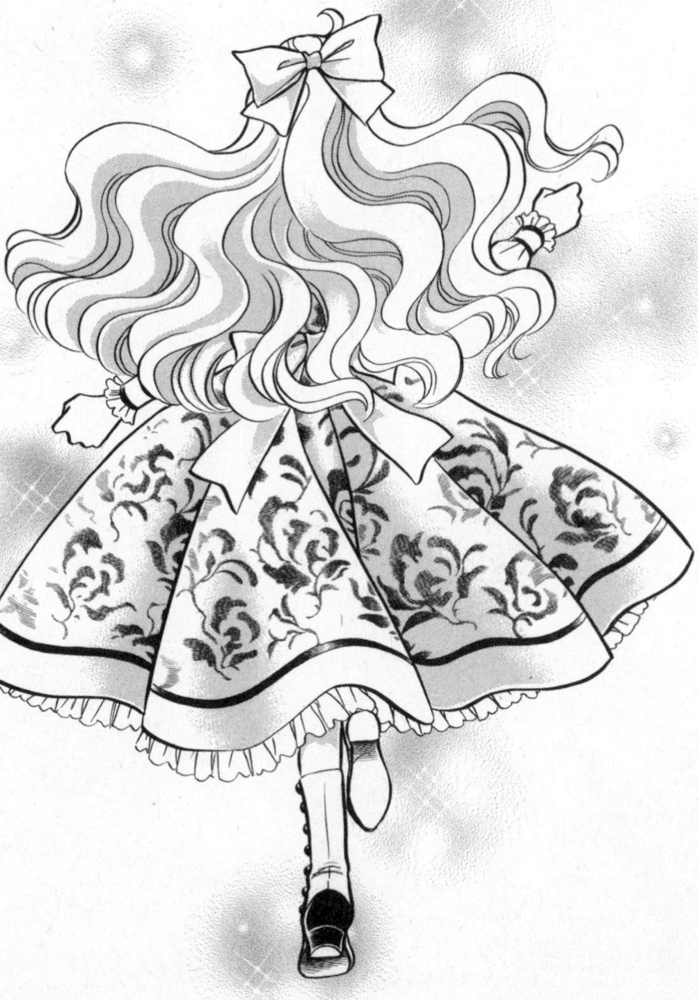

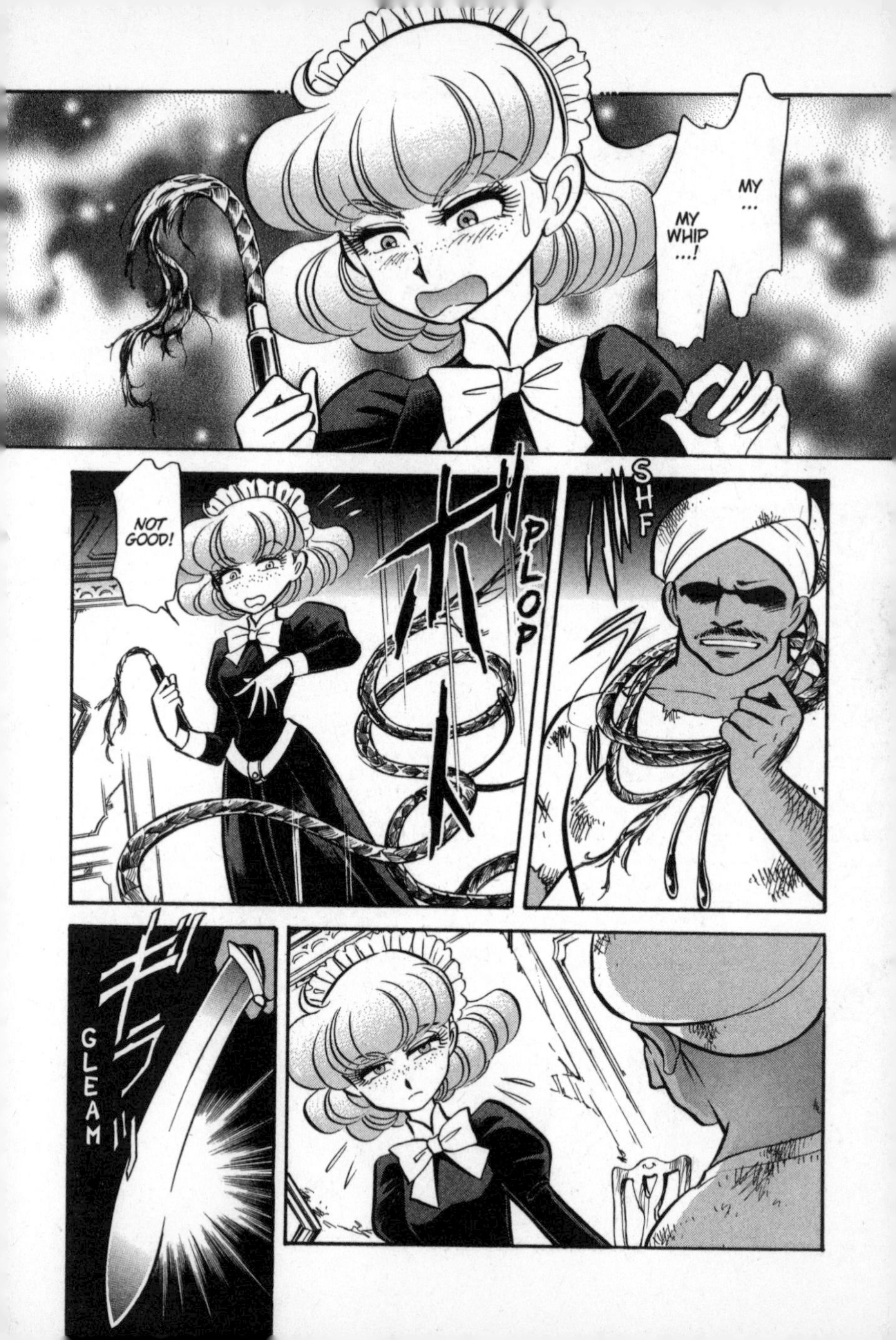
MY ...
MY WHIP ...!
SHF
PLOP
NOT GOOD!
GLEAM

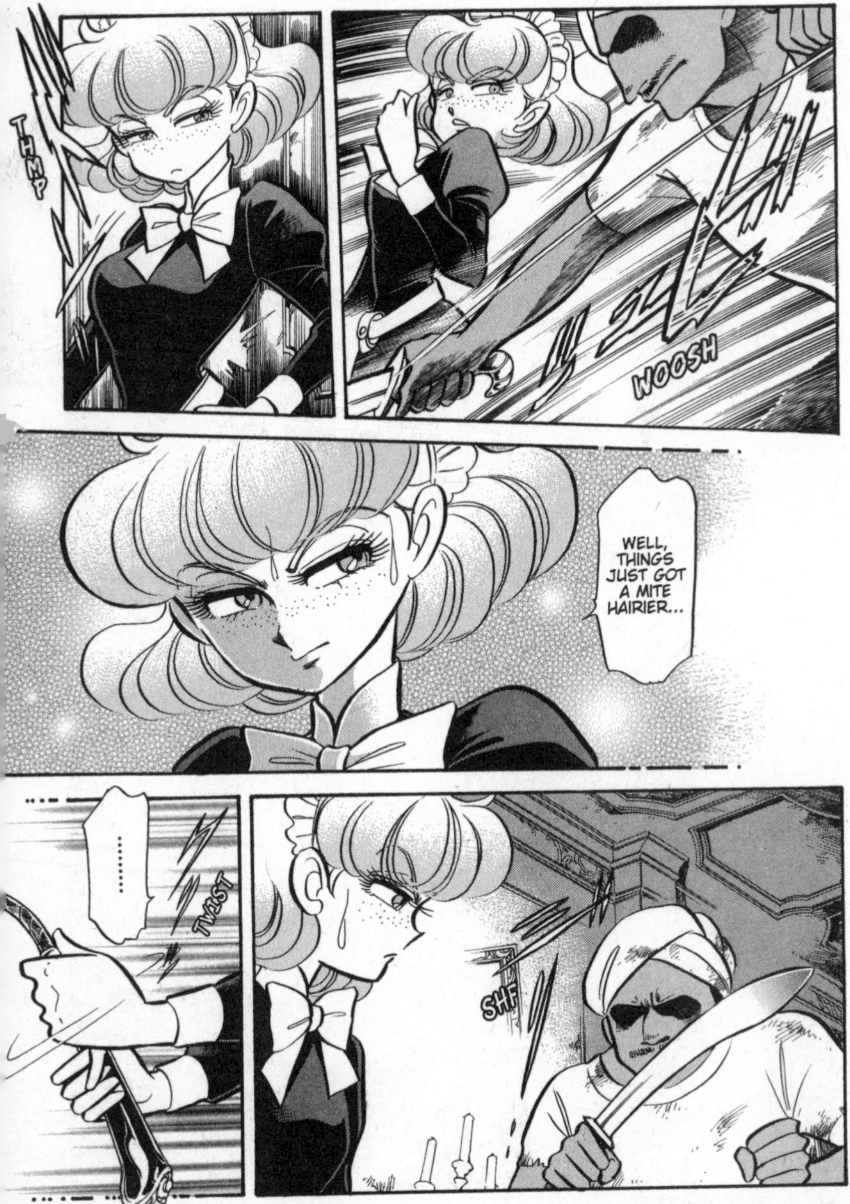
WOOSH
THMP
WELL, THINGS JUST GOT A MITE HAIRIER...
SHF
......
TWIST

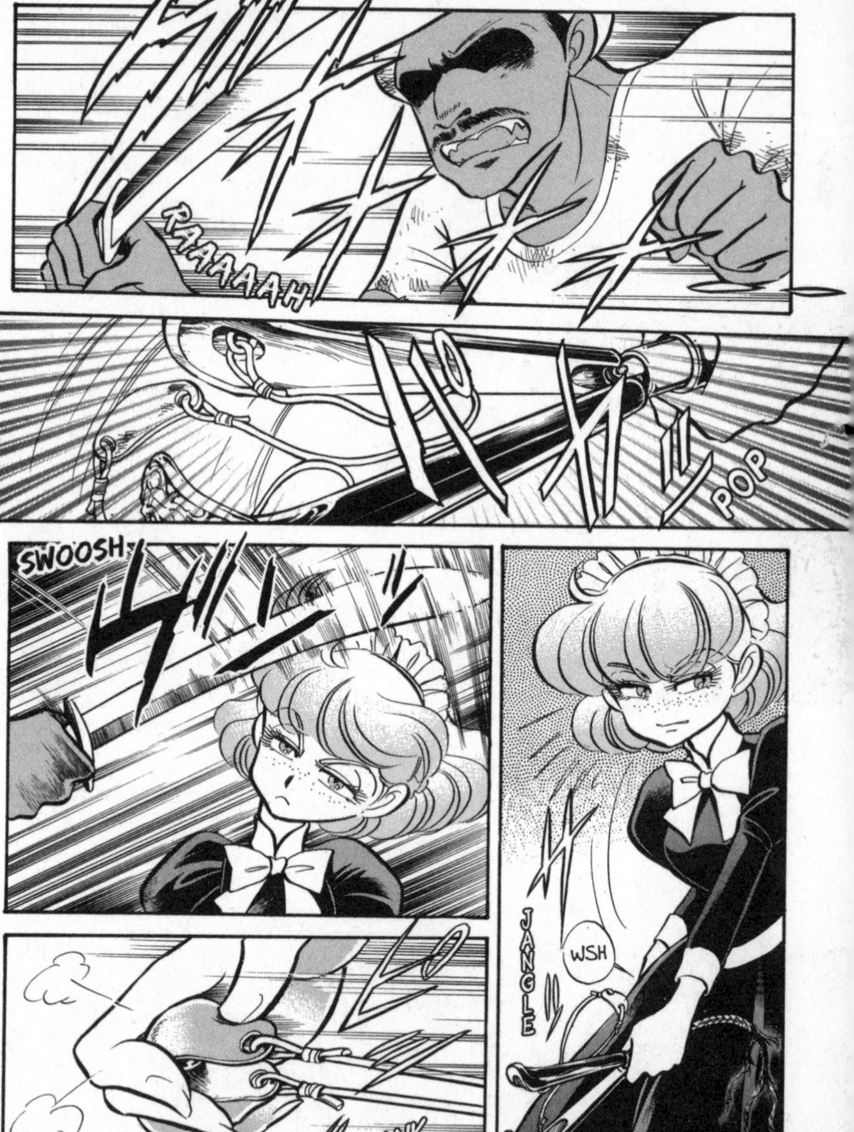
RAAAAAH
POP
WSH
JANGLE
SWOOSH
YANK

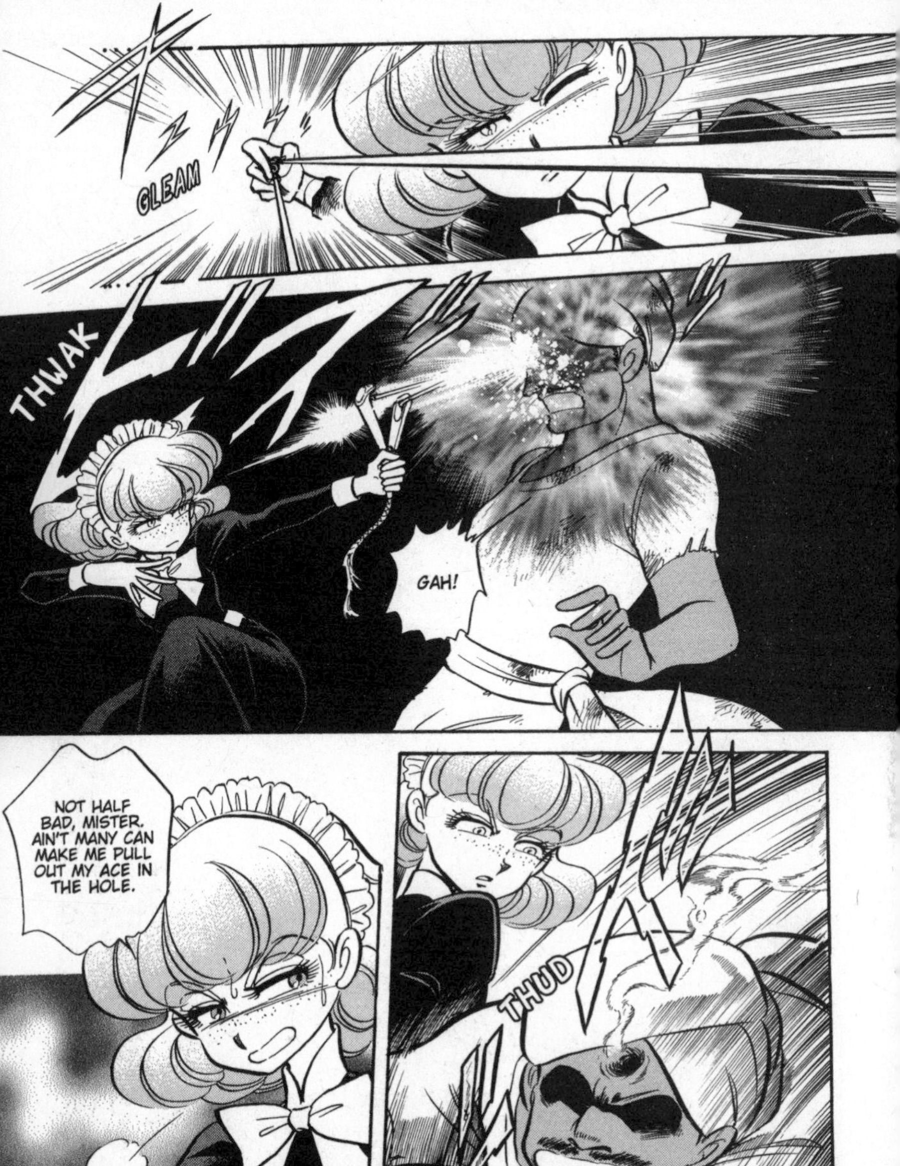
GLEAM
THWAK
GAH!
THUD
NOT HALF BAD, MISTER. AIN'T MANY CAN MAKE ME PULL OUT MY ACE IN THE HOLE.

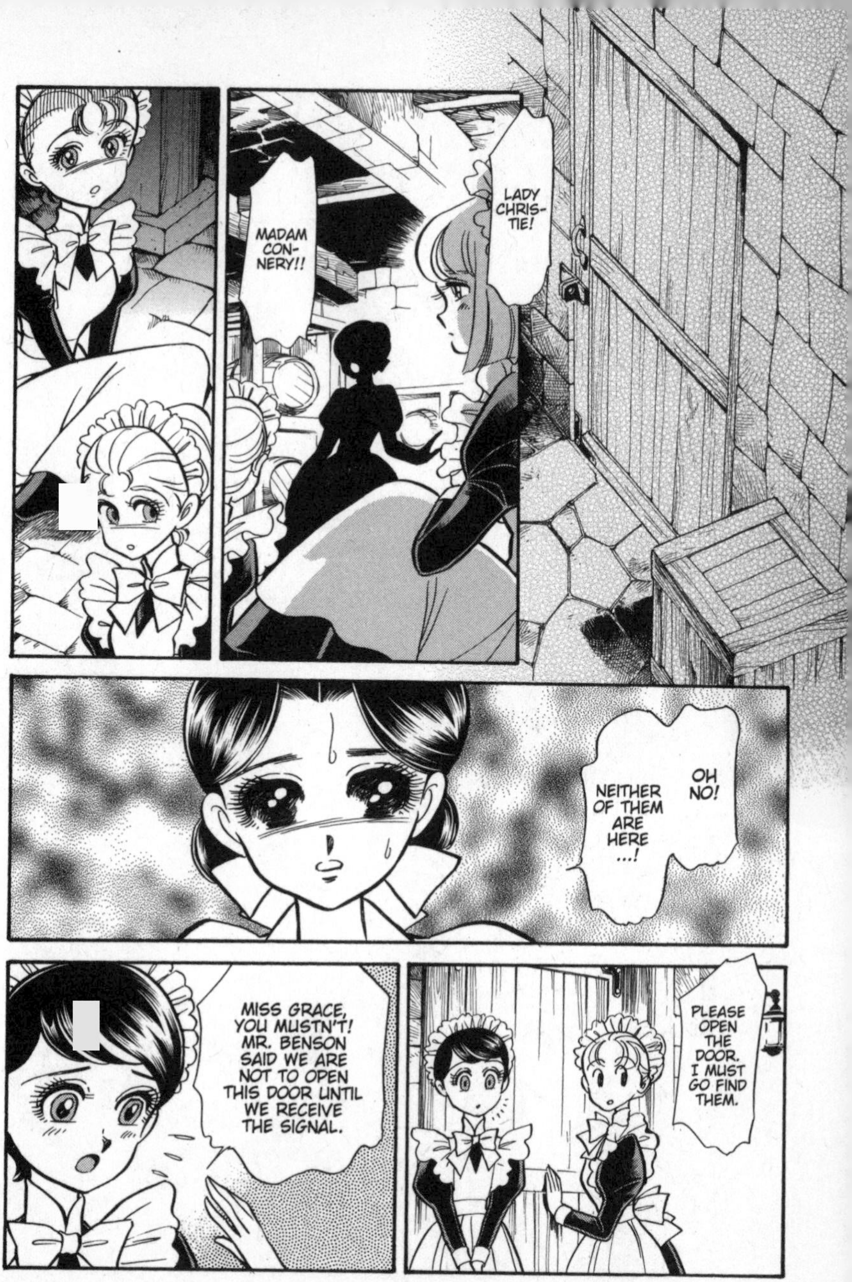
LADY CHRIS-TIE!
MADAM CON-NERY!!
OH NO!
NEITHER OF THEM ARE HERE ...!
PLEASE OPEN THE DOOR. I MUST GO FIND THEM.
MISS GRACE, YOU MUSTN'T! MR. BENSON SAID WE ARE NOT TO OPEN THIS DOOR UNTIL WE RECEIVE THE SIGNAL.

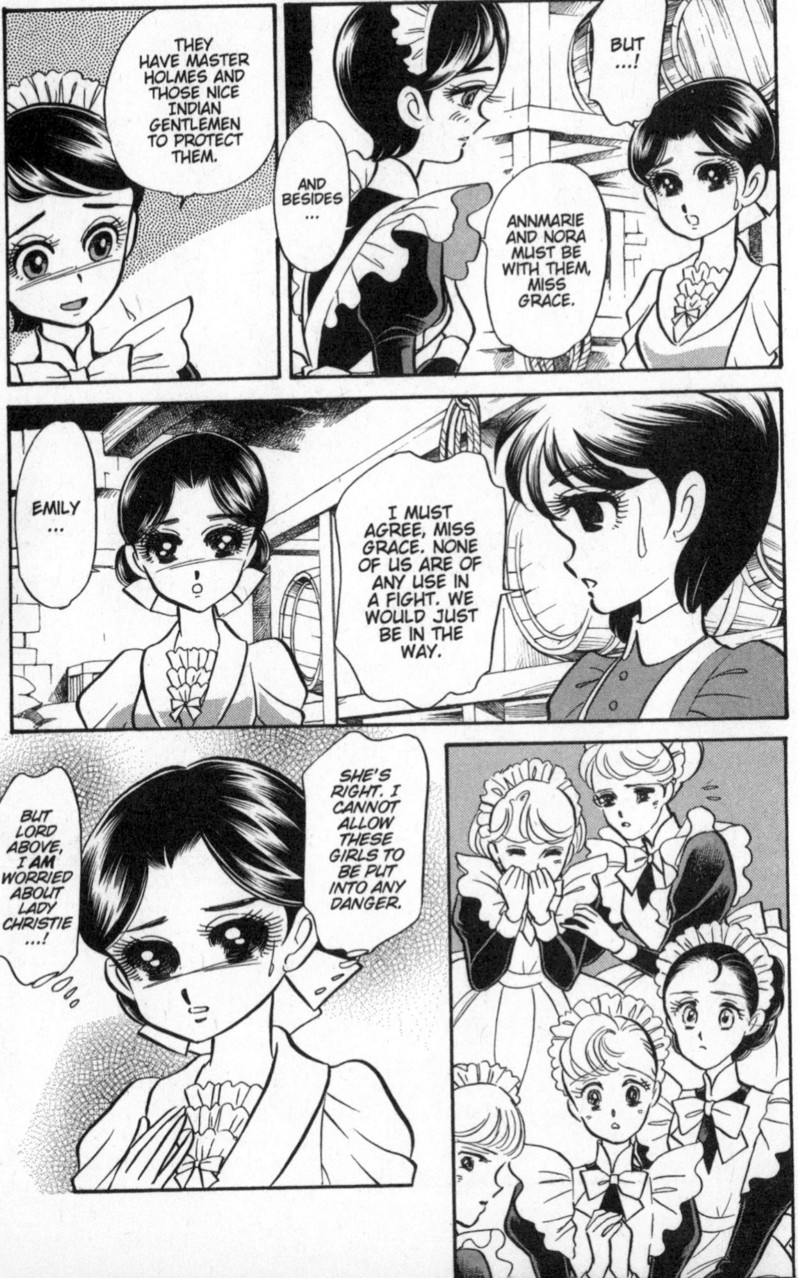
BUT ...!
ANNMARIE AND NORA MUST BE WITH THEM, MISS GRACE.
AND BESIDES ...
THEY HAVE MASTER HOLMES AND THOSE NICE INDIAN GENTLEMEN TO PROTECT THEM.
I MUST AGREE, MISS GRACE. NONE OF US ARE OF ANY USE IN A FIGHT. WE WOULD JUST BE IN THE WAY.
EMILY ...
SHE'S RIGHT. I CANNOT ALLOW THESE GIRLS TO BE PUT INTO ANY DANGER.
BUT LORD ABOVE, I AM WORRIED ABOUT LADY CHRISTIE ...!

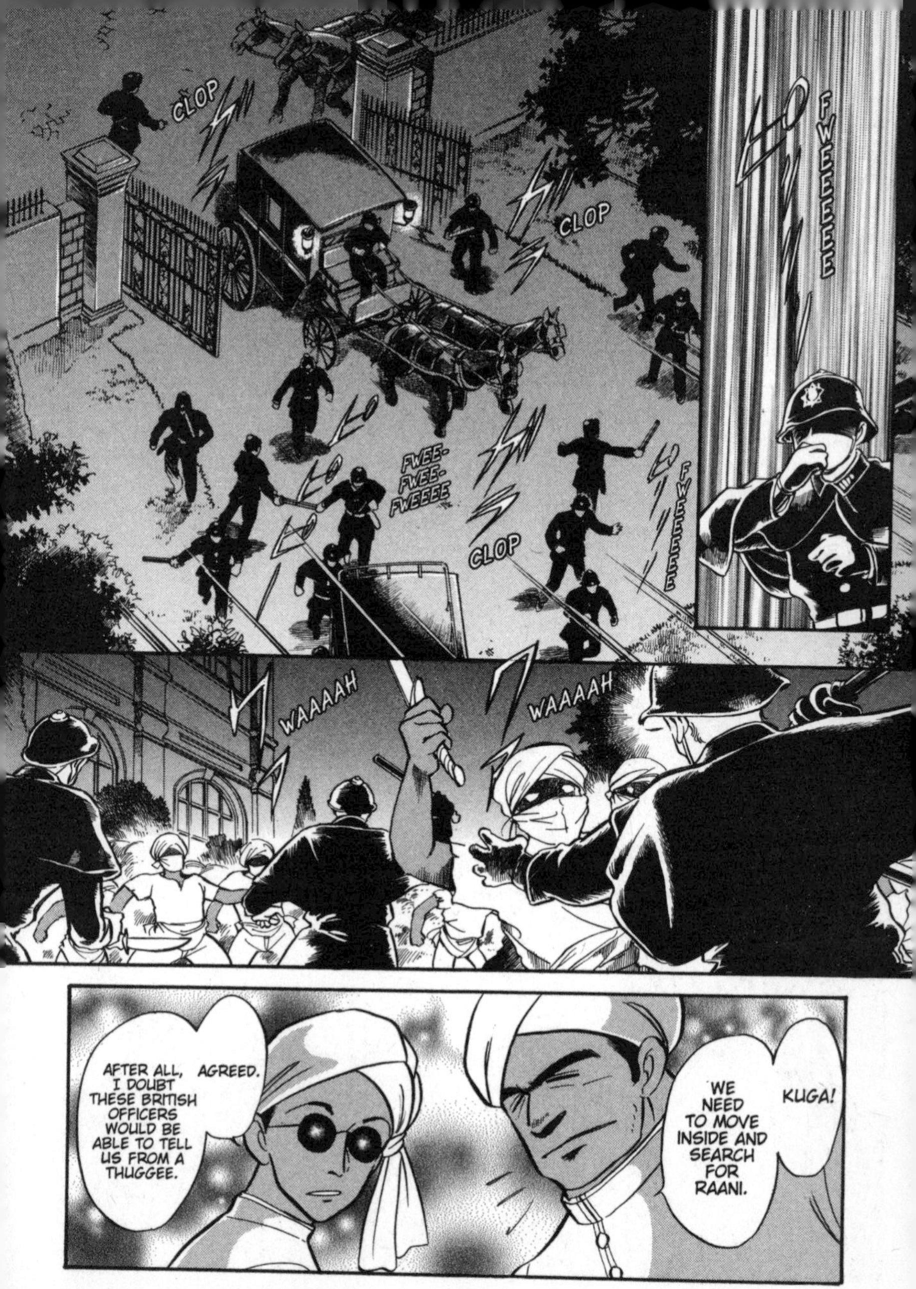
FWEEEEEE
CLOP
CLOP
FWEEEEEE
FWEE-FWEE-FWEEEEE
CLOP
WAAAAH
WAAAAH
KUGA!
WE NEED TO MOVE INSIDE AND SEARCH FOR RAANI.
AGREED.
AFTER ALL, I DOUBT THESE BRITISH OFFICERS WOULD BE ABLE TO TELL US FROM A THUGGEE.

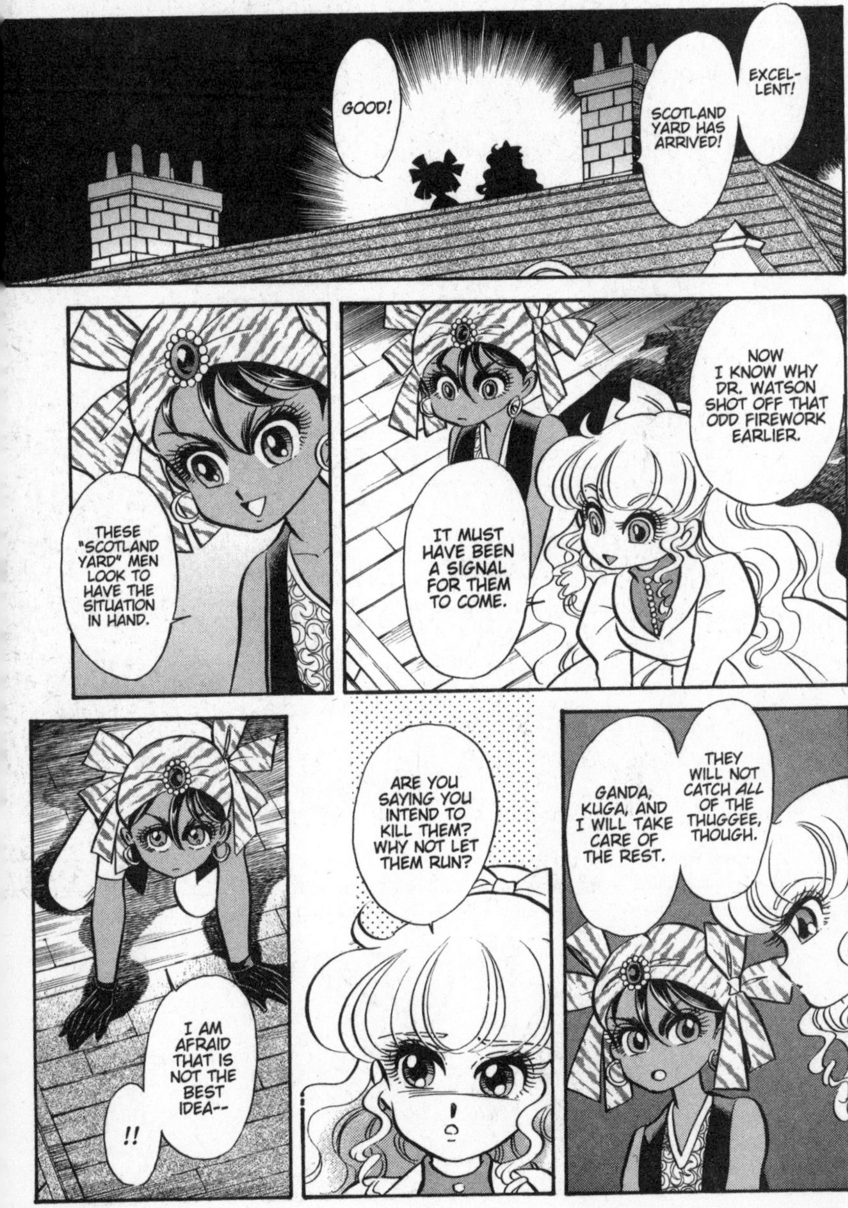
EXCEL-LENT!
SCOTLAND YARD HAS ARRIVED!
GOOD!
NOW I KNOW WHY DR. WATSON SHOT OFF THAT ODD FIREWORK EARLIER.
IT MUST HAVE BEEN A SIGNAL FOR THEM TO COME.
THESE "SCOTLAND YARD" MEN LOOK TO HAVE THE SITUATION IN HAND.
THEY WILL NOT CATCH *ALL* OF THE THUGGEE, THOUGH.
GANDA, KUGA, AND I WILL TAKE CARE OF THE REST.
ARE YOU SAYING YOU INTEND TO KILL THEM? WHY NOT LET THEM RUN?
I AM AFRAID THAT IS NOT THE BEST IDEA--
!!

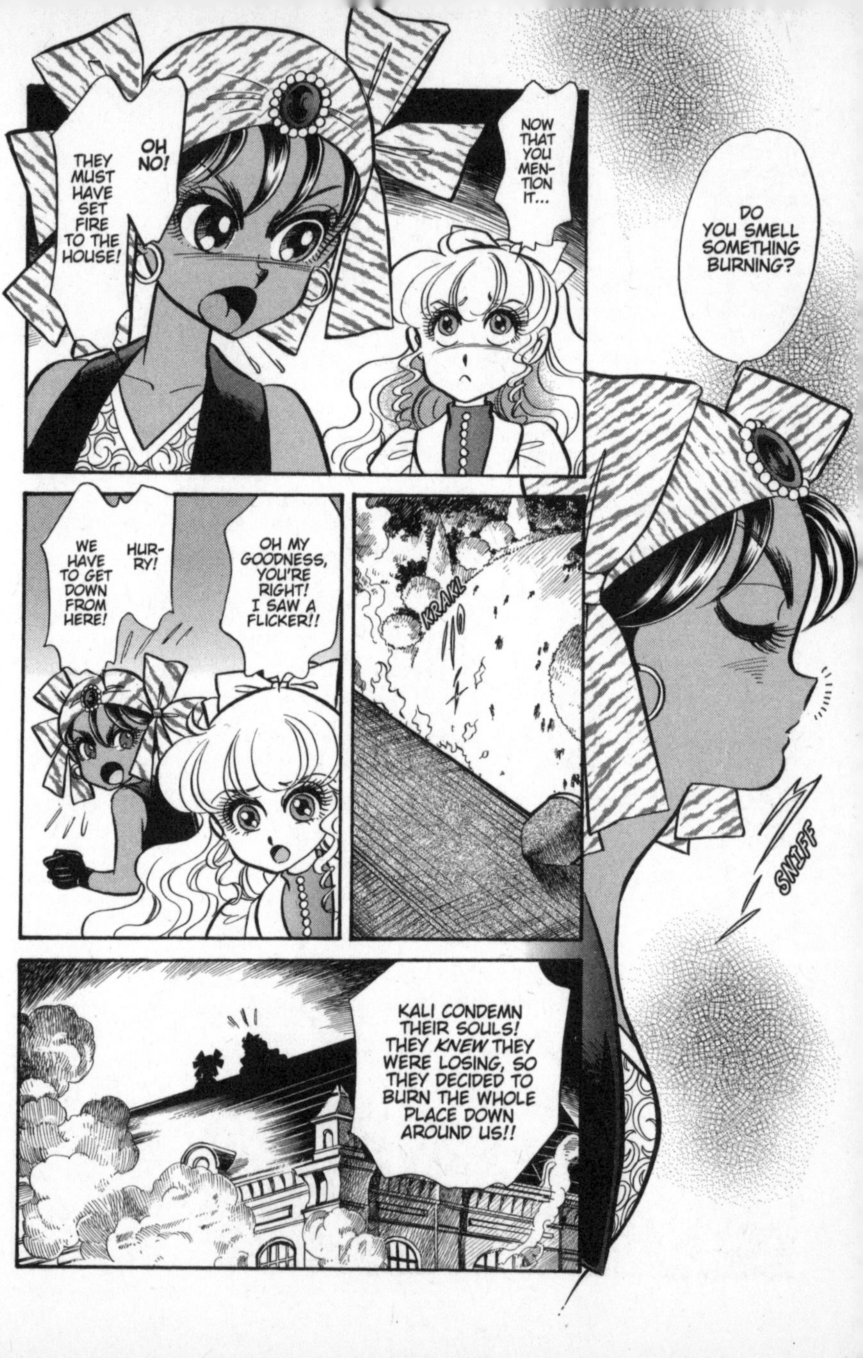
DO YOU SMELL SOMETHING BURNING?
SNIFF
NOW THAT YOU MENTION IT...
OH NO!
THEY MUST HAVE SET FIRE TO THE HOUSE!
KRAKL
OH MY GOODNESS, YOU'RE RIGHT! I SAW A FLICKER!!
HURRY!
WE HAVE TO GET DOWN FROM HERE!
KALI CONDEMN THEIR SOULS! THEY *KNEW* THEY WERE LOSING, SO THEY DECIDED TO BURN THE WHOLE PLACE DOWN AROUND US!!

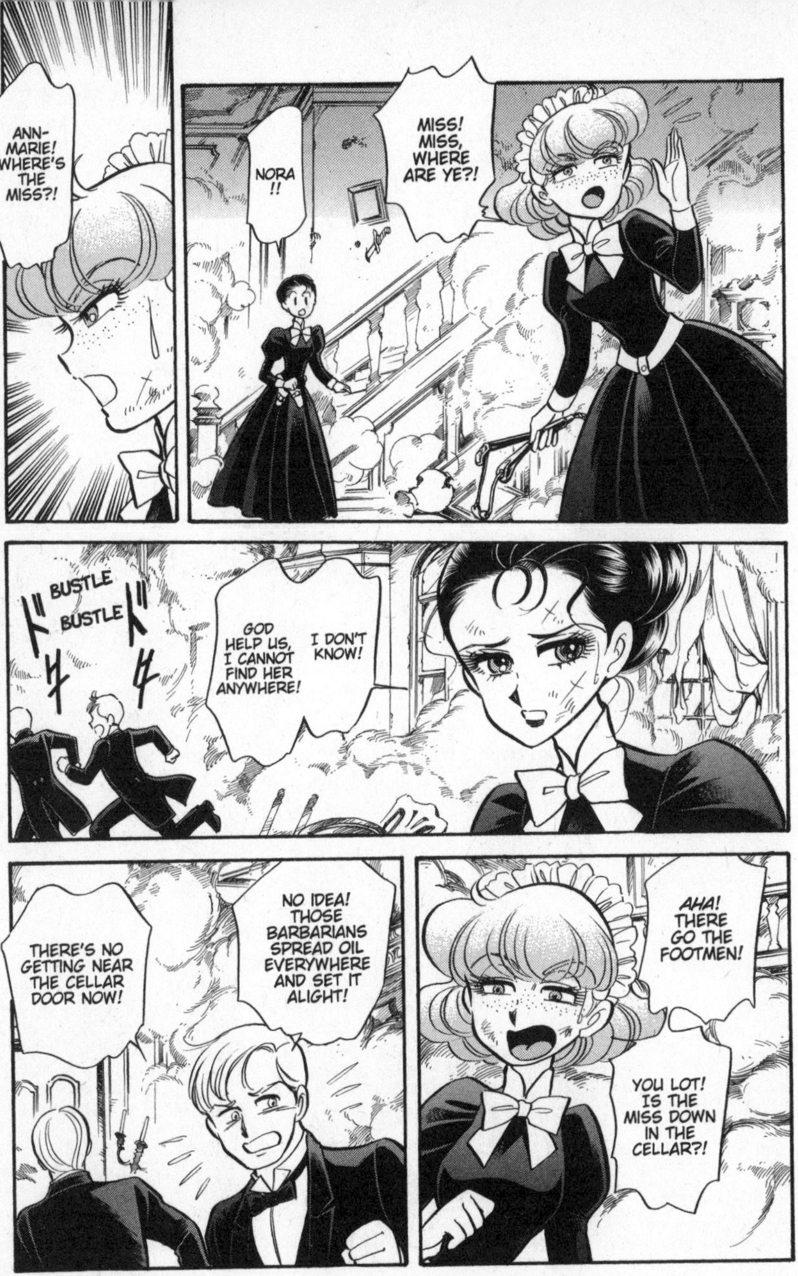
MISS! MISS, WHERE ARE YE?!
NORA !!
ANN-MARIE! WHERE'S THE MISS?!
I DON'T KNOW!
GOD HELP US, I CANNOT FIND HER ANYWHERE!
BUSTLE
BUSTLE
ドタ ドタ
AHA! THERE GO THE FOOTMEN!
YOU LOT! IS THE MISS DOWN IN THE CELLAR?!
NO IDEA! THOSE BARBARIANS SPREAD OIL EVERYWHERE AND SET IT ALIGHT!
THERE'S NO GETTING NEAR THE CELLAR DOOR NOW!

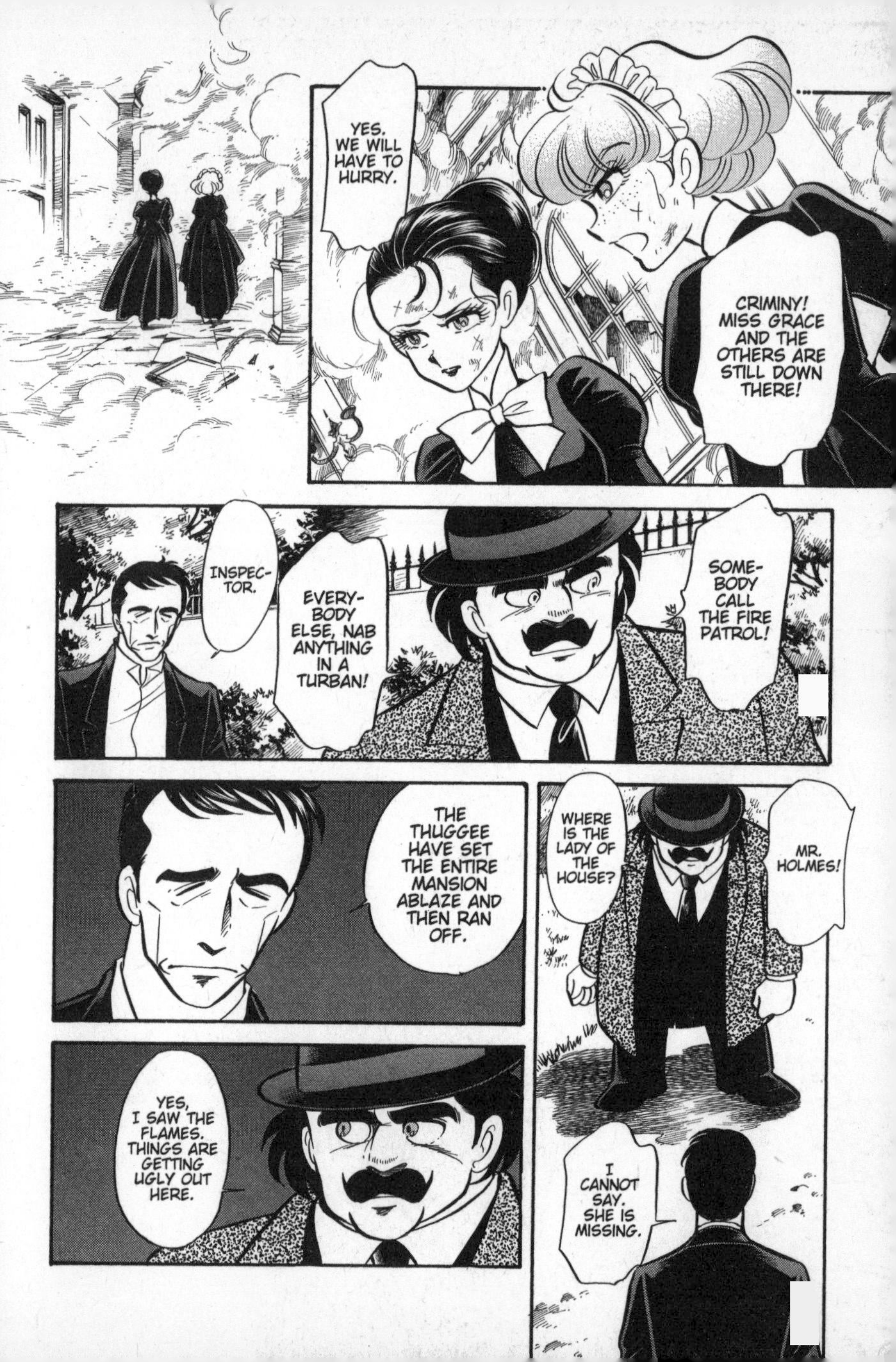
CRIMINY! MISS GRACE AND THE OTHERS ARE STILL DOWN THERE!
YES. WE WILL HAVE TO HURRY.
SOME-BODY CALL THE FIRE PATROL!
EVERY-BODY ELSE, NAB ANYTHING IN A TURBAN!
INSPEC-TOR.
MR. HOLMES!
WHERE IS THE LADY OF THE HOUSE?
I CANNOT SAY. SHE IS MISSING.
THE THUGGEE HAVE SET THE ENTIRE MANSION ABLAZE AND THEN RAN OFF.
YES, I SAW THE FLAMES. THINGS ARE GETTING UGLY OUT HERE.

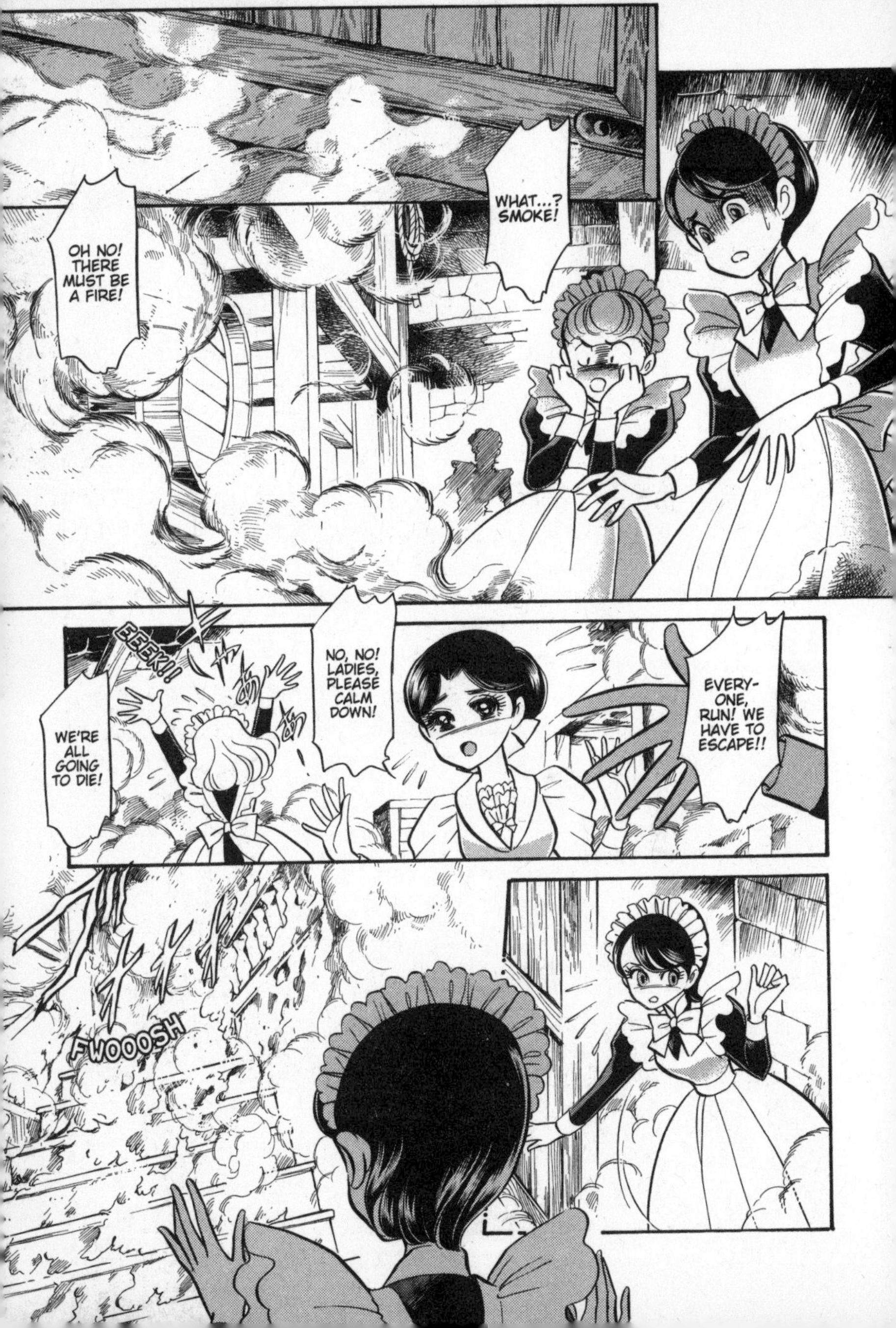
WHAT...? SMOKE!
OH NO! THERE MUST BE A FIRE!
EVERY-ONE, RUN! WE HAVE TO ESCAPE!!
NO, NO! LADIES, PLEASE CALM DOWN!
EEEK!!
WE'RE ALL GOING TO DIE!
FWOOOSH

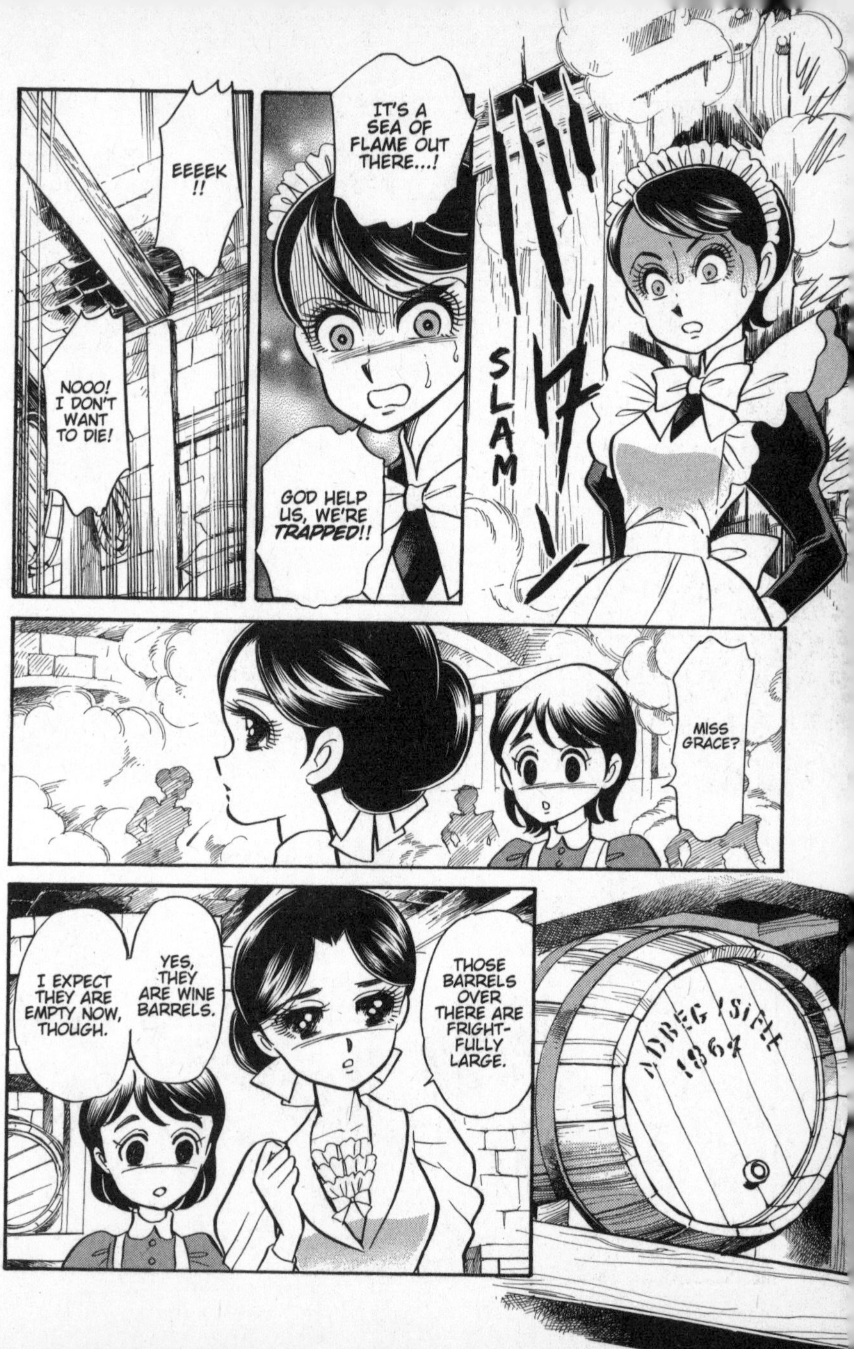
SLAM
IT'S A SEA OF FLAME OUT THERE...!
GOD HELP US, WE'RE *TRAPPED*!!
EEEEK!!
NOOO! I DON'T WANT TO DIE!
MISS GRACE?
THOSE BARRELS OVER THERE ARE FRIGHT-FULLY LARGE.
YES, THEY ARE WINE BARRELS.
I EXPECT THEY ARE EMPTY NOW, THOUGH.

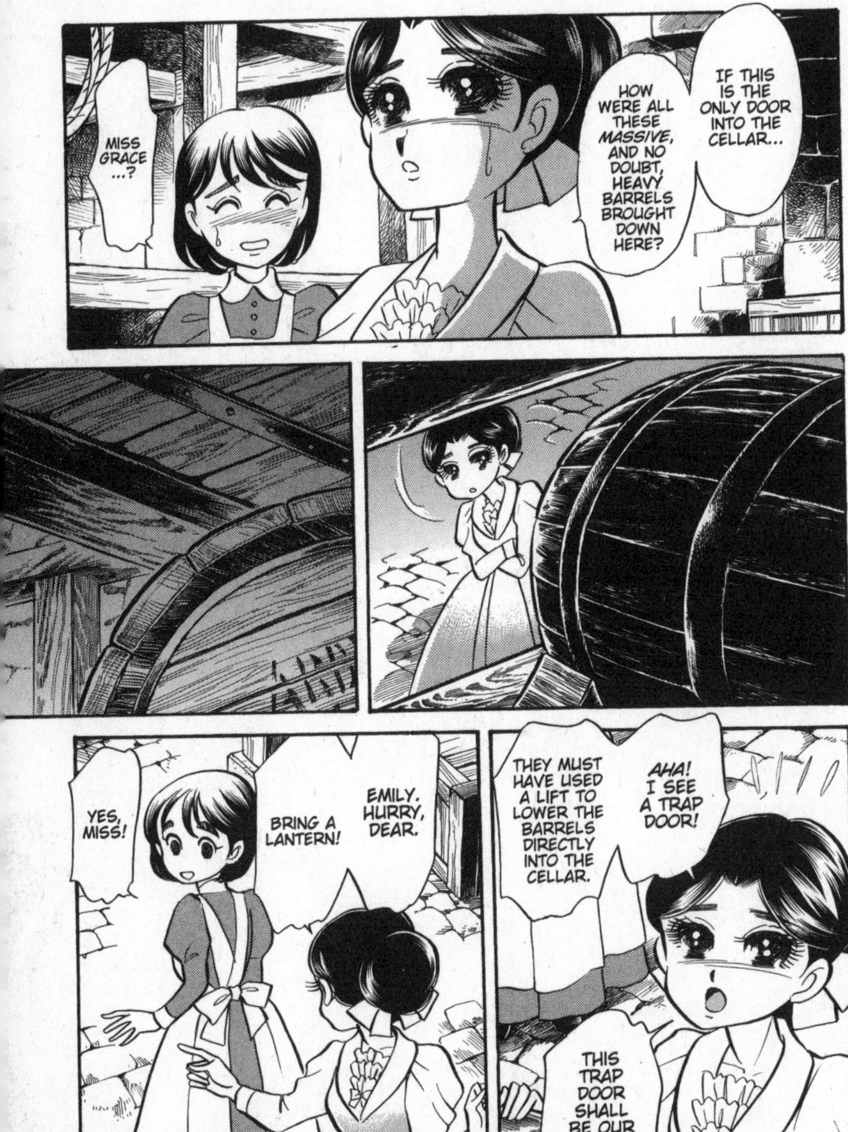
IF THIS IS THE ONLY DOOR INTO THE CELLAR...
HOW WERE ALL THESE *MASSIVE*, AND NO DOUBT, HEAVY BARRELS BROUGHT DOWN HERE?
MISS GRACE ...?
AHA! I SEE A TRAP DOOR!
THEY MUST HAVE USED A LIFT TO LOWER THE BARRELS DIRECTLY INTO THE CELLAR.
THIS TRAP DOOR SHALL BE OUR ESCAPE ROUTE!
EMILY. HURRY, DEAR.
BRING A LANTERN!
YES, MISS!

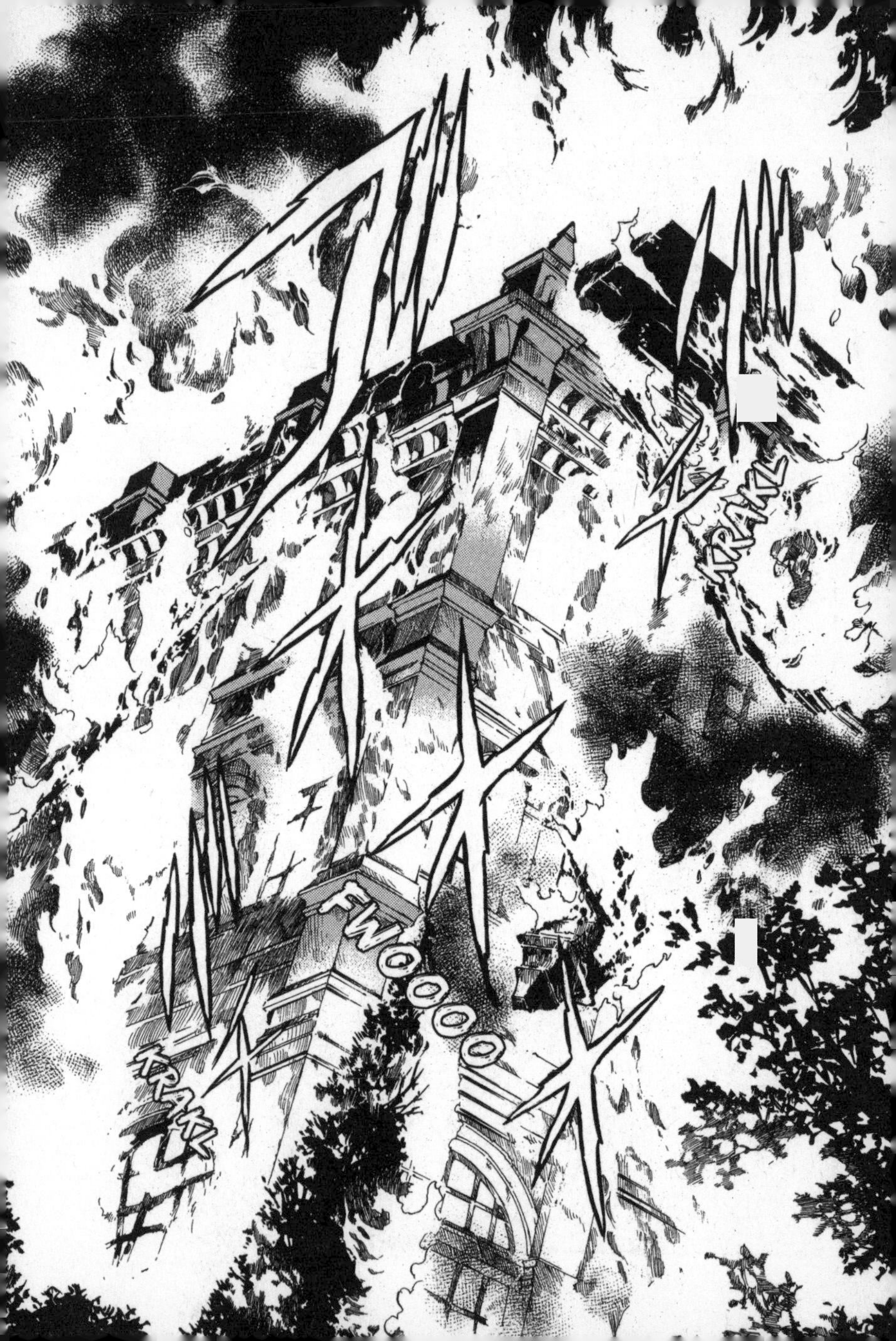
KRAKL
FWOOOOO
KRAKL

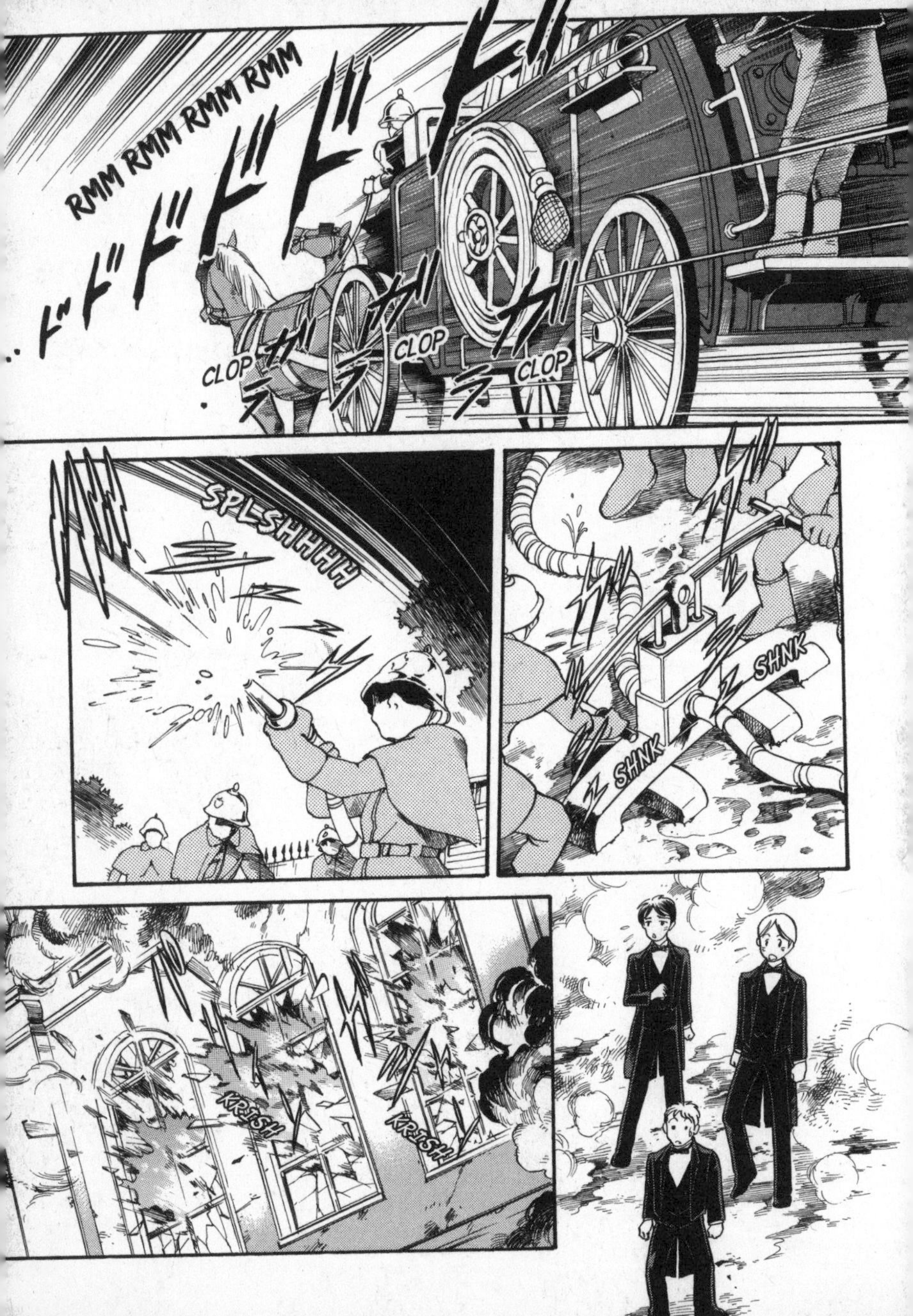

RMM RMM RMM RMM
…ドドドドドド!!
CLOP
ガラ
CLOP
ガラ
CLOP
SHNK
SHNK
SPLSHHHHH
KRISH
KRISH

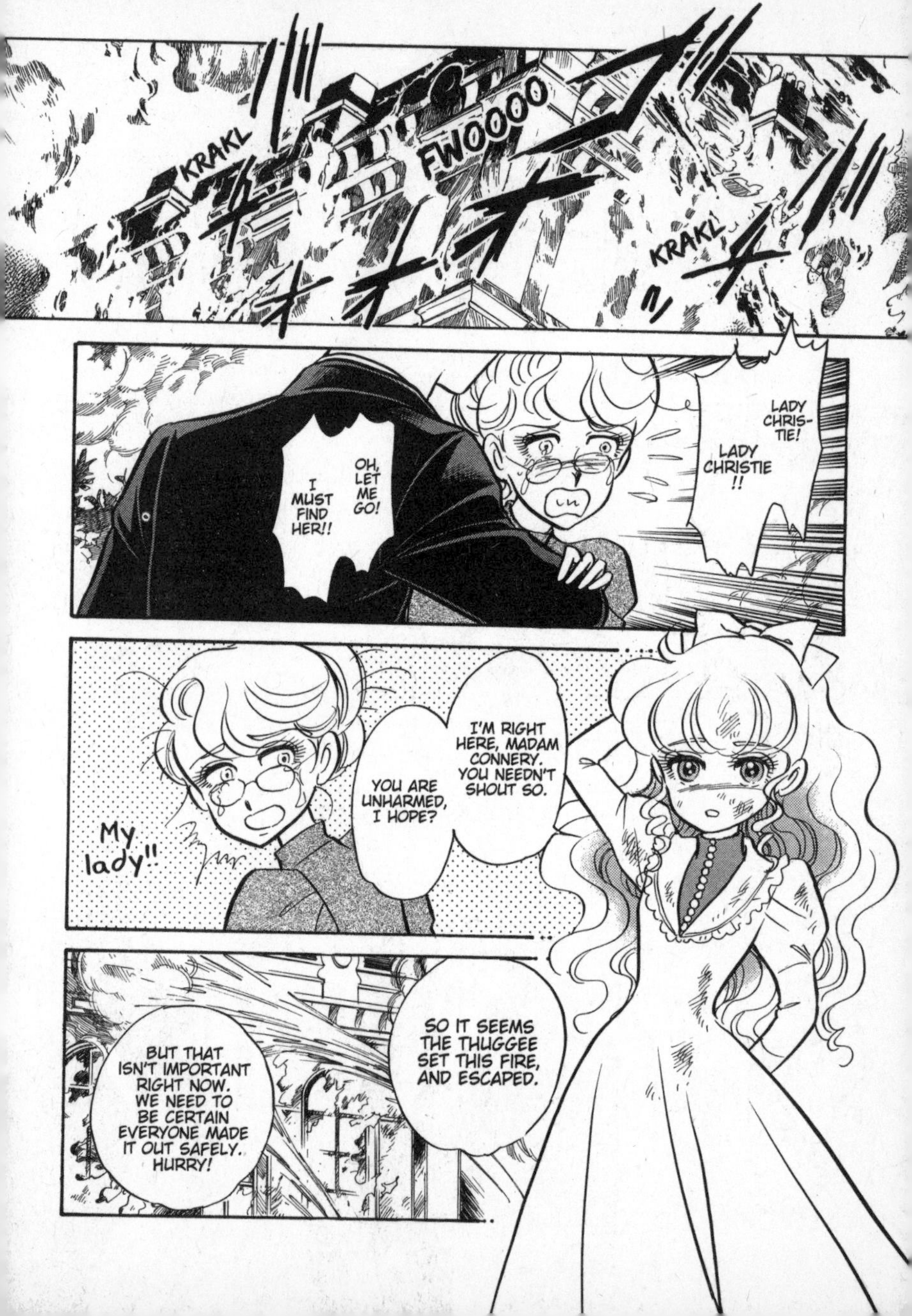
KRAKL
FWOOOO
KRAKL
LADY CHRISTIE!
LADY CHRISTIE!!
OH, LET ME GO!
I MUST FIND HER!!
I'M RIGHT HERE, MADAM CONNERY. YOU NEEDN'T SHOUT SO.
YOU ARE UNHARMED, I HOPE?
My lady!!
SO IT SEEMS THE THUGGEE SET THIS FIRE, AND ESCAPED.
BUT THAT ISN'T IMPORTANT RIGHT NOW. WE NEED TO BE CERTAIN EVERYONE MADE IT OUT SAFELY. HURRY!

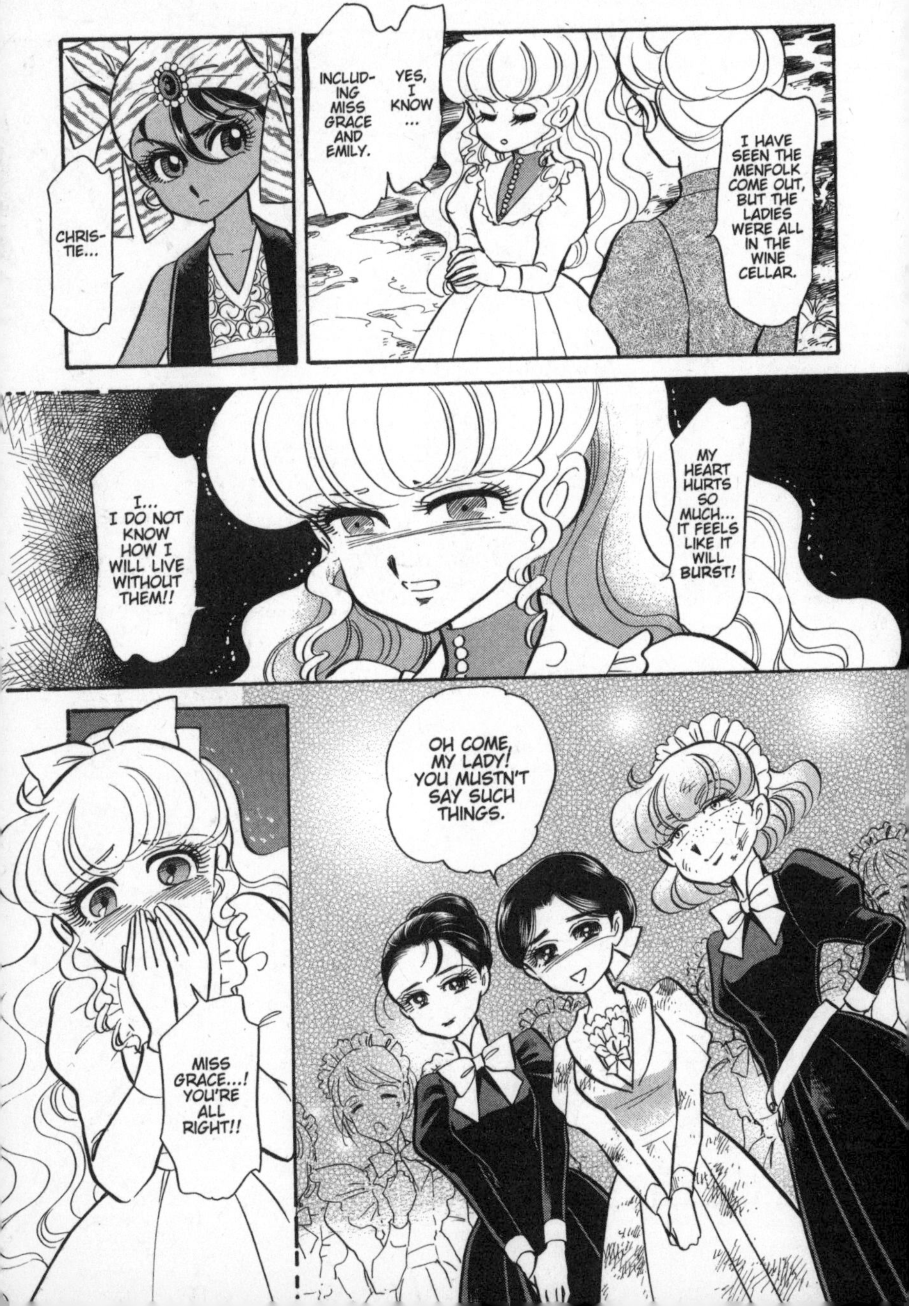
I HAVE SEEN THE MENFOLK COME OUT, BUT THE LADIES WERE ALL IN THE WINE CELLAR.
YES, I KNOW...
INCLUD-ING MISS GRACE AND EMILY.
CHRIS-TIE...
MY HEART HURTS SO MUCH... IT FEELS LIKE IT WILL BURST!
I... I DO NOT KNOW HOW I WILL LIVE WITHOUT THEM!!
OH COME, MY LADY! YOU MUSTN'T SAY SUCH THINGS.
MISS GRACE...! YOU'RE ALL RIGHT!!

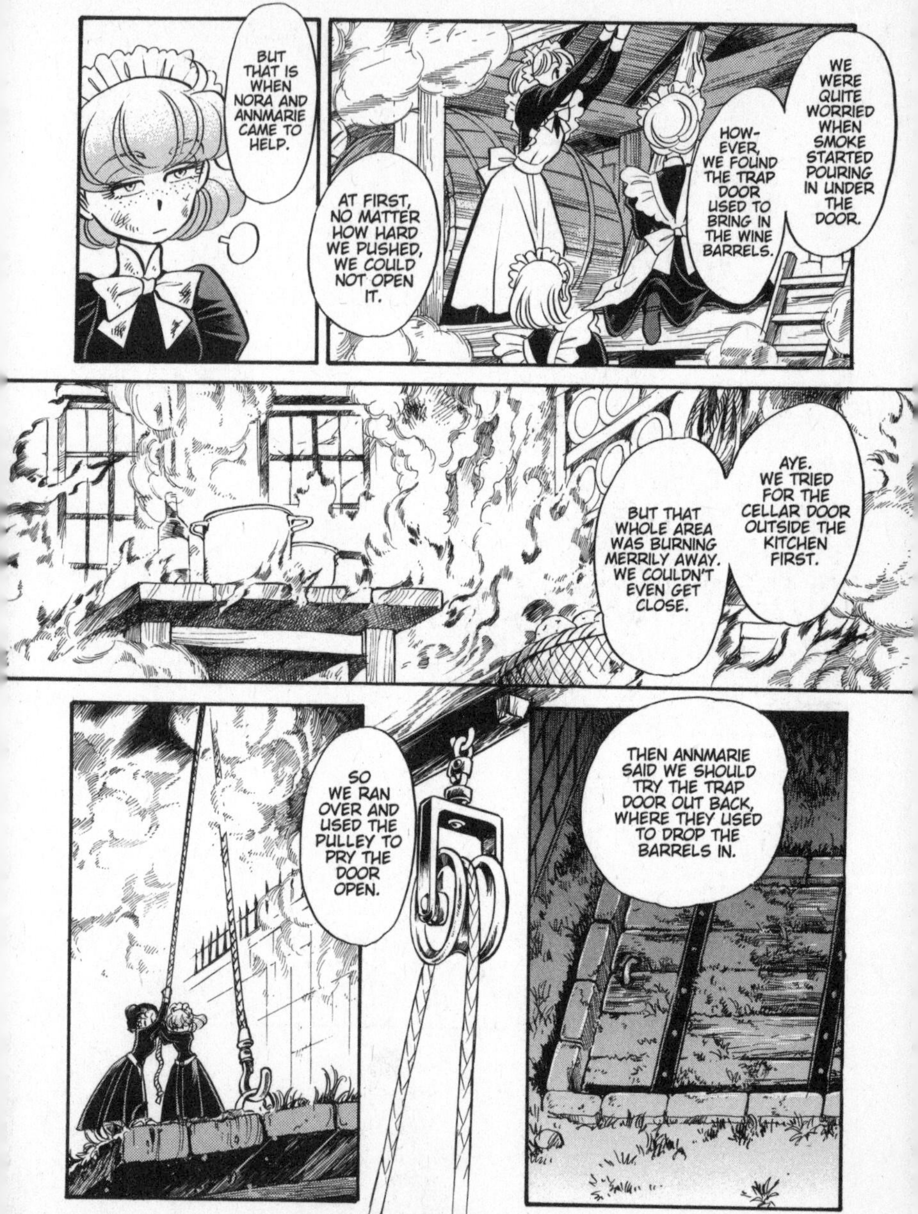
WE WERE QUITE WORRIED WHEN SMOKE STARTED POURING IN UNDER THE DOOR.
HOW-EVER, WE FOUND THE TRAP DOOR USED TO BRING IN THE WINE BARRELS.
AT FIRST, NO MATTER HOW HARD WE PUSHED, WE COULD NOT OPEN IT.
BUT THAT IS WHEN NORA AND ANNMARIE CAME TO HELP.
AYE. WE TRIED FOR THE CELLAR DOOR OUTSIDE THE KITCHEN FIRST.
BUT THAT WHOLE AREA WAS BURNING MERRILY AWAY. WE COULDN'T EVEN GET CLOSE.
THEN ANNMARIE SAID WE SHOULD TRY THE TRAP DOOR OUT BACK, WHERE THEY USED TO DROP THE BARRELS IN.
SO WE RAN OVER AND USED THE PULLEY TO PRY THE DOOR OPEN.

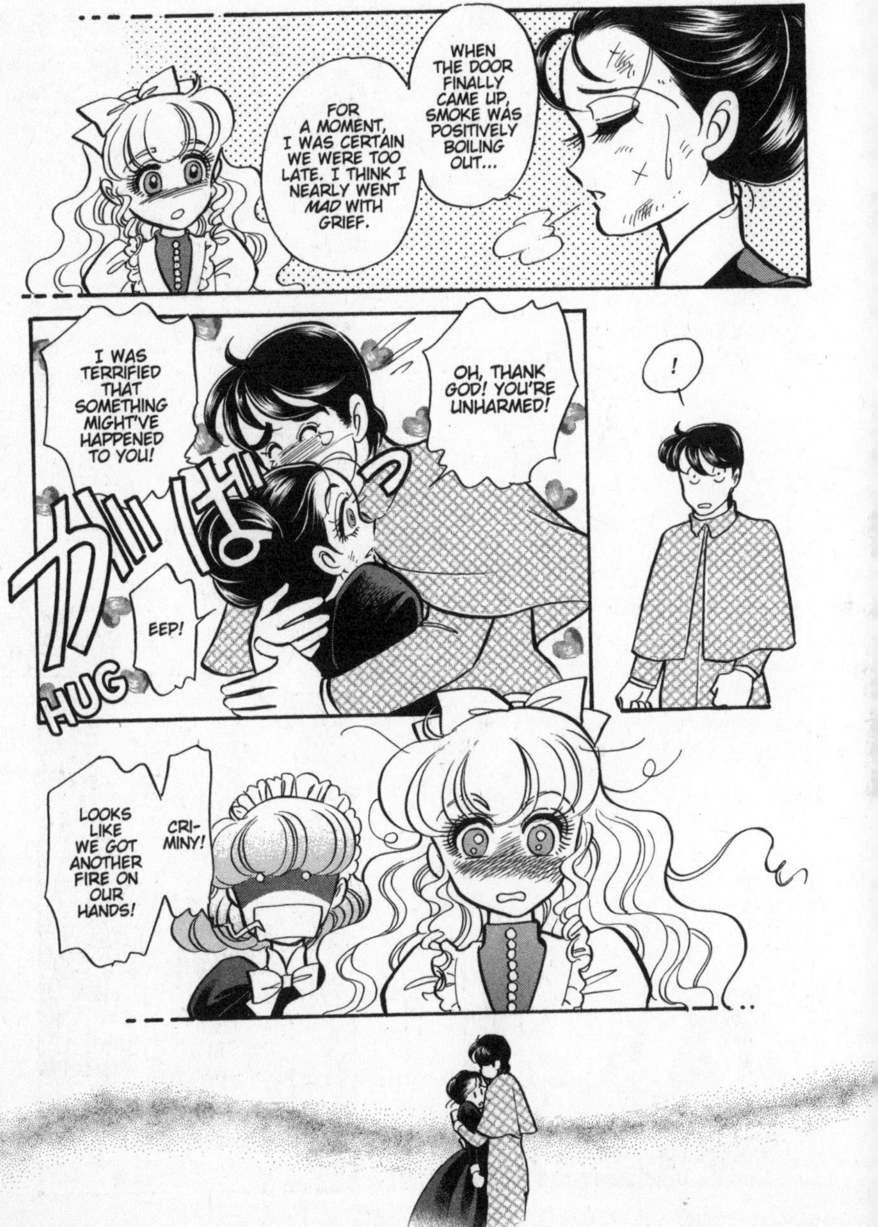
WHEN THE DOOR FINALLY CAME UP, SMOKE WAS POSITIVELY BOILING OUT...
FOR A MOMENT, I WAS CERTAIN WE WERE TOO LATE. I THINK I NEARLY WENT *MAD* WITH GRIEF.
!
OH, THANK GOD! YOU'RE UNHARMED!
I WAS TERRIFIED THAT SOMETHING MIGHT'VE HAPPENED TO YOU!
HUG
EEP!
CRI-MINY!
LOOKS LIKE WE GOT ANOTHER FIRE ON OUR HANDS!

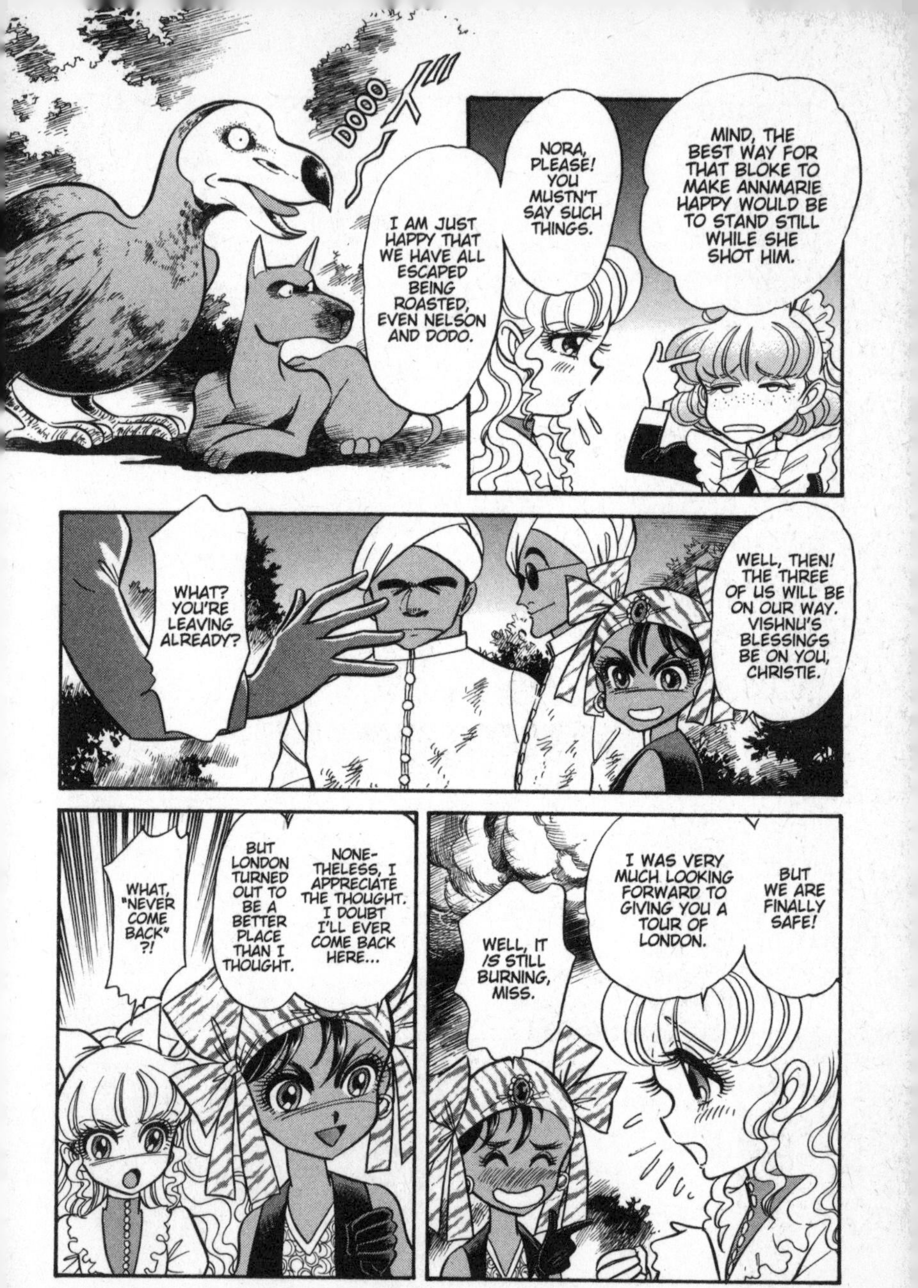
MIND, THE BEST WAY FOR THAT BLOKE TO MAKE ANNMARIE HAPPY WOULD BE TO STAND STILL WHILE SHE SHOT HIM.
NORA, PLEASE! YOU MUSTN'T SAY SUCH THINGS.
DOOO
I AM JUST HAPPY THAT WE HAVE ALL ESCAPED BEING ROASTED, EVEN NELSON AND DODO.
WELL, THEN! THE THREE OF US WILL BE ON OUR WAY. VISHNU'S BLESSINGS BE ON YOU, CHRISTIE.
WHAT? YOU'RE LEAVING ALREADY?
BUT WE ARE FINALLY SAFE!
I WAS VERY MUCH LOOKING FORWARD TO GIVING YOU A TOUR OF LONDON.
WELL, IT *IS* STILL BURNING, MISS.
NONE-THELESS, I APPRECIATE THE THOUGHT. I DOUBT I'LL EVER COME BACK HERE...
BUT LONDON TURNED OUT TO BE A BETTER PLACE THAN I THOUGHT.
WHAT, "NEVER COME BACK"?!

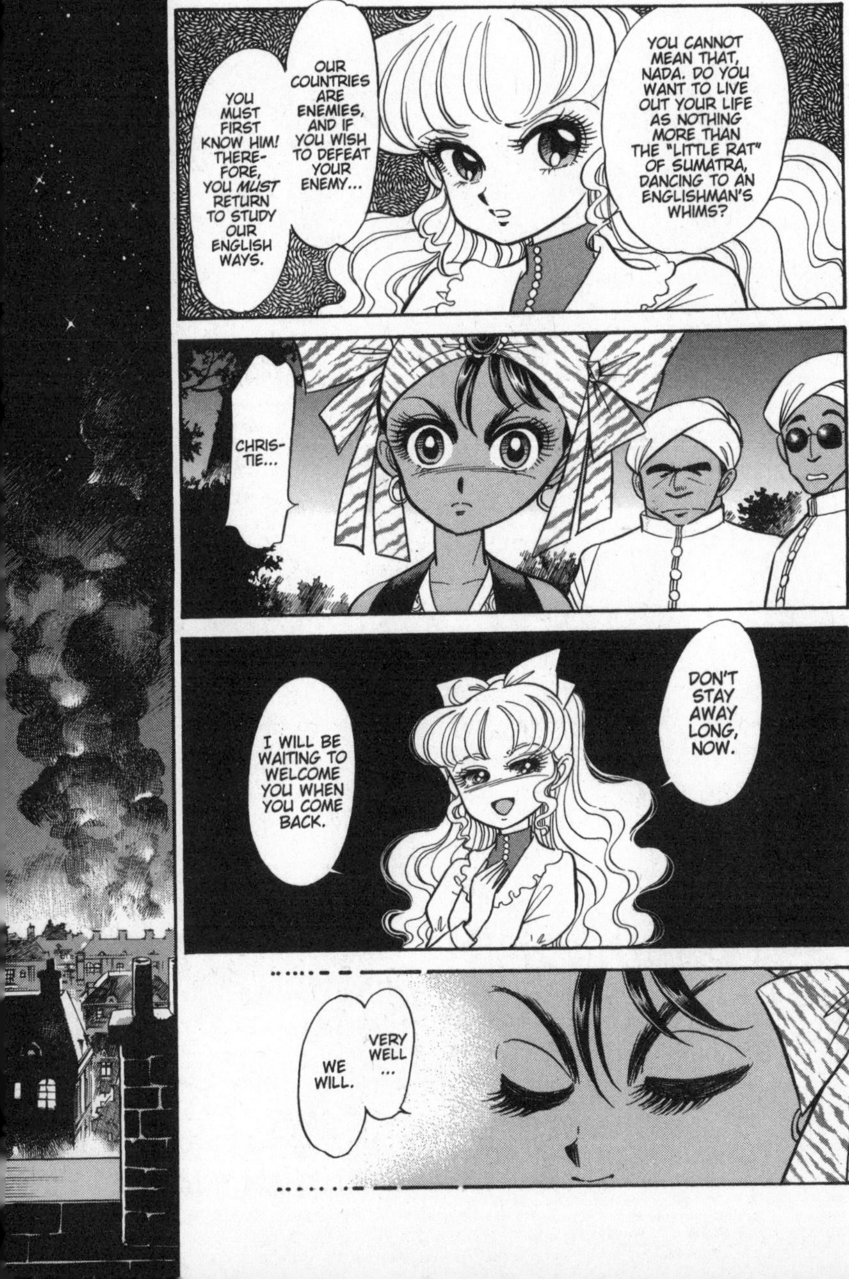
YOU CANNOT MEAN THAT, NADA. DO YOU WANT TO LIVE OUT YOUR LIFE AS NOTHING MORE THAN THE "LITTLE RAT" OF SUMATRA, DANCING TO AN ENGLISHMAN'S WHIMS?
OUR COUNTRIES ARE ENEMIES, AND IF YOU WISH TO DEFEAT YOUR ENEMY...
YOU MUST FIRST KNOW HIM! THEREFORE, YOU *MUST* RETURN TO STUDY OUR ENGLISH WAYS.
CHRISTIE...
DON'T STAY AWAY LONG, NOW.
I WILL BE WAITING TO WELCOME YOU WHEN YOU COME BACK.
VERY WELL...
WE WILL.

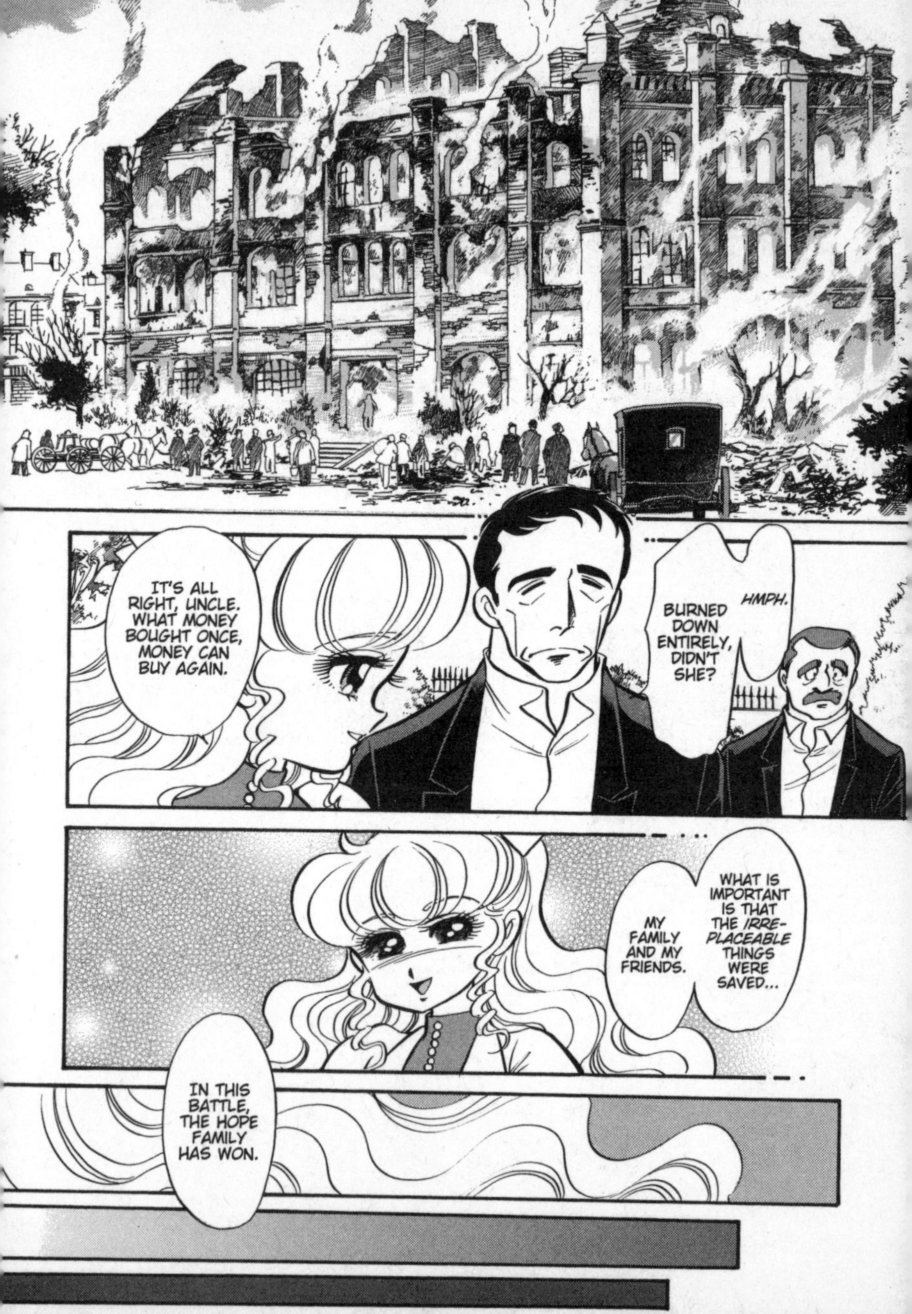
HMPH.
BURNED DOWN ENTIRELY, DIDN'T SHE?
IT'S ALL RIGHT, UNCLE. WHAT MONEY BOUGHT ONCE, MONEY CAN BUY AGAIN.
WHAT IS IMPORTANT IS THAT THE IRREPLACEABLE THINGS WERE SAVED...
MY FAMILY AND MY FRIENDS.
IN THIS BATTLE, THE HOPE FAMILY HAS WON.

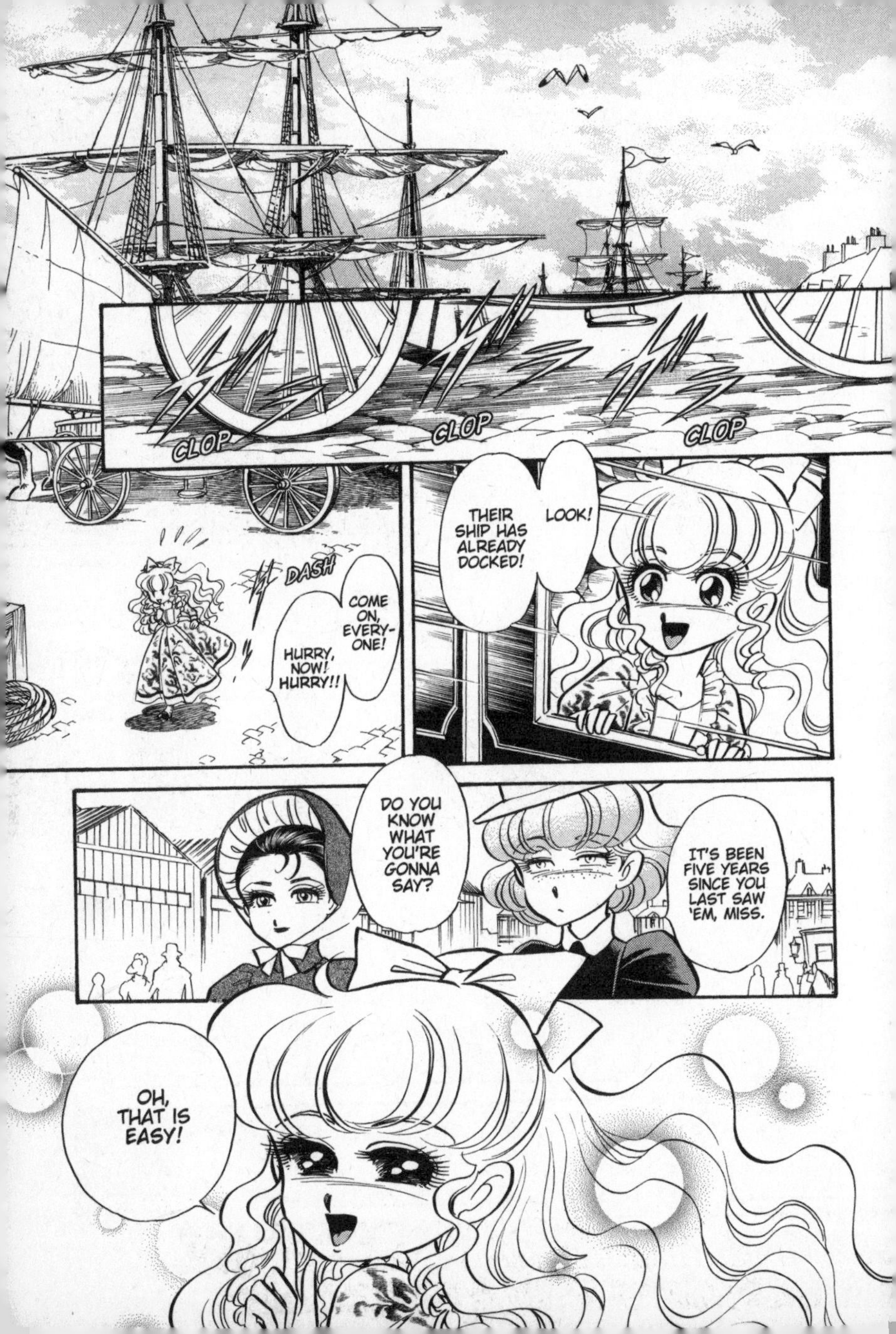
CLOP
CLOP
CLOP
LOOK!
THEIR SHIP HAS ALREADY DOCKED!
DASH
COME ON, EVERY-ONE!
HURRY, NOW! HURRY!!
IT'S BEEN FIVE YEARS SINCE YOU LAST SAW 'EM, MISS.
DO YOU KNOW WHAT YOU'RE GONNA SAY?
OH, THAT IS EASY!

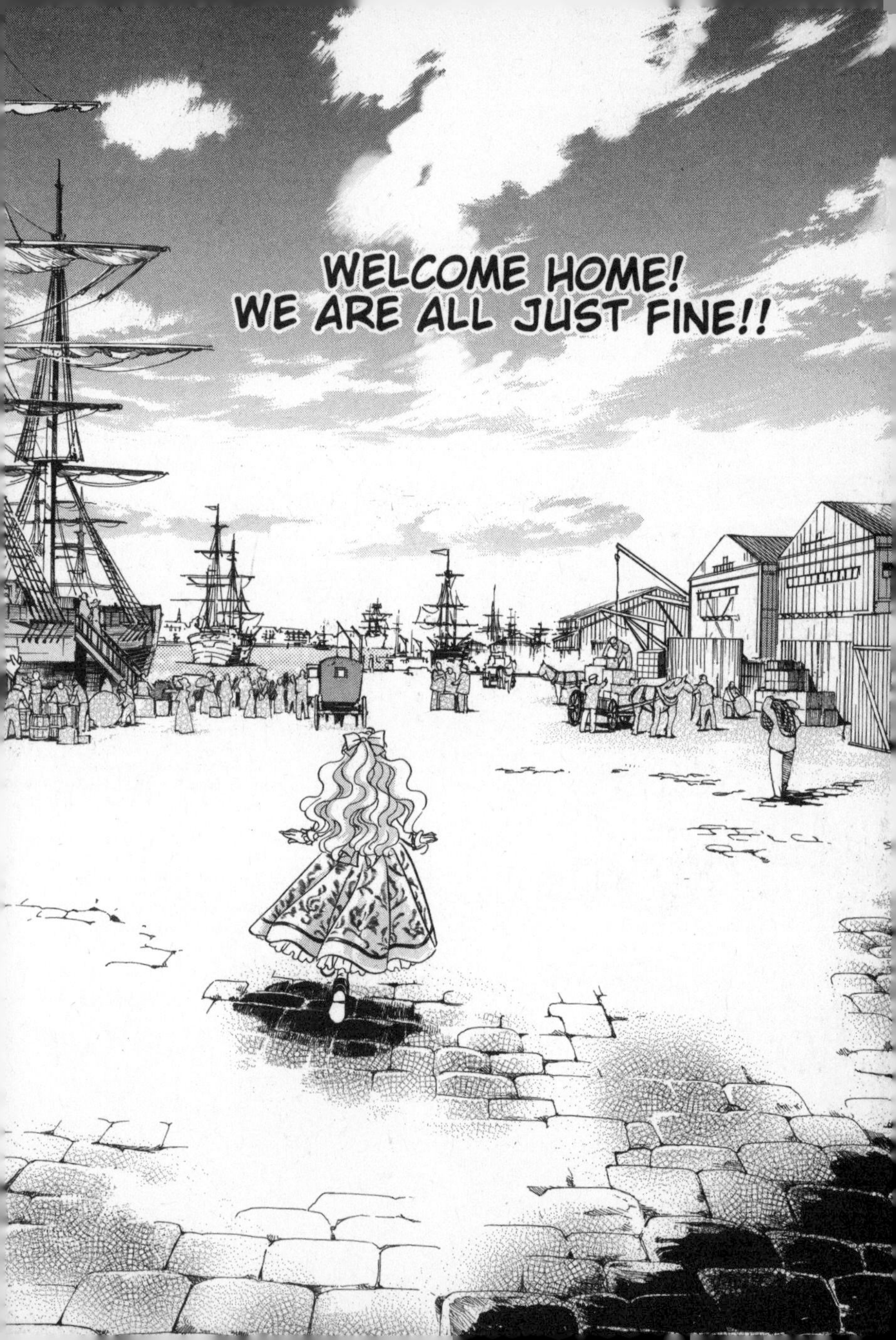
WELCOME HOME!
WE ARE ALL JUST FINE!!

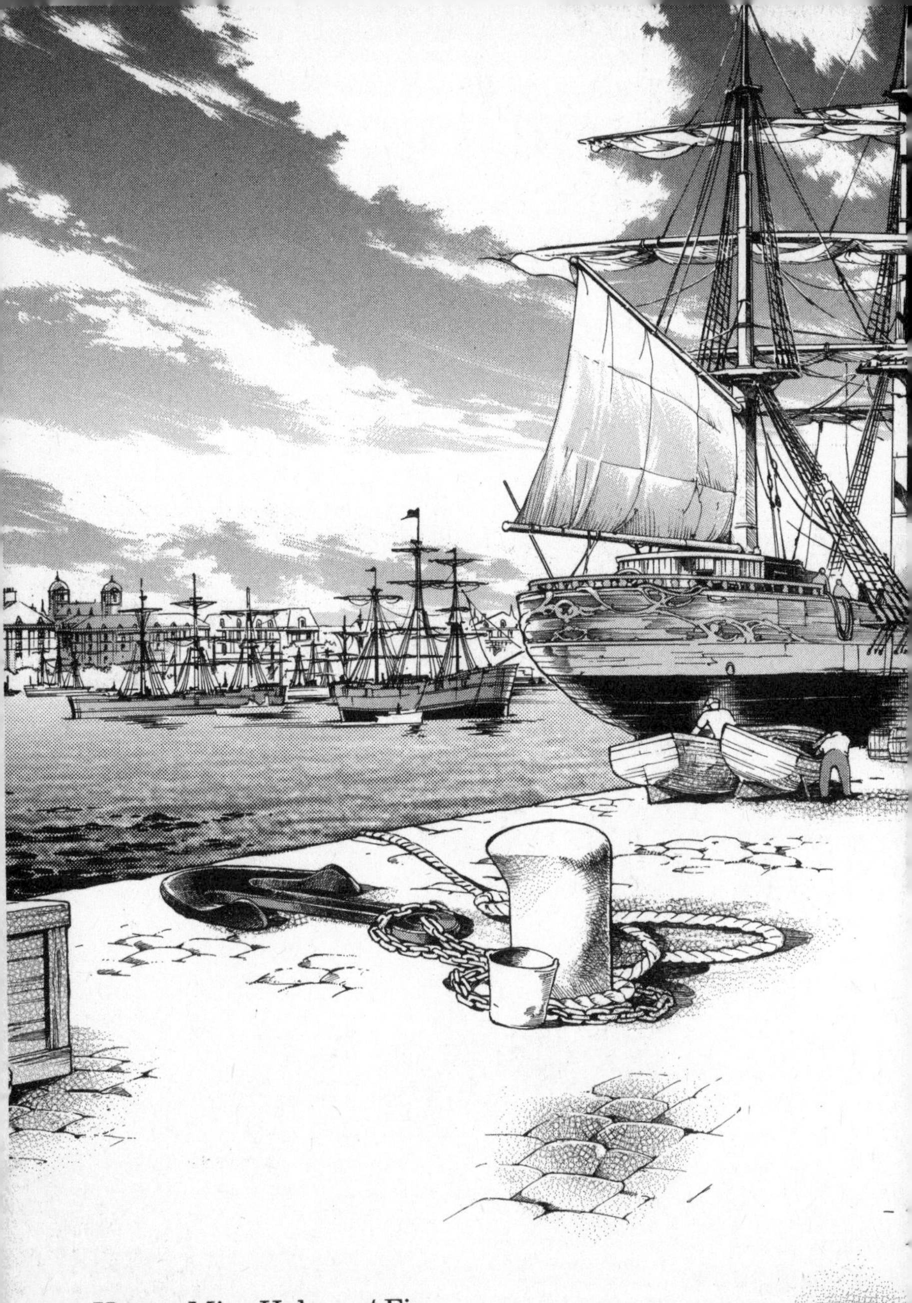

Young Miss Holmes / Fin

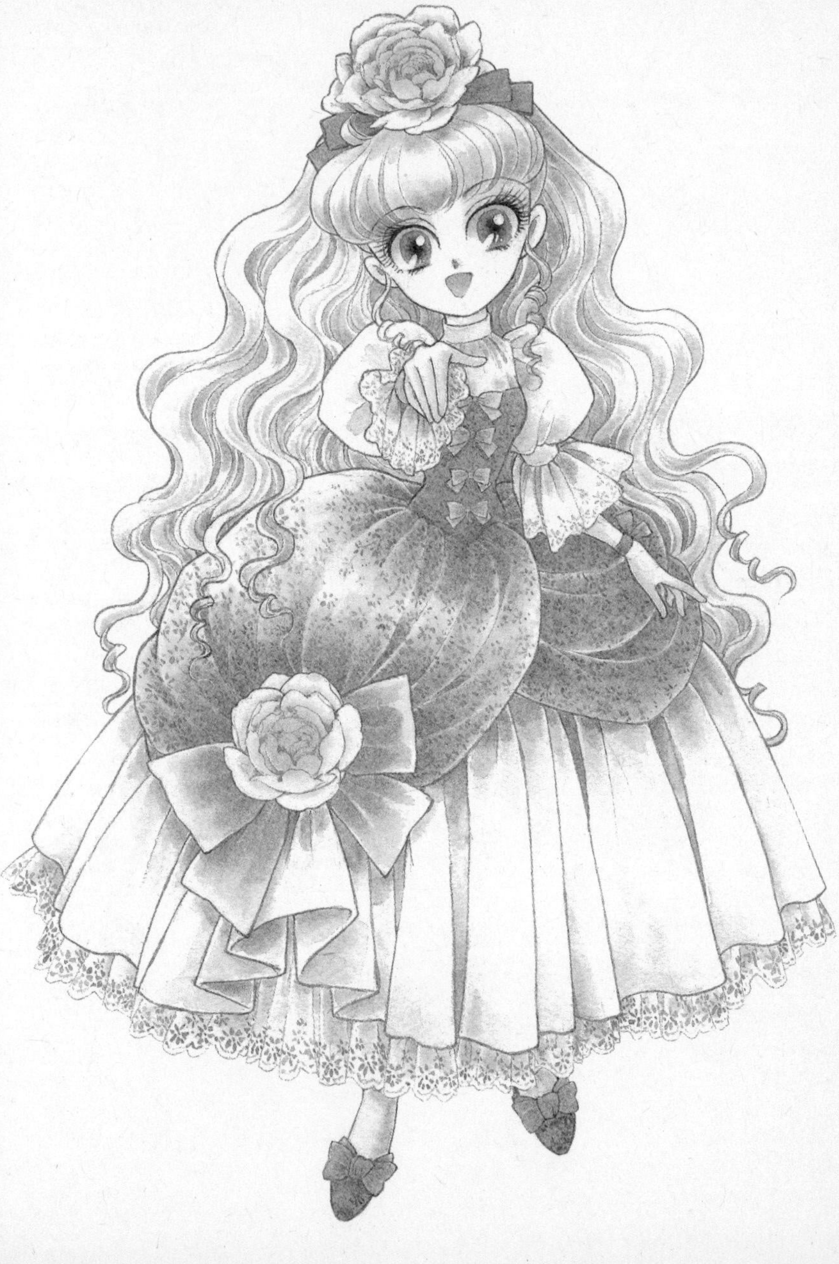

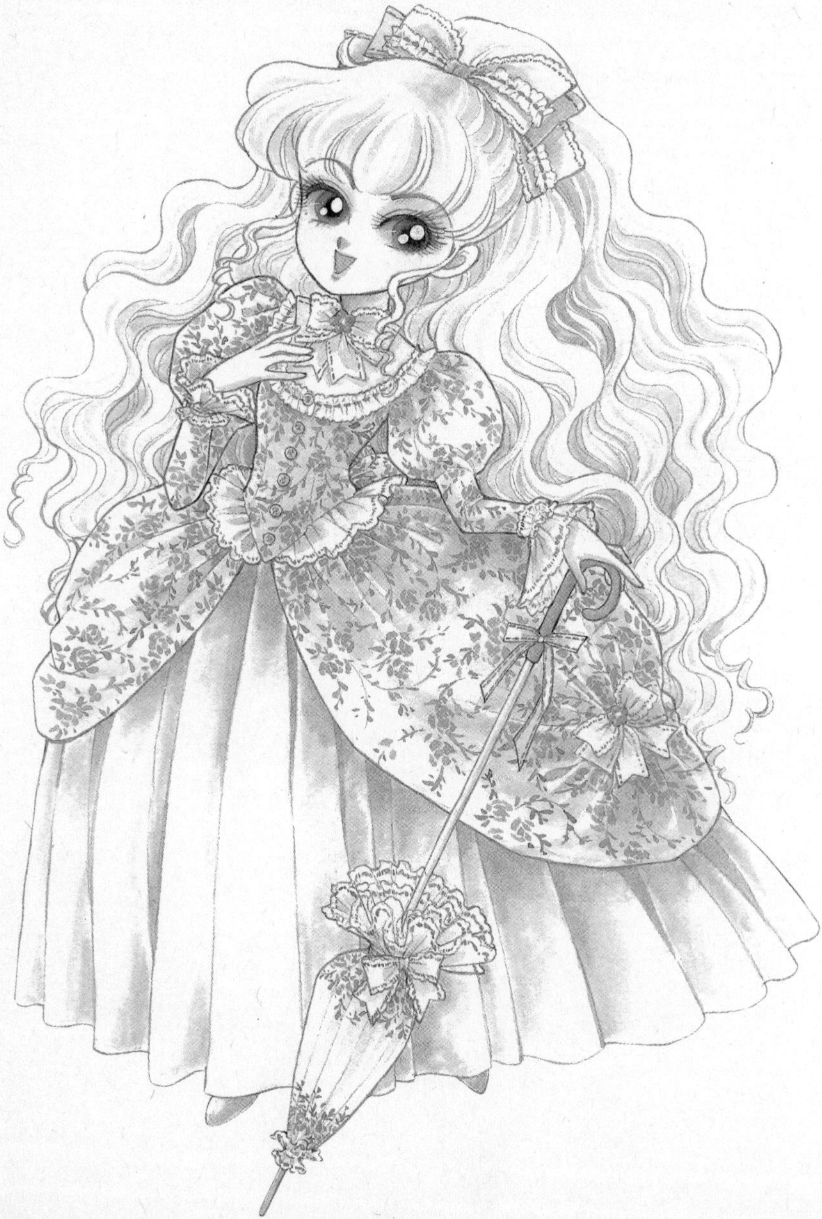

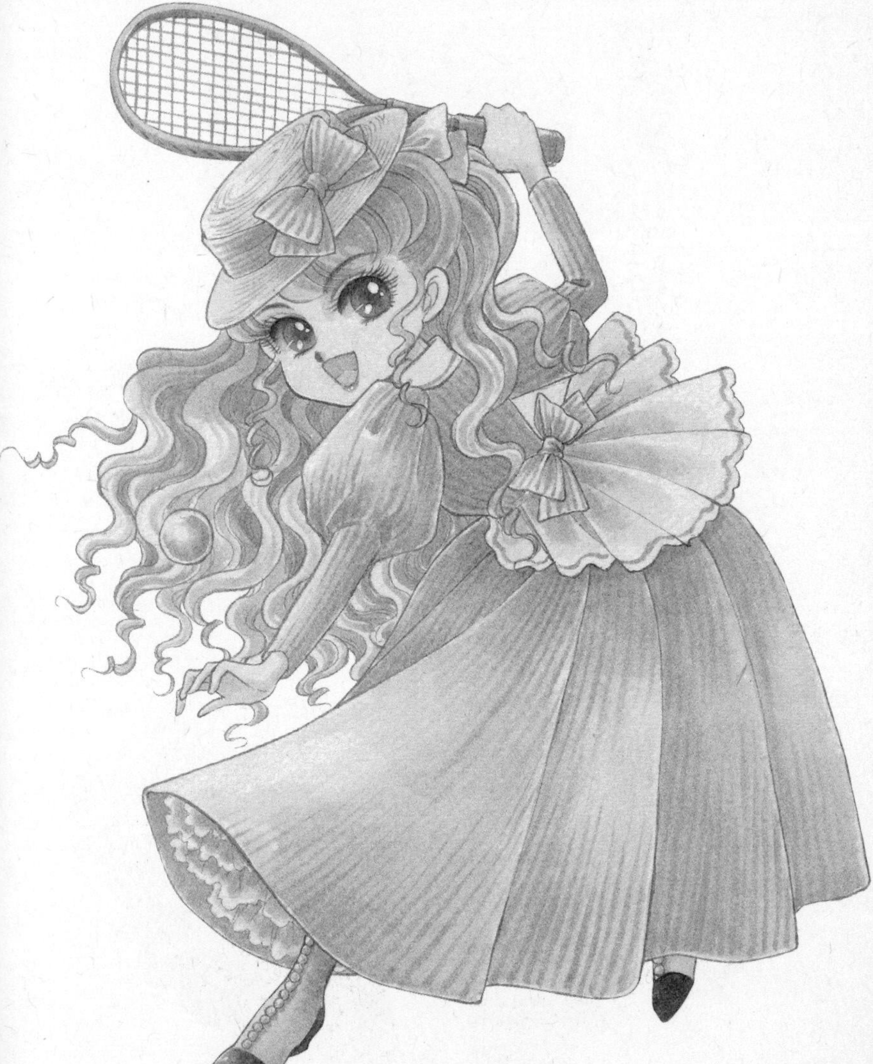

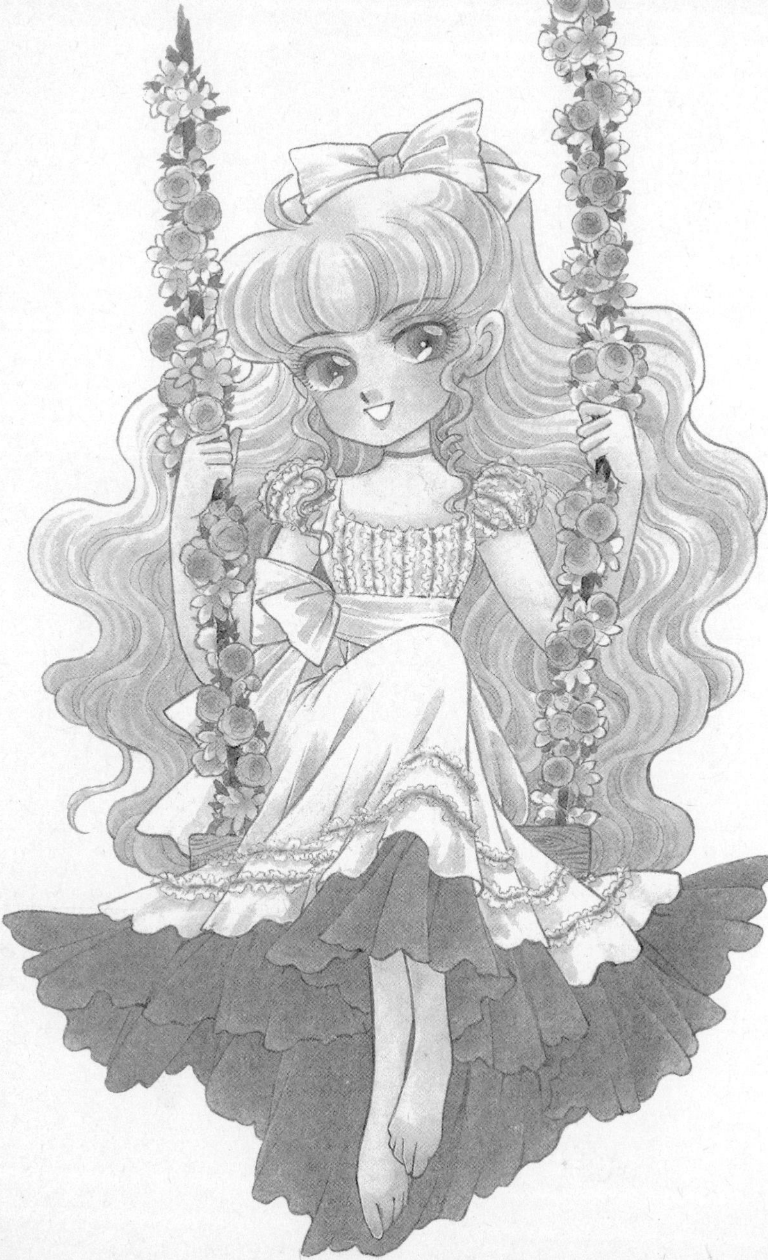

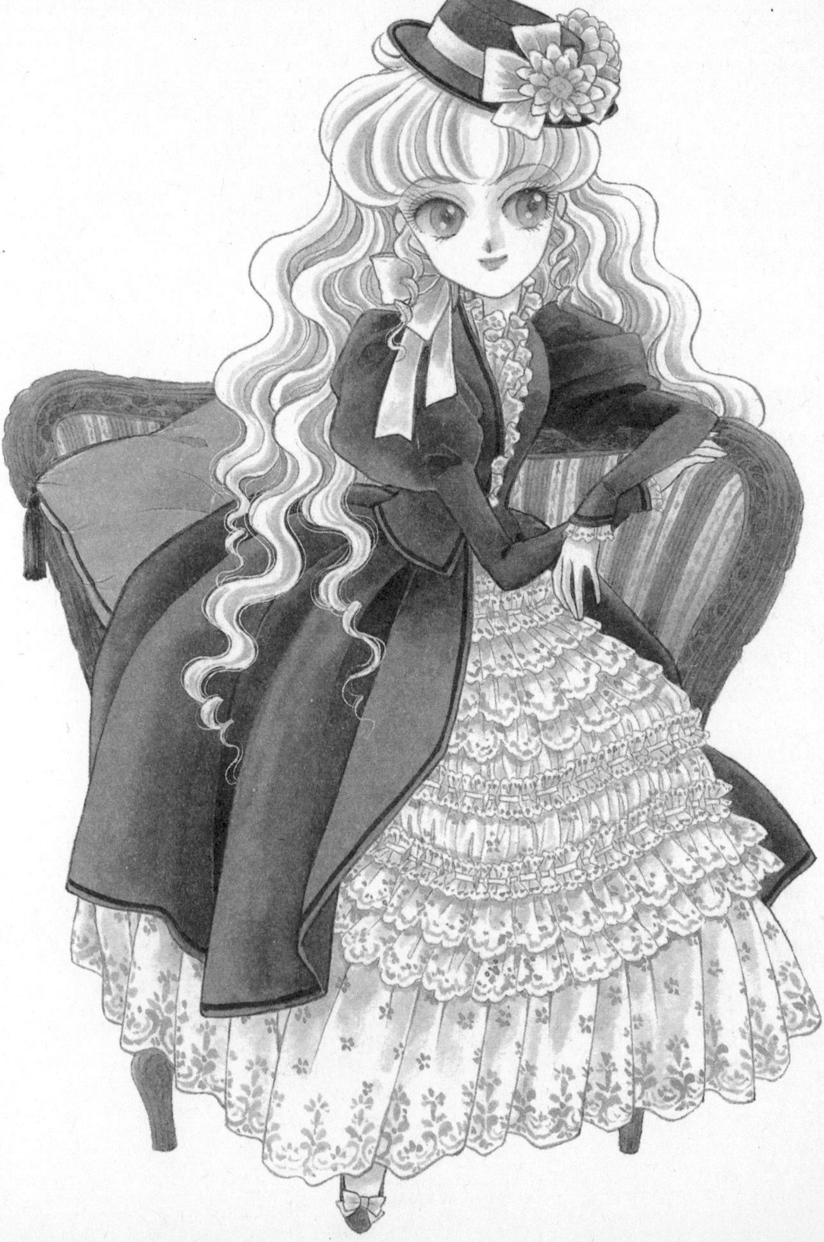

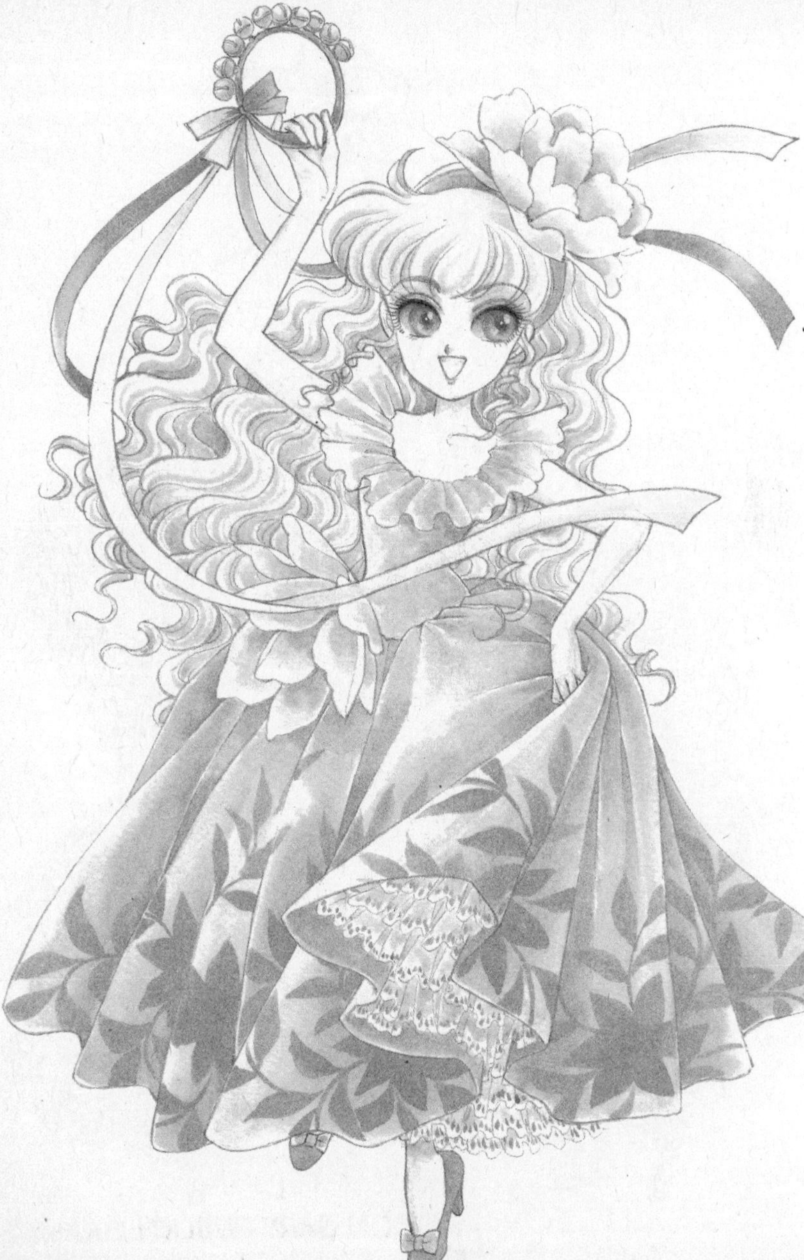

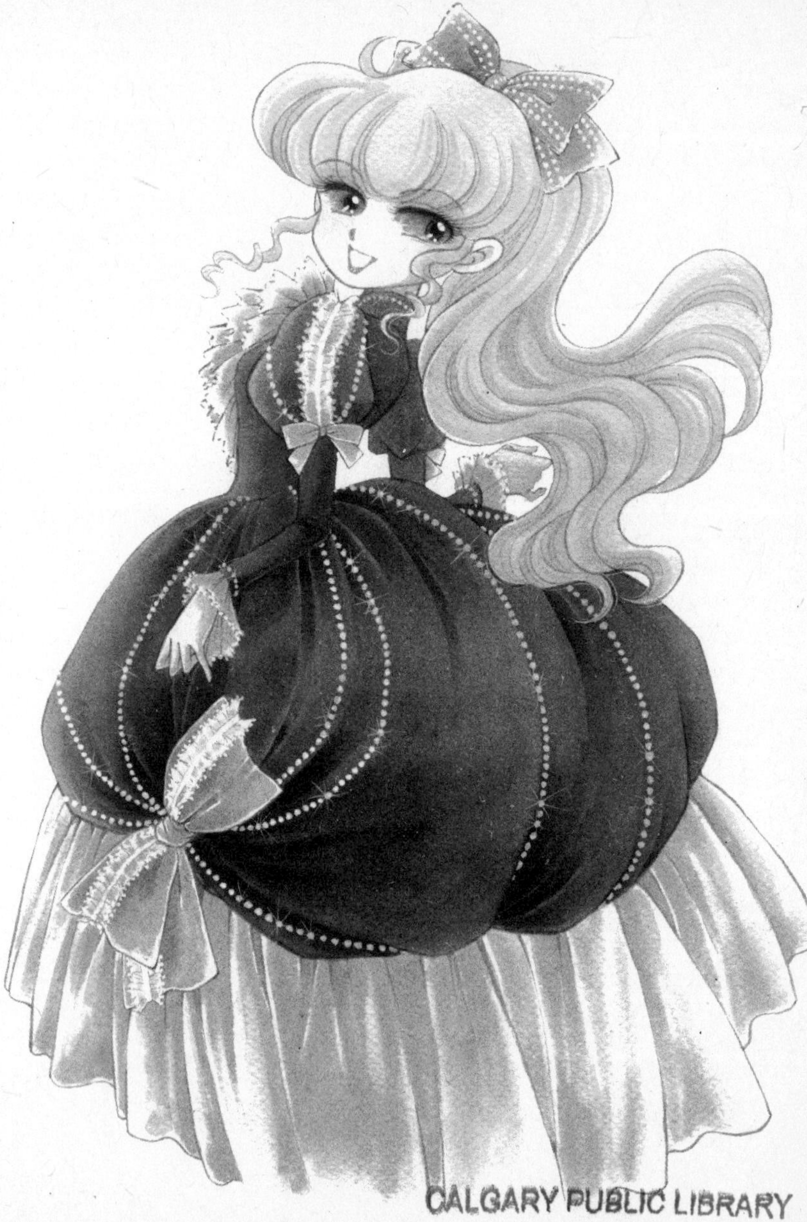